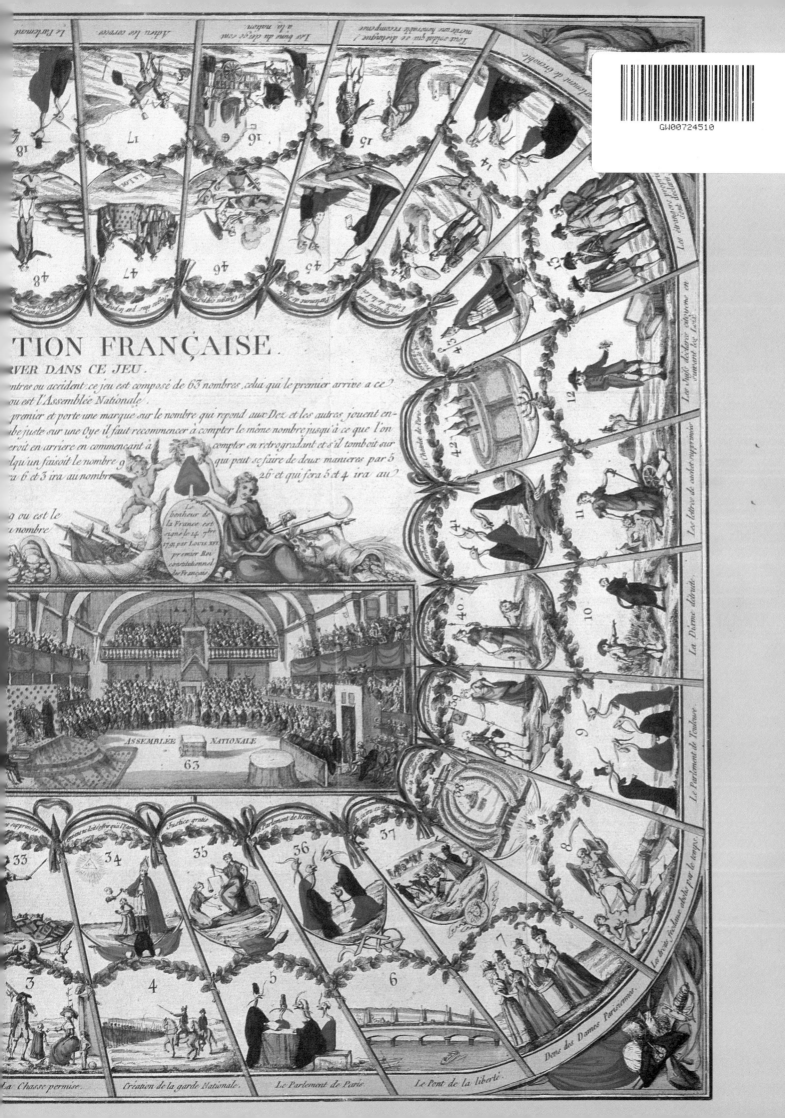

Chronicle of the French Revolution

Longman
Chronicle

Chronicle
of the
French Revolution

1788

1799

Longman
Chronicle

This book has been conceived and published by Jacques Legrand

Chronicle Communications Ltd.,
C/O Reader's Digest Ltd.,
Berkeley Square House,
14 Berkeley Square,
London WIX 5PD

I.S.B.N.: 0-582-05194-0

Typesetting: Berger-Levrault, Nancy – France
Color-separation: Christian Bocquez – France
Printed by: Didier, Château-Thierry – France
Bound by: N.R.I., Auxerre – France

Longman Group UK Ltd.,
Longman House
Burnt Mill,
Harlow
Essex CM20 2JE

Introduction

The French Revolution is one of those few events in the history of mankind whose seismic aftershocks continue to reverberate down the centuries and far beyond mere man-made borders. The tempest that was unleashed when the people of Paris finally erupted and stormed the hated symbol of the Bastille, on July 14, 1789, did not just mark the end of a weak-willed 18th century monarch.

Nor was it simply a case of a downtrodden, poverty-stricken population rising up against their despised rulers in a desperate attempt to both seek revenge for their woes and to improve their lot.

The Revolution was all these, but much more as well. The momentous events that shook France in the ten short years between 1789 and 1799 are among the most complex, fast-moving and sometimes contradictory of Europe's history.

In France itself, the Revolution brought profound political, social, cultural economic and even sexual changes. The birth of the "new order" was an agonising, bloody process, marked by a degree of violence that shocked many, both inside France and far beyond its borders. Hundreds, if not thousands, of innocents died. The old crowned heads of Europe trembled, watching in powerless horror as the guillotine efficiently carried out its grim task.

Yet from those days when the Reign of Terror stalked the land, new hope was born. A people had taken its destiny into its own hands and set about reshaping the future. Outdated political, judicial, cultural, educational and military institutions were torn apart and rebuilt, often from scratch.

In England, Germany, Austria, Italy, Spain and faraway America, the historic events underway in France kept people spellbound. Was the Revolution to be considered as a deadly threat to their very existence, or did it point the way to a future in which there would be equality, justice and opportunity for every citizen?

While that particular debate raged on both sides of the Atlantic, the Revolution's great leaders and thinkers worked tirelessly to incite others to follow their lead. The French Revolution, they argued, was a blueprint for all revolutions. Indeed, there was a startling degree of multi-faceted "cross-pollination" between France's revolutionaries and artists, politicians and intellectuals abroad.

In many ways, the Revolution's protagonists were right. The Revolution of 1789 has inspired revolutionaries the world over, not just in Europe, but in Latin America, Asia and Africa.

Two hundred years on, today's historians continue to debate the complex issues involved in the watershed events of 1789-1799.

Perhaps, however, it is necessary to view the Revolution not only as a major historical event, but also through the eyes of the men and women who lived through those ten fateful years: to see how they lived, played, loved, worked, fought and died. It quickly becomes apparent that not all aristocrats were "blood-sucking fiends" bent on exploiting the poor and that not all revolutionaries were saintly visionaries motivated solely by love of their fellow men.

Louis NEVIN

Chronicle of the French Revolution

Directed by	**Jean Favier,** *Director of the French Archives*
	Anik Blaise, Serge Cosseron, Jacques Legrand
Editorial Advisor	**Robert Maillard**
Assisted by	**Guy Chaussinand-Nogaret** **Françoise Kermina**
Specialists	**Hélène Coulonjou, Yann Fauchois, Philippe Faverjon, Evelyne Lever, Marie-Vic Ozouf,** **Anthony Rowley**
	Assisted by: Isabelle Calabre, Christophe Péry, Geneviève Reynes, Carole Thierry
Writers	Thomas André, Mathieu Arnoux, Nathalie Bailleux, Nathalie Bolgert, Henri-Philippe Boulard, Isabelle Calabre, Hélène Coulonjou, Hervé Darnajoux, Guy Defeyes, Gwenaëlle Fauchois, Philippe Faverjon, Nicolas Fouqueray, Catherine Glaser, Catherine Goussef, Jean-Louis Harouel, Frédérique Hatt, Barthélemy Jobert, Patrick Jusseaux, Bernard Klein, Jean-Louis Langlois, Roselyne Laplace, Bruno Lecestre, Bernard Lehembre, Donatella Marcuz, Catherine Menzaghi, Jean Modot, Philippe Niéto, Philippe Oval, Jean-Fernand Pelatan, François Pellissier, Christophe Péry, Nicolas Postel-Vinay, Geneviève Reynes, Guy Sabatier, Yves Sansonnens, Carole Thierry, François Vollhardt, Teresa Young, Isabelle Yvon
Chronologies-Index	*Chronologist:* Thomas André *Table of illustrations:* Frédérique Hatt *General Index:* Véronique Dussidour
	Chronicle of the French Revolution has been adapted and translated from the French under the direction of **Louis Nevin,** assisted by: Mark Hutchinson, Harold Lesh, John Meredith, Philippa Nevin
EDP	*Manager:* **Catherine Balouet** *Software Engineer:* Dominique Klutz *Assisted by:* Véronique Albert, Dagmar Collard, Martine Colliot
Artwork	*Manager:* **Henri Marganne** *Iconography:* Françoise Breton, Christian Danger, Frédérique Hatt *Maps:* Christian Baude, Michel Colley, Philippe Rekacewicz *Production:* Maud Escalona, Martine Toudert

CONTENTS

Foreword

A momentous event if ever there was one, in which each hour could at times be decisive, the French Revolution clearly gains an added dimension by being treated *from day to day,* using the formula which has already proved its merits in *Chronicle of the 20th Century.* The reader can see in action, within the framework of a strict chronology, the principal actors of these glorious and dramatic hours, beginning with the people who occupy the foreground: their leaders, orators, villains and, in all their astonishing diversity, their short-lived heroes. Nearly 3,000 facts, major and minor, anecdotal or decisive, are listed here in all the gripping immediacy of their unfolding. History itself is captured in the making.

This work spans the totality of the revolutionary cycle from 1788 to 1799 – in other words, in symbolic terms, from the "Day of the Tiles" in Grenoble to Bonaparte's takeover on Brumaire 18 (November 7th 1799).

As with other Chronicle books, this volume is composed of three distinctive and complementary elements:

A chronology, which gives the book its rhythm and which is divided (so as to adhere to the sequence of events as closely as possible) into periods ranging from one month to eight days. Nonetheless, for certain exceptional events – such as the Storming of the Bastille, the night of August 4th, the Festival of the Federation, the King's flight to Varennes, the fall of Robespierre or Brumaire 18, when events unfold dramatically – the chronology pauses to make room for more expansive coverage, with a different presentation, as if time were suddenly suspended.

Each sequence is introduced by graphic symbols indicating the political régime then in power: in turn, the monarchy (⚜), the Republic (𝔍), the various Assemblies (🏛): Constituent, Legislative, Convention, Directory.

Opposite this chronology are articles relating, in the manner of a newspaper, in a simple and direct style, not only the political facts, but also the daily life of the French. Indeed, while the Revolution pursued its often bloody course, men and women continued to live out their individual passions: their dramas, their loves, their extravagances, their distractions. Life went on.

Some 1,700 illustrations of the period, most often in colour, accompany these articles and make it possible to "visualise", as in a news story reported live, the movements of crowds and the actions of individuals.

In addition, a system of cross-references between the chronologies and the articles enables the reader to follow the different phases of the same event and thus to grasp all its implications better.

Finally, about 20 pages (printed on cream-coloured paper) are distributed throughout the book. They provide a sense of historical continuity by placing the facts in a coherent perspective. These pages are a summary of the transformation undergone by French society between Louis XVI's accession to the throne and the *coup d'état* of Brumaire 18, in the light of the major stages of the revolutionary process.

The reader will also find:

– At the beginning of the book, a portrait ot the main "actors" in, or witnesses to the Revolution, with their socio-professional and family background; maps illustrating the chief "sites" of the Revolution, both in Paris and the provinces, and also in far-away colonies; and the contemporary international situation.

– Appendices : Notes on what became of the protagonists who lived on beyond 1800; a list of government personnel in the years 1788-1799; a table of illustrations and finally an index listing characters, cities and principal revolutionary themes.

Robert MAILLARD

The France of Louis XVI

Louis XVI's reign began in 1774 amidst general rejoicing. It ended tragically after a short experiment with constitutional monarchy at the start of the Revolution. During that period, the traditional régime, of the patriarchal and aristocratic type, had to cope with difficulties that proved insurmountable because of the King's character and his advisers' personalities. Traditional types of opposition were made bolder by the power structure's weakness, the financial crisis and the constantly growing deficit, which rose to an intolerable level due to the enormous costs of French participation in the American Revolutionary War. Above all, there were profound changes in public opinion, which demanded the right to monitor state activities, abolition of the prohibitions and privileges that split society into groups with contradictory interests, and greater freedom. All this gradually forced Louis XVI to call on the Estates General to cooperate with him in reforming institutions to save the country from bankruptcy, even though, in the rush of events in 1789, this reform was actually made against his interests.

Popular sovereigns

France was tired of Louis XV's reign, and the kingdom breathed a sigh of relief when the King died on May 10th. 1774. The King left a country in good, vigorous health. The last years of his reign had brought some substantial reforms, and the minister Maupeou had crushed the parliamentary opposition that threatened the crown's authority and blocked any kind of change. However, public opinion paid more attention to the vagaries of Louis XV's love life than to his efforts to improve the way France was governed. People had high hopes for the new reign. They were already fond of their new sovereigns, the debonair and charitable Louis XVI and the young and pretty Marie Antoinette, whose gaiety and mischievous disposition delighted her subjects. People talked about the young couple's kind actions and felt they were likely to succeed. They were expected to do wonders for the country and to usher in a new golden age.

The King had announced some large spending cuts, above all in his own household, in order to lower taxes. He demanded that the poor be able to buy bread for two sous. He had even given up his right to a gift from the people to mark his accession in order to spare his subjects. Louis XVI's behaviour did honour to his wisdom in a France that was becoming more bourgeois. He had no scandalous involvements with women. People were glad to note the disappearance of the reign of ruinous "favourites" who were held responsible for all of the state's misfortunes. The King was not held hostage by the Court, but concerned himself with the welfare of the middle class and worried about the common people's misfortunes. There was every indication that the new reign would mark the start of a period of peace and prosperity.

However, Louis XVI's first act was a grave mistake, though it increased his popularity since public opinion generally favoured such a move. He recalled the parliaments, thus arousing a type of opposition that was very dangerous to his authority and to the required modernisation of the state, which that opposition was going to fight stubbornly (as it had already done in the past) by using the great resources available to it. At the outset, the philosopher and liberal minister Turgot undertook such reforms as freeing the grain trade and doing away with royal statute labour and other restrictions that paralysed the various trades. But he was unable to implement all of his projects: religious tolerance and buying back seigneurial rights. He was forced to resign in May 1776 due to opposition from a cabal of privileged people, the Queen and minister Maurepas. His successor, Necker, had to find money, especially since the American war was a major drain. He resorted to borrowing, and the government debt spiralled out of control. Despite some progress in the field of tax collection, Necker did not want to transform the tax system and did not touch privileges and immunities, a step that would have improved public finance. By publishing a "Report", a mendacious plea on behalf of his management, Necker displeased the courtiers by revealing the amount of their income. He had to withdraw in 1781 in the face of opposition from the parliaments, nobles and the Queen, giving way to some interim ministers until 1783, when Calonne tried a new approach. The issue of the royal finances was at the heart of the problem. Expenditures were rising constantly, but receipts were not keeping pace. Land income had been rising regularly since 1730, and that was where some new resources had to be found. Tax reform was needed, and Calonne decided to submit one to an "Assembly of Notables" that he called into session in 1787. However, the majority of the participants were princes, prelates or lords, namely, a privileged class that rejected the territorial subsidy that Calonne wanted to impose on all owners. In the face of resistance from people who did not want to lose their privileges, Calonne had to leave office, removed by the King at the Queen's suggestion. France then moved into a very turbulent period during which attempts at reform, opposition on the part of princes and parliamentarians, and demands expressed by ever more aggressive public opinion led to state paralysis and a pre-revolutionary crisis.

Wind of freedom

French participation in the American War of Independence had resulted in consequences and dangers of which the minister had not realised the extent. Aid sent to the rebels had worsened the royal finances and compromised the chances of recovery. Moreover, the monarchy had supported the rebels against their legitimate king, meaning that people could rebel against a king with the approval of the French monarchy. The fighters, La Fayette and Rochambeau's army, had come back from America strengthened in the views that had led them to embark for the New World. Had they not gone off to defend the cause of freedom and tolerance, reflecting the views of many courtiers and of wide segments of public opinion?

The Americans had been victorious, thanks to France. After their return to Europe, the fighters used their prestige to serve their ideal, freedom and republican equality, which they had admired in the young United States. La Fayette, Rochambeau and their officers had covered themselves with glory and became the young people's idols. They had borrowed the Americans' simplicity and democratic ways. They praised the beneficial effects of American institutions and indulged in republican remarks and behaviour patterns by comparison with which the French monarchy's pomp and prejudices looked very old fashioned.

Of course, the idea was not to overthrow it, but rather to dust it off, to tune it to the concepts of freedom and equality. La Fayette and his like carried on active propaganda in a receptive atmosphere. A wind of freedom had been blowing over the kingdom for a long time, and American independence strengthened it. The monarchy's difficulties and the feeling that it was working poorly and had no future in its traditional form created a pressure for change. New aspirations came into being in ever more extensive segments of the population under the influence of philosophy and the Enlightenment. Young officers spread their ideas in Masonic lodges. Clubs were established in which some reform proposals were prepared and a plan was developed that was to be put into effect in 1789: replacing absolute monarchy with a constitutional monarchy. La Rochefoucauld translated the American constitutions and offered them to the French public. There was a wave of emulation and of demands for new areas of freedom, beginning with such philosophers as Condorcet, members of the middle class who were angry at being kept in a subordinate position, such as Bergasse, and journalists (such as Brissot) annoyed by fetters on the Press. During the 1787 Assembly of Notables, La Fayette dared to demand a "National Assembly". The parliaments, a force opposing the régime as well as a citadel of the narrowest kind of conservatism, were conquered in turn by the new ideas and claimed to fight for freedom by humiliating the throne and attacking the majesty and the honour of royalty. The "necklace affair" had given them an unexpected opportunity to cast strong suspicion on the Queen. Revolt was in the air, fed by lampoons and the clandestine Press in an atmosphere of feverish demands.

The desire for equality got a receptive welcome from the Third Estate and the liberal nobility. The middle class was no longer willing to tolerate the humiliation it suffered from a society of orders and it struggled for recognition of its right to hold any civilian or military jobs that had been reserved to the privileged classes up to that time. All those people whose ability and fortune qualified them for responsible positions had become unwilling to passively accept the decisions of a power structure that acted without supervision and added a lack of ability to its arbitrary manner of acting. The state was on the verge of bankruptcy and had neither enough energy nor the imagination needed to resolve the crisis, reassure people living on private incomes and satisfy an impatient public opinion. Everybody viewed liberty as a panacea that would bring happiness and prosperity. The aristocracy yearned for it, the middle class, which had more to gain, was even more vehement and the word had a magical effect among the common people themselves.

On the eve of 1788

All this had created an unstable situation. There were growing signs of impending trouble, yet a revolution seemed quite unlikely. The leading agitators did not want one. The opposition elements in the parliaments that appeared most effective aimed only at substituting a judges' oligarchy for monarchical absolutism, fearing the latter's reformist whims and wanting to supervise the King's activities in order to prevent him from imposing solutions that might have ensured the régime's survival. The people who dreamed of major upsets and disturbances had only mediocre resources available to them and their efforts seemed sure to fail.

Still, it was impossible to delay reforms for much longer, as the state was threatened with paralysis and society with breaking up. At a time when the monarchy was foundering in impotence and bankruptcy, when it was reduced to stopping payments on its debts, the question was who would govern France, and for what purpose. The choice was clear. Was the state to remain under the control of courtiers backed in their conservative ways by battalions of magistrates hostile to reforms, desiring to maintain privileges and incomes and taking advantage of the monarchy's difficulties, to attempt to substitute their authority for the King's? Or would the élite of people with skills and talents, forcibly kept in a subordinate position by the monopolies and by the first group's desire to exclude them from power, manage to obtain some real control over the régime's workings? The humiliated dynamic elements of the Third Estate, the discredited nobility, and the middle class working in the administration and the bar but without any real future wanted to replace the reign of favouritism and injustice with emulation and competition on the basis of merit, save the régime by adapting it to modern conditions, and pluck it out of the hands of the people monopolising it for their own ends. As for the King, who was said to enjoy absolute power, he was actually held hostage by the privileged classes. Feeling the breakup of the power structure, the parliaments and those for whom they were the authorised spokesmen thought only of seizing power to satisfy their appetites. Paradoxically, they were helped in their efforts at sabotage by public opinion that still lacked guides and viewed them as natural defenders and the last rampart of freedom. Their opposition to the legitimate power structure, characterised as defence of the public interest, appeared to be a kind of backing for national resistance. In fact, the parliamentary opposition was only pursuing selfish goals and was indifferent to the people's demands and to the need for relieving the most obvious evils. While the monarchy was making a final effort to find solutions to the crisis and to reconcile progress with its tradition, the judicial and princely Establishment rejected this royal effort and any kind of concessions. The power structure naturally reacted vigorously against this provocation, but its authoritarian acts were immediately interpreted by poorly informed public opinion, lacking real leadership, as a coup d'état inspired by a despotism. The power structure had to backtrack, but then the masks were ripped off.

A society threatened with breakup

The crisis started by the parliamentary and aristocratic rebellion occurred in a society subject to violent upsets. The French population was still divided into orders: the clergy, the nobility and the Third Estate. But within each of them, there was an almost infinite variety of motivations and interests were often contradictory. Peasants and farmers accounted for nine-tenths of the population (26 to 27 million inhabitants) and the majority, who had not been affected by the century's currents and were slaves to routine, superstitious and technically backward, were involved in growing cereals and vines. Many of them were landless and exchanged their labour for starvation wages. Their fate was very different from that of the ploughmen, who farmed other people's land, had teams of horses, lived in comfortable circumstances, and encouraged their sons to move to the city, where they often enjoyed a career in office work. The large-scale farmers and the stewards of big estates constituted a rich and ambitious rural bourgeoisie. But the rural class led a miserable existence. It had to pay the bulk of the taxes, such as the "taille", the hated salt tax, as well as quarter troops, do road work, and make payments to the lord ("champarts" and "banalités") and to the clergy (tithes). Some aspects of serfdom survived in certain regions: the peasant was attached to the lord's land and could leave property to his children only by paying mortmain fees. Peasant discontent increased on the eve of the Revolution. Demands became more pressing. Peasants demanded the abolition of land-connected payments and the right to hunt, which was a seigneurial monopoly.

The anger that affected the rural world was even stronger among the urban middle class, which had enriched itself in trade, money dealing and manufacturing (large-scale industry began during the last third of the 18th century with the Creusot forges and the Anzin mines). The richest money dealers had become nobles and bought the large domains of debt-ridden aristocrats, whose titles they bore. But there was also a whole middle class of lawyers, notaries, physicians and administrators who were cultivated, aware of their merits, and resented their subordinate status. In the name of competition among talented people, they made loud demands for the right to hold all jobs, military, civilian and clerical that had previously been reserved for the nobility. They were leaders of public opinion and wanted recognition of their importance in a country that had so far given them only a minor role. They had a long way to go to catch up with the nobility, a class that consisted of only about 200,000 people but got the lion's share everywhere. Of course, the nobility was not all of a piece, and that class was also characterised by variety. Courtiers received large incomes, jobs and pensions from the King. They lived in luxury in Versailles and Paris. The provincial nobility displayed contrasts. The nobility recruited from the legal profession, which sat in the parliaments, had fine estates and showy town houses, while the rural nobility was often needy, poorly educated, and desperately attached to its privileges. The nobility also had a monopoly: regimental lieutenant's positions had been reserved to it since 1781. This did not satisfy the lesser nobility, since it had slim hopes of brilliant careers while the higher ranks were reserved for the high nobility.

The second order was not merely a force resisting political and social changes. The young nobles who took part in the American War of Independence brought back a wind of freedom from the United States, a simpler and more republican way of life. The enlightened aristocracy envied the English Constitution, and wanted the monarchy to evolve along British lines. The most dynamic part of the nobility contributed to the take off of industrial and commercial capitalism. It wanted to take a more active rôle in administration of the state and of the provinces and rebelled against government policy, which it considered despotic.

Thus, all classes of society were motivated by resistance or a desire for change in an intellectual atmosphere that profoundly modified attitudes, ways of thinking, and feelings. The rationalist current, illustrated by Voltaire, and Rousseau's romantic, sentimental and egalitarian thought, fused in the new generations, which recognised themselves both in Illuminism and in Raynal and Condorcet's progressive works. These contrasted the "Gothic" past with contemporary enlighten-ment, which favoured human progress. The new ideas were spread in society through the inter-mediary of schools, public courses, provincial aca-demies, libraries, and gazettes. Salons bringing intellectuals and aristocrats together and Masonic lodges (several hundred of them) were meeting places for the middle-class élite and the aristo-cracy. They promoted discussion among the soci-ety's enlightened classes. None the less, the ir-rational side of life also triumphed and there was great enthusiasm for Cagliostro's wonders and Mesmer's miraculous cures. A feeling of diffuse expectation spread throughout the kingdom. What were people looking for? Great upheavals, happi-ness, revolution? In any case, people were hoping, talking about a rebirth, about a new beginning, about regeneration.

At the crossroads

Ministers, paralysed by the parliamentary op-position, decided to change things, and to neutral-ise it by a sharp attack. In May 1788, the King deprived Parliament of the bulk of its judicial powers and of its right of legislative and fiscal monitoring. Public opinion's anti-absolutism led it to come down on Parliament's side. On occasions, in the Dauphiné, revolt turned into revolution. There were some deaths on the "Day of the Tiles", and the provincial estates met and made demands on the King: a meeting of the Estates General, a doubling of the Third Estate, and individual voting. The King had to give way, recall Necker, and an-nounce a meeting of the Estates General in 1789. Necker recalled the parliaments, which revealed their true goals, immediately demanding that the Estates obey the old rules, each order having one vote. That would mean that the privileged classes would win out over the Third Estate. Public opinion then veered away from Parliament and sought new leaders. A national party came into being, drawing members from throughout the kingdom. In Decem-ber, the King decided that the number of Third Estate deputies would be doubled. That move up-graded the monarchy's prestige, but France was demanding reforms.

Louis XVI and his ministers had so far tacked blindly between authority and surrender, between the use of force and weakness. Would they be able to make a skilful response to the dire threats piling up, to be brought to a peak by the economic crisis? Would they be able to make the right choice be-tween the inevitable reforms and the siren songs of conservatism? The year 1789, with its dramas and quickly dashed hopes, brought a quick and violent answer.

"Actors" and witnesses of the Revolution

A series of portraits of leading and less well-known figures involved in the Revolution, who had a direct bearing on events or who simply happened to witness them. These portraits show the people as they were in 1787, before the start of the Revolution.

The scenes and the places

Maps of the main French towns – Paris, Versailles, Bordeaux, Lyons and Marseilles – as well as of the French provinces and overseas colonies where decisive episodes of the revolutionary period took place.

The international scene

This section provides an overview of the international situation at the start of the Revolution, as the world's leading powers look on at the events in France in either horror or enthusiasm.

"Actors" and witnesses of the Revolution

Marie Antoinette and her ladies in waiting in the royal bed chamber.

The Comte de Provence.

The Comte d'Artois.

Louis XVI, Louis Auguste

Born at Versailles
Aged 33 on January 1st. 1788

Louis succeeded to the throne of France on the death of his grandfather on May 10th., 1774. His features were quite noble, and an indecisive look in his shortsighted eyes gave him a melancholy air. He was tall and well-proportioned, although he had a tendency towards plumpness. Very robust, he even managed to lift a pageboy on the end of a shovel held at arm's length. He had a passion for hunting, and carefully listed every piece of game that he killed. A graceful rider, he was somewhat less elegant on foot, for, like all the Bourbons, he waddled rather than walked. Extremely shy, he preferred to talk to his grooms than to converse with the great men of the court. To show his amiability, he would advance abruptly and, finding nothing to say, would cackle nervously. His voice was harsh, even nasal. He seemed bored at the meetings of the Council, where he paid less attention than when he was in his library, with its thousands of volumes. He was interested in everything, and especially in books on science. He spoke excellent English, and read the poems of Milton, as well as the English newspapers. When he wanted to relax, he retreated to a hideaway fashioned under the eaves of Versailles, and shut himself up there to make keys and locks. Fascinated by navigation, he closely followed the progress of the expedition of La Pérouse and wanted to make the Navy's modernisation the showpiece of his reign. At the

inauguration of the port of Cherbourg in 1786, the breadth of his knowledge won him the admiration of all the sailors. Pious like his father, and taught in accordance with the austere principles of his tutor, the Duc de La Vauguyon, Louis was as severe with himself as he was indulgent with others. Motivated by noble sentiments, he desired his people's happiness.

Marie Antoinette, Josèphe Jeanne de Lorraine

Born in Vienna, Austria
Aged 32 on January 1st. 1788

Married in 1770 to the Dauphin Louis, becoming Queen in 1774, Marie Antoinette, after having enjoyed great popularity both at court and with the people, soon faced increasing attacks from her brother-in-law and from her cousin the Duc d'Orléans. The notorious "Affair of the Necklace" tarnished her reputation considerably. Despite her sufferings, the Queen was considered to be among the loveliest sovereigns in Europe. When she walked across the Gallery of Mirrors, her proud and gracious carriage dazzled visitors to the Palace; her face had a soft, gentle expression which drew others to her like a magnet. Her smile was kindly, though she never lost her majestic air. She was seen as proud, although her tastes inclined her to simplicity. She never became used to court etiquette, preferring intimate circles to official receptions. At the King's Supper, she did not even deign to unfold her napkin; anyway she ate very little

and drank only water. In her youth she had loved parties and the gaming table, but her four pregnancies had made her more serious, and she spent her days with her children at the hamlet retreat of Trianon where, it appeared, the best butter in France was produced. Her frivolity lessened, and she was often criticised for dressing in an almost common manner. In 1783 she posed for Madame Vigée Lebrun in a simple dress of white muslin, and this "chambermaid's" attire was so derided that the painting was removed from the Salon. The Queen had little schooling, but she spoke Italian and knew how to read a musical score. A devotee of the Opera, she assured the success of Gluck in Paris; one of her intimates, he even had the right to enter her private dressing room. She also liked the theatre and often amused herself interpreting repertory roles, in private, on the small stage of the Trianon. Unfortunately her recent trials had saddened her, especially the death, the previous June, of Sophie, her little daughter, aged one, as well as her growing unpopularity. She knew that ever since the last Assembly of Notables she was openly considered responsible for the financial crisis, and was called "Madame Deficit".

Provence, Louis Stanislas Xavier, Comte de

Born at Versailles
Aged 32 on January 1st. 1788

A year younger than the King, the Comte de Provence reinforced the alliance with Savoy by marrying

Marie Joséphine de Savoie, eldest daughter of Victor Amadeus III. However, this mismatch produced no offspring. *Monsieur* nonetheless preserved his dignity, despite his obesity which made him nearly impotent. He was widely read, with a prodigious memory, liked to write light verse in a somewhat ribald vein, and was a contributor to various newspapers. The Luxembourg Palace was filled to overflowing with works of art: he had nearly 200 paintings, including a Raphael, and more than 3,000 engravings and his furniture was made by the Jacob brothers. A museum, a theatre, and a newspaper all carried his name; he financially supported quite a few writers, and thought of himself as a patron of letters. In spite of his awkward bearing, he was quite popular, for it was believed that he had liberal ideas. At the Assembly of Notables in 1787, he was widely respected for presenting himself simply as "the first gentleman of the kingdom" and for having favoured the doubling of the representation of the Third Estate.

Artois, Charles Philippe, Comte d'

Born at Versailles
Aged 32 on January 1st. 1788

He was the youngest brother of the King. In 1773 he married, like his brother, a daughter of the King of Sardinia, Marie Thérèse de Savoie, and fathered three children. Of all the princes, he was the one who most reminded the courtier of his grandfather, Louis XV. He had the

Mme. Victoire, the King's aunt.

Two of the Infants of France.

Louis Philippe d'Orléans.

same courtesy and good looks. However, he was often arrogant, even with the King. He was admired for his smart attire, his horses and livery, and the sumptuous castle of Bagatelle that he had built in one month, following a bet he made with the Queen. An opera fan, he also loved the theatre. Skilful in all sports and exercises, he excelled at dancing and riding. Generous with his friends and servants, he did not hesitate to spend money on luxuries and even his great fortune was insufficient to absorb all his debts, which the King had to pay regularly. He was loved by Parisians for his wit, but his absolutist principles damaged his reputation, and at a court session held in Parliament he was even booed. He returned to Versailles absolutely furious, swearing that he would never again let himself be so completely humiliated.

Elisabeth de France

Born at Versailles
Aged 23 on January 1st. 1788

The last child of the son of Louis XV, orphaned in 1767, she and her brother, the King, were bound by warm affection. Extremely shy with everyone, she spoke openly to him, and he listened willingly. She often stayed in Montreuil, near Paris, in a superb home that he gave her when she reached adulthood. There she divided her time between spiritual occupations and riding, in which she was highly skilled. Gentle and pious, the Princess took an interest in charitable works; she had 60 poor young girls vaccinated at her own expense.

Adelaïde, Madame

Born at Versailles
Aged 55 on January 1st. 1788

Louis XV's best-loved daughter, Madame Adelaïde was his sixth child. Very pretty in her youth, she later became a tall, harsh woman with a brusque manner and a grating voice. Her appearance was intimidating; she was over-conscious of her rank and did not even respond to the compliments of her visitors, except with unintelligible murmurs, on the pretext that these conversations were matters of pure form. She led a religious faction which her brother, the father of Louis XVI, had headed, and she even intervened in the choice of ministers. She disapproved of the marriage of her nephew, whose wife she would have liked to choose herself, in order to have had influence over her. She loathed the Queen and it was at her home that Marie Antoinette was first derisively labelled "The Austrian".

Victoire, Madame

Born at Versailles
Aged 54 on January 1st 1788

The youngest of the King's aunts ever since the death of Louise Marie (1737-1787), Madame Victoire was a plump, jolly woman who liked her comforts. She blindly obeyed her elder sister. Very pious, she was fond of rich food and, though she faithfully followed the rules of Lent, at the last stroke of midnight on Easter Eve she ordered chicken with rice in cream sauce. However, she showed courage when Louis XV was struck down with smallpox. Exposing herself to contamination, she closeted herself with her sister in the King's room and cared for the patient to the end.

Marie Thérèse, *alias* Madame Royale

Born at Versailles
Aged 9 on January 1st. 1788

Despite her youth, Madame Royale, the King's daughter, displayed signs of pride. Her pretty dimpled face, framed by blond curls, was in such contrast with her excessively grave demeanour, that her uncle, the Comte d'Artois, took to calling her "Muslin the Serious." There was at one point talk of marrying her to the Prince of Naples.

Louis Joseph, the Dauphin

Born at Versailles
Aged 6 on January 1st. 1788

By the time he was six, the Dauphin was in very poor health. He had a marked deformity of the hip. He was not expected to live long.

Charles Louis

Born at Versailles
Aged 2 on January 1st. 1788

Nicknamed "Honeybunch" by his mother, the Duc de Normandie was a handsome child with large blue eyes and a lively expression.

Orléans, Louis Philippe, Duc d'

Born at Saint Cloud
Aged 50 on January 1st. 1788

The Regent's great-grandson was a tall man, with a ruddy complexion and a noble air. Having been made very wealthy by his marriage to the Duc de Penthièvre's daughter, he led a grand life. For many years a style setter, it was he who introduced English fashions into France, notably horseracing. At first a close companion to the Queen, he was disgraced in 1775, when he was cheered in Paris for having refused to visit Prince Maximilian of Austria, who was staying at the court. After his mediocre performance in the battle of Ushant, the Duc gave up his naval vocation and began to speculate in property, renting out his gardens in the Palais Royal to merchants. This affair was a scandal and the King called the Duc a "shopkeeper". He handled criticism with wit. When told that he would never have enough money for so much construction, he answered: "But of course I will, everyone is throwing stones at me." He was once again made fun of when he appointed his former mistress, Madame de Genlis as tutor to his sons. The King never consulted him; he had all the less reason to do so as the Duc d'Orléans had long been an opponent of royal policies. He took advantage of the great scandal caused by the "Necklace Affair" to ermerge as the leader of the opposition. He professed to have very enlightened opinions and was even called the "Father of Reform". In 1771 he became a Grand Master of Freemasonry.

"Actors" and witnesses of the Revolution

The Comte de Fersen.

The Princesse de Lamballe.

Jacques Necker.

Bouillé, François Claude Amour, Marquis de

Born in Saint Eble
Aged 48 on January 1st. 1788

General de Bouillé was the strong man of the army. Always in favour of a forceful solution, he demonstrated his intransigence in Metz where he was Governor of the Trois Evéchés. He publicly stated his intention to apply rigorously the royal edicts demanding military surveillance of the Parliaments. The Chambers were placed under lock and key, the doors guarded by soldiers and the magistrates informed that any attempts to organise meetings would be punished by a sealed royal order. A veteran of the Seven Years' War, this energetic officer contributed to the American colonies' fight for independence, as governor of Martinique and of Saint Lucia. Despite his fiery temperament his loyalty to the King was unshakeable, and he demonstrated his integrity by declining Louis XVI's offer to pay his debts.

Calonne, Charles Alexandre de

Born in Douai
Aged 53 on January 1st. 1788

The former Comptroller General of Finances fled to London. Never had a bankruptcy been more total than that of the "Enchanter." On leaving his post, he had to give up the position of treasurer of the Order of the Holy Ghost. His creditors pursued him and he was even accused of having speculated with State funds. Even so, when he came to power in 1783, his talent, charm, wit and elegance were praised by all. This tall man, well built and agile, was capable of carrying on the most frivolous of conversations, all the while studying serious documents. He knew how to refuse requests pleasantly and all the ladies were mad about him. He juggled loans with ease. Unfortunately, in February 1787, he had to announce to the Assembly of Notables that France had accumulated a massive deficit of 115 million francs, and finally he was forced to demand strict budget cuts. This new policy of fiscal austerity united the Queen and the privileged classes against him. Even though at first she had borne with him, Marie Antoinette was in particular never able to forgive him for having strongly advised her husband against the purchase of the castle of Saint Cloud.

Condé, Louis Joseph de Bourbon, Prince de

Born in Chantilly
Aged 51 on January 1st. 1788

Faithful to the traditions of his royal blood, he was, of all the princes, the most skilled in war and the most courageous. Unimposing physically, short, redhaired and lame, his character was considered excessively proud. Nonetheless he showed great humanity to the peasants of his lands, as he did to the soldiers of his regiment. For example, he took care to reimburse them for the damage caused by his hunts and, during times of famine, he had wheat distributed to the country people. He resided chiefly in his palace of Chantilly, which he endlessly embellished and whose magnificence was reputed throughout Europe. Visitors came from far away to visit the marvellous English-style garden, the Natural History room, the menagerie with its extraordinary specimens, and especially the famous stables. Grand Master of the Royal Household at the age of 15, governor of Burgundy at 18, he continued to hold these functions though he was rarely to be seen at court, mainly because of his poor relations with Marie Antoinette.

Estaing, Charles Henri, Comte d'

Born in Ravel
Aged 58 on January 1st., 1788

After the taking of Grenada in 1799, Admiral Estaing became a national hero. On his return from America, after peace, he earned an ovation from the people of Passy, where he had a country house. Many Parisian theatres performed plays inspired by his exploits. He also had the knack of blowing his own trumpet. However, he was not liked by his peers, because he was not a professional sailor and had spent most of his career in the army, in India, under the command of Lally Tollendal. His appointment in 1763 to the post of Lieutenant General of the Navy was due to his friendship of the father with Louis XVI, rather than his knowledge of naval matters. Ambitious, but nonetheless superficial, he was, supposedly, open to new ideas.

Fersen, Hans Axel, Comte de

Born in Stockholm
Aged 32 on January 1st. 1788

This Swedish officer, in the service of the King from 1783, was very well regarded at Court. He was one of the few foreigners admitted into the Queen's circle. She greatly esteemed him and this aroused a great deal of jealousy. However, this distinction was well earned because the Comte de Fersen belonged to one of Sweden's most powerful families and was a personal friend of the King, Gustav III. His brilliant performance in America, as aide de camp to Rochambeau, earned him the rank of Colonel in the Royal Swedish, a prestigious regiment founded in 1690. In addition to his other qualities, Fersen had great physical attributes. An athletic bearing, the nobility of his handsome face and his perfect elegant manners seduced all women.

Lamballe, Marie Thérése de Savoie Carignan, Princesse de

Born in Turin
Aged 38 on January 1st. 1788

A widow at 18 after an unhappy marriage, she had been one of the first intimate friends of Marie Antoinette, who in 1774 appointed her superintendent of her household, a job fallen into disuse since the previous reign. Gracious, but not very pretty and without much spirit, she was only remarkable for her fine hair. From 1780, she lived away from the court and only appeared

The Duchesse de Polignac.

The Duc de Penthièvre's family, one of the wealthiest in France.

there to attend official functions, claiming that her poor health kept her away from Court. She may also have been angry at having been replaced by Mme. de Polignac as Marie Antoinette's confidante.

Loménie de Brienne, Etienne Charles de

Born in Paris
Aged 60 on January 1st. 1788

A prelate with up to date views, who was practically an atheist, even though an enlightened and philanthropic one, Loménie de Brienne ran his archbishopric at Toulouse more as an administrator than as a spiritual leader. He kept an eye both on charitable work and urban construction projects. He exerted considerable influence within his order, while at the same time being a very successful man in the secular world, in which the revenues from one of France's wealthiest sees allowed him to live well. He was a witty and highly cultivated man and a great lover of literature, who knew both Voltaire and d'Alembert and was made a member of the French Academy. He was always fascinated by politics, and in 1787 some clever plotting led to his appointment to replace his rival Calonne. He was backed by the Queen, and pushed through some badly needed reforms such as the abolition of forced labour and its replacement by a monetary contribution. However, his pet plan to create a territorial tax that would be equal for all met with some fierce opposition. When the Paris Parliament was exiled to Troyes for re-

fusing to rubber-stamp royal edicts, unrest spread to the provinces and to Loménie's own see. By 1788 his popularity was on the wane, and it looked as if he could be forced to seek a compromise.

Malesherbes, Chrétien Guillaume de Lamoignon de

Born in Paris
Aged 66 on January 1st. 1788

The Minister of the Royal Household was an independent man. His tolerance was legendary; in charge of censorship under Louis XVI, as director of the Library, he protected the encyclopaedia writers instead of hounding them. He wrote to Diderot, who was worried about a possible police raid: "Bring your manuscripts to my house, they won't think of looking for them here." He resigned in 1776 because of the dismissal of his friend Turgot. He then devoted himself to travelling and literature. He was from an ancient noble family, but lacked an imposing appearance. Small and fat, badly dressed, covered with snuff, he was "simply simple" according to Mme. Geoffrin. He was full of bonhomie and high spirits, with an inexhaustible verve. Louis XVI, who liked him, called him back. Malesherbes had several projects to improve the lot of the disinherited, in particular that of prisoners whom he personally visited. He wanted to abolish the King's Sealed Orders and had, for a long time, been one of a number of people who saw the need to convene the Estates General and to suppress privileges.

Necker, Jacques

Born in Geneva
Aged 57 on January 1st. 1788

His dismissal from the Ministry of Finances in 1781 did not permit him to apply his programme of reform, but he lost none of his great popularity. His own career was, moreover, a proof of his expertise in matters of finance. Beginning as a mere clerk in a Geneva bank, he quickly became an partner and amassed an immense fortune. His colleagues made a cult of him; he was praised above all for his integrity. When he was Minister, he refused to accept bribes and he always demonstrated complete loyalty to the King who, nonetheless, did not like him at all. His wife, daughter of a modest pastor, wrote works of great erudition and took under her wing the hospice of the rue de Sèvres, which she frequently visited with her husband. Their one and only child, Germaine, married Baron Erik de Staël, the Ambassador of Sweden. Necker did not have a very endearing appearance; he had a starchy manner and his slightly fleshy face, together with an air of gravity, gave an impression of a certain self satisfaction.

Polignac, Yolande Gabrielle de Polastron, Duchesse de

Born in Paris
Aged 38 on January 1st. 1788

She was an unpretentious and charming woman, who was always simply dressed and hardly wore any

jewellery. A blue-eyed brunette, she was a fine-looking woman with an excellent singing voice. In 1775 she became the Queen's favourite, and in 1782 was appointed governess to the King's children. Not an ambitious person, she allowed herself to be manipulated by her greedy family, which took advantage of Marie Antoinette's friendship for her. The Polignac family, which used to be relatively poor, later left the provinces to live at Versailles thanks to generous royal allowances.

Rochambeau, Jean Baptiste Donatien de Vimeur, Comte de

Born in Vendôme
Aged 62 on January 1st. 1788

A brigadier in 1761, Rochambeau was a cold man, distant, without any of the usual elegance of a man of his rank. His military career preoccupied him exclusively and, as one of his friends said, he made strategy "on the plain, in his bedroom, on his table and on your tobacco pouch, if you took it out of your pocket". Hero of the Seven Years' War, he renewed his victories in America, where he commanded the expeditionary force. He yelled "To me, Auvergne" on the redoubt of Yorktown, thus commemorating the gesture of the Chevalier d'Assas fighting under his command at Clostercamp in 1760. His wise and prudent behaviour delighted the Americans, and he was particularly loved by General Washington because he always took care to present himself as a simple auxiliary under Washington's orders.

"Actors" and witnesses of the Revolution

The toll-barrier at the Champs Elysées, built by Ledoux.

The painter Fragonard.

The composer Grétry.

Boullée, Etienne

Born in Paris
Aged 59 on January 1st. 1788

He built several large houses in Paris, notably the Hôtel de Brunnoy, in the Faubourg Saint Honoré and some marvellous castles in the country, particularly that of Tessé at Chaville in 1764; but, after 1770, he devoted himself above all to teaching. The most astonishing works of this visionary architect lay, in fact, in the varied compartments of his fertile imagination. The grandiose projects on which he worked from 1780 excluded all possibility of realising them, given the then existing techniques. No government was capable of ordering the *Palais National* or the *Bibliothèque* with its barrel vault, or the *Cénotaphe de Newton*, an immense sphere illuminated by a fire ball. Boullée dreamed of and imagined towns in a civilisation not yet conceived of.

David, Jacques Louis

Born in Paris
Aged 39 on January 1st. 1788

Despite a slow and difficult start he had to present his work four times before finally winning the Prix de Rome. David nonetheless managed to impose himself as a leading exponent of his field in 1785. His *Horace* was hailed at the Salon of that year as representative of neoclassical art and the painter himself as the renovator of historical art. From that day on, all elegant people wanted to be dressed in the *antique* fashion. An affable and generous man, David had his studios at the Louvre and had the habit of working in shirtsleeves, dressed in velvet. His studio was always remarkably neat and impeccably tidy.

Fragonard, Jean Honoré

Born in Grasse
Aged 55 on January 1st. 1788

Named by his friends the good Frago, he was no longer in fashion. His last important commission dated from the installation of Mme. Du Barry at Louveciennes. This had connsisted of four large panels illustrating the *Progrès de l'Amour dans le Cœur des Jeunes Filles* in 1772. The "Favourite" had, in fact, refused this work for unknown reasons. However, this did not change the optimistic and care-free outlook of the painter. In love with his models, he installed a swing in his studio for their use, in order no doubt to find the inspiration for *Hasards Heureux de l'Escarpolette*, one of his most successful paintings. Even so, he was a loving husband, while revering all women. It was rumoured, however, that he was taken with his young sister-in-law, Marguerite Gérard, whom he took as his pupil.

Gossec, *real name* Joseph Gossé

Born in Vergnies, Hainault
Aged 53 on January 1st. 1788

There was nothing more peculiar than the way he composed *O Salutaris Hostia*. While dining at the house of a friend at Sceaux, the village priest came to ask him for a motet for his parish. Gossec got to work, and two hours later the piece was being interpreted by three singers from the Opéra who happened to be there. He did not, however, just content himself with religious music. As Director of Music at the Paris Opéra in 1782, he composed several operas which had great success. In 1784 the King appointed him Director of the new Academy of Song. A wonderful career for the son of a labourer.

Grétry, André Ernest Modeste

Born in Liège
Aged 46 on January 1st. 1788

A little in the shadow of Gluck, Grétry stayed an idol of the public as long as he led the field of comic opera to perfection. Everyone hummed the famous tune: "Oh Richard, oh my king" from *Richard Cœur de Lion* created in 1784. Installed in Paris from 1768, a longwinded composer, he presented at least one new opera a year. The Queen appointed him director of her personal music and agreed to be godmother to his daughter, Antoinette.

Houdon, Jean Antoine

Born at Versailles
Aged 46 on January 1st. 1788

According to Grimm, friend of Voltaire and Diderot, Houdon was the first artist to be able to capture the look of a subject in sculpture. A student of Pigalle, he won the Prix de Rome at the age of 19. He made himself famous as a portraitist when exhibiting at the Salon of 1771 a terracotta bust of Diderot. The sculpture of Voltaire in marble, showing the writer seated and in Roman-style drapery, was not to be forgotten. Houdon travelled a great deal because he had a lot of foreign orders. He even went to America in 1786 to paint a portrait of George Washington.

Ledoux, Claude Nicolas

Born in Dormans
Aged 51 on January 1st. 1788

The King's architect, Ledoux, was appreciated by high society and had a lot of orders. However, the grandiose projects that he favoured made him an object of intrigue. The salt works of Chaux, at Arc et Senans, begun in 1775, stayed unfinished for almost ten years. As for the toll barriers, which, in his creative fervour, he named the Propylaea of Paris, he nearly finished them, but they were a grave disappointment. Ordered by the Farmers General, they were extremely unpopular.

Louis, Nicolas, *alias* Victor

Born in Paris
Aged 56 on January 1st. 1788

The architect of the superb Theatre of Bordeaux, built from 1773 to 1780, Victor entered the service of the Duc d'Orléans. He built for him

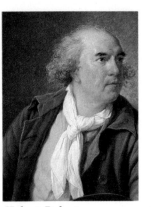
Hubert Robert.

The actor Talma.

A performance at the Comédie Française.

the Palais Royal arcades and started, at one of the corners of the Palace, the work on the future Théâtre Français, on the very site of the Opéra which had burned down in 1781. His career was not easy and his character was highly complex. He brimmed over with projects that he carried out with an extraordinary rapidity. He is said to have said of himself: "I'm always running".

Méhul, Etienne Nicolas

Born in Givet
Aged 24 on January 1st. 1788

His first opera, *Cora,* having had no success, Méhul threw himself into comic opera. This was hardly the field of a composer who had studied music at the Abbey of Laval Dieu and who at the age of ten had started playing the organ for friars and nuns. His talent lay in the dramatic expression that he had learned from his friend Gluck. His beginnings had been difficult and he had a residual melancholy: he worked with a skull on his piano.

Mique, Richard

Born in Nancy
Aged 59 on January 1st. 1788

Richard Mique was the King's chief architect from 1775, due to the favour of Marie Antoinette for whom he had re-arranged the Petits Appartements and designed the English garden of the Petit Trianon and his *Temple d'Amour* which was admired by visitors. He achieved the building of the Hameau de la Reine, started in 1783, but there was a rumour that it had cost a lot of money.

Montansier, Marguerite Brunet, *alias* Mlle.

Born in Bayonne
Aged 57 on January 1st. 1788

This audacious actress was afraid of nothing. The direction of the Théâtre de Versailles, of which she had charge from 1768, was not enough for her; she wanted to rule all the theatres of the kingdom. Even though she was neither particularly beautiful nor especially young, she had, above all, a talent for intrigue. She earned her privileges by proposing to serve the Queen a bowl of cabbage soup on the stage, during a performance of *Moissonneurs.*

Robert, Hubert

Born in Paris
Aged 54 on January 1st. 1788

A garden designer for the King from 1778, this painter, who specialised in the landscaping of ruins, was promoted in 1784 and took charge of the royal collection of paintings. The Queen, who protected him, often consulted with him. The grove of the *Bains d'Apollon* at Versailles was one of his masterpieces. His talent bordered on the prodigious; he painted just as quickly as he wrote a letter. He was a person full of charm, very Parisian in spite of an 11 year stay in Italy. He was welcomed at all parties, a handsome man usually accompanied by an elegant woman, worldly like him, who adored him. Naturally athletic, with an unshakeable gaiety, he was a brilliant conversationalist, with no hint of pedantry. He had a huge success at the Salon of 1787, where he presented four paintings.

Rouget de Lisle, Claude Joseph

Born in Lons le Saunier
Aged 27 on January 1st. 1788

Son of a Franche Comtais lawyer, he did brilliantly at literary studies before joining the Academy of Engineering at Mézières, where he left as a second in command Lieutenant in 1784. He then moved to the garrison of Grenoble. He used the long evenings to write pieces for the theatre; he also wrote romances, a field in which he excelled.

Talma, François Joseph

Born in Paris
Aged 24 on January 1st. 1788

This young actor, a former student of Fleury and Dugazon, had his beginnings at the Théâtre de la Comédie Française in *Mahomet* by Voltaire. His efforts to be realistic, his simple and natural diction, broke with the usual pomposity of tragedians of days gone by. He said the verse without any pretence of declamation. Talma had a superb head, a noble and expressive face, sombre blue eyes, and was tall, but slightly bowlegged. His bass voice predisposed him to dramatic works.

Vigée Lebrun, Marie Louise Elisabeth Vigée, Mme.

Born in Paris
Aged 32 on January 1st. 1788

She was only received into the Academy in 1783, but as early as 1779 she was already the official painter of the Queen, of whom she made more than 20 likenesses. The last of these portraits, which represented the Queen surrounded by her children, was much appreciated by the King who complimented her on the work. Even so the favours that she enjoyed caused hostility, and tongues wagged over a supposed liaison with Calonne. It was true that Mme. Vigée Lebrun did not get on with her husband, a rich seller of paintings, a man much older than her. They each led, separately, a life of fashion and high society.

Wailly, Charles de

Born in Paris
Aged 58 on January 1st. 1788

He first gained renown when he built the castle of Montmusard, near Dijon. A tireless worker, he devoted all of his life to architecture, accumulating honours and prestigious orders in both France and foreign countries. His masterpiece was the theatre of the Odéon, or the new Comédie Française, where the inauguration took place on April 9th. 1782. A modest and generous man, when he won the Prix de Rome he shared the three year stay with the candidate who had failed, the painter Moreau Desproux.

"Actors" and witnesses of the Revolution

A literary salon, one of Paris' favourite meeting places.

Beaumarchais.

Bernardin de Saint Pierre.

Beaumarchais, Pierre Augustin Caron de

Born in Paris
Aged 55 on January 1st. 1788

In April 1784 there was a great scandal surrounding Beaumarchais because of the first performances of *The Marriage of Figaro* by the actors of the Comédie Française. Following this he was jailed at the Saint Lazare prison for five days, and then the King ordered a performance of the opera at the Trianon, Marie Antoinette taking the part of Rosina and the Comte d'Artois the part of Figaro. From then on Beaumarchais could do as he liked, although, in fact, from when he left his job as a clock maker, he had always done as he pleased. He had been harpist to the daughters of Louis XV, a financier with the banker Paris Duverney, an arms dealer to the American rebels and a secret agent in England. He was also involved in colonial exploitation and the slave trade; in addition he was a shareholder in the water company. He got mixed up with all manner of things with a tireless passion. Women adored him because he was a tall and very handsome man.

Bernardin de Saint Pierre, Jacques Henri

Born in Le Havre
Aged 50 on January 1st. 1788

From the time of it's publication in 1787, his novel *Paul et Virginie* enjoyed a tremendous success. After many troubled years, which finished by making Bernadin de Saint Pierre as much of a misanthrope as his friend Rousseau, at last he tasted glory to such an extent that he almost complained about it; he received so much correspondence from all over Europe that he had to pay in one year nearly 2,000 francs in postage. Nobody before him had spoken of nature with such charm and eloquence. The former civil engineer had had a passion for botany since his youth. A great lover of women, Bernadin de Saint Pierre had many love affairs before marrying the daughter of the printer Didot, whom he made miserable. A demanding man for others, he was also intransigent with himself and was thus never satisfied: apparently he started the first page of his book 14 times.

Cabanis, Pierre Georges

Born in Cosnac
Aged 30 on January 1st. 1788

After passing a few years in Poland as secretary to the Prince Bishop of Wilno, Cabanis studied medicine but did not practise because he believed himself to be a poet. The influence of his father, a legal expert, gave him the entry into all the great literary salons. In 1778 he ended up living at Auteuil with Mme. Helvetius, the rich, beautiful widow of a philosopher farmer general. She had a crush on the subtle, but sickly, young man, who resembled one of her dead sons, and she smothered him with maternal love. At her house, Cabanis met everyone who mattered in Paris in arts and letters.

Cazotte, Jacques

Born in Dijon
Aged 68 on January 1st. 1788

Cazotte stayed for a long time in Martinique, where he was Controller of the Leeward Islands; he even opened fire on the English in 1759. That did not stop him from being a very cultivated man. The best of his fantastic stories was *Le Diable Amoureux,* published in 1772. After that he drifted into theosophy and lived, retired, at Epernay. He was an eccentric man, but lovable and generous; his conversation, studded with anecdotes, was an enchantment.

Chamfort, Sébastien, *real name* Roch Nicolas

Born in Clermont Ferrand
Aged 47 on January 1st. 1788

From humble origins, he gave himself the name of his place of birth in order to cut a fine figure in the world. Reader to the Comte d'Artois, he became secretary to Mme. Elisabeth. He was no longer the good-looking man, full of vigour, who had made so many conquests. His work became sombre and his wit, in the *Maximes,* sharp and biting.

Chénier, André de

Born in Constantinople
Aged 25 on January 1, 1788

The young poet was appointed in 1787 secretary to the Ambassador to London. He had no personal fortune, but came from a good family. His father had been a commercial agent to the ports of the Levant. His mother, of Greek origin, claimed descent from the Princes of Lusignan. He had not yet published, but his friends had faith in his talent. Obsessed by the ancient authors, it was said of him that he wanted to be the Lucretius of the century.

Chénier, Marie Joseph de

Born in Constantinople
Aged 23 on January 1st. 1788

More seductive than his elder brother André, he was no less enthusiastic about literature. Thanks to the support of the authors who came to their mother's salon, he was in 1783 able to get the Comédie Française to perform his play, *Edgar ou le Pape supposé.* The play was a flop. In 1785, his tragedy *Azémire* was performed at court and later in Paris. It too was not successful. The author was only aged 23 at the time.

Fabre d'Eglantine, *real name* Philippe François Fabre

Born in Limoux
Aged 32 on January 1st. 1788

He was the author of the famous song *Il Pleut, Il Pleut Bergère* in 1782. A poet and musician, a sad love affair made him an actor. He acted in the provinces, but settled in Paris where he staged, without success, one of his works, *Les Gens de Lettres.* His attractive name had its origin in the wild rose of gold, won

An author with his books.

André de Chénier.

Choderlos de Laclos.

Restif de La Bretonne.

at the floral games of Toulouse in 1775. An extremely seductive young man, he broke many hearts.

Florian, Jean Pierre Claris de

Born in Sauve
Aged 32 on January 1st. 1788

A protégé of Voltaire, his novel *Galatée,* published in 1783, classed him in the ranks of the pastoral authors. He had followed in the footsteps of his father, a noble officer of the Cevennes region, and served in the dragoons of the Duc de Penthièvre. Then he left the army and became secretary to the Duc. He assisted him in charitable works, living at Anet and at Sceaux, where he was very popular. He dreamt of joining the French Academy.

Laclos, Pierre Choderlos de

Born in Amiens
Aged 46 on January 1st. 1788

This modest captain in the army's corps of engineers unleashed yet another major scandal in 1786 when he married his mistress, Marie Duperré, after she had born him a child. In 1782 Laclos' novel *Les Liaisons Dangereuses,* in which the author bitterly criticised high society, had burst upon the literary scene like a bomb. People saw him as a dissolute man, although his sometimes unconventional behaviour was always marked by great dignity. The Minister of War, who was somewhat irritated by his literary fame, had him sent off to an obscure garrison at

Toul, where Laclos was bored and spent much of his time thinking about leaving the army.

Louvet de Couvray
real name **Jean Baptiste Louvet**

Born in Paris
Aged 27 on January 1st. 1788

He did not resemble the hero of *Chevalier de Faublas,* the adventures of whom he published in 1787. Small, bald, shortsighted, with an unhealthy complexion, this modest son of a paper manufacturer was, however, the hero of his own love story. He adored the wife of an old jeweller at the Palais Royal, Marguerite Cholet, who reciprocated. He even made her the heroine of his novel under the name of Lodoïska. In fact, he wrote the risqué novel, drawing inspiration from the works he sold as a book seller, in the hope of one day enticing his mistress away from her husband.

Mercier, Louis Sébastien

Born in Paris
Aged 47 on January 1st. 1788

The first two volumes of his *Tableau de Paris* were published in 1781 and had a considerable success. It was a work that evoked the daily life of Parisians and it was a sensation. However, it did not please the censor and Mercier was forced to seek refuge in Switzerland to write the rest. He missed Paris, the philosophical dinners with his friend, the poet-gastronomer Grimod de La

Reynière, and the evenings at the Palais Royal in the company of Restif de La Bretonne. He became extremely depressed and had bizarre ideas. In 1770, in *L'An 2440, Rêve s'il en Fût Jamais,* he thought that it was already possible to change the world one day.

Restif de La Bretonne,
real name **Nicolas Edme Rétif**

Born in Sacy
Aged 53 on January 1st. 1788

Restif often walked at night in the sector of Saint Denis, wrapped in a dirty black coat with frayed cuffs. Known as the "night owl", he wrote a work entitled *Nights of Paris.* He was of average size, but well-built; he had large eyes, and strong features with bushy eyebrows. He was a former typographer, the son of a well-off labourer, and was the author of many moralistic novels, such as *Le Paysan Perverti* (*The Perverted Peasant*) in 1775, followed by *La Paysanne Pervertie* (*The Perverted Peasant Girl*) in 1784. He wrote in bed all day and only ventured out at dusk to seek the raw material for his work in the streets of the capital. A disciple of Rousseau, he too dreamed of reforming man and undertook a series of curious works in which he proposed the transformation of morals, education, theatre and, amongst other things, spelling. However, he suffered from a particularly bad reputation; he was suspected of being a police spy and even a pimp because he was regularly seen in red-light areas and often frequented prostitutes.

Sade, Donatien Alphonse François, Marquis de

Born in Paris
Aged 47 on January 1st. 1788

The lively officer became a fat, greying man, somewhat bald, bent over a stick. He was reduced to this sorry state after having passed many years in jail for sodomy and "exaggerated debauchery". Because he had tarnished the family name with so many scandals, his mother-in-law, the Presidente de Montreuil, managed to obtain a Sealed Royal order against him in 1777. Even so, his wife Renée Pélagie, a sweet and virtuous person, always forgave him his many escapades and took loving care of him. She took snacks and, above all, books, which he devoured, to the Bastille prison to where he had been transferred in February 1784. He had spent the previous five years as a prisoner in the dungeon of Vincennes. He spent long hours writing, but his wife refused to place certain of his more obscene works with a publisher.

Volney, Constantin François de Chasseboeuf, Comte de

Born in Craon
Aged 30 on January 1st. 1788

His book *Voyage en Egypte et en Syrie* met with interest in 1787. Syria was a country that he had visited on foot, his bag on his back. His solitary travellings had not made him a savage; on the contrary, he was very assiduous at the homes of Baron d'Holbach and Mme. Helvetius.

23

"Actors" and witnesses of the Revolution

Chappe.

Condorcet.

Doctor Guillotin.

Bailly, Jean Sylvain

Born in Paris
Aged 51 on January 1st. 1788

This erudite man was famous throughout Europe for a monumental *Histoire de l'Astronomie Ancienne* in 1775 and *Moderne* from 1778 to 1783. He was a tall, thin man with a long nose, dark-skinned with an air of severity. He talked very little. If he was cold, he nonetheless had all the qualities of the heart, modesty, tolerance and goodness. In 1786 he married an elegant and beautiful widow, a friend of his mother. He lived at Chaillot and walked every day in the Bois de Boulogne, as he liked to reflect in the open air. A member of the Science Academy in 1763, he was also a French Academician in 1783.

Berthollet, Charles Louis

Born in Talloires
Aged 39 on January 1st. 1788

The son of a Swiss lawyer, this Savoyard studied at Turin and then became a naturalised French citizen in late 1787. A doctor, he was mostly interested in chemistry. In the year 1784, his *Treatise on Dyes* earned him the directorship of the Royal (carpet) Factory of the Gobelins. As a chemist, Charles Louis Berthollet was, at first, opposed to Lavoisier in the long-running argument over the vexing phlogistic question centred on the debate on the theory of combustion. However, Berthollet admitted his error in 1785 and they were reconciled.

Chappe, Claude

Born in Brûlon
Aged 24 on January 1st. 1788

As a child he had admired an astronomer uncle, who, in 1761, had travelled to Siberia to observe the passage of Venus in front of the sun. At the age of 20, Chappe was already a contributor to the *Journal of Physics*. He worked on perfecting a machine that, using pulleys and levers, would enable him to communicate with his friends who lived far away. He gave this ingenious device the name *télégraphe*.

Condorcet, Marie Jean Antoine de Caritat, Marquis de

Born in Ribémont
Aged 44 on January 1st. 1788

He was a child prodigy in science. Despite the military tradition of the family, he preferred to imitate his uncle Condillac. In 1765, he was the author of an *Essay on Integral Calculus* and quickly became a mathematician of European renown. After entering the Academy of Sciences in 1769, he was appointed secretary in perpetuity for a period of 30 years. Above all, his main preoccupation was the public good. An advisor of Turgot, from 1774 to 1776 he immersed himself in reform projects. From then on, he became fascinated by politics he fiercely defended Protestants, black slaves, women and the oppressed because of a strong belief in the progress of humanity. He had no religious faith, even though his mother

had dedicated him to the Virgin and dressed him in blue for ten years. Of a cold temperament, he remained unmarried for a long time; he even had a sad love affair. It was, therefore, surprising that, in 1778, he married, for love, Mademoiselle de Grouchy, 20 years his junior.

Fourcroy, Antoine François de

Born in Paris
Aged 32 on January 1st. 1788

This chemist was the star of the public school at the Palais Royal which had been founded by the brothers of the King. His beautiful voice and the elegance of his phrases fascinated everybody. Son of the apothecary to the Duc d'Orléans, he had a difficult start and talked of it gaily: "I never lacked for water!" evoked the time when he took care of his neighbour, a water-carrier. In order to pursue his studies, he became a transcriber and gave lessons. From 1784, he held the chair of chemist at the King's Garden. In 1787, along with Lavoisier, Berthollet and Guyton de Morveau, he contributed to the recognition of chemistry as a rational science.

Guillotin, Joseph Ignace

Born in Saintes
Aged 49 on January 1st. 1788

In 1784, Doctor Guillotin was part of a royal commission that included Franklin and Bailly; they examined the experiments of Mesmer on magnetism. He was, like his col-

leagues, very reserved in his judgement of phenomena. The son of a lawyer from the Gironde, he at first contemplated becoming a Jesuit priest, but abandoned this idea and became a doctor instead. In 1768, after defending his thesis at Reims, he became chief doctor at the faculty of Paris. He was a philanthropist, completely devoted to the suffering of humanity. Thus he strove to make the execution of criminals less barbaric.

Guyton Morveau, Louis Bernard

Born in Dijon
Aged 50 on January 1st. 1788

The son of a renowned legal professor of Dijon and himself an eminent jurist, having been appointed advocate general to the parliament of Dijon, he became interested in chemistry and finally, in 1782, gave up his work so as to devote himself entirely to it. A wealthy man, the installation of his laboratory was carried out at his own expense and visitors much admired it. Louis Guyton was renowned in Europe for his discovery, in 1773, of a new disinfection procedure and also for a masterpiece of an article about acid which appeared in one of the supplements to the *Encyclopaedia*. He had a lot of correspondence with foreigners. Guyton was an affable man, eloquent and interested in everything. In 1787, with Berthollet, Fourcroy and Lavoisier, he contributed to the *Method of Chemical Nomenclature* which broke with the language of rigmarole of the alchemists.

Monge.

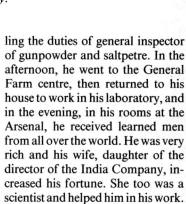

The chemist Lavoisier in his laboratory.

Hauy, Valentin

Born in Saint Just en Chaussée
Aged 42 on January 1st. 1788

At first he studied calligraphy and was a translator of coded correspondence at the Ministry of Foreign Affairs. There he met a blind pianist who read the notes of music by using pins on cards. It was this that gave him the idea for his *Essay on the Education of the Blind* in 1786, in which he proposed the method of raised writing that he had invented. In 1784, the Philanthropic Society had given him 12 pupils and he founded a small school in the rue Notre Dame des Victoires. In 1786, he held a demonstration of his methods at Versailles which aroused the interest of the King and the Court.

Jussieu, Antoine Laurent de

Born in Lyons
Aged 39 on January 1st. 1788

He became a botanist quite by chance, even though it was a family tradition. He was destined for a career in medicine when, at the age of 17, he went to Paris and lived with his uncle Bernard. The latter, who was by then old and nearly blind, had been in charge of replanting the garden of the Trianon in 1759, under Louis XV. He spoke only of plants to his nephew, and when he became incapable of carrying out his duties as professor at the Garden of the King, Jussieu became his successor. Since he knew nothing about botany, he studied the day before what he would teach the next day. This did not stop him from writing a work on the classification of plants that was renowned throughout Europe.

Lagrange, Joseph Louis

Born in Turin
Aged 51 on January 1st. 1788

This illustrious mathematician was called to Paris by Louis XVI after a 20 year stay in Berlin from 1766 to 1786. There he had succeeded Euler at the Academy of Sciences. Even though he was born in Turin, he was from a family related to Descartes. He had original ideas about everything. He refused to have his portrait painted because he felt that only ideas should be immortalised. He had fixations: he ate no meat, did gymnastics in the open air, and established a rigorous schedule for himself from which he never deviated. Every day he did the same thing at the same hour. A man of fragile health, he lived in seclusion in his apartment at the Louvre. He was a modest man who was not ashamed to say "I don't know". He prepared the publication of *Analytical Mechanics*.

Laplace, Pierre Simon

Born in Beaumont sur Auge
Aged 38 on January 1st. 1788

He was born into a poor agricultural family in the Auge valley. After intense study at the Benedictine college at Caen, he left for Paris and tried, without success, to meet d'Alembert. The next day, Laplace sent him such a brilliant letter concerning the general principles of mechanics that the learned man received him without hesitation. In 1769, at the age of 20, with the help of d'Alembert, he became a professor of mathematics at the Military Academy. He sent at least one memo a month to the Academy of Sciences about the most difficult subjects, such as celestial mechanics and the calculation of probabilities. The Academicians were impressed by the cleverness and working speed of such a young man and they elected him a member in 1783. He was not an easy writer to understand and he dismayed all those who attempted to rework his reasoning.

Lavoisier, Antoine Laurent de

Born in Paris
Aged 44 on January 1st. 1788

He was knowledgeable about all subjects, but it was chemistry which made him famous with his discovery in 1783 of the composition of water. The son of a rich merchant, he was a pupil of Rouelle and of Bernard de Jussieu. He multiplied his activities with an extraordinary capacity for work. He was only 25 when, in 1768, the Academy of Sciences made him a member. He ruined himself financially in order to conduct experiments with new agronomical techniques. He was an expert in public finance; he subscribed in 1779 to the lease of the General Farm's tax drive. A philanthropist, he prepared hospital reform. He had a heavy work load; he got up at dawn and spent the morning fulfilling the duties of general inspector of gunpowder and saltpetre. In the afternoon, he went to the General Farm centre, then returned to his house to work in his laboratory, and in the evening, in his rooms at the Arsenal, he received learned men from all over the world. He was very rich and his wife, daughter of the director of the India Company, increased his fortune. She too was a scientist and helped him in his work.

Monge, Gaspard

Born in Beaune
Aged 41 on January 1st. 1788

While at the college of the Oratorians of Beaune, he was already outstanding. He entered the School of Engineering at Mézières on the strength of his remarkable diagram of his native village. The son of a modest travelling pedlar, he was therefore not admitted into the officers' section, which was reserved exclusively for the nobility, but to the section of builders and outfitters, just good enough to form non-commissioned officers and foremen. Despite this handicap, his talent attracted attention and, in 1780, Turgot summoned him to Paris to teach hydrodynamics. He was extremely popular among his students because of his very lively courses. In addition he often took them for long walks in the country and, when he spoke to them, nothing could interrupt him, not even streams that he crossed whilst continuing to expound. Physically, he resembled a bear, but morally, he was all gentleness and honesty.

"Actors" and witnesses of the revolution

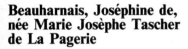

A festival at the Coliseum, near Lille.

Charlotte Corday.

Lucile Desmoulins.

Beauharnais, Joséphine de, née Marie Josèphe Tascher de La Pagerie

Born in Trois Ilets, Martinique
Aged 24 on January 1st. 1788

She came from a family that had lived in Martinique for 50 years; her father was a naval officer and a rich planter. At 16 she married an infantry officer, the Vicomte Alexandre de Beauharnais, but they did not get on very well. She found him pretentious, while he reproached her frivolity. Despite the birth of two children, Eugène in 1781, and Hortense in 1783, they frequently had extramarital affairs and subsequently separated. Joséphine was extremely attractive, with the easy, nonchalant grace of a Créole; she had the reputation of being "fast".

Cabarrus, Thérésa

Born in Carabanchel, Spain
Aged 14 on January 1st. 1788

She was a precocious child; at the age of 11, she was so seductive that her uncle, madly in love with her, wanted to marry her. François, her father, was a rich banker of French origin, but a naturalised Spaniard; the founder of the Saint Charles Bank, he sent his daughter to Paris. She made new conquests, especially among financiers. She married in haste the Marquis Jean Jacques Davis de Fontenay, aged 26, a councillor at the Parliament of Bordeaux. With her superb skin, jet-black hair and beautifully shaped body she was the centre of attention.

Condorcet, Marie Louise Sophie, Marquise de, née de Grouchy

Born at the Château Villette
Aged 23 on January 1st. 1788

Shortly after her marriage in December 1786 she opened a salon at the Quai de Conti, at the *Hôtel des Monnaies,* of which her husband was the director. This literary group was to become the "centre of an enlightened Europe". Many foreigners participated, above all the English, since she spoke their language fluently. Grouchette, her nickname derived from her maiden name, was a complete unbeliever. She was self taught, having listened to the tutors of her brothers and, above all, having read the Encyclopaedias during her stay at the convent of Neuville, where she was a canoness for two years. She was essentially a good person, as was her husband; it was when he saw her tending a rabid child that he fell in love with her. Physically, she was like an angel. She was as thin and ethereal as the Marquis was lumpish, but they were equally seductive in the force of their spirit.

Corday d'Armont, Charlotte

Born in Saint Saturnin des Ligneries
Aged 19 on January 1st. 1788

She was a descendant of the tragedian Pierre Corneille and had a strong character, in contrast with her gentle and self-effacing appearance. She was from a noble, if poor family and lived with an aged aunt, rarely seeing people. She was beautiful, but cared nothing for her looks. She devoted herself entirely to pious pursuits and to the reading of Plutarch, Tacitus and Rousseau. There were no apparent plans for her to marry.

Desmoulins, Lucile, née Anne Louise Duplessis Laridon

Born in Paris
Aged 17 on January 1st. 1788

She was an adorable brown-eyed blonde, small, with a fine face and a mutinous air. She was passionately in love with a half-starved looking young man, Camille Desmoulins, who was a frequent visitor to her mother's salon. He was hardly seductive, with a bilious air, hard eyes and hollow cheeks. A lawyer, he argued mostly in the cafés of the Palais Royal in addition he stammered. To make fun of him, Lucile called him "Monsieur Ha Ha". He returned her love and asked for her hand in marriage, but her parents would not consider it. M. Duplessis, a financier, wanted a son-in-law with a secure future and Mme. Duplessis was cautious of this man who had flirted with her before falling in love with her daughter.

Genlis, Stéphanie Félicité du Crest, Comtesse de

Born in Champcéri
Aged 41 on January 1st. 1788

This admirer of the authors of the Encyclopaedias knew everything about everything, science, the arts and technical matters. She spoke several foreign languages and knew how to calculate and how to garden; no-one wrote with more ease or more quickly and her playing of the harp was compared with King David's. Despite this, people did not find her pedantic because she was beautiful and spoke with such grace. As maid of honour to the Duchesse de Chartres in 1770, she wasted no time in becoming the mistress of the Duc, who subsequently became the Duc d'Orléans. Their passion was muted by friendship and in 1782 he appointed her "governess" of his sons. She brought them up with "ferocity": between study and practical work, they did not have a spare moment; she was inspired by the ideas of Rousseau concerning education. The children adored her. They had a pretty class companion in a little girl named Pamela, who was rumoured to be the bastard of the Duc and the governess.

Gouges, Olympe de, *real name* Marie Gouze

Born in Montauban
Aged 39 on January 1st. 1788

This tall woman, who was considered to have been one of the beauties of Paris, always wore ruffled muslin on her head, giving her a strange appearance. She believed herself to be an author of drama, and laid siege to the Comédie Française because they refused to perform her work. She wrote a lot, and talked even more, but she had generous ideas about improving the lot of women and black slaves.

Madame Roland.

Madame de Staël.

Women at work in a textile factory.

Kéralio, Louise Félicité de

Born in Paris
Aged 29 on January 1st. 1788

She was still single at the age of 30 because she thought of nothing but literature. From a noble Breton family, her father had, together with Condillac, been tutor to the Prince of Parma, then professor at the Military Academy. Both he and her mother were the authors of numerous works. She followed the family tradition and wrote her first novel, *Adélaïde*, at the age of 18. She translated many English and Italian authors and worked with difficulty for ten years on the *History of Elizabeth of England*. She was a member of both the Academy of Arras and the patriotic Breton Society. All this did not mean that she neglected female vanity; she wore make-up and at times feathers in her hair. She was small, rather spiritual and extremely talkative.

Lacombe, Claire *alias* Rose

Born in Pamiers
Aged 22 on January 1st. 1788

An actress, she appeared in provincial productions, mostly in southern France. She lived in Marseilles, in the Rue Rameau. She was talented and liked by the public. However, her clear-cut opinions, her critical spirit and her liberal opinions did not help her career. She was surrounded by women whom she dominated by her size, majestic beauty, proud look and dictatorial tone. She was generous in friendship.

Palm, Etta Lubina Johanna, Baronne d'Aelders

Born in Groningen
Aged 44 on January 1st. 1788

She was an imaginary baroness. Her husband, Ferdinand Palm, a student whom she had married at the age of 19, left for the Indies without leaving an address and never returned. She thought of living in Palermo with her lover, a lawyer, who had been appointed Consul there. However, whilst in Paris, she enjoyed herself so much that she stayed. She lived in the Rue Favart. Her own personal situation led her to a natural interest in the problems of divorce and of women's rights; she was militant about these issues, and was frequently to be seen in the society of thinkers.

Roland de La Platière, Manon, *née* Phlipon, *alias* Mme. Roland

Born in Paris
Aged 33 on January 1st. 1788

When Manon Phlipon, the daughter of a modest Parisian engraver, married, in February 1780, Roland de la Platière, who was aged 48, she herself was only aged 26. After the nomination of her husband to Lyons as an inspector of factories, the couple divided their time between Lyons and the family residence of La Platière, two leagues from Villefranche. Manon was a really erudite woman; as a devout disciple of Rousseau, she strongly believed that women should perfect themselves in order to insure the perfection of so-

ciety. She also made fun of the successful romanciers of the day and dedicated herself to collaborating in her husband's work. A serious soul, coupled with a strong character, the wise Manon despised frivolity, was proud to wear neither jewels nor extravagant hair styles, and voraciously read Plutarch. A very pretty woman, she had large black eyes and beautiful curly hair which she wore on her shoulders. She had a great series of admirers but, nonetheless, she stayed resolutely faithful to her husband, for whom she bore a great love. She adopted all the new ideas with lively enthusiasm and closely followed the events of the day.

Staël Holstein, Germaine, *née* Necker, Baronne de

Born in Paris
Aged 21 on January 1st. 1788

In December 1786 she married Baron Erik de Staël Holstein. The negotiations had been laborious because the young man, coming from an old Swedish family, was without fortune. The Neckers agreed to the marriage of their daughter on condition that Staël Holstein be appointed Ambassador to Paris. The young woman's presentation at Court was marred by a slight incident: she tore her dress, which was seen by some as either clumsiness or timidity. This was a total misreading of the young Baroness, who soon demonstrated an incredible self-assurance. Germaine was ugly, with a somewhat masculine appearance. She had opinions about every-

thing, got involved in things that did not concern her and committed blunders that worried the Swedish diplomats. Of an extraordinary intelligence, an amazing erudition, she held conversations that bordered on the prodigious. At the age of 15 she had written a commentary on the *Esprit des Lois* by Montesquieu. She was, in fact, very well aware of her talent, her parents having reared her as a prodigy. She returned their admiration; her love for her father was practically a religious cult. In contrast, her husband was a cold and cautious man, and the young couple did not get on. It occurred to Germaine to wonder if she would not have done better to have married William Pitt, the son of an English minister, as had been proposed.

Théroigne, de Méricourt, Anne *real name* Josèphe Terwagne

Born at Marcourt, Belgium
Aged 25 on January 1st. 1788

Her father was a wealthy grower from Wallonia, but she fled from the family home to escape from an unkind step-mother. Extremely small, she had a pretty little face, but irregular features, a burnished tint to her skin and a mass of brown hair, which did nothing but add to her charm. She was often to be seen at the Opéra, dripping with diamonds, with the Marquis de Persan. Apparently, she went out of her way to ruin as many important men as possible in order to avenge herself on her first lover, an aristocrat who had promised to marry her and who had then abandoned her.

"Actors" and witnesses of the Revolution

Barère de Vieuzac.

The Hôtel de Ville courtyard, headquarters of the provost of merchants.

Amar, Jean Baptiste

Born in Grenoble
Aged 32 on January 1st. 1788

A lawyer at the parliament of Grenoble, he was the son of a former director of the Mint and belonged to a rich bourgeois family. This gave him the opportunity, in 1786, to acquire for the price of 200,000 francs the sinecure as the treasurer of France for the tax region of the Dauphiné. After a rather stormy youth when he was always surrounded by pretty girls, he grew older and wiser and seemed to be very attached to his wife. He had a starched air, his manner was cautious and his speech soft and insidious. In spite of all his efforts, he did not manage to be appealing to those who met him.

Antraigues, Alexandre de Launay, Comte d'

Born in Antraigues
Aged 33 on January 1st. 1788

In his castle, set back from the Bastide, surrounded by a harsh backdrop of volcanic mountains, this landowner from birth wrote an explosive work about the political situation of the country. He led the life of a hermit, cultivated his garden and re-read Rousseau, but his background was that of an adventurer. Bodyguard at the age of 14, then a captain of cavalry, he was already considered strong-willed. Ill-intentioned people caused his retirement from the army in order to back out of a duel. He then left for the East in the company of his uncle, the

Ambassador to Turkey. Upon his return to France, he became interested in science. For a long time he had a relationship with an opera singer, the famous Saint Huberty, who had so often triumphed in the operas of Gluck. She was not very young, she had a difficult character and, while she dominated him, she called her lover the "badly-licked bear"

Babeuf, François Noël

Born in Saint Quentin
Aged 27 on January 1st. 1788

Poverty and bad luck were his lot. He himself said that he was "born in the mire". The eldest of 13 children of a modest exciseman, he taught himself and, proud of his beautiful handwriting, dreamt of "a place to write". He found his way as an expert in feudal law, and this inspired in him a passion for equality and the defence of the oppressed. His relations with his clients deteriorated, which, in turn, didn't help business; he wrote numerous reports defending his ideas. He married for love a former chambermaid. When his daughter died at the age of six, he was completely distraught.

Barbaroux, Charles Jean Marie

Born in Marseilles
Aged 20 on January 1st. 1788

Men saw him a fat, red figure, while women saw him as a Greek shepherd. It was true that he had large, black eyes, tanned skin, a

straight nose and a mass of black hair, but plumpness dogged him. He was a warm-hearted man of the south and a lover of the good life, whose voice seemed to be dedicated to eloquence. In fact, he was destined to use it at the Bar because he opened a lawyer's office. Passionately interested in physics, he could also be described as a man of science. He wrote a treatise about volcanos, corresponded with Benjamin Franklin and even boasted that he had personally discovered deposits of copper.

Barère de Vieuzac, Bertrand

Born in Tarbes
Aged 32 on January 1st. 1788

Barère de Vieuzac was a great speaker. He also wrote with the same prodigious ease. A perfect man of the world, he was liked in the provincial salons because of his courteous manners, his vivacious character and his well-bred attitude. Evil tongues wagged that he was a bootlicker; he adapted to any kind of company, giving the impression of knowing everything and of being capable of filling any function. Maybe, he had no original ideas, but he marvellously mirrored those of others, especially, as a typical Gascon, he knew how to use his warm and persuasive voice. If his character was weak, his intelligence and general culture were really out of the ordinary. The son of a magistrate, he was a lawyer at the Parliament of Toulouse and councillor at the seneschalsy of Bigorre. He considered standing at the convening of

the Estates General. His wife, who was a devout woman and a royalist, had made him promise to defend the King and religion.

Barnave, Antoine Joseph

Born in Grenoble
Aged 26 on January 1st. 1788

He was a lawyer attached to the bar of Grenoble. He had a tremendous gift of oratory; his voice was not loud, his elocution was at times confused, but he carried his audience with heart-felt improvisations which bore the mark of sincerity. A lawyer at the age of 20, he was always called "little" Barnave because he looked younger than his years. His expressive face and his large mouth with a seductive smile gave him even more juvenile charm. He had a lot of influence and was well aware of the unrest in the Dauphiné; he was amongst those who stirred up the quarrel at the Parliament. His Protestant family was rich and well thought of; his mother was a noble. Very early on, he believed in the new ideas of the day and revolted against the privileges that his birth had conferred upon him. He spoke of this frequently.

Barras, Paul François Jean Nicolas, Vicomte de

Born in Fox Amphoux
Aged 32 on January 1st. 1788

He almost lived in misery, due to a life of dissipation, but he was even more concerned about ruining the

Barnave.

Brissot.

Buzot.

family name. He was a descendant of a very noble family, one of the oldest in Provence. His uncle, Melchior de Barras, had commanded the French naval squadron sent to America. He himself joined the army as a sub-lieutenant in the Languedoc regiment at the age of 19. He left for the Indies and took part in the siege of Pondicherry as a captain. After that he saw action at sea, in a naval battle with the fleet of Suffren de Saint Tropez. An active, brave and generous man, he had a lot of adventures, including a shipwreck, from which he saved himself by building a raft. Unfortunately, his taste for pleasure and his disputes with the Maréchal de Castries, Minister of the Navy, forced him to resign. On his return to Paris it took him little time to spend all of his fortune. His reputation suffered; it was commonly assumed that he had been a croupier in a gambling-den. His future wife lived in seclusion in Provence.

Basire, Claude

Born in Dijon
Aged 23 on January 1st. 1788

The son of an honourable merchant from the Côte d'Or, he was brought up by the Oratorians, which gave him a vocation for the priesthood. He changed his mind and chose law and finally decided to become a lawyer. Unfortunately he was forced to interrupt his studies, and contented himself with a job as an archival clerk with the estates of Burgundy. He was somewhat bitter, since he was an ardent and generous

young man, with, sometimes, fits of violence. He had an energetic nature, which needed an outlet, but he was too fond of pleasure.

Billaud Varenne Jacques, *real name* Nicolas Billaud

Born in La Rochelle
Aged 31 on January 1st. 1788

He was ugly, sallow and sombre, yet he married for love a very pretty girl. She was a rather fat young woman, the daughter of a Farmer General; she helped him to forget his extremely strict upbringing. His father, a lawyer at the presiding headquarters at La Rochelle, was a rough and ready man, whose wife preferred her seductive confessor. As a small boy, Jacques had discovered the portrait of this man: that same evening, he was sent away to Paris as a boarder at the Harcourt College. It was there that he first tasted the delights of the theatre in all its forms, from comedies to tragedies. In 1781 he wrote his first comedy and had it performed at La Rochelle. He was dismissed from the college of the Oratorians, where he was teaching at the time. He was then obliged by his father to go into law, but he did not want to be in the town of his birth, where he had been booed. In 1785 he went to seek his fortune in Paris. Once there, he worked as a clerk in the office of a lawyer named Danton, who had his practice in the Rue du Commerce. Above all, Jacques concentrated on writing an essay, *The Last Blow to Prejudices and Superstitions,* which he signed Billaud Varenne, thereby

adding to his name the name of a village near La Rochelle, where his father had a farm.

Boissy d'Anglas, François Antoine

Born in Saint Jean Chambre
Aged 31 on January 1st. 1788

From 1785 he was the majordomo of the household of Monsieur, the brother of the King. He shared his taste for literature and science. He was very close to the Montgolfier brothers and collaborated in their research. He wrote an essay entitled *On the Advantages for Commerce of Balloons,* in particular for the transport of fragile products such as mirrors and wall-paper. Before he had bought his job, he had been a lawyer at the parliament of Paris. He was clever at spreading himself through all levels of society. From a Protestant family, he had friends in that religion.

Bonaparte, Lucien

Born in Ajaccio
Aged 12 on January 1st. 1788

This young, short-sighted boy had delicate health. He was remarkably intelligent and seemed to be destined for a career in the Church. He tried soldiering at the Military Academy of Brienne, which he had entered in 1784, following the example of his elder brother, Napoléon. He was then admitted to the seminary of Aix, but he did not much like it there.

Brissot de Warville, Jacques Pierre

Born in Chartres
Aged 33 on January 1st. 1788

He carried the name of a small family property, Ouarville, of which he anglicised the name in order to follow the fashion. He was a man of many projects, one for each day, that he undertook all at the same time. He made his living, rather badly, as a writer, even though he could have led a comfortable life as a merchant by staying in Chartres near his father, a wealthy hotelier. However, he said himself that he liked glory too "prodigiously". Glory was not always his lot because he was too disorganised. First, he wanted to start a newspaper in London which would have united together the most illustrious writers of Europe, but he only got into debt. Threatened with jail, he returned to France only to wind up in the Bastille, because of an anti-Queen pamphlet that he had published in England. Luckily, he was married to a remarkable woman, Félicité, who was teacher to Mlle. de Chartres and an intimate friend of Mme. de Genlis. Thanks to the influence of the Duc d'Orléans he was freed and got the job, in 1786, of Lieutenant General of the chancellery of that prince.

Buzot, François Nicolas

Born in Evreux
Aged 27 on January 1st. 1788

In his beautiful house at Evreux, in the Rue de la Petite Cité, he led the studious life of a man of the law. ▷

"Actors" and witnesses of the Revolution

Carrier.

Cazalès.

He was married to one of his cousins; she was rather rich, but deformed and 13 years his senior. He was very tall, had a noble, melancholic air and was constantly worried about his elegance, even though he was far from frivolous. In his youth, he deeply mourned the death of a very close friend and he was not known to have had any extramarital relationships. He said of himself: "I will never be a libertine and I have never been licentious in my speech." He loved solitude; he took long walks in the woods with, as his only companion, *The Life of Illustrious Men* - the very people whom he yearned to resemble.

Cambacérès, Jean Jacques Regis de

Born in Montpellier
Aged 34 on January 1st. 1788

In order to follow the tradition of his family, of the ancient nobility, he decided to go into the law. In 1771, however, he gave up the idea at the time of the Maupeou reform, because he did not want to plead before arbitrarily installed judges. In 1774, he succeeded his father as councillor to the accounts court of Montpellier. A single man, without a pronounced taste for women, he is not known to have had any affairs, although he did entertain to perfection and his food had a good reputation. He was a man with an imposing air, who had the habit of speaking with caution in a sonorous voice. His clients were mainly composed of influential men and the nobility of the Languedoc region.

Cambon, Pierre Joseph

Born in Montpellier
Aged 31 on January 1st. 1788

His father, who had made his fortune in the textile business, and more particularly in the manufacture of turkey-red cotton, took his retirement in 1784 in order to devote himself to public affairs. He left 50,000 francs to each of his four sons, who had succeeded him in his business. The eldest son, Joseph, who was amazingly gifted in finance, took charge of the accounts. He was a real work-horse. His reputation for probity was only equalled by that of his austerity; this was because he derived no pleasure from the normal pursuits of his age.

Carnot, Lazare Nicolas

Born in Nolay
Aged 34 on January 1st. 1788

His admission in 1787 to the Academy of Arras, of which Robespierre was the director, prevented him from being bored in the small provincial garrison, where he was billeted as an engineering officer from 1780. He mixed with good society and wrote verse in an attempt to forget his love affair with a young aristocrat from Dijon. He had been rejected on the pretext that he was a commoner. All of his genealogical research in order to try to find a link with nobility were in vain. On top of that, he had no hope of promotion since he had been appointed captain, by seniority, in 1783. He had already had the greatest difficulty in gaining

admittance to the very élite engineering school of Mézières. He was a specialist in fortifications and his *In Praise of Vauban* was very favourably received. However, he was so discouraged that he considered applying for a post in the Leeward Islands.

Carrier, Jean Baptiste

Born in Yolet
Aged 31 on January 1st. 1788

In 1785, in the little town of Aurillac, a new procurator was installed who had returned to the provinces after finishing his law studies in Paris. It was Jean Baptiste Carrier, who was, a few months later, married to the daughter of a local merchant. His practice prospered rapidly because he was active and fought law suits easily; he had inherited the laborious tenacity of his father, a landowning farmer. He was tall, thin and taciturn and, in addition, was a grasping man. His spine was a little bent, rather like that of a wasp. His bronzed skin gave him a sombre air and it was obvious, just from looking at him, that he was full of hatred for the feudal regime. It was also rumoured that he was not at all a temperate man.

Cazalès, Jacques Antoine de

Born in Grenade sur Garonne
Aged 29 on January 1st. 1788

This captain of the Dragoon Regiment of Deux Ponts was the most seductive of men. He was a descend-

ant of one of the most noble families of the Languedoc. His father was counsellor to the parliament of Toulouse, his mother was the daughter of a Knight of Saint Louis and one of his ancestors was the municipal magistrate of Toulouse. His education was rather neglected, as he joined the army at the age of 15, but he caught up for lost time by studying at night, sometimes until dawn. He studied primarily Montesquieu and the English writers of law and politics. He was won over by the principles of a constitutional monarchy of the English type. He was a very independent spirit and proved it by showing his opposition for many months to the reform of Maupeou. He also had a formidable gift for oratory and knew well how to make himself heard.

Chabot, François

Born in Saint Geniez
Aged 41 on January 1st. 1788

The Bishop of Rodez had forbidden him to preach, because his advanced ideas provoked a scandal amongst the congregation and he was considered a debauched priest. It was perhaps the job of his father, a cook in a college, which gave him the idea of becoming a Capuchin, for which he had manifestly no vocation, having a taste for women and being a greedy individual. In fact, he lost his faith whilst practising his ministry; he actually took it upon himself to check personally the sinful reading which his flock confessed to! Thus it was that he read all of the *Encyclopaedias*.

Etienne Clavière.

Georges Couthon.

Voltaire's ashes are transferred.

Chalier, Marie Joseph

Born in Beaulard, Piedmont
Aged 40 on January 1st. 1788

An Italian by birth, he was a passionate man, with a vehement expression. As a man who had travelled a great deal, going as far as Constantinople, he had acquired a violent desire to change the world, which seemed to him to be terrible when compared to ancient civilisation. He had, at first, thought of being a monk, like his teachers, the Dominicans, but he lost his faith. As a needy private tutor, he had the luck to meet a man, a silk dealer, for whom he became the representative. An easier life began, without ever changing his ideal of equality. He lived alone in Lyons except for his housekeeper, whom he had brought back from Italy; she bore the nickname of "magpie". He had built for himself, on the heights of the Croix Rousse, a hermitage in which, far from men, he devoted himself to animals and plants, in a life-style that was worthy of Robinson Crusoe.

Chaumette, Pierre Gaspard

Born in Nevers
Aged 24 on January 1st. 1788

His family, who were shoemakers, dreamed of his entering the Church, but he did not feel that he had the vocation. He obstinately refused and started off by seeking his fortune as a cabin-boy. After only reaching the level of helmsman, he returned to Nevers in order to study science and botany, and also fol-lowed courses in surgery at the hospital. He even did a long voyage in the company of an English doctor, in the capacity of secretary. After that, he became the surgeon of the Brothers of Charity at Moulins. He was small, with rather thick features, wore spectacles and neglected his hair.

Clavière, Etienne

Born in Geneva
Aged 52 on January 1st. 1788

This general administrator of the Life Insurance Company, a very clever financier of Geneva, was also a man of politics. He was forced to leave the country of his birth in 1782, following the revolution of Geneva against the Ancien Regime. The textile trade was not enough for his active and visionary temperament and he became one of the leaders of the democratic party. After the defeat of this faction, he took refuge firstly in Ireland, where he worked, without much success, as a watchmaker and where he hoped to find a small republic for the Geneva refugees. He hoped to reach Paris and so frequent patriotic circles. The writer Brissot was, in fact, an old acquaintance of his, and he proposed sending Clavière to America with the mission of buying land in his name. He was also very close to Mirabeau, who, inspired by him, published *Denunciation of Market Rigging* in 1787. He was said to be of a "ferocious" probity, with an irascible temperament. He was jealous of the successful rise of Necker, his compatriot. He was a very tall man, with a look of fragility; he was very deaf. However, his conversation was well informed because he had read an enormous amount.

Cloots, Jean Baptiste du Val de Grâce, Baron de

Born in Cleves
Aged 32 on January 1st. 1788

He had an immense fortune that he squandered. His father, privy councillor to the King of Prussia, wanted him to have a military career, but Cloots was only interested in the French Encyclopaedists. He arrived in Paris at the age of 21; he already had read the texts and then collaborated on the *Encyclopaedia*. Brought up by the Jesuits, he was an atheist and had convulsions at the name of Jesus Christ. He wanted to found a universal religion and meant it to be preached by an "orator of the human species". To this end he sought a Greek first name; he had a horror of the "barbarous"

Collot d'Herbois, Jean Marie

Born in Paris
Aged 37 on January 1, 1788

D'Herbois was the name that he used as both an actor and a dramatic author, and it could be said that his career was a success. At the age of 30 this actor with a travelling troupe had already written and played in ten successful pieces; in 1787 he became the director of the Carouge theatre in Geneva. He contributed a lot to the modernisation of that theatre, but the job disheartened him because he had difficulties with the actors. In fact, he was extremely irascible and had already been jailed for "violence, insults and threats". As an actor he pleased the public, being gifted with an arresting physique and a beautiful voice. He had a technique which departed from the usual provincial routine, and he improvised with talent. He was a big success in *Ladislas* by Rotrou. He nevertheless remembered being booed at in Lyons.

Couthon, Georges Auguste

Born in Crest
Aged 32 on January 1st. 1788

This young man was completely paralysed and only able to move around on the back of a man or in a wheelchair. It was said at Clermont Ferrand that this handicap was the result of an over-prolonged stay in a swamp, under driving rain, when he was on the way to the home of his fiancée, the daughter of a lieutenant general of the bailiwick. Far from helping the situation, a cure at Mont Doré rendered his affliction worse. Nonetheless, he was a good-looking man with a sweet and amiable character. He was one of the most brilliant lawyers of Clermont Ferrand ; he was a member of the judicial committee of the provincial Assembly of Auvergne and took an active part in it. He had many friends from all walks of life, particularly amongst the liberal aristocrats. He had a tireless willingness and was totally honest; he defended his poorest clients for nothing.

Georges Danton.

Camille Desmoulins.

Adrien Duport.

Danton, Georges Jacques

Born in Arcis sur Aube
Aged 28 on January 1st. 1788

In Paris, at the Café Parnasse, on the Place de l'Ecole, people talked a lot about this young man from the region of Champagne. He lived in the capital from 1785 and was married to Gabrielle, a pretty, brown-haired girl of 25. Danton was not at all handsome. He had more of a muzzle than a face; in his turbulent youth two enraged bulls had attacked him: one had crushed his lip and the other his nose; small-pox had done nothing to add to his allure. Even so, he was pleasing to women because he had character, a stentorian voice and overwhelming vitality. He had wide influence in the sector of the Cordeliers. Thanks to the manoeuvres of his father-in-law and a former mistress he was able to buy, in 1787, the post of lawyer to the King's Council. Thus he pursued the same profession as his father, who had died young, and he was a success early on in business affairs. He specialised in the verification of noble titles and he played upon it shamelessly, inscribing on the door of his office the legend: "Monsieur d'Anton, Lawyer and Doctor of Advice".

Desmoulins, Camille

Born in Guise
Aged 27 on January 1st. 1788

He was obsessed by the idea of having to return empty-handed to his father, the lieutenant general of

the bailiwick of Guise, a town which Desmoulins detested as "the opposite of reason and of philosophy". The people of Guise returned his scorn, he had so exasperated them with his subversive blusterings. A friend of Robespierre at the school of Louis le Grand in Paris, he enrolled, in 1785, at the bar of Paris. Despite his lively intelligence, he rarely had clients and he stammered. He only gave rein to his eloquence at the Palais Royal, where he spouted all day long and most of the night because he did not relish the thought of his miserable garret. His dream was to be a great poet and he did have great talent as a writer. For some time he was in love with a beautiful woman, Mme. Duplessis, the wife of a financial clerk, but she was virtuous and did not yield to the poorlooking supplicant, yellow and thin with straight hair and a black fringe. She accepted him as a friend of the family. He consoled himself by falling in love with her daughter.

Drouet, Jean Baptiste

Born in Sainte Menehould
Aged 24 on January 1st. 1788

Drouet returned to the small town of his birth after having served his time in the army. The son of a wood seller, he signed up at the age of 18 with the dragoons of Condé. He looked after his land and succeeded his father as postmaster. Drouet was an energetic young man. He was a partisan of the idea of the need for radical change in society; he was a good patriot, and, more than that, completely objective.

Dubois Crancé, Edmond

Born in Charleville
Aged 40 on January 1st. 1788

Even though his family belonged to the lesser nobility, the functions of his father, equerry to the King and administrative steward of war, enabled him to enter, at the age of 14, the prestigious corps of musketeers, and at the age of 29 he was made a lieutenant of the Marshals of France. He was a man of colossal size and extremely energetic. The royal army, in which he had so much experience, was the object of his severe critical judgement. He thought that there were too many bad elements in it; there were vagabonds, often without family and of no fixed address, who often only joined up to escape the law. He was in favour of compulsory military service.

Dupont de Nemours, Pierre Samuel

Born in Paris
Aged 48 on January 1st. 1788

He was re-engaged by Calonne in the post of commissary general of commerce; he had occupied the post before in 1774 owing to the influence of Turgot. He closely followed the meetings of the Assembly of Notables since he had the task of doing the minutes. He was back in public affairs after a long time in eclipse. He was said always to be ruled by his heart, he was faithful, and if he had retired for so long to his marshland property, where he devoted himself to literature and agriculture,

it was in order to follow his close friend, Turgot, in his disgrace. The reforming Minister had called him to his side in 1774 and Dupont de Nemours had gone with joy. In his new appointment, he thought he could reform abuse, prepare for a golden era, and, at last, apply the theories inspired by Quesnay, whose reputation he had contributed to by publishing, in 1767, a work on *Physiocracy*. Unhappily, the experience was too short to prove conclusive. He was an honest man and a hard worker, and had very many activities: secretary to the steward of Soissons, councillor for State Education to the King of Poland. He was loyal everywhere, imaginative, sententious but always with grace.

Duport, Adrien

Born in Paris
Aged 28 on January 1st. 1788

His immense fortune, his family, who were of the highest nobility, and his own talent made him a respected magistrate at the parliament of Paris. Even though he suffered from weak health — he had tuberculosis — he was a cold and ambitious character. He was one of the leaders of a group of parliamentarians and compared himself to Broussel, who had been the hero of the parliamentary Fronde of 1648. At his home, in the Marais, he organised a club in which he combined, along with his colleagues, the great liberal lords who had chosen as model the institutions of England. He wanted reforms more radical than those of the club. He repeatedly said "Work in depth!".

The mayor of Paris on the steps of the Hôtel de Ville.

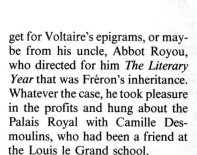

Fréron.

Eprémesnil, Jean Jacques Duval d'

Born in Pondicherry
Aged 42 on January 1st. 1788

Having been exiled to Troyes on August 14th. 1787, Duval d'Eprémesnil returned more insolent than ever. He was councillor to the parliament of Paris and led the resistance to the fiscal decrees that Loménie de Brienne imposed. He did not have any difficulty as he was one of the most brilliant magistrates of that court, where he had made the beginnings of his career. He had a loud voice, an attractive demeanour and the prestige of an vast fortune. He also had an immeasurable audacity. In November 1787, he had dared to demand the King to convene the Estates General and repeated that it was necessary to "de-Bourbonise" France. The Queen detested him, especially after the "Affair of the Necklace", because he had supported Cardinal Rohan. D'Eprémesnil, in his private life, lacked clearsightedness and did not follow through ideas. He was both devout and a follower of such charlatans as Mesmer and Cagliostro. He did not measure up to his duties and confused his ideals with the public good.

Fouché, Joseph

Born in Pellerin
Aged 28 on January 1st. 1788

He was the third child of a captain in the merchant marine who specialised in the spice trade. He entered the Oratory of Paris in 1781.

In September 1787, he became a teacher in the most brilliant of all the Oratorian schools, the Lycée Juilly. His pupils adored the "good father", the nickname that they gave to Fouché, because he amused them when he carried out experiments in class. In reality the pious individual, who wore a monk's habit and tonsure, was not a priest, but simply a "colleague of the Oratory". He entered the lay order of the Brothers because he suffered from sea-sickness and, therefore, in the long term, could not have become a captain in the family tradition. Fouché was a pale man and evidently in fragile health, but his intelligence was of the liveliest.

Fouquier Tinville, Antoine *real name* Quentin Fouquier

Born in Hérouël
Aged 41 on January 1st. 1788

He married his second wife in 1782. She loved him a lot, even though he was not very seductive, with his pock-marked face, his staring eyes and his bristling, black eyebrows. His colleagues appreciated him for his good humour and his generosity, but they missed the time when he had been happier for since 1783, his affairs had gone from bad to worse. He had to sell his office, liquidate the inheritance that his father, a rich farmer from Saint Quentin, had left him, and sell his beautiful country home in the Charonne. His creditors harassed him and he unfortunately had a lot of children. His procurator's office did well, though, because he worked very hard and was an excellent jurist. Finally, he was without resources and had to move house: gambling or women were the cause.

François de Neufchâteau, *real name* Nicolas Louis

Born in Saffais
Aged 37 on January 1st. 1788

This son of a village teacher was, in fact, the bastard child of the bailiff of Alsace, and it was to him that Louis owed his fortune. He could already write when a very young child and was acknowledged by the Academies at the age of 12. He published his first work, *Various Poems,* in 1765, when he was just 14. He was so diversely brilliant that he did not become a teacher, deciding instead to study law because "he wanted to unite the rose of literature with the thorns of jurisprudence". Then, in 1783, he accepted the function of procurator to the high council of Cap in Sainte Domingue. He arrived late at his post because, after nearly being poisoned by mushrooms, he was shipwrecked. He spent three years on the island and returned in 1786. He then remained at his house at Vicherey, whilst trying his hand at agriculture.

Fréron, Stanislas Louis

Born in Paris
Aged 33 on January 1st. 1788

It was possible that he got his vocation for journalism from his father, who had been a favourite target for Voltaire's epigrams, or maybe from his uncle, Abbot Royou, who directed for him *The Literary Year* that was Fréron's inheritance. Whatever the case, he took pleasure in the profits and hung about the Palais Royal with Camille Desmoulins, who had been a friend at the Louis le Grand school.

Gensonné, Armand

Born in Bordeaux
Aged 29 on January 1st. 1788

The legal bar of Bordeaux abounded with brilliant orators. Gensonné, the son of an army surgeon, was one of its brightest stars. However, he did not go off into flights of eloquent oratory; on the contrary, his wording was sober; his slender silhouette suggested a logical reasoner, even a severe moralist. But if his character was cold, he had generous ideals and called for the emancipation of the black slaves in Sainte Domingue. He lived comfortably with his family; he was happily married and the father of two children.

Gobel, Jean Baptiste

Born in Thann
Aged 60 on January 1st. 1788

He had a period of difficulties after a run of good luck. As a child, he was noted for his priestly qualities; he was pious, hard-working and had a charitable spirit. At first he succeeded brilliantly, in spite of his humble origins. After a stay of ▷

"Actors" and witnesses of the Revolution

Abbot Grégoire.

Hébert.

Hérault de Séchelles.

three years in Rome, where he earned for himself both a doctorate in theology and the applause of the jury, he returned to Alsace. There he was ordained, and was soon on the road to fresh honours. He was the Vicar-General of the Bishopric of Porrentruy and Bishop of Lydda in 1772, suffragan to the Archbishopric of Basel, charged with assisting the Bishop in his temporal duties to the French parishioners of the diocese. He was luxuriously installed in the episcopal palace and had all the trappings of a Prince of the Church, but still he showed such an edifying devotion that he was nicknamed the "Angel of Lydda". He led a very pleasant life, surrounding himself with pretty women, men of the world and valuable paintings.

Grégoire, Henri Baptiste

Born in Vého, near Lunéville
Aged 37 on January 1st. 1788

He installed a public library for the use of the surrounding country people in his parish presbytery of Embermesnil, where he had been the priest since 1782. The local people also found the best books, dealing with everything from moral politics to veterinary skills and medicine. This was because Abbot Grégoire gave himself the generous mission of improving the instruction of the poor. This philanthropist was born into a poor family from Lorraine. His father was a humble village tailor and it was by dint of hard work that Grégoire became a priest. In spite of deep theological studies, he did not want to make a career of the

Church because it pained him to see the high clergy betraying the evangelical ideal. A literary man, he wrote a *Eulogy to Poetry* which was honoured by the Academy of Nancy. He decided to participate in a competition organised by the Academy of Metz, the theme of which was "the means of making the Jews more useful and happier in France". To this end, he prepared an *Essay on the Physical, Moral and Political Regeneration of the Jews*. The subject was one that he had studied for many years; the sermon that he had preached in 1785 was remembered as a great scandal by the Catholics of Lunéville. He had regular features and a soft glance, which lacked neither authority nor humour.

Gaudet, Marguerite Elie

Born in Saint Emilion
Aged 29 on January 1st. 1788

He had a large head and black hair, just touching his shoulders, blue eyes and mud-coloured skin. His clothes were neglected but he didn't care. He was the son of a small land-holder of Saint Emilion; he had the luck to be adopted by a rich widow who left him 20,000 livres in her will. This allowed him to go and study law in Paris. When he went back to Bordeaux, he signed himself up at the legal bar of the city. He was a good orator, with an impressive voice and sober gestures. A hard worker, he liked rigorous reasoning and left nothing to chance. He married the daughter of a merchant and it was said that he was a tender husband and a good father.

Hanriot, François

Born in Nanterre
Aged 28 on January 1st. 1788

He was an unimportant clerk at the toll-office of Paris, who cut an effacing figure, but, despite a meagre way of life, wore rather fashionable clothes. It seemed that he had exhausted all possible alternatives since his childhood spent with his father, a poor grower from Nanterre who had ended up in domestic service in order to survive. As a child, François attended the local parish choir school and, with work and application, became the clerk to the procurator. He was fired, possibly because of pilfering, or, more probably, because he tended to drink when he got bored.

Hébert, Jacques René

Born in Alençon
Aged 30 on January 1st. 1788

In 1780 a ridiculous affair ruined his entire existence. When he was the lover of the widow of a pharmacist, who was 20 years his senior, she abandoned him for a wealthier doctor. In order to take his revenge, he had libellous posters pinned up, attacking his rival, who promptly took him to court. He was banished and had to pay the costs of the case; he was forced to flee the town in shame and disgrace, thereby losing the comfortable future which had awaited him as the son of a master goldsmith. After vegetating for a little while in Rouen, he finished by failing in Paris where he lived in

utter misery. He even considered going to China, but remembered at the last minute that he had written a comedy which he presented to the director of "diverting amusements" at the Palais Royal. The work was rejected, but he was hired as a ticket controller. He lived in a hovel at the Place Maubert; he often went hungry, and wore shirts which he had had lent to him by friends who took pity on him. He was a man in desperately straitened circumstances.

Hérault de Séchelles, Marie Jean

Born in Paris
Aged 28 on January 1st. 1788

From his cradle, he had everything. He was from the ancient nobility, a family that wielded great power and, in addition, he was very handsome. He was tall and athletic, with blue eyes, blond hair and a sweet face; he had exquisite manners and the natural elegance of a refined education. His beginnings, at the age of 18, as a lawyer of the King at the Châtelet had received as much attention as a theatre première. Women did not know which to prefer in him, his looks or his eloquence. This "divine" magistrate had, in fact, groomed his effect by taking lessons from the famous tragedienne Clairon. Neither had the Queen been indifferent to his charms when he was presented to her by his cousin, the Duchesse de Polignac. She gave him a belt, that she herself had embroidered and, above all, allowed him to obtain the post of

La Fayette.

Alexandre de Lameth.

The Altar to the Nation and monuments of Paris.

Attorney General, with 600,000 livres of income. Thus he was able to live a luxurious life, which was greatly appreciated by his women.

Jeanbon Saint André, *real name* André Jeanbon

Born in Montauban
Aged 38 on January 1st 1788

He was pastor at Montauban, after having been a sea-going captain; these were the two very distinct parts of his life. He was born into a family of small industrial Protestants and brought up by the Jesuits; he lived his childhood in a state of religious passion. A youthful taste for adventure gave him the idea of enrolling in the merchant marine, but in 1782, after three shipwrecks and the loss of all his savings, he left the sea for ever. He was a resolute man, with a yellow, bilious face, full of repressed ardour. His manners were rough and he had a tendency to sermonise.

La Fayette, Marie Gilbert Motier, Marquis de

Born in Chavaniac
Aged 30 on January 1st. 1788

His home, a large residence in the Rue de Bourbon, gave visitors the impression of being in America. His errand-boy was a costumed Indian who called him "father". Each Monday, at the La Fayette home, there was an "American dinner", to which all illustrious Americans were invited, such as the American Ambassador, Thomas Jefferson and even Englishmen, including William Pitt. Most of the guests amused themselves speaking English with the little daughters of their host, who spoke the language fluently. A copy of the Bill of Rights was affixed to the wall of the drawing-room and at the side there was an empty frame; La Fayette declared, when he was asked: "It is for the French Declaration of Rights." He himself prepared a draft. Everyone remembered how he had been acclaimed, both at Court and in the capital, when, at the age of 21, in February 1779, he had returned from America, covered with glory. He was profoundly affected by the War of Independence, in the course of which he had valiantly assumed the command of a division of insurgents. Everyone there was deeply grateful to him. He was very close to George Washington and the visit that he had paid him in 1784 was transformed into a tour of triumph. He and his descendants were granted American citizenship in perpetuity. His admiration for American democracy was so deep that he became an enthusiastic propagandist wherever he went. He had a fiery temperament and got worked up easily about utopian ideas. Mischief makers named him "Giles Caesar Esquire", alluding to the famous simpleton of the play, because La Fayette was also considered to be extremely ambitious. He had lost the ungainliness of his youth and he had a refined distinction. His marriage, at the age of 15, to the daughter of the illustrious House of Noailles, was very happy. His wife adored him. Their son was called George Washington.

Lakanal, Joseph

Born in Serres
Aged 25 on January 1st. 1788

A brillant pupil of the Oratorians, he became one of the most renowned teachers. At the age of 18 he already held the chair of grammar and, from 1785, he taught philosophy at the college of Moulins. He joined the seminary because of the influence of an uncle who was a priest; he did not have the slightest ecclesiastical vocation. He was a modest young man, studious, with simple tastes.

Lameth, Alexandre, Comte de

Born in Paris
Aged 27 on January 1st. 1788

From all points of view, he was a valuable addition to the Court. His mother was the sister of Marshal de Broglie and a protégée of the Queen, who gave her a pension from her own privy purse. Even so, Alexandre resented Marie Antoinette a little; he considered himself seductive enough for her to be attracted by him, but she didn't even look at him, which was a blow to his pride. He was in fact very proud of his appearance, because he was tall and slim with an elegance that was aristocratic. He loved all pleasures to excess, whilst remaining very brave under fire. A colonel of the Royal Lorraine regiment, he had been under Rochambeau's orders in the war in America, from which he returned with ideas about independence and social equality that he spoke about freely, intriguing actively in the circle of the powerful liberals who gravitated around La Fayette. People were wary of him because he was not an easy man and feared no adversary. He had several brothers, but he was so close to his elder brother, Charles, that they could hardly be told apart; they were known as "the Lameths".

Lameth, Charles, Comte de

Born in Paris
Aged 30 on January 1st. 1788

He was the eldest of the Lameth brothers, a colonel in the King's cuirassiers. He did not have the good looks of his brother Alexandre — he was even rather ugly — but his vivacity made of him one of the "lions" of the court. A hero of the battle of Yorktown in October 1781, during the War of Independence, his leg was shattered by a cannon ball and he virtually took no notice. So that no-one would forget his wound he used crutches, which made even the Queen laugh. She was attracted by him and enabled his marriage to a rich heiress from Sainte Domingue. The wealth did not stop Charles from posing as a democrat. After his return from America, he felt, he said, "a deep sympathy for the common man". This attitude served him well; it made him very popular. Indeed, he had a definite talent for making speeches to crowds. His witty eloquence always gained the hearts of the humourists, even though some found him a little too nasty, but that was a family trait that was willingly pardoned. In fact, his reputation for originality assured ▷

"Actors" and witnesses of the Revolution

La Révellière Lépeaux.

Le Bon.

Le Chapelier.

Le Peletier.

him total impunity from any hard words. He was a Knight of the Order of Malta, as was his brother. In addition, thanks to the Queen, he was a Knight of the Order of Saint Louis and a gentleman attendant to the Comte d'Artois.

La Révellière Lépeaux, Louis Marie de

Born in Montaigu
Aged 34 on January 1st. 1788

He detested priests so much that he blamed his hunch-back on the bad treatment that he had received from them at school. Sadly, his physical handicaps did not stop there; he had a large head with bulging eyes supported by a small body on stick-like legs, all of which made him look like a cork stuck on two pins. He had a sickly looking air; he was kindly towards everyone and often seemed to be alarmed. His youth was divided between a job as a clerk to a procurator to the parliament of Paris, music — he adored Gluck — and such pleasures as his physical handicaps would permit. He qualified as a lawyer in 1775 and returned home to his father, a magistrate in Anjou, where he met a very attractive girl with an extraordinary herbarium. It was thus that he fell in love with botany along with the young lady. After their marriage, they divided their time between country walks, studious pursuits and family concerts, in which he used to play the flute. He gave free lessons at the Society of the Botanists of Angers, of which he was a member.

Lebas, Philippe François

Born in Frévent
Aged 23 on January 1st. 1788

He was said to be cold and phlegmatic. Even so, he made a lasting friendship at school with a classmate, Maximilien de Robespierre. He was, like him, a lawyer and practised at Saint Pol. His father was a lawyer, but the family was large and the studies of Philippe rather laborious. He used his free time to read the plays of Racine, or to listen to music; he was a lover of Italian opera. He had a gentle and conciliatory character; he was also capable of being stern when he allowed himself to be influenced by those whom he loved.

Le Bon, Joseph

Born in Arras
Aged 22 on January 1st. 1788

The son of a sergeant of the town of Arras, he decided on the vocation of the Church without too much conviction. But, as the years passed, he became an excellent teacher of rhetoric and was unanimously acclaimed by the Oratorians of Beaune, where he had been installed since the age of 18, after finishing his studies at the college of Juilly, near Paris. He waited with impatience for the moment when he would be ordained priest, a function that would allow him to fulfil his taste for righteousness. He was a rather weak character, capable of excess and was not without a certain tendency towards eccentricity.

Le Chapelier, Isaac René Guy

Born in Rennes
Aged 33 on January 1st. 1788

At the end of 1787, the Breton parliamentarians started to demonstrate against the new taxes which had been proposed by the General Controller of Finance. There was none more tenacious among them than Le Chapelier, a lawyer from Rennes, as his father had been. He had great personal influence owing to his eloquence, his sage advice and his honesty in business. The slightest dishonesty was enough to make him reject a case and he only defended clients of whom he was sure. However, his career did not take up all his time. He was overflowing with energy and placed himself at the head of the bar in order to oppose privileges and to defend the autonomy of his province. His effort was backed by a group of friends who supported his ideas.

Le Peletier de Saint Fargeau, Louis Michel, Comte de

Born in Paris
Aged 27 on January 1st. 1788

From 1779, the year in which he had entered the parliament of Paris with a dispensation for his youth, he had a brilliant career, along with his childhood friend Hérault de Séchelles. This came naturally to him because he was from a long line of magistrates. He was High Court President, as was his father before him, affirmed himself particularly as a specialist in criminal law and

declared that he was against the death penalty. Seen from the outside, he was cold, rather haughty, as were all the Le Peletiers. He rarely intervened in the chamber's meetings; occasionally he got carried away, after which he recovered his usual calm. He was interested in universal education and, since he had imagination, he also had projects for reform. He was often to be seen in the society of the Palais Royal; he played billiards and lost a great deal of money, although he had at least 600,000 livres in income.

Lindet, Jean Baptiste

Born in Bernay
Aged 41 on January 1st. 1788

He was a lawyer born into a family of tradespeople; his father was a wood-seller. From 1776, he was the procurator of the King in the region of Bernay. In that town, which was a rival of Evreux, he was extremely active and defended its interests. He was a prudent and moderate man, though nonetheless authoritative; but he obliged when needed.

Lindet, Robert Thomas

Born in Bernay
Aged 44 on January 1st. 1788

Elder brother of Jean Baptiste, he was the priest of Sainte Croix de Bernay. He was a priest-philosopher and an adept of a Voltaire-like scepticism. Like his brother in civilian society, he, in the Church, believed in the abolition of privileges.

Marat.

Robert Lindet.

From the shop floor to the streets, newspapers shape public opinion.

Loustalot, Elisée

Born in Saint Jean d'Angély
Aged 25 on January 1st. 1788

In 1786 this young lawyer from Bordeaux went to Paris to seek his fortune. He was passionate about the people's welfare and felt great compassion for those living in tough conditions, such as the men employed in the charitable workshops of Montmartre, where he was often a visitor. Upset by the food problem and the high cost of bread, he tried to invent a machine that would produce ground flour more quickly. He wanted his philanthropic ideas to be disseminated by the press and collaborated with Prudhomme, a book dealer who also published pamphlets. The fiery Loustalot lived by a motto he took from Beaumarchais: "Great men only seem great to us because we are on our knees. Let us arise!" Unfortunately this generous man worked too hard, and his healt suffered.

Marat, Jean Paul

Born in Boudry (Neuchâtel)
Aged 44 on January 1st. 1788

Marat was one of the ugliest men of his time. His skin was copper coloured, he had a large, hooked nose and was cross-eyed. He was a small but sturdy man, whose pronunciation problems were made worse by a heavy accent. He used to gesticulate a lot to express himself. When he had nothing to say, he stood aside, crossing his arms as if he were trying to contain a simmer-

ing inner violence. His attire was often untidy, even dirty. Fear and disgust were the effects he had on others. Despite these handicaps, this son of a poverty stricken Sardinian family became a doctor and practised for 11 years in England, where he published *The Chains of Slavery* in 1774 and *Plan for Criminal Legislation*. On his return to France, he carried out research into electricity, but the Academy of Sciences took no interest in his work. When Lavoisier went to visit him, Marat, who was arrogant and cared nothing about what anybody thought of him, received his guest very badly. In 1777 he became doctor to the bodyguards of the Comte d'Artois. He only kept the position until 1783. By 1788 most of his projects had come to nothing, and he had no more money. Ill and forgotten by all, he then wrote to Frederick II, a backer of scientists. This appeal was not answered. Desperate, Jean Paul Marat wrote his last will and testament.

Maréchal, Sylvain Pierre

Born in Paris
Aged 37 on January 1st. 1788

The pseudonym he used as a poet aptly summed the man up: Berger Sylvain, or Shepherd of the Woods. He loved nature and saw himself as its servant. Literature was his first real activity. After giving up law, due to speech problems, he began writing light, pastoral poems in a style copied from the Latin author Lucretius. The public reacted coolly to his *Fragment of a Moral Poem on God*, published in 1781. As for his

Book Rescued from the Flood, which appeared in 1784, it was a parody of the prophetic style and attacked absolute power. Its publication cost him his post as assistant librarian at the Mazarin college. By 1788 he was finishing an *Almanach of Honest People*. He was a frequent visitor to the Duplessis salon, where he met Camille Desmoulins and Fréron.

Maury, Jean Siffrein

Born in Valréas
Aged 41 on January 1st. 1788

When he joined the French Academy in 1785, he achieved the ambition of a lifetime. However, he was not over impressed by this honour, as his vanity was only on a par with his ambition: "You can achieve everything that you really desire," he often said. He was not proved wrong, although his father was just a poor shoe-maker. A cunning man, Maury was built like Hercules, with wide and powerful shoulders, a piercing gaze and loud voice. He ate and drank an impressive amount, and his conversation was often very daring. "When he gives his jaws a rest, he can spout a sermon, a dirty story and a philosophical anecdote," his friends said of him. It was easy to forget that he was a priest, the senior vicar of Lombez, in Gascony, because he looked just like a grenadier. However, he never let people forget his position and guarded his prerogatives jealously. He was inordinately proud of the sermons he gave at Versailles during Lent, comparing them to the ones preached by John Chrysostomos at the court of Con-

stantinople. When asked if he thought highly of himself, this talented and aggressive preacher used to reply "Not particularly when I judge myself, but very much when I compare myself to others".

Merlin, Philippe Antoine, *alias* Merlin de Douai

Born in Arleux
Aged 33 on January 1st. 1788

Merlin did not disappoint the Benedictine monks of the school at Anchin, who admired the exceptional gifts of this lowly farmer's son whom they educated. From his early adolescence he showed a real vocation for the law. At the age of 20, he became a lawyer at the Flanders parliament. His reputation soon spread to Paris, and he was consulted by leading magistrates. The Duc d'Orléans selected him to be a member of his privy council. In 1782 he purchased a position as royal secretary at the chancellery of the Flanders parliament. He devoted all his time to the law and often rose at dawn to work on his legal documents. However, he did manage to find enough time to marry the sister of a monk of Anchin.

Merlin, Antoine Christophe, *alias* Merlin de Thionville

Born in Thionville
Aged 25 on January 1st. 1788

He was a lawyer, the son of a procurator of the Thionville bailiwick, but he had all the qualities of ▷

"Actors" and witnesses of the Revolution

Mirabeau.

Mounier.

Oberkampf.

a soldier; he was energetic and courageous, whilst also being sensitive. His father was determined that he should become a priest, but Merlin resisted with equal determination and registered at the bar of Metz. He was both slim and robust at the same time, with a loud voice and a mass of thick, black hair.

Mirabeau, Honoré Gabriel Riqueti, Comte de

Born in Bignon
Aged 38 on January 1st. 1788

His father was a forceful character, a "friend of man"; he was an economist as well as an extremely prolific writer, but an inflexible educator. Honoré was forced by him to join the cavalry at the age of 17, but it didn't make him any wiser. He was a typical rebellious son. He was in trouble for debauchery, adultery, literary piracy and even incest. Jail became a second home to him; the worst of his imprisonments was a period of 42 months in the tower of Vincennes. He flaunted his depravity despite impressive ugliness: a monstrous head and olive-coloured skin covered with scars. Nonetheless, women fell at his feet. The first of these women, Emilie de Marignane, he obtained in a scandalous manner, by standing outside her window in a state of near-nudity. Not only was this forced marriage in 1772 an unhappy one, each cheating the other, but, on top of everything, he ran through all the dowry of the rich heiress. The case went to trial and Honoré was banished. He also had a love affair with Sophie,

the virtuous wife of the Marquis de Monnier, a magistrate at Dôle. They were separated and jailed; she died from the shame. The intelligence of Mirabeau, his harsh voice with a southern accent and his ardent temperament made him superior to everyone. He was aware of it, but his genius was so disorganised that it never amounted to anything. He undertook important works that he hardly finished; he wrote *Essay on Sealed Orders and the State Jails* in 1782. He denounced ministers, argued, travelled and maintained the same life of excess.

Momoro, Antoine François

Born in Besançon
Aged 31 on January 1st. 1788

He came from an old Spanish family with not much money. He settled very early on in Paris, where he had been admitted into the community of printer-book sellers. He had a practical intelligence with ideas that were resolute. He was considered to be an excellent typographer; his business prospered and he had a few employees. As for Sophie Fournier, his wife, she appeared on the stage where she was, above all, remarkable for her beauty.

Mounier, Jean Joseph

Born in Grenoble
Aged 29 on January 1st. 1788

The son of a modestly comfortable draper, Mounier received a

solid education from an uncle who was a priest and extremely severe; he then went to college. He became a lawyer in 1779, after trying a military career and then renouncing trade. He was still a young magistrate when he gained the position of royal judge to the parliament of Grenoble. His colleagues, who considered him a specialist in English public law, esteemed him greatly. Although he had a talent for the law, he did not practise his profession because his voice was too weak. His honesty was proverbial, as was his sense of fairness. From the very beginning of his career, he only had one case that went to appeal. He was an admirer of English institutions, learning the language in order to understand the English. He was also a figure in the political circles of Grenoble. The influential men of the three orders often met at his house, where they prepared for the assembly of provincial states to be held at Vizille. Mounier was married at the age of 23.

Oberkampf, Christophe Philippe

Born in Wiesenbach, Bavaria
Aged 49 on January 1st. 1788

After having learned the rudiments of his profession from his father, a cloth-dyer domiciled in Switzerland, Oberkampf became an engraver at the printed cloth factory of the Court of Lorraine, at Mulhouse, and then a colourist at the Arsenal factory in Paris. He was sure of himself and an entrepreneur; at the age of 21, he founded his own business in a thatched cottage in

Jouy en Josas, with only 25 louis as capital. A remarkable technician, he took care of everything, design, engraving, dyeing, even building his own looms. Whilst facing all the difficulties, he continued to perfect the complex processes. Business went from strength to strength, especially when, in 1759, he obtained the cancelling of the old ban on the importation of calico and chintz. His cloth was purchased at the Court, as well as in the town; his agents travelled the world and he dominated the European market in printed cloth. He employed in all 20,000 people, thereby contributing to growth in a valley that had long been deserted and swampy. Oberkampf was naturalised in 1770 and was protected by Louis XVI, who, in 1783, ennobled him, while his business became a royal factory.

Pache, Jean Nicolas

Born in Paris
Aged 41 on January 1st. 1788

He retired to Switzerland, and resigned from all his positions, because he was a lover of country life and an independent character. He owed everything to the Maréchal de Castries, for whom his father, of Swiss origin, had been gate-keeper. The Minister of the Navy employed him initially as tutor to his children, then as his first secretary. General munitioner of the Navy commissary, then Controller of the King's household under Necker, his ambition stopped there, perhaps because the protection of a great lord weighed him down too much. He was of a

Blueprint for the Council of Five Hundred's hall at the Palais Bourbon.

Pétion.

Rabaut Saint Etienne.

modest appearance, with a taste for the simple; he preferred to live in the country with his family. He had all the attributes of a virtuous man, not without a few wily traits, which spoilt his personality. He spoke little and passed for an even cleverer man. His children missed France

Paine, Thomas

Born in Thetford, Norfolk
Aged 50 on January 1st. 1788

He stayed so often with the Condorcets that he was a part of the family. He spoke French badly, so it was Mme. Condorcet who interpreted in her salon where Paine held sway as a thinker of fashion. People forgot that he was English, he so wanted to be seen as an American; he said he was a citizen of the country with the most justice. He had many jobs, including that of his father, a corset-maker. He became a journalist in Philadelphia. In 1776 his work *Sens Commun (Common Sense)* was a considerable success. His support for the rebels dated from that period. In his writings he firmly defended both liberty and equality. A closeness with Franklin helped him in France, where his calm contrasted with the furore.

Palloy, Pierre François

Born in Paris
Aged 32 on January 1st. 1788

He was an architect, an intriguer and a social climber. He went from his father's wine depot to being

entrepreneur of the King's buildings. In between, he served in the Royal Dragoons. He married, in 1775, a woman 12 years his elder, whose attraction was her dowry: the clientele of her father, a master mason. Palloy was ruthless and took any opportunity to make money.

Pétion de Villeneuve, Jérôme

Born in Chartres
Aged 31 on January 1st. 1788

The Pétion family included men of the law, but they were not particularly wealthy. Jérôme was a mediocre lawyer and his business went badly. He was not worried, being an optimist; naive according to his friends, weak and vain in the opinion of those who did not like him. He was a tall man, with soft features and a permanent cordial smile. Sensitive, he cried at will and embraced easily. Convinced of his own charm, he thought that he was irresistible to women. He did not, however, have much luck, because he flaunted himself as a faithful and very attentive husband, with all the domestic virtues.

Prieur Duvernois, Claude, *alias* Prieur de la Côte d'Or

Born in Auxonne
Aged 24 on January 1st. 1788

He was the son of of a tax-collector for the bailiwick of Dole, but Prieur did not take up administration. He went to the engineering school at Mézières, where he met

Lazare Carnot, for whom he had an admiring friendship. He was a lieutenant of engineering; his speciality was making of gun-powder. He had a passion for mathematics and was an extremely hard worker.

Prieur, Pierre Louis, *alias* Prieur de la Marne

Born in Sommesous
Aged 31 on January 1st. 1788

He was a lawyer at the bar of Châlons sur Marne; he studied at the faculty of Reims, where the rights of man were much discussed, despite a repressive dean. There were many foreigners present and they were enthusiastic about the news of the rebellion in the American colonies. In the back of the shop of the baker, Fouet, in the Rue du Petit Cerf, where many students lodged, there was a lot of speech-making, especially by Prieur, whose sister was going to marry the son of the house. He was listened to with great attention because he had a strong voice and imposed himself.

Rabaut, Jean Paul, *alias* Rabaut Saint Etienne

Born in Nîmes
Aged 44 on January 1st. 1788

It was he who negotiated with Turgot, Malesherbes and Mgr. de la Luzerne the Edict of Tolerance of November 1787, thus obtaining the restitution of civil status for Protestants. Charged in 1785 by the consistories of the Midi with the pre-

paratory mission, he had already been well received by ministers. He was a pastor with a conciliatory character, and he had great authority amongst his fellow Protestants. He had a lot to cope with. His father, the pastor of Désert in the Bas Languedoc, had spent his life in work and being persecuted; he had taken refuge in the woods where he wrote his sermons and ate chestnuts. His son joined his ministry in 1763, after studying brilliantly in Geneva and Lausanne. His religious zeal was coupled with great literary culture. In 1779 he wrote a poem about the Protestants, *Le Vieux Cévenol*, which he published in Holland.

Reubell, Jean François

Born in Colmar
Aged 40 on January 1st. 1788

He was the son of a royal notary and from 1773 a lawyer to the sovereign Council of Alsace. He was one of the best jurists of Colmar and president of the barristers. Reubell was very cultivated and had a lot of spirit, but could be prejudiced. He hated everything which had to do with Germany, and opposed the vote for the Jews. He was a hard worker, whose energetic character pushed him to action. His qualities were spoiled by being an apoplectic loud-mouth. The slightest contradiction sent him into a fury: he swore and banged his hand on the table. He drank too much and was hardly delicate in his choice of acquaintances. His much-visited salon resembled an inn at the time of the arrival of a coach.

"Actors" and witnesses of the Revolution

Robespierre.

Roland.

Saint Just.

Robespierre, Maximilien Marie Isidore de

Born in Arras
Aged 29 on January 1st. 1788

His reputation in Arras dated from 1783. In that year he won his most important case since he had become a lawyer in 1780: he defended a doctor from Saint Omer who was being prosecuted for installing a lightning conductor on his roof. Robespierre became the chancellor of the town academy, a hotbed of philosophical propaganda, and belonged to the literary circle of the Rosatis. Nourished by the books of Jean Jacques Rousseau, he founded his ideal on the principles of liberty and virtue. Even though he was young, there was no known liaison, nor any vice. He led a very stable life in a modest house that was looked after by his sister, Charlotte. His time was divided between his office, the law courts, and evenings out. Even though he was small and narrow-shouldered, he was very smart: his wig-maker came to dress his hair each morning. Young girls were not fond of him: he danced badly and spoke of the law to them instead of singing songs. His business affairs were shaky; he had made the error of pleading against a powerful local abbey and was not invited to join the new judicial committee of the Artois council. These failures weighed upon him, because he had always possessed "infinite pride". Thus he became increasingly morose; his lips became pinched, he hid his green eyes behind dark spectacles and became something of a recluse who bit his nails.

Roederer, Pierre Louis

Born in Metz
Aged 33 on January 1st. 1788

He was an advisor to the Metz parliament, a function that he had purchased in 1780. He detested judicial procedure, but, after a long resistance, he finally obeyed his father by doing his law studies at Strasbourg. He much preferred the debate of ideas and philosophy. He was both rich and generous; he willingly subsidised the dissertation competitions. In 1784 he offered a prize of 400 livres and a medal to the best candidate in the following subject: *What is the origin of the opinion that all individuals of the same family share the shame of one of its guilty members?* It was a young lawyer from Arras, Maximilien de Robespierre, who won the prize, and he used the money earned to have his answer published. This was concrete proof that Roederer enjoyed encouraging the talents of the day; he himself composed a tract about the deputation to the Estates General, and he planned to present it to them in person.

Roland de La Platière, Jean Marie

Born in Thizy
Aged 53 on January 1st. 1788

From 1784 he was the inspector of arts and factories in the district of Lyons. He was a learned man of renown, he was widely-travelled and knew the cloth industry to perfection, in France as well as abroad. He used his leisure time to write technical books, in particular a monumental *Dictionary of Factories* in 1785, which was published as part of the *Methodical Encyclopaedia*. He came from an old family from the Villefranche region. His father was royal adviser to the bailiwick of Villefranche en Beaujolais. At the age of 19 he was not the administrator that he was to become. He even wanted to leave for India, but an illness kept him in Nantes where he found a job in a ship's outfitters. It was the influence of a cousin that gave him the entry into administration. He was tall and thin, afflicted by baldness, with yellow skin; he would hardly have been attractive if it had not been for his virile voice and his fine smile. He dressed simply and never powdered his hair. He was completely honest, but talked too much of himself and wanted people to listen. These habits were even more annoying after he gave himself the task of ridding the financial administration of Lyons of abuse; he had many enemies.

Romme, Gilbert

Born in Riom
Aged 37 on January 1st. 1788

After a prolonged stay in Russia where he had been tutor to the young Count Strogonoff, he returned to France with his pupil in 1787. He wanted to find a job as a teacher of mathematics. Behind an appearance of simplicity and sweetness he was a fervent admirer of the enlightened thinkers, and detested the Church and its pomp. He was single, as demanding of himself as he was of all the others, and a completely honest man.

Ronsin, Charles Philippe

Born in Soissons
Aged 36 on January 1st. 1788

Having decided not to be a cooper like his father, he at first hesitated between the army and a career in literature. He signed up at the age of 17, but did not manage to get further than the rank of a simple soldier. His literary career started in 1780 with a translation of a Latin poem by Claudian, *The Fall of Ruffin,* which described the crimes of an abject politician of the Lower Empire. In 1786 he published a book of plays, which included three tragedies, printed to raise money for his ailing grandmother. "I ease her pain with feeble gifts," he said as an epigraph. In 1787 he was unlucky: his *Jeanne d'Arc* was well received at the Comédie Française but unfortunately Mlle. Raucourt, who was supposed to perform the role, was quickly tired of the idea and he had to take away his play.

Roux, Jacques

Born in Pransac
Aged 35 on January 1st. 1788

This priest from Cozes proved to be very devoted to his parishioners and behaved in an exemplary way. However, he harboured a grudge against the church's hierarchy and claimed to be a victim of injustice.

Sieyès.

Talleyrand.

Demolition of the Cordeliers Church in Paris.

He was the last in a family of 12 children. Since his father was a mere infantry lieutenant, his career prospects were hardly brilliant. It was the priesthood that seemed to suit him best, as he had shown promise at the Angoulême seminary. Ordained in 1776, he taught philosophy and physics there. In 1779 he was involved in an unfortunate incident that forced him to spend a month and a half in jail. After his release he continued to teach until 1784, when he asked to be allowed to preach in the provinces, at the Saintes diocese. There, his behaviour was said to have been beyond reproach.

Saint Just, Louis Antoine de

Born in Decize
Aged 20 on January 1st. 1788

His wide and well-formed mouth seemed to have been made to smile, but he seldom did so. His gaze was sombre, peering out from under thick eyebrows. He suffered from boredom at Blérancourt, a small town near Laon. His parsimonious mother carefully counted out his pocket money. His father, who died a simple cavalry captain, did not instil in him a love of the army and he took a degree in law. He worked for a while as a public prosecutor's clerk, and then wanted to take over from the local notary public. However, the latter refused both this request and his daughter Louise's hand. To cure his broken heart, he took to writing poetry and reading philosophy. In 1788 he was working on a lengthy satirical and libertine poem, *Organt,* in which he denoun-

ced both rural poverty and debauchery in the convents. The work is similar to *La Pucelle* by Voltaire. Its publication was to give him enough money to quit the provinces.

Santerre, Antoine Joseph

Born in Paris
Aged 35 on January 1st. 1788

Santerre (Landless) was dubbed the "Father of the Faubourg". He was something of a philanthropist. In 1772 he took over the business run by his father, a master brewer from Cambrai who had settled in the Faubourg Saint Antoine. A wealthy man, as his business prospered, he was generous to a fault with his workers, regularly doling out tips, mugs of free beer and warm handshakes. While remaining popular with the workers, he was often seen among high society. He had an aristocrat's taste for English style horse racing. He also liked to be seen riding around the more fashionable streets of the capital and was considered an outstanding horseman. He was a tall, powerfully-built man whose voice carried a long way.

Sieyès, Emmanuel Joseph

Born in Fréjus
Aged 39 on January 1st. 1788

This former canon of Tréguier, who became a vicar-general and chancellor of the cathedral of Chartres in 1787, did not have a truly solid vocation. He was pushed to join the clergy by his father, a collec-

tor of royal dues and post office director. He often boasted openly of having neither preached nor taken confession. Emmanuel Sieyès preferred philosophy to religion, and he had a particular interest in metaphysics. He was a keen student, but did not go beyond Voltaire, whose works he read time and again, re-reading the first tome right after finishing the last. He also did a little writing, but was lazy about it. His later position as a councillor at the clergy's sovereign chamber meant he often had to travel to Paris, where he was seen as a friend of the Encyclopaedists, whereas he was considered a traditionally devout man in Chartres. Despite having a very comfortable income he dressed modestly, wearing a crumpled cassock. His health was far from robust and he was an aloof man, both speaking and moving slowly. He always acted cautiously. Sieyès was reputed to be a charitable man. He was never able to rid himself of his strong southern France accent. This made his conversation somewhat livelier.

Talleyrand Périgord, Charles Maurice de

Born in Paris
Aged 33 on January 1st. 1788

In late 1787 Talleyrand just failed to get himself appointed to the bishopric of Bourges, and his dissolute life-style was threatening to cost him the one at Autun. He became a priest against his wish, and had little religious faith. He rarely celebrated Mass. He was ordained at the age of 20. Even though he was an

eldest child, he knew that he was not destined for a glorious military career because of his limp. He therefore decided to make the best of his handicap. Abbot of the wealthy abbey of Saint Denis, in the diocese of Reims, he had an impressive income of 18,000 livres. In 1780 he became a senior church administrator, working efficiently thanks to both his razor-sharp wit and cynical cunning. His noble background — he was descended from the princes of Chalais and the sovereign counts of Périgord — opened up the doors of many salons for him. He had a lot of acquaintances, especially useful ones. He had Voltaire's blessing and courted Madame de Staël. He knew just how to behave in society, being both affable and gently mocking. Women found him attractive and he had many affairs, sometimes even seducing mother and daughter. This did not trouble him in the least. Adélaïde de Flahaut bore him an illegitimate child. He was a handsome and gracious man, who was able to conceal his physical handicap: a club foot burdened with an orthopaedic device. His trick was to lean nonchalantly against the backrest of armchairs.

Tallien, Jean Lambert

Born in Paris
Aged 20 on January 1st. 1788

The son of the Marquis de Bercy's major-domo, he was able to rise above his lowly rank due to his law studies, which allowed him to become a clerk at the public prosecutor's office. However, a boring job ▷

Target.

Vadier.

Vergniaud.

as a bureaucrat did not appeal to his fiery temperament. Intelligent, well turned out and a good speaker, he felt he was capable of far greater things. He tried business before seeking employment as a printer. He liked the good things in life, particularly gaming, culinary delights and, most of all, beautiful women. Ladies found his gracious ways and pleasant character irresistible.

Target, Guy Jean Baptiste

Born in Paris
Aged 54 on January 1st. 1788

A talented lawyer, one of the best at the Paris bar, he made a name for himself in 1771 by opposing Maupeou's reforms of the tribunals. His *Letter from one man to another on the extinction of the former parliament and the creation of the new one* was a sensation. On November 28th. 1774 he was asked by the Order of Lawyers to congratulate the parliamentarians who had been recalled by Louis XVI. He also took a brave stance in backing the Cardinal de Rohan during "the Affair of the Queen's Necklace". In 1785 he was unanimously elected to the French

Academy, and two years later he played an important rôle in the drafting of the Edict of Tolerance of Protestants. He was a fairly large man, who sometimes lacked tact. Once, during a party at the residence of the Maréchale de Bauveau, he even helped himself to snuff from his hostess' snuff box, thus scandalising a gathering reputed for its democratic ways. By the year 1788 his health was worsening.

Treilhard, Jean Baptiste

Born in Brive
Aged 45 on January 1st. 1788

He was a great jurist with a traditional sense of honesty. He was an eloquent man, but often clumsy, with an expressionless face and a habit of talking slowly. A lawyer's son, he became a lawyer at the parliament in Paris in 1761. Turgot, who was then a steward at Limoges, had noticed him and kept an eye on his early career. His clients were always important people. For example, he defended the town of Brive against Turenne's heirs. At the time of Maupeou's reforms, he shut his office and only reopened it in

1775. He later became inspector general of land and administered the Prince de Condé's affairs.

Vadier, Marc Guillaume

Born in Pamiers
Aged 51 on January 1st. 1788

He pursued his entire career at Pamiers, where he was councillor at the "présidial", a legal body that ruled on minor crimes and on cases that were of interest to the provosts. Despite his jolly appearance, he was a proud man who harboured fierce grudges. This meant that he had few close friends. He also lisped, and this made him less dignified. He hated pomp and always dressed with simplicity. An ugly man, he had a bony, balding forehead, and a prominent, hooked nose.

Vergniaud, Pierre Victurien

Born in Limoges
Aged 34 on January 1st. 1788

He had a difficult childhood. His father, who delivered supplies to the Limoges cavalry regiment, had been

ruined by the rise in grain prices. Thanks to Turgot, the steward of the Limousin, the young Vergniaud was awarded a scholarship to the Du Plessis college, in Bordeaux, which was run by Jesuits. For a time he was employed at the headquarters of the toll department. He resigned his position, thus losing the tax collector's post that had been earmarked for him. After considering a career in the church, he returned to Limoges. Reading was his one passion. His brother in law, a geographical engineer, took him in hand and paid for his law studies. In Bordeaux, where he studied law, he became secretary to Charles Dupaty, president of the local parliament and a magistrate known for his liberal ideals. In 1781, he became lawyer to the parliament. The following year, he took on his first legal case and won easily, as he was an excellent speaker, capable of brilliant improvisation. This talent was helped by his good looks: he had splendid, dark and passionate eyes, thick, sensual lips, abundant hair and an impressive forehead. Women were easy prey for him, but he had two major faults: he held most men in utter contempt, and was not tenacious enough.

Bonaparte.

Charette.

Dumouriez.

Hoche.

Bonaparte, Napoléon

Born in Ajaccio
Aged 18 on January 1st. 1788

He was the second son of a large family. His father, a Corsican lawyer of the lower nobility, who died in 1785, had backed France in 1770 after having fought for Corsican independence alongside Paoli. This helped the young "Nabulione" to enlist in the royal military academy as a gentleman-cadet. He left there with the rank of artillery lieutenant, and in November 1785 was posted to the La Fère regiment. He was a small, skinny and unkempt youth, with a broad accent, but he had a charming smile. The daughter of his landlady soon came to regret his departure from his garrison town in 1786. That was when he went on leave to Corsica. He was still there at the start of 1788.

Cadoudal, Georges

Born in Kerléano
Aged 16 on January 1st. 1788

His name meant "blind warrior" in Celtic dialect. In fact, at the age of 16, Georges already cut an impressive figure. Although his parents, well-off farmers, gave him a very religious education, he was afraid neither of God nor the Devil. When he enrolled at the Saint Yves college in Vannes, he refused to kneel at the entrance, as tradition required of all new students. However, his proud and haughty character was not evident in his kind and pleasant face.

Charette de La Contrie, François Athanase de

Born in Couffé
Aged 24 on January 1st. 1788

The "Knight Charette" was a strange looking man: he had a low forehead, a flat mouth, a prominent chin and an oddly-shaped nose. His bizarre looks, however, were found attractive by women. This former ship's captain was descended from a long line of shipbuilders. He was a solitary and proud man who spent much time hunting.

Dumouriez, Charles François du Périer

Born in Cambrai
Aged 48 on January 1st. 1788

The son of a war commissioner, he fought alongside his father in the Seven Years' War. The scar on his right temple came from a wound received at Clostercamp in 1758. The downfall of Choiseul, who was his backer and had given him several missions during which he lived very well, led him into a Bastille cell for several months in 1770. From the year 1778 until the start of 1788, Dumouriez was placed in command of the port of Cherbourg.

Hoche, Lazare

Born at Versailles
Aged 19 on January 1st. 1788

At the warehouse of the French Guard on the Chaussée Dantin, the grenadier Hoche, a heavy-set, five foot six inch lad with a piercing gaze, spent all his spare time studying and buying books. After his father's death he was brought up by an aunt, who cultivated fruit at Montreuil, near Versailles. He should have become a groom at the royal stables, like his father. But he chose instead to enlist, as he dreamt of going to India. He was a violent and aggressive man who chewed his knuckles when angry.

Kellerman, François Christophe

Born in Strasbourg
Aged 52 on January 1st. 1788

Descended from a noble family from Saxony, he was a career soldier who spent many years in the army. He fought during the Seven Years' War as a captain and distinguished himself at the battle of Bergen in 1759. In 1760 he became captain of the Dauphiné volunteers, and captured 300 enemy grenadiers at Orsten. Sent to Poland in 1765-66 to reorganise the cavalry, Kellerman finally returned to France in late 1787 as a senior officer in the Conflans hussars. His troops trusted him fully and he was able to lead his men wherever he wished.

La Rochejaquelein, Henri du Vergier, Comte de

Born in La Durbellière
Aged 15 on January 1st. 1788

Tall, blond, with a sharp gaze, a noble face and a very British elegance, he had a gift for physical activities and seemed destined for great things. He dreamt of military adventures and his hero was Turenne. In late 1787 he joined the Royal Polish regiment, of which his father was colonel.

Marceau, François Séverin

Born in Chartres
Aged 18 on January 1st. 1788

At the age of 17 he enlisted in the Angoumois infantry regiment, just because he had no intention of becoming a lawyer, despite the wishes of his father, a prosecutor for the bailiwick of Chartres. He was brought up by his sister, who taught him to be honourable and honest. His noble demeanour and gentle, generous character hid an extremely fiery temperament.

Pichegru, Jean Charles

Born in Planches, near Arbois
Aged 26 on January 1st. 1788

Pichegru was a complex man who was not easy to get to know. His austere looks gave him a cunning appearance. He was devoured by ambition, despite having parents who were lowly farmers. His exceptional mathematical gifts helped him to get the position of assistant at the Brienne school. Acting on the advice of one of his professors, he chose a career in the armed forces and enlisted in 1780 in an artillery regiment. He took part in the American War of Independence.

The scenes and the places

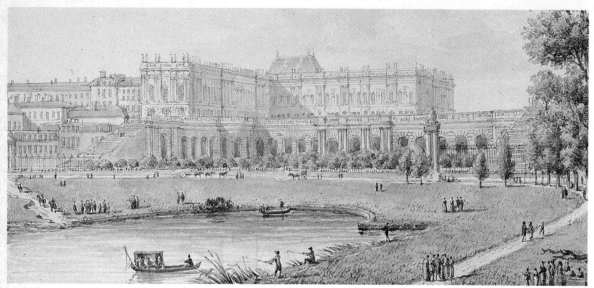

The Palace of Versailles, close to Paris, viewed from the Swiss Pond.

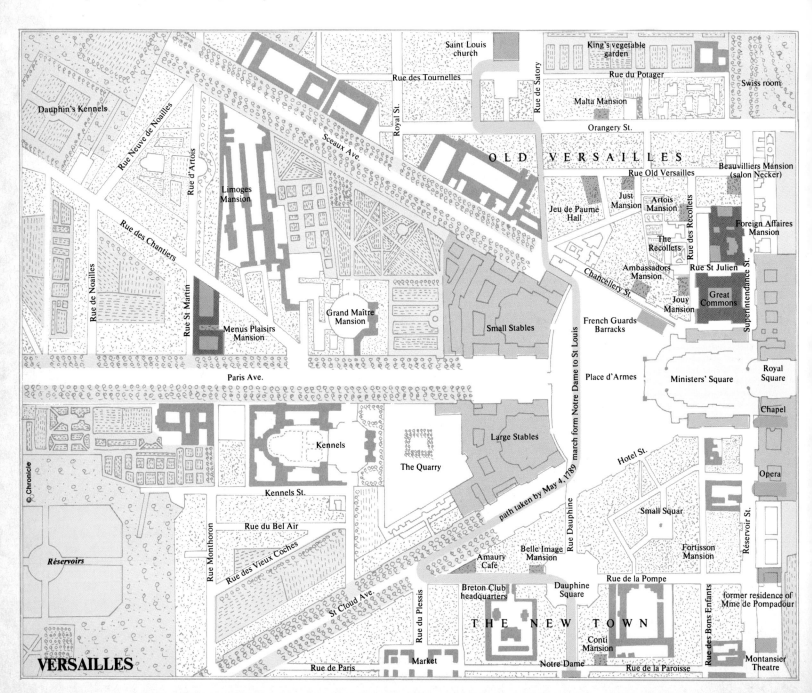

Dauphin's Kennels

Rue Neuve de Noailles

Rue d'Artois

Limoges Mansion

Rue des Chantiers

Rue de Noailles

Rue St Martin

Menus Plaisirs Mansion

Grand Maître Mansion

Paris Ave.

Kennels

The Quarry

Kennels St.

Rue Monthoron

Rue du Bel Air

Rue des Vieux Coches

Réservoirs

St Cloud Ave.

Rue du Plessis

VERSAILLES

Rue de Paris

Market

Sceaux Ave.

Royal St.

Saint Louis church

Rue des Tournelles

Rue de Satory

King's vegetable garden

Rue du Potager

Swiss room

Malta Mansion

Orangery St.

OLD VERSAILLES

Rue Old Versailles

Beauvilliers Mansion (salon Necker)

Just Mansion

Jeu de Paume Hall

Artois Mansion

Rue des Recollets

Foreign Affaires Mansion

The Recollets

Rue St Julien

Ambassadors Mansion

Superintendance St.

Chancellery St.

Jouy Mansion

Great Commons

Small Stables

French Guards Barracks

Place d'Armes

Ministers' Square

Royal Square

Large Stables

path taken by May 4, 1789 march form Notre Dame to St Louis

Hotel St.

Chapel

Opera

Rue Dauphine

Small Squar

Reservoir St.

Belle Image Mansion

Fortisson Mansion

Amaury Café

Rue de la Pompe

Breton Club headquarters

Dauphine Square

former residence of Mme de Pompadour

THE NEW TOWN

Rue des Bons Enfants

Conti Mansion

Notre Dame

Rue de la Paroisse

Montansier Theatre

© Chronicle

The skyline of Paris in the 18th. century viewed from the Sainte Geneviève hill.

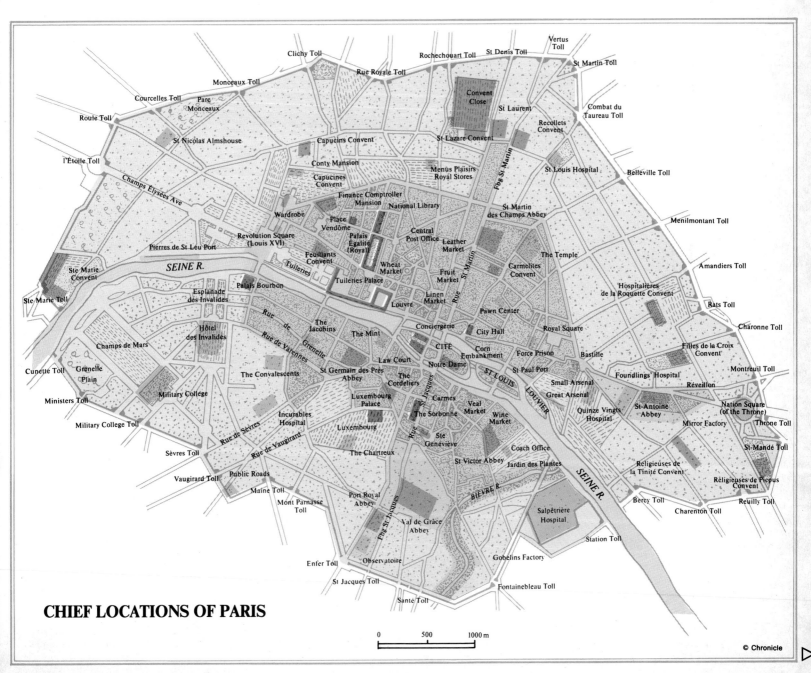

Vertus Toll

Clichy Toll
Rochechouart Toll
St Denis Toll
St Martin Toll

Rue Royale Toll

Monceaux Toll

Courcelles Toll
Parc
Monceaux

Convent
Close
St Laurent
Combat du
Taureau Toll

Roule Toll

St Nicolas Almshouse
Capucins Convent
St-Lazare Convent
Recollets
Convent

l'Étoile Toll

Conty Mansion
Menus Plaisirs
Royal Stores
St Louis Hospital
Belleville Toll

Champs Élysées Ave
Capucines
Convent

Finance Comptroller
Mansion
National Library
Fbg St-Martin
St Martin
des Champs Abbey

Wardrobe
Place
Vendôme
Central
Post Office
St Martin
des Champs Abbey
Ménilmontant Toll

Revolution Square
(Louis XVI)
Palais
Égalité
(Royal)
Leather
Market
The Temple

Pierres de St Leu Port
Feuillants
Convent
Wheat
Market
Carmelites
Convent
Amandiers Toll

SEINE R.
Tuileries
Fruit
Market
Hospitalières
de la Roquette Convent

Ste Marie
Convent
Tuileries Palace
Rue St Martin
Linen
Market

Ste Marie Toll
Palais Bourbon
Louvre
Pawn Center
Rats Toll

Esplanade
des Invalides
The
Jacobins
Concierge rie
City Hall
Royal Square
Charonne Toll

Hôtel
des Invalides
Rue de Grenelle
The Mint
CITÉ
Corn
Embankment
Force Prison
Bastille
Filles de la Croix
Convent

Champs de Mars
Rue de Varennes
Law Court
Notre Dame
St Paul Port
Montreuil Toll

Cunette Toll
The Convalescents
St Germain des Prés
Abbey
The
Cordeliers
ST LOUIS
Small Arsenal
Foundlings' Hospital
Réveillon

Grenelle
Plain
Luxembourg
Palace
Carmes
Great Arsenal

Ministers Toll
Military College
Incurables
Hospital
The Sorbonne
Veal
Market
Wine
Market
Quinze Vingts
Hospital
St-Antoine
Abbey
Nation Square
(of the Throne)

Military College Toll
Rue de Sèvres
Luxembourg
Ste
Geneviève
Mirror Factory
Throne Toll

Sèvres Toll
Rue de Vaugirard
Coach Office
Religieuses de
la Tinité Convent
St-Mandé Toll

Vaugirard Toll
Public Roads
The Chartreux
St Victor Abbey
Jardin des Plantes
SEINE R.
Religieuses de Piepus
Convent

Maine Toll
Port Royal
Abbey
BIÈVRE R.
Bercy Toll
Reuilly Toll

Mont Parnasse
Toll
Salpêtrière
Hospital
Charenton Toll

Enfer Toll
Val de Grâce
Abbey
Fbg St-Jacques
Gobelins Factory
Station Toll

Observatoire
Rue St Jacques

St Jacques Toll
Fontainebleau Toll

Santé Toll

CHIEF LOCATIONS OF PARIS

0   500   1000 m

© Chronicle

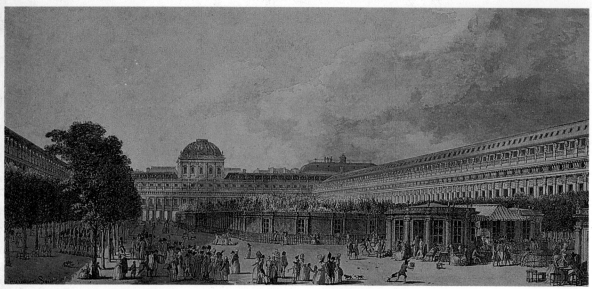

The Palais Royal and its gardens, one of the busiest parts of the French capital.

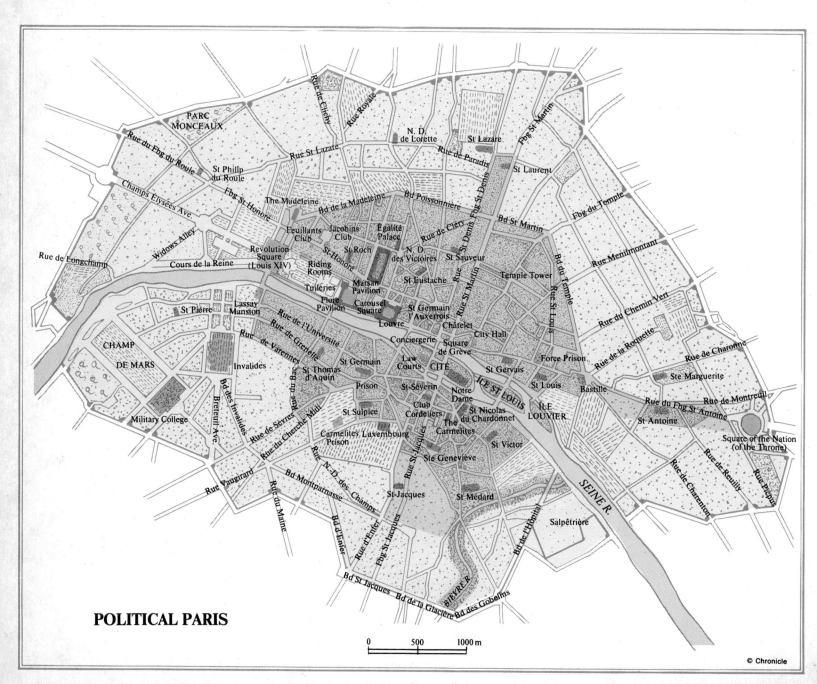

POLITICAL PARIS

0   500   1000 m

© Chronicle

Paris sets the example ...

... for the fashion-conscious.

Customers of the Palais Royal's Caveau Café read or chat.

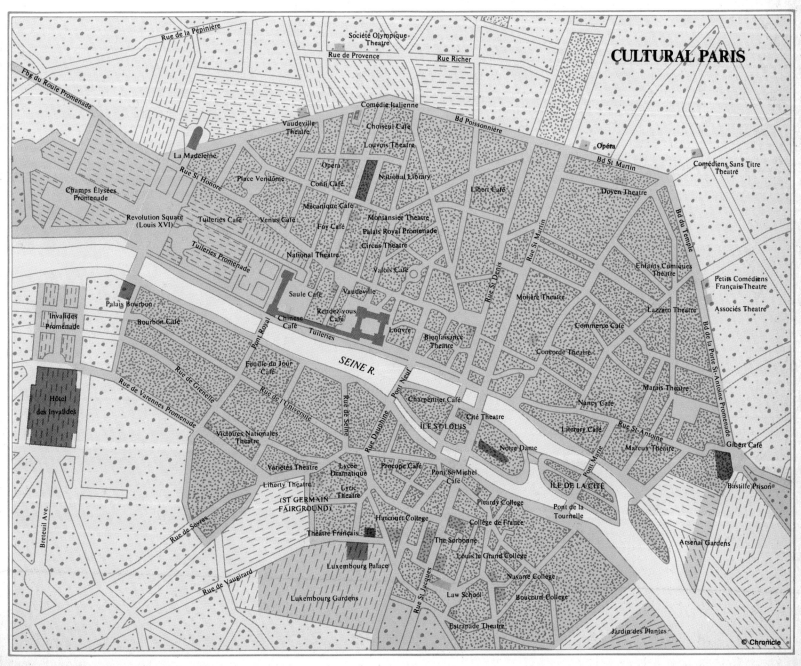

CULTURAL PARIS

Rue de la Pépinière

Société Olympique Theatre

Rue de Provence

Rue Richer

Fbg du Roule Promenade

Comédie Italienne

Bd Poissonnière

Opéra

Vaudeville Theatre

Choiseul Café

Bd St Martin

Louvois Theatre

Comédiens Sans Titre Theatre

La Madeleine

Opéra

National Library

Libori Café

Doyen Theatre

Rue St Honoré

Place Vendôme

Conti Café

Champs Élysées Promenade

Mécanique Café

Montansier Theatre

Revolution Square (Louis XVI)

Tuileries Café

Venus Café

Foy Café

Palais Royal Promenade

Enfants Comiques Theatre

Circus Theatre

Petits Comédiens Français Theatre

Tuileries Promenade

National Theatre

Valois Café

Molière Theatre

Lazzaro Theatre

Associés Theatre

Saule Café

Vaudeville

Palais Bourbon

Rendez-vous Café

Commerce Café

Invalides Promenade

Bourbon Café

Chinese Café

Tuileries

Louvre

Bienfaisance Theatre

Concorde Theatre

Feuille du Jour Café

SEINE R.

Marais Theatre

Hôtel des Invalides

Rue de Grenelle

Rue de l'Université

Rue de Seine

Pont Neuf

Charpentier Café

Nancy Café

Rue de Varennes Promenade

Rue Dauphine

ÎLE ST-LOUIS

Cité Theatre

Literary Café

Rue St-Antoine

Gibert Café

Victoires Nationales Theatre

Notre Dame

Mareux Theatre

Variétés Theatre

Lycée Dramatique

Procope Café

Pont St-Michel Café

ÎLE DE LA CITÉ

Bastille Prison

Liberty Theatre

Lyric Theatre

Picardy College

Pont de la Tournelle

(ST GERMAIN FAIRGROUND)

Breteuil Ave.

Rue de Sèvres

Harcourt College

Collège de France

Théâtre Français

The Sorbonne

Arsenal Gardens

Louis le Grand College

Luxembourg Palace

Navarre College

Rue de Vaugirard

Bourbon College

Luxembourg Gardens

Rue St-Jacques

Law School

Estrapade Theatre

Jardin des Plantes

© Chronicle

The scenes and the places

The harbour at Bordeaux with its ramparts.

The banks of the Rhône river at Lyons.

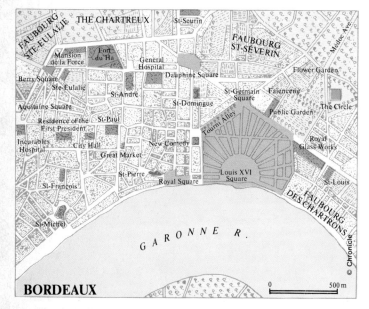

BORDEAUX

FAUBOURG STE-EULALIE
THE CHARTREUX
St-Seurin
FAUBOURG ST-SÉVERIN
Medoc Ave.
Mansion de la Force
Fort du Ha
General Hospital
Berry Square
Dauphine Square
Flower Garden
Ste-Eulalie
St-André
St-Germain Square
Faïencerie
Aquitaine Square
St-Domingue
Public Garden
The Circle
Residence of the First President
St-Paul
Tourni Alley
Incurables Hospital
City Hall
New Comedy
Royal Glass Works
Great Market
St-Pierre
Louis XVI Square
St-François
Royal Square
St-Louis
St-Michel
FAUBOURG DES CHARTRONS
GARONNE R.
© Chronicle
0   500 m

MARSEILLES

The Foundlings
St-Maur
The Preachers
Law Courts
Jangnin Square
Miséricorde Hospital
St-Laurent
St-Jaume
Fort St-Jean
St-Jean Square
New Square
City Hall
The Grands Augustins
Canebière
Monsieur Pier
Square of the Tower
HARBOUR
Carme des Chaux
King's Fountain
Oil Square
Calonne Pier
Comedy Square
Building Site
Dauphin Pier
Play House
St-Victor
St-Nicolas' Citadel
The Corderie
St-Roch
Monthion Square
The Piepus
St-Victor Gate
Gate N.-D. of the Guard
Paradise Gate
© Chronicle
0   200 km

LYONS

LA CROIX ROUSSE
St-Sébastian's Wall
VAISE
CONVENTION
The Two Lovers
Oratory Institute
SAÔNE R.
Liberty Square
Theatre
St-Vincent
Community House
Victories Bridge
St-Paul
St-Pierre
THE PELLETIER
Stone Bridge
Great College
N.-D. de Fourvière
St-Nizier
Small College
The Cordeliers
St-Barthélemy's Rise
CORN EXCHANGE
New Bath Rise
Flying Bridge
Hospice
RAISON
Gourguillon Rise
St-Jean
The Célestins
The Jacobins
St-Georges
Egalité Square
Arsenal
Guillotière Bridge
Ste-Irénée
Ainay Bridge
St-Jacques
Elders and Foundlings' Hospice
EGALITÉ
The Quarantine
Bertin Walk
GUILLOTIÈRE
RHÔNE R.
THE BROTTEAUX
© Chronicle
0   500 m

The port of Marseilles, protected by the Saint Jean and Saint Nicolas forts.

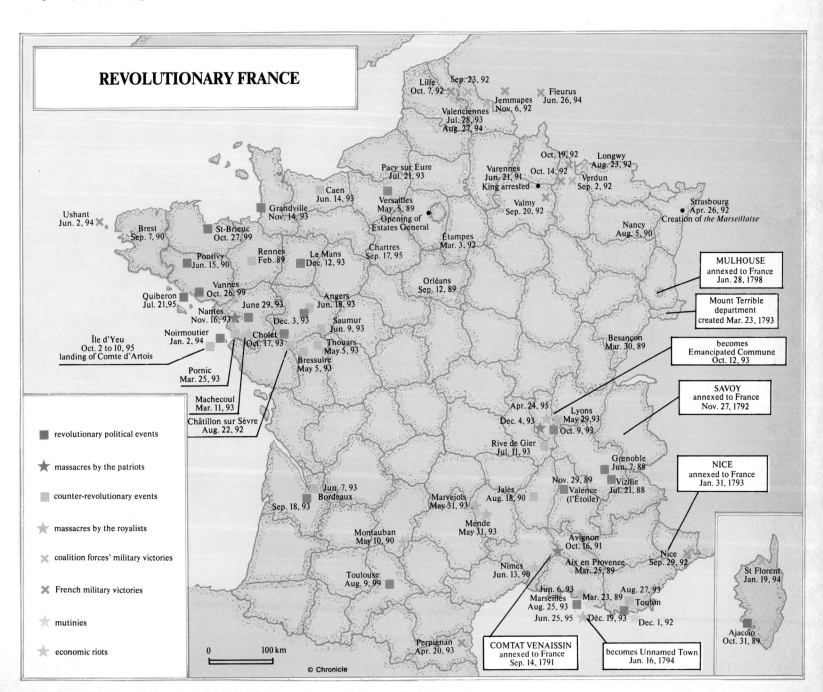

REVOLUTIONARY FRANCE

Lille Oct. 7, 92 / Sep. 23, 92 / Fleurus Jun. 26, 94 / Jemmapes Nov. 6, 92 / Valenciennes Jul. 28, 93 Aug. 27, 94 / Oct. 19, 92 / Longwy Aug. 23, 92 / Varennes Jun. 21, 91 King arrested / Oct. 14, 92 / Verdun Sep. 2, 92 / Valmy Sep. 20, 92 / Strasbourg Apr. 26, 92 Creation of *the Marseillaise* / Pacy sur Eure Jul. 21, 93 / Caen Jun. 14, 93 / Versailles May 5, 89 Opening of Estates General / Nancy Aug. 5, 90 / Grandville Nov. 14, 93 / Étampes Mar. 3, 92 / Ushant Jun. 2, 94 / Brest Sep. 7, 90 / St-Brieuc Oct. 27, 99 / Rennes Feb. 89 / Le Mans Dec. 12, 93 / Chartres Sep. 17, 95 / Pontivy Jan. 15, 90 / Vannes Oct. 26, 99 / Orléans Sep. 12, 89 / Quiberon Jul. 21, 95 / June 29, 93 / Angers Jun. 18, 93 / Nantes Nov. 16, 93 / Dec. 3, 93 / Saumur Jun. 9, 93 / Noirmoutier Jan. 2, 94 / Cholet Oct. 17, 93 / Thouars May 5, 93 / Île d'Yeu Oct. 2 to 10, 95 landing of Comte d'Artois / Bressuire May 5, 93 / Pornic Mar. 25, 93 / Machecoul Mar. 11, 93 / Besançon Mar. 30, 89 / Châtillon sur Sèvre Aug. 22, 92 / Apr. 24, 95 / Lyons May 29, 93 Dec. 4, 93 Oct. 9, 93 / Rive de Gier Jul. 11, 93 / Grenoble Jun. 7, 88 / Vizille Jul. 21, 88 / Nov. 29, 89 / Valence (l'Étoile) / Jun. 7, 93 Bordeaux Sep. 18, 93 / Marvejols May 31, 93 / Jalès Aug. 18, 90 / Montauban May 10, 90 / Mende May 31, 93 / Avignon Oct. 16, 91 / Nice Sep. 29, 92 / Nîmes Jun. 13, 90 / Aix en Provence Mar. 25, 89 / Toulouse Aug. 9, 99 / Jun. 6, 93 Marseilles Aug. 25, 93 Jun. 25, 95 / Mar. 23, 89 / Aug. 27, 93 Toulon Déc. 19, 93 Dec. 1, 92 / Perpignan Apr. 20, 93

MULHOUSE annexed to France Jan. 28, 1798
Mount Terrible department created Mar. 23, 1793
becomes Emancipated Commune Oct. 12, 93
SAVOY annexed to France Nov. 27, 1792
NICE annexed to France Jan. 31, 1793
COMTAT VENAISSIN annexed to France Sep. 14, 1791
becomes Unnamed Town Jan. 16, 1794

St Florent Jan. 19, 94 / Ajaccio Oct. 31, 89

- revolutionary political events
- massacres by the patriots
- counter-revolutionary events
- massacres by the royalists
- coalition forces' military victories
- French military victories
- mutinies
- economic riots

0   100 km
© Chronicle

49

The scenes and the places: the colonies

The fort of Martinique island viewed from the Flemish docks.

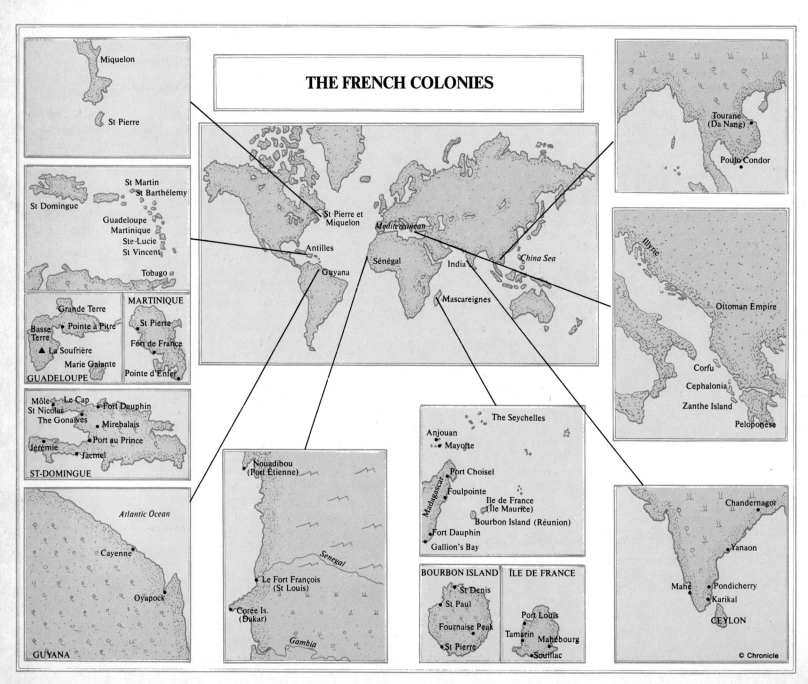

THE FRENCH COLONIES

Miquelon
St Pierre

St Martin
St Barthélemy
St Domingue
Guadeloupe
Martinique
Ste-Lucie
St Vincent
Tobago

Grande Terre
Pointe à Pitre
Basse Terre
▲ La Soufrière
Marie Galante
GUADELOUPE

MARTINIQUE
St Pierre
Fort de France
Pointe d'Enfer

Môle   Le Cap
St Nicolas
The Gonaïves   Fort Dauphin
        Mirebalais
Jérémie   Port au Prince
     Jacmel
ST-DOMINGUE

Atlantic Ocean
Cayenne
Oyapock
GUYANA

Nouadibou
(Port Étienne)
Senegal
Le Fort François
(St Louis)
Corée Is.
(Dakar)
Gambia

The Seychelles
Anjouan
Mayotte
Port Choisel
Foulpointe
Madagascar
Ile de France
(Île Maurice)
Bourbon Island (Réunion)
Fort Dauphin
Gallion's Bay

BOURBON ISLAND
St Denis
St Paul
Fournaise Peak
St Pierre

ÎLE DE FRANCE
Port Louis
Tamarin   Mahébourg
Souillac

St Pierre et
Miquelon
Antilles
Guyana
Sénégal
Mediterranean
India
Mascareignes
China Sea

Tourane
(Da Nang)
Poulo Condor

Illyrie
Ottoman Empire
Corfu
Cephalonia
Zanthe Island
Peloponese

Chandernagor
Yanaon
Mahé   Pondicherry
    Karikal
CEYLON

© Chronicle

The customs offices on London's River Thames. The Tower of London can be seen in the background.

England (Kingdom of)

Despite being the world's foremost power, England in the reign of George III (1760-1820) is still suffering from the effects of the defeat it suffered in America. Spain and France, the chief victims of the 1763 Treaty of Paris, are finally able, 20 years after the fact, to get their revenge on the wealthiest colonial empire. The English Navy's reputation for invincibility suffered badly and England's nine million inhabitants now have to face heavy war debts. On the home front George III is faced with a population that is better informed, thanks to the growth of the press and the publication of parliamentary reports. In a nation where monarchy is less absolute than elsewhere, the King's authoritarianism is being increasingly questioned, and England's setbacks in America have led to a constitutional crisis. In 1792 George III had to abandon his loyal minister, Frederick North, and appoint William Pitt of the Whig Party. In Ireland, patriots would have followed the American example if the King had not granted autonomy to the Dublin Parliament in time. Since George III began suffering bouts of dementia in 1785, he has delegated more of his powers to the cabinet. Despite the nation's industrial and commercial prosperity, Pitt has problems keeping finances on an even keel. Peace is needed for a healthy economy. After being the main rival of France, England signed a favourable trade treaty with Vergennes in 1786. This demonstrated a mutual desire for closer diplomatic relations between the two sides.

Austria (Empire of)

Faced with the spectacular rise of Prussia and Russia, Austria is desperately seeking to consolidate its empire. The reformist efforts undertaken during the reign of Joseph II (1765-1790) crown the achievements of Maria Theresa, adding a touch of enlightenment. The aim was to first centralise an empire that included the nations on the Danube, Lombardy and the Austrian Netherlands. By grouping the chancelleries, Joseph II streamlined an already large bureaucracy. He also imposed German as the administrative language for the 26 million Hungarians, Czechs, Rumanians, Slovenes and Poles living under his authority. However, such reforms did not always please the different states. The inhabitants of Lombardy, for example, were angered by the abolition of their senate. The kingdom of Hungary, which had no Diet or Palatine Prince, felt scant respect for Joseph II. The peasants were, however, much better off thanks to the abolition of forced labour. In Bohemia itself, Joseph ordered the abolition of serfdom in order to provide a major source of potential manual workers for the new manufacturing industries. By focusing on the development of industry in that region, the state demonstrated its desire to modernise the country, although it led to a larger economic gap between the east and west of the Empire. This does not worry the monarch unduly, as he measures the extent of his powers by the size of his territories. The key position Austria occupies in eastern Europe means that Joseph is faced by pressures from various quarters. Despite these, the sovereign prefers to trust France, his old ally, to keep the balance of power in Europe.

Spain (Kingdom of)

The empire on which the sun never sets cuts a poor figure in the gathering of great powers. Even though it is present on all continents, Spain has invested little of the profits from its colonies in the Peninsula. Under the reign of Charles III of Bourbon (1759-1788), the country has slowly progressed into the age of reform. However, with only nine million people, the country is sparsely populated. In addition to all the geographical and climatic problems there is the secular weight of an all-powerful church, crushing Spanish society. Influenced by the movement of enlightenment, the King tried to limit the power of the church by reducing the privileges and the number of clergy; but his initiatives were limited. He was, however, more successful in the economic sector, which until then had been the victim of colonial mercantilism. The development of irrigation, as well as the creation of factories, marked the beginning of a slight restructuring. Preoccupied by the management of its colonies, Spain takes very little part in European affairs, and then only indirectly through France. Because of a family pact with them, Charles III backed the French intervention in America. However, at the end of his life, he chose peace abroad, as well as peace at home where he left the door open to conservatives.

Italy

A victim, until 1748, of the conflicts between the great powers, Italy is enjoying a long period of stability. Peace and the absence of plagues have promoted a remarkable demographic expansion, which has swelled the country's population from 11 million inhabitants at the beginning of the century to 18 million now. Geographically, Italy is, since the treaty of Aix la Chapelle in 1748, split into 15 states of varying sizes, cultures and administrations. Between the large kingdoms of the Two Sicilies in the south and Piedmont-Sardinia in the northeast, the peninsula is dominated by the Papal States, the vast and rich Duchy of Tuscany and Austrian Lombardy. The republics of Genoa and Venice, powerful in the past, suffer heavily from the dramatic decline of Mediterranean commerce. Faced with political and economic stagnation in the peninsula, only Lombardy and Tuscany seem to be dynamic regions. Seduced by the movement of enlightenment, they have undertaken a series of reforms. They cannot stay the economic and social crisis threatening the population.

Austrian Netherlands

The Belgian territories are being rocked by unrest. Joseph II, who would willingly have exchanged them for Bavaria, has imposed reforms on two million Belgians which have angered everyone. While the patriots are indignant at the rise of absolutism, conservatives refuse to lose the privileges of their old

The international scene

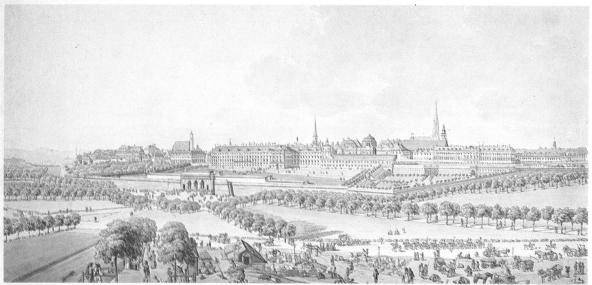

Vienna, the Austrian capital, as viewed from the Imperial Palace.

institutions. They also deplore the savage attacks against the clergy. Since 1787, public resentment has turned into open rebellion against the domination by Austria.

Poland (Kingdom of)

Not much is left of France's loyal ally in central Europe. After about a century of economic stagnation and political anarchy, Poland has become the victim of the greed of its powerful neighbours. In 1772, at the urging of Catherine II, Russia, Austria and Prussia each took their share of the Polish plains to the east, the south and the west. Even though the country has been able to hang on to its territory from the Bug to the Dnieper, Poland still feels threatened. Stanislas II, who was the ruler of four million people from 1764 to 1795, earned a reputation as a traitor working for Russia. His reforms were limited to just the education and administrative sectors. This did nothing to increase Poland's security. As a diplomat said after the first division of Poland: "Catherine of Russia has had her breakfast, but where will she dine?"

United Provinces

The economic and political rôles played by the United Provinces have been in constant decline since the start of the century. Holland, a seafaring and commercial power, has been unable to cope with the competition from England. It was forced to agree to England's protection, symbolised by the family ties linking the King of England and the Stadtholder William V, who has been in office since February 1751. The federation handed its powers over to the Stadtholder, but republican sentiment has remained strong among the Provinces' two million inhabitants. Republicanism is the root cause of the crisis in the country. Relying on their alliance with Paris, the Dutch tried to oust William V in 1787, the Anglo-Prussian intervention put paid to their plans. Dutch patriots were then forced to flee to France.

Prussia (Kingdom of)

The rise of Prussia to the rank of a great power over the course of the century shattered the balance of power in Europe. Under the rule of the ambitious Frederick II, the Great, who reigned from 1740 to 1786, Prussia spread over the whole of northern continental Europe, from the Electorate of Brandenburg to the borders of the Russian Empire. Being an enlightened despot, Frederick did not only seek to conquer territory. He also sought to reform the nation's administration. Under his leadership, agriculture went through a boom period, aided by the colonisation of virgin lands. The rich region of Silesia, seized from Austria, underwent a great industrial leap forward. However, military affairs were Frederick's favourite field. On seeing Prussia's army of 200,000 men out of a population of six million, Mirabeau said: "Prussia is an arrmy occupying a state." Frederick, like his successor Frederick William II, never hesitated to use his troops, particularly against Austria and Poland. Prussia was a constant threat to Europe's stability. France and Prussia's interests were diametrically opposed, and they clashed over the United Provinces in 1787.

Russia (Empire of)

From the Baltic to the Black Sea, from the Ural mountains to the Dvina river, Russia is on the move and growing constantly.

Faithfully carrying out Peter the Great's plans, Catherine II, who reigned from 1762 to 1796, has made territorial conquest her chief objective. At war against the Turks, from whom she is retaking the Black Sea coast, the Czarina scored a major victory in 1772 when she achieved a first partition of Poland. Even though Paris does not support such expansionism, France is still a model of modern civilisation for the Russians. The enlightened Empress looks west for political inspiration. Her main reforms have been influenced by the philosophers. In 1785, in order to breathe new life into a rigid and autocratic system, Catherine granted the nobility the right to take part in trade and industry. However, this move only affected a tiny proportion of her 26 million subjects. By distributing vast tracts of land to the nobility, she contributed to the spread of serfdom, which now exists all the way to the Ukraine. In a country where 95 per cent of the population is rural, agriculture has remained the chief activity. Despite this, the government wants to develop the vital military and industrial sectors. It is planning to encourage trade, and in 1787 Russia signed a commercial treaty with France. For Catherine, this pact brings hopes of French neutrality in Russia's conflict with the Ottoman Empire.

United States (Republic of)

The longing for independence and an affirmation of the rights of man were the main aspirations that led to the creation of the initial 13 United States of America in the year 1783.

The former British colonies which are stretched out along the Mississippi River, all the way from the Great Lakes to Georgia, defended their interests by force of arms. After a war in which the "insurgents" were helped by France, Spain and Holland, America's four million inhabitants now face the daunting task of organising their new nation. Lengthy and fiery debate led in 1787 to the adoption of a Constitution which appears to be a subtle compromise between two groups: the autonomists and the federalists. The freedom of the states was guaranteed by a double system of sovereignty. However, George Washington had to gamble on his huge popularity to get the Philadelphia Convention to approve the new institutions. These are admired from afar by the whole of enlightened Europe.

In France, which was the first ally of the United States, the reformists, particularly La Fayette, see the historic events in America as a victory for liberty and natural rights over conservative forces.

Chronicle of the reign of Louis XVI

The main political, economic, social and cultural events which marked Louis XVI's reign, from its start in 1774 to January 1st, 1788, the date at which this book opens.

1774

Versailles, May 10
Death of Louis XV. His grandson succeeds to the throne with the name of Louis XVI.

Paris, June 12
Louis XVI ends the exile of the Duc de Choiseul, a former minister of Louis XV famous for his reformist policies, which the King had condemned in 1770.

France, July 20
Louis XVI reshuffles his Council by appointing the Comte de Maurepas as Minister of State and the Comte de Vergennes as Foreign Affairs Secretary.

Compiègne, August 24
Louis XVI dismisses Abbot Teray and Chancellor Maupeou, whose reforms had caused public resentment the previous year.

Versailles, September 13
The new Comptroller General of Finances, Turgot, urges the King to restore the free circulation of grain in the kingdom.

Paris, November 12
The King recalls the magistrates who were exiled by Maupeou in 1771 and solemnly re-establishes Parliament.

Paris
The painter Jacques Louis David is awarded the Prix de Rome for his work *Artiochus et Stratonice*.

1775

France, March-May
The scarcity and constantly rising cost of bread, linked with the poor harvest, cause violent unrest to break out in the Brie, Champagne and Paris regions. This so-called "flour war" compromises Turgot's reform plans.

Paris, April 28
Jacques Necker, a Geneva banker, publishes a book on the grain trade and laws. In it he attacks Turgot's reformist policies.

Versailles, July 21
Malesherbes, a friend of the philosophers, is appointed Secretary of State at the Royal Household.

Paris, September 3
Turgot takes control of the postal administration.

Fontainebleau, October 27
The Comte de Saint Germain, an ardent supporter of Frederick II's military strategy, is appointed Secretary of State for War.

1776

Versailles, January 5
Turgot continues his reform policies by abolishing forced labour, the masterships and the guild wardenships.

Versailles, May 12
Louis XVI dismisses Turgot, whose reforms are angering noblemen and bourgeois alike.

Doubs, June
The Marquis Jouffroy d'Abbans gets a steam-powered ship to sail on the Doubs river.

Versailles, August 19
After having restored forced labour on August 11th., the King restores the guild wardenships.

Versailles, October 22
The bailiff Taboureau des Réaux becomes Comptroller General of Finance and Necker is made head of the Treasury.

Paris, December 31
Benjamin Franklin, the representative of the American Insurgents, arrives in Paris.

Paris
After publishing *La Morale Universelle*, Baron d'Holbach sets up the Nine Sisters Masonic lodge.

1777

Paris, January 1
First edition of the *Journal de Paris*, the first daily to be published in France. It will quickly be banned for publishing an article that is deemed offensive by the Chief Almoner.

Paris, January
Necker issues a loan that is attractive to the public but costly for the Treasury.

Paris, February 13
The Marquis de Sade is arrested.

Versailles, May 28
France signs an alliance treaty with the Swiss Cantons.

Versailles, June 29
Following the dismissal of Taboureau des Réaux, Necker is made Director General of Finance.

Unites States, July 27
The Marquis de La Fayette, the Vicomte de Noailles and the Comte de Ségur arrive in America to help the Insurgents.

Versailles, September 26
After the departure of Turgot and Malesherbes, Saint Germain's resignation marks the total failure of attempts at structural reforms in France.

Versailles, December 6
France recognises the United States of America.

France
The French chemist Antoine de Lavoisier perfects his theory of combustion.

1778

Versailles, February 6
France and the United States sign a bilateral treaty of friendship and commerce.

Paris, May 30
Death of Voltaire.

Ermenonville, July 2
Death of Rousseau, who had just finished writing his *Rêveries d'un Promeneur Solitaire*.

Versailles, July 10
The King declares war on England.

Paris, December
The King issues a loan of 80 million livres in an attempt to reduce the nation's deficit, which is being increased by France's aid to the rebels in America.

Paris
Madame Necker sets up a model hospital in the Saint Pierre du Gros Caillou parish.

Paris
Mozart performs the *Petits Riens* in the French capital.

1779

Africa, January 22-30
The Marquis de Vaudreuil conquers territories inland from the coast of Senegal.

Antilles, February
The English capture the island of Saint Lucia and force the French fleet led by Admiral d'Estaing to withdraw to Martinique.

Versailles, February
La Fayette returns from America and asks the King for further aid for the rebels.

Aranjuez, April 12
Spain and France sign a secret convention committing Spain to go to war against England alongside the American Insurgents.

Versailles, April 27
On the advice of Necker, a provincial assembly is created in the Dauphiné to reduce the powers of bailiffs and get local notables to take party in regional administration.

Versailles, August 10
Louis XVI frees the last remaining serfs on royal lands.

1780

Versailles, January
Necker starts reforming the King's Household in an attempt to improve the kingdom's disastrous financial situation.

Brest, May 2
Following La Fayette's latest departure for America, the King sends 6,000 men to New England under the command of Rochambeau.

Versailles, July
The assembly of the clergy votes for a free donation of 30 million livres to help the nation's finances.

Versailles, August 24
Louis XVI abolishes the "preliminary question", or torture, used to get a suspect to confess.

Versailles, August 30
Acting on Necker's advice, the King announces a reorganisation of the prison system in a bid to improve conditions in jails.

Versailles, October
Antoine de Sartine, the Minister of the Navy, is disgraced after being accused by Necker of being responsible for his ministry's debts of 20 million livres.

Versailles, December 23
The Upper Council is reshuffled. The Marquis de Castries becomes Minister of the Navy and the Marquis de Ségur is appointed Minister of War.

1781

Paris, January 19
Continuing with his major reform programme, Necker sets up the Hospital Administration.

Paris, February 19
Necker publishes his report to the King for the year 1781. It shows in detail the state of the kingdom's finances. This innovation is a big success, but financiers accuse the minister of having left out the arrears and the nation's special expenses.

Marly, May 19
After having sought the position of minister of state in vain, Necker foresees his fall from grace and submits his resignation. His departure shakes financiers' confidence in the Bourse.

Chaillot, August
The Perier brothers set up their first steam machine based on the principles of England's James Watt.

United States, October 19
Franco-American victory over the English at Yorktown.

Versailles, October 22
Louis Joseph, son of Louis XVI and Marie Antoinette, is born.

Paris, December 8
The publisher Panckouke announces the publication of a methodical *Encylopaedia*.

Paris
Condorcet's *Reflexions sur l'esclavage des Nègres* are published.

1782

Paris, April 10
Publication of *Les Liasons Dangereuses* by Pierre Choderlos de Laclos, which immediately causes a scandal.

Geneva, April
Beginning of the publication of the *Confessions* as well as *Rêveries du Promeneur Solitaire* by Jean Jacques Rousseau.

Versailles, May 7
Opening of peace negotiations between France and England.

Gibraltar, October
Franco-Spanish troops fail in their attempt to retake Gibraltar from the English.

1783

Versailles, February 23
The King creates a committee of finance. He appoints Vergennes as its head.

Annonay, June 4
The Montgolfier brothers succeed in flying a balloon for the first time.

Versailles, September 3
France, Spain and England sign a peace treaty.

Paris, October 29
Death of d'Alembert, author with Diderot of the *Encyclopédie*.

Paris
Lavoisier succeeds in the synthesis of water.

1784

Constantinople, January 8
Vergennes intervenes to settle the long conflict between the Ottoman Empire and Russia.

Versailles, January 18
Appointed Controller of Finance on November 3rd, 1783, Charles Alexandre de Calonne joins the Council and is appointed Minister of State.

Paris, May
After the performance of *Mariage de Figaro*, Beaumarchais is the object of violent attacks and is incarcerated in Saint Lazare prison. He is then released under popular pressure after five days.

Paris, December
Jacques Necker violently criticises his successor's financial management and performance in a treatise entitled *De l'Administration des Finances de la France*.

1785

Calais, January 7
The Frenchman Blanchard and the Englishman Jeffries succeed in the first hot-air ballon crossing o f the English Channel.

Paris, January 29
At the instigation of the Comtesse de Valois, Cardinal de Rohan buys, on behalf of the Queen, a necklace of diamonds and precious stone with a value of 1,600,000 livres.

Paris, April 14
Calonne restructures the French India Company.

Versailles, July 17
By order of the Council, the importation of goods from England is strickly limited.

Brest, August 1
Jean François de la Pérouse undertakes an expedition in the Pacific Ocean Which he has prepared with the King, with the aim of developing the fur trade with China and Japan.

Versailles, August 15
A scandal breaks out at court after the jewellers demand payment for the Queen's necklace. Marie Antoinette denies having bought it and Cardinal Rohan is arrested.

Versailles-Madrid, August 27
France and Spain sign a treaty redefining the border of the two countries.

Paris, October 30
Calonne undertakes financial reforms.

Fontainebleau, November 10
France signs an alliance with the United Provinces.

1786

Paris, May 22-31
Cardinal de Rohan's acquittal does not stop the suspicion that is discrediting the Queen in the public's esteem.

Savoy, August 8
A mountain guide from Chamonix, Jacques Balmat, becomes the first man to climb Mont Blanc.

Versailles, August 20
Calotte gives Louis XVI his *Précis d'un plan d'amélioration des finances*, in which he proposes reforms that he could have approved by an assembly of notables to avoid opposition in Parliament.

London, September 26
France and England sign a trade agreement.

Versailles, December 29
Louis XVI announces that a meeting of an assembly of notables is to be held shortly.

Paris
Supporters and opponents of a planned reform of the French justice system clash after the Paris parliament sentences three peasants from the bailiwick of Chaumont to death for murder.

France
The botanist Vilmorin introduces cultivation of the sugar-beet to France.

1787

Versailles, February 13
Vergennes, the Minister of Foreign Affairs, dies. He is replaced by the Comte de Montmorin.

Versailles, February 22
Opening of the session of the assembly of notables. Calonne admits there is a national deficit estimated at 112 million livres.

Versailles, April 8
Calonne resigns under pressure from the notables. He is replaced by Loménie de Brienne.

United Provinces, May
Rebelling against their Stadtholder, the Dutch call in vain for help from France, with whom they had signed a mutual assistance trealy.

Versailles, June
Loménie de Brienne replaces forced labour with a tax and allows the free circulation of grain.

Paris, July 30
After having demanded a meeting of the Estates General, Parliament refuses to approve a new tax, the territorial subsidy.

Versailles, August 30
Louis XVI decrees the Parliament's exile.

Versailles, August 27
The Council of Ministers is reshuffled. The Comte de la Luzerne is appointed Minister of the Navy and the Comte de Brienne, Loménie's brother, becomes Minister of War.

Versailles, September 4
Louis XVI recalls Parliament.

Paris, November 19
Faced with resistance from Parliament, the King holds a "bed of justice" in order to get approval for new loans. He promises to convene the Estates General in 1792.

Versailles, November 29
The Edict of Tolerance, promulgated by the King, grants civil status to Protestants, who did not previously have it.

Despotism charge enrages Louis XVI

"My subjects' legitimate freedom is as dear to me as it is to them."

Versailles, January 17

In its January 4 decree, the Paris parliament firmly condemned the system of sealed royal orders which allows the King arbitrarily to imprison unruly subjects. The crisis between parliament and the King, which has been dragging on for months, seems to have reached a point of no return.

This time, magistrates have no qualms about accusing the King of despotism. Outraged by such audacity, Louis XVI today summoned a parliamentary delegation to explain what he sees as a calumny. "The legitimate freedom of my subjects is as dear to me as it is to themselves. But I will not permit my parliament to denounce the use of a power ... which I have the sweet satisfaction of believing to have exercised with more moderation than any of my predecessors," the King drily told the delegation.

It is in fact difficult to see a tyrant in this easy-going monarch who spends more time hunting than dealing with the affairs of the kingdom. This, however, is not the question for the parliaments, particularly the capital's.

What they are questioning is the very concept of absolute monarchy that exercises power without a system of checks and balances. Using all of their traditional prerogatives, the parliaments have been seizing every conceivable opportunity to place obstacles in the way of Louis XVI's initiatives, but legally the King remains able to have the last word. Nonetheless, a trial of strength has begun today. The youngest and the most active of the magistrates, who include Jean Jacques Duval d'Eprémesnil and François Goislard de Montsabert, have dragged their elders down the path of rebellion. It therefore seems unlikely that parliament will sit idly by while the King annuls its decree. At the same time, the monarch appears unwilling to back down, an unusual attitude for Louis XVI.

Heir to the throne is critically ill

Versailles, January 18

The Dauphin, heir to the throne, is ill. Marie Antoinette, who has been following her children's education, is becoming more concerned every day.

The child is practically an invalid. His vertebrae have slipped and he limps because one hip is higher than the other. The pale and sickly boy has trouble walking from his room to the Trianon park. Every evening, he becomes feverish and looks weaker. The Queen seeks to avoid facing the truth and clings to a vain hope: "His teeth are troubling him," she says, although the Dauphin is seven years old. The worried Queen no longer resembles the fun-loving, party-going young woman she was (→ May 4).

Marie Antoinette keeps a close eye on the education of her children.

Lackeys go hungry at Swedish ball

Paris, January

The ball was in full swing when a group of lackeys brought the party to an abrupt end. They started protesting in the courtyard of the Swedish embassy, shouting insults. Their resentment had been caused by an oversight on the part of the ambassador, Baron de Stäel Holstein. Casting tradition aside, the ambassador had not served them a snack. Servants, who know all the latest gossip, should be treated with kid gloves.

For a successful party, one must be amongst trustworthy friends.

Rivarol pokes fun at famous people

Paris, January 20

Rivarol's stinging pen spares no one and nothing. Arguing that "France no longer knows how to laugh", this brilliant wit, known for his sharpness, has just published a *Little Almanac of Great Men* in which he scathingly satirises pillars of the literary establishment while simultaneously appearing to praise them. Reviewing in catalogue form and alphabetical order literary output over the past few years, he lists 516 widely differing authors whose only common trait is ... mediocrity.

Faced with such widespread literary senility, this daring author wonders what has become of the truly great intellects of the past. The sarcastic and scornful Almanac is not however published with Rivarol's name.

Lavoisier mixes powerful love potion

The famous chemist appreciates the assistance of his wife.

Paris, January

A marriage as successful as this one is unusual. The Lavoisiers are a happy couple, well-loved by their friends. Their marriage is different in part because it is a love match, rather than merely based on a financial arrangement.

Anne Marie Paulze was only fifteen when in 1771 she married Antoine Laurent de Lavoisier, then aged twenty eight. Moreover, the young woman quickly realised the exceptional qualities of her husband. A clever, lively and educated person, she learnt English and Latin in order to help her husband and translated several complex English works on chemistry for him. She is now a keen follower of his scientific experiments, working alongside leading researchers from France and abroad.

The Lavoisiers also share a taste for the arts: they have a box at the opera and regularly visit painting exhibitions. Anne Marie is not only an accomplished musician, she also has a real talent for painting and once studied under the great David. Her husband, who is both a farmer general in charge of tax collection and gunpowder manager, has become a very well known man. The Lavoisiers have made an exceptionally brilliant match.

Lagrange follows in Newton's footsteps

Paris, January

Thanks to Louis XVI, it is in France that the mathematician Joseph de Lagrange today published his *Analytic Mechanics*. The work is a major accomplishment. The scientist, who had been head of the Berlin Academy since 1766, came to Paris two years ago and became a member of the Academy of Science. His new treatise is a vast synthesis of all the major advances to date in the field of mechanics, but the brilliant mathematician has not been intoxicated by success, and tells his friends about the problems he had in finding a publisher for his work. Due to his new found fame, it is unlikely that Lagrange, who is already seen as Newton's equal, will have further trouble finding a publisher.

Protestants win civil status at last

Paris, January 29

The French church no longer has a total monopoly over civil status. From now on, non-Catholics will be able to register births, marriages and deaths with a royal judge.

The parliament has confirmed by a wide majority the decree which will allow Protestants to recover a legal status. Since the bill was submitted to parliament during the November 19 royal session, the clergy had done all they could to block the move.

The wife of Maréchal de Noailles even got a group of former Jesuits to write a lengthy anti-Protestant document which she then personally delivered to each member of parliament. As for the Archbishop of Paris, Monsignor le Clerc de Juigné, he went so far as to voice his opposition to the bill before the King himself. Despite this progress, the decree still does not officially recognise the Protestant faith and does not place French Protestants on an equal footing with the country's Catholics. Under the terms of the new law, Catholicism is to remain the only authorised public faith and non-Catholics are still barred from holding public office. The new legislation is a major disappointment for people such as the Pastor Jean Paul Rabaut Saint Etienne, who had negotiated the bill with its main architect, Guillaume de Malesherbes. However, the basic fact is that the improvement of the status of Protestants has finally been legally confirmed by parliament.

The King is praised for his decree on the civil status of Protestants.

Field guide for rich farmers launched

Paris, January 15

A newspaper aimed at farmers has just been launched, but the new journal is unlikely to be read by illiterate day labourers and farm workers who come home exhausted after spending a day in the fields. Rich farmers of the wealthy rural regions and well to do farm employees, who own their own land, will be able to read the new journal to keep abreast of the latest discoveries in agronomy.

Agronomy has become a favourite concept of physiocrats, who believe that the natural order of society is based on land and that its natural products are the only true form of wealth. Physiocrats are also strong supporters of advances in the field of agriculture, and are opposed to those who see business as the basis of society.

However, the state of French agriculture is such that technological progress is difficult to implement. The continuing use of traditional and inefficient methods means that the country's agricultural output remains relatively low. Output also remains linked to the whims of the weather. Moreover, fiscal and feudal burdens make it hard for peasants to dream of modernising their equipment. A few large landowners began to introduce physiocratic methods some years ago, but they remain exceptional cases.

A peasant is "born to suffer" ...

1. Versailles. A new ruling takes effect at the royal military school; the Abbot André Morellet and the astronomer Jean Sylvain Bailly become senior officials at the school.

3. Paris. A new agricultural machine is shown at the Louvre. It is a thresher that is equipped with 15 mechanical arms.

10. Alsace. An associate member of the Academy of Science sails up the Rhine on a steam-powered craft.

11. Versailles. A Council decree imposes controls on the import of muslin and cloth from Alsace, a region classed as foreign and under German rule.

13. Rome. The young painter Jean Germain Drouais, a favourite student of David, dies of smallpox. →

15. Versailles. A decree abolishes the use of preparatory torture.

17. Saint-Quentin. Death of the painter Maurice Quentin de la Tour, a brilliant portraitist whose works include paintings of major figures of the court and of the world of the arts. Since retiring to his birthplace, he had directed a drawing school.

19. Grenoble. Two Dauphiné parliamentarians, the president d'Ornacieux and councillor de Meyrieu, are summoned to Versailles to explain the parliament's behaviour to the King (→ 23).

19. Paris. The Abbot Grégoire, Jean Pierre Brissot and the Marquis de Lafayette found the *Society of Friends of the Blacks* to fight against the slave trade and get slavery abolished in the French colonies (→ March 3, 88).

19. Versailles. Summoned by Louis XVI, a delegation from the Brittany parliament is severely reprimanded for having dared to give its support to the principle of the equality of all the nation's parliaments.

23. Grenoble. The Dauphiné parliament fosters unrest by asking for the recall of parliamentarians summoned to the court.

24. Paris. The historian Dulaure publishes a new edition of his highly popular tourist guide, *A Description of the Sights of Paris*.

Brienne suspected of anti-parliament plot

Paris, February

Paris's parliament is worried: what can the King and his chief minister, the Comptroller General of Finance Loménie de Brienne, be up to in their secret meetings? Louis XVI and his chief financier have been spending hours discussing matters together without even consulting the royal Council. The other ministers do not like to be kept in the dark about major decisions or to learn of reform plans prepared by Brienne at the same time as the public.

It is true that in practice the growing autonomy of the Finance Minister has become institutionalised, but since the Assembly of Notables was informed of the deficit in the kingdom's budget, many had been expecting a little less secrecy. The parliaments have justifiably been suspecting Brienne of seeking to break them and take what little remaining legislative control they have away from them. There have been some alarming rumours. Some say that Brienne is planning to set up a plenary court which would become the only body empowered to register laws, while the parliaments would only keep their judicial powers. Such a move would be seen as a *coup d'état* by the executive branch, and that would be a dangerous step at a time when the weakness and lack of credibility of the absolutist system have become evident (→ Apr. 30).

David's most outstanding student dies

Rennes, February 13

Jacques Louis David is heartbroken: he has just heard that his best student has died. David felt both admiration and fatherly affection for Jean Germain Drouais. The Academy itself had reacted with great enthusiasm in 1784 when the work *Le Christ et la Cananéenne* had been presented. Thanks to this masterpiece, the young Drouais, brilliant offspring of a line of famous painters, had easily won the first prize and a stay at the Academy of France at Rome. He has just died at the age of twenty five of smallpox and the effect of three years of overwork. By far his most famous work is *Marius à Minturnes,* painted in 1786. Its subject matter, taken from Roman history, is treated in the great tradition of heroic classicism that is embodied by David: although he has vanquished the Cimbrian barbarians, the consul Marius is sentenced to death by his political rival Sylla. He is shown waiting for death at Minturnes, in Campania. Suddenly a Cimbrian slave enters to carry out the sentence and the condemned man asks him proudly: "Would you dare execute Caius Marius?" On hearing these words, the terrified slave drops his sword and flees from his intended victim.

The masterpiece of Louis David's most talented pupil, the young Jean Germain Drouais: "Marius à Minturnes".

The Paris carnival is in full swing

Everything is permitted: His Majesty Carnival is king of the streets.

Paris, February

It is the season for masquerades. Flirtatious women have taken to wearing jackets with long tails decorated with flounces and garlands. Each evening, they rush to the masked balls or to the theatre. There are plenty of attractions. A huge mounted parade brought a lot of famous people back to life: a person disguised as Henri IV had his hair torn out, while his mistress Gabrielle was slapped by an angry harlequin and the venerable Sully was hit with a walking stick.

The parliaments

The kingdom's 13 parliaments are essentially sovereign courts of justice. They deal with trials in which the Crown is involved. They also hear appeals in cases where crimes of blood have been committed.

However, their chief function is to register the King's laws, decrees and orders. The parliaments, in particular the capital's, which is the most powerful since it has the widest jurisdiction, have thus acquired a right to remonstrate with the monarch. Although in principle this only applies to technical aspects of the King's actions, magistrates can also express criticism of the executive and sometimes even stand in opposition to it. The country's parliaments thus play a role of middlemen that protect the traditional privileges from a centralised monarchy.

7. Paris. Before a group of experts and the commissioners of the Academy of Science, the industrialist Denis François Barneville demonstrates a new mechanical cotton loom which is based on some of the recent discoveries made by English engineers.

10. Paris. Louis XVI has come in person to get the kingdom's main parliament to register the prorogation of the unloved five per cent income tax, also known as the *vingtième,* or "twentieth".

11. Paris. Parliament drafts a call to the King asking for a pardon for the Duc d'Orléans. The King's cousin has been exiled to the village of Villers Cotterêts for having clashed in public with Louis XVI during the November 19 registration of the decree on the civil status of the country's Protestants (→13).

13. Paris. On the urging of Duval d'Eprémesnil, the parliament again issues an official protest against the use of sealed royal orders (→Apr. 17, 88).

14. Paris. Parliament registers the February royal decree ordering as an economy measure the sale or destruction of the castles of La Muette, Madrid at Boulogne, Vincennes and Blois.

15. Australia. Leading his two frigates, *L'Astrolabe* and *La Boussole,* French navigator La Pérouse sails from Botany Bay, in New Holland, for the last lap of his round the world voyage, Oceania.

17. Versailles. The Royal Agricultural Society approves a new type of bread oven based on a design submitted by a master baker of Paris' Saint Germain district.

19. Versailles. A Naval Council is set up on the urging of the Comte Loménie de Brienne, whose role is essentially consultative and legislative.

24. Paris. The music shop publishes three new piano sonatas by the composer and virtuoso Louis Adam.

24. Paris. The Queen's lute maker, Coussineau, sells a new type of pedal powered harmonica based on a design by the instrument maker Deudon.

25. Paris. New edition of the *Etudes de la Nature* by Bernardin de Saint Pierre.→

Noble blood talks on the battlefield

Paris, March 17

Has the army really become the private preserve of men of noble birth? Since 1781, only the sons of common officers who had been made knights of Saint Louis for their actions on the battlefield were exempted from having to prove four parts of noble blood before becoming sub-lieutenants. The exception made for sons of knights of Saint Louis is kept only for those whose fathers have served as titular captains. That requirement excludes practically all of them. The Baron de Bord, Major General of the *gendarmerie,* had written in 1781 that "the nobility is complaining, and rightly so, of not having an exclusive right to military postings". His complaint has been heard by the War Council.

Saint Pierre's new book hits the jackpot

Paris, March 25

Bernardin de Saint Pierre is no longer likely ever to be short of money. The third edition, published today, of his book *Studies of Nature* is promising to be as much of a success as the first edition, which appeared four years ago.

This time he has added a fourth volume entirely devoted to a charming, exotic pastoral entitled *Paul et Virginie.* Its sensitive and delicate tone is sure to please his women readers. Two bookshop owners have already ordered over three thousand copies of the new book.

New light thrown on great Louvre gallery

Paris, March 31

The King has just approved a new lighting plan for the great gallery of the Louvre, which is to be used for exhibiting royal art collections. The idea was proposed as early as 1776 by the Comte d'Angiviller, superintendent of the King's buildings.

There had been a multitude of problems because such a large building had till then never been used as a museum. Several options had been carefully examined, but lighting posed the most difficult problems. There were three main possibilities: lighting the gallery from the existing south-facing windows, from skylights cut into the vault or from glass panels built into the apex of the vault. This last option was the most ambitious and costly and Angiviller asked the Academy of Architecture for advice. After a lengthy debate, the academy chose the third option which provided the best lighting for the great gallery.

The Louvre's great gallery is now lit with a new apex-lighting system which was conceived by the painter Hubert Robert.

The colonial slave trade is targeted

Paris, March

The Society of Friends of the Blacks has launched a campaign. Set up by the journalist Jean Pierre Brissot and the Marquis de Condorcet on February 19, the group has decided to try to improve the fate of the 600,000 blacks living in the French colonies, but the chief aim of the many famous people who have joined the society is to get a total abolition of slavery and the slave trade.

The abolition of slavery is far from being a concept shared by all.

The nobility

France's 300,000 noblemen constitute in law the second order, coming after the clergy. There are few families who can boast they are directly descended from the nobility of the Middle Ages. A person can become a noble either through a royal decision or by purchasing an ennobling position, such as that of parliamentarian. Nobles are only allowed to occupy certain functions, under penalty of seeing their status withdrawn. These include the army, the King's service and wholesale trading. Most nobles live off the income from their properties when they have not been lucky enough to be presented to the court or to have royal grants. There is a huge gap between the country squire and the likes of the Duc d'Orléans who has an annual income of 680,000 livres.

4. Normandy. Towns are forced to collect funds for the unemployed after the coming into effect of the Eden-Rayneval Franco-British treaty of 1786, which has sparked competition between the two countries' industries.

15. Reims. The young Louis Antoine Léon Saint Just successfully gets his law degree.

16. Paris. The naturalist Georges Louis Leclerc, Comte de Buffon, dies. →

16. Versailles. The King decides to end the exile of the Duc d'Orléans, who had been ordered to remain at Villers Cotterêts. →

17. Versailles. In his reply to complaints from parliament, Louis XVI states he will never hand over the monarchy to "an aristocracy of magistrates so totally opposed to the interests of the nation and to its sovereignty".

17. Rouen. Officials in charge of mechanising the region's industries order from England 500 power looms of varying sizes for the local spinning mills.

18. Paris. The privately-owned water company, founded by the Perrier brothers in 1778, comes under royal administration.

22. Paris. Parliament registers the royal decree abolishing the military arsenal.

24. Amiens. The Picardy trade office refuses to recommend to local industrialists the new system for producing Javel bleach perfected by Berthollet, saying the process is too costly.

25. Switzerland. The French aeronaut Blanchard, living in Basle, is building a new hot air balloon.

29. Paris. The Italian theatre performs *Amphitryon*, an opera by André Grétry based on a libretto by Michel Jean Sedaine.

29. Paris. After a call by the councillor Goislard de Montsabert, parliament issues a decree opposing the King's right to create new taxes without the explicit consent of parliaments (→ May 8, 88).

30. Paris. Loménie de Brienne wants to set up a plenary court that would severely restrict the parliaments' few remaining powers. →

The rise and rise of Paris: a city gripped by speculation fever

The buildings on the Pont-au-Change are being demolished.

Paris, April

Paris is outgrowing itself! City limits, set by Louis XIII in order to avoid the enlargement of the capital becoming a threat to its security, are constantly being pushed further back. Brightness and sanitation are the order of the day in the new districts: the streets are wide and the aligned houses tall. The old houses of the Pont-au-Change over the Seine river have been torn down, the ossuary at the Saints Innocents, which was polluting the central market area, has been transferred to the catacombs and the insanitary Châtelet prison, by the Petit Pont, has been destroyed, but progress is not the only reason for all these changes.

For the past few years, Paris, a city of 600,000 inhabitants, wealthy capital of the arts, of trade, pleasure and finance, has been in the grip of speculation fever. Beyond the boulevards, the banker Laborde has had the Provence, Artois, Taitbout and Houssaye streets built. The Comte d'Artois has bought church lands in the area to build an "English style" neighbourhood. To the west, the matching façades of the impressive Rue Royale houses rise up. The rush to build is such that work goes on even at night.

However, there is disagreement among the population over the wall that the farmers general are having built around Paris, beyond the city's outlying districts. The purpose of the wall is to increase income from entry toll.

Abattoirs inflict grave wounds to central Paris

Paris, April

At the very foot of the Grand Châtelet, near the church of Saint Jacques, there is blood everywhere. This is where butchers slaughter cattle and where the animal fat is melted down.

There have been increasingly loud protests against the insanitary presence of these large slaughter houses within the heart of the capital. The lack of hygiene and the terrible smell are not the only problems. Every so often, an ox or a cow being driven through the streets to the abattoir escapes from the herd and injures somebody. Sometimes an entire herd wrecks a shop or ends up in the nearby Saint Eustache church, but public health officials also fear another danger. Streets close to the abattoirs constantly overflow with cow dung and blood which nobody dreams of cleaning up. Even worse are the butchers who throw animal remains into the street. These slowly rot, attracting hungry dogs and rats. People are asking when this dangerous and evil-smelling sector will be finally removed from the centre of the city.

Rent dispute at the Palais Royal

Paris, April

The shopkeepers and café owners at the Palais Royal have lost their court case. Their landlord, the Duc d'Orléans, will be allowed to increase their rents by over a third. Without this new income, the nobleman could not hope to pay for the luxury in which he has been living at his palace.

But the rent increase will prove to be a heavy burden for the tradesmen, already hard-hit by the cost of renovation work undertaken to keep the Palais Royal abreast of fashion. Ever since the Duc d'Orléans has had shopping arcades built in his palace gardens, the Palais Royal has become Paris' new centre of attraction. The public has taken a liking to this large walkway which is both an elegant bazaar and a meeting place for lovers.

Duchesses mingle with brightly dressed courtesans while men and women stare at each other more brazenly than anywhere else in the world. It has become the most fashionable place to be seen at. The new arcades, which are full of bargains and interesting objects, are making a good profit for the Duc d'Orléans, but his tenants will now be forced to pay a much higher price for the privilege of being in on the deal.

The Palais Royal gardens are surrounded by shopping arcades.

Finance minister's plan to abolish parliamentary powers sparks row

Paris, April 30

Duval d'Eprémesnil, a young councillor at the capital's parliament, is furious. He has just learnt that the ministry headed by Loménie de Brienne is seeking to eliminate the parliaments' powers. The Lord Chancellor, Lamoignon, is set to push through a radical judicial reform creating a plenary court and defining its jurisdiction. One of the main roles of this court will be to register royal decrees and all laws. The court will become the only body with the power to do so.

In other words, the parliaments will lose their chief role as well as the means of putting pressure on the exercise of royal power which they enjoyed through the system of remonstrances, but the magistrates have no intention of letting this royal *coup d'état* succeed. Duval d'Eprémesnil has just called on his colleagues to fight back and reminded them that the basic laws of the French monarchy guarantee the rights of the parliaments. The trial of strength between the two sides has begun (→Aug. 2).

Louis ends exile of the Duc d'Orléans

Philippe, Duc d'Orléans, in the uniform of a Hussar lieutenant general.

Versailles, April 16

Philippe, Duc d'Orléans, the unruly cousin of the King, is to be allowed to return to Paris. Louis XVI has cancelled the order that had exiled him to Villers Cotterêts since November 19. He had dared to stand up to the King in parliament by arguing that the ancient "bed of justice" procedure used by the monarch was illegal. "It is legal because I wish it to be so," the furious King had replied. There is little love lost between these two men and a small incident is enough to awaken old hatreds. There have

been rumours that Philippe has been supporting several pamphleteers who have been attacking the King, royal policy and the Queen's honour. People also whisper that he has been plotting to rule in Louis XVI's place. The prince does indeed enjoy plots, but he does not seem to have the desire or the power to become the head of a party. It is essentially because of a love of power that he has been supporting a meeting of the Estates General. It seems unlikely that this pleasure-loving prince has been secretly playing a major role.

French Jews find a new defender

Paris, April

"Monsieur de Malesherbes, I am naming you a Jew, go and take care of them," the King has said to his minister. After having granted a civil status to Protestants, the King now intends to do the same for the country's Jews.

But the problem is a far more complex one. There are in fact several rival Jewish communities with differing beliefs and customs. The Jews living in the southwest of France, who are mainly of Portuguese origin, enjoy considerable trade privileges and see themselves as fully-fledged French citizens. Above all, they do not want to be confused with less well off Jews from eastern France, most of whom have emigrated from Germany.

Malesherbes has therefore begun a wide-ranging inquiry into the way of life, religious customs and aspirations of the Jewish communities of France. He has been corresponding with their representatives, meeting with rabbis and writing reports. He is already convinced of the need to assimilate all the Jews. To reach that goal, it appears essential to Malesherbes to allow Jews to own and cultivate their land.

Buffon, celebrated naturalist, dies

Georges Buffon, a close watcher of the world of nature.

Paris, April 16

The King's gardens have lost their tireless steward, who had worked there for fifty years. The Comte de Buffon, Georges Louis Leclerc, died today at the age of 81. For many years, he had been suffering from stones in the bladder, and a sudden attack was fatal. This highly energetic worker spent his whole life doing scientific research and writing the 36 volumes of his *Natural History*. He was also a member of several European academies and was widely respected and honoured when he died.

Freemasons, sons of enlightenment

What lies behind the current success of Freemasonry? It is not due to their occult practices, as the less well informed claim. Rather, it stems from this century's enlightened philosophy, which has been shining on the kingdom's 600 masonic lodges. Even their names are a sign of their strong commitment to enlightened values: Perfect Union, Charity, Perfect Equality. The lodges bring together nobles, clergymen and members of the middle class. Tolerance is stressed during their debates. The real reason behind Freemasonry's new-found popularity is that it echoes the ideals of this urban elite. However, the secrecy surrounding Freemasonry has been fuelling the wildest rumours. People wonder what mysterious brotherhood unites Freemasons and what the secret initiation

ceremonies really involve. Newcomers are only allowed in with blindfolds and are submitted to strange rites before being allowed to "see the light". In any case, weren't the Comte de Saint Germain, who claimed to be immortal, and his disciple Cagliostro supposed to have been Freemasons? Such nasty gossip does not trouble France's 35,000 Freemasons.

Plate with masonic emblems.

1. Versailles. Acting on a call from the Lord Chancellor Lamoignon, the government decides to crush parliamentary opposition once and for all by stripping it of all its legislative and judicial powers and giving these powers to two newly formed bodies: the plenary court and the large bailiwicks (→2).

2. Pau. The Pau parliament is the first of several to draft a decree protesting against the royal reforms (→3).

3. Paris. The parliament issues a declaration of the kingdom's basic laws. It states that it is the laws' defender and sends remonstrances to the King at Versailles (→5).

5. Paris. During the night, the Marquis Vincent d'Agoult, acting on direct orders from the King, arrests at parliament the two main supporters of opposition to the royal reforms, the councillors Jean Jacques Duval d'Eprémesnil and François Goislard de Montsabert (→8).

8. Versailles. The King decides arbitrarily to register the Lamoignon decrees, disregarding the strong protests from magistrates.→

10. Rennes. On behalf of the King, the Comte de Thiard registers the royal reform decrees. A riot is narrowly avoided thanks to some very skillful manoeuvring by the steward of Brittany, Bertrand de Molleville (→31).

11. Grenoble. Parliament is dismissed after having finally approved the Lamoignon reform decrees under duress during a closed session held before the province's governor and its steward.

12. Paris. A total of 80 people taking first communion at the Barnabites church collect enough money to buy freedom for 18 people who had been thrown in jail for not having paid their debts.

14. Paris. The Italian theatre performs *Sargine ou l'Elève de l'Amour*, a comic opera by actor and playwright Jacques Marie Boutet, also known as Monvel, and Nicolas Marie Dalayrac.

31. Rennes. All the officers of the city's garrison inform the local governor, the Comte de Thiard, that they will categorically refuse to help him if the Brittany parliament is suspended (→June 2, 88).

King crushes opposition

Versailles, May 8

Parliament is rejecting judicial reform? Who cares! Disregarding protests from the magistrates, the King has just registered the decrees of his Lord Chancellor, Lamoignon, using the "bed of justice" procedure. Within three days, Louis XVI has crushed parliamentary opposition. During the night of May 4 to 5, he gave orders for the arrest of Goislard de Montsabert and Duval d'Eprémesnil. They had written the parliamentary decrees of April 29 and May 3 which strongly criticised the reforms of the Brienne ministry. However, the two fiery councillors escaped from the police and rushed to seek refuge with other parliamen-

tarians at the law courts. A crowd of Parisians has come from the suburbs to support them and form a barrier in order to stop any attempted attacks. After spending a night under siege, the two men agreed to turn themselves in while a delegation of magistrates went to Versailles. The magistrates begged Louis XVI to "listen in his wisdom to other advice than that which is about to drag legitimate authority and public freedom down into an abyss", but the appeal was in vain. The King has once again shown he is determined to break the parliamentary revolt. Despite this, opposition to the King has not been entirely broken and has won public sympathy (→May 31).

D'Eprémesnil and Goislard surrender as Parisians welcome their stand.

Florian elected a member of the Academy

Paris, May 14

The French Academy has elected Jean Pierre Claris de Florian a member by fifteen votes to fourteen which went to the naturalist Vicq d'Azir.

Following his election on March 6, the author today made his maiden speech, to which the librettist Sedaine responded. This is a personal triumph for a man who has friends at court and is protected by the Duc de Penthièvre. The playwright's success is also the triumph of a literary style: the tame and emotional bucolic one to which Florian gave full rein in his most recent work, *Estelle*, published last January.

Jean Pierre Claris de Florian.

Fury at Queen's spending spree

Everyone is talking about "Madam Deficit's" unfaithfulness.

Versailles, May 4

"Madam Deficit" is to join the Council! This groundless, though spreading, rumour has been doing the rounds of Paris since Marie Antoinette burst into the room where ministers were in session with the King.

It was not the first time that Marie Antoinette had involved herself in the kingdom's political affairs, but this time her actions have fuelled the public's anger. Pushed by advisors whose goals she knows little about, the Queen has been exercising a growing influence on Louis XVI, who has lacked the counsel of Vergennes since he died in 1787. Concerned about the future of the monarchy, she is hoping to save the throne for her son and inciting the King to adopt extreme positions in order to keep royal prerogatives at all costs. Since the unfortunate business about the necklace in 1785, the Queen's popularity has hit rock bottom. People are accusing her of squandering state funds on a spending spree aimed at "satisfying her unruly pleasures." The public has criticised her love of gambling, parties and finery. Some even say she has lesbian tendencies, while at the same time charging that she has many lovers. Although it is true that the Queen is still spending huge sums on clothes and jewellery, she has long since given up her past excesses, but the people take no notice of this. For the pamphleteers she is still Messalina, the Austrian, or Isabeau of Bavaria, another foreigner. They also dub her "Madam Deficit" (→June 88).

Poor prospects scare off school teachers

Le Mesnil Saint Loup, May

Despite what some people claim, school teachers are not all drunks and lazy. There are many teachers, such as Bernard Pénard, who seek through hard work to compensate for their students' ignorance and laziness. From morning till night, he patiently and kindly tries to teach a rudimentary learning to 50 farmers' children. He knows all about reading and writing, spelling, the handling of a compass, a circumferentor and a semi-circle. He also knows how to measure distances using a chain or an odometer, and division has no secrets for him. In exchange for all this knowledge, parents pay him an income of 25 écus and the community provides his housing. In other words, a teacher has trouble making ends meet. After a lifetime of devoted service, all he can look forward to is poverty, since there are no pension plans for teachers. The prospects are so bad that many a good teacher is discouraged from remaining in the profession, and goes to seek his fortune elsewhere.

The great majority of French people still don't know how to read.

It was Jules Hardouin Mansart who gave the castle of Saint Cloud its beautiful arrangements. Marie Antoinette purchased it in 1785. Shown on the left is the property, with a magnificent view from the hill overlooking the Seine. In the forefront is the Sèvres bridge also used by those travelling to Versailles.

Fever of revolt spreads to provincial parliaments across the country

The old nobility leads the fight against judicial reforms.

France, May 31

The parliamentary revolt has been spreading like wildfire. Only the capital's parliament has been holding its breath, somewhat tired by its abortive rebellion earlier this month.

But distance from the capital and the support of local populations have played a role in the provincial parliaments' open revolt. Officially, the parliaments have been told to take a vacation and all meetings are banned, particularly those held to discuss the validity of the widely criticised May decrees, but the Grenoble and Rouen parliaments have defied royal orders and dared strongly and personally to attack ministers.

The magistrates of Rennes and Pau disobey orders and hold public meetings. In a memorandum sent to the government, city officials of the capital of Brittany have expressed the anguish of all the lawyers, artisans and servants who have lost their jobs because of the suspension of parliamentary activities. Little by little, the fever of revolt has spread to all the parliaments and lower courts of the nation.

Queen backs new scheme to save children

Paris, May 1

There are currently over 30,000 abandoned children in the hospitals of Paris. Each year, some 3,000 babies are brought to the capital's centre for foundlings.

In order to reduce these dreadful statistics, Madame Fougeret has decided to set up the Society for Motherly Charity. Instead of devoting its energies to useless visits to hospitals, the society plans to get to the real root of the problem by giving assistance to mothers in distress. With the help of public donations begun a month ago, some 20,000 livres have been collected. That money will allow 129 mothers to care for their new-born children for two years. At least those babies will escape from the fate of the orphans, illegitimate or poor children who are given shelter at La Pitié and Bicêtre. The conditions at those centres are so awful that half of the children die before they reach the age of two. The Queen herself has already started helping the new society.

A child is a new mouth to be fed.

2. Rennes. His troops having refused to obey orders, the Comte de Thiard, governor of Brittany, cannot exile the parliament (→3).

2. Paris. The organist and composer Michel Corrette gets the bookseller Mercier to publish *Quatre Messes à Deux Voix*.

6. Grenoble. Overnight, an anonymous pamphlet, *L'Esprit des Edits* (written by Antoine Barnave), has been distributed in the town. It calls for the orders to unite against the reforms (→7).

7. Grenoble. The "day of the tiles" rocks the town as rioters take to the roofs and hurl tiles at royal troops, injuring several. →

10. Grenoble. The officer responsible for opening fire during the June 7 riot is arrested in a bid to calm the population.

11. Dijon. The introduction of the new jurisdictions sparks a revolt.

12. Grenoble. Magistrates obey the King's orders and finally leave the city.

14. Grenoble. An assembly of leading citizens calls a meeting of the province's orders for July.

19. Vannes. After meeting at Saint Brieuc on June 13, the nobles of Brittany elect the six last deputies to the delegation of twelve gentlemen that the nobility wants to send to the King to ask for the reforms to be dropped (→July 2, 88).

19. Pau. Local peasants, pushed by nobles, lay siege to the steward and force him to reinstate the parliament.

20. Versailles. The King's Council declares the nobility's assemblies illegal; the declaration will not reach Brittany as local priests don't dare read it out in church.

26. Paris. The naturalist Louis Jean Marie Daubenton begins teaching the natural history of plants at the Royal College of France.

28. Paris. Death of the German musician Jean-Christophe Vogel, composer of many famous operas.

29. Le Mans. The bishop holds public prayer meetings in a bid to get rid of the bad weather which is threatening the region's crops.

Street fighting erupts in Grenoble

Women are also active among the rioters hurling stones and tiles at the soldiers from the city's rooftops.

Grenoble, June 7

On this Saturday morning, the usual market day activity in the capital of the Dauphiné turned into a riot. The city's population, helped by peasants from the nearby mountains, rushed to nail the town's doors shut when they heard the alarm bells ring.

The people of Grenoble wanted to stop their parliamentarians from being sent into exile. Disregarding royal orders, these magistrates had gathered to criticise the forced registration of the May decrees on Lamoignon's judicial reforms. Reprisals were quickly taken: the rebels were ordered to return to their homes, but they had no intention of admitting defeat. An inflammatory pamphlet, *L'Esprit des Edits Enregistrés Militairement le 10 Mai*, which has been in circulation since last night, called on inhabitants to resist. Although the pamphlet is anonymous, everyone knows its author is a young lawyer named Antoine Barnave. Royal troops sent in to remove the magistrates were met by a hail of roofing tiles and stones thrown by an angry mob from the city's rooftops.

Blood was already flowing freely when the Duc de Clermont Tonnerre, who commanded the garrison, decided to give in. Wearing their robes of office, the parliamentarians could then return in triumph to the law courts (→June 10).

Anacharsis makes Greece fashionable

Paris, June

Cultured book-lovers are avidly reading the "Voyage of the Young Anacharsis to Greece". It is the only thing that is keeping their minds off politics.

The talented and erudite Abbot Jean Jacques Barthélemy is its author. He is a medal collector and a keen archaeologist who has spent thirty years of his life doing research for the book. It was during a trip to Italy that he first had the idea of bringing Antiquity back to life. He chose to focus on fourth-century Greece, which he knew a lot about, rather than on the Roman Empire.

Basing his tale on the fictitious journey of a young Scythian to the Athens of Demosthenes' day, he has sought to describe that forgotten world in great detail and using many quotations. His book has brought the Orient and Antiquity back into fashion.

Lawyers up in arms

Paris, June

The dissolution of parliament has meant that all the lawyers, court ushers and clerks find themselves out of a job. Since court employees have been supporting the magistrates, they now keep the unrest around the law courts going by lecturing the crowd about the kingdom's politics. The security forces are having a hard time keeping order without any blood being spilt.

Magistrates victorious after Rennes riot

Rennes, June 3

The magistrates of Brittany have won: they are not to be sent into exile. Yesterday, the people of Rennes rallied to block their departure by attacking the province's steward, Bertrand de Molleville. The riot broke out at nighttime, when news spread that sealed orders for the parliamentarians' exile had arrived. The magistrates had refused to obey royal orders to stop all activities. They had been meeting at the Cuillé mansion because soldiers were posted around the parliament. By the time the commander, Thiard, decided to use force, the steward had already been detained by the mob at the government buildings. The soldiers came across a group of unruly young gentlemen and Thiard had to force them to retreat. The magistrates were then able to parade in triumph, but Molleville is still being held by the mob.

The King's aunts entertain at Bellevue

Bellevue, June 16

Victoire and Marie Adélaïde have decided to give the "Austrian" a party worthy of her rank. Despite their dislike for this niece, which they were the first to dub thus, Mesdames, the King's aunts, treated the Queen with honour when she visited them at the Bellevue castle. About fifty guests came to the party. The two elderly ladies made an effort to be pleasant because they owe a debt of gratitude to the Queen. It was Marie Antoinette who persuaded Louis XVI to give them Bellevue, where they live a solitary life that is, however, more pleasant than the dreary apartment at Versailles to which their father had confined them.

It can be very expensive to invite 4,000 guests to the party.

Extravagance and profligacy rule at court

Versailles, June

Festivities at the court may be less ostentatious than they used to be, but the royal couple's palaces continue to swallow up vast sums of money.

Huge numbers of people work there, but most of them are not needed. Despite the hundreds of jobs scrapped in 1780, some of which dated back to the Middle Ages, far too many people are still employed at the palaces. Is it really necessary to pay high wages to a "royal business chair carrier"? The court's financial situation is getting worse every day. The ridiculously high grants that the Queen gives to her friends are unlikely to help balance the royal budget.

Church severs old ties with the throne

Clergymen still enjoy considerable standing in today's society.

Paris, June 15

The church has broken the old alliance between the altar and the throne. It is now backing the revolt of the old nobility. This became apparent during the assembly that has just been held. The clergy sent a series of remonstrances to the King in which they criticised the fiscal reform plans of Loménie de Brienne. The minister had been planning to entrust the future provincial assemblies with the task of evaluating church property on the same basis as the kingdom's other resources. It had traditionally been the church itself that had handed over part of its income to the King in the form of a "free donation". However, there seem to be no political motivations behind the clergy's opposition to fiscal reform. There are close family ties between the high clergy and the nobility. Taking advantage of the crown's current weakness, the nobility is seeking to recover its old powers. In its remonstrances, the church has taken up the call of the parliamentarians, who have been gagged by the King, and ask for parliaments to be restored immediately.

Malesherbes tells Louis to reform the constitution

Versailles, June

Is Louis XVI prepared to listen to his faithful minister? Malesherbes has been offering some very daring advice. "A King who offers a constitution to all his subjects achieves the greatest glory available to man," the minister has told the King.

Malesherbes believes that in order to survive, the monarchy must accept reforms and that Louis XVI must encourage changes. "Write a constitution for your century; take your place within it and do not be afraid to base it on the rights of the people," he added. This exceptional jurist has kept an open mind and is firmly convinced that it is high time to get rid of all the old traditions on which royal power is based and to which the sovereign remains so strongly attached (→July 5).

The clergy

Legally, the clergy form the kingdom's first order. Out of about 130,000 clergymen, half belong to the regular clergy, two thirds of whom are women. The church is a major land and property owner and has a large part of the nation's wealth. It keeps a close watch on collection of the tithe, taxes paid by peasants for their crops. The church also administers hospitals, schools and keeps the civil status registers, but it is divided into two very unequal groups. The high clergy, comprising 8,000 bishops and canons, usually of noble birth, dominate the order and take advantage of its power and wealth. But the lower clergy, made up of priests, chaplains and vicars, live such a humble existence that they differ little from the majority of their parishioners. The main difference is to be found in their learning.

1. **Brittany.** Deputies of the nobility set up a correspondence committee that will help keep gentlemen living far away abreast of all the latest events (→18).

1. **Grenoble.** In a bid to block public calls for the meeting of the three orders to be held at Vizille, the Duc de Clermont Tonnerre bans all irregular municipal assemblies.

2. **Paris.** A day after its arrival, the delegation of Breton nobles is informed by the secretary of the King's household, the Baron de Breteuil, that the King will not receive them at Versailles (→15).

9. **Romans.** The town's mayor, Claude Pierre Delay d'Agier, a strong supporter of the Vizille meeting, is thrown into jail at the Brescous fort.

13. **France.** An extremely violent tornado rips through the country from west to east causing extensive damage to crops.→

14. **Paris.** The Théâtre Français performs *La Jeune Epouse*, a verse play by the Chevalier de Cubières.

14. **Grenoble.** The King decides to name a strong military man, the Maréchal de Vaux, to replace the Dauphiné's lieutenant-general.

15. **Paris.** The delegation of twelve Breton nobles is arrested.→

16. **Dauphiné.** The Archbishop of Vienne intervenes on the political scene by publishing a pastoral letter in which he strongly criticises the forthcoming Vizille meeting (→21).

18. **Rennes.** The parliament responds to the jailing of the twelve nobles by sending a delegation to Paris, while the correspondence committee spreads the news of their detention and publishes a letter from the Breton prisoners to Louis XVI.

21. **Dauphiné.** The province's nobility, clergy and Third Estate meet jointly at Vizille and call for the Estates General to be convened.→

26. **Versailles.** To help provinces recover from the devastating hailstorm of July 13 (→), a Council decree allows the setting up of a 12 million livre lottery.

27. **Versailles.** A Council decree confirms the royal life and fire insurance company's monopoly.

Estates General poses dilemma for King

Versailles, July 5

When and how will the Estates General be convened? Such questions are troubling Louis XVI, who no longer knows whose advice to listen to. It was officially decided a year ago that the session would be held in 1792. Initially, the King had thought that by hurrying this national event along he could use the occasion to break the parliamentary revolt supported by the nobility and the high clergy, but now his ministers are advising him to delay as long as possible, while appearing to be willing to move ahead. This is apparent in the recently issued decree of the royal Council drafted by Brienne. It states that the monarch wants to "ask for his subjects' opinion before coming to any decision, so that they will be more confident of having a truly national Assembly". It is a matter of making haste slowly. Brienne believes that this will give him time to create a split between the nobility and the rebellious magistrates by offering what it wants most: provincial assemblies.

Soldiers must seek royal nod to wed

Paris, July 1

The latest decree is more than likely to cause deep resentment. All the military will in future have to ask for royal permission before they marry. The soldiers, who are already complaining loudly of being badly fed, badly housed, harassed and being subjected to degrading disciplinary measures, will now have yet another reason to protest. The Comte de Guibert, one of the main authors of the plan, based his ideas on regulations enforced by the Prussian army, which he considers to be the best in Europe, but the move has earned him the hatred of soldiers, officers and subalterns. The matter is hardly going to win support for King.

Written engagements, contract, banns: marriage is a complex business.

Free speech draws a shallow breath

Versailles, July 5

The government has just taken the unprecedented step of asking for the public's opinion. The Council decree, which today confirmed that the Estates General will be held soon, states that "His Majesty calls on all the scholars and learned people" to express their opinion on the convening of the Estates General. This does not mean that censorship has been scrapped, but the move appears to put an end to the need to have each publication previously approved. France is already flooded by a wave of pamphlets and political brochures. Their authors will no longer risk facing legal proceedings, and will take advantage of the new situation.

Wine by balloon

Paris, July 1

The alarm has just been sounded by the King's prosecutor, Louis Ethis de Corny. Fraud on city tolls is spreading and has become a cause for concern.

The cheats are becoming more daring every day: after drilling a hole in the ground, they use a metal pipe to channel wine from the suburbs into Paris, thus avoiding paying taxes. City tax officials are powerless.

Other cunning tradesmen prefer using aerial methods: after buying some land on each side of the toll barriers, they build scaffolding and when night has fallen they send hot air balloons carrying wine into their Paris property. In a single night, an innkeeper can get 5,000 litres of wine across the "border". Although city officials are complaining about the lost revenue, the people of Paris are glad to be able to get cheaper wine.

Twelve noble deputies sent to Bastille after Brittany protest

Paris, July 15

To hell with the nobility's revolt! The King has just had twelve gentlemen from Brittany jailed for daring to come to him with a memorandum protesting against the May decrees on judicial reforms. In Brittany, the fight between the monarchy and the nobility, which refuses to see its local privileges whittled away, has been going on for a long time. On that point, the Brittany nobles agree with the parliamentarians. That is why the victory won on June 3 at Rennes, from where the magistrates could not be exiled, has strengthened the gentlemen's resolve. They met at Vannes and at Saint Brieuc on June 19 to sent a delegation of twelve deputies. These travelled to Versailles aboard twelve carriages bearing only Brittany's coat of arms, but the minister, Breteuil, has informed them that Louis XVI would not receive them. Early in the morning, as they were returning from a banquet, the twelve were met by two soldiers who escorted them to the Bastille (→Sept. 12).

Troops called out as Paris unrest mounts

Over half of the workers' income is spent on buying bread.

Paris, July 6

Some twenty thousand workers of the Saint Antoine suburb are out of work and the cost of bread is rising all the time.

Fearing unrest, the government has called in ten thousand troops which have been deployed around the city. The move has, however, added to unrest in the poorer districts, which are always ready to rise up. A marble mason had resolved to assassinate the King, whom he blamed for all the prob-lems facing the poor. Before carry-ing his plans out, he confided in some close friends, who quickly turned him in. Warned about the attempted murder, Louis XVI gave orders that the mason should not be harmed, but locked up as a simple madman.

The Chief Minister, badly shaken by the incident, has called for the security measures around the King to be strengthened, but nothing has been done to help the capital's unemployed.

The small businesses of Paris

You don't need to own a fine shop to become a businessman in Paris. There is plenty of room to display your wares on the city's streets.

Strollers are offered a choice of low-priced goods everywhere. On the corner of the Petit Pont street and the Rue Saint Séverin, there squats a public scribe busy writing the letters which illit-erate maids and workers send home to their families in the provinces. Beside him there is a woman selling fresh oranges and a man selling the popular lottery tickets.

When you walk across the Pont Neuf bridge over the Seine, you find countless booksellers' stalls offering a wide variety of pamphlets and songs to those who are able to read. Near the Innocents cemetery there is a large and noisy crowd of travel-ling salesmen. From them you can purchase almost anything, from a broom to a chastity belt. Sitting on a stool, a woman earns her living by mending worn out clothes. There are also large groups of hucksters who provide the capital's poor with such essentials as wine, lard, eggs and coal, but the quality of their goods is low and the prices very high.

A huckster selling retail salt, spices and vegetables.

France blasted by devastating tornado

France, July 13

Nobody in France remembers ever having witnessed such a vio-lent and terribly destructive storm. The previous day and night had been unbearably hot.

Suddenly, this morning the wind began to blow hard from the west. The hail started soon afterwards, crushing countless fields, plains and gardens within eight hours. Hailstones as large as acorns were seen, some of them felling panicked rabbits and hares, while thousands of birds were killed. All the way from the Charente to the Escaut, the wheat and rye crops have been completely wiped out. At Ramb-ouillet, the storm has wrecked 11,000 of the castle's windows.

Throughout the country, countless roofs have been blown off, trees felled or ripped out and thatched roofs drenched. There have been floods in the regions of Poitou, Touraine, Beauce and Picardy as well as near the cathedral city of Chartres. A total of 600 parishes around the towns of Soissons and Chartres, as well as 78 around Lille, have suffered severe damage. The storm turned into a cyclone, devas-tating all that lay in its path. Told of the extent of the disaster, the King, who had gone hunting at Rambouillet with Monsieur, is al-ready planning to set up a lottery in a bid to help the regions which have suffered the most severe storm and flood damage.

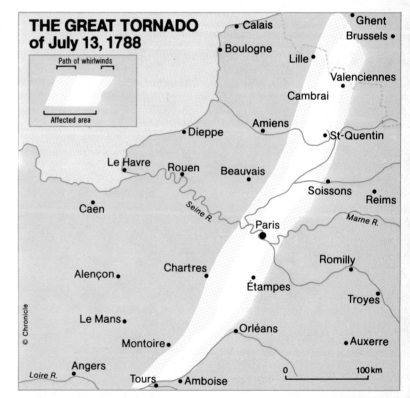

THE GREAT TORNADO of July 13, 1788

Path of whirlwinds

Affected area

Calais · Ghent · Brussels · Boulogne · Lille · Valenciennes · Cambrai · Dieppe · Amiens · St-Quentin · Le Havre · Rouen · Beauvais · Soissons · Reims · Caen · Seine R. · Paris · Marne R. · Romilly · Alençon · Chartres · Étampes · Troyes · Le Mans · Orléans · Auxerre · Montoire · Angers · Loire R. · Tours · Amboise

© Chronicle

0   100 km

Prices plunge on the stock exchange

Paris, July 19

Panic has struck the Paris stock exchange, or Bourse. Prices fell by half a percentage point again today despite the surprise visit of a comp-troller of finance who had come to attend the session. It is no secret that the Treasury is out of money and tax revenue has been slow in coming. In a bid to deal with urgent expenses, the comptroller general, Lambert, has committed the money donated to assist victims of last week's storm. Some are even saying that he dipped into the reserve funds of the capital's hospitals. Convinced that bankruptcy is just around the corner, shareholders are trying to sell all their holdings as fast as they can, even if it means making a loss. Given these circum-stances, who is going to lend money to the King? That is what a worried Chief Minister, Loménie de Bri-enne, is wondering. He had planned to finance half the state's budget this year through loans; but how can these be raised? (→ Aug. 16)

The three orders of the Dauphiné adopt joint demands at Vizille assembly

Mounier, defender of unity between the Third Estate and the nobility.

Vizille, July 21

Incredibly, the clergy, nobility and Third Estate are fighting together for the same cause.

This unexpected event has just occurred at Vizille. Following the "day of the tiles", about one hundred nobles representing the three orders met at Grenoble's city hall on July 14 to make preparations for a joint opposition to royal power. This move led to today's meeting, which the new lieutenant-general of the King, Maréchal de Vaux, has reluctantly authorised, on condition that it is not held in the city of Grenoble. Led by two young and fiery lawyers, Mounier and Barnave, delegates of the three orders jointly demanded that the Dauphiné's provincial estates be reinstated and called for the Estates General to be convened. Above all, they also demanded that the Third Estate be given equal standing with the other orders within these two assemblies.

Is this simply a sort of marriage of convenience aimed at defending the Dauphiné's local privileges against the monarchy? Or is it, as some Vizille delegates have been claiming, a lasting union which will set the example?

Cochin-China troop mission abandoned

Pondicherry, July 20

Plans to send troops to place King Nguyen Anh back on his throne have been dropped. The end of the monsoon season has forced the governor of Pondicherry, the Comte Thomas de Conway, to postpone the mission. All the necessary preparations to ensure the mission's success, had, however been made. The decision to send troops was taken by the King in November 1787, when a friendship treaty was signed between Cochin-China and France. It was all in vain, as the frigates needed to transport troops, expected since the start of the monsoon, have not arrived. Monsignor Pigneau de Béhaine, who dreams of setting up a Christian empire in the Far East, is dismayed. An opportunity to secure a trade monopoly sought by England has been lost.

Claude Périer takes power at Vizille

Vizille, July

Power at Vizille has changed hands. Until now, this small Dauphiné town's most important personage was the High Constable, Lesdiguières, who built the castle that now towers over the town, but today the new lord of Vizille is Claude Périer. Within the walls of the impressive feudal castle, he has set up a prosperous printed calico cloth factory.

Despite having decided to live in the midst of beautiful antiques, this dynamic son of a large family of local businessmen is above all a man of the future.

He was therefore the ideal person to host the important meeting of the Dauphiné's three orders, which are looking for new political institutions, although they still defend the old privileges.

Trianon opens to the public on Sundays

Versailles, July

Marie Antoinette has decided that anyone who has come with "honest intentions" will be allowed to visit the Trianon, the Queen's pastoral retreat near Versailles. Since she has had the hamlet built, there have been wild rumours about its cost and what goes on there. In a bid to stifle the rumours, Marie Antoinette has taken to opening the Trianon up to the public on Sundays and even presiding over a pastoral ball with the King. To please her guests, she sometimes joins in the dances. The Queen is hoping that this show of simplicity will boost her waning popularity.

The Queen's pastoral hamlet of Trianon, at Versailles, includes simple masonry or daub houses covered by thatched or flat-tiled roofs.

France's industries take off

Every region of France now has its own industries. The Loire and Rhône valleys, as well as Normandy, specialise in manufacturing cloth, while the regions of the Languedoc, Picardy and Champagne make sheets. In the Ardennes there are many foundries, countless coal mines in the Artois, while metal work is carried out in eastern France.

The growth of industry is such that is has led to the deforestation of entire regions. The wood-burning factories are great consumers of trees. Although mechanical inventions and mass production are spreading, most spinning is still based on the wheel. Like weaving, spinning is still done mostly at home by farmers' wives.

Metal founders shown hard at work at a blazing forge.

August 1788

from 1st. to 31st.

1. Paris. The players of the Théâtre Français perform Racine's tragedy *Athalie* to raise money for the regions that were badly hit by the devastating July hailstorms.

2. Versailles. The people of the Dauphiné score a point: they get Loménie de Brienne to agree to convene a consultative assembly to prepare for the reinstating of the province's estates.

3. Brittany. A food riot breaks out at Pontrieux after rumours of hoarding and grain seizures on behalf of the English (→19).

4. Rennes. Following the Dauphiné's example, an assembly of the three orders sends a memorandum to the King asking for sealed orders to be abandoned, the freeing of the twelve Breton gentlemen and a meeting of the Brittany estates.

8. Versailles. A decree stops the creation of the plenary court, thus marking the first time the court has backed down in the face of opposition to royal reforms.→

8. Grenoble. The patriots respond to the Archbishop of Vienne's July 16 letter by publishing a letter from the schoolmaster of the village of Moivieu, Michel Blanchard.

16. Versailles. Loménie de Brienne declares the state bankrupt.→

19. Rennes. Faced with a spread of food riots despite well stocked grain stores, the steward of Brittany calls on his aides to investigate.

25. Versailles. A day after accepting the resignation of Loménie de Brienne, Louis XVI asks Necker to take charge of the kingdom's finances.→

25. Vannes. Following false rumours that wheat had been removed from stores, an angry mob loots local grain warehouses.

27. Grenoble. The Dauphiné nobility protests against the jailing of the Brittany nobles and calls for their release from prison.

29. France. News of Brienne's resignation sparks outbursts of rejoicing in the provinces. In Grenoble, people place lights in their windows, while in Paris violent rioting breaks out and eight demonstrators are killed.

Estates General will meet on May 1, 1789, in attempt to ward off economic crisis

Versailles, August 8

Throughout the kingdom, there have been calls for a meeting of the Estates General to be convened. A decree from the King's Council has just set the date: May 1, 1789. The move should not, however, be seen as a capitulation by Louis XVI and his ministers in the face of the revolt by the orders. It is the economic crisis that has pushed Brienne to take the decision, which spells the end of his plan to set up the plenary court. The treasury needs 240 million livres and the announcement of the convening of the Estates General is the only thing likely to incite the bankers to provide the money.

Queen's infidelity sends Louis hunting

Hunting has always been one of the favourite pastimes of French royalty.

Versailles, August

Several days ago, during a hunting party, the King was found by his equerries weeping over some poison pen letters criticising the relationship between the Queen and de Fersen. To forget his marital problems, the King has become increasingly involved in his favourite pastime: the hunt. The violent sport helps him to forget all his worries and concentrate on his quarry. Some hunts go on for so long that he often spends the night at Rambouillet, arriving there late in the evening in a state of complete exhaustion. The Queen has spoken to her husband in an attempt to calm his fears: if he insists, she will stop seeing de Fersen, although isn't he their most faithful friend and the only one they can rely on?

Tippoo Sahib's new embassy in Paris

Versailles, August 3

The entire court has come to attend the reception given by the King in honour of the three ambassadors of the Sultan of Mysore, Tippoo Sahib. The lavish reception is in homage to France's ally and to the Sultan's epic fight to save India from being dominated by England, but all this pomp does not conceal the fact that the French monarchy throws parties when it should be sending assistance. Despite this, none of the King's councillors is prepared to admit that France has given up hopes of influencing events in India.

Tippoo Sahib, Sultan of Mysore.

Mirabeau's name dogged by scandal

Paris, August 18

Henriette Amélie de Nehra is fed up with having to share Mirabeau with other women: she left him this morning and has gone to live in England for good. Mirabeau had fallen in love with the beautiful Henriette, an orphan and the illegitimate daughter of a Dutch statesman, although she was just seventeen at the time. For five years Henriette, whom Mirabeau affectionately dubbed "Yet Lie", put up with her lover's shenanigans without complaining.

The straw that broke the camel's back was his year-long affair with his publisher's wife, a well-known and beautiful flirt, Evelyne le Jay. The scandal has once again marred Mirabeau's reputation, already tarnished by his elopement with the young Sophie de Monnier three years after his marriage to Emilie de Marignane. After having been jailed for four years for this, he stole Madame de Saint Orens away from her husband before dropping her in favour of Henriette. For the time being, this tireless Don Juan is seeking comfort at Madame le Jay's side, no doubt waiting for yet another amorous adventure to come along.

The peasantry

Over half of France's population, that is two thirds of those who live in the country, are peasants. They play a major role in the economy and their status varies considerably. Although there are only several hundred thousand serfs left today, there is a very wide gap between the farm labourer, who owns a bit of land, and the often impoverished small holder, who is forced to hand over part of his crop to the land's owner. Only half of the country's lands in fact belong to the peasantry. The rest is cultivated for the owners by farmers, or by share-croppers, who live mainly on the rich plains of the north as well as in and around Paris. On top of this, there are many day workers whose job often hangs only by a thread, as it depends to a large extent on the whims of nature.

France goes bankrupt

Versailles, August 16

The state has stopped making payments! The news has spread like wildfire through Paris. Furious and terrified savers have been rushing to the savings bank demanding that the royal bonds be reimbursed right away. They are even prepared to sell them at a loss. As from tomorrow, the state will only pay back in cash small sums as well as two fifths of its major debts. The remaining three fifths will be converted into a new obligatory loan, and nothing guarantees its value. Having failed to convince the financiers to provide new funds to the treasury, Loménie de Brienne has decided on a partial suspension of payments, but this daring ploy, which has meant a saving of 140 million livres for the state, has destroyed its creditors' confidence once and for all (→ Aug. 25).

Soldiers too hot for thermal springs

A stay at thermal springs can lead to some pleasant encounters.

Paris, August 12

The Army's headquarters is concerned about the increasing use of hot springs by soldiers. The War Council has informed the Health Council that doctors at the military thermal springs at Saint Amand, Barèges and Bourbonne were complaining about the number of visiting soldiers. Those spas have been in use since Roman times to cure war injuries. The doctors have said that some of the soldiers were perfectly healthy. Although the soldiers are only allowed to drink water while undergoing a cure, they will do almost anything to spend time relaxing alongside civilians.

Malesherbes resigns from the Council

Versailles, August 28

The wise old man has left the ministry. As a minister of state, Malesherbes had been isolated within the Council. He had always been firmly opposed to the authoritarianism of Loménie de Brienne, who worked directly with the King without informing his colleagues of his decisions. Such behaviour had upset Malesherbes. Before resigning, he was at least able to push through a law he cared about: the Tolerance Decree for Protestants.

The King recalls Necker

Versailles, August 25

Now that France is faced with the prospect of total economic collapse, Necker's name has come to the forefront.

Brienne himself has discussed the matter with the Queen. The news of Necker's recall has been warmly welcomed both by financial circles and the Palais Royal. The legal fraternity is overjoyed with the move and the ousted minister, Brienne, has been burnt in effigy. Necker, who had remained popular since his disgrace in 1783, has been biding his time. This Geneva-born Protestant banker does not, however, seem the ideal candidate to become the country's chief financier, but he is an outstanding financial operator who has pulled off some brilliant banking coups. His reputation is solid among businessmen, shareholders and government leaders. His wife's "salon" has meanwhile been attracting authors

The Geneva-born banker Necker is an admirer of England.

and scientists. The big question is whether he will be able to get the country out of its financial trouble. There seems little that Necker can do but wait for the opening of the Estates General.

Sale of black slaves continues to thrive

Bordeaux, August 13

The slaver *La Licorne* has returned. This 625 tonne ship, commissioned at Bordeaux by the firm Cochon, Troplon and Dupuy, has sailed back from Saint Domingue, where it had unloaded 390 Africans bought in Mozambique by its captain. The sale raised 723,000 livres for the company. Since the American War of Independence, Bordeaux traders have commissioned 120 slave ships. Bordeaux has become the most important port dealing in slaves from Mozambique and Zanzibar, but the volume of shipping is five times lower here than it is at Nantes and other ports.

Slavery booms despite efforts by the Society of Friends of the Blacks.

3. Quimper. New riots are sparked by false rumours that the export of cereals, a traditional activity of Brittany, has been banned.

5. Romans. The Dauphiné consultative assembly opens. It is to draft an updated constitution for the province.

11. Versailles. There will be no deputies representing the colonies at the meeting of the Estates General. →

12. Paris. The jailed Breton nobles, who have become symbols of despotism and the abuse of royal power, are released at Necker's request.

13. Versailles. A decree by the King's Council gives the go-ahead for the opening of a new canal to link the Ourq to the Marne.

13. Paris. The Théâtre Français performs *Lanval et Viviane,* a verse comedy by Murville and Stanislas Champein.

19. Versailles. One of Necker's opponents, Charles de Barentin, president of the customs and excise board, replaces Lamoignon, forced to resign on September 14.

23. Versailles. In a statement, the King orders the reinstatement of the prerogatives of parliament and sovereign courts. The move is the last step in the monarchy's capitulation (→24).

23. Paris. The Italian theatre performs *Les Deux Sérénades,* a lyric comedy by Nicolas Dalayrac.

24. Paris. Parliament's triumphant reassembly sparks popular demonstrations in which several people are killed or injured.→

25. Paris. Parliament registers the royal statement of September 23, saying the Estates General should meet in the same manner as they did in 1614, despite the risk that this could lose it the popularity won in the fight against royal authority.

27. Paris. Parliament bans the *Political, Civil and Literary Annals* by Simon Linguet, who poked fun at the government's economic and monetary policies.

28. Romans. The Dauphiné assembly breaks up after drafting a new constitution which will have to be approved by the King.

Parliament reassembles in triumph

Paris, September 24

The crowds of Paris have overcome the abuse of royal power. Yesterday a statement by Louis XVI announced that the judicial reforms have been dropped and the traditional role of parliaments been restored. The King has capitulated, disowning his ministers Brienne and Lamoignon, who have been dismissed. Today's new parliamentary session was held amid violent unrest which has been rocking Paris for the past month. The public rejoicing that had marked Necker's recall and Lamoignon's departure on September 14 turned into rioting two days later. On the Place Dauphine and at the Palais Royal fireworks were still blazing when a group of men armed with sticks and torches rushed towards the residences of the hated former ministers. That signalled the start of the clashes. The French Guards charged with drawn swords at demonstrators, killing and wounding several. Parliament has even launched an inquiry and is planning to punish the excessive use of force.

A fire at the guard post of the Pont Neuf bridge, a traditional gathering place for public rejoicing as well as angry demonstrations.

Parliament's reassembly sparks an outburst of public rejoicing.

No representation for colonies at Estates General

Versailles, September 11

Since the colonies are not provinces, they don't need to be represented at the Estates General! The King's Council has rejected a demand submitted by the settlers of the American islands. The Council has also rejected the request made to the Minister of the navy, the Comte de la Luzerne, by a delegation of large landowners, including the Marquis de Gouy d'Arsy and the Comte de Reynaud de Villevert, but the two men, who have been staying at the Massiac hotel, on the Place des Victoires, since July 15, are not likely to be put off by this setback.

The planters are determined to defend their concept of free trade. What they want is the right to trade with all nations. What they disagree with is the position of traders in mainland port cities who have been seeking to stop anyone who is not French from trading with the colonies.

Northern lights seen repeatedly at Metz

Metz, September 5

The people of Metz are again looking skyward tonight: two hundred metres above the ground, the night sky is veiled by a whitish and diffused light, like a huge phosphorescent sheet. Why is this atmospheric phenomenon, practically unheard of in these latitudes, repeatedly being seen here? Could there be a link between the aurora borealis and the meteorite showers that have been reported recently in several French towns?

Mme. Vigée Lebrun serves a Greek meal

Paris, September

Everybody is talking about the Greek meal that Madame Vigée Lebrun, the Queen's favourite portrait painter, has just served to some friends.

The famous artist, who loves to dress her models in ancient styles, invited her guests to arrive dressed as Athenians. They were offered a variety of Greek specialities and wine from Cyprus. Etruscan vases lent by a friend and special draperies helped to set the tone for the party. Annoyed at not having been invited, some ladies from the court have been spreading the rumour that the meal had cost a fortune, but it seems that more was spent on imagination than on the food itself.

Mme. Vigée Lebrun has dressed up in the ancient Greek style.

5. Versailles. Louis XVI decides to convene a new assembly of notables to discuss the make up of the Estates General.

5. Dauphiné. Hay de Bontville, the Bishop of Grenoble, commits suicide at his castle of Herbeys after his bid for the presidency of the consultative assembly had ended in total failure.

10. Versailles. A Council decree gives the go-ahead for the creation of a legal library which is to be attached to the French chancellery.

11. Quimper. A sudden rise in the price of bread causes a new food riot.

14. Versailles. Necker meets with members of the Dauphiné's nobility to inform them that the King has rejected the administrative demands of the province's estates and asks for the draft constitution to be changed ($\rightarrow$ 22).

17. Versailles. The diplomat Barthélemy de Lesseps is received at the court on his return from his adventures in Russia with La Pérouse.$\rightarrow$

20. Rennes. The patriots of Brittany get the city assembly to vote for regulations for Third Estate deputies to the Brittany estates which exclude nobles from the Third's future delegation.

20. Grenoble. The reassembly of parliament becomes a major success for the magistrates who are greeted as heroes.

22. Caen. The city council sends two municipal magistrates to Versailles to ask for a meeting of the provincial estates in Normandy.

22. Versailles. The King's Council declares the new Dauphiné constitution to be valid after amending parts of the text.

27. Essones. Berthollet tests a new type of explosive at the royal gunpowder factory.

31. Paris. The head of the bourgeois guard, the Chevalier Dubois, resigns. He had become extremely unpopular since the recent riots were quelled forcibly.

31. Caen. The steward of Normandy reports that the crops have not been good and warns that fear and hunger may causes new unrest in the province.

Marquis de Sade has visit from wife in the Bastille

Paris, October 20

Madame de Sade today visited her husband at the Bastille and saw his new accomodation on the sixth floor of the *Liberté* tower.

After spending the past four years locked up in the infamous jail, the Marquis de Sade has finally been allowed to change rooms and to arrange his new lodgings as he wished. Prison authorities allow detainees to bring in their own furniture if they want. The Marquis has even been allowed to hire an invalid to clean for him, do his shopping and look after him when he is ill.

The countless scandals that have marked de Sade's life had landed him in jail at the request of his mother in law, the Presidente de Montreuil. He was first jailed at Vincennes before being sent to the Bastille. Some say that to while away the time the Marquis de Sade writes books, but others have been whispering that if his books were ever to be published they would cause a far bigger scandal than the various minor misdeeds his family blames him for.

Inside the sinister prisons of Paris

Prison is basically a means of putting criminals out of circulation. For the poor it means overcrowding and often death from illness.

The way prisoners are treated depends on the size of their bank account rather than on the nature of their crimes. Some end up in the reeking cells of the Grand or the Petit Châtelet, where they are likely to die quickly of illness. Others who have a bit more money are held in the comfortable, furnished cells of Bicêtre or the Conciergerie, former princely residences. They are allowed to buy their own food and eat with the prison officials. Some people have paid up to 25,000 livres to become prison guards as the job can be most profitable. The Bastille, which only houses 42 prisoners, is in fact a luxury establishment.

La Pérouse exploits in Russia revealed by young adventurer

Versailles, October 17

The first member of La Pérouse's expedition to return to France is a 22 year old unknown: Barthélemy de Lesseps. The young vice consul taken along by La Pérouse to deal in Kamchatka furs is the King's guest today. He has returned with the expedition's mail and the log book of the famous navigator, but the epic adventures of the young messenger in Siberia are an exploit in themselves. After landing at Petropavlosk on September 30, 1787, Lesseps travelled for twelve months before reaching Moscow. He crossed the snowy wastes of Kamchatka by sled until he got to Okhotsk. Once there, he exchanged his dogs for horses and galloped off across the barren steppes of Asia to reach Moscow in only four months. Excited by the tale of Lesseps' adventures, the court is now anxiously waiting for the return of La Pérouse's frigates, which left Brest three years ago.

The expedition of La Pérouse and his companions to Russia was a major undertaking fraught with dangers.

Jean Blanchard parachutes into Potsdam

Potsdam, October 27

The physicist Blanchard had read somewhere that in certain countries slaves jumped from great heights holding umbrellas to amuse the king. He may well be thinking of this today as he prepares to perform the parachute experiments that have made him famous before the King of Prussia. He will be following in the footsteps of the Englishman Bates, who brought the kite to Europe in the 16th century, of the Frenchman Besnier, who in 1673 succeeded in flying by using flaps, and of the Marquis de Bacqueville, who flew for three hundred metres over the Seine in 1742. Blanchard has built a kind of flying ship equipped with six paddles. The discovery of the hot air balloon by the Montgolfier brothers in 1783 led Blanchard to hook up a balloon to his contraption. Since then, he has made up for the inconvenience of not being able to steer, despite having a rudder, by carrying out experiments in which he dropped animals in cages tied to parachutes.

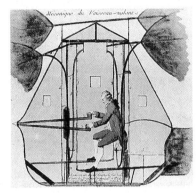

Blanchard hopes to take off aboard his "flying ship".

Man beats life expectancy by 80 years

Montaigu, October

France has at least one man aged over 100. He is called Jean Jacob and lives at Montaigu, in the region of Franche Comté. The old man has beaten all the longevity records. He was born in the year 1669 and this year reached the venerable age of 119. He is probably the oldest inhabitant of France, where the average life expectancy of the population hovers around 39 years. Despite its 28 million inhabitants, which places France in the ranks of "great nations", there have been growing fears of a drop in population over the past few years. The population rise and the increased birth rate recorded over the past thirty years have not been enough to reassure the economists. Even

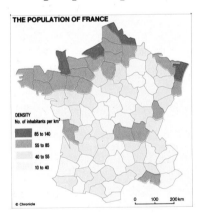

THE POPULATION OF FRANCE

DENSITY
No. of inhabitants per km²

85 to 140
55 to 85
40 to 55
10 to 40

© Chronicle

0   100   200 km

more than the high mortality rate, they fear the effects of the "deadly secrets", the contraceptive methods whose spread, particularly in Normandy, has been slowly changing urban behaviour.

A Polignac is sent to the convent

Paris, October 28

One of the Polignacs, an older brother of the one living at the court, is apparently planning to take advantage of the forthcoming Estates General session to complain of having been forced to enter a convent. The unfortunate man, who was born with a deformity, had been forced by his family to become a monk so that the family's good name would not be tarnished by his misfortune. Such practices remain common even today, despite being criticised by many. Some leading familites do not hesitate to send their children to a convent when they feel that their fortune or reputation is threatened. Girls are very often the victims of such practices, because it is usual to marry only one daughter, but boys sometimes suffer the same fate as the case of the unfortunate Polignac shows. The luckier boys are made abbots, which is a less unpleasant fate than becoming a monk.

Wig-keeping tips for the fastidious

Paris, October 28

Looking after one's hair is no longer just a matter of vanity but of hygiene. This is particularly true for those who wear a wig made out of real hair! The master wig-maker Dupuis advises his clients not to brush the curls, to powder them often and to back-comb lightly. He claims that this will help the wig stay in perfect condition even while its wearer is hunting.

Ribbons are also in fashion.

Toothpaste keeps teeth clean and white

Paris, October

The readers of the *Journal de Paris* have been reminded that teeth will only stay white if they are regularly cleaned, but there is no need to resort to the highly fashionable corrosive and bleaching substances. All that one has to do is to brush the teeth every day using water and toothpaste: but not just any toothpaste! It was recently demonstrated that most currently known toothpastes are much too acidic and can damage the teeth. Substances should not be applied directly to the gums. The attacks of "scurvy" such substances are supposed to cure are in fact only inflammations caused by a lack of dental hygiene and tartar.

Javel water bleaches clothes whiter

France, October

Javel water, which has been available for several years, is becoming increasingly popular with housewives and washer-women.

Even the *Journal de Paris* has been praising the qualities of Javel bleach that whitens cottons and linens. It is manufactured on the banks of the Seine river, at the village of Javel, not far from the capital. To make it, chemists use an acid which, when mixed with eight times its volume of water, acquires all the properties of a detergent but does not damage cloth. People's dirty clothes are soaked for thirty hours in large sandstone, lead, pottery or glass basins. Then they are dipped into a soapy liquid. After they have been carefully rinsed, the clothes will be clean and white. Once used only by professional cleaners, "Javel water" can now be bought in many shops. It can also be found in apothecaries' dispensaries among the countless phials of vitriol and acid.

The apothecary also performs the tasks of a dentist ... His job is to pull out the teeth that have not been regularly and carefully cleaned.

1. Versailles. A decree from the King's Council calls for the estates of Franche Comté to be convened.

3. Brittany. At Rennes, the election by the municipal assembly of four Third Estate deputies to the Brittany estates confirms the growth of a radical patriotism. Among the four are le Chapelier and Jacques Marie Glezen.

4. Paris. An order from the Châtelet calls on doctors to inform police of the identity of people wounded during street fighting. Any physician who refuses to comply will be fined.

6. Versailles. The second assembly of notables opens. →

6. Nantes. The patriots of the town set up a commune, occupy the city hall and pick twelve of their members to go to Versailles to hand a petition to the King calling for a doubling of the Third Estate and for noblemen to be excluded from the Third's elections (→18).

8. Romans. In a letter sent to the court, the Dauphiné assembly expresses the province's wishes for the Estates General, calling for free elections, joint deliberation and a Third Estate representation equal in size with those of the two privileged orders.

10. Paris. The vendors of novelty items sell a pamphlet that mocks the "hero" of May, the councillor d'Eprémesnil. This is a sign of the drop in the popularity of parliamentarians who have expressed opposition to the demands of the Third Estate.

10. Rennes. The first edition of *La Sentinelle du Peuple* is published. It is a patriot journal written by Constantin François de Chasseboeuf, the Comte de Volney.

15. Paris. The Théâtre Français performs *Le Faux Noble*, a comedy by Michel Paul Guy, violin player, intellectual and playwright.

18. Nantes. The Third Estate patriots set up a correspondence committee. Their delegation to Versailles has only been able to submit a petition to the King without obtaining anything.

23. Versailles. A decree from the Council reaffirms the principle of the free circulation of grain.

Necker opposes conservative line on organisation of the Estates General

Versailles, November 6

Who is to be sent to the coming session of the Estates General? How will the debates be organised? These are the main questions which the Assembly of Notables must answer. Necker opened the assembly's first session today. He said he was relying on their "thoughtful meditation" and "impartial study" for the preparation of a national election of which he has high hopes. He has chosen this option in response to the parliament of Paris, which asked in its September 25 ruling that the 1789 Estates General must be organised in the same way as the previous one, held in 1614. This conservative position is worrying

Necker. He wants the Estates General to be an opportunity for a national "renewal" and not simply confirmation of the privileges of the first two orders, but it seems unlikely that the notables will take any bold, innovative steps. It is hard to see why they must back the Third Estate's demands.

The assembly of notables is made up of a total of 150 magistrates, bishops, lords, princes of the blood and mayors of big cities. There are said to be only five commoners among them. It seems useless for the Third Estate to hope that the assembly will accept the doubling of its representation or agree to a vote by head (→Dec. 12).

King's brother aspires to patriotic image

Versailles, November 28

Monsieur, the King's younger brother, is siding with the Third Estate! The news has taken the court by surprise, since its members had become used to the the prince's usually reactionary statements, but at the Assembly of Notables, where he headed an office, the prince loudly proclaimed his support for the doubling of the number of Third Estate deputies to the Estates General. The Comte de Provence, which is another of his titles, seems to be extremely pleased with his attitude. He is looking after his public image and wants to appear to be a patriot prince. His friends believe that he has high ambitions. He has always felt a secret contempt for the King and wants to play a leading role. Louis XVI has until now carefully avoided giving him any responsibilities. He has not even admitted his brother into the

Council and hardly ever asks his advice. Louis XVI appears to be afraid of relying on this ambitious sibling who could one day overshadow him.

The Comte de Provence leads a showy life at the Luxembourg.

Six months' jail for stealing a chicken

Paris, November 14

A sense of humour is not much help when you stand before the judge. Jean Louis Aumont, an apprentice shoe-maker, has just discovered that sad truth. When a judge charged him with having stolen a chicken from a wine merchant, the young man simply denied everything.

The chicken, he claimed, had just dropped into his bag. Found guilty

of the theft, he has been sentenced to six months in jail. The motive for the theft was simple: to avoid dying of hunger. It has become a common sight to see women being arrested by police at the toll gates of Saint Denis or Aubervilliers because they are hiding a piece of stolen cabbage or some leeks. When there is no bread stored away, survival becomes a matter of begging for money or stealing food.

Liberals form their own club

Paris, November

Club fever has been sweeping the capital. Since the King allowed them to be set up, they have become the talk of the town. The most famous patriots, such as Condorcet, Mirabeau, Lacretelle, Target and Roederer have been gathering at the residence of the parliament's councillor, Duport. His club also hosts the liberal nobility and its leaders, Talleyrand and Lafayette, as well as leaders of rebel parliamentarians like d'Eprémesnil. The club has become a hub of opposition activity, a place where members voice sometimes contradictory political aspirations. The membership of some of the other clubs, such as the Duc d'Orléans' at the Palais Royal or the Enragés club of Abbot Sieyès, is more confidential.

The potato can be put to many uses

France, November

The potato has a wide variety of uses. Some have been using it as a cream, or as a makeup remover, or even as soap, but in France this vegetable is still not fully trusted. Despite Parmentier, who believes in it, and the heir to the throne, who eats it, the potato has not become a widely used vegetable. Only the plant's flower seems to have become popular: since Louis XVI wore one in his buttonhole, it is fashionable to decorate cloth and pottery with it.

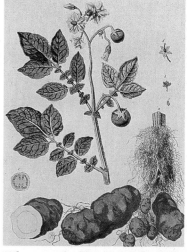
What people like most about the potato is its delicate flower.

Fragonard's tameness disappoints fans

"Le Baiser à la Dérobée": the master's style lacks passion.

Paris, November

The academy has been getting tired of waiting for the crowning work that would make Jean Honoré Fragonard a fully-fledged academician. The death of the painter's daughter last month could be one explanation for his reluctance to submit the work. Fragonard has never liked being hurried. He has been doing less and less painting, apparently getting his young sister in law Marguerite Gérard to execute certain paintings for which he only provides the composition and the idea. His *Baiser à la Dérobée* seems to be among the works that have been painted jointly. Its cold, smooth, and boring style is very different from the painter's usual voluptuous style. Fragonard really should get down to some serious work if he intends to remain popular with a public whose tastes have been evolving. Current fashion is focused on carefully-drawn "bourgeois" paintings in the style of the 17th-century Dutch masters.

Mme. d'Angiviller creates literary salon

Versailles, November

In order to get to know the great minds of today, one only has to go to the Rue de la Surintendance, where the Comtesse d'Angiviller has set up her "salon". Once a week, her residence becomes the meeting place for many outstanding people, who passionately discuss the latest fashionable novels or theatrical events. Eclecticism is the only rule that this self-styled liberal and enlightened group has set itself. The academician la Harpe, an apostle of good taste and a leading philosopher, rubs shoulders with Jean Baptiste Suard, the King's censor. The backbiting Marquis de Créqui, whose venom has replaced talent, holds conversations with Nicolas de Chamfort, whose wit helps people to forget about his unearned title of nobility. The salon is also visited by the author of *Les Liaisons Dangereuses*, Choderlos de Laclos. Women are well represented at the meetings by Madame de Genlis, a woman of letters and the governess of the children of the Duc d'Orléans.

The ladies of France love to wear hats. They have an amazingly wide choice of shape, colour and materials provided by milliners.

Axel returns to his Marie Antoinette

Versailles, November 7

The first thing that de Fersen did this morning was to rush to Versailles where Marie Antoinette was impatiently waiting for him. He had just returned from a lengthy stay in Finland and Sweden, where he had travelled with King Gustav III. The Queen is no longer trying to hide her feelings for the handsome Swede. She had shown an obvious interest in him as soon as he arrived at the French court in 1778, and their relationship has become even closer since he returned from America. The young man, who seems to be shy with women and unassuming with men, appears to hide a romantic spirit behind an icy facade. He always remains discreet with the Queen in public, but everybody is aware of their secret meetings at the Trianon and even at Versailles. In order to keep him at her side, Marie Antoinette has helped him to join the Royal Swedish regiment and has arranged for him to receive an allowance of 20,000 livres to help him live in great comfort at court.

The Swedish officer Fersen, a close friend of Marie Antoinette.

New papers flood onto the Paris streets

Paris, November 23

The readers of Paris will now have a chance to know *Everything that Crosses my Mind* by buying this new periodical. Its anonymous author has claimed that the new publication will be "neither as untruthful as the *Journal de Paris*, as boring as the *Journal des Savants*, nor as dangerous as the *Journal de Médecine ...*" The July 5 decree on the press has also caused a boom in the publication of pamphlets, some of which have even been appearing in instalments. Readers, who have been complaining about the lack of commentary on the preparations for the Estates General in the official reports, find the pamphlets satisfy their curiosity and hunger for satire and biting criticism. In the first edition of the *Sentinelle du Peuple,* a journal aimed at members of Brittany's Third Estate published on November 10, Constantin François Chasseboeuf, the Comte de Volney, wrote: "I have become a sentinel in order to shout Who Goes There!"

The Comte de Volney, philosopher, historian and scholar.

1. Romans. The session of the Dauphiné estates opens: 89 noblemen, 45 clergymen and 119 delegates of the Third Estate are to discuss the province's demands at the Estates General (→5).

2. Paris. A police ruling allows charitable centres to be set up to assist the city's poor.

5. Romans. The King allows the Dauphiné estates to elect the province's deputies to the Estates General from within the Dauphiné estates' own membership. This is a departure from traditional practice. (→Jan. 1, 89).

5. Paris. The Royal Academy of Music performs *Démophon*, an opera by Luigi Cherubini based on a libretto by Jean François Marmontel.

6. Paris. The steward of Brittany, Bertrand de Molleville, resigns. He had left Rennes in July.

9. Paris. The Seine has frozen over. The provost marshal makes it illegal for people to walk across the river, and those who are caught ice skating will be fined.

10. Paris. The city's six guilds of merchants publish a "Petition from Citizens Living in Paris" written by Doctor Joseph Ignace Guillotin. He calls for freedom of the press and the doubling of the number of the Third Estate's deputies to the Estates General (→19).

11. Paris. The physician and naturalist Felix Vicq d'Azyr joins the French Academy.

12. Versailles. The second Assembly of Notables breaks up after calling for the meeting of the Estates General to be organised in the ancient way. The move causes great disappointment.

19. Paris. Parliament replies to Dr. Guillotin by banning his petition and reaffirming that collective petitions are illegal.

23. Rennes. The *Héraut de la Nation* is published. It is a patriot journal edited by Michel Ange Bernard Mangourit du Champ Duguet, a diplomat and freemason.

27. Versailles. The King grants the doubling of the Third Estate.→

29. Rennes. The Brittany estates open at the Cordeliers convent (→30).

Devienne's new concerto pulls the crowds

Paris, December 8

François Devienne has delighted his admirers with his new concerto for bassoon and orchestra. An excellent bassoonist, this 30 year old composer, who plays the flute in the orchestra of Monsieur's theatre, has already composed a number of scores. They include concertos for his two favourite instruments. The fashion for concertos is relatively recent. It was perfected by the Italians, notably by Antonio Vivaldi, at the start of the century. Its spectacular nature and capacity to stress the performer's lyricism have made it a favourite with the public. It has largely replaced the concerto grosso, in which a group of instrumentalists carry on a dialogue with the rest of the orchestra. The concerto grosso also requires musicians to work hard, which few seem prepared to do.

A concerto is composed of a slow movement performed between two fast ones. These give the soloist a chance to distinguish himself.

Men of fashion wear warm clothes

Paris, December

This winter's fashions help well dressed people keep out the icy cold and avoid frostbite. The very latest fashion is for frock coats with tails made out of broad-cloth or velvet and decorated with brass buttons.

When the temperatures drop even lower than usual, gentlemen have taken to wearing a sleeve muff made of the finest Siberian fur and dyed a light puce colour.

The fashionable clothes shops of the Palais Royal arcades are full of a wide variety of warm winter headwear. This year, two models for women have in particular been selling like hot cakes. One of them, known as "La Courière", is completely round, with large pleats, decorated with gauze spikes and a crêpe tufted cockade. The other hat, which has been dubbed "the dragon", is festooned with golden acorns and fiery peacock feathers. Such exuberant headwear and the latest in winter fashions will help the well-dressed members of Paris society face the extremely cold temperatures. However, fashionable clothes are expensive and remain available only to the few who can afford such luxuries to stay warm. The poor will have little protection from the harsh weather.

Many fashionable ladies are keen on fur clothing this winter.

A saucy raconteur joins the Academy

Paris, December 29

The French Academy now has among its members one of the kingdom's most gifted and enchanting men.

Not only is the Chevalier de Boufflers a talented literary figure, he is also at very much at home in the capital's fashionable "salons", where he has become a focus of attention. He is extremely good at peppering his serious literary or political conversations with saucy and charmingly shocking anecdotes that ensure a rapt audience, but he had left Paris for three years to live in Senegal, where he acted as administrator. As France's official representative to African monarchs, he controlled the whole slave trade along the Senegal river from his fort at Saint Louis.

The sensitive soul of this libertine was apparently not shocked by the horrors of the slave trade, as he left behind a flourishing business that allows France to sell 31,000 slaves a year. Despite this, he ended his very well received inaugural speech at the Academy with a moving tribute to Africans, whom he termed "these simple and naive people".

De La Harpe is a hit at the Lycée

Paris, December 11

Jean François de la Harpe has been keeping abreast of current events.

For his fourth season at the Lycée, where he teaches literature, he has decided to concentrate on the philosophers whom everybody is talking about, notably Montesquieu. To counterbalance the recent Assembly of Notables, he has begun his new course with a discussion about the "intermediary powers". His daring theories are very popular with an audience which is wide open to new ideas and which attends the university in order to broaden its horizons.

But even his fame is not enough to balance the establishment's budget completely. Besides the subscriptions paid by its four hundred students the Lycée, conceived by Pilâtre de Roziers, had to seek urgent financial assistance from the freemasons in order to survive.

Bailiff de Suffren is killed in a duel

The bailiff Suffren.

Paris, December 8

The bailiff Pierre Antoine de Suffren de Saint Tropez died today of injuries suffered the day before yesterday in a duel against the Duc de Mirepoix. Before dying, he beg-ged his friends not to reveal the circumstances of the duel. The Duc de Mirepoix had two nephews who sailed in Indian waters on one of the ships of the squadron headed by Suffren. After their return, they were arrested on orders from the King based on a report by Suffren. On meeting Suffren at Versailles, Mirepoix asked him to have the two released. Annoyed by Mirepoix's pressing request, Suffren replied: "I won't do anything to help good for nothings!" Mirepoix challenged him to a duel and the bailiff agreed right away. Both men drew their swords, but the overweight Suffren had trouble defending himself and was injured in the lower stomach. His death is a great loss for the navy and the Order of Malta, of which he was bailiff. After winning three battles against the English in the Gulf of Bengal, he was promoted vice admiral after the Treaty of Versailles was signed.

Penniless French hospitals in dire straits

France's hospitals are in dire straights. Funds are desperately short and infection is spreading like wildfire. In his "Memorandum on Hospitals" published this year, the surgeon Jacques Tenon has lashed out against the situation, saying that hospitals are simply places to die in instead of being "machines to treat patients". Two, three and sometimes as many as six people sleep in a bed! Patients suffering from smallpox are sometimes not placed in isolation and even hospital workers are affected by the unhealthy conditions: nearly all of them catch scabies. This is a far cry from having individual, well-ventilated rooms reserved for "each type of illness" that Tenon wants. Despite a willingness to help the archaic system, the state lacks funds.

The Necker couple visits patients in hospital. The Geneva banker's wife had founded a hospital on the Rue de Sèvres eleven years ago.

Louis XVI agrees to double Third Estate

Versailles, December 27

The aristocrats are becoming worried. They have not been able to win the King over to their conservative policies. After the Council meeting held today, Louis XVI agreed to grant the Third Estate double representation at the Estates General. The decision came after lengthy hesitation and despite the advice of the Assembly of Notables. The move was based on Necker's urging. For the past two months, municipal petitions have been coming in from all over the kingdom calling for an increase in the number of Third Estate deputies, voting by head and joint debate by the three orders. Even the Paris parliament, frightened by this surge in public opinion, has finally joined in the demands. The King has, however, given way on only one of the three demands: the doubling of the Third. By doing this, he has managed to anger the privileged groups without satisfying the "national party" of the patriots. The latter are demanding an end to the separation of the orders at the Estates General.

The Third Estate is symbolised on the right by a sheaf of wheat and two horns of plenty. It has as many votes as the nobility and clergy together.

Brittany Third Estate splendidly isolated

Rennes, December 30

The unity of Breton deputies is at an end. When the provincial estates opened yesterday, the 54 delegates of the Third Estate announced that they would refuse to debate with the two other orders until their demands have been heard.

They are using the strategy of passive resistance launched in 1776 by the nobility, which was then openly fighting against royal administrators. In the past, the Third Estate has joined forces with the monarchy against the first two orders, but these groups are today resting on their privileges. It is against them that their former ally has called for the increase of the number of its representatives, fiscal equality and the abolition of feudal rights. The revolt that is taking place in Brittany is no longer purely a local affair. The Third Estate has just discovered its own strength there.

1. Romans. The notables of the Dauphiné elect their deputies to the Estates General. This move follows the adoption on December 31 of a programme of demands, formulated as an imperative mandate, that the three orders have promised to defend jointly (→9).

5. Caen. A violent riot erupts after authorities refuse to hand out portions of Twelfth Night cake to the poor of the town.

6. Besançon. The Franche Comté estates protest against the royal decision to double the number of Third Estate deputies at the Estates General.

7. Rennes. The three orders having completely failed to agree, the Comte de Thiard receives a royal order to suspend the meeting of the Brittany estates until February 3. This unleashes a storm of protest from the local nobility (→8).

7. Paris. The Théâtre Français performs *Le Présomptueux ou l'Heureux Imaginaire*, a comedy in five acts by Fabre d'Eglantine. →

8. Rennes. The Third Estate decides to obey the King's order and withdraws. Noblemen occupy the Cordeliers convent and solemnly swear an oath never to accept any change in the composition of the estates (→27).

8. Calais. The ice covering the sea up to eight kilometres from shore has paralysed all shipping.

9. Romans. In a bid to safeguard the political agreement between the three orders, Mounier adds to the imperative mandate a clause guaranteeing the payment of compensation when noble property has been abrogated.

9. Paris. To help the poor, the priest of the parish of Saint André des Arcs proposes an increase in the number of charity centres and the payment of an entertainment tax.

11. Versailles. The Council allows the payment of bonuses for foreign grain and flour imports.

11. Caen. The local parish priest hands out soup to the town's poor.

12. Montauban. The town hires unemployed men to build roads.

Women want jobs and enlightenment

Versailles, January 1

The women of the Third Estate also want their voices to be heard. They have sent a petition to the King to complain about their fate. While their husbands see themselves as victims of social injustice, the order's women live in a state of slavery. Only by having access to learning will their condition improve. "We are demanding to be enlightened, to have jobs, not in order usurp men's authority but so that we can have the means to live lives that are sheltered from poverty," the women wrote in their message to Louis XVI.

Vestris is injured in a stage accident

Paris, January 9

The dancer Auguste Vestris has fallen right through the stage. As he was in the middle of a performance of *Démophon* at the Opéra, the stage caved in under the weight of the star dancer.

The accident was due to a trapdoor breaking. The incident caused an uproar among the audience. Despite a fall of over two metres, the dancer was not seriously injured. After the shock was over, Vestris was hauled back on stage.

This "most amazing dancer in Europe" will probably not take too long to get over his unfortunate misadventure.

Fabre d'Eglantine is booed by audience

Paris, January 7

Fabre d'Eglantine is really not lucky. His latest play, *Le Présomptueux,* was greeted by such loud booing this evening that the performance had to be cut short. An actor of little talent and a regularly booed playwright, the poor Fabre has been leading a bohemian life without finding the success and glory he dreams about. Ironically, it was the words of his song "Il pleut, il pleut bergère ..." which made him famous, but Fabre is not easily discouraged and is already working on his new play, *Le Collatéral,* which he is sure will be a hit.

Flirtatious Madame de Genlis engaged as governess to sons of Duc d'Orléans

Paris, January 1

Félicité de Genlis was delighted today when she received some New Year's wishes at her Bellechasse residence from her students.

They had also sent lovely engraved rings. The ring given by Louis Philippe bore the inscription: "What would I have become without you?", while the one sent by the Duc de Montpensier said: "To love you is my duty". As for Beaujolais, the youngest of the princes, he had engraved by himself the words: "I am your handiwork and I give you mine". Far from complaining about the long hours they have to study, the children of the Duc d'Orléans adore their governess. In return for their affection, she spares no effort in their upbringing. After having been one of the most sought after young women of Paris, Madame de Genlis has given up flirtation to dedicate herself to her true vocation: edu-

Félicité de Genlis teaches the harp to the young Mlle. d'Orléans.

cation. Despite what some mean spirited people have claimed, her posting as governess is due to her merits and not to her relationship with the Duc d'Orléans.

Aristocracy remains blind to hardship

Paris, January

The famine, unemployment and unrest that have been stalking the kingdom have no effect on the quiet life led by most aristocrats, and not least by the Comte de Ségur. Last night at his residence a young and unknown poet, Marie Joseph Chénier, read out his new tragedy entitled *Charles IX*. The play is set at the time of the Saint Bartholomew massacres. The play did not move its audience, but everybody remarked on the talent of the author, saying he was sure to have a brilliant future. Conversation then turned to less weighty matters. Some played rhyming games, while others sang improvised madrigals. The pleasant evening was only slightly disturbed by the Duc de Brissac. When the Twelfth Night cake was served, he said it was useless to play the traditional game of choosing a king since "we now no longer have a king".

Dancing is one of the favourite social graces. It allows young women to show off their beauty as well as their fashionable clothes.

To avert a major famine, Necker has been buying grain from abroad

Versailles, January 11

Despite the pitiful state of the treasury, Necker has gone abroad on behalf of the King to buy over 140,000 tonnes of grain and flour. It is a matter of remedying the shortfall in the crops as quickly as possible. The floods of the spring of 1788 were followed by drought and summer heat which ended in hailstorms. The grain crop is therefore far below the levels required and the price of bread reached new heights as early as August. Since problems always come in groups, the bad weather has made travelling difficult for the convoys bringing food to the capital, while frost has stopped the flour mills from working. Necker is said to be having nightmares about famine reaching Paris. He is so obsessed by the food problem that he has himself woken up several times a night so that he can issue crucial orders. His political foes have unjustly accused him of making deals with grain hoarders and to be getting fat profits from this. Some are even speaking of a "famine pact".

The rotunda of Paris' new wheat market, built in 1767, where the grain needed to feed the hungry inhabitants of the capital is stored.

Icy weather tightens its grip on France

Louis XVI handing out alms to some impoverished peasants during the terrible winter of 1788-1789.

France, January

Snow has been falling non-stop for the past two months. Wine has congealed in jugs and clock mechanisms have frozen. The soil is so hard that the bodies of the dead cannot be buried. In the southern Midi region, fruit trees and vineyards have been destroyed. At Bordeaux, large fires have been lit on the city's public squares so that the poor can warm themselves. The Allier river can be crossed on horseback or in a carriage, while a baby in his cot died after falling through the iced Doubs river. At Lyons, the chief of police has ordered the ice broken around the flour mills on the Rhône. He also asked for eight hundred cartloads of charcoal to be brought to avoid half the town's inhabitants dying of cold or hunger. Food is running short everywhere, but temperatures are not rising.

Thanks to Lebon, people have gaslights

Le Havre, January

Are candles and oil lamps soon to become things of the past? The civil engineer Philippe Lebon is trying to convince people that gas will be the lighting of the future. He has just carried out an experiment at Le Havre using the "thermolamp" which he has worked on for several years.

The primitive mechanism consists of a metal box filled with wooden logs which are heated to a very high temperature. The burning wood gives off an inflammable gas which produces a bright and warming flame when it is piped to a burner.

The ingenious contraption is not only designed to light homes cheaply, but also to provide heat. Although the chosen few who had been invited to witness the experiment found it interesting, they nearly choked to death. Once the gas has been burnt, it must be carefully purified or it gives off a foul smell. Lebon's new system does not seem to be about to replace the traditional oil and candles.

The chemist Philippe Lebon.

Supplying the capital with food

Like a permanently hungry giant sitting astride the Seine River, Paris is a huge stomach that the country's provinces must feed.

The area that supplies it spreads well beyond the limits of the Ile de France region and reaches the farthest parts of the kingdom. Paris' food supply is provided by a large number of people. River barges must cross toll barriers and pay taxes. The goods are then unloaded along the banks of the Seine and carried to the central market place, known as the Halles. This is an intricate network of specialised markets surrounded by old houses dating from the 16th century. The impressive new wheat market that includes a huge rotunda built in 1767 is the only modern building in this outdated neighbourhood.

The Halles are in fact a total of 20 small, grimy and noisy markets. Aside from the professional tradesmen, there are hundreds of people cheaply selling what they have grown in their own gardens. Other more shady vendors try to sell food of doubtful quality. Wheat is ground into flour on the nearby hills of Montmartre and the Butte aux Cailles.

Cattle are slaughtered right on the street causing rivers of blood to flow. The area's 2,000 wine merchants belong to a privileged group, as the capital consumes 700,000 litres of wine a year. They easily outnumber the city's 600 bakers. The makers of lemonade, who have been experiencing a boom, have a monopoly over the sale of coffee, tea and chocolate.

Priest calls for elected Third Estate

Paris, January

Abbot Emmanuel Sieyès has just published a provocative pamphlet entitled *What is the Third Estate?* Last November, this brave priest had already lashed out against the nobility's vanity and selfishness in a pamphlet called *Essay on Privileges*. His new work kicks off on a biting note: "What is the Third Estate? Everything. What was it until today? Nothing. What does it want? To become something."

His statements go to the heart of the political issue of the hour: will voting in the Estates General be by class or by head? Sieyès stresses that the traditional class voting would ignore the wishes of 96 per cent of the population. For him, the Third Estate is the cornerstone of the nation, "the strong man with one arm still in chains. Nothing can work without him. Without the others, everything would work better." Sieyès states that members of the nobility "surely set themselves apart from the rest of the population by their laziness". The

"It won't last for ever": that is what the Third Estate, crushed by the heavy burden of poverty, feels about the privileged classes.

abbot saves his best barbs for the gentlemen, sparing the clergy. Above all, the troublesome priest demands that the Third Estate be given duly elected representatives in a National Assembly. This would pave the way for an entirely new political system akin to a constitutional monarchy, but without giving the privileged few as many advantages as is currently the case with the English system.

One of the last Encyclopaedists dies

Baron Holbach.

Paris, January 21

"Reason is simply knowledge acquired through experience of what is good or bad for happiness, for mankind's interest," the philosopher Baron Holbach was fond of saying. A co-author of the Encyclopaedia, friend and sponsor of his fellow philosophers, he died this morning.

His work, *The System of Nature*, was judged too materialistic and burnt. Nor did those in power appreciate the anti-religious aspect of his *Christianity Revealed*. His attacks did not spare members of the ruling classes, for Baron Holbach hated absolute monarchy, the feudal system and social injustice.

Electoral system condemned as unequal

Versailles, January 24

There are some who are more equal than others among those who are allowed to vote. Servants are not included. To be eligible to vote or to be elected to the Estates General, one has to be a man aged 25 or over, have a fixed abode and be subject to taxes. Nobles owning a fief are to be allowed to be represented by proxy, and certain paid clergymen are to have an individual vote. Other unpaid clergy will have to choose one elector for each 20 priests. Direct suffrage will be rare, and to complicate matters elections will not be held on the same day throughout the kingdom.

The Third Estate

The Third Estate is easiest to define by focusing on what it isn't. It includes those who are neither of noble birth nor members of the clergy, which is about 24 million people out of a total population of 25 million. It is a vastly diverse group. In the towns, there is a business middle class made up of bankers, tradesmen and manufacturers. However, all these groups have little in common with lawyers and those who have risen in standing through their talent. There is an even wider gap with inhabitants of small towns, such as day labourers, servants and beggars, who belong to a kind of "fourth estate" along with impoverished peasants. In rural areas, there are few large landowners, and most peasants are day labourers. Between these two extremes come the farmers, the small landowners and the tenant farmers. Basically, the only thing the Third Estate has in common is the feeling of being cut off from a privileged life by an accident of birth.

Breton patriots and nobles clash violently at Rennes

Rennes, January 30

After having been besieged by an angry mob in the Cordeliers monastery for three days and three nights, sword-wielding nobles succeeded in battling their way out early this morning. They had fled there after violent clashes between nobles and Third Estate patriots who were demanding equal representation with the two other orders. The nobility was furious over the royal decree adjourning the provincial estates assembly in a bid to put an end to the violence. The same nobles, supported by parliament, had started the January 26 clashes to inflame public opinion against the Third Estate.

That day, a large, unruly crowd of liveried servants marched down the streets of Rennes yelling anti-bourgeois slogans. The bourgeois are blamed for the rise of the cost of bread, but the unrest backfired on its organisers. On January 27, young Law School patriots came across a seriously wounded dye worker who claimed to have been attacked by nobles. Led by Moreau

Patriot caricature of the events at Rennes mocking the nobility.

and le Chapelier, the angry patriots then grabbed their weapons shouting "Death to the Nobility". Today the Comte de Thiard, military commander of the province, finally succeeded in arranging a truce, but several people have been killed in the clashes and the two opposing factions remain on a war footing.

Two hundred ships boost the slave trade

Nantes, January

The notorious "ebony wood" season has started. The first slave ships leave the Loire estuary, sailing from this busy Atlantic port. They wait in the Paimboeuf roads for the best winds to speed them straight to Guinea. Most of the vessels are two-masted brigs or store ships. Piled high on the quayside are locally-produced cheap jewellery, printed cloth, weapons and brandy, all of which are used to barter for slaves.

Brittany's former capital has become the most active French port involved in the three-sided trade between France, Africa and the West Indies: the slave trade. The ship-owners of Nantes have committed a fleet of two hundred ships to the trade.

At the Nantes shipyard, boats destined for faraway places are assembled on the docks, before being caulked while afloat.

Women declare war ...on each other

Brest, January 24

Shocked to the core by the effrontery of the Third Estate which dares to send envoys to Versailles to see the King, the city's noblewomen meet at the home of one of their own, Madame Dubosq, to decide what to do. They have drafted a *Decree* in which they solemnly state that the Third Estate consists only of persons "unworthy of being admitted into the ranks of honest people". The ladies pledge "on a gentleman's honour" never ever to "have any dealings with any wives, daughters or kin of these dishonoured persons".

They solemnly promise to walk out immediately if one of these women has the impudence to show up at the ball at the Comédie. They have also vowed publicly to brand with infamy any well-bred lady who violates the pledge. How dare these brazen Third Estate women rub shoulders with the other classes and transgress the most elementary rules of good taste!

Mirabeau declares war on fellow nobles

Aix en Provence, January 30

A nobleman has dared speak out in favour of the Third Estate before Provence's assembly of nobles! Not just any nobleman, but Honoré Gabriel Riqueti, Comte de Mirabeau, the famous tribune already revered by the people of Provence.

On a strenuous election campaign for the past two weeks, he speaks out today against the way in which Provence is represented at the Estates General. He stresses that neither the privileged nobility nor the bishops truly represent the first two classes. Taking up the arguments of the Third Estate, he demands the convening of an assembly grouping all three orders and infuriates his privileged audience by exclaiming: "Is it just that the two orders which are not the Nation should outweigh the Nation?" This declaration of war on the nobility of Provence makes him even more popular among the less privileged. Cheered by the inhabitants of Aix, the people's delegates triumphantly carry Mirabeau through the city's streets.

Royal connection makes theatre a hit

Paris, January 26

Monsieur's theatre is now open! The popular new establishment got its name because of the role played in its creation by the King's brother. Monsieur has chosen Léonard Autié, the brother of one of Marie Antoinette's hairdressers, and the violinist Giovanni Viotti as its directors.

The theatre is set up in the great hall at the Tuileries, after a total of 250,000 livres were spent on preparation work. The new theatre is given official permission to present the four fashionable styles of the day: French opera, French plays, vaudeville and comic opera. The theatre's directors travel to Italy to recruit large numbers of singers. Much of the hiring of performers is done by Viotti himself, who personally directs the orchestra. The inaugural performance, which includes both *Vicende Amoroso* and *Servanda Padrona*, is a hit.

1. Dauphiné. Mounier's conciliatory attitude towards the nobility is criticised by several local village communities, which accuse him of being guilty of treason.

2. Paris. Death of Armand Louis Couperin, the king's organist at the Versailles royal chapel and at the Saint Gervais church. His son then takes over from him.

4. Rennes. The assembly of Breton youths, which has been in continuous session since the start of the month, approves a support and unity pact in case of further attacks from the nobility.

5. Rennes. At the new session of the Estates, the Third Estate categorically refuses to approve taxes or even to continue debating the controversial issue. The Comte de Thiard orders the meeting to continue until new orders have come from the King.

7. Paris. Parliament hears the testimony of the Leleu brothers, millers from Corbeil, who have been accused by Paris' master bakers' union of contributing to higher bread prices (→Mar. 24, 89).

8. Versailles. Necker writes to the Third Estate deputies of Provence to warn them not to compromise future reforms by futile resistance at the forthcoming meeting of the region's estates.

8. Aix en Provence. Mirabeau is excluded from the order of the Provence nobility for not being the owner of a fief (→10).

8. Paris. Monsieur's theatre gives a performance of a comedy by Joseph Fiévée entitled *La Maison à Vendre ou la Nuit de Grenade*.

10. Paris. Parliament rules that Mirabeau's *Secret Story of the Berlin Court* is to be burnt after the work has deeply embarrassed the German monarchy and caused tension with France.

13. Grenoble. The parliament's president, Pierre Marie de Vaulx, informs Necker that peasants have been refusing to pay the feudal levies since the start of the month.

14. Rennes. Third Estate deputies approve the tax bill after Breton delegates sent from Paris read messages written by Necker and Villedeuil calling on them to agree to the plan.

Pressure for change mounts on Louis XVI

Versailles, February

Everything is moving too fast for the King! He no longer controls the reins of power. This man who has always had great difficulty in taking the slightest decision finds moves forced upon him which he does not approve of but which he is unable to block. He supports Necker, whose ideas are opposed to his, and is forced to convene the Estates General in a bid to solve the current financial crisis. The monarch is afraid of the slightest change and does not trust the nation's leading figures.

Louis XVI is desperately seeking ways to avoid the gathering of the kingdom's representatives at a time when the nobility is distancing itself from him and when there is rumbling among his "good people". He is discovering the existence of a monster, the nation, led by an elusive force: public opinion. The King is afraid!

Second American envoy arrives in Paris

Ambassador Thomas Jefferson.

Paris, February 3

Thomas Jefferson, the United States representative in France, is far from overjoyed by the arrival in Paris of the man he calls "peg-leg", Governor Morris. This former Convention member has been sent to France as trade representative. There is very little in common between the cultured, Virginia-born lawyer and admirer of France and the newcomer, a cynical, pro-English businessman. Moreover, Jefferson is aware that Morris is George Washington's secret representative. The only belief they share is that trade is the only way for the United States to repay its debt to France.

The nobility takes revenge and shuts out Mirabeau

The Comte de Mirabeau, a turncoat and Third Estate supporter.

Aix en Provence, February 11

The nobles of Provence have made a martyr of Mirabeau by excluding him from the order of the nobility because he does not own a land. Today, Mirabeau responds by publishing a *Call to the Nation of Provence*. Mirabeau claims in this hard-hitting pamphlet that the true reasons for his exclusion is the hatred of nobles for one of their own kind who has sided with the Third Estate and betrayed his class.

The Abbot Sieyès and his friends set up the Valois Club

Paris, February 11

A brand new club has opened at number 177 Valois Alley. Abbot Sieyès has picked ten of his close friends, who in turn picked ten of theirs, giving an initial membership of 100. Twice that number are expected to attend the next meeting. The club's members get together regularly to discuss current political and social issues. Its members belong to the liberal nobility and the upper middle class, people such as La Fayette, Talleyrand, Condorcet, Chamfort and the de Lameth brothers, two of whom were wounded in 1780 and 1781 while fighting alongside Rochambeau in America. The club's rooms, with a view over the Palais Royal gardens, include a library, a reading room, gambling rooms, its own letter-box and an excellent restaurant.

Those who do not belong to the Valois Club can meet at the nearby cafés of the Palais Royal.

February 1789
from 15th. to 28th.

16. Dauphiné. A majority of the people of the village of Saint Véran decide to oppose the policy of unity with the nobility that is being backed by the Provence Third Estate.

16. Paris. Three new sonatas for harpsichord and piano by the composer and virtuoso Muzio Clementi are published.

19. Paris. The Comte Henri du Vergier de la Rochejacquelein becomes a member of the Flanders regiment of chasseurs as a replacement officer.

20. Caen. Gangs of youths from Rennes who had been sent to meet groups of young patriots of Caen cause a disturbance during a performance at the Grand Théâtre.

20. Paris. The Théâtre Italien performs a new comedy by Collin d'Harleville called *Les Chateaux en Espagne*.

21. Paris. At the request of the Archbishop of Paris, the capital's parliament decides to allow eggs to be eaten by Catholics during Lent.

21. Paris. The former abbot Duperey is publicly executed on the capital's Place de Grève. →

25. Granville. The Third Estate's non-professional electors, or those with private means, meet in primary assembly to choose the delegates who will attend the order's secondary assemblies.

25. Vienne. A group of local noblemen decide to renounce their traditional privileges. This voluntary move is made in response to a call by Mounier.

25. Versailles. In a move aimed at avoiding widespread voting fraud, the King's Council decrees that in future debates should only be held in the parish or the professional assemblies.

16. Paris. The Duc François Henri d'Harcourt, governor of Normandy, tutor of the heir to the throne and the author of a learned treatise on gardening, becomes a member of the French Academy.

28. Lyons. The central France city's master weavers and workers choose their thirty six electors. All of those chosen are master craftsmen. However, some of them, such as Denis Monnet, had been sentenced to terms in jail after the August 1786 silk manufacturers' strike.

Lavoisier offers King his "Treatise on Chemistry"

Versailles, February 15

Yesterday the chemist Lavoisier received an unexpected invitation: "Your latest experiment still fascinates me," wrote the King. The Lavoisier couple have therefore taken a copy of their latest work, *Elementary Treatise on Chemistry*, to Versailles. The Queen congratulated the chemist's wife, Anne-Marie, on the quality of her easily understandable illustrations of the text. Fifteen years of work have thus paid off.

A chemist's tools and equipment.

A murdering priest is executed in public

Paris, February 21

The people of Paris enjoy executions, so there was a large turnout this morning on the Place de Grève for the execution of former abbot Jean Félix Duperey.

Earlier this month he had robbed one of his friends after beating him to death with a hammer. The condemned man endured the torture of the wheel with courage, although the executioner made a mess of his grisly task. A first blow with the iron bar landed on the victim's head instead of breaking a limb. Still alive, Duperey received a total of ten blows before being strangled. His body was then exhibited for two hours before being taken to the mortuary.

Faded frock coats are in fashion

Paris, February

Winter seems endless this year. To survive the freezing temperatures, the capital's well-dressed gentlemen have taken to wearing faded frock coats over special antiskid black cloth boots. Their winter headwear consists of a riding hat. To avoid catching potentially lethal head colds, fashionable ladies wear bonnets under a fairly long gauze shawl. Warm black stockings are also in fashion this season. It is considered in good taste to wear brass-edged buttons that match the outfit they adorn. The popular cotton and muslin clothes, which are all too easily set alight by sparks from a fireplace, are best left at home until spring arrives.

Fashion is blind to icy weather.

Laclos pushes Orléans to the fore in poll

Versailles, February

Choderlos de Laclos is believed to have pushed the Duc d'Orléans, leader of the "liberal party", to become a candidate in the elections to the Estates General. Laclos is both a talented officer and an author who in 1780 published a highly successful novel which is still shocking French readers, *Les Liaisons Dangereuses*.

The Duc de Biron had introduced him to Philippe d'Orléans and he soon became his private counsellor and influential advisor. While living at the Palais Royal, Laclos met Talleyrand and Sieyès, with whom he wrote the rules for the preparation of the Book of Grievances which is to be distributed throughout the Orléans lands. It is similar to books already being circulated in the kingdom.

The book is based on reforms which the Duc d'Orléans claims to support strongly. In the document the candidate demands, for example, that divorce be allowed, and

Choderlos de Laclos, an officer, author and politician.

calls for the nobility's hunting privileges to be restricted. He also states his readiness to pay taxes from which he has until now been exempt. Laclos is fully aware that fiscal inequality is what voters oppose above all.

The Books of Grievances

Ever since the Estates General held in 1484, assemblies entrusted with electing deputies have traditionally grouped the complaints and wishes of the people in special books.

In towns and villages, each parish or profession has its own book. The books of each of the three orders are grouped into a single book at the chief town of each constituency, known as a bailiwick or a stewardship. After this has been done, the deputies of each order submit their book to the King during the assembly of estates.

All the various demands made by voters are a kind of obligatory or imperative mandate for the elected deputies, but only those who have acquired basic learning, or who at least know how to write, are able to prepare books of grievances. These include members of the middle class, lawyers, priests or tradesmen. Complaints emanating from the poorest sections of society therefore rarely get as far as the assembly of estates.

Mounier calls for French Constitution

Grenoble, February

The lawyer Joseph Mounier has been sending messages to the King for over five months to demand a constitution that would "protect the monarch's rights as well as those of his subjects".

Mounier, who was the first deputy to be elected to the Estates General by the Dauphiné assembly last December, today published his *New Observations on the Estates General of France*. In it, he calls for the abolition of provincial privileges, as has happened in the Dauphiné, and the adoption of a constitution based on England's Basic Law system.

He strongly disagrees with Montesquieu's concept of monarchy, believing it gives too much influence to the nobility. Mounier does not, however, go as far as

Mounier, the chief instigator of the 1788 unrest in the Dauphiné.

Sieyès on national sovereignty. The lawyer's blueprint still allows a larger role for royal prerogative than Montesquieu's.

Madame's love life causes trouble

Versailles, February 19

Madame, the Comtesse de Provence, is heartbroken. The Foreign Minister has just exiled her close friend and personal reader, a certain Dame de Gourbillon. Over the past few weeks, the minister has had the Princess and her friend under close surveillance. However, the King and Queen had been turning a blind eye to the lesbian relationship between the two women.

Monsieur himself had tolerated the situation, having never felt the slightest physical attraction for his wife. Some even whisper that their marriage was never consummated. However, the harshness of the reader's punishment is probably due to something quite different: Gourbillon was in fact sent away from her mistress because she was spying on the royal family on behalf

Louis XVI's brother's wife.

of the English court. Madame used to keep her up to date on royal gossip and on what was said in private by the King.

A diplomatic row with the King of Prussia is narrowly avoided

Paris, February

Showing a lack of respect to royalty is a very serious matter. France's Foreign Minister, Montmorin, has been forced to convey his government's excuses to Prince Henry of Prussia, who is currently visiting Paris.

The Prince's brother, King Frederick William II of Prussia, is the unwilling hero of the *Secret Story of the Berlin Court*, a book that the people of Paris are reading avidly.

The anonymous work — although it is an open secret that it was written by Mirabeau — tells lively tales of unseemly goings on at the Prussian court, in particular the German monarch's passionate love affair with his current favourite, Madame de Voss.

A diplomatic row between the French and Germans has narrowly been avoided, but Mirabeau's problems are just beginning: the parliament has just condemned him.

Marquis is nearly lynched by a mob

Paris, February 23

A Paris gentleman has nearly been lynched by an enraged mob. The Marquis de la Grange had violently struck a coachman on the head with his cane after being accidentally knocked against a wall by a hackney carriage.

A crowd of onlookers formed immediately and a young butcher's apprentice called for the nobleman to be hanged on the spot. Only the prompt arrival of the guard saved the Marquis. The terrified nobleman was hurriedly taken to the nearest police station. The Marquis was allowed to get away through a back door after paying 12 louis.

Killers haunt the streets of Paris

Paris, February

Has the capital become a den for all the kingdom's bandits? In less than a week, two gruesome murders have been committed in Paris. The first victim was a Paris lawyer named Giraud. He was beaten to death with a hammer by a beggar to whom he had just given a few coins and who followed him home. The second crime is even more shocking. Mlle. Verrier, an elderly spinster, returned home after going out to look for her cat. Two men who had broken into her home and were lying in wait strangled her and stole her money and jewellery. The murderers are still being hunted.

Cabinet-makers designed for success

The renowned carpenters and cabinet-makers of the capital's Faubourg Saint Antoine district are being kept extremely busy. Demand for their work is on the rise. Famous carpenters such as Georges Jacob and Jean Baptiste Séné specialise mainly in unlacquered furniture.

Cabinet-makers also work with precious imported materials such as rosewood, mahogany, lemonwood and mother of pearl. Many of the leading cabinet-makers of the day are of German origin. The Queen herself has largely contributed to their success. After the death of Jean François Oeben, Jean Henri Reisener, who married his widow, and Jean François Leleu have become the royal household's main furniture suppliers. Their pieces avoid gilt and voluptuous shapes, stressing more severe, classic forms. The furniture they specialise in is square-backed, with straight legs, and is decorated with geometric designs and inlays.

Chest of drawers made by Reisener for the King's room at Versailles.

1. Dauphiné. The inhabitants of the community of Saint Vallier ask the provincial estates to allow the poor of the region, who are not entitled to vote in the elections, to express their grievances in a separate book.

2. Rennes. Deputies of the clergy and nobility jointly approve the prorogation of the 1788 tax base for 1789. The nobility of the region then decides that noblemen will refuse to attend the forthcoming meeting of the Estates General.

4. Paris. The huge book collection owned by the Maréchal-Prince de Soubise is broken up after his death in 1787. His ancestor, a cardinal, had started the impressive collection about two centuries earlier.

6. Paris. Parliament bans the publication of all reports about the recent and violent events in Brittany.

11. Reims. Hunger pushes local textile workers to loot the grain stores in the city's cathedral and abbeys. The riot continues to rock the town for a day and a night.

12. Aix en Provence. In a search for new allies, the Third Estate vainly asks fief-less nobles to join in the election of the province's deputies to the Estates General.

13. Paris. On a visit to the capital, Prince Henry of Prussia attends a performance of Antonio Gaspare Sacchini's opera *Arvire e Evelina*.

13. Paris. Parliament condemns a pamphlet, *La Passion, la Mort et la Résurrection du Peuple*, that predicted the end of the privileges of the country's nobility.

14. Manosque. Suspected of hoarding by local villagers, the Bishop of Senez is stoned by the angry mob. The hungry inhabitants of the province have been in an uproar ever since the start of the month (→27).

15. Bordeaux. A twice a month trans-Atlantic maritime postal service is set up between France and the United States.

15. Dauphiné. The town council of Saint Vallier calls for a protest meeting to show its strong opposition to any plans to compensate the dispossessed owners of noble estates.

Election fever hits the French for the first time

France, March

The local authorities at Gaillac, north of Toulouse, have been forced to set up a municipal militia since February 1 to cope with unrest caused by the elections.

The move came after the constabulary proved unable to handle the situation. For the past month, France has been in the grip of election fever in the run-up to the Estates General vote. The excitement is far from over, as royal orders calling together the bailiwicks are reaching their destination at irregular intervals. The province of Alsace was the first to receive the royal documents on February 7.

At the appropriate time, the electoral assemblies meet by parish or by trade guild. These unruly and noisy meetings, presided over by the seigniorial judge, are held in even the smallest village. They are usually held in church on Sunday, just after Mass.

At the meetings, participants elect by voice-vote the primary delegates who will then go to the county seat to choose the Third Estate deputies. The nobility and clergy also gather at the county seats to elect their own deputies. At the same time the Books of Grievances are readied, giving rise to heated arguments. Fears of food shortages between summer and winter crops have already been causing friction between the people, grain hoarders and tax authorities. Fierce, often non-partisan, competition between candidates for seats at the Estates General has been adding to the unrest, sometimes leading to riots.

Talleyrand impresses his faithful flock

Autun, March 15

Monsieur de Talleyrand has just arrived at his diocese. It was high time. The new bishop of Autun is hardly a young man: 35 is pretty late in life to get one's first diocese when one has the connections that go with the name of Charles Maurice de Talleyrand Périgord.

His flock was impatient. They still had not seen their new pastor six months after he was consecrated. However, the new bishop is a success. His flock has been particularly impressed by his interest in the diocese's income, but his hurry to leave Autun has surprised many parishioners. If only they knew how the bishop misses the fleshpots of Paris and the dancing girls of the Opéra. Although they are unaware

Autun's Bishop: Charles Maurice de Talleyrand Périgord.

of Talleyrand's private life, the faithful of Autun have noticed something strange: their good bishop does not know how to say Mass.

Rude words about royalty put Marat in the spotlight

Paris, March

Fame has come at last for Doctor Jean-Paul Marat. The supplement to his *Offerings to the Motherland, or Speech to the Third Estate*, aimed at widening discussion of the initial work, has just been impounded for offensive remarks about royalty. Inhabitants of the capital's Carmes district have been closely following the author's activities. He is about to be elected to the local electoral committee.

Marat has taken advantage of this to call for a French edition of his book *Chains of Slavery*, published in London in 1774.

Wine smugglers prove they have vivid imaginations

Cork, March

Irish customs officials still can't believe their eyes. The French wine was hidden inside the anchor cable and smuggled into the country under their very noses.

The enterprising captain of the *Marie Louise*, a French vessel that arrived recently in Cork harbour, managed to unload his whole shipment of wine without arousing the suspicion of local customs officers. Using the bad weather as an excuse, the clever captain had an extra-thick leather hosepipe strung along the anchor cable and lashed to the dockside.

With the help of a local wine merchant, the smuggling sailor succeeded in off-loading and selling his cargo without paying any customs duty.

After committing their crime, smugglers hide out in a hidden cave where they keep their ill-gotten gains and hold their hostages to ransom.

Revolt rocks Provence

The port of Marseilles, flanked by the Saint Jean and Saint Nicolas forts.

Aix en Provence, March 27

Mirabeau's skill at defusing the unrest currently rocking Provence has made him a local hero. The people have even dubbed him Provence's "saviour". Elected deputy of the Third Estate at Aix a week ago, he has just mediated in a dispute between local housewives enraged by the rise in the price of bread and the town's mayor backed by troops.

Mirabeau persuaded the soldiers to withdraw and persuaded the people of Aix to form a militia, as the inhabitants of the nearby port city of Marseilles had done a few days earlier. On the day when Marseilles electors were to meet to choose their deputies, an angry and starving mob poured into the city's streets, attacking the tax collector's house. The mayor and his assistant were forced to flee for their lives.

The city's military commander was about to order his troops into action to restore order when Mirabeau succeeded in calming the crowds. He then arranged for bills to be posted on the city walls telling people it was far better to accept higher bread prices and have a town militia than to rely on armed troops to keep order.

Starving crowds lash out at traders and food hoarders

France, March

Death to hoarders! Town and country dwellers are hungry. The poor 1788 crop is already nearly gone and the 1789 crop will only be harvested in July. In the interval, the scarcity of food has been made worse by the activities of speculators who hoard grain in a bid to get quicker price rises. Throughout the land, farmers, grain merchants, millers and even bakers are under suspicion, criticised and sometimes attacked. The army and constabulary have barely been able to maintain an uneasy order, except in the Dauphiné and Provence, where extremely violent rioting has broken out.

At Crest, landowners have been forced to sell their grain at 15 livres per "setier", or 15 to 20 sols below the current price. At Sisteron, the bishop barely escaped being thrown into the Durance river after he was accused of selling grain for profit outside the province. At Aix, local officials had to hide inside the city hall to escape from an angry mob. Starving crowds are looting public granaries everywhere and calling for the cost of essential necessities not to exceed a maximum set price.

Louvet de Couvray finishes writing a true-to-life love story

Nemours, March 20

Jean-Baptiste Louvet de Couvray has withdrawn to the tranquillity of Nemours to write the final section of his first novel, entitled *The Loves of the Knight of Faublas*.

Far from the bustle of Paris life, he is putting the final touches to the adventures of his young, handsome, wealthy and rakish hero. But the author's peace and quiet has just been shattered by the unexpected arrival of his young mistress, Marguerite Cholet. He has been madly in love with her since his youth. She has decided to leave her husband, a rich Paris jeweller, and move in with the author.

As a token of his affection, he has made Marguerite the heroine of his semi-autobiographical novel. In the book, Marguerite Cholet is given the name of Lodoiska. Astute readers have little trouble in identifying Faublas as the author himself.

The young woman with her shift off painted by Fragonard resembles all the Lodoiskas who have been at the mercy of Cupid's whims.

Priests, bishops, princes and dukes fight to become deputies

France, March

The elections have revealed unsuspected internal strife. Everybody expected that the nobility and the clergy would show strong class solidarity, but tensions run very high within these two groups, particularly among the clergy.

At Bellay en Bugey, diocesans voted for a parish priest rather than for their bishop, who then refused to hand the Books of Grievances over to the winner. The bishop's move had the backing of the cathedral's canons, but he had to give in when a crowd rushed to his house threatening to wreck his belongings. At Montfort l'Amaury, the Abbot of Espagnac has succeeded in beating his opponent, the popular Abbot Sieyès, by plotting and using bribes.

The same lack of unity reigns within the ranks of nobility. In the Clermont region, the Duc de Liancourt has ousted the Prince de Condé. At Bourges, the Comte de Guibert has been ordered to withdraw from the assembly. He was charged with having attempted to introduce Prussian military methods into France. Gentlemen such as d'Eprémesnil and Sémonville, as well as the Abbot le Coigneux, have all been defeated despite being parliamentary councillors. The new nobility of the Limousin no longer has an assembly to stand in. They have been rejected as members of the privileged class by the Third Estate as well as by the nobility, who see them as fakes. The elections to the Estates General are far from over, but feelings are already running high.

Passion shows in shady Palais Royal

Paris, March 20

Spring has arrived at last in Paris and the footpaths and shady alleyways of the central Palais Royal gardens are once again crowded with well-dressed ladies, busy gentlemen and noisy tradesmen selling their wares.

But many of those who are really in the know rush each day to a certain shady spot where a lusty couple is known to make passionate love in public. The man is called Constant, a huge, muscular blacksmith, while his willing companion is a plump local prostitute known simply as Marie Louise.

Their ardour is such that people claim they prove their love for each other 20 times a day for their appreciative public. The regular audience at the Palais Royal thoroughly enjoys the free open-air shows, often shouting encouragement from the sidelines.

Not so much a salon, more an academy

Auteuil, March

Madame Helvétius, who has lived here since her husband died in 1771, has been setting up gatherings of some of Paris' most outstanding philosophers and literary figures. Famous for her wit, intelligence and generous hospitality, she has turned her home into a charming and highly respected literary academy.

Benjamin Franklin, one of her many unsuccessful suitors, used to call her "Our Lady of Auteuil". She regularly plays host to her friends, surrounded by her twenty angora cats. Her two daughters, the beautiful Comtesses d'Andlau and de Mun, dubbed the two stars, help her receive guests in style. Often to be seen at Auteuil are the Baron Grimm, Abbot Morellet, the Marquis de Condorcet, the poet Roucher and the Abbot Lefebvre de la Roche. Condorcet has taken to bringing along his young bride, Sophie, who lends her beauty to the gatherings.

Colonial governor relaxes flour ban

Port au Prince, March 30

Saint Domingue lives in prosperity. Its warehouses overflow with animal pelts, sugar, coffee, cocoa, cotton and indigo. This wealthy colony of 523,000 inhabitants, of whom 465,000 are slaves, is, however, not safe from shortages. Therefore, in a bid to remedy the ban on the export of grain imposed by mainland France, the island's governor has just decided to allow flour to be imported. The move, which runs counter to current colonial regulations, is applauded by local settlers.

The colonial trade keeps the ports of France extremely busy.

Beaumarchais gives a house-warming party at his new home

Paris, March

Monsieur de Beaumarchais can throw quite a party. Parisians will long remember the one he gave as a house-warming when he moved into his new and palatial home in the capital's Saint Antoine district. Hundreds of people attended the house-warming, amongst them the Duc d'Orléans. The well-known author's house was the centre of attraction. Construction work, begun some two years ago, is still not completed, and the grandiose building has already cost the princely sum of over a million livres, but the results of all this work are impressive: the terraced gardens overlooking the boulevard attract many paying visitors. The gardens feature a Chinese bridge, a waterfall and a circular temple.

The house itself is already well known for its spacious halls and sitting rooms, its well-stocked library, its caryatids and English-style proportions.

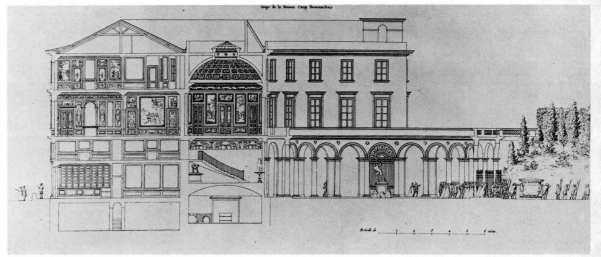

This cross-section view of the Beaumarchais residence shows the richness of the interior decoration.

Rivarol lashes out at Academicians

Paris, April

The wind of revolt currently blowing through France spares nothing, not even the prestigious French Academy. Until now the stately institution based at the Louvre had carefully avoided any involvement in political unrest, but today it is precisely this lack of involvement that has become the target of criticism.

Already charged with being outdated and useless, the institution is now being accused of lack of patriotism. In a biting attack entitled *Extraordinary and Secret Session of the Academy*, an anonymous critic writes that Academicians are indifferent to the wind of change blowing through France. Most well informed readers realise the author is none other than the polemicist Rivarol. In his pamphlet, Rivarol says that Academicians waste their time in pointless literary bickering while the whole nation is avidly following the opening of the Estates General. Rivarol adds that the sole concern of one of its most eminent members, the poet la Harpe, is carefully to pick candidates for literary competitions, using good taste as the sole criterion.

Antoine de Rivarol, brilliant talker and scourge of institutions.

Such pointless occupations seem out of place in a country riddled with political turmoil. Many are wondering what the French Academy's purpose is. Rivarol and others believe that the Academy has spent so much time posing as a defender of the French language and literature that it has become a graveyard for intellectuals.

Wealthy piano maker, Goërmans, dies

Paris, April

Jacques Goërmans, the wealthy piano maker, has died. He owed his fortune to the growing success of the piano, perfected in 1709 by Bartolomeo Cristofori and improved on ever since. In 80 years, piano makers have turned the unattractive sound of the early instruments into today's melodious and harmonious tones. The greatest composers of the day, such as Wolfgang Amadeus Mozart, are using its capabilities to the full.

A gentleman's prune cloak and a white taffeta skirt for the lady.

Talma brings new life to the Théâtre

Paris, April 1st

The arrival of François Joseph Talma at the Théâtre Français has just crowned a promising early career.

Ever since his first appearance on this famous stage, on November 21, 1787, in the relatively minor role of Séide in Voltaire's play *Mahomet*, his performances have been improving. His qualities include a fine voice, good looks, sensitivity, warmth, and highly expressive features which are capable of conveying great tragedy. The young actor seems destined to become a major star.

Talma playing the role of Titus in "Brutus" by Voltaire.

Locked-up wife is cleared of adultery

Paris, April 2

Justice has triumphed at last. Beaumarchais has just scored a major victory by winning the trial in which he had opposed the wealthy banker Kornmann and the lawyer Bergasse. Kornmann, who had had his young wife locked up for adultery, had in fact encouraged her to have an affair with a certain Daudet de Jossan in order to improve his business prospects.

Furious over repeated attempts by Beaumarchais to help his wife, Kornmann attacked and slandered him in scurrilous lampoons, aided by his friend Bergasse. The court sentenced both culprits to pay a fine of 1,000 livres in damages and the judge dismissed the charge of adultery against the young woman.

Peasant is elected to the Third Estate

Michel Gérard, deputy and peasant.

Rennes, April 13

Deputies to the Estates General elected by the Rennes assembly include three lawyers, a public prosecutor, a businessman, and the mayor of Vitré — but there is only one peasant among them. He is Michel Gérard, who has acquired some basic learning and become relatively prosperous. He is aware of the problems of his peers and will be well placed to become a strong defender of the rights of the Third Estate and of its role in society.

Taxes top complaints of Third Estate

France, April

Despite their diversity and their sometimes contradictory nature, demands made throughout the kingdom in the run-up to the meeting of the Estates General tally on several major issues. Even if the nobility is sometimes prepared to accept fiscal equality, it firmly rejects any weakening of provincial privileges in favour of centralised monarchy.

Thus, the gentlemen of Aix have stated that "the King of France will simply be known in Provence as a Comte de Provence". Clergymen in their Books of Grievances stress the social gap between the higher and lower clergy.

For its part, the Third Estate is unanimous in its condemnation of taxation, which it considers monstrously unfair and arbitrary. Members of the Third Estate are scandalised by the heavy tax burden on the poor and by the behaviour of those who are charged with the collection of taxes, such as provincial administrators. Tax collectors

"Soft boiled egg", symbol of a much sought after position.

are systematically accused of gross corruption. In the towns there is grumbling against the professional guilds' economic monopoly, while in rural areas most grievances are focused on feudal rights, but the criticism is harshest on the political front. Many Books of Grievances call for a Constitution which would impose limits on arbitrary royal power. They also stress the need for respect of the ideals of equality for all, the right to property and individual freedoms.

La Fayette torn between class and ideals

La Fayette dressed as a captain in the Noailles regiment.

Paris, April 17

La Fayette feels he is misunderstood by his American friends. Invited to dine with one of them, Governor Morris, he explains the wrench he feels between loyalty to his class, the nobility, and his pro-Third Estate ideals. La Fayette has been elected to the Estates General as deputy for the nobility by a narrow margin due to the unease felt by his peers over his politics.

But he is furious over having to hold to the nobility's imperative mandate to vote by class. He must have complained too loudly, because he is now being accused of preaching revolt. "One must be pretty evil to say on the eve of the Estates General that he who was the first to call for them plans to overthrow the kingdom and set it on fire," he exclaims.

Attacked on all sides, La Fayette finds little help among his American friends. Jefferson has written to say that he is becoming "very worried" about him. Morris, who claims to be "opposed to democracy due to a love of freedom", believes that La Fayette's plans are "incompatible with the basic elements that constitute the French nation". Could the royalist Marquis de La Fayette have become more of a democrat than his republican friends? Morris has sent a letter about him to George Washington: "He is at the moment as envied and hated as he may ever have wished."

Surprises in the Books of Grievances

Pont L'Abbé, April

The Books of Grievances do not just contain lists of complaints; some also suggest solutions. For example, a group of the artisans of Pont L'Abbé proposes that feudal levies be donated to hospitals to help the needy. Liberal ideas can be far-reaching: at Chalais, there are calls for all of the kingdom's priests to marry so that "the tenderness of their wives will awake in their hearts a compassion which has until now been crushed by their vows of chastity". Even more surprising is the very conservative content of some of the Books of Grievances. In the small Lorraine bailiwick of Mirecourt, the Third Estate has expressed its belief that "a proper social order requires differences in rank". At Orléans, the Third Estate says it will "always agree that the nobility remains superior to us". The French are truly a most amazing people!

The "bible" of French chemistry

Paris, April 3

The just-published *Annals of Chemistry* will tell its readers all they need to know about the medicinal properties of air, the chemical composition of cow's milk, cloth and thread, felt making, nitrogen, blue Roque-Fort cheese, sugar cane, prussic acid, phosphorus, tin and chloride. Among other things, it will also reveal the mysteries of adamantine spar and chrysoprase of gold.

The Marquis de Condorcet has just given the Science Academy's go-ahead for regular publication of the Annals. Its directors are to be Monge, Morveau, Lavoisier, Berthollet, Adet, Fourcroy, Hassenfratz and Dietrich. The Annals are soon to become a shining example of the dynamism of the French school of chemistry and have a wide impact throughout Europe. The Annals claim to be a compendium of major "new discoveries in chemistry and the related arts, written in a language that is familiar to all the knowledgeable nations of our continent".

300 killed as the Réveillon wallpaper factory is looted

The sacking by a mob of the residence, grounds and workrooms of the Réveillon wallpaper factory.

Paris, April 28

Three hundred people were killed today in the Faubourg Saint Antoine. A riot broke out in the district, which had been through a miserable winter followed by high unemployment. Rumours about the Comte de Réveillon's plans began spreading on Sunday. People claim that he has asked his district's

Looting outside the factory before the arrival of the troops.

assembly to cut his workers' pay to a mere 15 sous. On Monday April 27, groups of demonstrators marched near the factory, crying for blood while burning the owner in effigy on the Place de Grève. The demonstration broke up around midnight and the riot was thought to be over.

But trouble started anew this morning. A mob of several thousand people spread through the district's streets, blocking traffic. Fine carriages bound for the horse races at Vincennes were stopped and their passengers forced to get out and shout "Long Live the Third Estate". One of them, the Duc d'Orléans, was recognised by the crowd and cheered, but he proved unable to calm things down. The 30 or so guardsmen sent in to restore order have not been able to cope with the situation. At noon, the factory was broken into and looted. Three fires were lit and the mob threw books, sales records and even farmyard animals into the flames.

The looters emptied the barrels found in the building's basement and some unfortunates died after drinking the dyes they contained, thinking it was wine. The Swiss guard and the cavalry finally succeeded in quelling the riot by opening fire at the rioters, many of whom were throwing a hail of tiles from nearby rooftops.

Jean Réveillon

Within a few short years, Jean Baptiste Réveillon has risen from being a simple draper to a rich industrialist. The wallpaper manufacturer employs nearly 400 people in his "large and magnificent work-rooms open to the public". He has bought a paper mill in order to ensure a steady supply of raw material. Many envy his success, but his paternalistic attitude hides a harsh character.

Rioters face death sentence to set example to troublemakers

Paris, April 30

Two of the men who were involved in the attack on the Revéillon factory two days ago have just been sentenced to death by the court of the Châtelet.

Their fate is to serve as an ex-

ample to other potential troublemakers; but was the riot really as spontaneous as it might appear? There are many who support the theory that it was a plot. The bourgeois feel they were the target of an "aristocrats' plot", while the court

and the King believe that the Duc d'Orléans somehow had a hand in events. For many, it is easier to attribute the violence to a few hotheads than to admit that it was, in fact, a symptom of deep-seated social problems.

1. **Paris.** Following the looting and wrecking of his wallpaper factory, and fearing new reprisals from angry workers, the industrialist Jean Baptiste Réveillon has himself voluntarily locked up in the Bastille prison, claiming that it is the "only safe haven that I can find".

1. **Paris.** The artist Hubert Rodier, keeper of the King's collection of paintings, is requested to purchase for Louis XVI several drawings by Eustache le Sueur that currently belong to the Prince de Soubise.

2. **Versailles.** Deputies of the three orders are presented to the King at the palace. →

2. **Saint-Lô.** Faced with a chronic shortage of food, the local authorities are forced to allow the town's starving inhabitants to set off on armed grain and food hunting expeditions in the neighbouring countryside (→13).

2. **Paris.** The chemist Antoine François, Comte de Fourcroy, and the King's pharmacist, Antoine Louis Brongniart, start giving chemistry lessons at the capital's Royal Academy of Science.

3. **Versailles.** In the run-up to the forthcoming royal procession (→4), the people of Versailles who are fortunate enough to own property on the parade's path rent their balconies and rooftops to visitors so that they can watch the colourful event in comfort.

4. **Versailles.** A solemn mass is said before all the deputies, as well as the King, Marie Antoinette and the entire court at Notre Dame church. During the royal procession, some of the thousands of spectators dare to shout "Long Live the Duc d'Orléans" as the Queen is driven by in her carriage.

4. **Paris.** Monsieur's theatre performs *L'Impresario in Angustia*, a comic opera by Domenico Cimarosa and Carlo Goldoni, a Venetian author who has been living in France since 1787.

5. **Versailles.** Despite the political unrest, hunger and rioting that have been rocking the nation, the court continues faithfully to observe its age-old rituals: each morning, the superintendent of royal music, François Giroud, directs the special concert that marks the Royal Awakening.

Deputies are presented to the King

Versailles, May 2

The King has finally consented to receive the thousand or so deputies from the three Estates. The palace ceremony is grandiose. Cardinals wear red, archbishops purple and the other members of the clergy are in black. Noblemen are dressed in colourful outfits, white stockings, feathered hats and golden stoles.

Beside all this finery, the people of the Third Estate, dressed in black with a simple muslin cravat, look like court bailiffs. They were only told yesterday by the Marquis de Dreux Brézé what to wear and had problems finding clothes that fit in time for the ceremony. They were the last to be allowed into the great hall and the usher did not announce which province each came from. The King does not seem keen to get to know them.

Departure of the three orders for Versailles, led by Fame.

Thousands cheer the King's great parade

Versailles, May 4

It was the kind of parade the people of Paris love to watch. At precisely eleven o'clock, a huge, colourful procession marched slowly through gaily decorated streets, from the church of Notre Dame to the chapel of Saint Louis.

The King, followed by members of his immediate family, princes of the blood, the court, high dignitaries, deputies, military bands and the faithful, paraded under the arch where riders bearing hawks stood at attention. After the singing of a solemn hymn, *Veni Creator*, the Archbishop of Nancy delivered the sermon. It was late afternoon by the time Louis XVI finally left the chapel, cheered by the crowd of at least 10,000 people that had gathered outside.

Parade at the start of the Estates General, Place Dauphine, Versailles.

Breton deputies set up full-time office

Versailles, May

The reputation of the Third Estate deputies of Brittany has preceeded them to Versailles. They have been calling all the shots in Rennes since last winter. Moreover, they are in a unique position.

They are the only representatives of their region, since the nobility and the clergy of Brittany have refused to send delegates to the Estates General. They feel the burden of responsibility. The deputies of Rennes, including le Chapelier, Gérard and Lanjuinais, have rented the basement of the Amaury café, on the Avenue Saint Cloud, as an office from which they can ensure a permanent link between Versailles and their home region. Deputies from other provinces are always dropping in to congratulate them for their firm stand and to discuss the latest news.

Each day they faithfully send messages to Rennes, where a daily newsletter containing their correspondence is already being published. At Versailles their committee has been dubbed the "Breton Club".

Louis XVI prepares for the challenge

Versailles, May 4

For the past few days, the King has been working on the speech he is due to give tomorrow before the Estates General. He has been re-writing it endlessly, seeking advice from all around him. The Queen had advised him to take a solemn tone, but he would prefer to "let his heart speak". He has consulted his ministers, who disagree about how to handle the crucial speech. Barentin has advised the King to keep as much authority as possible, while the Duc de Nivernais and Montmorin tell him to give the deputies some legislative powers.

As for Necker, he is as usual calling for moderation. Finally, the King has written a rather vague speech in which he salutes the Estates General as a "new source of happiness" for the nation. In the evening, he asked his brothers to "correct my mistakes", but he left the text unchanged, being rather proud of it.

Formal opening at Versailles of the Estates General on May 5 1789, in the hall of the Menus Plaisirs.

93

May 5, 1789: The Estates General, a nation's

For the first time since 1614, a King of France is to speak publicly and solemnly to the representatives of the nation. The event has brought a surge of hope to country dwellers and city folk.

The dramatic event follows five months of preparations for the Estates General and the drafting of the Books of Grievances which have given each Frenchman an opportunity to express himself.

Gradually, hopes have turned into demands. People have had their fill of unjust taxes, of the iniquitous feudal system: they want their freedoms. There are great expectations. People hope that the King will agree to take the wishes of the Third Estate into account. The members of the Third Estate feel they have become the standard bearers for the aspirations and demands of the 27 million people they represent. All eyes are focused on the King.

The King presides over the opening of the Estates General at the Menus Plaisirs hall: in the forefront, the Third Estate deputies; at the back, the nobility; lower left are the members of the clergy.

The crowd has been gathered since dawn along the Chantiers street to watch the deputies to the Estates General pass by. They had been told to arrive at eight o'clock, and have come in small groups, meeting outside the Menus Plaisirs building. The Marquis de Dreux Brézé and the other two masters of ceremonies then ushered the deputies into the lobby.

The roll-call of the 1,200 deputies has begun, and the process takes three hours. Inside the building, a hand-picked audience of 2,000 have already taken their seats on the gallery. Some entry permits have fetched high prices.

The Marquis de Dreux Brézé seating the deputies.

Among those attending are the court, the cream of Paris high society and many of France's most famous names, such as Germaine de Staël, wife of the Swedish ambassador and Necker's daughter. The entire diplomatic corps is present. Soon, the messages sent home by the diplomats will inform the other courts of Europe of today's events. Neighbouring nations have been closely following the situation in France.

200,000 livres!

The meeting hall has been carefully prepared to receive over three thousand people. The huge room has been painted light green and white. The gallery is separated from the main hall by a double colonnade. The whole room is focused towards the impressive royal dais draped in purple cloth and decorated with golden fleurs-de-lis.

It has taken many months' work to transform what was originally a storeroom for the scenery of the King's opera. Hundreds of benches and chairs have been brought from Fontainebleau and Compiègne. Two workmen have been killed and six others injured during construction work. The whole thing will cost the Treasury the vast sum of 200,000 livres, but even that is in-

significant compared to the huge budget deficit, which is estimated by Necker at 56 million livres.

Cheers and jeers

The stately entrance made by the deputies gives the crowd a chance to observe them closely. Members of the Third Estate dressed in black have aroused a lot of curiosity, since they are largely unknown but much discussed. The deputies have been led to their respective seats: the clergy is on the right of the throne, the nobility on the left,

while the Third Estate is at the back of the room. Deputies from Brittany have received a lot of attention. Amongst them, many have noticed Michel Gérard, the sole peasant at the assembly, who is also the only one not to wear a wig or the costume that protocol requires.

Deputies from the Dauphiné have also been cheered, in particular their leader, Jean Joseph Mounier. The Duc d'Orléans, cousin of the King and deputy for the nobility of Crépy en Valois, has chosen to sit in the ranks of the nobility rather than with princes of the blood. His move

The complex subtleties of protocol

The organisers are having trouble choosing the correct protocol for the meeting of the Estates General. The only relevant material is over 150 years old. Lacking any instructions from the palace, the man in charge of protocol, Dreux Brézé, and the masters of ceremonies have found rules and precedents dating from the last meeting of the Estates General, convened by Maria de Medicis in 1614. There are problems to solve. Disputes over etiquette are delaying the meeting of the Estates

General. Should the Queen attend? Is the King to speak while sitting down or standing up, bare headed or not? Should the deputies' benches have backrests? These are vital issues for the country! Everybody wants to stand out: the representatives of the privileged classes want to distinguish themselves from Third Estate deputies, prelates from simple priests and dukes from lowly noblemen; will protocol officials dare ask Third Estate deputies to kneel when they speak to the King?

source of hope, are solemnly opened by the King

has been strongly acclaimed. A hostile silence followed by jeers has however greeted the arrival of the well-known defector from the nobility, Mirabeau. The Third Estate deputies, who consider him to be their spokesman, have escorted him to the minister's desk just below the royal dais. Members of the clergy have, meanwhile, been behaving strangely: bishops have refused to take their designated seats. They have instead occupied the front row, despite protests from the ousted priests who have been fighting back. Some of these manage to hang on to their seats, but none dare argue with the Marquis de La Rochefoucauld, the only cardinal to be a deputy.

Louis XVI left the palace shortly before noon, as the last few deputies were taking their seats at the Menus

ing between the representatives of one of the world's most enlightened, but also most unruly, nations and this monarch, heir to three races and 66 kings.

Peers and marshals, senior military officers, knights of the Orders, court ushers and halberdiers have all taken their places around the royal dais in an order clearly set out by etiquette. The elected members of the clergy, the nobility and the Third Estate all seem to be holding their breath.

The noon hour has struck, and suddenly the ushers kneel down. As the King slowly makes his entrance a huge cheer is heard, then silence returns. Wearing the large royal cloak and a wide feathered hat, the monarch salutes the crowd before taking his seat. Everybody has remained standing, even the Queen.

ties then had the effrontery to put on their hats, causing whispers to be heard among the crowd, but the King did not seem to hear the disturbance. He had again removed his hat to wipe his brow, forcing the nobles and the daring Third Estate members to remove theirs.

Disappointment

Then it was the turn of Barentin, the Lord Chancellor, to begin speaking, although few were able to hear his 30-minute long speech because of his low voice. Anyway, it was Necker the crowd was anxiously waiting to hear, expecting him to reveal at last what the King has decided about voting by head and the constitution. Necker's speech lasted three whole hours and was devoted entirely to complex financial issues. After a while he got one of his assistants to take over so that he could observe the crowd's reaction. Boredom could be read on every face. Some were even having trouble staying awake. The speaker did mention the need for reforms, but only in the context of taxation and the slave trade.

Only a few, extremely vague references to the constitution were heard. Moreover, Necker avoided the question of voting by head and postponed discussion of the issue. This won him cheers from the nobility. As soon as the speech was over, at around five o'clock, the King rose, thus putting an end to the session. This meant that there was

Michel Gérard, the sole peasant Third Estate deputy.

no speech of thanks from each of the orders. Was this done due to fears of what Third Estate deputies might say if allowed to speak?

Counter attack

Louis XVI left the hall amid loud cheering, but the cheers did not really mask the deep disappointment felt by a large number of deputies. Everybody then rushed off to dine and to discuss the day's events. Furious, but in fact secretly delighted, Mirabeau has decided to counter attack in his *Journal of the Estates General* which is to be published tomorrow. In it, he demands to be told whether the Estates General were merely a meeting of the chamber of commerce. Was it all a plot to silence the Third Estate? Doesn't that order represent the vast majority of the French nation? Voting by head is a matter of justice. These are issues that have to be decided urgently by the Estates themselves, Mirabeau writes.

Meanwhile, the deputies of the Dauphiné region have gathered to discuss how to react tomorrow. Deputies have been told to meet by order, but those from the Dauphiné, led by Mounier and Lefranc de Pompignan, Archbishop of Vienne, are obliged by an imperative mandate to oppose this. Can they really openly disobey the King's orders? They finally decided to go to their different assemblies in order to win acceptance for their views at each of them. Thus, the trial of strength is already under way. The basic question now is whether the harmony and wisdom called for by the King will prevail.

The ceremonial costumes worn by the three orders show the difference between the members of the privileged orders and the Third Estate.

Plaisirs. The princes of the blood were riding in the King's coach, while the princesses rode in the Queen's coach or in those carrying the King's aunts. No fewer than 38 coaches drove past the delighted crowd, accompanied by dozens of out-riders, grooms, page-boys and trumpeters. Men of the élite Gardes du Corps regiment, resplendent in their blue-trimmed red uniforms, marched alongside the monarch, forming an impressive and colourful procession.

A special moment

The excitement reaches a peak among the deputies when they hear the King is about to arrive at last. They all feel they are witnessing a major historical event. It is a meet-

All the men have doffed their hats. Then the King begins to speak in a loud, powerful voice. Calling on the nation's representatives to show harmony, he stresses that wisdom must prevail; but Louis XVI has not shown the slightest sign of being willing to abandon any of his sovereignty or powers. The already-tense ranks of the Third Estate grumble on hearing the King mention what he termed the "excessive desire for innovation".

But this did not really mar the crowd's enthusiasm, and the King's speech was interrupted by cheering several times. Once the speech was over, Louis XVI again saluted the audience and donned his hat. The nobility followed suit, as they are allowed to do when the King is not speaking. Some Third Estate depu-

The Comte de Mirabeau: the controversial leader is the focus of attention.

6. Versailles. The deputies of the Third Estate meet in the State hall at Versailles. Meanwhile both the clergy and the nobility decide to verify their respective mandates separately.

6. Versailles. The King's Council makes it illegal for journalists to publish any reports on the sessions of the Estates General (→ 19).

6. Paris. The first edition of Jacques Pierre Brissot's *Patriote Français* is published.

9. Paris. Death of Jean Baptiste Vaquette de Gribeauval. He was commander of the royal artillery. His reforms had helped to bring the elite artillery corps up to date.

11. Versailles. The nobility proceeds with the immediate verification of mandates in order to be able to issue legally binding decrees.→

14. Paris. Seeking the best possible education for their children, the Duc d'Orléans and the Duc de Bourbon enrol their sons at the Turquin swimming school, located on the Ile Saint Louis in central Paris.

19. Versailles. The royal Council decides to allow newspapers to print speeches made at the assemblies, but bans any editorial comment on proceedings there.

21. Paris. At the Palais Royal, the Austrian musician Frantz gives a demonstration of the "bariton", a stringed instrument that is still little-known in France: it is basically similar to the 'cello.

22. Versailles. The nobility accepts the principle of fiscal equality, thus following the example of the clergy, which two days ago agreed to give up its fiscal privileges.

23. Versailles. On the initiative of the lower clergy, a committee of priests is formed to discuss the means to join the assembly of the Commons.

25. Versailles. The Paris deputation joins the Estates General.

27. Versailles. Acting on the advice of patriot priests, the Commons sends a delegation to ask the clergy to join them.

30. Versailles. A third meeting of the arbitration committee, which has been held in the presence of the Lord Chancellor, fails.→

Dumouriez restores order at Saint Lô

Charles François Dumouriez.

Saint Lô, May 13

The worst has been avoided! In the Cotentin region, there is widespread hunger and unemployment due to construction work being stopped on the Cherbourg harbour. The Saint Lô marketplace is empty for the second consecutive year. The crowds have become more daring, knowing that the judges are safely at their country homes and the militia is leaderless. Cherbourg's governor, Charles François Dumouriez, has set up a public security and food distribution committee. Law and order seem to have been restored.

Third Estate starts crisis

Versailles, May 11

Debate at the Estates General has been stalled since May 6. Each order was to have checked the mandates of their deputies separately, but the Third Estate has refused, arguing that to do so would be to create a separate assembly and give implicit recognition to class voting. It therefore at all costs had to get each mandate checked prior to an individual vote. Pushed by deputies from Brittany and the Dauphiné, the Third Estate has confirmed that decision and named itself the Commons, like English parliamentarians. This move by the Third Estate has unleashed a crisis. The nobility has rejected individual mandate verification by 188 votes to 46. Today, the nobility has declared itself "constituted". The clergy is even more split. Several dozen priests have met privately to study moves to reconcile the three orders and their proposal has won nearly half of the votes cast, including those of three bishops. The clergy has therefore not declared itself "constituted" yet, but it is unlikely to give in to the demands of the Third Estate: a delegation sent to it on Mounier's initiative on May 7 has failed.

"The oppression of my chains gives me a terrible headache!"

Mirabeau shows skill at getting round the laws on the press

Anxious to learn the latest news, curious readers avidly read a wide range of newspapers outside printing houses.

Versailles, May 10

Mirabeau is not particularly impressed by bans imposed by Louis XVI. On May 7, an order issued by the Council of State banned publication of his *Journal of the Estates General*. Mirabeau's tactical mistake was to have printed a speech which he had been forbidden to make at the opening session of the Estates General. In order to get round the ban, he has just published a new journal called *The Letters of the Comte de Mirabeau to his Constituents*.

Although this publication plays exactly the same role as the first one, it cannot be banned because each deputy is allowed to inform his constituents of his mandate. To ban it would therefore constitute a crime and the government doesn't dare make such a move.

Paris deputies are finally elected

Paris, May 20

The Estates General have been in session at Versailles for over two weeks, but Paris' deputies have only been elected today. The delay is probably due to the lack of trust in the capital's inhabitants felt by those in power.

That same deep feeling of distrust has led the authorities to restrict suffrage severely: only those paying a minimum of six livres in poll-tax and having lived in Paris for at least a year are allowed to vote. This in effect means that the 20 representatives of the Third Estate are not a true cross-section of the capital's population. They include many lawyers and professionals, such as Sieyès, Dr. Guillotin, and Bailly, but there are only four tradesmen among them. Despite the delayed election, Parisians have been closely following the session. The assembly of electors decided on May 10 to continue meeting during the entire duration of the session.

Nobility and clergy reject all agreement

Versailles, May 30

The Estates General are again deadlocked due to the intransigence of the nobility and clergy, who still refuse to allow deputies of the three orders to verify their mandates jointly. Since a May 11 proposal by the clergy, committees set up by each of the orders have been seeking a solution. The committees had to wait for ten days to get the King's go-ahead before they could start work.

Meanwhile, the Third Estate deputy Malouet offered to mediate. He suggested that the Third Estate should proclaim it would "respect the properties, rights and prerogatives of the first two orders" in exchange for the clergy and the nobility agreeing to an individual, non-class vote. This offer was firmly rejected on May 14. By May 27, the failure of the first committees was obvious. At one point the clergy seemed prepared to join the Third Estate, but the bishops persuaded them to delay their response and called for the King to intervene.

The monarch suggested that the committees resume work today, but this time in the presence of his ministers. This latest attempt is unlikely to succeed otherwise than through a compromise that has little chance of being widely supported. The Third Estate will not give in, even though it has agreed to royal arbitration in order not to alienate the King. Its members hope the King will agree to their demands.

Fabre d'Eglantine chooses anonymity

People are flocking to theatres such as the Comédie Française (above).

Paris, May 26

At Monsieur's theatre in Paris, Fabre d'Eglantine's play, *Collateral or the Love of Interest*, is a big hit with the public. In a way, its success is due to a ploy.

Rehearsals were held in secret to avoid the public shunning a playwright who had just suffered three successive flops. An entirely different play, *Le Fabuliste*, was supposed to have been performed, but it had to be cancelled because one of the actors was unwell. The director, Saint Preux, offered the audience d'Eglantine's play instead, but carefully avoided revealing the author's identity. The play was an unexpected success and d'Eglantine was finally named by Saint Preux, although the playwright did not appear on stage. The audience called for a second performance on the following day.

Abbot urges some bishops to save corrupted Church

Paris, May

For the French Church, the time for the big test and regeneration has finally come. The Abbot Claude Fauchet has just written a new book, *Of National Religion*. Dismissed last year from his post as the King's preacher for having lashed out against the excesses of the court, the abbot has not lost his biting tone.

In his latest book, he states that the Church, thoroughly corrupted by luxury and easy living, can only be saved if it listens to the philosophers and returns to the purity of its earlier days. Fauchet says that the faithful must elect their bishops as part of a "State Catholicism".

A seducer is taught a tough lesson

Will these lovers be happier than Lazare Carnot and Ursule?

Béthune, May 29

The dashing Captain Carnot has been freed. An order from the minister of war has just annulled his jail sentence, imposed for the seduction of a young noblewoman, but Lazare Carnot is bitter: his sweetheart from Dijon, Ursule de Bouillet, is getting away from him. To stop her marrying another, he had told her fiancé the truth about his relationship with Ursule, in the hope that this would cement their love, but his move was a mistake: furious at having been fooled by a mere commoner, the young woman's parents arranged for the officer to be severely punished by his superiors. Desperate, Carnot then appealed to the minister for help, and vowed to think twice before falling in love again with a noblewoman.

Belgians want a national monarchy to oust Austrians

Brussels, May

Belgians have become weary of the despotism of Joseph II and of the Austrian domination. Liberal patriots, backed by most of the educated class, are calling for a national monarchy and for the population to be more widely represented at the assembly.

In the capital, the lawyer Verlooy has created a secret society, "Pro Aris et Focis" (For Altars and Homes). The group, which has set up branches throughout the country, is aimed at organising antigovernment propaganda and collecting the funds needed for an army of volunteers. French help has already been sought (→June 18).

Estates General

2. Paris. The operatic work *Prétendus* by Marc Antoine Rochon de Chabannes and Jean Baptiste Lemoyne is a major success at the Royal Academy of Music.

3. Versailles. The deputy d'Ailly, who was elected only two days ago, resigns for health reasons from the assembly of the Commons, where he was senior member. He is replaced by the well-known astronomer Jean Sylvain Bailly.→

4. Meudon. The Dauphin, Louis Joseph Xavier François, dies overnight at the age of seven. His heartbroken parents and the entire court go into mourning for two and a half months.→

6. Versailles. The nobility refuses the arbitration plan proposed by Necker two days ago, thus keeping the political situation stalemated.

6. Paris. At the electors' assembly, Nicolas Bonneville demands the arming of the capital.

8. Meudon. A delegation from each of the three orders comes to pay its last respects to the dead Dauphin.

10. Versailles. After the failure of the royal arbitration attempt, the Commons act on a suggestion by Abbot Sieyès and decide to constitute themselves immediately into an active assembly and to begin verifying mandates.→

11. Versailles. While deputies from the three orders attend the Corpus Christi processions, part of the clergy meets to debate the Commons' decision of the previous day. For a time, the assembly debates whether to go to the Commons, but it eventually decides to drop the plan.

12. Versailles. The Third Estate begins verifying its mandates and starts a roll-call of deputies.

13. Versailles. As the Poitou seneschalsy is called, the abbots le Cesve, Ballard and Jallet join the Third Estate.

15. Versailles. After the verification process has been completed, the assembly decides to change its name. It wants to choose one that stresses its widened representativeness. The Abbot Sieyès suggests the body should in future be known as the National Assembly.

An astronomer heads the Third Estate

Versailles, June 3

The Third Estate assembly has just chosen a new senior member, Bailly, a well-known astronomer and academician. His outstanding work has helped make him a member of the elite Academy of Science at the age of only 27. He also belongs to the French Academy and the Academy of Humanities.

His many talents have also made him a favourite among Paris' high society and he has decided to settle at Chaillot, with the assistance of numerous royal favours and allowances. He has been made a secretary at the cabinet of Madame, the wife of the Comte de Provence, who is one of the King's brothers. Although he is a liberal, Bailly is not much of an innovator and doesn't trust what he considers to be the ignorant masses. The capital's electoral assembly, chaired by the lawyer Target, has chosen him as its secretary. By electing him its senior

Honoured by the court, Bailly is now praised by the Third Estate.

member, the "Commons" of the Third Estate, in session at Versailles, have paid tribute to the crowds who come each day to support their representatives.

Sofas turn salons into boudoirs

The sofa, a favourite piece of furniture throughout France since the start of the century, has this year become even more widely used. The couch, known by its Arabic name of "sofa", adds a touch of comfort and luxury to the kingdom's sitting rooms. Always oval-shaped, it stands on finely-carved legs, is upholstered in brightly coloured material, and decorated with garlands and tiny, carved wooden medallions.

With the addition of a few contrasting cushions, the sofa can be transformed into a tasteful bed for courtesans, turning a living room into a stylish and fashionable boudoir.

This sofa, unlike Oriental ones which are simply carpet-covered platforms, is a comfortable seat which encourages friendly conversation.

The Dauphin has died of tuberculosis

Meudon, June 4

The young Dauphin passed away at one in the morning. His grieving mother, who remained by his side until the end, has reluctantly had to leave right away for Versailles. Etiquette demands it, just as it requires that the King and Queen let the Prince de Condé accompany the small coffin to Saint Denis. Louis XVI has asked the Archbishop of Paris to say 10,000 masses for his son's soul. "But who will pay?" the priest asked, knowing that the church's coffers are empty. A heartbroken King replied that the money would be taken from the royal court's own budget.

The King's eldest son dies aged seven (by Mme. Vigée Lebrun).

The Court of France is in mourning

Versailles, June

Fashionable ladies of the court are most upset. Strict mourning has been imposed on the court for two and a half months.

During an initial period, from June 7 to 19, they will have to wear woollen dresses and hats. Men are to wear "full court dress, black silk stockings, plain bronze buckles and sword". They will not be allowed to wear a feather in their hats. In July, women will be allowed to wear black silk dresses and diamonds, while men will once again be permitted to don their silver buckles and swords. During the hot August days, ladies will be allowed to wear their white silk dresses, but without ribbons.

The Third Estate scores some points

Cracks appear in the privileged group

Versailles, June 13

Three deputies of the clergy have just joined the ranks of the Third Estate! This totally unexpected move could help break the month-long deadlock within the Estates General.

A day after publication of a report confirming the failure of the efforts of the conciliation committees, the only option now left open to the "Commons" is somehow to regain the initiative. Sieyès has proposed that the Third Estate assembly "summon the two other orders to join it in the verification of the mandates of the nations' representatives". The call has been submitted to members of the clergy and the nobility by a Third Estate delegation.

The King has been informed of the move on the advice of Regnault de Saint Jean d'Angély, who was afraid that Louis XVI might take offence. Without waiting to hear the results of discussions within the other assemblies, the Third Estate today began the roll-call of all deputies by bailiwick and sene-

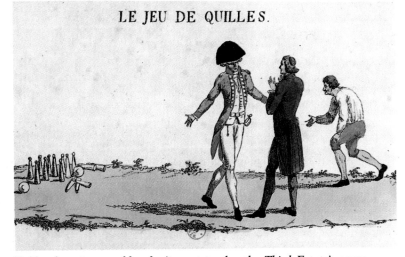

LE JEU DE QUILLES.

Unlike the priests, nobles don't want to play the Third Estate's game.

schalsy, without making any distinction between the orders. Barentin, the Lord Chancellor, commented ironically on the defection of the three clergymen, telling Bailly: "I congratulate you on your victory." To this, Bailly replied: "Sir, you may find it insignificant, but the move will be followed by many others."

Versailles, June 16

By today, a total of nineteen clergymen have defected to the Third Estate in response to its June 12 call to the other two orders. Some of the pro-Orléans deputies would dearly like to make the same move.

But a majority of the nobility and the clergy still refuses to accept the principle of individual voting and to meet in plenary session with the Third Estate. They would be prepared to agree to the fiscal equality of all, but reject any further basic reforms. The nobility in particular remains firmly attached to its age-old privileges, thus blocking any prospects of conciliation. Their only suggestion is that the King be the judge of the mandate verification system, an idea that has been rejected by the Third Estate.

Meanwhile, there have also been several defections from the ranks of the clergy, despite the strong pressures exerted on the order's deputies by the bishops. On June 14, Abbot Grégoire, priest of Emberménil in Lorraine, and five other clergymen followed the previous day's surprise defection by three priests of the Poitiers seneschalsy: le Cesve, Jallet, and Ballard. Frictions between the higher and lower clergy may well put an end to solidarity within the order. This could in turn quickly lead to cracks appearing within the ranks of the nobility.

Versailles and the Estates General

Versailles, June

The court has been pretending to ignore the presence of deputies in its midst, but these are demanding guests who must be made welcome, protected and entertained. The constabulary has stepped up its patrols and keeps a close watch on the royal street, which has become the scene of daily attacks.

At least the inn-keepers of Versailles are happy. Amaury, who owns a tavern on the Avenue Saint Cloud, has opened his Orient Café. The rental of rooms has become a flourishing business, since well over 1,000 people from the provinces have been seeking a place to stay. The Just Hotel, whose clients are mainly prelates and senior officers, is full.

In the market district, dressmakers and clothiers are offering accommodation to members of the lower clergy and Third Estate deputies, but money for rent is scarce, the comic opera is very expensive and the more earthy delights of Paris even more so. Luckily, one can dine free at the Chateau.

The everyday life of the deputies

Versailles, June

It is one thing to enjoy the prestige of attending the sessions of the Estates General, but quite another to cope with the new profession of being a deputy.

The day begins early and ends late, whether one is from Auvergne, Poitiers, Bourgogne or Paris itself. From eight a.m. untill ten in the evening, a deputy spends his time in the hall of the Menus Plaisirs. This room, used by the court's officials in charge of ceremonies, has become a centre of debate, voting and speech-making. Space is so short that some of the committees are forced to meet in the town. The hall is too hot and noisy for effective debate. Sessions are open to the public and debates are often interrupted by shouts from the ladies of Versailles and Paris. When the situation gets out of hand, many a deputy dreams of the two after-dinner hours during which he can work on his correspondence in private or stroll through the Trianon gardens which the Queen has made available.

Pottery centres slump in face of fashion

All of France's major pottery centres are on the wane. Most of them have not survived the fashion for fine china. Only Nevers and its region continue to prosper: the popular style of its output fits in with the revolutionary style of pottery. The manufacturers of Nevers have seized on the public's interest in simple, easily understood decorations reflecting the issues of the day. Following the session of the Estates General, decorations showing the three orders become widespread. They are symbolised by a sheaf of corn, a sword and a bishop's crook. Sometimes a crown surrounded by fleurs-de-lis is added, a sign of the public's lasting attachment to the King.

Given an appetite by seeing the three orders on their plate...

diners also find that the monarchy can be a very tasty dish!

Constituent Assembly

17. Versailles. The assembly aproves by a comfortable majority of 481 votes to 119 Abbot Sieyès' proposal to become known as the National Assembly, and decides to inform the King of the decision immediately.→

18. The Austrian Netherlands. The Emperor Josef II of Austria dissolves the Brabant Estates and orders his troops to occupy the capital, Brussels.→

19. Versailles. After a rowdy debate, the chamber of the clergy votes by 148 to 136 in favour of union with the Third Estate. The move succeeds largely thanks to the support of several leading liberal prelates such as the Archbishop of Vienne, Lefranc de Pompignan. When the results are announced, the crowd wildly cheers the winners.

19. Paris. The deputy from Bigorre, Bertrand Barère de Vieuzac, publishes the first edition of his newsletter *Point du Jour*.→

19. Versailles. In the evening, Louis XVI calls together a special council meeting during which it is decided to do all that is possible to block the meeting of the three orders (→22).

20. Versailles. The King tries to frighten the Assembly by closing the Estates chamber. The deputies therefore go to meet at the tennis courts of the Jeu de Paume, where some 3,000 deputies and spectators gather.→

22. Versailles. The National Assembly meets at the Saint Louis church, where it is joined by 151 members of the clergy and two nobles, the Marquis de Blacons and the Comte d'Agoult, gentlemen from the Dauphiné.

22. Armentières. The regiment of Condé intervenes to quell a food riot.

23. Versailles. Louis XVI, in royal session, orders the National Assembly to cease meeting immediately.→

23. Versailles. Despite the seriousness of the situation in France, many people have been singing a new song about today's proclamation of the inviolability of deputies: "Respectable senators, by all means become representatives, be inviolable everywhere. Jealous of such a privilege, your kind womenfolk will most prudently imitate you and will no longer let themselves be violated."

Third Estate forms an Assembly

Versailles, June 17

A new power is born, independent of the King. The Third Estate assembly has just approved a motion by Sieyès, supported by Target, by 481 votes to 119 and proclaimed itself a National Assembly.

It has used terms employed by Necker in his 1788 assembly plan and concepts spread by Abbot Sieyès in his treatise on the Third Estate. After lengthy debate, Sieyès succeeded in getting approval for the term of National Assembly, which had been suggested by le Grand, deputy from Berry. Sieyès stated that the deputies of the Third Estate, representing 96 per cent of the population, should "fulfil the wishes of the nation". Are their mandates not the only ones to have been publicly verified? All of the deputies have sworn to "faithfully fulfil their duties". The National Assembly has immediately taken crucial decisions, refusing to give legislative powers to the two other orders or to let the King keep the right of veto. Acting on a proposal by le Chapelier, it has decreed that only the Assembly could impose new taxes. It has, however, guaranteed the state's debts, which have been placed "under the safekeeping, honour and loyalty of the Nation". The National Assembly is already getting the support of the clergy, which has just agreed to join the Third Estate by a majority of three fifths.

The nobility remains undecided. Some say that the Duc d'Orléans has been trying so hard to persuade members of the nobility to join the National Assembly that he was taken ill and had to be carried from the hall. However, about 100 nobles had already agreed.

Revolt threatens Brabant Council

Brussels, June 18

An insurrection is at hand. The Belgian States have wielded their ultimate weapon and refused to pay taxes, to block increasingly unpopular decrees which Josef II had tried to impose by force in an excess of reformist zeal.

In response, Count Trauttmansdorff, Austria's minister plenipotentiary to the Belgian States, has just ordered the dissolution of the States, the banning of the Brabant Council and the annulment of the Joyeuse Entrée, the 500-year-old constitution guaranteeing the province's privileges. The astonished inhabitants of the Belgian capital watched the military occupy their city without reacting.

A Brabant aristocrat who had dared to tear up a patriot poster.

Restif de la Bretonne's wild nights

An illustration for the "Nights of Paris" by Restif de la Bretonne.

Paris, June

It is not simply to keep abreast of political events that Restif de la Bretonne has been spending every night he can at the Palais Royal in central Paris. He has also been keeping an eye on the capital's love life. In this notorious place of pleasure and debauchery, the self-styled "owl of Paris" likes to stroll along the Alley of Sighs with one of his many mistresses by his side, while marvelling at the scantily-clad and provocative beauties he finds along the way.

This pleasure-seeker sometimes has fatherly feelings for the ladies of the Palais Royal gardens, firmly believing that many of them are in fact his illegitimate daughters. He checks by looking up the relevant dates in his well-filled pocket book, a precise catalogue of his many encounters and mistresses.

The crafty Restif has assigned a day of the year to each woman he has known throughout his long and active love life. His carefully calculated paternity theories can't be entirely wrong, since he is welcomed as a long-lost father by many of the women he bumps into during his strolls.

Barère reports on the debates

Versailles, June 19

The young Third Estate deputy from Bigorre, Bertrand Barère de Vieuzac, has decided to provide daily reports on the previous day's debate.

Since his arrival at Versailles he had admired the Assembly's major speakers from afar, but today, armed with pen and notebook, he is quickly noting down the speeches and seeking information on the latest political developments. His politeness is much appreciated and he has already been dubbed the "nice Barère". Being too shy to be of much help to his political friends and allies at Versailles, Barère has decided to place his pen at their service. With the help of a young assistant, he published today the first issue of a daily newsletter, *Le Point du Jour*. He is extremely well suited to the task he has set himself, being both a political reporter and a deputy.

Deputies are sworn in at the "Jeu de Paume"

Bailly reads the text of the oath at the Jeu de Paume. The three people shown at the centre symbolise the clergy's move to join the Third Estate.

Versailles, June 20

The National Assembly deputies were surprised and very annoyed on this rainy morning to arrive at the Menus Plaisirs hall only to find their way barred by locked doors.

They were informed that the hall, guarded by sentries, had been closed in preparation for the June 23 royal session, but many deputies believe that this is just another step aimed at the dissolution of the Assembly. They decided that it was vital to find a suitable meeting place quickly in order to avoid falling into the trap. Dr. Guillotin suggested the nearby royal tennis courts of the Jeu de Paume. Mounier called for the deputies gathered in the large, empty room to take the oath, drafted by Target and formally read out by Bailly. They are to swear "never to separate and to meet whenever circumstances demand, until the Constitution of the Kingdom has been firmly established and consolidated".

All the Third Estate's representatives except one, Dauch, deputy of Castelnaudary, as well as seven representatives of the clergy, signed the oath, thus sealing the unity of the Assembly. Carried away by their enthusiasm, many of them exclaimed "Long live the King!". Despite this, the representatives of the nation have begun resisting the monarch by opposing the plot to dissolve the Assembly they believe the King to be hatching (→ June 23).

The King calls a special council

Versailles, June 22

For the third time, the King today called together an extraordinary council meeting to draft the speech he is to make tomorrow at the royal session before the Estates General. The King has sought help from the Queen and his two brothers. Thanks to them, the advice of the Lord Chancellor, Barentin, backed by Villedeuil and Puységur, has been taken. Despite efforts by Montmorin and Necker, the conservative programme proposed by the King will be adhered to. This favours fiscal equality, but says that the other privileges and voting by class must be kept.

Deputies defy King's order to leave

Versailles, June 23

The National Assembly will not accept its dissolution without reacting. "We will only leave our seats at the point of a bayonet," Mirabeau exclaimed as the Marquis de Dreux Brézé told the deputies after the royal session that the King had ordered them to leave. As for the reforms proposed by Louis XVI, they are but a caricature of the suggestions put forward by Necker, who has chosen not to attend. It appears obvious to many that the King, who has declared the Assembly's deliberations "void", is getting ready for a reactionary counter-attack.

Search begins for simpler measures

"Charlemagne weights" made up of units totalling 50 marks.

Paris, June 27

The French Academy of Science has set up a special committee in a bid to find a simpler, more unified system of weights and measures than the ones currently in use. This move has been called for in a large number of the Books of Grievances.

One thousand years ago, the Emperor Charlemagne created the "Livre de Paris", or Paris pound system. However, different systems are still being used nowadays in various regions of the kingdom. This has been making life difficult for all.

The King caves in to call a joint meeting

Versailles, June 27

A heavy-hearted Louis XVI has just called on his "faithful clergy and loyal nobility" to meet jointly with the Third Estate. The long fight over this issue has been won by the National Assembly; but did the King really agree to this move because his life was in danger, as the Comte d'Artois told the Duc de Luxembourg, or was it simply because he had no other option?

Since June 24, a majority of the clergy has been sitting with the Third Estate. The Archbishop of Vienne, Lefranc de Pompignan, announced that the clergy would accept voting by head. The following day, 47 nobles, including the Duc d'Orléans, Clermont Tonnerre and Adrien Duport, followed suit. There were further defections from the ranks of the clergy and the nobility on June 26, as deputies who obstinately continued sitting in separate rooms were booed by the

A wish is fulfilled: "That's how I always wanted it to be."

crowds. This left the King with only two options: either to carry out his June 23 threat and call in the army, or give in to the Third Estate's demands.

Coulomb claims major scientific discovery

Paris, June 28

Charles Coulomb claims to have become the first to identify correctly terrestrial magnetic forces which affect electric currents.

The *Annals of Chemistry* have just published extracts from the research done by this official in responsible for the royal fountains and water-works. He explains in the second volume of the Annals how the axes of poles exert a magnetic effect on electricity, either by attraction or by repulsion. Magnetised objects show the rule of polarisation on the molecular level. The experimental physicist has gone further than Benjamin Franklin.

Crowd frees French Guard soldiers from Abbaye jail

After invading the jail at the Abbaye of Saint Germain des Prés, Parisians give shelter to the soldiers they have released.

Paris, June 30

Someting unusual has happened: Parisians have attacked the Abbaye prison to free some soldiers, while dragoons and hussars refused to intervene. The mob succeeded in freeing French Guards jailed for protesting against their Colonel, whom they accused of being too strict. The mob's action is partly due to a friendship which has grown between the capital's inhabitants and members of this elite unit. Since the French Guards have been posted in Paris, links with the public have been created, with lower ranking officers finding they have much in common with artisans and tradesmen. Gradually won over to revolutionary ideas during public meetings, the Guards seem prepared to march with the lower middle classes (→July 1).

Constituent Assembly

1. Versailles. At the request of the patriots of the Palais Royal, the National Assembly decides to send a delegation to Versailles right away to seek the King's mercy for the jailed French Guards. Louis XVI agrees to the parliamentarians' request.

2. Versailles. The National Assembly elects its president. It had however previously adopted a rule limiting the duration of the president's mandate to a maximum of two weeks.

3. Versailles. After the Duc d'Orléans' refusal to become president of the National Assembly, the Archbishop of Vienne, Lefranc de Pompignan, becomes its first president. The old man welcomes the honour, saying: "I am slowly dwindling into my success."

4. Lyons. The arrival of a Swiss regiment from Sonnemberg puts an end to the city toll riots (→7).

4. Paris. Shouting from his well furnished Bastille prison cell, the infamous Marquis de Sade stirs up the crowd. →

4. Fougères. Local weavers and nailsmiths rise up against land owners who are suspected of selling their wheat outside the city limits.

4. Versailles. Deputies representing the island of Saint Domingue join the National Assembly.→

5. Paris. Antoine Joseph Gorsas publishes the *Paris to Versailles Post*, a newspaper which is soon to have a wide readership.

5. Paris. One of his plays having been censored, the poet and playwright Marie Joseph Chénier publishes a *Denunciation of the Inquisitors of Thought*.

6. Vitré. The town's workmen and artisans lash out at the local authorities, which are being blamed for contributing to the sharp rise in bread prices.

6. Versailles. Acting on a call by Mounier, the Assembly elects the thirty members of the committee which will be responsible for drafting France's Constitution (→9).

7. Lyons. The courts of the city start passing sentence on arrested rioters: a man from Savoie is found guilty of arson and sentenced to be hanged.

King finds satirical poem at the palace

Versailles, July 8

A satirical poem in which the King is "most humbly" called upon to become the willing "slave" of the people, and urging him to give up his crown in order to be known as "Christendom's foremost king", has mysteriously appeared on the walls of the royal palace. The poem also calls on the King to let himself be "defied".

This most disrespectful poem is said to be a translation of a work written by the Earl of Rochester for King Charles II of England.

There is, however, no record of how the French monarch reacted when he spotted the cheeky poem.

Saint Domingue to have own deputies

Paris, July 4

A total of six deputies are to be seated at the National Assembly as representatives of Saint Domingue. The Assembly reluctantly agreed to the demands of the island's settlers and large landowners, but the admission of the six deputies constitutes a major distortion of the Assembly's regulations, since not one of them was elected by a primary assembly.

Louis XVI gets ready to counter-attack

Versailles, July

Louis XVI has withdrawn to the privacy of his rooms to mull over the current deadlocked political situation.

He is now ready to break the National Assembly, having caved in to pressures from the Queen and some aristocrats, who advise him to dissolve the Assembly and set up a strong ministry in charge of restoring order and absolute monarchy. But there is continued unrest in the provinces and the slightest spark could set Paris alight with popular anger. Using the unrest as an excuse, the King has called in the old Maréchal de Broglie, who has begun massing 30,000 men around the capital.

When worried deputies demanded an explanation for the troop movements, the King replied that order had to be maintained. Yet few are fooled by the military activity in villages just outside Paris. Necker and the liberal ministers were the first to realise that the monarch is in fact preparing a counter-revolution.

When a major decision has to be taken, Louis XVI likes to meditate in the quiet of his library at the Palace of Versailles.

Parisians are running out of bread

Paris, July

"To be truly alive is to bite into a loaf of bread." Parisians have been repeating the old saying without really believing in it any longer. There are well over 600,000 mouths to feed in Paris and concern is growing daily.

Spring wheat has frozen, and the new crop will probably be a poor one as the summer weather is as dry as last winter was cold. Grain and flour stores are rapidly dwindling and fresh supplies are getting more difficult to find.

As bread prices rise, the number of hoarders increases. The queues outside bakeries are getting longer every day and anger is rising. The much sought after golden loaves baked by Gonesse are no longer available. Less expensive bread is difficult to find. Soon the city's poor will no longer have the lumpy bread, made from left-over dough, which is the only food for many. How much longer will the people of Paris put up with hunger?

Bread is becoming hard to find in the bakeries of the capital.

De Sade harangues the crowd from his cell in the Bastille

Paris, July 4

Parisians out strolling near the Bastille this morning were surprised to hear a loud voice coming from one of its barred windows, shouting that prisoners were being butchered and calling for help. However, it was only the notorious Marquis de Sade. Furious after having been forbidden to take his daily walk, he had grabbed a pipe used to drain his cell and turned it into a make-shift loud hailer. The nobleman, known as the "divine Marquis", was soon overpowered and silenced by his jailers. The Bastille's governor, de Launay, has decided to have the troublesome prisoner transferred to Charenton tomorrow.

9. Versailles. On behalf of the constitutional committee, Mounier submits to the Assembly the committee's programme, which includes plans for the drafting of a Declaration of human rights and the definition of the principles for a renovated monarchy (→11).

9. Versailles. The Assembly proclaims itself to be the Constituent Assembly.→

10. Versailles. Responding to Mirabeau's motion of the 8th., the King indicates that the current unrest in Paris has made it necessary for troops to be sent in. Louis XVI suggests that the Assembly should be transferred to Noyon or to Soissons.

11. Versailles. La Fayette proposes to the Assembly a first draft of the Declaration of human rights (→Aug. 1, 89).

11. Rouen. Driven by hunger, local textile workers cause a major riot.

11. Versailles. Under strong pressure from the Comte d'Artois, the King dismisses Necker, who is replaced by the Baron de Breteuil. Meanwhile, the Maréchal de Broglie is appointed to the Ministry of War (→12).

11. Paris. Acting in the name of the Duc d'Orléans, his secretary Choderlos de Laclos issues a motion proposing a tax of solidarity with the poor.

12. Paris. The journal *Les Révolutions de Paris* is published. It is headed by the printer Louis Prudhomme and the journalist Elysée Loustalot.

12. Paris. News of the dismissal of Necker causes anger among the people.→

12. Autun. Rise in grain prices unleashes popular uprising.

13. Paris. The assembly of electors sets up a permanent committee headed by Jacques de Flesselles. It decides to create a militia numbering 48,000 men.→

13. Sens. The grain warehouse is looted.

13. Paris. A mob loots the Saint Lazare convent in the hope of finding wheat.

13. Versailles. The National Assembly decides to remain in permanent session. Meanwhile, the Abbot Grégoire calls for those responsible for Necker's dismissal to be fired.

National Assembly creates a French constitution

Versailles, July 9

Most of the Books of Grievances show that the dream of Third Estate deputies was to give France a constitution. Today, the dream has become a reality: the National Assembly has proclaimed itself the Constituent Assembly; but the Third Estate did not win this victory easily. It had to resort to acts of revolt against the monarchy. Its deputies had to swear on June 17th. to remain in session until they had given the nation a constitution. On June 23rd. they had to make a show of their resolve by refusing to obey orders after the royal session.

The King sacks Necker

Versailles, July 12

The news spread like wildfire: this morning, the King demanded that the highly popular Necker should resign.

Necker has secretly set off for Brussels, as the court is afraid that his dismissal will spark off clashes. Both the other liberal ministers, Montmorin and Saint Priest, have also been forced to resign. The new ministry, which Louis XVI had been thinking about for the past few weeks, is headed by the Baron de Breteuil. The conservative Barentin remains Lord Chancellor and the Maréchal de Broglie, commander of the troops massed around the capital, has taken over from Puységur at the Ministry of War. The choice of Breteuil, a firm advocate of the restoration of absolute monarchy, is a major setback. The time for political concessions is over: the Assembly must be broken. Since early June, this former diplomat has been pushing Louis XVI to take repressive measures to put an end to the unrest in Paris.

In accordance with the plans proposed by the King on June 23rd., Breteuil wants the Assembly to return to the separation of the three orders. If necessary, he is prepared to dissolve it. He is relying on his troops deployed around the capital to restore order if a revolt breaks out. Breteuil is firmly resolved to stay in power, but this power play will cause deep resentment.

Minister's departure unleashes a storm of anger in Paris

Outside the Foy café, the young journalist Camille Desmoulins, standing on a table, shouts to the crowd: "To arms, to arms!"

Troops encamped at the Champ de Mars set off to the Louis XV square.

In the evening, the doors of the Opéra are shut to processions.

Paris, July 12, around noon

By the time the morning was drawing to an end, the news of Necker's dismissal had become the talk of the town.

The panicked population of Paris thinks that the great man's departure will surely signal the dissolution of the Assembly, starvation and total bankruptcy. The wildest rumours have been spreading: many claim that the city is about to be handed over to the surrounding troops and sacked. Ever since last May, Parisians have been keeping a worried eye on events at the Assembly. They have been kept informed hourly about developments there by the district primary assemblies. These had not been dissolved and have been holding repeated meetings. Since June 25th. a revolutionary municipality has been created, meeting in the great room of the city hall. Such autonomous political structures have kept unrest alive and today it has suddenly reached an unprecedented scale. In all the neighbourhoods people are meeting to discuss all the latest rumours. Concern is growing and mobs march to the Palais Royal, the capital's heart.

Paris burns after two days of non-stop rioting

Paris, July 12, afternoon

Paris has just lived through two days of rioting. There are no signs that the anger which has suddenly seized the people will die down.

At the Palais Royal, the crowd has been growing steadily, seeking plans for action. Stepping out of the Foy café, a young man, Camille Desmoulins, leaps onto a table brandishing a sword. He urges the people to rise up against the German troops who, he claims, have come to "butcher" the men and women of Paris. He grabs a leaf from a tree and pins it to his hat, using it as a crest. The crowd quickly imitates his move. Then the mob rushes to the wax museum to get the busts of Necker and the Duc d'Orléans, carrying them through the streets. The two busts are draped with black crêpe as a symbol of the death of Liberty. On the Place Vendôme, outside the residences of the farmers general, demonstrators clash with a detachment of the Royal German regiment and are forced to disperse, but there has already been one man killed, a member of the French Guard.

Meanwhile, at the Tuileries, another tragedy is taking place. Despite having received no orders, Colonel Besenval has massed his mounted troops on the Champs Elysées as a precautionary measure, in case there is a riot. This is the time when those who have been out for a Sunday walk return to Paris. Suddenly frightened by the size of

Run for your life! Innocent women and children in the Tuileries gardens are not safe from the brutal attack of Lambesc's mounted troops.

The toll barrier at the Conférence is set on fire and destroyed.

the crowd, which he believes is hostile, Besenval orders the Prince de Lambesc to move the strollers into the Tuileries gardens. The horses charge, trampling women and children. Enraged by the violence, many Parisians rush off to look for weapons; but where can they be found? Convinced that city authorities have been hiding an arsenal at the city hall, the rioters head there. The assembly of electors, which has been meeting non-stop in the building, cannot stop the mob from grabbing a few rifles, but it does not give its full support to the rioters. Meanwhile, the French Guard have escaped from the barracks to which they had been confined by Besenval. Around 6 p.m.,

the French Guard routs the Royal German regiment, killing three soldiers to avenge their dead colleague. Besenval no longer dares move his forces around. The town, now in the hands of the rioters, is set on fire. Toll barriers are burnt. By destroying them, Parisians hope to abolish taxes and force prices down. All night long, the sky over the capital glows red.

Paris, July 13

At Versailles, deputies are distressed to hear of the events in Paris and send envoys to the King to beg him to recall the dismissed ministers and to withdraw his troops from the capital, but the King, who feels his position has been strengthened by Breteuil and the German regiments, says that he has no orders to receive from the Assembly. Because of the extent of the danger, the Assembly decides to remain in permanent session, but nobody is now in control of the situation. Early this morning the alarm bells rang in Paris. Fearing military reprisals, the crowd demands guns. The mob loots the armouries and rushes to Saint Lazare looking for wheat. Prisoners are freed and join the crowds. Terrified by the events, the city's bourgeois heading the districts set up a permanent committee presided over by Jacques de Flesselles, the provost of tradesmen. To restore their control over the population, they decide to set up a militia to maintain public security, but panic is spreading: it is rumoured that guns are stored at the Invalides (→14).

The Saint Lazare convent is looted and its occupants are driven out.

On the afternoon of July 13th., a dense crowd desperately searching for weapons rushes to the royal furniture warehouse on the Louis XV square.

On the night of July 13th.-14th., the people walk the streets of Paris.

July 14th., 1789: the fall of the Bastille. While the French Guards are busy with the cannons, the people from the Paris suburbs enter the jail's forecourt.

July 14, 1789: The Bastille, symbol of royal

By taking the Bastille — symbol of arbitrary royal power and feudal régimes — Parisians changed the course of the Revolution. The people rebelled against the secular power of a régime seeking to return to a system which was already seriously threatened by uprisings and by an elected assembly that had proclaimed itself the National Constituent Assembly only a few days ago. The army is clearly supporting the cause of the people. Will the Revolution of July 14 remain a purely Parisian phenomenon, or will it have a nationwide effect? Is the Assembly, whose bourgeois leanings are obvious, prepared to back this revolt? Will the King make a last ditch attempt to stop the people?

Thousands of rifles, a few cannons: the spoils from the Invalides are impressive. Let's head for the Bastille!

A night of alarms

Around 2 a.m., a terrible rumour spread through the capital: 15,000 soldiers have been deployed on the Rue Saint Antoine and they have started butchering people! It was a false alarm. At 7 a.m., there was a new rumour. This time, the Royal German regiment was said to be heading for the Trône toll barrier, the men of the Royal Croatian for the Saint Antoine district, and other units for La Chapelle. Alarm bells ring out. To arms! An entire population was obsessed by just one idea: weapons must be found.

To the Invalides!

The Invalides are full of weapons. Yesterday, the governor, Charles Virot de Sombreuil, had prudently refused to hand over any of the thousands of rifles stored there to a delegation of electors, who wanted to arm the new militia. Quickly, a growing crowd headed from the capital's centre to the sombre Invalides building.

By 6 a.m., several thousand men had gathered on the huge parade ground in front of the Invalides. Sombreuil wanted to talk things over with them, but when he opened the gates the crowd surged into the courtyard, pouring into the buildings and even the basement. Systematic looting went on until 2 p.m. The demonstrators seized 32,000 rifles — without ammunition — as well as twelve cannons and a mortar. Gunpowder and cartridges were being stored at the Bastille, so the mob decided to rush there.

Not one of the occupants of the Invalides had put up any resistance to the looting. As for Besenval's troops billeted at the Champ de Mars, they hadn't moved an inch. The officers had told their superiors that their men would under no circumstances march against the people of Paris. This passive attitude, tantamount to tacit support, helped considerably in encouraging the rioters to head from the Invalides to the Bastille.

To the Bastille!

On the edge of the Saint Antoine district there stands a huge eight-towered fortress, which was used as a state prison. There a large crowd had been gathered since yesterday evening.

At dawn several hundred artisans, most of them furniture makers, armed with sticks and tools, had come to the Bastille to demand material needed to make cartridges. The tension rose quickly. People were aware of the fact that the prison's governor, the Marquis Bernard de Launay, had considerably strengthened the defences at the Bastille over the past few days. He had also stored in the jail's basement 250 barrels of gunpowder that his men had brought from the Arsenal. Thirty Swiss soldiers had been added to the garrison of eighty invalids posted to guard the prison.

The crowd became frightened, as people saw cannons aimed at Saint Antoine. The assembly of electors was immediately warned and it sent a delegation to meet de Launay. The envoys arrived at the Bastille around 10 a.m. The governor asked them in right away, inviting them to lunch. Meanwhile, the crowd was getting larger as tension grew. "We felt more daring," witnesses said. Suddenly, around 11:30 a.m., some shouts were heard. The cannons on the towers were being pulled back. Were they about to be loaded? Panicking, several men rushed to the headquarters of the neighbouring district warning that the people were about to be fired upon and claiming that the delegation was being held prisoner.

A second delegation, led by the lawyer Thuriot, went to the Bastille. It was allowed in. Outside, the crowd was becoming increasingly impatient. Finally, Thuriot came out again at about 12:30 p.m. and told the people that the cannons were not loaded and that the governor had promised not to open fire if the Bastille was not attacked, but this was greeted with booing: Thuriot had not managed to persuade the governor to surrender. "We want the Bastille! Down with the army!" the angry mob was now shouting.

Betrayal

Suddenly, around 1:30 p.m., first one, then three, then ten youths, who had climbed onto the roof of a perfume shop built against the ramparts, jump down into the Bastille's courtyard, landing just outside de Launay's residence. Using axes, they break the wooden beams holding the chains that support the draw-bridge. The heavy draw-bridge falls with a crash, killing a man by the prison's moat. Quickly, hundreds of screaming rioters rush

De Launay, last governor of the Bastille

Marquis Bernard de Launay, a victim of the mob's fury, did not really deserve such a terrible fate.

A long-serving officer aged 59, he had been governor of the Bastille ever since 1776. He was born when his father held the same post. His duties only consisted of keeping watch on the handful of prisoners jailed there on sealed orders. In fact, Bernard de Launay had very little actual military experience and no idea whatsoever of tactics. People have said that he only wanted to stop his residence being looted when he ordered his troops to open fire on the mob that had poured into the Bastille. He was unable to cope with the situation.

absolutism, is seized by the people

A certain Maillard, an usher, grabs the message of surrender.

The prison's governor is seized. He is to be executed summarily.

into the courtyard. A volley of gunshots rings out. Several of the demonstrators are hit by bullets and fall to the ground. The shout of "treason" rises up everywhere. The mob is sure that it has fallen into a trap set by de Launay.

There is no question whatsoever of surrendering, and the two sides start exchanging fire. News of the clash has spread through Paris like wildfire and men are rushing to the Bastille from all over the capital, armed with an incredible variety of weapons.

Around two o'clock in the afternoon, a third delegation arrives from the city hall to ask de Launay to cease fire, to hand over weapons to the people and to let a unit of the militia join the fortress's garrison. Despite the delegates' waving white handkerchiefs, nobody pays the slightest attention to them, and intense firing continues.

Ethis de Corny is then asked to demand a ceasefire and the hand-over of the Bastille to the bourgeois militia. He is accompanied by a flag bearer and a drummer. On arrival he succeeds in having the courtyard evacuated. A white flag is hoisted over the Bastille. As the delegation gets closer, shots ring out and a man drops dead. As the mob screams, the delegation withdraws. There is no more talk of negotiation.

The cannons arrive

Despite being enraged by the governor's betrayal, the rioters are starting to feel tired, but around 1:30 p.m. the five cannons arrive, dragged by some sixty members of the French Guard. With them are three to four hundred armed men

led by a certain Hulin, a former sergeant of the Swiss Guard. Simultaneously, another group of armed citizens arrives, under the orders of a man named Elie, a second lieutenant. They have come with the cannons that were seized at the Invalides. After having opened fire on the soldiers standing on the ramparts, they brave flying bullets to drag two cannons to face the drawbridge. "Blow the bridges down!" the mob screams. Inside the Bastille, the governor wants to give the order for the fortress to be blown up, but he is reported to have been

stopped by the invalids' bayonets. They are demanding a surrender, although the rioters are unaware of this.

Surrender

Just as the attackers are getting ready to use the cannons to force their way into the building, they see a piece of paper appear through a gap in the huge gateway; but how can this note be seized if the draw-bridge is not lowered? People run to a nearby carpenter's shop and come back with some wooden boards. As quickly as possible, the longest board is placed across the moat. As several men stand on one end of it, a shoe maker gingerly eases his way across to grab the piece of paper, but, as everybody is holding their breath, the unfortunate man slips and falls heavily. After this accident, the bailiff Maillard rushes across, takes the note and hands it to Hulin.

The message is brief and to the point. It reads: "Capitulation", but the mob is not satisfied with this surrender. It wants to take the Bastille. Hulin reluctantly gives in to the crowd's demands and is about to order the cannons to open fire when the draw-bridge sudden-

ly opens. Driven forward by the people behind, Hulin and Elie are the first to enter the fortress. They hope that further bloodshed can be avoided, but the mob attacks the invalids and, firing wildly, invades every part of the building.

The Bastille has fallen

The invading crowd loots and destroys everything in its path, throwing archives out of windows. It suddenly finds the prisoners it has been looking for. Among them is an accomplice of the regicide Damiens, held for 30 years, a mad aristocrat and a criminal, as well as four counterfeiters. Shortly afterwards, a shattered de Launay is brought out under heavy escort. Hundreds of enraged Parisians are baying for his blood.

A large procession of the conquerors of the Bastille then marches off, heading for the city hall as it drags its new prisoners along. For their part, the freed prisoners of the King are cheered enthusiastically and carried from the Bastille in triumph. At least, three of them are, since the four counterfeiters have already vanished, no doubt preferring to make the best of their new-found freedom right away.

A crude drawing by Cholat, one of the conquerors of the Bastille. In the fore-front, the barracks courtyard; on the right, the porch leading to the Arsenal; in the centre, the drawbridge leading to the Government yard. On its right, the governor's residence, and on its left, a bridge leading to the main draw-bridge.

July 14, 1789: The Bastille, symbol of royal absolutism, is seized by the people

Outside the city hall, the mob brandishes the heads of the Marquis de Launay, the Bastille's governor, and Jacques de Flesselles, provost of tradesmen.

Hulin and his men have a lot of trouble pushing their way through the crowds. The people are beating the governor and the disarmed soldiers, who, unlike some of their comrades, were not able to take advantage of the confusion to escape.

Vengeance

During the march, three officers of the Bastille headquarters and three of the invalids are killed. De Launay is beaten, despite efforts to protect him by Hulin. "We must chop his head off," some shout. "Let's hang him," scream others gathered outside the city hall. A cook rushes up to an already wounded de Launay. "Let them kill me!" he shouts, fighting back. He knees the cook, a certain Desnot, in the

groin. "Help me!" the latter screams.

Suddenly, a man stabs de Launay in the stomach with his bayonet. It is the signal for the butchery to begin. The governor is repeatedly stabbed before being finished off with a bullet as he lies in the gutter. The cook, who has got over his pain, grabs a knife and starts cutting off de Launay's head as the mob cheers.

At precisely that instant, Flesselles, the provost of tradesmen, walks out of the city hall. The crowd, which had accused him of having betrayed its cause by refusing to provide weapons, moves towards him. A unidentified man draws his pistol and shoots him down in cold blood. His head is immediately severed, just as de Launay's was. It is six o'clock. Amid the suffocating, damp heat of the city, the people are starting to celebrate their victory.

News of the fall of the Bastille has gradually spread through the capital. There is rejoicing everywhere. The severed heads of the "enemies of the people" are paraded around stuck on the ends of pikes, as crowds march from the city hall to the Palais Royal, but revolutionary joy is tinged with a feeling of disquiet and guilt.

Versailles waits

The day's events have been serious enough for the King to drop plans to go hunting, which remains his favourite sport. Besenval has come in person to warn him that his

troops have defected, and Louis XVI is very upset by the news. All through the afternoon, two delegations from the Assembly have been keeping him abreast of events in Paris. "The matter that concerns you is one that must surely move the hearts of all good citizens as it moves mine," the King said calmly. He has simply ordered the troops billeted on the Champ de Mars to withdraw to Saint Cloud. The King hopes to use other regiments that can be called in as reinforcements to put down the revolt in Paris. In his opinion, the latest events in the capital are simply a popular revolt similar to the ones Paris has known over the past decades. The impor-

tance of what has just happened is also being underestimated by the court. The Comte d'Artois, Louis XVI's youngest brother, thinks that the insurgents can be crushed and has offered drinks to two German regiments billeted at Versailles.

The King has gone to bed early, as he usually does. However, the Duc de La Rochefoucauld Liancourt, Master of the Royal Wardrobe, has come to awaken the King to inform him of the day's events and beg him to take control of the situation and to go to the Assembly tomorrow. "It is a rebellion," a shaken Louis XVI is said to have exclaimed. "Nay Sire, a Revolution," La Rochefoucauld replied.

Foreign reaction to the Revolution

There were many foreigners in Paris during this already historic day. Those who earned the name of "conquerors of the Bastille" knew they were involved in a major event, but foreigners also realised that July 14th. was a crucial day. They were all surprised by the discipline shown on that day by the people. It was astonishing to see how much simple artisans and shopkeepers could achieve. Everybody also wrongly believed in de Launay's betrayal, which is already the subject of widespread rumours. Foreign ambassadors in Paris have quickly drawn their own conclusions from the fall of the Bastille. Russia's ambassador,

Simolin, has written to the court at Moscow to report that "the Revolution has taken place in France". England's ambassador, the Duke of Dorset, a friend of the Queen who is not likely to have revolutionary sympathies, sent the following assessment of the events to London: "Thus, My Lord, the greatest revolution of our time will only, when you take into account the importance of the events, have cost the lives of a few men ... From now on, we will have to see France as a free country, the King as a monarch with limited powers and the nobility as being reduced to the level of the rest of the nation."

One of the big heroes of the day, Humbert, a simple watch maker.

Constituent Assembly

15. Versailles. Louis XVI, accompanied by his two brothers, arrives on foot to inform the National Assembly that he has decided to move the troops away from the capital. The King then returns to the palace surrounded by deputies.

15. Paris. A delegation of eighty eight deputies goes to Paris to calm the fears of the population, and reads out the King's speech of conciliation at the city hall. Acclaimed by the public, Bailly is elected mayor of the city and La Fayette is voted general of the National Guard. The reception ends with a *Te Deum* at Notre Dame cathedral. →

15. Le Havre. The port's armed inhabitants seize the François I tower.

15. Dijon. After having seized the Saint Nicolas tower, the patriots set up a permanent committee while a bourgeois militia is created under the leadership of the Capuchin friar Eugène Schneider.

16. Versailles. At the Assembly, debate on the possible dismissal of the ministers involved in the power play leads to a political break between Barnave and Mounier. Barnave blames Mounier for not realising that a revolution has taken place and for wanting to build a new state using material that has just been broken.

16. Versailles. Louis XVI recalls Necker.

16. Paris. The assembly of electors decides that the Bastille prison should be torn down right away and entrusts the task to the contractor Palloy. →

16. Saint Germain en Laye. A major hunger riot ends with the death of the miller Sauvage, who had been accused of hoarding and hiding wheat.

16. Rennes. Within the space of a few hours, youths and citizens led by Moreau and Joseph Marie Sevestre, a clerk of the court, seize control of the town. The town's garrison does not resist and sides with the revolution.

16. Versailles. The court nobility begins to emigrate from France. →

16. Lyons. Fearing a new revolt, the Consulate sets up a bourgeois militia.

La Fayette and Bailly, masters of Paris

On July 15th., the cannons of Paris are dragged up Montmartre hill.

Paris, July 15

Loud shouts of "Long live the nation and long live the deputies" greet the Assembly's delegation, led by La Fayette and Bailly, when it arrives at the capital's city hall, where electors have set up a "Commune of Paris". The electors see the two men as powerful symbols: Bailly represents the historic oath taken at the Jeu de Paume, while La Fayette is the hero of the American Revolution. La Fayette has been named general in command of the bourgeois militia, which has been called the National Guard, while Bailly had been made provost of tradesmen, but a voice of dissent is heard among the crowd, shouting "No, make him mayor of Paris", and the suggestion is warmly welcomed by all. The bourgeoisie has been badly frightened by yesterday's popular anger and is now counting on these new institutions to restore order.

The Bastille is torn down stone by stone

Paris, July 16

The breastwork has already been torn down and parts of the battlements are beginning to fall. It was not enough to seize the symbolic prison: every trace of it had to be wiped out quickly. That was the decision taken by the assembly of Paris electors, but the original idea of destroying the Bastille was not theirs: in May 1784, the King himself had asked the architect Corbet to tear it down and replace it with a public square where his statue could stand. However, the time for urban renewal projects is past.

The Bastille, symbol of oppression, is torn down by demolition experts.

The Comte d'Artois and the Polignacs set off into exile

Versailles, July 16

What a stampede! Versailles has become practically deserted over the past few days. The Comte d'Artois gave the example and many are following. The King's brother left in such a rush that he had to stop to borrow money in order to be able to continue his journey. His family will join him soon in Turin, at the King of Sardinia's palace. At midnight, it was the turn of the Polignacs, the husband, wife and sister in law. The Duchess had stayed behind, refusing to leave the Queen, who had tearfully to beg her to go and sent her a tender message of farewell. The noble fugitives are disguised as servants for fear of being recognised and attacked.

Charles de France, Comte d'Artois, is a supporter of absolute monarchy.

Jussieu finishes his dictionary

Paris, July

Although nature allows plants to grow wild, they are now to be placed in their proper order in a book. In his learned work, *Genera Plantarum*, the botanist Antoine Laurent de Jussieu has divided the vegetable world into three main genuses, from which stem seven species and one hundred groups; but a total of 137 genuses do not fit into in his "reasoned catalogue". These will have to wait to be given their proper place in the natural order, the great French botanist has humbly decided.

17. Paris. Louis XVI is handed the tricoloured cockade by Bailly.→

17. Rouen. The town's patriots set up a new local council.

18. Paris. Camille Desmoulins publishes the first republican manifesto of the revolution, *La France Libre.*

19. Le Mans. A violent riot forces the local authorities to free all the poor jailed for theft during the winter.

20. Bourgogne. News of the explosion yesterday of a barrel of gunpowder during a banquet held at Quincey in honour of the fall of the Bastille sparks off widespread fears in the province.→

20. Caen. An angry crowd chases the garrison out of the castle, while the Duc d'Harcourt forms a provisional committee in a bid to maintain order.

21. Cherbourg. The port's mayor is forced to flee from the town following serious rioting.

22. Paris. The financier Jean Louis Foulon de Doué and the bailiff Bertier de Sauvigny are murdered by a mob.→

22. Falaise. Fear of a riot forces the Marquis de Ségrier formally to renounce his feudal rights in five parishes.

22. Montauban. An assembly of citizens forces the former town council to share power with a committee of patriots.

23. Ballon. Peasants of the village assassinate the lieutenant of Le Mans, Cureau, and the Comte de Montesson.

28. Ruffec. After the regions of the Bourgogne, Champagne, Beauvaisis and Dauphiné, it is now the turn of the southwest of the country to be affected by the terrible panic, known as the "Great Fear," that began to sweep France just over a week ago and will last until August 6.

28. Versailles. The National Assembly forms a special committee to investigate the agrarian unrest.

29. Alsace. After having looted the local castles, the peasants of Sundgau attack members of the region's Jewish communities.

31. Luçon. The town council has a *Te Deum* said to express its gratitude for the restoration of order.

The King wears the colours of the nation

Arriving in Paris in the early evening, the King passes before the Louvre on his way to the city hall, where he will pin the tricoloured cockade to his hat.

Paris, July 17

The King crossed Paris surrounded by a large, silent, almost hostile crowd. The people had demanded that he come to pay homage personally to their victory of July 14th. La Fayette walked before the royal carriage carrying a drawn sword. Ahead of him, the cannons of Paris were dragged over the rough cobblestones. On each side of the procession there stood Parisians armed with rifles, sabres or pikes, forming a strange and threatening guard of honour. Afraid that he would not be returning, Louis XVI had named Monsieur the kingdom's lieutenant general before leaving Versailles. When he arrived at the city hall, Bailly handed him a tricoloured cockade, the new rallying sign of Frenchmen invented by La Fayette. The King, showing signs of emotion, silently pinned it to his hat and entered the building. That gesture, which marked the final humiliation of the monarchy, was greeted by shouts of joy. Citizens brandished their swords and the King passed under an arch of blades. Momentarily frightened by the clashing of steel and the shouts of the crowd, Louis XVI was soon reassured to see people hold out their hands to him and cry. There were many shouts of "Our King, our father!", but the King remained silent, unable to respond to the show of affection.

Tricolour Cockade

Yesterday, July 17, the King smilingly pinned the tricolour cockade to his hat. Now this song is going the rounds:

I love the bright and varied hue
Of the ribbons we all wear;
The citizen-King accepts them.
An emblem of equality
The cockade at once affirms
That gentleman of quality
And sweep are on equal terms.

To drive away the deadly foe,
All we needed was to show
Blue, red and purest white.
White's for the frank, open heart
Of republicans fair and true;
Blue skies promise a new start
And bliss long overdue.

So how do I the red explain?
I have it! The solution's plain!
Flowers from the earth grow:
O lovely womankind - how fair!

Robespierre backs the insurgents

Versailles, July 20

A certain Robespierre, a deputy from Arras, today made a speech that was supported by representatives of Brittany and attracted considerable attention. The Comte Lally Tollendal had suggested that the citizens be called upon to put an end to the unrest in Paris, but Robespierre strongly defended the insurgents and the principle of rebellion: "What was this Paris riot? Public liberty, a little blood spilt, some heads rolled, but they were guilty heads. Gentlemen, the Nation owes its freedom to this riot," he exclaimed. Convinced, the Assembly rejected Lally Tollendal's motion, although it had initially approved of it. The Assembly does not quite know what to make of the Paris uprising, even though the people were seeking to defend the constituent body. It sees such riots as somewhat terrifying and difficult to control.

Foulon and Bertier murdered by the mob

Foulon is hanged from a lamp post on the corner of the city hall square.

Paris, July 22

An empty belly is no aid to reason and rumours about who is behind the lack of food are easily spread.

Such a rumour today claimed two new victims: Bertier, bailiff of Paris, and his father in law Foulon, a little-loved financier who replaced Necker at the head of the Finance Ministry from July 12th. to 16th. Foulon was the first to be "arrested" at Viry Chatillon and brought back to Paris barefoot, with a collar of coal around his neck and bale of hay on his head. The old man was thirsty, but he was given vinegar to drink and his face was wiped with nettles. At the city hall neither La Fayette nor Bailly dared save him from the mob's fury. He was hanged from a lamp post, then beheaded. As Bertier arrived in Paris with an escort, he saw the mob carrying Foulon's head. He grabbed a gun, but was repeatedly stabbed with bayonets and his heart was torn out.

The Great Fear sweeps through the provinces

France, July

It all started in Bourgogne and Brittany. The cause was the same everywhere: rumours. At Nantes on July 20th., witnesses reported seeing a detachment of dragoons heading for the town. They were surely coming to put down the recent municipal revolt. Local men rushed to the armouries to grab weapons and set off to meet the soldiers, but peasants saw them as yet another dangerous armed gang. On the 24th., at Rumilly, in Champagne, a herd of cows was taken for a group of bandits! On the 28th., at Ruffec, in southwestern France, threats voiced by dissatisfied religious alms collectors were taken very seriously. In the regions of Maine, the Soissonnais and the Franche Comté, similar misunderstandings led women, children and farm animals to flee to the nearest woods while the menfolk set up defences. Only Brittany, parts of Normandy, the Ardennes, the Roussillon, the Landes and the northeast were spared by this wave of fear. Everywhere else alarm bells rang out, spreading panic from village to village. An agrarian revolt had been threatening to break out since the spring. The peasants had been waiting in vain for a reply to their grievances. Some of them attacked local castles, harassing their occu-

pants and burning the documents which backed up the hated feudal rights. The peasantry's misery was being made even more unbearable by hunger and unemployment. Growing numbers of drifters were taking to the roads, prepared to do anything to survive. People also said that bandits were being driven out of the cities by police action. Weren't the aristocrats likely to take advantage of such anarchy to restore their powers? Wasn't the enemy already at the borders? All of this was still just rumour, but the sight of the first armed gangs seemed to be confirmation enough and panic took hold. They have come, we've seen them!

It is difficult to know why this Great Fear spread so quickly. Was there an aristocrats' plot? Was it a move by the Assembly aimed at spreading the revolution? Or could it have been a show of solidarity in the face of what appeared to be a pre-planned nationwide action? Whatever the cause, the peasants are now armed, organised and ready to use force to liberate their lands from the nobles, who are sometimes being supported by the bourgeois. The deputies are wondering whether to give legitimacy to the movement or to let the gap between peasants and bourgeois widen further.

Started by a wave of rumours, the Great Fear is spreading to the country-side. Princes and courtiers are emigrating, castles are being looted.

The rebellion spreads to the towns

France, July

The revolt which spread through the countryside has now reached the towns. Newsletters written by deputies have kept the provinces abreast of events in Paris. The type of revolt differs from town to town, depending on whether the local authorities represent the majority of citizens. For example, in Stras-

bourg the former town council was eliminated by force. At Bordeaux the town council was placed under the control of a committee of patriots, while the one at Toulouse was kept unchanged. The representatives of royal power have been fleeing. Bourgeois militias are being set up everywhere. Priority is given to security and food supplies.

THE GREAT FEAR
of July 1789

Calais
Boulogne
Lille
Dieppe
Vervins
Rouen
ESTRÉE
Caen
Elbeuf
Châlons
Paris
Étampes
ROMILLY
Vitré
ST FLORENTIN
LA FERTÉ
NANTES
Loches
Sancerre
Dijon
Besançon
Autun
Bourges
LOUHANS
St Maixent
Surgères
RUFFEC
Limoges
Clermont
Belley
Ussel
Lyons
Bordeaux
Aurillac
Grenoble
Cahors
Privas
Valence
Briançon
Ager
Millau
Digne
Avignon
Castellane
Pau
St Girons
Marseilles
Lourdes
Prades

★ Places where panic started
→ Currents of fear
Regions in which agrarian riots occurred before the Great Fear
Regions not affected by the Great Fear

0   100   200km

© Chronicle

The Strasbourg city hall is sacked. All the archives are thrown from the windows and tiles are removed from the roof of the building one by one.

King backs down and recalls Necker

Versailles, July 29

An eerie silence greets Necker as he arrives at the palace of Versailles, which has been deserted by the court.

Deeply shocked by the uprising of July 14th., the King has given in to pressures from the Assembly and has recalled Necker to ask him to form a new government. Necker has therefore returned from his exile at Basel, although he hesitated for a long time before leaving. Whom is he to govern with? The only two ministers to answer the call are Montmorin and Saint Priest. The royal couple are lying low in their rooms and even their lackeys are showing a lack of respect as they perform their duties. Power has now moved to Paris. The whole kingdom has been rocked by the riots, as Necker was stunned to see during his return journey; but he also noticed that his popularity had remained unchanged. In even the smallest villages people rushed out to cheer him, and the deputies welcomed him warmly. Could he be the monarchy's last hope?

A victim of despotism is honoured

Thanks to these tools, Latude was able to build the rope ladders he used in his spectacular escape from the Bastille prison.

Paris, July

A prisoner can easily be turned into a martyr, but it is less common for him to become a hero. That is what has happened to Jean Henry Masers de Latude, who has gone from the gloom of his cell to the glow of glory.

He had been sent to the Bastille where he rotted for thirty five years before escaping. The people have now turned him into a living symbol of injustice. A woman, Madame Legros, was moved by a note he had managed to slip through the bars of his cell and had even undertaken steps to get the King to agree to his release. He had been jailed on the basis of a sealed order alleging that he had sent a parcel bomb to Pompadour along with a list of those who were supposed to be behind the attack. By this foolish stratagem, he had hoped to win the Marquise's favour, but the ploy cost him dearly. However, now that he is no longer behind bars, Latude has become a symbol of liberty for thousands. There is even a current exhibition about him in the courtyard of the Louvre. Crowds come to see his portrait painted by Antoine Vestier and the sawn iron bar of his cell.

Comédie Française responds to critics

Paris, July 21

The Comédie Française is to reopen. It is now to be called the "Théâtre de la Nation". The choice of the new name is probably a bid to calm criticism against the theatre. People have been charging it with abuse of privilege. The theatre depends entirely on the gentlemen of the King's Chamber, who hand out roles however they choose and set the prices and times of the performances. The Comédie Française has a monopoly over classic plays and no other theatre is allowed to perform them. The actors prefer to perform at Versailles and are often absent from work. The Academician La Harpe is quite right to speak out against the "haughty greediness of this usurping troupe". One of his main targets is Madame Comtat. Her success in the role of Suzanne in the *Mariage de Figaro* has gone to her head. Protected by the Comte d'Artois and Marie Antoinette, she thinks she can get away with anything.

August 1789
from 1st. to 4th.

Constituent Assembly

1. Saint Denis. The lieutenant of the town's mayor, Chatel, is killed during a distribution of bread to the poor which turned into a riot.

1. Lons le Saunier. The town's National Guard proposes to set up a "league against the enemies of the nation".

1. Versailles. A total of fifty six speakers have themselves registered at the Assembly's office to take part in the debate on whether or not to insert a declaration on human rights at the start of the constitution (→26).

1. Saint Malo. The national militia is entrusted with the custody of two burdensome prisoners captured at Dol, the Marquis de Bedée and the official receiver's attorney of the Brittany estates, the Comte de Botherel.

1. Valenciennes. Two peasants who had been captured by police during the recent rioting are hanged.

2. Rennes. On the Montmorin esplanade, the National Guard swears an oath of allegiance to the nation, to the law and to the King.

2. Avignon. There is unrest in the papal estates. →

3. Nantes. Acting on orders from the town council, a detachment of the local militia arrests the Marquis de Trémargat at the castle of Ponthue. By today, most of the Brittany noblemen who had led the 1788 parliamentary revolt have either been arrested or are being hunted down.

3. Rouen. During a workers' riot in which deserters from the Navarre regiment and army volunteers have taken part, a Parisian actor, François Bordier, is arrested (→4).

4. Rouen. A day after his arrest, the actor François Bordier is freed by his fellow rioters.

4. Rennes. The town council sets up a permanent committee combining youths, military personnel and city officials. Since July 14th. the former local authorities have been keeping a low profile, giving way to patriot town councils backed by militias that have been spontaneously formed.

4. Versailles. Despite recent events, the National Assembly confirms that it wants taxes and rents paid in the same way as before.

Ouvrard, a clever young speculator

Nantes, August

Although he is only 19 years old, Gabriel Julien Ouvrard is turning out to be an impressive financier. When he noticed that the revolution, in which he has no interest, had led to a huge increase in newspaper sales, he bought on credit all the available paper as well as the production of the Poitou and Angoumois paper mills for the next two years.

Then he cunningly spread the rumour that there would be a scarcity of paper. This quickly caused panic among printers and led to a sharp rise in the price of paper. The young man then sold off his stock for a high price, demanding immediate payment. Thanks to this clever and speculative ploy, Ouvrard made a nice profit of over 300,000 francs.

Two workmen placing sheets of paper on a drier.

Children play the revolution game

Paris, August

Angry mobs, shouting and bloodshed are grownups' business, but children can sometimes feel tempted to imitate their elders. Groups of young children have been spotted in the gardens of the Luxembourg playing with some very strange toys. They were carrying small drums and swords as they marched along the pathways proudly bearing a cat's severed head on a pike. Could the aristocratic cat have dared eat a patriot mouse?

Isnard's great organ plays at Pithiviers

Drawing of plans for a finely decorated organ chest (18th. century).

Pithiviers, August 3

The great organ on which Jean Baptiste Isnard has worked for five years is finished at last. It cost 90,000 francs — a fortune. Is such a huge expense justified at a time when French organ music is in the midst of a major crisis? There is nothing new being done in the field, either technically or in the repertoire of organ music. Today's cultured audiences prefer sonatas and secular music in general. Some composers have tried to keep the great tradition of masters such as François Couperin alive, but their work is weak. Others seek to draw audiences by resorting to superficial virtuosity. Michel Corrette even adapts some currently popular songs such as *Une Jolie Bergère*.

The peasants' revolt hits the Rhineland

The Rhineland, August

The nobility's privileges and the unjust distribution of taxes have been causing discontent in the Rhineland for a long time. News reaching there from France has added to the unrest. Peasants have been refusing to pay their rents, seizing feudal property and not carrying out their forestry duties. There have been several uprisings, including one in the diocese of Speyer, notorious for the Count of Limburg Styrum's corrupt administrative practices. At Boppard, unrest over local forestry rights suddenly turned into a riot. Frightened by events, princes such as the Archbishop of Cologne, Maximilian François, Joseph II's brother, have stopped supporting enlightened despotism. They now demand reactionary moves and call on the imperial army to quell the revolt.

The Revolution fires the imagination of Germany's intelligentsia

Germany, August

Many German intellectuals have been following events in France with feelings of sympathy. Since the announcement of the meeting of the Estates General, people have been crowding reading rooms to read the latest Paris newspapers and talk about the situation. The older rationalist generation sees the Revolution as an opportunity for legislation based on natural law and the ending of the arbitrary exercise of royal power. Younger people, disciples of Rousseau who feel ready for profound changes, are hoping for the end of all oppression. At Weimar, the author Wieland pays homage to the "necessary and salutary work of the Revolution". This gentle but sceptical sybarite is not one to be overcome by enthusiasm. An outstanding courtier, happy to live in a small principality, he is convinced that people are eternal minors and sees himself as an impartial judge.

The German author Christoph Martin Wieland.

Assembly rocked by provincial arson campaign and tax boycott

Versailles, August 2

As castles are being burnt to the ground and archives destroyed, the Assembly is becoming increasingly worried.

Its members are desperately looking for the best way to cope with the anger of the peasants. All the initial motions recommend repression. One of them, submitted by a deputy from Orléans, Salomon de la Saugerie, not only condemns the sacking of castles, but states that refusal to pay tithes and other feudal rents is a violation of the principles of public law. His motion was rejected. It would in any case have been extremely difficult to implement. Unless the Assembly is prepared to see widespread bloodshed, it now seems impossible to see how the peasants can be forced to pay the hated taxes and feudal rents. An Assembly which has adopted the principle of equality would only be going back on its word by delaying moves to abandon privilege, which seem inevitable (→4).

Madame Elisabeth has decided to change the "Turkish" room of her Montreuil residence: the walls will be covered in cretonne print.

Pope's subjects agitate for reforms

Avignon, August 2

The inhabitants of the papal estates have been closely following what their French neighbours have been up to. Are they not concerned about the abuses criticised at Versailles? This morning, the people of Avignon, who had already persuaded the town council to look into the trade guilds' grievances, found a notice posted on all the walls of the city. This "Notice from a Patriot to his Fellow Citizens" demands that an assembly of delegates of the trade guilds and heads of families be convened. It also calls for the formation of a bourgeois militia and tax reforms. A cautious deputy papal legate has said that he will give up some of his privileges.

Avignon, as well as the Comtat Venaissin, which includes Carpentras and Cavaillon, is part of the enclave of the papal estates.

Night of August 4, 1789: Privileges are abolished

The Constituent Assembly has done more work in six hours than it had in three months, getting rid of centuries-old traditions. Just one night, marked by great enthusiasm and unanimity, was enough to scrap the social structures of the Ancien Régime. First worried, then terrified by the Great Fear that has been spreading for the past two weeks throughout the countryside, the deputies have decided to take drastic measures. The most hated privileges have been abolished, from the most costly — such as tithes — to the most oppressive — such as hunting rights. However, in the weeks to come, these decisions in principle will have to be given a concrete form.

The "most revered and powerful lord of abuses" no longer exists...

The Duc d'Aiguillon.

The deputies gather around eight o'clock under the presidency of Le Chapelier. Allowed to speak, the lawyer Target submits the draft decree that was debated yesterday. It is aimed at putting an end to the unrest rocking the countryside. The draft text reminds all citizens that they must respect property and continue to pay rents and taxes. The Assembly had been getting ready to condemn the peasants' demands.

A stunning surprise

Target has hardly finished speaking when a man jumps up and begins to talk. He is well known: it is the Vicomte de Noailles, a member of the highest nobility of France. He states that if deputies really want to ensure public order in the kingdom, not only should fiscal privileges be scrapped, but feudal rights should be abandoned and peasants allowed to buy them back. As for all the individual servitudes, they should purely and simply be abolished. This statement causes an uproar ... Another deputy stands. It is Monsieur d'Aiguillon, duke and peer, a vastly wealthy man, unlike Noailles, who is a youngest child. In a fiery speech, the nobleman condemns excesses, speaks about "the unfortunate farmer who is subjected to the barbaric leftovers of feudal laws", and calls for the creation of "that equality of rights that must exist between men".

Enthusiasm

The deputies cheer the duke. For an important person to propose that the nobility should agree to such an act of generosity is a truly admirable thing; but the statements made by the two noblemen are not as strange as they might seem. It seems that the "Breton club" last night met Le Chapelier and decided to strike a major blow. Many agree that it is time to put an end to the shaky structures of the Old Regime and to proclaim loudly the principle of equality. Moreover, that would help to take the edge off the peasants' discontent, which has been increased by repressive measures. To get that result, what was needed was for the initiative to come from the ranks of the privileged themselves; but d'Aiguillon has calculated that it would cost thirty times a whole year's revenue to buy back the feudal rights. It is therefore out of the question to cast

At Versailles, where the Constituent Assembly meets, nothing like it has ever been seen. Deputies are trying to outdo each other. Suggestions fly thick and fast, each more generous than the last. Everybody wants to give up his privileges. Within a few hours, the whole edifice of the Ancien Régime is crumbling amid cries of joy. Some deputies are scared and leave the Assembly.

amid rejoicing - the Ancien Régime is dead!

"At long last ... to each his rightful share," the nation rejoices.

doubt on the principle of property. What d'Aiguillon specifically said was that a "just reimbursement" should be offered. Noblemen and bourgeois are in full agreement on this point, but at this emotional session of the Assembly gestures speak louder than cold calculations.

Shortly afterwards one of the Third Estate deputies from Brittany, Le Guen de Kérangal, lashes out against the "hungry monster of the feudal system" and describes the misery and injustice suffered by peasants.

Another deputy chills his audience by describing the horrors of the past in lurid terms: how lords used to walk over the disembowelled bodies of their vassals ... It is nearly eleven o'clock. Many deputies feel that the session should now be brought to a close. There are calls for the issues to be voted upon: fiscal equality, repurchase of duties on property and, most of all, the abolition of those duties that are a burden to the individual.

Even further

However, a deputy of the nobility from the Périgord, the Marquis Foucauld Lardimalie, is opposed to this. He is one of of those provincial squires who have always been opposed to the advantages that the wealthier nobles of Paris and at court have. He claims that there are even worse abuses: all those greedy courtiers who are given useless duties which are costly to the state must be the first to be forced to give up their privileges. He is cheered and the session is again in an uproar.

Everybody is trying to outdo his neighbour's generosity and daring. More cynical observers have noted that the deputies have a marked tendency to sacrifice what belongs to others. Then it is the Bishop of Chartres, who stands to propose the abolition of hunting rights, a privilege hated by peasants. All

The abolished privileges

Now that the people's will has been carried out, reconciliation is possible. Yesterday's snakes (the former privileges) are being trampled underfoot.

First to have been abolished are all the ancient and hated feudal servitudes: mortmain, which made it impossible for serfs to will their own property; serfdom, a status close to that of slavery; the duties of guard and

the noble deputies affected by this measure warmly welcome the suggestion. Those of the Third Estate rise and cheer the nobles wildly. During several minutes, the Assembly is in total uproar.

What about the clergy?

A short time later, the priest from Souples stands and states that he is renouncing surplice fees. A nobleman responds by proposing an increase in the income of the lower clergy. The deputies greet this with even louder cries of enthusiasm, but the Duc du Châtelet goes even further by suggesting that the highly unpopular tithe should be bought back and turned into a tax. Shouts of approval are heard. After this, there are proposals for the equality of punishment, equal access to the civil service and the abolition of mortmain.

A single France!

At this point, the deputies of the Dauphiné go a step further and

lookout, which had become an obligation for servants to guard the castle; statute labour, or days spent working for the local lord. Also abolished were the despised exclusive hunting rights and the right to breed fowl.

Then the following privileges of the clergy and nobility were abolished after being repurchased: the banalities, or the nobility's monopoly over the flour mill, the press house and the bread oven; the champarts, which were the part of the crop owed by dependent peasants to the landowner; taxes paid for authorisation to leave a region. Tithes collected by the clergy also disappear, as do surplice fees charged for christenings, weddings and funerals.

From now on, public office cannot be purchased, since the principle of the venality of office has been abandoned. Every citizen will have access to military and civil posts. Justice now being free, there will in future be no privilege due simply to birth.

announce that they are prepared to renounce all the privileges of their province. There are in France as many different statuses as there are provinces or towns. This proposal is a violation of the deputies' mandate, but who cares! If Frenchmen are equal and free, there can only be a single France, a single nation.

It is midnight and the uproar is total. Deputies from the Languedoc, the Artois, the Bordelais and Strasbourg are following the example set by their counterparts from the Dauphiné. A large crowd is milling about outside the offices of the Assembly's president, where deputies are registering the details of their sacrifices.

Equality and fraternity

After a chaotic hour, the Duc de La Rochefoucauld Liancourt, Master of the King's Wardrobe, suggests that a medallion be struck "so that the memory of the sincere union of all the orders and the renunciation of all privileges be kept forever". It is a question of principle. As a fitting end, the Archbishop of Paris gets approval of plans for a *Te Deum*. It is nearly 2 a.m. when Lally Tollendal calls on the Assembly to proclaim Louis XVI the "restorer of French liberty". Long live the King! The session can now end. Its president, Le Chapelier, reads out what has been achieved during this extraordinary night. It is an impressive list that marks the end of the France of the past. This remains to be confirmed and there is still some uncertainty, but a great principle has triumphed, one which will live on: the equality of Frenchmen.

Constituent Assembly

5. Versailles. After having done away with feudal rights, the National Assembly decides to give Louis XVI the title of "restorer of French liberty".

5. Bayeux. The high price of salt causes a riot to break out.

8. Versailles. The Marquis de La Coste Messelière calls for property belonging to the clergy to be declared to belong to the nation. Although the proposal enrages the clergy, Alexandre de Lameth goes even further by suggesting that the clergy's wealth be used to guarantee the nation's debts.

9. Versailles. The Assembly approves the 30 million franc loan requested by Necker (→26).

9. Fontenay le Comte. Overnight, a mob sacks the residence of the seneschal, who was under suspicion of food hoarding.

10. Versailles. The Constituent Assembly issues a decree entrusting the new town councils with the keeping of public order.

11. Versailles. The decrees of August 4th. are grouped into a single general decree.

13. Caen. The municipal committee resigns, deeply shocked by yesterday's assassination of Major de Belsunce, accused of having insulted the tricolour cockade.

14. Versailles. The King declares an amnesty for deserters. In Paris alone, over 3,000 soldiers are affected by the move.

14. Paris. Monsieur's theatre performs *Retour de Camille, ou Camille Dictateur pour la Troisième Fois*, a verse play by Joseph Audé.

15. Nantes. Soldiers of the Rohan regiment fraternise with the population.

18. Angers. The town's National Guard sends a plan for federation to the kingdom's militias.

19. Versailles. At the Assembly, Lally Tollendal proposes that the legislative body be split into two houses.

19. Marseilles. Bloody clashes break out between the people and the civil guard.

24. Versailles. A day after proclaiming the freedom of religion, the Constituent Assembly abrogates laws restricting the freedom of the press.

Homecoming of Jacques Delille

Auvergne, August

Chanonat has honoured its famous son. The brilliant Academician Jacques Delille, France's best-known poet, has once again become the boy from Auvergne who used to run through the fields or along the banks of the Auzon. All his former friends have come to welcome him back, from the old priest who cried when he hugged him to now-wrinkled Toinette, who used to look after his chilblains. The happy author of *Jardins* can now see how far he has come since the day he was just the illegitimate child of a well-born young woman who never even dared give him her name. Today she calls herself ... Madame Delille.

Despite all the honours, Jacques Delille is still a simple man.

Lavoisier arrested, then released

Paris, August 6

A threatening and over-excited crowd has gathered outside the Arsenal: rumour has it that the comptroller of gunpowder has removed ammunition stored there. Is Lavoisier trying to take away Paris' means of defending itself? Cries of treason have rung out. Lavoisier is arrested and taken to the city hall, but all can be explained: the gunpowder, which was of poor quality, was only being replaced with excellent battlefield powder.

The ladies of the Halle give thanks to God and to General La Fayette

Paris, August 5

What rejoicing there was among the ladies of the Halle when they heard at dawn about the vast revolution carried out overnight by the Assembly. Many of them marched off to the church of Sainte Geneviève to sing a *Te Deum*. They were followed by a procession of young girls in white wearing crowns of flowers, as well as by a detachment of the National Guard playing martial music. After mass had been said, they handed a home-made bunch of flowers to General La Fayette. Everything ended with some excessive drinking, but who can blame these patriotic women?

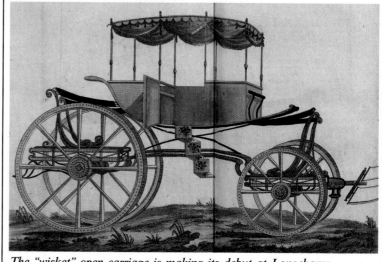

The "wisket" open carriage is making its debut at Longchamp.

Woman sets up a political newspaper

Paris, August 13

Despite her small size, Louise Felicité de Kéralio has her fair share of daring and ambition.

She has just set up the *Journal d'Etat et du Citoyen,* the first ever political newspaper written by a woman in the history of journalism. Her publicly proclaimed aim is to "spread the sacred principles of liberty, the eternal and sublime law of equality, the hatred of tyrants and the horror of prejudice".

A Breton on her father's side, this vivacious, witty and highly cultured woman in her thirties has been a involved in writing for a long time. By the time she reached the age of eighteen, she had already written a novel, *Adélaïde.* She then started work on a lengthy and erudite "History of Elisabeth", which took ten years to finish.

But her deep patriotic sentiments have led her to drop literature and take up journalism. Her example is followed by her future husband, the lawyer Robert, whom Louise fully intends to see involved in political activity.

The Orléans princes learn by experience

Paris, August 13

Madame de Genlis did not hesitate to choose a "field trip" rather than a boring history lesson. After having hurriedly left the castle at Saint Leu, she returned to Paris with her young pupils so that Louis Philippe d'Orléans and his brothers can witness the interesting sight of the Bastille being torn down. This real-life education is one of the basic rules of the governess. When the princes learn geography, they do so by travelling. When they study English, they speak the language during meals. As for physics, there is nothing as instructive as carrying out experiments. They are also tought carpentry, gardening and how to milk cows. All these are considered to be vital skills by their devoted teacher.

Crowds flock to realist art exhibition

Paris, August 20

The amazing success of this year's art exhibition in the capital is a sure sign of unexpected and radical changes in the taste of the public.

Until recently, art lovers preferred a rather delicate and figurative style, but today the taste is for meticulous realism, far brighter colours and moving expressions. Museum goers of today are particularly keen on portraits, and members of the bourgeoisie are avid collectors of such works. Other favourite contemporary styles are the still life and landscapes. Anything that touches on everyday reality seems certain of being a success. If the artist adds an edifying concept to his work, the public automatically sees it as a work of art. Antiquity is still the official theme for most paintings, although a growing number of historical scenes of the Middle Ages and the Renaissance are being shown in museums.

"Love Fleeing from Slavery" by Joseph Marie Vien, shown at this year's art exhibition. The public liked the brightly coloured painting.

David's painting, "Brutus", is a big hit

The painting "Lictors delivering the bodies of his sons to Brutus" by David is a homage to morality and republican self-sacrifice.

Paris, August 20

The huge success that *Serment des Horaces* had in 1785 has convinced the authorities to commission a new painting from Jacques Louis David. After having hesitated for a long time over what subject to treat, David finally chose the life of Brutus. The work is set in the 6th. century B.C.; the Republic of Rome has just been set up and Brutus has been named its consul. On learning that his sons have been plotting the restoration of monarchy, Brutus did his public duty and had the two young men executed. David has shown the moment when lictors bring the bodies of the two youths back to their father who is lying by the statue of Rome, while his wife and daughters give vent to their desperation. The composition of the work seems a little less taut than that of the *Serment des Horaces*, but it is more moving, and this is much appreciated by a public that is keen on dramatic scenes. David does not, however, go in for easy effects. The work retains a great dignity, using very few colours to achieve a sort of frozen beauty.

Danton provokes an uproar at the Théâtre Français

Paris, August 19

This evening, a member of the audience at the Théâtre Français dared to interrupt the performance by loudly demanding to see the play written by Marie Joseph Chénier, *Charles IX*, which has been banned since 1788. When the actor Fleury told the trouble-maker that he was not allowed to perform the play, the audience began to stamp its feet and to shout that there was no need to wait for official permission to go ahead. Security forces had to evacuate the theatre. The man who had been behind this public disturbance turned out to be a totally unknown lawyer named Danton.

Poet Florian joins National Guard

Sceaux, August 22

The gentle poet Florian is now wearing military uniform. He has just been named the commanding officer of the bourgeois militia of Sceaux. He could not refuse to say yes to a delegation from the town council which had come to see him with a military band. The post is mainly an honorary one, unless one wants to go into politics, which is not the case here. Every town has been seeking to follow the example of Paris and have its own National Guard, and the bourgeois of Sceaux did not want to be left out. They have formed a bourgeois militia whose chief purpose is to keep order and remain loyal to the nation, to the King and to the law. Florian was unable to refuse such an impressive offer.

Wearing a military uniform is a sign of great prestige.

Marie Antoinette scorns well-wishers from the capital

Versailles, August 25

Each year, the representatives of Paris have been coming to Versailles to wish the King a happy saint's day on the day of Saint Louis, but this year they were far from happy when they left. They were received by Marie Antoinette, who was covered in jewels and surrounded by her household. The Queen was annoyed because Bailly, the mayor of Paris, had not knelt before her. She replied to his speech in a scornful manner and said a few less than pleasant words to La Fayette, who had presented the National Guard to her. The Queen then dismissed them all.

25. Paris. The author of *Voyage du Jeune Anacharsis,* the Abbot Jean Jacques Barthélemy, is elected a member of the French Academy, in the seat of the grammarian Dom Nicolas Beauzée.

26. Versailles. The Constituent Assembly approves the final version of the declaration of human rights, which is the philosophical basis for the new social order.→

26. Liège. Frightened by the current revolutionary unrest, the Prince-Bishop decides to run away.→

26. Condé sur Noireau. The towns and villages of forty five parishes of the Normandy pasture lands form a defensive alliance.

27. Versailles. Following the failure of the first loan of 30 million francs, Necker issues a second one of 80 million francs. Despite having a guarantee from the Constituent Assembly, this loan will not be more successful.→

28. Versailles. At the Assembly, debate on the constitution opens with a speech by Mounier, who sums up the principles of monarchical government. The basic point of the new system is that the King is subordinate to the law.→

29. Versailles. Debate on the issue of the veto powers to be given to the King gives the right wing of the Assembly a chance to stabilise the political situation (→30).

29. Paris. The bakers of the wheat market start a riot and forcibly remove carts carrying wheat.

29. Versailles. The Assembly decrees that the grain trade will be free.

30. Paris. The veto issue causes great unrest in the capital.→

30. Cahors. The National Guard decides to support the federation plan for the city of Angers.

31. Versailles. Mounier and Lally Tollendal continue their offensive by proposing the creation of a hereditary senate. The plan gets a mixed response, even among the representatives of the nobility.

31. Paris. The town council decides to shut down three of the city's five charity centres set up for the unemployed.

Miners rise up against work conditions

In the bowels of the earth, underpaid miners work at the risk of their lives. The galleries are narrow and deep and fire-damp explosions are frequent.

Pyrénées, August 26

The miners of Rancié have rebelled against the awful working conditions imposed on them by the town, which owns the iron mine. The authorities have been unwilling to provide enough pit props to place in the mine and the miners have to pay out of their own pockets for the blasting powder and lighting oil. All this has to come out of their daily wage of twenty sous. To make matters worse, the baskets they have to carry are too heavy: 150 pounds for men and 75 pounds for ten year old boys! Accidents frequently happen and there are deaths and injuries. The situation can't go on. The 345 miners today went to the notary public to get him to note down their grievances. From now on, pit props and the use of explosives will be controlled by the workers, who will set a minimum wage and will handle hiring. Their demands are sent to the National Assembly to be confirmed as a new law. Will they be heard?

A song in honour of La Fayette

The Marquis de la Fayette, on August 13 last, attended the blessing of the flag of the sector of the Cordeliers. His charming wife was at his side. Imbert, the song-writer, has since composed a pleasant song about the event in which Mme. de La Fayette is not forgotten:

Ready to enjoy its noble conquest,
Liberty consecrates our flags:
Only that one must fly over the
Feast of he who was long heroic
Zeal and caution unite in him;
He proved it in America:
What his bravery has won,
His wisdom can preserve.
The lovely lady to whom he is wed
Smiles brightly upon us;
And beauty smiling at courage
Is, after glory, his chief reward.
Lord, grant Louis a guiding arm
He supports a worthy people;
Citizen-King, as our father lives,
And we will give him our lives.

MARIE, PAUL, JOSEPH, ROCH, YVES, GILBERT DE MOTTIER DE LA FAYETTE
Député d'Auvergne à l'Assemblée Nationale en 1789: Élu Commandant Général de la Garde Nationale parisienne le 15 Juillet.

The Marquis de La Fayette has become popular in France due in part to the rôle he played in the American War of Independence.

Necker urges issue of a new loan to cover public debt

Versailles, August 27

Is France going to have to live on credit? The government loan issued on August 9th. has only brought in two million francs out of the 30 million that had been expected. Necker therefore had to go back to the Assembly today. The minister begged it to issue a new loan to make up the deficit of the public debt, which is growing every day. Necker is hoping that the five per cent return offered to subscribers will make this loan more attractive than the previous one, because he is now calling for 80 million francs, but even if he succeeds in getting this amount into the state's coffers, he will not have solved the financial crisis. The treasury needs more than such stop-gap measures.

Prince-Bishop is driven from Liège

Liège, August 26

No one could have foreseen that a revolution was coming to Liège. Frightened by the recent turn of events, the Prince-Bishop, Constantin François de Hoensbroech, fled during the night.

Although he was not as enlightened as his predecessor, Velbruck, Hoensbroech was neither a tyrant nor a bigoted fanatic. He had a tendency to let things happen. It all started with a minor disagreement over the monopoly on gaming at Spa. Soon people were speaking out against the 1684 Constitution, which had increased the bishops' prerogatives and excluded the corporations from the states.

The unrest was compounded by external events such as the revolt of Dutch patriots, the convening of the Estates General in France and the opposition of Belgians to the edicts of Joseph II. Hoensbroech's clumsy actions only made things worse and a coup occurred on August 18th. The rebels seized the city hall and set up a new council. Hoensbroech was forced to sign the abolition of the 1684 Constitution and to recognise the new magistrate. The poor prelate finally decided he had had enough and fled from the city.

"Men are born free and with equal rights"

The Declaration of human rights and of the rights of the citizen is approved by the Assembly during its sessions of August 20th.-26th. 1789.

Versailles, August 26

Man has rights: this is an entirely new concept that is going to change people's way of thinking radically. After over a month and a half of debate, the Assembly has just approved the final version of the Declaration of human rights and of the rights of the citizen.

It was a matter of both sweeping away the theories justifying the old privileges and laying down the principles of the new regime that the Constituent Assembly is to set up. The amount of time spent in debate by the deputies is due to the extent of the task before them. Malouet did not believe that the people of France were yet ready to hear this text, while Mirabeau said: "This is a veil that it would be dangerous to lift suddenly, it is a secret that must be hidden from the people."

What could the terrible "secret" contained in the Declaration be? "Ignorance of, forgetfulness or contempt for human rights are the sole causes of the misery of the people and of the corruption of governments," states the preamble to the text. What is being proclaimed here are the "natural and indefeasible" rights of the individual — freedom, property, security and resistance to oppression. The concept of liberty constitutes a large part of the Dec-

laration. It is given an obvious practical aim, as all arbitrary practices of the monarchy are condemned. Individual liberty, particularly the freedom of thought, which includes religious belief, freedom of expression and the public freedoms are all enshrined alongside the principles of equality before the law and the taxman. The first article — "men are born and remain free and with equal rights" — sums up the thrust of the entire declaration. These new rights have not been invented by the French revolutionaries. The enlightened philosophers had already defined them and the American Declaration of Independence of 1776 recognised them.

But the text adopted today has a different significance. Barnave has called it a political "catechism" which creates public rights. These rest on the principle of the separation of the executive, legislative and judicial powers and on that of national sovereignty. Thus, "the principle of all sovereignty rests essentially on the Nation" and only it is empowered to delegate the exercise of power to its own representatives. The Declaration will thus acquire a sort of universal significance, and it seems more than likely that there will be many other nations which will decide to imitate it.

Royal prerogative debate splits the ranks of the patriots' party

Versailles, August 28

Is the King to be granted a right of veto? In other words, will Louis XVI be able to refuse to countersign laws approved by the Assembly in order to stop them coming into force? This is a hotly debated issue, as the King is still hesitating to approve the decrees of August 4th. and 11th. "Who is this Monsieur *Veto* who is upsetting everybody? Why don't we just string him up?" people asked this morning in the gardens of the Palais Royal; but the veto issue is above all the first question that has caused a split in the ranks of the patriots' party. On the right, moderates such as Mounier are in favour of an English-style system with absolute veto powers. Conciliators, like Pétion or Barnave, want a suspensive veto

allowing the holding of new elections when there is disagreement between the King and the Assembly. The democrats are the only ones to object strongly to any form of royal prerogative (→ Sept. 11).

The deputies Cazalès, Maury and Malouet: brilliant speakers.

People's march on Versailles blocked

Paris, August 30

Parisians have been overcome by a sudden rage today. A rumour had been spreading around the Palais Royal: the Assembly is getting ready to grant the King an absolute veto! This caused a surge of anger and some 200 men decided to set off for Versailles right away. They were talking about forcing the Constituent Assembly to dissolve itself and bringing the King back to Paris, but the grenadiers of the National Guard, acting on orders from the city hall, immediately blocked roads. The Commune of Paris had refused to sanction this handful of citizens by giving them official credentials. The march to Versailles therefore had to be called off, but the Parisians' anger has not been calmed.

The colours of the revolution are reflected in current fashions.

1. Lyons. The city's first ever daily newspaper, *Le Courrier de Lyon,* is published.

2. Saint Etienne. Workers wreck the hardware factory owned by a bourgeois, Jacques Sauvade.

9. Troyes. The town's mayor, Huez, is killed during a food riot.

10. Versailles. A day after having decreed the permanent nature of the legislative body, the Assembly votes against the creation of an Upper House.

10. Paris. The Commune increases the number of guards at the wheat market, which has been the target of daily rioting, to 600 men.

11. Versailles. An overall majority of the Assembly votes to grant the King the right to refuse to agree to actions taken by the legislative body. The King is also granted a suspensive veto (→14).

11. Paris. A new work by the composer Antonio Piccini, *Les Fourberies de Marine,* is performed at the Opéra.

13. Orléans. Violent rioting leaves 90 people dead. →

14. Versailles. At the Assembly, Barnave asks for debate to be suspended until the decrees of August 4th. have been sanctioned by the King, or until the Assembly has decided that it will not request the King's sanction for them (→22).

14. Trégier. The Bishop Le Mintier publishes a pastoral letter against human rights and the abolition of the feudal system.

16. Paris. Jean Paul Marat sets up the *Ami du Peuple.→*

18. Versailles. A decree from the Council frees the price of grain.

22. Versailles. The Assembly approves the first article of the Constitution. The previous day, the King had informed the deputies that he would have the August 4th. decrees published but not promulgated.

22. Paris. At the Opéra, a posthumous performance of the last work by Jean Christophe Vogel, *Démophon,* is a big success.

26. Versailles. Despite the failure of the loans, the Assembly places its trust in Necker's plans for economic recovery.

Artists' wives offer jewels to the nation

A delegation of artists' wives comes to Versailles to offer their jewels to the National Assembly. The generous ladies are shown their seats.

Versailles, September 7

A charming group came to the Assembly today. Dressed all in white and wearing the tricolour cockade as their only decoration, the wives of artists have come as a delegation to offer their jewels to the nation. Amongst them were Mesdames Vien, Fragonard, Lagrenée, David, Vernet, Gérard and many others. The youngest one solemnly handed over a chest containing their gifts to the deputies.

Before leaving, their leader, Madame Moitte, suggested that a fund should be started to receive new patriotic donations. As a reward for their generosity, the Assembly gave them the honours of the session and decided that their names would be added to the report of the day's proceedings. When they got back to Paris, a huge crowd was waiting for them to escort them triumphantly to the Louvre, where most of the ladies reside.

Riot at Orléans leaves 90 dead

Orléans, September 13

Not everybody is happy with the new institutions. The recently formed committee for security and food supplies of Orléans is responsible for the death of 90 citizens. It had been criticised for having too many privileged members. It had also angered country dwellers by keeping bread prices down only in the towns. Yesterday a grain convoy was attacked in the Bannier district. At the same time, the inhabitants of Olivet and Saint Sauveur tried to force their way past the gates of the town to loot the bakeries. Both times the guardsmen opened fire on the mob. Overnight, one of the leaders of the protest was judged and hanged. This morning people did not wear the cockade, to show their anger.

Mirabeau schemes at Palais Royal

Paris, September

What if the King were to disappear? Or if he were to flee with the Comte de Provence? Then the regency would belong to Philippe d'Orléans. Wouldn't that be the only way to save the Assembly and to avoid anarchy? Such a prospect does not displease Mirabeau. If the Duc d'Orléans were in power, he thinks that he would be able to govern as he wishes: this schemer, this puppet is unable of taking any personal initiative! Over the past few weeks the two men, whose ambitions are similar, have been seeing a lot of each other. Last night they dined at the home of the Comte de La Marck, where they are said to have spoken freely of their plans, but in public they are much more cautious and reserved.

Marat launches new daily paper, "L'Ami du Peuple"

Paris, September 16

Is Dr. Marat's destiny at last about to be fulfilled? For its fifth edition, his daily newspaper has been named *L'Ami du Peuple* and has adopted a more biting tone. His new pamphlet attacking the Assembly, which made the mistake of ignoring him, and the Commune, which did not elect him, will serve his ambition of becoming the herald of the Revolution better than his obscure theoretical writings. For months he has been trying to convince the people who matter — a group that he would love to belong to — that he is indispensable. Only one man trusts him: a printer, who in exchange gets 75 per cent of the paper's profits (→Oct. 8).

Marat is a very ambitious man.

Deputy slammed for swearing

Versailles, September 9

A scandal has broken out at the Assembly! Carried away by his fiery speech, a deputy, the Comte de Virieu, has uttered a resounding cry of "Hell and damnation!". This caused total uproar among those present. Indignant voices rose from all sides to call for the unfortunate deputy to be severely reprimanded. When he was finally allowed to speak again, one of his fellow deputies interrupted to say that he had "soiled his mouth with an oath". The poor orator was left with no other choice than to sit down and remain silent.

Louis tests loyalty of National Guard

The banner of the National Guard: Saint Marcel battalion.

Versailles, September 29

The Queen herself has graciously received the lieutenant colonels of the National Guard in Paris.

The court has every reason to be happy about the situation. There had been serious doubts about the National Guard's loyalty to the monarchy. To put this loyalty to the test, the King had sent the Guard to meet the Flanders regiment. By agreeing to honour this regiment, the Guard gave proof of its loyalty.

But will it be enough to give a flag to each company of the National Guard in order to keep it loyal to the royal cause?

The banner of the National Guard: Théatins battalion.

1. Paris. The writer Louis Sébastien Mercier, author of the highly controversial book *Tableau de Paris,* cooperates with journalist Jean Louis Carra to set up a new liberal newspaper, *Les Annales Patriotiques et Littéraires.*

1. Meudon. Despite the unrest rocking the kingdom, Louis XVI continues to practise his favourite sport: hunting. Today the King killed two stags.

1. Montpellier. Jean Jacques Régis de Cambacérès is elected vice president of the municipal assembly.

1. Versailles. A banquet, held at Versailles by officers of the Household Guard in honour of officers of the Flanders regiment, is marked by a fiercely anti-revolutionary demonstration. The banquet is attended by Louis XVI and Marie Antoinette (→2).

1. Versailles. Following an initiative by Baron Wimpfen, deputy of the bailiwick of Caen, the National Assembly decides to form a military committee to work with the War Ministry in the preparation of army reforms.

1. Fontenay le Comte. Local inhabitants hold a general assembly and set up a patriotic committee to replace the former town council.

2. Versailles. The president of the Assembly, Mounier, submits to the King the decrees of August 4th. and 11th. of the Declaration of human rights in order to get their promulgation. The King, however, delays his response.

3. Paris. Two papers, Gorsas' *Le Courrier de Versailles* and *Fouet National,* warn about the Household Guards' banquet and about military preparations that the court is said to be planning (→4).

3. Paris. At a meeting of the Cordeliers district, Danton urges Parisians to take up arms.

4. Paris. As crowds gather at the Palais Royal, there are non-stop district meetings at which the aristocrats' plot is condemned.→

5. Saint Etienne. A violent riot breaks out in the town over the amount of time spent by the town council in enforcing the long awaited September 23rd. Assembly decree lowering the salt tax.

Royalist officers trample tricolour cockades during Versailles "orgy"

Versailles, October 2

In Paris, rumours of a possible counter-revolution have been rife since last night's "orgy" at the palace of Versailles.

The King's bodyguards had held a banquet at the palace in honour of the Flanders regiment, which had been called in recently for use in case rioting should break out in the capital. Made cautious by recent events, the royal couple had not been quite sure whether to attend. The King and Queen's appearance at a balcony was, however, greeted by wild cheering. Guardsmen started singing the tune of "O Richard, O my King" as officers cheered. Deeply moved by this unexpected show of support, Louis XVI, Marie Antoinette and the Dauphin joined the guests. Emboldened by the wine they had been drinking, the officers tore off their tricolour cockades and trampled them underfoot, as they donned white cockades symbolising the monarchy. The hot-headed soldiers are obviously keen to see a full restoration of the King's powers, but the incident has led Parisians to suspect that Louis XVI is getting ready to make use of his faithful troops to break the revolution (→4).

The banquet offered at Versailles by the officers of the Household Guard to the Flanders regiment, during which tricolour cockades were trampled.

King suspected of military coup plot

Paris, October 4

An aristocrats' plot is said to be under way at Versailles. The alarming rumour, started by the press, is spreading. Gorsas, in his newspaper *Le Courrier de Versailles à Paris*, claimed yesterday that the King was getting ready to launch a coup d'état. In his *Révolutions de Paris*, Loustallot spoke of a "second wave of revolution". During the infamous Household Guard's banquet, the Flanders regiment plainly showed its attachment to the monarchy. Could the regiment really be planning to kidnap the King and take him to Metz?

Cockade is defiled

On October 1, officers of the French Guards gave a banquet for men of the Flanders Regiment. The cockade was trodden underfoot. Angry crowds are now singing this:
*Decent folk must bring
Their aid our dear France.
Men who guard the citizen-king
Are set on orgy-making.
With wine the madness flows
As brutish songs they bawl;
One voice is suddenly heard:
"Damn the tricolour cockade!"
Glass in hand all cry the word
And applaud the bold fellow.
In the trice the deed is done:
Shameless beneath ignoble feet
They stamp the emblem down.
Upon their hats
They pinned a black cockade.
These haughty gentlemen
Will need that somber sign again
When days of vengeance dawn.*

The capital has found its King again and Versailles is deserted. The march by thousands of Parisians has put an end to a century and a half of royal presence in the town of the Sun King. A 17th. century revolt by Parisians during the violent clashes of the Fronde had forced a young Louis XIV to settle outside Paris. Today, it is another revolt that has brought his descendant back to the Tuileries. The heart of the Revolution has moved from Versailles to Paris. In just three months, Parisians have acted thrice to speed up the pace of the Revolution. Within a few hours, the people have disarmed the King's party and taken control over the monarch. The Assembly, which will move to Paris in a few days, must take into account a power that is growing each day: the street.

It all started in the food queues. The women of Paris decide to go to see the King himself to ask for bread.

Yesterday at daybreak, around seven o'clock, as the capital was blanketed by fog, Parisians were on a war footing. The night had not helped to calm the revolutionary ardour, which had been given free rein on Sunday. On the contrary. They wanted to stop the King fleeing to Metz, as had been rumoured since the arrival of the Flanders regiment. "Let's march on Versailles" were the words that galvanised the entire city, which had been living in fear of hunger and of a royalist counter-attack.

The sun had barely risen when thousands, urged on by an irresistible force, gathered at the city hall. Thousands of women who had come in from the outlying districts were demanding bread and arms. Led by Hulin, the conquerors of the Bastille joined the women. Then one of them, the bailiff's clerk Maillard, began to harangue the crowd, offering to lead the people to Versailles. The women saw he was a true leader. Bedecked in tricoloured ribbons, armed with sticks, pikes and hastily grabbed pitchforks, the strange procession soon set off for the palace of the kings of France. A company of the Bastille's conquerors acted as rear guard to this highly unusual citizens' army.

To Versailles!

As deafening peals of alarm bells rang out all over Paris, groups were forming up and men were rushing to the city hall from every district of the capital. "To Versailles!" the mob roared. This cry was soon taken up by the grenadiers of the National Guard whose duty was to keep order.

By the time the morning was nearly over, La Fayette, who seemed unwilling to take sides, was desperately trying to calm his troops. His efforts were in vain. The city authorities finally gave in to the grumbling mob: it delegated two officials who were to bring the King back. Numbering 15,000 National Guardsmen and thousands of Parisians, the second procession gradually moved off under a heavy, driving rain around one o'clock, dragging the cannons of the capital's artillery behind it as if the people of Paris really intended to lay siege to the monarchy.

Versailles, where the two huge processions from Paris were to join up, saw the first women arrive around four o'clock. They immediately headed for the Assembly. A delegation of fifteen women, who were allowed in with Maillard, begged the deputies to take action against food hoarders.

Meanwhile, the King had hurriedly returned from the hunt. There was great concern at the palace, whose gates had been shut. The Council, which was holding an emergency meeting, didn't know what steps to take.

Women of Paris at the Assembly.

At Versailles, on the Armes square, the fighting is spreading. The people rush into the palace's courtyard.

Versailles, the King is forced to return to Paris

The rioters arrive outside Marie Antoinette's apartments.

"My friends, I will go to Paris with my wife and children," the King says.

The women go before the King

At the Assembly, deputies agree to back a delegation of women led by Mounier that is to be admitted to see the King, but the fishwives are awed by the splendour of the court and hesitate to speak. One of them faints. Reassured by their shyness, Louis XVI promises to see that the capital is provided with food and manages to calm them. Two hours later, the main contingent of the citizens' army gets to the huge Armes square at Versailles, spreading panic in the palace. The King decides to leave for Rambouillet with his family, but he has left it too late. The gate of the royal stables has been torn down and the mob has rushed in and taken the horses after cutting their harness. By nightfall, the mob controls the royal town; women invade the Assembly, some seek rooms at inns, while most settle down on the square for the night.

The King orders that bread be handed out to the people and the crowd calms down. La Fayette, who had left Paris around five o'clock, arrives at midnight: "Sire, I thought that it was better to come here to die at Your Majesty's feet than to perish uselessly on the Place de Grève," he tells Louis XVI. La Fayette then goes into Versailles to check on the situation there, returning shortly afterwards with some reassuring news. Calmed by the apparent quiet at the palace and around it, the King decides to go to bed, as does La Fayette. They both withdraw to their rooms and the palace rests for a few short hours.

The assault

It is now October 6th. The day has hardly begun when drums start beating on the Armes square. As if acting on a pre-arranged signal, tens of thousands of people form tight ranks. The huge, threatening crowd passes through the chapel gates, which have mysteriously been left open, and pours into the palace courtyard. The bodyguards are totally incapable of coping with the screaming mob, which heads for the rooms occupied by Marie Antoinette. One of the bodyguards rushes into the first anteroom. He has just enough time to shout "save the Queen, they want to hurt her", before being felled by a hail of blows. The Queen's ladies in waiting, who have spent the whole night outside her door, rush in, drag her out of bed and push her, still only half dressed, down the narrow secret passage leading to the King's rooms. Woken by the noise, the monarch's first thoughts are for the safety of his family. Using a dark underground passage, he manages to reach the Dauphin's bedroom, where his son is sleeping calmly. The King picks the child up and carries him in his arms back to his own rooms, but he is also worried about Marie Antoinette and rushes to meet her down the complex network of passages under the palace. After searching for a harrowing few minutes, the royal couple meet in the King's cabinet room, which is in an uproar. Outside, the mob is going wild. Men and women are hunting down palace bodyguards. They manage to grab two of them and fling them to the ground where, amid loud cheering, a huge man chops off their heads with a well-aimed blow from his axe. In all, some thirty other guards are to suffer the same fate. Warned about the massacres, La Fayette comes running to the royal apartments with a group of grenadiers who are sent off to attack the mob. Under the windows of the King's rooms the rioters, armed with rifles and aiming a cannon at the palace, are booing Louis XVI and demanding that he be taken back to Paris. La Fayette begs the royal couple to agree to the demand. Faced with such a huge and determined mob, the King reluctantly agrees and walks out onto the balcony to confirm his decision. This victory for the people is greeted by a salvo of shots fired in the air, but the mob is not satisfied. Parisians are also calling for the Queen. Marie Antoinette takes her two children by the hand and appears on the balcony. "No children!" the mob howls. Calmly, the Queen sends her son and daughter back inside and faces the crowd that a short time ago was calling for her blood. Time seems to stand still. "To Paris!" a voice shouts, and the cry is then picked up by thousands of others. Her ordeal over, the "Austrian" goes back, barely conscious, into her rooms.

The return to Paris

La Fayette immediately gives orders for the King's departure, as he is far too upset to handle the preparations himself. It is just one o'clock when the royal family leaves Versailles under pale autumn sunshine. The people are triumphant. The King's carriage, preceded by people bearing the severed heads of guards stuck on pikes, makes slow progress. Ragged, drenched and mud-stained men and women are singing at the tops of their voices and pointing derisively at the royal family they have dubbed "the baker, the baker's wife and their little assistant". After a harrowing six hour march, the capital's barriers are finally reached. The mayor of Paris, Bailly, greets the amazing procession with a speech of welcome to which Louis XVI answers in a dull voice, speaking of the trust he has in the city. After spending a short time at the city hall, where they appear on a balcony, the King, Marie Antoinette and the Dauphin are taken to the Tuileries.

Some very gory trophies for the return from Versailles.

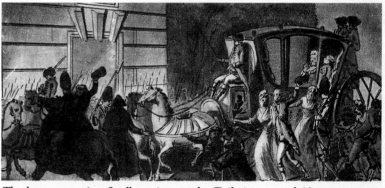

The long procession finally arrives at the Tuileries around 10 p.m.

October 1789

from 7th. to 23rd.

Constituent Assembly

8. Paris. In deep trouble with the authorities over his calls for insurrection, Marat goes into hiding.

9. Versailles. The Assembly issues a decree reforming criminal procedure and setting up police tribunals.

9. Paris. Louis XVI issues a conciliatory statement to explain the events that led to his decision to move into the Tuileries.

10. Versailles. Louis XVI is named "King of the French" by deputies. →

10. Versailles. After Lally Tollendal's exile in Lausanne, Mounier withdraws to the Dauphiné.

13. Lyons. Clashes break out between the bourgeois militia and the Consulate guard, made up mainly of the city's wealthy youths.

14. Grenoble. The parliament decides to convene the provincial estates to condemn the coup attempt of October 6th.

14. Versailles. The Assembly receives a delegation of Jews from the east of the country, which demands equal rights for their community.

15. Versailles. In the hope of playing the role of the prince's councillor, Mirabeau sends a first secret message to the King.

17. Rouen. Famine once again forces workers to sack six local weaving mills.

18. Lannion. A hungry mob seizes a wheat convoy meant for the city of Brest.

18. Paris. The city authorities ask provincial towns to keep their beggars and the unemployed from flooding into the capital.

19. Paris. The first session of the National Assembly is held at the archbishopric.

19. Paris. City authorities decide to forbid deserters from the army to join the National Guard.

20. Boulogne. The Duc Philippe d'Orléans sets sail for England. →

21. Paris. The killing of the baker François at the market on the Rue Pallu helps the right wing at the Assembly to get martial law approved. →

22. Paris. At the Constituent Assembly, debate begins on the electoral system.

King and Queen camp at Tuileries

Paris, October 7

When they arrived last night at the Tuileries, the King, the Queen and their children found a deserted and freezing palace. They had to spend the night in the rooms that Marie Antoinette used to sleep in after spending an evening out in the capital. The people who had accompanied the royal couple had to settle for the other rooms, hoping to find at least a bench or a table to sleep on. Today, the crowds that have filled the gardens are calling for the royal family to appear at a window. When he heard the crowd, the Dauphin whispered: "My goodness Mother, is today going to be like yesterday?"

King in Paris

The ladies of the Halle are going to praise the King

Louis XVI, Marie Antoinette and the princes are now at the Tuileries. A song in the language of the market-place, expresses the sentiments of the masses:

To Louis Paris is right dear.
This swells us hearts with pride.
And safe as houses he will be:
To stand on guard we take turns
And his protection guarantee
By love for him fast and firm.
That joy, long wished, I've found,
A peaceful happiness profound:
Our King will not his city flee.
His origins are here I'm told.
We'll look on him with glee
As did our dads King Henri bold.
That is why the King we prize
Cursed be he as 'gainst him rises.
For folk as hopes to trick him out
Will be trapped in their snare.
We'll whip 'em round the town about
And hang 'em on the lantern there.

Louis XVI becomes "King of the French"

Versailles, October 10

Monarchy by divine right no longer exists! Two days ago, the deputies decreed that Louis XVI would in the future be known as the "King of the French". He will have to abandon his title of "King of France and of Navarre", which has had no real meaning since the nation's sovereignty was proclaimed. The Assembly has, however, not dared abolish the sacred nature of the monarchy. It stated today that the sovereign's exact title will be "Louis, by the grace of God and the constitutional law of the State". The reference to God is probably only a temporary concession to tradition. Royal power is truly placed under the guardianship of the nation and of its laws. The little authority that Louis XVI retained has now been officially stripped from him, but the most recent riots in Paris had in fact put an end to the monarchy's prestige.

On this seal, the motto links the grace of God and secular law.

Guillotin says decapitation by a single blow of the blade is more humane

Versailles, October 10

The deputy who has just come to the rostrum is also a physician and a professor of anatomy.

Joseph Ignace Guillotin's profession and ideals are those of a humane man. In today's speech, he explains that there is a need to study plans for a reform of criminal procedure as well as methods of carrying out the death sentence. When a person deserves the death penalty, it must be carried out, but the end does not justify all means. Would it not be possible to find a way to make the punishment less terrible? Isn't it time that executions worthy of the Middle Ages were abandoned? Why not get rid once and for all of the wheel, the iron collar, quartering and the gibbet, which all seem designed to prolong suffering?

A murderer, a deserter or even a traitor is still a human being and should be treated as such. What is needed is a machine, similar to the ones that already exist in Italy, that is capable of chopping off a head with a single blow of a blade. Is the Assembly going to do something about Dr. Guillotin's plea?

The Paris deputy Joseph Guillotin shows off his uniform of a member of the French Guard to his admiring family. (Anonymous gouache.)

126

A disappointed Mounier quits politics

Grenoble, October 10

A tired and drawn Mounier has just arrived at Grenoble. The fiery speaker of Vizille has lost all hope of understanding a revolution that is quite beyond him. He had been one of those who had warmly welcomed the Third Estate's success in imposing the nation's sovereignty. Satisfied by that victory, he would have preferred to go no further and to reach an understanding with the King that could have been the basis for a constitutional monarchy, but this hope was dashed by Louis XVI's lack of trust and the people's impatience. The split within the patriot party over the veto issue has placed Mounier on the right wing of the Assembly, which he had presided over until three days ago. Even his friend Barnave has disowned him.

Mounier escaping. He is followed by a sinister lantern ...

Marie Antoinette drops escape plan

Paris, October 19

It was with a heavy heart that the Queen finally dropped the plans for escape suggested by one of her advisors, Augeard. According to the plan, she was supposed to disguise herself as a governess and travel to Austria with her two children to seek asylum from her brother, but Louis XVI was not to be told about her escape, so she refused to agree to the plan. "My duty is to die at the King's feet," she tearfully told Augeard.

Negroes and mulattoes visit Assembly

Versailles, October 22

The National Assembly has received a delegation of freed coloured people from the island of Saint Domingue. The negro and mulatto former slaves had been waiting impatiently for this moment for several months. Proudly, Julien Raimond, a wealthy mulatto, read out on their behalf the petition they had prepared. In this, they stress that they are landowners, free and French, just as the white settlers are. They too should be allowed to be members of the Assembly. They also state that they are in favour of slavery being practised in the overseas colonies. Deputies listened to them but made no firm promises.

In the West Indies, freed negroes, as well as white settlers, are opposed to the abolition of slavery.

Brutal killing of the baker François

Paris, October 21

The mob was after blood. Early this morning, a stone's throw from the archbishopric, where the Assembly has been meeting, some women started arguing with the baker François. They accused him of hoarding bread. He invited them into his bakehouse so that they could see for themselves that he had nothing to hide. Unfortunately, the women found three stale loaves that had been kept aside by the apprentices. The baker was dragged before the district authorities, who turned a deaf ear to his pleas of innocence. The mob threw itself on him and killed him. His severed head was paraded around the streets on the end of a pike, before the very eyes of his three months pregnant wife. The deputies, shocked by the murder, have imposed martial law.

The baker François is hanged before being beheaded by the mob.

War of cockades on Tobago Island

Tobago Island, October 23

Settlers have met at Port Louis to elect deputies to the National Assembly. The governor, Chevalier de Jobal, tried to ban the meeting, but it was held, although the proceedings were unruly. The island's inhabitants have been arguing fiercely over the wearing of the tricolour cockade: recently arrived Frenchmen wanted everybody to wear it, but this angered earlier, royalist, settlers, many of whom had come from Scotland.

Duc d'Orléans sent on secret mission

Did Philippe d'Orléans even have the time to pack one of these toilet bags without which no true gentlemen usually sets off on a journey?

Boulogne, October 20

Popularity sometimes has its drawbacks. Philippe d'Orléans is well placed to know this.

It all started on October 7th. On that morning, a clearly upset La Fayette turned up at his residence saying that there were rumours in Paris that he was behind a plot to overthrow the King. If he wanted to save himself, he had better leave right away for England, where the King was prepared to send him on a secret mission. The aim of the mission was to find out whether the English financed the march on Versailles. Without seeking to know more, Philippe d'Orléans packed his bags and arrived at Boulogne on October 16th., along with his secretary Choderlos de Laclos.

But, thinking that the King was sending him into exile, the people of the port city stopped him from leaving, keeping him a virtual prisoner for four days while delegates rushed to Paris to check that his passport was valid. It was finally this morning that the Duc d'Orléans could set sail for England, cursing both his popularity and Mirabeau, whom he suspects of having been behind the whole annoying affair.

24. Toulouse. Following the lead set by the nobility of the Languedoc region, which on October 16th. issued a statement strongly condemning the Constituent Assembly, the clergy criticises the scrapping of tithes.

24. Paris. The Military Committee decides to set up a corps of city barrier guards to try to stop the fraudulent import of goods into the capital.

24. Bavaria. The author Georges François Mareschal dies at Triesdorf. He was known as the "father of puns", for his habit of using many plays on words in his works.

24. Paris. Two members of the district of Saint Martin des Champs, the former notary Jean Maris Martin and the master chessboard maker Pierre Duval, alias Destin, are arrested. They had been behind a protest against martial law in the district.

24. Austrian Netherlands. The insurgents proclaim independence and strip Joseph II of his sovereignty over the country. →

25. Lannion. More than 2,000 national volunteers from Brest occupy the town and recover a cargo of wheat that had been confiscated by the inhabitants.

28. Paris. The Assembly provisionally forbids the taking of monastic vows after testimony by a superior on the lack of vocations (→ Feb. 13, 90).

29. Paris. The Assembly approves the decree known as the "silver marc", which limits eligibility to active citizens. →

29. Paris. The secretary of the Queen's commandments, Mathieu Augeard, is found in possession of a plan to kidnap the King. He is arrested after being denounced by the Commune's research committee (→ Mar. 29, 90).

29. Paris. The Academician La Harpe offers a voluntary contribution of 19 marks and one ounce of silver to the nation.

30. Austria. In a letter to the Comte d'Artois, the Emperor Joseph II, who seized Belgrade on October 9th., states that he has no intention of launching a military intervention in France.

31. Paris. The Italian theatre performs a comic opera by Giovanni Paisiello, *La Molinarella*.

Can the Americans find a solution to the financial crisis now rocking France?

Paris, October 27

There was no other option: Necker did not hesitate to set up a dinner at his residence with Morris, a businessman and one of George Washington's friends. He wants to open negotiations on the 24 million francs that are owed to France by America. France's Finance Minister and Montmorin, its Foreign Minister, wanted the talks to be held in secret. This is because the foreign bankers, heavily involved in efforts to get the debt repaid, are already concerned about the political situation in France. They must not be upset further by stormy debates at the Assembly. Morris has, however, refused to commit himself to a 10 million franc annual repayment over three years. He may be able to get 300,000 francs a month as from January, but this will not settle the deficit in the kingdom's budget. The two loans issued in August have not been covered and the deputies, who in June gave the nation's guarantee to the creditors of the state, are unlikely to declare France bankrupt.

Discord at the Academy of Painting

Paris, October

The venerable insitution of the Academy of Painting needs a new lease of life. When your name is Louis David and you are highly regarded in the world of the arts, it is tempting to find a new cause to fight for. David plans to make the best of his position to join in the debate launched by the Young Turks. The time has come to cast into doubt the system upon which the institution is based: the teaching of art, the selection of talented people and state patronage of the arts. Since 1785, the Academy and the Comte d'Angiviller, a great restorer of rules, have been very strict in the recruitment of artists. Faithfully applying its outdated principles, the Academy continues to reject everything that is not historical painting, either heroic or mythological themes. It has been obstinately refusing to make room for portraits, landscapes or genre painting. It has also issued a ruling that "a candidate whose reception work is refused will be struck" from the list of those admissible.

Young artists are worried about their future, as only the Academy can give the go-ahead for exhibitions at the Salon, which are the best way to find clients and to launch a career. A disagreement has just broken out over the case of Drouais, who died last year in Rome. This painter still had to submit his key work as an Academy candidate. David has demanded that Drouais be named an Academician posthumously, but the call has been rejected.

Houel paints everyday life. This work shows a cave carved in rock that is used near Rouen by the farmer general to store salt.

Restif is turned in by his son-in-law

Paris, October 29

Restif de La Bretonne has not spent the night at home. This was not because he spent it walking around the streets of the capital. He was, in fact, being questioned by the police committee of his neighbourhood about a charge made against him by his own son-in-law. The traitorous Augé had told the police that Restif was the author of three anti-patriotic pamphlets, including the pornographic *Dom Bougre aux Etats Généraux*. He went to the police as revenge for having been described as a brutal husband in his father-in-law's latest novel, but Restif was declared innocent early this morning. Augé has been charged with false accusation.

Restif de La Bretonne: freedom of expression can be dangerous ...

Turnhout is freed by its patriots

Turnhout, October 24

The Austrian officers guarding the border between the Belgian lands and the United Provinces have not been taking their duties very seriously, but it was a mistake not to have kept a closer watch on the region. Over 3,000 Belgian patriots have come from Breda and crossed the border behind their leader, Colonel van der Mersch. The volunteers today entered Turnhout, without having come across the slightest resistance. It is not enough to declare independence unilaterally: the Austrians must be forced to leave (→ Dec. 18).

Assembly opts for two classes of citizens

Paris, October 29

Sieyès' concept has triumphed: after having discussed the issue for an entire week, the Assembly's deputies have ruled that the right to vote would in future be reserved for a minority by adopting suffrage by property assessment.

The kingdom's seven million male citizens aged over 25 are now to be divided into two categories. The "passive" citizens only have civil rights, while political rights are limited to "active" citizens, that is those who provide a direct contribution equal to at least three days' work.

A total of only 4,300,000 men will thus be allowed to vote, but indirectly. This will be the case in particular for the choice of deputies. "Active" citizens will have to name second degree "electors" from their own group who pay direct taxes equal to at least ten days' work. It is these electors who will choose the deputies; but the group of eligible citizens is to be even more limited: in order to be able to aspire to being a deputy, a man will have to be able to prove direct taxation of at least one silver marc, or fifty francs and be the owner of landed property.

This "silver marc decree" limits the number of governors to large landowners, either noble or low born. This process is similar to the English system. Along with the distinction between active and passive citizens, this shows that the National Assembly still does not want a truly democratic political system (→ Jan. 25, 90).

Those who do not have a certain financial strength cannot be elected.

The misfortunes of the baker of Vernon

Paris, October 28

Discussion today at the King's Council was focused on the misfortunes of a well-off grain merchant, Planter. He is one of those responsible for the capital's food supplies. His operations at Vernon, in the Eure region, have for long caused hostility among the local population, who rightly claim that the feeding of Paris has been contributing to the scarcity of food in their town. A few days ago, a member of Vernon's permanent committee said that anyone who owns a grain store is a hoarder. All eyes immediately turned to the sinister dungeon where Planter has been storing his stocks of grain. That very evening, a crowd gathered outside. The guards were not able to stop the angry mob from grabbing the merchant and threatening to hang him from the nearest lamp post. It was only thanks to the fiery eighty year old local priest that Planter was saved. The mayor of Paris, Bailly, was told this evening about the attack against one of his officials. He interrupted the session of the Assembly to inform deputies of the case. In less than an hour, the Assembly issued a call begging the King to take all necessary steps to control the unrest. The Council has dissolved the Vernon committee and asked La Fayette to restore order there.

Madame de Staël guarantees her role as adviser to the constitutional "party"

Germaine de Staël also admires the ideas of Jean Jacques Rousseau. She has recently written an interesting book about the famous author.

Paris, October

Since the deputies have followed the King to Paris, Germaine de Staël has turned her home on the Rue du Bac into an annex of the Assembly, where people gather to discuss the latest political events. She has been lobbying parliamentarians to get support for the English type of constitutional monarchy that she would like to see in France. Necker's daughter loves to be surrounded by an adoring crowd which she delights with her charm and wit rather than by her beauty. As soon as she starts to speak, people forget all about her coarse features and her dull skin, seeing only her jet-black hair and magnificent eyes. Her words have a magic effect on her audience. Her husband, the Swedish ambassador, is starting to feel jealous of the young men who are always around her, but people say she keeps her favours for the Comte Louis de Narbonne, who has left his former mistress, Mademoiselle Contat, for her. When the beautiful actress heard of her lover's betrayal, she said the Comte had "chosen the bud rather than the rose".

When Pamela becomes Héloïse

Paris, October

Pamela, fellow student of the d'Orléans' children, could have inspired the author Rousseau with her large, languid eyes. Failing that, she has learnt how to imitate to perfection Rousseau's most touching heroine, Héloïse. Before the admiring glances of the visitors to the Salon, and acting on instructions from her tutor, Madame de Genlis, she knelt down raising an arm to the heavens in a passionate pose. She was like a living sculpture. The young orphan, who mysteriously arrived from England eight years ago to help the d'Orléans princes learn English, is a constant source of amazement to Parisians.

The lovely Pamela, whose beauty dazzles more than one Parisian.

2. Paris. The National Assembly votes by 568 to 346 in favour of the clergy's property being placed at the disposal of the nation.→

2. Paris. The first edition of the *Actes des Apôtres,* founded by Jean Gabrial Peltier, is published.

3. Paris. During the debate on the new administrative demarcation of France, Thouret proposes that the country should be split into 80 departments equal in size and arbitrarily drawn, but Mirabeau is opposed to this and asks that historical and regional considerations be taken into account.

5. Corsica. At Bastia and Ajaccio, clashes erupt between soldiers and the local patriot population which has just set up militias.

5. Paris. The town council receives a delegation of the deserters from the army who have joined the National Guard. In view of the services they have rendered, they ask that their new status be made permanent.

7. Paris. Acting on an initiative by Blin and Lajuinais, the Constituent Assembly approves a decree that makes it illegal for acting deputies to seek a ministerial mandate. The move is aimed directly at Mirabeau, whose political manoeuvring is worrying the Assembly.

11. Grenoble. Mounier publishes the *Exposé de ma Conduite à l'Assemblée Nationale et les Motifs de mon Retour en Dauphiné.* The text is a plea in favour of his policies (→15).

11. Saint Etienne. Rumours about the arming of nobles cause the town's population to loot the local weapons factory.

12. Metz. After repeated complaints by the Normandy parliament, the legistative body of Lorraine protests against the Constituent Assembly's decree of November 3rd., which prolongs the recess of the sovereign courts.

12. Paris. The Duc d'Orléans buys the exclusive rights of the new techniques of weaving and carding wool from the engineers Jack and John Milnes.

14. Paris. Necker asks for 170 million francs from the Assembly. He plans to raise the money by turning the Discount Bank into a national bank.→

The clergy's property is nationalised

Paris, November 2

If there is to be a solution to the financial crisis, this is probably it: the clergy's property has been put "at the nation's disposal". The state will from now on be responsible for the payment of priests and supporting religious establishments. The deputies have finally approved a proposal made on October 10th. by Talleyrand. The Bishop of Autun, as its former manager, is fully aware that the church's landed property is worth nearly two billion livres. The sale of the land would increase the number of landowning peasants and repay the public debt. Abbot Maury has indignantly complained about what he sees as a violation of the right to property, as enshrined by the Declaration of human rights and of the rights of the citizen. "If we are to be stripped of our property, it could be your turn next," he says. However, the lawyer Thouret replies that only individuals, as opposed to organised bodies, have an inalienable right to property. For now, it is only a vote of principle. The vital step is still awaited (→ 11).

The clergy's property is vast: 20 per cent of the kingdom's lands belong to the church. Their wealth is a choice target for many satirists.

Jean Jacques Rousseau's last confessions

Paris, November

The anxious wait of the pilgrims to Ermenonville has finally ended. Their idol, Jean Jacques, is again in the forefront of the literary scene since the publication of the second part of his *Confessions.* The first six volumes have been available for the last seven years. In them Rousseau told of his childhood in Geneva, giving an extremely sensitive and highly detailed account of the most insignificant events.

This entirely new undertaking had already shocked many readers, such as the Duchesse de Boufflers. When she read of a theft committed by the young Rousseau, she said the author had the "soul of a lackey"; but the early works lacked the hot blooded tales which his more recent works are reported to be full of. There are few things as risky as a man who has rubbed shoulders with high society and who is now ready to reveal all.

But the critics have been badly disappointed. The six previous books did not reveal anything that was not already common knowledge. Moreover, the subject of the work is the author himself. The disappointed readers have been forced to fall back on lamenting Rousseau's habit of harping on his "depravity", while paying scant attention to the astounding sincerity of the author's depiction of himself.

Jean Jacques Rousseau, by Quentin de La Tour.

Deputies condemn attitudes of the "cursed priests"

Paris, November 11

There was total uproar this morning at the Assembly when a statement from the canons of Autun attacking their bishop was read out. These dignitaries' fury against the man who had been behind the moves to nationalise and seize their property is as strong as the violence now rocking anti-clerical circles. At the end of each session, the deputies of the clergy are booed by the mob, which screams newly-invented insults, such as "calotin", or "cursed priest", at them.

Some members of the high clergy have indeed had a tendency to show strong opposition to the new political order. Le Mintier, Bishop of Tréguier, has been denounced as a counter-revolutionary by a large number of deputies. The bishop had had the effrontery to speak out against the abolition of privileges as well as the Declaration of human rights.

Cazotte translates tales from the East

Geneva, November

The translator's talent will help readers forgive him for his lack of faithfulness to the original text.

Jacques Cazotte is a good writer. This has been known since the publication of his small masterpiece, *Diable Amoureux*. He has now joined the current vogue for the East and for tales of fantasy by publishing four volumes of the Arabian stories of the "Thousand and One Nights". One of his predecessors, Antoine Galland, had in 1704 published parts of the tale, but Cazotte has sought to disguise the original manuscript completely, giving an even wider role to magic and benevolent spirits. For example, he tells the tale of a king of Syria who is terribly sad because he has no descendants. A magician, disguised as a repulsive creature, gives him a magic apple that will cure his sterility.

Thomas de Conway is named Governor

Port Louis, November 14

The main square of Port Louis was full of men in uniform this morning: d'Entrecasteaux wanted to honour his successor before the King's troops. The Comte Thomas de Conway has been named the Governor General of the French possessions beyond the Cape of Good Hope. The Pondicherry regiments and the men of the Welsh Infantry paraded before them after the ceremony. Conway then went to the government headquarters, where the magistrates of the Ile de France read out and confirmed his credentials as governor.

This Irish aristocrat, who is a former companion of La Fayette, has thus been placed at the head of the last French-held bastion in the Indian Ocean. However, his promotion has not surprised anyone: this soldier has been serving the King since he was twelve.

American land bargains lure the French

Paris, November

Land in the United States is being sold for only six livres per arpent, roughly an acre. This very interesting offer has been made by the Compagnie du Scioto, named after the tributary of the Ohio river, on whose banks the company has bought land in order to speculate in its resale value. Since the War of Independence, there has been great interest in America among the people of France. In these troubled times, it is wise to make good investments. A total of 50,000 arpents have already been sold. The agent of the company, an adventurer named Playfair, has, however, omitted telling the buyers that the firm's option on the land has just been cancelled because the first payments had not been made in time. Will the aspiring settlers ever see the land of their dreams, which is claimed to be "rich in fishing, has a tree that distils sugar, a bush that produces tallow, is free of wolves, foxes, lions and tigers", and where "a pair of pigs produces 100 offspring in three years"?

The many travellers coming from Europe disembark at New York, situated at the mouth of the Hudson River.

Politics bring chaos to the theatre

"The Cardinal of Lorraine blessing the Saint Bartholomew's Day killers". For Chénier, this historical event contains a lesson for the present.

Paris, November 4

There was a near riot tonight at the Nation theatre. The performance was loudly interrupted by both wild cheering and booing. It was more like being at a session of the Assembly, or a riot, than at a theatrical performance.

It was a young and hardly known playwright, Marie Joseph Chénier, who caused the uproar. His famous play, *Charles IX*, was being shown to the public. This verse tragedy lashes out against fanaticism and the bloody Saint Bartholomew's Day massacres, but another, although indirect, target of the play is Louis XVI's chronic weakness and his total submissiveness to his advisors. The veiled reference to a living monarch is clear enough to bring boos and screams of rage from the audience.

After the performance, Desmoulins, who liked the play, said that it would help the revolution more than the events that took place in October.

However, the uproar and the play's huge success are also due to the talent of the principal actor, Talma, who acted the difficult and unwanted title role to perfection. In turn violent or moving, his acting was greeted by a storm of applause when the final curtain fell.

A mayor for every single commune

Paris, November 12

The law must be applied. By a decree, the National Assembly has decided that the towns and rural parishes are from now on to have elected local councils. The move had been urgently needed as the countless revolutionary "communes" set up since July 14th. had to be recognised officially. They had replaced the elected "syndicates" in the villages, or the town authorities, usually designated by officials of the monarchy. The bodies were headed by former administrators and citizens chosen by the population. They are soon to be replaced by municipal councils, which are due to be elected between next January and March. Paris, however, will have a special system.

Dissent splits Belgian patriots

Breda, November

A row has erupted among conservatives and patriots. The committee of Breda, representing the leaders of patriots who have sought refuge in Holland, is now the scene of clashes. Conservatives, strong defenders of tradition, want power to be restored to the aristocracy and trade guilds. Their position is summed up in van der Noot's *Manifeste du Peuple Brabançon*. However, Vonck's democrats favour a constitutional monarchy, leaving the Emperor with the executive powers, but keeping the legislative powers within a single assembly elected by the provinces. Both sides disagree totally, but must remain allied to rid themselves of Austrian authority (→ Dec. 18).

Necker's loan plan does not succeed

Paris, November 14

A solution to the financial crisis is urgently needed! As the sale of property belonging to the clergy has still not started, some other means of finding funds must be found. Necker has come to the Assembly to ask for 170 million francs. The money could be loaned by the discount bank, which would then issue paper money worth 240 million francs in exchange for the new loan and the 70 million already owed, but Mirabeau is opposed to the plan: is the credit of the state to be submitted to the whims of a private bank with the authority to print money? He defeated the plan.

Polignac causes trouble again

Paris, November 11

Kicked out! The King really is a most demanding landlord. When he moved into the Tuileries, he forced all the tenants to leave right away. At the Tuileries, just as at the Louvre, the rooms have been rid of their unwelcome and troublesome guests. The Duchesse de Polignac is an example. She has now sought refuge in Rome, but when she was staying at the Tuileries the good duchess had insisted on repairs and improvements being carried out on "her" rooms. She also demanded that several paintings belonging to the royal collection be taken down. The keeper of the royal art collection, Hubert Robert, is firmly opposed to this.

The gorgeous Duchesse de Polignac, painted by Madame Vigée Lebrun.

Hérault de Séchelles exiled by his family

A fiery young aristocrat: Marie Jean Hérault de Séchelles.

Paris, November 3

Marie Jean is an unworthy son. At least, that is what all his family claim. This fiery young assistant public prosecutor has become an ardent revolutionary and shows utter contempt for his aristocratic background.

He spends his time preaching revolutionary ideas, even to his clients. Fortunately, parliament has seen to it that his holidays have been extended. This has given the family an excellent excuse to get him to leave town. If he refuses to obey, his funds will be cut off; but Marie Jean seems delighted with the punishment. He has gone to Strasbourg, a first stop on his road to exile in Switzerland.

Revolutionary tide wins support from English economist

London, November 4

Revolutionary ripples have crossed the English Channel. Several groups that had been set up to support American revolutionaries, but which had been dormant since that country's independence, are now resurfacing. At a meeting of one of these, the "Society of the Revolution", a young liberal economist, Robert Price, has spoken out in support of the latest events in Paris. He has called on his fellow citizens to follow the example set by France, which rid itself of despotism and "illuminated Europe".

Victims of royal imprisonment orders push for compensation

Paris, November

It is time to get rid of the worst abuse of the Ancien Régime: the sealed orders issued by the King to have unruly citizens jailed. The monarch has agreed to get rid of them and the National Assembly now wants damages paid to the victims of the system. A specially created committee has been inundated by demands for compensation and its members, Barère and the Comte de Castellane, are being kept busy. Advising them is an expert, Mirabeau, who boasts about the 54 sealed orders issued against his family, 17 of which were aimed at him! (→ Mar. 16, 90).

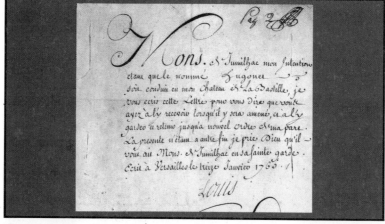

One of the countless sealed royal orders used by kings (Louis XV shown here) to have their subjects sent to prison.

Constituent Assembly

15. Grenoble. Seeing that he no longer has any control over events, it is now Mounier's turn to send his letter of resignation to the Constituent Assembly.

15. Le Mans. As the National Guard is swearing the oath of allegiance, three companies demand that the murderers of the Comte de Montesson be released. The move forces the patriotic committee to call in the dragoons to break up the gathering (→ Dec. 3, 89).

19. Paris. The National Assembly decides to set up an "Extraordinary Treasury" whose principal funds are to come from the sale of the church property.

20. Paris. The city's authorities charge the Baron de Besenval with the crime of outrage against the nation due to his attitude during the crisis of July 14th.

21. Paris. Lavoisier submits to the National Assembly the accounts of the discount bank, which has a deficit of 27.51 million livres. Six commissioners are named in a bid to draw up a recovery plan for the bank (→ Dec. 19, 89).

23. Rennes. Faced with an ever growing refusal to pay taxes in the countryside, the Provisional Committee bans gatherings and takes the farm administrators under its protection.

24. Paris. The bookseller Panckoucke publishes the *Moniteur*. He wants it to become the official record of the sessions of the Assembly.

26. Paris. The prosecutor of the Châtelet hears testimony by James de Rutledge, who was arrested for having offered a three million franc credit to bakers despite the fact that the town council is in charge of supplying Paris.

28. Paris. The journalist Camille Desmoulins, with financial support from La Fayette, sets up the *Révolutions de France et de Brabant.* →

29. Valence. In the village of Etoile, 12,600 National Guardsmen from the Dauphiné and the Vivarais celebrate the first Federation. →

30. Paris. The deputy Salicetti has Corsica decreed an integral part of the territory of France and gets a general amnesty for the combatants of the war of 1769.

National Guard pledges loyalty to Revolution

Valence, November 29

Unity is strength. Gathered at the village of Etoile, the 12,600 National Guardsmen of the Dauphiné and the Vivarais are set to defend the Revolution. Let no one doubt their resolve.

Behind this unprecedented gathering is that learned naturalist Faujas de Saint Fond. He had roused the men by saying that whoever stood against them would be betraying the homeland. The 118 delegates have all signed a commitment to "live in freedom" before swearing to be "loyal to the nation, to the law and to the King". This huge federation stems directly from events that took place a year ago: towns in Brittany, Ariège and the Rouergue had to join forces to fend off starving looters; but the movement in the Dauphiné is more than a simple imitation: through it, the nation has begun to feel that it is truly sovereign.

Crime flourishes in the streets of Paris

Paris, November

Con artists and criminals are doing extremely well in Paris. More and more often, people walking through the streets of the capital come across wandering gangs who are on the lookout for a new target. Nowadays, the criminals are the first to be pleased about the vogue for patriotic gifts. The naive citizen becomes an ideal prey for the troublemakers of the Halles or Courtille districts. It is enough to know how to ask a citizen to get a few coins that will not be donated to the nation.

If the unsuspecting client becomes a problem, a little violence can go a long way. People are roughed up or accused of being an enemy of the nation and soon hand over some money in the hope of being left alone.

But sometimes the criminals go even further and don't hesitate to grab earrings roughly — often with part of the unfortunate victim's ear still attached. If they still don't get what they're after, knives are pulled and blood is shed.

Rivarol: the King's good apostle

The "Actes des Apôtres": a firm stand against the Revolution.

Paris, November

Antoine de Rivarol, well kown in literary circles for his wit, is now making a reputation for himself thanks to his poisonous pen. Since the spring, he has been working on the highly monarchist *Journal Politique National*. He is now on the editorial team of the *Actes des Apôtres,* which has been appearing since the start of the month. This publication specialises in ridiculing the leaders and the institutions of the Revolution. This is done by using charades, anagrams and flowery compliments of doubtful taste. There is no physical handicap, no real or imagined marital problem that escapes the "apostles", who only respect the monarchy.

Sénac de Meilhan hosts a masked party

Paris, November

An aristocrat who is curious to know what is really going on in the streets of Paris and what the people are truly thinking can't really walk around the capital. He has to fall back on inviting to dinner the "owl" of Paris, Restif de La Bretonne; but it would not do to reveal one's true identity, one might appear to be too curious. Restif therefore attended a dinner party given by Sénac de Meilhan where not a single guest was showing his face. He found himself sitting next to a charming muslin merchant, who was in fact the Duchesse de Luynes. As for the man with a limp who was listening in closely to their conversation, why, he was none other than Monsieur de Talleyrand.

Panckoucke: the editorial baron

Charles Joseph Panckoucke, the founder of "Moniteur Universel".

Paris, November 24

Charles Joseph Panckoucke has been adding to his empire. Already known as the editor of the philosopher's *Encyclopédie* and of the magazine *Mercure de France,* he has just set up a newspaper, the *Gazette Nationale ou Moniteur Universel.* The neutrality of its title is a reflection of its basically informative content, for which Marcilly, a specialist of diplomacy, is responsible. Its large format helps the new publication stand out and allows it to print longer transcripts of debates at the Assembly, and more reports on the events in the capital or in the provinces, political and foreign news and literary criticism, than its competitors.

Gabriel Sénac de Meilhan, man of letters and administrator.

Desmoulins: the Revolution's voice

The "Revolutions of France": the monarchy not spared.

Paris, November 28

If Camille Desmoulins did not stutter, he would be a truly fearsome orator. His speech impediment has compromised a successful career as a lawyer. He therefore decided to start a career in journalism, which he considers to be a sort of public office. His *Révolutions de France et de Brabant,* for which he is practically the only writer, is a weekly pamphlet divided into three parts: France, Brabant and "other kingdoms wearing the cockade". It is not just in France and the Belgian lands that there are revolutionary rumblings and Desmoulins believes in its universal character. The first issue is extremely critical of the monarchy.

French patriots and partisans clash in papal states

Carpentras, November 25

The "French Party" has plenty of supporters in the papal estates. Interested by the reforms currently under way in France, these patriots have gone so far as to demand the outright annexation of the estates, but a proposal along these lines made by the deputy from Provence Bouche in the name of France's historic rights over Avignon and the Comtat Venaissin has just been blocked. The plan has brought a sharp reaction from the assembly of the Comtat. It asked Bouche why he did not listen to the will of the territory's majority.

Constituent Assembly

1. Grenoble. Publication of the first edition of *La Vedette des Alpes*, the newspaper of the patriotic society just set up on the initiative of patriots such as Amar and Réal.

1. Paris. A plan put forward by the Constitutional Committee to police associations and ban any numbering over 30 members enrages Mirabeau and the left wing of the National Assembly.

1. Toulon. Crew members of the fleet's ships revolt.→

3. Le Mans. The three murderers of the Comte de Montesson are executed amid rising tension. Dragoons are ordered to deploy throughout the town in case the people attempt to come to the condemned men's assistance.

3. Paris. The seascape painter Claude Joseph Vernet dies.

3. Dijon. The town's commune proposes a draft treaty of federation aimed at getting the decrees of the Assembly and the King's authority obeyed.

7. Paris. The court goes into mourning for a two month period following the death of Marie Anne de Lorraine, Marie Antoinette's sister and abbess of the chapter of Innsbruck.

8. Nîmes. An assembly of the town's Catholics meets to demand that religious establishments be maintained. This marks the start of a reactionary counter-offensive in religious politics.

9. Paris. The National Assembly decrees the principle of the division of France into departments (→22).

11. Paris. After the looting of the Bois de Boulogne and the Bois de Vincennes (→5), the Assembly decides to place forests, woods and trees under the protection of the nation.

13. Montélimar. A new federation is created forming 5,000 National Guardsmen.

14. Paris. The Assembly approves the law on a single municipal organisation which gets rid of the institutions of the Ancien Régime.

16. Paris. Augustin de Bétancourt y Molina submits to the Academy of Science a memorandum on two-stroke steam machines which he had seen in the Manchester workshop of the Scottish engineer James Watt.

Workshops for the unemployed

Paris, December 1

There are 100,000 people now unemployed and they are causing concern. To alleviate the problem, the city authorities have plans to set up charitable workshops where they can carry out jobs that are of use to the community. This ancient system that has been around as long as poverty has often been abandoned, but just as often restored, but the workshops are only open to workers who can prove that they live in Paris. The authorities don't want to see hordes of beggars and tramps rushing to the capital. The workers are formed into 100-strong groups and strict rules are in effect: their working day lasts from sunrise to sunset. There are four roll calls a day and complaints are forbidden.

"Poverty is not a vice," but *"a lazy youth leads to a hard old age".*

Peasants steal firewood from the Bois de Boulogne

Paris, December 5

It is terribly cold. Large numbers of peasants living outside the limits of the capital had no other choice but to cut dead branches off trees to use as firewood. The Bois de Boulogne and the Bois de Vincennes have been devastated by the freezing peasants. Faced with the extent of the damage to the two forests, the Commune has sent in a detachment of 400 National Guardsmen. In all, 57 looters have been arrested and sent to the Conciergerie. The real culprit is the icy weather.

The Assembly rejects a national army

Paris, December 12

Dubois Crancé has had to step down from the speaker's rostrum at the Assembly under a storm of shouting. This former musketeer of the King's Household was not able to persuade the deputies to support his plans for obligatory military service.

He had dared to say that the regular army is a "bunch of bandits". This sparked off cries of protest from several former officers who are now deputies. His plan for conscription is particularly ambitious, even though the parallel existence of the National Guard and the King's army is causing real problems. The National Guard had been formed spontaneously to protect the Assembly and the Revolution against the possibility of a counter attack by the aristocracy, which occupies all the higher ranks in the regular army. Although he felt that the new nation needed a

"We are also of the Third Estate," say the simple soldiers.

national army, Dubois Crancé has refused to fuse these two heterogeneous military groups into a single body. The time is not ripe for military reform (→July 29, 90).

The sailors of the port of Toulon munity

Toulon, December 1

The dismissal of two crew chiefs was enough to set the mutiny off. The squadron leader d'Albert de Rioms and several of his officers have been thrown into jail by the mutineers of the fleet.

Here and in other ports, workers at the arsenal, shopkeepers and small traders all remember the arrogance and the contempt shown by the noble-born officers. On the ships, subalterns and low-ranking officers whose promotion has been stopped by their birth, as well as seamen forced to endure the strict discipline, have all welcomed the political changes. The navy had for a long time remained untouched by the current unrest, unlike the army garrisons. Now the men refuse to obey orders. A crisis has hit the navy. Naval authorities have been taken by surprise by the new situation and are refusing to take even the slightest decision (→May 3, 90).

From this headland, the port of Toulon can be seen. Part of the French fleet shelters there. In all, the kingdom's fleet has nearly 14,000 cannons.

Marat is in trouble with the authorities

Paris, December 13

Marat is moving out. His biting pen had not been to everybody's taste. The court of the Châtelet has started legal action against him and he had to leave the committee of Carmes which had refused to give him its protection. He has placed himself under the protection of the Cordeliers district, presided over by Danton, who has offered him an office to publish his newspaper. The trouble started on October 8th. with a warrant for the detention of the *Ami du Peuple* pamphleteer. Marat had made the mistake of attacking Necker for "sacrificing the nation's happiness to bankers".

Victory for the Belgian patriots

Brussels, December 18

At last! The long-awaited day of the uprising has come. The exiles of Breda march through the capital, decorated with the national flag. An enthusiastic crowd has chased the governor out and proclaimed van der Noot "the father of the people of Brabant". After Turnhout, the Austrians had for a time forced the volunteers to go back to Holland, but they retook the offensive and marched on Bruges and Ghent, fanning the flames of revolt and freedom. The Austrians have given way. The patriots now also control the Limburg, Hainault and Namur regions (→ Dec. 11, 90).

Assignats: a new type of bond

The new assignats are "promised on the property of the clergy".

New-found fame brings its own rewards

Paris' "ladies of the Halle".

Paris, December 14

Why not take advantage of a new-found glory? That is precisely what Louise's father, Chabry, has been thinking. Louison, as she is known in the Halle district, was the shopkeeper who on the day of the march to Versailles had the honour of being received by the King and was so awed that she promptly fainted. Since then, the fishwives have been saying that she managed to get a tidy sum of money from the King. This morning, Chabry told the Commune's representatives that he had had to spend a lot of money to protect Louise from the gossip. Some form of repayment would be welcome ...

Give women a new deal, Assembly told

Paris, December

"From society's highest to its lowest levels, why is it that women, who are born to spread flowers on man's private life, only get torment and injustice from him in return?" The young woman who has come to ask the National Assembly this difficult question has asked not to be named.

But she said that she is "a wife and mother" and that her children are all boys. She is convinced that humanity cannot be truly happy as long as women are not given their rightful role in society. She has proposed that steps be taken to bring major improvements to the situation of women. In particular, she asks that young women without dowries should no longer be forced to remain single; that well-paid jobs usually reserved for men be made available to women; and that nuns without a true vocation be allowed to break their vows. She even demands that convents be scrapped.

"Gentlemen, in the name of my whole sex, who will not disagree with me, I am appealing to the tribunal of reason," she told the assembled parliamentarians.

But will the deputies take the trouble to listen to this moving appeal for equality and freedom, the two basic tenets of the Revolution that women want to share?

Paris, December 19

No solution has been found to the problem of the budget deficit. The National Assembly has now decided to create assignats, or promissory notes. Four hundred million francs worth of these bonds will be issued in denominations of 1,000 livres by a specially set up extraordinary treasury. Each assignat carries five per cent interest, and 170 million of them will be handed over to the discount bank to reimburse the money it advanced to the Treasury. The new state loan is an obligatory one which will help repay the national debt. The bonds are essentially to be used to pay for the nationalised church property. That will help convince creditors that a loan based on church property is bound to be a safe one.

Elegance costs a young woman her life

Grenoble, December 2

She was due to go out to the theatre with her husband after dinner, but all that remains of the young woman now are ashes.

The young wife of the prosecutor at the town's parliament has been burnt to death. She had been reading near a small metal stove that she had bought because she liked the fine tree, branch and leaf engravings on it.

Suddenly, as she was engrossed in her book, a spark leapt out and landed on a fold of her cotton dress. By the time she noticed the smell of burning, the dress was on fire and her muslin cloak was also alight. Panicking, she jumped from the sofa, desperately trying to undo her belt buckle and dress hooks, but her efforts were in vain. The heavy lined cloth could not be removed and she was quickly turned into a living torch. Her maid came rushing into the room, having been alerted by her mistress' screams. However, she too failed to tear off the fiery clothes and the young woman died a terrible death.

Constituent Assembly

22. Paris. The Constituent Assembly approves the decree on the reorganisation of the country's departments. Each will be headed by a council of 28 members, an eight-member directory and a prosecutor who will see that the law is applied. These will all be elected by active citizens (→Jan. 15, 90).

22. Paris. The city authorities decide to tear down the old Rouge bridge linking the Ile Saint Louis to the Ile de la Cité.

23. Paris. Abbot Charles de L'Epée dies. He had founded the institute for the deaf and dumb.

23. Paris. The Academy of Science approves the publication of *La Nouvelle Architecture Hydraulique* written by the engineer Marie Riche, Baron of Prony.

24. Paris. A decree from the Assembly allows non-Catholics to be candidates for elected office. The move affects Protestants, but no decision is taken regarding Jews, despite a speech in support of their case by Robespierre.→

24. Lille. A free performance of *Zaïre*, a tragedy by Voltaire, and of the *Retour Imprévu*, a comedy by Jean François Regnard, is given by soldiers of the garrison with the help of an actress of the Grand Théâtre, Mademoiselle Sainville.

26. Paris. The Comte de Provence appears before the assembly of the representatives of the Commune.→

27. Ile Bourbon. The inhabitants of Saint Denis demand that a single assembly be held for the island's whole colony.

29. Nantes. To reward the patriotism of its mayor, the town's authorities ask David to paint the portrait of Daniel Kervégan in exchange for a payment of 300 livres.

31. Paris. Louise Robert de Kéralio sets up the *Mercure National* with Carra, Masclet and Hagou de Basville. The paper will replace the *Journal d'Etat et du Citoyen*.

31. Bordeaux. Content with their status of second class citizens, the Portuguese Jews write to the Assembly to express their disagreement with the demands of the Jews of eastern France, saying that the latter could threaten the autonomy of their community.

French are unwelcome guests in Rome

Rome, December

The Revolution cannot justify everything! The people of Rome are starting to be fed up with the French living in their city, who are becoming more and more troublesome. Resident patriots or exiled refugees, students or princes, they have been causing problems and their growing numbers are worrying the authorities. More than 2,000 clergymen have had to be put up in the city's various convents and dioceses. Some of these, however, show their gratitude in strange ways: during the Holy Father's public prayer, they laugh openly when they see him kiss the feet of Saint Peter. The leading prelates have been behaving like courtiers, in particular Cardinal de Bernis, the French ambassador, who has seventy guests to dinner every day. The French ridicule the castrati at the theatre, complain that Rome's public baths are too expensive and its women too easy. As for those attending the Academy of France, they are supporters of the new revolutionary ideals.

The adventurer Cagliostro is chased by the Pope's police.

Pretending to defend freedom and equality, they cause arguments over nothing and are often in trouble with the papal police. Among these artists, one man in particular is being kept under close watch: the painter Augustin Belle, who is suspected of having loaned his studio to the adventurer Cagliostro for the purpose of holding orgies and witchcraft sessions.

An act of vengeance kills 23 people

The booby trapped house of the vengeance seeker kills many.

Senlis, December

Kicked out of the corps of the harquebusiers, the clock maker Billon has got his revenge. On December 13th., as his former companions paraded through the streets, he shot and killed their captain. Soldiers tried to detain the enraged man, but he had booby trapped his house and blew himself up, killing 23 people. His body was dragged from the rubble and stoned by the crowd. Despite his death, the court took legal action against Billon, whose corpse was sentenced to be left out for the crows. What remained of his house was razed to the ground and salt was spread on the land.

Segregation is over for Protestants

Paris, December 24

Protestants are now to be given the vote, on the same basis as Catholics. The decree that has just been approved also states that they can run for the public offices, either military or civilian, that have been created under the terms of the new Constitution. This new legislation, which makes Protestants equal to Catholics, was not opposed by the deputies of the clergy.

Since the Edict of Tolerance was promulgated in January 1788, the members of the country's Catholic majority had got used to the idea of Protestants being granted equal status.

Olympe de Gouges causes controversy

Paris, December 28

The audience is very restless this evening at the Théâtre de la Nation, where *L'Esclavage des Nègres*, a play by Olympe de Gouges, is being performed. Even before the curtain rose, there was unrest among the spectators, fuelled by agitators paid by the powerful anti-abolition coalition funded by the slave trade. Among the spectators, some are cheering wildly, while others are booing loudly. There is so much noise that a wit was heard to say that there should only be booing during the interval.

Olympe de Gouges, a woman of letters opposed to slavery.

David continues his fight against the Academy

Paris, December

Changes must be made. The fiery artist David, who has discovered that he has a talent for making speeches, has been lashing out at the Academy and its rigid, unchanging hierarchy. At the very top of the ladder, there is the body's director, then the vice-chancellors, the professors, the assistant professors and finally the councillors. All of these make up the group of the 52 officers. On a lower level, there are the 63 academicians, and finally, on the very last rung of the ladder, there are the candidates who have not yet submitted their required work for admittance.

David has already supported some who do not agree with the system. He is now writing a text with them. This proposes that the current structure be replaced by an egalitarian Fine Arts Society that would be "free and universal".

Actors are at last to become fully fledged citizens

Paris, December 24

Only a few short years ago, when comedians died their bodies were thrown into a common grave because they were said to have sold their souls to the Devil. The church and the monarchy kept actors out of the mainstream of society, but today the Assembly has shown its respect for them and recognised them. Thanks to strong action by Roederer, Robespierre and Clermont Tonnerre, and despite fierce opposition from Abbot Maury, a decree has confirmed actors' civil and military rights.

The King's brother denies being involved in the Favras plot

Paris, December 26

Paris is in turmoil! During the night, posters appeared on the walls accusing Monsieur, the brother of the King, of having plotted the escape of the royal family and the assassination of La Fayette and Bailly in order to be named regent of the kingdom.

The instigator of the plot, a certain Favras, allegedly a marquis and a former bodyguard of the prince, was arrested last night. To hire the manpower needed for the plan, Favras had gone to see the banker Chomel to ask for two million francs, but Chomel turned him in to the authorities. This morning there were rumours that Monsieur was about to be detained

at the Abbaye jail, but unexpectedly Monsieur himself showed up before members of the Commune, who were holding a special session. The room was packed. The prince, smiling calmly and soberly dressed, immediately won over the assembled officials.

He said in a sincere tone that the whole thing was simply a private affair. He had only wanted to get a loan to settle his personal expenses. "I did not see M. de Favras, I did not write to him and I have had no conversation with him," he said firmly. He ended his speech amid cheering by reiterating his total loyalty to the nation. "My feelings have never changed and they never will," he exclaimed (→ Feb. 19, 90).

Monsieur, the King's brother, is France's number two man.

Assembly deadlocked over role of Jews

Paris, December 24

The Assembly has been in session for the past four days, but has failed to reach any agreement. What is being debated is whether or not to allow non-Catholics, and especially Jews, to hold public office. Since the vote on the Declaration of human rights, which caused great expectations among the Jewish community, Jews have been sending a large number of requests to the Assembly asking for citizenship and civil rights, but most of them want to retain their own rights, language and religion. However, since the privileges of the orders and the provinces have been abolished, it seems difficult now to grant Jews what is being refused to the people of Brittany and Provence. Moreover, the deputies find they are caught on the horns of a dilemma: they are caught between the principles they have proclaimed and demands hostile to Jews contained in books of grievances. The Jewish

cause has been supported by Clermont Tonnerre, Custine and Robespierre, but to no avail. Robespierre had told the deputies: "Let us remember that it can never be politic, whatever one may say, to condemn a multitude of men living among us to oppression and degradation." Despite this, the Assembly has adjourned the debate. When will they finally solve the Jewish issue? (→Jan. 28, 90).

JEWISH COMMUNITIES IN 1790

- Ashkenazim
- Sephardim from Portugal
- Sephardim from the Papal States

Verdun · Metz · Paris · Nancy · Strasbourg · Bordeaux · Avignon · St Esprit (Bayonne) · Comtat Vénaissin

0   200 km

© Chronicle

A young patriot named Bonaparte

Ajaccio, December 27

The officer Bonaparte has understood that only the Revolution can free his island from French "occupation". He welcomed the abolition of privileges which made it impossible for lesser nobles like him to reach the higher ranks. However, he doesn't plan to make his career on the mainland. During a vacation spent at home, he was disappointed to find that Corsicans were still under the control of the royal administration. The Revolution has only encouraged the infighting between supporters of independence, who follow Paoli, and the pro-France party led by Salicetti. Bonaparte has chosen his side. He sent a message to the Constituent Assembly: "Take a look at our situation or we shall perish!" The first troubles on the island caused concern among deputies who, on November 30th., decided to integrate Corsica, an autonomous province, into the "French Empire". Bona-

Pascal Paoli, a strong supporter of Corsican independence.

parte has draped a banner over the family house saying "Long live the Nation, Long live Paoli, long live Mirabeau".

Restif calls for a new social order

Paris, December 21

Free medical care, a social welfare system with retirement benefits for workers, two rest days a week, free and obligatory schooling, a sewage system to keep the cities healthier: these ideas put forward by Restif de la Bretonne, who says they are those of an honest man, are truly revolutionary! After having proposed a land sharing plan in the

Andrographe, Restif today put forward, in the *Thesmographe,* plans for a general reform of social habits and laws, but the whole concept rests on the abolition of luxury, which he sees as the source of all evil. Although it was initially dedicated to the Estates General, this new work by Restif is intended for the "Federation of the United Nations of Europe".

Catholics urged to defend their religion

Poitou, late December

"Just one law, just one religion". This is the thrust of an anonymous Catholic pamphlet that has been handed out to the faithful in the main towns of western France.

The document comes at a time when there is likely to be growing concern over the Assembly's recent decisions. The Assembly has just proclaimed the freedom of religion

and given non-Catholics the right to be elected to all civilian posts. It is high time to react!

Quoting from Montesquieu at length, the author of the pamphlet criticises the Assembly's move. He warns his readers against the dangers of Revolutionary principles. Will his call to vigilance be heard by the nobles and the bourgeois it is meant for?

Year I of Liberty

The year 1788 ended with a council decision that disgusted noblemen and Parliament, but filled the rest of the kingdom with hope: the Third Estate would have a number of deputies equal to the number of the two privileged orders combined. One might conclude that there would be individual voting in the Estates General and hence that the Third Estate might be able to impose its solutions. The first effect of this measure was that the King, hailed as a benefactor, recovered his lost popularity. The year 1789 looked promising for him. He had recovered the capital of trust and prestige that he needed in relations with the Estates General, the calling of the latter into session came under promising auspices, and it would have taken a good prophet to foresee that before the end of the year, there would be a terrible revolution that would turn the political and social order upside-down.

Riots and violence

So France got down to work and the lists of grievances, aimed at informing the King of his people's wishes, were quickly drawn up. The wishes were unanimous in a rather general way, but passed over the subjects of friction, or even confrontation between the privileged classes and the rest of the nation. The election campaign and the elections themselves, which ended in April except in Paris, were marred by riots and violence. They were not the first such events in France, and the Ancien Régime had long been accustomed to these popular outbursts, but they now reached a scale explained by the excitement caused by hopes for a general consultation and by the severity of the economic and grain crisis that led to higher prices and misery, and the rising number of unemployed and vagabonds. Bread was short, and France rebelled. There were rumours that were unfounded, but hurt many: suppliers, helped by farmers of entitlement rights and municipalities, were hoarding grain and intentionally keeping food short. Granaries were looted, authorities came under attack, and one lord was assassinated in Provence. The frightened government, fearing that repression would worsen things, did not intervene. But could it have done so even if it had wanted to? All France had caught fire, there were too few troops to cover all regions, and the army was unreliable. Officers, and above all non-commissioned officers, were angry because of their blocked careers. Ordinary troops sympathised with the starving population. The situation in Paris was even tenser, despite the presence of the army and the authorities. The bread price was approaching a record high, to be reached in July, and the people crowded into the suburbs lived in misery. Anger grew, and riots broke out. On April 27th. and 28th., looting occurred in the Saint Antoine district. The Reveillon factory, a manufacturer wrongly accused of wanting to cut wages, was besieged and sacked, and horror soon succeeded this orgy of destruction. Security forces, attacked by looters who threw tiles and stones from the roof-tops and knocked down chimneys and eaves, suffered 12 killed and 80 injured, while the rioters had more than 200 casualties. It was among the Revolution's worst days from the casualty viewpoint

The opening of the Estates General

However, even though there were still outbreaks of anger here and there, things seemed to have quietened down. The Estates General were able to convene in Versailles on May 5th. in an atmosphere of apparent calm. The authorities were reassured. These was nothing about it to worry that Assembly, drawn from all France. It was composed of people with property and standing (the ordinary people were excluded), the élite of the royal administration and of its army, with a minority of representatives of the economic professions and of the bar, and it did not threaten the social order. There was, however, another threat: the deputies were divided by a barrier that some wanted to abolish and others to keep: the nobles' privileges. But the Court, ministers and the privileged classes still believed themselves strong enough to maintain them intact. The King's opening speech was characterised primarily by reluctance, and he spoke of the "exaggerated desire for innovation". Necker, considered by the Estates General as a genius whose skill would do away with all fears and open up great hopes, disappointed and worried them. He defended voting by orders, and indicated that the Estates General had not been convened to debate and make decisions, but simply to rubber-stamp decisions. The King had ordered each of the three orders to meet in its own chamber. This amounted to settling in advance the very question at issue. The Third Estate, a majority of the clergy and the liberal nobility wanted a single assembly, in which decisions would be made jointly with each deputy having one vote. But the dignitaries among the clergy and the majority of the nobility rejected this idea. Thus, the nobility, then the clergy, with some reluctance, went into separate session. The Third Estate avoided the trap. It waited. The reason was that it could hope for individual support from the moderate members of the nobility and the clergy, which would force the privileged orders to drop their resistance. But the Third Estate waited in vain, and as the threat of a royal move became stronger, it grew more urgent for the Third Estate to act. If it set up as a Chamber of Commons, would that not seal the division of the orders? Constituting a National Assembly would bring a royal response, and perhaps dissolution. The Third Estate decided on a bold course, called on the privileged orders to meet, began convening the bailiwicks and had the satisfaction of seeing some priests support it. It formed on June 15th. and claiming that it alone was entitled to represent France, called itself the National Assembly. To ward off dissolution, the Assembly prohibited tax collections if the authorities moved against it. The Court reacted hesitantly. Would dissolution not bring on civil war? There was support for the idea of a solemn session at which the King, surrounded by his soldiers, would state his will. Necker wanted Louis XVI to take advantage of the occasion to make some concessions, but the supporters of the Comte d'Artois, the sovereign's younger brother, who opposed any reforms, carried the day. While waiting for the royal session, which had been scheduled for June 23rd., the deputies of the Third Estate, prevented from sitting, met on the 20th. in the Jeu de Paume hall under the leadership of its oldest member, Bailly. It was determined not to yield to intimidation, and swore to remain in session until it could give France a constitution.

The royal session opened on the 23rd. Louis XVI made no promises and offered no hope, but he made a threat: if the Assembly disobeyed, it would be dissolved. And he ordered the three orders to separate and to go back into session the next day in their respective chambers. Thus the Third Estate's efforts had come to nothing, unless it resorted in turn to intimidation. It did. Inspired by Bailly and galvanised into action by Mirabeau's eloquence, it challenged the power structure to use force to try to make it give way. Would the King try this? The most nervous people advised him to do so, but Louis XVI was weak. He was hurt and depressed by the unpopularity he felt all around him. He preferred to yield, and Paris, the military, and all of France came to the Assembly's aid. On June 25th., the Parisian electors installed themselves in City Hall and decided to set up a "Bourgeois Guard". On June 27th., at the King's command, all of the members of the privileged orders rejoined the Third Estate, while power moved out into the streets. A riot freed some French Guards who had been jailed by their colonel in the Abbaye prison to punish them for disobedience. Unrest increased in the cities and the countryside. The day before, the King hastily ordered ten foreign regiments to move into Paris and Versailles. They were the only ones he fully trusted and they were headed by the Maréchal de Broglie, a level-headed soldier who always followed orders.

Necker's dismissal

The Assembly was a prisoner, watched by the army, and it felt threatened. Paris trembled, fearing a massacre and put all its hope in the Assembly. The Court was reassured by the presence of the regiments and was self-confident. The mistake came on July 11th. and the news reached Paris on the 12th.: Necker was dismissed and another cabinet was set up. The poor were worried because with Necker gone, there would be even less bread and it would be more expensive. People living on private incomes were afraid, thinking that bankruptcy was inevitable after Necker's removal. The Assembly feared for its very existence, seeing dissolution loom closer. Suddenly Paris caught fire. Some agitators at the Palais Royal, including Camille Desmoulins, proposed violent solutions, talked about arming themselves, and started organising what were still only disorderly demonstrations. At the same time, a parade of 6,000 men formed up on the Boulevard du Temple, marched to Vendôme Square and then on to the Tuileries, where it clashed with the Royal Dragoons Regiment. The latter had to withdraw, despite Swiss reinforcements, leaving the crowd victorious. Paris was already in the mob's hands.

The storming of the Bastille

When night came, the toll barriers were burned. The morning of the 13th. brought looting of houses suspected of having food stores. Oil, wine and wheat were taken from the cellars of Saint Lazare convent. Prisoners were freed from the jails. The fear of bread shortages was mingled with panic caused by the soldiers' presence and the political crisis that the Court had ushered in by dismissing the beloved minister. The Paris middle class was worried by the unrest and street violence. It decided to arm itself against both the royal troops and the risk to their property represented by the mobs. An organised militia of 48,000 men was set up. The stock exchange was closed. In spite of everything, Louis XVI did not yield. On the night of July 13th., there were rumours that 25,000 men were marching on Paris. Barricades immediately appeared in the streets, the militia went on alert, and the French Guards joined the Parisians. The morning of the 14th., the capital displayed all the signs of a city at war. Weapons were needed and people went to look for them at Hôtel des Invalides, which was captured without resistance, and then at the Bastille prison, which had large reserves of powder. The Saint Antoine suburb, helped by reinforcements from neighbouring districts, overcame the impregnable citadel, which surrendered after brief resistance. Even so, there were many casualties. The hated symbol of absolutism and arbitrary power had fallen, but this victory was not enough. The angry crowd, drunk with its victory, wanted more blood. It massacred the Bastille's governor, officers and soldiers, and for good measure the tradesmen's dean of the guild.

The King capitulates

The King was abandoned by his troops, who could have deserted at any time, and was no longer willing to act. Defeated, he went to the Assembly to announce the dismissal of the troops. Paris was still in a state of insurrection, despite the messages to it from the Assembly assuring the capital that the royal capitulation was complete. Parisians wanted more than mere words, demanding Necker's recall. Louis XVI no longer had any will of his own. He recalled the disgraced minister on the 16th. On the 17th., he placed himself under the Parisians' protection and confirmed their decisions and their victory. He approved the appointment of Bailly as mayor of Paris and that of La Fayette to head the National Guard. He was able to return to Versailles, but his palace now contained only the shadow of a king. The men who had advised him to resist realised his defeat, and theirs, so well that they began to leave the country immediately. What the Assembly had proved unable to obtain had been accomplished by insurrection, but this represented a terrible risk for the future. Would Paris not be tempted to resort to violence every time it felt it had grounds for discontent or wanted to counter the King or the Assembly?

The night of August 4

The first consequence of July 14th. was the abolition of the power of the King and of his representatives, while cities all over France organised themselves on the Paris model. The municipal revolution increased urban autonomy. The fears that had led to the capture of the Bastille persisted and a hunt was organised for hoarders due to widespread fears of bread shortages. There was also fear of robbers, criminals and vagabonds and a veritable panic spread through the land. This was the "Great Fear", a terrible outburst aimed at everybody suspected of being a supporter of the Ancien Régime. Castles were looted with a precise purpose: destruction of the records, the signs of feudalism ensuring the lords' control of the peasants. Property rights were threatened and the Assembly swung into action and decided to do away with feudalism. The night of August 4th. saw the abolition of all personal bondage, while seigneurial rights were made purchasable. All exemptions, privileges, inequalities and legal bars were done away with. Equality was proclaimed for taxes and punishments, government jobs were opened to all, the cities' and provinces' privileges were suppressed and the clergy's tithe was abolished. The people's revolt had given France a new face. The rural world was transformed and the church, deprived of its usual income, was soon to undergo thorough reorganisation. A start had been made to uniformity in the kingdom, and it was to be completed in the future by the establishment of departments. The Revolution brought on by the July crisis needed a consecration and that came on August 26th. with the Declaration of Human Rights, which proclaimed liberty, civil equality, and the principle of national sovereignty. The only thing left over from the Ancien Régime was a humiliated King and a decision still had to be made as to his place in the Constitution.

The King had executive powers. But was legislative power to be shared between the Assembly and the monarch, or should the latter be limited to approving legislation? The veto question came up on August 27th. The veto, meaning the King's right to accept or reject laws voted by the Assembly, was very unpopular. The Assembly, under pressure from the Press, clubs and the street, opted for a compromise solution that contained the seeds of future conflicts: the "suspensive veto", limited in time. While insufficient to ensure the authority of the executive, it was unpopular enough to compromise it.

October violence

The constitutional decrees did not need royal assent. The Assembly was categorical on this point. However, it made the mistake of sending them to the King for signature and he delayed his response. That was another error that was to have dramatic consequences. Since July, Paris had been in a state of continuous revolt, with some peaks of violence that culminated in October. This was due to the King's reluctance to sign the decrees, in days of violence that brought the Revolution temporarily to an end. A crisis atmosphere dominated, there were many unemployed, the bread price remained high and people in the trades were dissatisfied with their wages. At the end of August, Paris was threatened with food shortages and women besieged City Hall. In September, the agitation had spread to all of the ordinary people. A march on Versailles organised on August 30th. by one of the Palais Royal agitators, the Marquis de Saint Huruge, had failed, but in October the angry people were ready to act. There were rumours that the King was preparing to flee from Versailles. To defend itself, the Court called in a loyalist regiment. Its officers took the liberty of indulging in some provocations at a banquet on October 2nd. at which the King and the Queen appeared. Paris called this counter-revolution. Journalists seized on the event and Danton stirred up the districts. One slogan was widely heard: "Bring the King to Paris!"

On October 5th., some 6,000 to 7,000 women led by Maillard, one of the Bastille "victors", set off for Versailles, under good supervision from tested leaders. The National Guard, headed by La Fayette, also went there. It was a quiet night, but on the morning of the 6th., the palace was invaded, the Queen threatened, one young man killed and some bodyguards were beheaded. The King had to obey and return to Paris. He had now become a hostage and, installed in the Tuileries, he considered himself a prisoner. The Assembly, which had followed him, was still free, but would it always remain so? It might be feared that it would also fall into the rioters' hands. Some members, such as Lally and Mounier, fearing the future and believing that the "October days" marked the beginning of mob terror, gave up their seats and fled to the provinces or abroad, while others, such as Mirabeau, began drawing closer to the Court.

The Assembly had achieved its goals and was satisfied, so it no longer needed insurrection. Martial law was decreed, and steps were taken to ensure food supplies for the capital. The Constituents were then able to work on the major task they had set for themselves: drafting a constitution that would ensure peace and stable institutions for France. The year 1789 had experienced such profound upheavals that the kingdom had become almost unrecognisable, but it ended in a quiet mood. One could guess at more storms to come, but it was very difficult to tell just when.

Constituent Assembly

2. Grasse. Deeply upset by the death of his daughter, the painter Fragonard withdraws to his birthplace.

3. Languedoc. A royalist gathering is held at Pont Saint Esprit.

4. Paris. The *Cocarde Nationale*, a journal of correspondence of the kingdom's militias, is published.

4. Paris. The Théâtre de la Nation premieres *L'Honnête Criminel*, a drama written by Charles de Quingey, based on the story of a Protestant, Jean Fabre, who becomes a galley slave out of filial devotion.

4. Paris. A delegation of members of the Constituent Assembly goes to the King to ask him to calculate the amount of revenue that the state will spend on the upkeep of the royal household.

5. Strasbourg. Death of the organist and composer Philippe Schoenfeld.

5. Paris. The city of Bordeaux asks the Assembly to set a public holiday to commemorate July 14th. 1789.

7. Lyons. The local philanthropic society comes to the assistance of 25,000 poor people.

9. Paris. The parliament of Rennes having refused to register the decree ordering the suspension of the sovereign courts, the Assembly decides to forbid protesters to hold any public office.

9. Paris. The astronomer Pierre Méchain discovers the existence of a new comet in the constellation of the Ram.

9. Versailles. A crowd forces the local authorities to order a lowering of bread prices. →

10. Paris. A new auditorium of Monsieur's theatre is inaugurated at the Saint Germain fair. It is giving a performance of Paisiello's best known opera, *Il Barbiere di Seviglia*, based on the play by Beaumarchais.

12. Brussels. The proclamation of the "United Belgian States" confirms the victory won by the insurgents in the Austrian Netherlands (→Mar. 18, 90).

13. Paris. The Italian theatre premieres a new opera by Grétry, *Pierre le Grand*.

15. Paris. The Assembly rules that France will have 83 departments (→Feb. 26, 90).

Dauphin gets a patriotic New Year's gift

Versailles, January 1

When you are Louis XVI's son, you sometimes get some strange gifts. The Dauphin is still getting over his surprise. This morning, a unit of the National Guard solemnly gave him a game of dominoes carved out of stone taken from the Bastille. On the box, a patriot had carved some lines which he felt would be useful:

From these terrible dungeons, the terror of Frenchmen, you see what remains turned into a child's game. May it be a proof of your people's love and power as it serves for your childhood games.

The clear message is really meant for the prince's parents and the royal couple are not too happy about the gift. Not so long ago, Parisians had taken them to the Tuileries as virtual prisoners. The year is off to a bad start.

Ordinary people presenting their New Year wishes to the royal family.

Twelfth Night party at Danton's home

Paris, January 6

There is a party atmosphere at the Danton home. Guests are busy discussing local gossip or the latest events at the Comédie Française. Georges and Gabrielle Danton have gathered their friends Camille and Lucile Desmoulins, Louis Legendre as well as and Jean Paul Marat, around a good meal. When it is time for dessert, which has been proudly heralded by the lady of the house, the excitement rises. Today is the day that the Twelfth-night cake will be cut and passed around to see who finds the bean hidden inside. Georges cuts the cake and Legendre bites the bean. "Long live the King!" the guests shout as he drinks some mulled wine, but the women are worried that the cry will be heard by the neighbours and misinterpreted. "The Devil take me, but, by God, I have been at war with crowned heads for so long that nobody can misunderstand," cries Danton. Laughing, they all decide to go to Procope's café to end the evening.

Gambling becomes favourite pastime for the Parisians

Paris, January

Gambling and games of chance are everywhere, in the street or in the capital's estimated 4,000 gambling houses. Every night, as the sun sets, gamblers pull folding stools from under their coats and gather on the Quai Pelletier, the Boulevard du Temple or the Place Louis XV. When the money is gone, they rush to the mobile banks sponsored by the wealthy crockery merchant Souris. As soon as the gambler has found new funds, he goes to see "bulldogs", the touts who work for the bankers. Nobles play a game of "creps" with a former lackey of Madame du Barry's, while people from out of town who prefer court tennis meet at Madame Lafare's, where tea and cold food are served. Legislators play "trente et un" at the residence of a former actress, Madame Julien. Crooks go to the Radziwill hotel to play "passe dix", while servants prefer the Chocolat café, where they play dominoes. As for the poor, they play "biribi" at the Vertus, where benches can be used as beds.

Men and women of fashion really must be seen at the Palais Royal, one of the capital's most lively places.

La Fayette warns that unrest must cease

La Fayette manages to foil a plot hatched by some National Guard recruits and to restore order to the capital.

Paris, January

One of the main duties of the National Guard commander is to ensure that order reigns in the capital. Since early January, La Fayette has been kept informed about demonstrations that have broken out in various parts of Paris in support of demands for press freedom and the publication of even more papers. Fully aware of the danger, he has told the Assembly that unrest must be stopped before it goes any further, even if this means calling troops in. Is this one-time liberal, who welcomed the fall of the Bastille, going to remain a liberal? People say he is protecting the royal family and that his friendship with Necker is helping him at the court. Some even say power has gone to his head.

High price of bread causes new unrest

Versailles, January 9

For the past three days, there has been non-stop angry shouting and stone-throwing. The people of Versailles have been out on the streets to protest against the continuing rise in the price of bread. They are hungry and angry. This morning, they have gathered outside the city hall to demand the fixing of bread prices. Since the court and the deputies have left Versailles, the lackeys, artisans and innkeepers, who depended on them for a living, are in trouble. The mayor has promised to issue a decree that will set a fixed price for bread. He also wants to designate officials who will requisition grain to ensure that the markets are well stocked. He is hoping that his promises will be enough to calm the demonstrators, but if necessary he can always resort to force later.

The Nine Sisters' Masonic lodge wins new status as a national society

Paris, January

The nine Muses of mythology may have watched over the recent change in the status of the famous Masonic lodge that proudly bears their name.

The lodge of the Nine Sisters has just become a national society. It was always a special lodge. It was the Farmer General Helvétius who was the first to have the idea to set up an encyclopaedic lodge in which all the activities of the mind would be represented. After his death, his concept was carried out by his friend the astronomer Lalande. Since then the lodge includes men of letters, of science and a great many artists. The lodge's influence has spread well beyond the Masonic circles. It has focused primarily on spreading enlightenment by creating the Lycée, a sort of free university that numbers the King's brothers, the Comte de Provence and the Comte d'Artois, among its founders. Its other sphere of activity has centred on charitable works and the defence of innocents who have been unjustly condemned. The lodge has thus become a true heir of Voltaire, philosopher and tireless spokesman of the victims of injustice.

Théroigne gives up flirtation and goes into politics

Paris, January 10

The ravishing young Théroigne de Méricourt, a former lady of pleasure, has taken up the revolutionary cause.

She loves to wander around the capital to carry out her new political activities. Along with her friends, the doctor Lanthenas and the mathematician Romme, she has founded a new club called "The Friends of the Law". Its aim is to change the people's social habits and provide them with political know-how and information. She is convinced that there can be no lasting Revolution without a true education of the masses. Théroigne de Méricourt has managed to enrol about a dozen of her friends who share her ideals. The new club held its first meeting today. Coffee was served.

The decrees will be translated into regional dialects

Paris, January 14

The Assembly speaks French, but the people of Quimper speak Breton, those of Strasbourg speak Alsatian and those of the Aix region speak Provençal. How are the people of France to communicate and how can there be a truly nationwide civic education programme? Legislators are unhappy with a situation where half of France's citizens do not understand them, so they have approved a bill ordering that all their decrees be translated into the various regional dialects. Several translations will probably be necessary just for the Béarn region which has different local dialects. Some of the dialects used in the country are just oral ones. Something must be done, because a law common to all must be understandable by all.

This punch bowl of the India Company bears all the Masonic symbols used to lead the uninitiated layman to Wisdom and Enlightenment.

Constituent Assembly

17. Paris. A decree from the Assembly abolishes the royal administration of the water utility.

17. Saint Denis. The chemist Nicolas Leblanc sets up a factory to produce artificial soda, in association with the Duc d'Orléans.

18. Paris. The English traveller Arthur Young, who is sponsored by François Pierre Blin, attends a nighttime session of the Jacobins.

19. Pontivy. In session since January 15th., the Brittany youth renews its unity pact and swears to "live free or die". →

19. Brittany. Armed peasants spread out through the parish of Maure, looting castles as they go. The unrest hits several parishes of Brittany.

21. Paris. At the Constituent Assembly, Doctor Guillotin proposes a new method of executing criminals. It is a machine designed to cut off the condemned person's head as painlessly as possible. For his part, the Abbot Papin gets decrees approved stating that crime is a personal action and cannot be blamed on a guilty person's family.

22. Paris. The people of the district of the Cordeliers stop the authorities' attempts to arrest Jean Paul Marat. →

24. Brittany. At Yvignac, the dragoons of the Conti regiment kill 16 peasants who had been trying to set fire to the local castle.

24. Auvergne. The peasants of Allassac remove a bench reserved for the local lord and his family from their church.

25. Saumur. The population sets fire to toll barriers.

28. Saint Malo. About 1,000 National Guardsmen return with 80 prisoners after having restored order to the south of the region, where there had been an anti-nobility revolt.

28. Paris. The National Assembly decrees that the country's Sephardic Jews are to have the status of active citizens. →

29. Lyons. The National Guard, whose creation had been delayed due to opposition from the consulate, swears a civic oath.

31. Paris. As Mardi Gras nears, the city authorities ban masquerades and the wearing of masks.

Youths vow to "Live free or die!"

Pontivy, January 19

After Mass, Moreau, one of the leaders of the young patriots of Rennes, went up to the altar. He placed his sabre on the sacred stone and spoke these words: "We swear to remain united for ever by the links of the strongest brotherhood. At the first sign of danger, we swear that our armed ranks will rally to the cry of Live free or die!" The words aptly sum up what the 200 young National Guardsmen of Brittany and Angers feel. They have gathered at Pontivy to celebrate their federation. They are committed to the defence of the key ideals of the Revolution. These "strong defenders of freedom" have vowed to set the Revolution's "limits, correct its abuses and deliver it from the horrors of anarchy, a scourge that is a hundred times worse than despotism".

Parmentier watches over his ovens

Paris, January 16

For the past few days Antoine Parmentier, the chemist, has been worried about the security of his bakers' academy. In his laboratory he has been studying and testing flour made from potatoes. Every so often, a threatening crowd gathers outside warning that it will destroy everything. Parmentier has therefore sought protection from the National Guard: but will this be enough to overcome the prejudice against the potato? For the people of Paris, it is a disgusting object hardly worthy of being fed to pigs. They say it gives diseases and is being used in a plot to starve the people; but the potato has already become a staple in Lorraine.

The thieves of the Châtelet have kept their heads

Paris, January 26

From their dark prison cells Forget, Dubellet and Réville heave sighs of relief.

The three thieves have been sentenced to the galleys, but they are not to be hanged. On the night of December 20th. they had broken into the criminal records office at the Châtelet, near the guardroom, and stolen money and titles worth a total of 500,000 livres. Unfortunately, the alarm was given too soon and they were forced to flee. During the chase, the guards of the Châtelet arrested the most unlucky of the three robbers. They had little chance of getting away from justice as they had been caught red-handed.

Even the talents of the lawyer Vaudin were not enough to save them, so the desperate defence lawyers claimed that the police needed culprits and had planted gold in the pockets of the accused. It was all in vain. The court reprimanded Vaudin and sentenced the three to death. Fortunately for them, the Tournelle parliament reversed the sentence. They will be allowed to live.

Necker is a victim of the Inquisition

Valladolid, January

No one can escape the eagle eyes of the Spanish censors, not even a former minister — particularly when he has served France. The town's tribunal has ordered all the copies of Jacques Necker's *Observations sur la Religion* to be seized. These books, brought to Spain illegally, have been declared to be dangerous by the Inquisitors. They say the works contain new ideas that could sow the seeds of revolution. Since the events of July in France, the authorities of Madrid have been closely watching all goods and merchandise arriving across the border. They have given the order that any pamphlet or book containing a reference to the fall of the Bastille should be burnt. The authorities are even planning to expel any French national who does not have residence papers.

The Cordeliers fight to save Marat

Paris, January 22

"Let's stop them! Long live Danton! Save Marat!" The whole of the Cordeliers district is in an uproar since this morning.

The local inhabitants are firmly resolved to fight it out with the National Guard if they dare take one more step towards the house where Marat has sought refuge. The journalist is in trouble for having publicly attacked Necker in an article. The tribunal of the Châtelet has issued a warrant for his arrest and Marat has asked for Danton's protection. Danton wants to show that anyone who enters "his" territory must submit to "his" laws.

There is no question whatsoever of obeying an order that has not been confirmed by the Cordeliers. Danton remains determined to have his way, although he realises that resorting to violence is not the best way of getting what he wants. He has therefore asked the Assembly to try to settle the dispute. Will the deputies, who are usually so respectful of the laws, agree to play Danton's game? (→ Mar. 19)

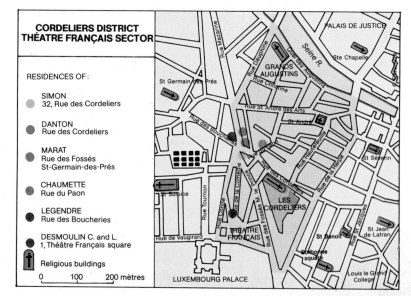

CORDELIERS DISTRICT
THÉÂTRE FRANÇAIS SECTOR

RESIDENCES OF:

SIMON
32, Rue des Cordeliers

DANTON
Rue des Cordeliers

MARAT
Rue des Fossés
St-Germain-des-Prés

CHAUMETTE
Rue du Paon

LEGENDRE
Rue des Boucheries

DESMOULIN C. and L.
1, Théâtre Français square

Religious buildings

0   100   200 mètres

Boos greet demand by Robespierre for universal suffrage

Paris, January 25

There has been uproar at the Assembly. Standing at the rostrum, Robespierre has demanded that the "silver marc" decree be abolished. This law means that only the rich are allowed to vote. The lawyer from Arras ended his speech amid a storm of insults and booing. The great majority of deputies have rejected universal suffrage and refused to be moved by Robespierre's calls in favour of "the defence of the interests of the people", but he knows that the people of the districts of Paris support him. His fellow deputies have not dared to reject his motion outright.

The Condorcet couple fall for the Revolution

Mme. de Condorcet hosts one of Paris' most brilliant "salons".

Paris, January

Like her husband, the charming Madame de Condorcet has become a real enthusiast for new ideas. It is in fact the only link remaining between the couple, who have a 20 year age difference. There was always more respect than love between the mischievous Sophie and the serious philosopher. It is said that their marriage was not consummated for a long time. At their residence in the Mint, many supporters of constitutional monarchy gather. These feel that the Assembly's programme is too moderate and would like to see more radical social reforms.

Constituent Assembly

1. Brittany. The militia of the village of Saint Péran, including its officers, takes part in the looting of neighbouring castles and parishes.

1. Paris. A new play by the Chevalier de Florian, *Le Bon Père,* is performed at the Italian theatre.

2. Paris. The school teacher Claude Dansart sets up the first ever mixed-sex Fraternal Society that is open to all citizens.

4. Paris. Louis XVI goes to the National Assembly to attend the ceremony of the swearing of the civic oath by the deputies. →

4. Paris. The sculptor Jean Antoine Houdon exhibits his latest work, a bust of Necker, at the city hall.

7. Lyons. The consulate is overthrown. The people and the National Guard unite to fight against the consulate's volunteers and force the consul, Imbert Colomès, to flee from the town. →

7. Jouey en Josas. The industrialist Christophe Oberkampf is elected mayor of the city, where he has set up his printed cloth factory. →

7. Aveyron. At Bournazel, the local peasants loot the castle following groundless rumours that the Assembly has ordered the residences of noblemen to be sacked.

8. Rouen. In a bid to help the poorest citizens, the town creates several charitable workshops which are financed by a special tax.

8. Paris. The Agasse brothers are executed for counterfeiting currency. →

8. Paris. The Jacobin society adopts its internal rules which have been submitted by Barnave. "Passive" citizens and women are not admitted.

9. Paris. The Abbot Grégoire informs the Assembly about the agrarian unrest that is rocking Brittany and the regions of Quercy, Périgord and Rouergue.

12. Paris. At the Théâtre de la Nation, *Louis XII Père du Peuple,* a verse tragedy written by Charles Philippe Ronsin, is performed for the first and last time.

13. Paris. A decree from the National Assembly bans monastic vows and abolishes contemplative religious orders. →

The King seeks to fool the Assembly

Paris, February 4

"I will maintain constitutional freedom." The King has spoken on Necker's advice. Speaking to parliament, Louis XVI is trying to pass himself off as a leader of the Revolution. The aristocrats present are amazed. Their surprise has helped to convince many of the King's sincerity, but Lameth is not the only deputy who is suspicious. Haven't some people been saying that the royal couple have been corresponding with Breteuil? He has emigrated to Brussels and is acting as a go-between for foreign courts. Breteuil, who is the former head of the "combat" ministry set up in July after Necker's dismissal, is the embodiment of the counter-revolution.

Louis XVI before the Assembly at the session of February 4th., 1790.

Sunday school starts lessons in civics

Paris, February 2

The artisans and merchants of the Saint Honoré district are to attend classes on Sunday evenings. A certain school teacher named Claude Dansart has just opened a new civics education society at the Capucins. There, people are taught to read and interpret the often complex decrees issued by the Assembly. It is a favourite course among women. So many of them have been attending that there are plans to call the group the Fraternal Society of both sexes. Despite the informal atmosphere, their teacher keeps an eye on discipline. A fatherly figure, he sometimes calls his students "my children". Also a practical man, he always has a candle, and the other night some of the students collected money to buy more of them so that they could burn the midnight oil.

The provinces take up arms: on February 7th., the patriots of Lyons armed with pikes looted the town's arsenal to find weapons.

The monastic vows are abolished

There are many temptations now that the orders are no more ...

The time for farewell hugs has come: a new life is starting for the former occupants of the monasteries that have been sold by the state.

Paris, February 13

It was a turbulent parliamentary session, but the decree has been approved. Monastic vows have been banned and regular congregations have been abolished. This means that their members will be able to leave them freely, simply by making a declaration to the local authorities. They will then receive a pension; but what is to become of those who wish to remain members? Those who belong to religious orders will by law be allowed to gather in a few monasteries. The nuns who so desire will be allowed to remain in their convents. This was the only concession that the clergy managed to get. During debates, clergymen had stressed that many establishments for nuns were not wealthy and that therefore their sale would not raise much money for the state. The move against monastic vows is directly linked to the nationalisation of the clergy's property. The deputies were very critical of the regular male orders, saying that they were of little use to society.

Oberkampf, mayor of Jouy en Josas

Jouy en Josas, February 7

Christophe Philippe Oberkampf has just been elected mayor of his village. Two of his clerks are assistant mayors and the 16 other members of the newly elected council are local worthies.

What a breakthrough for this Swiss immigrant who started off working in his family's printed cloth factory and has now set up a plant near Versailles. His cloth, bearing rural scenes, tinted blue, purple, red or black, soon became a commercial success. Oberkampf knew just when to increase production and hire more employees. Not only is he a smart businessman, he is also a good boss and a good patriot. He allowed his workers to take part in the procession marking the start of the Estates General and has been a generous contributor to the patriotic cause. His employees make up more than a third of the electors of Jouy en Josas, which may also explain why so many voted for him to become mayor.

Agasse brothers go to gallows amid tears

Paris, February 8

Two brothers, Augustin and Jean Baptiste Agasse, have just been hanged. The terrible sight moved the crowd to shout for mercy, while the prosecutor was crying and the condemned men fainted. Arrested on September 27th., the counterfeiters were unable to save themselves

After the hanging, the bodies of the Agasse brothers are handed back.

by their youth or by admitting their crime. On January 21st. they were sentenced to be hanged. The verdict immediately sparked off a wave of support for them. Their uncle, Pierre Agasse, who is the president of the Saint Honoré district, as well as all the members of his family, organised a demonstration at the district's assembly. The crowd, moved by the misfortune of the Agasse family, cheered them. A lieutenant of the National Guard resigned to offer his position to one of the brothers of the accused. Soon all of Paris was involved in the fate of the Agasse brothers. From the Récollets to the Sorbonne, and from Jussienne to the Cordeliers, the district assemblies have sent messages of support. Even commanders of the National Guard have shown solidarity with the parents of the condemned men. This morning, in a last desperate attempt to save the pair, children of the Agasse brothers' former school were sent to beg the King for clemency. Louis XVI was moved, but not sufficiently to save them.

14. Redon. Groups of angry peasants from neighbouring parishes set fire to the abbey.

14. Normandy. At Monts, the municipal elections are spread out over a week. This is because many of the inhabitants do not know how to read or write and bring in ballots which have been previously written on.

19. The Marquis de Favras is publicly executed on the Place de Grève. →

19. Paris. On the Champs Elysées, a pistol duel takes place between the Vicomte de Mirabeau and the patriot deputy Kervélégan. Neither of them is injured because both men are drunk.

20. Austria. The Emperor Joseph II dies in Vienna. His brother Leopold, Grand Duke of Tuscany, succeeds him. →

21. Dôle. Federation of the National Guards of the regions of eastern France: Alsace, Bourgogne and the Franche Comté.

22. Paris. The Théâtre de la Nation shows a first performance of a play written by Fabre d'Eglantine, *Le Philinte de Molière.*

23. Paris. The Constituent Assembly decides to reinstate the compulsory reading of decrees during sermons said in churches.

23. Paris. The Abbot Claude Fauchet says a funeral oration for Abbot de l'Epée at the church of Saint Etienne du Mont.

25. Paris. At the Jacobins, the deputy from Nantes, Mosneron de L'Aunay, asks that the slave trade be continued.

26. Paris. The Assembly gives a definitive ruling on the name, size and location of the 83 departments of France (→). At the same time, the Assembly votes for the abolition of mortmain, a remaining leftover from the days of serfdom in Franche Comté.

27. Paris. Departure for Switzerland of the deputy of the Vivarais region's nobility, the Comte d'Antraigues. He will be setting up an extremely active network of spies in southern France.

28. Paris. The Assemnly abolishes the military monopoly of the nobility, the only order to have access to the army's higher ranks.

France is split into 83 departments

Paris, February 26

To unify the kingdom's administrative districts, the Constituent Assembly has split the country into a total of 83 departments. The legislators had a tough job! For the past five months, the constitutional committee has been receiving several thousand petitions from all parts of the country. Provinces have asked that their traditional borders be respected. Towns have been competing with each other to become the new main departmental cities. Now all the newly created departments must be named. Names of major rivers and mountains are to be used.

This map shows the 83 departments created in 1790 and those of 1792.

Austrian Emperor dies at age of 49

Vienna, February 20

He was only 49 years old, but the death of the Austrian Emperor has not seemed to upset his subjects unduly. It is his brother Leopold, Grand Duke of Tuscany, who will succeed him. The change at the head of the empire has, however, deeply worried Marie Antoinette. She does not have the same friendly relations with her second brother as she had with Joseph, but, most of all, she has practically given up hope of seeing Austria intervene in her favour. Leopold is not in favour of the Franco-Austrian alliance being maintained. It was concluded on the eve of the Seven Years' War, in 1756. His country, threatened by Prussia, which has been plotting against him in Poland, Hungary, Turkey and the Netherlands, needs a trustworthy ally, but France is in the throes of political unrest and therefore not likely to be of much help. Also, the prince has not forgotten the trouble his brother had when negotiating with the French.

Joseph II, Emperor of Austria, embodied enlightened despotism.

Was Favras really the only culprit?

Paris, February 19

The Marquis de Favras was hanged by torchlight this evening. He died without revealing the names of his accomplices in the plot to help the King escape, and to kill La Fayette and Bailly, of which he was accused. Right until the end the condemned man believed that Monsieur would intervene to save him, because Favras claimed that he was only acting on Monsieur's behalf. When the journalist Suleau, who had been sent to see the Comte de Provence, returned around 8 p.m. saying "kiss your widow's friend", Favras realised that all was lost. As soon as Favras was dead, Talon, the officer in charge of the Châtelet prison, sent Monsieur a note saying: "He died but said nothing." Reassured, the prince is reported to have said to his friends: "Very well, we can sit down and eat heartily." Few people still believe that Monsieur was innocent. It is known that officers from his household had stood at the side of the condemned man to make sure that he said nothing. What about the two million francs borrowed by Monsieur from the banker Chomel? He swore it was all a private affair, but it is still a lot of money.

The Marquis de Favras is to be hanged. The execution satisfies the demands of the people and is a relief for many powerful men.

On Favras'death

A song about the last words of the Marquis de Favras:
Regrets are vain, no sighs for me,
For now my time is nearly o'er.
From my cares I'll soon be free
Ambition's dead, I hope no more.
Regrets are vain, no sighs for me,
For now my time is nearly o'er.
You seek a ready sacrifice,
And I the victim of your hate.
Pity Favras and his ill fate.
God, stretch forth thime arm
Save my poor soul from harm.
Citizens, I am innocent.
Care for my wife who weeps;
Now I must bear this punishment
That ends my brief years.
As you require my blood to flow,
I kneel to accept the fatal blow.

At Avignon, the consuls give up their positions

Avignon, February 22

A little shouting proved to have been enough to put an end to the Pope's secular power at Avignon. Could the pontiff continue to refuse to grant his subjects what the King of France was granting his? Tithes and feudal rights had already been abolished in the city. The National Guard and the spontaneously formed assembly of trade guilds were the only truly representative bodies at Avignon. Caught between obedience to Rome and pressure from the people, the council has agreed to approve a plan to reform the town's administration; but it is too late for reforms. Criticised by the trade guilds and booed by a few patriots, the consuls have had to give up their jobs (→ Apr. 14).

Théroigne scores a hit with the Cordeliers Club

Paris, February 27

Théroigne de Méricourt, the beautiful revolutionary, has been a big success at the Cordeliers club. She had gone there to propose that a palace for the Assembly be built of the spot where the Bastille had stood — a palace, or rather a basilica to honour the body responsible for the Declaration of human rights. Amid the cries of support, a voice was heard to shout: "She is the Queen of Sheba who has come to see the Solomon of the districts." A committee was set up right away to study the grandiose plan, but, unfortunately for Théroigne, her suggestion that she be allowed to join the club was greeted with less enthusiasm. Women are not welcome at the Cordeliers!

5. Paris. The Assembly orders the *Red Book* to be published. It contains details of royal pensions and gratuities.

8. Paris. A decree from the Assembly allows slavery to continue and orders the creation of colonial assemblies.→

13. Nantes. A total of 130 members of the Soleil reading association write to Jean Pierre Brissot to cancel their subscription to his newspaper, *Le Patriote Français*, which called for slavery to be abandoned.

15. Paris. Acting on a report from Merlin de Douai, the Assembly approves a decree abolishing seigneurial rights that are suspected of having been usurped or acquired through violence. No compensation is to be paid for them. The Assembly also rules that property rents, such as the champart and the feudal quit-rent, must be bought back.

16. Paris. An Assembly decree abolishes sealed royal orders.

17. Paris. Deputies decree that the church and domanial property will be put on sale by local athorities, who will be allowed to buy them.

20. Paris. A special delegation from Brittany and Anjou is admitted to the Assembly and proposes that all Frenchmen be asked to form federations.

21. Paris. The Constituent Assembly abolishes the salt tax.→

26. Nantes. The painter David, asked by the town council to do a portrait of its mayor, Kervégan, makes a triumphant arrival.

26. Algiers. A peace treaty is signed between France and the Dey of Algiers (→ Apr. 4, 90).

29. Paris. The secretary of the Queen's commandments, Jacques Mathieu Augeard, arrested for plotting, is acquitted by the Châtelet, which does not want the Queen involved in a trial.

29. Rome. During a consistory, Pope Pius VI criticises the Constituent Assembly's policy on the Catholic Church, but decides not to have his statement made public (→ July 23, 90).

31. Dauphiné. An agent of the Comte d'Artois, the Chevalier Henri Bonne Savardin, is arrested at the Bonvoisin bridge as he tries to cross into Savoie.

The Assembly votes for slavery to continue in France's colonies

Paris, March 8

The main demand made by the white colonial settlers has just been met. The decree that was approved today by the deputies has everything to please them: they are granted the right to hold colonial assemblies; but this crucial vote goes even further. It recognises the existence of slavery in the colonies. The fact that the text was approved without a debate shows that the Assembly is unanimous on the issue. The "Friends of the Black Man", who until recently were in favour of blacks' emancipation, have gradually toned down their position. By being silent, they seem to have joined the white settlers' side, but in fact they are waiting to defend the rights of the freed blacks and mulattoes who are not mentioned in the decree. However, they have taken note of the petitions sent by the coastal towns in favour of the status quo in the American islands. So far, none of them is yet prepared to support a policy that would harm the highly lucrative slave trade.

Freedom has not yet come for the slaves in France's colonies.

Mirabeau offers his services to the Court

Paris, March

Could the Comte de Mirabeau really be a secret schemer consumed by personal ambition? This noble-born man is a Third Estate deputy, a close friend of the Duc d'Orléans, a member of the Society of Friends of the Black Man, who in public makes his ideals plain to see. Despite all this, he also seeks to ingratiate himself with the King. In these troubled times, he may be trying to get an official posting. The King seems quite prepared to listen to his advice. Louis XVI had asked the Comte Mercy d'Argenteau, councillor to the Queen and the Austrian ambassador to Paris, to try to find out what Mirabeau's exact plans are. The latter quickly agreed to the apparent royal offer. It would seem to fit in with his plans to become prime minister. The deputy from Provence makes no secret of the fact that he would grant the King wide-ranging executive powers in a future constitution. He also vows to serve the monarchy loyally as long as he does not have to renounce his principles. The secret meetings are continuing. All that remains is to agree on the financial details and it looks as if that won't take long (→ May 22).

The King rejects an escape plan

Paris, March

Louis XVI has preferred to continue playing the game of whist with his family in the royal apartments at the Tuileries. He has just lost an opportunity, offered by the Comte d'Inisdal, to trick his guards and at last escape from his Paris "jail". When Monsieur Campan came to tell him that everything was ready and that he only had to agree to escape, the King hesitated and said simply: "Tell Monsieur d'Inisdal that I cannot agree to being kidnapped."

Journal launched to help doctors

Paris, March 5

Is your patient suffering from "congenital leprosy"? Treat him with mercury, sulphur and mallow mixed with rhubarb, cocoa butter and liquorice, says a specialist from Vienna.

But where can such valuable information be found? One such source is the first edition of the *Ephemerides*, published by the surgeons Lassus and Pelletan. This bimonthly publication is basically meant for practising physicians and it is the first of its kind. Its learned readers will be provided with a great number of clinical observations and details on the most efficient medication. They will be given information on how to diagnose ailments and, for example, on how to use the highly effective anti-venereal virtues of the plant *astragalus*.

Deaf and dumb orphans saved by state

Paris, March

The 50 orphans who had been cared for by the Abbot de l'Epée will not be abandoned. In the name of the state, the Academicians La

The Abbot de l'Epée had begun without any financial help.

Harpe and Marmontel have been requested to find a successor for the man who had been as much of a father as a teacher to his students. Before l'Epée, apart from some attempts to help the children of aristocrats, nothing had been done to aid children born deaf. People believed that it was no use trying to teach them anything, and they were condemned to a life of near-total isolation. By setting up an establishment open to all in 1756, Charles Michel de l'Epée proved that it need not be so. He rejected the lengthy teaching of speech or lip reading and focused on sign language, which he saw as the only natural way for deaf children to express themselves. He taught his students French by finding a hand sign for each word. The excellent results he achieved led to a visit by the King and royal funds. His most faithful disciple, the Abbot Sicard, is now likely to succeed him.

Tricoloured scarf for the officials of the city

Paris, March 20

French mayors and city officials will be given a new sign of office. A decree orders them to wrap a scarf bearing the nation's three colours around their waists when they carry out their duties. The knotted scarf will have a yellow fringe when worn by a mayor, a white one for his assistants and a purple one for the public prosecutor.

In every village of France, the national colours are now on show each time a ceremony is held.

Belgian democrats suffer a bloody defeat by mobs

Brussels, March 18

For the past three days, terror has ruled the streets of the city. At every crossroads, at the inns and in the town's basements, there are enraged mobs hunting for democrats, who are killed as soon as they are found. These "enemies of the Constitution and of religion must be strung up from lamp posts!" The clergy and some conservative members of the Estates have told the people to get on with the dirty work of getting rid of every one of the supporters of Vonck, the leader of the patriotic democrats. Their influence had been dwindling since January 11th., when the Constitution of the Belgian States had maintained the supremacy and privileges of the Estates and confirmed the principle of federalism. These concepts are favourites of the conservatives, but have caused the democrats to reject the new Constitution. On March 9th., the patriotic armed forces came out in support of the democrats and refused to take the oath of loyalty. Aware of the growing danger, the conservatives then resolved to take action.

The "Amazons" are insulted by soldiers

Aunay en Poitou, March 18

During a solemn ceremony held this morning, the town council heard the oath of allegiance of the "National Amazons", a sort of women's militia set up by the ladies of the city. They have sworn to remain faithful to the nation, to the law, to the King, and even, according to some wits, to their husbands and lovers. They then went to the church to have their flag blessed. They had made it themselves; but some soldiers, no doubt jealous that women were trying to compete with them, "plotted against the ladies' flag and their skirts". The flag was unharmed, but some skirts were damaged.

"We can handle weapons other than the needle and the spindle."

It can be risky to speak ill of deputies

Paris, March 17

One should know when to hold one's tongue: a Dutch sailor now has all the time in the world to meditate on this saying that he should have known. The unfortunate sailor, Curé, has been forced to kneel since this morning outside Notre Dame carrying a heavy Bible in each hand. Bareheaded and barefoot, he has been ordered to remain in this uncomfortable position for three days and will be whipped before spending the rest of his days working on the King's galleys. The court of the Châtelet has found him guilty of having spread insults about the Assembly as well as ugly rumours about the Revolution in the ports of western France, where his frigate had docked. The judges have been severe with this foreigner who had dared upset people and criticise new ideas.

Etiquette guide for revolutionary times

Paris, March

Despite the Revolution, some basic principles must be kept. Just because everybody is now dressing and speaking with considerably less formality than before, there is still such a thing as a proper way to behave.

At least, that is what an anonymous reader has just written to the *Cabinet des Modes et du Goût*. In today's civilised society, truly well brought up people should greet each other with bare hands. The doffing of hats is frowned upon, as they are ridiculous accessories left over from feudal times. One shows respect to a lady by covering one's face with a hand. Esteem for a lady is shown by placing several fingers in front of one's mouth before letting one's arm drop.

But to express a somewhat more tender feeling, the best way is to place one's fist as close as possible to one's heart. Last but not least, people should really learn how to bow more gracefully: men should avoid scraping the ground with their feet and women should not have to dip so low when they curtsey as this really is not very dignified.

Ladies, this is what is in fashion for the month of March 1790...

France's textile industry is booming

The textile industry is progressing rapidly. At the Duc d'Orléans' factory, in Montargis, steam powered machines work day and night to unroll 6,000 spools and they can weave 1,000 pounds of cotton over a 24 hour period. At Lyons, silk is spun using an industrial process in buildings that are several storeys high. In Alsace, the Dolfuss family has been enlarging its factories. In a cloth factory at Angers, 43 looms have been set up in the same workshop so that productivity is increased and it is easier to keep an eye on the work force. The poor peasants of western France, who used to do some weaving to get some extra money, have had to adapt to the progress. A cloth mill inspector has reported that there are more and more small weaving plants in the Normandy region. These are known as "jennys". Apart from lace made at Puy and Alençon, traditional textile craftsmanship nowadays seems to be a thing of the past.

Textile workers glazing cloth that has been roller-printed.

Mme. Vigée Lebrun is a hit with the artists of Rome

Rome, March

The life of a painter is not always a particularly restful one. As Madame Vigée Lebrun was recently painting the young Miss Pitt in the role of Hebe surrounded by clouds and giving something to drink to Jupiter's eagle, the ungrateful bird attacked her and gave her a bad fright.

Ever since she arrived in Rome, the famous artist has been working busily, as she has received a large number of orders for paintings. She started off with a self portrait that had been requested by the Duke of Tuscany. The painting shows her holding a palette while drawing Marie Antoinette's features.

The young artist has taken advantage of her stay in Rome to visit the ancient city's many monuments and museums. She prefers to do her sightseeing alone in order not to be disturbed when contemplating the beautiful works of art. Despite the huge success she is having in Italy, where she is already famous, she worries continuously about the situation in Paris, which she left in a hurry on October 5th. and where so many of her friends have stayed behind.

Badly frightened by the growing unrest in France and by the personal attacks against her, she chose to run away to Italy with her daughter, taking only a very small amount of money along. However, she is fully aware of the fact that she can easily make a good living out of her talent wherever she goes.

Mme. Vigée Lebrun has shown herself as she paints the Queen.

Ancien Régime's abuses are over

Paris, March 21

The Ancien Régime is well and truly dead! The three decrees that have just been approved by the Assembly mark the old system's end. Today, the abolition of the salt tax marked the end of an outdated system that cut the country up into as many regions as there were different tax rates on salt. This decree comes after the one approved on March 16th., which destroyed a symbol of the arbitrary exercise of royal power: sealed royal orders. On March 15th., the deputies also ruled for the equality of death duties. The "privilege of masculinity" and the law of primogeniture, upon which depended the death duties of nobles and of the commoners of Normandy and the Béarn, have been abolished. On the same day, the Assembly approved the law on the abolition of seigneurial rights. This had been agreed in principle on the night of August 4th., with the abolition of privileges, but what remained was to define which rights would be abolished without compensation and which would be purchased. The Committee of Feudal Rights led by the lawyer Tronchet is to handle this hard task. Rights considered to be "personal" will be abolished without compensation. These include mortmain, hunting rights and the right of banality. All others are assumed to be legitimate and the law states that peasants have to buy them back from the local lord, even if the rights are not being exercised, but most of them can't afford them, so the law seems to be a backward step (→ May 3).

A Protestant is to head the Assembly

The priest Jean Paul Rabaut de Saint Etienne, deputy of Nîmes.

Paris, March 15

It is a great honour for Jean Paul Rabaut Saint Etienne, a Protestant, to have been chosen to preside over the Assembly. Fourteen months after the Edict of Tolerance was registered by the parliament, the choice is a sign of the changing times. According to the rules currently in effect at the Assembly, the deputy from Nîmes will only remain in his new post for two weeks, but there have been strong reactions to his nomination. The Catholic party had done its best to block the election of this minister's son, even though he is a firm supporter of the monarchy. In his home town, insulting posters have appeared on the walls attacking the "infamous Assembly" that has just "put a final touch to its evil deeds". Worse, four Protestants have been killed.

Danton clashes with the court

Danton, a rousing speaker, is a scourge of all moderates.

Paris, March 19

It is a turning point in the battle: the Cordeliers have scored a point in their clash with the tribunal of the Châtelet. Their special assembly met and agreed on an extremely violent text rejecting the arrest warrant issued two days ago against Danton. On January 22nd., Danton had loudly spoken out on behalf of Marat, in violation of the court's ruling. Sent to the Assembly, the text issued by the Cordeliers district compares the legal tactics being used to an "attack" and proclaims that each citizen is inviolable because he represents part of the national sovereignty. The text has greatly impressed the other districts, which see it as a symbol of their opposition to city hall. As for Danton, he is turning out to be one of the capital's best agitators.

Robespierre leads the Jacobins

Robespierre has an amazing ability to persuade his listeners.

Paris, March 31

The deputy from Arras has just been elected the new president of the Jacobins Club. This group used to call itself the Society of the Friends of the Constitution. It owes its new name to the Jacobin convent on the Rue Saint Honoré, which it moved to in late November. This group is a successor to the Breton Club which had been founded at Versailles shortly before the opening session of the Estates General by the deputies of the Third Estate from Brittany. Robespierre has been a member ever since then, along with the Lameth brothers, Mirabeau, the Abbot Grégoire and Pétion. He spends most of his evenings now speaking at the club, in a small room that is more appropriate for his weak voice that the large hall at the Assembly.

Constituent Assembly

1. Paris. As the King has traditionally done on Maundy Thursday, Louis XVI welcomes 12 poor people at the Tuileries, washes their feet and serves them food.

3. Paris. The Assembly abolishes the commercial monopoly held by the Compagnie des Indes Orientales.

6. Nîmes. Clashes break out between Protestants and Catholics, who have been manipulated by agents acting on behalf of the Comte d'Artois (→ 20).

7. Paris. Marie Antoinette attends the First Communion of Madame, the King's daughter, at the church of Saint Germain l'Auxerrois.

9. Paris. The Assembly decides to consolidate the assignat rate by changing the clergy's debts into national debts (→ 17).

12. Paris. The new auditorium of the Montansier theatre, at the Palais Royal, is inaugurated.

14. Paris. Following the Assembly's refusal to declare that Catholicism is the state religion, as had been proposed by Dom Gerle two days ago, the right wing deputies walk out of the chamber. The remaining two thirds of the Assembly vote to approve the decree giving the state control over the expenses of the Catholic Church.

16. Paris. An anti-Jewish campaign in Alsace forces the Constituent Assembly once again to place the Jews of Alsace under its protection (→ May 90).

16. Paris. The Théâtre de la Nation shows a performance of a comedy by Pierre Laujon, *Fruits du Caractère et de l'Education.* The play only has roles for women.

17. Paris. The assignats become legal tender, but their use is not made compulsory. They bear an interest rate of three per cent. →

27. Paris. The Society of Friends of the Rights of Man and of the Citizen is founded at the Cordeliers.

29. Paris. The National Assembly allows military personnel to attend meetings of popular Societies if they go unarmed and not while they are on duty.

30. Paris. The Constituent Assembly decrees that juries will sit in criminal cases.

Has the Duchesse d'Orléans also been unfaithful?

London, April

The husband, the wife and the mistress. Until now, this love triangle had worked for Philippe d'Orléans. Did his wife ever so much as breathe a word of complaint about all his mistresses? However, a scurrilous pamphlet is being handed out in London. The document, entitled *La faction d'Orléans la Mieux Dévoilée*, warns Philippe that he has a new factor to take into account: a lover, named as the Comte de Ségur. His wife Marie Louise Adelaïde is supposed to be having an affair with the man. As for the author of the pamphlet, people are saying it is the Duc's ex-mistress, Madame de Genlis. What a complex situation!

Portrait of the Duchesse d'Orléans.

Papal Legate is taken hostage

Avignon, April 14

The Deputy Legate of the Pope, Casoni, has been overtaken by events. The last Papal representative at Avignon has had no instructions from Rome and has been signing all the decrees submitted to him to gain time. When he refused to agree to the adoption of the French Constitution in the Papal estates and to recognise the new town council, he was forced to go ahead. Since he has been under suspicion of wanting to flee, he has been locked up in his palace by patriots.

The "Red Book's" secrets are revealed

Paris, April 7

The mystery has now become a scandal. Since the Assembly had given the order on September 28th., everyone had been waiting impatiently for the publication of details of royal pensions, allowances and gifts. Camus, the president of the pensions committee, had been hinting that the King had been handing out secret funds that were only recorded in a mysterious account book known as the "Red Book". Despite efforts undertaken by Necker to stop it becoming public, the document has just been published. It has revealed to careful readers that since the start of his reign the King's secret expenses have totalled 228 million francs, but what has really shocked the deputies is that the money was spent using the procedure known as "cash orders". This means it was impossible to have any control over the money. The King's favours, which were notably granted to his brothers, are only a tiny part of the 100 million francs given away each year without any form of control. Where has

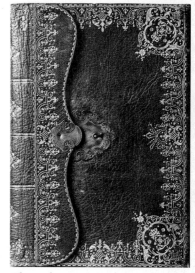

The infamous "Red Book" listing the gifts given by the King.

the rest of the money gone? Where is the illicit fund? Necker tried to explain that the accounts were secret not because they were in any way suspect, but because they were confidential. The matter has not helped the little credibility that Necker still had.

Luxury and lust go hand in hand

Paris, April

Do certain social habits really change all that much with the times? Not really. One only has to take at look at the private rooms of some of Paris' courtesans. Hidden away behind heavy velvet drapes, they seem to have an aversion to sunlight and spend all their time in private with their lovers. Sexually frustrated noblewomen and ladies of less noble birth all pay a great deal of attention to their looks. The boudoirs have become the centres of their lives, places where they spend endless hours looking at themselves in mirrors. They toy with the latest exotic perfumes and debate which part of their anatomy to place false beauty spots on.

The libertine theme used for "La Gimblette", an engraving by Bertony in the style of Fragonard, was often used by artists.

Measures taken against the clergy spark fresh clashes in the provinces

Nîmes, April 20

Is there to be a new War of Religion in the Languedoc? At first, the Revolution had brought the Catholic and Protestant churches of Nîmes closer together, but the fight for power in the town council, where Protestant patriots and Catholic conservatives have clashed, has renewed ancient hatreds. Decrees issued against the Catholic Church by the Constituent Assembly have been a last straw for the region. The Catholic people of the poor neighbourhoods, who are being helped by the town's parishes, are upset. Taking advantage of the situation, François Froment, a royalist agitator, has called on the Catholics today, Sunday, to gather

at the church of the Pénitents. He reads out a statement which he intends to send to the Assembly demanding that the "Catholic, apostolic and Roman religion be decreed to be the state's religion". He also demands that the "whole extent" of the King's executive powers be restored to him. His petition has been signed by 3,000 people. This former tax collector for the royal lands plans to start a revolt in the south of France. He has gone to Turin to convince the Comte d'Artois that "if the princes were to arm the supporters of the altar and the throne and get the interests of royalty and religion marching side by side, it would be easy to save both" (→May 1).

Church and state row rocks Assembly

Paris, April 13

The issue of religion has once again rocked the Assembly. Dom Gerle, a Carthusian monk, yesterday spoke out against the attacks launched by the Catholic party, which has accused the new regime of being anti-clerical. After having cried out "To say that the Assembly does not want religion is a calumny!" this deputy from the Auvergne, who is affiliated to the Jacobins Club, put forward an amazing motion. Amid cheers from the right wing, he asked deputies to

decree that "the Catholic, apostolic and Roman faith is, and will always remain, the religion of the nation and it will be the only one that can be legally practised". The astounded deputies have had the vote postponed. Dom Gerle today finally withdrew his motion amid an uproar. The Duc de La Rochefoucauld could only restore order in the chamber by proposing a compromise motion: the church must settle its own problems and the state must not get involved in religious issues (→Apr. 14).

Battle rages over the Paris commune

Paris, April 27

There was a lot at stake and the debating was tough. The members of the provisional commune have tried to hammer out definitive plans for the capital's council. The supporters of law and order are wary of the people of Paris who have shown they are always ready to rise up if necessary. They are attempting to set up solid central institutions that would be capable of coping with localised unrest. They also want to scrap the districts. On the other hand, democrats believe that the population should always actively participate in city affairs if the Revolution is to survive. They have sided with the districts. Since last summer, the districts have been fiercely demanding

their autonomy from the commune. Marat, openly hated by the mayor, Bailly, and Danton are now the districts' spokesmen, but Danton is in a difficult position: he is both president of the Cordeliers district and a member of the city hall.

Robespierre's membership card of the Cordeliers Club.

A century of Franco-Algerian peace

Algiers, with its casbah built on the heights and its fortifications that protect the port, where the fast feluccas of the Barbary pirates anchor.

Algiers, April 4

The hundred year old treaty of peace between France and Algeria has just been renewed. Under the new pact, which is to last until 1890, the Algiers Regency has guaranteed the security of French shipping and citizens in the Mediterranean. In exchange, the French royal navy will protect Algerian

corsairs. It is hoped that the treaty will ensure that relations between the two countries remain trouble free. The pact has pleased the shipowners of Marseilles and the merchant firm Compagnie d'Afrique, which has a monopoly over the coral trade. Talks lasted 18 months and the Dey Baba Mohammed was paid 800,000 livres.

Compensation bid to end Alsace row

Paris, April 28

The Assembly has proposed to offer compensation to the German princes owning fiefs in Alsace. These properties vary in size. Some are tiny, such as the seigneury of Horbourg, but others are extremely large, like the county of Hanau Lichtenberg, which belong to the House of Hesse and extends from the Vosges to the Rhine.

Treaties of 1648 which gave Alsace to France had recognised the rights of the foreign princes. When the Estates General were convened, the inhabitants of these territories had sent deputies to Versailles, while the princes were not represented. The princes now refuse to accept the abolition of feudal rights and are accusing France of treaty violation. Rather than getting involved in complex and lengthy legal discussions over the dispute, the Assembly has preferred to offer the German princes financial compensation.

The assignat is now legal tender

Paris, April 17

The Assembly decreed that the assignats created on December 19th. and 21st. will no longer be just bond certificates. They are also to be legal tender. Until now only banknotes issued by the discount bank were considered legal tender, but the public no longer trusts this bank, which will now have to hand over assignats in exchange for its own banknotes. The assignats are secured by the state on the basis of seized property.

A 1790 assignat with a face value of five hundred livres.

✚ 🏛 Constituent Assembly

1. Nîmes. Violent clashes break out between soldiers of the Guyenne regiment and the town's guards, which include some Catholics (→ June 15, 90).

2. Uzès. The publication of a declaration by the city's Catholic citizens, calling on the Constituent Assembly to proclaim Catholicism as the state's religion, widens the split between the Protestant and Catholic communities. In many parts of the Languedoc, both sides are arming.

3. Toulon. Workers at the arsenal demand the release of sailors who mutinied, and attack the head of the arsenal. The latter has to place himself under the protection of the city's authorities.

3. Paris. Acting on an initiative by Merlin de Douai and the deputy from Paris, Tronchet, the Assembly approves the decree on the repurchase of feudal and franchise rights. The move had been expected since March 15th.

15. Paris. The Assembly decrees the election of judges by active citizens.

6. Paris. Tolozan, the inspector general of factories, signs a contract on behalf of the government with the English worker Pickford, who is to build five mule-jennys of a new type.

8. Paris. A deputy of the Nivernais region, the Marquis de Bonnay, proposes the unification of the weights and measures system.

9. Paris. The Constituent Assembly declares that the crown's properties can be sold or transferred.

10. Rennes. The town council asks for a cavalry regiment to be sent to keep order in the countryside.

10. Montauban. The Catholics of the town chase patriots and Protestants away. →

11. Paris. The Italian theatre performs *Jeanne d'Arc à Orléans,* a verse comedy written by Pierre Desforges.

11. Ile de Ré. The monks of the Saint Michel en l'Herm abbey try to get 20 years of rent arrears paid to them before the old system is changed.

12. Paris. La Fayette, the Marquis de Condorcet, Brissot and Bailly found the 1789 Society. →

Massacre of patriots at Montauban

Montauban, May 10

In the southern provinces of France, known as the Midi, religious fervour and political feuds are turning the Revolution into a war of religion. After Toulouse and Nîmes, violence has now come to Montauban. For the first time in this area, blood has been spilt between Catholics and Protestants. Today there was a battle between the patriots of the National Guard and the Catholic supporters of the "aristocratic" town council, who were backed by the army. The clashes left five people dead and 16 others injured. Anti-religious measures taken by the Constituent Assembly had already been causing unrest for some time. Catholics claimed that the decrees were just a first step towards the handing back to Protestants of the churches that had been taken from them at the time of the Revocation of the Edict of Nantes in 1685. Aristocrats claimed there was a patriot and Protestant plot orchestrated by Jeanbon Saint André, aimed at gathering weapons. The local National Guard, against which a corps of counter-revolutionary volunteers has been set up, had gone into a federation with those of Cahors and Bordeaux and some of the Toulouse guards. Over the past few days there had been a growing number of clashes. This evening, as 55 patriots were thrown into jail, many worried Protestants began to flee from the town. The federated National Guards have been called in to help, but they may not get to Montauban to avoid a major new bloodbath (→ May 19).

At Montauban, Catholics and aristocrats clash with Protestants and members of the National Guard.

Capital of Tobago destroyed by fire

Tobago, May 3

The pretty Creole city has been reduced to ashes. Hundreds of exhausted settlers have set up camp in the nearby gullies.

Throughout the night the entire population of Port Louis has been fighting a huge fire. The causes of the catastrophe are still not clear, but what is certain is that the unrest that has broken out in the capital over the past few days has considerably hampered the authorities' attempts to fight the fire. Tension between the newly-landed royal French troops and the local National Guard had just caused a riot.

The authorities focused on restoring order and did not realise that a fire had started before it was too late.

Jews still under threat in Alsace

Alsace, May

Insults, violence and hatred: the renewed anti-Jewish flareup in Alsace is causing serious concern at the Assembly.

On April 16th., the Assembly issued a decree reminding all the citizens of France that "Jews are under the protection of the law" and ordering town authorities to "do all in their power to protect Jews and their property".

Already, in September 1789, hundreds of Jews had already been forced to flee from peasants who were looting and sacking their homes. Since then, they had gradually returned to their homes, but the recent events show that they are still in a difficult situation and that the Assembly's efforts to assimilate them will face obstacles.

A new club is born, the 1789 Society

Paris, May 12

Yet another club has been born in Paris. It has chosen a highly symbolic name: the 1789 Society, in honour of the Revolution. The high membership fees indicate that it aspires to be an elegant establishment that will rival the Jacobins Club. Its founders hope that only the best and the brightest will apply. The new club gave an inaugural banquet at the Palais Royal. There were 130 guests, including Bailly and La Fayette. After the meal, the two men drank toasts to the health of the nation, to the law, to the King, to freedom, to the Constitution and to the United States of America. Military music played at the banquet attracted a crowd of onlookers who cheered the members of the new club.

14. Paris. A letter sent to the Assembly by the minister Montmorin announcing that, by virtue of the "family pact", France can enter the war with Spain against England leads the Constituents to debate the right to war (→22).

15. Paris. Opening of the Variétés Amusantes theatre, constructed by the architect Victor Louis.→

19. Bordeaux. 1,500 National Guards march on Montauban to free jailed patriots (→29).

21. Paris. The Assembly approves the law to reorganise the municipalities, replacing Paris' 60 districts by a total of 48 zones.→

21. Paris. The old districts' saints' names are done away with.

22. Savoy. Mounier, travelling under the alias of Monsieur Duverger, leaves France for Savoy where his family awaits him.

22. Paris. At the end of the debate on the right to war, the Assembly solemnly declares it will "no more engage in a war of conquest nor ever employ its might against the freedom of any people".→

22. Paris. The people ransack the press of the royalist newspaper *La Gazette de Paris*, in the Rue Saint Honoré.

22. Paris. A tract circulating in Paris accuses Mirabeau of playing a double game.

24. Paris. The Assembly creates a court of appeal in each department: the Supreme Court of Appeal.

25. Saint Denis. The Isle of Bourbon is represented in the Assembly.

29. Montauban. Mediators sent by the War Ministry enter the city and free the imprisoned patriots.

29. Paris. The Royal Proclamation orders the tricoloured cockade to be worn throughout the kingdom.

30. Paris. The chemist Berthollet presents a new process for bleaching material to the Academy of Science.

30. Paris. The National Assembly creates new alms-houses.

31. Paris. In the Assembly Robespierre, in a debate on the clergy's future civil Constitution, says he favours priests marrying.

King and Assembly to share right to declare war

Paris, May 22

The deputies are past masters when it comes to a compromise. The text of the law just passed concerning the right of war and peace reads: "War may be declared only by a decree of the legislature after a formal demand by the King." A compromise between monarch and Assembly; but why? In fact, the two sides have been clashing for over a week to decide who has the right to plunge France into war. The debates have been a tonic to the crowds in the hall of the Manège, and people unable to find a place inside have been kept informed by a system of announcements on placards lowered from the windows on the end of a string. So everyone has been able to follow at first hand the intense personal struggle between Barnave from the Dauphiné and Mirabeau, said to be in the service of the Court. The right wing had hoped to give the King sole power to declare war, but the democrats claimed this for the Assembly. Mirabeau, with the cunning of a fox, kept a foot in each camp, proposing to give this right to both sides, but Barnave accused him of acting for the monarchy and Marat in his newspaper vented his spleen on this "traitor". These attacks have given Mirabeau the chance to appear as a victim. Today he finally managed to swing the Assembly round to his favour and got his proposals passed.

The women of the Paris market congratulate Barnave on his patriotism.

Bastille key for President Washington

The keys of the Bastille have now become a symbol of liberty.

Paris, May

A key which has opened the gates of the Bastille makes a wonderful present; and none better than the first American President, the hero of the War of Independence, to appreciate its true worth. So La Fayette has asked the famous journalist Thomas Paine to present George Washington with such a key. Paine, already highly popular on the other side of the Atlantic for his pro-independence articles, has shown great enthusiasm for the Revolution and is said to feel extremely honoured by this valuable gift; and even if the key is not a genuine one, it is the symbolic value which really counts.

Mirabeau accused of double-dealing

Paris, May 22

Mirabeau can shake his ugly head as much as he likes to deny he has sold himself to the King. He fools nobody. Already criticised for his life of notorious debauchery, he is now being decried for treason. A pamphlet circulating in Paris, "The Count of Mirabeau's treason revealed", accuses him of having received gold for his discreet service to the royal cause in the Assembly. One sure sign: his debts have been mysteriously wiped out. The living incarnation of the Revolution, Mirabeau is using his prestige and flagrantly playing a double game.

Victor Louis' magnificent new theatre opens to the public

Paris, May 15

Now the Palais Royal has its own theatre, known as the Variétés Amusantes, which opened its doors today. Started in 1786 at the instigation of the Duc d'Orléans, the building arouses general admiration for its classical architecture and bold proportions, but what are most to be admired are the superb interior decorations: the hall, with its blue and gold drapes, has four tiers of boxes with balustrades painted to look like marble. The candelabra has 40 lamps and all the staircases are made of white marble. One more splendid achievement for the architect Victor Louis to add to his list.

Almost finished! The newly constructed theatre in Paris, designed by the architect Victor Louis on the corner of Rue de Richelieu.

Paris zoned to defuse areas of unrest

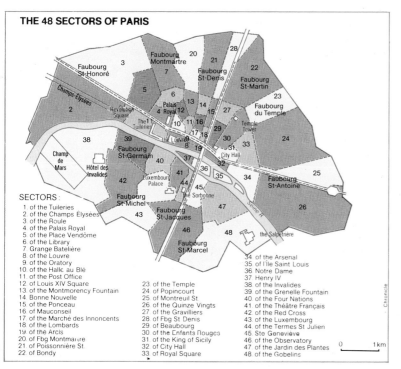

THE 48 SECTORS OF PARIS

SECTORS:
1. of the Tuileries
2. of the Champs Élysées
3. of the Roule
4. of the Palais Royal
5. of the Place Vendôme
6. of the Library
7. Grange Batelière
8. of the Louvre
9. of the Oratory
10. of the Halle au Blé
11. of the Post Office
12. of Louis XIV Square
13. of the Montmorency Fountain
14. Bonne Nouvelle
15. of the Ponceau
16. of Mauconseil
17. of the Marché des Innoncents
18. of the Lombards
19. of the Arcis
20. of Fbg Montmartre
21. of Poissonnière St.
22. of Bondy

23. of the Temple
24. of Popincourt
25. of Montreuil St.
26. of the Quinze Vingts
27. of the Gravilliers
28. of Fbg St Denis
29. of Beaubourg
30. of the Enfants Rouges
31. of the King of Sicily
32. of City Hall
33. of Royal Square

34. of the Arsenal
35. of l'Île Saint Louis
36. Notre Dame
37. Henry IV
38. of the Invalides
39. of the Grenelle Fountain
40. of the Four Nations
41. of the Théâtre Français
42. of the Red Cross
43. of the Luxembourg
44. of the Termes St Julien
45. Ste Geneviève
46. of the Observatory
47. of the Jardin des Plantes
48. of the Gobelins

Paris, May 21

Reorganisation is the answer to everything! In doing away with the capitals' 60 districts created in 1789 and replacing them with 48 zones, the deputies imagine that in one fell swoop they will wipe out the areas where public demonstrations flare up from time to time. Formerly known by the names of saints, these zones have been re-christened. Only Sainte Geneviève, the patron saint of Paris, has escaped this wave of secularisation.

Liberty takes root with planting of oak

Dancing round the tree of Liberty.

Saint Gaudens, May

The oak tree stands as a proud emblem for liberty. Impressive, robust and protective, it particularly symbolises long life. So on the day of the inauguration of the new town council Norbert Pressac, the priest of Saint Gaudens, uprooted the sturdiest oak tree from the nearby forest and had it planted with great ceremony in the square. Following this, he asked his flock to gather under its shade to settle their differences by legal procedures. The ceremony concluded amid handshakes, hugs all round and much joyful singing.

Lyons and Dijon celebrate the Federation

The Federates' camp in Lyons on May 30th. Above the altar to the Nation, the statue of Liberty dominates the ceremony.

France, May

The Federations are on the increase in reply to the attempts of the monarchist party to get the provinces to oppose the Revolution. In Dijon, on May 18th., 3,000 National Guards from the four departments which today make up Burgundy were sworn in before the temple of Liberty, decorated with scenes of the fall of the Bastille.

Vexed because other cities had taken the initiative and nettled by being reputed to be hostile to the Revolution, the people of Lyons have done things on a grand scale! On May 30th. no less than 50,000 volunteers lined up under 418 flags to swear allegiance to the nation, the law and the King on the huge plain of Les Brotteaux under the gaze of 170,000 spellbound spectators.

Dijon, May 18th: the walls of the Bastille have been rebuilt for the feast.

Isle of Bourbon gets its representative

Saint Denis, May 25

One year later than expected, the Isle of Bourbon is to have its own representative in the National Assembly. A total of 135 candidates met in general assembly to elect the one deputy who will represent them. This solemn meeting opened with a *Te Deum* and a salvo of 21 guns. Before leaving them to deliberate, the governor, David Charpentier de Cossigny, reminded them that their task ended there. He must be afraid that some revolutionary contagion might spread overseas!

Priest defrocked for love of his country

Beaune, May 19

He tore his habit into ribbons, swore and went off, leaving his superiors aghast. Father Joseph Le Bon slammed the door of the College of Oratorians, where up to now he had taught rhetoric. Leaving by night with his pupils, he made for Dijon, where a festival to celebrate the Federation was in progress. This fiery enthusiasm vexed the church officials, who then forcibly brought him back into their midst, but the young patriot has well and truly left the straight and narrow. We are sure to hear of him again.

1. Paris. Following complaints, police issue a order banning nude bathing in the Seine.

1. Paris. The priest Royou creates a monarchist news-paper, *l'Ami du Roi.*→

3. Paris. Publication of a letter announcing Louis XVI's plans to spend several days at Saint Cloud disturbs the people, who already fear the King's departure.

6. Paris. Nicolas André Castella, a lawyer from Freiburg, founds the Swiss Patriots' Club.

9. Paris. The Assembly votes 25 million francs for the upkeep of the King's house-hold and an allowance of four million for the Queen (→ May 26, 91).

9. The Antilles. A revolt of mulattoes breaks out in Martinique.→

9. Paris. The Assembly decides to organise a National Federation on July 14.→

11. Paris. The Constituent Assembly decrees three days' official mourning in memory of Benjamin Franklin.

12. Avignon. After driving out partisans of the Pope yester-day, the patriots of the Vaucluse ask to be linked to France.→

12. Orléans. Opening of a cotton mill built at the request of the Duc d'Orléans, who entrusts its management to English experts.

13. Rouen. Profiting from a local tradition on the feast of Saint Romain, two murderers are freed by the court.

15. Nîmes. Bloody clashes between patriots and Catholics leave 300 victims.→

19. Paris. The Assembly abolishes hereditary titles.→

26. Paris. Opening of the comic and lyric theatre at Saint Martin with a new opera by Giovanni Paisiello, *Les Trois Mariages.*

27. Paris. A National Assembly law reorganises the municipality of Paris.

28. Paris. The representatives of the Beaux Arts, David and Restout, express concern for the fate of the bas-reliefs representing the conquered provinces decorating Louis XIV's statue (the work of Desjardins) on the Place des Victoires, which the Assembly wants to remove.

National unity will be trumpeted at Paris festivities

In Lille, four obelisks and several antique temples have been erected.

In Besançon, the authorities have organised a federative camp on 16 June.

Paris, June 9

The country is caught up in a whirl of festivals to celebrate the Federation. Since the summer of 1789, these spontaneous demon-strations of brotherhood have pro-gressively spread throughout the kingdom, but in Paris it is thought that the time has come to call a halt. For these popular festivals go hand in hand with an increase in militia troops, created for the oc-casion to replace the traditional authorities which have been liter-ally dissolved in the revolutionary turmoil.

So the Assembly adopted Bailly's proposal of June 5th. to invite all the regional Federations to one great ceremony to honour "The" Federation in Paris on July 14th., the anniversary of the storming of the Bastille. Regiments of regular troops are to join forces with the National Guards of the different towns and villages to show that they must comply with the law. Are the deputies simply seeking to hon-our those who took up arms at the start of last summer in the cause of the Revolution? In fact, they are also hoping to stem a tendency, un-checked until now, which could prove dangerous: allowing men armed with guns to do what they like is never a good idea. Their energies should be channelled and used to proclaim the nation's soli-darity to the rest of the world. Whatever the case, there is no ques-tion of allowing this enthusiasm to degenerate into anarchy.

France mourns Benjamin Franklin, friend of the Revolution

Paris, June 11

"The American" is no more, and with his death liberty has lost one of its most ardent defenders.

Benjamin Franklin passed away today in Philadelphia at the age of 84. In sombre tones, Mirabeau announced his death this morning from the podium of the Assembly, which at once decreed national mourning. Revolutionary France has a duty to honour this physicist and philosopher who sat in the first American Congress, signed his country's Declaration of Independ-ence in 1776 with Thomas Jeffer-son at his side and, during his life-time, dedicated himself to mankind and its rights. He also negotiated the treaty of friendship with France

two years later. The news of his death spread round the capital like wildfire and the Friends of the Revolution and Humanity spon-taneously called a meeting of their members.

Among them, the regulars of the Procope café have organized a commemorative soirée. Zoppi, the owner of the café, has had it hung with black drapes, covering the medallions and their sculptured ribbons, the counter, the pilasters, the pillars, and even the little lava-tory, known as the "Spinney" be-cause of its mirrors painted with trees. At the entrance, reigning like a god, is the bust of Benjamin, with a chaplet of oak leaves around his brow and a compass in his hand.

Benjamin Franklin, the famous phy-sicist and friend of the Revolution.

Hereditary nobility dealt death-blow

Four villagers lash out in a mad frenzy at the emblems of the nobility.

Paris, June 19

The former Comte de Mirabeau is seething with rage! Journalists now refer to him by his ordinary family name, Riqueti. The deputies have just passed a bill to do away with hereditary nobility. Titles and family coats of arms can no longer be handed down from father to son. This is the death-blow to a once privileged class, but certain nobles have actually been in favour of this measure, such as La Fayette or the Vicomte de Noailles, who exclaimed: "The only distinction we recognise is that of virtue. Do we refer to Marquis Franklin or Count Washington?" There are many, however, who are pulling very long faces, including those who applauded the abolition of feudal rights on the night of August 4th. The death of the nobility is simply the inevitable result of the principle of equality as defined in the Declaration of the rights of man and the citizen, but the end of this breed could also herald the end of royalty. That at least is what the priest Maury believes, and today he has roundly declared: "If there is no nobility, there is no monarchy."

New monarchist gazette hits the stands

Paris, June 1

"Alarmed at the sight of an ocean of publications which print everything but the truth", the publishers of Elie Fréron's traditionalist *Année Littéraire* have decided to create a daily newspaper. The first edition of *L'Ami du Roi* was distributed today in the select quarters of Saint Honoré, Le Marais and Saint Germain. Its title and motto, *Pro rege, deo et patria* leave no doubt as to its contents. Its director, the Abbot Royon, attacks philosophers, rounds on Protestants and Freemasons, goes one further than Rivarol in criticising the Revolution, and warns the bourgeoisie. It already has one reader, the King himself, who was reported this evening to have read the tribute of his "friends" avidly.

"L'Ami du Roi", a monarchist daily headed by the Abbot Royon.

A bloody victory for the patriots in Nîmes

Nîmes, June 15

Civil and religious war has broken out again in the Midi! All day long the tough, hardy people of the Cévennes turned out from their villages with sabres to massacre the "aristocrats" of Nîmes, hanging them from lampposts. The number of victims is estimated at 300. It all started yesterday with a confrontation between the representative of the Comte d'Artois, François Froment's Catholic partisans, and Protestant volunteers. Froment's men were counting on the help of the Marquis de Bouzols, a military commander in the Languedoc, but he made no move. Only lightly armed, since funds promised by the émigré princes have not been forthcoming, they could not resist Protestant militiamen called out by the patriots to help. These attacked royalists sporting red pompoms in place of the forbidden white rosette. This evening the local population, mainly Catholic, has gone to earth. The Cévenols were rumoured to have been allowed to loot in exchange for their help!

Civil war breaks out in Martinique

Saint Pierre, June 9

Since dawn troops from Fort de France have surrounded the town, and the governor is ready at any moment to give his men the order to attack. It must be said that the behaviour of the whites of Saint Pierre has provoked the anger of the authorities. The trouble goes back to June 3rd. On the feast of Corpus Christi, the blacks wanted to organise demonstrations for equality. When the planters refused, the ceremony degenerated into bloody attacks on blacks after the white settlers lost all control, giving vent to their racial hatred. This morning the bodies of the mulattoes can be seen hanging at the entrance to the town, a macabre trophy for the soldiers.

Music and dancing are the slave's only remaining "liberties".

Avignon prefers to remain French

Avignon, June 12

The patriots of Avignon have got what they wanted! After a violent clash yesterday with the "aristocrats", during which several noblemen were hanged, they called a meeting of all the inhabitants who had not fled from the town in order to discuss recent events. A motion, passed unanimously, cynically records the inability of of the Vatican to guarantee the citizens' safety. It also states that the meeting at Avignon should exemplify what is in the public interest. Having broken off from Rome and from its moderate neighbours in the Papal state of the Comtat Venaissin, Avignon is left with only one option: to march on boldly (→Aug. 27).

Son and heir for Gabrielle Danton

Paris, June 18

Tyrants, stand in fear and trembling! Another Danton has just been born, soon to follow in his father's footsteps. While the bells of the church of Saint Sulpice were ringing out in full peal to announce the christening, delighted patriots gathered round the infant's cradle were making such comments as "He will grow up in better conditions than even the Dauphin!".

The very first thing Gabrielle Danton did was to pin the national cockade on the child's sleeve. Moreover, the proud father can hardly conceal his happiness, for he is certain that the first words of his offspring, Antoine, will be "Live free or die!".

▷

Barrel and blade for 954 Bastille heroes

"Conqueror of the Bastille": the certificate issued by the National Assembly.

Paris, June 19

The Nation is not ungrateful: it recognises and knows how to reward its heroes — and none more deserving than the conquerors of the Bastille! Accordingly, on the proposal of the deputy Armand Camus, the Assembly, amid cheers and with much enthusiasm, has passed a special decree to pay them tribute. A commission appointed to list the "candidates" reports that the official register numbers 954 combatants, who will each be pre-sented with a uniform and complete set of arms. The barrel of the gun and the blade of the sabre are to bear the inscription: *Presented by the Nation to ..., conqueror of the Bastille*. These 954 heroes are also to receive certificates recording the Nation's gratitude, and pensions for those who were wounded in the assault. Finally, during the Festival of the Federation places of honour are to be reserved for them so they can be admired by the crowd as living symbols of liberty.

Cloots stands up to speak for mankind

Paris, June 19

"We come from Europe, from Asia, from America, we represent Humanity!" Thirty-six foreigners, each wearing his own country's cos-tume, stood in the Assembly. You would have thought yourself at the centre of the world. There were Pio, the Neapolitan, Don Pablo Ola-vidès, the Spaniard, Trenck, the Prussian baron, the patriots of Hol-land, and many others. At their head was a young Prussian who wants to be known by the name of Anacharsis Cloots and has elected to be their spokesman. Jean Bap-tiste du Val de Grâce (his real name) was born in Clèves and has travelled extensively since his father's death in 1775. He has been to England, Italy and even Moroc-co before settling in France. With an African and an Arab at his side, he made his speech to an attentive audience. After congratulating the Assembly for its measures on the rights of man, he asked to be

A portrait of Anacharsis Cloots, the "spokesman of mankind".

allowed to take part in the Festival of the Federation which, he said, was not only that of the French but of all races. These words were en-thusiastically received by the deputies and, to general and warm applause, the Assembly welcomed "mankind" into its midst.

God guides Assembly, says prophetess

Paris, June 13

God inspires members of the Constituent Assembly! This reve-lation was made to the Assembly by Dom Gerle, the deputy for the city of Chartres. He came to this rather unexpected conclusion after having spoken to a saintly woman, Suzette Labrousse, who 11 years ago pro-phesied that the clergy would lose their wealth and that the Pope would have no more temporal power. To support his declaration, the Carthusian monk told his col-leagues of the astounding miracles which have marked the life of the prophetess. One example: when she was young, she spread quick-lime all over her face to avoid the temptations of love, but, amazingly enough, after this ordeal, her face was even whiter than before.

Jeu de Paume oath is commemorated by a bronze plaque and a banquet

Versailles, June 20

The walls of the hall of the Jeu de Paume will never forget the oath which has made them famous. A bronze plaque recording the text of the oath is now fixed on the walls, held in place by cement made out of débris from the Bastille. It was at the instigation of the Jeu de Paume Society that a delegation of deputies arrived today in Versailles to finish this symbolic act. With deep emo-tion, they intoned together the never to be forgotten declaration, thus affirming their faith to the nation. For greater precaution, and in order to preserve the memory of this historic day, the deputies re-quested that the walls which wit-nessed such a great event be pre-served for all time. Following this, the ceremony at Versailles was concluded by a splendid gesture of solidarity with a collection for the needy old people of the town; but the day was not yet over. Led by Gilbert Romme, the president of the Jeu de Paume Society, the depu-ties then repaired to the Ranelagh in the Bois de Boulogne for a ban-quet. There, in a lively and happy atmosphere, the guests, among whom Robespierre and Danton were to be seen, did justice to the fare and the many varied wines set before them.

Women clamour for right to bear arms

Paris, June 29

Weary of being for ever barred from taking an active part in life, women have at last dared to speak up! In the name of all those "who are tired of working, obeying and having no right to speak", a certain Madame de Vuignerais has written to the Assembly to ask that her sex should no longer be condemned to perpetual inactivity. Since the prin-ciples of 1789 proclaim the equal-ity of all mankind, why should women not have the right to take up arms and defend the country if it is in danger? For many, bearing arms has become more than a sym-bol: it is the very sign that they are playing a full and active role in the life of the nation.

Women want their voice to be heard above all others ...

"Land of Freedom begins right here!"

Strasbourg, June 14

At least 2,000 lusty voices were heard to shout as one "We do swear!". "Without any shadow of doubt," says the report on the Festival of the Federation in Strasbourg, "this patriotic fervour made itself heard on the other side of the Rhine. And may it teach despots that liberty is what empires are made of!" To confirm this, the volunteers from Lorraine, Burgundy and Champagne hoisted a red, white and blue flag on the Kehl bridge with the inscription "The land of liberty begins here!".

Marquis de Sade deserted by wife

Paris, June 9

For the Marquis de Sade the joys of family life are not the price of freedom. Released from prison on April 2nd., he had barely had time to walk the pavements of Paris before his wife informed him that she was not prepared to live with him again. Although previously she had fought tooth and nail for her husband, she now said that her decision was due to his behaviour at Arcueil and Marseilles, for which he was imprisoned. As de Sade has not condescended to reply to this, the Châtelet in Paris has today pronounced their separation by default and decreed that Madame's dowry be returned. Amid these tribulations, the Marquis has none the less managed to glean a few consolations. A charming lady, the president of Fleurieu, has provisionally offered him her hospitality, and her heart (→July 1).

Montmartre to join the Paris Commune

Paris, June 27

The rustics of Montmartre have shown little concern for the capital's problems up to now, being more interested in their gardens and windmills, but the men of Montmartre are going to have to take a closer interest in things for, from today, they will be invited to sit in the Commune in Paris, re-organised by official decree.

July 1790
from 1st. to 14th.

⚜ 🏛 Constituent Assembly

1. Paris. Publication of the first volume of *Bibliothèque des Villages* by Arnaud Berquin, a popular author of children's books.

1. The Marquis de Sade, freed from jail on April 2nd, is enrolled as an "active citizen" in the Place Vendôme sector (→Nov. 1, 90).

3. Paris. In an article published in the newspaper of the 1789 Society, Condorcet proposes giving women civil rights.→

4. Paris. The journalist Stanislas Fréron, son of the critic often trounced by Voltaire, joins Camille Desmoulins to publish *Révolutions de France et de Brabant.*

6. Paris. The première at the Opéra of a ballet by the choreographer and dance-master Pierre Gardel, *Télémaque dans l'Ile de Calypso.*

7. Paris. A Justice of the Peace created in each canton (→Aug. 16).

7. Paris. Choderlos de Laclos, anticipating the Duc d'Orléans' return to France, publishes an *Exposé de la Conduite de M. le Duc d'Orléans dans la Révolution de France* (→10).

8. Lyons. A new riot against taxation. Demonstrators and National Guards side together and wreck the barriers.

10. Paris. Première at the Comédie Italienne of *Le Chêne Patriotique*, a comic opera by Monvel and Nicolas Dalayrac.

11. Paris. On returning from England yesterday, the Duc d'Orléans goes to the Assembly and takes the civil oath (→20).

12. Paris. The Assembly adopts the civil Constitution of the clergy.→

13. Paris. Festivities for the Festival of the Federation begin in Notre Dame with the performance of a "sacred drama", *La Prise de la Bastille.*

13. Paris. A royalist conspirator, the Chevalier de Bonne Savardin, escapes from the Abbaye prison.

14. England. In a London tavern on the Strand, Lord Stanhope is guest of honour at a huge banquet to mark the storming of the Bastille.

14. Paris. The Festival of the Federation on the Champ de Mars.→

14. Paris. Louis XVI swears to uphold the laws of the State.

Condorcet champions votes for women

Paris, July 3

How is it that the principle of equality can be applied to men but completely ignored when it comes to women? With his publication in the press of "A memoire on admitting women to citizenship", Condorcet lends all the weight of his intelligence and fame to the feminist cause. This man of science, this brilliant mathematician, this philosopher of rigorous intellectual honesty declares that natural rights can be defended only in the name of all people. He considers that if the law is not to be guilty of flagrant injustice, it should recognize citizenship for women and, accordingly, the right to vote.

The Marquis de Condorcet's portrait by Jean Baptiste Greuze.

Fersen spotted on dark visit to Queen

Saint Cloud, July

Three in the morning: an hour when all is sunk deep in sleep; but no! A shadow slips furtively out of the castle and threads its way in and out of the bushes. A guard has spotted it. He rushes after it ... but stammers out his excuses on recognising Fersen. When the incident was reported the next day to the Queen, she merely laughed. Respectfully informed that the visits the handsome young Swede pays her every night are extremely imprudent, she replied airily: "Speak to him about it if you think it matters. I don't care one bit."

Marie Antoinette meets Mirabeau

Saint Cloud, July 3

This morning Mirabeau had himself driven to the park of Saint Cloud by his nephew, disguised as a coachman. He told him to alert the National Guard if he was not back within the hour. He got back in the nick of time, out of breath, but overjoyed at having had the pre-arranged meeting with Marie Antoinette. He was thus able to outline to her his plan to save the monarchy. "What a great lady! How noble! But how unhappy! But I shall save her. Nothing will stop me. I would rather die!" he repeated on his return.

Summer fashion: a bouquet of narcissi on a Phrygian or Liberty cap, which is worn with a light satin dress ...

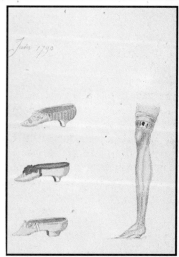

Light coloured stockings embroidered with a motif that matches with the shoes, which are worn with flowered garters.

Civil constitution transforms Church of France

Paris, July 12

From now on priests and bishops are to be elected! This is one of the measures resulting from the new civil Constitution of the clergy whose terms have finally been passed by the Assembly. By this law,

There are complaints over the new boundaries of the dioceses.

the Church of France is completely reorganised. The electoral body is composed of all active citizens whatever their religion, the one reservation being that they should have been to Mass before voting. On the other hand, the church's assets are placed at the Nation's disposal and the men of the cloth become civil servants. Their stipends, entirely adequate, will help the situation of the rank and file clergy. The Constituents have also simplified ecclesiastical geography: instead of 139 dioceses, there are to be only 83, each corresponding to a department. Has the Assembly overreached itself in passing these measures? This, at least, is what the opponents of the clergy's civil Constitution claim, criticising the independence of the new church in relation to the Pope. In fact, it is not from the Bishop of Rome but from one of the ten metropolitan bishops

Surrounded by wolves and serpents, the clergy spit out their "anticonstitutional venom" against the abolition of the clergy's temporal powers.

of France that the titulars of the new dioceses will receive their investiture. They will simply be authorised to write to the Holy Father to advise him of the fact. In the face of such measures, all the bishop-deputies in the Assembly abstained from voting.

Monster warship boosts naval power

Brest, July 1

Jacques Noël Sané's masterpiece has just been completed at the dockyard in Brest. The *Etats de Bourgogne*, the first of a new series of 118-cannon vessels, is at present only a magnificent oak hull measuring 64 metres, but once fitted out she will carry more than 5,000 tonnes and have sails measuring 4,640 square metres. The slings which held the launching cradle of this monster were severed at noon.

Once freed, the ship gradually gained momentum and glided gently down the slipway. The large crowd present waited patiently for the moment the stern made contact with the water to applaud and cheer with enthusiasm. Thanks to the efforts of the former minister Sartine in 1776, France is now one of the few great naval powers. Today her dockyards construct uniform fleets, made up of vessels of exactly the same type.

The fleet will soon have 82 large warships, 67 frigates, 19 corvettes, 29 brigs and sloops, 7 gun-boats, 17 store-ships and 16 transport vessels.

A scheme to check straying husbands

Paris, July 4

Reforms are the order of the day. Let's take advantage of the fact, says a young woman who in *Le Moniteur* has prudently signed herself by her initials. Her plan concerns one of the laws of civil status. She thinks it a shame that husband and wife cannot link their names in the same way they unite their destinies. One further advantage would result: the single person would stand out by having only one family name and be guilty of not founding a family for the Nation. More especially, it would keep an unfaithful husband at home: for with a dual name known officially by all, how could any scheming woman dare take him for a lover?

Royal cold shoulder for Duc d'Orléans

Paris, July 10

What a reception for Philippe d'Orléans! Arriving to report to the King on his journey to England, he did not expect to be received so coldly. He arrived at Saint Cloud with his usual bravado, but was surprised to see that several gentlemen took no notice of him and many of the women looked anything but pleased. These nobles at court rightly or wrongly consider him responsible for the troubles of October, the man who cut short their easy life at Versailles. The King received him coldly, showing him the door without even giving him a hearing. Pretending not to notice anything amiss, the Duc left, cut to the quick. Once more the court drives him against his will towards the Revolution (→11).

A satirical playing card showing the Duc d'Orléans.

Gossec's hymn breaks with tradition

Paris, July 13

On any solemn occasion, grand music is called for. To accompany the Festival of the Federation, the composer François Gossec has just elected to compose a *Te Deum* which breaks with all tradition. Its very title is in itself symbolic, for up to now this type of work has been played only on special occasions, such as coronations, or to celebrate great military victories. Now, under the guise of a religious hymn, it is in fact a real paean of civil faith which is to be sung before the thousands of people assembled on the Champ de Mars. Moreover, the orchestra is to consist of 1,200 players and singers, including some 300 wind instrumentalists and 100 drummers.

Gossec composed a "Te Deum" for the Federation celebrations.

Readers cash in on newspaper war

Paris, July 1

In these days of stiff inter-press competition, faithful readers are wooed by all means possible. The Chaignieau brothers, owners of the *Journal du Soir*, whose first edition comes out today, have invented a system which might not make them wealthy men but will surely bring fame to them and their newspaper. At a time when Paris is experiencing a cash-flow problem and even the smallest assignat costs 50 livres, they have announced they will accept subscriptions (considerably less than this sum) only in assignats and give subscribers the change in cash. The newspaper's offices are never empty!

Loyal sleepwalker falls to earth

Paris, July 10

Young Copinger arrived this evening from Bordeaux in a state of great excitement: in four days he is going to take part in the Festival of the Federation! Still with his boots on, he lay on the bed in his room in the Hôtel d'Aligre and quickly fell into a troubled sleep. Dreaming he was still in the stage-coach, he got up and jumped out of the second floor window shouting that the seat in the coach was too hard! When he was picked up in the street, he was fortunately still alive though badly bruised; but how surprised passers-by were to hear him declare he was going at once to swear faith to the Nation ...

Ah! ça ira, ça ira!

Everything can begin with songs. There is a verse which, exhorting citizens to act as one man, runs as follows:
"The French shall have their way!"
Both young and old to-day
Cry ceaselessly and say
"The French shall have their way!"
The rebels we'll allay
Our enemies waylay:
So let us shout hooray.
When Boileau to the priests
Spoke like a gifted seer
He foretold this right clear.
So with this song
These joyous words we say:
"The French shall have their way!"

Parisians feverishly prepare for Festival of the Federation

Paris, July 10

"For the Nation, nothing is too much trouble!" Fever is in the air, and everyone is busy with last minute preparations before the great day. For the whole country is to be honoured and this first celebration must be in the grandest style. Men of the National Guard, workers or deputies, all have their eyes riveted on the Champ de Mars where the ceremony is to take place. Under their various banners the corporations are hard at work, even at night, for time is getting short. In this vast open-air workshop, veterans from Les Invalides, pupils from the Academy of Art and actors from Mademoiselle Montansier's theatre can be seen wielding the pick and driving the heavy carts. A large crowd spurs them on while children hold torches. The earth which has been removed will serve to build an amphitheatre from which the orators and general parade can be viewed; but alas! not all the citizens are expending their energy in the same way ... for a hairdresser, with an old man as his attendant, was discovered hiding under the Altar to the Nation. They were busy looking up the skirts of the women passing by. They were both dragged out and beaten up.

All must be finished in four days.

Undeterred by the awful weather, all the people of Paris, armed with spades and barrows, work relentlessly to finish the work in time.

The huge celebration of the Federation held on Paris' Champ de Mars on July 14th. 1790, with the Altar to the Nation shown in the centre.   161

July 4, 1790: All the people of France

The festival which took place on July 14th. on the Champ de Mars was the culmination of a movement which sprang up in the provinces. On November 29th. 1789, some 12,000 National Guards from the Vivarais and the Dauphiné pledged a bond of mutual help and brotherhood. This idea spread rapidly and it was the men of Brittany who made the proposal of a federation covering the whole of France.

The Assembly adopted the proposition on June 7th. and La Fayette undertook its organisation. It was to be a grandiose demonstration of solidarity based on the achievements of the Revolution, hence the choice of July 14th., but it was also to serve to mask the growing differences between nobles and bourgeois, King and deputies, extremists and moderates. For many, the Revolution was accomplished. The unity between Constitution and monarch was the final proof; but today, enthusiasm prevailed.

The Festival of the Federation on the Champ de Mars, a show of national reconciliation.

Torrential rain poured down all morning, drenching the huge crowd gathered on the Champ de Mars, but it would have needed Noah's Flood to dampen the enthusiasm of the 300,000 spectators from Paris and all over France. Some were up before 3 a.m. to attend this festival of fraternity, the first since the new era of liberty.

France has never seen such an imposing gathering. The setting for the ceremony had been arranged to suit the occasion. What had simply been a piece of land used for military drill has today been turned into a huge esplanade nearly 1,000 metres long. On either side, banks of earth have been erected to support 30 rows of seats. At the far end, in front of the Military Academy, an enormous grandstand has been erected for the many officials and ambassadors who will attend.

In the centre is the royal tribune, which enables all the spectators to see the King clearly. At the other end of the esplanade the entrance is marked by an immense triumphal arch with three bays, 25 metres high, a magnificent observation post for those lucky enough to find

celebrate the Federation in Paris

places at the top. Above the main entrance, on one of the bays, these words can be read: "We who are dedicated to the duties of the Constitution will accomplish them", and above another bay: "With this defence, the poor man need fear no more that he be robbed by the oppressor".

A temporary bridge of boats, which the Federation's members will cross, has been built over the Seine. All this work has entailed removing tonnes of earth, erecting embankments 3,000 metres long and levelling nearly 250 acres of land. As there was a risk that the esplanade would turn into a quagmire, sand has been spread about; and all this has been achieved in just 28 days. People in the huge crowd protected themselves with coloured umbrellas and awaited impatiently the procession's arrival.

It assembled at dawn and moved off at eight o'clock. Seven and a half hours were needed to cross the capital. The assembly point had been fixed for six o'clock opposite the Champ de Mars on the boulevard between the Temple and the gate of Saint Martin. Entering by Saint Denis' Gate, people from Brittany, Marseilles and Flanders marched up the Rue Saint Denis to the Rue de la Ferronnerie, where a spontaneous and sincere homage was paid to Henri IV, assassinated nearly two centuries ago.

To the deafening sound of the cheers of the crowds leaning from the windows, delegations from all over the country then moved along the Rue Saint Honoré to arrive at the Place Royale before crossing the Seine. The deputies of the National Assembly joined in the procession, marching between the groups of old men and of children, on Louis XV Square.

The Federates' Procession

Several salvos of gunfire rang out as the detachments of cavalry were seen to move off. They lined up in a side lane to give way to a company of grenadiers, who had entered the esplanade amid tumultuous cheers and applause. Then came the electors of Paris, the representatives of the city and the presidents of the wards. After the battalion of the central military school, the deputies of the Constituent Assembly arrived, greeted with wild

enthusiasm. While the standard bearers of the Parisian National Guard were lining up along the grandstand, all these other groups moved slowly across the Champ de Mars to reach the official podium where the royal family was already installed. The Queen was wearing a large hat decorated with tricoloured plumes, a fact which did not go unnoticed by the spectators. One more battalion, and finally the first detachments of Federates, radia-

ting emotion, appeared. The Federates from Ain led the procession followed by those from the other departments, Yonne coming last as alphabetical order dictates. Each detachment of the Federate National Guards was preceded by a banner of white taffeta with a tricoloured bow and tassels bearing the name of the department and, framed in a crown of oak leaves, the words "Constitution and General Confederation. Paris, July 14th., 1790". In the middle of the procession of the departments were the delegates of all the regiments of

France and units of the nation's Fleet whose superb differently-coloured uniforms aroused general admiration.

Mass and solemn oath

The banners were solemnly blessed before the ceremony began. About half past three in the afternoon, surrounded by chaplains of the National Guard with their white albs and tricoloured belts,

La Fayette solemnly swears allegiance in front of the King and the Nation.

Talleyrand, the Bishop of Autun, celebrated High Mass. Largely responsible for the civil Constitution of the clergy, the bishop is said to have declared with a sigh: "I have done everything during my lifetime, even celebrated Mass." The end of the service was marked by salvos of gunfire, replacing the organ, and announcing to the whole country that the Federative solemn oath was about to be taken. In the name of the National Guards and troops, La Fayette then spoke these words: "We swear to remain faithful for ever to the Nation, the

Law and the King; by our authority to uphold the Constitution decreed by the National Assembly and accepted by the King ...; to protect the safety of person and property, the free circulation of corn ..., the collection of public taxes ... and to remain bound to all the people of France by the indissoluble bonds of Fraternity." With one voice, all the Federates replied: "I do so swear."

The King takes the oath

Next, all eyes were turned on the royal podium. The speaker of the National Assembly took the oath. Then Louis XVI rose. He held out his right hand towards the altar and swore "to use the power entrusted to him by the constitutional law of the State to maintain and see the laws upheld". The Queen was then seen to take the young Dauphin in her arms and show him off to the huge crowd. This unexpected gesture was warmly received. The ceremony was brought to a conclusion with a *Te Deum*. The esplanade resounded to a terrific shout of joy. At about six o'clock, everybody was able to go back home or to the Bastille Ball. On the site of the towers of the destroyed fortress, 83 trees had been planted, linked together by luminous garlands. In the middle, a flag with the one word "Liberty" flew from a huge pole. A sign at the entrance told all who came "You can dance here". By the light of lanterns, the dangers of the counter-revolution and the more daring proposals of the democrats seemed very distant to the dancers. As for the delegates of the departmental federations, before going to the ball they had been invited to the banquet for 22,000 people organised in the gardens of the Muette. All over the park, tables had been set up. This dinner, mainly cold meats, was so copious that the left-overs were able to be distributed to the people. All the officials were present and many a toast was drunk to the Nation, to Liberty and to the King. Despite the many guests, the banquet, one of the largest ever organised in living memory in France, was not marred by incidents. Instead, it took place in an atmosphere of friendship which swelled everyone's hearts, while all took advantage of the delicious food being served.

17. Paris. Two spinning-mills open, employing women and old people stricken by poverty as well as children under 16.

17. Paris. The première of a comedy by Collot d'Herbois, *La Famille Patriote*, is given at Monsieur's theatre.

18. Paris. To close the Festival of the Federation, a nautical contest is organised on the Seine while a hot air balloon is launched from the Military Academy.

20. Paris. The Court at the Châtelet dismisses accusations against the Duc d'Orléans of plotting against the King (→30).

21. Paris. The National Assembly agrees to absorb foreign regiments, who are, however, to wear French uniform.

22. Paris. Bailly, the mayor of the capital, orders the arrest of beggars of either sex who must be removed from Paris or employed in almshouses.

23. Paris. Despite the Pope's opposition, Louis XVI agrees to endorse the civil Constitution of the clergy.→

25. Lyons. Fresh disturbances break out. Workers loot the city's arsenal, compelling the authorities to declare martial law (→26).

26. Paris. As a result of the confrontations in May, the Assembly suspends the municipality of Montauban, now to be administered by government commissioners.

26. Paris. Marat brings out a pamphlet: *C'en est fait de nous!* (→31).

27. Reichenbach. Prussia, England and Holland jointly agree with Austria to undertake the reconquest of Belgium.→

28. Lyons. The Swiss of the Sonnemberg regiment search for weapons held by the people in the city's Pierre Scizes quarter.

29. Paris. Deputies disagree over the army's manpower. Comte Latour du Pin says France needs 250,000 men, but Lameth says 150,000 suffice.

29. Ile de France. The governor, Thomas Conway, resigns so as not to submit to the Assembly.

31. Saint Domingue. The quarrel between the two rival provincial assemblies turns into civil war (→Aug. 6).

The Festival continues in Paris ... but without the Royal Family

Nautical contests have been organised on the Seine, downstream from the Pont Neuf. The teams competed with élan and daring while the public on the banks watched the spectacle to the sound of small groups of musicians.

At nightfall, the Festival continues and the Champs Elysées are lit up with a thousand bright lights.

A placard on the site of the ruins of the Bastille announces "You can dance here". A huge ball has been organised where the high ramparts of "that appalling monument to despotism" stood not so long ago.

Saint Cloud, July 18

While in a festive Paris people continue to dance and drink to the reconciliation of King and Nation, the royal family have returned with relief to the castle of Saint Cloud where they are spending the summer. Far from Paris, they can rest and forget the anguish of the present, almost believing themselves back in the carefree times of the past.

The King has resumed hunting and riding, of which he is passionately fond. His face had become pallid during his long stay at the Tuileries, but it has now taken on its former colour and he seems in fine health. As for Marie Antoinette, she is happy to be organising, as she did last year, concerts and plays with her best friends. These distractions, which give her great pleasure, have restored some of her former high spirits. For the royal couple and their faithful followers, the Festival of the Federation will simply have been a disagreeable interlude which interrupted an almost trouble-free holiday. The people's exuberance, their shouts and noisy applause, this unusual ceremony in which the Nation played the leading role, have deeply shocked them. Despite a show of affection towards the King, Louis XVI and his wife hate these demonstrations of national joy in which they could take no part. They have been deeply embittered by being obliged to support a festival which to them is an abomination.

Danton a fresh victim of "Charles IX"

Paris, July 23

It is not only at the tribune of the Assembly that patriots and conservatives come into direct confrontation. The Revolution has now entered the theatre. Danton, who had gone to the Théâtre de la Nation to see Marie Joseph Chénier's inflammatory play, *Charles IX*, finished his evening out at the city hall. He and a few spectators had committed the error of keeping their hats on, but the new rules state that, while the play is on, men should remove their hats so as not to block their neighbours' view. The patriots with their round hats were unaware of this ruling, and claimed they thought it applied only to the conservatives' classical three-cornered hat. Taken to task, Danton defiantly pushed his hat further down onto his head and refused to comply with the rules. Following the public's lead, the actors then split into two camps and fighting spread: the conservatives, called the "blacks" (the majority) led by Naudet, against the "red squadron" whose leader was Talma. The police were finally called in and Danton was arrested.

A sketch of Danton by David.

Fine performance of a symphony by Cambini

Paris, July 24

This evening the public in the Hôtel du Musée has had a treat. Indeed, the music on the programme was particularly popular: a *sinfonia concertante* (the musical form currently most in vogue), written by a master of the style, Giovanni Cambini, and conducted by the great maestro himself. Since its appearance in about 1770, the *sinfonia concertante*, a dialogue between a group of solo instrumentalists and the rest of the orchestra, has had tremendous success in Paris. Although based on a principle identical with that of the *concerto grosso*, it is lighter, demands greater technique and has more varied melody. Living in Paris since 1776, Cambini, a richly inventive composer, has published 20 or so every month. He soon made his mark in the capital's musical circles, achieving fame and honours. Mozart himself, on a visit to Paris, spoke to him in flattering terms. By now, he has composed more than 80 such symphonies, and it is not an exaggeration to say that Cambini has a near monopoly which other writers do not seek to steal from him.

War minister calls for 250,000 soldiers

Paris, July 29

The euphoria of the Revolution has not made the deputies forget the country's defence. For over six months they have been discussing the size and nature of the troops to form the army. The abolition of the purchase of rank and the possibility for ordinary men to become sub-lieutenants have opened up the ranks of the army and, at the same time, led to debates. Once more the Comte La Tour du Pin, Minister of War, defended his pet project. At the podium in the Assembly he explained that 250,000 men were needed to defend the borders, to be cut back to 150,000 in peace time, but Lameth, speaking on behalf of the military Committee, said that a reserve of 50,000 men for a peacetime force of 150,000 men is quite sufficient. As the deputies wrangle without result, the émigrés in Chambéry and Turin remain under arms and are attempting to drag the King of Sardinia into their struggle against France.

Red belt on blue, close-fitting breeches: a becoming uniform.

A soldier puts his watch into pawn. His pay is so poor ...

Pope slams Louis XVI's impious reforms

Paris, July 23

Too late! Pope Pius VI's letter to Louis XVI arrived one day too late and the King cannot go back on his decision. Yesterday, after long hesitation, he finally made up his mind to announce that he would not refuse to sanction the clergy's civil Constitution. A scrupulous Christian deeply concerned for the salvation of his soul, he came to this decision only after consultation with the two most brilliant bishops at his service: the Archbishop of Vienne, Monseigneur Lefranc de Pompignan, and the Archbishop of Bordeaux, Monseigneur Champion de Cicé.

Now, scarcely 24 hours after this difficult decision, the Pope's letter, dated July 10th., has been a big shock: after recommending him to confer with the two prelates he has already consulted, the Pope asks Louis XVI to refuse this impious

Pope Pius VI's letter places the King in a delicate position.

reform which risks casting France into error and schism. The King is now a prey to anguish, all the more so because the letter should remain secret (→ Apr. 13, 91).

Is Laclos a mere tool working for the Duc d'Orléans?

Paris, July 30

The man responsible for the events of October? It's him! The brains of the Palais Royal? Him again! And this "him" is Choderlos de Laclos, accused in a violent campaign of pamphlets of pulling all the strings of the "conspiracies plotted by the Orléans faction". His widespread notoriety as the author of the *Liaisons Dangereuses* still persists. For his political enemies, he is the "power behind the throne" of that weak being who falsely embodies a hope of change, and it is true that the Duc d'Orléans owes much to his secretary and friend whose judgement and opinions are always more reliable and more firmly founded than his own.

Indeed, it was Laclos who drew up the *Explanation for the behaviour of the Duc d'Orléans* concerning the events of October, thanks to which the prince was able to hold his head up high before his judges; but even if Laclos, having seen Philippe d'Orléans at work, no longer has any illusions about the personal worth of his favourite, he still prefers him to the one currently in power, even if only because he is closer to him (→ Nov. 30).

Europe unites against French Revolution

Reichenbach, July 27

Fear of the French Revolution spreading has come to the leaders of the European powers. Anxious about a parallel development of the situation in France and Belgium, representatives of Prussia, Holland, England and Austria met in Silesia to discuss this eventuality. The matter being urgent, the four powers came to an agreement which masks their up to now divergent interests. It is imperative that the Belgian Sates, in revolt against Vienna for some months now, should return to Austrian rule. Accordingly, Prussia, England and Holland have decided to give the Emperor free rein to act as he thinks best, so resolving a long complicated diplomatic situation. Everyone will pretend to forget that, less than three months ago, the Prussian ambassador in Paris entertained cordial relations with certain members of the Constituent Assembly. This was at the time when Prussian officers were detached to serve with Belgian patriots, to resist the Austrians ...

Free trade war breaks out in West Indies

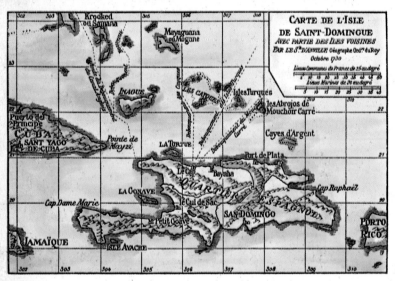

A view of the island of Saint Domingue, with its many inlets and channels and the narrow straits ships can take between the coral reefs.

Saint Domingue, July 31

Civil war has broken out between planters and traders. It was the colonial assembly, run by the settlers, which sparked things off by declaring the governor Du Peynier an outlaw. For more than a year, the "pearl" of America has been the site where two different concepts of free trade have been in conflict. The "red pompoms", the Creole planters, want to withdraw from the colonial protective system and open up the island's ports to foreign vessels. They are opposed to the Port au Prince traders who want to retain sole colonial rights. After the show of force by the Creoles, a face to face confrontation appears to be inevitable (→Aug. 6).

Assembly backs Belgian rebels

Paris, July 28

Treaties are no longer valid. The Assembly has dealt a death-blow to the 1775 alliance between Vienna and Paris. The Emperor of Austria will not be able to secure the right of passage over French territory he requested for his troops to put down the insurrection of the Belgian States. By its voice in the Assembly, the Nation has expressed its decision not to open up the frontiers to him so as not to be an accomplice in a show of force against the Belgian revolutionaries. How could it be otherwise when in France, every patriot dreams of one thing only: the spread of the Revolution! Although Leopold II is Marie Antoinette's brother, the Assembly will not allow ties of blood to prevail.

The counter-revolution is felt in Lyons

Lyons, July 26

The insurrection in Lyons was no more than a flash in the pan, but the National Guard had to put it down with loss of blood. More than a simple flare of anger, this riot was an attempt at a counter-revolution. The chief instigator of the trouble is none other than Imbert Colomès, the former municipal magistrate who has maintained close relations with the émigrés in Turin now headed by the Comte d'Artois. These conspirators were just waiting for the occasion to stir the region up against the new régime; but why at Lyons? Perhaps because the workers there are more ready than elsewhere to revolt because of the high cost of living. And, in fact, yesterday the people of Lyons came out onto the streets and destroyed the toll barriers where goods consumed within the town are taxed. The rebellion quickly took on a political turn: the crowd accused the Assembly of starving the people. This one-off alliance of people and counter-revolutionaries worries Paris greatly (→July 28).

Conus the conjuror amazes his audience

Lille, July 27

This evening, on the stage of the Théâtre de Paris, Conus made the dream of many a cuckold come true by magically making his own wife disappear. This disappearing act was the high point of a fascinating show. To carry out his tricks, this very famous conjuror, whose real name is Cote, unlike his fellow illusionists, uses absolutely no special equipment. Playing cards, coins, goblets and a few objects borrowed from members of the audience were his accessories all through the show. In this way, without effort and without any apparent trickery, he made coins pass through a table and even managed to remove articles of clothing, one by one, from a spectator. He was warmly applauded.

Malouet denounces Marat, Desmoulins

Paris, July 31

Jean Paul Marat and Camille Desmoulins are to share the same fate. Following accusations by Malouet, the deputy of Riom, the Assembly decided to charge them with having "incited the fury of the people". In Marat's case, no-one was surprised. Everybody had read his poster *C'en est fait de nous!* which appeared all over the walls of Paris on July 26th. On it the Friend of the People had issued what amounted to a call for massacre, inciting the citizens to seize arms and slay five or six hundred people to save the Revolution, but when it came to Desmoulins a questioning silence swept over the deputies. What was he guilty of? Indeed, Desmoulins had admitted that he disapproved of Marat's poster and even accused him of compromising his friends. So what was Malouet accusing him of? Simply of having attacked the King in one of the editions of *Révolutions de France et du Brabant* devoted to the Festival of the Federation. A slender accusation! In fact, Malouet was taking the opportunity of getting rid of an adversary who had already taken him to task several times and had even dubbed him "that infamous Malouet". It was to avenge this insult that the deputy of Riom linked the two men in the one charge. Marat at once wrapped himself in a cloak of secrecy. As for Desmoulins, the patriotic press has taken up his defence to have the charge dropped (→Aug. 2).

The threat of being sent to the gallows hangs over Malouet.

Constituent Assembly

1. Rome. France's Ambassador at the Vatican, Cardinal de Bernis, receives the King's order to get Pope Pius VI's blessing on the clergy's civil Constitution (→Oct. 6). The Assembly creates a diplomatic committee to restrict royal initiatives in this field.

2. Paris. Jean Sylvain Bailly's term of office as Paris' mayor is renewed.

2. Paris. Arrested for having interrupted Malouet's speech and having denounced him in his newspaper, Desmoulins is released thanks to Robespierre.

2. Paris. Because of his revolutionary opinions, Talma is snubbed by the present actors at the Théâtre Français, following similar action by its regulars.

4. Nancy. Two soldiers of the King's regiment are jailed, sparking mutiny among the soldiers who demand back pay (→15).

5. Paris. A police report condemns prison conditions in the women's gaol of the Salpêtrière.→

5. Saint Etienne. During a food riot, a mob kills a miller accused of hoarding stocks and organises a new municipality, broken up on August 6th. by the army.

6. Saint Domingue. The assembly of Saint-Marc is broken up by the troops. Its members are expelled from the island by order of the governor.→

6. Paris. La Fayette succeeds in getting a bill passed by the deputies, increasingly worried about the mutiny at Nancy. It bans soldiers' associations. Any refusal to obey orders will be considered as high treason (→16).

7. Paris. Workers in the alms-houses march to the city hall demanding a reduction in the price of bread.

9. Paris. Marat publishes a new pamphlet: *Beware, they are trying to fool us.*

11. Boulogne. Cazalès insults Barnave, as a result of which the two great orators of the Assembly fight a duel. Cazalès is slightly wounded.→

15. Nancy. After a brief respite, the rebellion spreads to all the Swiss regiments of the garrison. They decide to send a delegation to put their case to the Assembly (→16).

The capital's snare traps girls from the provinces

Paris, August 14

In the big city, Agathe Viton will see only the dim lights of a drawing room. This young orphan from the provinces has not found the job of housemaid she was looking for. Marguerite Cousin who took her in at her boarding-house soon found her another type of job. She must attend to every whim of the gentlemen waiting for her on the other side of the door. After all, why not? Her landlady has promised to feed and clothe her. So Agathe too will live in the sordid world of the "bawds". These brothel-keepers lure girls newly arrived in Paris with the promise of a job washing or mending clothes. In spite of a recent law against such activities, the police can do nothing. In the Rue Croix des Petits Champs, the girls wait in their lattice booths; on the boulevards, pimps furtively distribute their lists of addresses. The shop Trait Galant has become a meeting place for prostitutes. Even the garden of the Tuileries with its strolling, lightly-clad girls has become an open-air brothel.

Order returns to Saint Domingue

Saint Domingue, August 6

The "white pompoms" can claim victory. After a bitter battle against troops recruited by the colonial assembly, they got the better of the "red pompoms". In the face of this total defeat, 85 "red" deputies have been put on board the ship *Léopard*. They will have to answer for their conduct in Paris at the National Assembly. The hostilities between planters and traders are not of recent date, but, with the creation of the colonial assembly on March 25th., they have intensified. More numerous than the elected representatives of the town, the planters' representatives saw the assembly as the ideal tool for bringing about their economic freedom. They have sought to give Saint Domingue a constitution freeing it from the restrictions of metro-politan France. Their military collapse has ended their plans to achieve independence (→Oct. 29).

Pardon demanded for Salpêtrière women

The "ladies of pleasure" are among those callously taken to the Salpêtrière.

Paris, August 5

Of all the prisons in the capital, the Salpêtrière is certainly one of the most sordid. It is reserved for women, who generally have children and who rot in their cells, paying for their often minor offences with heavy sentences. Generally their one crime is that of having been unfaithful to their husbands or having committed petty theft. An official from the police department who paid them a visit in the context of an enquiry into prison conditions protested in great alarm: these shameful imprisonments must be stopped! He condemns the arbitrary nature of the punishments and the severity of the judges towards these unfortunate offenders. Public opinion, through its indifference, is also responsible, for the prisoners' complaints are too feeble to incite pity. So it is up to the legislators to act and ask the King to grant them a belated pardon.

The soul of an artist in search of Paradise

Switzerland, August

Leaving Paris for Switzerland has not been enough to bring him happiness. One month after marrying a young girl from Freiburg, more out of pity than for true love, the young Etienne de Sénancour dreams of only one thing: to leave again, but this time for one of those distant lands made fashionable by Bernardin de Saint Pierre. He has written to the author to ask if he can find him an island like the one described in *Paul et Virginie*. While awaiting a reply, he is rereading the novel, dreaming of a happiness he does not yet know.

The poet Etienne de Sénancour.

Two deputies fight a duel

Boulogne, August 11

Certain insults cannot be ignored and must be fought over. Following an insult hurled at Barnave by the royalist deputy Cazalès, the Assembly's two great orators arrived in the Bois de Boulogne each armed with his pistol. The duel was courteous, each begging the other to fire first. Barnave hit his adversary in the forehead and he fell. Fortunately, the brim of Cazalès' hat deadened the blow and he was only wounded.

**Constituent
Assembly**

16. Paris. By decree, the Assembly restores army discipline.→

18. Paris. La Fayette has the delegation of soldiers at Nancy arrested and writes to his cousin, the Marquis de Bouillé, asking him to put down the revolt in the garrison firmly (→31).

18. Ardèche. In league with the émigrés, 20,000 royalist National Guards create an entrenched camp at Jalès.→

21. Paris. The Assembly adopts the new disciplinary code for the army and creates military courts.

22. Paris. Mirabeau and Marat clash on the army issue.→

23. Paris. At the Favart theatre, a new comic opera, *Rigueurs du Cloitre*, with a libretto by Henri Berton and music by Joseph Fiévée, is performed.→

23. Paris. The Minister of the Interior invites manufacturers to employ workhouse children. Employers soon respond to the appeal: François Boyer Fonfrède takes on 400 children at his spinning-mill in Toulouse.

23. Paris. On the demand of the various districts, the town council decides to dissolve the corps of Bastille volunteers.

23. Nantes. The Society of the Friends of the Constitution organises a French-English festival in the presence of delegates of the British Societies (→Oct. 4, 90).

24. Pondicherry. The effects of the Revolution make themselves felt for the first time in the Indian settlements. The first mayor to be elected is Dunfort de Civrac.

26. Paris. The Assembly, refusing to recognise and honour the "family treaty", finally breaks with the Bourbons of France and Spain.

27. Paris. In the church of the Madeleine, the christening of the son of François, the baker killed in the riot of October 21st., 1789, takes place. The King and Queen, the child's godparents, send envoys.

28. Paris. Yet again, the Constituent Assembly adjourns the debate on the incorporation of the Comtat Venaissin.

31. Montauban. Garrison soldiers join forces with the patriots to ransack and loot the town's aristocratic cafés.

La Fayette calls for a "sanction to strike fear" against the Châteauvieux regiment

Paris, August 16

"The Nancy affair" has already lasted too long. The great general and "hero of the two worlds", La Fayette, has called for a return to order. The garrison at Nancy will have to toe the line and pay for its revolt. The matter calls into question the very existence of the army, although it is true that recent events are not particularly worrying. Since May the majority of soldiers at the garrison at Nancy, spurred on by the National Guard and the Jacobins, have been demanding better treatment and to be paid more regularly — but in vain! The situation deteriorated daily with arrogant officers who are hostile to the Revolution. A simple punishment of a soldier in the Châteauvieux regiment, which in other circumstances would have been a perfectly ordinary event, was the last straw. Taking up the cudgels for their comrade, the soldiers teamed up and confiscated the regiment's funds. This appropriation of the cash aroused indignation in the Assembly. After lengthy discussions, everyone fell into line with La Fayette's views. A return to dis-

The Swiss Guards are to have a red uniform. They receive double pay.

cipline will be by a "sanction to strike fear" as the decree passed today proves: those who incited the revolt will be declared guilty of high treason and punished with death. The military committee has ordered the Marquis de Malseigne, field marshal and governor of the province, to restore order, under the guise of mediation (→Aug. 18).

Chénier pleads for law and order

Paris, August 28

However justifiable and legitimate the Revolution may have been, it has lasted long enough. It is high time now to see "a return to law and order". The author of this *Opinion of the French people on their real enemies*, which dares to go against the ideas of the patriots, is none other than the famous Chénier. Moreover, he is the brother of fiery Marie Joseph, the author of *Charles IX*, but apart from family ties the two men differ greatly, particularly in their political views. Exalted for one brief moment by the winds of liberty which blew over France, André Chénier quickly saw his enthusiasm die away. Now he shares the same worries about the uncertain future as his friend Trudaine and his confidant François de Pange. In putting forward these "moderate" views, his *Opinion* risks having a considerable effect, the more so because it was published in the 13th. edition of the paper of the 1789 Society which, apart from André, counts among its members such people as Condorcet, Brissot, and even his own brother Marie Joseph ...

Marat and Mirabeau have a different conception of the army

Paris, August 22

Steps should be taken urgently. This is the one point on which Mirabeau and Marat agree. On all other matters, they differ. And the issue that separates them is the army — or rather, what is left of it!

Marat believes that noblemen must be purged from the army.

Of course, men are still to be seen in white attire with coloured markings denoting that they belong to such and such a regiment, but the army is no more: it has, so to speak, disintegrated from lack of discipline. In many garrisoned towns the grousing of the troops is getting louder every day. Even the Minister of War, La Tour du Pin, is forced to admit the army's deplorable situation; and that is not to speak of the affair at Nancy which comes up in every debate. In the face of this dangerous situation, which can only bring about confusion, Mirabeau proposed two days ago to disband the whole of the army. In his view, it would be best to recreate it with only the men who have sworn obedience to their chiefs, the aristocratic officers of the royal army. It was precisely on this matter of chiefs that Marat reacted with his usual vehemence. In his *Friend of the People* he proposed to purge the army of all its aristocratic officers so that they would no longer have

control. And in point of fact, when Mirabeau wrote that the most difficult thing "when you become involved in leading a revolution, is to contain it", Marat threw in his face the reproach that he was containing it far too well.

For Mirabeau, re-establishing the officers' authority can save the army.

Big shake-up of legal system announced

THE NEW JUSTICE

DISTRICTS COURTS	TO BE A JUDGE OF A DISTRICT COURT
5 titulars and 4 assistants elected for 6 years	Be over 30 Pay taxes equal to 10 days' salary Have practised law for 5 years

District court ← Appeal possible → District court

CANTON COURT (Peace court)	TO BE A JUSTICE OF THE PEACE
Presided over by a justice of the peace Before judgement, organises a reconciliation between the parties	Be over 30 Pay taxes equal to 10 days' salary

Election

PRIMARY ASSEMBLY	Election	TO BE AN ELECTOR
		Be over 25 Have lived in the Canton for over a year Pay taxes equal to 3 days' salary

ACTIVE CITIZENS

© Chronicle

Paris, August 16

Enough of arbitrary royal power, long live the new legal system! The Constituent Assembly has just approved a decree which completely restructures the judiciary. All judges will be elected, whether they be judges of the peace, called on to arbitrate in minor disputes between citizens, or those who sit in the district courts. Arbitration by the lords and the High Courts will disappear. This law also puts an end to buying legal authority. Magistrates will no longer wear the robe but the black habit and plumed hat like other civil servants. Juries made up of the public in general, selected by lot from the active citizens, will judge criminal affairs.

Avignon votes for new link with France

Paris, August 27

The demands of the Avignon envoys to reunite their town with France are a problem. Malouet was forced to tell them that France, having renounced all plans of pursuing wars of conquest, could not apply the principle of the right of peoples to self-determination without raising foreign powers against her. Was this the moment to antagonise the Pope, before he has even made an official pronouncement on the civil Constitution of the clergy? Moreover, the unanimous vote for reunion, obtained in dubious circumstances, is suspect. Can Avignon be reunited without the Papal estates of the Comtat Venaissin, opposed to such a move? (→ Aug. 28).

Pierre Malouet, deputy of Auvergne.

Convent drama wins praise for Fiévée

Paris, August 23

The Favart Theatre has just given us a new playwright, Joseph Fiévée. This former printer had won great success with his play, *The Convent and its Rigours* with music by Henri Berton. He was inspired by a real-life story of a young girl who had been put away in a convent against her will. Fiévée acquired a taste for literature from his contacts with books and pamphlets. He assuredly has a brilliant future ahead of him.

Census opens door to destroying dialects

Paris, August 11

Do people in the country like reading? Is local dialect spoken in the cities? Does every village have schoolteachers? These are three of the 40 questions to be answered by people in the provinces. The questionnaire has been drawn up by the Abbot Grégoire, a deputy in the Constituent Assembly, who begins his extensive survey today to get to know "country folk and all their habits". In this way he is hoping to monitor closely these regional dialects in which the Assembly is taking such an interest. However, his intentions are quite the reverse of those of his colleagues. Far from advocating the translation of laws into dialect, Grégoire wants to do away with these dialects in favour of "one national language", making French the language used in all the schools. Regional officials, clerks, priests or officials, chosen for their

The Abbot Grégoire, a promoter of the French language.

intimate knowledge of country life, will be asked to fill in the questionnaire and send it quickly back to the Assembly (→ June 4, 94).

Count Stroganoff visits Rousseau's tomb

Ermenonville, August

The isolated clearing sheltering Jean Jacques Rousseau's tomb is scarcely accustomed to such ceremonies: the usual pilgrimage of tearful disciples gave way to a solemn group of men, all visibly moved, as they stood round a young man. His name is Count Paul Stroganoff and he is Russian by birth. Today he has just completed his education in France. Around him are his friends and his tutor, Gilbert Romme. For both master and pupil, the parting moment has come: the Empress of All Russia herself has demanded that the young man should return to his country where he will be less exposed to the infection of those new ideas of which Romme is an ardent protagonist. The parting will be painful for, in the four years they have spent visiting Europe together, a true friendship has sprung up between them, but it was not just idle sorrow: the sanctuary rang to the vows of the two friends to remain faithful to their ideals of justice and liberty.

The tomb of Jean Jacques Rousseau at the park of Ermenonville.

Armed noblemen gather at Jalès camp

Gard, August 18

The counter-revolution is gathering strength. In the south of the Vivarais, traditionally the cradle of religious wars, 20,000 men mustered at Jalès. For these nobles and National Guards hostile to the Revolution, the National Assembly is abhorrent. Similarly, the efforts of the Constituent Assembly are considered invalid and its members are looked on as men having committed high treason. Acting in agreement and together with the Comte d'Artois and the émigrés, the federates of the camp at Jalès intend to stir up the south of France against the laws of the Assembly. On the initiative of Charles de Polignac and Laurent de Palarin, they have even drawn up a manifesto calling for resistance (→ Feb. 27, 91).

The faithful pray for rain to stop drought

France, August

The torrid heat at present afflicting the kingdom is a punishment from God. It is the only explanation for the heat wave which has caused wells and rivers to dry up over the last month and has killed off beasts and cattle. The parched land has turned to dust and the vine-growers watch their crops withering under their very gaze. In churches, prayers are said continually. In Saint Aignan in Loir et Cher, a pilgrimage had even been organised to ward off the curse. Wonder of wonders! A crowd of believers from all over the department saw the bishop simply raise his cross for rain to start falling abundantly. And all fell to their knees to drink the blessed drops. The prelate said: "Miracles exist."

Severe sanctions for the Swiss at Châteauvieux

Nancy, August 31

The Marquis de Bouillé, La Fayette's cousin, has carried out the National Assembly's orders to the hilt.

There are more than 300 dead bodies to prove it: the Swiss regiment at Châteauvieux has been brought to heel, as he intended. From August 16th., the Assembly, informed of the confiscation of the regimental funds by the soldiers in the garrison at Nancy, decided to restore discipline. A week later, the Marquis de Malseigne was on the scene. Although officially charged with settling the dispute between the officers and troops, the Marquis quickly realised that there was practically no possibility of coming to an agreement with the soldiers. The mutineers refused to obey his orders and leave the town. Called in to help, the departmental National Guard sided with the soldiers and even took Malseigne hostage. The Constituent Assembly then sent the Marquis de Bouillé, who set off immediately to settle the problem once and for all. Refusing to negotiate with the mutineers, he informed them of his conditions: the immediate release of Malseigne and the officers held prisoner; departure of the regiments in Nancy; but the final condition proved too severe: each regiment was called on to designate a certain number of soldiers to be hanged, as an example. Two regiments complied. Only the Swiss remained on the Place de Grève in the town and refused to pay such a price. This brought the "affair at Nancy" to a bloody end: a shot, fired from no-one knows where, started the massacre which apparently stemmed from the desire to suppress military and political officials rather than to hold any form of negotiation: 33 Swiss were put to death and 41 condemned to penal servitude (→ Sept. 2).

The Swiss Guards who are condemned to death are hanged or broken on the wheel. In the foreground, prisoners condemned to penal servitude move off.

The devoted young soldier Désilles rushing towards the rebels to avoid a bloodbath: "Don't shoot!" he shouts before being hit by a hail of bullets.

Constituent Assembly

2. Paris. Thousands of Parisians demonstrate in support of the rebel soldiers at Nancy.→

4. Paris. Jacques Necker resigns.→

4. Paris. Production at the Favart Theatre of *Euphrosine et Corradin*, a lyrical drama by François Benoît Hoffman and Etienne Nicolas Méhul.

4. Versailles. The communes round the royal palace demand that all the people under their jurisdiction be allowed the right to hunt freely outside the limits of the park.

6. Brest. The first mutiny takes place on board *América* (→17).

6. Paris. The Assembly approves the final suppression of the former parliaments.

6. Marly le Roi. The local priest has the laws on the civil Constitution of the clergy published and takes his own oath of allegiance in advance.

6. Angers. A demonstration of women from the slate quarries for a cut in bread prices ends in bloodshed: troops open fire killing 51 people.

7. Paris. A decree is passed establishing a centre for the National Archives.→

9. Corsica. In the consultative assembly of Orezza, Pascal Paoli is proclaimed president of the island's administrative council.

10. Lyons. First meeting of the People's Society of Friends of the Constitution, created after the Jacobins' refusal to accept inactive citizens in their society.

13. Paris. By a special law, the Assembly sets aside a hunting reserve for the King to be able to practise his favourite pastime.

15. Limoges. Fire ravages whole sections of the town, destroying 186 houses.

15. Besançon. The branch of the Society of Friends of the Constitution is denounced by citizens hostile to its increasing power.

16. Paris. *Le Misanthrope par Amour ou Sophie Desfrancs*, a play by the Marquis de Sade, has been received by the Comédie Française. As it will never be performed, Sade will be granted free admission until 1795, as compensation.

17. Brest. Mutinies break out on board the *Patriot* and the *Léopard*.

5,000 marchers protest Nancy massacre

Paris, September 2

With the announcement of the bloody reprisals against the mutineers at Nancy, the people of Paris have reacted violently. In the early afternoon, a band of 5,000 people set off from the Palais Royal for the Assembly. When they arrived at the Tuileries, there were already 40,000 people surrounding the hall of the Manège, shouting "String the ministers up!". This frenzied crowd demanded the dismissal of Necker and La Tour du Pin, the Minister of War. The demonstrators then wanted to go to Saint Cloud to blame the King himself and only changed their minds at the last moment. The speed with which this riot has come about and its size are surprising. The demonstrators do not seem to have gathered spontaneously and it is suspected that the leaders of the Jacobin Club could well have a hand in today's disturbances.

King, Assembly congratulate Bouillé

Paris, September 3

The Marquis de Bouillé can be proud. On a proposal by Mirabeau, the deputies have just passed a motion congratulating him on having put down the revolt at Nancy. The King sent him a letter of thanks for his courageous conduct, urging him to keep up the good work. Indeed, the least that can be said is that in taking the initiative for the massacre of the Châteauvieux regiment, the Marquis de Bouillé displayed authority. Robespierre unsuccessfully attempted to block the motion, crying: "In the end you will perhaps see all the patriotic soldiers on one side and, in Monsieur de Bouillé's army, all those whom despotism and the aristocracy have in their pay", but the Assembly wants law and order and so Robespierre was booed down, the deputies preferring to back Mirabeau and La Fayette. Rewards

The Marquis de Bouillé, commander in chief of Alsace and Lorraine.

were even voted for the National Guards who fired on the Swiss in Nancy. And what does it matter if the people of Paris revolt?

Fallen minister Necker forced to resign

Abandoned by the King, Necker is no longer Minister of Finance.

Paris, September 4

"How are the mighty fallen!" Yesterday adored by all, today Necker has been spurned by King, people and deputies. Moreover, the news of his resignation was coldly received in the hall of the Manège; but somebody has to be the scapegoat for the unpopularity of the affair at Nancy. The Minister of Finance fits the bill. For did he not fail totally to balance the nation's accounts? Assignats, his brainchild, are a fiasco of the first water; so much so that the Assembly decided just a short time ago that it would be responsible itself for the treasury. The darling of 1789 has turned into a symbol for the nation's bankruptcy (→Sept. 18).

Top musicians' precarious life

Paris, September 5

The musicians of the Sainte Chapelle have sent the authorities a pathetic petition. The loss of ecclesiastical earnings has plunged them into a dramatic state of penury. At the age of 69, after 22 years of loyal service, the 'cello player Nicolas Bidault from Gardinville has been reduced to begging for an allowance. Too old to live by his art, he no longer has the benefit of his little priory in the region of Caux, which has been confiscated by the state. By comparison, Gervais Couperin, the organist, is better placed: at least he has been given his own living quarters.

Assignats attacked by the English MP Burke

London, September

Beware! The system of assignats is a threat to freedom in France. Such a totally unexpected warning came from Edmund Burke, the English member of parliament and brilliant supporter of the American revolution. In his eyes, a state which interferes in the economy becomes a tyrant and, in the name of abstract principles, oppresses the individual. This is how he strongly denounced the artifical nature of this paper money whose value does not depend on public confidence but on an arbitrary decision by the government (→Nov. 1).

Burke, the English MP, is in favour of freedom of the economy.

After the mutiny in Toulon, the sailors of Brest follow suit

A battalion of National Guards arrives on the quays to disperse a mob of sailors.

Brest, September 17

Ten months after Toulon, the port of Brest is seething with unrest. On board the ships, the crews of the *Patriote* and the *Léopard* have rebelled against their officers. On shore, too, passions are roused and the gallows erected by the crowd in front of the house of the assistant admiral superintendent, Monsieur de Marigny, bears witness to a climate of insurrection. Revolt is everywhere. Deliberately fomented by members of the Society of Friends of the Constitution, defiance of the officers has become widespread. It only needed the revolutionary club to take up the cudgels for the Swiss condemned to penal servitude at Nancy to plunge everything into disorder. In the eyes of the soldiers, the officers are unscrupulous administrators of regimental funds. Since blood has flowed between soldiers and military officials, there is no more army. After the abolition of hereditary nobility, this wave of mutinies will increase emigration still further. The problem of reinstating these officials has now become a matter of great urgency.

A fusilier of the Fleet.

Is medical care adequate in France?

The doctors of today may not be as bad as those of the past, but being ill is still a problem. Despite recent progress in anatomy and knowledge of the human body, medicine remains a hesitant science. The different symptoms presented by patients often remain a mystery to the doctor who indiscriminately prescribes the same remedy for everybody. Anyone with a temperature is subjected to bleeding, supposed to purify the organism by eliminating malignant humours, but the sailor with his scurvy, the child with rickets and the old man crippled with gout remain an enigma about which the practitioner is still impotent, failing to understand the origin of the illness; and yet the microscope has enabled us to discover the secrets of anatomy. Following the example of the botanists' classifications, from now on illnesses will be listed and classified. It is now known that blood pressure can be measured precisely, and Lavoisier has proved that when we breathe, we consume oxygen, but these important discoveries have not changed the realities of medical care, and all too often at the patient's bedside, the practitioner's knowledge is called into question. Instead of a thorough examination, he is content to study urine samples before writing esoteric prescriptions. This is why many poor French peasants resort to charlatans, bonesetters and those self-styled miracle-workers popularly known as "faith healers".

Assembly sets up a National Archive open to everyone

Paris, September 7

It was high time to classify and file the Nation's acts and documents! The decree voted today by the Assembly established a new institution: the national archives. Five secretaries will be appointed to look after the acts, charters and documents concerning the state and the government. Under the direction of Armand Camus, the former legal adviser to parliament in Paris and deputy of Tiers, they will have to keep a register of all the documents entrusted to them and open up the archives to the public three days a week. Formerly private and secret, from now on the archives are to be centralised and accessible to everybody.

Necker quits Paris, his career finished

A retirement in the country awaits Necker at the château of Coppet.

Coppet, September 21

Neither satire nor eulogy. Not one word. What a sorry departure for this man who was everybody's hero only 15 months ago! Necker and his wife left Paris on September 18th., in an atmosphere of general indifference. Abandoned roads, full of pot-holes, ruts which bogged down and delayed their vehicle ... they were spared nothing. Even though he had a passport from the King and another delivered by the municipality of Paris, the former finance minister was right to be worried about the welcome awaiting him along the route. At Arcis sur Aube, the day after his departure, the crowd blocked his passage demanding his immediate arrest. He could only continue his journey after the National Assembly intervened. The same thing happened again at Vesoul, obliging him to give up the idea of going to the spa of Plombières to take the waters. From his vehicle, Necker sadly recalled his triumphant return to Versailles on July 29th. 1789, but this time everything is well and truly over. Meditating on his astonishing career, he arrived this morning at Coppet and has decided never more to leave this retreat.

Journalist Elisée Loustalot has died

Paris, September 19

Has disappointment hastened the end of Elisée Loustalot? The principal writer of the *Révolutions de Paris*, who was not yet 30, did not survive the grief he suffered at the Constituent Assembly's thanks to General Bouillé for his bloody repression of the mutinies at Nancy. This incorruptible defender of the Revolution and its press, from the *Ami du Peuple* to the *Ami du Roi*, wrote: "If there is only one man to stop abusing public feeling, we shall owe liberty to him! Who among us will receive this palm?" He was surely the one to deserve it!

"Solemn March" for the Swiss

Paris, September 20

There has never been a more approriate homage in music. To honour the memory of the victims of Châteauvieux, Gossec has written a *Solemn March*: as muffled drums mark time, the violins reply in high plaintive wails. It is not strictly a melody but rather a succession of poignant chords which strike the listener by their bold chromatic harmonies. To reinforce the effect, Gossec has not hesitated to enrich the tone colour of the military orchestra by the addition of trombones and even tomtoms, up till now unknown.

Oven-selling clown is new populist icon

Paris, September

Père Duchesne has now "gone public"! This popular personage, a sort of clown born in the fairs where he represented the traditional seller of ovens, is fast becoming a name which features in all the headlines of the newspapers read by the masses. At a moment when the democrats are openly breaking with the constitutional monarchists, it has become a matter of urgency to win over public opinion by a great show of demagogy. The *Hellishly patriotic letters of the real Père Duchêne*, inspired by the monarchists, was quickly followed by the appearance of the patriotic *Père Duchesne's anger*, also written in common, vulgar language. The author of this last periodical, Jacques René Hébert, the son of a rich Alençon goldsmith, has been eking out a living in Paris for some years after a sorry history. "Blood and sand! I'll bet you anything this will not be the last Père Duchesne," people say.

This huge gathering has nothing to do with the popular rejoicing of the celebrations for the Federation. It is a solemn funeral ceremony, held in Paris on September 20th. around the altar to the Nation, in honour of the "citizen soldiers" who died at Nancy during the reprisals against the Swiss of Châteauvieux.

Constituent Assembly

4. England. Jacobins of Nantes meet members of the Society of the Revolution in London.

6. Paris. The Academy of Sculpture and Painting asks to be allowed to remove works of art from religious institutions to exhibit them to the public in a suitable place (→Jan. 4, 91).

6. Saint Cloud. Louis XVI condemns the civil Constitution of the clergy in a private letter to the King of Spain.→

6. Paris. Antoine Augustin Parmentier founds *La Feuille du Cultivateur*, a newspaper intended to inform people in the country of innovations in the field of agriculture.

11. Joigny. The mayor asks the War Minister to send a squadron of cavalry to oversee the 3,000 workers from the workshops in Paris, currently working on the canal of Bourgogne.

13. Paris. Nicolas Bonneville and the priest Fauchet create the publication *Iron Mouth*.→

16. Paris. The National Assembly creates a special administrative office for the arts and professions.

18. Le Mans. Harvesting begins. Experts say this year's crops should be of excellent quality but limited in quantity.

22. Paris. At the Opéra, the première of *la Divinité du Sauvage ou le Portrait*, a lyrical drama by the composer Stanislas Champein, takes place.

22. Saint Jean d'Angély. The mayor of Varaize is killed in the course of a fight between the garrison and peasants who were looting convoys of wheat.

28. Paris. Merlin de Douai declares in the Assembly that Alsace will be French, as its inhabitants wish.→

29. Saint Domingue. The start of a revolt by mulattoes.

30. Paris. Archbishop Leclerc de Boisgelin, in a paper entitled *Exposition des Principes des Evêques Députés sur la Constitution Civile du Clergé*, asks that the Pope's sanction be awaited before the measure is implemented.

31. Paris. The Assembly decrees the suppression of internal customs toll barriers.

31. Aix en Provence. The priest Rive founds the Society of Anti-politicians, affiliated to the Cordeliers.

The King secretly hostile to the civil Constitution of the clergy

Saint Cloud, October 6

The King has embarked upon the the risky course of double-dealing. In a letter he sent to his cousin Charles IV, the King of Spain, he severely condemns the civil Constitution of the clergy although he promulgated this law on August 24th. It seems that it was under duress that he gave his approval to this reform. He will also have to approve new laws which he considers impious. Already, a year ago, Louis XVI had conducted secret correspondence with the sovereigns of Europe. In every letter, he explained that he was no longer free to act as he wished and that the different steps to which he had given his assent had been imposed on him. Moreover, on his forced return to Paris, Louis XVI had written to the King of Spain saying that by virtue of the "family pact" between the Bourbons of France and Spain, he was particularly counting on him to strive to unite the sovereigns solidly against the Revolution. Since that time the Spanish government has organised a network of spies in Paris, so ensuring that the King is very well informed.

Charles Surcouf is banned from India

Pondicherry, October 10

Charles Surcouf will not be governor. A bitter quarrel with an officer has ended the Indian dream of this sailor from Brittany and, by the verdict pronounced against him by the magistrates of Pondicherry, he is to leave India. Whatever the case, the monsoons have not blown in his favour, for during the crossing this summer he was shipwrecked and lost all he had.

The "Iron Mouth" speaks to France

Paris, October 13

Truth sometimes comes from the letter-box. The contents of the *Iron Mouth*, the organ of the new Social Circle, will be composed out of letters from the Friends of the Truth which have been placed in the suggestions boxes destined for this purpose. Their creator is the priest Claude Fauchet, a mystical patriot of esoteric speech who intends to "work in general concert of the human mind to create worldwide happiness"!

Title page of the "Iron Mouth", the "patriotic and fraternal" paper.

Exiled nobles set up court in Turin

Turin, October

Versailles is now dead, long live Turin! And if you have to live in exile, it is better to remain with people of high birth. Among the several hundred nobles in this seraglio are the Prince de Condé who has had his horses brought over from Chantilly, the Ducs d'Angoulême and Berry and the Princess of Monaco. Everyone wears state dress and every week they meet Victor Amedeus III, King of Sardinia. They go to the ball, or masquerades at the theatre. And when they are too bored, they play billiards. The uncontested sovereign of this new court is the Comte d'Artois, Louis XVI's younger brother. Living in the palace of Moncalieri, Victor Amedeus son-in-law, once such a feeble person, now takes an interest in politics: he wants to set up free groups of émigrés and establish a diplomatic network with foreign powers hostile to the Revolution — a plan which takes up all his time.

Via del Carmine in Turin where many French émigrés are to be found.

How to write at the speed of speech

Paris, October 1

At last there is no more risk of blunting your quill as you hastily take dictation! An end too to wrist cramp and incomplete copies! This is thanks to a brand new system of "tachography" perfected by its anonymous inventor. His original and astute method does not require any great powers of memory and does away with fatigue, but doubtless takes a short time to learn. Just imagine, for example, a debate in the Assembly when the speakers rapidly interrupt one another in successive uproar and with an unceasing flood of words. How can all this be recorded satisfactorily? First by splitting the work among a few seated round a table and then by each secretary nudging his neighbour to indicate which part he is going to copy, at what point he is going to finish and where he is going to take up again. It is up to each one to continue the chain (→Apr. 27, 91).

The people of Paris demand minister's dismissal

Paris, October 10

A crowd seething with hatred demonstrated today at the instigation of the different sectors. The people demanded the dismissal of the ministers whose unpopularity knows no bounds. Attempts at sedition are on the increase throughout the army, and the mutiny of the squadron in Brest proves yet again how little confidence the public has in the government. These events are not confined to the capital: tension is mounting in the very heart of the Assembly; but for the moment, unrest is on the streets. The people are screaming for the "traitors" to go. They particularly insist about La Luzerne, Minister of the Fleet and Saint Priest, Minister of the Interior. Only Montmorin finds favour in their eyes. It is certain that the replacing of districts by sections has not calmed the Parisians' frenzy.

King orders Sené's fine furniture

Paris, October

The state's finances do not appear to be in such bad shape after all. The Keeper of the Royal Chambers continues to give large orders to the best cabinet-makers in the capital. It is true that Jacob is less in demand than formerly, but this is because of his exorbitant prices. The latest order has been entrusted to Jean Baptiste Sené who has just delivered a magnificent set of armchairs and divans for the King's suite in Compiègne.

A chair by Jean-Baptiste Sené.

Jacques Réattu wins the prestigious Rome painting trophy

Paris, October

It is no easy matter to carry off the first prize in the *Prix de Rome* competition. Every year there are a hundred or so candidates, French art students who must be male and single.

The lucky winner this year is a young painter aged 28, Jacques Réattu, whose work called *Daniel silencing the assembly of elders accusing the beauteous Susanna* won first prize. The first round in the competition consists of painting in one day an outline of a given subject, so permitting a preliminary selection of the candidates. A fortnight later, they have four sessions of seven hours to paint a live model, in this case a nude male. The jury then retains only ten candidates for the final test: for 72 days, with the exception of Sundays and public holidays, the candidate is confined to his room in the School and has to execute a large painting of which the given subject is always drawn from ancient history or mythology.

One further difficulty is that the artist must remain faithful to the outline he executed on the first day of the competition or risk being eliminated. At the end of all these tests, the winner is decided by majority vote of the professors unless they consider that there is no work which merits the much coveted first prize. The winner of the laureate has the distinguished privilege of having his work exhibited for five years in the French Academy in Rome.

This painting by Jacques Réattu won the Rome painting award.

Inside the dark and humble homes of the French peasantry

The interior of a Brittany peasant's home. It is simply one badly lit room which serves as both living room and bedroom for the family.

In the peasant's home there is nothing superfluous, nor is there luxury: one single room, which is usually dark, set up to use the available space for the necessities of living, heating, eating and sleeping. A huge fireplace ensures heating for the whole of the room and serves at the same time for cooking. For sleeping, there are straw mattresses on a wooden bed with eiderdowns and pillows of down. The clock marks off the time, a chest serves to stow away the few belongings, a kneading trough is for making bread which is kept in a bin or a bread pan, depending on the region. The dresser, an essential element of any room, or at least the rooms of the better off, reigns in the centre. In it are kept china plates with family or patriotic designs, bought from pedlars, which are used only on high days and holidays. On normal days, glazed earthenware or ironstone china has to do.

Spinning wheel for flax or hemp, a vital piece of equipment.

Mother spins while gently rocking the cradle with her foot.

Resignation deepens government crisis

Between the people and the King, General La Fayette proves to be the man of the moment.

Paris, October 20

"Make the government resign": that is the advice given to the King by his two secret advisors, Bergasse, the lawyer and Paris deputy, and Mirabeau.

Both men are looking for ways to strengthen Louis XVI's position and have told the King to place the blame for the worsening government crisis on the Assembly. After Necker's resignation early this month, it is now La Luzerne, Minister of the Navy for the past three years, who has resigned. He based his decision on the wave of mutinies that has been sweeping through the navy since September and on the patriots' growing discontent. Louis XVI now has plenty of elbow room to call on the supporters of La Fayette. Names are already being bandied about: de Lessart, Duport Dutertre, Pastoret and Duportail. The King is, however, unlikely to satisfy the patriots, who have been unhappy with La Fayette since the Nancy affair.

Tricolour is chosen for new French flag

Paris, October 21

The royal fleur-de-lis is no longer in season! A few months after the fall of the Bastille, La Fayette offered the King the famous red, white and blue cockade. Since then, the tricoloured emblem has been worn as a victory sign and has become a symbol of the Revolution. France's national flag is also to be tricoloured. The traditional colours of the city of Paris, red and blue, will be placed on either side of a white strip, symbol of the monarchy. For a time there were plans to include green in the new flag, but people recalled that green was part of the livery of the Comte d'Artois, that most hated of princes.

The three national colours were dispersed: now they are joined together.

Louis XVI thinks about leaving Paris

Paris, October 22

The King is tired of the situation. He feels humiliated by his stay at the Tuileries, which was forced upon him by the Assembly. He also believes that he has forced to give his approval to the decree on the clergy's civil Constitution. The only remaining option seems to be escape. The King is convinced that, if he succeeds in fleeing from Paris, he will be able to recover his sovereignty. He is also certain that the army will obey him and that his people will once again support him. Louis XVI has therefore secretly written to Bouillé, who is in command of the troops in the east. This officer is prepared for everything and has already drawn up a plan that is supported by the Queen. Bouillé would be in charge of royal security during the escape. The plan would be overseen by Fersen, while Breteuil would negotiate with the Emperor of Austria to get him

The royal family takes a walk in the gardens of the Tuileries, while their escort keeps watch.

to intervene militarily in favour of his brother-in-law; but it is an extremely risky plan. Are foreign powers ready to risk war in order to save Louis XVI? (→ Nov. 26).

Cerruti's paper keeps villagers informed

"It is for you that we write, peaceful inhabitants of the countryside; it is high time for learning to reach you."

Paris, October 28

The title given to the weekly newspaper for rural areas is truly impressive: "Village newsletter sent each week to all the villages of France to inform them of the laws, events and discoveries that are of interest to all citizens."

Its founder, Joseph Cerutti, a former Jesuit, knows that most peasants are illiterate. He is therefore relying on priests to read out his publication from the pulpit. In the fifth edition published today, the village newsletter writes in its section on "universal geography" about France, which it says is a country that "has all that is best in Europe", particularly since the nation has given itself "the only thing it lacked: a Constitution". Today's edition also includes a brief "catechism on the French Constitution". This is presented in the form of questions and answers to make it easier to understand.

Bishops caught between Pope and nation

Paris, October 30

The bishops of the Assembly are asking that the Pope should at least be given enough time to state his position before the clergy's civil Constitution is enforced.

That is the thrust of the call they made in their text, *Exposition des Principes,* which was written by Boisgelin, Archbishop of Aix, and which only Talleyrand and Gobel refused to sign. Boisgelin and his colleagues condemn any reform of the church that is undertaken only by the civilian authorities. However, their position is relatively moderate and they do not rule out a compromise agreement, but it may be too late for that. At the Assembly, the patriots have charged that the text is just a dilatory move aimed at delaying the enforcement of the new legislation. However, the hard-line opponents of the Revolution see Boisgelin's text as being scandalously weak.

They claim that what happened at the start of the month during the funeral of the Bishop of Quimper proves their argument. Before a large crowd of faithful, a group of canons — who are to be dismissed under the terms of the new law — read out the dead man's "will" in which the dead prelate said the planned legislation constituted a mortal danger for the Catholic Church (→ Nov. 27).

No compensation for Alsace, says report

Paris, October 28

The German princes will not be given a penny in compensation. The deputy Merlin de Douai today submitted his report on the territories in Alsace which had been ceded to the princes by Louis XVI and have now been incorporated into France. Using some very subtle logic, this outstanding jurist demonstrates that the suppression of the fiefs is legitimate since treaties signed in the past are no longer valid. The Germans, therefore, are not entitled to receive compensation. All that matters is the will of the people of Alsace, who have chosen to be incorporated into France; but this is a double-edged argument that could result in the people of another region of France opting to join a foreign nation...

David gets an order from the Jacobins

Paris, October 28

The Revolution wants a work of art that will provide a truly worthy record of the momentous events of 1789.

Today Dubois Crancé suggested to his Jacobin friends that the oath taken at the Jeu de Paume tennis courts should be immortalised by a fitting painting. Whom should the work of art be commissioned from? The artist preferred by Dubois Crancé is David, who has already started to work on the project. Nobody has any doubts about the talent of David, particularly in view of his famous work *Serment des Horaces.*

Financing the painting and the reproductions should not pose any problems: a public subscription of 72,000 francs will be set up. It will be made up of 3,000 titles each giving the buyer the right to one printed reproduction of the work. This painting will be huge, 30 feet by 20, and will decorate the chamber at the Assembly. Some are, however, amused that David has been selected, as the artist was not even there on the day the oath was taken at the Jeu de Paume.

A preparatory sketch by David for his "Oath at the Jeu de Paume".

The Assembly adopts the decimal system

A litre (1), a gram (2), a metre (3), an are (4), a franc (5), a stere (6).

Paris, October 27

In future the system used in France for both weights and measures will be based on the decimal mathematical scale.

Following its decision, taken on May 8th., to unify the various systems of weights and measures, the Constituent Assembly has just confirmed a ruling by the Academy of Science, but it seems more than likely that a lot of water will flow under the bridge before the new decimal system becomes a reality, as there is such a wide variety of measures currently in use. Old habits are also hard to break. The Academy of Science had received details of the weights and measures still in use in the departments. It was an impressive list. The decimal reform is based on the efforts undertaken by Talleyrand, who was the first to propose the law. The Bishop of Autun was looking for a "natural, unchanging and universal system that can be adopted by all nations". Talleyrand even asked the president of the United Sates and the British parliament for advice. He stressed that it was in the "interest of international trade for all the civilised peoples to have the same measures". However, a great many small merchants in the provinces of France have already voiced strong opposition to the new system (→ Mar. 19, 91).

Mulattoes want to become full citizens

Saint Domingue, October 29

Either the decree of March 8th. is proclaimed, or there will be war: that is the choice given to the island's authorities by the mulattoes of the northern province. Here, as in Martinique, the freed mulattoes have decided to defend, with force if necessary, their demand that their rights as citizens should be recognised. These are enshrined in the decree, which states that they should be granted to all free men, regardless of colour. The mulattoes are led by Vincent Ogé, a brilliant lawyer and also a man of action. He has set up a militia of coloured men including veterans of the American War (→ Nov. 25).

The slaves want their freedom and free mulattoes demand citizenship.

Exiled minister criticises French economy

London, October

Charles Alexandre de Calonne is getting his revenge. He had been dismissed from the finance ministry in 1787 for having been unable to convince the privileged classes to drop their opposition to reforms. Later he was defeated in the elections to the Estates General, and decided to go into exile on the fateful day of July 14th. 1789. In his book *De l'Etat de la France*, published this month in London, he paints a dark picture of the state of the French economy: public expenditure is growing while receipts are dropping. He adds that the Estates General, who have since become the Assembly, had met to solve the problem, but had worsened it.

Babeuf defends the small tradesmen

Picardy, October 23

François Noël Babeuf has in the past been jailed for having called for the abolition of taxation, but he has not learnt his lesson. He has now come to the defence of small tradesmen. The butchers, innkeepers and café owners of Roye have been refusing to pay their indirect taxes ever since July 1789. The regional authorities have threatened to take legal action against them, so Babeuf has had a pamphlet printed that condemns the collection of these taxes. In the text he speaks out against the unjust way in which the taxes are assessed and the high cost of their collection. He knows what he's talking about: before the fiefs were abolished by the Revolution, this former landed property commissioner used to collect the seigneurial duties on property. Since then, he has become fascinated by politics and defends the cause of the people in his paper *Le Courrier Picard*.

Marie Antoinette is booed at the opera

Paris, October

How truly humiliating it was for the Queen! A few days ago, during a performance at the Paris Opéra of Gluck's *Iphigénie en Aulide,* the actor Laisné caused an uproar by singing the famous song "Let us praise our Queen" with a little too much conviction and gusto. However, according to tradition, the audience was supposed to pay homage to the Queen each time this opera was performed in public, but times have changed. This time, the unfortunate actor was not even able to finish his song. On the following Sunday, he was forced to apologise when he appeared on stage. On bended knee, he begged the audience to forgive him for having caused offence. He was also forced to tread on a crown to prove his patriotism. The incident was humiliating for the Queen and the monarchy and gave Marie Antoinette an idea of the full extent of the people's hatred of her.

1. London. The *Reflections on the Revolution in France,* by the British Whig statesman and conservative political theorist and orator Edmund Burke, are published (→ 29).

6. Paris. The Académie gives a performance of the opera *Iphigénie en Tauride* by Niccolo Piccinni to raise funds for the composer, who has fallen on hard times.

6. Sarlat. The general council decides to ban all the societies affiliated to the royalist club, Friends of Peace, in the department of Dordogne.

7. Ile et Vilaine. The National Guard of Bais intervenes at Gennes, following a call from a citizen who acuses the former president of the parliament of Brittany, Farcy de Cuillé, of hiding weapons and keeping his family's coat of arms at the church.

7. Paris. The Théâtre de la Nation gives the première of *Nicodème dans la Lune,* a successful play by Louis Abel Beffroy de Reigny.

9. Paris. The Assembly hears a message from the Dunkirk Society of Friends of the Constitution asking it for a decree placing club members under the law's protection.

10. Nantes. After a call from the Jacobins, a Requiem mass is said in memory of victims of the Nancy clashes.

10. Paris. A delegation from the Commune, led by Georges Danton, comes to the Assembly to demand the dismissal of ministers held responsible for the Nancy bloodshed.

11. Montauban. In agreement with the town council, the local people's society asks for the recall of the Royal Polish cavalry regiment, whose reactionary attitude is said to cause repeated clashes with the town's National Guard and the Tourraine infantry regiment.

12. Roanne. The Loire river, which has been rising steadily, floods low-lying parts of the city.

12. Paris. Charles de Lameth is wounded in a duel. →

14. Avignon. To avoid trouble during parades, the council orders the ghetto shut down.

15. Saint Domingue. Due to his anti-slavery stance, the commander of the Dauphin fort is ordered to be arrested by the Cap Assembly.

Church assets sold to highest bidder

Bordeaux, November 5

Going ... going ... gone! The first public auction of the clergy's property, which has been "placed at the nation's disposal", has just begun. Noblemen, members of the bourgeoisie, artisans, peasants and even clergymen are present in the auction room at the district's headquarters. Each successive sale, even when it reaches well above the reserve price, is welcomed by cheering and the buyer is congratulated for his patriotism. The proud buyer, however, often asks permission to have his payments spread over twelve months.

Young actress is de Sade's new love

Paris, November 1

The Marquis de Sade's latest conquest is called Marie Constance Quesnet. This young and good looking actress, who has been abandoned by an ungrateful husband, has stolen the nobleman's heart. Both of them are now living in a small house with a garden on the Rue Neuve des Mathurins. The Marquis has asked that furniture be sent from his castle at La Coste so that he can furnish his new home, where he feels as happy as "a big fat country priest in his presbytery". After spending years in captivity, he truly enjoys a little comfort. Could this be the start of a new life for the Marquis with the young woman he has dubbed "Sensitive"?

Alcohol and politics don't mix

Paris, November

Godet has suffered a bad bullet wound in the stomach. He had tried to get rid of a client who had been drinking heavily and was becoming uncontrollable, but the man returned with a group of his friends and waved his pistol around wildly, shouting "This is from La Fayette!". The man was a supporter of the Marquis and had been meeting friends of Marat at the lemonade vendor's café. The poor Godet has now sworn that no more politics will be discussed in his café.

Duc de Castries' house looted and burnt to avenge Lameth

The people find their own solution to discord among three noble factions: Castries, Lameth and La Fayette.

Charles de Lameth is wounded in his duel against the Duc de Castries.

Paris, November 12

"Let's all go to the Duc's house. Let us avenge Lameth!" At least 10,000 people gathered outside the Castries residence, on the Rue de Varenne. The angry mob was fully prepared to attack the building, but the Duc de Castries had cautiously decided to seek refuge at the residence of his good friend the Princesse de Tarente. He knew that he was in danger. The duel he had just fought with his political rival Charles de Lameth had placed him in a delicate situation. There are rumours that the Duc had dipped his sword in poison and that the wound suffered by his opponent is very serious. People are afraid that Lameth will die. Pamphlets handed out in the streets tell of the duel and strongly condemn the winner's attitude. While a delegation of patriots was on its way to the wounded man's home, the mob poured through the gate to the Castries residence. Everything happened very quickly. In less than half an hour the house had been sacked and reduced to ashes. Iron bars were used to shatter windows, furniture was thrown outside, the Castries coat of arms was torn down and tapestries ripped apart. The gold table-ware was stolen, while curtains were set on fire and mirrors broken. Not far from the scene of the violence, La Fayette was standing by with drawn sword, backed by a unit of his cavalrymen. He kept a close watch on events, but did not intervene.

Revolution bodes ill for the harpsichord

Paris, November 10

Will the harpsichord last until the end of the century? The piano's growing popularity is partly to blame for the sharp decline of the harpsichord.

The piano is also undergoing rapid technical advances and it has opened up new musical possibilities. The current political situation in France is not helping matters, as many people see the harpsichord as a symbol of aristocratic refinement. Many of the lovers of its music have been forced to emigrate. Louis Hénocq, the celebrated instrument maker, has just died leaving large debts behind.

A lot of other builders cannot survive, being unable to build pianos. Before he died, Louis Hénocq had barely been surviving by selling his wife's jewels at the local pawn shop. He even had to pawn the curtains of his apartment.

A harpsichord with two keyboards built by Jean Claude Goujon. It dates from the 1750s.

Corsican draws knife in Assembly debate

Paris, November 6

There were some angry exchanges at the Assembly during a particularly heated debate on Corsica. The patriots of the island had sent two emissaries to the Constituent Assembly to speak out against the behaviour of Matteo Buttafuoco and Carlo Peretti, respectively Corsican deputies of the nobility and the clergy, but the emissaries were not allowed to speak. Aristocrats accused them of insulting representatives of the people and demanded their expulsion, but Mirabeau read out two private letters from the Abbot Peretti proving the latter's hostility to the clergy's civil Constitution. The enraged abbot took a knife from his sleeve and would have struck Mirabeau if he had not been stopped.

Mirabeau defending the clergy's civil Constitution.

Smokers must pay the price for pleasure

The best snuff, chewing or smoking tobacco is made in the factories of the Belgian States, as visitors can see for themselves.

Paris, November 13

It would be highly unfair to force those who "take no pleasure from the habit" to carry the burden of 30 million livres in indirect taxes that tobacco raises each year for the state.

This is the argument that has been put forward by the Abbot Maury, against the advice of his colleagues who want the tax to be abolished. He states that the high price of tobacco helps stop women and children from becoming addicted to the harmful and unhealthy substance. Maury goes further: he wants the government to extend its tobacco distribution monopoly to the whole kingdom to stop any dangerous rotten or adulterated weed being available to French consumers.

A flood carries wine barrels away

Moulins, November 9

Three hundred large barrels of good wine have been washed away by floods caused by the overflowing Allier river. Local people say the water has reached its highest levels since the start of the century. It has been raining non-stop for 22 hours and all the rivers of central France have burst their banks, carrying away trees and bridges. At the town of Moulins, a regiment of the Royal Guyenne has had to move out of its barracks. When the alarm bells rang out, the population tried in vain to stop the hundreds of wine barrels placed on the river bank from being washed away.

Counterfeiters set up shop in jail

Paris, November

The convicts of the Force prison in Paris have been busily printing counterfeit money, no doubt as a way of helping the time pass while they serve their sentences.

Their daring project has been considerably helped by the prison authorities themselves: all of the convicted counterfeiters of the capital had foolishly been placed in the same section of the jail. After discussing their various techniques, the jailbirds got to work. By bribing some poorly paid guards, they were able to have tools, printing presses and special paper brought into the jail. All that remained to be done was to pick the very best specialists among them. Getting all the counterfeit money into circulation was no problem: visitors would bring in real money and leave with their pockets stuffed full of fake bills. The greedy and corrupt prison guards agreed to keep some of the profits in exchange for their continued silence.

Unfortunately, all good things must come to an end. Somebody finally told the prison authorities about the lucrative operation that was going on under their very eyes, and they decided to put an end to it by sending all the counterfeiters to different prisons.

 Constituent Assembly

17. Paris. Stanislas de Clermont Tonnerre sets up the club of the Friends of the Monarchical Constitution which groups conservative and strongly pro-English members of the Assembly.

19. Brest. Louis Antoine de Bougainville, commander of the Atlantic squadron, has 17 crew members of the frigate *America* arrested for gross insubordination.

19. Paris. The civic club of the Théâtre Français is founded. It is a fraternal society with a pro-Cordeliers position.

21. Paris. Acting on the advice of La Fayette, the King names Louis François Duport Dutertre as Lord Chancellor.

22. United Belgian States. The Austrian army starts to reconquer the rebellious provinces (→ Dec. 10, 90).

22. Paris. The city authorities order the expulsion of the canons from the chapter house of Notre Dame cathedral.

23. Paris. After having abolished the Ancien Régime taxes, the Assembly replaces them by a financial contribution.→

23. Uzès. Dozens of people are injured during violent clashes between the National Guard and the town's Catholic population.

23. Paris. A report on charitable workshops for the poor states that it would be profitable to have mechanical looms: a good worker can do four people's work on such a machine.

24. Lyons. The general council of the Loire et Rhône department orders that the girls who had been locked up for life on their parents' orders in the Visitation Sainte Marie reformatory should be allowed out.

25. Saint Domingue. After the mulattoes, the plantation slaves revolt and massacre several landowners (→ Feb. 26, 91).

27. Paris. A court of appeal is set up. The new judicial body is made up of 42 members elected for four years.

27. Lyons. On the Terreaux square, Jacobins exhibit a relief model of the Bastille built with stones from the fortress and sent by the contractor Palloy.

29. Paris. The Théâtre de la Nation shows Voltaire's tragedy *La Mort de César*.

Charlatans are on to a good thing

Paris, November 16

Success is guaranteed for those who know how to draw the gullible client.

Ever since newspapers have been printing more and more small advertisements, hundreds of small shop-owners, quacks and outright thieves have been doing good business. A certain Virfan, who claims to be a chemist, boasts in today's edition of the *Moniteur* that he has discovered a youth potion made from plants. The magic elixir can be used by both men and women. Meanwhile, Doctor Verdone claims that he can cure rickets ... with a correspondence course!

Some charlatans do house calls, like this quack medicine merchant.

Landowners face a tax on income

Paris, November 23

The land contribution will be based on both justice and equality. That is what is being stressed by the Duc de La Rochefoucauld. He is one of the main architects of this new fiscal move which has just been approved by the Constituent Assembly after lengthy and very technical debate. All landowners will in future be taxed on the basis of income from their land, which will be assessed by town councils. The tax will be collected by the departments and its annual amount will be set by the Assembly. This year the government expects to get between 240 and 300 million livres. It will help to cut the deficit.

Breteuil entrusted with a secret mission

Paris, November 26

Louis XVI has placed his fate in the hands of his former minister. He is now thinking of leaving Paris to place himself under the protection of the Austrians. He is in a hurry to flee because the religious crisis is getting worse daily. The King has therefore just written to Breteuil to ask him to open negotiations with the foreign courts. The former diplomat, who sought refuge in Switzerland in July 1789 after the fall of his counter-revolutionary government, has been granted wide powers for his secret mission. "I have chosen to entrust you with the interests of my crown. I approve all that you may do to achieve the goal I have set: the restoration of my legitimate authority and my people's happiness," the King states in his letter. He is convinced that he can legitimately resort to using foreign armies; but

Baron de Breteuil had told the King to flee on July 14th. 1789.

do the other courts of Europe share this opinion? Breteuil will have a hard time getting them to agree to Louis XVI's latest plan (→ Dec. 26).

Voltaire is more relevant than ever

Paris, November 17

The Théâtre de la Nation has just experienced one of its most unruly evenings ever.

Luckily for the audience and the actors, the posters advertising a performance of the play *Brutus* by Voltaire had ordered theatre-goers to leave their swords, walking sticks and other potential weapons at home. The revolutionary statements that abound in the play were loudly cheered. However, some of the lines spoken by the actors were

greeted with cries of "Long live the King!". These were answered with equally loud shouts of "Hurrah for Voltaire!".

When a bust of the author was brought on stage, there was loud clapping. Two grenadiers were placed in charge of supporting the heavy sculpture. There are now plans to show on stage a living reconstruction of David's painting showing the body of Titus lying on a stretcher that is being carried by lictors past a sombre Brutus.

A miniature statue showing Voltaire sitting at his work-bench.

Priests are forced to swear allegiance to the clergy's civil Constitution

Paris, November 27

What can be done to force the churchmen of France to submit to the clergy's civil Constitution? The radical solution that the Assembly has chosen is to force them to swear an oath of allegiance. The legislators were tired of hearing bishops, such as the Bishop of Nantes, protesting endlessly against the enforcement of the civil Constitution. Yesterday Viodel, a deputy, lashed out against these prelates he termed "unruly". He accused them of forming a cabal against the state "using religion as an excuse". All the members of the clergy have been given two months to swear to be "faithful to the nation, the law and the King and to do all they can to

support the Constitution approved by the National Assembly". If any of them should refuse, they will be considered to have resigned, and if they continue to carry out their duties they will be "charged with having disturbed the public order". It is important to remember that churchmen are now elected officials and are therefore subject to the laws of the land. The new decree could worsen the conflict that has been dragging on for several months. "Beware, it is dangerous to create martyrs," the Abbot Maury, a fierce opponent of the decree, has warned. The clergy is split. The Abbot Grégoire favours the oath, but there are many like Maury (→ Dec. 27).

Poland hears André Chénier's calm voice

Paris, November 18

André Chénier has been translated into Polish. The booklet he sent to the King of Poland has been appreciated. The Polish monarch found it "so moderate, so wise and so likely to calm unrest" that he decided to have it published in his country. In his letter of thanks to Poland's King, Chénier tells of the changes he has experienced since in August the 1789 Society published in its journal his *Avis au Peuple Français sur ses Véritables Ennemis*. In this he argued for "reason, justice and good sense", all of which he felt were threatened. France's "true enemies", he wrote, were not nobles who had emigrated and whom eight months ago he found "ridiculous and contemptible", but rather the watch committees that are starting to be set up. The success of his article had made him a spokesman for moderates.

Stanislas II Augustus Poniatowski, reformist king of a troubled state.

Immigrants to U.S. are disappointed

Paris, November

The romantic dreams that many French people have had about America have become somewhat tarnished over the past few months. The adventurers and settlers who had purchased land in the United States from the Scioto company had a nasty surprise when they finally reached their destination. They found out that their property

titles were worthless, and that nothing had been prepared for their arrival, but thanks to the generosity of George Washington they were able to settle on the banks of the Ohio River, in a log cabin village that they pompously named Gallipolis. The new settlers have, however, been advised not to put perfume in their hair: the Redskins like to collect perfumed scalps ...

Burke attacks revolutionary ideas

Paris, November 29

The French Revolution has not just been causing differences of opinion in France. It has also caused dissent among the subjects of King George III of England. This is clearly shown by Edmund Burke's "Reflections on the Revolution in France", a translation of which was published today in Paris. The pamphlet, which had first appeared at the start of the month in London, has had a devastating effect on public opinion here. Frenchmen may not agree on the merits of the revolutionaries, but they are generally in favour of their actions. The British Whig parliamentarian has said that the events in Paris are merely chaotic, while the so-called rights of man are aberrations and the sovereignty of the people just a trap. As for freedom, it depends above all on what is done with it. These ideas will no doubt cause

Edmund Burke, Whig politician.

angry reactions in French patriotic circles, while in London Thomas Paine, that ardent defender of freedom, is sharpening his pen to answer Burke (→ Mar. 13, 91).

Jews caught between yellow and black

Carpentras, November 18

Which to wear, a black or a yellow hat? The choice is a difficult one for the Jews of Carpentras.

Under the terms of a decree issued by the representative assembly of the papal state of the Comtat Venaissin, the town council yesterday allowed local Jews to stop wearing the humiliating yellow hat as a mark of their faith, but those who went outside this morning wearing black hats like those of the bourgeois were beaten up by the people.

The local authority is facing a dilemma. It finds itself caught between the inhabitants, who are opposed to the integration of Jews, and the sarcastic comments of its rivals, the Avignon revolutionaries, who accuse it of not being firm in its enforcement of the decree. Will Carpentras tolerate such an abuse of human rights when the Jews of

An old Jewish man of learning.

other towns of the Comtat have already dropped this "symbol of slavery and disapproval that is painful to see and saddens the soul" of honest citizens?

Shoe makers worry about their sales

Rennes, November

The workers of Rennes are pretty naïve. Some counter-revolutionaries managed to convince the town's shoe makers that the emigration of nobles was ruining their business. Their best customers were fleeing and it was the Revolution's fault. Afraid that leather shoes would be banned by law, the shoe makers took to the streets. In order to teach them a lesson, the patriot students of Rennes all started wearing clogs instead of shoes. The shoe makers soon went back to work.

Patriots threaten newsletter writers

Paris, November 18

The patriots of Zoppi's café, also known as Procope, are always on alert. Deeply upset by what they have read in the *Mercure de France,* the *Ami du Roi,* the *Actes des Apôtres* and other aristocratic newsletters, they have gone to see the authors of the articles to ask them to write "fewer calumnies, lies and insults". If they refuse, they have been threatened with being "led around the street on the back of a donkey facing the wrong way".

A Dutch noblewoman speaks out for the rights of women

Paris, November 26

Who was that lovely woman who bravely spoke out to defend a speaker who was being booed today at a society meeting? Despite the impressive tricoloured cockades pinned to his sword and his hat, the young man arguing in favour of women being allowed to take part in the political life of the nation was repeatedly interrupted by shouting and whistling. Suddenly, a woman stood up and demanded silence. After the session was over, she was surrounded by all the other women. Her name is Etta Palm and she says she is the Baroness Aelders from Holland. Her life in Paris is a bit of a mystery. She spends a lot of money, but nobody knows where it comes from. Before leaving, she told her admirers to imitate the "virtues and patriotism of Roman ladies" (→ Dec. 13).

A National Guardsman has at last returned to his village and found his family.

Laclos turns into a Jacobin propagandist

Paris, November 30

Choderlos de Laclos is at last in charge of a newspaper. A month ago he became a member of the Jacobin Club, but he quickly realised that he was not much of a public speaker. He is a man of action who also has dreams of inspiring public opinion. He has therefore offered to turn the correspondence committee he worked for into a newspaper that would provide information on the affiliated societies. Right from the first edition, the *Journal des Amis de la Constitution* has shown it has far greater ambitions. It is the propaganda paper of the Jacobins written by the Duc d'Orléans' man.

Laclos is now a journalist.

Aristocrats now prefer private luxury

A new vogue seems to have been born. Aristocrats are tired of pomp and ostentation. It was the Queen who set the example at the Petit Trianon. Nowadays, in noble residences, huge reception rooms are being shunned.

More intimate rooms are being used. Boudoirs filled with delicate pieces of furniture are all the rage. The aristocracy would appear to have taken to heart the old saying "to live better, live discreetly".

A sign of the times: pomp and ostentation, now no longer in vogue in society, is even being shunned in the residences of aristocrats.

"Young sirs" lose wigs, take low profile

France, November

Where have they all gone? It has become impossible to find any of those young gentlemen with such exquisite manners who only a short time ago crowded to the balls held at court and belonged to Paris high society.

These "young sirs," as they are still called, no longer wear their embroidered silk suits, their impressive wigs and their lace ruffles. They no longer make a point of being the ones to open the dances and always having a witty remark on their lips. The young swells have had to tone down their arrogance and flashy clothes. They have been forced to take a low profile. They now dress soberly, nearly like poor people. Those young members of the nobility who have not chosen to live abroad are now forced to go from door to door in search of assistance from the few friends they have left.

Police chief launches urban health drive

Tulle, November 26

The town of Tulle is currently in the throes of a fully fledged sanitary revolution, largely due to the health drive launched by its commissioner of police, Pierre Laval.

Laval has just given a fine to Mademoiselle Villadier because a certain liquid, easily identified by its smell, was seen flowing under her front door, but it is very difficult to fine all those who feel a pressing need to relieve themselves on the streets of the town. This is particularly so because the contents of privies regularly spill out onto the pavements. However, Laval has sworn to do all he can to convince the inhabitants that the Solane and Corrèze rivers could easily be used to clear the sewage away. The houses built on the banks of the rivers all have a special balcony that is used as a privy. Who cares if this allows the indiscreet to "see the moon at noon"!

Open sewers bring hazards to Paris life

Paris, November

"Watch out underneath!" That traditional cry is still heard each morning throughout Paris. At that time of day, anyone out for a walk is advised to have a good ear. The age-old cry warns people that someone is about to empty a chamber pot out into the street. Its contents will then mingle with the garbage and dirty kitchen water in the stagnant drainage ditch often dug in the middle of the street. These gutters flow into the sewage pipes, but these are often blocked by straw, cabbages, animal droppings, bandages and even rotting animal flesh. The disgusting state of Paris' streets is making a fortune for the "gutter leapers", who carry well dressed people across the stinking ditches on their backs. Even if some can afford to keep their shoes clean, nobody can avoid the awful smell. Those who want to escape from the capital's evil smelling streets and seek refuge in the countryside first have to cross the muddy wall, in places as high as a house, that has built up around Paris. Crossing the wall is a risky business and can leave permanent stains, as the mud contains diluted iron left there by artisans. Paris is really not a very healthy place and the city is often blanketed by "stinking fogs". Concerned sanitation experts have recommended that the houses crowded together on bridges be torn down and basements disinfected with lime. They have called in vain for windmills to be built to move the polluted air.

This situation shows that it is safer to stay away from the stinking ditch.

2. Rennes. The general council of Ile et Vilaine sees that it is losing control over the National Guard. It therefore issues a proclamation to stress that the Guard must in all circumstances remain under the orders of department authorities.

2. Paris. A decree from the National Assembly reorganises the artillery corps and sets its manning levels.

2. Paris. The man of letters Georges Desfontaines has the play *Le Tombeau de Désilles* performed at the Théâtre de la Nation. →

3. Cahors. The inhabitants of neighbouring communes collectively refuse to pay the seigneurial dues.

4. Le Mans. The town's municipal officials place seals on three churches: Saint Pierre, Saint Julien and Saint Michel.

5. Paris. The Assembly approves a decree setting the registry fees that must be paid in order to legalise births, marriages and deaths.

5. Perpignan. Two people are wounded by gunfire in a fight between Jacobins and members of the royalist club of the Friends of Peace.

6. Paris. The Constituent Assembly hears the report from the commissioners who had been ordered to inquire into the Nancy revolt. It is amazed to discover the extent of the plotting by the army headquarters, acting under the orders of La Fayette.

8. Rennes. 120 members of the Society of Friends of the Constitution leave the club because it allowed Le Chapelier to join. He had been rejected by the club's Paris headquarters for having "pro-Feuillants" leanings.

10. Lyons. Guillin de Pougelon, a former municipal magistrate, and two officers of the Maine regiment are arrested for being involved in a princes' plot aimed at getting the King to come to Lyons to lead an armed revolt.

12. Aix en Provence. Tension grows after clashes between patriots and royalists seeking to set up a Society of Friends of Peace and Order.

14. Aix en Provence. The former assessor to the Aix region, Mathias Pascalis, is hanged. →

Louis XVI appeals to the King of Prussia

Paris, November 3

Louis XVI has called for help from all the courts of Europe in a desperate bid to save the French monarchy. The King has secretly asked for assistance from Frederick William II of Prussia, begging him to try to set up a "European congress backed by armed forces".

What exactly does this mean? Does Louis XVI really want France to be attacked by foreign troops? Does he find an invasion preferable to the Revolution? The answer is no. The King will not hear of direct intervention. His moderation has, in fact, saddened the exiled nobles in Turin, who are busily working for a general uprising and trying to persuade foreign monarchs to go to war against France. The King simply wants a foreign coalition to be set up which would be sufficiently threatening to intimidate his subjects and force them to restore his sovereignty. The French journalist Jacques Mallet du Pan has

Frederick William II of Prussia, Louis XVI's best ally in Europe.

been sent to ask the King of Prussia for this. but there is no sign that the other European sovereigns are prepared to enter into such an alliance with Louis XVI.

Ladies risk their health for good looks

Paris, December

A sagging chin, crow's feet and nostrils that are either too wide or too narrow? All these problems that are a constant headache to fashionable ladies can be solved, or at least improved upon, by the use of modern cosmetics.

However, some of the new powders and creams can be dangerous, causing serious damage to the skin. The worst are those awful patches that are placed on the face to hide blemishes and dimples and end by irritating the skin and looking like spots. Many ladies now prefer to use the various unguents made from the essence of violets or from honey. Their use can improve ugly lips, although they do nothing to help damaged, blackened teeth. The use of makeup has become an art form and needs a steady hand. It is a little like a painter's task of making something more beautiful than it really is.

These ladies are comparing the results of their careful cosmetic work.

Jacobins call for people's alliance against monarchy

Lons le Saunier, December 5

Revolutionaries in the provinces are seeking to outdo their counterparts in the capital. Almost 900 Jacobin clubs have been set up this year throughout the kingdom. The inhabitants in the distant region of Franche Comté are just as Jacobin as those of Paris, sometimes even more so. In this border region, where soldiers regularly attend club meetings, the Friends of the Constitution feel particularly involved in military issues. They are extremely worried about rumours accusing the King of seeking assistance from the army and from the other European monarchies. The Jacobins of Lons le Saunier have therefore responded by suggesting a "holy alliance between peoples" to fight against any counter-revolutionary alliance of royalty.

French now prefer "tu" to "vous"

Paris, December 14

Everyday forms of speech can include outdated signs of respect. Attempting to combat "the influence of words and the power of their use", the *Mercure National* today publishes an article suggesting that the familiar form of address "tu", as opposed to the formal "vous", should be systematically used. The author of the article is identified only as C.B., a "free man", who could well be Madame Robert, the director of the newspaper. The author explains that "the 'vous' form used to be meant for a lord, and referred to both him and his vassals. The expression has since then spread to all those who own property or wealth. It is therefore just an insidious leftover from feudal times. Everyone knows that it is not enough to kill a snake, its eggs must also be wiped out! Let us therefore say "tu" to everybody, even to the King. Let us dare say to him: Louis, I order you in the name of reason to speak in the familiar form and to get your ears used to listening to it!" The author also proposes to drop *monsieur* and *madame* in favour of *citoyen* and *citoyenne*.

"Bourgeois" National Guard criticised

Paris, December 6

There was an unruly meeting at the Jacobins Club this evening. Robespierre spoke and strongly criticised the decree on the reform on the recruitment system used for the National Guard. Only active citizens, that is those who pay taxes, therefore the richest, will in future be allowed to join. By abolishing its popular nature, the deputies seem to have wanted to set up a bourgeois guard corps, basically designed to protect people and property from angry crowds.

They are, in fact, afraid to let the people have weapons, even though it was the people who were responsible for the creation of the National Guard by setting up militias to defend the Revolution. "The right to bear arms to defend freedom is as sacred as that of self defence," Robespierre cried out. Mirabeau, who was presiding over the meeting, then tried to put an end to the debate, telling Robespierre that he had no right to criticise a decree that had been duly approved, but all present supported Robespierre against Mirabeau. The split between them seems to have become total (→June 11, 91).

La Fayette, commander in chief of the National Guard.

Copper-bottomed success for "Le Solide"

Marseilles, December 14

The wealthy fur merchants of Spain will now have to compete against the traders of Marseilles. The Baux firm has just chartered a ship that will be commanded by Etienne Marchand. The firm wants to try to break the Spanish monopoly over the fur trade in the northern Pacific. The pelts are bought from the Nootka indians and then taken to Canton to be sold to the Chinese, who love fur. The dangerous aspect of this business is not the Indians or even the Spanish competitors, but rather the worms which feed off the ships' oak hulls during their two year journeys. The Baux brothers have therefore had a boat specially built for the trip. The 300 tonne, three masted ship has a hull that has been completely lined with copper. It has been christened *Le Solide*. This morning the vessel sailed for Gibraltar and Cape Horn (→June 24, 91).

Like this wealthy merchant, the trader Baux will soon be able to show his family the reason for his riches: the three-masted Le Solide.

Austria reconquers rebel Belgian States

The Belgian States' uprising against the Empire only lasted for a year.

The Hague, December 10

Diplomatically isolated, split by internal dissent, increasingly unpopular and lacking a true army, the insurgents were only able to offer feeble resistance to the Austrian reconquest. Following a painful string of defeats (at Namur on November 24th. and at Mons on November 30th.), Brussels fell on December 2nd. The Treaty of The Hague, signed by the Emperor Leopold, guarantees that Belgians will have their national institutions restored. His victory now assured, the emperor was able to show some generosity! He has promised never to enforce conscription in Belgium and to consult the assemblies of the states about all laws of public interest; but it has been a bitter disappointment for the friends of Jean François Vonck, now in exile at Lille. They had hoped that Leopold would set up a constitutional monarchy (→Jan. 12, 91).

Marechal wants corps of tyrant killers

Paris, December 4

In response to the large number of royalist pamphlets calling for patriots to be murdered, Sylvain Maréchal has suggested in the *Révolutions de Paris* the setting up of a "battalion of tyrannicides". The members of such an avenging corps would be responsible for putting to death all noblemen who try to subjugate the revolutionaries of France. This would help spare soldiers' lives. The new plan has already caused heated debate.

Furious mob lynches Royalist plotters

Aix en Provence, December 14

The aristocracy of Aix has paid its tribute to the Revolution. A former lawyer at the parliament, Pascalis, and two other nobles, rightly suspected of plotting an uprising in the Midi region on the orders of the Prince de Condé, have been hanged from trees. The National Guard, which has been in control of the streets since the recall of the royalist Lyonnais regiment, had arrested Pascalis and both of his accomplices. A mob rushed to the prison to lynch the captives. The powerless magistrates were forced to give in and hand the men over to the enraged crowd.

The first of the hangings at Aix.

Lieutenant Désilles, hero of Nancy, is immortalised on stage

The mutinous soldiers had not heard Désilles' heroic calls for calm.

Paris, December 2

In the capital, everything often revolves around the theatre. The Théâtre de la Nation was today showing a performance of a one act tale in prose entitled *Le Tombeau de Désilles,* written by Georges Desfontaines.

The new "martyr of Nancy", the "new d'Assas", the "Curtius of Brittany", as he has been dubbed by the press, is already part of the theatre's repertory. His actions on August 31st. during the revolt of the soldiers of Châteauvieux had been truly dramatic. After having in vain attempted to reason with the mutinied troops, the young officer, who was barely 22, had flung himself on a cannon aimed at Bouillé's forces, using his body to shield them from the full force of the blast. His fame is also due to the courage he showed during the time he spent in agony before his death. The play pays homage to his memory and to the deep remorse felt by the mutineers. They are shown guiltily weeping and repenting by the tomb of the young hero, as they sharpen their swords on his tombstone swearing they will always use them to defend freedom. The play was a great success.

Noverre's natural dance style means better ballet

Paris, December 14

A new style in ballet has come to the forefront with the performance of *Psyché*, which was directed by Pierre Gardel.

Part of a family of excellent choreographers, although he himself is a talented, precise and very technical dancer, Gardel is basically a direct descendant of Georges Noverre, who is currently working in London. Noverre has revolutionised contemporary ballet by rejecting the huge wigs and other aspects of the classical tradition, such as the monstrous hooped petticoats that got in the way of the dancers' moves, as well as heavily decorated costumes that princes and even peasants were supposed to wear; but what he has really changed are the very principles of ballet. He believes that each single phase of a ballet, every move and every step, must be directly linked to a dramatic and psychological requirement. The traditional and often unseemly entrechats had no real meaning. Modern ballet must be aware of feelings.

State to look after abandoned children

Paris, December 10

On top of all its other duties, the state will now handle one of the most worthy tasks: taking care of abandoned children. A series of decrees has filled the gap left by the abolition of the feudal system. The state will now be responsible for feeding children. In the past, it was up to the feudal lords to feed children found on their lands. In Paris, for the time being, newly born children are being cared for at the Vaugirard hospice or at the Maison de la Crèche until they are three or four years old. The ones who have not died from ill treatment or epidemics are then sent to various hostels, where they remain until they reach 14 or 16.

The nation pays its debts to the military

Paris, December 14

A nation must be prepared to repay soldiers for the sacrifices they have made for it.

That is why the Constituent Assembly has just decided to create a pension system on a national basis. Under the terms of the new legislation, soldiers will be entitled to a pension when they reach the age of 50. Thus, after serving for 30 years, non-commissioned officers and soldiers will receive a quarter of their pay, or a basic minimum of 150 livres. After 30 years' service, the amount of the pension will gradually increase. This system also encourages soldiers to serve longer terms. Pensions will no longer be seen just as favours.

Friends of empty Lycée launch rescue bid

Paris, December 1

The Lycée is no longer as popular as it used to be. The clubs, the Assembly and everyday political life have become its serious competitors. Despite the learned seminars taught by Chaptal, and La Harpe's erudite readings, the best brains are deserting what used to be one of the main centres of the capital's intellectual life. This is not entirely the fault of the Lycée's administrators. They have made sacrifices. In a bid to save the Lycée from financial ruin, they have even decided to set up a Society of Friends of the Lycée, whose capital will be based on 100 shares each worth 300 livres. La Harpe is one of those who have been asked to contribute generously, even though he still has not been paid the 1,200 livres he is owed for last year's lessons. Despite this, he bought one share. The contributions to the society will help pay for next year's courses, and maybe even for La Harpe's teaching fees.

Rousseau finds way to beat the hecklers

Paris, December 13

Charles Louis Rousseau — along with women — has had his revenge. The unfortunate orator and defender of the weaker sex who was so loudly booed last month when he spoke at the Cercle Social has not abandoned all hope.

Tonight at the Vauxhall, before a very attentive audience, he was at last able to make his speech on "the education and the civic and political existence of women under the French Constitution". Undisturbed by shouting, he was able to express at length his ideas on the usefulness of the education of women, the merits of divorce and the multiple adantages of breast feeding. His audience was extremely well behaved. He had taken a great many precautions: when he advertised the event in the press, he stressed that no men would be allowed in unless they came with a woman. His caution seems to have paid off as all the troublemakers stayed away (→ Feb. 8, 91).

The first music-café, where clients can listen to popular tunes while taking some refreshment, has just opened for business on the Champs Elysées.

Free trade threatens cosy coal monopoly

Anzin, December 9

The management of the very powerful Anzin mining company has been shocked by the news that customs tariffs are to be cut. The heavy import duties that until now had protected France's internal market from foreign competition are to be scrapped in the name of free trade. There will in future be nothing to stop businessmen from getting hold of cheaper and better quality coal from Mons, Charleroi or Liège. Both furious and very worried, the Anzin management has decided to alert public opinion by issuing a pamphlet reminding all of the good work that the firm has done for its employees in the past. One of its shareholders, a deputy from Calais, has even called for special legislation to protect northen France's mining industry from tough foreign competition.

Cross-section of a mine. An illustration from Diderot's "Encyclopédie".

16. Paris. The National Assembly grants financial assistance amounting to a total of 15 million livres to the kingdom's growing number of charitable workshops for the poor.

18. Paris. Jean Calas, who died a victim of the arbitrary use of power by the Ancien Régime, triumphs posthumously. A day after Lemierre d'Argy's play *Calas ou le Fanatisme* was performed by the troupe of the Palais Royal, the Théâtre de la Nation shows the drama *Jean Calas* by Jean Louis Laya.

18. Paris. A report by Voidel, deputy from Sarreguemines, on the plot at Lyons convinces the Assembly to dismiss the commander of the Lamarck infantry regiment, to move the unit to a different location and to transfer the people who had been arrested to Paris.

18. Paris. The Assembly rules that all ground rents can be bought back. It also bans the future creation of nonrepayable ground rent to make it impossible for feudal tenures to be reconstituted.

21. Paris. The Assembly decides to have a statue built that will bear the following inscription: "From the free French nation to Jean Jacques Rousseau."→

25. Tulle. The local people's society decides to forbid the use by its members of the term "Monsieur" and to use "Frère" (brother) instead.

26. Paris. Louis XVI, while still fiercely opposed to it, finally agrees to the decree approved by the Assembly on November 27th. →

26. Paris. The rise in the level of the Seine River causes serious concern. It is now 12 feet 11 inches, or 4.20 metres, above its normal level.

27. Paris. After lengthy resistance, deputies of the clergy finally swear allegiance to the clergy's civil Constitution.→

30. Paris. A decree issued by the Assembly provides guarantees that anyone who registers a new invention will have the full ownership and use of it.

31. Rouen. The organ player Broche inaugurates the new instrument at the Saint Pierre church. The organ has recently undergone restoration work by the organ maker Godefroy.

Poor are puzzled by new tax system

La Chapelle d'Aligné, December

After the general rejoicing over the abolition of the salt tax and feudal rights, there is now cruel disappointment. At the village of La Chapelle d'Aligné, taxation has gone up despite the fact that members of the privileged classes are now also taxed. Under the terms of the law, taxes no longer depend on a citizen's place of residence, but on the place where the property is located. The overall tax burden on some villages has therefore increased. The poor, who in the past did not pay taxes and who now have to hand over their money to the treasury, are annoyed by this "looting" by Paris. They are all the more angry since they found out that in a neighbouring village where the local lord is the main landowner taxes have gone down on average.

Radical priest is back on the scene at Cordeliers Club

Paris, late December

Jacques Roux has finally given signs of life. He has at last come out of hiding to join the Cordeliers Club. He will probably soon be making headlines.

Roux, who is also known as the "white wolf", is being sought by all the kingdom's clergymen. Just before the Revolution he was a priest, and had given lessons at the Angoulême seminary before being appointed priest at Saint Thomas de Conac. There, this less than orthodox priest became known for preaching "revolutionary" sermons. In particular, he said that the land belonged to all and that peasants should not have to submit to the seigneurial rights. Dismissed and banned for having been taken part in the looting of the castles of Saintonge, he was forced to leave that province in April 1790, as there were ugly rumours about him. A price was put on his head and he had to live in hiding, using the name of Renaudi.

Today a new life has begun for him: once again using his real name, the "red priest" has appeared at the Cordeliers, the most active of all the capital's clubs.

Jean Jacques Rousseau statue planned

Marie Thérèse Levasseur at Rousseau's tomb at Ermenonville.

Paris, December 21

It was only fair that the Revolution should honour its favourite philosopher. The Assembly has therefore agreed to erect a statue worthy of the author of the *Contrat Social,* Jean Jacques Rousseau. The nation also knows how to express its gratitude to the widows of its great men. Marie Thérèse Levasseur, who says that she does not have enough money to live on since the death of her famous husband, has called for the Assembly's generosity. The deputies have unanimously decided to grant her a yearly pension of 1,200 livres. Little do they know that these funds will partly go to the 35 year old farmhand whom the widow, now in her sixties, is living with!

Protective wing for France's works of art

Paris, December

Despite what the exiled nobles have been claiming from abroad, the Revolution has not been systematically damaging the country's priceless works of art. There have, however, been some acts of vandalism during the more violent clashes. Earlier this century, the deep contempt felt for all things related to the Middle Ages resulted in countless mediaeval churches being either transformed or mutilated in the name of aesthetics. The Revolution for its part has been trying to preserve the nation's rich common heritage. Therefore the Assembly, which in December 1789 had decided to sell off church property, has set up committees to draw up inventories and keep an eye on the clergy's works of art. The committees rule on whether a certain work should be protected or sold. To help in their choice, they hired specialists last October. This month, new artistic commissions will be also be involved.

954 honoured as victors of the Bastille

Paris, December 19

Marie Charpentier has officially been named a heroine. The Constituent Assembly has just agreed to her request and included her in the list of those considered as being victors of the Bastille. Marie will also be granted an annual pension of 200 livres because of the wounds she suffered on July 14th. 1789. She is the only woman to have been thus honoured. The title of victor of the Bastille is much sought after, and it would seem, from listening to the claims made by Parisians, that the whole city took part in the attack on the fortress. Latter day heroes have been popping up in the cafés and sitting rooms of Paris. All the claims and testimonies have been carefully looked into by ad hoc committees. A total of 954 people have been given the title of victor of the Bastille, but not all have come forward, for example, that young girl who, dressed as a man, was seen fighting beside her fiancé.

Some victors of the Bastille.

Louis forced to approve Church decree

Paris, December 26

Louis XVI has very few options left. He has already had to agree grudgingly to approve the clergy's civil Constitution, in spite of the advice of the Pope. Neither was the King able to stand firm against the Assembly, which demanded that he give his support to the decree on the priests' oath. The deputies even refused to wait until he had had a reply from Pius VI, who had been urged to intervene with the Church of France to help get the priests' assent. A deeply unhappy King has therefore caved in today, but harbours the secret hope of getting the decree cancelled as soon as he has recovered his powers. "I'd rather be King in Metz than King of France under such a situation, but it will soon be over," he said after signing the text. The King can see no way of compromising with the Revolution. Although he was able to deal with the "usurpation" of his power, he cannot accept the schism with the Catholic Church. His conscience is troubling him. This latest humiliation has still not moved him to action. This eternally wavering man has, however, resolved not to accept any further nibbling away at his power.

Churchmen split on whether to take oath

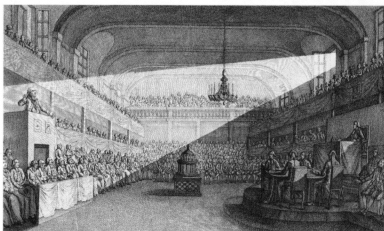

The Manège chamber where the Assembly has met since November 1789.

Paris, December 27

Who will be the first to take the oath? That question has been on everyone's lips ever since the date was set for the clergymen of the Assembly to obey the law. There was a deep silence when the Abbot Grégoire went up to the rostrum. After a short explanation, he spoke the words demanded by the law. He was followed by 62 other priests, among whom were the former president of the Assembly and vice chancellor of the University of Paris, Abbot Gouttes, but most of the clergymen of the Constituent Assembly abstained. If they continue to refuse to take the oath, the French clergy will be split down the middle! (→ Jan. 9, 91).

Families rent apart by progressive zeal

Paris, December

Exile has not taught a lesson to Hérault de Séchelles. A year ago, his family had sent him abroad in the mistaken belief that once far away from Paris he would forget all about his progressive theories.

But as soon as he returned, Marie Jean was elected to the post of judge in the capital's first "arrondissement", or district. This has greatly irked his family. He claims to have heard the call of the Nation. Whatever the case, he soon heard that of his parents! His grandmother cites the example of his friend, Louis Michel Le Peletier de Saint Fargeau, who refused the offer of being appointed a judge. All her efforts were in vain. Marie Jean is in total disagreement with his parents. Like so many others, the Séchelles family has been split by the Revolution.

Profitable liaison for fugitive count

Mendrisio (Ticino), December 29

Some noblemen will really do anything to restore their sagging fortunes. The Comte d'Antraigues, who has spent all his money, has married Madame Saint Huberty, a well-known opera singer, a woman of few morals who has been his mistress for a long time. It is a strange fate that this small country squire, who had tried but failed to become a member of the court at Versailles, has had. In fact, it was the Revolution that gave him his chance. This tireless pamphleteer became known throughout France after he published his *Mémoire sur les Etats Généraux* in 1788. He succeeded in getting elected to the Estates General despite the fact that nobody knew whether he was a supporter of the aristocracy or the Third Estate. Finding himself in trouble over the Favras affair, he chose to flee and seek refuge in Lausanne, where he was joined by his mistress. She has been supporting them thanks to the large sums of money she earns for her tours in France and the rest of Europe. The nobleman had decided to start writing again, but seems to have found a better job: spying.

Foe of priests choses church wedding

Paris, December 29

Holding Lucile's hand in his, Camille Desmoulins seemed to be deeply moved when he spoke the fateful words "I do" at the Saint Sulpice church.

One of the groom's witnesses, Robespierre, angrily whispered in his ear: "Cry if you really feel like it, you hypocrite!" The young journalist had a hard time winning the hand of Lucile Duplessis. He first had to convince her father, who was not at all happy about the match. Then this avowed mortal enemy of priests had reluctantly to agree to a religious wedding, which he saw as a blow to his self esteem, but all his doubts and worries vanished at the sight of his radiant bride in her tight pink satin wedding dress.

Camille had fallen in love with this beautiful, blonde and romantic young woman some six years ago. The priest has just declared them "united until death do them part", but such a sombre thought is very far from the minds of the happy couple.

Good food, lots of wine and pretty girls: a typical wedding meal.

Lucile Duplessis, who married Camille Desmoulins at St Sulpice.

Marriage for love gets more popular

France, December

Happiness seems to go hand in hand with the changes in society that have been brought about by the Revolution.

Until now, marriages such as the one recently contracted by the Comte d'Antraigues were nearly always more a question of interest than of sentiments. Money, inheritance or just survival on a day to day basis were considered far more important than love. By marrying his beloved Lucile despite all the obstacles, Camille Desmoulins has helped to show that in a more egalitarian society the wishes of the heart weigh more heavily. Since last year, there has been an extraordinary boom in the number of marriages. This can in part be attributed to the great changes that have been going on in the population of the country's major towns, but people have also been seeking a measure of individual happiness in these troubled times. A growing number of citizens have been lining up outside churches and register offices to get married.

But what about divorce? In a society based on freedom, why shouldn't divorce become a new option? If love contributes to the general happiness of a society, doesn't marital discord demoralise a good patriot, reduce the number of births and inevitably lead to adultery? For the good of the nation, harmony should reign over marital relations, but why should a marriage continue once it has gone? The divorce issue is under debate.

Fashionable bourgeois interiors reflect a lust for comfort

The members of the bourgeoisie make enough money to surround themselves with luxury and comfort. Even if he can't really afford to shop at the great cabinet makers such as Jacob or Reisener, the bourgeois manages to find some lovely, good quality pieces of furniture made by the artisans of the Saint Antoine district. For his sitting room, he picks armchairs made in natural wood, with straight feet and decorated with silk cushions. Sometimes, however, he prefers to buy lacquered grey or white wood furniture. As the modern bourgeois has nothing against novelty, he may place some of the newly fashionable Etruscan-style chairs copied from antique objects in the same room as the traditional bergère and small armchairs. The dining room, which is being increasingly used, includes a mahogany table and chairs. The walls of the house are covered either by wallpaper, often made by Réveillon, or by cloth from Jouy that matches the curtains. The bedroom contains a wooden or iron "Revolution" or "Federation" type bed, while the nearby bathroom has a huge wardrobe and a bathtub.

Bourgeois interior decoration: more comfortable than luxurious.

1. Paris. The royalist journalist Parisot sets up the *Feuille du Jour.*

1. Carpentras. Feeling threatened, Jews leave the town, which is occupied by "popish" troops.

2. Paris. The Society of Victors of the Bastille, led by Maillard and Santerre, becomes a fraternal society in Montreuil. Members say they are "Enemies of Despotism".

3. Paris. The Chevalier James de Rutledge, affiliated to the Cordeliers, publishes the first edition of *Le Creuset.*

3. Paris. The Assembly renews the order making it compulsory for clergymen to swear allegiance to the clergy's civil Constitution without any restrictions (→26).

4. Paris. The department of Paris holds its first electoral assembly.

4. Paris. The audience at the Théâtre de la Nation warmly welcomes a performance of *La Liberté Conquise ou le Despotisme Renversé,* a drama by Harny.

4. Paris. The convent of the Petits Augustins is chosen to house the works of art found in religious establishments.

6. Paris. The new auditorium of the Théâtre de Monsieur, on the Rue Feydeau, is inaugurated. The first performance is an opera by Guiseppe Sarti, *Le Nozze di Dorina.*

12. Liège. Austrian troops occupy the principality and restore the Prince-Bishop to power. He had been ousted by the revolution of August 18th. 1789.

13. Paris. The Assembly continues fiscal reforms, creating a personal contribution.→

13. Lyons. The city now numbers 31 clubs, comprising about 3,000 members. These are headed by a central body.

13. Paris. The Bishop of Autun, Talleyrand, who had sworn allegiance to the clergy's civil Constitution on December 29th., is elected administrator of the department of Paris (→20).

15. Paris. A comic opera, *Paul et Virginie,* by Edmond de Favières and Rodolphe Kreutzer, is a hit at the Favart auditorium.

15. Paris. The journalist Jean Joseph Dusaulx sets up the *Journal de Chirurgie.*

Oath of allegiance stirs up widespread priestly rebellion

Paris, January 9

The priest of the church of Saint Sulpice is a strong-willed man. He had already refused to celebrate Talma's wedding, despite the fact that actors have been granted all the civil rights. In spite of the pressures that have been brought to bear on him, Monsieur de Pancémont is one of those priests who have announced that they will not take the oath that has been imposed on the clergy. People had been awaiting this Sunday anxiously. The priest arrived at church with a crowd of the faithful. After the sermon had been read out, cries of "the oath!" and "string him up!" rang out as he was leaving the pulpit. Saint Sulpice was not the only church in the kingdom where people have been singing the revolutionary song *Ça ira* to encourage reluctant priests. Monsieur de Pancémont climbed back into the pulpit and said in a loud voice: "I will not take the oath, my conscience forbids it." If it had not been for the

"How to get the bishops and aristocratic priests to take the oath."

National Guard, the priest would have been torn apart. Later, he had to move his furniture out, as the mob was threatening to loot his home. People are saying that he ended up by fleeing to the dukedom of Luxembourg, where he became chaplain to the ducal garrison.

Mirabeau seizes crafty advantage

Paris, January

Mirabeau is overjoyed: he will at last be able to take action. From being just an advisor to a suspicious king, he has become the real power behind the government. The deputy from Aix last month submitted a plan for political action to Montmorin, who had asked him how to restore royal power over the Assembly. The current religious crisis has given him an opportunity to put the plan into effect. Even though Mirabeau claims to be opposed to any attempts at a counter-revolution and has asked the court to avoid such an option, he remains firmly determined to save the monarchy. The plan he has devised is very crafty: first ruin the credibility of the deputies by pushing them to make mistakes. This will create a crisis and the King will then be able to step in as a saviour and recover both his power and his popularity. The oath that the Assembly is demanding from the clergy is a heaven-sent opportunity. He knows that this issue could spark off a civil war. Mirabeau plans to get the deputies to take a tough stance on the oath question.

Queen pleads for aid from Spain

Paris, January

Who will agree to help the royal couple to flee? Marie Antoinette is now counting on Spain.

The Queen has sent a message to King Charles IV to beg his support. "We are no longer simply seeking your advice, we need real help. If the King manages to get out of here and seek refuge in a fortified town, can he count on your assistance?" she has written. Marie Antoinette has explained to the man she calls her "last friend", the ambassador of Spain to Paris, Fernan Nunez, the plan of escape drawn up by Fersen, Bouillé and Breteuil.

But how will she be able to persuade a king who feels he was "betrayed" by France last October? At that time, Spain was forced to give in to an English ultimatum because Louis XVI had chosen not to give it his support.

Nevertheless, diplomatic relations are one thing, but blood relations are quite another. Charles IV is the head of the younger branch of the House of Bourbon. The Queen's desperate appeal to her cousin is therefore based on family solidarity (→Mar. 7).

Butler's son nurses political ambitions

Paris, January 2

Men like his great energy, while women love to listen to a speaker who is only 23 years old. The young Jean Lambert Tallien has just been unanimously chosen to preside over the newly created Fraternal Society of Citizens of Both Sexes. His success has given Tallien, son of the head butler of the Marquis de Bercy, a desire to launch himself on a political career.

Jean Lambert Tallien, former clerk.

Bastille play set to heal breaches at Comédie Française

Paris, January 8

Both his pro-patriot beliefs and his talent have aroused pangs of jealousy among some of Talma's actor friends. Naudet has even dared to slap him on stage. It was high time to calm the situation down and there was an opportunity to do just that today. *La Liberté Conquise ou le Despotisme Renversé* was being performed. This play, based on the fall of the Bastille, has been having a great success. One evening, the audience nearly tore to pieces the actor who was playing the role of de Launay, the Bastille's hated governor. During another performance, a genuine victor of the Bastille who was among the audience was carried around in triumph as the spectators sang *Ça ira*. The play's success should help a reconciliation. The members of the royalist party, who are friends of Naudet, have mingled with the actors with convincingly apologetic looks on their faces. The public's silence was interpreted as forgiveness. Dugazon, of the patriot faction, then walked across the stage and said: "We have had our fights and differences, but now we shall embrace." However, Naudet did not seem to want to, so the crowd cried "Let them kneel and embrace", and he was forced to agree to the request (→ Apr. 10).

Universal tax on rent and property values introduced

Paris, January 13

In order to complement the land tax, the Assembly has just created a personal tax. Every citizen will in future pay a tax that is proportional to his rent or to the rental value of his residence. It will be up to the town councils to see to it that the assessments are done in good faith. This system appeared preferable to that of a declaration of income that would have allowed the state to learn "family secrets". In any case, don't people house themselves according to their means? This new tax will make the French fiscal system even fairer.

Huge population influx into Paris threatens to boost poverty

Near Notre Dame bridge, the people of Paris are always busy: small traders, workers, jugglers and beggars.

Paris, January

With its 600,000 inhabitants, Paris is by far the largest city in France and can only be compared to London. The kingdom's second largest city, Lyons, only numbers just under 150,000 inhabitants, while there are 85,000 people in Marseilles. Bordeaux, Rouen and Lille come far behind. Moreover, the capital's population is constantly growing. There are now some 20,000 christenings a year in Paris, a third of these being abandoned children. The number of deaths is slightly lower that this; but the difference in the total numbers of births and deaths is not enough to explain the city's dynamic demography. What is highly relevant is the fact that six of every ten Parisians were born in the countryside or abroad. In the capital, there are currently more Auvergnats than there are at Saint Flour and more Savoyards than in Moûtiers. Many people from the provinces were drawn by the hope of finding steady employment. The wiser ones, such as the young chimney sweeps from Savoie, only spend the winter in Paris, when it is too cold to work in the fields. The most ambitious dream of conquering the capital, but few make a living and they join the ranks of the poor.

Engineers' visions widen as Louis XVI bridge nears completion

The Louis XVI bridge is said to have been built with Bastille stones.

Paris, January

Bridges, like pieces of furniture, have their own styles. Those built in the Middle Ages, which are still in the majority, are getting old and are too narrow. The engineer Jean Rodolphe Perronnet is one of the men who have played a big role in the birth of the modern bridge. His latest work was the Louis XVI bridge which will give onto the Louis XVI square. Its structure is based on a simple concept. To cope with high water levels, Perronnet has built vaults that start above the water-line. In order not to have to raise the road too far, he used elliptical vaults instead of basket-handle vaults. Work on the bridge started in 1787 and is nearly finished. It will open in ten months. ▷

The delicate art of "hair sculpture"

Paris, January

Baron's is the capital's most sought after hair salon. This master craftsman says that he practises the demanding and delicate art of "hair sculpture".

Using his daring and quick-moving comb, he can create wigs for any occasion, day or night. The ladies who are lucky enough to be his clients can't get enough of his creations: toupées, false chignons, curls or hair pieces; but their favourites are without a doubt his "sleeping" and "semi-sleeping" wigs which appear so natural and can be stored under a pillow.

A wig gives that special touch.

Halle prostitutes starved of clients

Paris, January

The ladies of the Halle district are heartbroken. The King, whom they love as they would their own father, has been cruelly abandoned by his family and friends. How lonely he must feel in his huge palace at the Tuileries!

"Sire," the ladies have written, "we would like to express our sadness to see that all your family has abandoned you. We will take their place. Indeed, you will find among us one who will not leave you and who will always remain faithful." This very moving letter is signed, by, among others, Oudin, Petit Pas (Tiptoes), de Bartel, Minette (Pussycat) and Grosse Bonne (Fat Maid). More than the King's sad fate, these ladies are worried about their clients: the emigration of noblemen has meant that their wealthiest clients have left town.

Virgins of Nantes take a proud oath

Nantes, January

The people of Nantes can be truly proud of their daughters and wives. Their hearts will only throb for true patriots, not for those awful aristocrats. At least that is what the young women have solemnly sworn before the Society of the Constitution. The girls and women of Nantes have even written some verses based on their oath as a testimony of their patriotism, if not of their poetic gifts:

We, ladies of the Nantes region,
Wives, widows and unwed girls,
Let all Frenchmen know that
Being faithful democrats,
We see with horror those
Without wit, without heart
Who are called aristocrats ...
We would rather remain virgins,
Or faithful to our husbands,
Than see those bandits
Become tied to our families!

Soldiers finger too many foreign buttons

Paris, January 12

Army uniforms are a serious national matter, and the elected representatives should have a say in what is chosen. Basing himself on this principle, Delattre, a deputy from Abbeville, has drawn his colleagues' attention to the problem of buttons. The kingdom's button manufacturers have been having trouble with foreign competitors, in particular English ones. The government should order French-made uniform buttons mounted on wood or bone.

The ideal of federation on a button.

---

16. Paris. A decree issued by the Assembly organises the national gendarmerie.→

16. Lyons. The People's Society of the Friends of the Constitution publishes the first edition of its newspaper.

18. Paris. The deputy Martinneau having called for the rights granted to active citizens to be given to all the Jews of France, his colleagues Alquier and de Broglie get the debate adjourned by stressing the seriousness of the anti-Jewish activity in Alsace.

20. Paris. As part of the enforcement of the new judicial reforms, a criminal tribunal is created in each department.

21. Paris. The Assembly approves the *Instruction sur la Constitution Civile du Clergé* drafted by the church committee in response to propaganda from priests opposed to the oath (→26).

22. Quimper. Deputies of the Ile de France die in the sinking of the ship *Amphitrite* in the bay of Audierne.→

23. Ajaccio. Napoléon Bonaparte takes a clear stand in favour of Pascal Paoli in a *Lettre à Bottafuocu*.→

24. Nantes. The department enforces National Assembly decrees and reduces to eight the number of parishes in the town and its suburbs.

26. Paris. The Constituent Assembly calls for all the bishops and non-juring priests replaced (→Feb. 5, 91).

27. Troyes. Abbot Dubourg, priest of Saint Benoît sur Seine, submits a plan in favour of priests' marriage to the town's Society of the Friends of the Constitution.→

27. Paris. To replace the old consular jurisdiction, the Assembly sets up a trade tribunal.

28. Ebron. About 1,000 National Guardsmen, who had left from Saint Malo, restore order in the south of the department, where peasants had attacked castles and tax collectors.

28. Paris. The Favart auditorium shows *Convalescent de Qualité ou l'Aristocrate*, a successful monarchist comedy by Fabre d'Eglantine.

30. Paris. Death of the tragic actor Brizart, a strong patriot who excelled in the roles of kings and noblemen.

Gendarmerie takes over law and order

Paris, January 16

The old mounted constabulary no longer exists. From now on, the corps responsible for law and order is to be known as the national gendarmerie. Made up of men aged over 25 who have been involved in "at least one reproachless engagement in line troops", it will number a total of 7,450 men, in accordance with the decree that was approved today. The gendarmes will also be in charge of policing the army. Their motto is "valour and discipline".

Uniform of a gendarme in charge of order "in ports and tribunals".

Slave trade opened to competition

Paris, January 18

A new trading monopoly has just fallen. After the India Company, it is now the turn of the Senegal Company.

The National Assembly has just withdrawn the privilege it had been granted in 1786. Like trade with India, commerce with Senegal is now open to all of France's businessmen. The loss of this privilege means that the Senegal Company has lost the exclusive right to trade in black Africans between Cape Verde and the White Cape. This monopoly had caused a great deal of resentment and criticism in shipping circles, but the deputies have paid attention to the shipowners' complaints. However, instead of abolishing the slave trade, they have freed it.

Talleyrand resigns from his bishopric

Paris, January 20

It's official, Talleyrand has at last cut off all ties with his diocese at Autun. Relations between the old see and its young and fiery bishop had been worsening ever since Talleyrand had taken the oath for the clergy's civil Constitution, of which he was the main author. The clergy of Autun had been demanding the resignation of their bishop, whom they considered to be a traitor to the church. Talleyrand would have resigned earlier but for the fact that it provided him with an annual income of 18,000 livres. His new position as administrator of the district of Paris, which is a very well paid job, has made it easier for him to resign.

Talleyrand, one of the first bishops to swear the oath of allegiance.

Masked ball ban to stop impostors

Paris, January, 23

How does one know who is hiding behind a mask? Bailly, who is resolved to keep order in the city he controls, has forbidden disguises and masquerades. People will no longer be allowed to dress up as wolves, pirates or Harlequins. The municipal decree also states that police will have to be informed in advance before any public ball is held in the capital.

Bonaparte plumps to serve Corsica

Ajaccio, January

Napoléon Bonaparte made sure he was noticed at the first meeting of the "Globo Patriotico" club, set up to support the struggle led by Paoli in favour of the island's independence. He accused the Comte Bottafuoco, deputy of the aristocracy opposed to new ideas, of being "in France's service". The young officer seems to have chosen his camp: Corsica.

A true patriot pays back all his debts

Paris, January

Charles de Lameth will not leave his debts unpaid. He has just paid back to the Treasury the 60,000 francs he had received to pay for his education and that of his brothers.

Charles de Lameth.

In April 1790, the publication of the "Red Book" had revealed the amounts spent by Louis XVI since the start of his reign. Charles de Lameth and his brothers Alexandre and Théodore were educated at the royal military academy and received state funds during the whole time they were there. This created a moral dilemma for Charles: how could he support the Third Estate and fight against the monarchy's institutions while this debt was weighing on his conscience? Lameth is a deputy with strong moral principles. Elected to the Estates General as a deputy of the nobility of Artois, he was one of the first noblemen to give up his privileges during the night of August 4th.; but today he has finally repaid his debt and can concentrate on politics. If all noblemen were as honest, the Treasury would be rich.

Deputies on a mission drowned at sea

Quimper, January 22

There was a storm last night and two deputies were drowned at sea. A trader, the *Amphitrite,* which had been sailing to the port of Lorient, was flung onto rocks at Penmarch, on the storm-tossed Brittany coast. Aboard were two deputies from the Ile de France, Antoine Codère and Charles Collin. They had been elected by the colonial assembly to sit at the Constituent Assembly. They had sailed from Port Louis on November 2. Their voters had given them a double mission: defend the political emancipation of coloured people and fight against the abolition of slavery.

The cruel ocean can kill the innocent as easily as the guilty.

Inoculations used to combat smallpox

France, January

Smallpox is a truly democratic disease. It has no respect for social standing and can strike kings or peasants, in castles or hovels. Some die of it, while others are disfigured for life. Some victims of this terribly contagious disease are left permanently blind.

Nowadays, deaths from smallpox are estimated at between fifty and eighty thousand people in France each year. The disease had originally been brought to Europe by the Saracens in the sixth century. The country's medical profession is more or less powerless and can do little to cure the open sores or ease their patients' suffering.

Bloodletting, purging, applying poultices, or resorting to "cooling and warming" methods, all seem to have no effect. For their part, traditional healers, with their creams or salves made from such exotic ingredients as crushed slugs and onions steeped in urine, are no more effective. This often deadly disease has, however, had one positive result: it has led to a major medical advance, the prevention of sickness by inoculation. The technique, which originated in Turkey and has come to France via England, is based on injecting pus taken from a smallpox sufferer into the arm of the person who is to be protected. The process is being mainly used to protect children.

The injection causes a so-called artificial case of smallpox which is far less severe that the real disease and protects those who have been inoculated. However, it can sometimes be a risky process, and doctors have been arguing over cases where inoculation has led to death. The issue is also being discussed among philosophers. Thus, Diderot and d'Alambert's *Encyclopédie* sided with inoculation a few years ago.

Since the procedure has been saving a growing number of lives, its opponents are becoming less vocal and more and more inoculation centres are being set up throughout France. ▷

Bungled house search ends in bloodshed

City toll agents search a smuggler's store of illicit goods.

Two citizens are killed at the feet of the mayor of La Chapelle district.

Paris, January 24

The capital's unpopular city toll agents have once again caused trouble. This morning at 6 o'clock they came to search premises belonging to an innkeeper of the district of La Chapelle.

He was suspected of storing some smuggled goods. After their search, the agents were about to return to their barracks when the nearby alarm bells suddenly started ring-

ing. Always ready to defend a hard-working tradesman, a mob, which included members of the National Guard and armed citizens, quickly gathered. A gunshot rang out and the situation became ugly. There was a heavy exchange of gunfire between the toll agents and the smuggler's friends. Several people were killed or injured. The situation only returned to normal when reinforcements were rushed in.

Casanova spills the beans on sex life

Bohemia, January 23

Old age does not necessarily mean literary impotence. Now that he can no longer "have fun at all costs", Giacomo Casanova, who is 66 years old, has decided to take up writing in order to tell the story of his life. He chose to write the preface in French rather than in Venetian, although this is his mother tongue. He has just sent the manuscript off to his friend the Comte de Lamberg.

Casanova hopes that the tale of his countless adventures, mostly involving women, will help him forget all about his present misfortunes. What would his former admirers think if they knew what the world's greatest seducer has ended up as? Old and ruined, he is now working as a librarian at the Dux castle, thanks to the generous hospitality of its owner, the Duke of Waldstein. However, the duke is

often away and Casanova has to put up with the bad manners of the servants, who treat him as if he were an unwelcome guest. The old man prefers his memories.

Casanova in his prime.

2. France. The first constitutional bishops are elected by the electoral assemblies of the deparments (→24).

2. Aubagne. The bishop of Marseilles, De Belloy, whose bishopric has been abolished, says his final mass.

5. Paris. The order to take the oath is extended to include preachers, the itinerant priests who often belong to mendicant orders.

7. Aurillac. Acting on an initiative by Jean Baptiste Carrier, the Society of Young Friends of the Constitution decides to set up a watch society and offers to send officials to its parent group.

8. Lille. The priest and other officials of the parish of La Madeleine refuse to take the oath. The Nord department is one of the most strongly opposed to the religious decrees.

9. Lyons. Responding to a query from departmental authorities, 147 members of closed orders, out of a total of 241 members of the city's 16 religious establishments for men, say they want to leave their orders.

10. Paris. The Constituent Assembly receives a delegation from the Protestant Quaker sect.

10. Paris. The Assembly adds church buildings housing educational and hospital facilities to the list of church property to be auctioned off.

10. Nantes. A section of the Society of Young Friends of the Constitution is set up at the Carmes convent. Its motto is "Virtue does not depend on age".

11. Paris. Leading officials of the capital's coal port pay homage to Louis XVI who has come with his family to walk in the King's Gardens.

11. Paris. The Assembly decides to grant the free distribution of bread to soldiers. →

13. Vannes. Several thousand peasants demanding their priests, who refuse to swear to the clergy's civil Constitution, are dispersed by dragoons.

14. Montauban. Patriots win the new municipal elections.

15. Paris. The Opéra shows a performance of *Cora*, a lyric drama by Méhul based on a novel by Marmontel.

Capital punishment called barbaric and ineffective

Paris, February 7

Does the death penalty really deter criminals or is it just society's way of seeking revenge without feeling guilty about it?

The lawyer Vasselin discusses this complex issue at length in his work *Théorie des peines capitales ou Abus et dangers de la peine de mort et des tourments.*

He has just submitted the text to the Assembly. In it, he argues forcefully against the use of capital punishment. Vasselin states that the fear of execution has never stopped anybody from committing a crime. It is therefore high time to put an end once and for all to this outdated and barbaric punishment, he stresses.

Amazons of Creil honour Etta Palm

Creil, February 8

Solidarity among women is no laughing matter these days. Inspired by the forceful way in which Etta Palm has been standing up for the cause of Frenchwomen, the Amazons of Creil have sent her a medal and made her an honorary member of their group.

Etta Palm has graciously thanked her many admirers and congratulated them for their firm stand against prejudice. "This medal," she told the feminist group, "will be the sword of honour that will rest on my coffin." (→Mar. 22).

Wealthy American seeks Parisian wife

Paris, February 2

How times change! A sign of this appeared in a small ad just published by the *Courrier de l'hymen.* "An American, deputy of our colonies, who has not used his rights as a master to take advantage of his negro and mulatto women, wishes to share his fortune with a young citizen of Paris. All the dowry required is a pleasant face and a good character. Although he is a member of the legislative body, clear political opinions are not essential."

Fraud compels end of army bread war

Paris, February 11

The bread war is over. From now on, the precious loaves are to be distributed freely to all the kingdom's soldiers. This decision had become necessary because the notorious pay deductions for "munitions bread" had given rise to a great deal of fraud. In the garrisons of Flanders and Alsace, the soldiers were even compelled to buy their bread from the commissary, the official supplier of the army, at a higher price than on the open market. Moreover, the quality of bread was often poor. Loaves must now contain three parts of wheat to one part of rye.

Nantes takes pity on centenarian duo

Nantes, February 2

René Degro is 100 years old; Perrine Trouillard is at least 102. They have been married for over 73 years and had been living in squalor in a hovel not far from the Capucin convent, where the Nantes Society of the Friends of the Constitution holds its meetings. A generous citizen took them there. While they wait for the town to grant them a pension, a public subscription has been started to help them. Somewhat overcome by it all, the old couple have been dressed up in the national colours and taken to the Comédie Française to attend a benefit performance in their honour.

Food for the rich, food for the poor

A not very realistic image of the inside of a peasant kitchen.

France is a place where people eat well, and it is relatively easy to find good food; but, if one is hungry, it is better to have plenty of money at hand. A simple meal consisting of noodle soup and a piece of lamb costs 16 sols. Far more refined dishes can be found in city restaurants, which, for a more than respectable price, serve oysters, meat and fruit pies and roasts. From 11 a.m., a bourgeois usually goes to the restaurant to eat large quantities of cold meats. This midday snack will keep him going until the main evening meal. In the towns, poor people supplement their daily average of a pound of bread with vegetables, offal and sometimes some herring. This is washed down with half a litre of cheap wine. In the countryside, soup and bread are also the main staples, although cured pork meat can also be found. The most commonly served vegetables are cabbages, peas, beans and turnips. However, green beans and potatoes are becoming more popular.

France goes to polls to elect bishops

Autun, February 15

The congregation of the little church of Saint Vincent de Mâcon heard mass, making sure prayers for the nation, the law and the King were included.

As soon as mass was over, all the active citizens of Autun, both the believers and non-believers, went to vote for their bishop. A worthy successor has been found for Talleyrand. The Bishop of Autun, who had resigned on January 20th., has been replaced by the priest Jean Louis Gouttes. He was today elected constitutional bishop of the department of Saône et Loire. Gouttes, aged 51, is a model clergyman. He was one of the first to call for the three orders to meet jointly at the Estates General. He was also one of the first to take the oath of allegiance to the clergy's civil Constitution. He will now be an elected official of the kingdom, in charge of a department, just like all

Gobel is elected Bishop of Paris.

the other bishops who have been chosen throughout France since the end of last month (→24).

Bach, Gossec, Haydn under the hammer

Paris, February 10

One of the most impressive collections of musical scores ever put together has just been partly split up. Its former owner, the Comte d'Ogney, Claude François Rigoley, died a ruined man on October 4th., leaving debts amounting to nearly 100,000 livres to his wife, who is now forced to sell part of the wonderful collection.

On offer were works by all the great musicians of the century, including such names as Bach, Gossec, Niccolo Jomelli, Giovanni Pergolesi and Joseph Haydn. In 1789, Haydn had written three symphonies for the concerts held at the Olympic Lodge, opuses 90, 91 and 92. The last of these works was among the other treasures that were auctioned off today.

Du Barry jewel thieves caught in London

Louvenciennes, February 15

Her precious jewels have been found at last! Overjoyed, Madame Du Barry has been avidly rereading the letter she has received from England: the thieves who four days ago had stolen jewellery worth several million francs from her home have just been arrested. Immediately after the theft, she published a list of the missing jewellery and promised to pay a reward of 2,000 louis to whoever brought them back. The thieves were identified as they were trying to sell some of the precious stones to a London jewellery store. Louis XVI's former mistress just has one thing in mind now: she wants to get a passport so that she can travel to London to identify her beloved jewels (→Apr.).

The Comtesse Du Barry.

All hope of La Pérouse is abandoned

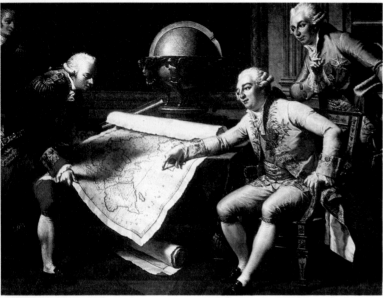

Louis XVI giving final instructions to La Pérouse before he set sail.

Paris, February 14

The Minister of the Navy, Claret de Fleurieu, has just announced that the expedition led by La Pérouse, the famous navigator, has been lost, but the official announcement will not stop search operations being set up to try to find any survivors. After a silence of three years, sailors and scientists are now convinced that both the frigates *L'Astrolabe* and *La Boussole* have sunk somewhere in the Pacific. Their disappearance is a great loss for Louis XVI and the royal navy. The expedition was supposed to have been far more important than a simple circumnavigation of the globe. The King had hoped it would be a major exploration of the Pacific. Preparations had been en-

trusted to Fleurieu, the Academy of Science and the experienced sailors Jean François de Galaup, Comte de La Pérouse, and Paul Antoine Fleuriot de Langle. The public's imagination had rapidly been fired by a trip that was presented as more of a philanthropic than a commercial venture. Royal officials had wanted to keep plans for fur trading between Alaska, Kamchatka and China secret, so they stressed the work that would be carried out by the gardeners and botanists who were sailing with La Pérouse. At each stop, they were supposed to sow and plant vegetables in order to teach agriculture to the local inhabitants. However, the Revolution had made many forget about the mission.

This piece of pottery dating from 1791 bears a very clear and highly patriotic message: Unity, the Nation, Strength and Freedom are placed above the drums and cannons that are both powerful symbols of war.

Slave with green fingers is freed

Saint Denis, February 12

Cloves are more precious than gold on Bourbon island, and the events that took place yesterday at the colonial assembly prove this. The agronomist Joseph Hubert had come to ask for freedom for his slave Jean Louis, who had spent years lovingly tending for the island's only clove tree. When they were shown the handful of cloves the slave had brought along as proof, the legislators quickly agreed to the request. They are hoping that cloves can be cultivated for export to mainland France.

Mâcon ploy secures chief town title

Mâcon, February 11

For over a year, Mâcon and Chalon sur Saône had been arguing over which one would be the chief town of the new department of Saône et Loire.

Mâcon has finally won after resorting to a last minute ploy. Last year, the situation had changed several times. The Constituent Assembly had decreed that the elections to the department's assembly would be held at Mâcon. A short while later, the voters decided that the assembly would be based at Chalon, although they were not empowered to do so. This move really set the cat amongst the pigeons! Finally, the Constituent Assembly today suggested that the criminal tribunal should be based at Chalon, which agreed before it had read the full text of the decree. When the text was published it said: "The criminal tribunal of Saône et Loire will be based in Chalon, while Mâcon will be the department's administrative seat."

Bishop hits back at gambling charge

Paris, February 8

It is one thing to criticise the morals of Talleyrand, but quite another to get one's facts wrong. That is the thrust of a letter from the former Bishop of Autun that was published this morning in the *Chronique de Paris*. The honest Camille Desmoulins had accused Talleyrand of having won 500,000 livres during one evening's gambling at Madame de Montesson's. Talleyrand cannot bear to see such lies said about him. He writes that, over a period of two months, his winnings were barely over 30,000 livres. He admits that gambling is wrong, but he can't have lies published. He did his gambling at the Chess Club, a favourite haunt of Paris gamers, but even that notorious club is better than to be associated with Mme. de Montesson, wife of the Duc d'Orléans. No great harm has been done to his reputation. Everybody was aware of his love of gambling and it hasn't harmed his political career.

A patriot woman, selling newspapers, dressed in the colours of the nation. Detail of a frontispiece of the "National Almanac" of 1791.

Troops deployed in Metz's Jewish ghetto

Metz, February 13

The city's Jewish community is worried by the presence of troops on the streets, but at least it feels a measure of security. Rioting lasted all day in the ghetto. After having been accused in the Books of Grievances of having lent money at exorbitant rates of interest, the Jews are now suspected of hoarding cash

and of making a fortune by claiming high exchange premiums on assignats. Crowds of irate citizens invaded their district and looted houses. The town authorities were forced to call in the army to restore order. When the mob had been driven out of the ghetto, soldiers were posted in the streets to make sure there was no further violence.

Constituent Assembly

19. Paris. The King's aunts, Adélaïde and Victoire, discreetly leave the country to seek refuge abroad (→21).

19. Vendée. The lawyer Charles Etienne de Villars sets up at the castle of Oie the Roving Society of the Vendée Friends of the Constitution.

19. Paris. The Assembly decides to abolish the city toll and entrance dues. The move is to become effective on May 1st.

20. Lyons. All the priests of the city's parishes are ordered to read from the pulpit the *Instruction sur la Constitution Civile du Clergé.*

22. England. The first part of the *Rights of Man* by Thomas Paine is published in London. It is the reply of a supporter of the French Revolution to Edmund Burke. The work is a major success (→Mar. 13).

22. Paris. The people of the capital invade the Luxembourg palace to stop any attempt by the King's brother, Monsieur, to leave.

23. Germany. The Prince de Condé settles at Worms to set up an army of émigrés.→

24. Lyons. The meetings of the Society of the Friends of the Constitution are to be open to the public. Men and women will be admitted on condition that they wear a patriotic ribbon.

25. Paris. The Théâtre de la Nation gives the première of an anti-clerical comedy by Claude Carbo Flins, *Le Mari Directeur ou le Déménagement du Couvent.*

26. Saint Domingue. The leaders of the mulatto uprising are executed on orders from the Cap provincial assembly. Vincent Ogé is broken on the wheel (→Mar. 4).

27. Jalès. The royalist camp is destroyed by National Guard troops.→

28. Paris. La Fayette orders the National Guard to put down a demonstration outside the palace of Vincennes. He then has the the "knights of the dagger" disarmed at the Tuileries.→

28. Paris. The new Théâtre des Petits Comédiens opens at the Palais Royal.

28. Paris. A deputy of the Périgord nobility, Foucauld de Ladimardie, asks the Assembly to ban clubs.

Royal aunts repeatedly harassed during hasty attempt to flee

The castle of Bellevue, built in the 1750s for Madame de Pompadour.

Madame Adelaïde.

Madame Victoire.

Arnay le Duc, February 21

The municipal officials who this morning carefully checked the passports of Mesdames at the gates of the village of Arnay le Duc were firm. Before allowing the King's aunts to continue their journey, they wanted instructions from the Assembly. Ever since Mesdames had left their castle at Bellevue the day before yesterday, they had been living in fear. Yesterday, their carriages were stopped at Moret and it was only thanks to the intervention of a military unit that they were able to proceed. Since the October events, they had been dreaming of leaving to seek refuge abroad. However, their excuse for leaving — to spend Easter in Rome — was greeted with suspicion and the authorities were reluctant to grant them a passport. Mesdames then decided to make a hasty departure. They had hardly left their castle when it was broken into and looted. Is their trip to end at Arnay le Duc? As a crowd surrounded the inn where they are staying, the Comte de Narbonne left for Paris. He is to remind the Assembly of the law which "lets every Frenchman go where he pleases" (→Mar. 1).

Marat's shirts

The precipitous flight and arrest of Mmes. Adélaïde and Victoire gave rise to this ironical song: (The Officers of Arnay le Duc:)

Hand us over Marat's shirts
Marat's shirts,
Marat's shirts.
We know you've got them,
Marat's shirts.
Hand them over!
(Mme. Adélaïde, amazed:)
I've not got your Marat's shirts,
Marat's shirts.
Search our bags for
Marat's shirts.
I've not got them.
(Mme. Victoire adds:)
What's with: "Marat's shirts,
Marat's shirts,
All make-believe, your
Marat's shirts.
He did not own one.
(The municipal officers:)
He had three grey Marat's shirts,
Marat's shirts.
Bought with cash, these
Marat's shirts,
Thanks to Pont Neuf.

King's brother suspected of escape plan

Paris, February 22

Monsieur, the King's brother, has the gift of being able to take advantage of the worst situations. This afternoon, a persistent rumour was heard in Paris: Monsieur was busy packing!

A crowd mostly made up of women went to the Luxembourg palace to try to find out what was going on. Monsieur, smiling and calm as usual, walked down the wide staircase to meet a delegation of citizens. "Is it true that you are planning to leave the good people who like you so much?" they asked him.

"Ladies," he replied, "I never had the slightest intention of leaving. You know how much the King respects the Constitution. Well, I respect the King and the Constitution and I will never leave the King." Despite this pledge, the people demanded that he accompany them to the Tuileries to repeat his promise. He agreed willingly enough, as he dines with his family every evening. His carriage, on which several women had climbed, could hardly clear a path through the growing crowd. Once he was at the palace, the National Guard had to disperse the crowd. It was a big triumph for Monsieur, but people still have their doubts: what will Monsieur do if the King decides to leave?

Monsieur going to the Tuileries.

Prince de Condé puts together ragtag army of French exiles

The Prince de Condé and the émigrés review an army of miniature soldiers.

Worms, February 23

There have been reports that an army of counter-revolutionaries is being formed in Worms.

The Prince de Condé is trying to put together an armed force in a bid to restore the authority of the French monarchy. Condé, who sees himself as the war-lord of the émigrés, has had an outstanding military career, at least for a prince. His moodiness and mediocre intelligence have, however, not allowed him to make the best of his expertise, but his subordinates like him and he looks after their well-being. An aristocrat and fierce defender of his privileges, Condé was one of the very first noblemen to emigrate

Condé, leader of an army of ghosts.

from France to be in a better position to fight against the Revolution. He is, however, finding it very hard to find good soldiers. He has managed to recruit Mirabeau Tonneau's two or three thousand "hussars of death", but the rest of his force is taking a lot time to get to him. Moreover, most of the men he has recruited are officers who had left their units to go abroad. That is one of his chief problems. Condé badly needs to find simple soldiers. The handful of deserters he has been able to pick up along the way are far from being sufficient. In order to pretend that he leads a real army, lower ranking officers will have to act as soldiers.

Abducted woman on murder charge

Belgian States, February 16

Poor Théroigne! She was kidnapped this morning, just as she was so happy to see her childhood friends again and to rest in her homeland after all her revolutionary activity. The man who forced her to go with him was the Chevalier de La Valette. He claimed that the émigrés had ordered him to take her to Fribourg en Brisgau to face charges of having attempted to assassinate Marie Antoinette. In spite of her pleas of innocence, Théroigne de Méricourt was not able to deter her kidnapper.

Mirabeau Tonneau heads fearsome hussars of death

Louis Mirabeau, the orator's brother.

Germany, February

A colourful man has now joined the émigrés. Louis Riqueti, the Vicomte de Mirabeau, brother of the famous Third Estate deputy, is in command of an armed force of French émigrés. The unit has decided to use the fearsome name of the "hussars of death". The former deputy of the nobility from the seneschalsy of Limoges has been dubbed Tonneau, or barrel, due to his shape and his drunken habits. He is a violent and coarse man who is always ready to pick a fight with anyone who stands in his way. He is also a fierce supporter of the monarchy, and had resigned last August from the Assembly. As he was to face charges the following month, he joined the exiled nobles.

National Guardsmen expel counter-revolutionaries from Jalès

Jalès, February 27

The counter-revolution has just suffered a severe blow in the Midi region of southern France.

Men of the National Guard have entirely destroyed the camp of Jalès, in the Ardèche. Last September, after the failure of the riots at Nîmes, Toulouse and Montauban, more than 20,000 men, all strongly opposed to the Constituent Assembly and to Protestants, had gathered at the camp. For these men, the counter-revolution is also a war of religion.

The insurgents of Jalès were hoping for Spanish military intervention.

La Fayette stops riot and royal plot

Paris, February 28

La Fayette has had an extremely busy day: he had hardly finished putting down a people's uprising at Vincennes when he had to rush back to Paris to disarm counter-revolutionary plotters.

This morning a riot suddenly broke out in the capital's suburbs. Several hundred members of the National Guards, who were being commanded by Santerre, had gone to the dungeon at Vincennes to destroy the hated fort, which they saw as just as much of a symbol of royal oppression as the Bastille. As soon as he was told about the march, La Fayette quickly rounded up a few battalions, leapt onto his horse and rushed to Vincennes. On arrival, he ordered his men to charge the rioters, several of whom were arrested. All in all, it was an efficient operation.

But as he was heading back to the city centre, the commander of the National Guard found the gates to Paris shut. This made him furious and he threatened to open fire with cannons. When La Fayette was finally able to enter the capital, a volley of shots was fired at him. La Fayette managed to survive the attempted assassination. Despite this, it was rumoured that he had been killed.

Later events seem to indicate that La Fayette had been deliberately diverted. While he was away at Vincennes, several hundred armed noblemen took over the Tuileries. The participants in the plot led by the Ducs Villequier and de Duras, who styled themselves "knights of the dagger", wanted to kidnap the King. Armed with guns and sword-sticks, they had broken into Louis XVI's rooms by using secret passages. They then overpowered the slightly inebriated guards.

La Fayette arrived in the nick of time to stop a bloodbath, but his loyalty has not been well rewarded. On one hand, at the Jacobins', Adrien Duport has said that he is making up imaginary threats in order to keep the army on a war footing. On the other hand, the court and Marie Antoinette in particular are extremely annoyed with him for having thwarted the plot aimed at getting the King and the Queen away from their palace in the capital (→ Mar. 13).

The "knights of the dagger" had hoped that La Fayette could not be in two places at once: putting down a riot at Vincennes ...

... as well as a counter-revolutionary plot at the Tuileries; but they had not taken into account the talents of La Fayette, head of the National Guard.

Condorcet calls for better schooling

Paris, February 26

Despite its many fine principles, the Declaration of human rights will never be enough to create true equality for all Frenchmen. Only learning can fill the gap that exists between citizens.

It is the Marquis de Condorcet who has spoken out in favour of such a daring concept. Today, his ideas have been published in the *Bibliothèque de l'Homme Public,* a journal which he founded a year ago. He believes that education is one of society's duties to citizens. It should be available to all, regardless of class or background. Condorcet, however, states that there are several educational levels. The basic one, which all children would be involved in, would be followed by a voluntary professional education. The most gifted students would be given a chance for higher education, notably in the scientific field.

Consecration of elected bishops gets under way

Paris, February 24

It was a decisive day for France's constitutional church. Its two first bishops have finally been consecrated. The Abbots Expilly and Marolles, who had been elected as bishops of Quimper and Soissons, had been waiting for weeks for a prelate to agree to consecrate them. In the end, it was Talleyrand who performed the ceremony, despite the fact that he had already resigned from his bishopric at Autun. Many leaders of the Assembly, such as La Fayette, Bailly, and Duport, were present.

All the rites were faithfully carried out, with the exception of the oath of allegiance to the Pope. The other unusual aspect of the ceremony was in no way related to religious matters: a military band took the place of the organ player, who was ill. The band even followed the two newly consecrated bishops home. After such a hectic morning, the two prelates, wearing their robes of office, went to the Assembly, where they were greeted by loud cheering (→ Mar. 10).

1. Fontenay le Comte. The electors of the department of Vendée vote for their constitutional bishop. A priest from the private chapel of Saumur, Jean Servant, is elected.

1. Paris. The journalist Poncelin de la Roche Tilhac establishes the *Courrier des Français*.

1. Paris. The King's aunts are allowed to continue on their journey (→Apr. 17, 91).

2. Paris. The National Assembly, acting on a proposal made by Pierre Gilbert Leroy d'Allarde, decides to abolish the trade guild-masterships and stewardships and approves a decree establishing trading licences.→

2. Sarthe. At Parcé, Claude Chappe carries out the first ever public test of an optical telegraph system.→

2. Lyons. The Abbot Adrien Lamourette, vicar-general of Arras, is elected constitutional bishop of Lyons. He takes over from Yves Alexandre de Marbeuf, who has emigrated.

3. Paris. Prugnon, a member of the Constituent Assembly, persuades the legislators to vote for the decree ordering churches and religious communities to hand over their silverware to the Mint.

4. Saint Domingue. Violent clashes break out: Colonel de Mauduit is killed by his troops.→

5. Paris. The Constituent Assembly decides to set up at Orléans a provisional tribunal that will judge crimes of insult to the nation.

10. Rome. In his brief *Quod Aliquantum*, Pope Pius VI condemns the clergy's civil Constitution. His move will persuade many clergymen to join the ranks of the nonjuring priests.

13. Paris. Nobles involved in the "knights of the dagger" affair are freed.

13. London. The second part of Thomas Paine's *Rights of Man* is published.→

14. Nantes. The department's electors replace the non-juring bishop, La Laurencie, and elect a priest, Julien Minée.

15. Paris. The royalist journal *Le Contre-Poison* starts a vicious press campaign to harass the journalist Camille Desmoulins by slandering his wife.

Marie Antoinette plots with the Emperor

Paris, March 7

Now more than ever the Queen is living up to the nickname of "the Austrian" which was given to her by the court. Hoping to put an end to the Revolution and to restore absolute monarchy, Marie Antoinette has been corresponding with her brother the Emperor. She has asked him to use his army to threaten France. A letter sent from Brussels by Mercy Argenteau, the former Austrian ambassador to Versailles, has just been intercepted and sent to the Assembly. It reveals that Leopold II will only agree to take action against France if the other main European states help him. He also wants assurances that there is a strong and influential royalist party in France. Major powers don't act without getting something for their trouble, so the Emperor wants both Alsace and Lorraine in exchange for Austrian intervention. The King of Spain wants part of Navarre, and the King of Piedmont wants some land along the Alps and in the Var region. This is enough to annoy Marat, a strong opponent of the "Austrian group" at court.

Saint Domingue: governor flees rioting

Colonel de Mauduit, the commander of the regiment of Port au Prince, is hacked to pieces by his own troops.

Saint Domingue, March 4

Violence has been getting worse at Port au Prince. For the past two days, the capital of Saint Domingue has been rocked by rioting settlers. The local garrison commander, Colonel Mauduit, was killed by his own men, amid a mob wearing red pompoms. The governor of the island, Blanchelande, was able to escape to the Cap. The outburst of mob violence had been sparked off by the publication of a fake decree from the Constituent Assembly congratulating deputies of the colonial assembly, which has been dissolved. A week after the execution of leaders of October's mulatto uprising, white men are terrorising wealthy neighbourhoods.

Free enterprise kills trade guilds

Paris, March 2

Supporters of a liberal economic system are overjoyed: the day of the trade guilds is over. Freedom of trade will no longer be hampered by the complex statutes which used to regulate trades. The suppression of guild-masterships and stewardships had not been a priority item for the Constituent Assembly. It was, however, called for by the deputy d'Allarde. He stressed that trade guilds were "exclusive privileges" which it was ridiculous to preserve since all privileges have been abolished. The approval of the measure will allow employers to set their prices, as well as the salaries of their employees, freely; but will workers in exchange now be able to organise in order to defend their rights? (→June 14).

Paine publishes his "Rights of Man"

London, March 13

Whether he is in England or in France, Thomas Paine is a firm supporter of the Revolution. His editor has just published the second part of his *Rights of Man*, a pamphlet in which he rejects the arguments contained in *Reflections on the Revolution in France* written by his fellow Briton Edmund Burke. Paine, who is steeped in the theories of enlightenment, speaks out in his work, soon to be translated into French, against monarchy, even constitutional monarchy.

Stylishness and good taste.

Optical telegraph sends message 15km

Sarthe, March 2

The rapid transmission of information will no longer be just a dream. Claude Chappe has just successfully tested an optical telegraph system. Over a distance of 15 kilometres, between Brûlon and Parcé, a message was transmitted in a few minutes. The engineer has at last found the answer he had been seeking for several years. He can now forget all about his failures over the acoustic and electric telegraph. He has managed to perfect a simple and reliable system: on top of towers built on open ground, machines equipped with mobile arms worked by an operator are placed. The arms can be moved into 196 positions, 92 of which represent the signs needed to transmit a message. Once the message has been sent, an observer on another tower reads it out to his own operator. This new method will allow messages of all types to be transmitted quickly. All that is left to do is to convince the authorities of the system's usefulness.

Claude Chappe has perfected an idea that was born a long time ago.

Slave traders of Nantes oppose Brissot

Brissot has angered slave traders by threatening their livelihood.

Nantes, March 13

"Keep your rag for your friends the Africans and don't bother to send it to us in future!" The members of the Soleil reading society at Nantes have written to Brissot to cancel their subscription to his newspaper *Le Patriote Français*. They accuse this "friend of the blacks" of being in fact "nobody's friend". Brissot's arguments in support of the abolition of the slave trade have greatly annoyed the slave traders and businessmen of Nantes. They say Brissot does "not care about the misfortunes" that would follow the ending of the slave trade. They also see the journalist as being responsible for "throwing thousands of men into misery and despair".

Stylish ladies defy the ban on carnivals

Paris, March

The ever-popular carnivals have been banned for the past several weeks. The mayor of the capital decided to forbid such events in a bid to avoid any trouble caused by crowds of over-enthusiastic merrymakers. The mayor of Paris, Bailly, is afraid that carnivals could be used as excuses for political gatherings which could give rise to fighting. Law and order must be enforced at all cost! — but high society ladies don't agree with him and have resolved to defy the ban. They have taken to wearing a kind of disguise, dressing up as lower class women. A so-called "peasant" outfit is now popular. It includes a striped satin corset, a large shawl, a small black ribbon worn around the neck and a conical hat with gilt piping, adorned with the red flowers of the pomegranate tree.

André Chénier dedicates a poem to David

Paris, March

André Chénier is far from being an ungrateful man. The ode he has written in homage to the "Oath at the Jeu de Paume", which he is just about to publish, has been dedicated to "Louis David, painter". It is his way of thanking the artist for the inspiration he has given him. Over several weeks, the poet spent long hours at the studio of his friend David. It was while he was admiring the preliminary sketches for the painting that had been commissioned by the Jacobins that Chénier decided to write an ode to celebrate the historic events at the Jeu de Paume, but Chénier's work also contains a warning that the deputies should not get carried away by their own self-importance.

André Chénier, both a polemist and a talented young poet.

Faster coaches slash journey times

Each evening, the large carriages of the central coach office set off from the Rue Notre Dame des Victoires. The coaches are packed with both passengers and baggage. They provide a regular service between Paris and the kingdom's main towns and can carry about ten passengers. Since Turgot, the coaches are a great deal faster and more comfortable. Nowadays, it only takes four days to get to Besançon, nearly six to get to Bordeaux or to Strasbourg. However, such journeys are relatively expensive: ten sols per league (four kilometres) and per person. Less wealthy people travel by wagon, cart or pony carriage. These vehicles are slower but cheaper, only six sols per league. The rich take the high speed mail coaches or rent carriages when they don't use their own transport. The French road network is one of the finest in Europe. It has no less than 25,000 kilometres of paved roads all converging on Paris. It also has many conveniently placed staging posts where travellers can eat and rest after a hard day on the road.

From Paris, it takes three days to get to Rennes by stage coach, four to Limoges, seven or eight to Toulouse and five to Lyons.

Flour milling gets all steamed up by the Périer plant on the Ile aux Cygnes

Paris, March 9

The mayor of Paris, Bailly, has just sent an official letter to the Academy of Science to invite its members to visit the new flour mills on the Ile aux Cygnes, under construction ever since 1789. The scientific community is fascinated by the "genuine experiment". Some 24 mills, each producing 72 "setiers" of flour a day, are to be powered by just two steam engines. This is the first time such a system has been tested in France. Jealous competitors have claimed that the Périer brothers have simply been exploiting an English invention, but in fact it was the Spaniard Bétancourt y Molina who found out about Watt and Boulton's secret and told the French engineers about it. The Périers were able to convince the French government to finance the project (→ March 17).

Paris' Ile aux Cygnes is neither inhabited nor cultivated. It is used to store the loads of firewood that have been shipped to the capital by barge.

Smugglers saved by the crowd

Annet, March 5

This time they were caught red handed. They had hidden some tobacco in bags. The two smugglers were immediately sent to jail. The customs officers were very pleased with their day's work.

But they had quite forgotten that smugglers often have friends and accomplices. These soon gathered on the town square, making a lot of noise and showing their weapons. Things would not have gone any further if a crowd had not mingled with the smugglers' friends. What united them was their hatred of excise men.

For local people, smugglers are not bandits. They are traders who provide goods that are heavily taxed at lower prices. Faced with the angry mob, the customs officers released their captives. Even more humiliating, they were forced to hand over the tobacco they had just impounded.

Goodbye to "Sir", hello to "Citizen"

Belfort, March 15

The Revolution will spread to all sectors: the law, social habits and even language. Now that fraternity and equality are the order of the day, it is time to get rid of aristocrats' pretentious and hypocritical politeness. Language must reflect the new relationships between people. The example was set by the Jacobins of Belfort: a month after their creation, they decided to stop calling each other "Sir" and to use "Citizen" instead. Isn't this the best form of address for the new society born in 1789? Moreover, the new style has a double advantage: it stresses the unity of the new nation, while at the same time putting an end to social discrimination and the need for formal bowing. Another positive aspect of the new system is that it serves as a reminder of the glorious Roman republic, on which Constituent Assembly members like to model themselves.

March 1791
from 16th. to 31st.

Constituent Assembly

16. Rhône. The priest of Saint Nizier, Abbot Linsolas, provokes a riot between patriots and supporters of non-juring priests when he says a sermon for Lent.

16. Douai. A hunger riot breaks out. Two people, a captain in the National Guard and a wheat merchant, are murdered (→ 19).

17. Paris. The Academy of Sciences visits the experimental steam-powered flour mill set up at the Ile aux Cygnes at the request of the government.

17. Toulouse. Three people are killed in clashes between patriots and troops of the royalist Saint Barthélemy force (→ Apr. 19, 91).

17. Paris. The capital's new bishop, Monsignor Gobel, takes up his office.

18. Paris. The Assembly decides to keep enforcing the system of monopoly of trade: overseas colonies can only trade with mainland France.

19. Paris. The Favart auditorium shows *Camille ou le Souterrain*, by Benoît Joseph Marsollier and Nicolas Dalayrac.

20. Paris. The Assembly decrees the abolition of the General Farm.→

20. Paris. A decree abolishes provincial militias, useless since the creation of the National Guard.

21. Vendée. Invited by the town of Sainte Florence, the Jacobins of the Mobile Society of the Friends of the Constitution hold their first public meeting and give a message to the people of Vendée explaining the Constituent Assembly's latest decrees.

21. Lyons. The former Primate of Gauls, Alexandre de Marbeuf, issues a ruling condemning the continued presence of non-juring priests and teachers at Saint Irénée seminary.

21. Lyons. As a sanitary measure, Jean Jacques Coindre asks the town to move cemeteries outside the city limits.

28. Paris. Mirabeau suddenly falls ill (→ Apr. 2, 91).

29. Paris. The Assembly issues a decree outlining regulations for the ownership of scientific and technological inventions. They will be protected by patents.

City fathers close right wing, pro-monarchist club

Stanislas de Clermont Tonnerre is a firm supporter of English-style constitutional monarchy.

Paris, March 28

Have the monarchists become enemies of the Revolution? Whatever the case, the city council of Paris has just ordered the closure of their club, the Friends of the Monarchist Constitution, which is led by Malouet and Clermont Tonnerre. It had been founded in September, after right wing deputies at the Assembly had failed to get support for a constitution based on two legislative houses with a major role given to royal power. However, this type of system seems outdated and suspicious today.

People must elect ministers — Laclos

Paris, March 19

Government ministers must be elected by the nation. That, at least, is what Choderlos de Laclos believes and has firmly told the Jacobins. A member of the club had initially suggested that ministers could be named by the King, who would be guided by a watch committee and a national verification committee. That was far from being enough for Laclos. Ministers must be submitted to the popular vote so that they faithfully represent the will of the people, he said. In that way, Frenchmen will no longer be the King's "subjects", a hateful term reminiscent of the slaves of antiquity, but free men who are freely governed.

Assembly votes to abolish General Farm

Paris, March 20

The General Farm has at last been abolished by a vote at the Assembly. This is the end of the line for one of the most hated institutions of the Ancien Régime. This private company had the right to raise taxes for a period of six years in exchange for the payment of a lump sum. It had been blamed for the big deficit in the Treasury's balance. The Books of Grievances had violently criticised the system of Farmers General, made up of the 20 families who shared the 40 jobs of Farmer General. They had become rich thanks to the salt tax, indirect taxes and city tolls. The Farmers General were held responsible for ruining the people without

making the King rich. There were hopes that it would be enough to abolish these go-betweens to settle France's financial problems. The patriotic donation of 22.5 million livres made by the General Farm at the start of the Revolution had aroused anger, as many were convinced that the money had been stolen from them. This just made people more wary of the institution, although it was envied by those who had a bit of money and would lend it to the Farm General. The deputies are to set up a committee to liquidate this financial body and look into its accounts. Six of the Farmers General will be members of the committee, as they know the ins and outs of the system.

Funeral procession for a farmer general who has "died of sorrow".

Medal marks end of priestly election

Paris, March 27

In all, it has taken two months to elect 17 priests. Since the start of February, the electors of the district of Paris have spent every single Sunday at Notre Dame to perform out their duty. After a while, the noble task became somewhat tedious. The day would start off with a mass, then voting would begin. Several rounds of voting were usually needed, and only about two priests would be elected at each session. Then came the speeches of those who had been elected. The tiresome proceedings were often not over until 7 o'clock. People are now so happy that it is all over with that a commemorative medal has been struck.

Brienne sends hat back to the Pope

Sens, March 26

Send your cardinal's hat back to the Pope! This was the advice that Beaumarchais sent to Loménie de Brienne, who took it with little hesitation. Severely criticised by Pius VI for having taken the oath of allegiance to the Constitution, the Archbishop of Sens wanted to show that he has no regrets whatsoever over his decision. Brienne, who used to be insulted when he was a minister of Louis XVI, has become popular since he got into trouble with the Pope. Delighted that his advice had been followed, Beaumarchais has written to Brienne again: "You have shown your enemies that here the head is worth more that the hat."

Douai officials on trial for mob lynching

Paris, March 19

It law and order an end unto itself? The Assembly today debated the clashes that have rocked Douai over the past few days. A wheat merchant was hanged by a crowd who wanted to stop grain being exported. The town council had refused to decree martial law. The Assembly's chairman proposed that the city officials of Douai be ordered to account for their negligence, and some deputies even called for their immediate arrest, but Robespierre then pointed out that the behaviour of the Douai officials should not be judged before they had been duly heard out. Law and order supporters, however, do not agree with him.

The people of Douai were quick to seek their own form of justice.

Abbot, father of two, seeks wedlock

Paris, March

Priests should be allowed to marry. Ever since members of the Constituent Assembly began to reform the church, one man has been in the forefront of the fight against enforced celibacy for the clergy. The fiery advocate of marital bliss is well placed to know what he is talking about: the Abbot Cournand has been living happily with a charming woman, with whom he has already had two lovely children. The only dark cloud on the happy couple's horizon is that they are not married and would dearly like to be. That is what has motivated the Abbot Cournand to go to the clubs and committees to press his case.

The monk's cowl is thrown away. The gate to freedom is open at last.

Imprisoned clerics gain their freedom

Paris, March 28

Large numbers of "cloistered victims" have regained their freedom since the Assembly ordered the monasteries to be opened. The heroine of a play with that name, which was shown for the first time this evening at the Théâtre de la République, had been locked up in a convent by a dissolute priest who forced her to hand over her property to the church. She is freed by her lover and a helpful National Guardsman. A member of the audience said that he had also been forced to become a monk.

Assembly boosts peacetime army

Paris, March 25

The army should remain strong, even in peacetime. That is what the Assembly believes and it has just issued a decree on the army's manpower needed to fight the enemies of the Revolution.

An active army of 150,000 men, to be increased by 100,000 men taken from the National Guard when necessary: that is what the deputies feel is needed. The National Guard is to continue to handle law and order.

Kings unite against the Revolution

Late March

The spread of the Revolution throughout France is causing serious concern among the crowned heads of Europe. They are forced to take steps to protect their nations. The Austrian Emperor and the King of Prussia have even settled their differences in order to unite against what they call the "revolutionary plague". As for Gustav III, King of Sweden, he is dreaming of leading a vast crusade of monarchs to restore Louis XVI's powers. Over the past few weeks, there have been major troop movements near the borders of France. The King of Spain, who doesn't particularly like the French anyway, has massed several thousand men along the Pyrenees. The King of Piedmont has done the same in Savoy. An Austrian army is occupying the borders of Franche Comté. The patriots of France are worried by all this. They have seen how firmly the Austrian Emperor restored his authority in the Netherlands; but Leopold II is by no means keen to go to war and all major military operations depend on him. He would rather see a weak France than a strong one and the Revolution in a way has served his purposes.

Despite the pressures from his sister, the Queen of France, and from the King of Prussia, who sees himself as the defender of monarchist Europe, Leopold II has not decided to head a coalition. Still, the patriots of France are not wrong to fear the consequences that an alliance between the crowned heads of Europe could have.

Queen stripped of regency powers

Paris, March 22

Despite the fact that women are playing increasingly active roles in society and politics, queens have just been stripped of a right they have had since time immemorial: the right to rule while their sons are under age if the king has died.

Most of the deputies want to stop women being regents, with the exception of Cazalès, but his colleagues have not listened to him and have decided that, if the king were to die, his closest male relative, as defined by the order of heirs to the throne, would become regent, on the conditions that he is aged over 25 and that he is a French citizen.

However, the mother will retain custody of a sovereign while he is a minor. Marie Antoinette had been keeping a very close eye on the debate at the Assembly. She knows she is directly concerned and has been deeply upset by the decree.

Lengthy debate chooses metre measure

Paris, March 19

The chaos that exists in the system of measures has continued to make life impossible for the French. Something is finally going to be done about the problem. A committee of learned men, which includes Borda, Lagrange, Laplace, Condorcet and Monge, has approved the concept of a universal measurement of length. In order that this can be used in all countries, thay have decided to choose a basic unit that is found in nature. After lengthy debate, they have agreed: it will be the metre, which will be equal to the ten millionth part of a quarter of the earth's meridian. To get an exact result, the committee has asked for a scientific mission to be sent to measure the meridian. As for the basic unit of weight, it will be the gram, equal to the weight of a cubic centimetre of distilled water at a temperature of four degrees.

Etta Palm sets up the Friends of Truth club

Paris, March 23

Loud cheering greeted Etta Palm when she spoke from the rostrum of the Confederation of the Friends of Truth.

For the past year the brave Dutchwoman has been playing an ever more active role in political life. She does not get involved in what happens in the streets, but spends her time attending club meetings and the Assembly, where she has been defending the cause of women. Today she proposed that, in each sector of Paris, women's clubs, to be called the Friends of Truth, be set up. These would give assistance to the poor, visit the sick and the handicapped and even take care of the education of children. Her proposal was so warmly greeted that Etta Palm has invited all the ladies present to come to the first meeting of the Friends of Truth next Friday.

Careful reading of the "Moniteur" is an essential part of every meeting held by the patriotic women's clubs.

April 1791
from 1st. to 15th.

1. Paris. The chemist Berthollet has his *Eléments sur l'Art et la Peinture* published by the editor Firmin Didot.

2. Paris. Death of Mirabeau: the authorities announce that an eight day period of mourning will be observed. →

2. Lyons. The book-seller Jean Louis Prudhomme and the Abbot Laussel set up the *Journal de Lyons ou Moniteur du Département de Rhône et Loire.*

3. Brédarieux. Four hundred citizens opposed to the clergy's Constitution ask the Assembly to hold a national vote on the issue.

6. Var. The department's authorities announce that 525 out of a total of 543 priests have taken the oath of allegiance to the clergy's civil Constitution.

7. Paris. On the urging of Robespierre, the Assembly approves a decree stating that no Constituent Assembly member will be allowed to become a minister for four years after the end of his mandate as a deputy.

9. Vendée. There is an attempt to assassinate the juring priest of the village of Saint Jean de Monts.

10. Nantes. The ship *Cerbère* is renamed *Mirabeau* and the white flag is replaced by a tricoloured one.

11. Paris. The department's authorities issue a ruling allowing individuals to meet to worship as they choose. This is aimed at giving non-juring priests some freedom of movement.

11. Lyons. The new bishop, Adrien Lamourette, is solemnly admitted.

12. Lyons. The Society of the Friends of the Constitution meets at the Plâtres district club. The Abbot Aymard, a missionary Saint Joseph priest, pays homage to Mirabeau.

15. Rouen. The constitutional bishop Charrier de La Roche is formally admitted.

15. Paris. Olympe de Gouges gets the Favart auditorium to show a lyric comedy, *Mirabeau aux Champs Elysées.*

15. Saumur. The constitutional bishop of Vendée, Jean Servant, is threatened, takes fright and sends his election certificates back to the department's authorities.

Mirabeau dies: poisoning suspected

Paris, April 2

The people have been heartbroken since Mirabeau's death. On March 28th. he made a speech at the Assembly and it was obvious that he was in considerable pain — death was already written on his face. That same evening, exhausted by his efforts, he went to bed, never to get up again. His friend Doctor Cabanis sat with him during his final hours, when he was delirious, with his eyes fixed on the window.

He died today at 8:30 a.m., as a silent crowd waited by his window. The news of his death at the age of 43 spread like wildfire throughout the kingdom. It was so sudden, so unexpected, that people had already become highly suspicious. The possibility that he had been poisoned had not been ruled out. Within a few hours of his death, posters had gone up all over the walls of the capital. Some proclaimed that the Lameth brothers were responsible for his death, while others accused Bar-

A dying Mirabeau hands over his work on successions to Talleyrand.

nave. In order to put a stop to all these rumours, the public prosecutor of Paris' first "arrondissement" ordered a postmortem to be carried out right away. It showed a serious inflammation of the stomach and liver, but no trace of deadly poison. The people of Paris won't be able to use revenge to help them get over their deep sorrow.

His tomb the first at Ste Genevieve

Paris, April 3

The temple of religion is to become the last resting place of illustrious men. Mirabeau's tomb will be an altar for freedom. The deputies have decided that the Sainte Geneviève church, built by Soufflot, will from now on be used as a burial place for glorious men. The following words are to be engraved on the church's façade: "To great men, from a thankful Nation". However, the honour given to Mirabeau by making him the first to be buried there has aroused some hostile reactions. Marat and the Cordeliers were the first to criticise the hero-worship of Mirabeau, whom they considered a schemer, but Robespierre has come to his defence. Mirabeau will be buried tomorrow.

A song about Mirabeau's death

Mirabeau was buried in the Panthéon yesterday. A weeping crowd followed his bier. Jacobins, suspecting him of having played a double game, want his remains taken to a cemetery outside Paris. A new song is circulating. It mentions Gobel, the first bishop to have sworn faith to the Nation, and Fauchet, the King's former preacher:

Rings doleful the knell
See yon Gobel
In Jacobin's dress
Feigns to honour with gloom
Mirabeau's tomb.
His soul must he bless.

Soft drums, bells and drone
Join with cannon:
In concert combine.
Their mourning declare,
Nobles where'er
In Paris repine.

Weep, Fauchet, deplore
His life now o'er.
The great man inhume.
And next year, so be,
In distant lea
We'll piss on his tomb.

National Guardsmen fire a salvo by the remains of Mirabeau. Dozens of constitutional priests stand around the coffin. More than 100,000 citizens of Paris pay their last respects to the great man.

Problems for the Duchesse d'Orléans

Paris, April 2

Poor Marie Adélaïde d'Orléans: it was the straw that broke the camel's back. It was one thing for the children's governess, Madame de Genlis, to have had an affair with her husband, but it was quite another for her to use her influence over the children to cause a rift between them and their very own mother. That is something she can't accept. Tired of being ignored, the duchess has gone to the boarding school to tell her former good friend that she is no longer in charge of the children's education.

Pope Pius VI lashes out against the clergy's civil Constitution

Rome, April 13

The Pope had been warning and threatening for several months. Now the head of the Catholic church has officially reacted: any juring priest who has not recanted within 40 days will be suspended. The new ruling that the Pope has issued to "the King, the bishops, the priests and all the people of France" is perfectly clear. It is, in fact, a total condemnation of the clergy's civil Constitution. The parish and episcopal elections have been declared void by the Vatican. As for consecrations, they are sacrilegious and all the bishops who have been involved in them are dismissed from the episcopal order. Gobel and Talleyrand are among those concerned by the move. Pius VI has blessed faithful Catholics and cited Saint Leon: "I praise you for having remained steadfast in the evangelical and apostolic doctrine." The only move left open to constitutional clergymen is to repent; in other words, to recant their oath of allegiance. There seems to be no hope of a compromise between the juring and non-juring camps. A schism seems inevitable. The Papal brief has been banned by the revolutionary authorities in France, as was a previous one, but it is circulating under the counter (→ May 3).

The Papal brief does not seem to worry this patriot unduly.

Chateaubriand sets off for America

François René de Chateaubriand leaves the Old World.

Saint Malo, April 8

True freedom is not to be found in France, but in the virgin territories of America that have been arousing the curiosity of explorers. That is what the Chevalier de Chateaubriand thinks. He is preparing to leave. He has no illusions about the revolutionary cause, nor about that of the émigrés, and he prefers to leave a France where it has become impossible for him to live. His aristocratic name has made him an object of suspicion. What will he find across the ocean? Adventure, a country that is three quarters unexplored and the hope of finding that celebrated northwest passage to the Pacific that so many navigators have dreamt about. As an avid disciple of Rousseau, he hopes what he will find in the forests of the New World will fire his imagination. He wants to paint the everyday life of the natives he is sure to meet. Before sailing, he has gone on a pilgrimage to his family's castle at Combourg where he spent his childhood. It is now deserted. He also went to Saint Malo to bid farewell to his mother (→ July 10).

Marauding harpies whip nuns in street

Paris, April 7

Despite their legendary strength, the ladies of the marketplace still have sore muscles. They certainly didn't spare the rod.

Groups of these women had spent the entire day going from convent to convent looking for nuns suspected of hiding non-juring priests. It all started at the monastery of the Filles de Sainte Marie. The women of the district of Saint Antoine thought that many more masses than usual were being said: by half past ten, they claimed, there had already been 22 masses, instead of the customary six or seven. They saw this as proof that non-juring priests were being sheltered there. After grabbing some whips, they demanded to be allowed in. Inside, a devout woman was confessing to a non-juring priest.

Seizing the unfortunate lady, they dragged her out into the middle of the Rue Saint Antoine and gave her a thorough thrashing. The two nuns who had opened the convent gates were also beaten. Similar scenes have occurred in several parts of Paris, in particular at Saint Roch, where it was claimed that the nuns wanted to pour boiling oil on any juring priests who were unlucky enough to pass under their windows.

A thrashing that was as unexpected as it was humiliating.

Oaths, oaths, oaths and more oaths

France, April

Everybody seems to be swearing an oath of allegiance at the drop of a hat. First there was the Oath of the Jeu de Paume, then the oath to the Federation and the oath to the clergy's civil Constitution. Every revolutionary act has given rise to some kind of oath. Kings, deputies, clergymen, National Guardsmen and simple citizens have been involved in the new patriotic fad, but not everybody is in full agreement and oath taking can cause tensions to surface between groups. An example of this is the conflict between juring and non-juring priests. Oaths can also help control the popular unrest that has worried bourgeois deputies. The oath to the Federation is one such case. Those taking the oath swore to be loyal to the Constitution and to "protect, according to the law, the security of persons and property and the free circulation of grain and essential goods". That is useful in view of the attacks against grain hoarders.

Good business for property developer

Grenoble, April

The sale of the clergy's property has been a godsend for Claude Perier. He used to be known in what was the Dauphiné province as Perier-Milord.

This financier has been buying up the clergy's property as fast as he can. First of all, he added a considerable amount of land to the grounds of his castle at Vizille. He also bought part of the Augustinian land at Voiron, a chapel at Laval and two handsome properties belonging to the Prémol Carthusian monastery at Vaulnaveys. One of these, worth an estimated 27,664 livres, includes a building, a garden, fields and meadows. He agreed to pay double the asking price and he does not seem to care how much he spends. He knows how to take advantage of the depreciation of the assignat and make the best of the conditions of payment. In his latest deal, he only has to pay 12 per cent within two weeks, while the rest is spread over 12 years. This means that he will have very little to pay right away. Perier is a supporter of revolutionary ideals, but he nevertheless is careful about how he invests his money.

Spy operation nets Madame Du Barry

London, April

Madame Du Barry has once again gone to London to try to get back her beloved jewels, which had been stolen, but the trial is dragging on and the judges do not seem inclined to give her what she wants. With all these worries to think about, Mme. Du Barry did not notice that she was being closely watched by a certain Blanche, an agent of the French police, who has been sending regular reports on her activities to Paris. She had already acted rashly by asking for letters of credit from the Vandenyver bank, which is suspected of having links with the émigrés, and by agreeing to take large numbers of letters to England. Since her arrival in London she has made matters even worse by being seen at meetings held at the club where the French émigrés gather. Meanwhile, her jewels are still under lock and key.

Voltaire fan renames Paris embankment

Paris, April 13

When they awoke this morning, Parisians found that the Théatins embankment had a new name. It was the Marquis de Villette, whose house sits on the corner of the embankment, who had erased the name during the night. He has renamed it the "Voltaire Embankment". The nobleman had wanted to pay homage to his friend and protector, Voltaire, for whom he had the greatest esteem. When he announced his action to the Jacobins' club, he said: "His memory is as immortal as his work. We will always have a Voltaire and there will never be any Théatins." The marquis had met the great philosopher in 1765. Since then, he had in a way become his adopted son. Villette has just asked the Assembly to have Voltaire's ashes brought back to Paris.

Voltaire's behaviour and his work broke new ground. For example, he used to dictate letters to his secretary while getting dressed.

Italian horseman is a hit in Paris

Paris, April 12

What a treat it is to watch the antics of the Italian-born rider Antonio Franconi.

Crowds of people have been flocking to Astley's riding school to see the acrobatic horseman, who has recently arrived from Lyons. On the covered arena that has been built on some waste land in the Temple district, he has performed some of the exploits that have already made him famous in the provinces.

With a gentle touch of his riding crop on the horse's flank, he got it to swivel round on its forelegs. He then leapt on the animal's bare back and stood up with his arms outstretched. Franconi kept the best for the end of the show: he got his dappled steed to stomp around the arena shaking its mane just as if it were a puppy following its master around.

Feudal inheritance laws are scrapped

France, April 5

Last-born children of common families at last have something to celebrate. From now on they are to be the equals of their elder siblings in matters of inheritance. That is what the Assembly, where last-born deputies are in the majority, has ruled. The law of primogeniture, which dates back to feudal times, had spread over the centuries to all levels of society. Not only did the first-born child get a large part of the inheritance, known as the "préciput", before any of it was shared out, he was also entitled to half of the remaining property. This system, designed to avoid the splitting up of a family's property, had for years caused disagreement within families. It meant that the youngest often were unable to marry and had a hard life. Thousands of young women were forced to become nuns because they lacked a dowry.

High drama marks theatrical move

Madame Dugazon playing Nina.

Paris, April 10

Talma has left the Théâtre de la Nation. Deeply upset about the petty moves against him, which are due to both his success and his revolutionary convictions, he has now moved to the Théâtre Français on the Rue de Richelieu. He has taken along with him the "red squadron" made up of famous actors such as Grandmesnil, the Dugazons, Mme. Vestris and Mademoiselle Desgarcins. Talma was only able to salvage his costumes, which were confiscated when he announced that he was resigning, by hiding them inside a dress stand that was carried by lictors while Dugazon marched ahead dressed as Achilles and carrying a spear.

Marie Rose Vestris.

Constituent Assembly

17. Paris. Clashes break out at the Théatins church, which is being rented by the non-juring priest of Saint Sulpice. A mob stops the faithful attending the service (→June 2, 91).

18. Paris. Louis XVI, who yesterday was given Holy Communion by the non-juring Cardinal de Montmorency, is forbidden to go to Saint Cloud by the National Guard.→

18. Caen. The Abbot Fauchet is elected Bishop of Calvados after failing to be elected at Nevers.

18. Paris. Doctor Pierre Cabanis reads a diary of Mirabeau's illness to members of the Lycée. The poet Marie Joseph Chénier recites an ode on Mirabeau's death.

19. London. The Protestant minister Richard Price dies. He was a member of the Society of the Revolution which had warmly welcomed the events in France.

19. Strasbourg. Sent to Alsace to enforce the clergy's civil Constitution, which has been rejected by much of the local population, Hérault de Séchelles receives death threats.

19. Toulouse. The Saint Barthélemy legion of the National Guard is dissolved. It had been recruited from parliamentary circles. The general council of Haute Garonne has thus punished those responsible for the riots of March 17th.

22. Paris. Timber workers go on strike to back their demands for higher daily wages (→May 4, 91).

23. Paris. La Fayette, who had tendered his resignation after the events of April 18th., agrees to resume command of the National Guard.

25. Paris. The patriot journalist Carra is attacked by National Guards who support La Fayette.

28. Paris. Despite strong opposition from Robespierre, the Assembly rules that only active citizens can become members of the National Guard.→

29. Paris. Acting on a proposal by Beauharnais, the Assembly grants soldiers the right to attend club meetings. Beauharnais based his call on the recent clashes between the soldiers and officers of the Beauvaisis regiment. The officers had tried to stop the lower ranks going to the Wissembourg club. In all, 12 people had been injured during the fighting (→June 7, 91).

National Guard prevents Louis XVI's trip

The royal family had to spend over two hours listening to the crowd's shouts.

Paris, April 18

On this Holy Monday, just as the King and his family were about to leave for Saint Cloud, the National Guardsmen posted at the Tuileries palace refused to let the royal family go. A crowd soon gathered and sided with the resolute guardsmen. There were rumours that Louis XVI wanted to go to Saint Cloud to pray alongside non-juring priests. People were also saying the King would take advantage of his trip to escape. La Fayette, who rushed to the scene of the trouble, tried in vain to talk some sense to his men. When he was unable to settle the problem, he advised the King to return to his rooms at the Tuileries. "It is up to you, Sir, to do what is necessary to enforce your Constitution," Louis XVI ironically told the commander of the National Guard (→Apr. 19).

Mesdames meet Pope Pius VI

Rome, April 17

Mesdames arrived in Rome yesterday. Today they were granted a private audience with the Pope. The princesses have not yet got over the trouble they encountered during their trip. Madame Victoire can't stop crying, while Madame Adélaïde can hardly say a word. They had been kept waiting at Arnay le Duc for about ten days because the local authorities would not allow them to leave. As soon as they were free to go, they hurriedly crossed the rest of France. When they got to the border at Pont de Beauvoisin, booing could be heard on the French side, while they were welcomed to Italy by salvoes.

"What can I say, my children, the French do what they please."

King, furious at detention, demands freedom for Easter travel

Paris, April 19

The King was most annoyed about the way the National Guard behaved yesterday. He came to complain about this outrage to the Assembly. He pointedly reminded the deputies that they had agreed to his trip to Saint Cloud. The deputies promised that they will do all they can to ensure the sovereign's freedom of travel. Apparently reassured, Louis XVI then reiterated his support for the Revolution and the honour he felt at being a constitutional monarch. After these solemn words, he left amid cheers from the legislators, with the exception of right wing ones, who were shocked by the King's words (→Apr. 25).

It was the people, not the Assembly, who stopped the King leaving Paris.

Louis XVI spends Easter in Paris

Paris, April 24

Where will the King go to say his Easter prayers? For the past few days everybody has been asking this question. At the Cordeliers they warned that the people would not tolerate the King celebrating Easter at the Tuileries, with its non-juring priests. Government ministers have been saying: "Sire, there is unrest in Paris. Can you continue to refuse to attend constitutional services?" For her part Madame Elisabeth, the very pious sister of Louis XVI, said: "The King attend a service held by juring priests? I'll believe it only when I see it." However, that was what the King finally decided to do. This morning he attended a mass said by the Abbot Corpet, the juring priest of the church of Saint Germain l'Auxerrois. In fact, ever since the National Guard stopped him going to Saint Cloud last Monday, Louis XVI had had no other option but reluctantly to demonstrate his loyalty to the Constitution. At Saint Cloud he could have attended a service held by a non-juring priest, but that option was ruled out.

Parisians celebrate Easter Day on the streets and in the cafes

Paris, Easter Sunday

Any holiday, religious or not, is a good excuse to go out for the people of Paris. The capital's poor will probably go to evensong, or "the beggars' opera" as the rich call it. Everybody is looking forward to spending a full day away from work and wondering how to make the best of it. The bourgeois are likely to go on a family outing along the alleyways of the Tuileries or of the Luxembourg. Some prefer to stroll down the boulevards or along the Arsenal embankment. These have all become favourite areas for their walks. The older bourgeois cast disapproving glances at the young women from the provinces, maids or seamstresses, walking around with smiles and their skirts hitched up slightly too far to show off pretty legs. There are crowds on the Champs Elysées, where the houses have terraces and there are cafes by the score. Workmen and artisans go from cafe to cafe, to La Courtille or the Porcherons. Many prefer the Nouvelle France sector, where wine is cheaper and flows in abundance.

Chairs have been placed on the Boulevard des Italiens so that people can chat and watch the crowds pass.

Politics comes to the confessional

Yvetot, April 20

Should politics be kept out of the confessional box? As Easter nears, the issue has become a burning one. After a large number of complaints, the town council has been looking into a matter that has shocked the village. Still shaking with anger, Félicité Aillard has told of her misadventure. She had hardly knelt down when the vicar, a notorious non-juring priest, had asked her opinion about "current affairs". "I have come to confess my sins, not to talk about all that," Félicité replied. "That is a typical thing for a woman to say," the priest responded, "you must tell me the truth: will you recognise the juring priests who will come to replace us? Are you going to abandon us?" To this, the poor woman exclaimed: "But you are the one who is abandoning us! I will obey the priests they send us and who look after us." Enraged by that reply, the priest sent her home after refusing to absolve her.

Church bells ring for Talma's wedding

Paris, April 19

The church of Notre Dame de Lorette is packed with flowers and the great organ is playing: François Joseph Talma is standing at the altar beside Julie Carreau, his new bride.

In order to be able to get married in church, Talma has had to give up his title of "actor" and take that of a simple "bourgeois of Paris". That was the condition set by the Abbot Lepipe, vicar of the parish. The priest of Saint Sulpice, who had earlier been asked to perform the ceremony, had been much more strict, stressing that under church law actors were not allowed to receive the holy sacrament.

These problems had only made Talma more impatient to wed Julie. The new Madame Talma is seven years older then her husband, and she is known to have had many previous love affairs, but she has a private income of 40,000 livres and has her own residence as well as several other buildings. Talma may be famous, but he is poor and heavily in debt. He was unable to withstand the lure of wealth and security. It was also high time that they were married: despite the threats of excommunication voiced by the priest of Saint Sulpice, their union has already been blessed and Julie is expecting a child (→ May 1).

Julie Talma, a former dancer with a busy love life.

Mob breaks up an aristocratic party

Paris, April 21

Some people found the incident amusing, but André Chénier has expressed outrage over what he has called the "altars of fear". In a private residence of the district of Saint Honoré, a charity concert attended by many aristocrats was held three days ago. Drawn by the noise and the bright lights, a crowd gathered under the windows shouting that a plot was being hatched. A local police officer was summoned and sent inside to take the names of those present, whose only crime was to wear the white cockade and to have aristocratic names. Despite this, they were forced to leave under the catcalls and insults of the angry mob. André Chénier's pen might not have been so bitter in writing about the event had it not been for the fact that among the unfortunate nobles there was a certain Madame de Bonneuil, whom he used to call Camille when he was her lover.

Louis XVI still plays a double game

Paris, April 25

After having told the Assembly how delighted he was to be a constitutional monarch, Louis XVI quickly wrote to Breteuil, his unofficial representative to the major European powers, to tell him not take any account of what he had said. The King and Queen have been doing their best to hide their true feelings by appearing to support the Constitution. The current unrest, in fact, does not displease them. The incident of April 18th. has helped their cause at the foreign courts. It has shown that the King of France is no longer free to go where he pleases (→June 15).

The National Guard will be bourgeois

Paris, April 28

Not everyone can join the National Guard. Membership of this militia is to be limited to active citizens, that is, those who can pay a direct tax equal to at least three days' wages for an unqualified worker. That means that some 40 per cent of the male population aged over 25 do not qualify. Robespierre has unsuccessfully attempted to remind the Assembly that the decree is a violation of the principle of citizens' equal rights. He knows that the basically bourgeois make-up of the National Guard makes it unlikely that it will become politically radical (→June 11).

The King finances "Le Logographe"

Paris, April 27

The quality of reporting on the debates at the Assembly is getting better. Today, the first edition of *Le Logographe* went on sale. Its title is based on the new system of shorthand being used by the newspaper's parliamentary reporters. They are the only ones to have access to a comfortable booth in the chamber from where they can follow the debates. However, patriots have already accused them of distortion of the debates. *Le Logographe* is funded by the King's civil list and this may explain their criticism.

May 1791
from 1st. to 15th.

Constituent Assembly

1. Paris. The decree on the abolition of the city tolls is enforced amid widespread rejoicing.→

1. Paris. Students of the Mazarin college attack their juring professors and the National Guard is forced to intervene. The young insurgents are disarmed and sent back to school.

2. Vendée. The election of the mayor of Saint Christophe du Ligneron causes a serious anti-patriot riot.→

3. Paris. Following the publication of the Papal brief of April 13th. on sanctions against juring bishops and priests, the Pope is burnt in effigy at the Palais Royal.→

4. Paris. After a wave of strikes, the city authorities decide to ban all meetings of workers.

4. Brabant. The former Bishop of Lyons, Marbeuf, now living at the Rêves castle where he has sought refuge, issues a pastoral letter condemning the seizure of his bishopric by the Abbot Lamourette.

4. Paris. The Academy of Science awards a prize to a memorandum on the resistance of fluids written by Charles Gilbert Romme.

7. Paris. Acting on a call by Talleyrand, the Assembly decides to apply to the whole of France the right of non-juring believers to worship freely in rented establishments.

7. Paris. Pressed by the journalist Robert, the Fraternal Societies for both sexes set up a central committee based at the Cordeliers.

9. Paris. At the Assembly, the deputies debate Le Chapelier's bill aimed at abolishing the right to petition of passive citizens and groups. Robespierre intervenes to stress the indefeasible nature of that right (→June 14, 91).

10. Paris. The bookseller Panckoucke issues an appeal by Necker, *De l'Administration par M. Necker lui-même.*

11. Caen. The Abbot Fauchet solemnly takes up his position at his new bishopric.

15. Paris. After a week of debate, the Assembly votes for a decree limiting the rights of freed coloured people: only those who were born of free parents will have the right to vote.→

Abolition of city toll sparks wild rejoicing

The "hellish barrier" has been turned into a place for merrymaking.

Paris, May 1

The abolition of the hated city toll by the Assembly has been greeted by a wave of wild rejoicing and drunken revelry in the streets of Paris. From now on the people of the capital will be able to bring in or take out as many barrels as they want without having to pay a penny in tax. The toll barriers set up by the farmers general are a thing of the past. To mark the happy occasion, groups of women have been riding around on donkeys laden with barrels of wine, while men have been carrying casks of wine on their shoulders. The deputy of Argenteuil and representative of French vine growers, Etienne Chevalier, finally convinced the Assembly. He had been complaining about the toll barriers that forced Parisians to buy cheap, adulterated wine that made them ill and gave them headaches. Along with bread, wine is still the main staple of the poor. The 600 officers recruited to stop fraud had proved inefficient for the past two years: smuggled wine had been easily available all over Paris. At Saint Lazare, an innkeeper had set up a 400 metre pipe under the toll barrier so that he could have wine pumped in from the other side. The new law means he will not be fined; but some say the move will boost drunkenness.

Temple of Health is popular retreat

Paris, May 8

Plenty of rest, fresh air and excellent care. That is what is being offered to a growing number of people by the Hygie "Temple of Health", located just beyond the Saint Philippe du Roule toll barrier, just a stone's thrown from central Paris. The facility, which has been licensed by the Assembly, is situated at the Ternes castle. Its clients are both French and foreign, and include convalescents as well as pregnant women. Young ladies who are "victims of seduction" also go there to find a discreet refuge. To help pass the time, clients at the "Temple" are offered a billiard room, a library, sitting rooms and a pharmacy.

Toll barriers end

The Assembly has decreed the end of the tolls in Paris as from May 1. Lines of carts were seen to be gathering at the barriers yesterday. At 12 p.m., a cannon shot announced the free passage of food in the city. The move gave rise to this song:
The Senate's decree
I tell you with glee:
That in the month of May,
In all France around
Victuals will abound,
All in the month of May.
Our famed Assembly
Now grants passage free,
All in the month of May.
You guards at the barriers
Repair to the frontiers!
All in the month of May.
Tolls now are o'er;
You'll search us no more,
All in the month of May.
Your furlough elect:
Goods travel unchecked,
All in the month of May.

Bishop Périer speaks out for unity

Clermont Ferrand, May 2

"Let's get together." That is the message that Jean François Périer, the constitutional bishop of Puy de Dôme, has sent to his predecessor, Monsignor de Bonal. The latter had refused to take the oath and was therefore dismissed in January by the department's authorities. Since his election in February the new bishop has shown moderation and has made repeated calls for unity, but his task is not an easy one in a diocese where there are nearly as many juring as non-juring priests.

Bishop Périer's initiative seems to be doomed to failure, as Bonal has already clearly stated his position: Périer is both an "intruder" and a "schismatic" with whom it is impossible to come to an understanding. Several constitutional prelates have also made unsuccessful attempts to heal the rift between the two sides. The bishop of Ile et Vilaine, Lecoz, has even promised to withdraw from his position if his predecessor will agree to take the oath of allegiance to the clergy's civil Constitution.

Vendée election fracas leaves four dead

Vendée, May 2

Four men have been killed. The peasants of the village of Saint Christophe du Ligneron had been sure that the local bourgeois were about to elect a committed revolutionary as mayor, so they grabbed some weapons and alerted the neighbouring parishes, but the peasants clashed with a detachment of dragoons that had been called in

by patriots. Since the decree on the clergy's civil Constitution has come into force, there has been a growing number of clashes in the region. A majority of priests have refused to take the oath and peasants have opposed, often by force, their being replaced by juring priests, whom they call "intruders". Last month one such priest suffered a gunshot wound at Saint Jean de Monts.

Patriot looting turns abbey into quarry

Dijon, May 4

The lovely Carthusian monastery of Champmol, which was built by Philippe le Hardi at Dijon to house the tombs of the dukes of Bourgogne, is to become a simple stone quarry. The monastery has become a victim of the zeal of the patriots of Dijon. After kicking the monks out, they looted the treasury and the library and sacked the chapel, of which only the door now

remains. They also knocked down the cross that stood over the *Puits de Moïse,* the masterpiece by Claus Sluter. There is nothing to be done with the now useless buildings other than to sell them off to the highest bidder. The contractor Emmanuel Cretet, a deputy at the Constituent Assembly, has just bought them: he has decided to quarry their stones for other building projects.

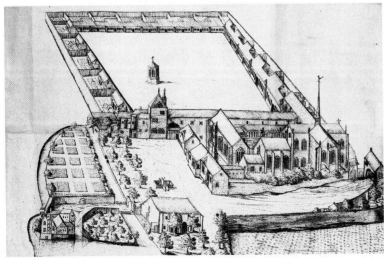

The Carthusian monastery of Champmol before it was destroyed.

Pope burnt in effigy at the Palais Royal

Paris, May 3

The recent Papal brief condemning the civil Constitution has been greeted with a spectacular show of anger in Paris.

An eight foot tall straw effigy of Pius VI was burnt by an angry crowd that had gathered at the Palais Royal late this morning. The effigy had been carefully dressed in all the Papal finery, and two posters stating "civil war" and "fanaticism" had been hung from its neck. In its right hand, people had placed the text of one of the two Papal

briefs, while the left hand brandished a dagger. Just before it was set alight, the effigy was sworn at and spat on by the angry mob, then beaten with sticks.

As the straw dummy was blazing fiercly, the crowd threw hundreds of copies of *L'Ami du Roi* onto the flames. At no time during the noisy incident did the security forces intervene. What happened today at the Palais Royal is hardly likely to improve the already tense relations between revolutionary France and the Vatican.

Everyone rejoices: the straw effigy of Pope Pius VI is being burnt.

Assembly votes to deny black freedom

Paris, May 15

The slave trade is not likely to be abolished in the near future. The issue was not even brought up during the debate on the status of inhabitants of the colonies that has just been held at the Assembly. Barnave spoke out in favour of the slave traders and the big colonial landlords. This man from the Dauphiné is a close associate of the Lameths, who have invested a fortune in the colonies. He told the deputies that under no circumstances should the status of coloured people be changed before white settlers had been asked for their opinion. This was tantamount to calling for the status quo to be kept. It was Barnave's bill that was approved today, despite protests from the extreme left, which Sieyès himself supported. Robespierre, a member of the Society of the Friends of the Blacks, demanded that they be granted civil equality in the name of human rights. His call

was in vain: the white settlers are to keep their political rights, which will only be granted to a minority of mulattoes born of free parents.

Barnave as the two-faced Janus: a man of the people and of the court.

Poland votes for its own Constitution

Warsaw, May 3

Like France, the Polish state is to be based on a Constitution, but in Warsaw this reform has caused a profound political upheaval. King Stanislas Poniatowski and his patriot friends did not trust the Diet, or parliament, where they were not assured of a majority. They therefore decided to use the element of surprise and placed the army on alert, while the bourgeois were occupying the streets and the parliamentary chamber. Based on the ideas of Montesquieu, the Constitution confirms the separation of powers. The executive belongs to the King, who is assisted by ministers and five central committees, for finance, foreign affairs, war, education and justice. The Diet holds legislative powers, while judicial power will be exercised by independent tribunals. What is new about the Constitution is that it

Stanislas II Augustus Poniatowski, a king elected with Russian support.

creates an hereditary monarchy. It was the elected nature of royalty that had led to unrest and intervention by foreign powers.

Castor and Pollux, Talma's twin sons

Paris, May 1

A mere ten days after his wedding Talma has already become a proud father. Today was the christening ceremony for his twin sons, Henri Castor and Charles Pollux. However, when she decided to name the two children after the

Dioscuri, the mythical sons of Leda, Julie Talma was thinking more of her own personal memories than of the gods of Greek mythology. When she was starting out on her stage career, she had been very successful acting in Rameau's play *Castor et Pollux*.

The many problems of childbirth ...

There is not much a midwife can do if there is a problem during childbirth. The midwives of today are a considerable improvement over those of the past, who were ignorant and superstitious; but things have changed for the better. At the request of the King, all midwives have studied a text on the art of childbirth written by Mme. de Coudray. Some have even attended lessons where they practised with a silk life-like model. Each year a group of 150 graduate midwives is being taught by the specialist Jean Louis Baudelocque of the Port Royal maternity clinic. However, if problems arise, all they have are the forceps invented by the surgeon Levret. The practitioners who are being called upon by those with money

favour Caesarians, but there are a lot of deaths. The last successful Caesarian was done three years ago!

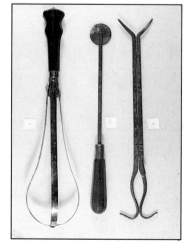

Midwives only have a few very rudimentary bits of equipment.

 Constituent Assembly

16. Paris. Legislators decide that members of the Constituent Assembly will not be able to seek re-election at the next legislative elections. →

17. Saint Malo. The town council sends a letter to departmental authorities to express concern over the emigration of priests and noblemen to the island of Jersey.

17. Paris. The Cordeliers Club is expelled from the Cordeliers convent and bases itself at the Genlis residence, on the Rue Dauphine.

20. Mantua. The Comte d'Artois tries in vain to convince Leopold II to launch a military intervention against France.

20. Paris. The Théâtre de Monsieur performs *L'Ecole des Jaloux*, by Antoine Jacob, with a score by Antonio Salieri.

22. Martigné. The parish priest Guillou, who refuses to take the oath, is replaced by a juring priest.

22. Paris. Despite repeated calls from Robespierre, Pétion, Grégoire and Dubois Crancé, the Assembly allows individual petitions, but forbids collective petitioning by sections and people's societies.

22. Colmar. Local people stop the departure of priests of the Capucin convent, who have been placed under house arrest at Neuf Brisach and Belfort by the departmental authorities.

25. Paris. The bookseller Onfroy publishes the *Vie de Joseph Balsamo*.

26. Paris. The National Assembly decides that "all objects of science and of art" will be stored at the Louvre.

28. Paris. Robespierre asks the Assembly to cancel the decree on the silver marc issued on October 29th. 1789.

30. Paris. At a debate on a penal code bill submitted by Le Pelletier de Saint Fargeau, Robespierre calls for the ending of capital punishment. →

30. Rouen. A local custom, the Saint Romain privilege, is abolished. Once a year it allowed the release of prisoners held for murder.

31. Paris. Abbot Guillaume Thomas Raynal sends a letter to the National Assembly calling for the restoration of monarchical institutions.

Deputies of the Assembly cannot seek re-election

Paris, May 16

The legislators of the Constituent Assembly have ruled that they will not be able to seek re-election. A vast majority of them have been convinced by the arguments that were brilliantly put forward by Robespierre. In a long speech, Robespierre stressed the need for integrity and self-sacrifice by his fellow deputies. In fact, the aim of his speech was to get rid of the representatives of the former privileged orders and the lawyers who served the Ancien Régime. There are still many of these around. The right wing deputies agreed to the move because they hope that the new assembly will undo what was achieved by the present one.

Tallien meets Thérésa Cabarrus

Jean Lambert Tallien.

Paris, May

"Tell me, who is that young man?" asked Thérésa, the young daughter of the Spanish banker François de Cabarrus. She had gone to spend some time with her friend the Comtesse de Lameth. The young woman is married to the Marquis de Fontenay, a councillor at the city's parliament, but their match is not a very happy one. Tallien was spotted as he walked in the garden picking white roses for the pretty guest. Despite Thérésa's interest, Madame de Lameth finds that her brother-in-law's secretary is lazy, has no name, no money and not much future.

The abbey at Royaumont is to be sold

This Cistercian abbey had been founded by Saint Louis in 1228. All that now remains of it are the cloisters, dining hall and some convent buildings.

Royaumont, May

The Marquis de Travannet, who was Marie Antoinette's banker, has just come across a bargain. He has bought the abbey at Royaumont, near Senlis, for a pittance. He plans to turn the convent buildings into a cotton mill. In order to prove his patriotic feelings, he has also torn down the beautiful church that had been built by the "tyrant" Saint Louis. To speed the demolition work up, the nobleman has had the bases of the pillars supporting the church beams weakened. Then chains were tied around them and when oxen heaved, the whole structure came crashing down.

The Louvre palace is in a pitiful state

Paris, May

What has become of one of the wonders of French architecture? For decades, the façades of the palace of the Louvre have been cluttered by dozens of huts and dirty, smelly stalls that have made a bad impression on many a foreign visitor to the capital.

Already, around the year 1750, Soufflot and Gabriel had tried to restore the building, but a lack of funds had put an end to their efforts. It was only in 1776 that the area between the colonnade and Saint Germain l'Auxerrois was finally cleared, but the other areas are still eyesores, with fences and piles of filth in places. The interior of the Louvre is not much better off: the artists and hangers-on who live in the Grande Galerie have no qualms about hanging their belongings, food and plants from the ceiling. This habit has caused considerable damage.

Corridors are blocked by the works of artists living at the palace.

Louis XVI is housed and fed by the state

Portrait of the King dressed as a sovereign. His hat has been decorated with a tricoloured cockade and he holds a sword bearing the words "The Law".

Paris, May 26

Louis XVI is going to hand over all the assets of the crown to the nation.

This wealth, along with that seized from the clergy, will form a public collection that all will soon be able to view. This move is not, however, due to a sudden generous impulse on the part of the King. He was more or less forced to do so by the Assembly. The King is, in fact, getting rid of all the attributes of his former position in order to become a true constitutional monarch. The state will in exchange grant him a "civil list", or pension, of 25 million francs a year. He is also to be provided with a residence worthy of a sovereign, the Tuileries palace. The move just taken by the Assembly confirms that the King is now the nation's chief civil servant, getting a sort of wage.

But Louis XVI has kept the right to take decisions about the kingdom's finances. It is the King who twice a month will continue to sign the orders that authorise public funds to be disbursed.

The royal couple's life at the Tuileries

Paris, May

Nowadays, the royal family's life at the Tuileries is a far cry from what it was at the palace of Versailles. The King and Queen used to complain bitterly about being crushed by the weight of palace protocol, and the prying eyes of so many jealous courtiers, but today there are only a loyal few left. As for court protocol, it has been cut down to the bare bones. No more balls, no more huge parties, just a few outings aboard carriages and the occasional evening's visit to the theatre. Louis XVI and Marie Antoinette are now living very private lives with their children. They are taking care of the children's education themselves and the King often leaves his map room to check that the Dauphin has learnt his lessons. The Queen goes for walks with the young princes in the gardens, which are now open to the public, and encourages them to speak to strangers. Each time her son speaks to somebody, he rushes back to his mother asking: "Was that the way to do it?" Despite their happy family life, the royal couple have never felt less free. They no doubt even miss the hustle and bustle of Versailles.

▷

Robespierre opposes capital punishment

Paris, May 30

His talents as a speaker and his technique as a lawyer were not enough to convince his audience. Robespierre has had to give in on an issue he cares deeply about, that of the abolition of the death penalty. After having condemned this "barbaric routine", he stressed that capital punishment was not necessary since some societies had done away with it, even despotic Russia.

On a matter as serious as this, all that should be heard are the voices of justice and reason, he said, adding that deputies must respect human dignity; but they did not listen to such vague concepts. The law they have approved does not go as far as Robespierre wanted: the death penalty will be applied, but only in cases where the head of a party is "declared a rebel by the legislative body".

The former lawyer of Arras argues in vain for the end of the death penalty.

Beaumarchais says No to suitors

Paris, May 21

Once and for all, the answer is no! Pierre Caron de Beaumarchais is not looking for a husband for his daughter Eugénie. He is tired of having to cope with the dozens of suitors who have been turning up on his doorstep. He has even written a circular letter for them; but he is partly to blame for all this. He had brought his 14 year old daughter home from a convent. In order to celebrate, he wrote a song that circulated as a pamphlet. It was so full of praise for the young girl that many thought that her father was seeking a son-in-law.

Lazare Carnot is married at last

Saint Omer, May 17

He is getting married after 17 years in an army garrison. As an officer in the corps of engineers in the north of France, Lazare Carnot was badly wounded while working on the lock at Asfeld. Taken to his brother's place at Saint Omer, he was cared for by his sister-in-law and her sister, Sophie, who wrote music for him and learnt to play backgammon to keep him amused. His convalescence has led to marriage. At the age of 38, Lazare is settling down in the area and will be able to lead a comfortable life thanks to his wife's fortune.

June 1791
from 1st. to 25th.

Constituent Assembly

1. Paris. During the debate on the penal code, the deputies decree the abolition of all forms of torture.

1. Paris. The collection of stones and precious minerals that had been put together by the mineralogist Jean Baptiste Romé Delisle is broken up.

2. Vendée. The National Guard of Angers searches the premises of the Saint Esprit missionaries and those of the sisters of Sagesse. Two priests are arrested and pamphlets used by non-juring priests sre seized.

5. Paris. The Assembly issues a decree abolishing the King's right to grant clemency.

7. Paris. At the "Grands Danseurs du Roi", on the Boulevard du Temple, two pugilists, Partner and Fewtrell, give a first demonstration of English boxing.

8. Arles. Violent clashes break out between the royalist "Chiffonistes" and the patriot "Monnaidiers".

10. Brest. Death of Toussaint Guillaume, Comte Picquet de La Motte, the lieutenant general of the royal navy.

11. Paris. The Molière theatre, founded by the actor Boursault Malherbe, opens for business on the Rue Saint Martin.

13. Paris. From now on, officers will have to sign a declaration of obedience and loyalty to the Constitution.

14. Paris. The Le Chapelier law abolishes corporations and all workers' associations.→

15. Montauban. The printing presses of the *Journal National* are sacked by the town's patriots.

15. Paris. Fabre d'Eglantine shows a new comedy, *L'Intrigue Epistolaire,* at the Théâtre Français.

16. Paris. The Assembly decides to shut down aid centres, which are costing too much to run.

19. Paris. Abbot Sieyès is criticised at the Society of the Friends of the Constitution for a draft statement. It is to be addressed to patriots of the 83 departments and opposes the principle of a unified legislative body.

24. Paris. Following the flight of the King, the Assembly cancels the primary elections for the next assembly.

Strikes banned and coalitions outlawed by Le Chapelier

Le Chapelier was the founder of the Breton Club in the year 1789.

Paris, June 14

The Le Chapelier law has been approved without major problems. It makes it illegal to set up professional associations or to form coalitions. As for strikes, which had been tolerated until now, they are also banned. This vote paves the way for a return of the trade guilds, a development hinted at by the appearance of mutual aid societies. At the headquarters of one of these, the Union of Paris Carpenters, papers were found that revealed the existence of plans for a vast nationwide movement in favour of a minimum wage and guarantees for workers. The new law will be a big boost for an unfettered economy and individual enterprise.

Marat condemns bourgeois laws

Paris, June 18

"In Paris, there are 20,000 of us workers and we will not let the bourgeoisie put us to sleep." In the *Ami du Peuple,* Marat used these words to lash out against the new law which leaves each worker to face his employer alone and gives no guaranteed wage. For a democrat like Marat, production should be in the hands of those who do the work and not those with money. Marat is, in fact, attacking the bourgeois traders, who see the Revolution as a way of getting rid of the nobility's privileges, but who care nothing for the people.

Volunteers are to defend the Revolution

Paris, June 11

Certain priorities are absolute. Faced with growing military dangers, Robespierre and Lameth have decided to put an end to their endless quarrels over the role of the National Guard.

The Assembly has just asked the King to launch a training programme for line troops at special instruction camps, to put all the border troops on a war footing, and to ensure that the nation's arsenals are well stocked with ammunition, weapons, kitbags and clothing. Last, but not least, deputies have taken decisive steps to solve the chronic lack of military manpower. They have ruled that each department will set up a system of "free conscription of national guardsmen of good will". One man out of every 20 will be drafted. These "volunteer national guardsmen" will be paid by the state.

However, they will only be able to gather or designate their officers on the basis of a decree by the legislative body. The deputies do not fully trust the regular royal army, so they have created a sort of parallel force of volunteer battalions whose chief task will be to defend the Revolution (→ July 22).

Louis XVI secretly prepares his escape

The cage symbolises the Tuileries: "I am doing penance," says the King.

Paris, June 15

Over the past few weeks there have been countless discreet meetings in the Queen's apartments. The King has been convinced that he has become the prisoner of the nation. He has finally agreed to Marie Antoinette's wishes: he will leave the capital in secret with his wife, his sister and his children. He plans to seize power in the provinces, where there are still troops that are loyal to him. He will do this without the help of the nobility. The King is certain that, once he is free, he will once again find his "good people" and will be able to return to Paris in triumph. "As soon as my backside is back on the saddle ..." he keeps repeating. The plan of escape has been drawn up with the help of Bouillé, who has insisted that the royal family go to the fortress at Montmédy, near the frontier. Outside reinforcements can be quickly sent there and, if things go wrong, Louis XVI can always seek refuge outside the country. Given the crooked line of the border, it would be easier for the royal party to cut across some foreign provinces to get to its destination, but the King has insisted that the entire journey should be made on French soil. He wants to avoid annoying an already grumbling public opinion by travelling through foreign lands; but the King has not once thought that his departure could cause trouble.

One is never too young to learn about weapons to defend the nation.

Robespierre slams aristocratic officers

Paris, June 7

Robespierre has violently criticised aristocratic army officers, saying they embody the counter-revolution. "You have destroyed the nobility, but the nobility is still alive at the head of the army," he said. At a Jacobin gathering he called for the dismissal of officers opposed to the Revolution, who should be replaced by officers taken from the people, but his call is unlikely to be heard by deputies who have for months tried to stop soldiers joining political clubs. Although Robespierre seems to be having difficulties getting his views across at the Assembly, his portrait is selling like hot cakes in the street. People call him "incorruptible".

Religious clashes at the Théatins church

Paris, June 2

There has been fighting again at the Théatins church. During the morning, large numbers of patriots gathered outside the church doors and demanded that they be opened. They had been told that inside several non-juring priests had met to hold a religious service. When they were finally allowed to enter, they dispersed the faithful and the priests before knocking over the altar and other religious items. Already, in April, an angry crowd had stopped the faithful from attending a mass said by a nonjuring priest. To make their warning perfectly clear, the patriots had pinned whips to the door, as well as the following inscription: "Note to devout aristocrats, purgative medicine distributed freely here."

Services held by non-jurors are seen as provocations by patriots.

Bailly is told of the royal escape plans

Paris, June

A certain woman, Rochereuil, who is Marie Antoinette's official "stool carrier", or person in charge of the royal toilet, has revealed to Bailly that the Queen is getting ready for her family's flight. She had overheard secret discussions between the Queen and her chambermaid, Madame Campan. One evening she had seen Marie Antoinette carefully packing all her jewels. Using the pass-key she has in order to carry out her work, she noticed that a corridor linking the royal apartments to an empty house had been built. Seeing that Bailly seemed to ignore her, she then went to warn Gouvion, La Fayette's aide de camp. ▷

Bullfights are cruel, says police official

Paris, June

There are some so-called sports which should really be banned: a police official has sent a thinly veiled warning to the departmental authorities. The public has a right to its pastimes and distractions, but some limits must be respected. It is high time to put an end to those circus games where the public is shown violent and cruel fights between various types of animals. It is also a scandal that the arena built at Belleville has still not been torn down. That is where people go to watch two bulls fight to the death, goring each other as bloodthirsty spectators cheer the gory sight. Such barbaric practices are immoral because people pay to see blood, the policeman added. Steps must urgently be taken by the appropriate authorities to put a stop to all this.

Lavoisier finances Dupont de Nemours

Paris, June 8

It is an interesting business deal: with the 71,000 livres loaned by Antoine de Lavoisier, the deputy Pierre Samuel Dupont de Nemours has bought a printing works on the Ile Saint Louis from a certain Lemesle. Turgot's former advisor is going to set up his newspaper, *La Correspondance Patriotique*. As he used to be a journalist he is aware of the fact that press ventures can be risky, but he hopes to get public opinion to support moderate ideas and thus avoid the Revolution getting out of control. Thanks to his friends Lavoisier and Condorcet, he will be able to print reports of the committee debates at the Assembly and memoranda from the Academy of Science. Such official orders will help his business.

A national fine arts school is needed

Paris, June

The famous David seems to have sworn to ruin the reputation of the Academy of Painting. It is true that he has plenty of reason to dislike the institution. The academicians refused to grant him the prestigious Rome prize three times, before they finally awarded it to him in 1774. The painter never forgot that triple humiliation. David's hatred alone is not enough to destroy such a venerable institution. However, its reputation is waning. People say students have been wasting their time at the Paris Fine Arts School and the region's small municipal arts schools. All too often, teachers just keep an eye on their students instead of imparting the knowledge that they do not always possess. Quatremère de Quincy, the art critic, has just published his *Considérations sur les arts du dessin en France* in which he criticises the teachers for neglecting classical art. More and more people are now

This self portrait painted by David stresses the vivid intensity of the eyes of the famous artist.

calling for the creation of a more open, less outdated art academy whose students would also be regularly taken to visit the main art museums.

At the Louvre's vaulted entrance, art lovers and strollers are drawn to look at the print vendors' wares. On the right, a flower seller is shown.

June 20, midnight: Louis XVI is ready to flee

Fersen has prepared a fake passport in the name of the Baronne de Korff.

and National Guardsmen were even sleeping in the corridors. On the evening of June 20th., La Fayette personally carried out a tour of inspection, as he sometimes does. Everything appeared to be in order.

A carefully laid plan

Despite all these precautions, the unexpected has just happened: the King and his family have managed to get out to the street by using an unguarded exit. The plan had been carefully worked out over several months. Secret passages had been built linking the rooms, using two-sided cupboards. The route had been checked a hundred times by Axel de Fersen. Over the past few days, a man about the size of the King had made a point of being seen around the palace, so that no suspicions would be aroused at the critical moment. By 1 a.m., the royal family is supposed to meet a carriage that awaits them in the Saint Martin district. A gig with two of the Queen's chambermaids will be waiting at Claye, on the road to Metz. As the first part of the trip is to be made at night, no escort has been provided before the group reaches the staging post at Pont sur Somme Vesle. There a unit of the cavalry is to meet the King around 3 p.m. After that, small military units will be waiting at each staging post until they reach their temporary destination, the fortress at Montmédy, commanded by Marquis Amour de Bouillé. A passport signed by La Fayette, in the name

King Louis XVI hurriedly does the hair of his wife Marie Antoinette prior to their departure.

of a certain Baronne de Korff, has been drawn up. It is in fact for Madame de Tourzel. The King will pass himself off as his own valet. Only three bodyguards, all loyal, will travel with the fugitives.

Mistakes are made

Some surprising decisions have been made: the King chose to use a heavy, slow coach in spite of its six horses, instead of one of the light carriages recommended by Bouillé. Also, the bodyguards wore the easily recognised and hated Condé livery. Finally, the crucial passport stated there were five people travelling, although there are six fugitives. At least the first part of the plan was a success.

The King and Queen went to bed at eleven thirty p.m., as court etiquette requires. The King's man-servant has fallen fast asleep in the antechamber. Total silence reigns in the Tuileries palace. At half past midnight a large, heavy-set man, dressed as a valet, greets a simply dressed woman and the pair climb aboard a carriage, which immediately sets off for the Saint Martin city gate. They are the King and Queen of France. The carriage's other passengers are the Dauphin, the King's daughter, their governess Madame de Tourzel and Madame Elisabeth, the King's sister. The coachman is none other than Axel de Fersen, the Queen's confidant. The fate of the royal family is at stake.

A risky venture

The flight had been discussed in royal circles ever since October 1790, but in fact it was the Queen who urged Louis XVI to take action, as the King had once again shown his usual lack of resolve. Their goal is to meet up with the border troops, where the monarch can count on a few loyal generals. Once their aid has been enlisted, they can march on Paris to restore royal authority. If need be, the King can always call on other sovereigns for help. For the Queen, the main problem was to find a way of avoiding the tight security that surrounds the King, which has been stepped up since April 18th. On that day the royal family tried to leave the Tuileries to go to Saint Cloud, but the people of Paris stopped them. Since then, journalists and pamphleteers have constantly been writing about the secret royal escape plans. More guards had been posted at the Tuileries. All the exits from the royal apartments were being watched

The impressive carriage awaits the royal family at the Marigny gate. One of the bodyguards carries the Dauphin, who is disguised as a girl.

All France had learnt of the King's flight by the time the royal family, which was arrested on the night of June 21st. to 22nd., neared Paris on the evening of June 25th. Louis XVI himself had said that he had attempted to "get his freedom back" and defy the Revolution. For two days, the people of Paris more than others believed that the King had managed to reach the border, but several missed appointments led to the pitiful failure of the escape plan. During those crucial days, the King realised how isolated he had become. The soldiers who were to have escorted him onwards from Somme Vesle showed hostility to their officers. Everywhere town councils reacted firmly. At first fear spread through Paris and the provinces, but this quickly turned into a mobilisation of the people, who are already calling for the King's deposition. Only a fear of uncontrollable unrest drove the moderates to save the monarchy

Patriots burst into the grocer Sauce's shop and think they recognize the King. Sauce is the local prosecutor.

The King's hackney carriage had passed through the Saint Martin gate without any trouble shortly after half past midnight. Luckily, the guards posted at the gate were celebrating a wedding and had not paid any attention to the carriage. A short distance from there, the large travelling coach waited to pick up the royal family. It then set off on the road to Metz, although it was over an hour late. Around 4 a.m., they met the gig carrying the Queen's chambermaids at Claye. As Paris faded into the distance, Louis XVI started to feel more secure and began to speak about his plans for the future. "Once my backside is back in the saddle, everything will change," he said. The day had barely risen when the two carriages crossed Meaux around six o'clock. The initial delay did not seem to be important and nobody decided to hurry the horses along, although the heavy coach was only travelling at ten kilometres per hour. Changing horses every so often took time and the King carelessly talked to some people passing by. Twice he even ordered a halt so that he could relieve himself. Everything was going well and the royal party crossed Chalons around four o'clock in the afternoon. Nothing

could go wrong after this stage: soon they would meet the first unit of troops at Somme Vesle.

Paris without its King

It was 7 a.m. precisely at the Tuileries when the royal man-servant Lemoine drew the curtains of the bed to wake the King up. The bed was empty! The alarm was quickly sounded and it was discovered that the entire royal family had disappeared. It was learnt later that the Comte de Provence had also fled. La Fayette was informed as he awoke by the deputy d'André. Calmly, he gave the order for couriers to set of on northern and eastern roads to look for the King, claiming that he had been "kidnapped". Around 9 a.m. the National Assembly held an urgent meeting, fearing that there would be a popular uprising. Some men working on the river docks had shouted treason.

A bit later, La Fayette was insulted and accused of having allowed the King to flee as he went to the city hall to discuss security issues with Bailly. Panic was in the air. Some checked the sewers and underground passages. Others claimed that noblemen and non-juring priests were gathering at La Cour-

neuve and planned to attack Paris. National Guardsmen grabbed their weapons. The Assembly decided it was dealing with a kidnapping, and the moderates were afraid of being overtaken by revolutionary unrest. Emissaries were sent to the chief towns of all 83 departments. A new development came at midmorning as the minister Duport Dutertre told deputies that Louis XVI had left a document behind. The text caused consternation. In it, the King said he was "getting his free-

dom back" and withdrawing all the concessions he had made since May 1789. This proved that the King had lied and that the Revolution was threatened. The Assembly ended the debate at 4 p.m. All were convinced that the King was already under the protection of foreign armies.

Problems arise

In fact, the royal family had only reached Chalons and only got to

On hearing news of the King's escape, people rush to the Tuileries.

People of Varennes placing stones under the coach's wheels. Alarm bells sound, National Guardsmen arrive.

Somme Vesle at six o'clock, three hours later than had been planned. The fugitives were astounded to find that the Duc de Choiseul and the troops they had expected to find were not there. Choiseul had waited, but his soldiers had first aroused the curiosity, then the anger, of local peasants and he had decided it was better to leave. Even worse, thinking that the plan had been dropped, he informed the other unit commanders of this and they ordered their troops to stand down.

The royal coach resumed its trip towards Sainte Menehould. The sight of units of 50 dragoons posted along the way was begining to worry the people of the region. The royal party stopped at the Sainte Menehould staging post, run by a certain Drouet, to change horses. The officer in charge of the military unit whispered to the occupants of the coach that it was time to leave quickly because Drouet seemed to have noticed that something was amiss. The clever innkeeper was said to have recognised the disguised King by comparing the royal portrait on a coin.

Badly shaken by their close call, the royal fugitives finally arrived at Clermont around 9:30 p.m. and went on towards Varennes, leaving the main Metz road and veering towards Montmédy, which was

only 50 kilometres away. Night had already fallen at Varennes when the convoy stopped just outside the village at 10:30 p.m. Several minutes were wasted as the bodyguards looked in vain for soldiers and the fresh horses that should have been prepared by the Marquis de Bouillé. At his wits' end, the King decided to go to the Grand Monarque inn, where he hoped to change horses. Just then, two riders galloped past the coach: it was Drouet and a friend.

The trap is readied

Drouet's worst suspicions were confirmed when he met couriers from Paris who told him of the King's "kidnapping". He had set off after the convoy, although it was an hour ahead of him. At Clermont, he and his friend were told of the new route taken by the convoy as they were about to take the Metz road. As soon as both men got to Varennes, Drouet rushed to the village's prosecutor and had a bridge blocked. It was the only road head-

ing north. Meanwhile, the gig and the coach had set off again, even though the postilions hired at Clermont had been unwilling to go further. As the convoy reached an arcade standing across the main street, it was stopped by the National Guardsmen who had been alerted by the alarm bells. The prosecutor, a grocer named Sauce, demanded to check identity papers, then ordered the passengers to go into his shop. Till then, nobody was aware of the King's and Queen's true identities.

But soon after midnight Louis XVI was identified by the judge Destez, who had been to Versailles. All hope seemed to have vanished, as Bouillé's troops were fraternising with locals, but an unexpected opportunity arose when the Duc de Choiseul arrived with his mounted troops. Could he save the King? This was not to be, as Louis XVI refused to resort to force, fearing that the Queen and his children could be hurt. All night long he tried to convince the people holding him to let him go, saying he had no evil intentions. "I don't trust him!" a peasant cried. While a messenger was sent to Paris, the envoys from the Assembly, who had travelled since the previous afternoon, arrived at 6 a.m. Two hours later the royal party set off again, back to Paris, where the Jacobin and Cordeliers societies had started meeting overnight. The people attending shouted: "Live free or die!" The abolition of the monarchy is now being openly discussed.

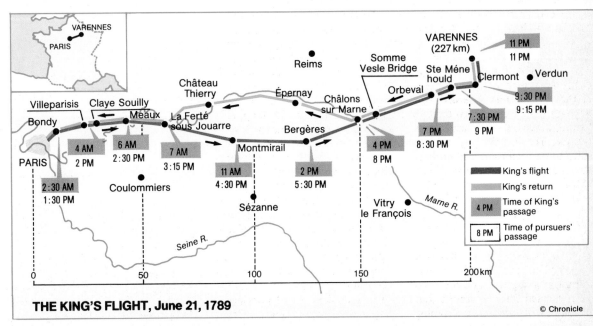

THE KING'S FLIGHT, June 21, 1789

© Chronicle

June 25 1791: The royal coach, escorted by National Guardsmen, arrives back in the capital amid and is greeted by a huge, silent crowd.

The royal family's dramatic return to Paris

Paris-Varennes, June 22-25

"They must go! They must go!" screams the crowd gathered by Sauce's shop. Since the National Guards have arrived from Paris to arrest the King on behalf of the Assembly, there is no longer any question of the royal fugitives being allowed to continue their trip. The people of Varennes feel a surge of panic at the thought that at any moment Bouillé, the "butcher of Nancy", could arrive with his men to help Louis XVI. The King is trying to stall, in the hope that his saviours will come in time to free him. The King, Marie Antoinette and the royal children all need to rest, but the Varennes town officials are as worried as the crowd and want to see the royal party leave as quickly as possible. All of a sudden, Louis XVI opens a window as if he is about to speak to the population, which is worried about possible reprisals. The move is greeted by silence, but the King does not say a word. The shouts start up again and the King closes the window. It is all over; Louis XVI has given up hope. He and his family will go back to Paris. The Queen, tears flooding down her cheeks, takes her tired children's hands and starts walking down the stairs. Dazzled by the bright sunlight, the King blinks and climbs aboard the coach that the crowd has already hitched up and parked outside the grocer's store. The carriage sets off, as an escort of peasants armed with rifles, sickles and scythes runs alongside.

The fateful journey begins

Late in the morning, the convoy arrives in a cloud of dust at Sainte Menehould, where a sea of people waits. Moved by the fate of the royal couple, the town's mayor wants to offer them the use of his house so that they can rest and wash, but cries ring out: "We have been betrayed, Bouillé is on his way!" Faced with an angry mob, the King and his exhausted group tiredly head back to their coaches. Suddenly they stop in horror. Just beside them, standing behind some thick iron bars, they see dozens of haggard faces belonging to the prisoners of the town. The local jail and the town hall are linked to the passage they had been made to use. The King and the prisoners stare at each other for a long time without

a word being said. Finally, the King takes his purse and hands it to the unfortunate men. Outside, the crowd is getting impatient, despite the terrible heat. Once again the convoy sets off, followed by an ever growing number of people. Hundreds of peasants who have come from neighbouring villages mill around the carriage, trying to catch a glimpse of the King. At Chalons, where the convoy finally stops around 11 p.m., the coachman unhitches the horses outside the administrative headquarters. It was there that the Queen had been cheered in May 1770 as she arrived in France to marry the future monarch; but today, a few loyal royalists tell the King to use the cover of darkness to escape by a hidden staircase that leads to the gardens. However, the plan calls for Louis XVI to leave his family behind and he firmly rejects it.

Guardian angels for the King

It is the dawn of June 23rd. As he leaves the town, the King sees that the people are increasingly hostile. Four leagues from Epernay, he is extremely relieved to meet the officials who had been sent by the Assembly: the royalist Latour Maubourg, the moderate Barnave and the democrat Pétion. The three men from Paris climb aboard the crowded coach. "The King did not try to leave France," the Queen nervously tells them. "No, gentlemen, I was not leaving," Louis XVI stresses. At first the officials don't get a chance to speak, but after a

while they strike up a conversation. The Queen tells Barnave about the Dauphin's education. Pétion is amazed by how informal the royal family is. Elisabeth, the King's sister, has taken her niece on her knees, and several times the King passes the chamberpot to his son without showing the slightest embarrassment. When he wakes up at Meaux on Saturday, June 25th., the King asks an usher to give him a clean shirt as his is dirty. None of the coach's passengers has been able to change for the past five days!

Return to Paris

Fearing that clashes could break out, the Assembly has ordered the convoy to drive through the less busy outer streets. At Bondy, then at Pantin, tension is rising. The

coach is moving slowly, surrounded by an increasingly threatening mob. Women rush forward to hurl insults at the King and Queen, but when the convoy enters the capital there is an eerie silence. On the walls there are notices saying: "Whoever claps the King will be beaten, whoever insults him will be hanged." A journalist of the *Bouche de Fer* says: "Keep your hats on, he is about to stand before his judges." The crowd has been waiting for hours under a driving rainstorm to see the dazed looking monarch drive by. When Louis XVI gets out of the coach by the steps of the Tuileries Palace, he doesn't even seem to notice a group of enraged men who are trying to shove their way through the security cordon in an attempt to strike a blow at the hated monarch.

As the convoy passes by, young men wipe the eyes of the statue of Louis XVI that they believe is annoyed.

The King's coachmen and bodyguards are assaulted by the Paris crowds.

Assembly and clubs argue over the King's fate

Paris, June 25

The King's flight has caused consternation among the deputies, particularly as it came at a time when most of them thought that the worst of the Revolution was finally over. Their masterpiece, the Constitution that they have nearly finished drafting, has been endangered by a sovereign whose trickery seems obvious now that the document he left behind has been found. Many members of the Constituent Assembly, who are opposed to a return of the Ancien Régime while being deeply hostile to the establishment of a republic, are supporting the unlikely theory of the King's kidnapping, so they have simply temporarily suspended Louis XVI's powers, hoping that he will easily exonerate himself before a pro-monarchy committee. Led by Robespierre, the deputies of the left are not prepared to support such a transparent move. At the Jacobins' club the deputy from Arras has clearly stated his desire to set up a true democracy, but at the Manège hall his colleagues did all they

The people's anger against their King is at a peak. They feel they have all been betrayed by the monarch's barefaced lies and trickery.

could to stop him from speaking. "The Assembly is betraying the interests of the nation!" he exclaimed, while accusing the moderates of being willing to reach a compromise with the King and ministers. For the clubs and societies the King's escape was, in fact, a very positive event. "At last we are free and rid of the King," members of the Cordeliers said. At the Assembly, a petition calling for the establishment of a republic, that was signed by over 30,000 patriots over the past two days, has been submitted. For his part, Danton said that regardless of whether Louis XVI is a traitor or an imbecile, he can no longer reign. It would be enough to proclaim him legally "banned". To take the place of royal power, there should be an executive council chosen by representatives elected in the departments. At the Jacobins, Chaumette made a strong speech against the monarchy, saying it had violated the pact linking it to the nation. Chaumette, who commands a lot of attention among the people of Paris, said the King should be stripped of his power and royalty should be abolished for ever. The people's societies could be asked to call for this at the National Assembly. It appears that the Cordeliers want the King's fate to be settled by the nation, while the people's societies favour much more radical solutions. They want to get rid of both Louis XVI and the Assembly. They say the legislators' behaviour is a betrayal of the state. The idea of resorting to a nationwide uprising to achieve their goals does not frighten them in the least.

"I'm happy to be back," says Louis

Paris, June 26

Practically held prisoner at the Tuileries palace since their return to the capital, the King and Queen have spoken to three deputies who were nominated by the Assembly to question them about their strange journey. Louis XVI had already met them briefly yesterday, but Marie Antoinette asked them to come back, claiming that she was in the bath. Today, the King calmly told the three men that he was happy to be back among the people of Paris. However, he did not have much to say about the reasons for his unexpected trip. He talked about his faith in the Constitution, but it was hard to believe him after reading the handwritten document he had left behind. The legislators for their part asked their questions in such a way as to make it easy for the King to find excuses for his actions. As for the Queen, she said that as a good wife she had followed her husband, adding that neither of them had had the slightest intention of going abroad.

How the royal flight was seen abroad

London, June 25

The French émigrés living in England felt a surge of renewed hope when they learnt that the royal family had escaped from the Tuileries. They told themselves that they had been quite right to rent their rooms by the week rather than on a monthly basis, to show that they were always ready to return to France. The women of the aristocracy would soon forget the lives they have been leading here, dancing all night long after spending the day working to earn some money; but at eleven o'clock this evening their dreams were shattered. They discovered that the King and Marie Antoinette have been arrested near Metz.

According to this etching, the Queen set up the escape from the Tuileries.

The return from Varennes

The royal family returned to Paris from Varennes. They were badly received by the people who see their flight as a betrayal. A song which expresses Parisians' feelings has been heard since this morning:

The city they left,
So let them go,
They'll not go far.
Desertion is base.
Their journey cut short,
And caught unaware
They fall in the trap.
By floods of false tears,
The traitors intend
To win back our hearts.
In secret their soul
Is torn by our sneers.
How it smarts under
The weight of their shame!
Perfidious regents,
Your tears now reserve,
Soon comes the time
To settle your debt.
A free people the charms
Will enjoy of renouncing
Their faith in your throne.

26. Rhône. As the city of Lyons itself remains relatively calm, news of the King's escape from the Tuileries palace sets off serious unrest in the Lyons region. At Chasselay, peasants and National Guardsmen attack the castle of Marie Aimé Guillet du Montet, the former governor of Senegal, who is killed and thrown onto the blazing ashes of his home.

26. Luxembourg. Bouillé sends a threatening letter to the Assembly in which he states that he is fully responsible for the King's flight. In Paris, the deputies Tronchet, d'André and Duport are placed in charge of hearing testimony from the King on the circumstances of his so-called "kidnapping".

26. Montauban. Following the King's escape, the town council bans all public gatherings and starts controlling the mail.

26. Paris. In response to a motion by the National Assembly, which has openly named the Duc d'Orléans as the successor to Louis XVI, the nobleman publicly renounces the regency. →

28. Paris. A delegation of men from charitable workshops go to the National Assembly to protest against the closure of the workshops (→July 3, 91).

28. Paris. Jean François Ducis presents a new tragedy, *Jean sans Terre*, at the Richelieu theatre.

28. Bordeaux. During a party thrown by the Bordeaux Friends of the Constitution, women patriots pay homage to the constitutional bishop. Only half of the priests of the department have sworn allegiance to the Constitution.

29. Paris. As a protest against the June 25 Assembly decision to suspend Louis XVI, 290 royalist deputies state that they will no longer take part in debates. They will however continue to sit in the Assembly in the interests of the monarchy.

29. Aix en Provence. Local authorities order peasants who own more than six rifles to hand over their weapons within 24 hours.

30. Paris. Like those of the navy, the army's flags and standards will in future have to be tricoloured.

Monsieur manages to flee and becomes leader of the émigrés

Brussels, June 29

On the same day that Louis XVI was arested at Varennes, his brother, the Comte de Provence, was able to cross the border into the Austrian Netherlands. He had also left Paris secretly on the evening of June 25th., and was luckier than his elder brother. Monsieur has now settled in Brussels, where he has been joined by the Comte d'Artois. The latter is, however, more popular among the émigré community than the Comte de Provence and this could have harmed his brother's position. Monsieur is seen as being too liberal by many émigrés. To solve this problem, Monsieur had the idea of making a speech to the exiled French noblemen in which he lavished praise on the Comte d'Artois. This forced the Comte d'Artois to respect protocol and to reply: "I only did what I had to and I will be the first to obey you as our leader." That was precisely what Monsieur wanted. He had been dreaming of being recognised by the émigrés as a sort of regent in exile (→July 5).

Late arrival makes trouble for Florian

Sceaux, late June

Florian is now convinced that having the rank of commander of the National Guard is not in itself a guarantee of being a good patriot.

The poet had just been passing through Paris on the day that the King and his family escaped from the Tuileries. What was only a coincidence for Florian could have cost him dearly. As soon as the King's departure had become public knowledge, all the gates of the capital were closed as a security measure. Florian was unable to return to his post as head of the National Guard at Sceaux until June 24th. That was enough to arouse suspicion that he had been involved with the royalist party. In any case, isn't this notorious aristocrat the secretary and close friend of the Duc de Penthièvre?

Philippe d'Orléans refuses the regency

The Duc d'Orléans, the King's cousin.

Paris, June 26

A totally unexpected event has just rocked political circles. In a statement that he has just had published by the newspapers, Philippe d'Orléans has solemnly refused the regency. Future prospects of the King's cousin had looked good. The escape of Louis XVI had given him high hopes. According to the Constitution, the Duc d'Orléans was, in the absence of the King's brothers, a potential regent. He had been triumphantly received at the Jacobins' club on June 24th. and had been dubbed "the first Frenchman". When the King returned to Paris, both Danton and Laclos had urged him to demand the regency while Louis XVII was under age. There was nothing to stop him, but nobody had taken his weakness and lack of true ambition into account. Under the influence of Madame de Genlis, Philippe d'Orléans preferred to remain a simple citizen. For his part, Laclos is furious. He sees eight months of careful plotting going up in smoke (→Sept. 15, 92).

In Strasbourg, people burn effigies of the Marquis de Bouillé, commander of the eastern armies, and of the Austrian commanders Klinglin and Heyman, who are all suspected of involvement in the King's escape.

Two Pacific islands join the kingdom

Marquesas Islands, late June

The kingdom has become larger with the addition of new territories in the Pacific Ocean. The captain of the ship *Le Solide,* Etienne Marchand, was unable to resist the temptation of taking possession of the archipelago that he had just discovered. The islands, which have become French, were immediately named by him as the Revolution Isles. The impromtu ceremony was held in the presence of many local inhabitants, who were amazed by the arrival of the French but did not show hostility. They have sworn to keep the sealed bottle that the captain gave them, without realising that it contains the document linking their fate to France (→ Nov. 21).

Young Saint Just's literary success

Louis Antoine de Saint Just.

Paris, June

Only a few days have gone by since it was first published, but it is difficult to find even a single copy of Saint Just's book, *L'Esprit de la Révolution et de la Constitution de la France.* This may be because it is hard to resist his fiery style and theories.

This is not a particularly complex work, but a hymn to the achievements of the revolution and the republican ideal. Behind the excessive sentimentality of the 24 year old author, readers discover that each page is marked by his boundless admiration for his political mentor, Robespierre.

 Constituent Assembly

1. Vendée. At Saint Fulgent, officials arrest the Baron Robert de Lézardière, his two sons and 33 other plotters who wanted to make Châtillon sur Sèvre the base of the counter-revolution in the Anjou and Poitou regions (→ Sept. 18, 91).

1. Paris. The National Assembly is upset by the appearance on the city's walls of a republican poster written by the American Thomas Paine and probably translated by Condorcet.

1. Paris. Pierre Henri Lebrun Tondu and the Belgian printer J.J. Smits resume publication of the *Journal Général de l'Europe,* which they had been printing in Liège.

2. Paris. At the Assembly, a list of governors whom the Constituent Assembly could provide for the young Dauphin is read out. Among them is the Marquis de Bouillé.

2. Montauban. The King's escape leads the Jacobin Daunous to suggest that the throne be declared vacant. His proposal is not acted upon.

3. Paris. In a bid aimed at shoring up the defence of the kingdom's northern and eastern borders, the Assembly decides to mobilise 26,000 National Guardsmen immediately (→ 22).

3. Drôme. Twenty two Jacobin clubs of the Valence region hold a congress.

5. Aix la Chapelle. On the way to Coblentz, the Comtes de Provence and d'Artois meet the King of Sweden, Gustav III. The monarch proposes that a coalition of all major powers be formed against revolutionary France.

6. Padua. In a statement, Leopold II calls on the sovereigns of Europe to join him in demanding the King of France's freedom. →

7. Paris. The Feydeau theatre shows a performance of a new play, *Calas ou l'Ecole des Juges,* by Marie Joseph de Chénier, based on the wave of religious intolerance.

9. Paris. A decree from the Assembly gives émigrés a month to return to France, failing which they will have to face sanctions. →

9. Paris. At the Social Circle, Condorcet makes a speech about the need to set up a republican system in France quickly (→ 10).

Will the royal family's arrest now force the Emperor Leopold II to take action?

Padua, July 6

Although Leopold II is not one to be easily impressed, he has been deeply upset. The arrest of the French royal family has made him truly angry. His dear sister Marie Antoinette and his brother-in-law Louis XVI have been imprisoned by scum! Forgetting his usual caution, the Emperor has given in to anger and mobilised the monarchs of Europe against what he sees as the "amazing attack" on the French royal couple. However, it seems unlikely that the events of June will be enough to get this peaceful sovereign to go to war. In any case, Austria is not certain of being able to win a conflict against France (→ 25).

Marie Antoinette's elder brother.

Charitable workshops have been closed

Paris, July 3

Since this morning, women and children dressed in rags have been facing National Guardsmen on Paris' Place de Grève and Place Vendôme. The unfortunates are protesting against the closure of the charitable workshops. Created by the Constituent Assembly, they employed 28,000 jobless people to do navvying work for 15 sous a day — a worker's average daily wage is 36 sous — but there have been scandals. People were being paid for doing no work and building materials were sold on the black market. To restore calm, the city council has promised demonstrators it will provide a 96,000 livres credit; but there is no work.

The émigrés will have to return to France

Paris, July 9

There must be no pity for the enemies of the Revolution who have left the country. The debate on emigration, which has been at a standstill since March, has been revived since the recent events at Varennes.

The deputies have just decreed that they will give émigrés just one month to return to France. Those who do meet this timetable will have their civil rights suspended and their property taxed. If they are still not back by next October, these taxes will be tripled. The move was supported by Barère, who solemnly told the Assembly that whoever "abandons an endangered city will be stripped of his rights". So the members of the Constituent Assembly finally ruled in favour of sanctions against the émigrés. It was not an easy decision, as it contradicted a basic revolutionary principle: freedom. Is the Revolution to go back on its own principles? However, truly exceptional circumstances require equally exceptional measures (→ Oct. 14).

Birds of a feather flock together: two noble émigrés at Aix la Chapelle.

10. Paris. Thomas Paine, Condorcet and du Châtelet publish the first edition of the *Républicain ou le Défenseur du Gouvernement Representatif.*

10. Auray. Georges Cadoudal starts working as a clerk for the notary Glain.

11. Paris. The ashes of Voltaire are transferred to the Panthéon. →

11. Paris. The *Gazette de Paris* publishes a statement from a group of royalists who offer themselves as guarantors so that the King is allowed to leave the capital.

13. Paris. Gorses' *Courrier des Départements* publishes a poem on the placing of the ashes of Voltaire in the Panthéon written by Marie Joseph de Chénier, with a musical score by Gossec.

13. Les Sables d'Olonne. Brigadier Dumouriez and some of his officers go to the town's club where he makes a strongly worded speech about the unrest rocking the Vendée region.

13. Paris. The debate on the King's flight opens at the Assembly. Robespierre calls for the nation to be consulted over the question of the inviolability of the King's person.

14. Paris. The second anniversary of the Federation is celebrated on the Champ de Mars. →

15. Paris. In order to preserve the monarchy, endangered by the King's flight, and to avoid passing judgement on him, the National Assembly decrees the inviolability of the royal person and rules that Bouillé should in his absence be judged by the High Court for having attempted to kidnap the King. →

15. Paris. At 10 p.m., hundreds of citizens rush into the Jacobins' convent and ask the society to join them tomorrow when they go to the Champ de Mars to demand Louis XVI's deposition. Brissot, Danton and Laclos write a petition asking that the King be replaced by "all constitutional means". For their part, the Cordeliers issue another petition demanding the abdication and judgement of Louis XVI.

15. Lyons. The city's authorities send a republican manifesto to the Assembly, but its members refuse to support it.

Voltaire's ashes go to the Panthéon

In the procession there is a model of the Bastille (10); the people of the Saint Antoine district carrying the portraits of Rousseau, Franklin, Désilles and Mirabeau (11); the statue (13) and the works (14) of Voltaire.

Paris, July 11

The procession set off from the Place de la Bastille at 2 p.m. and only reached the Panthéon at 10 o'clock. The nation has once again demonstrated the respect in which it holds its great men. David has shown his ability to organise impressive revolutionary ceremonies. The people had been expecting a lot of the moving of Voltaire's ashes to the Panthéon. Yesterday, the great philosopher's coffin was placed on a special dais erected among the ruins of the Bastille, where the dead man himself had once been imprisoned. The coffin was then placed on a carriage pulled by 12 grey horses. Today it was escorted by many delegations who had come to pay their last respects: the National Guard, the Jacobins' Society, the strong men of the marketplace, the sections, the electors of 1789, and the men working on the demolition of the Bastille who were led by Palloy. After them came the Academicians carrying a coffin which contained all the 70 volumes of Voltaire's work. Behind them came the deputies. Despite an overcast sky, there were large crowds standing all along the procession's route across Paris.

Twelve grey horses decked out in blue cloth sprinkled with golden stars were used to pull the carriage bearing Voltaire's coffin to the Panthéon.

Royalists depict Mme. de Condorcet as a prostitute

Paris, July 14

The royalist press has unleashed a vicious campaign against the Condorcets. Today the *Journal Général de la Cour et de la Ville* printed a cartoon showing the lovely Marquise in the nude and being courted by La Fayette. The drawing bore the inscription *res publica*, or public property. Her husband is the target of daily insults in newspapers close to La Fayette, whose friend he was before the King's escape. All this is because this man of science, who became politically active along with his wife at the onset of the Revolution, supports republican ideals. He has called for the abolition of the monarchy and set up a newspaper, *Le Républicain*. Their residence on the Rue de Lille has become a hotbed of "subversive" ideas. The mathematician's former muse, the Duchesse d'Enville, has had a bust of Condorcet buried under a heap of manure. Malesherbes has sworn to kill him on sight.

Chateaubriand's first contact with the New World

Virginia, July 10

"Land ahoy!" the ship's lookout cried and François René de Chateaubriand's heart started to beat faster. He had been waiting for this very moment since he set off from Saint Malo for the New World aboard the *Saint Pierre* over three months ago. America was still just a lush, wooded coastline around the huge Chesapeake Bay, but the young man would soon see the first houses in Virginia and the port of Baltimore. Although lengthy, the ocean crossing was not unpleasant. As a native of the port town of Saint Malo and the son of a privateer, Chateaubriand enjoyed his trip across the Atlantic. During the journey he even dived into the ocean for a swim, not caring about shark attacks or the strong currents, although at one point he had to be hauled back aboard before he drowned; but now he can't wait to set foot on American soil for the first time (→ Aug.).

Unrest and anger continue in the capital

Paris, July 15

Unrest is continuing to rock the capital. Several thousand demonstrators, mostly members of clubs and people's societies, gathered today on the Champ de Mars, precisely where yesterday's celebration of the anniversary of the fall of the Bastille was held.

Rejoicing has turned into anger. The people of Paris are unhappy about the deputies' attitude towards the King. In the early afternoon the members of the Cordeliers drafted a petition demanding that the King be judged by the nation, but the speaker of the Assembly, Charles de Lameth, has refused to publish it. The decree exonerating the sovereign after the events at Varennes has just been approved and it is illegal to issue a petition opposing a decree. However, this did not satisfy the crowd. The demonstrators have gone to the Jacobins' club to see Robespierre and convince him to draft another petition.

The current wave of popular unrest is starting to worry the deputies, who have asked the city council to take special security precautions to ensure public order in the capital.

The Chinese lanterns on the Bastille's ruins were quickly extinguished.

Madame Roland's political salon

Paris, July

The Roland couple have been back in Paris since last February, and have settled at the Britannique residence, on the Rue Guénégaud. The move was made after the commune of Lyons named Roland as a special deputy and placed him in charge of efforts to get the city's debts nationalised. For his delighted wife, Manon, this is the start of a new life. She loves to have guests and has been inviting to her salon all the left wing deputies and journalists. Her home has become a meeting place for all the most progressive members of the National Assembly: people such as Pétion, Buzot and Robespierre as well as Jacobins such as Bosc, Brissot, Bancal des Issarts and Lanthenas.

Since the start of the Revolution, the young woman has been fascinated by politics and has turned into an ardent patriot. Taking advantage of her return to the capital, she has been attending all the debates at the Assembly, going to the clubs and the Social Circle. Since the King's escape, she has been frustrated by the weakness shown by the Jacobins. She is convinced that the time has come to proclaim the republic and to put Louis XVI on trial. This would be "the greatest and most just move", she says. On this point, she agrees with her husband, who is also suffering from political fever. In spite of the great difference in their ages, the Roland couple are very happy indeed.

King is inviolable, so he is innocent

Paris, July 15

Louis XVI has been exonerated and Bouillé is the only one responsible for the "kidnapping" that ended at Varennes. That is what the Assembly has decided, and it has saved the monarchy. It has decreed that the King was not responsible for his actions. He could only be put on trial after his abdication and not for crimes committed during his reign. "Everybody must see that it is in the general interest for the Revolution to come to an end," Barnave exclaimed. The Assembly has shown that it does not want too much more democracy.

Banquet wrecked in Birmingham

Birmingham, July 14

Celebrations to mark the anniversary of the fall of the Bastille caused a riot in Birmingham. The pro-liberal British chemist Joseph Priestley had organised a banquet for his friends to celebrate the events of two years ago in Paris, but Anglican clergymen incited the crowd against Priestley, a strong supporter of Protestant dissidents. An enraged mob poured into the scientist's home, wrecking the banqueting hall, burning his library and destroying his laboratory. At no time did the authorities do anything to stop the mob.

Royal excesses are decried on stage

Paris, July 13

It can be extremely pleasant to live at a time when the freedom of thought is a fundamental right. Some of the plays currently being shown are based on the hated days when tolerance only existed in the wildest dreams of philosophers. Two such plays, *Le Chevalier de La Barre,* by Benoît Joseph Marsollier, shown at the Italian theatre, and *Jean Calas ou l'Ecole des Juges,* by Marie Joseph de Chénier, shown at the Théâtre Français, are based on famous legal and religious cases in which Voltaire played a major role. The great philosopher remains very much in people's minds.

16. Paris. While some 3,000 people are gathered on the Champ de Mars to call for the King's deposition, the Assembly decrees that the sovereign's powers have been suspended. →

16. Paris. A major split appears within the ranks of the Jacobins' club. →

17. Rouen. A Reformed form of worship is created in a church that previously used to be Catholic.

17. Paris. Collot d'Herbois presents a new and successful performance of a vaudeville play, *La Famille Patriote ou la Fédération*, at Monsieur's theatre.

17. Paris. Dozens of republicans are massacred on the Champ de Mars. →

18. Paris. Following a proposal by Regnault de Saint Jean d'Angély, the Assembly issues a decree sanctioning the publication and distribution of any written material that calls for laws to be violated.

18. Paris. The Assembly grants a 200,000 franc reward to the people who helped arrest Louis XVI at Varennes. Drouet is given a 30,000 franc share of the total reward.

19. Bayeux. Club members are arrested for having torn down plaques commemorating Louis XVI's visit to the town in 1786 (→Aug. 29, 91).

22. Paris. Military volunteers recruited on the basis of the decree of June 11th. are increased from 26,000 to 97,000. They can be put under the orders of army generals just like line troops.

22. Montauban. The town's people's society receives a letter from the Feuillants informing it of the split at the Jacobins. Like most provincial societies, it decides to correspond with both rival clubs.

24. Paris. At the Jacobins, Robespierre forces the rejection of the unification conditions (membership of the society would be restricted to active citizens). He has the internal rulings changed and gets provisional approval for a purge to be led by a 12-member committee. →

25. Austria. In Vienna, Chancellor Kaunitz opens negotiations with Prussia aimed at setting up a European congress to oppose the Revolution. (→Aug. 27, 91).

The King is suspended from office until he agrees to ratify the Constitution

Paris, July 16

The Assembly has just shown the people that it can act firmly, but the decision it has just approved is only superficially severe. Acting on a proposal by Démeunier, the deputies have decided that the King's powers will be suspended until the drafting of the Constitution is completed and he has agreed to ratify it. The decision means the King no longer has any say in legislative matters, but is has no effect on the monarchy's authority as it is only a provisional measure. It is essentially aimed at calming the anger aroused among the people by yesterday's decree on royal inviolability. As for Louis XVI, he is waiting resignedly for the final text of the Constitution to be submitted to him.

Moderates break away from the Jacobins

Paris, July 16

The break is final: the Jacobin deputies have deserted their club. There are some who have remained, grouped around Robespierre, but most of the members of the Assembly who belong to the Society of the Friends of the Constitution have just noisily walked out. They haven't gone far, only across the Rue Saint Honoré to settle at the Feuillants convent.

The royal issue is behind the split sought by the moderates of the constitutional party, led by Duport, Lameth and Barnave. In the wake of the royal couple's escape to Varennes, these men had stated that they wanted the monarchy maintained as they believed it was the best guarantee of order. However, a minority within the Jacobins had been demanding the King's deposition. The latter asked Laclos and Brissot to draft a petition stating their position so that it could be signed tomorrow on the Champ de Mars. In this text they say they no longer recognise "neither Louis XVI, nor any other

"I've come from the Feuillants."

king". They don't go as far as calling for a republic, as opposed to the Cordeliers, who will also take a petition to the Champ de Mars calling for the King's deposition.

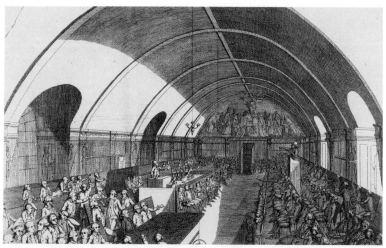

A meeting at the Jacobins Club in the former convent on the Rue Saint Honoré.

A new address for Robespierre

Eléonore, Duplay's daughter.

Paris, July 17

Robespierre has found a brand new family. An arrest warrant was issued against him after the bloodshed on the Champ de Mars, so the deputy from Arras was no longer safe at his home on the Rue de Saintonge. The Jacobin Duplay, a carpenter by trade, therefore offered to put him up on the Rue Saint Honoré, where his wife and three daughters warmly greeted him. This closely knit family with revolutionary ideals liked Robespierre even before meeting him. He need no longer be a lonely man.

Republicans massacred on the Champ de Mars

The crowd of petitioners had gathered on the steps of the altar to the Nation to add a note of formality to their protest and republican demands.

Paris, July 17

Nothing will ever be the same again: a lot of blood was spilled today.

The deputies, who feared a riot, had ordered the National Guard to keep public order. The people of Paris had been called out to the Champ de Mars to sign petitions drafted by the Jacobins and the Cordeliers, which demanded the deposition of Louis XVI. The dramatic events began unfolding early in the morning. Two men were found hidden under the altar erected in honour of the Nation, upon which the petitions had been placed. The restless crowd immediately grabbed them and cut their throats, claiming that they were royalist agents. News of the murders stunned the Assembly. Its speaker, Charles de Lameth, immediately sent a message to the city council to demand action. Then the deputies issued a decree stating that the petitioners were all criminals guilty of "insult to the nation". Robespierre, who wanted to stay within the bounds of the law, sent Santerre to withdraw the Jacobins' petition. This, however, left the Cordeliers' petition, which large numbers of Parisians were about to sign. La Fayette and his men, who had been sent in by the Assembly, were just arriving on the parade ground when a gunshot

was fired at them. The commander of the National Guard remained calm and did not give his troops the order to retaliate, but as soon as they were told of the incident the deputies panicked and demanded that the city hall do something. Bailly immediately had martial law

proclaimed and sent in reinforcements. Marching behind their red flag, the troops poured into the Champ de Mars from all sides, shoving aside the thousands of men, women and children who had come to sign the petitions. Suddenly, another gunshot rang out. That

provoked the troops into charging the crowd. When the smoke cleared, several dozen bodies were found. Many other people lay on the ground bleeding and badly hurt. City officials and members of the clubs were unable to agree on the exact number of the victims.

A mixture of horror and anger can be seen on the faces of these innocents, among whom are many women and children. No prior warning was given before the shooting started.

A wave of repression hits democrats

Paris, July 20

Fréron has just been arrested. The editor of the violent newspaper *L'Orateur du Peuple* was one of the authors of the petition sent by the Cordeliers to the Champ de Mars. The Assembly has decided to take action against those it sees as being responsible for the bloody massacre. It is also after the republicans who were fired upon by the National Guardsmen. The very next day after the terrible events, the deputies admitted that what had happened was not caused by simple "unrest", but was due to provocation. That assessment was based on Bailly's report, which whitewashed the security forces. Some tough repressive measures have been taken. Regnault even wanted anyone who had ever called on the people, in writing, to disobey the law to be put in irons for three years, but Pétion opposed this in the name of the

The man with two faces, half Bailly and half La Fayette.

freedom of the press. The hunting season for democrats is now open and the supporters of the King appear to have won (→Aug. 10).

Queen offers Emperor opposing views

Paris, July 30

The Queen has just written a letter to the Emperor, her brother, dictated by Barnave. In it she asks him to remain France's ally. It was during the long journey back from Varennes that the young deputy met Marie Antoinette and was moved by her charm and misfortunes. He has since become her secret advisor, and spends all his time trying to save the monarchy, but although the Queen pretends to listen to him she secretly writes to the Emperor to tell him to ignore what has been dictated to her (→Oct. 5).

Mass expulsions from the Jacobins Club

Paris, July 24

Robespierre has decided to take action. As the Feuillants are refusing to rejoin their parent society, he has decided to expel them. A committee that includes deputies who have remained loyal to the Jacobins, such as Grégoire, Pétion, Prieur and Robespierre, has been set up to expel all members of the society opposed to the principles of the Revolution — in other words, those who have broken away from it. Robespierre has said that the people who are supporting right wingers at the Assembly against democrats are "seditious". He has also sent a letter to ask the provincial societies not to accept any offers from the Feuillants.

"Their Jacobin Majesties' great funeral procession." Satirical engraving.

August 1791
from 1st. to 31st.

Constituent Assembly

1. Paris. Robespierre publishes a "message to the French" defending the policies he has been backing since the King's escape. The message is an immediate success.

3. Caen. Club members destroy a statue of Louis XVI which stands on the Royal Square (→29).

3. Paris. Tallien begins publication of a new paper, *L'Ami des Citoyens,* which is printed only on one side so that it can be posted up on walls for all to read.

5. Paris. Thouret submits to the Assembly a draft French Constitution that is to be revised article by article, starting on August 8th.

5. Arcis sur Aube. Danton, who is being sought by police since the shooting on the Champ de Mars, decides to travel to England (→Sept. 9).

9. Paris. At the request of Rabaut Saint Etienne, the Assembly decrees that France is indivisible.

10. Paris. Brune, Momoro and Saint Félix are arrested. They are all members of the Cordeliers. Santerre and Legendre, who are also being hunted, go into hiding.

11. Loire Atlantique. While on an inspection tour at Machecoul, Dumouriez notes that the country would already be in the throes of an insurrection if it were not for the army and National Guard.

11. Paris. The historian Jacques Antoine Dulaure starts a patriot newspaper, *Le Thermomètre du Jour.*

21. Avignon. The troops led by General Jourdan seize the town hall and the Papal palace, forcing the mediator, Abbot Mulot, to flee.

22. Saint Domingue. The slaves of the northern province revolt (→24).

28. Angers. The department's authorities call for cavalry reinforcements to cope with non-juring unrest in the Mauges region.

29. Caen. An arrest warrant is issued for Bishop Fauchet, who had defended the club members of Bayeux, as well as for the heads of the people's societies of Bayeux and Caen.

31. Paris. The Marais theatre is opened. It has a gothic auditorium made out of stones taken from the Bastille.

Mme. Du Barry and English justice

Louvenciennes, August 26

Madame Du Barry's third visit to England has proved to be as useless as the two previous ones. When she returned empty handed, she finally started losing all hope of ever seeing her precious jewels again. The English judges don't want to know about the theft that was carried out in France. They have ruled that the trial will not resume for a long time. The accused have even been freed due to a lack of conclusive proof. As for the jewels, they are still locked up in London banks. Mme. Du Barry has pleaded with senior members of the British court, but to no avail.

An elegant patriotic reaper.

Some greedy water vendors are jailed

Paris, August 10

People have a right to drink water, even if for some this means making a loss. That is what the judges at the police court of the city hall have ruled. In order to set an example, they have sentenced two water vendors, Jean Monpechin and Jean Canel, to a two week jail term. That will teach them to stop forbidding, sometimes by force, people of their neighbourhood from getting water at the Montmorency fountain. The two men claimed they were only protecting their livelihoods; but water belongs to everybody. The culprits will also have to pay for posters denouncing their shameful behaviour.

Chateaubriand meets the Iroquois

United States, August

Chateaubriand is disappointed. His first ever encounter with the "savages" did not go at all as he had expected.

True, the Iroquois were half naked, with rings in their noses and cut ears, just as the travel books had said, but when he met them they were involved in an unexpected activity: in the heart of the forest, they were dancing to the strident music of a violin played by a white man. He was wearing a powdered wig and a green frock coat with lace sleeves, and was calling out the steps in a high pitched voice. This former cook in the French army had stayed behind after the troops left. Poor Chateaubriand, a loyal admirer of Rousseau's "noble savage", was most upset to see these Indians behaving just like Frenchmen who were having fun.

The Assembly leans towards a constitutional monarchy

Paris, August 8

It is hard to see whether it will be the Feuillants party or the diehard royalists who will get the upper hand. The debate that has just opened at the Assembly on the review of the Constitution, in fact the text's final drafting, is sure to be a rowdy one.

The Feuillants are concerned about the wave of republican feeling that is sweeping the country. They have therefore decided to reach a tacit agreement with the royalists, aimed at giving the King a major role in the new Constitution. Barnave met the Queen at the Tuileries on July 25th. Marie Antoinette assured him that she wanted to be saved only by him and the Constitution, rather than by the sovereigns of Europe and a war. So Barnave has brokered a new deal between the Feuillant Le Chapelier and the royalist Malouet. The two deputies have agreed to hold a fake debate that would discreetly lead to reinforcing the royal prerogatives in the Constitution. They thought that this trickery would not be noticed by the Assembly, which has grown very tired of the endless procedural discussions and wants to get the debate over with once and for all, but their plan was foiled when the highly sensitive issue of religion arose. Today the royalist d'Eprémesnil protested, on behalf of the right wingers, against the repression that the Assembly is planning against the non-juring priests, whose activities are causing grave tensions to continue throughout the country. Although they have broken away from the Jacobins, the Feuillants have not forgotten that they voted for the clergy's civil Constitution, but that no longer really matters. A majority of deputies still supports constitutional monarchy. The democrats, who are in a minority, have

"I can eat gold and silver, but I can't swallow the Constitution."

no way of getting the other deputies to support their views. In the end, the text will anger the royalists, who in any case don't want to hear of a constitution, as well as the moderates, who already feel they have made too many concessions.

Exiled French aristocrats meet in London

London, August

It seems as if the entire aristocracy of France is now living in London, where life can sometimes be quite hard. There are some wealthy families living in large and fancy homes in London's West End, but they cannot always find enough money to pay the rent.

However, the great majority of the French émigrés are forced to live in garrets in the poorer neighbourhoods and have trouble hiding their lack of cash. The men are bored and depressed, while the women usually work to support their families. Madame de Pange gives French lessons, Madame de MacMahon paints portraits, but most of the other noblewomen earn money by sewing or doing needlework. They spend their days making muslin dresses or lace, the same tasks which they used to watch their private dressmakers perform, but unfortunately they are not so efficient. An English lady, however, bought one such dress and wore it at a reception given by the Prince of Wales.

Monsieur has a fine time at Coblentz

Coblentz, August

Monsieur and his brother, the Comte d'Artois, are being royally housed at the residence of their maternal uncle, the Archbishop of Trèves, who has decided to pay for all their expenses during their stay with him. He has placed his castle at Schönbornlust, near Coblentz, at their disposal and Monsieur holds court there. The prince invites émigrés and other important men. Based on the traditions that used to be observed at Versailles, everyday life at the castle has already taken on age-old rhythms: at 10 o'clock the prince rises, Mass is said at 11 a.m., dinner is at 9 o'clock sharp. There is, however, a bourgeois novelty: lemonade and almond milk are served before bedtime. The Comte de Provence is playing the role of an exiled sovereign. He has formed a government that meets every morning to discuss the need to resort to force against the Revolution. It also discusses the need to set up a military organisation for the émigrés, and how to manage relations with European powers.

France gradually loses all its nobles: Luxembourg sails for London where Calonne is waiting for him, while Polignac has already set off for Spa.

A church is razed and the Virgin is taken to Vendée

Bellefontaine, August 26

The miraculous Virgin of Notre Dame de Bon Secours has changed sides. The small chapel at Bellefontaine that shelters the statue had become one of the centres of the opposition of the peasants of the Mauges region to the new religious legislation.

On the night of August 14th., a huge torchlit procession had been held there. The *Salve Regina* had been sung by the faithful and there had been prayers "for the preservation and the restoration of the Catholic faith". Eight days later, after a new procession, the local authorities decided it was time to take some firm measures. The National Guard today destroyed the tiny chapel. The authorities have also asked the constitutional priest of Notre Dame de Cholet to pick up the statue and take it to his own church.

The removal of the Virgin was carried out with great ceremony as National Guardsmen stood by in case of trouble, while the people sang ... *Salve Regina*.

The Pillnitz declaration: a cautious threat to the Revolution

Pillnitz, August 27

Is war likely to break out? Is the coalition of the European powers against revolutionary France that is being talked about so much about to become a reality? Leopold II of Austria and Frederick William II of Prussia have met at Pillnitz, the summer residence of the court of Saxony, near Dresden. Worried about the fate of the King of France after his escape failed at Varennes, and under pressure from the émigrés to launch a military offensive to restore the French monarchy to power, the two sovereigns have drafted a joint declaration, but the text is far from being the definitive and firm commitment that the Comte d'Artois, who attended the meeting, had hoped for. The Emperor and the King of Prussia state that "the situation in which His Majesty the King of France currently finds himself is of common interest to all the sovereigns of Europe". They even threaten to use, including in France if necessary, "the most effective means" of consolidating "the basis of a monarchical government in accordance with the rights of the sovereigns". However, they specifically state that they will only intervene with

The Prussian King, the Emperor and Saxony's Prince Elector at Pillnitz.

the assent of the other powers. This clearly shows that neither Leopold nor Frederick William is keen to take action. They know that Spain, England and Sweden, not to speak of Naples or Piedmont, are not prepared to take any steps against the French revolutionaries. Nevertheless, their declaration has caused great concern in France.

People of the Ile de France remain loyal to Louis XVI

Port Louis, August 25

The Ile de France has forgotten its differences long enough to pay homage to the King. In the capital's packed church, all the island's political parties have jointly celebrated the day of Saint Louis. The ceremony began early this morning, as the colonial Assembly went to the church. Ushers led to their respective pews the governor, de Cossigny, civil and military officials and the bailiff.

But behind this apparent show of unity there is a deep sense of unease: the island's Assembly has just abolished the governor's power of veto. Cossigny has not reacted to this move yet, although he will do so soon. After Mass was over, the priest turned to face his parishioners, who roared: "Long live the King, long live the nation, long live the law!"

Do French people bath regularly?

There are only about 150 bathtubs in all of Paris. Unlike the public baths, these remain a privilege reserved exclusively for the very wealthy. To own a bathtub, one has to be able to afford to pay the water carriers who deliver by the pail.

A day-worker would have to spend several days' wages to go to one of the public baths that operate on the banks of the Seine.

These are very efficient establishments. Special boats pump water from the river into the comfortable private cabins. A new room is also being added to many of the luxurious homes that have been built over the past few years: the bathroom. Its most revolutionary item is the bidet, used for intimate ablutions. However, washing is not an everyday thing for the great majority of French people. In fact, for most of them an occasional wash simply involves dashing some cold water onto their face. For truly special occasions such as public holidays, the feet are also washed. It is high time for there to be a revolution in the sanitary habits of the people of France.

This bathroom is shown as an idyllic part of a modern home.

The Louvois theatre opens as a new centre for comedy

Paris, August 16

There has been a major advance in theatrical design. The awful establishments of yesteryear have gradually been changed into beautiful public monuments.

The architect Alexandre Théodore Brogniart is now focusing on building theatres, because current events have made his usual clients, the aristocrats, unwilling to invest in new luxury houses.

Brogniart had therefore drawn up the plans for the new Louvois theatre, which opened its doors to the public today in the street with the same name. The theatre can seat a total of 1,435 spectators and will specialise in showing both comedies and comic operas. The formal, austere style of the building's facade is much appreciated at a time when the stern classicism of ancient Rome is in fashion.

The Salon is now open to all artists

Paris, August 21

The Salon was created under the Ancien Régime. It was born in 1648 in the square chamber at the Louvre which was itself known as the Salon, or living room. Until now, it has only been open to artists who had been certified by the Academy. It was a rare privilege to be granted the right to compete, and a severe handicap not to be able to exhibit works there, as much of a handicap as when an author cannot find a publisher; but the Assembly has decided to change all that. In the name of equality, it has now decreed that "all French and foreign artists, whether or not they are members of the Academy of painting and sculpture, will be allowed to exhibit their works". This move is not going to please everybody. However, the deputies are convinced that this is a good way to help

Alexandre Roslin will exhibit this portrait of the naturalist Daubenton at the Salon in September.

French art "find its freedom". The system will bring fame to many artists and allow the public to judge the quality of their art (→ Sept. 8).

New representatives are to be elected

Paris, August 29

More than two months later than expected, the people of France are at last to elect their deputies to the legislative Assembly.

The primary assemblies have been meeting since June, but the King's escape and the massacre on the Champ de Mars forced the authorities to delay the elections. A total of 745 representatives is to be elected, with so many for each department, depending on the size of its population and the amount of taxes it pays.

While the voters of the Hautes Alpes, Lozère and the Pyrenees Orientales will only elect five deputies each, those of Aisne will have 12, those of the Calvados, the Manche and the Somme 13, those of Seine et Oise 14, those of the Rhône et Loire 15 and those of Seine Inférieure 16; Parisians will

have 24. The election will be indirect and based on property assessment. Only active citizens, those who are listed on the National Guard rolls, who have taken the civic oath and who pay a direct contribution equal to three days' work, will be able to take part in choosing the electors. These will in turn elect the nation's representatives and their substitutes. About a third of the total number of voters is expected to stay at home due to lack of interest.

Those who do take the trouble to vote are likely to be influenced by the recent events. The moderate candidates should be helped by the fact that the Assembly has aided the monarchy and placed responsibility for the bloody events of July 17th. on the democrats. In Paris, Danton himself is worried that he will not be elected.

The Duc d'Orléans sells his art works to raise money

Paris, August

The Duc d'Orléans is short of money. His creditors are demanding that he repay some of his gambling debts. However, Philippe d'Orléans wants to use his wealth to finance a political campaign that he hopes will sooner or later bear fruit. He has therefore decided to sell his collection of paintings, considered to be one of the finest in Europe. It was started by Richelieu who had collected 485 works at his gallery in the Palais Cardinal, which later became the Palais Royal and was handed over to the Orléans family. The collection has continued to grow, thanks to royal contributions, and its quality is as high as its diversity is wide. There are works by the great French masters and by the famous Italian, Dutch, German and Flemish artists; but to whom should he sell all this, and for what price? Offers made by one potential buyer, the Englishman Thomas Moore Slade, seemed too low to the Duc, though he did not really know what price to ask for. The powerful Brussels banker Walkuers was a bit more generous, offering 700,000 livres just for the French and Italian works. Philippe may well accept this offer.

An uprising by the black slaves of the Cap Français is a failure

Saint Domingue, August 24

The countryside near the Cap Français has been ablaze for the past two days. Thousands of rebellious black slaves have spread out through the white-owned plantations, setting fire to all they found. A huge pall of smoke has spread from Port Margot to Rocou and the northern capital is totally isolated from the rest of its province. Faced with such devastating anger, the governor, Blanche-

lande, has turned the town into an armed camp and ordered all the slaves of the Cap to be put in irons. Leading his troops, he has so far managed to repel all the attacks launched by the rebels, but his forces are not strong enough to chase them through the nearby hills. Many farmers have been massacred by their own slaves. The island's white population is living in fear. This is obviously not just a simple revolt, but a general

uprising. In fact, the black people of Saint Domingue had waited for months to get the go-ahead from their leaders, Jean François, Boukman and Biassou. The uprising was set off by the break that came in late July between the black and white communities. Their chief goal was to destroy the Cap. However, Blanchelande has temporarily foiled the rebels' plan by using the town's 12,000 black people as hostages (→ Sept. 20).

The houses on the plains that surround the town and port of Cap Français will burn non-stop for 40 days.

1. Paris. Beaumetz, the chairman of the committee on the Constitution, gets the Assembly to agree in principle that the Constitution should be submitted for royal approval.

1. Saint Domingue. After the revolt by the black slaves, the military now take up arms. They rout the patriots of Port au Prince near their camp at Croix aux Bouquets.

2. Paris. The Assembly approves the principle that there should be national holidays to celebrate the Revolution.

2. Rennes. Several priests are killed at the Carmes convent.

3. Paris. Following the dismissal of the troops of the Royal Household, the Assembly proposes to provide the King with a constitutional guard to ensure his security. →

3. Paris. The debate on the Constitution at the Assembly ends. The revamped Constitution is immediately submitted to Louis XVI.

4. Ile et Vilaine. At Etrelles, a unit of the National Guard loots the house of the non-juring parish priest.

7. Paris. A decree from the Assembly orders that departmental authorities must outfit the volunteers who cannot afford to buy their own equipment.

8. Paris. The Salon opens at the Louvre palace. 247 artists, including 19 women, exhibit their works. →

9. Paris. Danton returns after spending a month in England.

9. Arles. Royalists take control of the town and barricade themselves inside it after having seized a convoy of artillery.

10. Ile de France. The mandate of the substitute deputies who were elected to the Constituent Assembly in July 1790 is extended.

11. Paris. The order of lawyers is abolished as a guild and the Assembly states that everyone is free to choose his own defence lawyer.

12. Paris. The rank of commander of the National Guard which La Fayette used to hold is abolished. The position will be filled in turn by the heads of the six legions (→Oct. 8, 91).

13. Paris. Louis XVI decides to approve the Constitution (→14).

France finally has a Constitution

Paris, September 3

The kingdom of France now has its first ever Constitution. The long awaited document has finally been approved by the deputies.

Every single law voted into force since 1789 is either explicitly included in the crucial text or at least summed up in it. It sets out the way the nation's powers are organised. First there is royal power. It has been reduced to its simplest form: the only means of action left to the King is the right of a three year suspensive veto over decrees issued by the Assembly. The monarch is now just the country's first public servant.

Even the right to declare war and to conclude international treaties now belongs, in the last resort, to the deputies. These are the representatives of the nation, although significantly they are only elected by some of the citizens. The right to vote is limited to people who have an income of over 250 francs a year. Although it is set fairly low, this financial condition makes the system less than totally democratic. The French are bound to get used to the new regulations, but they will not be enthusiastic about them, particularly after all the aspirations aroused over the past three years by the Revolution. The time has obviously come for the deputies to be replaced by a new generation of legislators (→Sept. 13).

An allegorical monument to the Constitution. Its base is made of stones taken from the Bastille. On top, the 83 departments support the tablets of the Law. The Nation drafts the laws with its legislative sceptre.

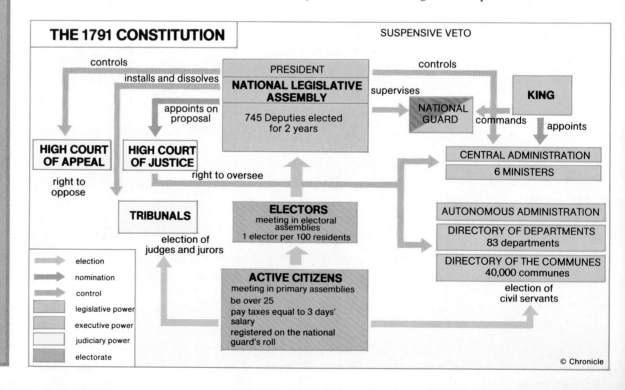

THE 1791 CONSTITUTION

SUSPENSIVE VETO

controls — installs and dissolves — appoints on proposal

PRESIDENT
NATIONAL LEGISLATIVE ASSEMBLY
745 Deputies elected for 2 years

controls — supervises — commands — appoints

KING

NATIONAL GUARD

HIGH COURT OF APPEAL
right to oppose

HIGH COURT OF JUSTICE
right to oversee

CENTRAL ADMINISTRATION
6 MINISTERS

TRIBUNALS
election of judges and jurors

ELECTORS
meeting in electoral assemblies
1 elector per 100 residents

AUTONOMOUS ADMINISTRATION

DIRECTORY OF DEPARTMENTS
83 departments

DIRECTORY OF THE COMMUNES
40,000 communes
election of civil servants

ACTIVE CITIZENS
meeting in primary assemblies
be over 25
pay taxes equal to 3 days' salary
registered on the national guard's roll

- election
- nomination
- control
- legislative power
- executive power
- judiciary power
- electorate

© Chronicle

Louis XVI is to have a constitutional guard corps

Paris, September 3

It seems that the King's failed escape attempt has not caused irreparable damage to his prestige. Only two months after the King's return from Varennes, the Assembly has decided to reorganise the royal household's military corps. Louis XVI's 1,124 personal bodyguards had been dismissed on June 25th., and the Assembly has just assigned him a personal guard unit made up of 1,200 infantrymen and 600 cavalrymen. The chief task of this "constitutional guard" is to ensure the King's security both inside and outside the palace. The moderate majority at the Assembly has been aligning itself with the King, due to its fear of republicans. Since July it has attacked some of the more progressive newspapers: Marat's *L'Ami du Peuple* has been seized and Camille Desmoulins' *Révolutions de France et de Brabant* has ceased publication. By taking steps against the most fiery patriots and giving the King his personal guard corps, the constitutional majority has dealt a severe blow to the people's societies. These remain committed to the Revolution and their rallying cry is "No more tyrant, no more monarchy!".

David's "Oath at the Jeu de Paume" is a big hit at the Salon

David's sketch, which he has reworked dozens of times, shows the crucial moment at the Jeu de Paume.

Paris, September 8

A simple sketch is drawing the most attention at the Salon. David has only just started work on the final version of the "Oath at the Jeu de Paume". Art critics have expressed surprise over the way the painting is to be structured. They say: "Bailly is standing too far forward, where there is hardly anybody else, while there is a large crowd behind him." It seems as if Bailly is speaking to the wall. David has done this to give the impression that the dean of the Third Estate is speaking directly to the viewer. This is not the only bit of artistic licence. In the forefront David shows the Carthusian monk Dom Gerle, Abbot Grégoire and Pastor Rabaut Saint Etienne, who symbolise the clergy's support of the Third Estate. However, Dom Gerle only came to Paris in December 1789 (→ Sept. 28).

The problems of women authors

Being the source of inspiration for male authors and poets can have its rewards, but some women prefer to seek fame on their own merits.

The 17th. century had already produced several major women authors. There are even more of them nowadays: poetesses such as Madame Du Boccage, fiction writers such as Madame de Genlis or Madame Riccoboni, playwrights such as Olympe de Gouges.

However, the fate of women of letters is not always an enviable one. Public opinion often has difficulty in accepting a woman who has dared publish her works. A lot of courage is needed to persevere.

A declaration of the rights of women

Paris, September

"Woman is born free and has the same rights as man." That is how the declaration of the rights of women that has been drafted by Olympe de Gouges begins. It is modelled on the Declaration of human rights. This fearless author has placed her literary talents in the service of the Revolution and of her own sex. Olympe, a playwright who has so far had little success, has written countless political pamphlets in which she shows a strong attachment to the monarchy, even though she is an ardent patriot. In her declaration of the rights of women she argues for the totally revolutionary and highly controversial concept of the equality of the sexes based on both "nature and reason", but Olympe has very few illusions about how her declaration will be greeted by the public. "As I read this strange text," she writes, "I see the clergy, the hypocrites, the prudes and all the rest of the infernal crowd rise up against me."

Olympe de Gouges has left her husband to live freely in Paris.

Women's rights

Olympe de Gouges is launching out into politics. Extolling the emancipation of her sisters, she has just drawn up a *Declaration of the rights of woman and citizeness*. Marchant, the song writer, has penned these ironical verses:
That all my voice admire,
Of late did I rehearse
The Rights of Man upon my lyre
In patriotic verse.
But soon my feeble muse,
Must change perforce her tune:
And now 'tis Women's Rights,
In song I importune.
To make us yield more to Love
And turn our chains to flowers,
And o'er our hearts to wield
A female's sovereign powers;
Ready e'er to charm and light,
Soon as love's flame doth shine:
That is man's idea finite
Of woman's rights condign.
That they serve the Nation well
Our mentors dignified
The compass of their laws will swell,
Their scope extending wide.
Soon in France, I do declare,
A fickle dame we'll see
Swap husband 20 times a year;
With Women's Rights she's free!

14. Paris. The National Assembly approves the decree joining Avignon and the Papal state of the Comtat Venaissin to France.

15. Bouches du Rhône. 4,000 National Guardsmen gather at Tarascon to march on Arles, where a former brigadier has taken over command of the royalist troops (→27).

18. Les Sables d'Olonne. The Baron Robert de Lèzardière is released and celebrates his freedom by giving 400 livres to the poor.

20. Saint Domingue. The colonial assembly of the Cap calls on all mulattoes to unite with whites in fighting rebellious blacks. In exchange, they are promised that the decree of May 15th. will be enforced (→Oct. 19).

23. Paris. An Assembly decree lays down regulations for the registration of land.

24. Paris. The debate on the colonies ends. The deputies drop the progressive articles of the May 15th. decree.

25. Paris. The new penal code is promulgated.

26. Rome. Because he has sworn allegiance to the clergy's civil Constitution, Pope Pius VI dismisses Loménie de Brienne, strips him of his decorations and condemns him for apostasy and perjury.

27. Paris. The Minister of War, Delessart, orders the dismissal of the National Guards of the Bouches du Rhône who had mobilised against Arles.

27. Paris. The Constituent Assembly decrees the emancipation of the Jews of eastern France, despite opposition from the deputies of Alsace, but it does not rule on the status of coloured people in the colonies.→

28. Paris. The deputy Bertrand Barère gets the Assembly to grant funds so that David can finish his "Oath at the Jeu de Paume". A studio is set up for him in the church of the Feuillants convent.

29. Paris. A decree supported by Le Chapelier, which aims to restrict the activities of clubs, is approved.

30. Paris. During its final session, the National Assembly decrees a general amnesty for all those sentenced for rioting since 1788.

Louis XVI solemnly swears allegiance to the Constitution

The new Constitution has made Louis XVI "King of the French".

The Constitution is submitted to the King: the Third Estate is willing to try it, while the two other orders inspect it very closely.

Paris, September 14

No royal throne had been set up for Louis XVI at the Assembly. The King walked forward slowly past the deputies, who were standing bare headed, until he reached an ordinary chair. As he was about to start saying the oath of allegiance to the Constitution, everybody sat down. Slightly bemused, the King sat down as well, although he seemed to have been deeply humiliated by the deputies' lack of respect. Loud cheering and cries of "Long live the King" did not help much. Louis XVI is past caring. At the same time, many a deputy is wondering whether the King is really sincere, if he really accepts the principle of the nation's sovereignty which is embodied by the Constitution. The monarch is said to be privately horrified by the text. Could this chronically hesitant man simply be seeking to gain time until he can find a way of destroying the Revolution once and for all?

Joyful Parisians celebrate the King, the Nation and the Law

Paris, September 20

Night has fallen over the city, but the merrymaking goes on unabated. The wild rejoicing has been going on for the past two days and nobody knows when it will come to an end.

A lantern has been hung from every tree. There is an orchestra playing at every street crossing. People everywhere are singing *Ça Ira* and shouting "Long live the Constitution!". All of Paris has been celebrating the uniting of the King, the Nation and the Law. The whole city is waiting to catch a glimpse of its sovereign and watching for his carriage to appear on the Champs Elysees, where the royal family is to salute the people. They have just left the Opéra, where they attended a performance of the ballet *Psyché*, in which witches are seen to dance with torches. An even worse omen has shaken the Queen: as people cried "Long live the King" a man jumped onto the step of the royal carriage and with an evil grin said "Don't listen to them, long live the Nation!". At this, the Queen and her husband paled and quickly forgot to smile at the crowds.

Proclamation of the Constitution on the Marché des Innocents square.

An ode to freedom by Rouget de Lisle

Strasbourg, September 25

Strasbourg is second only to Paris for the great richness of its musical contribution. Ignace Pleyel has played a major role in the eastern city's fame, and music lovers travel long distances to listen to the orchestra of the cathedral. An ode to freedom for orchestra and choir that had been commissioned from him some time ago was played for the first time today on the Armes square, to mark Constitution day. The words were written by Rouget de Lisle, who has simply adapted a hymn he had written at the start of the Revolution.

Ignace Pleyel, born in Austria, was taught by Haydn and by Cimarosa.

Volney tells of the fall of empires

Paris, September 25

"All is saved if the people have been enlightened," writes Volney in his book *Les Ruines ou Méditations sur les Révolutions des Empires*. He supports new ideas based on the freedom of the individual.

In his work he artfully mixes tales of travels to exotic lands, philosophical considerations, violent polemics and lyrical passages. He tells the story of how the narrator sits one evening at sunset on a fallen stone column, contemplating the ruins of the once prosperous city of Palmyra, and sees the spirit of the tombs.

He is taken up into the sky by the spirit and shown what causes great nations to fall: tormented by the evil of tyrants and priests, entire populations sink into ignorance and poverty.

The Assembly's last session

Paris, September 30

The Constituent Assembly has just held its final session and there is a general feeling of relief. The King closed the session amid the somewhat contradictory shouts of "Long live the King" and "Long live the Nation".

The speaker of the Assembly, Guillaume Thouret, told the deputies: "The Constituent Assembly states that its mission has been completed." Legislators are relieved at having managed to avoid the pitfalls of both an aristocratic counter-revolution and republican "anarchy". They feel they have succeeded in setting up a moderate and lasting system. However, this system is far from being solid, given the unrest that is still rocking the nation. On the one hand there is the religious dispute, which is worsening daily. On the other, the clubs and people's societies are all dreaming of getting their revenge. The Jacobins, who were for a time severely hurt by the bloodshed at the Champ de Mars, are starting to strengthen their position. The legislators' last decree, issued yesterday by the Assembly, condemns collective petitions, but it is unlikely to stop the Jacobins pushing for their demands to be met.

Jews are at last French citizens

Paris, September 27

France's Jewish "nation" has now become one religious group among others. The decree granting French citizenship to the country's Jews has been approved by the Constituent Assembly. However, they must swear allegiance to the Constitution and give up the status of a community. For the past two years, and despite the fact that it was based directly on the Declaration of human rights, the Assembly had been unwilling to approve the measure, fearing anti-Semitic demonstrations. Today Duport stressed that, since equal rights are guaranteed by the Constitution, there can be no discrimination against Jews. Reubell was the only one who tried to protest, but he was not allowed to speak. The decree was approved by a massive majority.

Entrecasteaux searches for lost explorer

The two aptly-named frigates: Rear Admiral d'Entrecasteaux's vessel, the "Recherche" and Captain de Kermadec's ship, the "Espérance".

Brest, September 30

The leader of the expedition that set out from the port of Brest this morning is already worried. His main concern is whether the two heavy scows under his command, the *Recherche* and the *Espérance*, will be able to stand up to the long journey to the South Pacific. The vessels will be difficult to handle in rough seas and among the coral reefs of southern latitudes. The aim of the expedition is to search for any traces of La Pérouse's ill-fated journey of exploration. It is in itself amazing that the search mission was able to be organised during the political upheavals of last summer. Rear Admiral d'Entrecasteaux had only a few weeks to hire the crews for his two ships. Ever since February 15th., the Assembly had not entirely given up hope of doing something to find the La Pérouse expedition. It approved the funds requested by the Navy Minister, Claret de Fleurieu: 400,000 livres for the first year and 300,000 livres for the following years. The ships under d'Entrecasteaux's orders are setting off for a minimum of two to three years.

After the King, it is now the turn of the National Guards of each district to swear allegiance to the Constitution. Clergymen preside over the joyful public ceremonies attended by many onlookers.

The Constituent Assembly's work

The storming of the Bastille on July 14th., 1789 and the night of August 4th. had toppled the Ancien Régime. The "October days" seemed to have broken the King's resistance for good. It was up to the Constituent Assembly to complete the work for which it had been elected and thus give the kingdom the institutions needed to organise it on a new basis. But the Assembly was not unanimous and parties bickered. On the right, the "Blacks" tried to block debate. The left, deploring the fact that the King still had too much power, wanted to do away with his most effective weapons. In the centre, La Fayette, who had become very powerful since October, and above all Mirabeau, who was trying to establish a parliamentary régime, were caught in a cross-fire. A debate got under way and the issue was resolved on November 7th. Mirabeau had proposed choosing ministers from among the Assembly members. The deputies rejected this idea, fearing the influence that Mirabeau might acquire if he became a minister, and this refusal prevented the establishment of trustful relations between the Constituent Assembly and the King's ministers, who remained suspect, as did the monarch himself.

However, in spite of disputes among the parties and some violence that troubled the kingdom's calm here and there, there was a drive for unanimity. The great Festival of the Federation on July 14th., 1790 was a kind of apotheosis of fraternity and reconciliation. Delegations of middle-class militias came from all over France and mingled with the National Guards and the Paris crowd gathered on the Champ de Mars. The delegations swore fidelity to the nation, to the laws and to the King. The latter, having sworn to uphold the Constitution, was acclaimed in an atmosphere of enthusiasm that seemed to wipe out all earlier conflicts But this beautiful feeling of union was only a façade, for France was profoundly divided. Counter-revolutionary sentiment was growing in the south, the west and Alsace. Troubles were breaking out in such major cities as Lyons and Toulouse, while a camp of a few thousand men backed by the Turin émigrés took form at Jales, in the Vivarais, with a view to a coup. The patriots themselves suddenly found themselves divided when the King fled in the middle of the night on June 21st., 1791, trying to get abroad. He had accepted the Constituent Assembly's reforms only because he was forced to do so and his troubled conscience disapproved the religious policy that the Pope had condemned. His abortive flight, his arrest at Varennes, and his return to Paris brought about an entirely new situation that led to clashes. While the majority of the Assembly, worried about things getting out of

hand, invented the fiction of an abduction, the most radical revolutionaries, with the Cordeliers Club in the forefront, demanded the King's ouster. The conflict wound up in a massacre: on July 17th., after proclamation of martial law, the National Guard led by La Fayette fired on a crowd that had gathered to sign a republican petition. The King was restored and exculpated. As if nothing had happened, he swore allegiance to the Constitution on September 14th., 1791, a few days before the Constituent Assembly broke up, making way for a new body, the Legislative Assembly, composed of newcomers. The reason for this was that at Robespierre's request, the deputies had decided not to run again.

The session, which had seen so much and had witnessed a revolution, could point to the accomplishment of a considerable body of work. It had not only torn down everything left over from the Ancien Régime, but had also given France a Constitution, built a new state on foundations that were sometimes fragile and contained the seeds of future conflicts, and above all had proclaimed principles that were to constitute the universal basis of freedom.

Declaration of Rights

The Americans had already drawn up some declarations of rights that were known in France. Numerous lists of grievances had urged called for such a move, and La Fayette had made a proposal along those lines to the Assembly as early as July 1789. The document that was finally approved on August 26th. was in the form of a statement of principles based on natural law, the philosophy of the Enlightenment, and the desire to replace the inequality and fetters of the Ancien Régime with citizens' equality and freedom, to define human rights and the nation's rights. First of all, it proclaimed human and citizens' freedom, individual freedom of opinion, of belief, of thought and of expression, as well as equality before the law, justice and the taxation system. It stated the right to resist oppression and the right to property, which was called "inviolable and sacred". It also set forth national sovereignty, the exercise of authority in the interest of all, and the separation of powers in order to avoid aonfiscation in the interest of one or more such powers.

The Constituent Assembly tried to bring the laws into harmony with its principles. Criminal proceedings were modified so as to protect individual freedom. Freedom of conscience and of religion was confirmed by enfranchising first the Protestants

(on December 24th., 1789) and then the Jews (on January 28th., 1790). On the other hand, it is true that the concern with individualism and freedom led to weakening the defences of the most disadvantaged and of the workers, who were delivered into the employers' complete power by the ban on "forming coalitions". Nor did the election law guarantee equality of rights, since the French were divided into passive and active citizens. The former, those not making a sufficient contribution, which was set at the equivalent of three days' work a year, were excluded from voting. Despite these contradictions, the Declaration of Human and Citizens' Rights gave rise to a new political philosophy, which had vast effects in Europe and was to dominate all later history.

The nation and the King

The Constituent Assembly had shared out powers in such a way that the Assembly exercised close supervision over the King. The hereditary monarch under this constitutional monarchy had great prerogatives from the formal viewpoint, as the nation's first magistrate, but there were many obstacles preventing him from actually enjoying freedom of decision. He had a substantial civil list, was head of the executive branch of government and appointed ministers. He was responsible for diplomacy, and was also commander in chief of the military services. He could even use his veto right to delay the Assembly's legislative measures for the duration of two legislatures. In May 1790, there had been a great debate between Mirabeau and Barnave on the issue of the right to make peace and war and it ended with a compromise. It led to recognition of the nation's right, as well as of the King's right to take initiatives in this domain: war was to be declared by an Assembly decree voted on the basis of a formal proposal from the King, who would also have exclusive responsibility for the kingdom's internal security.

The provisions on organising powers left little freedom for the ministers to adopt initiatives. They were responsible to the Assembly and could be hauled into the High Court of Justice at any time. They were chosen from outside the Assembly and were at its mercy, and they had no way of putting pressure on it. But the Assembly could not be dissolved. It already enjoyed the power of initiating laws and regulations, and encroached on the executive branch's responsibilities by setting up committees with extensive powers. It had the real power in France and one could predict that there would be conflicts of jurisdiction and that the King, already mistrusted, would have to give way. If he resisted, he would risk destroying his credibility. The ministers, who were also mistrusted by the monarchy, were all the more unable to act effectively in that the kingdom's administrative reorganisation deprived them of all resources of authority.

The kingdom's new organisation

The Constituent Assembly actually reshaped France on the basis of a double principle: decentralisation and election. The task of imposing uniformity on the country, already undertaken under the Ancien Régime, was completed. The kingdom was divided into 83 departments, which in turn were divided into districts, and the latter into cantons. A department was administered by a general council consisting of members elected by the department's electoral assembly from among second-degree voters, making a contribution equal to ten days' work a year. The general council named a "directory" with executive powers. The King was represented by a trustee-general prosecutor elected for four years. Hence the King's authority could be exercised in the departments, and he was obeyed to a large extent, though there was resistance here and there. District organisation was modelled on departmental organisation. The communes, which replaced the former parishes, also had their general council, mayor and public prosecutor representing the King, as well as the taxpayers. These municipalities often resisted the authority of the district or of the department, but above all, in rural areas marked by extensive illiteracy, it was often difficult to recruit people with the skills needed for training them.

Judicial organisation was very similar to that of the administration. On the civil side, there was one justice of the peace for each canton and one court for each district. On the criminal side, a municipal court of justice constituted the "first degree", while each canton had a correctional court and the departments had a criminal court. Thus careful steps were taken to keep the parliaments under the Ancien Régime from reconstituting themselves. There was general satisfaction with the establishment of justices of the peace, while corruption was done away with, judicial administration was made subject to the elective principle and the judges were made more independent.

Finances and national property

The lists of grievances had demanded a reformed taxation system. But it was not easy to reform taxes and the collection system, draw up a land register, and in the meantime pay the "rente" incomes and reimburse the people who had lost offices. This was particularly difficult since the taxpayers often proved reluctant, and borrowings were hard to place. The Constituent Assembly undertook a complete recasting of the taxation system. The land tax remained the heaviest tax, but all owners without exception were made subject to it. A personal and securities contribution was instituted, as was a "patente" tax on industrial and commercial income. The new taxes and the patriotic contribution established as early as 1789 did not bring in as much money as anticipated, while the funds previously coming from the financiers in the form of advances dried up together with the disappearance of the "venal charges" that had been abolished.

To overcome such difficulties, the Constituent Assembly came up with a measure that had the advantage of being popular and of supplying resources viewed as almost unlimited: nationalisation of the clergy's property. This step had to be justified before it was carried out. The property was not owned by the church, which only had use of it. Moreover, there were precedents. Had the King himself not seized the goods of the abolished congregations? Despite opposition from certain clergymen and the danger that such a measure might represent for all other types of property, which caused some alarm, the Assembly approved a law putting ecclesiastical property at the nation's disposal (November 2nd., 1789). The sale of such property was associated with the issue of assignats (December 10th., 1789), which were initially simply an acknowledgement of debts offered to state creditors enabling them to buy national goods. Assignats then became real paper money. The Constituent Assembly issued a total of 1.3 billion livres worth. This, however, led to rapid depreciation.

The sale of national property had substantial consequences on the distribution of property. The Revolution had freed land by doing away with feudalism. The sale of the clergy's property might have offered an opportunity for increasing the number of landowners among the poor peasantry. But the sale terms were unfavourable to people lacking considerable capital. The buyers were recruited primarily from among the middle class, the nobles and rich farmers. The proletarians, journeymen and small farmers were excluded from the advantages of redistribution. In their disappointment, they began to turn away from the Revolution that had not given them anything.

The sale of church property, which made it necessary to turn the clergy into a group paid by the state, led the Assembly almost in spite of itself to remodel the French clergy and give it a new constitution. The clergymen, who had given tokens of good faith to the Third Estate and the Revolution by waiving their tithes and "casual rights" on August 4th., 1789, were not rewarded for their zeal. With the exception of the educational and charitable houses, the orders and congregations were abolished at the same time as monastic vows were suppressed. But the Constituent Assembly felt a need to go farther and to carry out a thorough reorganisation. An Ecclesiastical Committee was set up, with members favouring reform and it drew up the clergy's Civil Constitution. The principles it followed satisfied almost everybody: Gallicans, Jansenists and philosophers. The principles were a return to the primitive church, independence of the Papacy, and association of the clergy with the state's life. Discussion of the clergy's Civil Constitution began in the Assembly on May 29th., 1790, and it was approved on July 12th.

First of all, the document transformed the country's ecclesiastical map. To adapt it to the new administrative districts, it was decided that there would be one bishop for each department, entailing the disappearance of many dioceses and of parishes that were too small. The greatest difficulties stemmed from the question of appointing bishops and parish priests. It was decided that, as happened in the primitive church, they would be elected by the faithful, more exactly by the department's electoral assembly for prelates and of the district for the parish priests. Such assemblies could contain a variable number of non-Catholics. The Metropolitans (there were ten of them) were to confirm the election of the bishops, who were to give the parish priests their canonical investment. In addition, the Constituent Assembly granted the democratically elected members of the clergy, like other civil servants, to swear fidelity to the nation, the King and the Constitution. They received remuneration of 12,000 francs a year for a small-city bishop, with up to 50,000 francs in Paris. The parish priests received 6,000 francs in Paris, and 1,200 in the countryside. Teaching and assistance, which had previously been the specific tasks performed by the clergy, became public services.

The Civil Constitution was approved by Louis XVI on August 24th., 1790. Since the Pope refused to approve, many priests began to denounce that constitution as heretical. The King unwillingly approved the decree on December 26th. At the start of 1791, a good half of the clergy had sworn their oaths, and it was decided that the "non-juring" priests would be dismissed. So two churches came into being and tension grew. The Constituent Assembly proclaimed in vain that it did not want to change doctrine or the faith. Anger grew among members of the clergy and the faithful, who were led to reject the Revolution as a whole. When the Pope condemned the clergy's Constitution in April 1791, and all revolutionary principles along with it, the schism was complete. The measures adopted by the Constituent Assembly to try to restore calm and make earlier measures more flexible could not quiet resentment. Religious war soon broke out.

Summing up

The Constituent Assembly had carried out a considerable task. Even though its work was often positive, it remained fragile and sometimes represented a threat to the future. It had offered the Declaration of Human Rights, which remains its greatest claim to glory, releasing citizens from various prohibitions affecting them, and freeing the economy and individual initiatives. But was the drive to reform the church not a mistake? In any case, it meant running the risk of dividing France and triggering civil war. Even if the kingdom's administrative organisation had made it possible to combat the excessive diversity of the former France and often proved effective, the fragile political balance that had been achieved was already compromised in 1791. The King's flight had shown the weak point. The constitutional monarchy had stepped off on the wrong foot because of mutual lack of trust. Moreover, the vast hopes that were born in 1789 had not become a reality. The passive citizens excluded from voting felt unwanted, while democratic ideas were spreading in the clubs, the "popular societies", and even in the Assembly, where Robespierre demanded universal suffrage. Such journalists as Marat kept agitation going, while François Robert's "Mercure National" was already calling itself republican. The structure started to crack. Even though the leaders of the Constituent Assembly thought the Revolution had already gone too far, the democratic movement expanded. Furthermore, the "Constituents" would no longer be present in the next Assembly to see to the future of their work, as Robespierre had pushed them into declaring themselves ineligible for re-election. Would the Legislative Assembly that was to succeed the Constituent Assembly and consist of new people, younger and more progressive, have its heart set on preserving a constitution that already seemed outdated in many respects?

Is the French Revolution over?

Paris, October 1

With a feeling of a job well done, the members of the Constituent Assembly wound up their work yesterday; but have they really succeeded in consolidating what was achieved by the Revolution? Does the fact that France now has a Constitution mean that political unrest will come to an end? The few who believe this have conveniently forgotten all about the rage of the non-juring priests in the west of the country. Neither are they aware of the fact that, on the very evening they were swearing allegiance to the Constitution, the King was writing to foreign leaders saying that he did not feel bound by the text. The Revolution is still being threatened from nearly every side. To begin with, financial problems are getting more acute every day. The number of assignats in circulation has grown a lot, starting an inflationary spiral which could easily be halted if anybody took the trouble to do so. Then there is the political unrest focused around the King, the non-juring priests and counter-revolutionary noblemen. Strong, but not united, pressure from the émigrés and European sovereigns could lead to a war that would be fatal to revolutionary France. Last, but not least, the clubs' one-upmanship, in particular by the Jacobins, is a threat to the cohesion of the revolutionary ranks. These supporters of a republic will never be happy with a constitutional monarchy. The situation remains precarious.

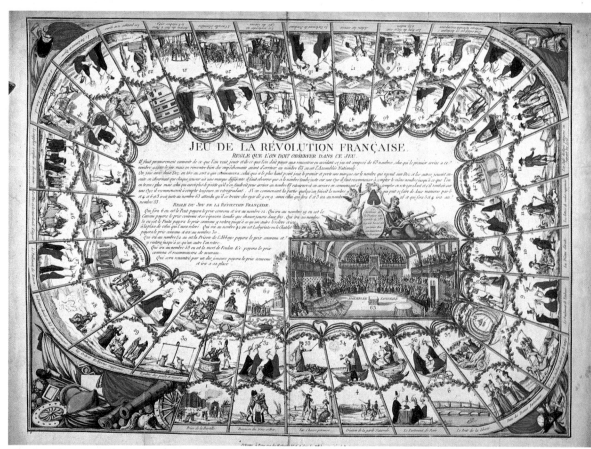

The Revolution game starts with the fall of the Bastille and ends with the King's acceptance of the Constitution.

Jalès camp rebuilt

Jalès, October

Royalists can sometimes be very stubborn. They have just rebuilt the camp at Jalès, which had been broken up once already. The mountainous region of the Vivarais is ideally suited to serve as a base for resistance groups.

The royalists have not given up all hope of setting up a centre for opposition to the Assembly on French soil, similar to what the noble émigrés have created abroad at Coblentz.

Revolutionary waves reach Irish shores

Belfast, October 14

The French Revolution has won quite a few supporters in Ireland. Their interest is based on both the religious issue and that of the sharing of power.

In Ireland it is the Catholics who are denied the right to vote, or to be elected, by the English. The people of Ireland also feel they are not properly represented at the parliament in London. Why not unite? That is precisely what has been suggested by a fiery young Protestant lawyer, Theobald Wolf Tone, who is active in politics. He has just set up in Belfast the first united Irish club: the Belfast Society of United Irishmen. It is to call for the emancipation of Catholics and parliamentary reform.

But what is really at state in the Irish political debate is the independence issue. Many people there feel that an independent republic is the only real alternative to continued and total submission to English rule (→ Nov. 6).

240

King makes inaugural speech to new Assembly

Louis XVI tells the Third Estate he backs the Constitution, while telling the clergy he will destroy it.

Paris, October 7

Could the new deputies be more royalist than the King himself? Louis XVI was certainly happy that the new Assembly dropped its decree of October 5th. which ruled that there would be no throne in the chamber, that the term "Majesty" would no longer be used, and that deputies could sit down and put their hats back on as soon as the King had entered.

The deputies felt that they should show some respect to their sovereign. "Sire, we need to be loved by you," the moderate speaker of the Assembly, Pastoret, told the King on behalf of his colleagues. In his inaugural speech, Louis XVI told the assembled deputies that it was time to get to work. The Revolution is over, he said. Now that the country had a Constitution it needed legislation. The King then outlined the major areas where action was needed: finance, justice, education, trade and industry and aid to the poor. He sought to show firmness on two issues. "I will let the army know that I have resolved that order and discipline must be restored," he stressed, adding, "I have taken appropriate steps to ensure that harmony and good relations are maintained with foreign powers so that we are guaranteed peace." These royal statements were greeted with cheering.

The Dauphin and human rights.

A love-lorn knight travels to Prussia

Paris, October

The Chevalier de Boufflers has set off for Prussia. This man of the court, happy and carefree, has now left a France he no longer recognises, after having tried to play a role at the Assembly following his election to the Estates General; but the real reason for his departure is that the knight misses his beloved mistress. Eléonore de Sabran left some time ago to stay as a guest of Prince Henry of Prussia. Boufflers was most unhappy without her. They have known each other for ten years, although his friends were amazed that he had remained faithful to her; but Eléonore is not like other women. She was dubbed "the country flower" because of her simplicity and openness which were unusual for a courtier.

Who are the new deputies?

The new Assembly has been formed. The members of the Constituent Assembly were not allowed to be reelected, so it is an entirely new group of men which makes up the Legislative Assembly.

Most of them are unknown quantities, young, without great political experience, but all are in favour of the principles of 1789. On the right wing, there are no more counter-revolutionary aristocrats. Instead, there are 160 constitutional royalists close to the Feuillants and grouped around Jaucourt and Théodore de Lameth. In the centre, there is a floating group of approximately 250 independents.

It includes such people as Pastoret and Lacuée. This group has the capacity to make or break the majority. However, it is closer to the right wing than the left. The left wing, led among others by Brissot, groups over 300 pro-Jacobin deputies.

Most of them are provincial lawyers or department administrators, but the left is, in fact, led by a small faction of men of letters. As for the extreme left, it groups the Jacobins, notably Chabot, Cambon and Hérault de Séchelles. These fiery supporters of a republic exert their considerable influence by using the press, rather than at the Assembly itself.

La Fayette wants to be mayor of Paris

Paris, October 8

The "hero of the Old and the New Worlds" is resigning from his post as commander of the National Guard. La Fayette today came to see Bailly, who is himself resigning as mayor of Paris, to tell him of his decision. Bailly was practically weeping when he heard the news. As a farewell gift, the city offered La Fayette a gold-hilted sword with an inscription on it. Can La Fayette, who is still only 34, really be thinking about quitting the political scene? Not really, since he plans to run in elections to choose a new Paris mayor, despite the fact his popularity suffered badly from the Champ de Mars massacre.

The Chevalier de Boufflers.

An alarming parliamentary report on the situation in Vendée

Paris, October 9

The slightest incident would be enough to set off a civil war. That was the alarming thrust of the report made by Armand Gensonné when he returned from Vendée, where he had been sent to investigate the unrest, along with the legal expert Jean Antoine Gauvin, also known as Gallois. Throughout their long mission they discussed the situation with a wide variety of people, but they have not brought back any concrete plans on how to deal with the crisis. Gensonné explained to his fellow deputies how the people of Vendée remain closely attached to traditional religion. He believes that the root of the trouble is the decree on the obligatory oath of allegiance to the clergy's civil Constitution. Prior to that, the Revolution had not been badly greeted in Vendée. Gensonné added that most of the peasants and non-juring priests he had spoken to had seemed sincere in their beliefs. However, he said the non-juring bishop and his priests had led an intense anti-oath propaganda campaign which had fuelled the unrest. The question now is whether the authorities should opt for tolerance or for a hard-line approach.

The Girondin Armand Gensonné.

The Queen secretly meets Barnave

Paris, October 5

Barnave finally had a secret meeting this evening with Marie Antoinette at the Tuileries palace. The meeting had been planned for a long time, but was not held due to the risks it involved.

Only three days ago Barnave was forced to turn back at the last moment after he saw somebody he knew near the Queen's apartments. It was Marie Antoinette herself who started the secret correspondence that has been going on ever since last July between the Queen, Antoine Barnave and his friends Adrien Duport and Alexandre de Lameth.

However, the Queen is only pretending to listen to their advice, as she tells them that she is being

Antoine Barnave, the recipient of Marie Antoinette's coded letters.

quite sincere. Instead, she is only seeking to gain time while she is secretly negotiating with her brother. In order to keep her correspondence secret, Marie Antoinette has been using an extremely simple code. She uses numbers instead of letters: 2 (or B) means Barnave; 1-12 (AL) stands for Alexandre de Lameth; 4-16 (DP) designates Duport, etc.

It is the Comte de Jarjayes — codename 10 — who acts as the Queen's go-between and "mailbox". He is a friend of the Queen and married to one of her ladies in waiting. It is usually Jarjayes who writes the letters that Marie Antoinette dictates, so that the Queen's handwriting will not be recognised.

Legislative Assembly

16. Marseilles. Violent clashes break out between soldiers and citizens after the arrest of four officers of the Ernest Swiss regiment, who had insulted local patriots. The town council demands the regiment's departure from the port city.

17. Avignon. Sixty one people are executed as a reprisal for the murder by women yesterday of the patriot secretary of the commune, Lescuyer. →

19. Saint Domingue. An alliance is signed between the leaders of the mulatto revolt and the royalist commanders who protect the white planters of western regions. The latter have agreed to the mulattoes' demands: disbanding of the colonial assembly and the rehabilitation of Vincent Ogé (→24).

20. Paris. At the Assembly, Jean Pierre Brissot openly supports a war during a debate on émigrés (→25).

21. Paris. Symptomatic of the moral crisis of the revolutionary movement, Camille Desmoulins makes a disillusioned and pessimistic speech about the Revolution at the Jacobins.

22. Paris. The Marquis de Sade organises a performance of a drama, *Le Comte Oxtiern ou les Effets du Libertinage* at the Théâtre Molière.

24. Saint Domingue. Whites and mulattoes fraternise in the streets of Port au Prince after the signing of the treaty of October 19th.

25. Limoges. Named captain of the second battalion of the national volunteers, Jean Baptiste Jourdan sets off to join the army in the north of France.

25. Paris. The deputy from the Gironde, Pierre Victurien Vergniaud, also calls for firm measures against emigration and foreign powers.

31. Paris. A Legislative Assembly decree requests that Monsieur, the King's brother, return to France within two months, failing which he will be stripped of any right of becoming regent. →

31. Paris. First perfomance at the Théâtre Molière of an anonymous play, *Le Retour du Père Gérard à sa Femme.*

31. Paris. The Comte de Montmorin resigns from his post as foreign minister.

Civil war at Avignon

Murder of the patriot Lescuyer on October 16th. at the Cordeliers church.

Avignon, October 17

This morning the bodies of the 61 victims of the night's massacre were found covered in quicklime in a cell at the Glacière prison. The terrible mass murder was committed by the most extreme patriots of Avignon to avenge the killing of one of their number.

Yesterday posters had appeared on every wall of the former Papal city. They were a "notice to good patriots", both calling on the people to rise up, and violently attacking the anti-religious policies and corruption of the Jacobin administrators of Avignon.

Alarm bells were rung at the Cordeliers church, where a large crowd had gathered. Attacked as he was walking in the street, the commune's secretary, Lescuyer, was taken to the church, where he was killed by a group of enraged women. His friends were quick to

Jourdan "beheader".

seek revenge. Last night dozens of prisoners, who had been arrested last August when the patriots took control of Avignon, were dragged from their cells and systematically beaten to death.

"Justice to the law!" and the massacre of the Glacière prisoners begins.

Père Gérard is rewarded by the Jacobins

Paris, October 23

Collot d'Herbois, the secretary of the Jacobins, has had a brilliant idea: use the celebrity of Michel Gérard, the well-known peasant from Brittany, to distribute a popular version of the Constitution throughout the provinces so that the people continue to support it. His *Almanach du Père Gérard* has just been given a prize by the Jacobins Club. Collot d'Herbois had a great deal of trouble convincing the suspicious peasant, who has gone back to his land, to take part in the scheme, but how could Gérard refuse to help again the cause to which he has contributed so much? Isn't the best way to preserve the achievements of the Revolution to give new hope to the peasants?

Engravings from the Almanach ...   *... show Père Gérard's role.*

Monsieur is ordered to return to France

Paris, October 31

The Legislative Assembly has had just about enough of the émigrés' counter-revolutionary activities — particularly the activities of Monsieur. The Assembly has just approved a decree that should put an end to the endless provocations of the King's brother. The Prince has been ordered to come back to France within a maximum of two months, failing which he will lose all rights to the throne. The way his brothers have been behaving has made the King's relations with the deputies even more difficult. They have been doing their best to convince the Emperor of Austria to lead an anti-France coalition, as well as having officially protested against the Constitution. Louis XVI has decided at least to appear to be going along with the Constitution. He has therefore written to the Comte de Provence to beg him to return to Paris: "The Revolution is over, your true place is to be at my side. Your interests, your feelings tell you to return to your place.

I ask you to do so, and if necessary I order you to.": but will the Prince listen to a King whom he considers a prisoner and whose place he is prepared to take even if this is a violation of all the Assembly's decrees? (→ Dec. 6).

An aristocratic émigrée makes a face when the Revolution is discussed.

The Queen's best friend returns to court

Aix la Chapelle, October 16

Before setting off to return to Paris, the Princesse de Lamballe wrote her last will and testament. She had fled from the Revolution and has now bravely decided to go back. It was Barnave who managed to convince the Queen's former favourite to set an example for the émigrés by returning to her place at court. It should also reassure the people. Madame de Lamballe is not too optimistic. She knows that her return will not save the monarchy, but, since she was Marie Antoinette's closest friend when her glory was at its peak, she has chosen to help the Queen in her misfortune. Their close friendship had sparked off a lot off ugly rumours. It was in 1774 that Marie Thérèse de Savoie, Princesse de Lamballe, became the favourite of the young Queen, who was bored and wanted a "kindred spirit". Their relationship was so close that it fuelled gossip. This did

The Princesse de Lamballe.

not stop the Queen making her superintendent of her Household. She was later replaced by Mme. de Polignac.

Sade, Justine or the misfortunes of virtue

Paris, October

Virtue is punished, while vice is triumphant: that is the theme that the Marquis de Sade has dared to use for his first published work of fiction, "Justine or the Misfortunes of Virtue". Its prudish heroine is the victim of a whole series of outrageous attacks, becoming the plaything of depraved men and finding herself in the most demeaning situations. The author acknowledges that the story is a departure from the usual work of fiction, as the novelists of today tend to prefer less shocking subjects. A scandal erupted as soon as the book appeared, although the critics admit that its author is an exceptionally gifted writer. It was during the time he spent in a cell at the Bastille that the Marquis wrote the amazing tale. It had started out as a short story, but was gradually turned into a novel. His work had hardly been published when Sade rejected it, telling his friends to throw it into the fire without reading it. He said that he had only written the immoral novel, which "stinks of the devil", to please his editor and because he urgently needed money. However, the care he took writing it proves this is not so.

Strange poem with two interpretations

A curious poem entitled *A two-faced Civic Oath* is now cirulating clandestinely in Paris. Read from left to right, it appears to be a straightforward declaration of Republicanism. However, when it is read from top to bottom, it conveys an entirely different meaning. Anyone found in possession of this strange poem risks being sent to jail.

Loyalty I'll no more give
To those who rule us now
For in my heart I love
Both King and Queen. I vow
God's blessing alight on
The noble families
The Lord send his blight on
The elected Deputies

To those who ruled us once
I'll ever faithful be
"The new laws": I renounce
They're no good as I can see.
All the new democrats
Can take themselves to hell.
The old aristocrats
Are guardians of all that's well.

4. Caen. The Marquis d'Hericy and 84 other noblemen involved in a royalist plot are arrested. This marks the start of the "case of the 84". (→11).

5. Lille. Troops intervene at Quesnoy, where local people have stopped a convoy that was transporting grain.

6. India. The Chandernagore colony promulgates its own constitution despite orders issued by the Constituent Assembly. Natives are not allowed to exercise any of their civil rights.

6. Ireland. The patriots of Ireland set up the Dublin Society of United Irishmen.

6. Paris. A report to the Legislative Assembly from the authorities of the Mayenne department warns that the department is in a pre-rebellion situation.

7. Paris. Under the terms of a new contract signed with Panckoucke, the Academician La Harpe becomes chief editor of the *Mercure Français*.

8. Saint Etienne. The industrialist Jacques Sauvade patents a machine with two rolling mills that can mass produce hardware.

9. Paris. Taking advantage of his recent successes, Collot d'Herbois has his play, *Le Procès de Socrate ou le Régime des Anciens Temps*, shown at Monsieur's theatre.

9. Paris. The Legislative Assembly calls on émigrés living abroad to return to France before January 1st. 1792 (→11).

11. Paris. Louis XVI vetoes the Assembly's decrees on the émigrés.→

11. Paris. The deputy Cambon proposes to the Legislative Assembly that the nation's High Court should meet to judge the noblemen of Caen (→Jan. 19, 92).

12. Melun. Rioters loot the local wheat market.

24. Austria. Théroigne de Méricourt is freed. She had been held for many months at the Kupfstein fort.

25. Paris. The Assembly sets up a Watch Committee to gather information about plots against the Constitution.

28. Paris. After returning from a trip to Arras, Robespierre is elected president of the Jacobins Club (→Dec. 14, 92).

Trial of strength starts between Louis XVI and the Assembly

The two forms of royal veto.

Faced with Mr. Veto, the peoples' only option is to resort to force.

Paris, November 11

This time, they have gone too far! The King had forced himself to swear an oath of allegiance to the Constitution that meant nothing to him, but he absolutely refuses to place his signature on a text which he does not approve. Therefore, he has just vetoed the decrees of October 31st. and November 9th. that ordered the émigrés, and specially his own brother, to come back to France. He refuses to sanction laws which, once they have been voted on by the Legislative Assembly, can only come into force when they have been signed by the King, as is stipulated by the Constitution. The King has therefore chosen to make use of the few powers he still retains. The monarch's opposition to the Revolution, which has now become constitutional, is now plain to see. Behind the King's usual lack of resolve, there is a stubbornness that could well be a surprise to many of his opponents (→Dec. 19).

Non-juring priests must take the oath

Paris, November 29

The hunt is on for non-juring priests. Those who stubbornly continue to refuse to swear allegiance to the civil Constitution, as is now required of all who receive an income or a pension from the state, will no longer get the money they were entitled to until today. They will also risk being chased away from their own churches and could even be placed under house arrest. Under the new legislation, they cannot buy or rent a place where they can practise their religion. Life is likely to become very difficult for non-juring priests.

"Vanitas vanitatis." All is vanity in this poor, Godforsaken world.

Historical painting is complex work

Paris, November

A lot of preparatory work is needed for an historical painting. After having determined the main outline of the composition of his *Jeu de Paume*, David is now busy filling the sketchbook that never leaves his side with all kinds of drawings.

He has just written a letter to the Abbot Grégoire asking for a meeting with him. David has great respect for the classical tradition. He began by sketching some naked human figures before clothing them with carefully drawn outfits. Bit by bit, his sketchbooks were filled with drawings of ... Spartan warriors! These are to serve as models for the deputies who will people his finished work. Later on, David will transpose his final sketches onto the canvas. To do this, he resorts to a much used method of cross-ruling the sketches so that they can be copied on a far larger scale. Then all that will remain to be done will be to paint the composition colour by colour, from the darkest shade to the lightest.

A song about the emigrants

People suspected of wishing to emigrate can now face a death sentence. Those who are abroad have until January 1 to return. This has inspired a song:
Dear Friends, must our France
Hold fast from prudence
To people discontent?
No! Show them the door.
Hell curse evermore
Each perfid emigrant.
If arouse our laws new

A rebellious crew
Of Frenchmen discontent,
Let them change their address
And let Heaven bless
Each perfid emigrant.

In far distant shore
Their wailings outpour,
These people discontent!
But these my regrets:
The now lost assets
Of each perfid emigrant.

Pilgrims claim they see the Virgin Mary

Maine et Loire, November

It was a total waste of time tearing the chapel down. The department's authorities had ordered the chapel at Saint Laurent de la Plaine to be destroyed in a bid to put an end to the large religious gatherings that were being held there, but now they have to cope with a much more unexpected and delicate problem. The Virgin Mary in person, carrying Her child and with a crown of stars around Her head, has been appearing every day in the branches of an oak tree growing near the ruins of the chapel; so now twice as many people are coming to Saint Laurent to see the wonderful sight.

Each day, large groups of peasants gather under the miraculous tree for lengthy prayer meetings. Whether or not they actually see the Virgin, the pilgrims all go home with renewed faith and even more hostility to the Revolution. The local authorities have decided to take some drastic action: all future gatherings are to be banned and the tree will be cut down.

Jérôme Pétion elected Paris' mayor

Paris, November 14

A totally unexpected event has just rocked Paris: La Fayette has been beaten in the municipal elections! He was beaten by the Jacobin Pétion, who scored 63 per cent of the vote. Many people had been certain that the election would be easily won by the former commander of the National Guard. He was being supported by the capital's former mayor, Bailly, who hoped that La Fayette would ensure the continuation of bourgeois rule. La Fayette's lack of popularity among the lower classes is not enough to explain his big defeat. According to the latest rumours, the Queen herself had advised her friends to vote against La Fayette, whom she deeply hates, but that was not in itself sufficient to change the will of the majority. In fact, only a tenth of the voters actually cast their ballots, nost of these being the democrats. In the popular district of Saint Antoine, 90 per cent of the votes went to Pétion. The revenge of the losers of the Champ de Mars has already begun.

Jérôme Pétion de Villeneuve.

"Beware of mistakes!" says Bailly (2) to Pétion (1) before La Fayette (3).

"Le Solide" makes record ocean crossing

Macao, November 21

Captain Marchand has made a new record: the crossing of the Pacific Ocean from north to south in an amazing 60 days. His ship, *Le Solide*, was built by the Baux firm in Marseilles. It has just sailed non-stop from Alaska to southern China. Speed was necessary due to the strong competition. Captain Marchand wanted to get to Macao before the Spaniards or the English did so that he could sell his cargo for a better price. He carried some bcautiful otter pelts, as well as seal skins, and blue fox furs which Indians had traded for some weapons made at Saint Etienne.

This autumn's fashions call for high waists and busts ...

... while the revolutionary colours are always in fashion.

The wild dreams of a visionary architect

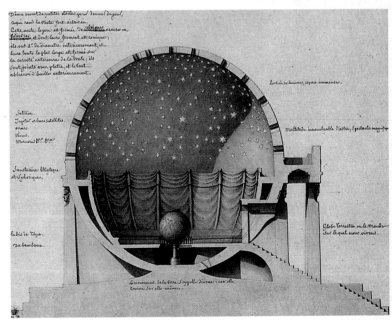

The temple of the Earth, also dedicated to Wisdom, is shaped like the world and shows a vaulted ceiling sprinkled with stars.

Paris, November

Jean Jacques Lequeu believes that architecture must also be open to symbolic forms. His latest plan involves a temple of the Earth with a vaulted ceiling that looks like the night sky full of stars. Lequeu's projects are, however, not particularly popular and his ambitious blueprints seldom become reality.

2. Paris. After having deserted the Jacobins Club for six months, Hérault de Séchelles rejoins the Society of the Friends of the Constitution.

5. Paris. The Théâtre Molière shows a performance of the *Suisse de Châteauvieux,* a play written by Louis François Archambault Dorvigny.

6. Paris. After failing to be elected to the Assembly, Danton is elected deputy public prosecutor of the commune.

6. Perpignan. Royalist officers mutiny, but they fail in their attempt to get the soldiers to support them.

7. Paris. The King names the Comte Louis de Narbonne as the new Minister of War. He is to replace Duportail.

8. Cluny. The town council is upset about damage done to the abbey and decides to keep it under permanent surveillance.

12. Paris. Camille Desmoulins stops publication of the *Révolutions de France et de Brabant.*

14. Paris. Louis XVI announces to the Legislative Assembly that he is ordering the Archbishop-Elector of Trier to disperse all gatherings of émigrés before January 15, 1792.→

15. Paris. Disgusted by the warlike policy backed by the Assembly, Marat puts an end to *L'Ami du Peuple.*

19. Paris. The King refuses to approve the decree of November 29th. on the nonjuring priests.→

21. Paris. Claude Chappe, who has settled in the capital, sets up his optical telegraph system at the Etoile city barrier.

21. Paris. The Assembly learns that the Emperor Leopold II has ordered his troops to stop French soldiers entering the Trier electorate.

21. Paris. The author Arnaud Berquin, or the "children's friend", dies of "putrid fever".

29. Paris. The Assembly approves credits of 20 million francs for war expenses.→

31. Paris. The Legislative Assembly decides to grant an amnesty to the soldiers of Châteauvieux. The move disregards the special legal status of the Swiss regiments serving France.

Must there really be a war?

ROBESPIERRE: Absolutely not.

Paris, December 12

Robespierre and his followers want to avoid a conflict at all costs. They firmly believe that a war would endanger the Revolution's success. If there is a victory, the King will once again have an obedient army and will recover his prestige and his power. If there is a defeat, it will spell the end for revolutionary aspirations and the monarchy would be restored anyway. Robespierre is convinced that it would be ridiculous to try to attack the European sovereigns while the war against the enemies of the Revolution at home is not over. Not being a deputy, the former lawyer from Arras can only express his views from the podium of his club. That is where those who oppose him within his own camp, who are grouped around Brissot, argue against him. The Jacobins of Paris are split over the war issue. But most of the affiliated clubs and provincial societies are backing Robespierre's pacifist theories.

LOUIS XVI: Yes, maybe.

Paris, December 14

The King is not afraid of war. But he is not looking forward to one. On one hand, he is trying to convince Frenchmen that he is a sincere constitutional monarch, committed to the defence of the realm. On November 12th., he had said that he disagreed with the émigré nobles. On the other hand, he is trying to gain time, hoping for an intervention by the European powers to restore his sovereignty. The foreign powers don't know what to make of all this. Louis XVI wrote to the sovereigns of Prussia, Sweden and of Russia to ask them to launch a military operation against France. That is a strange way for a King who claims to be a patriot to behave. He finally told the Assembly today that he has asked the Prince-Elector of Trèves to get rid of the émigrés who had sought refuge on his territory by January 15th. If he refuses, he will be "treated as an enemy." Could this threat just be a ploy?

BRISSOT: Yes, absolutely.

Paris, December 18

The Jacobin Brissot is a man who doesn't mince his words. "We need great betrayals. War is actually in the nation's advantage," he proclaimed today from the podium of the Legislative Assembly. Brissot and his backers strongly favour a conflict against the major European powers. They are afraid that the King will gradually win back the confidence of his people if he is allowed to calmly play the role of constitutional monarch. Nothing would be better than a good and bloody war to give renewed vigour to Frenchmen's patriotic ardour. A war would also provide a timely and useful opportunity to take the Revolution beyond the borders of France. Isnard is by far the loudest advocate of the crusade that Brissot is carefully trying to organize. The warmongers believe that war and freedom can live side by side. They have so far succeeded in getting the majority of the Jacobin deputies to support their cause.

New actor appears on the political scene: the sansculottist

A sanscullotist wields a sabre ...

"They are just sans-culottes," or men without breeches, the aristocrats sneer at the extreme republicans. "Yes, we are the sans-culottes," the patriots retort proudly. Gone are the golden breeches and the silk stockings. No more perfume or fancy clothes. The friends of the Revolution now wear simple breeches held up by braces, a short jacket known as the carmagnole, a scarf around the neck, a Phrygian, or liberty, cap and they always carry a long pike. Their clothes have become symbolic of the new order. Their simplicity echoes the principle of equality. The sansculottist does not use the term "Monsieur", but that of "citizen". The traditional formal forms of polite address are abandoned and the novel habit spreads quickly among the people. The sansculottists are basically people of the street, who are becoming aware of their power. The sansculottists are notably demanding autonomy for all of Paris' 48 sectors.

... her husband carries a gun.

Counter-revolutionary style, but the cockade is still worn.

The King again resorts to using his veto

Paris, December 19

The Assembly greeted the news of the royal veto of the decrees of November 29th. with an icy silence. The parliamentary session was interrupted when a letter from the Keeper of the Seals was delivered to the speaker. The letter stated that the King was sanctioning several less important measures; but the veto of the decree on the non-juring priests was carefully hidden among all the rest.

This ploy did not succeed in masking from the deputies the full importance of the King's move. Particularly sensitive to religious issues, the King has attempted to use this matter to improve the balance of power between himself and the Assembly. Those who have advised the monarch to oppose the decree include the usual defenders of the non-juring priests, such as the extremely pious Madame Elisa-

"Capet the elder flies into yet another fit of fury."

beth. Therefore, in the name of the principles of 1789, the members of the Paris departmental authority begged Louis XVI not to give his approval to this decree.

Assembly approves new war credits

Paris, December 29

Twenty million francs have been earmarked to pay for war preparations. Narbonne has won. The new War Minister, who took over from Duportail on December 7th., is a warmonger. Since that date, he has been putting pressure on the Assembly. Today the deputies finally accepted his arguments, supported by Hérault de Séchelles. The latter became a Jacobin again after December 2nd. As for Brissot, he is torn between being happy to have what he has been asking for over the past two months and fearful of seeing the moderate Constitutional Party take over "his" war.

A future leader of black rebels

Saint Domingue, December 22

As a token of peace, the black rebels have handed over to the authorities the white prisoners they had been holding hostage. They were escorted to the Cap by the doctor of Biassou's army, Toussaint Bréda, a black man who had joined the revolt in November. When he got back from the Cap after the failure of the talks he had held on behalf of the leaders of the revolt, Toussaint decided to set up an elite cavalry corps. He believes that the fight for the freedom of the blacks can only be won by force.

Monsieur sneers at the Assembly

Coblentz, December 6

Monsieur is convinced that he is in the right. He has just sent a response to the Assembly, which has ordered him to go back to France. "People of the so-called National Assembly of France, logic demands, by virtue of Title 1, Chapter 1, Section 1 of the indefeasible laws of common sense, that you go back into yourselves, failing which you will be considered as having given up all claims of being reasonable entities and will be judged as madmen only worthy of being locked up forever in an insane asylum." (→Jan. 18, 92).

La Rouërie's plans to reconquer France

Coblentz, December 5

The Marquis de La Rouërie's busy love life had made him the talk of the nation, but all that has now changed and he has joined the fight against the Revolution. This Breton gentleman has just submitted a plan for the reconquest of France to the King's brothers. It involves a landing of armed émigrés on the western shores of France, followed by an uprising in Brittany. The fiery nobleman has set up a "Breton association" whose aim is to restore traditional monarchy. The group relies on several committees based in fairly large towns of the regions from Poitou to Normandy. It is being supported both by nobles and peasants. Its shock troops are a militia of former contraband salt dealers. The King's brothers found the plan to be most interesting and encouraged La Rouërie to continue working on it in the hope that it will soon be put into action.

A good year for the theatre in France

Paris, December

Nineteen new theatres opened to the public this year. The decree issued on January 13th. on theatrical freedom has been a great boost for the Revolution, which has had a big success on stage. There have been countless patriotic and anti-religious plays. The titles of some of them are pretty explicit: *Le Mari Directeur ou le Déménagement du Couvent,* a comedy by Flins; *La Liberté Conquise ou le Despote Renversé,* a drama by Harny; *Les Victimes Cloîtrées,* by Monvel. Even the rivalry between the Théâtre de la Nation and the Théâtre Français has political overtones.

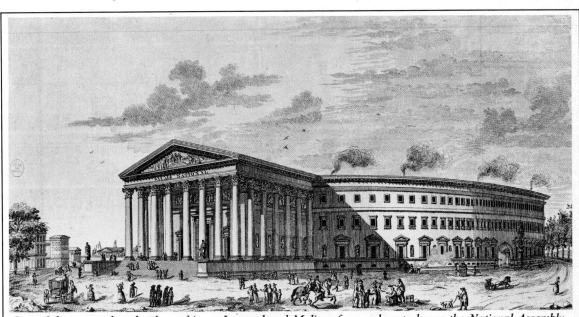

One of the many plans by the architects Legrand and Molinos for a palace to house the National Assembly.

Legislative Assembly

1. Paris. Marat is officially engaged to be married to Simone Evrard.

2. Paris. The Legislative Assembly decrees that the "era of liberty" began on January 1st., 1789. This means that the year 1792 becomes Year IV of Liberty.

2. Le Havre. François René de Chateaubriand has returned from a failed voyage of exploration to America.

3. Paris. During a debate at the Assembly on the mutiny of royalist officers seeking to seize the Perpignan citadel, Carnot proposes that all the kingdom's fortresses be torn down.→

9. Jassy. The second treaty between Russia and the Ottoman Empire is signed. It gives Catherine II of Russia free rein to act in Poland and against France.

11. Paris. The Favart auditorium shows *Cécile et Dermancée ou les Deux Couvents*, an opera by Grétry and Rouget de Lisle.

11. Paris. France's Minister of War, the Comte de Narbonne, calls on the Assembly to launch hostilities, despite the fact that the Elector of Trier decided on January 6th. to get rid of the émigrés staying on his territory.→

12. Paris. The Vaudeville Theatre is inaugurated on Rue de Chartres Saint Honoré. It is directed by Augustus Piis and P.Y. Barré.

13. Paris. Speaking on behalf of the diplomatic committee, Gensonné asks the Assembly to send an ultimatum to the Emperor (→25). At the same session, the Assembly declares any Frenchman who directly or indirectly either takes part in a meeting aimed at changing the Constitution, or in mediation between France and rebels plotting against it, a traitor to the nation.

15. Paris. An Assembly decree places David in charge of the artistic education of two children from the Drôme who show great promise.

17. Paris. At the Assembly, Brissot begs deputies to ask the King to declare war on the Emperor.

18. Paris. Monsieur, the King's brother, is stripped of his right to the regency because he has not returned to France within the time allotted by the decree of November 7th. 1791.

Everyday life of a front-line soldier

Moselle, January 17

All the soldiers are fast asleep. This is the time of day when the army volunteer Gabriel Noël likes to write to his family. There are many tents at the camp, most of them shared by seven or eight soldiers. The men have to bend down to enter their tents, where they rest on straw or hay beds. These must be aired often and changed every once in a while. The men complain bitterly that their beds are "flea palaces". The authorities have tried to convince soldiers to shave their heads, but they all refuse, saying that they would look like common criminals. For the time being, there is no news of the enemy. The young soldier only has the crash of ice floes breaking up on the Moselle river nearby to keep him company. The intense cold is what he finds most difficult to bear; but Gabriel Noël wants to reassure his parents: "The more you must do to serve your country, the happier you are," he writes. He is lucky not to be on guard duty this evening. That unpleasant chore happily only comes round once a week.

Blacksmiths are demanding a fair deal

The preparation of iron ore is a difficult and very badly paid task.

Isère, January 8

The blacksmiths of Rives are demanding justice. Despite the high price of bread, their employers have been refusing to increase their wages. They have been out of work for three or four months each year without compensation, while the bosses speculate on the price of coal and iron. The men are furious about having to live in misery and have asked the town council to settle the dispute. They have prepared a petition which 83 of them took to the town hall. In it, the blacksmiths say that if their grievances are not heard, they will leave the region and find work elsewhere.

Patriot fashion is for bright colours

Paris, January 1

The brighter the colour the more fashionable the garment. Winter fashions this year are focused on garish colours. Dull, traditional clothes are definitely out. The well dressed Parisian patriot is now opting for white and red, as well as the brightest yellow and purple. The ladies have taken to wearing flashy wimples and shawls and rainbow-hued hats.

Catherine of Russia's victory over the Turks: a fascinating sight.

Adoption is proof of love and virtue

Paris, January 18

The lessons taught by Madame de Genlis have been bearing fruit. Her daughter Pulchérie de Valence today put into practice one of her mother's most innovative ideas by adopting Hermine Compton, who is eight years younger than her. Ever since September 29th., 1783, she has been nearly a mother to the young English-born girl.

From today on, she will in the eyes of the law be Hermine's real mother. The fatherless girl had been "ordered" by Madame de Genlis from Nathaniel Forth, the same man who had brought Pamela to help teach the children of the Duc d'Orléans, but Hermine and Pulchérie were soon the best of friends, spending all their time together.

Just as soon as it was legally possible to adopt her Pulchérie went ahead, thus proving her love for the child as well as her public-spiritedness.

Clergymen can be good with money

Orléans, January 9

The clergy's civil Constitution is not a bad deal for every man of the cloth. Some clergymen at least have been able to take advantage of it, like the master of music of the cathedral of Orléans, the Abbot Charles Hérissé. Having paid his musicians out of his own reserve funds, the Abbot, who is now just an official paid by the state, has lost no time in claiming the money back from the authorities of the department. The officials in charge of the district quickly agreed to the crafty request. A clever financier, Charles Hérissé is also a talented musician who composed a famous motet.

Sackcloth habit is frowned upon

Amiens, January

The mayor of Amiens, Le Roux, really does not like "fanatics". Two former priests of the Carmelite convent have just discovered this. They had come to ask him for a certificate of residence. This is a vital document which allows the members of a regular order disbanded by law to receive a state pension. The mayor, however, was not pleased to see that the two men were still wearing their sackcloth habits and had dared come to the city hall dressed like that. In order to make his feelings perfectly clear, the good mayor flatly refused to grant the certificate.

The "stay behind" aristocrats are Robespierre's real enemies

The Jacobins, shown as cowards, fearfully listen to the "minister Linotte" announce that war is coming.

Paris, January 11

This evening, at the Jacobins Club, Robespierre made up his mind to oppose Brissot firmly. Once again, he has attacked him over the issue of war. This morning the Minister of War, Narbonne, submitted an extremely optimistic report on the military situation to the Assembly. The speech enraged Robespierre, particularly when the minister said: "When the national will is as strong as it is in France, nobody can stand in its way." In other words, that meant that a conflict between the European powers and revolutionary France was now inevitable. Robespierre believes, however, that the true enemies of the Revolution are inside France rather than abroad. It is vital to quash quickly and efficiently the many royalist plots that are being hatched, he believes, at the Feuillants, at the court and among the people close to La Fayette and Narbonne. The Girondist Party, and Brissot in particular, are in a sense indirectly aiding these plots by pushing for war abroad. Given all this, it would be madness to entrust the conduct of a war to a government that is prepared to betray the nation and that should not be trusted. As he argues for peace, the leader of the Jacobins knows that the public backs him, especially among the provincial societies and the press (→ Jan. 26).

The French ought to speak French

Aveyron, January 5

The administrators of the district of Sauveterre are fed up with the "cursed dialect" that is spoken by local inhabitants. They want all to speak the "national language". They wrote to the Assembly this very morning to tell legislators of the serious problems posed by the lack of French speakers in their region. How can they be expected to try to administer peasants for whom the law remains a total mystery because they simply cannot understand it? How can the officials enforce texts which some of them cannot even decipher? Two years ago, there was a decree from the Assembly ordering laws to be translated into all the kingdom's local dialects, but this ambitious decree was never fully carried out. In any case, the officials of Sauveterre feel this is entirely the wrong way to go about things, placing the cart before the horse. The "awful jargon" that the locals speak is far from being as effective as French, they say. The officials are now demanding that French be taught from the earliest age in the smallest and most isolated village schools. To achieve this goal, teachers who are perfect French speakers are needed and this is unfortunately not the case in the district's six schools.

Deputy Lazare Carnot has a hard time

Paris, January 3

The maiden speech of the deputy Lazare Carnot has not exactly had the effect he had hoped for. His proposal that all the fortresses of the kingdom be torn down so that their officers cannot hand them over to the enemy was greeted by jeers and laughter. The legislators showed little respect for the orator's military expertise. Lazare Carnot is in fact something of an unknown quantity. Even his colleagues at the Legislative Assembly can't tell the difference between him and his brother Claude Marie, known as Carnot the Young. The Carnot brothers, both deputies of the Pas de Calais and officers of the corps of engineers, are inseparable. Some observant people have noticed that Carnot the Young speaks loudly and what he says is often beside the point, while his brother Lazare is more reserved and has a methodical mind. As the brothers gradually become better known, it appears that they belong to no particular political tendency. Lazare Carnot's strange proposal is probably based on his undeniable patriotism rather than on the traditional hostility of army engineers towards the officer corps. Such military rivalries are, however, difficult to explain to civilians, as Carnot has noted.

19. Paris. Gaudet submits to the Assembly the committee of inquiry's report on the plot at Caen. The people who had been charged are finally acquitted.

20. Paris. During a riot against grocers, a fire destroys part of the prison at the Hôtel de la Force (→21).

20. Vendée. A detachment of front-line troops is sent to the Ile d'Yeu, where a revolt has been raging since the start of the month.

21. Saint Domingue. Saint Léger, the governor, leaves the town of the Cap to try to restore peace to the southern and western provinces.

22. Paris. The rise in prices leads the people of the Saint Marceau district to call for the taxation of sugar.

24. Paris. A final day of rioting ends five days of looting of groceries.

25. London. Talleyrand arrives in the English capital. He has been given an unofficial mission to seek closer links between France and England.

25. Paris. The Assembly approves a proposal from Gensonné to send an ultimatum to Leopold II.→

26. Paris. At the Jacobins Club, the pro-Brissot group succeeds in getting Robespierre to put an end to his speeches against war.

26. Paris. Back in the capital after being detained in Austria, Théroigne de Méricourt gets a triumphant greeting at the Jacobins.

28. Saint Domingue. The rebellious slaves launch a major offensive against the city of the Cap.

28. Paris. The section of the Croix Rouge district tells the Assembly that its members will boycott sugar and coffee to punish speculators. It calls on other sections to follow its example (→30).

29. Nantes. Despite the royal veto, the authorities of Loire Inférieure approve regulations on the detention of non-juring priests who cause a public nuisance or who are suspected of lack of patriotism.

30. Paris. At the Jacobins, the novelist Jean Baptiste Louvet de Couvray gets club members to swear that they will not eat sugar sold for over 20 sous a pound.

The price of sugar soars: Parisians blame the grocers and speculators for the rise

Paris, January 21

The cost of living is getting higher every day. This hard fact is one of the effects of the policy of trade liberalisation. Yesterday the inhabitants of the Saint Marceau and Saint Denis districts rushed to the wholesale groceries, destroying all they came across, in an attempt to get them to sell the goods more cheaply. Yesterday evening, the people even set fire to the Hôtel de la Force and the blaze nearly spread to the entire area. Since this morning, the riots have been spreading. Why are the people so angry? The reason is that the cost of a pound of sugar has just risen from 22 sous to over three francs. Grocers have been explaining that this is due to a scarcity of produce from the colonies caused by the civil war in Saint Domingue, but the poor claim that the rising prices are due to speculation by the owners of sugar warehouses. To make matters worse, the hoarders, condemned by Hébert in *Le Père Duchesne,* are genuine revolutionaries such as the former Constituent Assembly members

Constituent Assemblyman d'André, charged with sugar speculation.

d'André and Laborde, or the banker Boscary, a deputy at the Legislative Assembly. How can the crisis be resolved? If prices are not controlled this could lead to new rioting and looting, but to restore price controls would be to act against the principle of economic liberalism (→Jan. 24).

Germaine de Staël draws up a plan for the royal family's escape from France

Paris, January

The two ministers, Bertrand de Molleville and Montmorin, who have been shown Mme. de Staël's

Mme. de Staël has always dreamt of playing a major political role.

plan to save the royal family, have rejected it out of hand. Simple and practical, the plan's main defect is that it has been drawn up by a woman who is hated at the court because of all her plotting. The young ambassadress had suggested that some land be bought in Normandy where she could go often with people closely resembling the King, the Queen and the Dauphin in order allay suspicions. On the chosen day, the royal family would have taken their places in the carriage and gone to the coast of Normandy, from where they could sail to England. Madame Elisabeth and Madame Royale, who have nothing to fear for the time being, would have remained in Paris. The two ministers did not even want to tell Louis XVI about the plan, which they said was "as dangerous as it is adventurous, and hardly decent". In any case, it is likely that the King, always suspicious and hesitant, would have rejected it, as he has done with earlier plans.

Revolutionary names are in

Paris, January 21

Christenings are no longer very Catholic affairs. The priest of the capital's district of Saint Antoine today saw a family from his parish come rushing into his church.

All the women were wearing tricoloured ribbons in their hair while the men proudly wore cockades pinned to their lapels. As the congregation sang a lusty rendition of the revolutionary song *Ca Ira,* the mother placed her newborn infant on the baptismal font. Then she curtly nodded to the priest, ordering him to get on with it; but the clegyman's surprise turned into amazement when the father said his daughter was to be named ... Pétion Nationale Pique!

Monsieur Danton, who are you?

Paris, January 20

From now on, Danton will have to be considered as being a truly hard-line patriot. In his inaugural speech at the Commune, the orator gave a fiery presentation of his past life and future plans. He said he had always fought against the enemies of freedom, adding that he lived according to one simple rule: to act as his heart told him to. He stressed that he is ready to die for the people. "That is what my life has been. From now on, it will be devoted to the defence of the Constitution." Who dare doubt this huge man's commitment?

Danton, the new assistant public prosecutor of the Commune.

Narbonne under fire at War Ministry

Madame de Staël's creature, Narbonne, is held on a leash.

Paris, January

The Comte Louis de Narbonne is not a universally popular man. He has been head of the ministry of war since last December, and some say his nomination was due to the friends he has rather than to his performance. Some critics have even claimed that Mme. de Staël played a major role in his promotion. Everybody in Paris knows that this former military man, who was once commander of the National Guard at Besançon, is her lover. More serious people worry, however, that his arm will prove too weak to wield the sword of France (→ Mar. 9).

France sends an ultimatum to Austria

Paris, January 25

There can no longer be the slightest doubt: the Assembly wants war. Over the past few weeks, however, the prospect of a conflict had seemed to lessen. The Elector of Trier, obeying the demands made in December by Louis XVI, had given assurances that the groups of émigrés living on his territories, notably at Coblentz, had been dispersed. Acting on the advice of Leopold II, the Elector of Mainz had also followed this example and ordered the Prince de Condé to get out of Worms. The Assembly was informed of these moves on Jan-

uary 6th. There no longer seemed to be any risk of war breaking out, at least for the time being, but now the deputies have sent an ultimatum to Austria, on the urging of Hérault de Séchelles. In their message they ask the Emperor to disown the Convention of Pillnitz, adding that his silence, or any attempt at evasiveness, would be considered as "a declaration of war". The Girondists, who are in the majority at the Assembly, still hope that a war will contribute to the overthrow of the monarchy and help them get their hands on all the reins of power.

Jacobin-style club is set up in London

London, January 25

Across the English Channel, fans of the French Jacobins can be found. A group of eight London friends has just set up a club that is similar to the Jacobins. The brand new political society, called the London Corresponding Society, is to seek to speed up the revolution-

ary process in England. Its policies and bye-laws are openly based on those of the Jacobins Club in Paris, with which the new society is to correspond. Open to all, without exception, the English society will defend the rights of the poor and oppressed, and already hopes to serve as a model for other groups.

Madame de Beauharnais' strange salon

Paris, January 21

Lights have been burning all night long at the Paris residence of the Comtesse de Beauharnais, on the Rue de Tournon, just as they do each Friday. Fanny has been meeting her friends, who include the former Constituent Assembly member Rabaut Saint Etienne, the author Cazotte, the anatomist Vicq d'Azyr, the publicist Bonneville, and the author of *Tableau de Paris,* Louis Sébastien Mercier. The latter has brought along his friend Restif de la Bretonne. What brings such different people to the salon is their common taste for esoteric ideas, notably the illuministic doctrine of the philosopher Saint Martin, seen as a hero by Mme. de Beauharnais. She also welcomes many gnostics and cabalists, some of whom are even able to get tables to turn. This evening the strange gathering listened to the first eight chapters of Restif de la Bretonne's new book, a novel which is to be called *Monsieur Nicolas.*

Captain Malingre, a hero of the high seas

Galicia, January 19

It is just 8 a.m. and the storm is getting worse. The captain of the brig *Alexandre,* Michel Philippe Malingre, who is sailing to Marseilles, has decided it would be safer to seek shelter for his ship in the bay of El Ferrol. Suddenly one of the lookouts spots a corvette, flying the Spanish flag, in serious trouble. The captain immediately orders his ship to help the stricken vessel. The dinghy thrown overboard breaks up. As soon as they are close enough, the French crewmen throw ropes across to the sinking ship. Risking their own lives, the crew of the brig save ten sailors before the Spanish corvette is torn apart by the rough seas and sinks.

Storms are often deadly for the heavy and hard to steer sailing ships. There are many sailors who have been involved in more than one shipwreck.

1. Paris. The Opéra Comique shows a performance of *Charlotte et Werther*, the first time that Goethe's novel has been adapted for the stage. The opera is presented by Dejaure and the composer Kreutzer.

1. Paris. The Legislative Assembly decrees that anybody travelling within the kingdom's borders must in future have a valid passport or risk being arrested.

3. Paris. The Italian man of letters Joseph Cerutti dies. A deputy at the Legislative Assembly, he also directed the very popular weekly *La Feuille Villageoise* with the help of Rabaut Saint Etienne.

6. Noyon. Local people stop four ships loaded with grain from leaving. During the whole month, France is rocked by violent unrest caused by the high cost of wheat.

7. Vienna. Austria and Prussia sign a new military convention against France.

11. Paris. The King gives his approval to the decree voted on at the Legislative Assembly on February 9th. The property of émigrés will be seized.

13. Oise. 30,000 armed peasants gather around the Ourcamps abbey, where grain seized at Noyon has been stored.

14. Dunkirk. The homes of the port's grain merchants are sacked by the people, worried about grain being shipped to other regions. The authorities kill 14 rioters.

16. London. The publisher Jordan starts selling the second part of Thomas Paine's book *The Rights of Man*. The author has dedicated his work to La Fayette and donates his profits to the Constitutional Society.

21. Saint Malo. Giving in to pressure from his family, Chateaubriand finally marries Céleste Buisson de La Vigne during a secret ceremony held by a non-juring priest (→March 19, 92).

28. Aix en Provence. 4,000 National Guardsmen and Marseilles patriots disarm the soldiers of the Swiss regiment of Ernest.

29. Paris. Couthon calls on the Assembly to abolish the feudal rights that had been declared re-purchasable by the Constituent Assembly. However, the proposal is adjourned.

Fersen's secret advice to the Queen

Paris, February 14

Fersen is prepared to risk his life for Marie Antoinette. Although there is an arrest warrant out for him, he arrived in Paris yesterday with false identity papers and disguised as a courier. This morning he discreetly entered the Tuileries, resolved to convince the Queen and, above all, Louis XVI that their salvation rests on his plan. The Swede urges the royal couple to escape, as they did last June, but this time by faking their own kidnapping in order to try to start a war between France and the European powers. He believes this is the only way to save the monarchy. He knows the Queen is wrong to rely on the peace-loving Leopold to declare war. For their part, the émigrés are not likely to be of much use. Supported in Paris by Mme. Elisabeth, the Comtes d'Artois and de Provence are active in Coblentz, but their efforts are in vain. Their interests and those of Austria are too contradictory for them to agree. The King is backing away from his brothers' ideas, which are dreams of the restoration of absolutism.

Marie Antoinette, accompanied by Madame Elisabeth, the King's young sister, walks with her children in the gardens of the Tuileries.

Due to his indecisiveness, he has rejected Fersen's plan. Could he still be hoping to unite monarchy and Revolution, despite his vetoes at the Assembly?

Jews banned from the National Guard

Metz, February 21

Although Jews are now fully fledged citizens of France in the eyes of the law, their integration into society is not easy. This is not due to a lack of good will on their part. For example, many of them have signed up to join the town's National Guard, set up at the start of the month, but faced with violent protests from the local population the commune has decided to change its mind, and is now refusing their applications for membership. The town's citizens have expressed great reluctance at the idea of serving alongside Jews. This attitude, the people claim, is not based on any shameful prejudice, but on "physical causes". Most Jews, people say, suffer from a contagious hereditary disease. This mysterious ailment is caused by the Jews' special lifestyle and could quickly spread to the rest of the population. Prejudices, even when people prefer to use another word, are indeed deeply rooted and very difficult to get rid of.

Royalists clash with patriot troops

Mende, February 27

The royalists are triumphant. The three companies of grenadiers who came to Mende two days ago at the request of local patriots were forced to leave this morning.

They had been given a very bad time during yesterday's rioting. As soon as they arrived, National Guardsmen made no secret of their dislike of the grenadiers. "Long live the nation," the grenadiers shouted as they entered the town, to which the National Guardsmen boldly replied "And the King!". The bravest ones just shouted "Long live the King". On Sunday, a day after their arrival, the grenadiers went to the cathedral to attend a constitutional Mass, while the National Guardsmen attended a service held by a non-juring priest. The fighting broke out that evening. The soldiers had to take shelter inside their barracks. Threatened by both the royalists and local peasants, who wounded three of the soldiers, the grenadiers decided to leave the town.

The logotype: a new, faster way to print words

Paris, February 16

The printer François Hoffmann is pleased with himself. He has just been granted a 15 year special privilege for his new type-setting system, which is known as the logotype. Ever since Gutenberg, characters have been assembled one by one in a sort of ruler called the composing stick. Hoffmann's idea is to cast the most commonly used characters together to speed the process up.

The "Journal of Fashion" ceases publication

Paris, February 15

The capital's ladies of fashion are in despair. The *Journal de la Mode* today announced that it would no longer be appearing. Nobody seems to know why the journal is to cease publication. Le Brun, who set up the illustrated periodical over three years ago, had made a career of the art of pleasing people. As the journal's only writer, he knew how to flatter people's tastes, and stressed the need for proper clothes and refined conversation. His nimble pen and good eye for detail made him a much read chronicler. His review was also known for its excellent drawings. Its passing will be greatly mourned in the world of Paris fashion.

Where will the ladies of fashion go now to seek inspiration?

Rabaut becomes an historian

Jean Paul Rabaut Saint Etienne.

Paris, February

Rabaut, the former speaker of the Constituent Assembly, is now leading a quiet life, far from the clamour and bustle of politics. He has been on leave from the Assembly since last September and refused an offer to become administrator of the Gard region in order to spend his time writing. He has just finished a "Précis of the History of the French Revolution" in which he writes very positively about this "drama, with its beginning, middle and end". "The King finally accepted the Constitution and the move was decisive for the Revolution," he writes. Even if things have not completely settled down, he adds, "the Revolution will now survive everything".

No Revolution without the people!

Paris, February 6

The fraternity and equality of the Revolution must not be threatened. That is the main point made in a letter sent by the mayor Pétion to the Girondist Buzot, which has just been published by *Les Révolutions de Paris*. "The bourgeoisie and the people made the Revolution: only their union can save it," Pétion stresses. He criticises the growing gulf between the wealthy and the poorest members of society. The poor feel they have been badly rewarded for their contributions to the Revolution of 1789. How can such a social gulf be bridged before it is too late? The people must be given arms to prove to them that their representatives really trust them. Pétion does not explicitly argue for this option in his letter, but he hints at it. The idea of giving guns to the people of France is already a widespread one. The Girondists have been encouraging it openly. If this were done, the passive citizens would be on the same footing as the active ones, those who are wealthy and who can become members of the National Guard (→11).

The Empress of Russia, the Emperor, the King of Sweden, the King of Prussia and Monsieur cheer the masterly play of the Comte d'Artois, who is good at the "émigré game". In one stroke, he has knocked down the patriot skittles with a ball named after an Austrian general, Bender.

Joseph Sec, the rich benefactor of Aix

Joseph Sec's motto: "Having come from a cruel enslavement, I am now my own master, but I wish to use my freedom only to obey the law."

Aix en Provence, February 26

After leading a full life, what is more natural than to think of one's death? At the age of 77, Joseph Sec, the son of a family of peasants of the Luberon region, has reached the heights of success. He started off as a master carpenter at Aix, and gradually became wealthy by trading in wood and speculating on the price of stone. Today, an entire neighbourhood of the city belongs to him. However, the rich man also sees himself as the benefactor of his commune. He has therefore decided to set up a "monument dedicated to the town council, which respects the law". That is what has been inscribed on the strange mausoleum, decorated with revolutionary and Old Testament designs. It is to be his tomb.

Paris mayor bans illegal weapons

Paris, February 11

The city council is worried. In the past four days, there have been persistent reports that scores of Parisians have managed to get hold of rifles and pikes. What can be done to control the people? In order to limit the spread of weapons, the authorities have decided to forbid anybody to own a weapon that has not been officially declared and duly registered. Any citizen who breaks this new ruling will be immediately disarmed and placed under arrest. The city council has also made it illegal for the people of the capital to wear any badge or insignia other than the cockade or the national colours (→Mar. 6).

Dead woman really was in the coffin

Bordeaux, February 1

Revolutionary zeal can sometimes cloud the mind. There had been a rumour that the relatives of a dead woman had placed a log in her coffin, while the body was being secretly laid to rest at the convent where she wanted to be buried. The false coffin was to be taken to the constitutional church of the district of Sainte Eulalie.

Suspecting a trick, the women of the city decided to act: several dozen of them went to the cemetery, stopped the funeral procession, opened the coffin and finally removed the shroud — but instead of a log, they found the body of the dead woman.

⚜ 🏛 **Legislative Assembly**

1. Upper Rhine. There has been a miracle at Blotzheim: the crucifix of the Capuchin convent used to drip tears of blood. Since the departmental authorities have transferred it to the constitutional parish church, it has stopped dripping blood.

2. Paris. The Théâtre de la Nation shows the premiere of a new comedy by Colin d'Harleville, *Le Vieux Célibataire.*

4. Paris. Hébert, the editor of *Père Duchesne,* faces legal problems for having written that Marie Antoinette is a "crowned whore".

4. Rouen. A Free Society is set up to help those who seek to modernise the country's industry.

5. Vendée. The region's authorities order the expulsion of every single non-juring priest who does not reside in the department.

9. Paris. Louis XVI dismisses the Minister of War, Narbonne, after he had sent the King a memorandum calling for a purge in royal circles.

10. Paris. The Assembly brings charges against the Minister of Foreign Affairs, de Lessart. He is accused of not having reported officially Austria's and Prussia's military preparations. All the ministers resign.

11. Loire Inférieure. A new type of gunpowder is tested at the Indret arsenal.

12. Cantal. The former royal judge Coligny is assassinated. He had been arrested yesterday for having opened fire upon national volunteers. Gangs of armed peasants spread throughout the department, looting the castles.

12. Coblentz. The Marquis de La Rouërie is named leader of the Brittany plot.

12. Paris. At the theatre of the Rue Feydeau, *Cadichon ou les Bohémiennes* is shown. It is a comic opera by Pujoulx about the popular Cadichon, a big hearted innocent.

15. Paris. Louis XVI names as ministers several Jacobins who are members of the Girondist faction: Lacoste becomes Navy Minister, Duranton goes to Justice and Dumouriez gets Foreign Affairs. All of them favour war (→23).

Leopold II is dead, long live Francis II of Austria!

Marie Antoinette's late brother, Leopold II, "aristocrat of Tuscany, self-styled philosopher, then self-styled emperor of the Romans and now less than nothing".

Paris, March 8

The news has just been brought all the way from Strasbourg by special courier: the Emperor of Austria, Leopold II, died suddenly on March 1st. in circumstances that remain unclear. He will be succeeded by his son Francis II; but the new ruler has not inherited his father's caution and pacifism. Leopold II was able to avoid a conflict with France, as his views about Poland did not allow him to become too closely allied with his direct competitor, Prussia. In the absence of any agreement with Prussia, an attack against France remained out of the question. A liberal, Leopold also believed that there would eventually be a reconciliation between Louis XVI and the Revolution. The arrival on the throne of Francis II is likely to result in a war. It also means the end of the subtle plan drawn up by the Feuillants and approved by the court. The plan was to get the European sovereigns to arm themselves in order to intimidate the Assembly, without going so far as declaring a war that Louis XVI dreads. For their part, the pro-war Girondists are delighted.

Simonneau, mayor of Etampes, is killed

Etampes, March 3

The very high cost of living has claimed a victim this morning. An enraged crowd representing six communes suddenly poured into the market square at Etampes. The mob wanted to force the traders to lower the price of grain, which has been rising non-stop ever since it could be freely set. The security forces, led by Simonneau, the city's mayor, were about to stand between the traders and the demonstrators when the rioters flung themselves at him and killed him.

The incident has caused strong feeling. It is a sign of the conflict that is growing between the people, fed up with the hardships of everyday life, and a bourgeoisie which is tempted to use force to put down unrest. What has just happened at Etampes could occur anywhere in France. The whole of the country is being rocked by sudden and violent clashes. This evening, while some are shocked by the murder, others say that the mayor deserved to die as he was a hoarder and depriver of the people (→April 16).

Louis David also paints on commission

Paris, March 10

Louis David's portraits are much sought after by the high society of the capital. He is often asked to paint portraits of aristocrats and wealthy bourgeois. Some of his works are done on commission, like the painting he is currently finishing for Madame de Pastoret, but there are also works he does for love, such as the one that was ordered today. For his friends, the Trudaine de Montigny, he will paint the portrait of the wife of one of them, Charles Louis. The two brothers, whose father was one of Turgot's friends, have both chosen careers in the law. They were the King's lawyers at the Châtelet, then became councillors at parliament. They met David in 1786, when Charles Michel ordered a painting, the "Death of Socrates". They are great admirers of the painter and have also bought two prints of the "Oath at the Jeu de Paume".

An unfinished portrait of Madame Trudaine by her friend Louis David.

Police break up a gang of assignat counterfeiters

Passy, March 11

It is easy, far too easy, to print fake assignats. This has just been proved by the discovery of yet another clandestine workshop in which police found fake paper money. Acting on an anonymous tipoff, police burst into a luxury residence at Passy. There, they found machines used for printing assignats. Not only had the counterfeiters produced fake bills worth 13 million livres, but they also had enough barrels of paper paste to print another 100 million livres' worth of assignats. All the gang's members were placed under arrest. However, they are not just common gangsters: Sauvade is an abbot, Guillot is a librarian and Dufour is a merchant — honest citizens by day, counterfeiters at night. They are perfect examples of the new type of "clean" criminal, usually small businessmen or impoverished men of letters. The authorities have a problem: there are more and more counterfeiters and the flood of fake bills on the market is becoming a grave threat to the assignat, a currency that is already in trouble.

Jacobin leaflets are found in Aragon

Aragon (Spain), March

"Your parcel has arrived. It was immediately distributed and was a great success. Continue. We feel we can rely on an entire region of Aragon, near here. According to some reports, it is already about to explode."

The members of the Jacobins Club of Paris may find that their correspondent in Spain is a little over-optimistic. Hatred for the powerful minister Floridabianca, a strong opponent of the Revolution, had led the population of Aragon to feel sympathy for the French. The situation improved when the minister was replaced in February by Aranda, the head of the Aragon Party.

He put an end to Spain's policy of systematically harassing the citizens of France. Now may be the time to step up the spread of Jacobin propaganda in Spain.

Violent brawling breaks out in a bar

Paris, March

Wine can make people lose control, but so can politics. The clients of a Paris bar, known as the *Café Mécanique* because it boasts a mechanical piano, have just been involved in a violent brawl. It was set off by politics rather than a dislike for the monotonous piano music. The innkeeper Tanrès has learnt that it is better for his customers to leave their politics in the cloakroom. The other night, as the clients were glancing through the newspapers while sipping their mocha or wine, a patriot started singing *Ça ira* at the top of his voice. Tanrès got him to shut up, but not before several customers had jumped up and surrounded the trouble maker. Chairs and tables were broken. As he tried to break the fight up, Tanrès was knifed in the arm and his pregnant wife received a bad injury to the stomach.

Women of Paris want to have weapons

Paris, March 6

It is not just the men of Paris who are excited by the prospect of war. The women of the capital are also wrought up about it. Thus, Pauline Léon, a chocolate maker who is proud of the rôle she played in the taking of the Bastille, today went to the Legislative Assembly to submit a petition signed by 315 women of the Fraternal Society of Minimes. The signatories are asking for pistols, sabres and rifles, even though some of them are not really strong enough to handle them. They also want to train every Sunday on the Federation grounds. "Please, Pauline told the deputies, don't think that we want to stop looking after our families and our homes. No, gentlemen! We simply wish to be able to defend ourselves in case our enemies are victorious because our side has betrayed us, or due to a clever ploy by the other side." But the fiery Pauline's arguments did not convince the deputies.

A young Frenchwoman armed with a pike going to a training session.

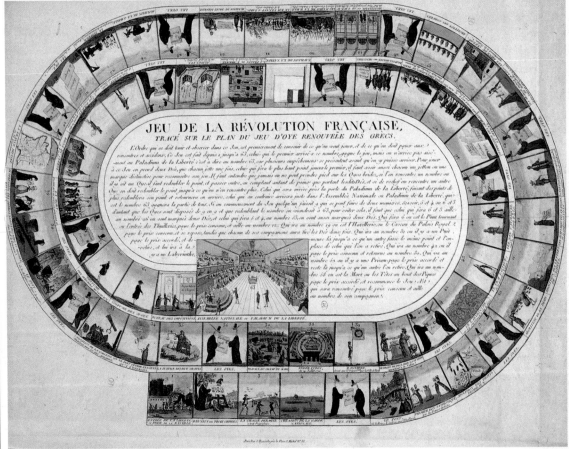

The search for liberty is a long and arduous one, according to this "game of the French Revolution". Its 63 boxes represent the steps that lead from the seizure of the Bastille to the Liberty Hall, the Assembly. If a player lands on a box marked by a goose — symbol of a member of a provincial parliament — he is allowed to have another turn; but beware of the labyrinth of the Châtelet, of the Abbaye prison, or, even worse, of the death of Foulon, Bertier and de Launay. If that happens, the player must start anew.

Legislative
Assembly

16. Sweden. King Gustav III of Sweden is attacked by a nobleman during a masked ball (→ April 15, 92).

16. Paris. The Comte Henri de La Rochejaquelein becomes a member of the Constitutional Guard, which, along with the National Guard, is in charge of protecting the King.

20. Paris. The Legislative Assembly approves the new technique of "mechanical separation" in a bid to make the death penalty as painless as possible.→

20. Ile et Vilaine. The National Guardsmen of six parishes take control of Saint Jean sur Vilaine to close the church down.

21. Lyons. The Jacobins of the Porte Froc section, upset over the death of the mayor of Etampes, hold a memorial service in his honour at the cathedral.

22. Paris. Claude Chappe presents his invention, the optical telegraph system, to the legislative body.

23. Paris. The Girondist ministry is completed.→

23. London. A pro-Jacobin demonstration is held at Drury Lane theatre, where spectators call for *Ça Ira* to be sung in place of the English national anthem.

24. Paris. By a wide majority, the Legislative Assembly grants political rights to free coloured men.→

26. Paris. As soon as it has been drawn up, the French battle plan is sent by Marie Antoinette to the governor of the Austrian Netherlands, Mercy Argenteau.

27. Clamecy. Demanding better salaries, hundreds of woodcutters of the Morvan region, on strike since March 20th., invade the town.

30. Vivarais. The peasants of Villeneuve de Berg set fire to the castle of La Bastide, residence of the Comte d'Antraigues, who emigrated in 1790.

30. Paris. On their return from the galleys, the Swiss of Châteauvieux are received triumphantly by the people of Paris (→ April 9, 92).

31. Saint Domingue. The Confederates seize Port au Prince and ask the governor to oppose the manoeuvres of the colonial assembly at the Cap.

The Girondists join the government

Etienne Clavière heads Finance.

Paris, March 23

This time the Girondists have done it. When the last Girondist minister was appointed, Brissot had pulled off a master-stroke: he had led his party to power. On March 10th. he had made a crucial speech, backed by Vergniaud. With proof in hand, Brissot accused the Minister of Foreign Affairs, de Lessart, of treason. By denouncing the tacit peace agreement fostered by de Lessart between Vienna and the Tuileries, Brissot was also criticising the Queen, whose approval was needed for any accord with Austria. Once de Lessart had been ousted, the entire government was forced to resign. On March 9th. the War Minister, Narbonne, had been dismissed by the King for having asked for a purge of aristocrats from royal circles. The defeated court was forced to agree to a Girondist ministry. Brissot could not seek the post for himself, as he badly needed to keep his place at the Assembly as a power base, but he was able to pick his men. A Geneva banker, Clavière, has been given the Finance Ministry, while Dumouriez, a former hussar aged 56, has replaced de Lessart. A brave and able man, he proved during his diplomatic career that he is capable of duplicity. Roland, the new Interior Minister, was told of his nomination this evening at 11 p.m. This virtuous and enlightened man from Lyons has been active in Girondist circles with his wife since he came to Paris.

A Jacobin crusade against Arles

Bouches du Rhône, March 25

The patriots of Marseilles want to enforce revolutionary order in the department. There was news today that National Guardsmen who had set off from Marseilles three days ago are heading for Arles and not for Avignon as had been thought. Since last summer that city has been in the hands of counter-revolutionaries, known as the Chiffonistes because of the name of the house where they meet. Scandalised by the lack of action taken by the department, the Jacobins have decided to take matters into their own hands.

Is the pox curable?

Paris, March 17

Shameful diseases need no longer be so. Better still, cures are being found for some of them. Doctor Nauder has informed the Academy of Medicine of a preparation he concocts with vegetable extract which cures venereal disease. The balm, which is easy to apply discreetly and requires no special diet, is currently being successfully tested by the navy's health services. In addition the Assembly has just classed the cure as being in the public interest, but will it be enough to combat an ailment that is spreading all the time?

Louis XVI discusses the guillotine

Paris, March 20

This evening, at the King's residence, the talk was of medical and technical matters: the guillotine was being discussed. Earlier, at the Legislative Assembly, the debate was focused on a "Detailed memorandum on the separation method" which had been drafted by Doctor Antoine Louis, a senior official of the Academy of Surgery. Since the proposals made by Guillotin in 1789 the Assembly had shown great reluctance to discuss such a grim issue, but now it must decide in what way "any person sentenced to death will have his head cut off". Louis helped the debate by calmly giving his medical opinion. He

The anatomist Joseph Guillotin.

simply explained why he sees the guillotine as the most suitable instrument of "separation". Its angled blade "penetrates the neck along the side and exerts an oblique slicing action that surely works efficiently". Moreover, he added, "since the structure of the neck is composed of several linked bones, one is not certain of achieving a truly prompt and perfect separation when the task is performed by an agent whose ability may vary due to physical and moral reasons". It is therefore necessary "to rely on invariable technical means in order to ensure efficiency". His demonstration has convinced the deputies, who have approved a decree on the use of the guillotine.

Before being called the guillotine, the machine was dubbed the "louison" after Antoine Louis.

The Brissotins

"To brissot" is the new verb in fashion. It is used derogatively to denote a person who flits about, constantly doing something and quite prepared to scheme in order to achieve his ultimate goal: power. This could be due to the fact that Brissot, the Paris deputy who has given his name to the new word, is a man often apt to change political direction. In a pamphlet published last March, Desmoulins had even accused him of financial wrongdoing. This, however, did not stop Brissot from becoming the leader of a group of his colleagues at the Assembly who are known as the Brissotins. They include Isnard, Buzot and Louvet. All of them are Jacobins, but the war issue, which they back, has split them from Robespierre and brought them closer to the Girondists in general and Brissot in particular.

Algerian wheat feeds Provence

Algiers, March 24

If Provence has managed to stave off starvation, it is thanks to the Dey of Algiers. He has granted France a loan of a quarter of a million livres, which was handed over today to the French Consul, Vallières, by Baba Mohammed's treasurer. This will now enable the consul to go to the markets of Constantine and Mascara to buy the wheat and corn that the people of Provence badly need. This aid from the Algiers regency is an act of gratitude to the National Guards of Cavalaire. On March 18th. they had protected two Algerian privateers which were being chased by a Neapolitan frigate. The help was much appreciated by the Dey of Algiers; but the consul knows that the loan is also part of Algiers' new economic policy. The Dey is encouraging Arabs to grow cereal for export in a bid aimed at bringing in money from abroad.

For or against the red wool bonnet?

A sansculottist places a red wool bonnet over Voltaire's bust.

Paris, March 19

Not everybody is overjoyed at the initiatives taken by the new Minister of Foreign Affairs. In order to prove his patriotism to all, Dumouriez has felt it fitting to go to the Jacobins' while wearing the red wool bonnet favoured by peasants, which is seen as a sign of equality. This enraged Robespierre, who is saying that "it is degrading for the people to assume that they can be moved by such signs of respect". He disdainfully condemned the bonnet as a "ministerial bauble", saying it has nothing to do with true revolutionary feelings. Dumouriez reacted calmly, expressing his great friendship for the leader of the Jacobins, but his move is also a sign of the times. After a performance of a play based on the Swiss of Châteauvieux, who were the first to wear the red bonnet, a propaganda campaign has been waged in Paris for the past week to make the wearing of the red hat obligatory for all patriots.

Chateaubriand misses his wedding

Saint Malo, March 19

The marriage of François René de Chateaubriand and the young Céleste Buisson de La Vigne seems to have got off to a bad start. Even though the second wedding Mass has been said, the couple have still not met each other. The first Mass was celebrated by a non-juring priest at the request of the bride-groom's mother. It was held on February 21st. in the absence of the bride and her family, who support the Jacobins, and who replied by organising a second wedding, this time celebrated by a juring priest, at which the groom was not present. Yet all this political and religious strife is over a simple match based on wealth.

In the eyes of the law, a marriage is a civil act from now on. This does not stop the bride and groom from getting a priest to bless their union.

The "freed coloured men" are to become fully-fledged citizens of France

Paris, March 24

The anti-mulatto coalition has broken up. A new majority, led by the supporters of Brissot, who set up the Society of the Friends of the Blacks, has approved the decree granting equal rights to freed coloured people. It has taken a total of three years to solve the issue finally. Up to now the colonial deputies, who were opposed to the emancipation of mulattoes, were being backed by the representatives of big business, but the spread of the revolt of the Saint Domingue slaves has led to a sudden change of opinion among the deputies representing French port cities. They now hope that the white landowners and mulattoes will join forces to fight against the rebels and save the "pearl of the Antilles".

Legislative Assembly

1. Corsica. Back in his native land, Napoleon Bonaparte decides to stay in Ajaccio, where he is elected lieutenant colonel of a battalion of Corsican volunteers.

1. Paris. The student is playing the master's music: during a concert at the theatre on the Rue Feydeau, the violinist Pierre Rode plays the concerto in E minor composed by Gian Battista Viotti.

4. Paris. The King gives his approval to the decree of March 24th. granting equal political rights to freed coloured men.

5. Paris. The Sorbonne and the faculties of theology are banned.

5. Paris. The Cordeliers Club votes in favour of a motion giving its total support to Marat, who is to resume publication of his newspaper on April 15th.

6. Ile et Vilaine. National Guardsmen of 20 parishes launch a major operation against the non-juring priest of Acigné. Bertin, the president of the departmental authority, tries to stop the operation, but is forced to flee after the National Guard refuses to obey his orders.

7. Vitré. Arrival of a detachment of dragoons which is to capture the commander of the National Guard of Bais, Pierre Jameu. The latter is a strong opponent of the clergy.

8. Lyons. The Easter Mass, celebrated at the Clarisses church, is disturbed by Jacobins, who expel the participants.

9. Paris. The Legislative Assembly pays homage to the 40 Swiss of Châteauvieux. Collot d'Herbois makes a speech praising them and is cheered (→ 15).

11. Paris. On behalf of the feudal committee, the deputy Latour du Châtel submits to the Assembly a report and a draft bill on the abolition without compensation of the redeemable feudal rights.

15. Paris. The capital celebrates a Liberty feast in honour of the Swiss of Châteauvieux.→

15. Rennes. The department's authorities refuse to agree to a request from the city's Jacobins, who want the non-juring priests of Rennes to be jailed.

Louis XVI and Marie Antoinette lose a useful ally, the King of Sweden

Paris, April 15

Louis XVI and his wife have received some bad news at the Tuileries: Gustav III of Sweden is dead. The news came in the night by a courier. The Swedish King had been attacked on March 16th. by a nobleman, Ankaeström. He finally died on March 29th. In the letter he sent to Marie Antoinette today, Fersen was unable to hide his concern. "With his death, you lose a strong supporter and a good ally, while I lose a protector and a friend." The King of Sweden was one of the firmest backers of the restoration of absolute monarchy in France and a loyal supporter of French émigrés. This tough but enlightened despot had planned to launch a naval operation against France, along with Prussia. The plan has been dropped now that Gustav IV is in power.

Gustav III: Sweden's nobility never forgave him for his reforms.

The women of Saint Antoine district get into big trouble

Paris, April 12

In the capital's Saint Antoine district, the armed women's club has badly misfired. Its founder and president, Théroigne de Méricourt, only just managed to escape from the anger of local husbands, who are fed up with seeing their wives abandon the home to attend all sorts of political meetings. As soon as she returned to France last January after her release from detention in Austria, Théroigne resumed her revolutionary activities with her usual zeal. Her recent misfortunes have made her a martyr and brought her a degree of glory. She has even been acclaimed at the Jacobins Club, where members begged her to read a tale about her "persecution". Emboldened by all this fame and success, she was full of new plans, including one to mobilise all the women of Saint Antoine, but little did she know the trouble this would cause. She was attacked by the mob and only saved when the local constabulary rushed in. She was escorted to a carriage by 12 National Guards, who made her promise that she would stay away from the area.

A strange case of Satanic exorcism

Aveyron, April 10

The police constables first asked the man if he really was Lavergne, who has been claiming to be possessed by the Devil for the past two years. He replied that he was, adding that Abraham, who lives in the nearby village of Asprières, had sent him the demon, Beelzebub. Despite this tall tale, he was not officially classed as being mad and was jailed by the district's police commissioner. When he was arrested, Lavergne was about to be exorcised for the fourth time by the priest of Saint Martin de Bouillac. In fact, the exorcism sessions gave local parishioners a chance to listen to Lavergne claim he was possessed by a "juring demon" and make speeches attacking the constitutional clergy. The police chief has really had enough of all these religious shenanigans.

Widespread clashes mar Easter prayers

Calvados, April 9

The faithful parishioners of the town of Verson are not going to forget this year's Easter celebrations in a hurry. A total of some 3,000 people had come yesterday from all the nearby towns and villages to attend an Easter Mass, one of the last to be celebrated by a non-juring priest in the region, but today, Easter Monday, another type of visitor has come to the local church. Four hundred National Guardsmen have come from Caen to settle a score with the religious "fanatics". Although they did not open fire with the cannon they had brought, they violently arrested about 15 people. Such incidents are not uncommon. In many parts of the country, Holy Week has been marred by violent clashes between members of the revolutionary clubs and the supporters of non-juring priests. In a number of departments, the district authorities have even been forced to decide, despite the royal veto, that all non-juring clergymen should remain in the regional chief towns.

One can avoid a lot of unpleasantness by getting rid of clerical robes.

The Jacobins pay homage to the Swiss of Châteauvieux

Preceded by a long procession, the huge Liberty float arrives at the Louis XV square amid loud cheering.

Paris, April 15

The procession slowly begins moving off around midnight. Ever since this morning, a huge crowd gathered around the Trône barrier had been waiting for this moment. The long wait for the start of the Liberty feast in honour of the Swiss of Châteauvieux, who have been freed from the galleys, has been worthwhile. The procession is led by four citizens carrying a "Declaration of the rights of man" that has been engraved on two stone tablets.

In the middle of the procession, wearing their yellow epaulettes, are the 41 soldiers rescued from the galleys, where they had been sent by Bouillé. Then come two coffins which symbolise the massacre of August 31st. 1790: one coffin for the Swiss, one for the National Guards they clashed with. After that there is a grandiose Liberty float, drawn by 20 horses, draped in a scarlet cloth painted by David. On one side it shows Brutus and on the other William Tell. David had

planned the entire, and very symbolic, procession. Right at the back there is a group of young women dressed in white and brandishing the rusted chains of the unjustly condemned men. Several hundred thousand spectators watch as the procession crosses half of Paris. However, the members of the Feuillants, who are totally opposed to the rehabilitation of the mutineers of Châteauvieux, see the Jacobin-backed procession as an outrageous provocation.

The communes fail to impose land and property taxes

France, April

The results of the efforts of the authorities are very slim. Out of a total of 40,911 communes in the country, only 5,448 have managed to draw up the fiscal registers for the payment of land and property taxes. This means that, instead of the 300 million livres expected, a little less than 175 million have been collected. Knowing that a delay was likely, the finance minister, Clavière, had proposed that the communes be helped by special officials, who could have estimated the net income from each piece of land in order to calculate the tax base, but he was opposed by the Jacobins, who say that it should be up to the people themselves to set their tax contributions. The Assembly, faced with the problem of many illiterate municipal officials, has reluctantly agreed that each commune should hire its own officials in charge of estimating taxes, but these experts, mostly former tax collectors, are only to have a consultative rôle. In some areas nothing is being done, while in others endless, and often unruly, arguments block any decision. Elsewhere, people complain of being overtaxed. Meanwhile, the budget deficit is growing.

Hymn to Liberty

Marie Joseph Chénier: Hymn to Liberty, set to music by Gossec.

Innocence is back in France,
Its victory is here to stay;
Come Liberty,
This is your chance,
Come fill our hearts to-day.
The tyrants are defeated now.
Praise Liberty,
And raise your voice;
French hands have set upon her
Brow the immortal crown:
Let all rejoice.

André Chénier: A hymn to the Swiss of Châteauvieux.
These forty murderers,
Robespierre's own,
He wants us all to worship now...
Come, Arts, on canvas, in stone
Set life immortal on each brow,
On Collot d'Herbois
And his Swiss.
To such heroes
He grants his love;
They drink, they kill,
Yet naught's amiss.
Let them be as stars above,
So when all weary mariners
Look up to the sky, they'll see
Collot's Swiss murderers.

Poetry and politics cause a rift between the Chénier brothers

André Chénier owes his fame to his talents as a polemist.

Paris, April 15

The Chénier brothers no longer find anything to agree on. Their literary rivalry has over the past few months led to a fierce political dispute. This came to light during the feast in honour of the Swiss of Châteauvieux. The elder brother, an ardent patriot, was one of the organisers of the ceremony, which his younger brother disapproved of. Marie Joseph, a strong supporter of the Swiss mutineers, composed a "Hymn to Liberty" in their honour. Meanwhile, André today published in the *Journal de Paris* an ironic and stinging "Hymn to the Swiss of Châteauvieux" which is in total contrast to his brother's song of praise. The loser, Marie Joseph, chose to ignore his brother's victory and spent the day in the country with friends, the Trudaine family.

Marie Joseph Chénier has become famous for his tragedies.

Legislative Assembly

16. Paris. In response to the feast held in honour of the Swiss of Châteauvieux, the Feuillants decide to organise a celebration in honour of the mayor of Etampes, Simonneau, in June (→June 3, 92).

18. Paris. The Academy of Sciences awards its astronomy prize to Jean Baptiste Delambre, who has just completed a list of the satellites of Jupiter and Saturn.

19. Paris. The owner of the ship *Le Solide* donates to the Assembly maps drafted by Captain Marchand of the Marquesas Islands, which he has re-named Revolution Islands.

20. Paris. The Legislative Assembly approves by an overwhelming majority the King's proposal to declare war on Austria.→

21. Paris. The Périer brothers take out an import licence for the double-injection steam machines invented by James Watt.

21. Paris. Condorcet ends the presentation to the Assembly of his plan for public instruction. He had started yesterday but had been interrupted by the declaration of war.→

23. Paris. At the Legislative Assembly, the deputy Antoine Merlin de Thionville asks for non-juring priests to be deported. A committee of 12 is ordered to investigate unrest caused by non-juring priests (→May 27, 92).

23. Avignon. A procession of Jacobins goes to the Saint Lazare gate, also known as the Royal gate, to get its name changed to Liberty gate.

25. Paris. The guillotine is used for the first time on the Place de Grève on a condemned murderer.→

27. Rouen. The town council asks all inhabitants to wear the tricoloured cockade.

28. Lille. General Théobald Dillon is killed by his own troops.→

30. Maine et Loire. Representatives of 34 parishes of the Mauges region meet at La Pointevinière to draft a petition calling for the return of non-juring priests and the disbanding of clubs.

30. Strasbourg. Rouget de Lisle's *Chant de Guerre pour l'Armée du Rhin* is sung for the first time in public.

Louis XVI declares war on Austria

Paris, April 20

An overwhelming majority of deputies has decided to declare war on Austria. Louis XVI had himself told the Assembly that all French citizens "prefer war to seeing the dignity of the people of France being trampled and its security threatened". The King, on the urging of Dumouriez, who wants to fight against the Emperor in order to negotiate with Prussia, has now decided to attack his own nephew, Francis II, thus violating the alliance that has linked France and Austria since 1756. It was easy to find an excuse for war. On March 25th. the Foreign Affairs Minister had sent a message to the Austrian Chancellor demanding that he dissolve the Congress of European sovereigns. Prince Kaunitz simply replied to this on April 7th. that the kings' intentions had not changed. That was sufficient. Judging by the large majority of the vote, the deputies welcome war. Only the supporters of Lameth, including the deputy of the Haute Marne, Becquey, tried to oppose the move.

At the Jacobins', Robespierre for his part is continuing to speak out against a conflict which he says can only benefit La Fayette and the army's generals.

Dressed in purple, the colour of mourning, Louis XVI appeared sombre.

Rouget de Lisle composes a war song for the army of the Rhine

Strasbourg, April 26

Military music was played this evening at the residence of the mayor of Strasbourg, Philippe de Dietrich. Accompanied by his wife on the harpsichord, the host sang a rousing and lusty war song which delighted his guests. The composer of this warlike *Chant de Guerre pour l'Armée du Rhin*, in honour of whom the dinner was held, is a young captain of the engineer corps, both a poet and a music-lover, called Rouget de Lisle. Yesterday, when news of the declaration of war reached Strasbourg, the mayor had asked him to write a fitting song. Fuelled by patriotic sentiments, Rouget de Lisle composed the song overnight. He hopes it will be more of a success than the "Hymn to Liberty" he wrote last year. That song is still unknown outside the Strasbourg limits (→April 30).

Rouget de Lisle sings before the mayor of Strasbourg: "Soldiers of France, the day of glory dawns at last!"

Condorcet shows the principles of public instruction to the Legislative Assembly

Paris, April 20

Schooling for all? That is now possible. This is what Condorcet explained today at the Assembly, stressing that it is just a matter of providing sufficient funding. His plan for public instruction, based on a memorandum he had drafted on February 26th. 1791, provides for a system of schooling open to both girls and boys. It should be free and secular in order to be in accordance with the principles of equality and the unhindered development of talent. Adults are not forgotten by his plan. For them there is to be a system of permanent training, focused on one weekly session with the schoolmaster on Sundays. However, the deputies hardly listened to Condorcet's very ambitious plan. He spoke in a low

The Marquis de Condorcet.

voice and his colleagues were more concerned about the declaration of war on Austria than about the education of children (→ April 21).

The guillotine has cut off its first head

Paris, April 25

The condemned man placed his head between the upright runners down which flashed the weighted blade, neatly chopping off his head. The "separation" of the highwayman Jacques Pelletier was carried out without a hitch, like the tests performed on 15 bodies provided by Bicêtre hospital. The authorities did not know how the large crowd that had come to watch the execution on the Place de Grève would react. La Fayette was therefore asked to make sure no damage was done to the expensive machine.

French troops around Mons are routed by the Austrians on April 30th. 1792. Monsieur de Beauharnais can, however, be proud of his men. Brigadier Pie, dying from an enemy bullet, has spoken to him with bravery and loyalty: "Sir, I am about to die alongside my rifle and the only thing that I regret is that I am no longer fit enough to carry it."

General Dillon is killed by his own troops

Lille, April 28

The military career of General Comte Théobald Dillon has gone up in flames. Hit in the head by a gunshot, finished off with a blow from a bayonet, the unfortunate officer's body was thrown into a fire by his own soldiers. The incredible chaos the army is currently in has cost him his life. Yesterday Dillon was ordered to launch a fake attack on Tournai, in order to stop the town's garrison from heading to Mons, which was being simultaneously attacked by the French troops led by General Biron. All was going according to plan when suddenly the cavalry squadrons turned back, screaming "Every man for himself, we've been betrayed!". Pushed back by the cavalry, the demoralised infantrymen began to flee in all directions. When they got to Lille the furious soldiers attacked their officers. The situation on the northern front is now disastrous. Eight days after the declaration of war, the volunteers have still not received any rifles. They have no food and less hope.

The body of General Dillon is thrown on a fire by his own troops.

The outbreak of war is announced

Epinal, April 29

Bells have been ringing out ever since early this morning. Once in a while the sound of a cannon shot is heard above the sound of the town's bells. The authorities of the department of the Vosges were informed of the declaration of war three days ago, but decided to wait so that they could make the public announcement during a fitting and patriotic ceremony. The National Guard gathered this morning at 7 o'clock on the Champ de Mars, by the Altar to the Nation, along with local dignitaries bearing the banner of the Federation. The commander of the Epinal guard read out the proclamation and said France was at war against tyrants. He was cheered, but the people remained sombre. It was not an ordinary celebration.

The Jacobins now control Avignon

Avignon, April 29

The patriots are once again in control of the whole sector. Taking unjust advantage of the amnesty law that came with the decree setting up the French administration of the Comtat of Avignon, those responsible for the massacre that took place at the Glacière have joined the Marseilles patriots who are enforcing Jacobin rule throughout the region. Today the patriots marched into the city with the two proconsuls named by the authorities of the Bouches du Rhône to restore the Avignon district to the department. They are none other than the heads of the Marseilles army. Over the past few days all those who feared the return of the "men of the Glacière" have fled the city, and the Royal gate has been re-named Liberty gate.

1. Rome. The Abbot Maury is consecrated Archbishop of Nicaea at Saint Peter's Basilica by Cardinal Zelada, in the presence of Mesdames Victoire and Adélaïde.

2. Paris. The composer Devienne writes the score for the *Hymn to the Red Bonnet*, which is sold to raise funds for the poor of the Bonne Nouvelle sector.

5. The Legislative Assembly issues a decree ordering the creation of 31 new battalions of national volunteers.

9. Paris. Following the resignation of Colonel de Grave, Louis XVI appoints Joseph Servan de Gerbey as Minister of War without consulting La Fayette.

9. Neukirch. Three weeks after the declaration of war, the hussar regiment of Saxony defects and takes its weapons and equipment over to the émigrés. Two other regiments, the hussars of Bercheny and the Royal German, joined the enemy at the start of the month.

15. Paris. The *Moniteur* publishes a report that there is an "Austrian committee" at the Tuileries which is helping the enemy (→23).

17. Paris. Robespierre publishes the first edition of his *Defender of the Constitution.*

18. Valenciennes. During a meeting of the army's leaders, La Fayette says that the offensive is impossible. The generals decide to send a message to the King urging him to seek peace immediately.

18. Belleville. Charles Simon Favart dies at the age of 82. →

24. Paris. Jacques Roux publishes a "Speech on the means of saving France".

25. Rhône et Loire. At Roanne the constabulary arrests counterfeiters who were producing assignats in five-livre denominations.

27. Paris. A new step is taken in the fight against the non-juring clergy: the Assembly decides that non-juring priests can be deported if at least 20 active citizens in their place of residence demand it. →

27. Paris. The Assembly decrees the disbanding of the King's Constitutional Guard, which had become a nest of royalist activists.

"L'Ami du Peuple" is banned again

Paris, May 3

The Girondists are starting to lose patience with the Cordeliers. In an unusually violent speech to the Assembly, Lasource has just lashed out at Marat. He called for legal action to be taken against the newspaperman who had dared mock the government in *L'Ami du Peuple,* which was allowed to resume publication on April 15th. The government had claimed that the war would allow it to crush all the counter-revolutionaries still within France. The early military defeats have proved it wrong. The government's embarrassment has fuelled Marat's attacks on it. Since Dillon was killed by his troops, Marat has slammed "traitorous" generals and urged soldiers to mutiny. The Girondists find such charges outrageous. In a bid to calm the growing dispute the depu-

Doctor Jean Paul Marat.

ties have decided to ban *L'Ami du Roi,* which was founded by the royalist Royou at the same time as Marat's paper, but they are also out to discredit Marat.

A priest speaks out against property

Paris, May 1

An embarrassed silence greeted Dolivier's speech to the Assembly. The priest from Mauchamp, a small village not far from Etampes, read out a petition condemning the repression that followed the murder of the mayor Simonneau. In his speech, Dolivier accused the victim, a wealthy tanner, of having enforced the law with brutality and a total lack of flexibility, instead of seeking to ease the concerns of a people burdened by poverty. The plea made by this revolutionary priest, who is also something of a philosopher, goes beyond a simple protest. Speaking on behalf of all peasants and workers, Dolivier said it is "revolting and unnatural that the rich man lacks nothing in his idleness while he who earns his life by working is being crushed by the burdens of misery and hunger". What he is opposed to is nothing less than property, especially land. It is therefore not surprising that his speech has worried deputies, as most of them are property owners. However, the same speech was very well received by the Jacobins two days ago.

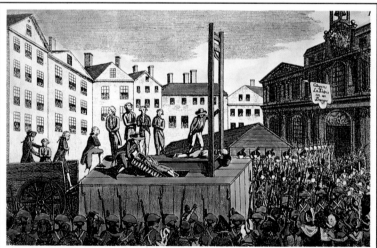

One of the first times the guillotine is used on the Place de Grève. Nine young émigrés captured in Strasbourg while carrying weapons are executed. A banner reminds the spectators that "the Nation is being threatened".

Liberty is not always in season

Libourne, May 6

Corporal Dupré has spoiled the party. The current fad of planting Liberty trees everywhere has come to the town of Libourne. Its citizens wanted their tree to "grow and flourish like the liberty it stands for", but Dupré told them it was far too late in the season to plant trees. Anything planted now would be bound to die, he said. However, he reassured the crestfallen inhabitants by saying that, if they were to plant another tree in the autumn, it would give them a good excuse to have another party.

Paris declares war on the city's rats

Paris, May 7

The capital has become a haven for all sorts of sharp toothed, dirty rodents. Paris has countless tiny and filthy courtyards giving onto its thousands of narrow alleyways. It is a city of damp staircases and rotten lofts where bursting sacks of grain are stored alongside pots of rancid lard. The capital's sanitation services are unable to cope with the millions of rats. If hundreds of the rodents are burnt, they are replaced by thousands more. In an attempt to solve this dangerous problem, a shopkeeper called Brignoul has started selling a clever trap: it uses candles to attract pests, who are killed by a firecracker when they get too close.

The "Sentinel" warns of traitors

Paris, May

For the past few days, a pamphlet known as *La Sentinelle* has been posted on all the walls of Paris. Its banner headlines scream: "War has been declared; the court obviously backs Austria and is betraying our army. The people must be told all about such plots." This dire warning was written by its editor, Louvet de Couvray. He was urged to go ahead by his friends among the Girondist government ministers. Dumouriez got the funds to print the pamphlet from the foreign ministry's secret account.

La Fayette drops the Brissotins

Paris, May 23

The court has been betraying the nation ever since France has been at war with Austria. This betrayal was denounced today at the Assembly by Brissot and Vergniaud. They spoke of a so-called "Austrian committee" which they said had been negotiating with the Emperor from its headquarters at the Tuileries. Its aim is to start a counter-revolution with help from abroad and from senior army officers. This grave charge is also aimed at La Fayette, said to be involved in the plot. This general has a widespread reputation as a plotter. Some even claim that he wants to become a dictator. The Jacobin Chépy swore to Brissot that La Fayette sent a secret envoy on May 16th. to see Mercy Argenteau, the Austrian ambassador. He is said to have asked Vienna to stop military operations so that he can march on Paris and seize power. This has enraged the Girondists. They had briefly felt they they could count on La Fayette's support. But he has moved closer to the Feuillants since he settled his dispute with Duport on May 13th. He was furious about not having been consulted over the appointment of the new War Minister, Servan. On May 21st. La Fayette sent Roland, the Minister of the Interior, an insulting letter in which he refused to accept the government's authority. The break between La Fayette and Brissot now appears final.

Brissot, leader of the Girondists.

Despite the war and the problems faced by the army, Paris' high society is making the best of springtime. People go for walks in the gardens, where flirting is rampant, or sit for a chat and cold refreshments.

A sad day for the Comic Opera

Favart, "Apollo's Florist".

Belleville, May 18

The world of entertainment is in mourning. Charles Favart, the director of the Opéra Comique and talented playwright, has died. He has just been killed at the age of 82 by a bout of pulmonary catarrh. He had begun his long career at the Foire theatre and his first play was written for puppets. He was soon introduced to Louis XV and to Madame de Pompadour. In 1745 he was married to the actress Marie Justine Duronceray, and became director of the travelling company that followed the Marshal of Saxony to Flanders. His works, about one per year, were always well received by audiences, and he was a favourite among directors. He was an uncontested master of the art of comic opera.

Two killed in ammunition dump blast

Paris, May 26

A huge explosion has just rocked the district of the Halle au Drap. The ammunition dump has blown up, killing two people outright and sending rifles, cartridges and barrels flying in all directions. Three people were also injured by the blast. After an inquiry, investigators ruled that it was an accident rather than a criminal act. They found the explosion was caused by a clay pipe that was carelessly smoked by Captain Beudon, the officer in charge of cannon crews posted in the area. The soldier had simply dropped his trusty pipe in the wrong place.

The Madrid château is to be burnt down

Neuilly, May 27

One of the most beautiful 16th. century castles is to be destroyed. It stands close to the forest of the Bois de Boulogne. In 1788, Louis XVI had decided to have the castle torn down. Its façade, richly decorated with ceramic medallions, was no longer fashionable. It was finally auctioned off for 648,000 livres to Leroy, a demolition contractor, who is to strip the building of its decorations before burning it. This will save demolition costs.

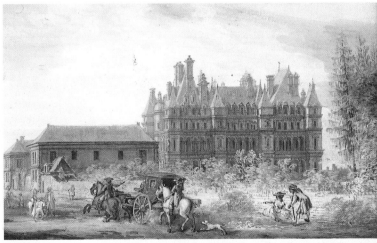

Begun during the reign of François I, the Madrid castle was one of the jewels of Italian-style architecture, with its decorated polychrome exterior.

The non-juring priests are to be deported

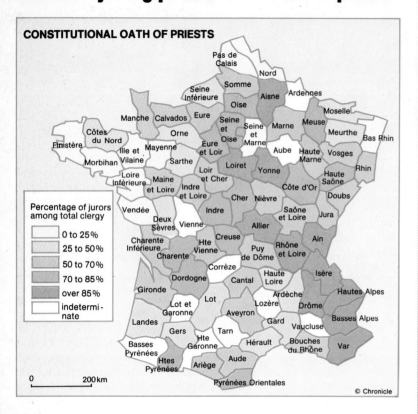

CONSTITUTIONAL OATH OF PRIESTS

Percentage of jurors among total clergy

- 0 to 25%
- 25 to 50%
- 50 to 70%
- 70 to 85%
- over 85%
- indeterminate

0   200km

© Chronicle

Paris, May 27

Things are getting extremely difficult for non-juring priests. The decree approved by the Assembly states that all non-juring priests risk being deported if such a move is requested by at least 20 active citizens. If any unrest is caused by a non-juring priest, he can be deported if just one active citizen makes a complaint. The new ruling is to be enforced by the departmental authorities on the basis of advice given by local districts. In cases where a dispute has arisen, an inquiry will be held. A priest will, however, be able to choose which country he is to be sent to. If he violates his sentence by remaining in France or by returning, he risks

spending up to ten years in jail. Since the start of the war, patriots have become increasingly hostile towards non-juring priests. They are now simply seen by a majority of people as enemies of the revolution and agents of Austria. Over the past few weeks, the Assembly has received several petitions from soldiers about to go to war calling for action to be taken against the "fanatics". For the priests, the situation is worse in some regions than in others. It all depends on the attitude of the local population and the authorities. If the King decides to veto the new decree, the authorities could play an even bigger role, as most of them are strongly in favour of the deportation measure.

La Rochejaquelein, supporter of the King

Paris, May 29

Henri de La Rochejaquelein is wondering whether he should not have followed his father into exile. The Assembly has just disbanded the King's Constitutional Guard, of which he had become a member. This corps was felt to be too loyal to the King, with its officers chosen by the Queen. It does not even use the tricoloured banner, and the Jacobins were unhappy with the unit's uniform, blue with a yellow lining, similar to the one used by

the émigrés at Coblentz. To make matters worse, many of its men had tied black crêpe bands around their left arms when the death of the Queen's brother, the Emperor Leopold, was announced on March 8th. The King wants to keep his guards, and has ordered them to stay in Paris, but to wear civilian clothes. The Queen knows that it will be difficult to keep these gentlemen in France. Henri believes, however, that "the defenders of the throne must stay by the King".

1. Ile et Vilaine. The National Guard and front line troops carry out a fruitless search at the castle at Saint Ouen belonging to the Marquis de la Rouërie, which is rumoured to be a nest of anti-revolutionary Breton plotters.

7. Upper Rhine. The mutiny of troops at the Neuf Brisach military camp comes to an end. It was sparked off three days ago by the passage of a convoy of arms destined for Switzerland.

8. Paris. On the urging of the Minister of War, Joseph Servan, the Assembly decrees the creation near Paris of a military camp for 20,000 Federate soldiers. This will enable the capital's line troops to be sent to the front.

8. Paris. The city authorities rule that two bells must be kept in each church.

8. Paris. A ruling orders the King's Library to be re-named the National Library.

9. Lyons. Lange, the municipal officer, publishes a report called "Simple Means of Ensuring Plenty", in which he suggests that a national ceiling be set for grain production.

10. Paris. A petition signed by 8,000 active citizens of the capital opposed to the creation of the Federation camp is taken to the Assembly.

11. Paris. Roland, the Interior Minister, orders the King to agree to the decrees on the deportation of non-juring priests and on the creation of the Federation camp.

12. Paris. Louis XVI refuses to agree to the demands of the Interior Minister, who is dismissed along with Servan and Clavière. The Minister of Foreign Affairs, Dumouriez, replaces Servan as Minister of War.

13. Paris. The Assembly again expresses its full confidence in the dismissed ministers and threatens to take action against Dumouriez.

13. Paris. At the Jacobins Club, Robespierre condemns all rebellious activity aimed at getting ministers recalled. Meanwhile, the Brissotins are seeking to get the King to form another Jacobin cabinet.

14. Paris. Danton suggests that Louis XVI should repudiate Marie Antoinette to put an end to Austrian influence at the Tuileries.

Former transvestite spy wants to fight

Paris, June 11

A ghost of the Ancien Régime was discussed by Carnot today at the Assembly. The former transvestite secret agent who worked for Louis XV, the Chevalier d'Eon, has just sent a proposal to the deputies. He has been living discreetly in London, where he is known as the "Lady Knight". He has offered to recruit a legion, "like the Roman ones, strong and disciplined", and place it at the Assembly's orders. The deputies cheered the generous offer, although the ex-spy is known to have a great thirst for fame and glory. It is highly likely that the Assembly's military committee will quietly forget all about this potentially embarrassing offer.

Charles d'Eon, transvestite knight.

A young musician's "De Profundis"

Paris, June 11

The French Revolution has not yet brought to light any great musical geniuses. However, it has made a number of young people more aware of music. One of these is Charles Simon Catel. At the age of just 16, this disciple of Gossec enlisted in the capital's National Guard in July 1789. He joined the Guard's corps of musicians. Now, after having composed two military marches, he has started writing religious music, including a *De Profundis* for choir and orchestra. The new piece was played for the first time today. It is the work of a composer whose talent has not yet fully matured.

The Feuillants turn Simonneau into a martyr of liberty

Funeral pomp in honour of the mayor of Etampes. A statue of the Law followed the procession.

Paris, June 3

The Jacobins have their own martyrs: the Swiss of Châteauvieux. The Feuillants are now also to have theirs: Simonneau, the mayor who was assassinated during a riot on March 3rd. A monument is to be erected in his honour on the Champ de Mars. The procession that has been organised for him by the deputy Quatremère de Quincy is very reminiscent of the feast held by the Jacobins six weeks ago.

Again there are many things to remind the spectator of the dead hero. Simonneau's sash, wrapped in black, and a bust of him have been placed before the grieving family. Young women dressed in white and wearing crowns of oak leaves, who march behind Olympe de Gouges, are like the ones who took part in the patriot procession. Right at the rear of the procession there is a huge and somewhat threatening statue of the Law bearing the ins-

cription "Liberty, Equality, Property". On a golden chair carried beside the statue there is the book of the Law, alongside a silver Minerva. The whole thing looks more like a military show than a fraternal event. At the head of the procession, the constabulary marches before the banners of the capital's 48 sectors. Red bonnets have been placed atop the banners. All the leaders of the sectors wear black, while the soldiers are in white.

Astronomers are under suspicion

France, June 1

The astronomers who are busy between the two ports of Dunkirk and Boulogne, measuring a quarter of the earth's meridian — of which one ten millionth is the new unit of length — are having a hard time. In these troubled times, when there is unrest throughout France and in many European countries, people can easily become suspect. When Jean Baptiste Joseph Delambre put a white rag on a geodesic marker to make it easier to spot, he was accused of flying a counter-revolutionary banner. He only managed to avoid further trouble by replacing it with a tricoloured flag. As for Pierre Méchain, he has just been arrested by suspicious patriots who don't like the look of his astronomy instruments.

Smallpox spreads to Ile de France

Port Louis, June 14

The smallpox epidemic that first started a month ago on the Ile de France has been spreading. At first it was limited to one plantation, but it has now reached all of them. What is new about this epidemic is that the disease is affecting the white population. Concern is such that the colonial assembly held a 48 hour session to organise the fight against the disease. According to Doctor Léonard Laborde, there is only one solution: healthy people must be inoculated. Using a lancet, those who are to be inoculated are cut twice on the arm and some pus taken from an affected patient is injected. The deputies have ruled that everybody must be inoculated and that all the sufferers must be quarantined.

The tragic fate of an overzealous forest ranger

Eure, June 3

Justice has been done. The forest ranger Cousin has been executed as many onlookers cheered. He had been accused of having beaten a woodcutter who was caught chopping down the best trees of the Brotonne forest. Local people had come to hate this zealous ranger, who was not born in the same region. Cousin had a reputation for showing no mercy to any poachers unfortunate enough to be caught red-handed by him. His tough policy had the full backing of the local authorities. But Cousin's brutality is only partly to blame for the sad business. Since the country's finances were reorganised, money made from forestry on public land is supposed to belong to the state, and this year the government has budgeted for an income of 15 million livres. However, local people cut and sell trees privately, keeping the profit for themselves. Over the last two years there has been no income from forestry whatsoever, while forests have been decimated. The rangers have been powerless to do anything about this theft — that is unless they overstep the mark. That is precisely what Cousin had taken to doing.

A singer who loved the Queen too much

Paris, June 1

Marie Antoinette is not known for being a particularly loyal friend. The singer Rosalie Dugazon has just been forced to retire at the age of only 37, although her voice has lost none of its power or charm. Her mistake was to have foolishly and repeatedly made her affection for the Queen known.

For example, during a performance of *Evénements Imprévus* on February 20th., the singer's behaviour on stage sparked off demonstrations. During her duet with the valet, she had turned to face the royal seats and passionately sung the words "Oh, how I love my mistress!" while clasping her hands on her heart. She was nearly lynched on the spot by the Jacobins present, who leapt onto the stage. Later, the angry Jacobins tried to seek revenge by demanding that she

sing a revolutionary song. She refused, but has now decided it may be a prudent move to take early retirement. She has been an idol of Parisians for the past 20 years.

Rosalie Dugazon, the famous opera singer and actress.

15. Paris. Nicolas de Bonneville publishes the *New Conjugal Code* which groups all legislation concerning civil marriages.

15. Paris. Dumouriez resigns. Louis XVI forms a cabinet made up of many unknown Feuillants: Lajard becomes Minister of War, Chambonas is Minister of Foreign Affairs, Terrier de Monciel Interior Minister and Beaulieu Finance Minister.→

16. Maubeuge. La Fayette sends a threatening letter to the Assembly. On the same day, military operations are suspended (→18).

17. Paris. The few remaining royalist officers in the army are infuriated by a decree making the wearing of the red bonnet, a symbol of liberty, obligatory. Some 600 royalist officers have left the army in less than a month.

17. Paris. A delegation of the sector of Croix Rouge comes to the Assembly to criticise Louis XVI, accusing him of perjury. Meanwhile, members of the wheat market sector call for the resignation of the leaders of the Paris National Guard.

17. Paris. The Assembly creates a special committee to oversee the activities of the new ministers, which it doesn't trust.

17. Brussels. The royalist journalist Rivarol arrives. He has been forced into exile by growing political tension in France.

18. Paris. The Assembly learns of La Fayette's letter in which he lashes out at the army's lack of discipline and the unrest caused by the clubs.

18. Dijon. A rumour about the presence of non-juring priests among enemy ranks results in the arrest of priests by the National Guard.

19. Paris. The Assembly is informed of the King's veto of the decree on the deportation of non-juring priests.

19. Paris. The Assembly rules that all genealogical documents kept in public store-rooms must be destroyed.

20. Paris. A huge mob overruns the Tuileries during a demonstration organised by the Brissotins to demand that the royal veto of the latest decrees be withdrawn and the ministers recalled.→

The King recalls the Feuillants to power

The outgoing Minister of War is ironically shown climbing out of a pile of dung that is being swept out through the door of the King's stables.

Paris, June 15

The hesitant policies practised by the Girondists were their undoing. Louis XVI got rid of them at the first opportunity. Today, Dumouriez was the last of Brissot's men to leave government. It all began with the letter sent by Roland to the King on June 11th. It was a veritable republican manifesto demanding that the sovereign renounce his veto powers. Louis XVI had opposed the decree of May 27th. ordering the deportation of the non-juring priests, and that of June 8th. proposed by the Minister of War, Servan, on the creation outside Paris of a military camp for 20,000 Federates. On the 12th. the King dismissed Roland, Clavière, Servan. The latter was replaced by Dumouriez, who hoped that he could stay in power. But he was booed yesterday by deputies angered by the government reshuffle. He had to resign after unsuccessfully asking the King to change his mind about the veto. Only two Girondists ministers are still in place. The others are unknown members of the Feuillants: Lajard is War Minister, Terrier Interior Minister, Beaulieu Finance Minister and Chambonas Foreign Minister.

Santerre, leader of the sans culottists

Paris, June 19

There is tension tonight at the meeting of the Enfants Trouvés sector. The leader of the neighbourhood's National Guard battalion, Santerre, has met the sans culottists, or extreme republicans, in the cafe he runs. With his companion Alexandre, a commander at Saint Marcel and notary's clerk, he is trying keep the sectors aware of the counter-revolutionary peril. They said that the people will use force instead of legal means to get what they want, since the deputies are unable to impose their will on the King and the government has been dismissed. Santerre plans to cause unrest tomorrow (→20).

Santerre, "neighbourhood leader".

The Legislative Assembly abolishes the last feudal rights

Paris, June 18

It was a very tough battle, but the democrats ended up by winning it. The final decree on the abolition without compensation of all the feudal rights has just been approved. In fact, the fight ended on June 14th. On that day, the moderates, led by the deputy Deusy, had said that the remaining feudal rights could not be abolished because they were the property of the nobility and the right to property was sacrosanct. They really feared that such a move would pave the way for egalitarianism. On June 12th. the deputy Louvet had called for the abolition of feudal rights, saying it was necessary to fight against all "excessive fortunes". But those opposed to the bill drafted by the feudal committee were taken by surprise. They had walked out of the Assembly to show they did not agree. The democrats then took advantage of this and approved the most important clauses of the law. This was done quite legally as more than 200 deputies were still present. The abolition of the last feudal rights, which Mailhe has called "the missing stone in the foundations of the Revolution", has now become a fact of life.

The Assembly's generosity: "My dear colleagues, the people are suffering, what will we sacrifice for them? All! Except my castle (1), my tithe (2), my pride (3), my game (4), my rights over my vassals (5) and my lard (7)."

A mob from the suburbs overruns the Tuileries

Paris, June 20

The Assembly was right to be wary. Today marks the anniversary of the oath at the Jeu de Paume. It is also the anniversary of the King's flight to Varennes. As if that were not enough, the population has been further stirred up by Louis XVI's veto on the latest decrees approved by the deputies. For the past few days, the wildest rumours have been circulating: people were saying that a plot was being hatched at the Tuileries and that the King's guards wanted to murder patriots. As a precautionary measure, the department's authorities yesterday ruled that "any gathering is against the law". But the people wanted to go to the Assembly to demand that the veto be abolished. Woken abruptly this morning at 9 o'clock, Terrier, the Minister of the Interior, asked the authorities to "order the troops to march to defend the palace", but all that was done was to shut the main gates. By

10 a.m. a large crowd was already gathering, although so far it was only asking to march past the Manège hall. People were calling for caution: "The blood of patriots must not flow to satisfy the pride and the ambition of the perfidious palace of the Tuileries". But suddenly, in the early afternoon, citizens begin to arrive from all the sectors, along with units of the National Guard armed with pikes, sabres and sticks. Most have come from the Saint Marceau and Saint Antoine suburbs, from the neighbourhoods of Montmartre and the Observatoire: some 20,000 of them, led by Santerre and Saint Hugue. They wave threatening banners proclaiming "Liberty or death!". The mob then goes into the Manège and passes through the Feuillants alley to pour into the Tuileries. That is when some panicking municipal officials rush to the King's rooms to beg him to open the gates. But it is too late: a

People from the neighbourhoods march to deliver a petition to the Assembly.

roar rises from the gardens, the gates have broken. Part of the crowd has gone through the Louvre to reach the Carrousel, outside the palace. Santerre faces the mob and screams that the people must get into the King's rooms. A group

from the Val de Grâce sector seems aggressive. It has dragged along a cannon. The King, surrounded by his wife, his sister and his two children, listens to the roar of the mob as it gets closer. He doesn't know what is going on. It is just 4 p.m.

The gates of the Tuileries palace have broken and the mob rushes in, armed with pikes and sabres. Santerre's men have even brought a cannon.

The King dons a red bonnet and calms the rioters

Paris, June 20

The rioters have succeeded in getting inside the Tuileries. With a loud crash, the palace doors are broken down with axes. The big cannon that the people from the Val de Grâce have brought is dragged slowly up to the first floor and its heavy wheels wreck the fine wooden floor. The few National Guardsmen left to defend the palace are powerless to stop the huge tidal wave of people. On the ground floor, groups of men brandishing pikes are noisily milling about, searching for the Queen's rooms. One of them finds the way and they start to tear the doors down. Marie Antoinette is sobbing and frozen with fear.

She rushes off with her children to seek shelter, running down a secret passage linking the King's room to the Dauphin's. She finally finds a refuge in the Council chamber, guarded by the royalist grenadiers of the Filles Saint Thomas sector. As for the King and his sister, they are now completely surrounded by rioters, but have not yet been found. Suddenly the head of the second legion rushes up to the monarch and begs him to show himself in order to avoid the worst. Louis XVI, escorted by grenadiers, reluctantly agrees to appear before his people in the parade chamber. The mob is still ugly, but silent, as if impressed by the grand surround-

Louis XVI takes the hand of a grenadier and places it on his heart, asking: "Do you think I am trembling?"

ings and the sight of the sovereign. The King starts speaking in a calm voice, asking what they want and proclaiming his loyalty to the Constitution. He dons the red wool bonnet worn by patriots that is handed to him and even drinks from a proffered bottle of wine. But he will not say that he agrees to withdraw his veto. The butcher Legendre then says to him: "You are falsehearted. Take care, the situation is grave and the people are fed up with being your toys." Sitting on a bench by a window, the King watches the men and women of Paris file past slowly as they snigger or insult him. "National justice for tyrants! Down with Veto and his wife!" say the banners they brandish under his nose. Meanwhile, Marie Antoinette is also being humiliated as she is guarded by Santerre, who points to the Queen as if she were a circus attraction. "This is the Queen, this is the royal Prince!" he tells the mob. Standing on the Council table and wearing a red bonnet, the Dauphin watches the miniature gallows on which tiny figures of women have been hung. "Beware of the gibbet!" say the notes attached to the gallows. It is all over by 10 o'clock. The mob has left the palace, its gardens and courtyards, leaving piles of broken glass behind. The deputies have not done a thing. Around 6 o'clock Pétion had gone to the Tuileries, where he said: "The people have done what they had to. But enough of this now, let everybody depart." The King's authority is now in tatters (→June 21).

Madame Elisabeth is briefly mistaken for the Queen. She tries to cope.

The King drinks the rioters' wine.

June 1792

from 21st. to 30th.

🏛 Legislative Assembly

21. Paris. The frightened Assembly forbids delegations of citizens to come to its podium. Brissot's supporters call for the leaders of the rioters to be punished.

22. Paris. Louis XVI issues a proclamation to the nation on the events of June 20th. in which he says he will not give in to pressure.

22. Marseilles. During a patriotic banquet, a Jacobin from Montpellier sings the *Chant de Guerre de l'Armée du Rhin*, popular among the Federates.

22. Paris. The Legislative Assembly approves the decree placing town councils in charge of civil status.

22. Amiens. The authorities of the Somme department criticise the events in Paris and issue a statement declaring that the nation is in danger, requisitioning the National Guard and issuing plans to send delegates to the King to help protect him.

24. Paris. Appointed lieutenant of the 58th. infantry regiment by Servan, the War Minister, who had noticed him during manoeuvres, Lazare Hoche goes to Thionville, his garrison town.

26. Paris. The Assembly orders each commune to set up an altar to the nation.

26. Paris. The Marais theatre performs a new drama by Beaumarchais, *The Guilty Mother*. It is not very successful. It has a hateful character named Begearss, an anagram of Bergasse, the lawyer who had given Beaumarchais a hard time during the Kornmann trial. →

27. Eure. Under pressure from Buzot, the Evreux town council refuses to issue the counter-revolutionary and royalist statements of the authorities of the Eure department.

28. Paris. La Fayette, who has left the army without warning, goes to the Assembly to demand that clubs be banned (→ 29).

29. Paris. The Assembly rejects by 339 votes to 234 a proposal made by Gaudet calling for La Fayette to be reprimanded.

30. Paris. After his failure, La Fayette returns to his headquarters. Brissot and Derby ask the Assembly to file charges against the general (→ July 17, 92).

Was the mayor of Paris in league with the rioters?

Paris, June 21

What on earth was the mayor of Paris doing during the riot? In a short statement, Louis XVI did not hesitate to complain bitterly about the way Pétion behaved yesterday. The mayor, who must have been aware of the violent unrest rocking the capital, only reached the Tuileries in the late afternoon. When the King met him in the Oeil de Boeuf chamber, he told him that he had only just been informed of what was happening. Louis XVI curtly replied that the incidents had started two hours earlier. Also, on June 19th., Pétion had been warned that "the citizenry appears to have the most peaceful intentions, but is in fact seeking weapons". However, Pétion had not requisitioned the troops, despite a request from the department's officials. Instead, he even tried around midnight to confer legality to a movement he could not control by allowing a crowd to "march and meet under the command of its leaders". Such passive collusion has enraged the King. Today, Louis XVI sent a letter to the Assembly to demand that repressive measures be taken right away. Tomorrow, Pétion must explain himself to the deputies.

Liberty bonnet

The appearance at a window of the Tuileries of the King wearing a red bonnet was so striking that it immediately inspired a song:

This bonnet!
What dignity it gives us French!
How fine it looks on our heads!
The faces of nobles blanch.
It fills their hearts with dread,
This Bonnet.

This Bonnet,
Ladies: your only trimming;
Kids: your best-loved plaything;
Husbands: put on no other hat,
Sign of a true democrat,
This bonnet.

With this bonnet
All men we now command,
With this bonnet
Cover your heads proudly.
One day soon someone, we hope
Will crown his Holiness the Pope
With this bonnet.

The provinces are not backing Parisians

France, late June

Could the King's revenge come from the provinces? From all over France, the Legislative Assembly is receiving protests against the action taken by the people of Paris during the events of June 20th. Not only are the supposedly moderate departmental authorities expressing distrust about Paris, but so are the provincial town councils. The bourgeois are frightened. The citizens of Le Havre are calling for "revenge upon the scoundrels who have violated the home of the hereditary representative of the nation". They ask that "the Assembly benches be silenced, as they do not represent the people, while their indecent rumblings are rejected by all honest citizens". The statement made by the authorities of the Eure was seen as so eloquent that it was printed and sent to all the other departments. The Somme, the Meuse, the Gironde, the Var and Abbeville, Strasbourg, Tarascon, Bastia — all congratulate the King on his courage and dignity. Only a few, such as Buzot in Evreux, are shocked that "the victors of the Bastille, the Frenchmen who laid the foundations of our Constitution" are being called "scoundrels".

Theatregoers shun some of the new plays

Paris, June 23

Some playwrights have been trying far too hard to follow the fashion of the day. A new work by Charles Philippe Ronsin, *Arétophile ou la Révolution de Cyrène*, a tragedy in five acts, was only a moderate success. Ronsin had been careful to stress the virtues of the nation and of liberty, both themes that are much appreciated by the patriots, but his increasingly revolutionary stances have not had the desired effect. He was luckier last year when the same theatre on the Place Louvois showed his play *La Ligue des Fanatiques et des Tyrans*, another tragedy in verse and in three acts, which was a big hit. As for his other plays, they have been printed but none of them has been performed.

The army lacks both soldiers and officers

Paris, June 26

Accounting can be a depressing job. Two months after war was declared on Austria, there are still 72,000 men missing out of the 250,000 which had been expected. Emigration has hit the officer corps hard. Just in the infantry, there are 3,000 officers less than there should be. The situation is only good for the non-commissioned officers. For them, the emigration of their superiors has often meant a quick and welcome promotion. In accordance with measures taken last year, the national volunteers have been used to beef up the regular army. But the administrators in charge of recruitment have been slow to act. Only 83 battalions are organised, although 169 had been expected. Moreover, the Assembly is still refusing to integrate the volunteers into the line troops, due to a fear of aristocratic military leaders. As for their equipment, money, rifles and uniforms are still sorely lacking, despite the many decrees that have been issued about this by the deputies.

Some volunteers still wear parts of their civilian outfits.

▷

A major setback for Beaumarchais

Paris, June 26

The wild acclaim that greeted Beaumarchais' *Barber of Seville* and *Marriage of Figaro* now seems only a distant memory. His new work, *The Guilty Mother,* which was supposed to be the final part of the trilogy, is far from being as brilliant as the two earlier plays. The first performance tonight was an awful flop. The unfortunate actors of the Marais theatre could hardly make themselves heard. The audience didn't stop whistling and booing. Supporters of the rival Théâtre de la Nation added to the din. The play was bound to be a bad one, since its author had not entrusted them with it, they claimed.

A dishonest baker is punished

Montpellier, June 26

It is getting harder every day to cheat over the quality of bread. A local baker has just been reminded of this fact. He has been sentenced by the police tribunal to pay a fine of five livres after angry customers lodged a complaint against him. But there is worse to come for him: 50 banners are to be posted all over town so that everybody can be told of his dishonesty. Anyone who tries to sell mouldy bread must be severely punished. Bread is the people's basic food.

An English caricature showing the joy of Parisian aristocrats on hearing news of French defeats: "We will keep our rights!"

The royalists are active around Jalès

At Jalès, the monarchists' fortified camp will be overrun and set on fire.

Ardèche, late June

The royalists have once again gathered on the Jalès plain. The castle that stands over it has been a base for noblemen planning an uprising twice in the past. Tension grew suddenly in the region on June 21st., when the inhabitants of the village of Berrias trampled a tricoloured cockade underfoot. For his part the Comte François de Saillans, who leads the royalists of the Vivarais, had organised a major uprising for early July. When he heard the news about the events in Paris, he decided to move sooner than planned, but the plot was discovered. The authorities of the Ardèche department mobilised all available battalions of national volunteers to crush the uprising before it had a chance to get under way. This was not an isolated plot. Taking advantage of the growing clashes between Jacobin-controlled town councils and Feuillant-led departmental authorities, many nobles and non-juring priests have been trying for months to restore the monarchy's powers (→ July 12).

Volney's farming innovations fail

Corsica, June 22

What a bitter disappointment for such an advocate of new ideas. Volney had wanted to experiment with the cultivation of tropical plants on his new property at La Confina, near the port of Ajaccio. Full of hope, he had planted several banana, sugar cane, coffee and date trees. He then enclosed his land to stop local peasants from grazing their animals on it. But they are mocking him and getting their goats into his plantation. Volney, who had hoped to be a deputy for Corsica at the Convention, has not been any luckier in politics. Instead of votes he got threats. Local rivalries are far too complex for mainland people.

Flowers are worn in a hat.

Marquis de La Fayette launches an unsuccessful coup attempt

Paris, June 29

A disappointed La Fayette has had to return to his troops at Maubeuge. He had come to Paris to order the Assembly to restore the King's power to him by interpreting the Constitution in a very moderate way, as do the Feuillants. Already, on June 18th., a letter had been read out at the Assembly in which he called for the withdrawal of the decrees against the émigrés and the non-juring priests, the free use of the royal veto, the dissolution of clubs and the outlawing of popular gatherings. Booed by the Girondists, the letter was, however, cheered by quite a few deputies. In the wake of the riot of June 20th. at the Tuileries and the royalist reac-

La Fayette shown as a burnt candle.

tion that followed it, he thought that his proposals had a chance of being accepted by the Assembly. In fact, a majority of deputies had backed him yesterday when he called for the arrest of any deputy suspected of the slightest degree of collusion with the rioters of the Tuileries. But La Fayette wanted to go further and was planning a veritable coup d'état. Today, he even attempted to mobilise the National Guard and get it to march on the Jacobins Club to break it up by force. Alas, the move has failed. Faced with the hostility of the court and of the Girondists, the general now only has the political support of the Feuillants. This was not enough for his bid to succeed (→ June 30).

♦ 🏛 Legislative
Assembly

1. Paris. A delegation of the sector known as the Croix Rouge comes to the Assembly to ask it to declare the nation to be in danger and to dismiss the Paris National Guard commander. At the same meeting, the petition, or the "call of the 20,000", condemning what took place on June 20th. is submitted to the legislators.

2. Paris. Overnight, the Assembly decrees that meetings of administrative bodies must be made public, and dismisses the commanders of the National Guard in cities with 50,000 inhabitants or more.

2. Marseilles. Ignoring the King's veto against the arrival of Federates, the Marseilles battalion sets off for Paris.

2. Paris. The Assembly by-passes the royal veto against the setting up of the Federates' camp by ruling that they may attend the Federation feast on July 14th. and can then go to the Soissons camp.

3. Dourdan. The English engineer Pickford sets up a cotton mill.

6. Paris. The department's council dismisses the capital's mayor Pétion and the Commune's prosecutor Manuel (→13).

7. Paris. The musician François Devienne scores a big success with the first performance of his comic opera *Les Visitandines* at the Rue Feydeau theatre.

8. Lyons. A Liberty tree is planted on the Terreaux square, which is then re-named Liberty square.

11. Paris. The National Assembly declares the nation to be in danger.→

12. Ardèche. The castles of Bannes and Jalès, occupied by royalist National Guardsmen, are liberated by members of the National Guard of the Gard supported by line troops.

13. Paris. The Assembly decides that Pétion and Manuel can now return to their posts.

14. Ireland. The Dublin Corps, a militia of Irish patriots, holds a procession to celebrate the anniversary of the fall of the Bastille.

15. Paris. The Cordeliers club approves a proposal calling for a Convention to be set up.

The Assembly lashes out against the King

Paris, July 3

"You no longer mean anything to this Constitution that you have so unjustly violated, nor to the people you have betrayed in such a cowardly fashion!"

With that terrible charge against Louis XVI, Vergniaud ended his speech to the Assembly today. His eloquence was such that the deputies stood to cheer him warmly. This Girondist deputy has just clearly raised the issue of the monarch's future: if Louis XVI does not whole-heartedly defend liberty and the nation against the external threats facing France, he will be considered as having abdicated under the terms of the Constitution. The fiery speaker has therefore proposed outright that the nation be formally declared to be "in danger". Vergniaud has also demanded that the ministers be held entirely responsible for the current internal unrest caused by religious troubles, and in the event

Pierre Vergniaud, a great orator.

of a foreign invasion. In short, Vergniaud has issued a final warning to Louis XVI. As leader of the army, the King has a duty to lead patriotic resistance, but everything points to the contrary.

The Girondists

The region of Bordeaux has given its name to the most influential political group at the Legislative Assembly, the Girondists. Initially, this party had formed itself around the new representatives of the department of the Gironde: Gensonné, Ducos, Grangeneuve, Guadet and Vergniaud. All these men are lawyers and brilliant orators whose eloquence makes up for their lack of political experience. Brissot and his friends then came to join the group, which is on the left of the Assembly and broke off from Robespierre over the war issue. In favour of war, the Girondists often advocate vague policies, simultaneously backing the King and the democrats. Girondists meet at the salons of Julie Talma, Condorcet or Madame Roland, who is an avid supporter of these philosophy-loving republicans.

Bishop Lamourette calls for politicians to end their feuding

Paris, July 7

It was an extremly moving call. Lamourette, the deputy of Lyons and constitutional bishop, has just made a highly eloquent speech. In it he appealed to all the political parties to settle their differences once and for all. His call for peace and harmony has had a big effect amid the current tense atmosphere. The deputies hardly knew what to do. When the speaker asked them to stand up and show that they rejected both the republic and constitutional monarchy, which he said were the chief sources of discord, they all jumped up and started embracing each other in a great show of emotion. Can such a spontaneous accord last? Some are already expressing their doubts.

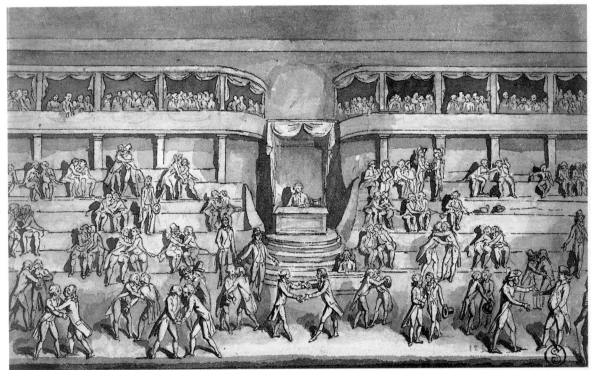

In a wave of patriotic emotion, the deputies embrace each other: this is known as the "Lamourette hug".

An uneasy calm has marked this year's Federation celebrations in Paris

The symbols of the aristocracy are burnt on a huge fire.

Paris, July 14

Today's celebrations in Paris for the Federation have been held amid a tense calm that hardly masked underlying anger. Large numbers of Federates came to join in this year's celebrations. A highly revolutionary Federates' Committee was even set up earlier this month. On July 11th. Robespierre had termed the committee members "defenders of liberty". He warned them to be suspicious of royal power and advised them to be cautious. However, Marat has never been one for caution. He has written an article calling on the people to rebel against the King and his accomplices who betray the Revolution, but the printer refused to publish it. The militants of the Paris sectors are the ones showing the most anger. They have been issuing petitions demanding the rehabilitation of the mayor Pétion and of the Commune's public prosecutor Manuel, suspended for their role in the riot of June 20th. (→July 20).

Two priests are massacred in Bordeaux

Bordeaux, July 15

Non-juring priests are no longer safe. An opponent of the clergy's civil Constitution, the vicar general Langoiran had felt he was in danger since he had become one of the chief targets of speeches by members of revolutionary clubs. As a precaution he had sought refuge at Caudéran, on the outskirts of Bordeaux, where he lived in hiding with two other churchmen. But he was not cautious enough: this morning armed men came to arrest him. Posters immediately appeared on walls calling on people to come and insult him: "Langoiran has been arrested and will be taken from Caudéran to Bordeaux this evening. Let all good patriots be informed." This call had its effect. As the National Guard was busy elsewhere, the "good patriots" were soon able to take action. Abbot Langoiran and one of his companions were killed.

Luckner, an over-talkative marshal

Paris, July 17

Marshal Luckner is in very deep trouble. The Federates have now demanded that charges be brought against La Fayette and that the army's aristocratic general staff be dismissed. Luckner, a Prussian nobleman friendly with La Fayette, is a high profile target. People have expressed surprise at seeing him in Paris at a time when the enemy is threatening France's front lines. He even had the temerity to reveal La Fayette's plan to march on Paris during a dinner. Luckner, who used to say his "heart was more French then his accent", will have a hard time convincing the revolutionaries that he is on their side (→July 21).

Luckner, marshal since 1791.

Horace Desmoulins' civil christening

Paris, July 8

The tiny Horace Desmoulins is one of the first infants of his generation to have had a civil baptism. The new procedure has just come into force. His father told the registry official that he wanted to avoid being blamed later by his son for having "committed him to religious opinions" at a time when he was too young to choose for himself. The father, flanked by two witnesses, placed the baby on the Altar to the Nation and had his birth registered on the civil status register instead of in the parish archives.

The King's Garden has a new steward

Paris, July 16

Bernardin de Saint Pierre, the author of *Etudes de la Nature,* has just been chosen by Louis XVI as a truly worthy successor to the great Buffon. The King had been impressed by Bernardin's moral and civic qualities and has appointed him as the new steward of the King's Garden. It was not his scientific competence, but the pamphlet attacking club members, which was published yesterday, that particularly impressed the King. The naturalist Daubenton and the botanist Lamarck are slightly jealous. But despite his lack of technical knowledge, Bernardin has a deep and real love of nature. He has another virtue that the government should appreciate: he is extremely good at avoiding unnecessary expense.

The alleys of the Jardin des Plantes are a favourite place for walks.

Legislative Assembly

19. Paris. The author Pierre Desforges has a comedy called *The Altar of the Nation* performed at the Théâtre des Amis.

18. Paris. Death of John Paul Jones, commander of the American Navy during the War of Independence.

20. Paris. The Federates' central committee, which is based at the Jacobins Club, issues an "Address to Frenchmen of the 83 departments" announcing that the Federates intend to remain in Paris (→Aug. 25, 92).

20. Paris. Vergniaud, Guadet and Gensonné offer their mediation to the King.

21. Paris. At the Assembly, the deputy Lasource calls for charges to be lodged against La Fayette for having suggested that Marshal Luckner should march on the capital.

22. Paris. The decree proclaiming the nation to be in danger is read on public squares as cannons fire hourly shots of warning. →

24. Paris. The Assembly lowers to 16 the age at which boys can enrol in the army of the Republic.

25. Coblentz. The Duke of Brunswick, commander in chief of the Prussian army, publishes a manifesto. The text, written by an émigré, the Marquis de Limon, threatens Parisians with exemplary revenge if they do not submit to their sovereign (→Aug. 1, 92).

25. Paris. The Legislative Assembly issues a decree authorising the sectors to meet permanently. Also, the battalion of Federates of Brest and the Finistère sets up camp in the Saint Marceau suburb.

26. Paris. At the Assembly, Brissot makes a speech violently attacking the groups calling for the King's ousting.

27. Paris. The sectors of Paris set up a central correspondence office to enable them to communicate with the provinces and among themselves.

27. Paris. The Federates hold a civic banquet on the ruins of the Bastille.

31. Paris. The Mauconseil sector rules that on August 5th. it will come to inform the Legislative Assembly that it no longer recognises Louis XVI's authority (→Aug. 5, 92).

France is declared to be in danger

This martial procession on the Pont Neuf encourages many patriotic citizens to rush to the enlistment centre.

Paris, July 22

Calls to arms and noisy martial songs have been ringing throughout the capital.

The Assembly declared the nation to be in danger on July 11th. and the city council today began enlisting the volunteers. A grandiose ceremony has been organised to make the event more impressive. For a day, the city has become a huge stage on which civic and republican heroism is playing the lead role. Two large processions have been gradually winding their way along the streets. At the head of each one, a mounted National Guardsman carries a large banner bearing the words "Citizens, the Nation is in danger". At the end of the day, the banners will be placed at the city hall and the Pont Neuf, where they will remain for the entire duration of hostilities. Eight vast amphitheatres have been set up in Paris. The awnings that cover them have been decorated with oak leaf crowns and tricoloured banners. A makeshift table placed on two drums is used to register the names of the citizens who volunteer. The impressive and colourful ceremony has sparked off a wave of popular enthusiasm and martial fervour among the population. With breasts swollen with patriotic pride and devotion, some 15,000 men, young and not so young, are all set to sign up.

A volunteer sets off to fight for his country: both bourgeois and peasants volunteer to join the army.

Volunteer son makes his father proud

Clamecy, July 31

The young man from Nevers who is walking so quickly along the main road has chosen to spare his family painful farewells. Martin Bellanger decided alone to enrol in the volunteer battalions and is now in a hurry to reach the border where the patriots are fighting for their country. He walks with a resolute step, carrying his few belongings wrapped in a sack attached to a stick. It is hot and his shirt is open to the waist. Suddenly a man pops out of some bushes along the road. It is his father, who embraces him, saying: "Go if you must, because you are doing the right thing, but take this purse and jacket as you will need them both badly." The young man then sets off again, a broad smile on his face.

A Russian plot against Poland

Warsaw, July 24

If there was one thing that scared Poland's neighbours, it was the prospect of a strong Poland united by its new Constitution and its hereditary monarch. The Prussians, and particularly the Russians, were extremely worried, but they needed an excuse to intervene. Such an excuse was provided by a few members of the Polish nobility opposed to the Constitution, which limited their prerogatives. They formed a league called the Confederation of Targowica and asked Russia to intervene to save the country from the threat of "the monarchical and democratic revolution of May 3rd". Catherine II reacted promptly to this call. On May 18th. Russian troops marched into Poland. The King of Poland, Stanislas Augustus Poniatowski, today was forced to join the confederation of his opponents. This truly marks the death of the Polish Constitution.

An illustration from the "Story of Sergeant-Major Orson".

High speed writing with shorthand

Paris, July 21

It has become as easy as pie to write shorthand. In just a few hours, people can learn the basic rules that will allow them to turn a lengthy speech into a set of easy to translate symbols. The translator Pierre Bertin has adapted the principle discovered by the English expert Samuel Taylor so that it can be used in French. Stenography, with its geometric characters which "are linked one to the other", will make deputies' work easier, save authors and court officials from writer's cramp and will "even be a useful pastime for the rich".

Carnot tells soldiers to fight with pikes

Paris, July 25

Courage is not enough to fight a modern war. Today's soldiers also need weapons. However, French patriot troops are sorely lacking in both rifles and ammunition, and some are wondering how they can continue fighting. The enemy is brave and armed to the teeth.

The officer Lazare Carnot has just told the Assembly that he supports the theories of a certain Scott, a former colonel of dragoons who has written a book stressing the importance of the pike as a weapon of war. The lowly pike, which started off as the homemade weapon of peasants in the early days of the Revolution, must now become the soldiers' weapon. The pike has a double advantage: it can be quickly built and can also be found easily, for example on castle or park railings. At least 300,000 more pikes must be quickly made by weapons factories, and local ironsmiths must get to work right away, Carnot said. But Carnot's appeal in favour of the pike has not been greeted with enthusiasm by the deputies (→ Aug. 1).

The pike is a fearsome weapon.

Everybody must do their utmost to contribute to the war effort

Paris, July 30

The huge esplanade outside the Invalides has become a hive of frantic activity. No less than 258 forges have been working non-stop, producing four cannons every day. The work for the war effort has even spread to the Seine river, on which boats have been tied up near the Tuileries gardens. Aboard, some 90 workshops are busy building badly needed rifles. There is a great sense of urgency. Over the past two years, the arming of the National Guard has caused a big drop in the number of weapons being delivered to the army. Even the army's takeover of the rifle factories has not resulted in each soldier having his own gun. A desperate effort is being made. Saltpetre is being scraped from city walls for gunpowder and there are even plans to melt down church bells.

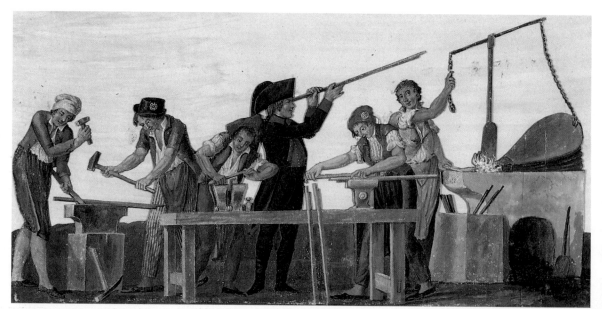

Workshops have been set up on the Invalides esplanade to produce rifles badly needed by the volunteers.

A young woman fights the tyrants

Paris, July 25

"Born with the courage of a Roman and a hatred of tyrants, I would be happy to contribute to their destruction. Let the last despot perish!" The beautiful young brunette wearing a riding outfit who spoke these words before the Assembly today was very warmly cheered by all those present. She is not wealthy enough to give funds to her country, so she is offering to take up arms to defend it. Her name is Claire Lacombe. She used to be an actress in the provinces before coming to Paris, where she is currently unemployed. But she added that instead of worrying about her lack of work, she feels the "purest joy" because it means that she is free to offer her services to the nation. However, the Assembly's speaker thanked her before graciously rejecting her generous offer. He told the other deputies after she had left that Claire was so lovely that she would "be better at softening up tyrants than at fighting against them".

A private academy of music has major money problems

Marseilles, July 23

This evening, the Concert of Marseilles is to play some very classical pieces, as it is offering works by Lully and Gluck.

In Marseilles, this academy of music is the oldest and most famous. It was founded in 1719 by Marshal de Villars, the then-governor of the region of Provence. Each Monday and Friday evening it holds concerts which have always been of high quality. The Concert gets no financial assistance whatsoever from the city and survives only thanks to contributions from its 350 relatively wealthy members, who pay a yearly subscription of 75 livres each.

The rest of the money needed to keep going is provided by subscriptions to concerts costing a modest six livres per season. The Concert has always had a hard time making ends meet, particularly as guest performers have a tendency to ask for high fees.

The 500 Federates of Marseilles sing the "Marseillaise"

Paris, July 30
Soldiers of France,
The morn is breaking,
The day of glory dawns at last!
See the tyrant's banner shaking
As it basely streams in the blast.
The field of battle lies before you,
Fierce foes advance in their pride,
Confusion spreading far and wide
While for aid your children
Implore you to arms
And hence away
To arms this glorious day.
March on, march on
Brave sons of France
To fame and victory.
Ye tyrants quake,
Your days are over
Detested so by friend and foe
Who your base designs discover,
Ye shall die as traitors do.
Each gallant heart
With zeal o'erflowing goes eagerly
Forth at the call.
Though some may
For their country fall,
Others will hear bugles blowing.

During its long march to the capital, the battalion of 500 Federates from Marseilles sang this song. They were still singing the *Marseillaise* when they reached Paris. The song tells of combat and of tyranny, of the motherland and of liberty. The Revolution has at last found its anthem, a hymn to war, but also to brotherhood and to the sacred love of country. The song is uniting all of France in a wave of patriotic fervour. The fiery patriots of Marseilles were the first to adopt this song whose origins are to be found in eastern France.

The war song of the army of the Rhine becomes the "March of Marseilles".

A big banquet held on the Champs Elysées ends in fighting

Violent fighting rages amid the pastoral setting of the Champs Elysées.

Paris, July 30

The Federates had only been waiting for the arrival of the battalion from Marseilles to launch hostilities. The first clash came this evening. At the end of the banquet held in their honour by the city, the men from Marseilles attacked the National Guardsmen of Filles Saint Thomas, all strong supporters of the monarchy, and forced them to flee. Over the past few days, the Federates had been champing at the bit. They have picked some delegates as members of a secret leadership which is planning a major uprising. Their ranks are now full: 5,000 men ready to leap into action at the slightest excuse.

1. Paris. The National Assembly orders all the town councils of the kingdom to produce pikes of the "Marshal of Saxony" type. They are to be distributed to every single citizen.

1. Montélimar. The special tribunal set up to try the patriots involved in the massacre at the Glacière acquits all those charged.

3. Paris. At the request of 47 out of 48 sectors, Pétion comes to the Assembly to ask that the King be stripped of his crown.→

3. Toulouse. Like the capital's society and all of the provincial societies, the Jacobins Club demands that the King be immediately stripped of his powers.

4. Paris. The court orders the Swiss to be stationed at the Tuileries. They are usually stationed at Courbevoie and Rueil. Large numbers of armed noblemen arrive in the capital.

4. Paris. Awaiting a decision over the ousting of the King, the Quinze Vingts sector sets a deadline for the "people's patience" that will expire at midnight on August 9th.→

5. Paris. In response to an invitation from the Mauconseil sector, the other sectors come to ask the Assembly to rule that Louis XVI is no longer King of the French.

6. Paris. A new petition, brought to the Champ de Mars, calls for the King to be stripped of his crown.

7. Paris. The Théâtre Français on the Rue de Richelieu shows the premiere of a new tragedy by Jean François Ducis.

7. Paris. Marat appeals to the "Federates of the 83 departments". In this appeal, he formulates the concept of a monarch elected by a national convention.

8. Paris. The Legislative Assembly, acting on a proposal by François Amédée Doppet from Savoie, who had set up the Foreign Patriots Club, decides to create a legion of Allobroges grouping patriots of Savoie.

9. Paris. The Legislative Assembly ends its session without having dared to debate the petition from the sectors calling for the King's ousting. In the evening, calls to open revolt are issued among the sectors.

The Brunswick manifesto is seen as an affront to Parisians

Paris, August 1

It is anger rather than fear which has been spreading like wildfire through the capital. The text published on July 25th. by the Duke of Brunswick has just been sent to the Assembly. The deputies feel that the document's insolence is only surpassed by its absurdity. The commander of the Prussian army has deeply involved the King at a time when the people of Paris are calling for his ousting. The Duke states that the goal of the war is to "put an end to attacks against the altar and the throne" and to allow the French monarch to exercise his legitimate powers. In short, it is in the interests of Louis XVI that the European powers are preparing to invade France. The text is seen as final proof of the close links between the Tuileries palace and foreign powers. The manifesto is based on direct instructions issued by the King of France. Even more serious is the fact that Brunswick threatens to lay waste to France, as he sees the revolutionaries not just as simple enemies, but as dangerous men who must be eliminated. He states that if the slightest outrage is committed against the royal family, he will take exemplary revenge by "carrying out a total military execution of the city of Paris".

The Duke of Brunswick is in favour of an "exemplary revenge."

The day of a sansculottist

An artisan by day and a militant by night, the sansculottist is an ardent republican activist who gets up at dawn, works hard all day to feed his family and tries to be a "good son, good father and good husband". At the end of his long day's work, he goes to his sector bringing his membership card to talk politics and vote. On his way home, he stops to listen to a street speaker or to attend a public reading. Back at his garret with his family, he likes to read almanacs or play cards.

The sansculottist wears simple breeches and carries a pike.

The sectors demand Louis XVI's ousting

Paris city officials: Pétion stands between Manuel and Chaumette.

Paris, August 4

The Assembly only has five days left in which to decree that the King has forfeited his rights. That is the deadline set today by the Quinze Vingts sector of the Saint Antoine district. If the deputies have not forced Louis XVI to abdicate by August 9th., the people of Paris will rise up. On July 25th. the Croix Rouge and Mauconseil sectors came to call on the Assembly to strip the King of his powers. They felt that this move was based on the Constitution, given the obvious treason committed by the monarch. On the following day, the committees of the capital's 48 sectors met at the city hall, now known as the "Community House". Yesterday they agreed to approve the text issued by the Grenelle sector which demands the King's ousting. All the sectors signed the petition, with the exception of the one at the Filles Saint Thomas, known for its royalist views. The mayor, Pétion, was chosen to take the petition to the Assembly. However, the deputies decided to follow the suggestion made by Vergniaud and refuse to act on the sectors' call (→Aug. 9).

Master craftsman Nicolas Fourneau dies

Paris, August 4

Nicolas Fourneau died quietly, just as he spent his life. He was never seen at the Assembly's podium or among the Paris crowds on the Champ de Mars. However, in his own way he also worked for the Revolution. This self-taught master carpenter from Rouen, an expert at cutting wood, had come to Paris at the age of 50 to set up a carpentry school and teach a new generation of young artisans the secrets of the art of carpentry, about which he had even written a treatise. This became the chief goal of his life, and his knowledge spread far and wide as his students left the capital to start practising what they had been taught in the provinces. His contribution to the craft earned him a yearly grant of 10,000 livres from the state. But Nicolas Fourneau never cared much about being wealthy. He was in love with his craft.

The journalist Louise Robert is attacked

Paris, August 6

Speaking from the podium of the Jacobins Club, the journalist Louise Robert, née de Kéralio, has caused shudders to run down her audience's spines by telling of the terrible attack she has just been a victim of. Three "aristocrats" had attempted to tear off her revolutionary cockade and she fought back fiercely. "A small knife, a firm reponse and a roll of sheet music" were the only weapons she needed to rout her cowardly assailants, she said. Who now dare speak of the weaker sex? Louise Robert has in the past also shown great physical bravery and has managed to win victories over many an unsuspecting male opponent.

Racial violence continues to rock Saint Domingue

Saint Domingue, August 6

The situation is still extremely confused in the three provinces of the French part of Saint Domingue. For the time being, only the mulattoes who are in control of the west of the country accept the governor's authority. They laid down their weapons after the promulgation of the law of March 24th. which recognises their rights. Elsewhere, the authorities are powerless to restore law and order. In the north, the rebellious slaves have been resisting for a year. In the south, the white settlers today won a decisive battle near Jérémie. This give them renewed hope that they will be able to fulfil their dream and set up an independent state in the south.

Enemy soldiers are incited to desert

Isn't it better to get a grant of 100 livres than blows from a stick?

Paris, August 2

A special grant of 100 livres is being offered to each foreign soldier who agrees to "gather under the banner of Liberty". The speaker of the Assembly has finally got what he wants. Ever since last April he had been asking for a special grant for deserters. The offer which has just been approved is for a life-time grant of 100 livres to be paid every three months. The decree also provides for a guaranteed pension similar to that of French soldiers, as well as help and protection all over France. Yesterday a letter from a northern army officer was read out at the Assembly. He said that 700 Austrian deserters had just come over to the French side. This was welcome news for the deputies who approved the grant decree. Despite the propaganda campaign conducted by France to try to spread revolutionary ideas throughout Europe, it seems unlikely that the reward offered to deserters will convince the majority of France's enemies to rush to join the Revolution. The money involved is substantial, but it could still be not enough to do the trick.

Land values remain a good investment

Le Mans, August 8

Barbet has just passed away. This muslin merchant, a supporter of revolutionary ideals, has left his heirs one of the biggest fortunes in the city.

Apart from his shop in Le Mans and a branch in Cadiz, Spain, he owned shares in many other businesses in which he was a partner. Overall, more than 420,000 livres are owed to him this year. Moreover, a year and a half ago he had purchased state-owned property worth a total of 120,000 livres. The astute businessman knew that it was wise to invest in land. It was also a good way to prove his social success. Like so many noblemen of the Ancien Régime, Barbet had always done his utmost to become a major landowner.

On August 9th. the royal family attends Mass at the Tuileries on the eve of a decisive day. Just Madame Elisabeth and Madame de Lamballe remain to share the King' and Queen'ís everyday lives.

Alarm bells start ringing out while the Assembly continues to hesitate

Paris, August 9, evening

It is midnight. The King hears the alarm bells ring out throughout Paris to signal the start of the uprising. Their sound makes him shudder. The deadline granted to the deputies by the sectors of Paris ran out this evening. The monarchy has been the victim of the Assembly's hesitation. Overwhelmed by petitions demanding Louis XVI's ousting, it chose to bury its head in the sand instead of taking action. The deputy Viennot Vaublanc went so far as to say that the legislators could flee to Rouen in order not to have to debate under pressure from the people. However, it is too late for such advice. The people from the suburbs are calling for the King's blood, saying he has betrayed the nation. They want to take revenge on the moderates at the Assembly who last year whitewashed the shooting on the Champ de Mars. The deputies decided to remain in session, as the uprising is getting under way. People are grabbing weapons wherever they can. As drums beat, men load rifles, sharpen sabres and ready cannons. The Federates' Committee intends to play a major role in the events. These soldiers who have come from the provinces are to give the revolt against the monarchy in Paris a nationwide resonance. The Federates from Marseilles have gathered at the Cordeliers club, listening to Danton. In the Saint Antoine district, Santerre has grouped units of sector militants.

The fall of the Tuileries palace on August 10th. 1792: The final assault takes place under heavy fire from the Swiss Guards.   279

The fall of the Tuileries, after a three hour battle, left more than 1,000 victims. It has virtually ended the eight centuries' old Capet dynasty. The King has been made prisoner and suspended from office. It is the decisive step towards his ousting which has been called for since June and demanded since August 3rd. by the sectors of Paris. Nothing had been sure when the alarm bells started ringing at midnight. The King was prepared for the clash. If he were to win, he would be able to play on internal disputes within the Assembly, and the foreign armies, which he hoped would win, would have come to help him. But only the Swiss were there today to defend desperately a palace already deserted by the King against federates, sansculottists, the sectors and the National Guardsmen of the poorer districts. The people of Paris were armed with patriotism, a deep fear of counter-revolutionary plots and aspirations to equality. They were victorious. The people are now represented by a Commune and able to impose a Republic.

Federates, National Guards and sansculottists clashing with Swiss troops.

The ultimatum set by the sectors was due to expire at midnight. If the deputies did not strip the King of his powers, the people of Paris would take matters into their own hands. Alarm bells started ringing in the Saint Antoine district, on the right bank of the Seine, and in the Cordeliers, on the left bank. These were the two gathering places for the armed columns that were to march on the Tuileries. The Federate battalions, mainly from Marseilles and Brittany, had already formed up and 18 sectors were ready. In all, 30 sectors had promised to help. Out of the 48 sectors of Paris, 44 had decided to take part in the action. In the poorer districts everybody had grabbed pikes, while National Guardsmen were trying to form groups. There was a bit of trouble because not all the guards were in favour of the sansculottists. Everything would depend on their attitude and on that of the authorities. Would they try to stop the people from marching? The 100 or so deputies still at the Legislative Assembly were being extremely cautious. The public prosecutor of the department, Roederer, was at the King's side. Louis XVI wanted to avoid a clash. As for the mayor of Paris, Pétion, he fled around midnight. Only Mandat, the commander for August of the capital's National Guard, was resolved to defend the Tuileries.

The opposing forces

Events were to happen quickly. By 3 o'clock, an insurrectional Commune had been formed at the city hall with the sector delegates and against the wishes of the Paris authorities. Around 5 a.m., the Commune summoned Mandat and accused him of treason. He was arrested and butchered as he was being dragged off to jail. Mandat was replaced by Santerre, one of the leaders of the revolt. The insurrectional Commune, which now held the reins of power, had dealt a severe blow to its opponents by eliminating the man in charge of defending the Tuileries. By around 6 o'clock, the Federates and sector members from the left bank had managed to cross the Saint Michel bridge without firing a shot, as the National Guard unit wanted to avoid bloodshed. Gradually, they got to the small Carrousel square opposite the main courtyard of the Tuileries. The insurgents, still few in number, were surprised by the security precautions. Over the wall, they could see the Swiss in their red uniforms, a large unit of National Guardsmen, cavalry and cannons aimed at the Carrousel. Mandat had called in nearly 4,000 men. Apart from the 900 Swiss, led by Lieutenant Colonel de Maillardoz, there were 2,000 National Guardsmen and hundreds of mounted men of the constabulary. In response to a secret appeal from the King, some 200 to 300 noblemen and loyal former royal bodyguards had also come to join the defenders of the palace, but they were only carrying crude arms and ceremonial sabres.

The King leaves the Tuileries

As the insurgents were getting ready for battle and waiting for reinforcements to arrive, the King inspected his forces around six in the morning. The monarch was tired, having stayed up all night, and his clothes were rumpled.

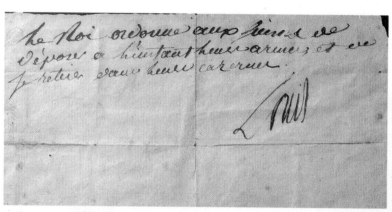

King Louis XVI's last written command.

the Tuileries and oust the King

Louis XVI is loudly cheered by a battalion, while other soldiers shout "Long live the Nation!". On the esplanade behind the palace, the King is booed and gunners scream insults: "Down with the filthy pig!" A short time later, the order is given to resist at all costs and to use force if necessary. But some gunners are spotted unloading their cannons. A feeling of uncertainty is also noted among the constables. At last, Roederer manages to convince the King to seek shelter at the Assembly because it seems too risky to try to resist. One hour later, the King goes there with his family. They are escorted by Swiss Guards amid hostile shouts from the mob massed at the terrace gates. The Assembly greets the King perfunctorily and he is led to the record keeper's office.

A vicious battle

Meanwhile, the Federates and the National Guards from the district of the Gobelins have managed to get into the courtyard. There were still only a few thousand men at the Carrousel. However, the constables, brandishing their hats on their bayonets, quickly began fraternising with the insurgents. Many National Guards joined in, among them the gunners of Val de Grâce, whose cannons were dragged onto the Carrousel square. The Swiss, who had pulled back inside the palace, protected the entrances as the insurgents reached the main staircase and tried to get in. As discussions continued amid great confusion, all hell suddenly broke out. A terrible barrage of shooting was heard. A hail of bullets, fired from every door and window of the palace and from the barracks on the river side, slammed into the insurgents, dozens of whom were cut down. The rebels fell back toward the Carrousel square, leaving the screaming wounded behind. About 200 Swiss, taking advantage of the element of surprise, rushed after the insurgents. Men from Marseilles and Brittany fought back, angered by the betrayal of the Swiss, who were pushed back. Then the units from the Saint Antoine district arrived: thousands of National Guards, flanked by a crowd of men and women armed with knives and pikes. The fighting became intense and the insurgents soon reached the palace doors. Cannons opened fire, spewing thick smoke and flame. At the Assembly the King was told of the bloodshed and issued a ceasefire order, but the messenger, General d'Hervilly, was unable to transmit it. Vicious hand to hand fighting raged on with pike and sabre. Some of the Swiss troops regrouped at the palace's main entrance and kept on firing at the mob until their ammunition ran out. Apart from a group which managed to reach the Assembly, they all died.

The massacre of the Swiss

The enraged attackers entered the palace around 1 p.m. That was when the real bloodbath started. The surviving Swiss were stripped naked and castrated. Some of them were beheaded, others impaled on pikes or thrown out of windows. Many nobles, servants and women were also butchered. The mob rushed around breaking furniture. However, whatever money was found was taken to the Assembly. Nearby, about 60 Swiss who were trying to get back to their barracks at Courbevoie were arrested by the mob and taken to the city hall. Huguenin, one of the leaders of the new Commune, had them tried. Their nude and mutilated bodies were thrown onto dustcarts. People everywhere were brandishing severed heads. When the massacre finally came to an end, nearly 1,000 of the defenders of the place had been

Bodies litter the ground.

killed. Among the insurgents, 390 were left dead, 90 of whom were Federates, while the remaining victims were members of the sectors, in particular those of Saint Antoine and Saint Marcel. In the wake of the battle, people were tearing down royal statues everywhere as the Assembly decreed that the King was now suspended from office. Louis XVI will spend the night locked up with his family at the Assembly, which has decided to replace the government with an executive committee. Danton is appointed its Justice Minister.

The insurrectional Commune

A new power was born on August 10th., the Commune which set up its base at the city hall. It is a grassroots body and claims to hold the reins of power in Paris, taking over from the city authorities immediately. The sectors' assemblies had approved the march on the Tuileries and allowed passive citizens to join. Every sector elected three commissioners, like the Théâtre Français sector to which Danton and Marat belong. However, the elections last till August 13th., when the Commune will number 288 members. On the evening of August 10th. it was led by Huguenin, a city toll official. Robespierre, Chaumette, Billaud Varenne and the Jacobins will later become its leading members. Less famous men also belong, like the jeweller Rossignol and the shoemaker Simon.

The mob bursts into the Assembly, where the King has sought refuge in the official recorders' box.

11. Paris. The Assembly elects an Executive Council which groups the following ministers: Danton, Minister of Justice, Servan, Minister of War, Roland, Minister of the Interior, Clavière, Minister of Finance, Lebrun, Minister of Foreign Affairs, and Monge, Minister of the Navy.

11. Paris. Voters are asked to elect the Convention by universal suffrage. The legal age limit is lowered from 25 to 21 years.

11. Paris. The city's commissioners place seals on the Tuileries palace.

12. Somme. The department's general council refuses to obey the new authorities.

14. Paris. The Assembly decrees that priests must swear a new oath of allegiance to "Liberty and Equality" (→26).

14. Sedan. La Fayette orders the arrest of the Assembly commissioners who had been sent to explain the measures taken by the provisional executive powers since the King was suspended (→19).

14. Strasbourg. The mayor of the city, Dietrich, tries in vain to get the garrison to revolt against the Paris authorities.

15. Paris. Following the arrest of Charles de Lameth in Rouen on August 12th. for having protested against the insurrection of August 10th., his brother Alexandre is also charged.

16. Nord. The French army deployed in the north starts to withdraw for no apparent reason.

16. Paris. The Commune decides to set up an entrenched camp by the capital's outer walls.

18. Paris. The actor Charles Ronsin says a eulogy for the dead of August 10th. at a meeting of his sector. He ends his speech by demanding a terrible punishment for "the traitor Louis XVI".

18. Paris. The Legislative Assembly bans the remaining religious orders: the teaching and hospital congregations.

19. Isère. The Constituent Assembly member Barnave is arrested at Saint Egrève on orders from the Legislative Assembly. This comes after documents showing that he plotted with the royal family are found at the Tuileries.

Royal family is taken to the Temple

"Louis the Last and family are taken to the Temple." The King, in shirtsleeves, wears a jailbird's bonnet.

Paris, August 13

It is six o'clock. The mayor of Paris, Pétion, is waiting for the arrival of the royal family so that he can take them to the Temple, the new residence that has been chosen for them by the Assembly. The King, the Queen and their children as well as Madame de Lamballe and Madame de Tourzel climb aboard one of the court's large carriages. In a second vehicle, the six servants which the Commune has allowed the royal family to keep are seated. During the trip, a large crowd of onlookers insults the royal party as it passes. When they arrive at the Temple, the royal couple is led to the Comte d'Artois' former palace where a decent meal awaits them. Pétion has not yet dared tell them that they will not be living there, but in the sinister dungeon nearby. Louis XVI shows no emotion. He is led to a small tower next door because nothing had been made ready for his arrival. That is where the King and Queen are to spend their first anguished and uncomfortable night as prisoners.

The provinces react to the Paris events

France, August

"Legislators, we have welcomed the caution and firmness of the measures you took." Not a word of reproach for the Paris uprising or support for the King. The Assembly heaved a great sigh of relief when the letter of support for the events of August 10th. sent by the Eure department was read out from the podium. At Amiens, the department's authorities are not in a hurry to issue the unsigned decrees of the Legislative Assembly and have sent a commissioner to Paris to find out what is going on. At Epinal, people have other things on their minds: the enemy is at the border. There the slogan being used is "unity and patriotism".

The Commune sets up its own tribunal

Paris, August 17

The Assembly has been forced to obey orders from the Commune. Led by Ollivault, a delegation from the insurrectional city council came to ask that justice be done to the counter-revolutionary criminals who were arrested on August 10th. The delegation warned the deputies there would be a riot if they did not immediately agree to set up a special criminal tribunal elected by the militants of Paris' sectors. On the 15th. Robespierre had already called for such a tribunal to be set up. He didn't just want a simple court martial. He demanded that all the supporters of the King be punished, not just the Swiss officers or the aristocrats of the Tuileries. Robespierre was offered the post of president of the new tribunal, but he refused, saying that he prefers to remain a member of the general council of the Commune. The insurrectional city council claims to be the true embodiment of national sovereignty. It refuses to be under the Assembly's control.

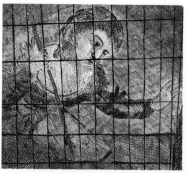

Liberty has been jailed by tyranny. Will it see justice done?

"Le Solide" sails round the world

Toulon, August 14

Mission accomplished: after a journey lasting 20 months, the ship *Le Solide* dropped anchor this afternoon at Toulon. Its 50 crewmen are overjoyed. They are the first Frenchmen since Bougainville 25 years ago to have circumnavigated the globe without any major incidents. Their trip was completed in record time. They had left Marseilles on December 14th. 1790 aboard the three masted ship commanded by Captain Marchand. They only stopped once, when they rested for ten weeks on the Ile de France. They did put into other ports, but only for a few hours at a time, even when Marchand claimed the Revolution Islands on behalf of France. His mission was above all a trade one. He was to trade fur from Alaska at Macao and Canton. But the sales did not bring in the hoped for profit. The captain had trouble getting 15 piastres per pelt, although he asked for 100 piastres.

Some scientists fear reprisals

Paris, August 11

There is suspicion, fear and hatred everywhere. At the Academy of Sciences, like elsewhere, each man's political zeal is weighed and analysed. Revolutionary ardour is seen as being more important than scientific excellence. During today's meeting at the Academy, the chemist Antoine de Fourcroy suggested that members known to lack civic pride or to have counter-revolutionary tendencies should be kicked out of the august body. Is he acting out of fear or seeking to save the Academy from disaster? In fact, more than half of the academicians are no longer attending the weekly working sessions. They have gone to live in the provinces, emigrated, or abandoned science to start a career in politics. Fourcroy is insistent and his frightened colleagues call on the minister to decide the issue. Their chief argument is that the progress of science must remain their only goal.

Royal statues are torn down by mobs

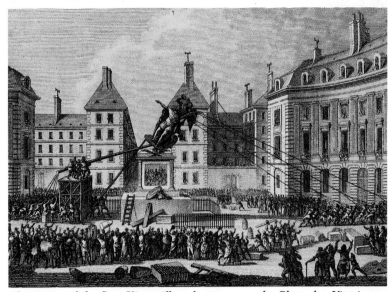

The statue of the Sun King will no longer grace the Place des Victoires.

Paris, August 19

The people themselves "take revenge on bronze kings". The large statues of kings, on foot, on horseback, crowned with laurels or wearing wigs, have been torn down one after the other. They no longer grace the squares of Paris. There was Louis XIII on the Place Royale and Louis XIV on the Place Vendôme and the Place des Victoires, as well as Henri IV at the Pont Neuf and the city hall. The statue wreckers hesitated when it came to knocking down Henri IV, as he was a popular king, but then they recalled that he had not been a "constitutional monarch" so down he went. On August 14th. the Assembly decreed that the bronze used for these monuments to "prejudice and tyranny" should be turned into cannons. Statues are also starting to bite the dust in the provinces.

"The greatest despot is overthrown by Liberty", on the Place Vendôme.

The deserter La Fayette is arrested

Austrian Netherlands, August 19

This evening La Fayette is being held prisoner by the Austrians, not by the Assembly, despite the charges it placed against him today. The events of August 10th. marked the final split between La Fayette and the Revolution. "The unrest in the capital is probably being financed by foreign powers trying to help the counter-revolution," wrote the commander of the northern army in Paris the day after the fall of the Tuileries palace. He was asked to hand over his command to Dumouriez. His troops were no longer following his orders. La Fayette then joined Alexandre de Lameth, who is also facing charges, and crossed the border with 21 officers from his headquarters. They chose to desert rather than face the guillotine. When they were stopped by some Austrians, they explained that they weren't enemy soldiers since they had left the army. They said they weren't émigrés either, but men "torn away from the joy of serving Liberty". That is not likely to endear them to the Austrians.

La Fayette flees from Sedan accompanied by some staff officers.

The Academy of Medicine is dissolved

Paris, August 18

In the great hall of the college of medicine, examinations are no longer conducted as they used to be in years past, under the watchful eye of deans wearing long-sleeved gowns, square hats and red hoods. A simple decree was enough to mark the end of a celebrated institution, with five centuries of history behind it. Generations of French and foreign students pored over the theories of Galien and Hippocrates before being allowed to do any dissection of corpses. How will the doctors of the future now be trained? The deputies must seek an answer to this problem.

20. Paris. The lowly police clerk Antoine Quentin Fouquier Tinville asks for help from his distant cousin, Camille Desmoulins, a senior official at the Ministry of Justice since August 11th., in order to get a position in this ministry (→29).

21. Paris. The royalist Collenot d'Angremont is executed on the Carrousel square. He had been sentenced to death by the criminal tribunal.

22. Paris. As the fortress of Longwy continues to be besieged by the Prussians, the Assembly decrees that any citizen of a town under siege who offers to capitulate will be sentenced to death.

25. Paris. The Legislative Assembly abolishes without compensation the remaining feudal ground rents that were subject to repurchase.

25. Huningen. Captain Rouget de Lisle, who has once again refused to swear allegiance to the Republic, is dismissed for lack of patriotism.

25. Paris. Servan, the War Minister, tells the Assembly of the dismissal of Marshal Luckner, who he says is senile. Kellermann takes over as commander of the Metz army.

26. Paris. As soon as news of the fall of Longwy becomes known, the Assembly decrees that 30,000 more men are to be recruited.

26. Paris. The Legislative Assembly approves the final draft of the law ordering priests who refuse to take the oath of August 14th. to leave France within two weeks. Those who refuse will be deported to Guyana.

27. Paris. An executioner falls off the scaffold and kills himself when he tries to show the crowd the head of one of the three counterfeiters he has just executed.

28. Paris. The Assembly allows the Commune and town councils to carry out house searches to find suspects.

30. Paris. Using the legal action taken against the Brissotin journalist Jean Marie Girey Dupré as an excuse, Guadet and Roland get the Assembly to approve the dissolution of the insurrectional Commune of August 10th. (→31).

31. Paris. The Assembly cancels yesterday's decree.

Royalist newsman du Rozoy is executed

It has been decided to keep the scaffold permanently on Carrousel square.

Paris, August 25

All monarchist newspapers have been banned and their printing presses seized, but journalists had not been guillotined until now. Du Rozoy, the director of the *Gazette de Paris,* who had been charged with collecting funds for émigrés and trying to start a civil war, went to the scaffold today. His last words were: "A royalist such as I should die well on the day of the feast of Saint Louis." His was the third death sentence passed by the tribunal set up on August 17th. to try accomplices of the Tuileries. The two men already executed were the steward of the civil list, Laporte, and d'Angremont, an official of the royal court.

Fouquier Tinville is a very tough cross examiner

Paris, August 29

The new head of the jury of the Paris criminal tribunal, Antoine Quentin Fouquier Tinville, has proved he is an able official. All day long, he cross examined the author Jacques Cazotte, who had been charged, along with his daughter, with being involved in a counter-revolutionary plot and with having corresponded with émigrés. The old man — he is aged 73 — was arrested on August 16th. after police discovered his correspondence with a certain Pouteau, secretary of the former steward of the civil list. In letter after letter he expressed his royalist fervour and his hatred of the Revolution. In one letter he went so far as to offer to shelter the King if he decided to flee from the Tuileries palace. The old author has admitted all. He is not likely to be considered much of a patriot.

Paternal rights are trimmed down

Paris, August 28

Paternal authority is now seen as a reflection of royal power and is being whittled down by the nation's legislators. A decree has just been issued ruling that children will no longer be subject to their fathers' authority when they reach the age of 21. This move is to prove particularly important for the women of France, who will now be able to marry without parental consent as soon as they reach their majority. Yet another of the many shackles on the freedom of choice has been scrapped. The latest move by the Assembly is bound to have a profound effect on society.

ICI
ON S'HONORE
DU TITRE
DE CITOYEN

Citizen is not just a new way to call oneself, it is a title with its own rights and duties.

Longwy surrenders to the Prussian troops

Longwy, August 26

A house has just been burnt to the ground. It belonged to one of the city officials who had refused to surrender to the enemy. But in fact Longwy has surrendered without honour. It was only a week ago that the Prussian troops turned up outside the city walls. Longwy, with its large stores of ammunition, 72 cannons and more than 1,800 garrisoned soldiers, could easily have resisted longer. However, the Prussians only had to fire a few cannon shells to win. The Duke of Brunswick may be pleased with himself: his "military walkover" has got off to a good start.

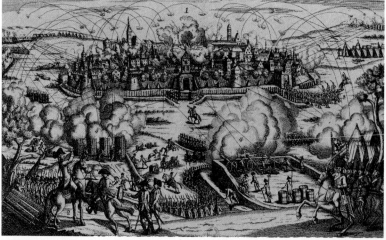

The fortified French town under heavy crossfire from Prussian troops.

Paris honours those killed on August 10

The large crowd attends the solemn ceremony in the Tuileries gardens.

Paris, August 27

A strange celebration has just been held in the garden of the Tuileries. It was as if a solemn memorial ceremony had suddenly turned into a funeral. The function was organised by Sergent, an engraver of little talent and one of the administrators of the Commune. Several thousand armed men marched for three hours to pay homage to the citizens who died in the name of Liberty during the attack on the royal palace on August 10th. But the very presence of these soldiers unsettled the spectators, reminding them of the war raging on France's borders. With solemn looks on their faces, they slowly filed past the towering pyramid that had erected over the pond and which was draped in black cotton serge. They bowed before the widows and orphans, all dressed in white with black sashes. During the entire ceremony the crowd listened to some harsh music composed by de Gossec, while the air was thick with smoke from the many incense burners which had been lit.

The Commune is declared illegal by the Assembly

Paris, August 30

Tired of having to submit to pressures from the insurrectional Commune, the Assembly has just decreed that it is to be dissolved. Even the most progressive democrats were furious over the daily humiliations that the deputies had to put up with. The straw that broke the camel's back came when the provisional town council tried to take legal action against the journalist Girey Dupré, a friend of Brissot. He was accused of having attacked the Commune's general council. The Girondist newsletter, *Le Patriote Français,* yesterday said the municipal commissioners were plotters, adding they were guilty of seeking to set up a "harsher and even more hateful despotism than that of the monarchy". The deputies therefore decided to put an end to all this by ordering the municipal commissioners to prove that their powers were legal or be considered as being usurpers. Also, they ordered the sectors to elect new delegates to the Commune. A veritable trial of strength is under way.

A group of famous foreigners becomes French citizens

Paris, August 26

The Revolution wants to be an international movement. A group of 18 foreigners, Americans, Poles, Britons, Germans and Italians, has just been made French citizens by the National Assembly. They are known for their revolutionary ideals. Among them are Bentham, Cloots, Paine, Hamilton, Klopstock, Washington, Madison, Kosciuszko, Priestley, Pestalozzi and Schiller. Some live in France to avoid harassment at home.

The Pole Thadeusz Kosciuszko.

Unrest shakes the region of Vendée

Châtillon sur Sèvre, August 22

The National Guard once again arrived too late this morning. When they entered the town, Lieutenant Boisard and his men found that the district headquarters had been sacked. In the courtyard, all that was left of the town's administrative archives was a pile of ashes. The documents had been burnt by the insurgents. Not far from there, on the road to Bressuire, one could see the rearguard of the 8,000 peasants armed with pitchforks, old guns and scythes, who for the past three days have been wandering around the region attacking representatives of the new political authorities. Their adventure ended this evening when Boisard caught up with them and opened fire with cannons. The men, led by Baudry d'Asson, were herded towards Bressuire, where local authorities had taken steps to defend the town, calling out the National Guards from the area.

Municipal officials like the mayor of Rouen, shown here, need nerves of steel to face with dignity the riots caused throughout France by the sudden, sharp rise in the cost of grain.

1. Paris. The sectors increase the number of citizens who are members of the Commune's general council to 288.

2. Verdun. Commander Beaurepaire dies in suspicious circumstances. He was governor of Verdun and a supporter of the resistance. He died as the fortified town was surrendering to the Prussians. →

3. Paris. Marat, Panis and Sergent write a circular letter on behalf of the Commune in which they announce the executions being carried out in Paris jails.

4. Paris. The toll of the September massacres is set at from 1,100 to 1,300 victims, three quarters of whom were common criminals.

4. Meaux. A unit of the constabulary from Paris harangues the mob, which butchers 13 prisoners, including seven priests.

4. Reims. Nine non-juring priests are murdered by volunteers from the Soissons camp.

4. Gisors. The population, led by volunteers, massacres the Duc de La Rochefoucauld, who was being taken to Paris under escort.

4. Brest. Ship's lieutenant Aristide Aubert du Petit Thouars sets sail to explore the coastal regions of America.

4. Charleville. Lieutenant Colonel Juchereau, commander of the town's fort and director of the weapons factory, is killed by volunteers from Seine et Oise.

5. Paris. The Paris deputies are elected to the Convention. Robespierre is the first to be elected, followed by Danton and Collot d'Herbois.

6. Caen. As a result of the events in Paris, the local public prosecutor is murdered by an angry mob.

8. Paris. The Minister of Foreign Affairs, Bigot de Sainte Croix, appointed on August 1st., orders the invasion of Savoy (→24).

8. Puy de Dôme. The department's electoral assembly writes to Thomas Paine, who is still in London, to inform him that he has just been elected to the Convention. Three other departments are vying with each other for the honour as having him as their representative.

Verdun surrenders to the Prussian troops

Verdun, September 2

The inhabitants of the town have all agreed to surrender, despite the Assembly's decree that anyone contributing to the surrender of a town under siege would be sentenced to death. Verdun's council has chosen to open the town gates. This means that the road to Paris is now clear for the enemy. For the past three days, the Prussians had been methodically bombarding the fortified town's weak defences. The local inhabitants, the majority of whom are opposed to the Revolution, soon started looting the soldiers' stores. As for the bourgeois, they were afraid of the effects of a long siege on their businesses. The commander of the garrison, Colonel Beaurepaire, was killed when he tried to stand firm against capitulation. It appears that it was the royalists of Verdun who were responsible for this murder, which was made to look like a suicide.

An illustration of the theory that Commander Beaurepaire killed himself.

"Boldness and yet more boldness ..."

Paris, September 2, noon

The enemy is marching towards the capital and will soon be at the gates of Paris. In the city, panic has reached a peak. Everybody is trying to get out as quickly as possible. Around noon, Danton, who has been Minister of Justice since August 11th., starts speaking at the Assembly. He is desperately trying to save the situation, to stop a panic flight which would leave the city deserted and defenceless in the face of the Revolution's enemies. He tries to give new hope and resolve to the citizens. "The nation will be saved! Everything is now moving, all are burning with a desire to fight! We need boldness, yet more boldness and even more boldness and France will be saved!" His words spread quickly through the city. Danton is now seen as the daring man of the moment, the man who cries defiance when others tremble in fear.

The capital will not die of starvation

Paris, September 4

If it comes to being besieged, the people of Paris will not starve to death. The Legislative Assembly has just approved a credit of 12 million livres for the import of wheat to feed the city. Ever since the enemy set foot in France, the authorities knew that grain would play a crucial role in the war. The officials of the supplies bureau, who had been dismissed by the insurrectional Commune, are back at their posts. Efficiency is more important than ideology. They told Pétion that the city's current reserves could last six weeks. If there is a siege, plans must immediately be made to feed 150,000 soldiers, their horses and cattle as well as the capital's population. The deputies were fully convinced by these arguments.

A terrible massacre after a parody of justice

Paris, September 2, evening

People have already forgotten how the bloodbath started. The orgy of murder that swept over the people of Paris seems to have been set off by a sudden panic. The Commune had agreed with the Assembly to have the capital's alarm bells rung this afternoon to order the recruitment of 60,000 volunteers, needed to keep the invading enemy troops at bay. At 3 p.m. the cannon on the Pont Neuf was fired to give the signal and the bells of all the churches started tolling. But there were worrying rumours sweeping through the capital: the traitors jailed in Paris cells were said to be plotting against the Revolution. A wave of panic soon spread among Parisians. Men did not want to leave for the front lines before having purged their city of the non-juring priests and royalists who had not yet been put to death by the courts. Marat and above all Fréron wrote strongly worded articles calling on the population to execute prisoners summarily. This "people's justice" spread quickly. At the Abbaye, the bailiff Maillard set up a "revolutionary tribunal". This fiery man from the Saint Antoine district is far from being a humanist, but he wanted aristocrats to be executed legally. The Commune and the Assembly, who do nothing to stop the killing, simple sent commissioners to ensure that only those jailed for unpaid debts are spared the mob's fury.

Stanislas Marie Maillard, hero of the Bastille and a murderer today.

A wave of massacres spreads to the jails of Paris

The first victims of the bloodbath were part of a convoy of prisoners being taken to the Abbaye jail, near Saint German des Près.

The people's commissioners judge the prisoners on the basis of their records of custody and a short interrogation. Those found guilty are executed.

At the Châtelet prison.

Paris, September 3

The murderers want to get rid of the capital's scum. A mob has just rushed to the Bernardins prison, where it butchered around 60 men who had been sentenced to the galleys. The killers are not just murdering so-called counter-revolutionaries. Most of their victims are the common criminals that Paris jails are full of. The murderers aren't gangsters. Most of them are usually honest and hard working shop-keepers who live near prisons and who have been swept up in a wave of collective madness. Some Federates had gone to the city hall to get 24 prisoners, including several royalist priests, and take them to the Abbaye prison. When they reached the Buci crossroads, they handed the 24 over to the mob, telling the people to kill them. The enraged crowd then went to the Abbaye to kill more prisoners. Gangs of killers then formed, going from jail to jail. This morning the toll had already reached nearly 1,000 dead. But the bloodbath is not yet over.

At the Bicêtre prison.

At the Force prison, the killing will only end on September 6th.

The killers, "drunk on wine and smoke", ironically agree with those prisoners who claim they are innocent and ask them to get out of their cells. As soon as they cross the thresholds, they are butchered on the spot.

A close friend of the Queen is killed and beheaded

Paris, September 3

"Get up, Madam, you must go to the Abbaye." It is just eight o'clock in the morning. At the Force jail, where she has been locked up since she was separated from her friend the Queen, Madame de Lamballe is roughly woken up by two National Guardsmen. Trembling with fear, she stutters: "If I had a choice of jails, I would rather stay in this one." But she must obey. At the

The Princesse de Lamballe as seen by one of her assassins.

foot of the stairs, she is horrified to spot the sinister tribunal that awaits her. The men are armed and their hands are covered in blood. Unable to answer the judges' questions, she is dragged outside. They want to force her to swear allegiance to the nation as she stands by a pile of bodies. As she looks away in horror, the killers attack and plunge their long knives into her. Stripped naked, her body is mutilated. Her head is then severed and a wig maker forced to curl her hair. The head is then carried on the end of a pike to the Temple. The King has convinced his wife not to look out of the window, and she does not see the terrible sight of the mob brandishing her friend's head.

Prostitutes are killed at the Salpêtrière

Women are killed at the almshouse-prison after the custody papers are read.

Paris, September 4

The gangs of crazed killers, who had been turned back yesterday evening by units of the National Guard, came back today to the Salpêtrière and found the way was clear. After knocking down the doors they rushed through the building armed with sabres and staves. They raped and killed all those who were in their way. The

Salpêtrière is an almshouse and jail which houses prostitutes, madwomen, women held on criminal charges and young orphaned girls. The men, soaked in blood, did not spare anyone. They left behind them 35 dead, including elderly women. Several young girls and children simply disappeared. When they had finished, the killers went to Bicêtre in search of new victims.

A glass of human blood to save a life

Paris, September 3

At the Abbaye prison, all is blood and carnage today. The former governor of the Invalides, Monsieur de Sombreuil, who is very old, was being judged along with his young daughter. When she saw that the judges were not keen to sentence an old man, she threw herself at their

feet and begged for mercy. The laughing executioners were reported to have handed her a glass full of human blood and told her that her father would be spared if she drank it. She is said to have gulped it all down! News of this heroic act has spread like wildfire through Paris. But is it true?

Mademoiselle de Sombreuil is said to have agreed to the killers' sinister demands in order to spare her father the fate of other prisoners.

Jailed priests are massacred at the Carmes

Paris, September 2

The massacre has begun in the garden of the Carmes, where all the jailed priests have been grouped. A clergyman stands quietly by the pond holding his breviary. His head is split open by a blow from a sabre and he is finished off with a pike. The orgy of killing is under way, blood is flowing freely and there are bodies all over the place. Suddenly a man comes forward. "Stop," he shouts to the murderers, "that is not the way go go about it." He adds that things must be done in an

The priests are held in the church.

orderly fashion and a tribunal must be set up, as at the Abbaye. The surviving priests are gathered in the church and called forward by twos to stand before self-appointed judges. Then they are sent out to the garden. As each one comes out, the killers waiting for them on the threshold cut them to pieces with their sabres and pikes. Within two hours, 114 priests are murdered. Most of them were only poor country priests who had come to seek shelter in Paris. A unit of the National Guard has been sent in to find out what is going on, but it cautiously withdrew without taking any action. Its commander said nothing could be done as the people had decided to "carry out their own just revenge on unruly priests".

Chateaubriand owes his life to his manuscript

Thionville, September 5

A man who is hit in the back by two bullets and continues to fight must truly be a hero. However, in this case he is an author. Chateaubriand, who had joined the Princes' royalist army on July 15th., had been marching to Thionville with his unit. When the men were about to cross the Moselle river, they were forced to attack because the forces led by Kellermann were getting too close. The patriot forces, which had come from Metz, were trying to outflank the royalist troops and were wheeling their cannons to face them. Fighting broke out amid a great deal of confusion. The noise of shooting and the cries of the injured were deafening. During a manoeuvre, Chateaubriand suddenly found that his back was facing the enemy. This made him an easy target for the French patriot sharpshooters. But, miraculously, he was hardly wounded even though two bullets hit him. His thick backpack, which contained the manuscript of his book about his adventures in America, had saved his life. This is definitely an excellent omen and the author is now sure that his forthcoming book will be a great success.

The royalist Princes' army gets into trouble outside Thionville

Prussians shell Thionville, which fights back. In the left of the foreground, the attackers are shown retreating.

Thionville, September 6

The time for braggadocio is over. What the Duke of Brunswick, who is commander in chief of Prussian forces, had termed a "military cake walk" is turning into a nightmare. After a siege lasting two days, the émigrés who had come to swell the ranks of the enemy troops were forced to admit that Thionville was not going to surrender as easily as Longwy. The wealthy Princes, army had been very sure of itself when it set off from Coblentz last July, with its magnificent equipment and its many camp followers and servants. Its commanders believed that they would be able to win just by making an appearance. But this was not to be. Even the weather came to dampen the army's enthusiasm. Ever since the start of operations, a nonstop downpour has made it extremely difficult for the soldiers to move around. Their heavy equipment gets bogged down. Prussian soldiers and officers, who had been led to believe that they would be welcomed with open arms, have found only open hostility.

The advantages of using bayonets

Paris, September 5

"Let's attack our enemies with bayonets fixed to the ends of our rifles, let's attack them without fear three times and they will then run away like children," the Minister of War, Servan, tells his troops. He wants General Dumouriez to get his men to make greater use of their bayonets. As Montesquieu used to say, "the French soldier is a fearsome fighter". All the military strategists are in full agreement: lining up fusiliers is a good way to face the "robot-like Prussians". The hard to please common soldier wants a "democratic" weapon that is easy to handle. Bayonets are also a good way to save precious gunpowder, of which the country's arsenals have already become dangerously short.

Start of a new wave of emigration

"For me, there is no longer a France," Madame de Staël said unhappily as she set off into exile on September 3rd.

This feeling is currently shared by countless other people in France. Like her, there are many who are now leaving the country.

The fall of the monarchy and the bloody massacres carried out in September have started a new wave of emigration. But the new émigrés are very different from those who left in 1791. The noblemen who emigrated in the wake of Varennes had gone to seek help for their cause from abroad. Today, those leaving are constitutional bishops, liberal aristocrats, moderate politicians and supporters of a constitutional monarchy, men such as Charles de Lameth and Duport who took part in the Revolution. Some of them feel they are threatened, others are simply disappointed by the turn of events.

They have gone to live either in the French provinces or abroad. For many of them the road to exile is not without risk. Madame de Staël preferred to leave Paris openly, aboard a fine carriage with its liveried footmen, but her coach was stopped at the gates of Paris by an angry mob. As she cowered inside, people grabbed the horses and insulted her. Necker's daughter was finally forced to wait until the following day to set off again, more discreetly this time, for Switzerland, where she plans to join her parents.

Literature, war are not incompatible

Northern France, September 6

It is possible to be a warrior and also have a love of literature. General Miranda, who has just joined the French army in the field, has given General Dumouriez a rare edition of the works of Plutarch which he had brought along with him. At an earlier meeting between the two men, Dumouriez had taken a liking to this strange man. Miranda, who was born in Venezuela, spent a total of 22 years fighting in America and in Africa, where he served Spain. He then resigned his commission to join the French army, saying he wanted to "serve the cause of Liberty". Francisco Miranda's intelligence and wide knowledge of politics, of science, of poetry and literature always amaze the people he meets.

9. Lyons. As a result of the events in Paris, a mob overruns the Pierre Scize fort and the Saint Joseph prison, seizes the aristocratic prisoners and kills 11 of them.

9. Versailles. A total of 53 prisoners, whose cases had been submitted to the high court of Orléans, are massacred during their transfer to Paris.

9. Paris. A decree issued by the Assembly authorises the district authorities to carry out a census of grain stocks. This is a first step towards control and taxation.

9. Lille. Austrian troops led by General Clerfayt start besieging the city.

9. Nantes. The local mayor, Giraud, celebrates the first civil wedding, in accordance with the decree of June 22nd. 1792 ordering that civil status registers be handed over to municipal officials.

10. Paris. The Assembly orders the requisitioning of all gold and silver religious objects so that they can be melted down.

10. Paris. A month after his appointment as Minister of Foreign Affairs, Le Brun asks France's ambassador in Madrid, Bourgoing, to set up "a small espionage operation" in Spain.

11. Saint Malo. 180 non-juring priests are detained prior to being expelled to the Channel island of Jersey.

11. Paris. Malesherbes writes to the Convention to defend Louis XVI in case the King is put on trial.

14. Meuse. The Prussian army fights its way through the strategic Argonne gorges, forcing the French troops to withdraw towards Châlons sur Marne.

14. Lorient. As a result of the Paris events, the merchant Gérard, who had been accused of attempting to ship rifles to the Ile de France, is murdered by a mob.

15. Paris. Following a ruling by the public prosecutor of the Paris Commune, Louis Philippe Joseph d'Orléans and his descendants will in future bear the surname "Egalité".

17. Paris. The crown jewels are stolen by burglars. →

20. Valmy. Kellermann's army wins a victory over the Prussians. →

Trial of strength continues between the Commune and the Assembly members

Paris, September 10

The recent massacres have not ended the vicious infighting between the Paris Commune and the Assembly. On the contrary, the bickering has been getting worse. The insurrectional authorities have just been accused by Brissot of being responsible for the massacres. This is just the latest incident of the no-holds-barred dispute between the two bodies. As early as the evening of September 2nd., as the orgy of killing was rocking the capital, Robespierre and Billaud Varenne of the Commune's general council had criticised by name several of the Girondins at the Assembly, who they claimed were accomplices of the Duke of Brunswick, the leader of Prussia's forces. The next day, municipal commissioners searched Brissot's residence. On September 4th., the Commune redoubled its attacks on the deputies and issued an arrest warrant against Roland. The Interior Minister had complained about the abuse of power by city hall and stressed that revolutionary power must be provisional if it is to avoid being destructive. Danton, Justice Minister, had the move stopped, but the fight has only just begun.

A most unwilling gift to the nation

Young women donate assignats and jewels to outfit a volunteer.

Eure, September 9

A mayor must always set a good example and be a patriot. The mayor of the village of Beaumont le Roger, Hinoult, nearly paid a high price for not living up to this duty. Having summoned the women of the village so that they could hear the latest laws being read out, he made the mistake of glancing at his watch. The ladies immediately ordered him to donate the timepiece to the nation. Hinoult, who tried desperately to get away from them, was nearly hung from a lamppost for his reticence.

The Revolution causes splits in America

Philadelphia, September 9

Thomas Jefferson and Alexander Hamilton are apparently not going to change their minds one bit. Even though both men are members of the cabinet of George Washington, they do not share political views. Hamilton, leader of the Federalist Party, is a great admirer of English institutions and does not really trust the people. On the other hand Jefferson, a liberal and a democrat, favours enlightenment. He is a great admirer of France and places a great deal of trust in the intelligence of the people. Once again, President Washington has just tried and unfortunately failed to get the two men to reconcile their widely differing political views.

Crown jewels have been stolen

The "Régent" weighs 140.5 carats.

Paris, September 17

The diamonds have vanished. The "Régent," the "Sancy" and the "Golden Fleece": all these priceless stones, which used to belong to France's royal family and had been stored at the national repository, were stolen sometime during the night of September 11th. to 12th. Roland, the Minister of the Interior, has just told the Assembly. He also had more criticism for the provisional Commune and its governing body, the oversight committee. They, along with the Paris National Guard, which is under their control, had been entrusted with the diamonds' safekeeping. Roland also asked the Assembly to take control of watching over the nation's property. This may allow it to recover the authority which the Commune is trying to usurp.

The Duc d'Orléans had asked the Commune to give him a name. The one chosen suits him well: "Philippe Egalité".

The French are victorious at Valmy

Cannons played a big rôle in win

Cannons played a major rôle in the French victory at Valmy, even though most of the cannon balls fired at the Prussians ended up in the muddy ground. This meant that there were fewer deaths and injuries from flying shrapnel. However, the roar of the larger cannons and the sound of the projectiles were enough to terrify the most hardened soldiers. A single well-aimed, 12 pound cannon shot that slams into a column of enemy troops can kill dozens of men. A 12 pound shot can pierce a two metre wall of earth at 500 metres, or a 40 centimetre thick wall. The French victory at Valmy was won by revolutionary troops, but the equipment they used had been inherited from the monarchy.

From a hilltop near the Valmy windmill, the French headquarters directs the cannon fire at the Prussians.

A museum opens at the Louvre palace

Paris, September 19

The Louvre is now to become a national museum. A decree on the setting up of the museum, which came after the law of May 6th. 1791 for the building of a central arts museum, was today approved by the Assembly. The idea of having a hall open to the public was not a new one. The success of the exhibitions to the public of the most beautiful paintings in the royal collection, held ever since 1750 at the Luxembourg palace, had convinced Louis XV's steward of buildings of the need to have some kind of permanent museum. The plan, taken up by Louis XVI, was easy to put into effect because the royal collection included countless masterpieces by such artists as Titian, Leonardo da Vinci, and Raphael. Most of these works had been acquired by François I, Louis XIV and Louis XV. The Assembly has agreed to have a large museum open to all at the Louvre, but the palace is unfortunately in a terrible state. Since its occupation by a destructive mob, it has fallen into disrepair. The ground floors are covered in débris, the main hall's floor has been ripped up and a tenant has planted a garden on a terrace.

Valmy, September 20

"We won't be able to beat them here," the Duke of Brunswick said as he reluctantly decided to give the order for his troops to withdraw from Valmy. He was faced with the daunting sight of 50,000 French soldiers waving their hats on the ends of their spears, as deafening roars of "Long live the Nation" echoed through the valley below. The French had been determined to beat the Prussians and they had the advantage of superior numbers. Kellermann did not have as many artillery pieces as Brunswick, although they were of better quality. Also, the Prussian troops were exhausted after several long, rainy marches through muddy terrain and they were fighting at a disadvantage on enemy territory. The battle, in fact, simply consisted of an exchange of cannon fire between the two sides, which left a total of 200 French and 300 Prussian soldiers dead.

Divorce is now to be made fully legal

Paris, September 20

The marriage vows can from now on be legally dissolved by divorce. That is what the Legislative Assembly has ruled. It is a further step towards a more liberal society. A divorce can be decided on the basis of mutual consent in cases of irreconcilable differences. Divorce can also be obtained on the grounds of madness of one or other of the parties, physical abuse or serious injury, sexual perversion or of desertion of the home.

A judge can sometimes get husbands and wives to avoid a divorce.

The new divorce legislation

The Assembly's decision making divorce possible has incited many a joke. One songwriter imagined this conversation between two fish-wives:

Madame Bigmouth
My vows I now can break
Despite the pious brood.
With one short Latin platitude
A hell they wedlock make,
With a Mass our fate they seal
In death to hell's ordeal.

With divorce, my man will play
At ducks and drakes no more;
And bed will cease to be a chore
His poteen to allay.
He'll know I can my vows revile
And that'll cramp his style.

Madame Carper
And my old man! He gives his bit
My wages, even my skirt.
I'll sort her out, the wanton flirt:
You'll see this dressed up pig
Divorce, it's thanks to you I dare
Her eye black'd and arse bare.

The Legislative Assembly's work

The new Assembly, from which the members of the former Constituent Assembly had voluntarily excluded themselves, met on October 1st., 1791, and was composed of new and mostly rather young men. They belonged to the middle classes of intellectuals and lawyers that had approved the work of the Constituent Assembly, had introduced the new institutions in the departments, but often wanted to go further. The 740 deputies were divided into three groups. On the right, there was a party, unconnected with the former right in the Constituent Assembly, that thought only of ensuring observance of the Constitution and of defending it against its enemies. It did not enjoy any great prestige in the Assembly, but outside it, was supported by the Feuillant Club, which resulted from a split among the Jacobins after the King's flight. The three men ("triumvirs") who inspired the club — Lameth, Barnave and Duport — ensured contact with the Court. The Feuillants had a strong influence in the ministries and were supported by some members of the National Guard and by some top officials in the departments. But they soon lost one of their trump cards, the Paris City Hall.

The left, which consisted essentially of the Girondist party, which was to lead the centre (the "Marais") rather easily, was under strong pressure from the extreme left in the form of a small, more "popular" party that based itself on the powerful Jacobins Club, of which Robespierre had seized control, on the democratic Cordeliers Club dominated by the powerful Danton, and on the districts ("faubourgs"). The Girondists, who were to dominate the Legislative Assembly, were both legalminded and idealists. They included some of the Revolution's strongest personalities: the philosopher Condorcet, the journalist Brissot, who extended his parliamentary influence through the columns of the *Patriote Français,* and the fiery, young Girondist delegation led by Vergniaud.

Increased violence

This Assembly was to sit for less than a year, declare war abroad, and witness the fall of the monarchy. First of all, it was to try to get the Constitution to work, and the majority of the deputies were determined to do so, though with differences of approach. In Paris and in France as a whole, in the cities as well as the countryside, a kind of "popular dynamics" was developing that endangered the precarious balance that had been attained. For the counter-revolutionaries, as well as the masses who felt excluded from the benefits of 1789, there could be no question of locking the Revolution in place on the foundations set up by the Constituent Assembly. The people who rejected both the constitutional régime and the clergy's Civil Constitution began to make threats. The opposition of the south's royalist regions was backed by the west, Brittany and the Vendée, with a non-juring majority, in which the religious issue sparked off conflict. The discontent of the urban and rural masses was the main force making for radicalisation of a Revolution that had not met their hopes. Shortages and inflation had brought higher prices during the 1791-92 winter, a process that continued until spring. Endemic unemployment was worsened by emigration, which affected luxury goods trades and building. The peasantry, which was supposed to have been satisfied by being authorised to buy seigneurial rights, was unhappy about its continued subjection to feudal practices, while the poorest peasants, who did not benefit from the sale of national prosperty, became involved in localised uprisings.

During the winter and spring, both the cities and the provinces suffered from disorders and violence. Paris groceries were looted because of suspicions that they were hoarding such products as spices, sugar and coffee. In such wheat-growing areas as the Beauce and the northern plains, gang with varying degrees of organisation invade markets, arbitrarily set wheat and flour prices an sometimes even killed people who opposed suc measures. Lords were attacked in the south, an castles were burnt.

While such outbreaks of violence were occurring the masses began to organise themselves. The frequented sections and clubs that welcomed them such as the Cordeliers. Some leaders, such as Jac ques Roux in Paris, preached the use of force Certain Jacobins, such as Robespierre, thought i necessary to make use of the popular covenant t ensure the Revolution's success. The Montagne (Mountain) party began to take shape. Sans-culottists, egalitarian and violent, started to demand state economic intervention and the extermination of the "aristocrats".

Given such a complex situation, one that was tense and apparently offered no way out, every-body was thinking about the same solution: wa would make it possible to take a stand, to come out clearly for or against the Revolution. This question came up during the initial meetings of the Legislative Assembly. Other countries took steps that actually helped the counter-revolutionaries. The imperial princes welcomed the émigrés plotting against France. Thus, on November 29th., the Assembly urged the King to call on the Electors of Trier, Mainz and the other princes to disperse the units of émigrés which had formed up on the border. There was a gradual movement towards direct conflict. Everybody wanted war. The Girondists, and Brissot above all, viewed it as the way of unmasking traitors, and why not the King himself? They saw it as an opportunity to assert the nation's freedom, stimulate the economy and open up markets, spreading the Revolution throughout Europe. La Fayette dreamt of the opportunity war would give him to keep the influence that was scaping him. The King welcomed the possibility that armed conflict would enable him to recover his authority. The Jacobins were generally favourable to war and Robespierre, who denounced the dangers of such a development, was quite isolated throughout Europe.

The winter was spent in debates between pacifists and the pro-war factions, but there was such an imbalance between the two camps that the pro-war groups were sure to win out, since France was multiplying demands on the Emperor' who was negotiating an offensive agreement with Prussia.

The Girondist cabinet and the declaration of war

The Girondists had called for a holy war against kings. On their part, Berlin and Vienna had signed an "alliance of kings" against the Revolution on February 7th., 1792. War was decided. But while the Girondists were sure of the Assembly's backing and were cheered by the street mobs, they had no influence on the cabinet, which was suspected of secretly seeking Austrian intervention in order to restore royal prerogatives. The Girondists attacked the ministers and threatened the King, who had to call in a new cabinet in March. Roland and Clavière, pushed by the Girondists, were appointed along with Dumouriez. On April 20, war was declared on "the King of Bohemia and of Hungary". This fiction actually concealed a conflict with Austria and Prussia, its ally. But the indiscipline of the army, which was still disorganised by the departure of certain officers and many others' lack of enthusiasm, as well as by the fact that the high command was in the hands of Rochambeau, who was very old, of Luckner and of La Fayette, who were unreliable, brought initial reverses on the northern border, where Dillon's troops massacred their general while withdrawing. Certain units went over to the enemy, while La Fayette considered turning his army against Paris to set up a régime more to his liking. Such journalists as Marat and some club members condemned that, viewing it as treason and the people became suspicious.

As for the Girondists, they suspected the Court, priests, and the King himself. They adopted a series of decrees to deal with the danger. On May 27th., they decided to deport non-juring priests denounced for counter-revolutionary activity. May 29th. brought the dismissal of the 6,000 men constituting the King's Constitutional Guard. On June 8th., there was the formation of a camp of 20,000 Federates near Paris. The King vetoed the first and last of those decrees, angering the Girondist cabinet, which strongly criticised his decisions on June 10th. in a statement written by Roland. Louis XVI, thinking he could rely on the army, responded by dismissing the ministers, and Dumouriez, who wanted to avoid compromising himself with the new Feuillant cabinet, resigned and rejoined the northern army. Even if the King planned to re-establish his authority and La Fayette was beginning to appear threatening, the Girondists did not give up, and the people of Paris, who were agitating violently in the sectors, were continue to put pressure on Louis XVI.

On June 20th., shouting "Down with Mr Veto!" the sansculottists invaded the Tuileries. Louis XVI, who put on his red bonnet that day, remained faithful to his rôle, claiming the rights he enjoyed under the Constitution and refusing to drop his veto. His courage impressed the rioters, but his position did not improve. From then on, he was tossed to and fro by events, while the Girondists in turn lost the initiative to "people's insurrection". While the sectors were growing by taking in hosts of passive citizens, battalions of Federates were setting out for Paris. Officially, they were going there to celebrate July 14th., but many did not arrive until later. The Marseillais, arrived on the 30th., singing *La Marseillaise*, in which patriotic themes mingled with threats to "tyrants". Paris was living in a feverish atmosphere.

The June 20th. events had upset the émigrés, and the foreign kings issued a statement, known as the Declaration of Brunswick (July 25th.), written by an émigré, that threatened Paris with merciless repression if there were any outrages against the royal family. This angered a population that was thinking about removing the King. The massing of enemy troops on the borders, the Assembly's proclamation of "the nation in danger" (July 11th.) and unrest due to fear aroused great patriotic enthusiasm and led many men to sign up: 15,000 in Paris alone. The capital was again seized by an atmosphere of revolt. The most active elements, the sectors, clubs and Federates, were determined to get rid of the King. Petitions arrived from the provinces demanding his removal. On July 31st., the Mauconseil sector declared that it no longer recognised Louis XVI. On August 3rd., the mayor of Paris demanded his removal in the name of the Paris sectors. Faced with the Assembly's hesitations, the mob took the initiative.

August 10

On August 9th., the sectors' delegates set up an "Insurrectional Commune" that replaced the regularly elected Commune. On the morning of the 10th., some National Guards coming from the suburbs, Federates and sansculottists marched on the Tuileries. The palace, abandoned by the National Guards who were supposed to defend it, was guarded only by Swiss and faithful royalists. An attack was launched, and the defenders resisted, but at 10 a.m. the King ordered them to stop fighting. Louis XVI put himself under the Assembly's protection. Vergniaud, who was chairing it, did not yield to the petitioners' demand for the King's immediate removal. He had measures adopted that authorised the mandate that the deputies had received from the voters: temporary suspension of the King and election of a Convention that would be called on to determine Louis XVI's fate and the nature of the future régime. The Insurrectional Commune, which the Assembly had recognised, immediately incarcerated Louis XVI in the Temple prison.

The Legislative Assembly was already moribund and subject to pressure from the Commune and street demonstrations and it had hastily appointed a cabinet. The Girondists, who had been kicked out by the King in June, had recovered their portfolios. Danton's appointment to the justice ministry on July 11th. was of special importance.

Far from restoring calm and resolving the difficulties, August 10th. had stirred people up and turned the capital into a centre of continuous agitation, which the Insurrectional Commune intended to use to give itself a leading rôle. Moreover, the enemy was advancing and Paris was afraid. The Prussians had entered Longwy on August 24th., and Verdun on September 2nd. The road to the capital was open and there were fears that the victorious troops and the royalists would take revenge. Steps were taken against all suspects. On August 26th., the priests, viewed as potential counter-revolutionaries, were forced to swear allegiance under penalty of deportation. On the 28th., home searches were authorised and the jails filled up. A special criminal court had organised as early as the 17th. These strict measures, which could be justified by the approaching danger, were quickly made redundant by the "terrorist" activity of the hysterical sansculottists, which was facilitated by the Paris Commune's laisser-faire attitude. There was a widespread fear that was to lead to massacres: could one leave for the front, go off to defend the homeland, leaving alive so many conspirators who might get out of jail and kill women and children? On September 2nd., gangs of killers went to the jails and indiscriminately murdered common-law criminals, priests, counter-revolutionaries and "suspects". Half of Paris's prison population was butchered in cold blood, with nearly 1,400 victims in the capital alone. The provinces were not spared by the crime wave and there were massacres in Reims as in Marseilles, in Lyons as in Soissons, in Charleville as in Toulon. The reason was that the Commune's Supervisory Committee and the sombre Marat had called on the provinces to follow Paris's example. While these tragic events were occurring, France was electing its deputies to the Convention. On September 20th., the day on which the Legislative Assembly broke up to give way to the new Assembly, the revolutionary troops won the victory of Valmy. That victory led Goethe to say: "A new era in world history will be dated back to this spot and this day." Democracy had won its first battle. It was to follow up that win by setting out to conquer Europe.

End of the Legislative Assembly

The constitutional régime set up by the first assembly, which the Legislative Assembly was called on to implement, had lasted for only about ten months. The rules of the game applying to that régime had been made null and void by the day of August 10th. However, the Legislative Assembly did not break up until September 20th. and it was not inactive during the last two months of its existence. Its decisions determined the nature of the new France, which was no longer a real kingdom but was not yet a republic.

Above all, drawing a lesson from the August and September events, it modified the voting system, which had previously divided the population into two classes: active and passive citizens, who were distinguished on the basis of income level. The result was to make the poor a separate class, but this distinction now disappeared, and universal suffrage was established. The conditions governing eligibility were also modified. The new rules required only that the candidate be a citizen and be at least 25 years old. Democracy seemed to have made perceptible progress, but the new arrangements had little effect on voter turnout. The Convention was elected by a minority of the population, as nine-tenths of the voters abstained. There were various reasons for this low turnout. It probably indicated political immaturity on the part of a large portion of the population, as well as disapproval and resistance. The electoral assemblies were held at the time of the massacres and a large number of people were kept away by anxiety, fear or disgust.

21. Paris. During its first public session, the Convention acts on a proposal submitted by Collot d'Herbois and Grégoire and decrees the abolition of the monarchy. A day later, it proclaims a Republic (→22).

22. Paris. The Convention decides that all official rulings will from now be dated from the Year I of the French Republic.→

24. Paris. The Convention approves a plan to set up a federal guard whose duty it will be to protect it from pressure from the people.

24. Savoy. The French troops march into Chambéry.→

25. Paris. Following a request from Couthon, the Convention declares that the Republic is "one and indivisible".

25. Paris. The author Jacques Cazotte, who had been accused of involvement in royalist plotting, is executed at the age of 73.

27. Vendée. For the seventh time, non-juring priests are shipped off from the port of Sables to Spain.

28. Paris. The Convention decides that the *Marseillaise* is to replace the traditional *Te Deum* during the celebration to be held on October 14th.

29. Paris. The Convention sets up a constitutional committee to draft a new constitution.

29. Paris. The son of Fragonard, Alexandre Evariste, aged 12, joins the school for special students directed by David.

30. Paris. Since the plurality of mandates is forbidden, Roland resigns from his post as a deputy in order to keep his job as Minister of the Interior.

30. The Rhineland. The Rhine army, led by Custine, seizes Speyer before heading towards Worms.

30. Paris. The National Guard's director of music, Gossec, performs at the Opéra an "Offering to Liberty", which includes a tune that is to become famous: *Veillons au Salut de l'Empire.*

Prussia. On being told of the proclamation of the Republic, the German philosopher Emmanuel Kant says: "Now I may speak like Siméon; Lord, let your servant die in peace as he has lived to see this memorable day!"

The French Republic is proclaimed!

Paris, September 22

Year I of the French Republic is starting. It was today that the term "republic," suggested by Billaud Varenne, was approved by the deputies. However, it was yesterday that the Assembly acted on a proposal made by Collot d'Herbois and unanimously voted for the abolition of the monarchy. This move, in fact, simply gave a legal basis for an existing situation. Joyful cries of "Long live the Nation!" greeted today's move. "Morally speaking, kings are on the same level as monsters are in the physical order," Grégoire said. He added that "the history of kings is that of the martyrdom of nat-

A republican breast offered to all.

Under the tree of Liberty, the armed Republic holds the Constitution.

ions." Such eloquence was hardly necessary to convince members of the Convention. The 749 elected representatives are republicans at heart. The Feuillants and aristocrats have been dismissed or sent to prison. Democrats have got the upper hand everywhere and have expressed support for the events of August 10th. Less than 100 deputies from the Constituent Assembly have been reelected. Among them are Robespierre, Barère, and Grégoire. Nearly 200 were already members of the Legislative Assembly, most of them Girondists such as Brissot, Condorcet and Carra, but on the whole most of the deputies are new, bourgeois from the provinces, often lawyers. They are about to shoulder a heavy burden: the drafting of a constitution while governing until the new régime can be enshrined by law.

A dispute at the Comédie Française

Paris, September 30

There has been a major split at the Comédie Française. Its patriot members finally have walked out on their royalist colleagues and gone to work for the Théâtre de la République, as Talma has named it at the Rue de Richelieu. An entirely new era has begun for theatre. The well known actor has stressed that "genius will find new paths, the time for truly national plays has come".

Song to the glory of the Republic

From the moment the new régime was proclaimed, poets have been praising the advent of the Republic:

Hail we the great Convention
Whose energetic force
Teaches our new-born Nation
(A view which all endorse)
Kings to abhor,
Love of the Law,
And of the French Republic!

Mock their deuced commotion!

The nobles' rule is through.
Sometimes pretending devotion
('Tis prudent so to do)
They murmur this cry,
A tear in their eye:
"Long live the Republic!"

Retake we our rights undisputed,
Our former powers of yore.
Now is the tree uprooted
Of kingly lineage sore.
Consecrate be
The sacred tree
Of our new French Republic.

Lavoisier leaves Paris to study

Lavoisier at work.

Blois, September

The famous scientist Lavoisier has moved out of Paris. He has gone to stay on his property at Fréchines, near Blois, where he feels he will find peace and quiet to continue his research. The great chemist has resigned as commissioner of the national treasury and rejected the ministerial post he had been offered. He is still steward of saltpetre and gunpower, a subject about which he will write a treatise.

Rivarol emigrates with his mistress

Brussels, September

Rivarol has left France, but he did not leave his mischievousness behind. He is full of tricks. The lovely Manette, his mistress, is furious over a recent argument they had and threatening to sell herself to the first man she finds. "Madam", he tells her calmly, "the greed of Belgians is hardly conducive to immorality." The two lovers have been living together since they arrived in Brussels four months ago. The well known polemist has left his son, Raphaël, and his wife in Paris. He had never got on well with her. She is a proud, self-centred woman, who believes she is witty and beautiful. People laughed at her and pitied her husband when she announced she wanted to write. As for Manette, she is lively and unselfconscious. Rivarol says she "tastes like a nice fruit and is as witty as a rose". He has found friends in Brussels, émigrés like himself. He is a popular man at literary meetings and social events.

A patriot priest's strange sermon

Cher, September 23

The priest of Epineuil is a good patriot, but he is fed up. Since his parishioners are such sheep, he has decided to play the wolf during a Sunday Mass. From his pulpit, he shouts and waves his arms around madly, as the worshippers look on in utter amazement at their red faced priest. There was no sermon today. He spoke instead of more urgent matters: the petition that is to be sent to the local mayor, Jamet. He must allow the citizens to be represented at the municipal council. Also, all the village's property, including the church, must belong to everybody. The 90 people attending Mass agree wholeheartedly with him and cheer. The priest is right. But shouting is heard outside. The doors open and Jamet comes in followed by his supporters and the commander of the guard. The loud shouting turns into a riot and stones are flung. However, the priest manages to escape into the nearby church gardens.

Triumphant French forces arrive in Savoy

The people of Savoy rejoice as French troops arrive at Chambéry.

Chambéry, September 24

The royalist cockade has been tied ignominiously to the tails of dogs. That is how the people of Savoy chose to show their hostility to the monarchy and the King of Sardinia. They were overjoyed to greet the revolutionary troops led by General de Montesquiou. The conquest was not marred by violence. The many émigrés living in Chambéry had preferred to flee before the arrival of the French and they were quickly followed by the people of Piedmont. That was why Montesquiou had no trouble in capturing the opposition's forts. Without awaiting the rest of his troops, the General entered the city practically by himself. Won over by revolutionary ideas, Savoy has fallen like a ripe fruit.

The new Republic's army easily conquers the Comté of Nice

Nice, September 29

The conquest was carried out without violence. Nice fell with practically no resistance. It was the capital of the county bearing the same name, which had become a haven for non-juring priests and noblemen from Provence and the Comtat Venaissin. The revolutionary troops of the Var army, led by General Anselme, marched into a nearly deserted city. For his part the King of Sardinia, Victor Amadeus III, had only deployed a few troops in Nice and Savoy. Lacking support from Piedmont, unpopular among local inhabitants, his men preferred to pull back and avoid a battle that they were unlikely to win. General Modeste Anselme is an ambitious man. In particular, he hopes to be appointed a marshal and dreams of taking the Revolution to Italy.

Nice and its citadel besieged by the fleet of Rear Admiral Bruquet and the troops led by General Anselme.

1. Paris. A general security committee is set up. It is responsible for security throughout France.

2. Nice. Local revolutionaries form the Club of Defenders of Liberty and Equality.

2. Paris. The musician Gossec composes a an orchestral score for the *Marseillaise*.

3. Switzerland. French troops seize Basel. A Republic is immediately proclaimed.

4. Paris. Danton suggests in vain that the Assembly declare that the nation is no longer endangered.

5. Rouen. The Jacobins enforce the ruling that all symbols of royalty are to be removed from public places. Two statues of Henri IV and one of Louis XV are destroyed.

5. Germany. Troops led by General Custine seize the town of Worms.

7. Northern France. The Austrian army ends the siege of Lille. →

8. Paris. The Girondist Buzot proposes that the Assembly be provided with 4,500 guards. This would mean four infantrymen and two cavalrymen per deputy. →

9. Paris. Garat is appointed Minister of Justice in place of Danton.

9. Paris. The Convention decrees that any émigré found bearing arms is to be executed within 24 hours (→ 23).

10. Paris. The Girondist leader Brissot is accused of having insulted the Commune. Since he does not come to explain himself, he is expelled from the Jacobins Club.

11. Paris. Santerre, the commander of the National Guard, resigns following a mutiny of Guardsmen entrusted with guarding the Temple.

11. Paris. The Convention elects its constitutional committee. Danton and Lavicomterie are its only members belonging to the extremist Montagnard group.

12. Paris. The Convention appoints Pache as Minister of War. He replaces Servan, who has taken over command of the Pyrenees troops.

13. Paris. General Arthur Dillon is dismissed on suspicion of having corresponded with a foreign monarch.

The Austrian siege of Lille has ended

The end of the siege gives the people of Lille the incentive to hold a celebration amid the debris of the city.

Lille, October 7

The defeat of an ally is never good news. When Duke Albert of Saxe Teschen was told about the retreat from Valmy of the Prussians led by the Duke of Brunswick, he decided it was time to end the siege of Lille, which he had begun on September 26th. The fighting in and around the city had been extremely difficult, but the people of Lille remained steadfast right to the bitter end. An intense seven day long bombardment did not succeed in breaking the resolve of the town's garrison, commanded by General Rual, or of its mayor André and his officials. The inhabitants' will to resist redoubled when the Archduchess Marie Christine, the "Governor of the Netherlands" and Queen Marie Antoinette's sister, aimed the cannons at the town herself to encourage Austrian soldiers. In particular, the daring of the local barber Maës increased the citizens' resolve. His stall was destroyed by cannon fire, so he took a piece of shrapnel and used it as a shaving dish. In all, the brave barber managed to shave 14 men while a constant barrage of cannonballs landed all around him.

A petition calls for public schooling

Avranches, October 11

The Convention has just been sent a pressing call from a group of patriots. The authorities of the district of Avranches have mailed a signed petition to the Assembly asking it to drop everything and give total priority to the pressing issue of public schooling. The petition says that if children are not given proper education, they will fall prey to the dangerous influence of priests and counter-revolutionaries. It is high time for the deputies to debate the problem and take all necessary steps to find a solution.

Common-law union is all the rage

Bondy, October 12

A great many couples, mainly in the poorer strata of society, live together without being officially married. What is new is the desire to regularise such unions without going to the trouble of an official wedding. Etienne Pascal, a farrier's mate aged 26 and 17 year old Marie Louise Buffon have gone to the sector headquarters of Bondy to proclaim their love for each other and register their newly born son, for whom they want a civil status. The officials, embarrassed, nonetheless decided to register the declaration.

It won't last

Since the September killings, many Parisians have shut themselves up in their homes. Some invite friends to sing counter-revolutionary songs. The author of these has been hanged!

Though on every side we hear
The French shall have their way!
I'll tell you now what I esteem:
'Tis but a golden dream.

And if you think that long can last
These infamous decrees,
I'll say again what I esteem:
'Tis but a golden dream.

In the end, from madness cured,
The people will arise.
I believe that then will reign
The status quo again.

Girondists seek support in the provinces against the revolutionaries of Paris

Paris, October 8

Is France in danger of being hit by a wave of anarchy due to the activities of the revolutionaries of Paris? That is what the Girondist Buzot has been claiming. He accused the capital's revolutionary leaders of subversion. To foil their plans, he suggested that a law be passed against any incitement to murder. The elections have shown that the Girondists have lost the backing of the people of Paris, and they are worried. Last September 24th., Buzot had called for the creation of an armed federal guard unit made up of men from all over France. It would protect the Convention from unrest. The Girondists want help from the provinces.

François Buzot, lawyer and deputy of Eure, one of the Girondist leaders.

Private royal grants no longer exist

Paris, October 13

The nobleman La Tour du Pin, a former Minister of War, has just had some bad news. Following the discovery of the "Red Book" listing royal expenses, grants and gifts, he has been sentenced by a Paris tribunal to give back to the national treasury the sum of 30,000 livres, with interest, which had been a loan from Louis XVI. On September 19th. the Assembly abolished all private treasuries and put an end to the grants they distributed.

Could the Papal palace end up like the Bastille?

Avignon, October 1

The Jacobins are now in full control of Avignon, which has become part of France. They want to get rid of every single remaining trace of the Ancien Régime. Some symbols, such as seals and documents, are easy to destroy, while others are harder. The leader of the general council has called for the destruction of the Papal palace. "This Bastille of southern France that still stands should have been given the same fate as the one in Paris a long time ago." The palace was "the terror of patriots; it used to be their tomb when the enemies of Liberty were triumphant". Its destruction would have another advantage: the demolition work involved would provide employment and the jobless "would earn enough to stave off hunger". The council has asked for permission to go ahead from the departmental authorities.

Séchelles builds a fancy love nest

Chaillot, October 1

Despite being elected as a deputy to the Convention in September, Marie Jean Hérault de Séchelles has not abandoned his pleasure seeking and frivolous ways. But now he has to be more discreet. His reputation could be damaged by his extremely active love life. After searching far and wide, Hérault has just found in Chaillot a small suburban house.

It is far from prying eyes and suits his purposes perfectly. This bachelor's residence has a boudoir shaped like a small cave, a fireplace that looks like a sea shell, curtains made out of leaves, and a bed made out of reeds which is surrounded by mirrors. Marie Jean has let his fantasies run wild and covered the wooden floor with grass and tiny flowers. There is even a small indoor stream that runs into a pond where goldfish and shells have been placed. The handsome young rake has left nothing out in order to attract his willing victims. No doubt countless lovely brunettes and blondes have been enticed into this fancy love nest.

Goethe loves eating French beef stew

Meuse, October 5

Poets don't always spend their time writing, locked up in their ivory towers. Goethe, a volunteer in the Duke of Brunswick's army, has been stationed in the Meuse valley. When he was granted some leave, he visited the French countryside and was given a taste of the hospitality of the inhabitants of the village of Sivry. He was warmly welcomed by a family of peasants and showed great fondness for the traditional French beef stew they gave him. This rich and tasty peasant dish is cooked for hours in a thick stock to which a clove has been added. It is served by pouring it over a large slab of country bread. After he had eaten his fill, Goethe looked around him and was impressed by how clean and well organised the home of his hosts was. In a corner of the house's only room, which also serves as the bedroom, he saw a sink, shelves and a sideboard. A large fireplace provides heat to keep out the winter chill. Their only luxury is a round chest used to keep the salt dry and as a chair for the man of the house.

In the Ardennes, the Prussian troops are being routed and chased by men led by Dumouriez. Some of them withdraw through the Granpré Gap. "On top of the firm resistance of the French there also came the season's bad weather and disease which afflicted them and they were all forced to retrace their steps."

16. Paris. The deputy of Yonne, Bourbotte, calls on the Convention to sentence Louis XVI to death without any trial (→Nov. 7, 92).

18. Paris. The Brissotin Rebecqui asks Danton for his ministry's accounts. But Danton can't explain a deficit of 200,000 livres in his special expenses (→25).

18. Brest. During a ceremony marking the proclamation of the Republic and the abolition of the monarchy, the navy's warships are given new republican names.

18. Saint Domingue. News of the Paris events of August 10th. leads to the arrest of the governor, d'Esparbès, and of Admiral de Girardin and 25 officers, who are immediately sent back to France.

19. Longwy. After having evacuated Verdun on Oktober 14th., the Prussian troops pull out of the city.

19. Paris. The Jacobins set up their own auxiliary constitutional committee which groups Robespierre, Couthon, Danton, Collot d'Herbois, Chabot and Billaud Varenne. This body is responsible for keeping an eye on the Convention's drafting of a new constitution.

21. Germany. The troops led by General Custine capture Mainz.→

22. Chambéry. During an Allobroges national assembly session, the representatives of Savoy call for their region to be united with France (→Nov. 27, 92).

23. Paris. Nine émigrés are caught with weapons and sentenced by virtue of the decree of October 9th. which gave the death penalty to any who serve foreign powers.

24. Paris. Brissot publishes a pamphlet entitled "To all the Republicans of France". In it he states that, if the people are there to serve the Revolution, they should go home once their task is completed.

26. Paris. Acting on direct orders from the government, Kellermann and one of Dumouriez's officers open peace talks with Brunswick and Hohenlohe.

27. Northern France. The French forces led by Dumouriez invade the Austrian Netherlands and march on Mons.

The Order of Saint Louis is abolished

The decorations of the Ancien Régime must he handed in at the city hall.

Paris, October 15

The Cross of Saint Louis is no more. Following a brief debate, the Convention has just decreed its abolition. "The Cross is a stain on clothes, it must be rubbed out." It was the death warrant for the most popular decoration of the Ancien Régime. This order of knights was founded in 1693 by Louis XIV. It was aimed at honouring military achievements and it could be awarded to anybody, regardless of birth. It had a hierarchy of three groups: knights, commanders and the great crosses. Now, the deputies will have to find a republican equivalent to replace this award, which has contributed a lot to the morale of French troops over the years.

General Custine marches into Mainz

Mainz, October 21

Surrender can be contagious. The capture of Speyer, followed by that of Worms by the French army of the Rhine led by General Custine has convinced the garrison defending Mainz that it would be useless to resist further. As he marched to Mainz, Custine personally explained to his troops the tactics he planned to use to defeat the enemy forces. His plan was a particularly daring one as it called on the tired French troops to march a distance of 18 leagues only in 24 hours. This would get them across the Rhine earlier than expected, thus taking the enemy by surprise. Custine's easy victories have not brought much glory on the patriots, but they have helped to fill the state's coffers: the general imposed war taxes on all the conquered cities. This forced contribution system affects everybody, instead of just the magistrates and officials. The inhabitants of Mainz even saw groups of French soldiers break into local homes and businesses and openly loot them.

General Custine opens the Liberty Ball at Mainz.

Florian thinks he is La Fontaine

Paris, October 21

The mild-mannered Florian has changed. After having tried the theatre and writing historical novels and poetry, he is now following in the glorious footsteps of La Fontaine. Didot l'Aîné has published a collection of five books of *Fables* written by him. The work owes a lot to the master, but it is far from being as good as La Fontaine's. An excessive taste for pastoral images often spoils the graceful and witty fables based on human morals. The author of *Galatée* is not quite as good as his mentor. But at least he is good at describing a species that has become rare: the great noblemen he knew well.

Jacobins have also spread to Germany

Georg Forster, a German naturalist seduced by the Revolution.

Mainz, October 23

The democrats of Mainz have set up their own club, the "Society of German Friends of Liberty and Equality". It has some 200 members and groups the city's intellectual élite. One of its dominant members is Georg Forster, even though the scientist did not seem destined to play a big revolutionary role. He had joined James Cook in his round the world trip before becoming a professor of natural science at Cassel and a librarian at Mainz. His research has made him famous in Germany. In 1790 a trip through Europe took him to Paris, where he attended the Federation celebration. This deeply moved him. On his return, he decided to become a champion of the Revolution in Germany (→Nov. 6).

Danton is ordered to explain his fortune

Jean Marie Roland de La Platière is leading the attacks on Danton.

Paris, October 25

People are wondering where all Danton's money has come from. He owns a house at Arcis sur Aube and the priory lands at Saint Jean du Chesne. He has, however, sold his legal practice for 69,000 livres and gets an annual income of about 100,000 livres. But people are asking whether he is not involved in some kind of shady fraud with public funds. On October 6th. he submitted to the Convention a detailed accounting of his expenses since he left the ministry. However, a deficit of 200,000 livres has come to light. The former Justice Minister said he couldn't give details about secret ministerial expenses. Despite this, the Roland couple and their friends are sure Danton is guilty. They criticised his financial dealings and asked him to explain the discrepancy. He was helped out by the ministers Lebrun, Monge and Clavière, who said that Danton had provided them with details of expenses. People are not convinced.

Marat accuses Dumouriez of treason

Paris, October 16

There was a shocking scene at Talma's this evening during a party honouring Dumouriez, the general who led the victorious troops at Valmy. Marat suddenly burst in and publicly accused the guest of honour of being a counter-revolutionary. He said he suspected the officer of having plotted to discredit the battalions of Paris volunteers. On October 4th. two volunteers had massacred French émigrés who had come to Rethel to surrender. Dumouriez has asked for the murderers to be severely punished, and his call has been firmly backed by the Convention, but Marat is convinced that the authorities are not telling the whole truth about the incident and believes it is all a plot hatched by the general and his Girondist friends. The Girondists have in fact been opposing the representatives of Paris and their supporters, the volunteers.

Treading on symbols of the Ancien Régime before the Liberty Tree, Marat threatens attacking aristocrats with his mighty pen.

Paris rejoices over the liberation of Savoy

The actor Chenard, dressed as a sansculottist, carries the flag during the celebration of October 14th. at Chambéry of the liberation of Savoy.

Paris, October 28

The liberation of the province of Savoy called for a celebration. All the Savoyards now living in Paris met at the Champs Elysées to attend a huge banquet honouring the recent liberation of Savoy by French troops. Among the guests were five members of the Convention, including Lequinion, the deputy from Morbihan. All drank a toast to what is to become France's 84th. department and cheered the principle of universal brotherhood. During the feast a child opened a cage, setting free several dozen birds. When the banquet was over, the merry Savoyards went to the Jacobins Club, where they were given an exceptionally warm welcome (→ Nov. 11).

Lowly priest "borrows" archbishop's bed

Maubeuge, October 14

Austrian troops have left a trail of devastation behind them. When they passed through the tiny village of Brettignies they sacked every single house, helping themselves to whatever they wanted. The local priest, Guyot, can't even find a bed to sleep on, as his mattress has been carried off on horseback. Luckily his aristocratic archbishop's bed happened to be free, so Guyot did not hesitate. He spent the night in the luxurious four-poster bed, with its fluffy cushions and fine curtains. Just in case anybody were to look in and find him there, the priest had hung a tricoloured sign from the bed which said simply "They had taken mine".

▷

A violent diatribe against Robespierre

Jean Baptiste Louvet de Couvray, a man of letters and an orator.

Paris, October 29

The author of *Les Amours du Chevalier de Faublas* has dared to attack Robespierre. Encouraged by the Roland couple and the Girondists, Louvet de Couvray openly accused the deputy of Arras of being a verbal despot and of only wanting power for himself. The charges were made during a session of the Assembly. A passionate and violent man, Louvet used all his powers as an orator rather than concrete proof. He craftily hit out at Marat in order to blacken Robespierre's name. Louvet was cheered by the deputies. His attack has apparently been successful: Robespierre has asked for eight days to prepare his reply (→Nov. 5).

France's national heritage finds a saviour

Paris, October 18

An outhouse is to be turned into a museum. The warehouse set up in November 1790 at the Petits Augustins convent, near the Louvre, will become a museum to house works of art that are France's heritage. Initially works that had been confiscated by revolutionaries had been stored there, but as time passed many other masterpieces were added, chiefly dating from the Middle Ages and the Renaissance. The official in charge of the warehouse, Alexandre Lenoir, always tried to protect the works. This intelligent man has just convinced the Convention to support his plan to turn the warehouse into a small museum (→Sept. 1, 95).

Religious objects are to be confiscated

Beaune, October 30

The Republic is short of money. The nuns of Hôtel Dieu have been visited by two municipal officials who removed all the holy vases and reliquaries to send them to the mint. This move was also a response to the nuns' open hostility to juring priests. Ever since their chaplains had to leave the capital after refusing to swear the oath of allegiance to the clergy's civil Constitution, they have been calling on clandestine non-juring priests.

The courtyard and main building of the Hôtel Dieu at Beaune.

November 1792
from 1st. to 12th.

Convention

1. Paris. The Convention approves the decree giving the state control over the property of all the émigrés and absent citizens.

2. Paris. The general assembly of the Piques sector decides to print and distribute to every other sector a speech by Citizen Sade entitled *L'Idée sur le Mode de la Sanction des Lois.*→

2. Saint Domingue. The three commissioners of the Republic take up their posts on the island.

3. Paris. Several battalions of Federates demonstrate in the capital's streets to demand the heads of Marat, Danton and Robespierre.

4. Paris. A delegation of citizens from Nice comes to ask the Convention that Nice be made part of France.

4. England. At the royal castle of Winchester, which has been turned into a sanctuary for priests who have fled from France, 16 priests and the superior of the seminary of Lisieux, Monsignor Martin, are installed.

6. Belgium. At Jemmapes, the French army commanded by Dumouriez beats the Austrian forces led by Duke Albert of Saxe Teschen after two days of combat.→

7. Paris. Mailhe, the deputy from Haute Garonne, writes a report on the issue of a trial of the King and states that Louis XVI should be judged by the Convention, as it represents the nation's authority (→13).

8. Rouen. The rise in the price of many basic foodstuffs causes a riot. The town council proclaims martial law.

9. Paris. Facing charges for having hesitated instead of seizing control of Geneva, General de Montesquiou escapes to Switzerland.

11. Paris. A delegation of Savoyards asks the Assembly to agree to make Savoy part of France.

11. Paris. The Minister of Foreign Affairs, Lebrun, has his daughter christened in a civic ceremony. She is named Civilis Victoire Jemmapes Dumouriez.

11. Lille. The Convention's decree stating that Lille and its inhabitants are owed a debt of gratitude by the nation is solemnly read out.

People of Mainz must choose which side they back

Liberty that is forcibly imposed is likely to be only "a bonnet without a head atop a rootless tree."

Mainz, November 6

The revolutionaries of Mainz have really put the cat among the pigeons. They organised a solemn demonstration during which they handed the people two symbolic books. One of them was black and wrapped in chains and the other red, known as the "book of life", representing the Revolution. The inhabitants of the city were told they must choose publicly which side they were on by writing their names in one of the two books. This daring idea was not welcomed by all, and even some democrats were not happy about it. Very few people agreed to sign. For the first time, a dispute has arisen between the vast majority of the people of Mainz and Georg Forster and his Jacobin friends. The liberal bourgeoisie had welcomed the French troops led by General Custine and the abolition of feudal rights and the more scandalous abuses of the Ancien Régime, but it remains opposed to violence, and the news of the massacres of September caused a wave of fear. Only a part of the intellectual élite is prepared to press ahead. The Jacobins of Mainz are now seen as fanatics (→Nov. 21).

Robespierre launches a counter-attack

Paris, November 5

Loud cheering greeted Robespierre's response to the attacks that Louvet had launched against him on October 29th. Louvet had said that the Jacobin had been guilty of "insulting for a long time the most pure and the best patriots". He had also accused Robespierre of having acted as a criminal agitator in the provisional Commune after August 10th., of incitement to murder and of seeking to wield tyrannical powers. Point by point, Robespierre demolished the so-called proof on which the attack against him had been based. His measured but firm defence deeply impressed the spectators and the Assembly. But what had the most effect was when he posed a question that went to the heart of the issue: "Citizens, do you want a Revolution without revolution?" In other words, the question is whether the Girondists want to end the revolutionary process by turning the "missionaries of the Revolution into arsonists and enemies of public order". A majority of deputies then backed Robespierre. In its attempt to destroy Robespierre by using false charges, the Girondists have in fact helped him and lost credibility.

Each volunteer costs more than 230 livres

Paris, November 3

A fighting man needs to be properly equipped. The Convention has ruled that the Republic must in future bear the cost of outfitting its soldiers, although it can deduct some money from their wages. A lot of money is involved. A cloak, a jacket and two pairs of trousers currently cost 129 livres; a hat costs 7 livres; three shirts cost 24 livres; two pairs of stockings, two pairs of shoes and two pairs of gaiters cost 39 livres; two collars cost two livres; three brushes cost one livre; a leather bag, a cloth sack and a cartridge pouch cost 32 livres. At the start of the year there seemed to be no equipment problem. As they had come from the National Guard, the volunteers still had their outfits: blue jackets with white trousers and waistcoats. But many National Guardsmen did not have any uniforms, because they wore what they had on when they joined up. Some of them were very poorly dressed indeed.

"Patriotic citizens bring shirts, shoes, stockings and overcoats to be sent to the army's volunteers." But will that be enough to equip them?

The priest Le Bon marries his cousin

A happy juring priest: "I get a shave this morning, tonight I get married."

Saint Pol, November 5

The city's faithful were horrified and the bride's mother is extremely upset. Joseph Le Bon, a constitutional priest, today went to the city hall to marry his cousin Mimie, a strong 20 year old girl. This former Oratorian father of the Beaune college is an ambitious man of few morals, who is used to scandal. When his career failed, he took the oath of allegiance to become a simple village priest. But he is full of bitterness against his former superiors and has found a way to get his own back. As he was elected last September as an alternate member of the Convention and mayor of Arras, he hopes the Revolution will give him a chance to seek revenge on those responsible for humiliating him. It was the first civil wedding, and the first time a priest had got married, in the region. In his speech, Le Bon said he was an example for other juring priests and asked them to follow in his footsteps.

Married priests

More and more priests are getting married. Their wedding is generally accompanied by a thousand and one jests by the commoners. Here, for example, is a facetious song which has been particularly popular:

My priest is a good patriot,
A dutiful citizen priest,
A really true sansculotte,
A brick, to say the least.
To each parishioner does he spell
The paragon of living well.
His image must our love compel.

No cassock does this man wear;
He affects a layman's gait.
Whene'er he sees a sheep to err,
To tries to put him straight.
To all children he's well known.
His seeds of love are nightly sown
Whereby he will beget his own.

Marquis de Sade or Citizen Louis Sade?

Paris, November 2

During a meeting of the Piques sector, Citizen Sade read out his speech entitled *L'idée sur le Mode de la Sanction des Lois*. In it he states that legislators cannot do without the people's assent. The audience was most impressed by this idealistic principles and decided that the text should be printed right away and sent to the other sectors. The aristocratic Marquis, who has been appointed secretary and, later commissioner in charge of investigating hospitals, is becoming more popular every day among members of his sector. This exemplary sansculottist has become an ardent revolutionary and patriot. When people dare remind him of his noble background, he indignantly replies that he is the son of poor peasants and has always been known simply as Louis Sade.

Dumouriez triumphs at Jemmapes

Women go off to do battle

How proud they looked, the two Fernig sisters, as they ran around the battlefield, both doing their duty as aides de camp. The young women had already made a name for themselves at Valmy, but they really distinguished themselves at Jemmapes. Félicité, who is only 16 years old, fought bravely alongside the young Duc de Chartres. As for Théophile, who is two years older, she led a unit of cavalrymen which routed a whole battalion of Hungarians and captured its commander. They joined the militia of their village, led by their father, a few months ago. After that they enlisted in Dumouriez's forces before serving on his headquarters staff. Both young women had willingly volunteered to fight against the enemies of the nation. There are dozens more like them fighting for France in the north, many of them coming under fire daily and dressed only in rags.

France's 10th. light infantry battalion fights ruthlessly in the Fiana woods of Belgium, near Jemmapes.

Jemmapes, Belgium, November 6

"War is absurd, but victory is magnificent." The Austrian forces led by the Duke de Saxe Teschen will have plenty of time to think about this paradox as they pull back. A major battle has just taken place on the boggy, damp Belgian lowlands. Early this morning, the French forces saw through thick fog the six awesome redoubts that had been set up by the enemy on a wide, watery prairie. The soldiers of the French Republic are mostly badly dressed and ill-trained. They are far from being battle hardened troops. Under a hail of gunfire and the roar of cannon volleys, they had to attack the six fearsome forts which were claimed to be impossible to destroy. The Austrian soldiers did not give up easily and continued firing down at the assailants. Some of the many French battalions were forced to fall back; some even ran away. But others pressed on regardless, as the men sang the *Marseillaise*. At last General Fernand La Caussade, who was in command of six of the French infantry units, managed to push through the enemy's left flank. This move was decisive. The battle was won thanks to a direct and simultaneous attack on the entire Austrian front. But the fighting was far worse than it had been at Valmy. The French were victorious because they outnumbered their opponents and because they knew when to take the offensive. The hero of the hour, General Dumouriez, fully intends to make the best of the difficult but rewarding success (→ Nov. 12, 95).

Fighting on the road from Mons to Jemmapes, near the Cuesnes lock.

The strategy is simple: the French launch a frontal attack on the Austrians.

French troops advance through Belgium

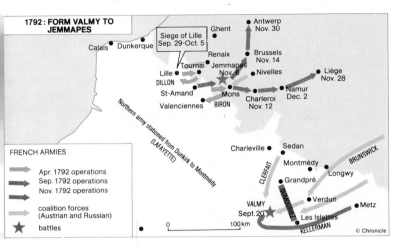

1792: FORM VALMY TO JEMMAPES

FRENCH ARMIES
- Apr. 1792 operations
- Sep. 1792 operations
- Nov. 1792 operations
- coalition forces (Austrian and Russian)
- ★ battles

© Chronicle

Belgium, November 12

The advance of the French forces has been unstoppable and their reputation travels ahead of them. The Republican troops' glory has been boosted by their victory at Jemmapes. The high command has decided to move Dumouriez's men forward on two fronts: some of the troops are heading for Antwerp, while others head for Liège via Charleroi and Namur.

The French enter Mons after in November the Austrian withdrawal.

Two French patriots face the Inquisition

Rome, November 10

The people of Rome have never really got on well with the French. Now they really hate them. Many Romans, in particular the authorities, have been upset by the activities of some French people who have been trying to spread the revolution to Italy. Two French sculptors, Chinard and Rater, were arrested as they were on their way home and taken to the Saint Ange castle. Both are members of the National Guard of Lyons and ardent patriots. They soon became suspect. They were charged with having offended religion, and are to be tried by the Inquisition. One of their French friends has been warned he will go to the galleys if he does not testify against them.

The Republic, a sculpture by the patriot Lyons artist Joseph Chinard.

 Convention

13. Paris. A former employee of the journal *Le Moniteur*, Charles His, and a newspaperman, Jacques Gouget Deslandres, set up a new publication, *Le Républicain Universel*.

13. Paris. At the Convention, Pierre Joseph Cambon calls for the immediate abolition of the budget for French religious orders.

13. Paris. Debate begins at the Convention on the King's fate. After Saint Just has spoken (→), Pétion requests a prior debate on the issue of royal inviolability.

13. Sarthe. Groups of peasants and wood-cutters, who are already known as "taxators" by local people, gather at Montmirail and decide to march on the towns of Loué, Sablé and La Flèche to impose a maximum price on essential commodities.

13. Germany. The inhabitants of the county of Saarwerden, a German enclave on French territory, ask that their region become part of France.

14. Ghent. A group of Jacobins close to Jean François Vonck set up the Society of the Friends of Liberty.

14. Brussels. The French army marches into the city. →

15. Paris. Grégoire is elected speaker of the Convention. He reiterates the call for the King to be put on trial, but says he opposes the death penalty for the monarch. →

15. Mainz. Georg Forster states in a speech on the future of relations between city of Mainz and France that the Rhine river is a natural border for France.

19. Paris. Following a proposal by La Révellière Lépeaux, the deputy of Anjou, the Convention approves the decree stating that France will grant "brotherhood and assistance to all those peoples who want to win their freedom back".

19. Paris. The Minister of the Interior, Roland, approves a 10,000 livre grant to the Lycée, but warns that some of the teaching being done there is not quite revolutionary enough (→ Jan. 12, 93).

19. Toulouse. A big patriotic celebration is held in honour of the visit to the port city of the representative from the capital, Lazare Carnot.

Saint Just calls for King's execution without trial

Saint Just, a very young deputy.

Paris, November 13

Saint Just has committed himself at last. He chose to make his first public statement before the Convention during a debate on a very sensitive issue: the fate of the King. He began his speech in a low key, but this soon changed: "As far as I am concerned, I see no middle way, this man must either rule or die." The firmness of the young deputy over the fate of Louis XVI is clear. He has rejected the arguments of supporters of the King's inviolability and of those who want him to be tried as a common citizen. He is opposed to both these positions, even though, as he wrote in *L'Esprit de la Révolution*, the King is incompetent rather than guilty (→ Dec. 3, 95).

Border information: "Travellers, this land is free."

The émigrés flee from Brussels as they hear that the French are coming

Dumouriez is greeted at the gates of Brussels by the city's magistrates.

Brussels, November 14

It is every man for himself for the émigrés living in Brussels. Local inhabitants had welcomed Dumouriez when he entered the city, but news of the general's victory at Jemmapes on November 6th. had caused a wave of panic to spread through the émigré community. All those who were able to tried to get hold of transport to flee the city. The smallest carts were being snapped up for amazing prices. Entire families piled in, carrying their weapons and belongings. They then set out on the road to Maastricht. Not all arrived safely. Cart wheels broke, fancy carriages overturned and fell into ditches. Some beautiful aristocrats, followed by their servants carrying luggage, were even spotted walking by the roadside carrying young children in their arms.

Prussia's King and Marshal Brunswick return ignominiously to Germany.

Cross-border love affairs can be risky

Maurienne, November 13

The Republic is safe. Letters that had been sent from Piedmont to a quiet young woman were only full of endearments. The mail had been intercepted by the watchdog committee of Saint Jean de Maurienne. It takes its responsibilities very seriously and is constantly on the lookout for counter-revolutionary activity in the border regions. Just across the border, émigrés are busy plotting against the republic. The amorous young woman could have loved her young man more than the nation. She has been told to go to the city hall twice a week to report on what her lover tells her about "what is going on over the mountains concerning the Revolution".

A new miracle cure is on offer

Paris, November 16

There is new hope for all those who suffer from flatulence, whose nerves are shot or who can't stop spitting. The good Doctor Dubreuil is selling a cure for all their ailments. It is a plant-based medicine, but its exact ingredients are being kept secret. It is claimed to be very effective against all sorts of problems and is being widely advertised. It can cure gout, rheumatism, epilepsy, heartburn and much more. These are all ailments for which no remedy has yet been found. However, the vaunted miracle cure may simply be a hoax. Each treatment costs the princely sum of 40 livres. What is more likely is that the medicine will turn out to be an excellent remedy for the doctor's ailing bank balance.

The Girondists are losing steam

Paris, November 15

The Girondists have just suffered a major setback. The Jacobin Grégoire has been elected speaker of the Assembly, winning 246 votes out of a total of 352. This has confirmed that Brissot and his supporters at the Convention are losing their influence. Deputies are begining to turn away from their policies, to weary of their endless attacks on the Paris Commune, and to be fed up with accusations that Robespierre, Marat and Danton are all "dictators". Even Condorcet seems to be disgusted by the Girondists' behaviour, particularly by Roland. The decline of the Girondists is starting to help the opposing group known as the Montagnards. They are seated on the extreme left and are supporters of Robespierre.

The republicans are truly on the warpath

Paris, November 16

The Cordelier Chaumette has just made a rousing speech. "The territory that lies between Paris and Saint Petersburg as well as Moscow will soon be made French, municipal and Jacobin," the fiery revolutionary, who is also a member of the Commune, has told his rapt audience.

Such a thirst for conquest has become a source of embarrassment to the Convention. The war against the tyrants of Europe is no longer limited to defending the borders of France and has turned into a policy of conquest. But what can be done with territory once it has been occupied? The government and a majority of deputies are rejecting all negotiation. Brissot and the Girondists believe that the Revolution will only be fully safe once republican forces are in control of all of Europe. But should defeated nations be occupied or annexed or should sister republics be set up there? Simple annexation will be chosen for Savoy, which has asked to be joined to France. As for Nice, which was conquered by General Anselme's troops, it is a far more complex problem. The republicans are on the warpath and their desire to conquer new territory seems be unquenchable (→ Nov. 19).

This "bombardment" of the crowned heads of Europe and the Pope by the Republic shows its self-confidence and contempt for the enemy.

A personality cult among Girondists

Anacharsis Cloots calls himself the "orator of the human race".

Paris, November 18

Neither Marat, nor Roland!, a pamphlet by the philosopher and Convention deputy Cloots, has just confirmed the break with the Girondists. He criticises the "contemptible" personality cult that he says is corrupting the Girondists who hold the reins of power. The head of the government, Roland, is one of the main victims of this cult, as is his friend Brissot, according to Cloots. He adds that the Girondists are playing into the hands of the counter-revolution by seeking the backing of the departments to put an end to revolutionary militancy in Paris. Cloots has been sure this was the case ever since he saw the Federates from the provinces come to the capital on the urging of the Girondists to demand the guillotine for Robespierre, Danton and Marat. Cloots also sees Marat as a dangerous "anarchist" who is no better than the Girondists.

A home for young female workers

Paris, November

A group of ladies concerned about the education of young girls of the capital is now planning to open a special home for them. The girls would not only be taught to work on textiles, but also reading, writing and basic mathematics. The plan is even more ambitious: the ladies want the new home to be a place where every woman, regardless of her age, can be provided with both medical help and moral counselling by other women.

Convention

20. Paris. Roland, the Interior Minister, tells the Assembly of the discovery at the Tuileries of the "iron strong-box". →

20. Paris. The War Minister appoints the actor Charles Ronsin to lead the forces in Belgium.

21. Paris. A new comic opera by Joigny and Trial, *Cécile et Julien ou le Siège de Lille*, is performed.

21. Germany. At Mainz, the naturalist Georg Forster, in a message to his fellow citizens calls for the Rhineland to be joined to France, saying this is the only way to guarantee the people's sovereignty.

22. Spain. In Madrid the new Prime Minister appointed on November 15th., Manuel Godoy, decides to place French clergymen who have sought refuge in Spain under house arrest. He has forbidden them to speak publicly about events in France.

23. Loir et Cher. 3,000 peasants meet at Vendôme, shouting "Long live the Nation, the price of wheat is to go down!". They then head for Le Mans, imposing taxation as they go (→ Dec. 1, 92).

24. Paris. The Théâtre des Amis de la Patrie shows a patriotic play by Citizen Gamas, *Les Emigrès aux Terres Australes*.

27. Paris. Following a proposal by Grégoire, the Convention decrees the incorporation of Savoy into France. Only Marat is opposed to this as he doesn't back the Convention's thirst for conquest. →

28. Liège. The French army marches into the city.

29. Paris. The Girondists get the Convention to abolish the criminal tribunal set up on August 17th.

29. Antwerp. The South American General Miranda, who leads a unit of French troops, captures the city.

30. Paris. The Girondist Chambon de Montaux is elected mayor of Paris, beating Lullier, a backer of Robespierre. The vote follows the resignation of Pétion, elected to the Convention by the department of Indre et Loire.

30. Liège. Publication of the first edition of the *Gazette Nationale Liègeoise*, a Jacobin journal in favour of France's annexation of the principality.

The "iron strong-box" is discovered

Roland discovers the King's secret correspondence implicating Mirabeau.

Paris, November 20

There was a major upheaval at the Assembly today: Roland, the Minister of the Interior, told the stunned deputies that a locksmith named Gamain had asked to meet him to convey information of vital importance to the nation's security. Gamain, who had been wracked by guilt for several months, had finally decided to admit that he had built a secret hiding place for the King in his rooms at the Tuileries, a large locked box hidden behind panelling that could be moved on its hinges. Secretly Roland then went to the palace and opened the strong-box.

Inside he found a great many papers. These did not prove that the King had been in collusion with any foreign powers, but they did show that he had not been telling the whole truth since 1789, that he had sided with counter-revolutionaries and attempted to bribe deputies, in particular Mirabeau. The Convention now has grounds to charge the King. The discovery of the documents means his trial can no longer be put off. A commission of 12 men, all Girondists, has just been formed to inventory the contents of the "iron strong-box".

"Would you like to learn English?"

Paris, November 20

It is no longer enough to be able to speak intelligently in one's own language. People nowadays need to be able to converse fluently in a foreign language. That is what an advertisement paid for by a certain Monsieur Daix has been telling his readers. Daix is an interpreter and English teacher who has just set up

a special dining establishment for a few lucky bourgeois. His students are to pay three louis a month for lessons and three livres per meal. They will speak English as they dine. The advertisement states that students will drink tea, read English newspapers and soon be able to express themselves perfectly in English. ▷

A new French department: Mont Blanc

Paris, November 27

The former Duchy of Savoy has become the French department of Mont Blanc. By doing this the Convention acted in accordance with both revolutionary law and military strategy. Dumouriez's military plans called for the defence of France's natural borders along with an attack on Belgium as well as the Sardinian States. On November 19th. the deputies approved a decree stating that France is prepared to assist all who want to "recover their freedom". So it was simple for them to agree to the request of the Allobroges — the name given to the patriots of Savoy taken from the ancient Gauls who used to live in that region. One month ago those patriots wrote to the Assembly, saying: "By becoming French, we would be worthy of those Frenchmen who have won their freedom." A man named Savoye has even asked to be called Montblanc (→ Dec. 8).

The highest peak in Europe is now a part of France.

A patriot bishop gets married

Evreux, November

The bride and groom went first to the city hall, then to the church. Robert Lindet, the first bishop to get married, has made sure that he did everything in accordance with the new legislation on the civil status. This believer in the Revolution has turned his wedding into a big event, saying that he was setting a moral and political example. He explained his position in a letter to his congregation: "I have practised all the religious and civic virtues. I still had to set an example and that was to rise above those superstitious priests. That I have now done and I have chosen a mate with whom I will demonstrate to all the domestic virtues." Most of the constitutional prelates were extremely upset by the news of his wedding and have sworn never to follow in Bishop Lindet's footsteps.

Royalist peasants, republican workers

Mayenne, November 27

The men who work in the forges at Port Brillet, Chaillard and Moncors are all proud republicans, but the local peasants have kept their Catholic faith and continue to support the monarchy. So the workers have decided to organise against the peasants. Their ironworks have been turned into garrisons where they can produce their own weapons. They feel safe there. The workers have been keeping in touch with the patriot troops and have begun chasing royalists. They know all the local forests and pasture land so they have been able to provide some useful information to the soldiers, showing them where the counter-revolutionaries had made their hideouts. There is a great deal of bad blood between the two sides and the opponents are getting ready for a final showdown.

Royal family lives in the Temple prison

The royal family is being kept under close watch. Cléry, the Dauphin's former manservant who followed Louis XVI to the Temple, serves dinner.

Paris, November

In the dungeon of the main tower of the Temple, the royal family lives a strange life under the ever watchful gaze of their municipal guards. Louis XVI, his wife, their two children and the King's sister, Madame Elisabeth, have no idea what is in store for them. They are housed in two four-room apartments, one above the other. The place is not very grandly furnished. The King lives alone in the upper flat, where the wallpaper at the entrance shows the inside of a jail. There are huge bars on his windows and the shutters keep fresh air out. Despite the stove that has been installed, it is cold. Louis XVI has just had an "inflammation of the head" and was forced to spend several days in bed. His wife and his sister are there constantly to watch over him.

The King has been allowed to keep his manservant, Cléry, who does the housework and looks after his master with great zeal. Now it is Marie Antoinette who washes her son and helps him get dressed. The days all seem to be the same. The King awakes at 6 o'clock. When he has said his prayers, he reads a book until 9 a.m. His family then joins him for breakfast. After that, they go for a walk in the courtyard if the National Guard commander says they can. When the walk is over, they go to the Queen's room which is also their sitting room. There, the children learn their lessons while Marie Antoinette and Elisabeth do some needlework. After supper, the King goes back upstairs and reads till midnight. Downstairs, the princesses are locked up in their room for the night.

Tight security measures have been taken to keep people away from the big medieval tower of the Temple. The gaolers fear an escape attempt.

Louis XVI readies his son for life as a monarch

Paris, November

Louis XVI, who believes in divine providence, has convinced himself that the Dauphin, now seven years old, will one day reign over France. Ever since he has been locked up in the Temple, the overthrown King has been preparing the young prince to become a monarch. He often tells him about the

Louis XVI's young son ...

... discovers the world from a cell.

misfortunes of kings, including the story of Charles I of England who was beheaded in 1649. The awestruck child listens closely to his father. Louis XVI used to be far too busy for such lessons, but now he patiently gets his son to read, count and write, and gives him a grounding in geography, his favourite subject. The King even draws maps for the boy, telling him about far-away places and Captain Cook's travels.

🏛 **Convention**

1. Lille. The leader of the Belgian patriots, Jean François Vonck, dies in exile.

1. Berlin. After Austria on November 27th., now Prussia dismisses the army corps set up by the émigrés. The only remaining unit is the one led by the Prince de Condé, which is backed by Austria.

2. Belgium. Following the surrender of Namur to troops led by General Valence, Dumouriez decides to stop the offensive.

2. Paris. The renewal of the Commune's general council sees the arrival of many Hébertists. Hébert himself, as well as Chaumette and Jacques Roux, are among the 122 representatives.

3. Paris. At the Convention, Robespierre calls for the King to be executed (→6).

4. Paris. The Convention rules that the death penalty will be enforced against those who call for the restoration of the monarchy in France or who seek to diminish the people's sovereignty.

5. Paris. After examining the documents found in the King's strong-box, the Assembly places charges against Talleyrand. He is already abroad on a diplomatic mission (→12).

5. Rethel. Four émigrés are caught by national volunteers and killed.

6. Paris. The Convention decides to summon Louis XVI to interrogate him. Marat gets approval for a voting procedure: names are called out and deputies state their vote.→

7. Belgium. In Brussels, French troops cause bloodshed when they quell a demonstration calling for the independence of Belgium.

7. Paris. Acting on the basis of a report from Viard, a secret agent, Marat and Chabot accuse Fauchet, Roland and Roland's wife of plotting to restore the monarchy.→

8. Paris. A decree from the Convention bans the export of grain but restores the freedom to trade grain in France.

10. Avignon. Members of the "Enragés", or extremists, are punished after being arrested for having extorted money claiming that it was needed to equip volunteers.

The French are kicked out of Frankfurt

Violent reprisals are taken against the French who remain in Frankfurt.

Frankfurt, December 2

The French army didn't manage to stay for long. Only 40 days after having easily marched into the city, Custine's troops have been kicked out, just as easily, by the Duke of Brunswick's Prussians.

Custine is entirely responsible for the French setback. When the Prussian troops arrived at the walls of Frankfurt, the French general left the city taking with him nearly all the artillery. He withdrew behind the Nidda river and didn't cover his move. Even worse, he left his flank open to the enemy. It was almost as if the general was perfectly prepared to sacrifice the 2,000 men defending the city. The French commander had even ordered the garrison's chief, Van Helden, to resist as long as he could and, if necessary, to burn the city if he could not control it.

Van Helden was mistaken to think that the general would come to his aid. In fact, it would have been far better for Custine to have gone to Coblentz two months ago to stop the enemy there instead of trying to gain territory on the eastern bank of the Rhine.

A revolt in the Beauce region is put down

Chartres, December 1

The regular troops posted in the town have gone on the offensive after being besieged since November 24th. At dawn, they caught by surprise and immediately disarmed 3,000 "taxators". In the wake of this successful operation, they deployed throughout the Beauce region to restore calm by force. For the past two months, the departments of Eure et Loir, Loir et Cher, Indre, the Loire and the Sarthe have been rocked by unrest. Gangs of several thousand peasants have been roaming the countryside and villages imposing their own "taxation" of goods. To shouts of "Long live the Nation, the cost of wheat will go down", they took control of the cities of Vendôme, Le Mans and Tours. At the village of Courcelles, they even forced three envoys from the Convention to support them by threatening to kill them if they refused. This grassroots movement is calling for a maximum price for essential goods and lower

The lack of food is making peasants increasingly hostile.

land rents. However, some of their leaders are priests who see a direct link between the cause of the poor and that of the Church. They have criticised the Assembly for being anti-clerical. This is not likely to please local republicans.

▷

The Convention decides to try the King

Paris, December 6

After a rowdy debate lasting several days, the deputies decided that Louis XVI would have to appear before them to answer to the crimes they have accused him of since they read the documents found inside the secret strong-box. However, the legislators spent a long time arguing over whether or not the King should be arraigned. The Girondists, who up till now had done all they could to avoid such a move, believed an arraignment risked provoking other European monarchs at a time when peace negotiations were in the offing. But they were forced to acknowledge that a trial had become inevitable. The Montagnards want the Temple's royal prisoner sentenced. They support a democratic revolution and have close ties to the sansculottists and the Paris Commune. For them, a refusal to declare the ousted King's guilt would be tantamount to a disavowal of the events of August 10th. At the Convention on December 3rd. Robespierre used the arguments wielded by Saint Just last month. "The King is not a defendant. You are not to pronounce sentence on a man, but rather to take action in the public interest, to accomplish an act of national salvation," he cried. Robespierre's eloquence was not powerful enough to get a majority of deputies to declare the King a traitor and a criminal without due process. Pétion, who had argued against Robespierre violently, won the battle and the Convention decided to back him: it ruled that there would be a trial and that it would itself be the tribunal (→ Dec. 11).

There is disagreement between the Convention and the sansculottists.

Mme. Roland accused of royalist plotting

Paris, December 7

The wife of the Minister of the Interior was called in to explain herself to the Convention today. Speaking in a firm, clear voice, Madame Roland had quite an effect on the assembled deputies. Even Marat, who had accused her, along with Chabot, of being involved in a royalist plot, agreed. "The lady, who had rehearsed her rôle, has played it well," he said. Swearing that she only looked after her family and was "not involved in business", Manon Roland said she was a victim of "envy and spite". The deputies were charmed by her and cheered. "Look at how quiet the spectators are, they are better than you!" Marat chided the deputies.

Manon Roland, the seductive advisor to the Girondist Party.

The Republic's earthenware is popular

Utensils that are needed around the home can also be used to help spread the ideals of France's new political system.

The earthenware makers of Nevers are extremely lucky. There have been so many important events this year that they have found plenty of inspiration for the elaborately drawn decorations they use on their pots, plates and serving dishes. Soon after war was declared on Austria last April, their wares were decorated with angry, warlike fighting cocks proudly proclaiming "I keep watch over the Nation." In July, when the nation was declared to be in danger, the cock appeared astride a cannon and looked even more threatening. Finally, in September, when the French Republic was proclaimed, all the emblems of royalty disappeared and were replaced by symbols of liberty. This was shown as a bird escaping from an open cage.

Mirabeau falls off his pedestal

Paris, December 10

Even dead men owe the Republic an explanation. The royal iron strong-box has revealed its secrets and because of this Mirabeau's bust was burnt today on the Place de Grève. Five days ago, at the Jacobins', Robespierre denounced the plotting that went on between the court and Mirabeau. As Robespierre was cheered, club members smashed Mirabeau's bust as well as that of the philosopher Helvétius, Jean Jacques Rousseau's persecutor. Things have really changed since the days when the grief-stricken people of Paris had marched alongside Mirabeau's coffin as it was taken to the Panthéon.

Nantes prospers, Bordeaux suffers

Western France, December

The year 1792 is ending very differently for France's two main ports on the Atlantic coast. Both have been severely hit by the effects of the war and the unrest due to the Revolution in France and in Saint Domingue. However, Nantes, in the northwest, is still a very busy port. Despite a sharp drop in the slave trade, its total trade volume of 26,000 tonnes is higher than during the last few years. But Bordeaux, in southwestern France, is stagnating, partly because of the poor grape harvest. Exports have dropped from a high of 86,000 tonnes in 1788 to only 58,000 today. The people of Bordeaux have a tough year ahead.

The Belgians want their independence

Paris, December 4

The Belgian issue had not been on the agenda and the delegation of Belgian autonomists was unable to get what it wanted: that France should not sign any peace treaties before it has recognised the absolute independence of Belgium. One month after Jemmapes, the Convention has still not decided what its policy is on France's neighbours. Anyway, these countries don't all agree what their future should be. Some want autonomy with moderate reforms, others are demanding radical changes, and some want to be linked to France.

Beaumarchais: an arms trafficker?

Paris, December 1

Beaumarchais, the ardent patriot and successful author, is worried. He has been accused of having conspired agaist the Republic and of having attempted to sell arms to the enemies of the state. He has refuted the charges, saying that it was the Legislative Assembly that asked him a few months ago to import into France 60,000 rifles which had been seized in the Netherlands and were being held in Holland. But unfortunately for the author the Convention is now in power, and it doesn't want anything to do with the weapons.

Federation of the English reformists

Edinburgh, December 10

The French Revolution has been gaining supporters abroad. Since the events of June 20th. and August 10th. these men have been getting bolder. The reformist societies in Great Britain, which have been set up since the start of the year on the initiative of the Scottish shoemaker Thomas Hardy, have more than 20,000 members. They have decided to become federated, and to act rather than just talk. The days of debate at the House of Commons between Fox, the cautious backer of the Revolution, and Burke, its opponent, are over.

Wallpaper with France's national colours

There is red, white and blue for the wallpaper as well.

Who would think that some of the wallpaper being produced by Messrs. Bénard and Jacquemart is actually made in the factory that used to belong to Réveillon? He was the one who sold them the factory in 1791, as he never really recovered from the dramatic looting of April 1789. Nowadays there is a new fashion: people are clamouring for wallpaper with tricoloured cockades, red bonnets and other revolutionary or republican symbols. These are needed urgently to decorate government offices.

The people of Savoy celebrate their incorporation into France

Maurienne, December 8

The town council of Saint Jean de Maurienne has taken a leaf out of the book of the French Revolution and decided that it must have a fitting celebration for the linking of Savoy to France. Since France's troops "liberated" Savoy, its inhabitants could hardly have kept the Revolution from reaching their territory even if they had wanted to. The entire population and the unarmed French soldiers had been invited to gather on Liberty Square, which used to be known as Cathedral Square. The ceremony organised by local officials was practically a carbon copy of similar ones held in France, but that did not stop people from thoroughly enjoying themselves. Red wool bonnets were worn, a *Te Deum* was sung, and there was plenty of music, as well as fireworks, Liberty trees, flags and rousing revolutionary songs such as *Ça Ira*. The people of Savoy, each one personally escorted by a French soldier, filed out of the cathedral as new converts to the Revolution (→Jan. 10, 93).

Victor Amedeus III flees from Savoy carrying his luggage on his back as if he were a common footman.

11. Paris. The sector known as Mirabeau, or Grange Batelière, informs the Convention that it is dropping its name and will be called in future the Mont Blanc sector.

11. Paris. Louis XVI appears for the first time before the Convention, where he is questioned by Barère.→

12. Paris. Following the Convention's ruling that any Frenchman can defend the King, the monarch picks his former minister Malesherbes and the former Constituent Assembly member Tronchet to be his defence lawyers.

12. England. From his new sanctuary in London, Talleyrand writes to the Convention to plead innocent to the charges against him.

13. Martinique. On the urging of the governor general, de Béhagne, the colonial assembly declares war on the French Republic.

13. London. The British parliament unanimously decides to support William Pitt's war preparations against France.→

14. Paris. 300 million new assignats are issued.

15. Paris. Cambon gets the Convention to approve the decree placing territories occupied by French troops under revolutionary administration.

15. Paris. Olympe de Gouges offers to defend the King.→

16. Paris. The Convention decrees the death penalty for whoever "suggests or attempts to break up the unity of the Republic, or to separate its integral parts from it".

16. Paris. To divert attention from the King's trial, Buzot suggests that all the Bourbons, including Philippe Egalité, should be arraigned.

17. Naples. The French fleet from Toulon arrives at Naples to force King Ferdinand IV to recognise the ambassador of the Republic, Mackan.→

17. Paris. The Convention allows the lawyer Raymond Romain to join the King's defence attorneys (→26).

20. Paris. On behalf of the public education committee, Romme gets the Convention to approve principles outlined by Condorcet on unified free education and equality of the sexes.

People vote to kill off smallpox

Port Louis, December 13

The Ile de France has voted to stamp out the smallpox virus once and for all. The unanimous verdict was delivered on December 5th. As a first step, the colonial Assembly has decreed that the contagious disease must be eradicated, but did not specify exactly how. Measures that have been taken since June to control its spread have had little effect. The idea of holding a vote on the issue came when doctors asked the deputies whether they should try to do anything about the virus that was killing off the population. The legislators decided that too many people were affected by the epidemic for them to act unilaterally. The toll is already heavy: 4,000 people have died out of a population of 58,000. The disease has serious economic repercussions. Not one foreign ship has anchored in Port Louis over the past six months. The French inhabitants of Bourbon island have forbidden all ships out of Port Louis from getting provisions there. This is partly due to the fact that the move will help Bourbon island's economy. But it also means that the Ile de France is now threatened by famine as it can't get hold of grain.

Girondists leave the Jacobin Club

Only the Montagnards have remained with the Jacobins. The Girondists have left the club, either willingly or by force. As early as October 10th., Brissot was expelled and Manuel was dismissed. Vergniaud, Guadet and Gensonné simply "forgot" to renew their membership cards. Robespierre is therefore the only one in control and the Society of the Friends of the Constitution has become the Society of Jacobins, Friends of Liberty and Equality. This club will allow him to strengthen the influence of the Montagnards at the Assembly, which had been dominated by Girondists. There are currently some 100 Montagnards at the Assembly, including Danton, Marat and Saint Just. They are not trusted.

William Pitt prepares England for war

British Prime Minister William Pitt during his speech at the Commons.

London, December 13

Britons can be extremly stubborn people. After two months of non-stop effort, Prime Minister William Pitt has finally succeeded in getting the House of Commons and the House of Lords to support his preparations for war against France. The French victories at Valmy and Jemmapes have upset the balance of power in Europe. Now that the French control the Austrian Netherlands, the port of Antwerp looks likely to see an economic boom. Vienna had always been opposed to this, not wanting the port to compete against London. Moreover, Batavian patriots in Holland are calling for French republicans to enter their country. Finally, Pitt is afraid of the emergence of closer ties between Prussia and Russia, following the Prussians' setback in France. Fox, the leader of the opposition, was the only one to try to block Pitt's plans.

Will the French navy bombard Naples?

Naples, December 17

The French Republic's honour is at stake. The Convention has therefore ordered Admiral de Latouche to drop anchor in the harbour to force the King of Naples to agree to meet the French ambassador. In fact, Ferdinand IV, his wife Marie Caroline and their minister Acton had refused to recognise the republican government of France. A lowly grenadier was told to take the French demands to the sovereign. Ferdinand IV finally agreed, thus avoiding French reprisals which could have resulted in bloodshed.

The grenadier Belleville conveys French demands to the King of Naples.

Anaxagoras: the prosecutor's name

Paris, December 12

The general council of the Paris Commune was most surprised to be told that the Christian name of the capital's new public prosecutor, Chaumette, was the tongue twister Anaxagoras. He explained to them that he had taken the name from a martyr of the ancient Athenian republic. It was, he said, far preferable to the Christian sounding Pierre Gaspard. The self-styled Anaxagoras is a sansculottist with a vivid imagination and a gift for speaking in public.

Anaxagoras Chaumette.

Olympe de Gouges offers her services to defend the King

Paris, December 15

When the letter that was sent to the Assembly by the young Olympe de Gouges was read out there was an uproar of protest. While the deputies were busy debating the technicalities of Louis XVI's trial, the brave young woman dared offer her services as his lawyer. He may be guilty as a King, but he is innocent as a man, she writes. "He was weak, he was duped, he duped us and he duped himself. That is the trial in a nutshell," she said. He doesn't deserve the death penalty but exile, which is more humiliating for him and more honourable for the Republic. The outraged deputies have decided to get on with their previous discussions and treat this impudent offer with all the contempt it deserves.

The King's trial: charges are read

Paris, December 11

An increasingly large crowd was fighting for room this afternoon in the public gallery of the Manège auditorium.

An ominous silence greeted the King's arrival. The monarch was led in by Santerre. Everybody was trying to get a close look at the man who had ruled France for 18 years, but who is now simply known as Louis Capet. He is charged with "having committed a multitude of crimes in order to establish his tyranny and by destroying the freedom of the people of France".

The King cut a far from impressive figure. His plump body was clothed in a simple brown broadcloth coat worn over a white waistcoat. His face was covered with several days' growth of beard, as he has been forbidden to use a razor. He is short-sighted and squints to see better. In fact, he looked like a tired and ill bourgeois who had just been dragged from his bed. He calmly listened to the charges being read out. They were based on the report drafted by the deputy Lindet on behalf of the special committee in charge of the trial.

The text was a detailed list of the King's activities since June 1789. It said he was guilty of having organised the counter-revolution from that date, of the violence at Versailles on June 23rd., the ordering

The ex-King is led to the Convention by Chambon, Paris' mayor, and Santerre.

of the troops to march on Paris in July, the arrival of the Flanders regiment, the "orgy" of October 3rd. when officers trampled on the tricoloured cockade, the violation of the oath of the Federation, the attempts to bribe deputies, the collusion with Bouillé in the affair of the Swiss of Châteauvieux, the plot of the "knights of the dagger", his escape to Varennes on June 20th. 1791, his own admission of duplicity since the start of the Revolution, the massacre at the Champ de Mars, the funds given to the émigrés, the backing given to the royalist camp at Jalès, his plotting with his brothers, the support of non-juring priests, the betrayal of Longwy and of Verdun, and finally

the crimes of August 10. Throughout it all, the King did not bat an eyelid. However, his main tactical blunder was to behave not as a king but as an accused man, thus playing into his opponents' hands. Louis Capet did, however, face embarrassing questions, basing his arguments on his rights as an absolute monarch or on the rights granted to him by the Constitution, depending on which period of his reign each specific charge referred to.

When asked whether he had had the notorious iron strong-box built, he amazed everybody by claiming he knew nothing about it. Before he left the auditorium at the request of the speaker, Louis XVI simply asked for a lawyer.

Interrogated by Barère, the speaker of the Assembly, Louis Capet has to face some embarrassing questions.

Convention

21. Paris. The Convention decrees that the wages of line troops are to be aligned with those of national volunteers.

23. Paris. The societies affiliated to the Jacobins Club now call themselves the "fraternising societies".

23. Evreux. The criminal tribunal of the Eure sentences to death 16 people found guilty of having murdered a forest ranger on June 3rd. The ranger had beaten a woodcutter who was chopping down trees without permission.

23. Sens. After having refused the post of mayor to which he had been elected on December 2nd., the Constitutional Archbishop Loménie de Brienne agrees to become a member of the Commune's general council.

25. Paris. Despite being banned by the Commune, midnight Masses are celebrated in many parts of the capital with the backing of sansculottists.→

25. Paris. Louis XVI writes his last will and testament.→

26. Paris. Louis XVI appears before the Convention for a second time.→

27. Paris. The Girondist Salles suggests that the Convention should ask the people to judge the King. The proposal is violently opposed by Saint Just.

27. Paris. The Théâtre de la République shows "Catherine or the Beautiful Farm Girl", a pastoral play by Julie Candeille. It is an immediate success.

28. Paris. The Minister of Foreign Affairs, Lebrun, tells the Convention that Spain's continued neutrality will depend on Louis XVI's fate.→

29. Guadeloupe. An uprising breaks out in Point à Pitre, which decides to back the French Republic.→

30. Paris. Buzot, on December 28th., and now Vergniaud, favour asking the people to decide the King's fate.

30. Paris. The Convention hears a member of the Polish Diet ask for France's help against Russia.

31. Paris. Marat accuses Dumouriez of plotting against the Convention.

31. Paris. 12 theatres opened this year in the capital.

The lovely Pamela gets married

Tournai, December 27

It is to be the most unusual and romantic wedding of the year. The bride, Pamela, born to an unknown father and a poverty-stricken mother, had been "sold" at the age of seven to the Orléans family. She is marrying a Scottish gentleman, Lord Edward FitzGerald, the son of the Duchess of Leinster. The groom had fallen madly in love with Pamela when they met only three months ago at the theatre. The young woman had just got back from a stay in London with her governess, Madame de Genlis. Unfortunately, the two women left Paris two days later for Belgium and Edward had to catch up with them to propose to Pamela.

Jean Marmontel, a timeless author

Paris, December

All's well that ends well. This is especially the case in the *New Moral Tales* by Jean François Marmontel. At the age of 69 this friend of the encyclopaedists, who was once employed by Madame de Pompadour, is still writing. The political upheavals have not had the slightest effect on his work. His tales are still full of the gentle, smiling wisdom that had delighted the readers of his *Moral Tales*, which were first published 30 years ago. A prudent man, he has gone to live in the Eure region with his family. He doesn't seem to have noticed that times have changed. He may, however, be saving his comments on the revolution for the memoirs he is said to be writing.

Marmontel, a protégé of Voltaire.

Guadeloupe wants to be republican

Pointe à Pitre, December 29

The red, white and blue flag of France is once again flying over Pointe à Pitre. After nine days of fighting, the republicans have been able to chase the royalist forces, led by General Arrost, out of the city. Less than one month after his arrival in the Caribbean aboard his ship the *Félicité*, Captain Raymond Lacrosse has already been successful. His calls for a revolt issued from the island of Dominique had the desired effect on the inhabitants and seamen of Guadeloupe. But his task is far from over. He wants to get all the islands in the region to join forces with the Republic, but he will need many reinforcements to achieve that goal.

Should Christmas Mass be banned?

Paris, December 25

The bells of Paris did not ring out tonight. The city authorities were afraid that unrest would break out and therefore ruled that all churches must be closed from yesterday at midnight until this evening. This move sparked off several angry gatherings.

At one point, dozens of enraged believers knocked down the doors of Saint Merri church. All over the city, crowds went to see priests to ask them to celebrate Mass in their parishes. However, the unrest did not go any further. In most cases, people went home to celebrate Christmas with their families as soon as Mass had been said by the priests.

Spain attempts to save Louis XVI

Paris, December 28

The Convention is furious. It has been deeply offended by the letter that has just been handed over by Ocariz, the Spanish consul, on behalf of his prime minister. In it, the Spanish premier says he is prepared to guarantee Madrid's neutrality, to mediate with European powers and to recognise the French government, but only on condition that Louis XVI and his family are freed. Thuriot has warned the deputies against being influenced by any "crowned bandits" who want to impose their will on France. The Spanish offer seems likely to be rejected out of hand by the Convention.

The purity of the geometric forms of this project is a typical example of the visionary style of Etienne Louis Boullée. The plan for a new National Palace to house the Convention has been submitted to deputies.

The ex-King's defence lawyers

Guillaume de Malesherbes.

Raymond Romain de Sèze.

François Denis Tronchet.

Paris, December 26

Three men are to defend the King: Tronchet, whose help the King has personally asked for, the venerable Malesherbes, who was twice his minister and who has volunteered to defend Louis XVI and the young lawyer from Bordeaux, Romain de Sèze, who was recruited by Malesherbes. De Sèze has links with several Girondist deputies. They have been working nonstop for the past 12 days to study the huge file. The Convention has rejected their request for a postponement to give them more time.

The King's trial: the defence speaks

Paris, December 26

At nine o'clock this morning, the King appeared for the second time before his judges. "Louis, the Convention has decreed that your testimony will be heard today," the speaker said as soon as the King walked in.

Then Raymond Romain de Sèze spoke. The lawyer is pleading not guilty on behalf of his client. He spoke for three solid hours amid a deep silence. His purely legal argument was flawless when he spoke of the inviolability of the King's person. He took the analysis to its limits: not only has the King been stripped of the inviolability conferred on him by the Constitution of 1791, but he doesn't even have the same rights as any French citizen. "I look among you for judges, but I only find accusers. Is Louis to be the only Frenchman for whom there exists no law and no procedure? Is he to have neither the rights of a citizen nor the prerogatives of a king?" the lawyer cried loudly. His words troubled the deputies. Taking advantage of this, de Sèze then discussed the deeds with which the monarch is charged, starting with those that took place prior to the Constitution before

coming to those that came after, which he said were covered by the inviolability. He justified the King's every action, sometimes resorting to specious arguments. "Citizens, I am not finished, but I pause before History. Remember that it will judge your verdict and that its judgement will be that of the centuries," he finally said. After the lengthy speech, Sèze sat down, completely exhausted. Louis XVI asked for a fresh shirt for his lawyer as his was drenched with sweat. "He has done a good job," the King said. Then he asked to be allowed to speak.

He told the deputies that he had a clear conscience. "My heart is torn to see that the charges against me give the impression that I wanted to shed the blood of the people and above all that I am held responsible for the misfortunes of August 10th.," he said. "I was convinced that the many demonstrations of my love for the people that I gave time and time again and the way in which I behaved were proof enough that I never feared to take a risk to save their blood and get rid of such impressions," he added. Neither de Sèze's speech for the defence, nor the King's statement, however, see-

med to convince the deputies, who resumed their debate after the former monarch's departure. Many of them have been offended to hear someone defend the King and to watch Louis dare to absolve himself of all the crimes he is charged with (→Jan. 4, 93).

The testament

It has been a sad Christmas for Louis XVI. Separated from his family, resigned to his fate and having "only God as my witness", he is writing his testament after lengthy prayers. He forgives his enemies, his false friends and his wife "if she feels she has something to reproach herself for". "I advise my son, if he ever has the misfortune to become king, to remember that he must devote all his to efforts to ensuring the happiness of his fellow citizens, that he must forget all hatred and resentment, in particular concerning the misfortune and heartbreak I experience, and that he can only make people happy by reigning in accordance with the law."

Louis Capet surrounded by his lawyers: "I was never afraid of my life being examined in public."

Citizen Palloy's miniature stone Bastilles

Chambéry, January

The main town of the new department of Mont Blanc has just been given the Bastille on a tray. It is a miniature scale model of the Paris Bastille allegedly made out of "material coming from the demolition that has been put together with plaster". The model is identical to the 93 others that Palloy, the demolition contractor who had been hired to take the famous fort apart, had sent to the other departments in 1790. The model's base has some handles so that it can be easily carried during official festivities. Apart from miniature Bastilles, the enterprising Palloy also sells engraved or decorated stones and iron medallions which he claims are made from the metal used for the chains of the notorious Bastille. By

A Bastille stone given to Chambéry on January 1st. 1793.

selling such items, Palloy hopes not only to spread the revolutionary message, but also to make money in the process.

France wants to help the Irish

Paris, January 1

The best way of causing problems for the English is to help the Irish patriots fighting against England's domination of their island. The French deputy Kersaint, a former ship's captain who once fought against the English, today put forward a plan to help the Irish fighters for independence and supporters of the French Revolution. The plan will also allow France to spread revolutionary ideas, while at the same time embarrassing a potential enemy. It would be a disaster for France if England were to join in the war alongside the continental powers.

Dysentery is raging through Valmy

Champagne, January 1

More and more people have been dying at Valmy. Six months ago, the Prussians arriving in France did not suspect that they would not just be facing those devilish republicans but also another fearsome enemy, dysentery. Brunswick's soldiers, who had already suffered from the bad weather, were hit by the disease. One out of every eight of his men was affected. Although the Prussians have now left, the disease has stayed behind. At Sainte Menehould the mass graves for fallen soldiers are to be covered up. Local inhabitants have been given garlic and vinegar to fight the disease.

"I won't become the Belgian Attila!"

Paris, January 1

With these words, Dumouriez a few days ago expressed his refusal to enforce the Convention's instructions in Belgium. He added: "I don't wish to be considered as a traitor by a nation to which I have spoken only of French loyalty." The decree of December 15th. on the occupied territories had made him extremely angry. He has just arrived in Paris to try to get the decree abrogated. With that aim in mind, he met Cambon, the man responsible for this law which notably rules that national authori-

ties will be dismissed and that all taxes and privileges are to be abolished in conquered lands. As for public and church property, they are to be placed "under the protection of the French Republic", that is to say confiscated. Dumouriez sees the law as tyrannical and in violation of the ideals of liberty and brotherhood. The law would be outright exploitation of Belgium, he says. The over-ambitious Convention is acting as if it wants to become master of Belgium, he told Cambon. However, the latter was not convinced.

Censorship hits the Paris stage

Paris, January 5

The comedy nearly turned into drama at the Vaudeville theatre during a performance of *La Chaste Suzanne*.

An actor had simply cried out "You are accusers, you can't be judges!". Immediately, the Jacobins saw this as a reference to the trial of Louis XVI. They leapt up on stage, stopped the play, and ordered the audience to stop applauding the actors.

Angry Savoyards rise up in revolt

Saint Jean, January 10

The people of Savoy have only been French for two months, but they have already had enough. They are angry about the system of spies and informing that has been set up by the Society of the Friends of Liberty, the growing religious persecution, the searches and night-time visits.

A few days ago, the citizens of Saint Jean de Maurienne rang the alarm bells and invaded the town hall to demand the resignation of the councillor Marcoz, who immediately took their advice. His fellow councillors today met the commissioners, who had hurriedly come over from Chambéry. When they were accused of having given in to the rioters too easily, the councillors replied that this was because they had been repeatedly told ever since the Revolution that "the people were in control".

An elegant young bourgeois.

La Harpe, a fair weather patriot

Paris, January 12

Some people are Jacobins out of a deep conviction, other just due to circumstances.

La Harpe belongs to the latter category. A few months ago the great success won by the French army during the battle for Valmy had inspired the poet to write a fiery and enthusiastic "Hymn to Liberty". But La Harpe would never have dreamt of publishing this work if he had not been asked a few days ago, when the Lycée reopened for the year, to show a little more patriotic and republican spirit. At the request of the Lycée's administrators he read his hymn out during the opening ceremony. It is now to be published.

Free information and aid available

Paris, January

The notary Degasne has turned his office into a centre for free services. He now provides information and assistance to all those who know neither how to read or write, or who have trouble coping with the mysteries of official forms. Negotiating a complex contract of sale, renting an apartment or getting a subscription to a newspaper are some of the services he offers. He is only paid by commissions from the firms he sends his clients to. If a deal is successful, he gets a bonus. This is a good way of making money without taking it from the poor.

Farmers protest

Vaucluse, January 9

Out of work farm workers and jobless men from Avignon this morning invaded the tiny village of Mazan. The were resolved to stop attempts to use draught horses to work in the fields while they have no jobs. They blocked the local stables, then grabbed the carts and dragged them to the fields where they got down to work. That was their way of protesting against the farm owners' decision to carry on using animals instead of men to work the fields, even though there is chronic unemployment.

The King's trial: people to decide?

Paris, January 4

The independent moderate legislators of the Plaine group today voted against the Girondist call that the people be allowed to decide the King's fate.

The vote was taken on the urging of Barère, the representative of the Hautes Pyrénées department. Although they hadn't been convinced by de Sèze's defence speech, most of the Plaine deputies were opposed to pronouncing a death sentence on a man who was the kingdom's absolute ruler for many years and who is still seen by many as a sacrosanct and unassailable personality. Regicide is an unforgivable crime and

The moderate Barère is against.

there are well-hidden feelings of guilt. On December 27th. the Girondists had suggested that the people should be asked to decide Louis XVI's fate, feeling that it would be safer in the long run to spare the King. Vergniaud stressed that the nation was sovereign and only it could decide what punishment could be inflicted on the former monarch.

He added that the primary assemblies should be consulted on the issue. But if this procedure were to be used, and if, as seemed highly likely, it led to a verdict of clemency, the Republic and the Convention could be endangered. Indeed, petitions and calls in favour of the King have been flooding in to the Convention from all the departments. Aware of the danger of this, Robespierre spoke out strongly against plans for a people's verdict on December 28th.

"In my heart of hearts, I have felt the republican nature wavering in the face of the guilty man's humiliation before the sovereign power," he told the Assembly, adding, however: "But, citizens, the final proof of devotion to the nation is to stamp out these natural feelings for the sake of a great people and oppressed humanity ... Clemency that aids tyranny is an abomination." For Robespierre, as for the Monta-

gnards, the people's verdict is simply a "means of bringing despotism back through anarchy". Today, in an extremely tough speech, Barère brilliantly outlined all the legal and political arguments and demanded that the proposal to call for the people's verdict be dropped.

He also demanded that the Convention keep overall powers in the matter of the King's fate. He used some of Robespierre's arguments. He stressed, however, that while a law can be submitted to the people's approval, a trial cannot. His speech could well be decisive and push the moderates of the Plaine over onto the side of the Montagnards.

The Girondist Gensonné is for.

Mobs of Romans nearly massacre several French residents

Rome, January 14

The students of the Academy of France in Rome narrowly escaped being massacred. The Convention had ordered the removal of the royal shields that decorated the front of the Academy and of the French embassy in Rome. The artists studying at the Academy were hard at work when an anti-French mob of Romans, who have been increasingly opposed to France over the past months, attacked the school overnight. They forced the students to run for their lives. The painter Anne Louis Girodet and some of his friends managed to rush down alleyways, chased by a crowd screaming for blood. But luckily, they managed to lose their pursuers and reach the French embassy, run by Hugou de Bassville, the French representative to the Holy See. But they were too late: Bassville had

been lynched by the mob. This morning, the young painter cautiously returned to the Academy, which had been set on fire by the

mob. Fortunately, a man came up to him and said: "Come with me, you'll be safe." Girodet recognised one of his models.

The assassination of Bassville, France's representative in Rome.

Paine opposes the death of Louis XVI

Paris, January 15

"As a true republican, I see kings more as objects of contempt than as objects of vengeance. I will never believe that we have been empowered to pass the death sentence on a man." Paine did not mince his words when he spoke from the podium of the Convention. What he had to say enraged the Montagnards, particularly Marat. The Englishman fears that the execution of Louis XVI would lead to a spiral of violence. He has therefore suggested that the King's fate be submitted to the new Assembly, as the Convention's only mandate is to draft the Constitution.

André Chénier tries to help the King

Paris, January 15

There are few people who now dare to state publicly their support for Louis XVI. André Chénier is one of them. As his brother seems to be about to vote in favour of the death penalty, he has decided to side with the King's defenders. At the request of the monarch's lawyers, de Sèze and Malesherbes, he is trying to write a pleading letter that the King could read out if a majority votes for a death sentence. This may move the Assembly to change its mind. The poet is trying to use all his skill in a desperate attempt to save Louis XVI.

Philippe Egalité becomes a regicide

Paris, January 17

"I vote for death," said Philippe in a wavering voice. These words were greeted by silence at the Assembly. The daring man who has just spoken is none other than the King's own cousin. The Convention was today judging Citizen Capet, and all the representatives of Paris had already voted for the death penalty. Just one name had still not been called out, that of Philippe Egalité. His vote was unexpected and Danton was heard to whisper: "He was the only one who could have refused to vote and he didn't dare do that."

The King's trial: the death sentence

Paris, January 17

Since dawn, all of Paris has known that the King has been sentenced to death by a majority of 53 votes. The news spread like wildfire through the city, which is strangely silent. It is almost as if Paris is in a state of total shock. Three days ago, the Assembly decided on the three questions the deputies should try to answer: the first was about the King's guilt, the second about the issue of the people's verdict and the third was what the punishment should be. An overwhelming majority replied "yes" to the first of the questions. On behalf of the French people, Louis was declared guilty of "conspiring against the liberty of the nation and the security of the state".

The plan to ask the people for its verdict was rejected by 424 votes against 287. But it was yesterday that the deputies had to respond to the crucial question: "What punishment does Louis deserve?" Ever since this morning, a large crowd had gathered in the Manège hall. There were several lovely women present. Jokes and banter among the spectators did not hide the growing sense of unease. Garat, the Minister of Justice, opened the session by speaking about all the troubles that have taken place in Paris. The debate lasted for a long time. Finally, at eight p.m., the roll-call of deputies began and each was called on to state his verdict. "Death." Throughout the night, that fateful word was spoken 387 times in the large, cold and badly lit hall. At dawn all the votes were counted, although the final result was hardly in doubt. But among the deputies who voted for the death penalty, 26 had asked for a further debate to decide whether the sentence should or should not be suspended. It is supposed to be carried out the day after tomorrow. It is now up to Malesherbes to give the dreadful news to the condemned man (→Jan. 20).

Marat votes for the King's death.

THE KING'S PROSECUTORS	VOTED FOR DEATH
VOTED FOR DETENTION Boissy d'Anglas, Defermon, Fauchet, Gorsas, Kersaint, Paine, Peraldi, Villette... **VOTED FOR THE HIGHEST PENALTY** Condorcet. **VOTED FOR A SUSPENDED DEATH SENTENCE** Brissot, Cambacérès, Guadet, Louvet de Couvray, Treilhard, Vergniaud...	Amar, Barbaroux, Barère, Barras, Basire, Bourbotte, Buzot, Billaud Varenne, Cambon, Carnot, Carra, Chabot, Chasles, M. J. Chénier, Cloots, Collot d'Herbois, Couthon, Danton, David, Desmoulins, Drouet, Fréron, Dubois Crancé, Gensonné, Isnard, Lavicomterie, Lebas, Fabre d'Églantine, Lequinio, Marat, Jeanbon St André, Lindet Robert, Petion, Prieur, Philippe Égalité, Robespierre, La Réveillère Lepeaux, Romme, Saint Just, Sieyès, Soubrany, Tallien, Thuriot, Vadier...

A deputy and former nobleman dies for voting for King's death

Paris, January 20

People are shocked and deeply upset. The deputy Louis Le Peletier de Saint Fargeau was murdered this evening as he dined at Février, a restaurant at the Palais Royal. The restaurant owner said afterwards that, around six o'clock, a tall young man with a beard and dark skin had walked up to the legislator and asked: "Are you Le Peletier de Saint Fargeau? — Yes — Did you vote in favour of the King's death? — Yes — Very well then, here is your reward!" With that, the assailant stabbed the parliamentarian with his sword before running away. He can only have been a royalist hit man, people are saying. Many such counter-revolutionaries are known to hang around the prostitutes of the Palais Royal. Along with the Duc d'Orléans, Le Peletier embodied all that such men hate. They saw him as a traitor to their class.

The former nobleman used to support the King. He had been a devoted and loyal royalist. But the times changed and so did his political convictions. He came to back Robespierre and sometimes stood in for him at the Jacobins. Little did he know that he was signing his death warrant by voting for the King's execution (→Jan. 24).

Nobody was able to stop the killer of Le Peletier de Saint Fargeau.

The King's trial: reprieve is rejected

A banned play is read in public

Paris, January 14

There has been yet another incident at the Théâtre des Nations. This evening the plays that were supposed to have been performed, *L'Avare* and *Le Médecin Malgré Lui*, are to be replaced by a play written by Laya. The author of *L'Ami des Lois* had written a cheeky work attacking both Marat and Robespierre, who were called Nomophage and Duricrâne in the play. So three days ago, the Commune decided to ban the play. However, the actors decided to read the play out in public rather than to perform it. The audience was content and no laws were broken.

Manon Roland's love for Buzot

Paris, January

"The fear of death is the least of my worries," Roland told a friend. Increasingly unpopular, fearing for his life and that of his family, the minister has serious domestic problems on top of everything else. With her usual candour, his wife has just told him she is in love with Buzot. Since the young deputy of the Eure came back to Paris, their friendship has turned into a passionate, but platonic, love affair. When she gave her husband the bad news, Manon swore that she would remain faithful to him, even though her heart belongs to another.

M. Clochard fights against poverty

Bordeaux, January 18

The official in charge of the poor-house, Monsieur Clochard, is a man who takes his work seriously. This authoritarian puritan wants to fight against laziness and vice by giving the unfortunate work to do. The elderly and invalid people in his establishment are all treated decently in exchange for work that is tailored to their physical capabilities. The able-bodied poor must sweep the port and the city's streets, as well as doing other useful jobs, in order to earn the meagre food they are served and be given an uncomfortable bed to sleep on.

The last portrait of Louis XVI.

Paris, January 20

At 3 a.m. this Sunday, the tired deputies wound up the long session after having approved a final decree concerning Louis. The former King is to be executed within the next 24 hours, they decided. As for the "appeal from the nation against the judgement handed out against him by the Convention", which has been submitted by the King's defenders, it was ruled to be invalid. These decisions were not easily reached by the Assembly. The debate on a reprieve had begun yesterday morning at 10:30 under the chairmanship of Barère. The Montagnards said at the outset that they were firmly opposed to any such move. The Girondists were split on the issue: Barbaroux was against, but Buzot, Condorcet and Brissot were for. The latter argued on the basis of France's foreign policy interests. An execution may lead to a dangerous coalition of European sovereigns, he warned. "Are you now prepared for such a universal war?" he asked his colleagues. However, Barère found the decisive words: "Republics are only born out of effort, we must be up to facing the governments of Europe." The roll-call started right after Barère's speech. Those who were in favour of an immediate execution won, getting a total of 380 votes against 310 (→ Jan. 21).

Louis XVI's heartrending farewells to his wife and family

Paris, January 20

Since Malesherbes informed him of the fateful verdict, Louis has been preparing for his death. This evening he was allowed to see his wife, their children and his sister. He had been separated from them ever since December 11th. The moment they walked into his room, they rushed sobbing into his arms. Then the King sat down between the Queen and the princesses and the Dauphin stood by his father. They remained close to each other for nearly two hours, whispering and weeping. Finally, Louis XVI tore himself away from his loved ones and promised that he would be seeing them again tomorrow. He then went to see Abbot Edgeworth who had been allowed by the Convention to be at the King's side even though he is a non-juring priest. "What a meeting I have just had! How much I love them and am loved by them," the deeply upset King told Edgeworth.

The condemned man promises his family he will see them again tomorrow before mounting the scaffold.

January 21st. 1793: The death of Louis Capet, the 16th. King to bear that name, on Revolution Square. 319

Paris, 10:22 a.m. — King Louis XVI is guillotined

At the foot of the scaffold, Louis XVI has removed his robe himself. His hair is going to be cut. Abbot Edgeworth gives the King the last rites.

Paris, January 21

Nothing has moved in Paris. And yet, this morning the regicide desired by the nation's representatives took place. At 10:22 a.m., the guillotine blade fell on the royal neck. An hour earlier, leaving the tower of the Temple, Louis XVI, who had just received communion from Abbot Edgeworth de Firmont, had turned down an opportunity to bid a last farewell to his family. "Tell them I wanted to spare them the pain of so cruel a separation, and how terrible it is for me to leave without their final embraces," he murmured to his confessor through his tears.

Then then King left on his last voyage, between two ranks of National Guards holding back a silent crowd, as cries of "mercy!" went up from time to time. Louis XVI recited prayers for those about to die with the priest. When he arrived at Revolution Square, the King cast a confident glance at the scaffold facing the Tuileries gardens, removed his coat and opened his shirt collar. When he saw the executioner's assistants come forward to tie his hands, he stepped back indignantly. People even thought for a few seconds that he was going to resist, but in a mood of sudden resignation he let them tie his hands and cut his hair before climbing the scaffold steps. But at the top of the steps, escaping from his guards, he ran to the balustrade. Just as he was going to speak, Santerre ordered the National Guards to muffle the King's voice with some drumrolls. Before he was seized again, he had enough time to shout: "People, I die an innocent man! I pardon the authors of my death! I pray to God that my blood shall not fall on France."

He was attached to the plank, which tipped, and he cried out in fear. Sanson, the executioner, then seized the bloody head and displayed it for a long time to the crowd, all of whom shouted together "Long live the nation!" followed by a heavy silence. People then rushed up to touch the victim's blood or take clothing and hair, which were then sold off at very high prices. At last, the crowd went its way without a word.

Louis XVI's death

The King's death has inspired two very different songs. One, composed by Ladré, the author of *Ça Ira*, is being sung in the streets. Here is an extract:

In January's third week
In seventeen ninety three
The tyrant foul Capet
The sixteenth King Louis
Received his guerdon dread;
His treachery was seen
When from Varennes he fled,
And guillotined he's been.

His efforts base to plot
The fall of our dear France
'Gainst liberty's proud lot
'Twas this his worst offence.
His sovereign power withal
His judgement did ensnare.
'Twas at the queen's fond call
That blood flowed everywhere.

While he on earth was king,
He reigned in bliss purblind.
But this the saddest thing:
His feebleness of mind.
Forsooth, a crown to wear
A man must have brains keen;
No wits he had whate'er,
And guillotined he's been.

The other is a rather moving lament. It is being sung *sotto voce* in royalist families:

O my people, are you grieved?
I loved justice and virtue.
To your welfare e'er I cleaved;
A heinous death is all my due.

Was it not, O Frenchmen dear,
That amongst you I was born?
And neath France's sky so clear
Our youth reached its bourne

O my people, fare you well!
Have no fear, I painless die.
May my spilt lifeblood spell
The end of hate and life awry.

The spectators did not hear the King's last words, which were muffled by the guard's drumrolls.

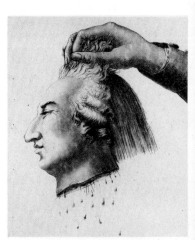

"Something to think about for all crowned charlatans."

January 1793
from 22th. to 31st.

Roland is forced to resign as minister

Roland is downtrodden by fate.

Paris, January 22

The Interior Minister is certainly plagued by misfortune. Betrayed by his wife, whose passion for the Girondin Buzot is known to him, he is also isolated in public life. Robespierre has accused his propaganda departments of having been involved in Le Peletier's assassination, and Roland was forced to resign this morning.

England breaks with France

London, January 24

"You have one week to leave England." Those were the terms used to inform Chauvelin, the representative of the French government in London, that he was being expelled from Great Britain. The English were horrified by the news of the execution of Louis XVI. As early as last December, two Members of Parliament had spoken out in the House of Commons to ask the English government to intervene with the Convention to prevent the King of France from being guillotined. However, the indignation that was caused by the monarch's death is not the only reason for Chauvelin's expulsion. The British Prime Minister, William Pitt, explained to the House of Lords that the ambassador from Paris was a very dangerous man because he might spread revolutionary ideas. Actually, England is seizing on this occasion to break diplomatic relations with France, as the British government now wants war (→ Feb. 1).

A celebration at the Carrousel is raided

Paris, January 27

The charms of fraternity are not always spread equally. Thus the Commune of Paris took advantage of a celebration to be held at Carrousel Square, where a tree of fraternity was to be planted, to "clean up" the area, which was "contaminated" by the nearby gambling and amusement houses of the former Palais Royal. The ceremony began in solemn fashion, in the presence of municipal officials and a delegation of deputies. Once the tree was planted, the deputy Maure exhorted the crowd to display republican virtues: "Let us swear to maintain freedom and equality, even at the risk of our lives." They all swore at once and broke out into a *Carmagnole*. They began dancing a round, led by the mayor, and they were still dancing at 8 p.m. But suddenly the square was surrounded by soldiers and anybody who could not show a citizen's card was arrested. Interrogations, searches and arrests continued until morning.

Funeral is held for Le Peletier de Saint Fargeau

Paris, January 24

No such funeral had ever been staged before. The still-bloody corpse of the deputy Le Peletier de Saint Fargeau, who was stabbed by one of the King's guards three days ago, was carted all through Paris to the sound of cannon-fire, lying on a bed with a civic crown on his pale head and his soiled clothing hanging on the end of a pikestaff decorated with cypress branches. On that occasion, David proved his brilliance when it comes to organising funerals.

The martyr's body shown on the base of Louis XVI's statue, on Place des Piques, formerly Place Vendôme.

Convention

1. Paris. France declares war on England as well as on the United Provinces.

4. Paris. In the wake of attacks by Dumouriez and Custine, War Minister Pache is replaced by General Beurnonville.

4. Paris. Premiere at the Théâtre de la Nation of Louis Benoît's play *Le Conteur ou les Deux Postes.*

5. Lyons. The General Council is having raids made on homes, and 150 suspects are arrested (→7).

6. Paris. Death of the Venetian writer Carlo Goldoni. He settled in France in 1787 and leaves some *Memoirs*, which he wrote directly in the French language.

7. Paris. Dubois Crancé proposes to the Convention that the army should be reorganised by combining national volunteers with line troops.

7. Lyons. Mayor Nivière Chol resigns after coming under attack from the Commune's General Council for having authorised the searches carried out on February 5th. (→18).

12. Paris. A delegation from the 48 sectors reads the Convention a petition in favour of passing a law concerning military supplies. The petition was drafted by Jacques Roux.→

14. Paris. The former War Minister, Pache, who has joined the Montagnards, is elected mayor with 12,000 votes out of 15,000 cast. He is to replace the Girondist Chambon, who resigned on February 2nd.

14. Paris. A decree is issued to annex the Principality of Monaco to France.

15. Paris. Anacharsis Cloots brings out the first issue of *Batave*, the organ of the Dutch refugees.

15. Paris. Condorcet submits a draft *Declaration of human, natural, civil and political rights* to the Assembly, together with a draft constitution that has been approved by the majority of the Girondists.

17. Belgium. Dumouriez's army penetrates into Holland.

18. Sardinia. The French army makes an unsuccessful attempt to land.

18. Lyons. Nivière Chol's re-election as mayor of Lyons triggers a violent royalist riot.

The Court of Spain goes into mourning

Madrid, February 8

Indignation is at a peak at the Court of Spain following the announcement of the execution of Louis XVI. Charles IV, determined on a solemn display of his hostility to the French Revolution, decreed three days ago that the whole Court should go into mourning, while the newspaper *la Gazeta* noted the "great heroism" of the "very Christian King of France" and exposed "the atrocious inhumanity characterising the attack on his person". The paper is publishing the guillotined French King's will today.

Instrument-maker was also a faker

Paris, February 9

With the death of Pascal Joseph Taskin, two great names in the world of harpsichords have just disappeared. The fact is that, in the face of a dwindling clientele, Taskin had followed a very common practice these days and become a counterfeiter to save his workshop from bankruptcy. He turned out original instruments bearing his name, but also some fake Ruckers. The harpsichords made by those famous Antwerp craftsmen of the 16th. and 17th. centuries are considered masterpieces, and they are the only ones that still sell.

Portrait of Fénelon as a revolutionary

Paris, February 9

Fénelon was not only a philosopher, but also a patriot. At least, that is the case if we believe *Fénelon or the Nuns of Cambrai*, the latest work of Marie Joseph Chénier. The late prelate, already popular because of his statements against Louis XIV's absolutism, and still bathed in his glory as a pedagogue, is portrayed in the book as a veritable precursor of revolutionary ideas. He is a hero with a pure and divine soul and uses his authority as a bishop to end the torture of a nun condemned by her order. Nothing could be more pleasing to the audience in attendance at the Théâtre de la République.

War deprives the Parisians of their fish

A sansculottist faces the coalition of nine foreign forces, all of whom he hopes to be able to mow down with a single shot.

Paris, February

There is no more sea-fishing, and hence no more fish on Parisian tables these days. The war that was declared a few days ago on England and Holland is having some marked effects on supplies for the capital of France. Previously, the food shortage that has affected France for five years had been greatly attenuated by large-scale imports of grains and a certain number of other foods, but that trade most often involved the efforts of English and Dutch traders and shippers, who have now become enemies of France. All of the many goods imported by sea, and not just fish, are going to suffer from Anglo-Dutch hostility.

Le Peletier's assassin commits suicide

Forges les Eaux, February 1

It will never be known whether the assassination of Le Peletier de Saint Fargeau was an isolated act of an impulsive individual misled by hate, or the result of a royalist plot of which the assassin was only an instrument. Pâris, Louis XVI's former King's bodyguard who killed the regicidal deputy 12 days ago, will never speak again. The killer of that revolutionary, who had forgotten he used to be a noble, killed himself as the gendarmes, who had tracked him down, were trying to arrest him.

The gendarmes did not have enough time to capture killer Pâris alive.

Extremists defy the Montagnards

Paris, February 12

The Montagnards now risk being overwhelmed by revolutionaries who are even more virulent than they are. The agitators from the Paris sectors have just submitted a petition to the Convention. They want to put an end to rising prices and to the monopolists' activities. They are therefore demanding abolition of free trade in grain. Together with the Federates belonging to the group of united defenders of the 84 departments, these sector militants constitute the spearhead of the Enragés (extremists), vehement revolutionaries led by Jacques Roux and Varlet, who demand an end to social inequalities. They attack the moderate Girondist policy, needless to say, but also have an ambiguous position with respect to the Montagne, which is dominated by the Jacobins. The latter welcomed them to their premises on the Rue Saint Honoré, hoping to control the popular revolt against the high cost of living, or, at the worst, to use them to destabilise the Girondists. But now the Enragés are attacking the Jacobins themselves, and especially Saint Just, who opposed any regulation of trade. Their political positions are making a lot of waves. The Montagnards are worried, fearing that they may lose their popular legitimacy. As for Marat, he hates those "disguised royalists".

Danton weeps over his wife's death

Gabrielle Danton, née Charpentier.

Paris, February 17

Gabrielle Danton died while giving birth to her fourth son. Danton will never see again the woman he married for love in 1787, when he was still a mere notary's clerk without real prospects. When he learned the tragic news, Danton was on a mission to Belgium. He returned to Paris as quickly as possible, but it was too late. When he arrived at Rue des Cordeliers, he learned that his wife had already been buried. He did not react to his friends' signs of friendship, and then indulged in a wild act of love and despair. He looked up the deaf mute sculptor Deseine, whom he dragged off to Sainte Catherine cemetery. At night he dug up Gabrielle and got the artist to make a moulding of her face. The fact that, without thinking of his reputation, he dared to violate his wife's grave in order to see, for the last time, the face of the woman he had loved so shows the depth of his sorrow.

The Girondists defeat Chalier in the Lyons city hall elections

Joseph Chalier, tribune of Lyons.

Chalier exhorting his friends while he was president of the Lyons district.

Lyons, February 18

Only one thing is sure: Nivière Chol, the Girondist mayor who was re-elected today, has defeated the Jacobins. But it is very hard to say whether the Girondists or the counter-revolutionaries really won the election battle. In Lyons, the Girondist groups not only timid republicans and royalists who favour order, but also many counter-revolutionary provocateurs whose only concern is defeating the Jacobin camp. To complicate the situation, further, Nivière Chol finds the majority of the municipality against him, as it supports the Jacobins and their leader, Chalier. This Piedmontese, a mystical revolutionary with florid speech, has constantly tried to clear counter-revolutionaries out of Lyons. But the house searches ordered by the municipality at his request have annoyed the population more than they have intimidated it. Nivière Chol seized this opportunity. Claiming a Jacobin plot, he did not hesitate to resign, rightly believing that he could personally benefit from the resulting panic. The election results show he was right. But the most opportunistic of his backers then unmasked themselves. Laying siege to the Jacobin Central Club, they sacked it and then dragged Jean Jacques Rousseau's bust through the dirt before burning the tree of Liberty (→ Mar. 8).

Monte Carlo is to become French

Paris, February 14

The French Revolution doesn't just annex territories. It calls such moves restoring France's ancient "natural" borders. That was the formula used by Carnot in speaking to the Convention to justify attaching the Principality of Monaco to France. He said that "the old and natural limits of France are the Rhine river, the Alps and the Pyrenees". Hence there is "no infraction in taking them back". On this point, Carnot fully supports Danton, who also claims that maintaining France within those natural borders will reassure Europe. For if France contents itself with annexing the territories located within its "ancient" limits, Europe no longer needs to fear the revolutionary war that the Girondists wanted.

The difficulties of the priests in exile

London, February 18

For the French priests who have found refuge in London, salvation comes from the "Freemasons' Tavern". The committee that manages the fund for helping non-juring priests holds its meetings in that establishment. But this evening, the meeting ended on a note of concern. The Bishop of Saint Pol de Léon, who is responsible for distributing financial aid, faces the problem of the very fast increase in the number of exiled priests. The latter already have to agree to a humiliating examination of the condition of their wardrobe by a tailor if they want to get new clothes. Despite the English subscribers' generosity, the funds are running out and the committee has found itself forced to call on public charity again.

Convention

19. Strasbourg. Euloge Schneider is appointed public prosecutor at the revolutionary Tribunal. →

21. Paris. The Convention approves the decree on the organisation of the army's regiments.

22. Paris. The première at the Théâtre de la Nation of a comedy by Louis Boissy, *The Village Mayor, or the Force of Law*, which puts a virtuous nobleman on stage. The performance triggers the audience's anger.

22. Paris. In the struggle against rising prices, the sectors demand a "maximum" value to be respected. Some meetings are being held in the suburbs.

23. Paris. Le Peletier de Saint Fargeau, the recently assassinated deputy, is celebrated in an historical play staged at the Favrart auditorium.

24. Paris. The Convention decrees a call-up of 300,000 men (→), as well as the amalgamation of regular troops and national volunteers. It also provides for election by the soldiers of part of their officers. But the generals are to refuse to apply this measure until the winter of 1793-94.

24. Paris. Paris women seize two boats loaded with soap. It is then sold cheaply.

24. Paris. Philippe Egalité, Grand Master of the Grand Orient Lodge of France, refuses to carry out his Freemasonry duties.

24. Bordeaux. The very active Society of Women Favouring Freedom and Equality, established by the female citizens of the Gironde, congratulates the Convention on executing Louis XVI.

25. United Provinces. Breda is captured by Dumouriez.

25. Ille et Vilaine. The administrators of Bains district inform the department that the levy in mass risks causing an insurrection.

25. Ile de France. The Republic is proclaimed. →

25. Philadelphia. President Washington adopts Jefferson's view and decides on gradual repayment of the American debt to France.

26. Paris. A riot breaks out in the Halles, where women pillage the grocery shops. →

Is Corsica going to remain French?

Corsica, February 23

War has been declared between Pascal Paoli, friend of the English, and the Francophile Napoléon Bonaparte. A long-time nationalist Paoli had gone into exile in England so as to avoid French domination. He returned in 1789, thanks to the Revolution, and is now supported by the whole population. He is worried about the way things are developing on the mainland and is conspiring to win independence for his island, which became a French department in 1790. But Bonaparte, who is determined to make his career in the French army, is hostile to any idea of autonomy. Paoli has just won an initial victory. Paris had ordered him to occupy Sardinia, a possession of King Victor Amadeus of Savoy. Bonaparte was in charge of operations. But once the plan was well under way, Paoli gave the order to retreat on the grounds of having insufficient forces. What an affront to Bonaparte, who was counting on his first military success! Now nothing can reconcile the two men (→June 10).

Well-dressed pries

Mont Blanc, February 25

The priest of the small town o Viry had a fine wardrobe, at leas according to the inventory mad soon after his departure. Peopl found no fewer than eleven chasu bles, five silk tunics, two stoles, fiv surplices, six albs, and 36 of th small handkerchiefs know as "lava bos" that the priest uses to wipe hi hands before the consecration. O the other hand, the priest had a rather small income: only 384 livre and 10 sols in money, and a few deliveries of wheat, oats and barley

Trouser-like stripes are now used for elegant ladies' dresses.

The irresistible rise of Euloge Schneider the Jacobin in Strasbourg politics

Strasbourg, February 19

The Strasbourg Jacobins have never been so close to power as now. They have finally managed to get rid of their most determined and most influential opponent, Dietrich. The former Girondist mayor, in jail in Besançon, is awaiting trial on a charge of having tried to deliver the city to the Austrians in April 1792. Euloge Schneider, who was made the city's new mayor by this development, has been named prosecutor of the Upper Rhine criminal court. This odd character, a defrocked priest and former professor at the Bonn seminary, took refuge in Alsace after the publication of one of his poems hailing the capture of the Bastille. He became a journalist in Strasbourg before joining the radicals. In September 1791 he brought about the breakup of the Society of the Friends of the Constitution to form the Jacobins' Society, while the Girondists, in the minority, set up the Society of the Congregation of the New Temple.

This magnificent wallpaper with its republican emblems will strengthen citizens' patriotic spirits.

France mobilises 300,000 men

Paris, February 24

The French Republic has not got enough arms. Widowers and childess married men, as well as single people between the ages of 18 and 40, are going to find this out, since the Convention has just decided that 300,000 of them are needed to help defend the borders. At a time when almost all the parts of Europe ruled by kings have joined Austria and Prussia against France, the shortage of troops is creating a crucial problem, and a remedy has to be found at once. The levies have been volunteers so far, but now, at least in principle, every Frenchman can be called up to meet the needs of defending the Revolution.

But the legislators do not consider it useful to spell out the recruiting procedures. If one does not rely strictly on volunteers, there are three possible procedures: volunteers receiving bonuses, an election, or a lottery. Granting bonuses is up to the urban authorities, a fact that prevents extending the system to rural areas. As for the election of "volunteers", one can easily imagine the various difficulties. The rich will want to send the poor, while patriots will be ready to elect the aristocrats, who in turn have the same kind of plans for the others. Hence a drawing or lottery would seem the fairest and most pratical system. But the way these future soldiers are to be incorporated into the army is still the subject of debate. Some people question the idea of amalgamating them with regular troops, especially since there are fears that they may be incited to desertion.

Seasoned officers will be called on to train the new recruits.

A father proposes joining up, replacing his sick son, who cannot serve.

Paris housewives sack the grocery shops

Paris, February 26

Paris housewives have decided to deal out justice themselves. In exasperation at the rising prices of soap, sugar and candles, they stormed the shops in order to make the merchants sell them their goods at lower prices. Everywhere in the capital there were scenes of pillage, even though the Convention decided yesterday to subsidise the Commune in order to maintain existing bread prices. It all began on February 22nd., when a delegation of women from the Quatre Nations sector went to the Jacobin Club to discuss the subsistence issue, and were refused the premises they wanted. Two days later, faced with a group of angry laundresses who brought a petition to the Convention demanding the death penalty for monopolists and speculators, the deputies adjourned their debate, and that was too much! The riot that broke out yesterday, with great violence, scared everybody, from the Girondist and Montagnard deputies to the Commune's General Council.

Yet Hébert and Chaumette, the municipality's prosecutor and deputy prosecutor, are not the last to thunder against the "rich fattened on the blood of the poor", as *le Père Duchesne* wrote in December. But they also fear popular movements getting out of control. Even Marat, whose article yesterday seemed to urge the people to loot, took his distance from such activities today. As for the Jacobins, they made a quick job of claiming that they had absolutely nothing to do with it all. Only Jacques Roux, of the Gravilliers sector, cries out for all to hear that, in doing all this, the people are defending the "real principles" of the Revolution.

The Ile de France is shaken by a riot over the Republic

Port Louis, February 25

The proclamation of the Republic in the Ile de France almost had an unhappy ending. Shortly after the official *Te Deum*, sung together by all of the island's authorities, an anti-royalist riot broke out in the port. Without the intervention of the National Guard, several naval base officers, including Major Denis Decrès, would have been killed. Yet all precautions had been taken to avoid such disorders. The colonial assembly, for instance, had hastened to adopt the decrees instituting the Republic as soon as the *Beauté* arrived. That vessel had come from France just to bring the decrees. The island's assembly, always eager to reaffirm its loyalty to the mother country, had even voted a motion urging the governor and all civilian and military officials to appear immediatly to swear allegiance to the new régime.

French Revolution is very unpopular in the Rhineland

Rhineland, February 24

Roving commissioner Forster and his Jacobin friends have been disavowed in a cutting fashion. By a decree of December 15th. the Convention decided to organise elections for the Rhineland convention, as a prelude to France's final annexation of the Rhineland. Forster had made every effort to ensure success for this effort, multiplying his articles in the *Gazette Rhénane* and criss-crossing the country to persuade his compatriots. But in Mainz, only 375 voters went to the polls. They refused to vote at all in Speyer, while in Worms and Bingen people voted only at gunpoint. Altogether a mere 106 out of 900 communes took part in the vote and there were many acts of resistance, sometimes violent. Still, this failure will not prevent the Rhineland convention from meeting. If need be, Forster is determined to impose the Constitution by force. He says that the Jacobins, as the country's political élite, are entitled to force the majority to accept their will.

Convention

1. Paris. A decree issued by the Convention defines the status of émigrés.

2. Paris. While Miranda's army has lost Maastricht and is withdrawing, the Convention is turning the county of Hainaut into the department of Jemmapes. It is also adding the territories and cities of Stavelot, Franchimont, Longe, Salm and Ghent to France.

4. Cholet. The conscripts' lottery degenerates into a riot.

7. Paris. The Convention declares war on the Kingdom of Spain (→April 8, 93).

8. Lyons. After the decision made by the Girondist Nivière Chol, the businessman Bertrand, one of Chalier's friend, is elected mayor of the city.

10. Paris. Creation of the revolutionary Tribunal of Paris, of which Fouquier Tinville is the public prosecutor.→

11. Loire Inférieure. Beginning of the Vendée insurrection: the insurgents seize Machecoul.→

14. Vendée. Saint Gilles sur Vie and La Roche sur Yon fall into the Vendean insurgents' hands.

14. Morbihan. Some insurgent peasants besiege Vannes.

15. Cholet. Nicolas Stofflet and Jacques Cathelineau, at the head of 15,000 Vendeans, seize control of the city.

16. Pontivy. The city is attacked by bands of peasants.

16. Orléans. Léonard Bourdon, a travelling representative, is bayoneted by some young people refusing to be signed up.

17. Parcé. A force of 2,000 armed men is dispersed by the National Guard, eight kilometres west of Rennes.

18. Ille et Vilaine. After Redon on March 17th., Fougères comes under siege from a peasant uprising.

18. United Provinces. Defeat of Dumouriez at Neerwinden.→

18. Paris. The Convention decrees the death penalty for anybody proposing agrarian law. At the same session, it decrees that taxation shall be progressive, depending on each taxpayer's fortune.

19. Paris. The Convention decrees the death penalty for all rebels who are captured with weapons in their hands.

Imperial forces recapture Liège

Liège, March 5

Dumouriez' army has had to beat a retreat. The French, crushed by the Prince of Coburg's troops, have left Liège, which the Austrians have just seized. Here, as everywhere in the Low Countries, the French régime collapsed in just a few hours. The fact is that it was installed hastily, and in four months was only able to shake up the old institutions, without uprooting them, and their restoration was immediate and complete. But unlike what happened in the Belgian provinces, it is accompanied by severe measures in Liège. The sovereign Prince Bishop has refused to grant a general amnesty and ordered the execution of ringleaders.

Things look dark for the schools

Paris, March 8

The situation is disastrous. But it is not a question of threats to the French borders or of internal disturbances. What Fouché, the deputy, denounced in a speech to the Convention was the state of education. His report is a damning indictment. Since the abolition of the tithe and of the municipal grants on which their income was based, the schools have been labouring under severe difficulties. The sale of the clergy's property did not help. The Assembly is submerged with complaints from moneyless teachers whose salaries, for which the communes and departments are officially responsible, are no longer being paid. The law approved today makes them the nation's financial and moral responsibility.

The Assembly dispatches travelling representatives to each department

Milhaud, a Convention member, in a travelling representative's uniform.

Paris, March 9

Patriotism has got to be stimulated. At Danton's suggestion, a commissioner will be sent to each department to organize citizen mobilisation. This travelling representative will be the Convention's main weapon. Judging by the alarming description made by Danton and Delacroix upon their return from Belgium and from the northern front, such steps must have top priority. Even though the two envoys noticed the low level of Dumouriez' revolutionary zeal, they still think, along with the Girondists, that he is the only man able to resolve the military crisis.

Massacre of patriots in the West

Loire Inférieure, March 11

"No lottery and give us our good priests!" With this cry, 3,000 to 4,000 men armed with scythes, pikes and hunting rifles took over Machecoul. Rejecting the idea of levying new soldiers by means of a draw among single men, the farmers decided to attack the district authorities directly. Wasn't it said, after all, that those authorities were having handcuffs made to drag the recruits to the borders, cuffed in pairs? So they immediately massacred some of the small city's most notable patriots: National Guard officers, the local post office manager, and the parish priest. Others owed their very temporary salvation to the fact that they were locked up in jail. This, however, is a most unenviable fate because of the notorious cruelty of the rebel leader René François Souchu.

Carnot at front

Paris, March 12

In Carnot, the Assembly quickly and unhesitatingly found a good travelling representative for the northern front. This officer of genius is well acquainted with the region, since he lived there for many years. He even drew plans of all of the border fortifications. His recent assignment to the Pyrenees army showed his energy and his intransigent patriotism.

An open-air "Te Deum" to celebrate the Vendeans' victory

Vendée, March 14

No church was big enough to hold all of them, so the peasants who had seized the town of Chemillé yesterday heard Mass in the cemetery. The fervour was heightened by the fact that many of those men had not attended a religious ceremony for a long time. They were all fiercely attached to their "good priests" and had deserted the Church when they were replaced. They were greatly comforted today by having the holy mysteries celebrated by Abbot Barbotin, one of the most popular members of the non-juring clergy, who had been living in concealment for several months. But when it was time for the *Te Deum* to be sung, people were no longer looking at the priest, but at the man serving the Mass. This very tall man, with a powerful voice, is the one the insurgents have elected as their leader. He is a cart driver and door-to-door salesman from Pin en Mauges named Jacques Cathelineau. Yesterday morning, while he was kneading his bread, a few of the men who had beaten the republicans at Saint Florent the day before came to ask him to become their leader. He did not hesitate to agree to their request, despite the supplications of his wife and his five young children: "God, for whom I am going to fight, will take care of you." And off he went to war, leading his Vendean fighters to victory, first at Jallais and then at Chemillé.

The same religious fervour unites peasants and nobles against the Republic.

A revolutionary court is set up by the Convention

Paris, March 10

After yesterday's riots, which found the sansculottists destroying the offices of the Girondist newspapers, the Convention has decided to react. To avoid anarchy and punish the "traitors", it has set up a special criminal court. Five judges and 12 jury members appointed by the deputies will be responsible for considering counter-revolutionary undertakings and attacks against the Republic or state security. A public prosecutor and two deputies, including Fouquier Tinville, will draw up the indictments. According to Danton, joined by Marat and Robespierre, the point is to be "terrible, to dispense the people from being so".

Public Safety Committee emblem.

Tallien recruiting some "volunteers"

Tours, March 18

It is far from being an easy assignment, but young Jean Lambert Tallien does not lack energy. In accordance with the law promulgated on February 24th., he was assigned by the Convention to recruit 3,418 "volunteers", in the two departments of Loir et Cher and Indre et Loire, for the Moselle army. He is lucky to know the region already, as he spent part of his childhood there. In view of the insurrectional disturbances that have just broken out in the neighbouring departments of Deux Sèvres and Vendée, he decided today to assign the Loir et Cher recruits there. He left orders along those lines for local authorities (→ April 23).

General Dumouriez is beaten by the Austrians at Neerwinden

Neerwinden, March 8

The enthusiasm of the Republic's troops did not make up for their total lack of experience. And, despite being stronger numerically, they had to give way to the professional soldiers under the command of Frederick of Saxe-Coburg. General Dumouriez, who had been led into Holland by his personal ambitions, had come back down hastily to take his scattered units in hand. But it was too late. The fact that his subsequent retreat was a model one is small consolation for the French army, which suffered 4,000 killed and the discouragement of a lost battle, not to mention the desertion of some 10,000 soldiers. It is a disaster for the Republic's army, and the French will be unable to remain in Belgium any longer.

The first important defeat of General Dumouriez' troops in Belgium.

20. Fougères. The National Guard launches a counter-offensive, as detachments criss-cross the countryside looking for insurgents.→

20. Paris. Annexation by French troops of the German Duchy of Zweibrücken.

20. Lyons. Establishment of a cannon foundry at Perrache.

20. Paris. Creation at the Opéra of the *Marriage of Figaro* in a French adaptation, with spoken dialogue from the work by Mozart.

20. Louvain. Dumouriez meets Danton and Delacroix, sent by the Convention to get the General to retract his letter of March 12th. in which he held the Assembly responsible for his defeats. But he refuses to withdraw his accusations (→25).

21. Paris. Establishment of revolutionary watch committees in each commune and each sector.→

23. Paris. The Convention decrees the annexation of the former bishopric of Basel, the Republic of Raurarcie.→

23. Côtes du Nord. At Bréhan, farmers from about 15 parishes led by Charles de Boishardy march on Saint Brieuc.

25. Rennes. The guillotine is installed permanently on the town's Palace square.

25. Ille et Vilaine. Some armed gangs which were trying to seize Romillé are repelled. Except in a few districts, the insurrection is marking time because of the National Guard's presence.

25. Hainaut. Dumouriez meets the Austrian Colonel Mack at Ath and suggests a joint march on Paris to him (→26).

26. Ille et Vilaine. Some 200 soldiers seize Tinténiac to monitor the conscript lottery. Their dissuasive presence makes it possible for the recruits to leave.

26. Paris. At a meeting of the General Defence Committee, Robespierre requests the recall of Dumouriez, whose duplicity is now known (→April 1, 93).

29. Paris. David gives the Assembly his painting of *The Assassinated Michel Le Peletier.*→

31. Lyons. The establishment of the Jacobins Club, replacing the Central Club of the "Concert", causes splits within the people's societies dominated by the moderates.

The Assembly deals severely with the Brittany agitation

Rennes, March 20

The West is rebelling. The counter-revolution is shaking Brittany, as well as the Vendée. The Marquis de La Rouërie, an ardent royalist, had organised a vast plot against the Republic in his province, which is so attached to monarchical and religious principles. He died without having been able to carry out his plan, but the uprising, which had long been scheduled for March 10th., set Brittany ablaze in a day, as if the Marquis's soul were still presiding over this outburst of anger. Billaud Varenne, sent by the Assembly, arrived in Rennes this morning, quite determined to restore order. Denouncing the laxity of the departmental authorities, who had been warned of the existence of La Rouërie's plot in 1792, he demanded reinforcements of 6,000 men. But it is already very late in the day to act.

Anything goes in churches ... except gross indecency

Paris, March 23

Circumstances lead to churches being used in highly varied ways. Very often the election meetings for the Convention are held in them, and it is not unusual for the members of the clubs to have developed the habit of meeting there, too. In war-struck areas, the religious buildings may be turned into infirmaries, supply depots, or even camps for the troops.

But the parish priests' repeated complaints have finally had an effect on the Convention, which has decided to meet their demands in part. The deputies voted a decree today that now makes acts of "indecency" committed in the churches subject to prosecution. People now hope there will be no repetition of the profanations committed by the National Guards of the small city of Teste, in the department of the Gironde. To carry out exercises sheltered from the elements and manoeuvre at their ease, they found no better spot than the small village church ...

Vendée: now it's war!

Pont Charrault, March 20

The republicans are totally stunned this morning. A column of line troops, more than 2,000 men, was routed yesterday by some Vendean "brigands". General Marcé's men had moved into a narrow valley right in the heart of the high woodlands and came under fire from snipers who had taken up positions on the wooded heights overlooking the road. The republicans had too little space to deploy and use artillery against the elusive enemy, so they finally broke ranks. The rebels already the masters of Machecoul Saint Florent and Cholet, are going to be able to organise themselves Now the entire region has escaped from the Republic's control. For members of the Convention, who were sent to the area immediatly. Marcé's incredible defeat casts doubt on his loyalty. Rather than accepting the rout, people prefer to think that the Vendeans owe their success to a yet another counter-revolutionary plot.

One Watch Committee for each commune

The Revolutionary Committees check the good citizenship certificates.

Paris, March 21

You have to have order, even in a revolution. That is why the deputies have decided to legalise the Revolutionary Watch Committees. This is the only way to have a say in the way they operate. Established nationwide just after August 10th. at the initiative of the sectors, with the Committee of the Commune of Paris as a model, these institutions have gradually acquired actual police powers. While stating that the committees will be elected from now on, the law voted today limits their powers to the right to check suspects and foreigners. Again, the Convention is confirming a spontaneous popular movement it could not prevent.

Franconi's circus draws young and old

Paris, March 21

The rider Franconi has made his dream come true. By buying the amphitheatre from Astley, his former boss, he has become his own master and can finally manage a circus. But Franconi does not plan to stop there, and there is no question of merely putting on some horseback riding exercises. Now there will also be some pantomimes to make people laugh and horse dances to amaze them. Among the troupe, in addition to Franconi, the public can now admire the English rider Saunders and his wonderful aerial acrobatics. The public's favourite is the clown Gontar. His grotesque appearance makes old and young laugh till they cry.

Charette scores a resounding success

Loire Inférieure, March 25

The men under the command of Charette have just had their first success against republican forces. The republicans, who had initially blocked the rebels' path, were forced to flee when Charette made his men set fire to the thatched roofs of the houses on the Place du Marché, where the enemy had been posted. The town of Pornic is now in the hands of the insurgents, whose leader was only barely able to stop them ending the day with an orgy of drinking and looting. Ten days ago about 100 peasants from the Marais and the region of Retz went to the Fonteclose manor to ask Charette to be their leader. At first the former navy officer categorically refused, saying that their revolt was pure madness. But he finally accepted and solemnly swore to "only return here in death or in victory" (→April 22).

Death of a famous porcelain maker

Paris, March 28

France's porcelain industry is in mourning: the great artisan Antoine Guerhard is dead. He had set up his factory in Paris in 1781, first on the Rue de Bondy, then on the Rue du Temple. Thanks to the quality of its porcelain and the protection granted by the Duc d'Angoulême, son of the Duc d'Artois, it had become one of the chief competitors of the royal factory at Sèvres. Even though it has lost its owner, the factory will stay in operation under the leadership of Catherine Guerhard, Antoine's widow, and her associate Christophe Dihl.

A water jug and basin made at the Guerhard and Dihl factory.

Raurarcie joins the French Republic

Paris, March 23

The Convention has ruled that Raurarcie, a tiny chunk of land on the edge of the upper Doubs region, is to be a part of France. The propaganda efforts undertaken by Bishop Gobel, the former assistant, the Bishop of Basel who is now the Constitutional Bishop of Paris, have been successful. At his urging, the capital of Raurarcie, Porrentruy, rid itself last autumn of the Prince Bishop of Basel's control. It also cut all its links with the Holy Roman Empire. It proclaimed the Republic on November 27th. and asked for French protection. Then annexation followed.

Avignon people prefer to set their own tax levels

Avignon, March 26

The community chest is empty and the patriots running Avignon are wondering what to do about this. Some are saying it would be a counter-revolutionary act to impose direct taxes on the Pope's former subjects, who never paid taxes. This delicate issue must be decided by the people of Avignon themselves. The Avignon Club has just proposed to create a department around the city. This would include the former papal lands, which in 1791 became districts of Ouvèze and the Vaucluse and were respectively attached to the Bouches du Rhône and the Drôme.

Deserters hide out in forests

Haute Marne, March 25

A group of about 30 young men from the village of Corginon has gone to hide out in the woods to avoid being drafted into the army. They are fiercely opposed to conscription and have been writing anti-patriot posters which have been appearing all over the region. The patriots are becoming worried about their activities and have now asked for aid from the army. This was not much help since the runaways are being helped by locals.

Cathelineau observes an Easter truce

Jacques Cathelineau, the hero of the Vendée, as shown in legends.

Vendée, March 31

The village of Pin en Mauges will long remember this year's Easter Mass. It was celebrated by Abbot Cantiteau, the non-juring priest who was able to come out of hiding after the Vendeans' recent victories. Mass was sung by Jacques Cathelineau. Following a succession of military victories over the past two weeks, Cathelineau, known as the "Saint of Anjou", had wanted to go home for Easter. It was time for a rest, and anyway his men were deserting him. As the republicans have been pushed back, the Vendeans all wanted to go home to see their families. They said they would come back if there was more fighting to be done against republicans.

David had suggested to the Convention that he should paint Le Peletier de Saint Fargeau as a martyr to Liberty. On March 29th. he presented the work to the Assembly, which decided to hang it in the main session hall. The work has been lost and only the etching remains.

Convention

1. Saint Armand. Threatened with arrest, Dumouriez hands over to the Austrians the four commissioners from the Convention and the Minister of War, Beurnonville, who had come to inform him that he was summoned to appear before the Convention (→4).

3. Paris. The Convention declares that Dumouriez is a traitor to the nation.

3. Paris. The Convention rules that any person found walking the streets without a red, white and blue cockade will be arrested.

4. Paris. Colonel Jean Baptiste Noël Bouchotte is appointed Minister of War, replacing Beurnonville who has been handed over to the Austrians.

4. Vendée. The leaders of the Vendean rebels meet at the camp of Quatre Chemins de l'Oie and set up a council for the Catholic and royalist army.

4. Saint Amand. Unable to convince his troops to march on Paris, General Dumouriez defects to the Austrians along with his headquarters staff and Louis Philippe d'Orléans, the Duc de Chartres.→

5. Saint Domingue. Clashes resume at Port au Prince between settlers and mulattoes.

5. Paris. Elected as president of the Jacobins Club, Marat signs a ruling calling for the arrest of counter-revolutionaries and of "suspects". He also orders the ousting of the main Girondist deputies (→13).

6. Paris. The Convention sets up a Committee of Public Safety grouping nine members who must be changed each month.→

7. Paris. Following the desertion of his son Louis Philippe, the Duc d'Orléans and Choderlos de Laclos, now under suspicion, are jailed at the Abbaye.→

8. Marseilles. The French refugees expelled from Spain arrive.

8. Paris. The sector of Bon Conseil draws up a list of 22 Girondist deputies who are denounced as counter-revolutionaries.

8. Paris. From now on, prices at all public marketplaces will be posted in assignats (→11).

8. Antwerp. Diplomats representing the nations at war with France hold a meeting.

Danton attacked by the Girondins

Paris, April 1

The Girondist Lasource has just attacked Danton. He accuses him of conspiring against the Revolution with Dumouriez, who seems more and more suspect. The General reportedly sent the Assembly a letter on March 12th. that has not been made public, but according to rumours the letter held the Convention responsible for the army's defeats, and the General said he wanted to make Belgium an independent state under his authority. But some claim that Danton is involved in this plot. Didn't he support Dumouriez at the height of the crisis? Danton counter-attacked, saying that Dumouriez' real accomplice was the Gironde, which has always left the road open for him.

The hero of Jemmapes has become a political outcast.

Stage cavalry strongly applauded

Paris, April 1

To increase its box-office receipts, the Favart auditorium management hit on an original idea. Right in the middle of *Déserteur de Hamm*, an opera by Rodolphe Kreutzer, the audience was surprised to be offered a large-scale cavalry fight simulated by the famous equerry Antonio Franconi as part of the show. That was really something new! Of particular interest was a clash between two riders who were isolated from the main body of troops, but the whole fight won great applause. This astonishing mixture of horses, music and patriotic prose was a big hit.

Dumouriez' treason

Dumouriez acknowledged his treason by arresting the Convention's envoys.

Saint Amand, April 4

The commander in chief of the French armies has gone over to the enemy. For several weeks Dumouriez had been making threatening remarks about coming back to re-establish order in France, to rid the country of the "idiots" and the "scoundrels" who govern it. He had even started secret negotiations with the Austrian Colonel Mack, whom he had promised he would evacuate Belgium without a fight. During that time, the outraged and worried Convention sent to Saint Amand the Minister of War Beurnonville and four commissioners — Camus, Lamarque, Quinette and Bancal — to summon Dumouriez to appear before it. When the envoys arrived on April 1st., showing the Assembly's decree, Camus asked Dumouriez to go with him. Since the latter refused flatly, he told him calmly: "I suspend you and arrest you." The General immediately ordered that the five envoys should be seized and delivered to the Austrians. He is determined to restore the monarchy and put a member of the Orléans house in power, and wanted to get his army together and march on Paris. But he had no luck haranguing his troops, who refused to follow him. The traitor Dumouriez, outlawed by the Convention, has now found refuge in the Austrian camp with a few faithful supporters, including Valence and the Duc de Chartres.

The devotion of a patriotic mother

Manche, April 1

Recruitment in the countryside does not always arouse indifference or hostility. Take the woman from Gonneville who proposed having four of her sons sign up for enlistment when the whole commune was to supply only five men. She said: "They are my whole joy and my consolation. They are my whole fortune. They want to serve the motherland, so they should go. They are young and vigorous, and will behave well." If her fifth and youngest son had not had to stay on the neighbouring island of Aurigny, all of the Gonneville volunteers would have been Delaunays.

Beautiful Thérésa gets a divorce

Paris, April 5

The most beautiful woman in Paris is free. Thérésa Cabarrus, aged 19, and her husband, Marquis Jean Jacques Devin de Fontenay, aged 31, signed their divorce document in the presence of the public officer Antoine Jaquotot. Thérésa was given custody of little Théodore, aged 4. She was 15 when her family made her marry the marquis, but the couple could no longer stand each other by the following year. She was disappointed in her short, ugly and arrogant husband and granted her favours to one of his friends, while the marquis consoled himself ... with her chamber-maid.

330

La Harpe returns to Lycée thanks to admiring women

Paris, April 8

La Harpe is back in the capital. That piece of news delighted many hearts, especially the ladies'. The most popular of all the Lycée teachers had been absent for almost a month. Rather than wrangling with the management about the content of his courses, he had preferred to resign. But his female admirers did not agree with this one bit, and while La Harpe's replacement was absent himself because of illness, they sent a petition to the establishment to demand the immediate return of their favourite poet.

Committee of public safety is set up

Paris, April 6

The Girondists are yelling about dictatorship. But Marat replies: "Freedom must be established by violence, and the time has come to organise the depotism of liberty for the time being." The establishment of the Committee of Public Safety does not leave anybody indifferent. Actually, since the traumatic news of Dumouriez' treason reached Paris, and the Vendée has been up in arms, the main thing is effective action in order to resolve the crisis threatening the Revolution. Since the General Defence Committee, the Convention's executive organ, proved to be ineffective, a new committee has been set up. It deliber-ates secretly, and monitors and stimulates the action of the ministers on the provisional Executive Council, whose decisions it can speed up or suspend. It consists of nine members, renewed every month and designated by the Convention. Its powers are making it the country's main political organ and a focus of the power struggle. But the initial appointments to the Committee, scheduled for April 11th., will probably not favour the Girondists. Danton should influence them, since he has started championing defence of the Republic. And at the times of crisis, the Plaine centrist deputies follow the Montagnards more than the Girondists.

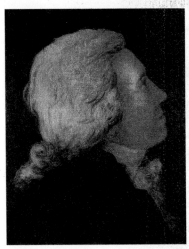

Barère is among the men who will sit on the committee with Danton.

The Prussians were unable to stand up to French artillery at Landau: "They don't have enough legs to make off." But is it a decisive victory?

No taxes due on patriotic beer

Paris, April 6

To the public's warm ovation, the Convention has granted citizen Santerre a tax rebate of 49,603 livres, 16 sous and 6 deniers. According to a law with retrospective effect specially voted to pay homage to this master brewer's good citizenship, he is to be reimbursed for all duties paid on every litre of the beer he brewed from 1789 until March 1791. The measure was demanded by the whole of Saint Antoine district. It must be noted that, since the start of the Revolution, the Santerre establishment in Reuilly Street has been a veritable meeting place for the area's patriots. It was here that the brewer, commander of the capital's National Guard, made the preparations for June 20th. and August 10th. His partisans say the measure is only fair, since for the last five years Santerre has been distributing his beer free every day to the glorious suburb's craftsmen. And some citizens go so far as to urge that the nation should compensate him for the beer consumed "on the occasion of the movements to which the Revolution has given rise".

Women working for the nation even on Sunday

Besançon, April 15

The Republican Women's Society of the eastern French city of Besançon was honoured today at the Convention. The commissioner who read out a homage to them informed the admiring deputies that those good patriots had not only sent the troops hundreds of shirts, shoes, stockings, gloves and hand-kerchiefs made with their own hands, but also spent their Sundays putting on plays to collect badly needed funds for the nation. The receipts amounted to between 12,000 and 15,000 livres for each performance, and the women put it all into equipping the soldiers.

Philippe Egalité and his friends are behind bars

Paris, April 7

There is no more Orléans faction. After the desertion to Dumouriez of General Valence, Mme. de Genlis's husband, Sillery, and the eldest son of the former Duke, Louis Philippe, all the faithful followers of Philippe Egalité as well as his youngest son, Beaujolais, have been charged, and the majority are already behind bars. The first one to be jailed, five days ago, was Choderlos de Laclos. His release two days later must have been a mistake, since he has now been jailed again. The Abbaye prison will be a change for the d'Orléans from the Palais Royal (→April 22).

A citizen being forced by some sansculottists to pin a cockade to his hat immediately. It is not unusual for such people to be held at the guard offices for several hours for such negligence.

9. Lyons. Following the sectors, it is now the Jacobin Club's turn to call for the creation of a revolutionary army.

10. Paris. At the Assembly, Robespierre denounces the links between General Dumouriez and the main Girondist leaders, Brissot, Guadet and Vergniaud.

11. Paris. An obligatory rate for assignats is established. The practices of using double pricing and of trafficking in currency are forbidden. This satisfies one of the demands made by the Enragés.

11. Paris. The nine first members of the Committee of Public Safety are appointed. They are: Danton, Barère, Cambon, Debry, Delmas, Bréard, Guyton Morveau, Delacroix and Treilhard.

13. Vendée. The young Vendean leader Henri de La Rochejaquelein defeats republican troops at Aubiers.

13. Paris. The Convention approves the arraignment of Marat which was submitted yesterday by the Girondist Gaudet. The move follows the publication of a Jacobin pamphlet signed by Marat (→24).

14. Antilles. The English seize control of the island of Tobago without meeting any resistance.

15. Paris. The capital's mayor, Pache, comes on behalf of a majority of the Paris sectors to demand the dismissal of 22 Girondist deputies.

18. Paris. *Le Moniteur* announces the publication of the French edition of "Voyages in France", by the English agronomist Arthur Young.

20. Perpignan. Spanish troops lay siege to the city.→

21. Paris. At the Jacobins Club, Robespierre reads out a draft declaration of the rights of man and citizens. This includes limitations on the right to own property and society's duty to provide for all its members.

22. Machecoul. The town is recaptured by troops led by General Beysser. The Vendean leader Souchu, responsible for the massacre of republican prisoners, is beheaded with an axe.

22. United States. The American government proclaims its neutrality in the war in Europe.→

The Port au Prince rebels are wiped out

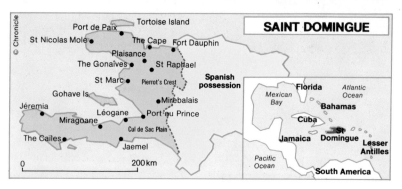

Saint Domingue, April 14

Félicité Sonthonax and Etienne Polverel did not hesitate for a second. They used everything at their disposal to crush the resistance of the royalist rebels in Port au Prince fighting against the republican and mulatto forces. On March 21st. they had ordered the war-fleet to stand by in cannon range of the city. In the final days of the siege, they ordered intense shelling which destroyed parts of the capital of Saint Domingue. This victory is significant. On a military level, they have just wiped out the main anti-mulatto stronghold in the west. On a political level, they have won the trust of the coloured citizens by soundly defeating the "aristocrats of skin colour", namely the whites opposed to equal rights.

Vosges inhabitants are true patriots

Paris, April 12

The people of the Vosges are not in the habit of resting on their laurels. Twice already the Convention has been moved to congratulate them for their high patriotic zeal after many local men and boys had willingly signed up as volunteers. Today, the deputy Poullain Grandprey once again described to the Convention how the entire city of Epinal rose up as one man when the news of Dumouriez' betrayal reached it. As for the department's council, it decided to go into permanent session, declared the nation to be in danger and, amid scenes of patriotic fury, swore "an implacable hatred of tyrants, constant support of the Convention and to preserve until the last drop of blood the Republic, united and indivisible".

A group of royalists is arrested

Vendée, April 9

The guests gathered at Madame de Lescure's home were unable to finish their Sunday lunch. A unit of 20 mounted policemen burst into the courtyard of the Clisson castle. Monsieur de Lescure, an ardent royalist, is on the list of those who are considered suspect. He had already attempted to defend the King on August 10th. in Paris. Moreover, barely a few days ago, he welcomed into his home his cousin and friend Henri de La Rochejaquelein, a former member of the King's guard. Lescure and his wife, along with her parents, M. and Mme. Donnissan, and a friend, M. de Marigny, have been arrested and taken to Bressuire, where they are being held in a patriot's home.

Perpignan is under threat from Spain

Perpignan, April 20

Spanish troops led by General Ricardos are at the city walls. Within just three days, the Spanish army has carried out attacks against Saint Laurent de Cerdan and at the Portell mountain pass, just west of Bellegarde. The Republic's troops have been having a rough time. They were forced to pull back hurriedly behind the city's walls. This setback is due to chronic desertions, the Convention's over-confidence, and lack of organisation.

The promotion of a "red" general

Paris, April 16

Ronsin, known as the "red" general, has now become one of the Republic's most important public officials. He had been sent to the northern border region to keep an eye on officers suspected of being secret supporters of Dumouriez. Now the new minister, Bouchotte, has just appointed him chief of the Ministry of War's 2nd. division. At the request of Robespierre, all the royalist and Feuillantist elements in the ministry have been purged. The ministry has been transformed into one of the most trustworthy bastions of republicanism.

Generously, Maurice d'Elbée, the recent victor at La Chapelle du Genêt, orders his men not to execute a group of republican prisoners who have had the misfortune to be captured during the fighting.

Talleyrand is forced to sell his library

Talleyrand Périgord, disliked by both émigrés and revolutionaries.

London, April 12

As incredible as it may seem, Talleyrand is short of money. His large collection of books is being auctioned off today. It is advertised as "the entire, elegant and not inconsiderable library of Monsieur the Bishop of Autun". Life in exile had seemed pleasant to this fun-loving man of the cloth, especially while he had the generous assistance of his friend Germaine de Staël, the muse of liberal émigrés. But ever since she left life has been hard for Talleyrand, who must now rid himself of his cherished books brought from Paris. They are the last sign of his past wealth. But he has little hope of raising much money at the auction. The other French émigrés aren't even coming. They like to see he is in trouble and some have promised to have him beaten when they return to power.

Philippe Egalité is taken to Marseilles

Marseilles, April 22

The Abbaye prison was just one step on the ladder. As was ordered by the government, Philippe Egalité, as the Duc d'Orléans is now known, arrived last night at the Notre Dame de la Garde fort, along with his sister, Louise Bathilde, his cousin, the Prince de Conti and his son Beaujolais. It had been a very tiring journey. Philippe and his family had to face the hatred of the population. People threatened and insulted them everywhere. On top of that, they had to cope with the danger of a journey where ambushes had been set, particularly near Lyons. Their arrival at the fort was a sad affair. Bare rooms with just straw pallets awaited them. The only thing to cheer Philippe up was finding his second son, Montpensier, who was arrested in Nice on April 8th.

United States proclaims its neutrality

Philadelphia, April 22

There will be no global war. The American government has just officially proclaimed its neutrality in the conflict between England and France. The United States had not taken sides when France declared war on England. It was a matter of deciding whether to help the government of France fight against the allied powers, or that the conflict was a purely European one. It was a delicate issue as many remembered the help provided by France during the American War of Independence. The trade and friendship treaty signed in 1778 states that the United States must support and assist France. However, George Washington was not willing to rush into an overseas adventure whose outcome remains uncertain. Despite his sympathy for the reforms carried out by the Revolution in France, the United States did not approve of the execution of Louis XVI. Since that day, it has been following the violence with concern. The decision to remain neutral was approved by a large majority. The only leader to favour intervention was Thomas Jefferson.

The Vendean leader holds court at Legé

Vendée, April 22

The republicans have retaken Machecoul, but they have failed to recapture Legé where Charette, the Vendean leader, has set up his camp. That small village has been turned into Charette's headquarters while he and his men await new operations. There is plenty of food as local peasants have been delivering cattle in exchange for coupons which can be cashed "when peace returns". Plenty of wine has been flowing too: the cellars of patriots who have fled were well stocked. "I want there to be rejoicing wherever I go," Charette likes to tell his friends. He is both brave under fire and in bed. Dubbed the "King of Legé", Charette spends a lot of his time merrymaking.

François Athanase de Charette, the Vendeans' commander in chief.

Hébert's men control the Cordeliers Club

The pro-Hébert faction has been in control of the Cordeliers Club ever since the end of 1792. The "Hébertists" are revolutionary extremists who owe their name to Hébert, assistant public prosecutor of the Paris Commune and director of the fiery newspaper *Le Père Duchesne*. Hébert and Chaumette, its public prosecutor, exert considerable influence within the Commune. Over recent weeks, the Hébertists have turned the Ministry of War into their own stronghold. The "red" general, Ronsin, head of the 2nd. division, and Vincent, the secretary of the new Minister, Bouchotte, have gradually taken over the ministry. Thanks to them, *Le Père Duchesne* is being widely distributed to the army. This is not due to chance. For the Hébertists, a true revolutionary carries a sharp sabre and boasts a fine military moustache. As for the others, their agenda depends largely on circumstances. They are firm supporters of the policy of de-Christianisation and of the fight against the "filthy rich". They closely follow popular trends and often clash with the Enragés to see which group can control the people. They are always there to foment unrest, unless it is a matter of fixing food prices. They remain firmly opposed to this.

Marat defeats his accusers

It was a victory: Marat is carried in triumph by the people, who see him as their only true spokesman.

Paris, April 24

It was not just an acquittal, it was a triumph. Marat left the revolutionary Tribunal on the shoulders of two burly workers from the marketplace as a large crowd of militants from the sectors cheered his victory. On April 12th. he had personally demanded to be put on trial during a stormy session at the Convention. This was because Pétion had called him a "vile scoundrel who has preached despotism". This followed the publication of a Jacobin text, signed by Marat on April 5th., that included a call to arms to "exterminate the traitors to the nation", namely the Girondists. On the very next day, the Assembly decided to have him arraigned. Marat did not turn himself in until he had been informed of the exact charges. Given the many expressions of support he was receiving from patriots, Marat was certain he would be not only declared innocent but also congratulated. "It is not a guilty man who stands before you, but an apostle and martyr of Liberty," he cried at the start of the proceedings. In fact, Fouquier Tinville himself described the charges as a disgraceful plot hatched by Brissot and the Girondists. As for the verdict from the jury, it was full of praise for the accused man.

Cupid's arrows strike at the Convention

Paris, April 24

The Duplay family is in total uproar. Elisabeth, the youngest daughter, has fallen in love. She didn't have to look far to find the right man. The two met at the Assembly. Elisabeth had gone there with Charlotte, Robespierre's sister. They were greeted by a young deputy. It was Philippe Le Bas, aged 28, with blue eyes, brown hair and an open, frank look. He is the representative of the Pas de Calais and Robespierre's best friend. It was love at first sight. Robespierre has been living at the Duplay home for a year so Elisabeth knows she'll see Philippe often (→ Aug. 26).

The handsome Philippe Le Bas.

Tallien in action

Tours, April 23

The special envoy from Paris, Tallien, is indefatigable. His job is to organise supplies of food, arms, ammunition and clothes for the army and to try to put a stop to thieving by volunteers, who send their weapons off to Paris so that they can be sold. Moreover, he is enforcing obligatory military training in the departments for which he is responsible. Thus, all citizens of Indre et Loire and Loir et Cher who are aged between 16 and 50 must do weapons training three times a week in the chief towns of each district, and on Sundays and holidays in the villages.

Non-juring priests face more repression

Paris, April 23

Death within 24 hours: that is the fate that will be meted out to any priest due for deportation who is still on French territory or who has returned. The new decrees on non-juring priests state that, when they are arrested, they are to be taken immediately to the district detention centre and on the same day brought before a military jury. Death sentences are to be carried out right away. As for the priests who were until now bound neither by the oath of 1790 nor by the "civil" oath, if they want to avoid deportation, they must take the oath of "liberty-equality" of August 13th. 1792 and make sure they commit no unpatriotic acts.

The lightning of Reason protects Liberty from Ignorance and Fanaticism.

A wealthy banker's strange marriage

Paris, April 24

In these troubled times, there are many unusual marriages being celebrated. Thus, the hugely wealthy banker Récamier today married the young Juliette Bernard, who is barely aged 15. A former lover of the girl's mother, Récamier has always had fatherly feelings for her. The family's closest friends are convinced that Juliette is in fact the banker's daughter. They say he offered to wed her, but not bed her, in order to be able to bequeath his fortune to her, thus making sure her future was guaranteed. This is a wise precaution at a time when to be rich is enough to make one suspect.

Anacharsis Cloots' universal republic

Paris, April 26

The Republic will be universal or it will not survive. That was the ambitious concept put forward today at the Convention by Anacharsis Cloots. According to him, man cannot achieve freedom by himself any more than a small group of people can remain free for very long. Therefore the republicans of France and those of the rest of Europe, America, Africa and Asia must all unite around a single government. The larger the geographic area covered, the stronger the new government will be, he said. This startling proposal was greeted with total indifference. There were no cheers and no boos, just silence. The main reason for this was that nobody had been listening. During Cloots' speech the deputies had been laughing and chatting among themselves about the latest show at the Opéra. Who could be insane enough to listen to such a wild plan for a universal republic? Just a year ago, however, Cloots had been carried in triumph as the ambassador of the human race. Deeply hurt and disappointed by all this indifference from his colleagues, Cloots has had his speech printed and distributed. He now hopes that the plan will be given a more positive welcome by the Parisians.

Marie Adélaïde will get no inheritance

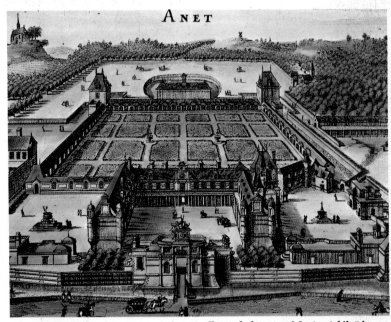

The castle of Anet, in Eure et Loir, will not belong to Marie Adélaïde.

Paris, late April

It is all over for the huge widow's dower left by Louis Jean Marie de Bourbon, the Duc de Penthièvre. His lands have been seized, split up and decreed to belong to the state. The son of a legitimised bastard of Louis XIV, the Duc was one of the kingdom's wealthiest landowners. Until his death on March 3rd. he had been able to keep a large part of his wealth, thanks to the respect people had for him. He notably owned the castles of Sceaux and Rambouillet, of Chanteloup and of Anet — a Renaissance masterpiece that was built by Philibert Delorme for Diane de Poitiers, Henri II's mistress. But there is nothing left of this vast fortune today. That is a great pity for his daughter Marie Adélaïde, who is the wife of Philippe Egalité, the Duc d'Orléans. She will not be able to get her hands on the massive inheritance she had been hoping for.

Women are dismissed from the army

Paris, April 30

Even when it is endangered, the nation has no need of women. The decree approved today by the Convention dismisses women permanently from the army. It is not just the wives, legal or common law, of the soldiers who are to go. The ruling also applies to all the women who joined up in 1792. Each of the latter will receive five sous for each league they have to travel to return home. What is to become of them, these women such as the Fernig sisters, Reine Chapuy and Rose Bouillon, who fought so bravely for their country? The deputies don't seem to care much about that. They are scandalised by the very existence of women soldiers. Ever since Carnot wrote to the Convention to criticise the "herd of women and girls" who follow the troops, the deputies have been doing their best to get rid of them (→ June 26).

The Fernig sisters are "demobbed".

Convention

1. Paris. The capital's sansculottists demonstrate and march to the Convention to ask it to enforce the maximum, as well as an obligatory tax on the rich and the abolition of leases (→4).

1. Rouen. During a riot caused by the rise in the price of bread, National Guardsmen and volunteers clash violently.

1. Paris. The Commune's General Council decides to set up an army of 12,000 men to fight against the rebels in Vendée.

2. Bressuire. La Rochejaquelein captures the town. The Vendean forces currently number more than 22,000 men.

4. Paris. Under heavy pressure from the people, the Convention decrees a maximum national price for grain.→

5. Paris. Youths demonstrate against military recruitment on the Champs Elysées. The issue had also caused unrest yesterday.

5. Vendée. Thouars falls into the hands of the insurgents. General Quetineau surrenders with his 4,000 men.

9. Valenciennes. General Dampierre, the commander of the northern France army, is mortally wounded during an Austrian offensive.→

9. Bordeaux. A petition from the western port city's citizens calls for the withdrawal of the list outlawing 22 Girondists and the establishment of a Constitution.

10. Paris. The Convention holds its first session in the former Machines hall at the Palais National, which used to be the royal palace of the Tuileries.

10. Paris. Claire Lacombe sets up a club for women, the Society of Revolutionary Republican Women, which will support ideas similar to those backed by the Enragés.→

14. Lyons. The town council orders all local citizens to be disarmed and decides to set up a special revolutionary army numbering 6,400 men. This entirely new force will be financed by an obligatory tax on the rich.

15. Lausanne. Joseph de Maistre begins the publication of the *Letters of a Royalist of Savoy to his Fellow Citizens*.

The priest's wife causes a stir

Paris, May 9

The parish of Saint Augustin has a new priest, Abbot Aubert. The consecration ceremony, which was attended by the Bishop of Paris, was held today amid great pomp at Notre Dame cathedral. All eyes turned to Madame Aubert, who has been the priest's wife for the past few months. She had been given a special seat by the choir. When he was just a simple vicar, Aubert had come to the public's attention due to his fights with the priest of Sainte Marguerite, who had tried to stop him living with his new wife at the presbytery.

Laclos' home is now his prison

Paris, May 10

For the second time in a month, Choderlos de Laclos has been let out of jail. He is happy to go home again and see his wife Marie Solange. But he is also bitter. He is not really a free man. He is only allowed to remain a prisoner in his own home, where he is being watched by a special guard that he pays out of his own pocket. This is not an unusual situation in Paris. It is better than jail, but the prisoner is often spied on by his guard. That can be most inconvenient, but Laclos is still overjoyed to be back among his loved ones.

The Convention sets a maximum price for the price of grain in France

Paris, May 4

The policy of revolutionary liberalism has misfired. Once again, economic controls are the order of the day. The Convention has just decreed a maximum price for grain, although it did not want the move to become an issue of principle. Deputies saw this simply as a response to a crisis situation. The repeated issuing of new assignats has sparked off an inflationary wave in France and this has meant the depreciation of paper money. In turn, this means a constant rise in the cost of living. Machines at the mint have been working night and day, but prices have been rising just as fast. This has forced the head of the Finance Committee, Cambon, to wage a constant struggle in order to avoid bankruptcy. But what got the deputies to approve the grain price measure was public protest against the high cost of living. This economic issue has become a political one. The Montagnards, seizing on the Enragés' arguments, have found an opportunity to attack the Girondists. Although they have long favoured economic liberalism, they fought to get the new law on the statute books. A bit of demagoguery can go a long way.

What do the Enragés want?

Jacques Roux, who is known as the "red" abbot, the young Varlet and Leclerc are the main leaders of the Enragés. Even though they were born into the bourgeoisie, they claim to be representatives of the people and social demands are at the top of the revolutionary agenda they have set themselves. The fight against hoarders and the high cost of living, economic equality and the destruction of property, are their objectives. They are always to be found on the front lines when urban riots break out or when prices are unofficially forced down, as has been the case over the past two months. At Lyons, Leclerc supported Chalier, the leader of the revolt in Paris, while Varley was unable to organise an insurrection and lost the Commune's support. In fact, the Enragés' real strength is to be found in the Paris sectors, notably the one at Gravilliers, Jacques Roux's stronghold. As do the Cordeliers, with whom they are competing, the Enragés dream of a government by sansculottists. Their dealings with the Convention are tense. As opponents of the Girondists, they are sometimes backed by Montagnards.

Lazare Hoche, a clever young officer

Hoche is only 25 years old.

Paris, May 15

Lazare Hoche is a far-seeing man. He is aware of the dangers that high office can bring, so he has cautiously refused an offer from the Committee of Public Safety to become adjutant general in charge of a battalion. He prefers to keep his rank of aide-de-camp to General Le Veneur. The members of the Committee had wanted to reward him for the brilliant report he submitted last month. Lazare Hoche had boldly described the privations suffered by so many soldiers and criticised the inefficiency of some of the Convention's special envoys. His daring report does not seem to have harmed his career prospects one bit.

A volunteer's equipment

Vendée, May 14

The "Vendean bandits" may not be particularly well equipped, but the Convention's volunteers are hardly better off. The rifles, of poor quality, the screwdrivers and the wad extractors are all provided by the state. The rest of their equipment is provided by the town councils. This has led to great variety in the outfitting of volunteers from different regions. Their patriotic zeal has to replace their lack of proper training and poor equipment. They have a hard task ahead of them. The Vendeans aren't going to give up, as the recent republican defeat at Thouars has shown.

Large farmers clash with small ones

Eure, May 14

The situation can't go on any longer. In a bid aimed at ending unrest in the countryside and guaranteeing production, an agronomist from Evreux, Morize, has sent a request to the Convention. He is asking for enforcement of a rule to force the wealthy farmers to rent their horses to the small farmers who need the animals to cultivate their lands. When he was sent by the departmental authorities to examine the food production situation, Morize noted that a great deal of land was lying fallow due to a lack of animals to plough it. The poor peasants are afraid of famine or a rise in the cost of living, and they sometimes use force to seize animals to plough their land. There have been many clashes between rich and poor farmers.

A new women's club: the Revolutionary Republican Society

Paris, May 10

Some women are tired of always being kept away from the front of the political stage. So a group of particularly active women has set up its own club, the Revolutionary Republican Women's Society. According to its by-laws, the club is to have a president picked by a democratic election each month. Throughout the duration of her mandate, the president will wear a red bonnet. Club members must be aged at least 18. They will have to give proof of their good morals and be sponsored by three citizenesses. On the day of their admission, they will have to take the following oath: "I swear to live for the Republic or to die for it; I promise to abide by the Society's regulations so long as they exist." The first president was elected today: Pauline Léon. It was she who in March last year went to the Assembly to read out a petition on behalf of women calling for the right to bear arms to defend the Constitution. At her side stood Claire Lacombe, whose aims are just as warlike. The two women have another thing in common: they are both in love with the Enragé journalist Leclerc.

Women patriots meet twice a week at their new club in Paris.

General Dampierre's heroic death

His leg has been torn off by a cannonball. General Dampierre will soon die.

Valenciennes, May 9

It was his last operation. General Marie Picot de Dampierre died at the age of 37 as he attempted to break out after being surrounded by Austrian troops. He played a major role in the French army. He knew when to be bold. In 1788, he was one of the first men to climb aboard a hot air balloon. He knew how to be innovative: as a great admirer of the Prussians, he showed up one day wearing a long pigtail, like the ones worn at the court of Frederick of Prussia. When Louis XVI saw this, he exclaimed: "Have you seen that madman with his Prussian habits?" He was also pragmatic: knowing that his career was likely to be slowed by the pigtail affair, he left the army. He was stubborn: he went back into active service in 1791, showed daring at Valmy, and his bravery played a big role in the victory at Jemmapes. He was also a republican. At the time of Dumouriez' betrayal he came out in favour of the Convention, and was then appointed commander in chief of the army.

A spanking for Théroigne de Méricourt

Paris, May 15

The proud Théroigne was outnumbered. She fought her attackers like a demon, screaming that she would force all of them to "bite the dust". But they were stronger and she had to suffer the humiliation of being whipped. For the past few days a gang of women Jacobins has been policing the corridors of the Convention, where they check the tricoloured cockades and entrance tickets. They soon spotted Théroigne de Méricourt and called her a Brissot supporter. Their poor victim would have had an even worse beating if a guard had not intervened. Some people say, although they can't prove it, that Marat, who was passing by at the time, had gallantly tried to come to Théroigne's assistance.

On May 5th., at five o'clock in the morning, the Vendean leader Lescure climbs under fire the barricade erected across the Vrine bridge, near the village of Ligron. La Rochejaquelein and others soon follow his lead.

General Miranda is acquitted

Paris, May 16

General Miranda successfully refuted all the charges against him and he has been acquitted. He was able to save his life without using lies or trickery. Miranda had been facing an extremely serious charge. His friend Dumouriez had come to hate him after he refused to join the enemy camp with him. Dumouriez never forgave him for this and, on March 25th., he got the Convention commissioners to rule that he was responsible for the loss of his army on the battlefield at Neerwinden. Soon after that, Dumouriez was to betray the Republic and Miranda, who was being held at the Conciergerie, was charged with being the accomplice of a traitor to France. But fortunately for him, he has now been declared not guilty.

La Pérouse is still reported missing

Vanikoro Island, May 19

Life has been getting drearier every day aboard the ships that had set out to find La Pérouse, who is still missing. D'Entrecasteaux has been hopping across the Pacific from one archipelago to the next, but his efforts are in vain. A few miles from the Santa Cruz Islands he has just discovered an islet which he named "Ile de la Recherche", but he didn't anchor there. However, that was where the two frigates led by La Pérouse sank. He has lost all hope of finding him.

Elegant despite everything!

The Vendean generals can be reckless

La Rochejaquelein widening a breach in the walls of Thouars.

Vendée, May 25

Was it a case of courage or just recklessness? The generals of the Catholic and royalist army took all sorts of risks in order to win the battle at Fontenay le Comte. When he saw that his men's morale was sagging, Lescure rode forward all by himself under enemy fire. He was shouting "Long live the King". He was fired at by six cannons and it was a miracle he was not hurt. He then turned around to face his men and cried: "You see, the republicans don't know how to shoot. Forward!" As for La Rochejaquelein, his contempt for danger is becoming legendary. Wearing three red handkerchiefs — on his head, at his waist and around his neck — he refused to remove them even after the enemy gunners were ordered to "aim for the red handkerchiefs". After their victory, his friends decided they would all wear three red rags so their leader can't be spotted.

Love and politics sometimes mix well

Mont Blanc, May 18

Marie Jean Hérault de Sechelles left Chambéry this morning. He was accompanied by the beautiful Adèle de Bellegarde. There are many around who have already noticed that the young woman, who is the widow of the late Marquis de Bellegarde, is attracted to the handsome representative, currently on an official mission in the department of Mont Blanc. Adèle has been going out with him to all the official dinners and ceremonies held over the past six months. Marie Jean is also captivated by the young woman. He has been frequently visiting the salon of the former noblewoman, who has become a republican out of love.

Cabarrus, a wealthy Bordeaux family

Bordeaux, May 21

Paris was just too depressing for a 19 year old divorcée. Thérésa has therefore decided to return to Bordeaux where she still has family and live there until she can go to Spain to join her father, the rich banker François de Cabarrus. She is now staying with her two servants at the home of her uncle Dominique. The 70 year old man is helping his son, Jean Valère, aged 35, to run the family business, "Cabarrus and Sons". The two men are among the four or five wealthiest shipbuilders in Bordeaux. Jean Valère, who recently got married, has just launched a 500 tonne ship, and as a wedding present he named the new vessel after his wife.

Saint Pierre and Miquelon are again English

The Girondists' ultimatum to Paris

At the Jacobins Club, charges against the Girondists are already drawn up.

Saint Pierre, May 24

The cod fishing monopoly has been seized by the English. None of France's naval or land forces were able to stop the troops led by General Ogilvie, landing. Ten years after it was handed back to France under the terms of the Treaty of Versailles, the archipelago of Saint Pierre and Miquelon has been recaptured by the English. The loss is a severe blow to the French fishing fleet. The islands had become a centre of operations for cod fishing. Every March to April, some 10,000 to 12,000 of them come ashore to dry the codfish they had caught. The so-called *French Shore,* which granted them exclusive fishing rights off Newfoundland, has been scrapped. As for the Acadians who lived near Saint Pierre, they are once again facing deportation. A fleet is due in to take them to Nova Scotia.

Paris, May 25

"If an insurrection were to harm the national representation, then Paris would be wiped off the face of the earth." That is the terrible threat which has just been uttered before the stunned delegates from the Commune by the Girondist Isnard. They had come to ask for the release of Hébert, the assistant public prosecutor who was arrested yesterday on orders from the Convention. They did not get what they came for. Isnard's ultimatum is another step in the vast offensive launched a week ago by the Girondists, who suspect the city hall and the sectors of seeking to get rid of them. Thus, in order to escape from the "tyranny" of the people, on May 18th. Guadet called for a meeting at Bourges of all the deputies' assistants. Guadet, who saw this as a precaution, also said that all the constituted authorities of Paris should be abolished. But Barère stood firm against these extremist demands. In a bid aimed at ending

the hostility between the Assembly and the Commune, he suggested that a Committee of Twelve be formed. It would be given the task of keeping an eye on all plots threatening the law and liberty. But this body, made up exclusively of Girondists, is also turning out to be a major threat to the Commune and the sansculottists. Yesterday, claiming there was a city hall plot, Viger called for a decree to outlaw the Commune's armed forces. Then Hébert and Varlet were arrested. But the Girondists are taking a risk by threatening to crush Paris.

Beaumarchais is a poor secret agent

Paris, May 25

Beaumarchais is not a very lucky man. He caught a disease just as the problem over the guns for Holland is being settled. He had been charged with arms trafficking in December 1792, but had always claimed to have acted in good faith. In February he even had 6,000 copies of a document defending him distributed. He states that the

rifles were never delivered because Paris had not given him the money he needed to buy the weapons. The author was finally proved right. The Committee of Public Safety has restored his good name and asked him to resume his negotiations with Holland, which now has the 60,000 guns. But his illness could wreck everything. It's a bad start for a secret agent.

Lyons' Jacobins are ousted from power

The roles have changed: the Jacobins were the judges, now they are in jail.

Women cause trouble at the Assembly

The fearsome knitting women.

Paris, May 18

It was hard to hear oneself think at the Convention today. The deputies debating the Constitution were rudely interrupted several times by fights that broke out among the public. For the past three days Jacobin women, who feel they have the right to check who goes in or out of the gallery, have been causing disturbances at the Assembly. During a session one of them even caused a big row by trying forcibly to eject Bonneville, the former Girondist editor of *La Bouche de Fer.* Some deputies believe it is all a sinister plot to stop the Assembly doing its work.

Lyons, May 30

The city hall has been under Jacobin control since last March. But the people of Lyons have been voicing growing opposition to the various excesses of the policies drawn up by the Jacobin administrators. The Jacobins had accused the Girondists of fomenting the counter-revolution, to which the Girondists replied by criticising Chalier and his friends. The situation took a turn for the worse yes-

terday. A delegation of sector members, who have been holding nonstop sessions, came to ask the Convention's representatives, Nioche and Gauthier, to dismiss the entire city council. But some rebels had seized the arsenal and the Jacobins had holed up at the city hall. This morning at 5 o'clock the city hall was recaptured. The Jacobin leaders were all arrested and the council has been suspended. Lyons is once again in Girondist hands.

May 31-june 2, 1793: Girondists are ousted from

The Girondists have been kicked out of power following three days of street demonstrations. Thirty one of them were arrested on the evening of June 2nd. For the first time since 1789, the people have risen up against their representatives to dictate solutions to the major crisis that is rocking the nation. The enemy is at the borders, the Vendeans are winning victories and prices are on the rise. All this has led the sansculottists to demand the resignation of their administrators. Urged on by Marat, led by Hébert and Varlet, helped by a minority of Montagnard deputies, they are about to impose a revolutionary government made possible only by their revolt. That was how the Girondists, moderates, opposed to any social measure and claiming to represent the whole nation, were finally defeated by the capital's sansculottists.

The evening of June 2nd., shortly before the arrest of the Girondist deputies.

On May 31st., at about 3 a.m., the alarm bells rang out at Notre Dame cathedral. The ringing soon spread to the other neighbourhoods. Soon after that, drums called the National Guard to arms. Around 11:30 a.m., eighteen cannon shots were fired from the Pont Neuf bridge: it was the alarm cannon that can be used by the Convention only in cases of extreme emergency. But the Convention had nothing to do with all these events. They marked the start of the insurrection. Since May 29th. sector members had been meeting at the bishopric, in central Paris, to plan the move that was to force the Convention to outlaw the Girondists. A secret committee had been formed to carry out the operations. Late on May 30th., while Marat was busy making speeches to rouse the sansculottists, the committee decided to start operations the next day. It already had the support of most of the sectors, of the mayor, Pache, probably also of the Committee of Public Safety, of Marat and of the Montagnards. Paris had to rise up against those who had sworn to destroy it. At 6:30 a.m., the secret committee went to the community hall and, acting on behalf of all the people, set itself up as an Insurrectional Committee. The first thing it did was to appoint Hanriot as head of the National Guard and place him in charge of organising a general mobilisation.

The Convention yields

Alerted by the alarm bells which had not stopped ringing, the Convention started meeting at 6 a.m. A lengthy and rowdy debate quickly led to clashes between the Girondists and the Montagnards. The public galleries were full of people opposed to the Girondists. When the alarm cannon boomed out, Danton called for the people's demands to be satisfied. "What people?" his indignant enemies asked. All sorts of delegations kept coming forward, applying increasing pressure on the legislators. A mob gradually gathered around the Palais National. Around 5 o'clock that evening, a delegation from the Insurrectional Committee came in, demanding the charging of 22 Girondists, an far-reaching purge and the sentencing of all suspects. They also demanded an obligatory tax of one billion livres on the country's rich, public assistance and funds, a freeze on bread prices and the creation of a revolutionary army of sansculottists for every town.

Hanriot

Hanriot was appointed commander in chief of the National Guard by the revolutionary Committee at the age of only 34. In 1789 he was just an official involved in the collection of city tolls. He later became the leader of the battalion of the sector of Sans Culottes. He is a short man but has a lot of energy.

On May 31st., the Girondist deputies Fauchet, Brissot, Buzot, Pétion and Vergniaud, among others, are grouped behind Hérault de Séchelles, who stands with open arms. They are cheered by the crowd of sansculottists.

the Convention by the Montagnards

The delegation from the Insurrectional Committee was allowed in and mingled with the deputies seated on the left. Despite a forceful speech by Robespierre, the Convention only gave way partly. It just decreed the abolition of the Committee of Twelve and agreed upon an inquiry. This gave the uprising a certain degree of legitimacy. The Convention members then left the session hall, cheered by the crowd. The long day was drawing to a close amid considerable enthusiasm.

The day of June 1

The next day, the Revolutionary Committee decided to take action and arrest the suspects. Roland had already fled, but his wife was detained. The ministers Lebrun and Clavière were placed under surveillance. But there was still a major issue to be settled: agreement had to be reached on a list of the main Girondist leaders whose arrest was to be demanded. In all, 25 names were drawn up, including Brissot, Guadet, Pétion, Vergniaud, Isnard, Lajuinais and Rabaut Saint Etienne. To mark the event, alarm bells were rung, a call to arms was issued and the alarm cannons fired. As it was Saturday evening, workers responded massively to the new call. At the Convention, where only about 100 deputies were sitting, the seats on the right were practically empty when

The tragic trial of strength between Girondist deputies and National Guardsmen, on the evening of June 2nd.

the petitioners arrived. On behalf of the Committee of Public Safety, Barère agreed to give a report on the petition. However, the people were asking for more.

The Girondists are arrested

At 4 a.m. on Sunday, the Revolutionary Committee met and gave orders to Hanriot for the troops to march on the Palais National. An ultimatum would be issued to the deputies to demand the arrest of "sedition-mongers". When the Convention began its session, around 10 o'clock, the Palais National was already surrounded. Cannons were aimed at it, ready to be fired. The main hall and corridors were full of people. The deputy Lajuinais bravely called for something to be done about the insurgents. He even said Hanriot should be executed. Some deputies came forward as if they were about to drag him off the podium. As the tumult grew, the delegation from the general council was allowed in. It demanded the arrest of the Girondist deputies. As

no decision was forthcoming, the petitioners threatened the right wing deputies. "To arms!" people cried and the hall quickly emptied. The time had come for the Convention either to give in to the people or risk a fearful explosion of anger. Barère went for a compromise: the deputies on the list were asked to request their own temporary suspension. Isnard accepted and came to stand alongside the petitioners. Three others followed suit.

Then there was an incident which made the tension grow: Delacroix was stopped from leaving the hall by armed sansculottists, even though he was Danton's friend. As for Boissy d'Anglas, he was also turned back and his clothes were torn. It soon became obvious that the Convention was being held prisoner. The whole Assembly rose to leave and followed Hérault de Séchelles out into the courtyard to ask Hanriot to withdraw.

But neither the troops nor their cannons budged an inch. After having walked around the Tuileries, past the massed ranks of soldiers shouting "Long live the Montagnards! We want the traitors," the deputies returned to the main hall. There had been no violence, but the Convention was defeated. After an hour-long debate, 29 deputies and the ministers Clavière and Lebrun were arraigned. There was no roll call, as this might have incited some moderate deputies to change their mind. Only a few of them actually protested.

A dramatic and tumultuous session at the Convention. In the foreground, Danton leans on a walking stick, while Marat is seen on the right, his head swathed in a turban.

Convention

3. Paris. The Convention decrees that illegitimate children are to have the right to inherit. Under the Ancien Régime, illegitimate children cound not succeed their parents *ab intestat*.

5. Paris. The Assembly issues a decree authorising community property to be shared out, with the exception of forests, footpaths and buildings.

6. France. The insurrection of June 2nd. sparks off a series of open revolts against the Convention: Marseilles, Nîmes, and Toulouse rebel.

6. Evreux. A special meeting of the authorities and inhabitants of the Eure issues a ruling against the Convention calling for an army to be formed and march on Paris. However, the town council and the other towns of the department do not back this initiative (→17).

7. Paris. The Convention arraigns Buzot, suspends and summons the administrators of the Eure and stops Evreux being the main town of the district and the department. These roles are given to Vernon and Bernay respectively (→11).

7. Paris. From now on, all criminal tribunals will, like the one in Paris, be able to hand out deportation sentences.

9. Bordeaux. In a state of revolt since June 7th., the city authorities announce that they are now a popular committee of public safety for the Gironde.

9. Saumur. The city is captured by the Catholic and royalist army.→

9. Niort. General Biron takes over command of republican forces along coastal regions.

9. Martinique. General Rochambeau defeats the royalist troops at Gros Morne and captures all their artillery.

10. Paris. The Convention decrees the creation of a museum of natural history.→

10. Saumur. During a meeting of Vendean leaders, Stofflet proposes to march on Paris (→12).

10. Port Louis. The first corsairs of the Ile de France set sail to take part in the war against the English and Dutch fleets. This follows a decision by the governor of Mascareignes, the Comte de Malartic.

The King's garden becomes a museum

Paris, June 10

The Jardin des Plantes is not to be used for cultivating potatoes, despite a request from the Paris Commune. Acting on plans drawn up by Joseph Lakanal, the Convention has approved a project for a reorganisation of the King's garden, which was founded by Louis XIII and whose existence is now threatened. The new establishment is to be known as the national museum of natural history. Existing facilities are to be enlarged. The underpaid scientists are to have their salaries doubled, they will be made professors and will be able to teach mineralogy, chemistry, botany and human and animal anatomy. Directors will no longer be appointed by the King, but elected. Daubenton is currently the director.

Vergniaud agrees to face his judges

Paris, June 3

Vergniaud decided not to try to escape. Having been arraigned at the same time as his Girondist friends, he has now chosen to stay in Paris to face the Convention's justice. From his residence on the Rue de Clichy, outside which a policeman stands guard night and day, he has just written to the Assembly to say he never harboured evil intentions. He has refused a request to resign, but says he will submit to all the Assembly's decisions. This loyalty is the only guarantee that he won't try to flee by jumping over his garden wall.

Vergniaud, a Girondist leader.

The Vendean forces capture Saumur

Lauzun, the republican, pulls back.

Saumur, June 9

Nothing seems capable of stopping the Vendean advance at the moment. They had never until now attacked such a large city, but it only took a day for them to capture Saumur. Led by Cathelineau, Lescure and La Rochejaquelein, the Vendeans inflicted heavy losses on the city's defences. Many of its people were forced to flee to Tours. Large number of prisoners were captured and some of them even joined the Vendeans. Most of all, the fall of Saumur allowed the rebels to seize huge amounts of guns, cannons and ammunition. The Vendeans have now become stronger than ever before.

Lescure is collecting victories.

The Bonapartes in exile on the mainland

The Bonaparte family home in Corsica, where Napoléon was born.

Toulon, June 10

Young Napoléon Bonaparte's Corsican dream has been shattered for good. That homeland which he loved so deeply does not feel like home to him any longer. In order to escape assassination, the Bonapartes reluctantly decided to leave Corsica. As a result of the events of February, Pascal Paoli had outlawed the family in May. Their home at Ajaccio had been sacked and they were all forced to seek refuge in Calvi. But the Bonapartes were running out of money and had to leave. "This country is not for us, let us prepare to leave it," Napoléon told his relatives. That was done and the Bonaparte family is living in exile on the mainland.

Lakanal opposes "cultural vandalism"

The "vandals" want to erase the past with blows from their cudgels.

Paris, June 6

Lakanal has not forgotten that he used to teach Roman history before the Revolution. Referring to the Germanic people who devastated Gaul in the fifth century, he used the term "vandalism" at the Assembly to denounce the wanton destruction of works of art that has become the hallmark of many a revolutionary event since 1789.

"Citizens, the masterpieces that grace a great many national monuments suffer the outrage of vandalism every day. Priceless masterpieces are broken or mutilated ..." Lakanal cried from the podium. He called for courts to hand out a sentence of "two years in irons for whoever damages works of art that are the property of the nation". His proposal was approved.

Charette wins a decisive victory

Machecoul, June 10

The battle was long and bloody. In order to defeat the republican enemy, Charette had to lead his cavalry to the top of the hill where they had deployed their artillery. Once the Vendeans had entered the city, the republicans continued to fight in the streets and gardens. Many died in hand to hand fighting after being chased and caught by local peasants. This difficult victory means that Charette can now boost his standing within the Vendean camp. It is high time for him to do so, as last month his troops had panicked and fled several times. There had even been rumours that he was just a "whipper-snapper" who was too young and inexperienced to lead the rebel forces.

Long live the Montagnards

The Montagnard movement is very popular, according to the designs on humble china plates. It is usually depicted as a mountain surrounded by a symbolic revolutionary red bonnet and tricoloured flags.

The Assembly determined to reassert its power despite grass-roots pressure

Paris, June 8

The Convention is under fire from two sides. It must cope with the ousting of the Girondists and the unrest caused in the provinces by the events of June 2nd., while at the same time being careful not to let itself be overtaken by pressures from the Insurrectional Committee and the Enragés. Robespierre is determined to maintain the legislative body's authority despite the strong grass-roots pressure upon it. But he won't go so far as to make deals with the right wing and he is demanding that the Girondists be tried by the revolutionary Tribunal. For their part, Danton and Barère are in favour of a policy of appeasement. Barère, in his report dated June 6th. and drafted on behalf of the Committee of Public Safety, asked the Montagnards to give some "hostages" to the departments, namely special Convention envoys who would be held as guarantees of the safety of the arrested deputies. Danton offered to become such a hostage in order to reassure the provinces. He stressed yesterday that everything possible must be done to avoid a civil war. He is opposed to the use of force against the Girondist supporters, which he does not consider to be a major danger. He wants reconciliation. But it was Robespierre's argument that won. Strongly opposed to the humiliating plan to deliver hostages to the departments, he got deputies to reject the moderate line backed by Barère and Danton.

Girondist resistance in Normandy

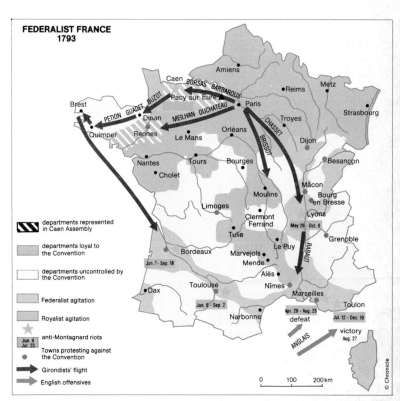

Caen, June 11

The insurgents of Normandy needed a leader, so Buzot has set off for Caen to organise resistance against the extremists in Paris. A departmental force has already been set up to "protect" the Convention. Things are different at Evreux, where Buzot failed to convince local people. Despite the popularity of this outlawed Girondist, his proposal to take up arms against the Assembly's decrees did not meet with a great deal of support in a town where many back the Montagnards. Moderates such as the Bishop of Evreux, Thomas Lindet, the deputy of the Eure, and his brother Robert, the deputy of the Calvados, even condemned his actions, which they said were bound to fail in Normandy "where heads are cold".

12. Albi. During a general assembly meeting, the local sectors strongly protest against the elimination of the Girondists.

12. Saumur. The leaders of Vendean uprising elect the coachman Jacques Cathelineau as commander in chief of the anti-revolutionary Catholic and royalist army. →

13. Paris. Following a request from Robespierre, the Committee of Public Safety is reorganised. →

13. Paris. Louis Deschamps Destournelles is appointed Minister of Finance, taking over from the Girondist Clavière.

13. Caen. The representatives of the insurgent departments set up an army in order to march on Paris. A former Constituent Assembly member, General de Wimpffen, is appointed its commander. In all, some 60 departments are affected by a royalist or Girondist revolt.

14. Paris. The Committee of Public Safety dismisses the authorities of the Somme which had called for armed opposition against the Jacobin Convention (→27).

15. Paris. The Rights of Man sector calls for the creation of general taxation and the voting and enforcement of a law against food hoarders.

16. Paris. The Cordeliers Club asks the Convention to set up the internal revolutionary army as quickly as possible.

16. Wissemburg. General Alexandre de Beauharnais is asked to replace Colonel Bouchotte as Minister of War, but he refuses the offer.

17. Paris. A Convention decree orders the temporary closure of commodities' exchanges.

18. Maine et Loire. The rebellious Vendeans led by d'Elbée and Stofflet capture Angers. They free the Prince de Talmont, who takes command of the Vendean cavalry.

18. Paris. The troupe of the Théâtre de la Nation performs *Bourru Malfaiteur* and *Le Méchant* to raise money for the widow of Carlo Goldoni.

18. Paris. On the capital's Place de la Révolution, 12 members of the Breton plot that was led by the Marquis de La Rouerie are publicly executed.

After the Girondist crisis, Public Safety Committee is beefed up

Paris, June 13

The Committee of Public Safety is getting bigger. Five new members have just been appointed. Three of them are Montagnard deputies who distinguished themselves fighting against the Girondists: Saint Just, Hérault de Séchelles and Couthon. The Committee is also to be divided up into six sections, each of which will correspond to a ministry. It now numbers 12 members after having undergone two reorganisations. On June 5th., Berlier replaced Bréard, who had left due to "illness". Then Gasparin and Jean-bon Saint André were elected yesterday to the posts held by Jean Baptiste Treilhard and Robert Lindet. This gives the Committee a greater control over government.

The Committee of Public Safety meets twice a day, morning and evening.

Haggling over holy relics in Savoy

Mont Blanc, June 14

The patron saint of Saint Jean de Maurienne has lost none of his prestige. The village's public prosecutor was ordered by the department authorities to hand over the silverware from local churches as soon as possible. But he replied that some of the local officials wished keep the silver arm, a relic of Saint Jean, until the next saint's day. The mayor even offered to pay for it in the form of a "patriotic gift". His generous offer may not be too well received by officials who think that a couple of chalices, a monstrance and a ciborium are quite enough for a church.

Trousers are too costly for a soldier

Northern border, June 17

It really has become too expensive to go to war. Sergeant Jannin of the 1st. Haute Saône battalion is up in arms over the cost of proper clothing in the region: 32 livres for a piece of cheap material. He has therefore written to ask that trousers be sent to him urgently. The good sergeant is not the only one to complain. Too many soldiers are poorly dressed. Many of the men are already dreading the end of summer and the icy weather that is sure to follow.

The Vendeans have found a leader at last

Saumur, June 12

The noble generals of the armies of Anjou and the upper Poitou have met at Saumur and preferred to pick a commoner as their leader rather than choose one of their own. Jacques Cathelineau has just been elected generalissimo of the Catholic and royalist army. The lack of a single, unified command had repeatedly made itself cruelly felt. Internal rivalries have been rife among the Vendean leaders, so the nobles decided to agree to pick a coachman from the village of Pin en Mauges. This choice was also a good political move, particularly at a time when "equality is on everyone's mind", they told each other. However, the generals were unable to agree on a military strategy. In order to keep the enemy under pressure, La Rochejaquelin wants to set off right away to march on Paris. But he was told that the peasants would never agree to fight so far away from their homes and so his plan was rejected.

The French troops under the command of General Ferrand put up a brave fight at Valenciennes against attacks from the Austrian forces.

Danton remarries before a priest

Paris, June 12

Love can lead a man to all sorts of places, even to church. Just four months after the death of his wife, Danton has married Louise Gély, a frail girl aged only 16 who has been brought up by bourgeois and deeply religious parents. Initially, her family had not welcomed the planned wedding. In order to try to put an end to the couple's plans, they had demanded that the marriage be blessed by a non-juring priest after the bride and groom had gone to confession. But Danton is in love and prepared to do whatever is necessary. However, he asked that the religious ceremony be held in private so that his political image should not suffer. It was held in an attic, far from prying eyes. As far as

Danton's son and his stepmother.

his colleagues are concerned, Danton got married at a civil ceremony held at city hall. Danton is now a happily married man.

Franco-American ties are under threat

Philadelphia, June 18

Relations between Philadelphia and Paris have soured, even though Thomas Jefferson has done all he can to keep relations between the two countries on an even keel. It all started going wrong last February, when Tenant, the French ambassador in Philadelphia, demanded the immediate repayment of the American debt to France. This currently stands at an impressive 554,500 dollars. Faced with a categorical refusal from the American Secretary of the Treasury, Alexander

Hamilton, Jefferson then suggested a phased repayment. But Genêt, the newly appointed French ambassador who has taken over from Tenant, firmly rejected the compromise offer. In spite of all his efforts, Jefferson has been unable to get George Washington to agree to repay the entire debt simultaneously, so he has just announced that America will only honour 20 per cent of the debt, not a dollar more. This is hardly likely to be deemed acceptable by the government of France.

Two Paris envoys held hostage at Caen

Caen, June 14

The Convention has just received a letter from two special envoys it had sent to Normandy. They are Romme and Prieur de La Côte d'Or and they have written to say they are being held hostage at the Caen castle. Their mission had been to go to Normandy to try to block any attempted federalist secession. But on June 9th., they were stopped at Bayeux and taken to Caen on orders from the department's assemblies. These bodies have stated that they are in a "state of insurrection and resistance against oppression".

Normandy, which backs the Girondists, has always distrusted the Paris Commune and its sansculottists. It rebelled openly against the French capital on May 31st. The two envoys have asked the deputies to consider them as hostages. They are to be held as a guarantee against the enforcement of plans to execute the Girondists held in Paris. As for the Caen authorities, they have sent a proclamation to the other departments in the region urging them to rise up. However, nobody knows if Romme and Prieur are to be freed.

A British setback in Martinique

Saint Pierre, June 19

The British expeditionary force has sailed from Saint Pierre amid great confusion. The Creoles who had called in the British frigates have now gone back aboard them to escape from republican reprisals. Admiral Alan Gardner is furious: the royalists on the island had guaranteed that they were in full control of Martinique. He did not expect to fall into the ambush laid south of Saint Pierre by the mulatto forces and General Rochambeau. Adm. Gardner made the mistake of believing that the mulattoes would welcome him. They intend to defend their new French citizenship.

A young sergeant-major risks his life to destroy a bridge and block the Vendeans' path.

Queen at Temple

Since the execution of Louis XVI, people have been gathering daily under the windows of the Temple prison to sing songs hostile to Marie Antoinette. In one of these, the former queen is supposed to confess her crimes. Reference is made to Cardinal de Rohan, who was involved in the infamous royal "Necklace Affair".

When Rohan Collier
Some years back
Took me from my mother's arms,
What Louis should have done,
He did first, whith no qualms.
That holy man,
His prowess hid
From Louis' eyes.
Brought before this
Foolish cur, my beauty
Conquered this numbskull;
Rohan slipped a world to infer
That pure and chaste I was.
Through d'Artois and his friends
I did to Louis a son present
When I left my mother's house,
In her presence I did swear
In the blood my hands to souse
Of France's citizens everywhere.
And La Fayette and Bailly true
Have promised me
The same thing too ...

Marie Antoinette's bleak days in detention at the Temple

Concern over Madame Royale's health adds to the Queen's worries.

Paris, June

Dressed in the black mourning gown that was given to her by the Convention after the execution of the King, the "Widow Capet" leads a solitary life on the third floor of the tower of the Temple. She even refuses to go down to the garden in order to avoid walking past the door on the second floor that leads to the rooms where Louis XVI had been housed. Weighed down by worry and anguish, she spends her long, lonely days knitting as she sits in an armchair by the window. Her rooms are not uncomfortable. She has a harpsichord, furniture and even a bathtub, but Marie Antoinette is deeply unhappy and her only remaining consolation is to look after her children and teach them their lessons.

Convention

20. Paris. At the urging of Jacques Roux and the "Enragés", or extremists, the Cordeliers launch a campaign of protests against the lack of food and hoarding.

20. Saint Domingue. The city of the Cap is destroyed following an attempted royalist uprising. →

21. Paris. The Convention orders Kellermann to march against Lyons. What was initially an anti-Jacobin uprising has become openly royalist since the arrival in the city of General Louis François de Précy.

21. Haute Marne. The local steel industry is called upon to provide rifles for the army. It is only surviving thanks to such government orders.

22. Paris. Failure of the plot by Baron de Batz, who wanted to get Marie Antoinette to escape from the Temple.

24. Paris. The Constitution of 1793, known as Year I, is finally approved by the Convention. →

24. Nantes. The commanders of the Catholic and royalist army order the city's mayor, Baco de La Chapelle, to surrender. If he refuses, they threaten to massacre the garrison.

24. Drôme. At the request of the Jacobin Joseph Payan, the representatives of 48 popular societies of southeastern France meet at Valence to organise resistance against the offensive of the Federates of Marseilles and Nîmes.

24. India. An English naval squadron blockades the port of Pondicherry (→ July 11, 93).

25. Paris. The Convention creates a new department, Vaucluse, in a bid to get Avignon away from the influence of Marseilles. →

25. Paris. Jacques Roux is booed at the Convention when he presents a petition criticising the shortcomings of the new Constitution. →

26. Paris. The deputy from Ariège, Lakanal, submits to the Assembly a new national education plan. This calls for the building of one new school for each 1,000 inhabitants, with top priority being given to primary schools (→ July 2, 93).

26. Paris. At the port of Saint Nicolas, a mob loots ships at anchor loaded with soap. The unrest is to last three days.

Slaves clash with royalists at Saint Domingue

Le Cap Français, June 20

The city of the Cap is ablaze, but the commissioners Sonthonax and Polverel, who have been on a mission on Saint Domingue ever since September 1792, have had a new success. After having put down the white settlers' revolt at Port au Prince, they have just crushed the royalist uprising led by General François Thomas Galbaud du Fort. The rebellion was nearly successful yesterday. The General, leading a group of mutinied sailors and white National Guardsmen, was able to chase the commissioners and the mulatto forces from the city. The anti-royalist forces only had one option if they wished to avoid being wiped out: order the arming of the insurgent Cap's slaves who were living around the city. The operation against Gen. Galbaud was swift. About 10,000 blacks rushed down from the hills and attacked the drunken sailors who had just finished looting the city.

Vendeans resort to guerrilla tactics

Vendée, June

A moment ago, there was nothing to be seen. But suddenly as if they had appeared out of thin air, a large group of Vendeans fell upon the Republic's forces. It was a truly classic case of guerrilla tactics. The republican troops have a lot of trouble knowing who or where the enemy is. It is extremely difficult to spot the Vendean symbol of a red heart on the clothes worn by the peasants of Vendée as they lurk behind bushes ready to attack. As soon as they meet strong resistance, the anti-revolutionaries pull back and disappear so quickly that even the cavalry can't catch up with them. Nature is their best ally. Each Vendean knows the local countryside like the back of his hand. Regardless of whether they win or lose an engagement, they rarely agree to bear arms for more than a few days at a time, going back regularly to tend to their animals and crops. They were badly armed during the first clashes, but have since captured enemy arms.

The Constitution of Year I is approved

A text aimed at giving the executive enough powers to cope with the crisis.

Paris, June 24

The Montagnard Constitution is considered as a highly democratic document. It is largely based on ideas developed by Robespierre and stresses the people's sovereignty, rather than the sovereignty of the nation as was the case for the 1791 Constitution. The executive powers are subordinate to legislative powers, which are embodied by a single assembly elected through direct universal suffrage. The 24 ministers of the Executive Council are appointed by the assembly and by the duly elected departmental authorities. This shows a certain desire to decentralise power. Moreover, all laws voted by the deputies must be approved by the electors' primary assemblies during a referendum. Although it was drafted in a totally haphazard way, this Constitution is a complete text that includes as a preamble a new Declaration of Human Rights. This is based on the Declaration of 1789, but also includes the right of the people to assistance, to education and to welfare. It also proclaims the right to petition, to resist oppression as well as the right of insurrection, which is termed "the most sacred of rights and the most vital of duties", when a government "violates the people's laws". In its first Article, the Constitution states that "common happiness" is society's supreme objective. The new institutions do not respect the principle of the separation of powers, but they at least provide the means for the people to exert almost permanent control over elected officials.

The Enragés' petition

Paris, June 25

Jacques Roux is perfectly clear: the new Constitution is no good for the people. It only contains formal declarations that have no real purpose. "Liberty is just a vain illusion when an entire class of men has the means of starving the people with impunity," the "red priest" cried out from the podium of the Convention. He had come to present the petition sent by the Gravilliers sector and the Cordeliers Club. Both are strongholds of the "Enragés", or extremists, who are demanding that provisions against food hoarders and speculators be included in the new Constitution. They accuse the Montagnards of not attacking the centres of wealth and of accepting social inequality. Jacques Roux added: "It is the wealthy who have taken advantage of the Revolution and the trading aristocracy that is oppressing us." His speech was greeted by howls of protest. The deputies are furious to be the targets of such insults and have had Roux expelled. Thuriot even called him an anarchist who was as much of a fanatic as the Vendean priests. However, he acknowledged that some of the demands made by the Enragés are justified. Thuriot has asked the Assembly to draw up a report on how to get food prices own. The Convention has been shocked to hear a man question the very integrity of the new institutions.

Madame Roland is freed, then rearrested

Paris, June 24

Madame Roland was allowed to walk out of the Abbaye jail this morning, but she was rearrested this evening and taken to Sainte Pélagie. Since her first arrest on May 31st., she had not stopped complaining about her arbitrary detention. As a ploy aimed at putting an end to her protests, the Security Committee decided to free her and then to detain her again right away with all the legal formalities. During her imprisonment at the Abbaye, Mme. Roland had used the long days to write her memoirs. The manuscript has been given to trusted friends.

In her cell, Madame Roland writes her memoirs for her daughter.

No women soldiers, even heroines

Women of the army in action during the siege of Valenciennes.

Paris, June 26

The women in France's army are up in arms. A decree approved on April 30th. has ordered them to return to their homes. Some are simply afraid that when they leave the army they will have to survive with no job and no money. But many others had really come to like the military life and they now fear the boredom of civilian life. However, the Convention is adamant: no women in the army, regardless of their past military record. The woman gunner Catherine Pochetat today asked the deputies to let her continue serving in the Ardennes and showed them some glowing certificates to prove her bravery under fire. She was even promoted to the rank of sub-lieutenant for her behaviour at Jemmapes. The Convention refused to budge, but granted her a 300 livre pension.

A new French department: the Vaucluse

Paris, June 25

France has 87 departments now that the Vaucluse has been added to the list. It will include the districts of Carpentras, Orange, Apt and Avignon, which will be its chief town. The decree approved by the Convention only gives geographical reasons for the move, but the real reasons are quite different. The move is aimed at blocking the "fateful influence of the Marseilles sectors". If these sectors and the federalists of Nîmes were to join forces with the rebels of Lyons, the Assembly would lose control of the entire region. In reality, the Vaucluse was set up to reduce the size of the department of the Bouches du Rhône while also creating a buffer zone that remains loyal to the Convention.

A prisoner fools Fouquier Tinville

Paris, June

A woman prisoner has escaped from the Conciergerie. To make matters worse, she was able to flee thanks to Fouquier Tinville. One evening, as he was on one of his regular inspection tours of the jail, he came across a young guard. He asked him to take a message to his wife to say that he would be late home and tell her not to worry. The young man tried to explain that he was not allowed outside. But Fouquier Tinville would not listen. He grabbed the youth by the arm and took him to the gate, where he gave orders for him to be let out. When he got home, his anxious wife told him that no message had been delivered. Furious, he went back to the Conciergerie the next day to have the youth punished for his laziness, but found that he had disappeared. To his horror, he discovered the youth was in fact a woman prisoner who had stolen a guard's uniform.

27. Paris. The Convention decides that the new French Constitution must be submitted to the people's ratification through a "plebiscite" (→Aug. 4, 93).

27. Paris. The Convention rules that the Paris Bourse, or stock exchange, is to be closed to avoid speculation.

27. Paris. The deputies meet a delegation of farmers who complain about the scarcity and cost of soap and candles.

27. Paris. The Convention approves a law stating that those who have been sentenced to life terms in jail or in prison camps before the Revolution may seek a retrial.

28. Paris. At the Jacobins Club, Robespierre violently attacks Jacques Roux and the Enragés, accusing them of playing into the hands of the enemies of the French Revolution (→30).

28. Paris. The Assembly decrees that each district will have a home to shelter unsupported pregnant girls, who will be allowed to stay there until they give birth.

28. Bordeaux. The department's authorities ask the envoys from Paris, Mathieu and Treilhard, to leave the city as soon as possible.

29. Loire Inférieure. Some 40,000 Vendeans try to seize control of Nantes, but the city manages to hold out. Since it can't gain access to the sea, the Vendean uprising is now condemned to slowly die out.→

29. Paris. The Convention decrees the death penalty for anybody caught disseminating a constitution that is not the one approved on June 24th.

29. Paris. Now it is the Commune's turn to attack the Enragés. It decides to sanction Jacques Roux.

30. Saumur. General Menou recaptures the city after royalist peasants have gone home to harvest their crops.

30. Germany. The philosopher Joseph Fichte publishes his *Contributions Aimed at Correcting the Public Assessment of the French Revolution.*

30. Paris. Hébert, Robespierre and Collot d'Herbois go to the Cordeliers and get Jacques Roux and Leclerc expelled from the club. Varlet is placed on suspension.→

A dispute surfaces between Amiens and the Somme

Paris, June 27

The commune of Amiens and the town's peoples' society have just shown great revolutionary zeal. They complained to the Convention about the actions of the department's authorities, which had issued a statement by eight deputies of the Somme opposing the events of June 2nd. The Assembly immediately approved a text congratulating all the patriots of Amiens. The Committee of Public Safety dismissed the department authorities. Worried, the Somme officials denied such "slander" and said they had no reason to feel guilty. They got their jobs back.

Chateaubriand has problems in London

London, June

For the past month, the French poet Chateaubriand has been at death's door in London. He had not got over the smallpox he caught on the battlefield at Verdun and his health deteriorated as soon as he arrived in London. He doesn't have enough money to live without working and he quickly spent his savings. Exhausted and delirious with fever, he would have died of hunger if it hadn't been for the British Literary Fund. This group gave the unknown poet 10 guineas.

This card is most useful for all revolutionaries.

Nantes resists a Vendean assault

The Vendeans are blessed before going into battle.

Nantes, June 29

The economic capital of western France has been saved. The people of Nantes, who for weeks had been living in fear of the "bandits" of Vendée, have successfully fought back against a Vendean assault. The patriots from nearby regions who had sought refuge in the city had told chilling tales about the cruelty of the Vendeans. Some of the Vendeans' victims at Machecoul were said to have had their hands chopped off before being dragged before a firing squad. Some even claimed that patriot soldiers had been nailed alive to farm doors as if they were owls. These tales gave the people of Nantes all the more reason to fight bravely to defend the city. They were helped by their mayor, Basco, who stood on a dustcart which he called the "chariot of victory" to urge the townspeople on, even after he had been badly wounded in a leg; but the victory is also due to the lack of co-ordination among the four royalist armies numbering 40,000 men. The armies were led by Charette, Bonchamps, Cathelineau and by Lyrot. The one led by Cathelineau was delayed by fierce fighting along the Erdre river against a republican battalion under the command of an ironmonger. But Cathelineau was hit by gunfire just as he had led his men to the Viarmes Square at Nantes. This broke the men's spirits and they retreated.

Jacques Roux ousted from the Cordeliers

Paris, June 30

The "red priest" has just been disowned by his own supporters. He and Leclerc have been kicked out of the Cordeliers Club, while Varlet was placed on suspension. Jacques Roux owes this humiliating expulsion to the Jacobins. After the Enragés had submitted their violent petition to the Convention, Robespierre finally decided to get rid of them. On June 28th., as there were signs of a new riot against hoarders in Paris, Robespierre launched a strong attack on the petition. He denounced Jacques Roux, saying that "this man wearing the mantle of patriotism...is insulting the majesty of the national Convention". In particular, he accused him of plotting against liberty by urging the people to revolt, and called on citizens to be "extremely circumspect". Today, Robespierre led a delegation of Jacobins and went to the Cordeliers to ask them to disown the Enragé manifesto. Collot d'Herbois convinced the club's members that Jacques Roux's policies would lead to total anarchy, adding that this would end up having counter-revolutionary effects. First, the leader of the Enragés was expelled from the Assembly and now he has been banished from his club. People are even saying that Hébert is planning to have Jacques Roux kicked out of the Commune.

Marat clashes against the "red priest"

Paris, July 4

Marat's attacks against Jacques Roux are tantamount to libel. The editor of the *Ami du Peuple* today accused the leader of the Enragés of having taken a false identity by using the name of an assassinated priest. This came after Marat had said the Enragés were "false patriot fanatics who hide behind their mask of patriotism to lead good citizens astray and into violent activities". Marat has been using all the arguments at his disposal to lash out at the "red priest's" popularity and credibility. Roux has been leading the fight against hoarders and encouraging unofficial price fixing. However, for Marat, all such spontaneous expressions of the people's anger against the high cost of living are irresponsible acts and help the counter-revolution. He could also be annoyed at having come across a man who is even more revolutionary than he is.

The young Agricol Viala's heroic death

Avignon, July 5

You don't have to be full-grown to be brave, people say. A boy from Avignon aged only 12 has died a hero's death while trying to defend the city against the federalist army from Marseilles. These forces, who had already captured Arles and Tarascon, were preparing to cross the Durance river. The boy, Agricol Viala was the only one to volunteer to cut the rope that was used for the river ferry. But he was said to have been hit by a bullet as he tried to hack through the thick rope with an axe. By this evening, his uncle and godfather, one of the patriot leaders of Avignon, were spreading the tale of the boy's heroic deed throughout the besieged town. But there was another version of the story: The boy was killed by the ferryman after he and some friends had shown the man their backsides when he scolded them for trying to damage the ferry.

The young Agricol Viala was a victim of his own heroism.

A potter is given aid by the Convention

Clamecy, July 7

Citizen Nolet has been extremely persuasive: he has just been given a grant of 2,400 livres by the Convention so that he can carry out repairs on his workshop.

His place of business had been badly damaged in a recent fire. The money was granted in view of the artisan's "great services to society by setting up a pottery works in this town". He was also rewarded for his "talent and integrity" and for his "pure patriotism". Pottery from Clamecy, like that made at Nevers, is an excellent way of spreading revolutionary propaganda far and wide.

Marie Antoinette's son is taken away

The cobbler Simon was entrusted with the care of the young prince.

Paris, July 3

At the Temple prison, the Queen is getting ready to go to bed. It is 10 o'clock. The children are already fast asleep. Suddenly, there is a knock at the door. Five municipal officials come in and tell Marie Antoinette that the Committee of Public Safety has decided that her son is taken away from her. She looks at them without understanding before screaming "Never!" The child, who is now awake, starts to cry. The officials threaten to call the guards and take the boy away by force. After pleading in vain for an hour, the Queen has to give in. Weeping, she hugs her "beloved darling" one last time. In the rooms below, which were used by the King, the cobbler Simon is waiting for his new charge.

Today, the Dauphin is just the son of the late Louis Capet.

Condorcet is forced to go into hiding

Paris, July 8

It was only thanks to some fast footwork by his friends that Condorcet was able to avoid being put in jail. The Assembly ordered his arrest this morning because of his pamphlet attacking the Constitution. The police immediately went to the residence of the deputy of Auteil, but he was not there. The mayor, one of Condorcet's friends, kept the policemen waiting a long time, thus helping him to get away. Meanwhile, his brother-in-law, Cabanis, helped by his friends Pinel and Boyer, also doctors, had been hiding the fugitive in Paris. Now it is Madame Vernet who is sheltering Condorcet at the Rue des Fossoyeurs, near Saint Sulpice, just as she used to shelter her medical student friends. When the doctors asked for

Cabanis, doctor and philosopher.

help, she agreed right away. All she knew about the fugitive's real identity was that he was a "virtuous man" (→ Mar. 29, 94).

Robespierre presents the education reform plans drawn up by Le Peletier

Paris, July 13

Robespierre has spoken very convincingly. The deputies have overwhelmingly approved the national education reform plans drawn up by Le Peletier before his death. This martyr to liberty was also a daring educationalist. Basing his plan on ancient Sparta, he suggested that common education establishments be set up. Attendance would be obligatory for all local children aged between five and 12. They would be fed, clothed, housed and educated so that they could become perfect republican citizens as quickly as possible. This truly national system would fill the gap left by the abolition of small village schools that were run by priests.

Danton suffers a major setback

Paris, July 10

It looks as if Danton is going to have to retire. The Convention has failed to re-elect him to the Committee of Public Safety and this is a big setback for him. The move benefits the supporters of Robespierre. Danton had been a member of the Committee ever since it was set up. He had come to play such a major role there that some called it a "Danton ministry". He was only backed by one Montagnard deputy, Delacroix. All the other members were part of the Plaine group, moderates who supported the Montagnards or the Girondists depending on the circumstances. But since the events of June 2nd. and the ouster of the Girondists, Danton had lost his influence over the Committee. His policy of seeking accommodation with the Federalists was rejected. As the man in charge of military affairs, his position was weakened by France's defeats. He had trouble coping with the attacks from Marat, who on July 4th. wrote a sarcastic article on the "Committee of Public Loss" and blamed its failures on Danton. He was also compromised by the plot involving Dillon, a friend of the Danton supporter Desmoulins. It is a tired, disheartened man who today leaves the Committee.

The Normandy army of Federates suffers a crushing defeat

Pacy sur Eure, July 13

The Federalists have suffered a stinging humiliation. The mere sight of several hastily recruited units of armed men from the Paris sectors was sufficient to force them to withdraw, and there was no real bloodshed. The troops who were so easily defeated were the spearhead of the army formed by Wimpffen, the former commander in chief of the army of the Côtes de Cherbourg who had joined the Girondists sheltering in Caen after June 2nd. They were led by Puisaye, another officer who had rallied to the camp of the enemies of the Convention. Today's humiliating setback is highly significant. Unless they ally themselves with the royalists, which seems extremely unlikely, the Girondists will probably not be capable of liberating the capital from the tyranny of the Jacobins.

Despite being popular in the provinces, the Girondist rebels are routed at Pacy by the troops from Paris.

The Lyons rebellion is spreading

Rhône et Loire, July 11

It is best not to be a Jacobin when the army of royalist and Girondist rebels is heading your way. The Lyons insurrection is spreading quickly. The rebels have begun moving to meet up with their supporters in Saint Etienne. Among the column of 1,200 men marching towards Forez there are quite a few young aristocrats and sons of the rich men of Lyons. When they marched through Rive de Gier, these violent upper class youths gave free vent to their hatred and sacked the local Jacobin Club as the inhabitants looked on in absolute horror (→Aug. 25).

Dupont de Nemours to be arrested?

Paris, July 13

Pierre Dupont de Nemours, who was denounced on April 4th. by the sectors of the Finistère, was the target of a violent attack by Danton at the Convention yesterday. Danton accused that "old rascal" of plotting to help the rebels of the Eure and Calvados. The General Security Committee has given orders for the immediate arrest of this notorious anti-Jacobin. Even though he has withdrawn to his lands at Montargis, de Nemours is seen as an active opponent. He still runs his Paris printing works and is suspected of anti-revolutionary propaganda.

The telegraph is successfully tested

Paris, July 12

One of the few benefits of a war is that it can lead to technological progress. The initial tests of the new telegraph have been a success. They were carried out between Belleville and Montmartre before three commissioners from the Convention: Joseph Lakanal, Pierre Daunou and Louis Arbogast. The engineer, Claude Chappe, had already offered his invention to the Legislative Assembly, but it was rejected. The Convention saw it as a means of fast communication with the army in the north and 6,000 francs were earmarked for further tests.

Marat stabbed to death in his bath

Marat is stabbed to death by Charlotte Corday as he sits writing in his bathtub.

Paris, July 13

The whole neighbourhood came running when the terrified screams of Marat's woman friend rang out. The police commissioner is already on the scene. He is astonished to see the murderess calmly standing at the window as if nothing has happened. There are National Guardsmen posted all around to protect her from the crowd. The surgeon was not able to help. Marat died nearly immediately. It was 7 p.m. when the blonde, well-dressed young woman entered the first floor appartment at number 20, Rue des Cordeliers. Marat was busy writing while sitting in his bathtub, where he had to spend a lot of time due to a skin inflammation. Unsuspecting, he welcomed the young woman, who claimed she had the names of a group of Girondist conspirators in the Calvados. All of a sudden, she pulled a knife out of her bodice and plunged it into Marat's chest. Charlotte Corday had left Caen, where she lived with her aunt, four days ago. She arrived in Paris the day before yesterday, determined to kill the man she considered to be an enemy of the human race. She had initially planned to murder him in public on July 14th. on the Champ de Mars, to make the crime even more symbolic. But the festivities were cancelled at the last minute so she decided to go to his home. To look at her, it is not hard to believe that Charlotte, who is a great grand-niece of the playwright Corneille, acted alone (→July 17).

Charlotte Corday is interrogated about the crime after her arrest.

Marat's death

Marat's death has evoked much comment. His friends have had a song of vengeance compsed and handed out to the people who bewail his murder.

By patriotism great
And staunch love the laws,
By these virtues, Marat
Prepared for France her Weal,
And by his constant care
Our love won, deep and leal.
Marat, thy fate is seal'd;
Thy courage be thy shield.
A harpy, fell and dread,
A hell-cat, Satan's slave,
Thy lifeblood now hath shed
With ignominious glaive.
Dear Heaven! Can this be true?
Marat is dead and gone.
His ashes all will rue,
In vain our tears forlom.
We pray thee, God of Wrath,
Revenge this heinous deed,
And of our star henceforth
His blessings crown, we plead.

Charlotte Corday is sentenced to death and guillotined

Charlotte Corday.

Which seems the more inhuman, the court or the accused?

Paris, July 17

With her hair cut short under her white bonnet and her hands tied securely behind her back, Charlotte Corday climbed slowly up to the scaffold as if she was in a daze. She appeared calm and seemed to have accepted her terrible fate. Throughout the trip from jail, Marat's assassin stood upright in the cart, beside the executioner Sanson. The rain made her long red wrap stick to her body. Moved by her youth, the president of the revolutionary Tribunal, Montané, tried in vain to save her life. But the judges refused to declare her mad, which would have meant that she could have been locked up at the Salpêtrière asylum instead of facing a death sentence. Even her defence lawyer, Chauveau Lagarde, had been half-hearted in his efforts. What can be said when the accused admits everything and there are no extenuating circumstances whatsoever? When she left the tribunal, Charlotte simply asked for permission to get her portrait painted by an amateur artist so that she could leave a final memento for her family. After the sentence was carried out, one of Sanson's assistants dared pick up her head by the hair and wave it at the crowd. This was greeted by a shout of horror. The same people who only a few moments ago were singing and dancing around the guillotine were all shocked by this lack of respect.

The deputies scoff at proposals made by Sieyès

Paris, July 14

Something unusual has taken place at the Assembly. A speech by Sieyès has made the deputies laugh. The educational plan proposed by the man commonly known as the "metaphysician" was quite a surprise and the deputies quickly censored its weirdest elements. His list of 40 public holidays was greeted by roars of laughter, especially the holiday for "man's friends, the animals". That was immediately dropped. Ten other suggested holidays were cancelled, as was his plan for obligatory teaching of dancing and singing. Sieyès is silent, angry and sulking because his proposals were so badly received. He is convinced that his fellow deputies are not intelligent enough to recognise his true genius.

Cathelineau dies from his battle wounds

Saint Florent, July 14

"The good Cathelineau has just given his soul back to God, who had granted it to him so that he could avenge His glory." With these words, the anxious crowd that was waiting outside the home of the Vendean leader was told of his death by a man who had been at his bedside to the last. As soon as Cathelineau was wounded, on June 29th., those close to him knew how serious it was. The bullet had shattered his elbow before ending its flight in his chest. His men had been so upset that they were unable to continue their attack on Nantes. Marching alongside the stretcher on which he lay in great pain, they had pulled back to Ancenis. From there, the injured man was taken across the Loire river so that his own people could look after him at Saint Florent. His condition improved slightly after the bullet was extracted by a surgeon, but then the "Saint of Anjou" caught a fever. Knowing that the end was near, he asked Abbot Cantiteau, his village priest, to hear his confession before he died.

D'Elbée takes over from Cathelineau without Charette even noticing.

Momoro: a very successful printer

Paris, July

It is easy to spot something that has been made by a really good printer. Momoro's success is not simply due to the political influence he wields within the Cordeliers Club. It is also based on the exceptional quality of his goods. He uses only the most modern production methods and has copying presses and reversing presses which can reproduce four pages in less than two minutes. Writing paper, pencil lead from England, vellum, erasing rubber, China paper, multicoloured waxes — bronze, puce, light brown and even transparent — nearly everything can be purchased at Momoro's store. For his more refined clients, he has perfumed wax.

Antoine François Momoro, "Liberty's foremost printer".

Guillotin, cautious but unfortunate

Arras, July 18

The unfortunate Guillotin was warned about his imminent arrest and joined the army as a military doctor to escape from Paris, but was terrified when he was told where he had been posted. He is to go to the Saint Vaast hospital at Arras, whose mayor is none other than the sinister Lebon. He still hopes to be able to avoid being arrested. The Republic needs good doctors too much to get rid of him. But how long can this last?

Is Jacques Roux to be the new Marat?

Paris, July 22

The Enragés are jockeying to see who is to succeed Marat. Jacques Roux has just said the funeral oration for the murdered man at Saint Nicolas des Champs. Roux intends to continue the famous newspaper in which Marat had again criticised him just a few days before he died. On July 16th., Roux published *The Shadow of Marat*, which is supposed to be a follow-on to the *Ami du Peuple*. But Roux is not the only one to want to bask in the dead man's glory. Yesterday, Hébert told the Jacobins: "If a successor to Marat is required, I am the one!" Robespierre is irritated by the praise being heaped on Marat by his former rivals (→Aug. 8).

Marat at the Panthéon? The Cordeliers are for, but Robespierre is not.

Lyons challenges Paris

Lyons, July 16

For the past month and a half Lyons has been in defiance of Paris. The counter-revolution is making giant strides there. The opponents of the Convention are seeking to purge the city of all the republican supporters. They had Chalier beheaded in Lyons today. The Convention had none the less ordered that this extreme Jacobin leader should be spared. He had been in charge of a special tribunal set up to try the émigrés and royalist priests.

The Convention even sent a special envoy, Buonarroti, to take an official decree on the affair to Lyons. Chalier's execution was spectacular. The executioner, an incompetent beginner, had forgotten how to place the guillotine's blade properly. After three vain attempts, he finally had to use a knife to chop off the condemned man's head. The Lyons authorities, who wanted to make an example of Chalier, only succeeded in making a martyr out of him (→Aug. 14).

Even in death, Chalier is the object of the people's veneration.

Authors are to get new rights

Paris, July 19

The time of easy pickings is over for those who make a living by infringing the rights of authors. Anyone who publishes a book without its author's permission can be punished by law. For the first time, a decree controls literary and artistic property. In future, the author can do what he wants with his rights. He can be his own publisher or get his work published professionally. Printers must pay the author his rights. If he is dead, the money goes to his heirs (→July 24).

Death of Admiral d'Entrecasteaux

Molucca Islands, July 21

The expedition that had set out in search of La Pérouse is in mourning. Its leader, Rear-Admiral Antoine Bruny d'Entrecasteaux died yesterday evening. His funeral took place this afternoon off the shores of the Moluccas. The expedition's two store ships, *Recherche* and *Espérance,* heaved to while his coffin gently lowered overboard. The cause of his death is not obvious, but after two years at sea, all the crewmen are in a very poor state of health.

23. Mainz. The French garrison capitulates and is allowed to leave the city.→

25. Avignon. The republican troops push the Federate forces back beyond the Durance river.→

26. Paris. The Convention grants Chappe the title of "telegraphic engineer" and orders that optical telegraphs be set up all over the country.

26. Vendée. The leader of the Vendeans in the Fontenay region, Chevalier Sapinaud, is killed during a clash with republican troops at Pont Charrault.

26. Paris. Acting on a report by Collot d'Herbois, the Assembly decrees the death penalty against hoarders. They are traders who don't declare their stocks.→

27. Paris. The Abbot Grégoire, a member of the colonial committee, obtains the abolition of the government subsidy of 2.5 million francs granted to the slave trade.

27. Paris. Robespierre becomes a member of the Committee of Public Safety, where he takes Gasparin's place.→

27. Evreux. The Girondist Buzot is burnt in effigy at Evreux.→

28. Northern France. Valenciennes surrenders to the allied troops led by the Duke of York. In the occupied territories, the Austrians set up a junta which restores the Ancien Régime and hunts down revolutionaries.

29. Mont Blanc. Sardian troops launch an offensive against the Republic and recapture the valley of upper Maurienne (→Aug. 22, 93).

20. Luçon. The Vendeans launch a first assault against the city.

31. Paris. The Ministry of War turns the Val de Grâce convent into a military hospital.

31. Rome. Pope Pius VI publishes a short address to the French clergy in which he states that the bishopric of Agra does not exist and that the head of the ecclesiastical council of the Catholic and royalist army is an impostor (→Jan. 5, 94).

31. Paris. The Convention decides to withdraw from circulation all assignats worth more than 100 livres that were issued under the monarchy.

A copyright for all books

Paris, July 24

Since the abolition of the trade guilds, anybody has been able to open a workshop and to produce and sell any kind of book without any kind of prior authorisation. All that is now about to change. A law now protects artistic property: any citizen who produces a work that can be copied, either literary or artistic, will have to send two copies to the Bibliothèque Nationale in Paris. Only when this is done can any unauthorised reproduction be punished by law.

Citizen, watch your language!

Paris, July 23

"Madame, Mademoiselle, Monsieur ...", these words are now taboo in France. An actor at the Favart auditorium was unpleasantly surprised this evening when he discovered this. He made the mistake of using the banned words when he spoke to the audience, who forced the foolhardy actor to start again. It was only after he was interrupted a second time by the angry spectators that he consented to use the approved term of "citizens".

Beaten, the French withdraw from Mainz

The intensive Prussian bombardment of Mainz finally defeated the French garrison. The time for revolution is over for the Rhenish town.

Mainz, July 23

The French garrison was unable to hold out any longer, despite having put up a brave fight. It had suffered heavy losses and was forced to surrender to the Prussian troops. The garrison could not count on getting any reinforcements as so much of the French army was committed to the defence of the country's borders. Since the start of the siege by the King of Prussia himself last month, the city had been surrounded by a ring of steel. In spite of this, the French continued to launch attacks on the enemy. But there was little that the garrison's 22,000 men could do against the 80,000 Prussian soldiers. Not only were cannonballs raining down on Mainz, but there was also a severe famine to cope with. People started eating the horses, before having to feed on cats and dogs. The garrison is now to be sent to Vendée because the Prussians have ruled that it can no longer fight along the border.

Buzot is burnt in effigy at Evreux

Evreux, July 27

The people have burnt the man they used to adore. The effigy of the Girondist deputy Buzot, who was once the pride of the town, is just a pile of ashes surrounded by a frenzied mob on the main square. Several days after the defeat of the Federate army at Pacy sur Eure on July 13th., representatives of the Convention had been warmly welcomed by the town's inhabitants. On July 23rd., the Convention celebrated the rehabilitation of the rebel town. It decided that the department's administrative headquarters would be based there. To mark the return of liberty, six young couples were married and each was granted a sum of 2,400 livres in assignats and property as a wedding gift. Buzot's creditors are worried by the deputies' decision to have his house burnt down. But the Assembly has firmly swept away their protest, saying: "If the house were to belong to another, they would be happy to see such a den of crime burnt down."

Buzot, Mme. Roland's good friend.

Avignon resists against Federates

Avignon, July 25

Twice invaded and twice liberated, Avignon has become a major problem for the Federates. Its inhabitants have become martyrs of the revolt in the Midi region of southern France. The troops from Marseilles met no resistance when they marched in on July 7th., but they had to flee on the 14th. in the face of the Convention forces. The next day, they marched back into the city, but were pushed back behind the Durance river on the 25th. Throughout all this, the people who had stayed behind hid in their homes. People were careful which side they were seen to back as they didn't want to be massacred if the other side won. Some of those who had remained uncommitted made the mistake of leaving their homes too soon and were killed anyway.

Louvet, Lodoïska marry in secret

Vire, July 31

Louvet de Couvray has just wed Lodoïska, for worse rather than for better. The marriage ceremony was a sad affair, with Buzot, Pétion, Salle and Guadet as the only witnesses. They are on the list of outlawed people and had left Paris to save their skins. Meanwhile, Lodoïska, whose divorce has just been formally announced, was busy selling her jewellery to pay for her trip to England. She finally met up with Louvet and will now share his exile as an outlaw's wife.

A new law against hoarders

Paris, July 26

Under pressure from massive demonstrations ever since last February, the Convention has just approved a decree against hoarders. In future, all traders in goods that are considered as "useful for life", wholesalers and retailers alike, have to inform the municipal authorities and the public about their stocks. These are to be sold "without any delay or postponement, according to demand". Special commissioners have been appointed to enforce the new law, which also states that goods can be seized and that people caught hoarding can face a death penalty.

Robespierre is now a member of the Committee of Public Safety

Paris, July 27

The man they call the "Incorruptible" has finally decided to face up to his political responsibilities. He has just been appointed a member of the Committee of Public Safety to replace Gasparin. This move was proposed by Jeanbon Saint André. Along with Saint André and Saint Just, Lindet, Barère, Herault de Séchelles, Couthon, Prieur de la Marne and Thuriot, Robespierre will for the first time hold an official post of political influence. It is a vital post as the Committee in fact directs the actions of ministers. But to listen to him, the lawyer from Arras was unwilling to accept the honour: he only agreed to join on the urging of his friends and not out of a lust for power. At the Assembly, he always preferred action to administrative responsibility. He saw this as limiting his freedom. That is probably why he refused to head the revolutionary Tribunal when he was asked to do so in August 1792. He was not part of the Legislative Assembly and until last spring only had little influence at the Convention, dominated by Girondists. However, he has always been extremely popular among the people and the clubs. The Girondists were suspicious of this popularity and thought that Robespierre wanted to make use of it to set up a "dictatorship". But the leader of the Jacobins is a man who has a deep respect for the law and parliamentary institutions and it is most unlikely that he ever dreamt of making such a move. Despite this, he is good at political manoeuvring and has a gift for convincing deputies to support his policies. He is aware today of the fact that most members of the Committee back him. This means he will not have to reach any compromises in order to push his policies through.

The first problem facing Robespierre at the Committee is that of the war.

Joseph de Maistre, a royalist of Savoy

Lausanne, July 30

Counter-revolutionary ideas are also spreading. They have found a new advocate in the magistrate from Savoy, Joseph de Maistre. He is now living at Lausanne, where he had sought refuge along with King Victor Amadeus after the invasion of Savoy by the Convention's forces. He is just finishing the publication of his *Letters of a Savoy Royalist to His Countrymen*. In contrast with other royalist polemists, Maistre doesn't just berate the rationalist philosophy of Enlightenment, which he believes was a cause of the Revolution. He also wants to know why some of the people of Savoy were led astray, and criticises the passivity of the former government of Piedmont. He has found a clever way to fool the revolutionary censors: his works are distributed inside missals.

The philosopher Joseph de Maistre.

The ambassadors Sémonville and Maret, sent by France to Tuscany and Naples to negotiate the freeing of the royal family in exchange for the neutrality of those states, are arrested by the Austrians in Piedmont.

Convention

1. Paris. The Convention continues enforcing its policy of destroying all symbols of the monarchy by ordering that the tombs of the kings of France at Saint Denis be opened.

1. Paris. The new system of weights and measures, based on decimal units, comes into force.→

2. Paris. Theatres in Paris that are specified by the city hall are ordered to perform, three times a week starting on August 4th., the tragedies *Brutus, William Tell, Caius Gracchus* and others. These plays are based on glorious republican political events.

2. Paris. Marie Antoinette, her daughter and Madame Elizabeth are transferred to the Conciergerie jail.→

2. Paris. Sade, who has become president of the Pique sector, saves his parents-in-law as well as President de Montreuil and his wife.

3. Paris. The Convention orders the nationals of all countries at war with France to leave France within eight days except those working in factories and those whose patriotism cannot be doubted. They will need a special certificate.

4. France. Following a referendum, the Constitution of Year I is ratified by 1,800,000 votes for and 11,600 against. However, it will never be enforced.

5. Maine et Loire. The general and former jeweller Jean Antoine Rossignol defeats the Vendeans outside Saumur.

6. Bourg en Bresse. Kellermann takes command of the army unit in charge of putting down the revolt in Lyons.

8. Paris. At the request of Abbot Grégoire, the Convention abolishes academies and literary societies.→

8. Saint Denis. The royal tombs are destroyed.→

9. Paris. Barère gets approval for the decree creating storage granaries in each district and the building of public bread ovens.

10. Paris. The Constitution is promulgated before deputies from the departments at the celebration for the first anniversary of August 10th.→

The Convention decrees the total "destruction of Vendée"

Paris, August 1

The fate of the Revolution hangs on the result of the war being waged in Vendée. It is essential to destroy this fanatic region which is allied with the English enemy and has become a symbol of plotting against the Republic. That is what Barère has just said in the report he wrote on behalf of the Committee of Public Safety. That was enough to get the deputies to immediately approve a decree calling for the total "destruction of Vendée". The army is to be beefed up by troops from Mainz. The general staff will be purged and military discipline will be strictly enforced. The Convention also decided to burn down forests, destroy rebel hideouts and crops and confiscate cattle. The property belonging to counter-revolutionaries will be seized. As far as the deputies are concerned, no move is too strong to fight against the gangs of Vendean peasants who are still defying the Republic.

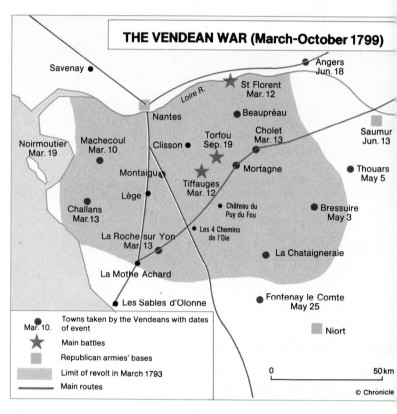

THE VENDEAN WAR (March-October 1799)

- Mar. 10. Towns taken by the Vendeans with dates of event
- ★ Main battles
- ▪ Republican armies' bases
- Limit of revolt in March 1793
- Main routes

0   50 km

© Chronicle

A unified weights and measures system

Paris, August 1

Like the Ancien Régime and inequality, all that is arbitrary in the field of weights and measures must be abolished. The aune, the fathom, the foot and the span are no longer to be used. Neither are the arpent, the league, the rod, the rood or the acre. These measures all vary from one region to the next. The Convention has just approved the weights and measures system proposed by the Academy of Science. In future, the basic linear measure will be the metre, or the 10 millionth part of a quarter of the meridian.

Marie Antoinette at the Conciergerie jail

Paris, August 2

Helped by Madame Elizabeth and her daughter, Marie Antoinette hastily packed the few belongings she has been allowed to take with her. In the middle of the night, four police officials had come to take her away. Trying to hide her emotions, she kissed the little Marie Thérèse, telling her to "be brave". Then she entrusted the girl to her sister-in-law before leaving without a backwards glance. Yesterday, the Convention decided to transfer the Queen to the Conciergerie where she will be held pending her summons to appear before the revolutionary Tribunal. The discovery of plots to help the royal family escape, such as the one by Baron de Batz, has proved that the Temple was not secure enough. At dawn, Marie Antoinette discovered her new prison. It is nothing like her comfortable room at the Temple: a damp cell, two chairs, a table, a wicker armchair and a camp-bed.

The King's widow in mourning.

The academies are abolished

Paris, August 8

Only four people attended the last session of the French Academy on August 5th. Disenchantment had taken a heavy toll. The Convention today put an end to a dying institution. By virtue of the principle of equality among citizens, the deputies voted unanimously in favour of the abolition of academies and literary societies. It was the Abbot Grégoire who fired the first shot, lashing out at these "gangrenous assemblies afflicted with the disease of incurable aristocracy". Who can need such dusty and falsely elitist institutions nowadays, he asked. "I will say frankly that true genius is nearly always sansculottist," he added. Then David spoke, thus fulfilling an old desire: to trample on the corpse of the Academy of Painting. He denounced the privileges granted to its members and the strict conditions of admittance. These included prior acceptance, approval of a special work of art and submission to outdated aesthetic rules. The burden of such demands had become unacceptable, all the more so because an artist could not hope to become a success unless he was accepted by the Academy.

Marat's widow accuses the Enragés

Paris, August 8

Simone Evrard spoke with such conviction and indignation that she easily convinced the deputies. She had gone to the Convention to accuse the Enragés Leclerc, Varlet and Roux of using her dead companion's name without permission. She had been urged to do so by Robespierre. The Jacobin leader is worried that the Enragés will make use of Marat's memory to rouse the people. As the celebration of the Federation draws near, he is afraid that there could be violent unrest. Robespierre has scored a point over his rivals by sending Marat's widow to the Convention. The deputies have now asked the Security Committee to deal with both Roux and Leclerc.

Marat's prestigious mantle is now much sought after.

An improved military health service

There is only an uncomfortable straw mattress aboard army ambulances.

Paris, August 7

The French Minister of War is now to have three doctors, three surgeons and three chemists as special advisors. This is because practically as many soldiers have been dying from disease as from the wounds suffered on the battlefield. The sanitation and health situation in the army is terrible. This new central health team is to oversee the Convention's earlier attempts to remedy the grave military health problem. It was thanks to a competition set up by the Assembly to see who could design the best "covered vehicle equipped with suspension for the transport of the ill and wounded" that the first rapid ambulances were created.

A violent "chicken war" rages in Savoy

Mont Blanc, August 4

The chicken breeders and sellers of Viry are up in arms. They have come before the municipal authorities to complain bitterly about the behaviour of the inhabitants of the neighbouring village of Carouge. They accuse them of imposing, sometimes through force, unfair and ridiculously low prices on the chickens that the people of Viry bring in to Carouge to sell on market days. The town council has now ruled that the delegates who will be chosen to go to celebrate the anniversary of August 10th. at Carouge would be well advised to call on the officials of that village to put an end to such outrageous practices before there is any further trouble.

Napoléon Bonaparte, a Jacobin militant

Avignon, August

Napoléon Bonaparte prefers the democratic freedoms to the constraints of aristocracy. *Le Souper de Beaucaire,* which was published early this month by the young officer, supports some very republican concepts. In this political pamphlet written as a dialogue, an officer in the army led by Carteaux, a Marseilles Federalist, a Girondist from Nîmes and a Montagnard from Montpellier discuss the problems in their regions. Speaking through the army officer, Bonaparte violently attacks the Marseilles Federalists. But Napoleon has always been an opportunist and one is allowed to doubt the sincerity of the feelings he has the officer express.

Saint Denis royal tombs are desecrated

Saint Denis, August 8

The ancient basilica of Saint Denis has for the past two days seen some pretty gruesome goings on. Officials from the commune of Franciade, acting ahead of the deadline, have been opening up the royal tombs. The Convention had ordered that "the tombs and mausoleums of former kings placed in churches, temples and other parts of the Republic must be destroyed by August 10th." to celebrate the first anniversary of the fall of the monarchy.

The breaking open of the royal tombs has given officials "plenty of material for anatomical and chemical observation due to the gradual process of decomposition of human bodies over many centuries", Dom Poirier, the basilica's learned archivist, noted down coldly. The operation, however, did not just arouse scientific comment. Local inhabitants were deeply shocked to discover crowns, tiaras and other precious ornaments that had been buried along with the "rotten corpses". The locals insulted the "vile remains of all those proud monarchs", which are to be gathered up and thrown into a common grave that has been dug in the small cemetery next to the basilica. Then the sacking of tombs got under way with a vengeance.

In only two days, a total of 51 monuments have been destroyed. Iron tombs have been dismantled and are to be melted down. Alexandre Lenoir was the only one to voice opposition. He managed to save the large stone Renaissance mausoleums of Louis XII, François I and Henri II. These were taken to the Petits Augustins warehouse he is in charge of. The inhabitants of Franciade have a big plan: They want to use the stone from the royal tombs to build a huge pyramid in honour of Marat and Le Peletier de Saint Fargeau, two martyrs of the Revolution (→Oct. 24).

Coffin by coffin, stone by stone, the basilica's crypt is emptied out.

August 10: anniversary of the monarchy's fall

On the ruins of the Bastille, the fountain of Rebirth is a stop along the route taken by the procession.

Paris, August 10

It wasn't really much of a celebration. The cannons were fired regularly throughout, but it was not a particularly joyful sound, as all those present were fully aware that the allied forces were steadily marching on Paris.

People sang the martial tune *Chant du Départ* instead of the *Marseillaise*. The large crowds that were out in the streets were not as boisterous as those who had attended the earlier Federation celebrations. The mood was extremely sombre. The Federates were some-what taken aback when they had to allow themselves to be searched on entering the city. Despite all this, the Convention has spared no effort in its preparations for the first anniversary of the fall of the monarchy. It had resolved that the occasion would be a memorable one. A budget of 1.2 million francs had been allocated. Two huge museums were opened, the Louvre and one for French monuments. David had been one of the chief organisers. The big show, awesome in size, was held in five acts centred around five monuments. It started at dawn on the ruins of the Bastille with a huge plaster statue representing Nature. From its 200 breasts the water of life poured. The Speaker of the Convention, Hérault de Séchelles, filled a cup and drank from it before handing it over to the 87 old men bearing the banners of each department. The procession then moved off down the boulevards. It was led by Jacobins carrying their flag showing one eye emerging from clouds. Behind them were the deputies surrounded by a tricoloured ribbon that was held by the Federates. After them came the Paris Commune, the ministers and magistrates and the people of the capital. On several decorated carts, blind people and orphans rode, while a carriage was used to carry urns containing the ashes of martyrs.

A dustcart full of crowns and sceptres was overturned at the foot of a giant statue of Liberty. When Hérault set fire to the symbols of royalty, no less than 3,000 birds were set free. The procession passed along the Boulevard des Italiens, under the triumphal arch dedicated to Equality before arriving at the Invalides.

There it came across another giant statue, the People slaying the Dragon of Federalism. The procession finally halted at the Champ de Mars before the Altar to the Nation that had been erected atop a Holy Mountain. Then, each one of the 87 old men gave the pike he carried to the Speaker of the Assembly, who tied them together. Hérault announced the departments' acceptance of the Constitution: "Never has a more unanimous desire created a greater or more popular Republic. Let us swear to defend the Constitution to the death!" At this, hundreds of thousands of people roared as one.

Reason festival

The festival of the Goddess of Reason, held today on the Place de la Bastille, was a big success. The crowd sang this song to the tune of the "Marseillaise":

O sister dear of kindly nature,
O wise and powerful deity,
Reason, lay low base imposture
And crown serene verity.
Wrest from papism shameful
Its mask stained blood-red,
The cruel serpents downtread
Of its bigotry and ideas baneful.
O Reason, we entreat:
Our minds now subjugate;
Now may thy bright flame
Our errors dissipate.
Trick'd by kings and priests
The French have lived too long
Neath their masters' yoke
And downtrod by charlatans.
They held in shame
Such heinous bondage:
Cast off the chains of its curse;
To the god who rules all
They present their homage.
O Reason, thou who didst bring
Retiring, modest equality,
Let thy presence overwhelming
Brace the reign of true liberty.
As brothers bind men together,
Proof 'gainst false joys,
And cast away our fickle toys;
Guide thy friends
Sincere and true for ever.

Royal symbols are burnt and birds are set free on Revolution Square.

A triumphal arch on the boulevard.

The Salon of sculpture and painting grows ever more popular

Fouché's daughter to be called Nièvre

Paris, August 10

The crowds visiting the Salon of sculpture and painting, which has been open to all ever since 1791, have been getting bigger every day. The former exhibition hall, known as the square Salon, has now become too small and the works of art are beginning to spill over into the other rooms, particularly into the Apollo gallery.

Its walls are covered with works of art, while miniatures are hidden away in the corners by windows and carved busts are lined up on a huge makeshift table. It all looks like a vast, untidy oriental bazaar and the artists have been fighting tooth and nail to see who can claim the best place for his work. A well-placed work gets noticed by the visitors and the judges.

This overcrowding, which some had warned about in 1791, is a direct result of the policy of giving all the possibility to exhibit. The preface of the Salon's booklet is quite explicit about this issue. "Artists are by definition free: genius itself is independent. Genius must live

A very popular work: the "Sommeil d'Endymion" by Girodet Trioson.

forever in France and bring itself up to the level of Liberty." To better serve the cause of free art, the authorities have restored the system of official funding. Some of the exhibited works will be picked out

and "purchased by the nation". Among these paintings there are the portraits of the famous Jacobins Robespierre and Couthon that were painted by the pastellist Ducreaux, a student of Quentin de La Tour.

Nevers, August 10

If there is one revolutionary who is popular among all others it is definitely Fouché. Since he came to Nevers on July 29th., the Convention's new commissioner and the people under his administrative care have been congratulating each other on their good luck. Fouché, a kindly and warm local official, relies more on persuasion than force in his fight against federalism. His faultless family life has added to his reputation and the recent birth of a baby daughter has provided the people of Nevers with an opportunity to demonstrate their friendship for him. A special civic christening ceremony has been held on Federation Square. The National Guard and department authorities stood around Citizen Damour and Citizeness Champrobert, the baby's godfather and godmother. Deeply moved by the ceremony, Fouché has decided to dedicate his child to the friendly department, naming her Nièvre after the region.

Pleyel is forced to prove his loyalty

Strasbourg, August 10

Compose or die: that, in a nutshell, is the choice that was given to Ignace Pleyel by the town council. He was under suspicion. The Austrian-born composer, whose talent for writing religious music has won him a great many friends among the clergy, had been denounced to the authorities seven times before he was finally arrested. As they were not convinced by his protestations of patriotism, the officials ordered him to compose a symphony celebrating the fall of the Tuileries. Relieved, the musician then withdrew to Dorlisheim where he composed the *Tocsin Allégorique* in ten days, under the watchful eye of a guard. The new piece was played today.

Pleyel wrote a dramatic score on the capture of the palace. Seven bells, cannons and rifles were used to make it more realistic. It begins with the people's awakening, gradually building up to a thunderous storm: the attack itself. Amid this noise, royalist songs are drowned out by revolutionary tunes.

The French Monument museum is now open to the public

Paris, August 10

Alexandre Lenoir's day of glory has come at last. His museum on the Rue des Petits Augustins has finally opened its doors to the public. On show are sculptures and pieces of architecture. Few would suspect that this modest but stubborn man sometimes risked his life to save works of art from certain destruction.

For example, when even bronze was being requisitioned by the government, Lenoir hid away two silver angels by Sarrazin and Coustou. In order to save some of the tombs at Saint Denis, he braved the sansculottist mob. As a result, he now has collected 256 works. They include some of the most famous names in sculpture: Germain Pilon, Girardon, Coustou.

The collection even boasts works by the great Michelangelo himself: numbers 98 and 101 on the catalogue are two of his works which were to have been placed in the tomb of Julius II and were given to François I. Alongside such prestigious names, there are numerous anonymous works dating from the Middle Ages.

Alexandre Lenoir trying to stop the destruction of Louis XII's tomb.

11. Paris. The Convention orders each commune to carry out a census of the local population.

12. Paris. The department of Rhône et Loire is split into two parts by the Convention. Lyons used to be its chief town. Two new administrative zones are created: the departments of the Loire and the Rhône.

13. Vendée. The Catholic and royalist army suffers a second major defeat when it tries to capture Luçon.

14. Paris. The Committee of Public Safety recruits two engineers: the military engineer Lazare Carnot and Claude Antoine Prieur Duvernois, known as Prieur de la Côte d'Or.→

15. Besançon. Lack of bread sparks off violent riots.

15. Paris. The new Théâtre National on the Rue Richelieu is inaugurated. It performs a patriotic play, *La Constitution à Constantinople*.

16. Paris. The capital's 48 sectors and the departmental representatives ask the Convention to decree mass levy (→23).

17. Paris. A decree from the Convention orders a general grain stock-taking and rules that any false declaration will mean a ten year jail term.

22. Lyons. The republican artillery starts bombarding the city.

22. Gironde. The supporters of the Convention leave Bordeaux and seek refuge at La Réole, which has been turned into a fortified camp.

22. Mont Blanc. As the royalist supporters in Chambéry, Rumilly and Annecy cause violent riots, the Sardian troops led by the Duc de Montferrat and those under the command of General de Magland occupy Moutiers and Cluses (→Sept. 12, 93).

23. India. Informed of the fall and execution of Louis XVI, General de Clermont hands Pondicherry back to the English forces.→

23. Paris. The Convention decrees a mass levy of all Frenchmen. The young men aged between 18 and 25 and who are either single or widowed without any children, will be among the first to be enrolled in the armed forces.→

Powerful republicans surround the besieged city of Lyons

Lyons, August 14

The Republic has deployed an impressive array of forces around Lyons city, in central France. There is heavy artillery lined up in the plains of Bottreaux and La Guillotière. In all, 10,000 men under the command of General Kellermann are standing by, waiting for the order to overrun the city. Their target is the people of Lyons themselves, who seceded from the Republic last May after the city, tired with being dictated to by extremists, finally rebelled. All the different groups, from the royalists to the moderate republicans, were involved in rising up against the municipal authorities, whose leader, Chalier, was beheaded. The revolt was initially led by the Girondists, but in July control was seized by Précy, an ardent royalist and former officer in the royal army. He was in command of some 10,000 men who had been recruited and armed in the best traditions of the bourgeois militias of Lyons in the Middle Ages. The men have worked tirelessly to build up the city's crumbling fortifications and to set up a defensive perimeter around the Guillotière bridge.

Convention can't have France's second largest city rebel, on top of problems with Vendée and the allies.

Two military men, Carnot and Prieur, join the Committee of Public Safety

Paris, August 14

The nation is in grave danger. Barère has convinced the Committee of Public Safety that the military situation is so serious that army specialists should be called in and entrusted with high political office. Therefore, Prieur de la Côte d'Or and Carnot have just become members of the Committee. Prieur, first elected to the Legislative Assembly then to the Convention, was a special envoy when he was captured by the Caen Federalists last month. Both men are officers and military engineers.

A new clock to save the church's bell

Aveyron, August 15

The old church of the village of Pachins will be allowed to keep its two bells despite a July 25th. Convention decree ruling that a commune cannot have more than one bell. Faced with a flood of angry petitions, the local authorities have agreed to let churches also have a bell that chimes the hours. This was no sooner said than the people of Pachins decided to build a clock so their beloved village church can keep its two bells.

Hollow cannonball is being tested

La Fère, August 20

The concept may have been a simple one, but its practical application was far from easy. Choderlos de Laclos had the idea of having hollow cannonballs which could be filled with the nitrate powder that was invented by the chemist Berthollet. This would make them far more devastating explosive weapons than the traditional solid cannonballs. But the test carried out today by the artillery officer François Fabre as Berthollet and Laclos stood by was not particularly satisfactory. The hollow cannonballs only worked over a short range. However, the inventor has not given up hope (→Oct. 20).

Madame Manon Roland's coded secrets

Paris, August 15

From her prison cell, Madame Manon Roland has again been able to write a letter full of endearments to Buzot. Ever since she realised that she was to be permanently kept away from her beloved, who is in hiding at Caen, she no longer feels any guilt about loving him. Despite the danger they are both in, the two lovers are able to keep in touch. As a precaution, Manon uses a secret code which only they can decipher. For herself, she uses the code name *Sophie* and writes of her imprison-

ment as a *disease* for which there is no known cure. Her poor husband Roland, who is dying of jealousy in his Rouen hideout, is described as her impotent *old uncle* who is in very bad health. As for Buzot himself, he has been turned into a businessman who is unfortunately experiencing some financial problems. "Farewell, thou most beloved man of the most loving woman," she writes. "Ah, let me tell you, all is not yet lost, with such a heart, whatever fortune may bring, it is yours forever."

Girondists set sail for Bordeaux

Brest, August 21

A small boat has just sailed from the port of Brest under the cover of darkness. On board, there are nine Girondists, including Girey Dupré and Cussy. They hope to reach Bordeaux soon. They were forced to flee from Normandy on foot to seek refuge in Brittany, where their friend Kervélégan, who is also the target of an arrest warrant, gave them shelter. Pétion, Guadet and

Buzot decided to remain with their companion Barbaroux, who is now recovering from the fatigue of their long march. Hidden inside an isolated house near Quimper, they will wait for him to get better before they too set sail. For the time being, they feel safe in Brittany, where the people do not like the Montagnards and the commissioners of the Convention don't yet dare to enforce the laws dictated by Paris.

Bordeaux kicks out envoys from Paris

Gironde, August 22

The climate in the Gironde is not always suitable for Jacobins. Two special envoys from the Convention, Baudot and Ysabeau, had been sent to Bordeaux to restore order following the attempted revolt in the region, but they soon found out they were not welcome. The local people's Public Safety commission, set up after the events of June 2nd. in Paris by the Girondist members of the General Council, has resigned. It did not have

enough members to be able to plan to march on Paris. Some of the more hot-headed young men in Bordeaux would like the Jacobins to stay there a long time. The Convention had angered the people of Bordeaux by declaring that the members of the "so-called people's commission" were traitors to the nation. Faced with such hostility from the local population, the two emissaries from the Convention have decided to leave Bordeaux to seek refuge at La Réole (→ Sept. 21).

Pondicherry surrenders to the English

Pondicherry, August 23

The people have been cheering the English, an unheard of sight in Pondicherry. A great cheer went up this afternoon when the siege of Pondicherry was finally lifted. The town only surrendered to the English after news of Louis XVI's death had reached it. All land and sea exits had been blocked by English forces since June 24th., but the French held out until August 13th. hoping that reinforcements from

the Ile de France would arrive. That day, however, the colonial assembly ordered the fighting to stop and asked the governor to negotiate the town's surrender. The deputies had just read newspaper accounts of the King's execution. When the English marched in, they heard shouts of "Long live Louis XVI!" The act of surrender signed yesterday states that the colony will be British until order is restored in France.

The mass troop levy

"Sacred battalion defending the Constitution against the tyrants' slaves."

Paris, August 23

"From this moment on, and until all the enemies have been chased off the territory of the Republic, all Frenchmen are under permanent requisition for service in the army." Those were the words used by Barère when he spoke before the Convention to submit his report and propose a draft law for an immediate mass levy of soldiers. When Robespierre said it was enough to "punish the traitors" to save the military situation, Barère replied that all France's energy must be mobilised to defeat the enemy. The decree stipulates that "the young men will go into combat, married men will produce weapons and transport food and equipment, women will make tents and work in hos-

pitals, children will shred old linen, old men will get themselves carried to public places so that they can stir up the warriors' courage, preach the hatred of kings and the unity of the Republic".

The nation is calling for everybody to play a role in the conflict. Such a move has been demanded by the sectors of Paris for several weeks. Danton has suggested that the requisition of manpower be carried out directly by the primary assemblies in order to avoid administrative delays. The decree approved today also defines the new strategy for the waging of a revolutionary war. The French army will focus on the tactic of mass offensives that are designed to crush the enemy as quickly as possible.

Markets are empty despite good crops

Paris, August 20

Only one bag of wheat was delivered today at the noon market, although the harvest has been plentiful. Despite the law, peasants are refusing to sell their crops in exchange for assignats that are worth less with each passing day. The loss of this currency's value has been making trade between towns and the provinces more difficult and people are resorting to barter. Starving, the poor of Evreux are increasingly angry with those responsible for their misfortunes. Some are accusing wealthy farmers of counter-revolutionary hoarding.

Jules François Paré, the former head clerk in Danton's office, is appointed to the Interior Ministry on August 20th.

Convention

24. Lyons. The explosion of the arsenal, caused by the bombardment of the city by republican troops, sparks off a huge blaze.

24. Paris. Following a proposal made by Cambon on August 15th., the Convention draws up a vast Register of Debts on which all the Republic's debtors are to be listed.

24. Toulon. Admiral Hood, who yesterday contacted the general security committee that governs the port city, sets conditions for an intervention by the Anglo-Spanish fleet. He demands that the forts be handed over, that the squadron be disarmed, the sharing of the city's defence and the proclamation of Louis XVII as the new King (→28).

25. Marseilles. The republican forces led by General Jean François Carteaux capture the town as it was about to be handed over to the English by the royalists.

25. Paris. Doctor Philippe Pinel, a respected mental health specialist, is appointed to the capital's Bicêtre hospital (→Sept. 11, 93).

25. Saint Emilion. The former mayor of Paris, Jérôme Pétion, finds shelter at the home of the wigmaker Troquart.

25. Versailles. The public auction of the contents of the palace begins. It will take one year to sell all the lots. →

26. Paris. Gossec plays the famous *Marche Funèbre* at the Tuileries in honour of the victims of August 10th. 1792.

27. Charleville. Departure for Paris of 1,200 workers of the Maubeuge arms factory who had sought refuge at Charleville. They are to repair damaged rifles.

28. Paris. The revolutionary Tribunal sentences General Custine to death. He is guillotined at once.→

29. Saint Domingue. The commissioners of the Republic, Sonthonax and Polverel, proclaim the immediate freeing of all slaves.→

29. Toulon. Admiral Hood and Admiral Langara of Spain are officially received. Betrayed by their leaders, many French sailors try to join the republican camp.

30. Paris. At the Jacobins Club, Abbot Royer asks that the Terror be debated.

The furniture of the palace of Versailles goes on public auction

A list of the objects on sale.

The contents of Marie Antoinette's golden dressing-room draws admirers.

Versailles, August 25

It is 10 o'clock on a Sunday morning and there is already a large crowd at the palace. They have all come to attend the first public auction of the contents of Versailles: furniture and precious objects that used to belong to Louis XVI and Marie Antoinette. All is to go under the auctioneer's hammer. The most exceptional objects have already been taken to the Museum. The rest have been grouped in lots and a list of them was published by French and foreign newspapers. The advance publicity has brought many English lords, Russian and Polish princes and representatives of the courts of Europe. They have been told that the objects may be taken abroad "without any taxes" being paid. Among those attending, there are former noblemen who have not emigrated but chosen to "democratise" their names, as well as many speculators.

A pigeon makes his nest on Liberty

Paris, August

It looks like a common pigeon will succeed in stealing the great David's limelight. A lot of people have been coming every day to gaze at the statue of Liberty that was erected for the celebration of August 10th. on Revolution Square. However, their admiring glances have been focused not on David's work of art, but on the pigeon that has built its nest in the folds of the statue's veil. It was one of the birds that had been released during the celebrations and had landed on Liberty's giant shoulders.

The India Company is in deep trouble

Paris, August 24

Like all the insurance firms and those with shares, the hugely rich India Company must go into liquidation. Since it had lost the monopoly on trade with the Far East in 1790, the financial firm had mainly invested in shipbuilding. The deputies Pierre Cambon and Joseph Delaunay have been appointed by the government to oversee this liquidation, as well as that of the other firms. The law banning trading companies was approved thanks to Delaunay's efforts. For the past six months, he had been criticising the "capitalism and speculation" that had been going on for the benefit of Austria and the Vendeans. He had accused the firms of having stolen 40 million livres from the nation and of being involved in speculation to lower the value of assignats. Philippe Fabre d'Eglantine, another of Danton's friends, even claimed that some companies had agents in London who were acting on Pitt's orders and seeking to ruin France. The former Capuchin, François Chabot, and Jean Julien, a member of the Committee of Public Safety, also accused the India Company of falsifying its accounts. But some deputies are sceptical about their zeal, as all four of them are linked to the founder of a life insurance firm, Baron Jean de Batz. They were once guests of this daring speculator who hardly hides his royalist opinions (→Sept. 18).

The fops of Lyons are massacred

Loire, August 25

A group of "Muscadins," as the young dandies of Lyons are known, have been killed and butchered. Their column, which had set out from Saint Chamond under the command of the young Servan, was unable to cross the Gier river. When they spotted the men from Lyons approach, the local villagers rose up and rushed to defend the Egarande bridge at Rive de Gier. They were helped by the dragoons from Lorraine. The sansculottists gave the Muscadins a thrashing and forced them to pull back. The Lyonnais then sheltered inside a barn at Logis des Flaches. Hemmed in, Servan's small group fought back for several hours, but they were totally outnumbered. Some of them managed to escape into the woods, but they were soon caught and their throats were slit. Servan was captured by the dragoons along with 13 of his companions. The others were massacred. That was when the butchery started. Their bodies were stripped and a woman, Tatasse, emasculated them.

Robespierre's best friend gets married

Paris, August 26

Philippe Le Bas has just married Elisabeth Duplay with the blessing of Robespierre. The secret had been kept right up to the last moment. Philippe had proposed six days ago and the bride's parents had asked Robespierre what he thought of the suitor.

Robespierre was only too happy to see his best friend get married to the woman he has always considered as his own sister. The republican wedding ceremony was celebrated privately at the local community hall. There were four witnesses present: the painter David, Hébert, Robespierre himself and the young woman's uncle.

A former minister defends his record

Sens, August 30

It was not for being an archbishop that Loménie de Brienne was arrested on orders from the Convention earlier this month, but for his record as a former minister of Louis XVI. He is accused of having made a decision on July 31st. 1788 which is claimed to have cost the Treasury eight million livres. He was summoned to Paris to explain himself before the Finance Committee. The old prelate was able to explain matters and the arrest order, temporarily suspended on August 19th., has now been permanently lifted.

The Federalists of Provence hand Toulon over to the English

Toulon, August 28

The English have achieved a foothold in the Mediterranean. That can easily be seen by looking at the flags flown by the ships now at anchor in Toulon harbour. The English did not have to resort to force: Admiral Hood was invited in. For the past several months, the port city has been turned into a powder keg by the intense rivalry between the Jacobin town council and the department authorities, who are royalist. At the urging of the Jacobins, 17 people, including four departmental officials, were killed in September. In response, 24 Jacobins were massacred. Feeling threatened by the arrival of Convention troops, the port's inhabitants chose to hand the city over to the English. At Marseilles, more or less the same sequence of events took place, except they ended in a different way. Three days ago, the Convention's troops seized control of the town just before the arrival of the English, who had been called in to help. The Federalists of Marseilles who managed to escape have sought refuge in Toulon. The loss of Toulon is serious: it means that the English now control the forts, the ammunition dumps, the warships and cargo vessels of France's leading port ($\rightarrow$ Aug. 29).

The French fleet and the navy shipyards are now in the hands of the English, greeted as liberators.

Saint Domingue frees its black slaves

Saint Domingue, August 29

Some 500,000 blacks are expected to take advantage today of the decree abolishing slavery that has been promulgated by the civil commissioners Polverel and Sonthonax. One year after they arrived in the French colony, these two envoys who wield considerable power have finally decided to free all the slaves. They hope that this humanitarian move will help keep Saint Domingue within the French Republic. The war against Spain and England has made it practically impossible for France to defend its colony. The English could land troops there whenever they wish as there is no French navy squadron in the Caribbean. As for the Spanish, they already own the eastern part of the island. If it is to be defended, all republican forces must be mobilised. The troops led by General Laveaux were unable to defend the territory so long as the black insurrection continued to rage. For the past month the two commissioners have been trying to negotiate with the rebels through the priest of Dondon. Until today, the leaders of the black slaves had rejected all offers. But the freeing of the slaves should help change that. However, the leaders did say that only the decrees from Paris mattered.

Windward Islands are defenceless

Barbados, August 27

The frigate commanded by Captain Lacrosse, *Félicité,* has set sail for Brest. Its crew is refusing to stay in the Caribbean Sea any longer. This departure has put an end to a successful campaign. It was the same frigate that had got the Windward Islands, Martinique and Guadeloupe to rally to the French Republic. Now it has gone, the governor has no naval protection: the squadron led by Morard de Galles, expected since January, is still blocked by the English on the coast of Brittany.

Accused by Hébert of spying for the Prussians, General Custine was guillotined on August 28th.

1. Ille et Vilaine. Jean Baptiste Carrier and Pierre Pocholles arrive in Rennes. They have been ordered to "wipe out all traces of federalism".

2. Paris. At the Convention, Billaud Varenne attacks the Committee of Public Safety for not having informed the public of the arrival of the English in Toulon and of the attempts by the insurgents of Marseilles to hand the city over to the enemy.

3. Paris. The Théâtre de la Nation is shut down for having performed *Paméla*, a play by François de Neufchâteau deemed to be counter-revolutionary. Barère states that the theatre must be the "primary school of enlightened men".

5. Paris. Under pressure from the sansculottists, the deputies agree to place the Terror on the agenda. →

6. Paris. Billaud Varenne and Collot d'Herbois join the Committee of Public Safety.

6. Nantes. The vanguard of the Mainz army led by Jean Baptiste Kléber arrives.

7. Paris. The Convention orders the arrest of foreign bankers and rules that seals are to be placed on their documents.

8. Hondschoote. The victory of General Houchard over the Anglo-Hanoverian army led by the Duke of York forces the Duke to end the siege of Dunkirk. →

9. Paris. Admiral Trogoff, commander of the squadron of Toulon, is declared a traitor for having handed his fleet over to the English.

9. Paris. The Convention musters an internal revolutionary army led by the supporter of Hébert, Charles Ronsin, to ensure that supplies reach the capital (→ Oct. 3, 93).

11. Paris. A decree from the Convention sets a maximum price limit for grains at a national level (→ 29).

12. Toulon. The authorities publish a declaration of allegiance to Monsieur, the Comte de Provence and Regent of France.

12. Lyons. General Kellermann, commander of the forces in the Alps, launches an offensive against Sardian troops which have reoccupied Savoy. The region will be liberated within three weeks.

Concern grows and people call for action

The sansculottists: a street army.

Paris, September 4

This evening, a huge crowd invaded the Commune. The thousands of Parisians who this morning had gathered on the boulevards and the Place de Grève have come to complain that they can no longer stand the burden of the cost of living and the scarcity of food. Public anger and grumbling increased in August and things have finally come to a head. On top of everything else, there is the war. People have just found out that Toulon has been handed over to the English following a royalist trick. The already poor political climate is being poisoned by a feeling of betrayal. The sansculottists are demanding that the government deal mercilessly with traitors, starting with those of the Gironde. Faced with the crisis, the government doesn't appear to be doing anything, which is why today's demonstration was held. Taken aback by the invasion of their offices, both Chaumette and Hébert moved fast and took control of the situation. Hébert asked the people to go to the Assembly tomorrow and to besiege it "until the nation's representatives have taken steps to save us". But the Jacobins are not about to be outdone. They too have decided to go to the Convention to demand action (→ Sept. 5).

Two commissioners on holiday in Nice

Nice, September 1

Some official missions can turn out to be far more pleasant than others. Last March, Fréron and Baras were appointed commissioners of the Convention for the departments of the Hautes and the Basses Alpes. Since then, the two men have been inseparable. They both work and relax together. Before setting off for Toulon, they decided to take some well-earned time off in south-eastern France, in the seaside town of Nice. The two friends are making the best of the sunny weather and the sea air. They are also spending a lot of their spare time with some lovely ladies.

The deputy Stanislas Fréron.

Doctors voice opposition to the policy of locking up mentally ill

Paris, September 11

Change is also coming to the sad world of mental asylums. Doctor Pinel and some of his colleagues are looking into the possibility of actually trying to cure the mentally ill. Until now, the policy had been simply to lock them up so that they could not harm society. But times have changed. Jacques Tenon, the surgeon, has just stated in his report on hospitals that: "It is only after all possible recourses have been exhausted that one can consider the unpleasant necessity of depriving a citizen of his freedom." For his part, Doctor George Cabanis, in his *Rules on the Admission of the Mad*, recommended that mental asylums should be made more humane and medical facilities there be improved. Philippe Pinel is one of those who consider mental illness as a disease and want to treat it "morally" rather than just "physically". Appointed to the infirmary of Bicêtre hospital last month, he found it was full of "criminals and fierce men", but also of victims of "arbitrary power, the tyranny of families and paternal despotism". These men are "our equals whose freedom has been taken". His first move was to remove their chains.

Doctor Pinel ordering mental patients to be freed from their chains.

Steelworkers don't have to go to war

Dordogne, September

There are many able-bodied men who are jealous of those who now work in the nation's steel mills. Their work is considered to be of vital importance to the war effort and so they don't have to go to the front. There is increasing rivalry between steelworkers and peasants. At the demand of the local inhabitants, the town council of Mareuil has decided to check every factory to see if the men working there are really helping the war effort. In some firms, they found under paid workers, while in others there were "tall, strong and fortunate youths" who are paid to do nothing.

Conscripts murder and cause havoc

Saint Dié, September 4

The people of the region of the Vosges are not about to forget the mass levy.

Blood has been spilt there for the first time since 1789. One year after the September massacres in Paris, the same kind of atrocities have been committed at Saint Dié. On the eve of their departure to the war front, the town's inebriated volunteers decided to kill the prisoners so that there would be "no enemies left behind". For four whole days, a bloodthirsty mob of drunken conscripts seeking revenge laid waste to the town, killing the prisoners. It was only when a new detachment of (sober) volunteers marched into town that a semblance of order was restored.

The Terror is placed on the agenda

Jacques Billaud Varenne.

Paris, September 5

The people of Paris have jammed the Convention's main hall, led by the capital's mayor, Pache, and the public prosecutor of the Commune, Chaumette. "No quarter!" Chaumette screamed. During yesterday's demonstrations, the mob had demanded bread, and death for the "starvers". These demands have been heard by the Commune. It ordered the deputies to set up by decree a special tribunal for food hoarders, a revolutionary army and to ensure that as much grain as possible be made available. Also yesterday, Robespierre condemned the unrest and attributed it to the action of "a few plotters". It is Robespierre who is today presiding over the session of the Assembly. In order to keep a measure of control over the situation, he allowed a Jacobin delegation join the representatives of the city. The Jacobin demands had not been directly connected to the current food crisis. Initially, they demanded the immediate sentencing of the Girondist prisoners, then the man who spoke on their behalf cried: "It is time for equality to wield its scythe over all the heads. Very well, legislator, place Terror on the agenda!" His words were greeted by loud cheering. This morning, the deputies approved the division of the revolutionary Tribunal into four bodies that are to meet non-stop to make sure that the prisoners are judged more quickly. After the demonstrators arrived, the deputies approved in principle the plan to set up a revolutionary army, the arrest of all suspects and the reorganisation of the Committee of Public Safety.

Jean Marie Collot d'Herbois.

Two supporters of Robespierre, Billaud Varenne and Collot d'Herbois, have joined the Committee. Danton was also asked to join, but he refused. He had been the one who had taken steps to put an end to grassroots pressure on the Assembly. He also got approval for a special bonus to be paid to all participants in sector meetings to counteract the influence of the Enragé minority, thus giving the Jacobins and the executive more room to manoeuvre (→Sept. 6 and 9).

General Houchard defeats the allied troops at Hondschoote

Hondschoote, September 8

French troops have just won a victory. The Anglo-Hanoverian forces led by the Duke of York have retreated so quickly that they left behind 52 heavy cannons as well as ammunition and equipment. General Jean Nicolas Houchard can be proud of his men. During a battle that raged for two days, he was able to get his 45,000 men to outfight the 35,000 enemy soldiers. The French victory has come at a good time as the situation on the northern front is critical. Since the start of the month, the Prince of Saxe-Coburg has been in control of the forts at Condé, Valenciennes and Cateau Cambrésis. Moreover, the French army's morale is low: the defeat suffered by Dumouriez at Neerwinden had dealt a severe blow to French hopes in Belgium and the memory of the setback at Mainz was another burden. There is one more reason for the French to be pleased: the English troops preferred to head for Dunkirk rather than Paris although the road to the capital was clear.

Spain is afraid of French Constitution

Spain, September 4

The royal Spanish court is afraid of the spread of revolutionary politics. The royal household has just ordered that the text of the French Constitution is to be banned in Spain. The authorities had heard of an imminent delivery of some 3,000 copies of the text. It was high time to do something as several Barcelona lawyers have already seen the text, which they found to be particularly interesting.

England's Duke of York.

The battle's death toll is heavy: a total of some 6,000 men killed.

13. Paris. The Committee of General Security is reorganised. A deputy from the Ariège, Vadier, the painter David and Amar from Grenoble become members.

13. Paris. An actor from the Théâtre de la Nation, Larive, is arrested. He is suspected of having sheltered the former mayor of Paris, Bailly, who is being sought for his rôle in the shooting on the Champ de Mars.

14. Paris. Churches are stripped of all coats of arms and any other signs of monarchy or feudalism.

15. Corsica. The republicans besieged inside Saint Florent by supporters of Paoli reject an offer from Admiral Hood to follow the example of Toulon and rally to Louis XVII.

15. Austrian Netherlands. General Houchard, the recent victor at Hondschoote, is defeated by Anglo-Hanoverian troops at Menin.

16. Montaigu. The forces led by Charette, which operate independently from other Vendean troops, are routed by republican soldiers.

17. Paris. The Convention approves the law on suspects. →

18. Maine et Loire. The Catholic and royalist army defeats the republican forces led by Santerre at Coron. →

18. Bordeaux. Sansculottists overthrow the federated municipal authorities as the representatives Tallien and Ysabeau unleash the Terror.

18. On the orders of the Committee of General Security, the supporter of Hébert, Varlet, is arrested for having led the Droits de l'Homme sector's opposition against the decree of September 9th. on the sectors' assemblies.

18. Paris. At the Convention, there is a clash between Billaud Varenne and Collot d'Herbois, who states that "we must fight with pikes and stop relying on rifles".

18. Paris. The Revolutionary Republican Club asks the Commune to ensure that prostitutes are detained in state-run homes, where the wives of émigrés can also be held.

19. Maine et Loire. Forces led by Kléber and Marceau are defeated by the Catholic and royalist army. →

An "anti-suspect" law is approved

The first "suspects" are summoned before the revolutionary committee.

Paris, September 17

All enemies of the Revolution, be they real or simply presumed, are to be placed under arrest and held until the war is over. This draconian law, proposed by Merlin de Douai, has just been approved. Its definition of what constitutes a "suspect" is sufficiently vague for the law to act as a catch-all. Obviously, it is in part aimed at the émigrés, but it also includes all their relatives "who have not demonstrated a constant attachment to the Revolution". It targets the ousted public officials and all those who have been refused certificates of patriotism. But it also affects "those who by their behaviour, their relationships or what they have written have shown themselves to be supporters of tyranny or federalism and enemies of liberty". In other words, people who will be considered "suspect" are those who "cannot justify having acquitted themselves of their patriotic duties and who cannot justify their livelihood". The Revolution has no time for tramps. The new law is to be enforced by revolutionary committees and this is to give them tremendous power. The new committees will only have to account for the arrests they carry out to the Committee of General Security. This is a decisive move that is to mark the birth of a sort of legalised Terror that will sweep the country.

Many of the "suspects" are arrested after having been informed on.

An abbey is to be a military hospital

Aisne, September 13

Citizen Acloque, the official in charge of military hospitals for the northern army, has agreed to have the former Thénailles Abbey turned into a military hospital. The building had been sold in 1792 to an innkeeper after it was seized by the state. He tore down large parts of it to sell the stone. A lot of work will have to be carried out before it can serve as a hospital. However, there are so many wounded or ill people that there is no time to be lost. Ten heavy covered carts, each pulled by four horses and with some straw in the back, have already brought the first patients to the rudimentary and ill-equipped hospital.

French war effort: roof-lead needed

Bournazel, September 17

The roof of the ancient castle of Bournazel, parts of which are lined with lead, had escaped serious damage during the riots of 1790. But it will not escape from the war effort. The local district council met today and decided it was "not enough to levy men for war, they must have ammunition to fight with". It has ruled that the castle's occupant must now tear the lead down from the roof so it can be melted down and made into bullets. It based its ruling on article 19 of the 1793 Constitution which states: "a citizen may be deprived of his property when this is required by public necessity".

A deputy suspected of shady deals

Paris, September 18

The Convention has given orders for the residence of the deputy Jean Julien to be thoroughly searched. He was ousted from the Committee of General Security four days ago. Documents were found proving that he had been involved in suspicious deals with the army's supplier in the Alps, while at the same time he had publicly criticised the greed of businessmen. Other papers revealed that he had accepted money to protect aristocrats in trouble. The officials also found piles of shares in the insurance firm owned by Baron de Batz, known to be an acquaintance of his, worth a total of 100,000 livres.

"Monsieur Henri" is hit by a bullet

The injured young Vendean general continues to fire with his good hand.

Maine et Loire, September 13

Wounded but victorious. It was with a thumb that had been shattered by a bullet that La Rochejaquelein led his men and after a long, bloody battle managed to beat a republican army from Saumur at Martigné Briand. At one point, "Monsieur Henri" had been alone with his aide-de-camp and his bat-

man when three republican soldiers suddenly appeared. As they were running away, one of the three fired wildly, hitting La Rochejaquelein in the right thumb. The young General said the painful wound "spoiled the joy of victory". He fought bravely till the enemy had been beaten and has begun to teach himself to shoot with his left hand.

A volunteer's child gets a godfather

Aveyron, September 19

A baby who was just born at Saint Aubin has been given a good republican start in life. The president of the departmental authorities has agreed to be godfather to the child, whose father is a volunteer. "Law and fairness make it the administration's duty to replace his father, who, forgetting all about

nature's sweetest affections, has torn himself away from his family to rush to the defence of the nation." The people of the Aveyron are not at all keen about joining the army, so this was a good opportunity to encourage local fathers to enlist by showing them that their children would be well taken care of during their absence.

Former Mainz troops are among the best

Maine et Loire, September 19

The anti-republican Vendean forces have good reason to fear the army troops that had to surrender at Mainz.

These republican soldiers are now considered to be among the most fearsome and efficient of the nation's fighting men. They had only surrendered Mainz after putting up fierce resistance and suffering heavy losses. Now they have been sent to Vendée to fight against the Catholic and royalist army. Their vanguard, under the command of Kléber, has suffered a temporary setback at Torfou. This was not just due to the considerable bravery and skill of the Vendean forces. Kléber's men found themselves totally isolated because of a lack of proper coordination among the leaders of the republican forces. Despite this problem, the pull-back of the men from Mainz was orderly and they intend to come back to the attack and win a decisive victory against the enemies of the Republic.

Gen. de Charette

The Vendean victory at Tiffauge has made de Charette a popular man. A song has been composed about him which the Chouans know off by heart:

*In every province
You hear people say
That there's a new prince;
And they say in Vendée
That his name is Charette.
May God bless his soul!
And with this octet
His fame we'll extol!
This friend of the king
A hindrance did bring
To France's fair land
In England, with cheers,
His praises they tell;
On all the frontiers,
And in Paris as well.
Despite cannonade,
He strikes with intent,
And neath fusillade
He cries: Regiment!
Your voices let ring,
Exacting vengeance
For the death of our king.*

A republican retreat turns into a rout

Maine et Loire, September 18

Republican hopes have just been cruelly shattered. When Antoine Joseph Santerre had set out from Saumur leading a large force of republican troops, he had been sure of victory. But when he sent his men into a narrow valley near Coron, the unfortunate General was ambushed by a horde of men who had been lying in wait in the woods overlooking the valley. As they tried to retreat, Santerre's

troops were hampered by their own artillery which was blocking the narrow road along which they had marched. The defeat soon became a rout as many of the republican soldiers had never fought before. Santerre had to run for his life, although there were rumours that he had been killed. This gave birth to an ironic epitaph for Santerre, once a Paris brewer: "Here lies General Santerre, whose only god of war was beer".

Santerre may be a good brewer, but he is not a very good general.

Convention

20. Paris. The Convention decrees that all those who attempt to avoid the draft will face jail sentences.

21. Paris. Threatened with arrest, the Cordelier Club member Leclerc, a friend of Marat, is forced to suspend publication of his newspaper *L'Ami du Peuple par Leclerc*.

21. Nevers. Fouché and Chaumette inaugurate a bust of Brutus at the Nevers cathedral. This marks the beginning of a wave of de-Christianisation in France (→Oct. 9, 93).

21. Paris. In response to the move to stop British grain exports to France taken on June 8th. by William Pitt, Barère gets the Convention to pass a navigation act which states that all imports must be shipped aboard French ships.

22. Paris. The Constitutional Bishop of Dordogne, Pontard, presents his young wife, the clairvoyant Suzette Labrousse, to the Convention.

23. Paris. The Committee of Public Safety orders all the workers of Paris to manufacture rifles.

23. Paris. Perrin, the deputy of the Aube, is sent before the revolutionary Tribunal on charges of hoarding.

24. Paris. The Convention places the northern army under the command of Jean Baptiste Jourdan.→

25. Paris. At the Convention, Robespierre clashes violently with backers of Danton, who have proposed the appointment of Briez, responsible for the surrender of Valenciennes, as assistant head of the Committee of Public Safety.→

26. Paris. Changes are made in the revolutionary Tribunal: the judges and juries are chosen from a list submitted jointly by the Public Safety and General Security committees.

28. Paris. Abbot Grégoire, who has been asked to record heroic acts inspired by the Revolution, gives the Convention a draft of his "Annals of Patriotism".

29. Paris. The Convention decrees the nationwide General Maximum fixing a top price for most goods and a maximum for wages.→

29. Lyons. During their advance, the republican troops arrest Bishop Lamourette.

The Convention does not forgive failure from those who command the army

Houchard will face treason charge.

Paris, September 24

Heads are going to roll. General Jean Nicolas Houchard is already certain to lose his own. The revolutionary Tribunal is blaming him for having been too slow to come to the help of the troops at Mainz. Worse still, he is charged with being totally responsible for the rout that followed the capture of Menin. His successor as leader of France's northern army, the newly appointed General Jean Baptiste Jourdan, a man who has risen through the ranks, was not too sure about accepting the promotion. But one can hardly refuse a request from the Convention as this may brand you as a counter-revolutionary. Houchard's case is far from being an isolated one. The men in charge of the Moselle and Rhine armies, Schauenbourg and Landremont, have both been relieved of their duties, the first for not having defeated Pirmasens 10 days ago and the second for saying he could not hold the Wissembourg lines.

Chabot adores both women and wealth

Paris, September 23

The Frey brothers have discovered Chabot's Achilles heel: he can't resist women or money. Two weeks after they first met him, the two bankers succeeded in getting their hooks into the former Capuchin turned deputy. They offered him their sister and her fortune. The marriage contract was signed this morning and it is most appealing for a penniless man: a dowry of 250,000 livres, food and housing and an annual pension of 4,000 livres for the couple. This was a pact linking the bankers to an elected official. Nobody asked for the bride's opinion (→Oct. 5).

Chabot, deputy of Loir et Cher.

Robespierre beats Danton's friends

Paris, September 25

Robespierre has just outfoxed a plot against the Committee of Public Safety hatched by Danton and his friends. Unhappy about being cut off from power by the supporters of Robespierre, they had decided to get the emissary Briez to be appointed assistant to the head of the Committee. Urged on by Merlin de Thionville, Briez immediately started lashing out at what he said were the Committee's arbitrary methods. Thuriot, a Danton supporter, went even further: "We must stop this impetuous torrent that is dragging us all down into barbarity." The Assembly was upset by these attacks, but then Robespierre stood up and said clearly: "Whoever seeks to divide the Convention is an enemy of the state." This was enough to swing the deputies and silence the accusers.

Bordeaux remains under suspicion

Bordeaux, September 21

The emissaries from Paris were refusing to enter Bordeaux as long as the former rebel town council was not dissolved. That has now been done. The port city's new administrators, whose politics are Jacobin, have claimed that "perfect unity now reigns" in Bordeaux. This assurance did not fully convince the envoys, particularly after events there. In place of words, they have called for concrete steps: armed men must be sent to the borders and those suspected of federalism must be dealt with.

The symbols of the French Republic are used to decorate patriotic red, white and blue wallpaper.

Laclos wants to be forgotten by all

Paris, September 20

Choderlos de Laclos has now left the army. He has given up his rank of brigadier, which he was awarded exactly a year ago for his very useful contribution to the victory at Valmy. He hopes that by leaving the army he will avoid becoming a target for the revolutionary forces that were unleashed by the terrible law on "suspects". Laclos could indeed become a target, chiefly because of his notorious links with the Orléans faction. Also, since he is a military man who was recently freed from jail, he could now be placed in the same boat as those public officials who were suspended from office and kept out.

The General Farm on the way out

Paris, September 26

The Convention has appointed the deputy Antoine Dupin to keep an eye on the commissioners who have been ordered to dismantle the General Farm. He was a former official of the General Farm, who not so long ago called himself Dupin de Beaumont. The only problem now is that Antoine hates his former employers. He has never hesitated to call them crooks at the Assembly. He often acted as if he was the people's spokesman against this hated symbol of arbitrary taxation and the injustices of the Ancien Régime. He is now doing his best to demonstrate how corrupt the farmers general are.

Plant wheat in your gardens

Saint Etienne, September 28

These are lean and hungry times and the local district administration has issued the following ruling to the people of Saint Etienne: "We request all those who own gardens to plant March wheat in them, given that the luxury of gardens makes useful and vital production impossible and instead covers with flowers a soil that regretfully gives forth its nourishing juices for plants whose sole use is to be caressed lovingly."

The General Maximum is decreed

Paris, September 29

The Convention has taken one more step towards enforcing a far stronger economic policy. Despite being in favour of the freedom of trade, it has grudgingly decided to vote for the law on the General Maximum.

From now on, the price of most foodstuffs and consumer goods will be set by department authorities. They will have to ensure that prices do not rise more than 30 per cent above what they were three years ago, in 1790, despite the effects of inflation. However, wages are to be allowed to be 50 per cent higher than they were in 1790. The legislators were fully aware of the arbitrary nature of these decisions, but they acted under strong political pressure and on the basis of the measures approved on September 5th. First of all, their moves are aimed at restoring calm and satisfying pressing demands for higher wages by the people of Paris. Ever since last February, the people had been calling for such moves, as were the Enragés, now safely under lock and key. Some kind of decisive action had been urgently called for as the economy had to be placed on a war footing to help defend the nation and pay for military equipment. As Barère pointed out when he summed up the law: "The Republic is the temporary owner of all that is produced on the territory of France by commerce, industry and agriculture."

Patriot arrests Speculation thanks to the Maximum brandished by Wisdom.

France's higher education in art keeps its traditional values

Ancient themes and neoclassical designs are taught at the Academy.

Paris, September 28

The Republic's authorities may have attacked and defeated the academies, but they carefully avoided doing anything to breathe new life and change the institutions of higher art education. Among the most notable of these is Paris's special school of painting and sculpture, and the one devoted to architecture. These hold an regular entrance examination every six months. The school of painting and sculpture teaches the drawing of models or of ancient stonework, as well as the study of anatomy and perspective. France's future architects learn the history and theory of their chosen discipline. They are also given lessons in mathematics with practical work done on the behaviour of building materials. For the most part, their professors used to be members of the former academies who are firm believers in the old traditions. But since the academies have been dissolved, it doesn't seem necessary to change the time-tested teaching methods. That would be a difficult task.

Convention

1. Paris. A delegation from the people's societies asks the Convention to put Brissot and the imprisoned Girondist deputies on trial.

1. Paris. The Convention urges the army in western France to get the war against the Vendeans over as quickly as possible.→

2. Paris. The Convention decides that the ashes of René Descartes are to be honoured and placed in the Panthéon.→

3. Paris. On the basis of a report from Amar, 46 deputies, most of them Girondists, are charged and 73 others are arraigned. Robespierre had been opposed to all the protesters being charged. On the same day, the deputies decide that Marie Antoinette is to be brought before the revolutionary Tribunal as soon as possible.

4. Paris. The Commune's general council forbids prostitutes from soliciting in the streets and bans erotic books and engravings.→

4. Paris. After his appointment as commander of the Rhine army on September 28th., Jean Charles Pichegru is promoted to the rank of major general.

5. Paris. The Convention adopts the new republican calendar drawn up by Gilbert Romme (→ Nov. 24, 93). Since the republican era is supposed to have begun with the founding of the Republic on September 22nd., 1792, the calendar that is to be used starting tomorrow will begin at Year II.

7 (Vendémiaire 16, Year II) Reims. The special envoy Philippe Jacques Ruhl breaks the Holy Ampulla used during the consecration of the kings of France.→

7 (Vendémiaire 16, Year II) Paris. The Girondist Gorsas is arrested, tried and executed all on the same day.

8 (Vendémiaire 17, Year II) Paris. Delaunay d'Angers presents the decree on the liquidation of the India Company, a process from which he hopes to benefit. Fabre d'Eglantine gets approval for an amendment stipulating that the liquidation will be carried out by the state and not by the Company itself (→ Oct. 17, 93).

9 (Vendémiaire 18, Year II) Lyons. The city capitulates to the republican army.→

How can the Vendée war be ended?

Paris, October 1

It is absolutely essential for the terrible war with Vendée to be over before winter comes. That is what Barère told the Convention as he submitted the report he had drafted on behalf of the Committee of Public Safety. He just can't understand how the Catholic and royalist army can still fight eight weeks after the "systematic destruction" of the entire region was called for. The republicans are baffled. There are regular announcements of republican victories over the rebels, but the Vendeans always come back for more, increasingly determined and more numerous. Their stamina is a real mystery, but Barère is not a man who believes in miracles. He has a very rational explanation for the republicans' failure to stamp out the endless Vendean revolt: "Too many representatives, too many generals, too many moral and military divisions, too much lack of discipline in victory, too much love of money among administrators — those are the problems." He has put forward plans to deal with such lack

Charette wants to get the soldiers born in Vendée baptised in Paris.

of proper organisation. First, the number of representatives who are sent off on missions must be cut down. But most of all, he wants to unite the four republican armies of Saumur, the Brest coast, Nantes and La Rochelle into a single fighting body with just one commander, General Léchelle. He has also asked the deputies to severely punish anybody caught looting or spreading false rumours about the military situation. Barère will not allow the young Republic to be defeated by some armed bands of fanatical peasants.

Madame Roland goes on hunger strike

Paris, October 8

There is no hope left for Madame Roland. On October 3rd., the Convention outlawed the deputies who are in hiding and carried out mass arrests of those still in Paris. In a final show of courage, Manon has taken a decision worthy of her: she is determined to starve herself to death so that her enemies do not have the satisfaction of dragging her ignominiously up to the scaffold. In her cell, she is writing her *Last Thoughts*, a moving testament in which she bids farewell to all the people she loves. "My example", she tells her daughter Eudora, "will stay with you. Now that I see myself at death's door, I feel that this is a rich heritage."

Silhouettes of the Roland couple and of their daughter Eudora.

A former actor now a revolutionary army commander

Paris, October 3

It is a great day for Ronsin. This former actor turned soldier, then captain of the National Guard, has just been made commander of the new revolutionary army of Paris. In his brand new uniform, he reviewed what troops have already been mustered. In fact, it is a strange army with widely differing weapons and equipment: there are more pikes than rifles and more men wear the revolutionary jacket than the regulation blue coat. This is partly due to the fact that the army was only set up one month ago. Each department now has a similar force to put down counter-revolutionaries, fight against food hoarders and enforce the Maximum. They are composed of volunteers and members of people's societies, but recruitment is a slow and chaotic process. Ronsin, however, takes his new job very seriously and is already trying to organise the battalions and provide them with regulation uniforms.

Pornography and prostitution are banned

Paris, October 4

Sansculottists take matters of morality extremely seriously. This is proved by the Commune's latest ruling making it illegal for prostitutes to solicit in streets and banning the sale of pornographic books or etchings. The text of the ruling condemns the districts of Paris that are "poisoned by debauchery" and where good republicans fear for their children's safety. The Commune has declared war on licentiousness, which is "more harmful for the Republic than gold, plotting and the armies of despots". The law has, however, been toned down by Chaumette, who was told to "paint virtue alongside vice and do justice to the city, which harbours both".

An English hairstyle.

Descartes honoured

Paris, October 2

When he created the Panthéon, the deputy Pastoret only wanted it to be for three men of the Ancien Régime: Descartes, Rousseau and Voltaire. It was therefore high time for the first on the list to join the other two famous men. The plan to send the great philosopher to the Panthéon was warmly applauded by the deputies. The bid to honour Descartes was put forward to the Committee of Public Education by Marie Joseph Chénier. He believes that the Republic should honour the philosopher who was always treated with indifference by kings.

Another stage performance is disrupted

Paris, October 6

The Théâtre de la République in Paris has been presenting a tragedy in five acts by Marie Joseph Chénier, *Caius Gracchus*. But when one of the actors on stage said the line "Give us laws and not blood", the Montagnard Albitte, the deputy of Seine Inférieure, jumped up from his seat and stopped the play. The contested line had been cheered by most of the audience. Albitte said that such a concept was reprehensible and a clear sign of "diehard moderationism and Feuillantism". The playwright was not allowed to explain his position on the matter. The performance later resumed.

The cathedral at Reims is desecrated

Reims, October 7

What a terrible sacrilege: the Holy Ampulla has been publicly destroyed by a commissioner from the Convention. It was in Reims, the city where kings of France had been anointed ever since Clovis was christened by Saint Rémi, that the precious container of holy oil was kept. The oil was used to anoint the forehead of each new king. However, that symbol of the ancient traditions of royalty had to be destroyed. The patriots' anger also turned against the saint's tomb, which had stood behind the altar of Saint Rémi Church ever since the 16th. century.

Saint Rémi's tomb at Reims.

The Republic's forces recapture Lyons

The Convention is thinking about renaming Lyons as Ville Affranchie.

Lyons, October 9

The "Vendée of the south" is now finished. After 60 days of fierce, bloody fighting, the city's inhabitants, who had been convinced by Jacobins to rise up against the Convention, have laid down their arms. On August 22nd., the besieging republican army led by Kellermann attempted to crush the city of central France under heavy artillery fire. The terrible damage done by the cannon fire was made even worse when supporters of the Jacobins infiltrated Lyons and were able to blow up the arsenal. In spite of the determination of the people, the attackers captured Sainte Foy in late September and then reached the gates of Saint Just, thus posing a direct threat to Lyons. The leader of the revolt, Louis François de Précy, a former officer in the King's army and an ardent royalist, decided the game was up and managed to flee across republican lines.

Chabot defends his wealthy marriage

Paris, October 5

The newly-married Chabot is a man with a certain style. When he announced his wedding at the Jacobins Club, the former Capuchin was perfectly frank. People have accused him of loving women too much. Very well, he said, I have now wed Léopoldine Frey to put an end to such insulting lies. He even admits that he is not in love with the young woman, whom he only met three weeks ago. He picked her because of her virtue, her wit and her patriotism, he said. The fact that she is rich also helped. To prove what he said, Chabot read out the marriage contract. A delegation from the Assembly has been picked to attend the wedding that is to be celebrated tomorrow.

"Death is eternal slumber"

Nevers, October 9

At Nevers, the Terror is not sparing anything, even cemeteries. Since Chaumette came to teach him all about real revolution, Fouché, who used to be such a kindly soul, has become truly implacable. He has decided to purge Nevers of all remaining traces of superstition. The ruling he has just issued has stunned local inhabitants, not so much by its restrictions on the freedom of religion, but by the nitpicking way in which it states that funerals are to be held. All funerals must in future be stripped of religious ritual. And, in order to make things perfectly clear, the gates to all the town's cemeteries are now to bear a sign saying simply: "Death is eternal slumber".

10 *(Vendémiaire 19, Year II)* Paris. After a long speech by Saint Just, the Convention decrees that "the government of France will be revolutionary until peace has come". →

10 *(Vendémiaire 19, Year II)* Montbéliard. The principality is occupied by French troops and immediately annexed by the Republic.

11 *(Vendémiaire 20, Year II)* Paris. Dismissed from the Convention, Danton goes to live at his home in Arcis sur Aube.

12 *(Vendémiaire 21, Year II)* Paris. The Convention decrees that Lyons must be partly destroyed. →

13 *(Vendémiaire 22, Year II)* Lower Rhine. The Austrian army led by Wurmser breaks through French defences, directly threatening Strasbourg.

14 *(Vendémiaire 23, Year II)* Paris. David informs the Convention that he plans to exhibit his just completed painting of Marat's death in the Louvre's courtyard.

15 *(Vendémiaire 24, Year II)* Strasbourg. As part of the de-Christianisation campaign, the authorities shut down the town's churches.

15 *(Vendémiaire 24, Year II)* Maine et Loire. The Vendean leader Lescure is seriously injured during combat not far from the castle of La Tremblay (→ Nov. 4, 93).

16 *(Vendémiaire 25, Year II)* Paris. The deputy Basire reads out a report from General Desmarres praising the death of the young soldier Joseph Bara.

16 *(Vendémiaire 25, Year II)* Lyons. Repression starts and four rebels are executed in Terreaux Square.

16 *(Vendémiaire, 25, Year II)* Paris. A new comedy by Monvel and Dalayrac, *Urgande et Merlin*, is performed at the Favart auditorium.

16 *(Vendémiaire 25, Year II)* Northern France. The victory at Wattignies won by Jourdan and the representative Carnot forces the Austrian troops to end the siege of Maubeuge. →

16 *(Vendémiaire 25, Year II)* Paris. Condemned to death at four o'clock in the morning by the revolutionary Tribunal, Marie Antoinette is guillotined the same day at 12:15 p.m. →

Emergency government is formed

Saint Just attacks the bureaucrats.

Paris, October 10

The end justifies the means. The first article of the decree that has just been approved by the Convention states that "the government will be revolutionary until peace has come". The vote was pushed through by the Committee of Public Safety after the reading of the terrible report by Saint Just. He lashed out against the current government, saying that "all the enemies of the Republic are in the government". He accuses the bureaucracy of having become a paper tyranny that has "replaced the monarchy". He added that "the Republic is now facing 20,000 fools who corrupt it, fight against it and bleed it dry". The food crisis, speculation and the chaos within the army, in short all that is going wrong in the country, is due to the slackness, inertia and corruption of government officials. The real problem is that "the laws are revolutionary but those who enforce them are not". From now on, the ministers and their officials, as well as all the legal authorities will be placed under the direct control of the Committee of Public Safety. It will be the Committee that will get the Convention to appoint generals. Strict time limits will be set for the enforcement of laws and whoever does not respect them will be punished as if he had violated Liberty. "Liberty must vanquish, whatever the cost," Saint Just cried at the start of his speech. The price to be paid may be that of a dictatorship.

Drunks are banned from town council

Mont Blanc, October 12

The town councillors of Viry kicked off the meeting with an issue that is both unusual and worrying: the town's representatives are to stop systematically turning up at local meetings when they are dead drunk. After some debate and for the sake of public order, they have ruled that "any man who is found to be under the influence of wine" will have to pay a fine of three francs and will be sent home immediately until he sobers up.

Saints banned from place names

Now is the time to act to change the names of towns and villages and give them truly republican names. From mainland France to the colonies, hundreds of towns and villages have erased out the names of saints and regional apostles from their signposts, just as they have already done with their calendars. Thus, Saint Rémy de Provence has become Glanum, Saint Dié has become Ormont and Saint Etienne is now the Commune d'Armes. Saint François de la Guadeloupe now bears the name of Egalité.

Limoges honours the memory of Marat

Limoges, October 14

The shops are closed and local citizens are wearing their Sunday best. The "disorderly, majestic and impressive" procession slowly files past the bust of Marat, whose death is being commemorated. Behind the statue, there stands a pike on which there is a banner bearing the following inscription: "To Marat, the friend of the people, this is how the people honour their friends". The man who was assassinated three months ago has earned such honours. The Convention wants each city to pay its respects to him. In Paris, a sculptor is making a wax mould of his face that will be taken around the land so that people don't forget what he looked like.

Marat, the Republic's martyr.

Problems arise over fusing army units

Nice, October 10

Some things are easier said then done. General André Masséna is trying unsuccessfully to fuse the battalions of volunteers with the front-line battalions, but he is having a lot of trouble. Such a "mixture", which is stongly favoured by Dubois Crancé, the Convention's recorder for the decree of February 1793 aimed at "nationalising the army", is turning out to be far easier to achieve on paper then on the ground. Masséna is just finding out how hard it is. It is impossible to achieve the apparently ideal model called for by Paris: form single units of three battalions and mix veterans with volunteers in each of these. The General also has another reason to be worried: one of his army doctors has just been kidnapped by a group of the rebels who are known around here as "barbet". These peasants of the Nice region have stepped up their resistance against what they see as foreign occupation of their land. The Convention's attitude and the looting done by some of the volunteers in the Republic's army are partly responsible for their feelings.

Arras celebrates the new calendar

Arras, October 10

The authorities of Arras have decided to use mathematics and astronomy as the themes for their celebrations for the new calendar. Thousands of people who had come from all over the region were divided into 12 groups to symbolise the months. Leap days in the calendar were embodied by old men and the day added every four years was shown as a 100-year-old man who placed the book of the Constitution under the Liberty tree (→ Nov. 24).

Tallien seduced by the lovely Thérésa

Bordeaux, October 16

Fate itself seems to be trying to unite them. This evening at the Théâtre de la République, Tallien is not paying the slightest attention to the play *Plantation de l'Arbre de la Liberté*. Uppermost in his mind is the sweet memory of the lovely lady he has just seen. He had briefly met her two years ago at the Lameth residence. Her name is Thérésa Cabarrus. The young woman was also impressed by the handsome representative from the Convention who arrived in Bordeaux this morning with his three associates.

Rebellious city of Lyons is to be torn apart "stone by stone"

The representative Couthon (A) striking the first blow for the demolition of the Bellecour Square façades.

Paris, October 12

No mercy is to be shown to the cities in revolt. Lyons had surrendered on October 9th. but the city is not to be forgiven for its revolt against a united and indivisible Republic. Barère today got approval on behalf of the Committee of Public Safety for a decree on Lyons. In his report he stressed that the city "must be buried under its own ruins". The text of the new law states that all the homes of the rich and of counter-revolutionaries are to be destroyed. The only houses that will be left standing are those belonging to patriots and to the poor. Industrial buildings and the public monuments are, however, not to be torn down. In a bid to underline the Revolution's final victory over its enemies, a column bearing the inscription "Lyons waged war on Liberty, Lyons is no more" is to be erected on the ruins. In short, the city is to be gone over with a fine tooth comb by envoys from the Convention. They will draw up lists of the buildings that are to be destroyed. After that, Lyons will be renamed Ville Affranchie. All this is aimed at wiping out all traces of the city's shameful past. The punishment meted out to Lyons is also meant to be seen as an example to all (→ Oct. 26).

Jourdan wins the battle of Wattignies against the Austrians

Wattignies, October 16

The French troops were helped by the fog that blanketed the battlefield. This unexpected ally has allowed the forces led by Jean Baptiste Jourdan to inflict a defeat on the Austrians. More than 6,000 of the soldiers led by the Duke of Coburg and the Count of Clerfayt lost their lives in combat against Jourdan's and Carnot's men. Their strategy had been to weaken their centre and left defences in order to concentrate most of their forces on the right. This was a daring and highly dangerous gamble that only succeeded because of the weather. If the visibility had been good, the French troops would have been in deep trouble. The element of surprise also played a role, but the battle really hinged on actual combat. As the fog was lifting, a heavy artillery barrage started. It soon became so intense that the Austrians admitted they had never heard anything like it before. Nothing could stop the French advance. Heavy fighting continued as men sang the *Marseillaise*. The enemy troops, pushed back on all sides, were finally forced to admit defeat. They will have to try again elsewhere to beat the French.

After Hondschoote, this new victory is a boost for French morale.

Robespierre hits out at Chabot

Paris, October 16

There seem to be spies everywhere. Robespierre has just criticised the deputy Chabot at the Jacobins Club, accusing him of being the leader of an Austrian faction. Chabot does indeed have close links with the Austrian banker Frey, whose sister he married on October 5th. He is also involved in some dubious financial dealings which may lead him to become a traitor. Suspicions about his behaviour grew today with the mysterious disappearance since yesterday morning of Desfieux, a former spy acting for the Committee of Public Safety and friend of the Jacobin Collot d'Herbois and Hébert. Desfieux used to share rooms with an Austrian called Proly, who has business dealings with Chabot.

Marie Antoinette is executed after a rigged trial

Marie Antoinette defends herself as Fouquier Tinville looks on.

Paris, October 16

The day was just barely dawning when the Queen heard the young servant girl Rosalie enter her cell at the Conciergerie. She had come to tell her the time had come. Right up until the end of the two exhausting days of her trial, Marie Antoinette had hoped that she would be spared the guillotine. Her guilt, her betrayal, her plots with foreign leaders were obvious to all, but were never fully proven. She was accused of having squandered vast sums of money on her close friends, of having urged the King to stand against the Revolution and even of having treated her son as a king after the death of Louis XVI, but there was no clear proof. The worst was when Hébert dared accuse her of having had sexual relations with her own son. Horrified, the Queen cried out: "I appeal to all mothers" and many a woman among those present was deeply moved by her distress. Her lawyer, Chauveau Lagarde, spoke on her behalf for two hours. He was so eloquent that he was arrested on the spot. In spite of this warning, his assistant, Ronson du Coudray, also made a fiery speech for the defence. He too was arrested. All their efforts were in vain. Around four o'clock in the morning, the sentence was proclaimed: the Tribunal, acting on its deep convictions, sentenced "the widow of Louis Capet to death". The Queen listened to the verdict in total silence and with downcast eyes. When she was brought back to her cell, she was unable to go back to sleep. At dawn, the executioner Sanson came to fetch her and she had to cross all of Paris as the mob screamed "Death to the Austrian bitch, long live the Republic!" Looking dazed, the Queen did not seem to hear any of the insults.

When the cart stopped before the scaffold, she climbed down from it so quickly that she lost a satin shoe and stepped on the executioner's foot. "Sir", she told him politely, "please pardon me, I did not do it on purpose." She was then strapped down on to the wooden plank. It then tipped and the blade fell. One of the executioner's assistants bent down to pick up her head with its white hair and brandished it so that the crowd could see.

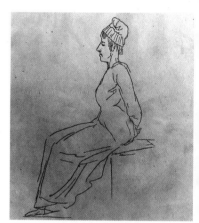
Marie Antoinette, drawn by David.

After being dubbed "The Austrian", "Madame Veto" and "Madame Deficit" throughout her reign, Marie Antoinette is insulted right until the last.

October 1793
from 17th. to 24th.

Laclos works on hollow cannonballs

Paris, October 20

Despite the disappointing results of the first tests, the Convention has decided to press on with the testing of hollow cannonballs. Choderlos de Laclos has been put in charge of the tests as assistant commissioner. He started work on the project three weeks ago, helped by the scientists Berthollet and Fourcroy. As he had to find a building and a firing range, he picked Meudon and its park. However, Laclos' prestige in scientific matters has not improved his political reputation. The authorities are still watching him closely and he is still subject to the law on "suspects".

Jean Carrier calls for swift action

Carrier, deputy of the Cantal.

Nantes, October 20

The new delegate from the Convention is a man who knows what he wants and how to achieve it without wasting any time. Jean Baptiste Carrier, aged 37, is a former public prosecutor from Aurillac. Now he is here, he firmly intends to track down and deal with all the enemies of the Revolution. In order to do this, he has already contacted the city's revolutionary committee and informed it of his plans to reorganise local government. During his inaugural speech this evening, he lashed out against the "futile deliberations" at the town council. Carrier also ordered the immediate enforcement of the September 29th. decree on prices.

Vendeans suffer major setback at Cholet

The Vendean leader General Bonchamps is to die of his wounds.

Cholet, October 17

"Vendée is no more!" The joy of victory has made the envoys from the Convention under estimate the still dangerous Catholic and royalist army, even though it has just suffered an unprecedented defeat. Following the failure of their badly planned offensive last September, the republican troops this time had three armies converge on Mortagne and Cholet, in the very heart of rebel country. After a first clash on October 15th., during which Lescure was badly injured, the Vendeans moved out of Cholet and pulled back to Beaupréau in the north, not far from the Loire river. But there disagreement between the leaders made the situation worse. Talmont and Donnissan wanted to get the men across the river, while the others said it would be madness to leave Vendée. It was finally decided that the majority of the army would return to face the republicans outside Cholet, while a detachment of 4,000 men would seek to establish a bridge-head north of the river in case a retreat was necessary. This turned out to be a fatal move: the men sent across the Loire were sorely missed by the rest of the Vendean army fighting at Cholet. After a long, indecisive battle, the republicans, who were brilliantly led by Kleber, finally routed the enemy. Bonchamps and d'Elbée, two of the most popular Vendean leaders, were both badly wounded. Their men then panicked and fled.

The India Company goes into liquidation

Paris, October 17

Politicians are troubled by a complex problem. A decree voted on October 8th. calling for the break up of the India Company has just been published in the official *Bulletin*. There is nothing very unusual about that. The Company is specialised in insurance and discount. It had been accused of tax evasion because it hid its profits behind imaginary investments. On July 16th., the Montagnard deputy Delaunay was the first to speak out against the Company at the Convention. The India Company was forced into liquidation. But Fabre d'Eglantine revealed on August 3rd. that despite everything it was still involved in fraudulent specula-tion. The deputies have therefore decided to break up the firm once and for all. To make doubly sure, they have ordered state commissioners to keep an eye on the process. During the vote, many were surprised to learn that the one who was most opposed to the break up of the company was Delaunay. Also, the text of the decree that was published today differs from that of the October 8th. decree. It stipulates that the liquidation of the Company should be carried out by the firm and not by the state. If the new decree has been tampered with, it must have been with the help of the secretary of the Finance Committee, Fabre d'Eglantine, who signed the decree (→ Nov. 14). ▷

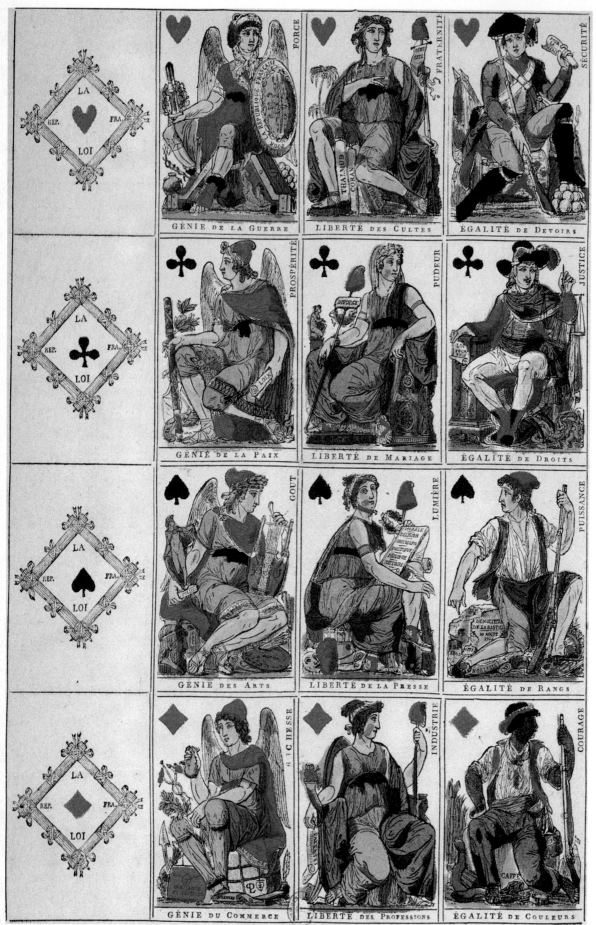

GÉNIE DE LA GUERRE — LIBERTÉ DES CULTES — ÉGALITÉ DE DEVOIRS

FORCE — FRATERNITÉ — SÉCURITÉ

GÉNIE DE LA PAIX — LIBERTÉ DE MARIAGE — ÉGALITÉ DE DROITS

PROSPÉRITÉ — PUDEUR — JUSTICE

GÉNIE DES ARTS — LIBERTÉ DE LA PRESSE — ÉGALITÉ DE RANGS

GOUT — LUMIÈRE — PUISSANCE

GÉNIE DU COMMERCE — LIBERTÉ DES PROFESSIONS — ÉGALITÉ DE COULEURS

RICHESSE — INDUSTRIE — COURAGE

Card games with the colours of the French Republic

France, October

Kings, queens and jacks are all being reshuffled. France's playing cards are changing because of a decree from the Convention. Card designers have been working hard. It was the pack of cards designed by the Comte de Saint Simon which were the most sensational. His new cards will probably outsell the others. This liberal aristocrat who had refused to emigrate and became rich thanks to the purchase of nationalised property, has designed a revolutionary pack of cards. The high-scoring ace is shown as the Law, while kings are replaced by the spirits of peace, the arts, war and trade. The queens have been turned into Freedoms — of the Press, of profession, of religion and of marriage. Finally, the jacks have become Equalities — of rank, of duty, of colour and of rights. In this game, the Law of clubs can outbid the Liberty of the Press. But there are other types of cards where the kings are called Cato or Brutus and the jacks are Hannibal or Horatio. Philosophers also appear on cards. In one such game, the sansculottist of hearts, formerly the jack, looks on as battles are fought between the Rousseau of spades and the Voltaire of diamonds. As for chess, there are no longer any kings or queens, but standard-bearers and sergeant majors. Castles are cannons and knights are light cavalry. Pawns are infantrymen. People no longer say "check" but "to the flag" and "victory" instead of "mate".

"If the real friends of philosophy and humanity noticed with pleasure, among the cards of Equality, the Sansculottist and the Negro, they will be delighted to see the Law, only sovereign of a free people, standing by the ace with its supreme power whose rays are its image and give it its name." This is a strange thing for the former nobleman Saint Simon to say. But he now simply calls himself Citizen Bonhomme.

Claude Henri de Saint Simon.

The Vendean army is forced to retreat

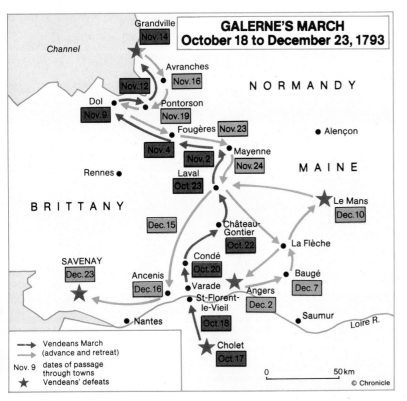

GALERNE'S MARCH
October 18 to December 23, 1793

- → Vendeans March
  (advance and retreat)
- Nov. 9 dates of passage through towns
- ★ Vendeans' defeats

0   50km

© Chronicle

Kings, even stone ones, are beheaded

Paris, October 23

The "executioners" lashed a rope around their necks and pulled them down to the ground, where they all shattered. These are bad times for crowned heads, even if they sit atop stone statues gracing the entrance to the capital's monuments. A decision by the Commune is being systematically enforced: "considering that it is our duty to get rid of all monuments that bring back the execrable memory of kings", the Commune decreed that the 28 royal statues that stand around the three doors of Notre Dame Cathedral must be destroyed. Not one of these "gothic effigies" is to be spared, even if some of them are not statues of kings of France.

The fleur-de-lis: a nation's emblem?

Paris, October 24

A wave of iconoclasm has been sweeping the country, destroying all symbols of the monarchy and the Church in the name of great revolutionary principles. The men of the revolution did not just want to get rid of the Ancien Régime, but also of all visible signs of it: churches have been devastated, castles looted and emblems of royalty broken or burnt. Abbot Grégoire and Alexandre Lenoir have done all they could to save some of the treasures of Gothic art. Now the deputy Romme has just been defending the fleur-de-lis. "It was to honour French industry abroad that our artists stamped a fleur-de-lis on their work. Are we to destroy what they made just because this symbol is now banned?" he asked. Why shouldn't this symbol be used on objects of value? The fleur-de-lis could even become a symbol for all that is made in France.

Food supplies are still a big problem

Paris, October 23

The Convention has set itself a new priority: food supplies must be brought efficiently to the towns, and particularly to Paris, where hunger stalks the people. Therefore, a Committee for Supplies has just been set up. It includes three administrators who are not elected but who are known for their revolutionary zeal. It will enforce the Maximum law, requisition grain and whenever necessary buy it from abroad. This will be a difficult task, so five officials have been appointed so they can be sent out to the provinces. Along with the Committee of Public Safety, this new body has been given wide-ranging powers. It will even be empowered to call for force to be used if this proves to be necessary.

Maine et Loire, October 18

"To the Loire!" With that cry, the Vendeans defeated at Cholet fled north towards the river. The fear of the republican troops, whose advance seems unstoppable, has pushed thousands of soldiers as well as women, children and old men to gather at the beach at Saint Florent. There, amid chaos and confusion, people tried to find a place aboard one of the small and crowded boats used for crossing the river. There were so many people that Lescure's officers had to draw their sabres and threaten the crowd before they could get their badly wounded commander on to one of the boats. Lescure was opposed to crossing the Loire, as was his cousin Henri de La Rochejaquelein, who has been appointed generalissimo despite being aged only 21. He will be replacing d'Elbée, who is

A republican innkeeper's plaque.

dying. Other army officers urged civilians and soldiers to head for the northwest of the river. They feel this will help spread their revolt to Brittany and the Maine and put them closer to any help from England, just across the Channel.

German thinkers and the Revolution

The events in France over the past year have become increasingly incomprehensible to German public opinion. The constant use of violence has upset the philosophers Fichte and Kant. When their initial enthusiasm had melted away, they slowly came to believe that the Revolution should have stopped with the principles enshrined in the Constitution of 1781. As for August Rehberg, a careful reader of all that is published on either side of the Rhine, he has just written a long article voicing his countrymen's growing discontent with the Revolution.

Twenty one Girondist deputies were brought before the revolutionary Tribunal, headed by Herman, on October 24th. Fouquier Tinville leads the prosecution. Among the accused are Vergniaud, Gensonné, Brissot, Carra, Valazé and Sillery. Many of their friends have fled.

25 (Brumaire 4, Year II)
Sumatra. The frigates involved in d'Entrecasteaux's expedition overseas are seized by the Dutch. Their crews learn that France has now become a republic and that it is at war with Holland.

25 (Brumaire 4, Year II)
Mayenne. La Rochejaquelein crushes the republican troops that had been sent in to block the road to Entrammes.

26 (Brumaire 5, Year II)
Nantes. The representative Carrier rounds up a company of 60 men whose task will be to arrest suspects. The unit calls itself the Marat Company.

26 (Brumaire 5, Year II)
Lyons. The special envoy Couthon strikes a first blow with a hammer at the façade of a house on Bellecour Square. This is the signal for the start of the destruction of Lyons buildings.

27 (Brumaire 6, Year II)
Paris. The writer Bernardin de Saint Pierre gets married at the age of 56 to Félicité Didot, the sister of the famous printer. She is 30 years younger than her husband.

27 (Brumaire 6, Year II)
Paris. At the Jacobins Club, Alexis Thuriot calls for the de-Christianisation movement to spread: "We must kill off all religions and create a population of philosophers."

28 (Brumaire 7, Year II)
Paris. The Convention decrees that in future no man or woman of the church will be allowed to become a teacher.

26 (Brumaire 7, Year II)
Paris. A comedy by Rosalie Dugazon, Les Modérés, is performed at the Théâtre de la République.

30 (Brumaire 9, Year II)
Paris. The Committee for Supplies, which was set up to enforce the Maximum law, gets down to work.

30 (Brumaire 9, Year II)
Paris. Brissot and the Girondists are sentenced to death by the revolutionary Tribunal (→31).

30 (Brumaire 9, Year II)
Paris. A decree from the Convention bans all the women's revolutionary societies.→

31 (Brumaire 10, Year II)
Strasbourg. Saint Just imposes a tax of nine million livres on the rich. Part of the money raised will go to help poor patriots.

The painter Hubert Rodier is arrested

Paris, October 29

His friends were all stunned by the news: Hubert Rodier has just been arrested and dragged off to the Saint Pélagie prison. What are the charges against this talented painter who has made a name for himself by painting landscapes with ruins. There are rumours that he had not renewed his citizen's card. Some even claim that his fellow painter Louis David is to blame for the error. But the most likely reason for Rodier's arrest are his old links to the court. He was named designer of royal gardens in 1770 and had subsequently remodelled the gardens of Versailles.

The remodelling of Versailles' gardens as seen by Hubert Rodier.

Republican women's clubs are banned

Paris, October 30

Robespierre, Hébert as well as the Paris Commune had found it most useful to use revolutionary republican women when they wanted to overthrow their enemies the Girondists. But now that their foes have been silenced, they don't know how to get rid of these cumbersome allies. The ladies of the marketplace at the Saints Innocents will provide them with an excuse: yesterday they came to the Convention to complain angrily about the way they had been insulted and mistreated the day before by women of the republican clubs. Brandishing pistols, the republican women had tried to force the fishwives to wear the revolutionary red bonnet. The clubwomen said the ladies of the marketplace were unpatriotic and wrong to complain about the lack of business. The deputies have decided to seize this opportunity to keep women out of politics. They have approved a decree banning all the republican women's clubs.

A priest marries out of "patriotism"

Champigny, October 27

"Ye true sansculottists, representatives of the people, a thankful couple gladly pays tribute to you." During the unusual wedding ceremony celebrated today, it was the groom himself who preached the sermon to the faithful. This is due to the fact that the groom is the local parish priest. He quickly told the congregation that it was not "the heat of passion, but the sacred love of nation" that had convinced him to take a wife. Nowadays, many priests see marriage as a patriotic duty that must be done to prove one's loyalty to the nation. Some of them are certainly happy to forget their vows of celibacy, but others see it as a simple precaution that could save them from the guillotine or at least from being drafted into the army. Thus, there have been several cases where young village priests have married their elderly governesses. This has the advantage of guaranteeing them a peaceful life while at the same time ensuring that they won't become a target for angry republicans.

The victory at Laval gives the Vendeans a road to the sea

Laval, October 25-27

The Vendeans are still a force to be reckoned with. They had no problem reaching Laval and brilliantly succeeding in pushing back the republican troops chasing them. The republicans had once again under-estimated their opponents. There were 60,000 Vendean men, women, children and priests when they crossed the Loire. In all, they had 30,000 combatants. The republican generals were over-confident. Not all of them were good soldiers and they often disagreed. Mistakes were made. Westermann tried to take the rebels by surprise on the night of October 25th. to 26th. He did not wait for reinforcements to arrive and failed abysmally. But the mistakes by General Leclerc, the man in overall command, were even worse: having ordered his troops to attack on October 27th., he told them to advance in just one column without bothering to deploy. His officers warned him, but they had to obey their leader, who only owes his command to his political friends. The republicans were routed.

The Sansculottists

Sansculottists have made the stage. At the Vaudeville, a play shows them in a saucy light in this finale song. It is being sung by all Paris. The point of the song relies on the literal translation of "sans-culottes" (without pants).

Our foemen hostile to subdue
Frenchmen, dear friends true,
Are thorough patriots.
But if success you wish to ensure,
Be it in love, be it in war,
Long live the sans-culottes!
Tis false to say the Prussians,
The English and the Austrians
Are not true patriots.
I swear we in each campaign
Their men time and time again,
Have made real sans culottes!
If ever I a lover choose,
Said Jane, I want a man who's
A thorough patriot.
His clothes count not,
For his own good and mine too
I want him sans culottes.

"My name is no longer Louis!"

Paris, October 29

It is neither wise not safe to bear the same name as France's dead King nowadays. This morning, a Paris citizen went to see the representatives of the Commune saying: "I now want to be called Mutius Scevola because he was a brave Roman and a hero of the people." He was congratulated for his patriotism but told that if his request was granted thousands of others would come pouring in to change their names. There are a great many French mothers who have chosen to call their sons Louis, he was reminded.

A village is to be named after Brutus

Paris, October 31

The Convention has just agreed to grant the two requests made by a delegation from the people's society of Ris Orangis. The village will in future be called Bourg Brutus in honour of the hero of the Roman Republic. They also said they had decided to outlaw the Catholic faith from their village. The delegates had seized the silver from their church and given it to the Convention. The fate of the statue of Saint Blaise, the village's patron saint, was decided by the inhabitants: they tore it down and plan to use the wooden statue as firewood when winter comes.

It can be risky to be a priest's maid

Mont Blanc, October 31

Some political accusations are sometimes simply based on neighbourhood quarrels. Marie Antoinette Richard, who used to be the maid of the priest of Montgilbert, was arrested by the National Guard after being informed on by Pierre André, a municipal official. He claimed that she was "fanaticising" the women of the village. But in fact, Marie Antoinette had just asked him to pay the 200 livres he owes her. Pierre was jealous because after the priest's departure she had been allowed by the mayor to keep the presbytery (→ Jan. 9, 94).

The Girondists are put to death

Leaving the Tribunal, the condemned men are taken back to the jail.

Paris, October 31

"Soldiers of France...the day of glory dawns at last": the first verses of the *Marseillaise* were sung under the arcades of the Conciergerie when the five carts carrying the prisoners to the scaffold set off. In a final show of defiance, the Girondists were trying to prove their patriotism. They sang the song all the way to the guillotine and this made a deep impression on the many people who had turned out to watch, but that was the only show of emotion. Today's executions did not cause any tears to be shed and there was no unrest. The death of the Girondists was greeted with indifference. It came after a procedurally flawed trial that lasted a week. People wanted to get it over with. Since the arrest of the 21 men, there had been delays in the legal process, possibly due to a lack of proof or because the Convention did not want to reopen old wounds. But as soon as the trial began before the revolutionary Tribunal, everybody knew that the verdict would be death. There was no other solution as the execution of the Girondists was the logical culmination of all that the Convention had done since June. To let them live would be to admit that mistakes had been made. Moreover, not one lawyer had volunteered to defend the prisoners. Fouquier Tinville had charged them with a wide variety of crimes. He accused them of having been accomplices of La Fayette, of Philippe d'Orléans and of Dumou-

riez. He also said they had declared war on all the kings of Europe. Two men from the Commune, Hébert and Chaumette, acted as prosecutors on behalf of the Tribunal's president, Herman, a friend of Robespierre. It was a slow process and there were fears that it would never end. Fouquier Tinville called for a decree aimed at speeding things up to be approved. The day before yesterday, the Convention decreed that the jury could hand down its verdict right away. This was proclaimed yesterday: all the accused were sentenced to death. Some of them started weeping, while others like Vergniaud showed no reaction whatsoever. As for Valazé, he was unable to bear the stress any longer and stabbed himself with a knife right where he stood.

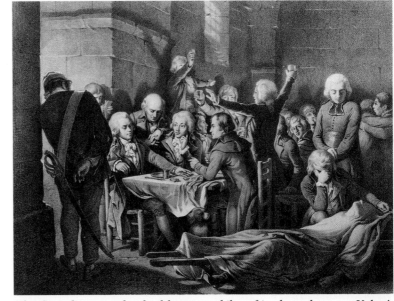
The Girondists attend a final banquet while a friend watches over Valazé.

The 21 condemned men are guillotined on Revolution Square.

1 *(Brumaire 11, Year II)*
Paris. The Convention decides to have a prison built at Lorient where the non-juring priests who have been sentenced to be deported from France can be held.

2 *(Brumaire 12, Year II)*
Paris. The Convention decrees that both legitimate and illegitimate children are equal in all matters of inheritance.

2 *(Brumaire 12, Year II)*
Rouen. The young composer Adrien Boieldieu gets his first opera, *La Fille Coupable*, performed at the Théâtre des Arts.

3 *(Brumaire 13, Year II)*
Paris. Olympe de Gouges is executed.→

4 *(Brumaire 14, Year II)*
Mayenne. Death of the Vendean General, Lescure.→

4 *(Brumaire 14, Year II)*
Paris. The painter Fragonard becomes a member of the Art Commune, which includes many revolutionary artists.

4 *(Brumaire 14, Year II)*
Paris. A zoo is built at the Jardin des Plantes in southeastern Paris.→

4 *(Brumaire 14, Year II)*
Ille et Vilaine. Vendean forces capture Fougères.

5 *(Brumaire 15, Year II)*
Paris. At the Convention, Marie Joseph Chénier proposes that existing religious holidays be replaced by patriotic and revolutionary ones.

5 *(Brumaire 15, Year II)*
Meudon. Choderlos de Laclos is arrested again on orders from the Committee of General Security.

6 *(Brumaire 16, Year II)*
Gironde. The special envoys from Paris change the department's name to Bec d'Ambès.

6 *(Brumaire 16, Year II)*
Paris. Philippe d'Orléans is executed.→

6 *(Brumaire 16, Year II)*
Paris. In response to a request from a delegation that has come from the village of Mennecy, Barère gets the Convention to approve a decree allowing French villages to renounce the Catholic faith and choose the one they prefer.

7 *(Brumaire 17, Year II)*
Paris. All the clergymen who are deputies at the Convention, with the exception of Abbot Grégoire, solemnly renounce their faith.

Philippe d'Orléans dies on the scaffold

Orléans, who voted for his cousin the King's death, is in turn executed.

Paris, November 6

In the end, Philippe d'Orléans' decision to renounce his title as a nobleman was no help whatsoever. He was guillotined this morning as the same people who used to cheer him booed loudly. At the start of the Revolution, the people had carried his bust triumphantly along the streets. On April 6th., the Convention had ordered the arrest of all Bourbons. They could serve as hostages for the Revolution. Philippe d'Orléans was dragged before the revolutionary Tribunal six months later and accused of having had links with Mirabeau and Dumouriez and of seeking the throne. This was despite the fact that he had voted for the death of the King, his cousin. He fought bravely to save himself, but knew all was lost. The man who was born the Duc de Montpensier, then Duc de Chartres, before becoming the Duc d'Orléans when his father died, was today using the name he chose in 1792: Philippe Egalité.

Marquise is said to starve the people

Marne, November 1

The Marquise Henriette de Marbeuf has just been arrested on orders from the Committee of General Security. The farmers Rolpeau and Loiseleur, whom she had dismissed, have got their revenge. They went to the people's society at Gournay and accused her of being an aristocratic hoarder. They also said she was unpatriotic. She is an enterprising woman who has had a cotton mill built on her land and turned the 1,500 acres she owns into grazing land. People say that she prefers to sow alfalfa to feed her 150 horses and 700 sheep rather than the wheat that is so necessary to feed Paris. Some people are even claiming that along with her farm supervisor Payen she is storing grain, not to wait until prices rise, but to give or sell it to the Prussian army with which she is said to have close ties (→Jan. 12, 94).

The Vendean chief, Lescure dies of his injuries

Mayenne, November 4

The carriage bearing the dying man only stopped for a few minutes at La Pellerine. Nothing must delay the long Vendean lines marching from Ernée to Fougères. Riding just behind her husband, Madame de Lescure hears someone sobbing. She gets down off her horse and she tries to get closer. She sees the surgeon step down from the carriage. She now knows all is lost. Again, she tries to climb into the carriage, but she is held back. Her husband is no worse, they tell her. The column must press on because the republicans are very close and there will be no mercy for those who are caught. It was only that evening, when they had reached Fougères, that she was told the truth. For the Catholic and royalist army, the death of Lescure is a heavy loss. He was probably the most far-seeing of the Vendean leaders and his death could lead to further dissent among his men. His cousin, Generalissimo Henri de La Rochejaquelein, is a good leader of men in the field, but he is too young to impose his own views on his officers.

The armies of the Republic have plenty of heroes: an example is the bravery of Baralliev, a soldier in the 5th. Rhône et Loire Battalion.

A huge Hercules is to replace Henri IV

Paris, November 7

What is to be done with all the remains of the statues of kings that the Commune has had torn down from the façade of Notre Dame Cathedral? All the bits and pieces are lying about in a pile by the cathedral walls. Louis David, the painter, has had an idea which he outlined today before the Public Education Committee. He is proposing that the remains be used to make foundations for a huge statue of Hercules which would symbolise the people of France trampling on "the heaped rubble of the double

A broken Notre Dame king's head.

tyranny of kings and priests...Thus, the statues mutilated by national justice would today serve Liberty." The new statue would be built by the Pont Neuf, exactly where the statue of Henri IV used to stand. Hercules would be 15 metres high, with one hand resting on his club and holding Liberty and Equality in the other. It would be made in bronze seized from the "allied despots" and show Hercules treading on the remains of "Capet's predecessors". Ironically, however, it was Henri IV who first started the vogue for statues of Hercules.

"The sovereign people" as Hercules.

A zoo opens at the Jardin des Plantes

Paris, November 4

Going to the zoo will no longer be a luxury reserved only for the nobility. The people will be able to take a close look at real wild animals and exotic species from far away. That is why Lakanal and the professor of zoology Geoffroy Saint Hilaire have built a menagerie at the Jardin des Plantes. Its first customers will be the survivors of the royal menagerie at Versailles: a lion, a zebra, an antelope and a dog. All the other animals, gifts from foreign monarchs, had been massacred in 1789. They were seen as living examples of wasteful royal habits. Animals are food, people had said. The new zoo is also to house dromedaries from the private game parks of émigré nobles as well as bears. A recent ruling makes it illegal to exhibit live bears in public places because of the danger to children and spectators.

Olympe de Gouges is guillotined

Paris, November 3

The woman who had once tried to defend Louis XVI was unable to find even one lawyer to act for her. After spending long months in jail, Olympe de Gouges appeared before the revolutionary Tribunal yesterday. She was sentenced to death. In a bid aimed at delaying her execution, she lied and told the judges that she was pregnant. However, this claim was greeted with howls of unbelieving laughter. The doctor who was ordered to examine her did not even want to commit himself. The sentence was carried out today. After looking disdainfully at the guillotine, Olympe turned to face the crowd and cried: "Children of France, you will avenge my death!" Those were the last words of a woman who had bravely fought for the rights of women and whose mistake was to trust freedom under the Revolution.

Priestly deputies renounce the clergy

Paris, November 7

There was an important session at the Convention this afternoon. Wearing the red bonnet, Gobel, the metropolitan Bishop of Paris, solemnly placed his ring of office and his heavy pectoral cross on the desk of the speaker to show to all that he was renouncing his position. Yesterday evening, a delegation from the Commune led by Hébert, Chaumette and Cloots had come to demand that he publicly forswear the Catholic faith unless he wanted to be put to death by the people. Gobel had refused that particular demand, but he did agree to abandon the episcopate. This morning, he went to the city hall with 11 of his vicars before going on to the the Convention. They were mocked by the people along the way. He finally said he renounced Catholicism and would now place his faith in "Reason". All the deputies from the clergy quickly followed suit amid rowdy scenes. Abbot Grégoire, wearing his full episcopal finery, was the only one to stand firm and refuse. He stolidly remained deaf to the entreaties from his fellow clergymen.

The "left-overs of superstition", such as gold, silver and all sorts of church ornaments, are brought to the Convention by the Paris sectors.

Restif has another narrow escape

Paris, November

"Open up, in the name of the law!" When he heard those fateful words, Restif de la Bretonne must have been terrified. Without giving Restif time to think, the judge Hué rushed into his rooms and started searching everything in silence. He seemed to be looking for some kind of compromising documents. Restif did not dare say anything, as he was afraid to make matters worse. As far as he knew, he had done nothing wrong, but in these times of Terror, how can one be sure? Fortunately, after a while the problem was solved. Before she sued him for divorce, Restif's wife had wanted to find out exactly how much her unfaithful husband was worth.

Is the singer Garat a secret royalist?

Rouen, November 5

Music lovers are most upset: their idol Pierre Jean Garat, the man they consider as the most perfect singer that France has ever known, has just been arrested. The singer is suspected of having sung a song that people thought contained references to Marie Antoinette. His fondness for the late Queen is well known. He had been recommended by the Comte d'Artois and the Queen had allowed him to play music with her. During parties at the Trianon, the singer and his sentimental songs were much appreciated by the Queen and her friends who all hope that Garat's disappearance from the stage will not last too long.

"Liberty, what crimes are committed in your name!": Mme. Roland's last words

"You deem me worthy of sharing the fate of those you have murdered?"

Paris, November 8

Proud and smiling, wearing a white dress with a gay, flowery pattern, she climbed up into the cart with the dignity of a queen. When the executioner tried to tie her hands, she told him haughtily: "Excuse me, I am not used to that sort of thing." During the journey across the city, Madame Roland never lost her calm, smiling demeanour. This made a strange contrast with the trembling man standing beside her, a condemned criminal named La Marche whom she tried to cheer up. Madame Roland was sentenced this morning, after a rushed trial at which she was not even allowed to speak. She had been steeling herself for death for months. At the end of the trial, she had promised her judges that she would remain brave right until the very last. The Girondins' muse kept her promise. As she climbed the

Buzot mourning his dead friend.

steps to the scaffold, she paused for a moment to gaze at the tall statue of Liberty that towers over Revolution Square. After a while she exclaimed: "O Liberty, what crimes are committed in your name!" These were her last words.

Roland kills himself after his wife's death

Rouen, November 10

Roland left the residence of the Malortie sisters, where he had been hiding, during the night. He spent a long time walking aimlessly. At last, he stopped by a wood, drew out his dagger and stabbed himself in the left side. To make sure, he pulled the knife out and stabbed himself again before collapsing. Roland had been shattered by the news of his wife's execution and vowed not to go on living. His suicide also means he can escape from his tormentors and will his money to his daughter.

Roland's body was discovered by peasants from the region.

A National Music Institute to open

Paris, November 8

Despite its many worries, the Convention also finds enough time to deal with cultural matters. It has approved a plan to create a National Institute of Music in order to encourage music and the teaching of music. The musician Bernard Sarrette is behind the plan. It was he who as early as July 13th. 1789 had set up a special orchestra for the National Guard of Paris. Then, on June 9th. 1792, he founded a non-paying school of music for the Guard which was approved by the Commune. What was needed now was a truly nationwide music education system. Sarrette had brought his music professors to the Convention to plead his cause: "Public interest as well as that of the arts must make you realise the usefulness of my request," he said, stressing the work that has already been accomplished over the past six months. He also stressed that the new Institute was to play a big role in fostering the kind of powerful, nationalist music that is "demanded by the sacred cult of Liberty".

Sansculottists are motivated men

Colmar, November 10

"Our sons are shedding their own blood on the borders so we are only too pleased to work for them and for the Republic." That was how the sansculottists from the village of Saulxures explained the feat they had just performed. A group of 16 patriot fathers spent four days dragging two heavy carts loaded down with animal fodder. The carts had been stuck in their village due to a lack of available horses, so they decided to drag them for 22 leagues until they reached Colmar. During their long, slow journey, they had to cope with heavy rains, mud and hostile villagers. As they arrived, two envoys from Paris, Hérault de Séchelles and Ehrmann, set out to meet them with all the members of the local people's society. After embracing them warmly, Hérault de Séchelles promised the 16 exhausted men from Saulxures that "this sublime act of republican virtue" would not pass unnoticed by the Convention.

Armed gangsters strike again

Normandy, November 13

In the Eure region, vicious gangs of armed men have been looting houses and torturing the peasants. What is most frightening about them is that they seem to be impossible to stop. Nobody knows where they come from or where they will strike next. At Fidelaire, they came disguised as National Guardsmen and surrounded an isolated farm belonging to a local farmer, Juin. They knocked on his door and ordered him to tell them where the Chouans were, saying they wanted to search the house. The poor man was terrified, believing they were real Guardsmen. But as soon as he let the men in they started destroying everything. They didn't use their usual trick of putting their victim's feet on hot coals to make him speak. Instead, they put a sharp knife to his throat and demanded to know where the farmer kept his money. The trembling man did not take long to tell his torturers just what they wanted to know. He showed them where his gold was hidden and they stole 7,000 livres.

Reason is now worshipped at the former Notre Dame Cathedral

Mlle. Maillard, goddess of Reason.

The German cartoonists mock this "idolatrous feast" in a sacred place.

Paris, November 10

Citizeness Maillard of the Paris Opera was picked to play the rôle of the goddess of Reason because she is "a masterpiece of nature". The ceremony was held in what used to be Notre Dame Cathedral. In the large transept, a miniature mountain had been built. It was topped by a Greek temple bearing the inscription: "To Philosophy". The choir was hidden behind huge drapes, while busts of Benjamin Franklin, Voltaire and Rousseau had been given pride of place. The celebration of Reason, attended by the Convention members, started at around 10 a.m. It was organised by the Paris Commune and consisted mainly of a succession of revolutionary songs and speeches. What those present enjoyed most was the moment when the goddess, who wore a long white dress, suddenly appeared. After sitting still "in an impressive and graceful posture that commanded respect", she then walked slowly back into her temple, smiling at the audience as she vanished from sight.

On November 12th., the former mayor of Paris, Bailly, is executed on the Champ de Mars. The spot is chosen in memory of the massacre of July 17th. 1791 for which he was held responsible.

A church becomes a revolutionary court

Rochefort, November 10

"We are going from miracle to miracle and soon there will just be one temple left in this town, the temple of Truth," the Convention's two envoys to Rochefort have reported proudly. The town's parish church today opened for business as a revolutionary tribunal. This was not the only "miracle" brought about by the two envoys, Lequinio and Laignelot. Using both thinly veiled threats and bribes, they also managed to get two clergymen of Rochefort, a priest and a pastor, to renounce their faith. These highly efficient emissaries from the capital have also succeeded in turning a local temple into a prison as part of the de-Christianisation policy.

"Vous" is a banned word in Paris

Paris, November 12

One of the last remaining bastions of the Ancien Régime has just fallen. The formal form of address used throughout France for centuries has just been declared a taboo word. The decision was taken by the department's authorities on the urging of all the capital's people's societies. The deputy Basire even proposed a law that would force all citizens to replace the "aristocratic vous" with the more "democratic tu". Robespierre had tried to oppose the linguistic change, saying it was not appropriate. However, the authorities remained deaf to his arguments.

The de-Christianisation campaign throughout France includes parodies.

David presents his painting of Marat's death to the Convention

Paris, November 15

"David, we need you! You have given the picture of Le Peletier to posterity, now you still have one painting to do: the one showing the assassination of Marat." David said in response: "I will certainly do it." That exchange took place at the Convention the day after Marat was killed by Charlotte Corday. Three months later, the work was completed. Today, David presented it to the Convention, after having exhibited it to the public at his home and in the courtyard of the Louvre. The work is to be hung in the hall where sessions are held, right beside the one David had done of Le Peletier de Saint Fargeau. The two paintings are equal in size and they are both mute testimonies to the Revolution's two chief martyrs. Alongside the body of Le Peletier, which lies on its deathbed, Marat is shown at the moment of his dramatic death, as he holds a pen in one hand and in the other the note written by his murderess. On the floor, David has painted the blood-stained dagger used by Corday. In the sombre, dark brown-background, the only thing that stands out is the bust of Marat, the People's Friend, whose expression is marked by a calmness that probably he never achieved in his lifetime. On a plain wooden box, the artist has simply written the words: "To Marat, David".

The assassination of Marat, the People's Friend, painted by Louis David.

The Jews of Metz still face problems

Metz, November 10

Although France's Declaration of Human Rights has by now been translated into Hebrew, the Jews of eastern France are still experiencing major integration problems. Ever since the start of the year, they have had to cope with yet another wave of anti-Semitism, not only from local inhabitants, but also the authorities. House searches and petty persecution have been on the increase. Like French Catholics, the Jews have been careful to avoid any outward show of their faith, cautiously preferring to remain discreet. However, they continue to observe Mosaic laws. This summer, Jews who were members of the city's National Guard asked the Commune's council to be allowed not to serve on the Sabbath but their request was turned down. Even worse, the council decided on September 13th. that all citizens "professing the Law of Moses" must come in on the following day to register their children and male servants. But as September 14th. was the day of Yom Kippur, the Jews sent a delegation to the council to ask for a one-day delay. However, this request was curtly rejected by the Commune and all the members of the Jewish delegation were arrested on charges of rebelling against authority.

The Convention banned the national lottery on November 15th. The game, claimed to be immoral, used to bring in a lot of badly needed money.

Mme. Montansier is locked up

Paris, November 15

The Théâtre National does not have a director any more: Madame Montansier has been arrested and taken to the Petite Force prison. She had always been willing to show her patriotism by helping to fund the war effort and putting on revolutionary plays. Her theatre even became a rallying point for the sectors at the start of Marat's funeral procession. But she had many determined enemies such as Hébert and Chaumette, who yesterday denounced her to the Commune. It is claimed that she had taken money from the English and from Marie Antoinette to pay for the building of her theatre near the Bibliothèque Nationale, which she is suspected of wanting to burn down.

Volney is jailed for unpaid taxes

Paris, November 16

Volney was arrested on orders from the Committee of General Security just as he was leaving the Ministry of Foreign Affairs, where he had gone to discuss a mysterious mission to the United States. He is to be held at the Force prison, not on spying charges, but simply due to a dispute with the income tax administrators. He had not yet paid for land he purchased in Corsica. This was quite legal. However, he was forced to flee from the island after being threatened by Paoli, who confiscated his lands. Even though he no longer owns the land in Corsica, Volney is supposed to have paid the debt as soon as it was due. He now knows that the tax men take their work seriously.

Convention

17 *(Brumaire 27, Year II)*
Paris. At the request of the Committee of General Security, all the people involved in the India Company scandal are to be picked up. Chabot, Basire and Delaunay d'Angers are arrested, while Julien de Toulouse, Batz, Proly and Boyd manage to escape.→

17 *(Brumaire 27, Year II)*
Paris. On the urging of Thuriot, the Tuileries sector announces that it is renouncing the Catholic faith (→19).

17 *(Brumaire 27, Year II)*
Paris. Robespierre tries to reassure neutral nations about France's foreign policy, in a report to the Convention on the Republic's external relations.

18 *(Brumaire 28, Year II)*
Paris. The National Museum opens at the Louvre.→

18 *(Brumaire 28, Year II)*
Paris. In a report on a system of provisional revolutionary government, Billaud Varenne joins politicians already calling for several centralising measures (→Dec. 4, 93).

19 *(Brumaine 29, Year II)*
Paris. It is the Gravilliers sector's turn to renounce Catholicism (→23).

20 *(Brumaire 30, Year II)*
Paris. Danton returns hurriedly to the capital after learning that some of his friends involved in a foreign plot have been arrested.

21 *(Frimaire 1, Year II)*
Paris. The Théâtre des Variétés, which specialises in both political plays and farces, performs *A Bas la Calotte* by Pierre Rousseau, a defrocked priest.

21 *(Frimaire 1, Year II)*
Paris. At the Jacobins, Robespierre, who considers the de-Christianisation policy to be a dangerous political mistake, speaks out forcibly in favour of the freedom of religion.→

23 *(Frimaire 3, Year II)*
Paris. The Commune orders all the capital's churches to be closed, in a move to back the wave of de-Christianisation that is spreading throughout Paris.

24 *(Frimaire 4, Year II)*
Paris. The Convention sets up an institute at the palace of Versailles which will house paintings by artists of the French School for which there was not enough room at the Louvre.

Brainwashing hits Strasbourg

Strasbourg, November 17

The first "Propaganda Session" was held today in the cathedral. As a cowed audience of local people listened, the best speakers of the Jacobin Clubs of neighbouring departments spoke at length about the main themes of the Revolution. Such sessions have been set up to encourage the inhabitants of Strasbourg to be good patriots. These sessions are far from being the most unpleasant of the steps taken by Saint Just and Le Bas, the two commissioners sent to represent the Convention at the Rhine army. They both believe in fighting fire with fire. Entire local Catholic villages had fraternised with the Austrian troops and waved the white anti-revolutionary banner. As soon as they arrived, Saint Just and Le Bas ordered the Committee of General Security to provide them with a list of "suspects". They also called on the people's society to evaluate the politics of the administrators of the Lower Rhine and purge the district, town and department councils. Over the next few days, they imposed an obligatory loan of nine million livres. Speculators were severely punished and the town council was ordered to confiscate the shoes of 10,000 aristocrats overnight and give them to the barefoot soldiers of the Republic.

Bibles to be used to make bullets

Angers, November 19

Some booksellers are true patriots, for example, Charles Pierre Mame, a printer with a good reputation. He was most concerned over the unrest in Vendée and the anti-revolutionary Catholic uprisings, so he decided to do what he could to help. Instead of offering some money, he suddenly had an even better idea. Since the Republic is desperately short of weapons and ammunition, why not fight the enemy with his own weapons? The bookseller has decided to donate every single religious book he has in stock to the government. They can be used for the manufacture of cartridges. When the young Republic is fighting for its life, one has to use imagination to find ways to help.

The Art Museum is open to the public

Paris, November 18

It had first opened its doors on August 10th., but only for a day. However, the Art Museum is ready to greet its first visitors today. So far, it only occupies the Louvre's Square Salon and a small part of the Great Gallery. But other exhibition halls are to be prepared. As for the choice of works to put on show, the organisers have had to do some fast footwork. The paintings and what few statues are on show have been placed any which way. There seems to be no logic to the way which the works are being exhibited. For the time being, the Museum is offering a sampling of royal collections, which are still widely dispersed, and works of art that were seized by revolutionaries. Despite teething problems, people are flocking in.

The exhibition of masterpieces fascinates not just the curious, but also the art students who carefully copy paintings on show in the Great Gallery.

Montagnard deputies are arrested for being involved in a financial scandal

Paris, November 17

The India Company scandal has spread to the world of politics. The Montagnard deputies Delaunay, Basire and Chabot have just been thrown into jail. Another Montagnard, Julien de Toulouse, had been arraigned, but he fled with the Baron de Batz, the counter-revolutionary financier. All of them are involved in the India Company scandal and have been charged with corruption. It was Chabot who blew the whistle to Robespierre on November 13th. By doing this, he had hoped to steer blame away. He told Robespierre that he had been given 100,000 francs which were to be handed to the secretary of the Finance Committee, Fabre d'Eglantine. The latter was to forge the decree approved on October 8th. ordering the Company to be put into liquidation. The fake decree was drafted by Delaunay and Julien de Toulouse. Chabot said he was overcome by guilt and didn't accept any money. But knowing him to be a man who loves money as much as women, the deputies agreed to Robespierre's calls and ordered an inquiry. As far as they are concerned, Chabot is as guilty as those he is denouncing. The Convention is to look into the matter, but has asked Amar and...Fabre d'Eglantine to investigate. The latter could well be an accomplice as his signature is on the fake decree. The scandal could reach Danton, a friend of Fabre, and be used to compromise all Montagnards (→Nov. 20).

▷

Robespierre condemns atheism

Many people could be upset over anti-religious extravagance.

Paris, November 21

Tonight, Robespierre explained to the Jacobins at the Assembly that his belief in God is based solely on natural reason. He firmly condemned all those who "are trying to turn atheism itself into a form of religion simply because they say they want to destroy superstition". The main target of Robespierre's pointed criticism was Hébert, who was at the Assembly, but who did not dare respond. It is Hébert and the Enragés who are behind the efforts to de-Christianise France by persecuting believers and desecrating churches. Robespierre is warning of the dangers of such extremist policies. He said that he who seeks to stop priests from officiating "is even more of a fanatic than the man who celebrates Mass". Robespierre is neither an atheist, nor a fully-fledged Christian, even though he does believe in God. He says that the people need God.

Vendean troops win another victory

Ille et Vilaine, November 22

Once again, the Vendeans have been successful because of the dire lack of coordination among the republican forces. In a clash at Dol de Bretagne, they managed to repel two charges launched by General Westermann and two offensives led by Marceau and Rossignol. The outcome could have been very different if Westermann, who had marched from Pontorson, and the other two leaders, who came from Antrain, had attacked at the same time. The fighting was extremely tough. Early on November 21st., the royalists nearly panicked. But local women and priests waving crucifixes rushed up to urge the frightened men to go back into the fray. Today's victory means that the road back to the Loire is now open for the Vendeans. Since the siege of Granville, their morale has taken a beating and most of the anti-revolutionaries just want to go home.

The Vendeans had failed to win at Granville last November 14th.

A republican calendar to celebrate the start of a new era in French history

Paris, November 24

The leaders of the Revolution have decided to leave their mark not just on France, but on History itself. The Convention today gave its final approval to the plan for a new calendar that was drafted by an *ad hoc* committee that included David, Fabre d'Eglantine, Romme and Marie Joseph Chénier. The plan is far from being a novel one. The habit of calling 1789 "Year I of Liberty" was well established by 1792, when it started being used to date coins and assignats. On September 22nd., 1792, the Convention decreed that all official documents would in future be dated from "Year I of the French Republic". That meant that 1789 and the Con-

Fabre d'Eglantine, a political poet.

stituent Assembly were cast back into the mists of time, like the Ancien Régime. In his report to the Convention, Romme, the chief artisan of the calendar's reform, has summed up the plan thus: "Time opens a new book for History; and in its new march, as majestic and simple as equality, it must use a new etching needle to record the annals of a regenerated France." The traditional calendar is "a monument of slavery", just like the historical periods it covered. This outdated system must be replaced by a rational, more "natural" calendar. On the very day that the Convention issued its decree abolishing the monarchy and marking the end of the "vulgar era", the sun reached its autumn equinox, Romme noted. "Thus, the equality of days and nights occurred in the heavens at the very moment when the people's representatives did proclaim the moral and civil equality of every Frenchman." The new system is supposed to be both more natural and more scientific than its predecessor. It is also resolutely secular: there are no more anti-revolutionary Sundays or religious holidays. Time, just like the new system of weights and measures, is to be decimal. The week, called a *decade*, will now last 10 days: primidi, duodi, etc. That means there will be a lot of extra days to work for the good of the Republic. The year will be split up into 12 months, each having three decades, to which five days, known as the "sansculottides", will be added so it all adds up. Names of plants, tools or animals, such as tomato, cart and goat, will now replace the names of Catholic saints. New words with links to nature will be used to name the 12 months: Vendémiaire for the new month of the "vendanges", or vine harvest, Nivôse for "neige", or snow, Floréal, for the month of flowers, Messidor for "moissons", or crops, Thermidor for the hottest month and Fructidor for the month when fruit is ripe...

The new calendar

The republican calendar is a bit confusing for ordinary folk. But since it is forbidden, under penalty of death, to live in the "old style", the people put up with it. Some even find that the new revolutionary names are very poetic. A song has been written about therm:

The changes made by Fabre now
Will benefit us all, I trow.
This student keen of Molière
The names engraves in letters or,
From gay Vendémiaire
Until the splendid Fructidor.
None is sweeter than Germinal;
None more gay than Floréal:
After they did metamorphose,
Each month has a novel name
Nivôse, I cite, and Pluviôse
These names we acclaim.
Primedi leads to duodi,
Tridi, quartidi, quintidi;
Sextidi then and septidi blest,
Followed by cotidi and nonidi;
And after these we all can rest
In hallowed bliss of décadi.

The Republic, leaning on its knowledge of astronomy and trampling on the Gregorian calendar, proudly presents Fabre d'Eglantine's calendar.

PLUVIOSE

Janvier. Le Soleil est au Signe du Verseau.

Sous un leger nûe s'achemine au Bocage.
La Nymphe au doux Nectar apportant son trousseau.
Bravant Pluie et Hiver, brulante en ce bel âge
Des feux qui vont Fouir à son cher Pastoureau.

VENTOSE

Fevrier. Le Soleil est au Signe des Poissons.

La Nymphe du Rivage aux Poitçons fait la guerre.
Dans ce Mois ou les Vents dechaines fur les eaux.
Les font rentrer au Fleuve & rendent à la Terre.
La Prairie ou les Fleurs ramenent les Oiseaux.

GERMINAL

Mars. Le Soleil entre au Signe du Belier c'est l'Epoque de l'Equinoxe du Printems.

Tout végète & s'anime au retour du Zéphire.
La Nature à ses Loix ramene nos desirs.
Et l'Age le plus pur apprend des Tourterelles.
Qu'il est doux de s'unir & de s'aimer comme elles.

FLOREAL

Avril. Le Soleil entre au Signe du TAUREAU.

Si-tôt que FLORE en Sa magnificence,
Promet dans Ses présens des tresors aux Humains;
On aime à voir la candeur, l'innocence,
Que la Jeune Beauté couronne de Ses mains.

PRAIRIAL

Mai. Le Soleil correspond au Signe des Gemeaux.

Ma faulx m'a fait goûter les fains de la Prairie
Que pour nourrir l'hiver, les vilès trompeaux;
De même j'aurai soin des caresses nouvelles.
Que ton brulant amour fait echapre à la vie.

MESSIDOR

Juin. Le Soleil correspond au Signe du Cancer.

Quel repos plein d'attraits goûte la Moissonneuse.
Quand aux travaux du Jour succede un doux Sommeil.
Cérès par tes présens te rends la vie heureuse.
Jamais on ne les voit s'evanouir au reveil.

THERMIDOR

FRUCTIDOR

VENDEMIAIRE

BRUMAIRE

FRIMAIRE

NIVOSE

Bucolic allegories that represent the 12 months of the new revolutionary calendar which was approved by the Convention on November 24th. 1793.

Convention

25 *(Frimaire 5, Year II)*
Paris. Nineteen of the country's 27 former Farmers General are arrested. They are jailed at the Port Royal convent, which has been turned into a prison (→30).

25 *(Frimaire 5, Year II)*
Paris. Mirabeau's remains are withdrawn from the Panthéon.

26 *(Frimaire 6, Year II)*
Paris. At the Convention, Danton follows Robespierre's lead and protests against "anti-religious charades". He states that: "We did not seek to wipe out the reign of superstition in order to establish the reign of atheism" (→28).

28 *(Frimaire 8, Year II)*
Paris. The Convention finds out that the text of the decree on the liquidation of the India Company is different from the text it approved on October 17th. (→Dec. 19, 93).

28 *(Frimaire 8, Year II)*
Bordeaux. Tallien orders the arrest of 86 members of the troupe of the city's Grand Théâtre, which he considers to be a nest of aristocrats.

28 *(Frimaire 8, Year II)*
Paris. Feeling there is a change in the air, Chaumette gets the Commune to confirm the freedom of religion.

29 *(Frimaire 9, Year II)*
Paris. The former Constituent Assembly member Barnave is guillotined after spending 15 months in jail. The former Minister of Justice Duport Dutertre is executed on the same day.→

29 *(Frimaire 9, Year II)*
Paris. The Théâtre de la Cité shows *Les Vous et le Toi*, a comedy by the Jacobin Aristite Valcourt based on the new vogue for informal speech.

30 *(Frimaire 10, Year II)*
Paris. In a speech to the Convention, Prieur de la Marne stressed the lack of education of Bretons, saying this makes them prey to counter-revolutionary ideas.

30 *(Frimaire 10, Year II)*
Alsace. Hoche is defeated by the Prussian forces at Kaiserlautern as he attempts to break the siege of Landau.

30 *(Frimaire 10, Year II)*
Paris. A delegation from the Convention attends the Feast of Reason at Saint Roch Church, during which the first republican hymn by Méhul is played.→

Carrier announces that 84 non-juring priests have drowned

Paris, November 28

"A total of 84 of the people we call non-juring priests were being held aboard a ship on the Loire river. I have just been informed, and the information is most trustworthy, that every single one of them has perished." This letter has been read out to the Convention. It is signed by the special envoy from Paris, Carrier and dated November 17th. Behind the announcement there lies a terrible fact: the ship aboard which the priests were being held because of over-crowding in the city's jails was purposely sunk by Carrier's men. The priests were mostly old or crippled and they had been held for a month aboard a barge tied up at the port. The ship was pulled out to the middle of the river and scuttled. Only one of the priests, who were tied together, was able to escape (→Dec. 14).

Scuttling barges is an efficient way of drowning the non-juring, rebellious, or simply suspect clergymen.

The speculator Ouvrard prefers to work in Paris rather than in Nantes

Nantes, November 27

In all, 132 tradesmen have been arrested and charged with being hoarders. The rough justice that the Convention's special representative Jean Baptiste Carrier is becoming famous for doesn't leave them with much hope of avoiding the death penalty. Among those arrested is a friend of Gabriel Julien Ouvrard.

When Ouvrard found out about this, he asked General Boivin for a safe-conduct so that he could go to the capital. Aged only 23, this young man is known in Nantes for having already made huge profits by stocking colonial imports and then selling them off when prices had risen. He has now gone to Paris to seek his fortune.

A mass execution of Vendean prisoners under the walls of Nantes.

French soldiers are fed up with their old equipment

Arras, November 25

The Republic's fighting men are increasingly fed up with their military equipment and uniforms. It is not much fun to march off to war without even a flag or a drum, but it is a scandal to expect men to fight when they aren't given any shoes. The new recruits are a pitiful sight without their shoes, stockings or proper trousers. The situation is having a serious effect, as has been pointed out by the commander of the 1st. Battalion of Arras: "The soldiers are deserting because they are disgusted at still not having uniforms." In Paris, Carnot continues to think that the half-brigades still number 3,000 men. In fact, there has been so much desertion that it is now impossible to carry out the recommended tactics: focus most of the troops on one spot. As the year closes, there are more than 60,000 missing.

The chemist Lavoisier turns himself in

Paris, November 30

An excess of honesty is not necessarily a good thing. The chemist Antoine de Lavoisier has turned himself in at the Port Libre jail, which used to be the Port Royal convent and was recently turned into a detention centre. He is prepared to share the fate of all the other Farmers General. Five days ago, Bourdon de l'Oise got legislators to approve the decree on the arrest of 27 Farmers General. But Lavoisier was warned by a friend and decided to hide at the home of his old friend Lucas, the former usher at the Academy of Science. He then sent letters to the Convention stating that he had quit being a Farmer General long ago to devote himself to science, but there was no reply. When told of the arrest of his father-in-law and the other Farmers, he surrendered.

Lavoisier lives only for chemistry.

Antoine Barnave's final moments

Paris, November 29

Antoine Barnave was executed today on Revolution Square. The crowd made no noise when he was beheaded. The condemned man, who was popular in 1789, also kept silent. However, some claim to have heard a group of royalists shout: "Is your blood pure, Barnave?" Nobody was later able to confirm this. A lot of people had forgotten all about Barnave, who was jailed after August 10th. 1792 on orders from the Legislative Assembly. He was still young and the crowd felt sympathy for him. When he was called in to testify before the revolutionary Tribunal, he had vigorously and ably defended monarchist ideals, so much so that even some of the court's hardened jury members were for a while unsure of themselves. But as he was driven to the scaffold in a cart this morn-

Barnave, killed at the age of 32.

ing, he hardly said a word. The man who used to say "I would rather suffer and die than lose my moral and political convictions" died quietly.

Some detainees are housed in a castle

Aveyron, November 28

The first "suspects" were placed under house arrest at the Firmy castle. This was because there has never been a proper jail in the district of Aubin. It was therefore necessary to find quickly a suitable place to house the many "suspects" who have already been arrested since the law of September 17th. came into force. The only places that could conceivably be suitable

were the castles. Preparation work took eight days and the one at Firmy is now ready to welcome 80 guests. The most "dangerous" suspects had been temporarily housed in private homes until construction work was completed. The authorities sent less dangerous prisoners to the village inn. Despite their relatively pleasant surroundings, the prisoners haven't forgotten that they face a long jail term.

Wealthy Bordeaux traders are arrested

Bordeaux, November 30

A total of 200 Bordeaux merchants were arrested overnight as a "security measure". The port city's revolutionary Tribunal has acted on behalf of the Committee of General Security. The Tribunal's members had told Paris that they would do their best to "bring the public's mentality up to the level of current events" and to "put a big squeeze on the purses of wealthy egotists

and help sansculottists, who have been betrayed by scoundrels, to enjoy the fruits of their labours". Two days ago, the Tribunal ordered the imprisonment of the Grand Théâtre's actors, saying they had incited the audience to shout "Long live the King!" Today, it was the wealthy Bordeaux merchants who were detained. It looks like the authorities are planning to put a "big squeeze" on their purses.

The streets of Paris are renamed

Paris, November 30

Ever since the beginning of the month, the names of the capital's streets have been undergoing some changes to fit in with the winds of change sweeping the nation. In a bid to stop the Revolution's most famous names from being forgotten so quickly that the young would not even have a chance to learn them, they are now to figure prominently all over Paris. The move is based on proposals made at the Assembly by the deputy Chamoulaud. Why not call the Palais National the Temple du Républicanisme? The Hôtel Dieu could be renamed the Temple de l'Humanité Républicaine, and the Halle could become Frugality Square. The streets nearby could then be called Temperance and Sobriety. The Place Vendôme can

be renamed the Place des Piques and streets leading into the square could be the Rue du 10 Août, Rue du Patriotisme and Rue du Jeu de Paume. As for the sectors, those hotbeds of revolution, they more than any other must be given names that speak directly to the people and fan their revolutionary zeal. The King of Sicily sector is dead, long live the Human Rights sector! It is high time for the Croix Rouge sector to become the Bonnet Rouge sector. As for the one known as the Observatoire, it must henceforth be renamed the Sans Culotte sector. The new, patriotic and republican names are springing up all over the French capital as each neighbourhood tries to outdo the rest. The renaming frenzy will soon spread to the provinces.

There are many in Bordeaux who have made money from colonial trade.

Convention

1 *(Frimaire 11, Year II)*
Paris. According to the decree on public education, gatherings of citizens in the form of popular societies, theatres, civic games, military manoeuvres and national and local celebrations are integral parts of civic education.

1 *(Frimaire 11, Year II)*
Paris. At the Convention, Danton manages to win rejection of Cambon's project for forced exchange of metallic money for assignats.

3 *(Frimaire 13, Year II)*
Paris. Danton suffers an initial setback at the Jacobin Club. In opposing turning over a church in Le Havre to popular societies, he is sharply criticised by Chasles, and must personally ask for an investigatory committee in order to clear himself. Robespierre saves him from being purged.

4 *(Frimaire 14, Year II)*
Paris. The Convention adopts the measures proposed by Billaud Varenne on Brumaire 18.→

4 *(Frimaire 14, Year II)*
Angers. The Vendeans are defeated outside Angers and must fall back toward the Sarthe river.

5 *(Frimaire 15, Year II)*
Appearance of the first edition of Camille Desmoulins's *Le Vieux Cordelier.*→

5 *(Frimaire 15, Year II)*
Paris. Robespierre gets the Convention to adopt a *Response to the Manifestos of the Kings in League Against the Republic.*

6 *(Frimaire 16, Year II)*
Paris. The Jacobin Philippeaux publishes a letter criticising the control of republican military operationing in the Vendée. The letter attacks the Ministry of War and the Generals Ronsin and Rossignol, as well as questions the policy of the Committee of Public Safety.

8 *(Frimaire 18, Year II)*
Paris. Former minister Etienne Clavière commits suicide in his cell after being informed that he would have to appear before the revolutionary Tribunal.

10 *(Frimaire 20, Year II)*
Paris. After Hébert, Desmoulins violently attacks Cloots and Chaumette in the second edition of the *Vieux Cordelier* (→ 15).

12 *(Frimaire 22, Year II)*
Mayenne. After occupying Le Mans on the 10th., the Vendeans are crushed by Marceau and Kléber.→

Charette escapes from his pursuers

Vendée, December 6

Charette is certainly elusive. He had taken refuge in the town of Bouin, built on an island amidst swamps. The republicans, controlling the only four roads leading to the town, were sure that, this time, he was "caught like a rat in a trap". But remaining true to his taste for pleasure and bravado, the knight had spent the whole night dancing with his women friends. When the Blues surrounded Bouin in the morning, Charette was not there. Guided by a villager, he had fled with his men by way of the inextricable neighbouring canal system.

Shoemakers serve their fatherland

Paris, December 8

The shoemakers have been requisitioned. From the last week in December until the first one in February, they will have to devote themselves to a single task: making shoes for the military. The services are so short of shoes that the country has to resort to such "encouragement" of patriotic gifts. Any shoemaker who works for an individual during that period will have to pay a 100-livre fine. The law has foreseen all contingencies. For instance, the shoe tips will be square, so soldiers cannot sell them.

Repression becomes a massacre in Lyons

Lyons, December 4

The guillotine, supplied by the Commission of People's Justice, was not working fast enough. Couthon had already been recalled to Paris last month for having rejected strict application of the terrible decree of October 12th. providing for the destruction of Lyons, the city of central France. Fouché and Collot d'Herbois, who replaced him, do not have the same scruples. This morning, 64 prisoners were shot on Esplanadè des Brotteaux. "I would like this day of justice to be a day of celebration," the Commission chairman had written to the representatives. The dragoons took two hours to finish off the wounded.

Vengeance of the sansculottists.

One of the shootings ordered by Collot d'Herbois at the Hôtel de Ville.

Desmoulins launches a Press campaign against the Terror

Desmoulins's accusatory article.

Paris, December 5

Camille Desmoulins is not a man to be afraid of going too far in his use of language. In his newspaper *Le Vieux Cordelier*, the first issue of which comes out today, he does not hesitate to compare "exaggerated" patriots, Hébertists and supporters of the reign of Terror to agents of British Prime Minister Pitt, to whose "genius" he pays ironic homage. This surprisingly bold attack is not aimed at the Enragés alone. An indirect target is the policy followed by the Committee of Public Safety, and it is part of the "indulgent" campaign against the Terror. Dantonist Desmoulins thus lines up with the people preaching moderation: one might think that he is playing Robespierre's game. The latter, in fact, has launched out into a merciless struggle against the Hébertists, whom he wants to exclude from the Jacobin Club. To this end, he has joined up with the Dantonists, the leaders of the indulgent offensive and fierce opponents of the Hébertists. At the Jacobin Club last December 3rd., he defended Danton, who had returned to Paris two weeks previously and was the target of a barrage of criticism for his moderate policies. Yet paradoxically enough, Desmoulins's pamphlet might well work against Robespierre's policy and compromise his relatively fragile alliance with Danton. The reason is that it is so violent it gives Hébertists an opportunity to defend themselves and regain the initiative.

For Mr Louvet, all roads lead to wife Lodoïska

Paris, December 6

Louvet de Couvray cannot live without Lodoïska. He took refuge in the autumn in the Bordelais area with the other outlawed Girondins, but he could not stand being without news of his wife. Worried to death, he finally left his hiding place and braved a thousand dangers to rejoin her in Paris. He crossed France using a wide variety of disguises, sometimes on foot, sometimes by coach. At the end of three long weeks of travelling, he finally reached the gates of the capital. He got through the last police roadblock hidden under a cover, while the other passengers in the coach were called on to identify themselves. Of course, life is not a bed of roses when one is outlawed. But life has no meaning for Louvet if he cannot hold his Lodoïska in his arms.

The pastor Rabaut mounts the scaffold

Paris, December 5

The ardent defender of freedom of worship is no more. The Protestant minister Rabaut Saint Etienne was guillotined this morning. He was a deputy to the Convention and made the mistake of backing the Girondins. Fabre d'Eglantine denounced him. Since June 2nd., he had been hiding in the home of the Payzacs, a Catholic couple who were friends of his father. They were arrested with Rabaut and suffered the same fate. When she learnt the news, his wife killed herself.

Jean Paul Rabaut Saint Etienne.

New government installed for war

Paris, December 4

The new government has been installed promptly. The fact is that the extraordinary circumstances associated with the Revolution demanded a powerful authority with "more activity and nerve". Hence Billaud Varenne, in the name of the Committee of Public Safety, presented a definitive decree on the organisation of the revolutionary government to the Convention today. This institution, announced as provisional, is specially designed for the period of war France is going through, pending the possibility of applying the Constitution of the Year I once peace has returned and the counter-revolutionary dangers have been averted.

In accordance with the wishes of the Committee of Public Safety, which drew up these special measures aimed at restructuring the public authorities, the executive branch is more highly centralised. National agents will be appointed in the districts and the communes to pass on the Convention's directives directly. In the same spirit, the deputies voted for the abolition of the departmental directories, the wide ranging autonomy of which has sometimes favoured the Girondists since last June. As to the representatives on mission, they are now forbidden to delegate their powers, and they will have to see to a strict purge of all constituted civil authorities. Bourdon de l'Oise even wanted to do away with the ministers, whom he considers as "aristocratic agents who halt the electric fire of the Revolution". But Robespierre replied that there was no point in that since ministers "cannot abuse the authority entrusted to them, being carefully watched". Barère added that in any case, they would come "every day, and at the indicated times, to receive the orders of the Committee of Public Safety.

Actually, the decree that has been adopted considerably strengthens the Committee's power. Even if Billaud Varenne affirmed that this does not risk leading to despotism, the moderates greatly doubt that. As a technical, but also highly symbolic measure, the decree equally provides for transmission to all of the country's authorities of all the laws adopted by the Convention, by means of a numbered bulletin called *Bulletin of the Laws of the Repub-*

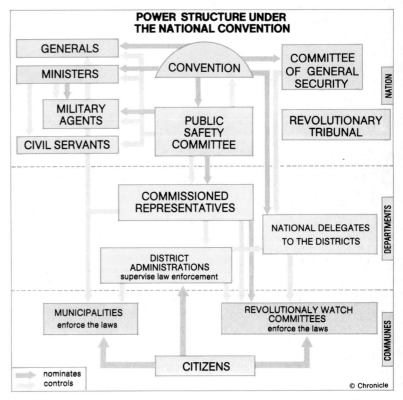

POWER STRUCTURE UNDER THE NATIONAL CONVENTION

lic. This veritable official journal of the Republic will be produced by a printing shop that will have to devote itself to that task alone. To avoid any possibility of falsification and give the documents solemnity, they will use special paper with the Republic's seal.

The executive as seen by opponents: a machine for issuing arrest warrants.

The young Joseph Bara's heroic death

The young man reportedly died for refusing to cry "Long live the King".

Vendée, December 8

The Adjutant-General Desmarres, displayed some emotion in reporting to the Convention on yesterday's ambush. Among the many soldiers killed by the Vendeans during the occupation of Jallais, north of Cholet, was Joseph Bara, the young son of the gamekeeper of the former lord of Palaiseau, whom he had known as a boy. He wrote that "that boy was too young to join the Republic's troops, but was extremely eager to serve, and he accompanied me, mounted and equipped as a hussar. The entire army was astonished to see a mere 13 year old boy confront all dangers." He asked the state to be responsible for the boy's family.

Thérésa triumphs as goddess of Reason

Bordeaux, December 10

The whole city is celebrating the feast of the goddess Reason. The representatives of the Convention, Tallien and Ysabeau, parade in blue uniforms at the head of the vast procession crossing the city to a background of patriotic banners. On the Military Committee's banner, one can read: *The Law: tremble, conspirators*. On the one belonging to the Vigilance Committee, a big open eye has been painted and underlined with these words:

Traitors, I see the bottom of your hearts. Some girls dressed in white and wearing tricoloured scarves accompany the parade, which now arrives in front of the stand reserved for the authorities, where Ysabeau is to make a speech. Thérésa Cabarrus, glowing and more beautiful than ever, appears as the goddess of Reason. Shouts go up, and applause breaks out. She is named queen of the feast, a way to let Tallien make his liaison with her official.

Woe betide cutters of the Tree of Liberty!

Somme, December 8

One must not pass up any opportunity to "terrorise". During the night, in the town of Crécy, somebody pulled down the Tree of Liberty, a fact that gave rise to the appointment of an investigatory committee. That body has already ordered a large number of house searches. The representative on mission, Dumont, considers that measure insufficient. He has ordered that any clergyman found in the street between 6 p.m. and 7 a.m. is to be arrested, as is any citizen as of 10 p.m. More generally, anybody caught criticising any revolutionary measure is to be arrested.

A halt is made to de-Christianisation

Paris, December 6

Is Robespierre to be viewed as a protector of Catholicism? A decree that he has put through the Convention condemns "any measures and any violence contrary to freedom of religion", but without repealing the laws aimed at non-juring priests. This initiative is a move against the powerful movement of de-Christianisation, accompanied by some anti-religious masquerades and church closings, that got under way at the start of autumn. Robespierre had taken a stand on this issue on November 21st. He is a Deist and moved away from Catholicism while still in secondary school. Hence he cannot be suspected of any liking for "fanaticism", but he thinks the de-Christianisers' zeal will be sure to bring the Revolution into disrepute, or even "awaken" expiring religion. Danton expressed the same feelings in the Convention on the next day. The Paris Commune, a direct target of these speeches, initially seemed to choose confrontation by issuing an order on the 23rd. closing all churches in the capital. But Robespierre's determination forced it to cancel that decision as of the 28th. With the December 6th. decree, the "Incorruptible One" scored again in his conflict with the Commune's "zealots", as they are often called. He said that their exaggerated views supplied arguments to foreign sovereigns, who constantly denounce the Revolution's supposed impiety.

The fabulous "Régent" diamond found

Paris, December 10

The *Régent* has been found. That fabulous diamond of around 140 carats had disappeared on September 12th., 1792. It was stolen from the royal wardrobe, along with the *Sancy*, the *Diamant bleu*, the *Toison d'or* and all of the crown jewels. It had remained hidden since then, despite all the efforts of the police to track it down. The investigation which has been headed by Vadier brought the diamond to light in the attic of a Paris house on Allée des Veuves, near the Champs Elysées where it was concealed by somebody in a hole of "an inch and a half" in a beam. The capital's police have not yet managed to discover who hid it there.

Du Barry pays dearly for a King's love

The seductive Mme. Du Barry.

Paris, December 8

As the guillotine blade came down on the back of her neck, Mme Du Barry cried out like an animal having its throat slit. The knife had difficulty cutting into her neck because of all the fat. The woman who had loved life passionately was dragged to the execution site half dead of terror, and the executioner had to carry her in his arms to the scaffold. She had vainly tried this morning to save her life by giving her judges a list of her hidden wealth. Her statements delayed her execution by only a few hours. She had been denounced for well-known lack of public spirit and aristocracy, and Louis XV's former favourite was arrested on September 22nd. She had never fully realised the nature of the danger. She had naively believed that to be acquitted, she need only deny having supplied London émigrés with funds. She did not know the result of her trial was a foregone conclusion.

Marceau and Kléber crush Vendeans at Le Mans

Le Mans, December 12

"Ah, I wish I were dead!" The despair that has seized the Vendeans is summed up in that reply made by La Rochejaquelein to Lescure's widow, who expressed surprise to find him alive after the battle. The fact is that the defeat at Le Mans put an end to the Catholic and royal army's long wanderings north of the Loire river. Since their victory at Dol, the Whites have followed the opposite path to the one that had led them to the coasts of the English Channel. Their only goal was to get back across the Loire, but their failure outside Angers forced them to head back north, still harassed by their republican pursuers. They still con-stituted a substantial body of sol-diers, though haggard and famish-ed, when they seized Le Mans on December 10th. to seek food and rest. But after barely two days of respite, the Blues were there. The Whites managed to repulse the van-guard commanded by Westermann, but they succumbed when Marceau and then Kléber arrived. There was terrible bloodshed in the narrow little streets in the old town, cram-med with women, children as well as the wounded. However, between 20,000 and 30,000 Vendeans man-aged to flee, following the Laval road. They are only a fleeing rem-nant, whom people nearby are help-ing to track down, out of fear or because of a hatred of royalism.

The battle while at its peak in the countryside around the city.

Faulty procedure at Babeuf's trial

Sylvain Maréchal, atheistic writer.

Paris, December 7

Sylvain Maréchal has proven his effectiveness. By getting the trial quashed on the basis of faulty pro-cedure, he enabled his friend Ba-beuf to get out of jail after three weeks' detention. The affair dates back to last January. Babeuf was accused of having produced a forged signature for an auction of national property, and he had to flee from the Somme and take ref-uge in Paris, where Maréchal got him a job at the "Administration des Subsistances". But Babeuf had been sentenced in absentia by the Somme court and was jailed on November 14th. Now he hopes to be acquitted (→ July 18, 94).

Oberkampf's factory is going through a difficult phase

Jouy en Josas, December 11

For the first time since the start of the revolutionary torment, Chris-tophe Philippe Oberkampf, the di-rector of the printed-fabrics factory in Jouy en Josas, is worried about his business. Previously, business had not suffered from the political situation. On the contrary, that si-tuation had brought higher con-sumption by the lower classes, and his fabrics had even become some-thing of a fad among the well-off classes. In the face of higher de-mand, Oberkampf had undertaken construction of additional work-shops, which are on the way to completion. But since then, the warehouse has emptied out rapidly. The stocks of white fabrics are com-pletely exhausted, the "Maximum" law has driven up the prices of all raw materials, dyes are no longer to be found, and Oberkampf has had to cut his prices by 20 to 40 per cent to maintain sales. In addition, the war is not helping matters. Many workers left for the front, the result being that the workshops were left empty.

J. B. Huet drew, for Oberkampf, the motifs of this Jouy fabric representing the factory's work.

14 *(Frimaire 24, Year II)*
Paris. At the Jacobins Club, Robespierre defends Camille Desmoulins, who is threatened with being purged.

14 *(Frimaire 24, Year II)*
Nantes. Members of the Marat Company take custody of 129 prisoners at du Bouffay prison, who are put on launches and drowned during the night.

15 *(Frimaire 25, Year II)*
Paris. In the third edition of the *Vieux Cordelier*, Camille Desmoulins attacks the system of terror made into a principle of government.

15 *(Frimaire 25, Year II)*
Bas Rhin. The combined offensive carried out by Pichegru and Hoche causes a veritable exodus. Nearly 40,000 people take refuge in Germany, fleeing from the French.

17 *(Frimaire 27, Year II)*
Paris. At the Convention, Fabre d'Eglantine wins approval for the arrest of Vincent and Ronsin.

19 *(Frimaire 29, Year II)*
Paris. In the sealed property of Delaunay, one of the accused persons in the India Company affair, Amar discovers the original of the fake liquidation decree bearing the signature of Fabre d'Eglantine (→ Jan. 13, 94).

19 *(Frimaire 29, Year II)*
Toulon. Dugommier chases the English out of the city.

20 *(Frimaire 30, Year II)*
Paris. At the Convention, Robespierre, eager to avoid a major split in the Montagnards' ranks, proposes the establishment of a special committee responsible for seeking out suspects who have been unjustly jailed.

21 *(Nivôse 1, Year II)*
Paris. Collot d'Herbois returns from Lyons to justify his repressive activities. In defending the terrorists, he turns the situation around in their favour, both in the Convention and at the Jacobin Club.

23 *(Nivôse 3, Year II)*
Loire Atlantique. The remnants of the great Catholic and royalist army are crushed at Savenay (→ 24).

24 *(Nivôse 4, Year II)*
The Convention rechristens Toulon, a major port in the south, Port de la Montagne.

25 *(Nivôse 5, Year II)*
Paris. Robespierre submits a report to the Convention outlining the principles of the revolutionary government. →

Dugommier and Bonaparte recapture Toulon from England

The Republic's troops have just recaptured a war-ravaged port city of Toulon and a decimated fleet.

Toulon, December 19

In the port, ships and arsenals are burning out. After five days and five nights of non-stop vigilance and battle against the Anglo-Spanish forces, General Dugommier's army entered the city. The day before, the enemy had set fire to the French ships before fleeing by sea. Actually, the die was cast two days ago on Aiguillette promontory, where the English had built a vast redoubt.

It was defended by 3,000 men and was considered impregnable. But that view neglected the will-power displayed by Dugommier and a young artillery captain, Napoléon Bonaparte. In a driving rain, the republican troops had to finish the battle in hand-to-hand combat. Inhabitants who turned the city over to the English last August are trembling at the idea of republican punishment (→ Dec. 24).

A fan showing one episode in the French victory over the English.

No more roads now leading to Bourges

Centre, December 21

The poor condition of the roads is seriously worrying the authorities of the departments of Cher and Indre. Whenever the weather takes a hand, horses get bogged down and carts wind up in the ditch. For instance, the road from Bourges to the Allogny forest collapsed, cutting the city off from its wood reserve. More serious is the fact that the diligence providing connections with the capital was sidelined by the fall of a chestnut tree uprooted by the wind. The boxes contained official mail and missives from the Revolutionary Court. Berry is cut off from the world more than ever before.

Free, obligatory primary schools voted

Paris, December 19

The local popular associations' agitation has paid dividends. Public education has become a topical subject. After three months of confrontation following abandonment of Le Peletier de Saint Fargeau's proposal, the deputies have finally just reached agreement. Determined not to leave children to their own devices because of the disorganisation of the religious schools, they have approved and voted Deputy Gabriel Bouquier's education project. Primary education will be lay, free and obligatory for all children aged six to nine. The teachers, who must have a certificate of "civism", will be paid by the state as a function of the number of their students, and will be subject to the active vigilance of the popular associations. It is a sign of the times that ecclesiastics are also authorised to open schools, provided they meet the same requirements as "lay" teachers. In view of the fact that freedom of worship was solemnly declared on December 6th., the legislators do not want to ostracise the clergy in any way. This political will is also the result of a practical consideration. The Assembly knows that clergymen are almost the only citizens now with enough experience and knowledge to be able to teach. Moreover, there is the fact that establishing a state monopoly would be a risky undertaking, particularly in the countryside, in which the "little schools" are really flourishing institutions.

Saint Just orders arrest of Schneider

Strasbourg, December 14

After his return to Strasbourg following his report on his activity to the Committee of Public Safety, Saint Just decided to settle matters with Euloge Schneider. The Strasbourg public prosecutor perverted his functions by handing out extremely unfair judgements during his inspection "tours". He even attracted attention to himself the day of his wedding. The couple returned to Strasbourg in a *chaise de poste* drawn by six horses and escorted by National Guards, and they had the guards of the Porte Nationale honour them. Referring to this "insolent luxury", Saint Just immediately had Schneider arrested (→ April 1, 94).

Robespierre joins the camp of advocates of Terror policy

Paris, December 25

Robespierre has taken a clear position. In his *Report on the Principles of the Revolutionary Government* read to the Convention, the "Incorruptible One" condemned the partisans of moderantion and supported the Terror policy. Distinguishing the constitutional government, made for peace, from the revolutionary government prevailing in wartime, Robespierre stated: "Those who call the revolutionary laws arbitrary or tyrannical are stupid and perverse sophists." Why has Robespierre suddenly changed? It was thought that he had joined the Indulgent campaign led by the Dantonists against the Terror and the Hébertists. In fact, during the whole month of December, he constantly attacked "exaggerated" pa-

triots. On the 12th. he had Cloots expelled from the Jacobin Club, and Cloots was then able to point to his humanistic beliefs only by publishing an *Appeal to the Human Race*. On the 14th., Robespierre came out in defence of Desmoulins, who was being attacked because of his pamphlets against the Terror that appeared in *Le Vieux Cordelier*. Finally, on the 17th., he supported Fabre d'Eglantine who had the Hébertists Vincent and Ronsin arrested. But on the 21st., Collot d'Herbois, who had returned hastily from Lyons to combat the Indulgent offensive, made Robespierre change his mind. Even if he has fallen away from the advocates of clemency, he still opposes the Hébertists. He will have to maintain a stand between two camps.

Robespierre fears losing influence.

It is recommended to say "tu" at work

Paris, December 25

Silence is golden...and especially when one still has the Ancien Régime's detested formulas on one's lips. A waiter at the Procope Café learnt this fact at some cost to himself. While serving two customers who wanted some refreshment, he was so imprudent as to use the "vous" form in talking to them, whereas for a month now, the "tu" form has been obligatory in Paris. Even worse, he called them "messieurs" as if he did not know that this term has been banished from patriots' vocabularies. The two citizens reacted sharply, insulting him and calling him a "slave".

The Vendean army is dispersed after its defeat at Savenay

A soldier of the Vendean army.

Loire Atlantique, December 24

Mme. de Lescure spent an anxious night in Prinquiau. She had taken refuge with some peasants after the destruction of the Vendean army at Savenay, and had trouble sleeping despite her exhaustion. On the humble share cropper's farm where she was staying, her room was separated from the stable only by a wood partition, and the noise of the cattle striking their horns on the floor made her awaken with a start several times. Was it not the Blues, knocking on the door to announce a search? Hiding and escaping the pursuers is the only thing that matters now to the survivors of

the campaign, following the Vendeans' defeat by the republicans yesterday at Savenay. After the defeat at Le Mans, the "brigands", harassed by General Westermann, exhausted by hunger and suffering from dysentery, again moved out toward the Loire river, which they finally reached at Ancenis. But due to a lack of boats, they were unable to cross it, except for La Rochejaquelein and Stofflet, who set out like scouts in a canoe and were pursued by "Blue" soldiers on the far bank. The Vendeans, deprived of their leaders, then began to disperse. Savenay, where they were defeated, was their last battle.

The principles and the symbols of the French Republic.

Members of the former French Academy petition to receive the right to pensions

Paris, December 23

Farewell pensions and other income! The French Academy is dead, and with it the former Academicians' means of existence. They have been reduced to telling the Assembly that they might starve to death, in the vain hope of regaining at least a little of their former incomes. They are headed by the most brilliant one among them, the poet La Harpe, who submitted a petition in the name of his colleagues explaining their complaints. If the last "symptom of decay" has been done away with, so

be it. But is it fair, is it republican, all the same to deprive honest writers of their means of existence? The abolition of pensions has already ruined many of them. In the past, a writer only needed to make an honourable name for himself and then wait for the king or some important lord to grant him the funds needed for his talent to blossom. If they are deprived of their income as Academicians, what will become of them? That is why they are demanding that they be paid the 25,000 livres that used to go to the defunct Academy.

Geneva watch with portraits of Robespierre and Marat.

Convention

26 (*Nivôse 6, Year II*)
Paris. The Convention decrees that due to the war, no foreigner may represent the French people from now on (→28).

26 (*Nivôse 6, Year II*)
Alsace. Lazare Hoche's victory over General Wurmser's Austrians at Geisberg makes it possible to relieve the city of Strasbourg from the enemy threat.

26 (*Nivôse 6, Year II*)
Paris. An order allows women to attend meetings of the Commune and they will also be allowed to knit there.

26 (*Nivôse 6, Year II*)
Paris. Billaud Varenne gets the Convention to reject the proposal by Robespierre for the establishment of a "justice committee" responsible for checking on whether arrests are justified.

27 (*Nivôse 7, Year II*)
Bas Rhin. Hoche enters Wissembourg, reinforcing the French positions on the Rhine. Desaix meanwhile captures Lauterbourg.

28 (*Nivôse 8, Year II*)
Paris. Robespierre has the honours of the Panthéon awarded to the young Bara. The artist David is requested to paint his portrait (→July 11, 93).

28 (*Nivôse 8, Year II*)
Paris. The former Girondist minister, Lebrun, and the Feuillant mayor of Strasbourg, Dietrich, are sent to the guillotine.

28 (*Nivôse 8, Year II*)
Paris. In application of the decree of December 26th. against foreigners, Thomas Paine and Anacharsis Cloots are arrested and jailed in Luxembourg jail.

28 (*Nivôse 8, Year II*)
Paris. Divorce proceedings are simplified. The courts will now have to rule on divorces within a month after they are requested, and men will then be entitled to remarry immediately.

30 (*Nivôse 10, Year II*)
Rouen. The first civic feast is celebrated in the city's cathedral, which has been turned into a Temple of Reason. It is followed by the installation of busts of some republican martyrs on the four sides of the fountain on Marché Neuf Square, which is renamed Montagnards Square.

31 (*Nivôse 11, Year II*)
Paris. Execution of General Biron, who proclaims his royalist beliefs while on the scaffold.

All of the peasants must have ability to be land owners

Haute Saône, December 26

Such unjust practices have to stop. Speaking to the Favernay People's Association, citizen Lebichet denounced the administrators of Vesoul district. In wishing to sell national property only *en bloc*, they prevent poor peasants from buying any, while at the same time, they also allow the new "privileged class" to become even richer. To patriots' applause, he urged cancellation of the sales and proposed a fairer distribution of lands so as to enable everybody with such a desire to become the owner of an estate.

Hérault: "Yes, I'm noble. So what?"

Paris, December 29

In some cases, attack is sometimes better than defence. His realisation of this fact has just helped Hérault de Séchelles save his head. On December 16th., he was accused by Bourdon de l'Oise of collusion with foreign agents. That was one way of reproaching him for his origins. "Yes, I'm noble. So what?" he told the deputies. He offered his resignation to the Commitee of Public Safety, with his hands stretched out toward the portrait of Le Peletier, a nobleman and a martyr. It was rejected.

De Wendel property seized by Republic

Hayange, December 30

The Convention reacted immediately. To punish the de Wendel family's flight to Luxembourg, the Republic nationalised their forges and mills at Le Creusot and in Lorraine, and sequestered their property. This Draconian measure is proportional to the offence. The Assembly is certain that Ignace de Wendel is now acting against the interests of the Revolution. This gifted engineer is the main artisan of the modernisation of the French steel industry, but now he has put his knowledge at the service of the enemies of France.

The peaceful life of a painter in prison

Painter Hubert Robert depicted himself in his cell at Sainte Pélagie.

Paris, December

"My father says that you were a companion in misfortune." The daughter of poet Jean Antoine Roucher wrote these words to the painter Hubert Robert, who shares her father's cell. At Sainte Pélagie, well-off prisoners may live with only two or three in a cell. That is fine for the two men since they are friends, so their fate is less bitter. Actually, if it were not for anxiety about the future, life there would almost be pleasant. With the antiques' expert Millin, Joseph Audran of the Gobelins factory and the painter Restout, they are in good company, and the detention rules are not too strict. They can receive food and books, have visitors, and fill their hours in whatever way they like. Hubert Robert spends his time drawing. He always has a pencil or a brush in his hand, and he even indulges in decorating the plates.

Loménie de Brienne forswears, is freed

Sens, December 26

After a long 41-year career, the metropolitan of the Yonne, Loménie de Brienne, has given up his clerical garb. A letter from England was the origin of this about-face. The letter arrived a month ago at the home of the former cardinal, addressed by Mr de Canisy to his wife, indicated as "residing at the bishop's home". As Mrs de Canisy's uncle, Loménie de Brienne was immediately suspected of involvement in complicity with "foreign conspirators". He was arrested and thrown into Sens prison on the basis of an order issued by the Vigilance Committee. But then one week later, the city's General Council received a letter in which Loménie de Brienne gave up all of his ecclesiastical functions and duties. He even went so far as to say that his decision was not due to being jailed, but that he had wanted to resign as archbishop for a long time. He said that the reason was that for a long time, his only cult had been the cult of Reason. Still, he had to wait almost another two weeks for his release. His home is still watched by a guard.

The former minister of Louis XVI.

🏛 **Convention**

1 *(Nivôse 12, Year II)*
Paris. The Committee of Public Safety criticises the excessive de-Christianisation measures adopted by the representative Lequinio in Charente Inférieure.

2 *(Nivôse 13, Year II)*
Paris. A Convention decree orders the dispatch of the *Collection of Historic Actions* by Léonard Bourdon to popular associations and to schools.

3 *(Nivôse 14, Year II)*
Vendée. A republican column seizes Noirmoutiers, where d'Elbée is taken prisoner.

4 *(Nivôse 15, Year II)*
Paris. The Committee of Public Safety orders the production of bayonets, rather than pike-staffs, which are considered ineffective.

5 *(Nivôse 16, Year II)*
Angers. The chaplain of the royalist and Catholic army, Guillot de Folleville, arrested near Ancenis, is shot at the order of the Military Committee. He is better known as the Bishop of Agra.

6 *(Nivôse 17, Year II)*
Corsica. In Murato, the English representative, Gilbert Eliott, is negotiating with Pascal Paoli on the terms of English aid for the Corsican separatists (→June 15, 94).

6 *(Nivôse 17, Year II)*
Paris. A Convention decree authorises the destruction of the Marseilles churches that have been used for federalists' meetings.

7 *(Nivôse 18, Year II)*
Rhineland. Pichegru claims credit in contacts with War Minister Bouchotte for the capture of Landau, to Hoche's detriment.

9 *(Nivôse 20, Year II)*
Noirmoutiers. The execution takes place of Maurice Gigost d'Elbée. Several hundred Vendean prisoners are shot with him.

10 *(Nivôse 21, Year II)*
Paris. Death of Rhineland revolutionary Georg Forster. He had become embittered about the trend followed by French policy with respect to the German patriotic middle class.

10 *(Nivôse 21, Year II)*
Paris. Camille Desmoulins, who is continuing his attacks on advocates of the Terror in *Le Vieux Cordelier*, is expelled from the Jacobins Club at Robespierre's personal suggestion.

Bonnefoy lambastes prison conditions

Paris, January 1

He has nothing more to lose. Tomorrow, former War Commissioner Charles Bonnefoy will lose his head, and in his cell in the Conciergerie, he thinks mostly of Fouquier Tinville. The public prosecutor can do anything, except prevent a prisoner from sending his last letter to him, and from denouncing the detainees' living conditions. He describes the drunken keepers who shamelessly steal the "residents'" property, as the *concierges*, the Richards, look on benevolently. With cold irony, Bonnefoy adds that the prisoners never know under what law sentence has been passed on them, and that the majority of them have probably wound up in jail by mistake.

Fouquier Tinville, the accuser.

The tragic resistance of Mrs Lavoisier

Paris, January

Mrs Lavoisier has destroyed her husband in trying to save him. The scientist will be tried at the same time as the other jailed tax farmers for "abuses and malfeasance". That is precisely what his wife wanted to avoid, and that is why she called on Antoine Dupin, Convention Commissioner. He had promised her that the famous chemist's case would be dissociated from the one involving his financial colleagues. One could also try to arrange his escape during a transfer to another prison. But far from producing the anticipated results, the talk turned to the prisoner's disadvantage. Mrs Lavoisier was bitter and insulting. She did not hide her indignation, saying haughtily that she was not asking for pity, but for justice, since her husband was innocent and "his only accusers were scoundrels". The furious Dupin dismissed her at that point, and he is now quite determined that he will turn a deaf ear to any approach that may be made to him in the future on behalf of the chemist.

A bitter return for maid of a priest

Mont Blanc, January 9

Marie Antoinette Richard has no intention of letting people impose on her just because she has just gotten out of jail. She was released after having been found innocent on a charge of "fanaticism". But when the maid of the former parish priest returned to the town of Montgilbert, she found that her house had been looted, and her furniture, effects and money had vanished. Marie Antoinette immediately filed a complaint before the judge who had just acquitted her. Neighbours' testimony and her own underlying conviction indicate that the looter and the person who denounced her to the authorities are one and the same.

Luckner, commander of the French forces, was guillotined for treason on January 4th.

Georges Cadoudal becomes engaged

Morbihan, January 7

After 44 days of war against the republican forces, Georges Cadoudal went back home, to Kerléano, accompanied by his comrade-in-arms Pierre Mercier. While fighting side by side against the Blues, the two young men pledged never to leave each other. They want to liberate Brittany together. Furthermore, they will soon belong to the same family. During their military campaign, the two friends stopped off several times at the Merciers' home, in Château Gonthier. There, Georges met Lucrèce, Pierre's sister. She is 17 years old, while he is 23. He was won over by the girl's grace. She loved his courage and his royalist faith. They won the parents' approval, and a non-juring priest came to bless their modest engagement ceremony. The wedding, however, will be some time later. The reason is that Georges does not want to marry Lucrèce until the King is back on his throne. He says that will not be long now.

Republican Carol

Curious songs called civic or republican carols are going the rounds. This one is particularly popular.
Changed to sans-culotte lowly
God plans His heaven to show.
Of a pure virgin lowly
Born here on earth below.
And as to His Conception,
'Tis true all know the way :
The husband was not there,
He was so heard to swear.
Rumours run everywhere;
That's how it's done to-day.
A darksome stable : therein
The Christ-child saw the day.
Royal purple and sheepskin
Come nigh and homage pay.
Princes and legislators
They trace the Magi's way.
And all as one combine
Before the sacred shrine
Where lies the Child divine,
Their homage due to pay.
Lord of the sans-culottes,
Robespierre bold entered in.
"I here denounce you all!"
(A fit the orator threw).
"Christ! What schemers base!
It's naught but a disgrace!
The worship You embrace
To me is rightly due!"

Convention

11 *(Nivôse 22, Year II)*
Paris. Bishop Lamourette, who was taken prisoner during the siege of Lyons, city of central France, is tried and guillotined.

12 *(Nivôse 23, Year II)*
Champs sur Marne. A detailed investigation carried out by the Committee of General Security confirms that Henriette de Marbeuf did plant a total of 287 arpents of land with lucerne, rather than with wheat as she should have done (→ Feb. 5, 94).

13 *(Nivôse 24, Year II)*
Paris. The Convention grants the honours of the Panthéon to Deputy Fabre, who was killed while on a special mission on December 20th. 1793, during the French troops' retreat after they were defeated by the Spaniards at Banyuls.

13 *(Nivôse 24, Year II)*
Paris. The Feydeau theatre, which refuses to put on plays that are too political, schedules *Paul et Virginie*, an opera by Alphonse Dutheuil and Jean Lesueur, based on the book by Bernardin de Saint Pierre.

14 *(Nivôse 25, Year II)*
Paris. Amar reveals to the Convention the ins and outs of the India Company scandal, and especially dwelling on Fabre d'Eglantine's embezzlements.

14 *(Nivôse 25, Year II)*
Auteuil. Since her husband is regarded as a fugitive, Sophie de Condorcet very reluctantly files a divorce petition with the municipality so that her daughter will not suffer from the law calling for disinheriting the children of émigrés.

16 *(Nivôse 27, Year II)*
Paris. A decree issued by the Convention renames Marseilles Ville sans Nom, or The Nameless City.

16 *(Nivôse 27, Year II)*
Paris. Divorce of the Restif de La Bretonne couple. →

16 *(Nivôse 27, Year II)*
Rochefort. Execution of seven sailors who could have borne witness to the inaccuracy of the charges made against Admiral Grimoard, who was guillotined on January 8th. in connection with what is known to be a case of personal revenge.

17 *(Nivôse 28, Year II)*
Vendée. Applying the slogan that the Vendée region must be destroyed, General Turreau organises the "infernal columns" that are going to ravage the strife-torn department (→ 21).

Fabre d'Eglantine put under arrest

The cause of the scandal.

Paris, January 13

The long-running financial scandal involving the India Company has become a political affair. There is nothing surprising about that. It compromises some prominent men suspected of having been corrupted, including Fabre d'Eglantine. He was the man who signed the fake decree ordering liquidation of the Company, to his own benefit. In November he stated that he did not know anything about the forgers, and protested he was innocent. But Fabre is a Dantonist opponent of the Terror and supports the Indulgent campaign led by Desmoulins, and the Committee of General Safety viewed this affair as a good way to eliminate him from the political arena. It asked Amar, who was responsible, along with Fabre, for investigating the case, to push ahead with his probe. Amar arranged for removal of the seals placed on the papers of Delaunay, who drew up the fake decree, and in them, he actually found the text of the document, corrected by Fabre in pencil. That proves that he did indeed know what he was doing when he signed the forgery. These facts led to Fabre's arrest during the night. His friend Danton, indirectly affected by the accusation, wanted to defend him today before the Convention, but Billaud Varenne and Vadier did not leave him enough time to do so. Just as Danton was getting up, Billaud Varenne said to him: "Woe to him who has sat beside Fabre d'Eglantine and who is still his dupe!" As for Robespierre, he is waiting, impartial, condemning the Dantonist faction as well as Hébertists (→ 14).

What Parisians eat these days

Even if they are equal in rights, Parisians are not equal when it comes to eating. To the poor man with just a few sous, the strolling merchants at Pont au Change offer herring roasted with scallions, cooked prunes and lentils. That is the sombre and often the only meal of the working-man. But as soon as you go into one of the fashionable restaurants, it is quite another kind of menu. Véry, for instance, offers its customers 44 side-dishes, 31 poultry dishes and 28 fish dishes. At Beauvilliers, *boudin d'écrevisses* rivals with *tourte de rognons*. Despite food shortages, some people indulge in carousing. Thanks to the black market, meals with more than a score of courses are not rare. Among other exquisite dishes, the guests sample *saint-pierre sauce aux câpres, anguilles à la tartare* and *culs d'artichauts à la ravigote*. More modest circles content themselves with beef with pickles and ray with black butter. The prisons have not been spared by this culinary frenzy. Chabot, jailed at the Luxembourg, has a fattened pullet and stuffed chickens delivered to him every day. Meanwhile, the queues are getting longer in front of the bakeries.

A butcher is fined for price violations

Montgeron, January 15

Butcher Robillard has got into trouble. He is accused of having tried to starve the community by violating price controls, having refused to sell his meat at the set price. And to boost his profits, he slaughtered his herd of sheep and sold the meat in Paris for five sols more. He tried to explain that price controls were making him lose money, but the court paid no attention to this claim. It sentenced him to a 100-livre fine and had his name put on the list of suspects. If he falls from grace again ...

Happy the tradesman who escapes from the hunt for speculators!

The divorce of Restif de La Bretonne

Paris, January 16

Agnès Restif has finally got her way. The divorce of the Restif couple, issued today on the grounds of separation and misunderstandings, gives her back her freedom. Husband and wife have lived apart for almost nine years now, and they do not at all suffer from this fact. Their love match did not survive 15 years of conjugal life, nor Agnès's infidelity. Restif strongly suspected her of having deceived him in the past, and what is even worse, under his own roof. The lucky man is said to have been a young poet, Joubert, whom Restif had taken in out of friendship. To wipe out the memory of that sad experience, Restif is thinking of marriage again ...

Forced conversion of an Epinal craftsman

Epinal, January 13

Jean Charles Pellerin, one of Epinal's most famous artist-craftsmen, had some very unwelcome callers today. To check on proper observance of the law of last October 22nd. ordering the abolition of all emblems of royalty on playing cards, the mayor and his clerk made the rounds to inspect all the places in town that might have them. In Pellerin's establishment, they found some "criminal" plates, which were immediately destroyed. Now, in order to earn a living, he will have to limit himself to engraving pastoral scenes, shepherds, and such, or to making clock faces on paper. Fortunately for him, he is also a clock-maker.

Music at the service of the Republic

Paris, January 18

It is necessary to institutionalise music's role in popular festivities. That was the idea that led the musician Sarrette to make a proposal to the Committee on Public Education on January 10th.: the creation of an association that would print patriotic hymns and songs and send them to all districts in the Republic for performance at national and other festivities. Since hand-written scores are enough for performance, the works would not be engraved or kept. The Committee was taken with the idea after reading this report, and it approved the plan today. The musicians of the National Institute, who have an obvious interest in the matter, will be asked to supply the Association every month with some 50 to 60 pages containing four or five works. The profits from subscriptions will be paid over to musicians' widows and children.

Students of David enter the Muséum

Paris, January 11

For a long time, the artist David had wanted to control the choices of the Muséum, even if only by means of intermediaries. Now he has had his way. The Museum Committee has been replaced by a new committee with ten members, all of them beholden to the painter. Even though it had led in the long run to the opening of the Louvre museum last November 11th., the defunct institution was condemned to death. Its awkward classification system, unfortunate restorations and "colourless patriotism" made it suspect in the authorities' eyes. The new curators, paid 2,400 livres, all share a passion: Antiquity.

A collection of heroic acts for edification of all the young people of the Republic

The young drummer Darrudder avenging his father, slain by a Vendean.

Paris, January 16

Children like stories, and they like stories of heroes more than any other kind. While amusing themselves, they will now also be able to learn, since the Conventionals have decided to make obligatory the *Collection of Heroic and Civic Actions* that Montagnard Léonard Bourdon has been preparing for several weeks. The Committee on Public Education has even set the press-run at 80,000 copies so that, in accordance with the recent Bouquier decrees, it may be present in every primary school. This new-type school manual consists entirely of virtuous and patriotic recitals honouring the Republic's civic values. It is also original in the way it has been drawn up. Since October, the popular associations and the citizens themselves have been sending Léonard Bourdon accounts of heroic deeds in which they participated or which they witnessed. In this way, the devotion of a Joigny farm worker or the bravery of the young Armand Sailland in combat will come down to posterity. Examples are the best possible teaching device.

A scene of heroism in Vendée: two young Republicans, whose village has just been burnt, risk their lives in trying to restrain the peasants in revolt, who are attempting to chop down the Tree of Liberty.

Blessed Tree

O blessed tree,
How famed you be,
A-telling me of Liberty.
And we who set thee here
Admire with pride sincere.
Thy stately height,
Thy colour bright,
Thy graceful sight,
A thousand charms diverse
Which nothing in the universe
Can ever disunite.
But I espy up there on high,
Kissing the sky, I specify,
Three objects all sublime,
The symbols of our time.
An ensign clear, a flag so dear,
A trusty spear.
True French, with love aflame,
A thousand times proclaim
That they these signs revere.
What king in palace bright,
His power despite,
Could see this bonnet unafraid?
It doth the Crown o'ershade!
Courtiers allege
That in this age
It doth outrage;
Behold it then, and may you all,
On seeing it, caught in its thrall,
Expire in fits of rage!

Convention

19 *(Nivôse 30, Year II)*
Paris. As the Arts Commune was dissolved due to lack of patriotism, Paris's patriotic artists, led by the engraver Antoine François Sergent, found a new group, the Popular and Republican Society of the Arts.

20 *(Pluviôse 1, Year II)*
Paris. At the Jacobin Club, Couthon opens a debate on the English Constitution.

21 *(Pluviôse 2, Year II)*
Toulon. Special envoy Albitte has the anniversary of Louis XVI's death celebrated by having wax figures representing a variety of European kings decapitated in public.

23 *(Pluviôse 4, Year II)*
Paris. Barras and Fréron, who led repression in Toulon, are both recalled by the Convention.

24 *(Pluviôse 5, Year II)*
Lyons. The architect Jean Antoine Morand, a student of Soufflot and responsible for the redevelopment of Quai Saint Clair, is guillotined.

26 *(Pluviôse 7, Year II)*
Paris. The Committee of Public Safety establishes a Revolutionary Agency for Powders and Saltpetre in order to supply the Revolution's forces with gunpowder.

27 *(Pluviôse 8, Year II)*
Paris. The Convention orders that French-speaking schoolteachers should be moved into regions in which vernacular languages dominate.

28 *(Pluviôse 9, Year II)*
Maine et Loire. Death of La Rochejaquelein at the battle of Nouaillé.→

29 *(Pluviôse 10, Year II)*
Saône et Loire. The People's Association of Autun arranges republican soirées at which Voltaire's *Death of Caesar* is performed.

30 *(Pluviôse 11, Year II)*
London. Charles Maurice de Tallyrand Périgord, accused of Jacobinism, has to leave England and goes to the U.S.

30 *(Pluviôse 11, Year II)*
Paris. The deputy, Coupé, of the Oise gets the Convention to approve the establishment of district libraries, which will receive books, paintings, prints and medals.

31 *(Pluviôse 12, Year II)*
Paris. Collot d'Herbois submits a report to the Convention on assistance and indemnities for the defenders of the fatherland.

"Infernal columns" of General Turreau ravage the countryside in the Vendée

Neither women nor children are spared by the Republican repression.

Vendée, January 21

One week for sacking la Vendée, that is the mission assigned to the 12 columns that followed up the Blues' latest military victory at Savenay by setting out from Cholet to devastate the rebellious area. This plan of systematic destruction is the work of General Turreau, the new chief of the Army of the West. The plan, which is considered barbarous and useless by many Blue generals, has not been explicitly approved by the Convention, but Turreau can portray it as a simple application of the measures adopted by the Assembly last August with respect to "destruction of the Vendée". Cynically calling this campaign a "military stroll", Turreau sent the following instructions to the generals commanding the columns: "All brigands who are found with arms in their hands, or are convicted of having taken up arms, will be bayoneted to death. You will act in the same way with the women, girls and children who are in the same category. Nor will persons who are merely suspect be spared. All of the villages, towns, crops and everything else that can possibly burn will be consigned to the flames."

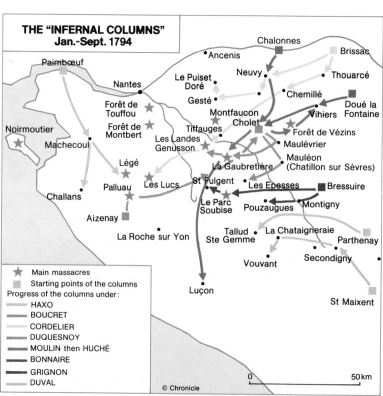

THE "INFERNAL COLUMNS"
Jan.-Sept. 1794

★ Main massacres
◼ Starting points of the columns
Progress of the columns under:
— HAXO
— BOUCRET
— CORDELIER
— DUQUESNOY
— MOULIN then HUCHÉ
— BONNAIRE
— GRIGNON
— DUVAL

0   50km

© Chronicle

The tribulations of Girondins in hiding

Saint Emilion, January 20

The lives of the outlawed are not sinecures. The Girondist deputies who have been hiding out for several days awaiting the end of the Terror know all about that. They spent the start of the winter in the small Bouquey cave, and endured many sufferings in that cold and humid hideout. They got up at noon, so that they would not have to have lunch. That's how scarce food was. They did not leave their prison until evening, to dine with the Bouqueys. Then, too, their refuge was becoming dangerous. Salle, Guadet, Louvet and Valady left on November 15th. Pétion, Buzot and Barbaroux decided to leave today. They took refuge in the home of the wigmaker Troquart, one of Guadet's friends. Fortunately for them, there are still some brave people, ready to risk their lives to help outlawed people who have to remain concealed in order to survive.

The contents of a Paris peddler's box

Paris, January

The overwhelming majority of the population does not know Florian's *Fables,* Delille's poems or Bernardin de Saint Pierre's exotic novels. It knows nothing of Diderot's *Encyclopaedia* or Voltaire's writings. What the masses read, when they know how to read, are mainly the things carried about by peddlers. And alongside Racine's works, Laclos's *Liaisons Dangereuses* or adaptations of great literary documents appreciated by the middle-class clientele, one finds primarily insipid and tear-jerking stories, which are imitations of English "black" novels, such as *Le Souterrain* or *Mathilde*, or recipes for obtaining material wealth or some other means of success. At least, this is what was contained in the box of the Parisian peddler Buy, which was seized during a search and was inventoried by the Revolutionary Committee of the Montagne. Other great successes are the revolutionary poems and songs that have replaced the lives of the saints, formerly very popular. These are small, anonymous books with a blue cover that is a firm emblem.

French is language of liberty: Barère

Paris, January 27

One knew the enemy was everywhere, both inside and outside. But before the Barère report to the Assembly, nobody suspected the enemy might also lurk in words. Yet that is what the deputy demonstrated today in speaking to the house, throughout a brilliant speech that aroused his listeners' enthusiasm. Using his finger and his voice, he singled out for public condemnation the four languages to be rooted out: Bas-Breton, German and its Alsace and Lorraine derivatives, Basque, and finally Corsican, a language close to Italian. These four languages are like the heads of a detested hydra that is constantly reborn and which is called, depending on the case, fanaticism, despotism, federalism or superstition. Freedom, according to Barère, will be unable to prevail over the whole national territory as long as such survivals of barbarism persist. How can people obey the laws if they do not know them and be trained without a national language? Hence he asked that a French-speaking teacher be named in each of the nine departments in question to teach children to read and speak French by using the *Declaration of Human Rights*. Thus the Tower of Babel raised by tyrants will be replaced by the only universal language of freedom.

Some laundresses running short of soap

Paris, January 23

Rebellion is brewing on Square des Tripes, in the Saint Marceau district. The local laundry-women are angry. Soap prices have been going up constantly for a year. The product is now at 25 sols per livre, and the authorities are very parsimonious in doling it out. When they have to waste a whole day to get soap, it winds up costing these poor women more than one ecu per livre. They can no longer continue to work under such circumstances. They are determined to defend themselves and their livelihood, and are going to pay a visit to city hall to protest.

Thousands of Paris women depend on doing laundry to earn a living.

The Vendeans lose their generalissimo

La Rochejaquelein's friends waste no time in avenging leader's death.

Maine et Loire, January 28

"Monsieur Henri" is dead. He set out on a reconnaissance trip leading a few armed horsemen and spotted two isolated republican soldiers on a road near Nouaillé. In a desire to capture them for intelligence purposes, he rushed at them, shouting: "Surrender, and I won't kill you." The two Blues then pretended to surrender, and one of them offered him his rifle. But just as the young general was stretching out his arm to take the weapon, the soldier fired, hitting him in the forehead. The general's companions rode up a few seconds later and massacred the two men on the spot, before proceeding with the burial. It was necessary to disfigure the Vendean hero to prevent the Blues from identifying him. Since he had recrossed the Loire river with Stofflet, he had harassed the Blues constantly by attacking isolated convoys, but sometimes his operations were on a much larger scale. As an example of his operations, he took a few hundred farmers and attacked several small republican outposts that were located rather far from each other, so that the republicans thought that they were having to deal with several roving gangs (→ Feb. 6).

A very strange "nursing home" indeed

Paris, January 24

Doctor Belhomme's so-called nursing home, at the top of Charonne street, is certainly a very strange establishment. Public prosecutor Fouquier Tinville has just assigned one of his deputies to investigate this luxury prison, to which the rich suspects held in Paris jails can ask to be sent if they are found to suffer from rheumatism. Once there, they are sure of escaping the scaffold as long as they tip well and pay the charges. The fact is that Belhomme has a lot of pull with the local watch committees, which make him pay through the nose for their tolerance, in that he has to give them a cut of his profits. But things have not been going well since the doctor boosted some of the charges to line his own pockets. For instance, Citizen Tissier revealed that he was paying 400 livres for an attic room, but that Belhomme had advised him to say it was only 200 if he were questioned about the matter. While she has occupied an identical room for 20 days, Mrs. de Breteuil complained that she had to pay 2,000 livres, and like the other inmates, also had to pay for food, heating, laundry, furniture, hair-dresser ... A number of detainees, who have unfortunately been unable or unwilling to satisfy their jailer's growing cupidity, have already been transferred to the Conciergerie.

2 *(Pluviôse 14, Year II)*
Vendée. The column led by Adjutant-General Lachenay burns Soubise Castle and kills 200 prisoners in the park.

3 *(Pluviôse 15, Year II)*
Paris. Robespierre and Danton attend the first performance at the Théâtre de la République of *Epicharis and Nero*, a tragedy by Gabriel Marie Legouvé.

4 *(Pluviôse 16, Year II)*
Paris. The Convention abolishes slavery in the French colonies. →

5 *(Pluviôse 17, Year II)*
Corsica. The English fleet anchors in the Bay of Mortella, bringing Paoli's militiamen the artillery they need to capture the ports remaining in the republicans' hands.

6 *(Pluviôse 18, Year II)*
Anjou. Stofflet, who has been the Vendeans' generalissimo since February 1st., secretly buries the body of La Rochejaquelein at the spot known as La Haye de Bureau, near Nouaillé. Stofflet is waiting for February 8th. to inform his men of their commanding general's death.

6 *(Pluviôse 18, Year II)*
Paris. Major Napoléon Bonaparte is promoted to brigadier general at the age of only 25.

7 *(Pluviôse 19, Year II)*
Paris. Louvet de Couvray leaves the capital secretly for Switzerland. →

8 *(Pluviôse 20, Year II)*
Paris. On the basis of a report from its agent in western France, Julien de la Drôme, who noted the pointless cruelty of repression in Nantes, the Committee of Public Safety has Carrier recalled to the capital (→21).

10 *(Pluviôse 22, Year II)*
Paris. Jacques Roux, one of the leaders of the Enragés, commits suicide in jail. →

11 *(Pluviôse 23, Year II)*
Paris. The manufacturer Périer is authorised to set up a rifle production unit in Notre Dame de Lorette Church.

12 *(Pluviôse 24, Year II)*
Paris. The Convention authorises Ville sans Nom (The Nameless City) to resume its former name of Marseilles.

12 *(Pluviôse 24, Year II)*
Paris. At the Cordeliers Club, Momoro denounces the Jacobins' moderation and the "Revolution's broken legs", thus attacking Robespierre but without naming him.

Paris Convention abolishes slavery

The whole world appears to be transfigured by the Assembly's decrees.

Belley, a Saint Domingue deputy.

Paris, February 4

The Blacks' cause has finally won in the Convention. The deputies from the French part of the island of Saint Domingue took their seats yesterday and had the Assembly approve a decree satisfying the demands of the leaders of the insurrection. Freedom and French citizenship are granted to all slaves in the colonies. The decree, which abolitionists had awaited for five years, was approved at a session devoted entirely to the political and military situation on Saint Domingue, which ended in an apotheosis of the island's three deputies: Louis Pierre Dufay, Jean Baptiste Belley and Jean Baptiste Mills, respectively White, Black and Mulatto. Their success was due to the fact that they used very clear language with respect to England. They say that abolition will win the Republic the allegiance of the Black insurgent forces, which have sworn to chase the English off the island. It will also make the slaves in the English colonies rise up. Considering such a possibility, Danton cried: "Today Pitt died." Actually, what the island's deputies did was to get the Convention to approve the policy that is already being enforced out there by civilian commissioners, one of whom, Sonthonax, is a member of Friends of the Blacks.

Two arrested Hébertists are released

Paris, February 2

The Parisian sansculottists' campaign has borne fruit. The two War Ministry Hébertists, Ronsin and Vincent, have just been released. The Committee of Public Safety stated that it did not have sufficient evidence against them. They had been arrested on December 17th. at the request of Dantonist Fabre d'Eglantine, who accused them of having demanded merciless repression in Lyons. That event caused a great stir among the lower classes, and since then, the Cordeliers and the National Guardsmen have agitated constantly for the release of their friends. But that release was due above all to the change in the Jacobins' attitude and to Collot d'Herbois's intervention. Since he returned from Lyons, the former Cordelier has made great efforts to show that jailing the Hébertists was unjustified. Did he himself not make exactly the same kind of remarks as Ronsin and Vincent? But let us be clear about one thing: the fact is that the struggle being waged between the Jacobins and the Enragés is far from being over yet (→ March 2).

Agriculture can also lead to the scaffold

Paris, February 5

The Marquise de Marbeuf and her steward, Payen, are going to be guillotined. Yet they are not guilty or treason, nor of plotting against the Republic with royalists or Prussian agents. All those accusations turned out to be false. But the court condemned them for having turned wheatfields into grassland. Even if the law allowed them to do this, their action contributed to starving the people, so the result is that they are major criminals.

When love is in control of politics ...

Bordeaux, February 4

A veritable palace revolution took place at the end of the afternoon. Tallien removed the Bordeaux watch committee, ordered the arrest of its members, and appointed a new three-member committee to carry out the interrogations. The official grounds for this decision were the arbitrary nature of arrests and the pointless severity of the prison system. But the real reason is Tallien's passion for the beautiful Thérésa Cabarrus, his mistress. At noon, the furious Tallien burst into her residence, threatening to have her guillotined. The watch committee had just intercepted a package containing a portrait of her and a rather tender letter addressed to Félix Le Peletier de Saint Fargeau. It took Thérésa several hours to calm her lover's terrible jealousy and then to persuade him to arrest the committee members for all the abuses they had committed. By six o'clock in the evening, they were behind bars.

General is waiting for glorious scars ...

Puy de Dôme, February 13

"If you want a portrait, bear the image of Freedom." That was not much consolation for General Desaix's sister. She and her mother had been jailed as suspects on November 15th., and she asked for a portrait of her brother to make her cell a less depressing place. But how was Desaix to have his portrait painted in Schifferstadt, a war-devastated village? The liberator of Alsace came up with an excuse to explain his refusal: he will soon have some glorious scars on his face, a proof of patriotism. Therefore, he will wait for the end of the war to have his portrait painted.

Jacques Roux kills himself in prison

Paris, February 10

The "red priest" preferred death to the humiliation of a trial with a foregone result. Arrested on September 5th., Jacques Roux was supposed to be tried by the Paris Correctional Police Court. However, after five months of proceedings, that court said it lacked jurisdiction and it sent his case back to the revolutionary Tribunal. To escape the guillotine, Jacques Roux stabbed himself five times in the chest. But since he had only injured himself seriously, he tried again. The second attempt was more successful: he perforated a lung and died during the day.

Terror and virtue, in Robespierre's view

Paris, February 5

Robespierre is a fierce champion of political balance, and the speech he just made to the Assembly proves that fact again. In his *Report on the Moral Principles that Must Guide the Convention*, Robespierre met the challenge of attacking both the Dantonists, who are favourable to indulgence, and the Hébertists, advocates of the Reign of Terror, blasting both factions in order to put over his own political line. This critique supplied him with an ideal opportunity for explaining his own conception of popular government in wartime and revolution. Then, he launched into a brilliant demonstration, explaining that this kind of government is based on two inseparable principles: "virtue, without which terror is fatal, and terror, without which virtue is powerless", and which is "a consequence of the general principle of democracy applied to the fatherland's most urgent needs". Robespierre had in the past already been heard to justify revolutionary dictatorship by invoking the necessities of national defence, but he has never gone as quite as far in the field of political theory in dealing with this particular point.

Louvet leaves capital for Switzerland

Paris, February 7

Ever since Louvet de Couvray came back to Paris, Lodoïska has been having a hard time. She had to find a way to hide her husband very quickly to save him from the guillotine. They were forced to leave their first refuge, as the friend who was putting up Lodoïska was unwilling to risk his life for an outlaw. In their new apartment, she handled the plane, hammer and plaster, making a fake closet in which to hide Louvet. The outlaw spent his days reading and writing his memoirs. At the slightest noise, he scurried back into the hiding place, waiting for the scare to blow over. But people cannot live for a long time with such anxiety. The couple had to look for another solution, and they found one. Lodoïska managed to get her husband into Switzerland, which welcomes immigrants from France. When he left her this morning, she promised to join him soon. She is two months pregnant, and if everything goes well, Louvet will be able to be present for their child's birth.

No death sentence for stubborn nuns

Paris, February 9

The eight nuns appearing before the court managed to escape the death penalty. Yet the charges were extremely serious. Despite the dissolution of their religious order, they had continued to live together on Cassette Street. Furthermore, they had taken in some non-juring priests, of which there are a large number in the Saint Sulpice area. A fanatical brochure was seized on their premises. And finally, they had stubbornly refused to take the liberty-equality oath. When they persisted in their attitude at the hearing, the judges were moved: "Swear, and you will be freed!" Everybody, including the police, gave them the same advice, but the nuns refused to be shaken. The troubled jury then showed its clemency, deciding to substitute deportation for the death penalty.

This montage of a Phrygian bonnet on a landscape background is a homage to the Republic, the mother of sciences. Recent discoveries make it possible to use balloons to make war and liberate other peoples.

A lullaby

Here is a republican lullaby which patriotic baby-sitters and good citizen-mothers sing to lull babies off to sleep. It is sung to the tune of "La Carmagnole".

To the tune of this warsong
Which taught tyrants a lesson,
I love to sing in unison
To my son, dearer than anyone.
And never more will baby weep
In fear of things that creep;
Hearing the Carmagnole
His eyes grow dim,
Hearing the Carmagnole,
His eyes grow dim with sleep.

Sleep little darling, do not cry,
And close your foxy little eye;
And as I sing my lullaby
You'll fall asleep by and by.
He's a dear sweet sugar bun,
Good as gold and weighs a ton,
Who'll be a big brave soldier,
Never afraid, never afraid,
Never afraid of the gun.

When you leave me my son,
To go out to the bright sun,
As soon as in the street you run,
'Tis not time for play and fun :
The little drum you'll beat,
The Carmagnole will help your feet;
Just like a duteous mother,
I'll put you in step.

15 *(Pluviôse 27, Year II)*
Paris. The Convention votes to do away with the old French navy flag and to replace it with a red, white and blue flag having the stripes arranged vertically.

17 *(Pluviôse 29, Year II)*
Corsica. The English capture Saint Florent, which they will in future use as a naval base.

19 *(Ventôse 1, Year II)*
Paris. The Small Arms Agency decides to appropriate the churches' lead roofs. The lead will be melted down to be used for the purpose of making bullets.

19 *(Ventôse 1, Year II)*
Paris. Opening of the Saltpetre Workers' and Gunnery School, where Monge and Berthollet, among others, are going to be teaching. →

19 *(Ventôse 1, Year II)*
Sumatra. The members of the Entrecasteaux expedition who came out in favour of the Republic are arrested at the order of the royalist d'Auribeau.

20 *(Ventôse 2, Year II)*
Bourbon Island. In application of the decree of March 19th., 1793, the colonial Assembly decrees that the island will be called Réunion Island from now on. But Governor Vigouroux du Plessis refuses to give his approval (→April 11, 94).

26 *(Ventôse 8, Year II)*
Paris. Saint Just has a decree issued sequestering suspects' property. →

26 *(Ventôse 8, Year II)*
Paris. The Opéra Comique creates an opera, *Congress of the Kings*, with music written by a dozen fashionable composers. Notable among them are the names of Grétry, Méhul and Kreutzer.

27 *(Ventôse 9, Year II)*
Paris. The Cordeliers once again demand the arrest of traitors they say are unworthy to sit in the Convention, including Camille Desmoulins.

27 *(Ventôse 9, Year II)*
Paris. Death of the architect Jean Rodolphe Perronet. Along with Trudaine, he had created the Bridges and Roads School, which he directed until his death.

28 *(Ventôse 10, Year II)*
Vendée. General Cordelier's column massacres a total of 468 inhabitants at Lucs sur Boulogne, including 110 children aged from three months to seven years.

Pius VI makes Abbot Maury a cardinal

Rome, February 21
Abbot Maury is getting his reward. Pope Pius VI has just made him a cardinal for his services to the cause of the Church and kings. The famous orator of the Constituent Assembly, detested by the revolutionaries, is enjoying a triumphal reception in all the courts of Europe. When he left France in November 1791, Maury already had a high reputation. For instance, when he went to visit the princes in Koblenz, 600 French gentlemen in two rows applauded him as he went by. Then the Pope invited him to Rome, where cardinals and Roman princesses vied for the honour of inviting the abbot. Maury, who was named Archbishop of Nicaea by Pope Pius VI, was sent as ambassador of the Holy See to Frankfurt, where Holy Roman Emperor Francis II and the King of Prussia rendered him the same homage he

Maury is a shoe-maker's son.

had received in Koblenz. Later, at the very time at which the Convention decreed his arrest, he received the bishopric of Montefiascone, which is a town in the province of Tuscany that is quite well known for its wines.

Civic education continues on days off

Gironde, February 18
The Revolution is giving rise to some real devotion to teaching. The teachers in Libourne, not content with devoting themselves to the children just on workdays, are pushing their efforts to the point of working even on "décadi", which is supposed to be their day off. As desired by the people's associations, they take their pupils to the Temple of Reason and have them sing republican texts and patriotic songs, thus edifying their parents.

Saltpetre and powders are on the agenda

Paris, February 19
National defence needs are a controlling factor. Where the Ancien Régime would have taken three years, 30 days is enough for the Republic. A month is all aspiring arms-makers will have for learning how to turn out powders and saltpetre. The idea came from Barère, who submitted it and had his colleagues on the Committee of Public Safety adopt it on February 2nd. As of today, a thousand strong citizens, gunners or National Guardsmen from every corner of the country, will attend intensive courses that will be taught by some of France's greatest chemists.

Some students sent by various departments are going to bring the Assembly some powder and saltpetre they have made and a gun they cast.

Dancer recovers her civic spirit paper

Paris, February 22
The famous dancer Marie Madeleine Guimard, who is now retired, has had her civic spirit certificate returned. It had been taken away from her by the Commune on the 14th. of this month because of her past affairs with high-ranking men, especially Marshal de Soubise, which made her suspect. Fortunately, the Commune changed its mind, and the unforgettable creator of *Mirza* and *Déserteur* has recovered her peace of mind.

Guimard, painted by Fragonard.

Saltpetre

The requisitioning of saltpetre ordered by Carnot for making gunpowder has suddenly put this salt in the limelight. It is called the "patriots' ally". A song praises its qualities:

Dear Saltpetre,
How shattering is your effect;
Your charms for me
Could not be sweeter;
Your praise my songs reflect,
Dear Saltpetre.

Loud Saltpetre,
How noisy your cannon sounds;
You split in two each tyrant who
The weak man hounds,
Loud Saltpetre.

Thanks Saltpetre,
How randy now I am in love:
I'm said to be record-beater;
I satisfy each ladylove.
Thanks Saltpetre!

Triumphant return for a rich corsair

Ile de France, February 25

The entire city of Port Louis was on the docks to welcome Captain François Thomas Lemême. He did not simply content himself with boarding the ships of the India Company, but he also launched a major operation. On November 15th., with the complicity of a Danish pilot, he headed for Sumatra and captured the Padang fort and trading post. After filling the holds of his ship, the *Ville de Bordeaux*, he was even granted a ransom for not destroying the things he could not carry away. On the way back, he seized a Portuguese vessel, the *San Sacramento*, and her ten million francs' worth of cargo. That is a real fortune for the captain.

Punishment milder in cruel Black Code

Ile de France, February 28

Runaway slaves will no longer be mutilated. That cruel punishment is abolished. The Colonial Assembly is studying new regulations softening the hardest punishments contained in the famous Black Code, which has governed slaves' lives since 1723. The Ile de France colonists want to show mainland France that the latter has no monopoly on humanism. Because of the distance involved, they are unaware of the fact that slavery has just been finally abolished in the colonies by the Convention.

Can slavery be "humanised"?

For Saint Just, the Revolution must be carried on to the end

Paris, February 26

When you start a revolution, you have to carry it on through to the end. At least, that is Saint Just's opinion. He has just told the Convention: "What constitutes a republic is the total destruction of the things opposing it." He thinks that by showing "metaphysical luxury in the display of their principles", certain revolutionaries are too easy on the worst enemies of good patriots. Those revolutionaries are Danton and his friends, called the *citras* because, contrary to the *ultras*, they advocate clemency and a degree of moderation. The speaker then mentioned "the force of circumstances", namely, the logic of republican defence, to justify the bloody Reign of Terror, and especially the decree he got approved. This states that the property and assets of all arrested "suspects" must be confiscated, which tends to expropriate the rich to the benefit of the poor. In sketching out this social policy, the Robespierrists want to defuse popular pressure used by the ultras, especially the Cordeliers, who criticise the Committee of Public Safety for "putting people to sleep". The decree is aimed at Hébertists as well as Dantonists.

How artist David sees Saint Just.

Tallien disavowed by "Incorruptible"

Bordeaux, February 23

Bordeaux is breathing easier, but Paris is alarmed. Tallien has set out for the capital to explain his position in person. He knows Robespierre is angry with him, and also knows what that might mean. The "Incorruptible One" disavows the arrest of the members of the watch committee, reproaches him for his moderation and the softening of repression, and finally is worried about his liaison with a woman, "one Cabarrus, an ex-noble, who gets him to pardon many enemies of the Republic". As he was leaving for the capital, Tallien gave a final token of affection to his beloved Thérésa. Standing on the coach footboard, he cut off a lock of his hair and gave it to her.

The peculiar tomb of a citizen of Aix

Aix en Provence, February 25

Even dead, citizen Joseph Sec will not be forgotten. The strange "cenotaph garden" he had built, where he is now resting, bears eternal witness to his acceptance of the ideas of the Revolution and of Masonic principles. Over his eternal rest watches the law, omnipresent, a statue of which tops the edifice. Moses presents the Tablets of the Law to Europe, symbol of freedom, and to Africa, symbol of slavery. As to the person responsible for this law, it is none other than God, the Great Architect.

Convention approves Carrier's behaviour

Paris, February 21

Carrier has managed to convince the Convention that his expeditious methods were proper. The local revolutionary committee, mistreated by the representative, had finally got scared. Three weeks ago, it sent three of its members to Paris to request Carrier's recall. The latter arrived in the capital after a five-day trip. He had hardly dismounted from his horse when he went to the Convention to read the report on his mission. He said that the Vendean revolt had almost been crushed, and confirmed the execution of many children who had been guilty of helping their parents in the fighting. "Let us kill all of the rebels, showing no mercy," he said. He was unanimously approved by the Convention.

Redevelopment of Odéon Square in Paris

Paris, February

Architect Charles de Wailly, who won fame under the Ancien Régime, has managed to retain the esteem of the revolutionary authorities. He has been entrusted with the task of redeveloping Odéon Square, which he knows well since he built Théâtre Français there in 1779-82. Using one of David's ideas, he wants to devote Odéon Square to popular festivities in the ancient style, and with this in mind, he plans to install rows of seats and a stand harmonising with the theatre's neo-classical style.

One of de Wailly's architectural projects, with a tricolour awning.

Convention

1 *(Ventôse 11, Year II)*
Paris. Saint Just is elected presiding officer of the Convention.

2 *(Ventôse 12, Year II)*
Paris. At the Cordeliers Club, the commandant of the Paris Revolutionary Army, Ronsin, says that in his view, a new insurrection has become necessary (→4).

3 *(Ventôse 13, Year II)*
Paris. Speaking to the Convention, Saint Just declares: "Happiness is a new idea in Europe." He has a decree voted, supplementing the one of Ventôse 8 and providing for distribution of condemned persons' property to indigent patriots.

4 *(Ventôse 14, Year II)*
Saône et Loire. The Committee of Public Safety requisitions the Le Creusot foundry, whose blast furnaces are no longer operating after having cast many cannons from bronze scrap.

5 *(Ventôse 15, Year II)*
Paris. The refusal of the Commune's prosecutor, Chaumette, and of the head of the National Guard, Hanriot, to lend themselves to a possible uprising prevents the Hébertist protest movement from growing (→6).

6 *(Ventôse 16, Year II)*
Paris. At the Convention, Barère denounces the various factions which he believes to be threatening the Republic, linking the fate of the Indulgents with that of the Cordeliers (→9).

7 *(Ventôse 17, Year II)*
Paris. Jean Marie Collot d'Herbois, heading a delegation of Jacobins, goes to the Cordeliers Club. The two clubs decide to conclude what they call an "indissoluble union".

9 *(Ventôse 19, Year II)*
Paris. At the Cordeliers Club, Ronsin resumes his attacks against the Cromwellites, Robespierre and his partisans, as well as on Collot d'Herbois (→2).

10 *(Ventôse 20, Year II)*
Paris. Hoche is appointed to command the French forces operating in Italy, and Jourdan to lead the Moselle army.

10 *(Ventôse 20, Year II)*
Paris. Louis David protests to the Temporary Arts Committee against the acts of vandalism perpetrated on the capital's ancient monuments. The committee's members have been selected, and they include, among others, Fragonard and Le Sueur.

The Cordeliers call for an insurrection

Paris, March 4

At the Cordeliers Club, the table bearing the *Declaration of Human Rights* was covered with black crêpe. The militants solemnly declared that it would remain out of sight until the people have recovered their rights. All of the Hébertist leaders were present for this "declaration of war", and all of them made violent speeches against the "faction", the Dantonist clemency party that they associate with Robespierre, though without naming him. Vincent castigated the "destructive system of moderantism" that, in his view, governs the Convention and the Committee of Public Safety. He called on the Cordeliers to use "all of the terror that the guillotine inspires in the people's enemies" against those traitors. In turn, Carrier cried; "Insurrection, that is what you have to use against the scoundrels." Hébert chimed in by shouting: "The Cordeliers will not be the last to give the signal that will slay the oppressors!" But it seems very likely that these ultras will confine themselves to verbal attacks. The reason is that they do not have a big enough hearing among the lower classes to be able to spark off a Paris uprising alone, even if people are really exasperated by scarcities. But the accusation they make is a serious one, since it casts doubt on all of the principles of the revolutionary government (→March 5).

The words of "la Marseillaise" bring all citizens together in the same kind of fervour. And the better the wine, the louder they sing.

The women of Aveyron save their church bells by resisting a destruction order

Aveyron, March 4

Laroque Bouillac will keep its church bells. The special envoy from Paris, Chateauneuf Randon, who had ordered the demolition of the belltowers, acknowledged this fact with a touch of humour after reading a report from the municipal officers sent to carry out his order. "Today, 14 Ventôse, in Year II of the one, indivisible and imperisha-ble Republic, we the undersigned went to the place in question. And as we were getting ready to get to work, suddenly a group of women appeared on the rock overlooking the church, and they made the direst possible threats against us, and so we thought that it was much more prudent to give up or to suspend the implementation of the order in question."

Celebration of the cult of Reason in Catholic Catalonia

Perpignan, March 7

With songs, a procession and a banquet, the Republic is sparing no effort to inculcate the cult of Reason in Catholic Catalonia. General Dugommier, commander of the army of the Pyrénées Orientales, as well as Milhaud and Soubrany, representatives on mission, can be proud of the inauguration of Perpignan's Temple of Reason. After the troops paraded, the city's population went to the nation's altar, with children dressed in white preceding the republican old people. The centrepiece of the festivities was a bonfire of "100 quintals of pictures of former angels and men and women saints of Catalonia", lighted by the young Marie Antoinette, who was rechristened Virginia this morning in honour of Washington. After the ensuing fraternal banquet, the soldiers returned to camp, since they have to go out tomorrow to combat "the monsters of the Castiles".

Poet André Chénier makes a fatal visit

Passy, March 7

A friendly call wound up in a dramatic arrest. Poet André Chénier paid an evening call on his friend Adélaïde de Pastoret, who was also being visited by her childhood friend François de Pange, but André Chénier finished the night in Saint Lazare prison. At 9.45 p.m., five men burst into the residence with an arrest warrant for Claude Emmanuel Pastoret, Adélaïde's husband. They were greatly disappointed not to find their prey — the former general prosecutor having considered it prudent to take refuge in southern France — and policeman Guennot then started to check out the other "suspects" who were there. What was supposed to be a very ordinary identity check for Chénier turned into a very fierce interrogation. He was soon suspected, despite his denials, of having corresponded with enemies of the Republic, and then of "picking a fight" with citizen Guennot, and worst of all, of having been ill on August 10th., 1792. He was arrested "as a general security measure".

11 *(Ventôse 21, Year II)*
Thionville. General Lazare Hoche marries citizen Anne Adélaïde Dechaux.

12 *(Ventôse 22, Year II)*
Paris. Warned the day before about preparation of an insurrection by the Cordeliers, the Committees of Public Safety and General Safety meet and decide to adopt repressive measures (→ 13).

13 *(Ventôse 23, Year II)*
Paris. Following the reading of the Saint Just report, Hébert, Ronsin, Momoro and the main Cordelier leaders are arrested. →

13 *(Ventôse 23, Year II)*
Paris. After the decree of the 8th., publication of a second decree organising "sorting" of suspects by people's committees.

14 *(Ventôse 24, Year II)*
Paris. To contain the Indulgents, the Committee of Public Safety orders seizure of the proofs of the seventh issue of *Vieux Cordelier*.

15 *(Ventôse 25, Year II)*
Paris. Speaking in the Convention, Robespierre declares that "All factions must perish at the same time", and he threatens Dantonists.

16 *(Ventôse 26, Year II)*
Paris. Amar submits a report to the Convention against Fabre d'Eglantine and Chabot.

17 *(Ventôse 27, Year II)*
Paris. Saint Just obtains confirmation of the arrest of Hérault de Séchelles, which occurred on the 15th., after having accused him of maintaining contacts with counter-revolutionaries sought because of emigration.

18 *(Ventôse 28, Year II)*
Paris. Chaumette is arrested at the order of the Committee of Public Safety.

20 *(Ventôse 30, Year II)*
Paris. Even though he was assigned on the 10th. to command the Army of Italy, Hoche is charged on the ground of Cordelier sympathies. The move comes as a result of a proposal by Saint Just, who prefers Pichegru to Hoche.

20 *(Ventôse 30, Year II)*
Paris. Robespierre wins a cancellation of the charge brought the day before against the Jacobin Héron, principal agent of the Committee of General Safety. He had been denounced by Bourdon de l'Oise for his many exactions.

Hébert and Hébertists are arrested

Paris, March 13

Saint Just has just struck a mighty blow. After his report was read to the Convention, Hébert and the Hébertists Momoro, Vincent and Ronsin were arrested. Saint Just accuses them of hatching a plot in conjunction with parties abroad to overthrow the Republic. He also suspects them of having prevented supplies from reaching Paris in order to starve and excite the population. Actually, this is the Robespierrists' response to the insurrectional call made by the Cordeliers Club on March 4.

One must say that this response was made easier by events. As of the 5th., the Commune prosecutor, Chaumette, and the head of the National Guard, Hanriot, broke with the Hébertists by refusing to cooperate in a popular uprising. On the 6th., Barère attacked "factions" in the Assembly, condemning both the Insurgents, i.e., the Hébertists, and the Indulgents or Dantonists. To make the advocates of insurrection see the light, former Cordelier Collot d'Herbois went to see his former friends on the 7th., heading a Jacobin delegation. Momoro, Ronsin and Hébert seemed ready to accept a reconciliation with the Robespierrists, but Vincent dissuaded them. The Com-

Old Duchesne seems to be "mad as a wet hen" about getting arrested.

mittee of Public Safety, at which Robespierre and Couthon reappeared, both having been ill for a month, then decided to order the arrests. In agreement with the Committee of General Safety, it approved Saint Just's report yesterday. But the latter speaks not only of the Hébertists' treason, but also of the plot of the Indulgents' faction. When will their turn come? (→ 24)

Deputy La Révellière Lépeaux in refuge

Montmorency, March

"We'll all be going to prison." When he spoke those words last year, La Révellière Lépeaux did not realise how much truth there was in them. Since his Girondin friends were outlawed, his life had been hanging by a thread. He was outlawed on August 14th. and preferred to escape the capital's dangers. He has just found refuge with the naturalist Bosc, a friend of Mrs Roland and of all of the Girondins. The former deputy's life is not in danger for some time. He could not find a better hideout than that Sainte Radegonde hermitage, in Montmorency Forest. And since he has pledged not to reappear in the Assembly until he is free to speak his mind there, he is not ready to go back there.

Not all of the poor deserve to be given public assistance

Le Havre, March 19

Lacking sufficient funds to help all indigent people, the city's Welfare Office has decided on a strict selection process. To receive a subsidy, one must now be a good patriot unfairly reduced to living in misery and give Republican answers to the following questions: what should one think about the King's execution, the assassination of Marat, closing the churches, and deporting priests? The numerous applicants who may prove unable to pass this "test" will be able to prove their revolutionary zeal by denouncing some émigré who has returned to the country secretly or people plotting against the Republic. This is likely to win them the jury's indulgence.

Tallien wins his case in the Convention

Paris, March 19

Being audacious paid off: all accusations against Tallien have been dropped. Knowing that Robespierre's informers were accusing him of moderatism, he appeared voluntarily before the Committee of Public Safety to report on his mission to Bordeaux and confound the people slandering him. In his speech, he boasted of having returned the city of Bordeaux "to the Republic without a single drop of patriotic blood having been shed". He offered attestations from committees and cleverly attacked his detractors. But Robespierre is mistrustful. He has decided to send a trusted man to Bordeaux to check on its revolutionary zeal.

Are the Dantonists now threatened?

Paris, March 18

A touching scene just took place in the Assembly. Alsacian deputy Ruhl, who was chairing the meeting, threw himself into Danton's arms as a sign of his friendship. He is, in fact, among the rare people who have dared to approve the speech Danton made in defence of the Paris Commune. Public prosecutor Chaumette is behind bars. He seems to have been arrested because he is close to the Hébertists. But the grounds for his indictment remain obscure, since he seems very harmless, in spite of his virulent anti-clericalism. That is what Danton wanted to show. Replying to a delegation that appeared in order to justify the prosecutor's arrest to the Convention, he said that almost the entire Commune was "pure and revolutionary". In adopting this position, Danton is playing with fire, since he is in great danger of annoying the Robespierrists. He must suspect that they are ever more hostile to him. He knows that the Hébertists' arrest can be interpreted as presaging a vaster purge, as Saint Just indicated in the indictment by saying: "All of the plotters have got together, the Indulgents' faction, which wants to save the criminals, and the foreign faction." The latter term designates the Hébertists, but also the Indulgents,

Danton is unworried by danger.

namely, the Dantonists. Robespierre's supporters now seem to have a clear position. If they really want to maintain their power, they must not limit themselves to simply striking at the ultras, to their left. They also have to criticise the moderates, Danton's friends, who are to their right. Indeed, it is known that Camille Desmoulins has already been bothered. A search was made of his printer's shop and the printer was arrested. And yesterday, two moderate deputies, Hérault de Séchelles and Sismond, were thrown in jail. Even though it is a fact that Danton is too popular to be attacked directly, he is still in serious danger (→ March 31).

A reconciliation try proves unsuccessful

Paris, March 20

The miracle did not take place: Danton and Robespierre did not manage a reconciliation. The efforts of their mutual friends, including Camille Desmoulins, proved unavailing. They had arranged a dinner at Humbert's, Maxililien's former host. The meal lasted until late at night. There was champagne, but the two men's political differences are too marked. Danton does not want any more blood, while Robespierre wants to give the Republic a firm foundation by using any available means. Nobody knows what was said around the table, but Robespierre came out first, obviously disappointed. Will he drop Danton, or remain faithful to their former solidarity? It is hard to say, but there seem to be too many dead dividing the two men.

Two thousand oxen are lent to farmers

Mont Terrible, March 19

The farmers will at least be able to do their ploughing. The Mont Terrible administration requisitioned the 2,000 oxen now moving through the department for two weeks, for the farmers' use. These draft animals, bought by the Convention in Switzerland and on their way to the military services, will be made available to farmers who have applied for them, with their municipality's approval. It is hoped that this will lead them to put fallow land back into cultivation. The amount of such land has increased the last few years due to a lack of resources. To keep from being accused of seizing property, the department has sent a representative to Paris. He will have to justify the plan, stressing that farmers involved are all good Republicans.

21 *(Germinal 1, Year II)*
Paris. The trial of the Hébertists gets under way. For good measure, the charges against them lump together the leaders of the plotters' movement and such highly unscrupulous businessmen as the bankers Kock and Proly, as well as a number of aristocrats (→24).

24 *(Germinal 4, Year II)*
Vendée. The Republican garrison of Mortagne sur Sèvre, besieged by Sapinaud's armed bands, has to leave the outpost.

24 *(Germinal 4, Year II)*
Paris. Those among the Hébertists who have been sentenced to death are guillotined.

24 *(Germinal 4, Year II)*
Poland. Kosciuszko takes command of the insurrection.

26 *(Germinal 6, Year II)*
Paris. Bishop Gouttes, who was one of the artisans of the meeting of the three orders at the Estates General, is sentenced to death and quickly executed for having dared to criticise the Convention's religious policy.

27 *(Germinal 7, Year II)*
Vendée. A republican column discovers the hospital being used to treat the injured soldiers of Stofflet's army in the Vezins forest. Some 1,000 to 1,500 wounded soldiers are massacred by Crouzat's troops.

27 *(Germinal 7, Year II)*
Paris. Acting on the basis of a report submitted by Bertrand Barère, the Convention decides to dissolve the Paris Revolutionary Army. →

28 *(Germinal 8, Year II)*
Paris. The Paris Commune is reorganised. The Hébertists are replaced by supporters of Robespierre. Payan replaces Chaumette as national agent, assisted by Moënne and Lubin.

28 *(Germinal 8, Year II)*
Philadelphia. The American Government decrees a 30-day embargo on all French goods.

29 *(Germinal 9, Year II)*
Bourg la Reine. The Marquis de Condorcet is found dead in his cell.

29 *(Germinal 9, Year II)*
Northern France. General Pichegru launches an all out offensive against Austrian-held Le Cateau (Cateau-Cambrésis).

30 *(Germinal 10, Year II)*
Paris. The Committee of Public Safety attacks the Indulgents and orders the arrest of Danton and his supporters, Desmoulins, Delacroix and Philippeaux (→31).

Army costing state less to maintain

Paris, March 22

The Treasury is saving money. The chairman of the Committee of Finance was satisfied to find that maintaining one and a half million men now costs only 180 million a month. "A year ago, we were spending twice as much, on fewer men." Too much government money was being squandered, and there were well-known supply shortages. A start was made by cancelling all contracts for baggage trains, food and ambulances, replacing them with a state-management system. But that is not the only thing explaining these marked savings. Systematic exploitation of occupied countries makes a large contribution to feeding the nation's armies. According to a report recently submitted by Baudot, for instance, the Palatinate has been "profitable beyond all our hopes".

Monge name is cut from émigrés list

This certificate is obligatory.

Paris, March 28

"I was appointed Minister of the Navy, and that is why I left the Ardennes." It took Monge five months to get this obvious fact accepted. But today, he finally managed to get his name removed from the list of Ardennes émigrés, to which it had been added on November 27th. Since he was not at home, the hasty conclusion was drawn that he had emigrated. Absorbed in his new duties, Monge had simply forgotten to send in a certificate of change of address.

Hébertists are guillotined for "deceiving people"

The tumbrel taking Hébert, Vincent, Chaumette, Gobel...to the scaffold.

Paris, March 24

The Paris patriots are in extreme disarray. They no longer know whom they should trust after the deaths of the Hébertists, accused of having deceived the people. A large crowd witnessed the executions. It did not hesitate to boo Hébert, who tottered so much that he had to be supported when mounting the scaffold. The pale Ronsin displayed remarkable courage. Cloots insisted on being guillotined last. Hébertists Ronsin and Vincent, as well as their leader, were convicted of the worst possible kinds of treason at their trial. To be sure, the revolutionary Tribunal was not at all choosy about proceedings in order to get death sentences. It combined a number of cases on the ground that some of the defendants had personal links with a few schemers. The main defendants were tried at the same time as banker Kock and financiers Pereyra, Proly and Dubuisson, all of whom were agents of foreign enemies and were involved in Dumouriez's treason or in financial scandals. For the occasion, the authorities had lumped in some mere suspects, such as General Quétineau's wife and Laumur, the governor of Pondicherry. They also tossed in some ultra patriots, especially the militant sector member Leclerc, of the Ministry of War. The Prussian Cloots, who billed himself as the "friend of the human race", was also in the dock for having tried to save an émigré. He maintained his dignified demeanour and cried that he did not want his case to be mingled with those of people he called "brigands". And then, when the sentences were read out, defendant Momoro shouted: "They accuse *me*, I who have done everything for the Revolution!" But such bravery left the judges unimpressed. After all was said and done, the death verdict was final.

Hébert's death

The hanging of the bombastic Hébert, whose scurrilous articles in the "Père Duchesne" were beginning to annoy the people, has inspired this "Impromptu on the cutting-down of the Père Duchesne and his accomplices".

Père Duschesne bids us adieu :
He is for the guillotine due.
Hear him curse, rant and rave;
His poor head he cannot save.
Ah, ah, ah, I tell you true,
Père Duchesne is feeling blue!
In his wretched morning rag,
His filth became a right drag.
The blade will absolve his debt
And all his petty little set.
Cut heads off, neat and clean.
Duchesne from Normandy came
Far and wide spread his fame.
Said he was a true sans-culottes
And was but a false patriot.
Pray, this way! O Domine!
To the guillotine, and no delay!

The English easily recapture Martinique

Martinique, March 23

The English, expelled on June 19th. 1793, are back in Martinique. The absence of French naval forces made any resistance absurd, and the island's representatives surrendered. Since the forced departure of Captain Lacrosse's frigate, the Caribbean had come under the control of Admiral Gardner's fleet. The English blockade of French Atlantic ports prevented any rescue expedition, and hence indirectly delivered the French islands in the Antilles to England. The slaves, for whom the mulattos on the island have rejected freedom, were unable to defend the Republic.

The English forces' offensive against Fort Royal encounters little resistance.

Is France going to Poland's assistance?

Poles prefer the tricoloured cockade to the attributes of royalty.

Krakow, March 24

Poland is rising up against its oppressors. Tadeusz Kosciuszko, leader of the patriotic army, has just proclaimed the "Insurrectional Act", a provisional constitution giving him dictatorial powers. The émigré patriots had started to prepare the insurrection immediately after the 1792 Russian invasion. While Kosciuszko was in Paris demanding French assistance, in Poland the rebels were setting up secret organisations and were putting pressure on the émigrés to speed up the pace of the insurrection. They rose up on March 12th., and Kosciuszko soon joined them.

The Committee of Public Safety dissolves the sansculottist "Revolutionary Army"

Paris, March 27

The Convention is laying people off. In accordance with the decree submitted by Barère in the name of the Committee of Public Safety and adopted by the Convention, the Revolutionary Army is dissolved, and its volunteers are to be sent home. However, the ones who want to continue their service are to be incorporated individually into the Republic's armies. Actually, the Committee has no doubts about the patriotism of the sansculottists, who make up the bulk of that army. Even if they have sometimes indulged in abuses and exactions, the Committee thinks their leaders were responsible for this, meaning the Hébertists France has just got rid of. This decree is aimed mainly at strengthening centralisation. The Committee wants no special military group that might oppose it.

Prieur and Monge go up in a balloon

Meudon, March 29

This morning, people saw the Committee of Public Safety in a balloon. To convince his Committee colleagues of the military interest of this invention, Prieur of Côte-d'Or had invited Barère to attend trials of the balloon, which had been made at the Meudon camp under the supervision of Conté, the inventor of the pencil. Prieur himself ascended to a height of 150 *toises* above the ground. To show that the device was safe, the mathematician Monge took his daughter along in the balloon.

Art has to be virtuous and instructive

This reign of pleasure shown by Boucher does not meet today's standards.

Paris, March 29

While the Muséum was saved from "clumsy" people, it has now fallen into the hands of David's followers. An aesthetic purge is the only thing on the agenda. Thus the only things selected for display in the galleries are civic and edifying works able to contribute to the people's intellectual and moral progress. Everything has got to be imbued with old-time order and virtue. So it is hardly surprising to find a ban on Flemish canvases, Boucher's "erotically Mannerist" works, and porcelain that does not conform to "the simplicity and the purity of an Etruscan vase". At their meetings, which David never misses, the curators agreed on a proposal to the Committee of Public Education to install the "censured" works, when they deserve it, in a place which only artists would be allowed to visit. The same fate would be reserved to paintings on subjects seen as possibly "maintaining fanaticism".

Condorcet's suspicious death in prison

Did Condorcet take the poison that his friend Cabanis gave him?

Bourg Egalité, March 29

The outlawed philosopher's wanderings are over. Condorcet was found dead in his cell at Bourg Egalité prison in the town formerly known as Bourg la Reine, where he had been held under the pseudonym of Pierre Simon. To keep from compromising Mrs Vernet, who put him up, the outlaw fled from Paris on March 25th. Weakened by his seclusion, he reached Clamart with some difficulty. There, his highly cautious friends, the Suards, refused to take him in. The desperate man, at the end of his rope, was then questioned as a suspect in a Clamart inn. Thrown into jail without having been recognised, he was later found dead there. While some people think he committed suicide, his anxiety and exhaustion may explain the death of a man who had become disappointed in humanity.

Cover up that stag — I can't stand it...

Anet, March

Diane had a close call. Ever since King Henry II offered his mistress, Diane de Poitiers, the bronze bas-relief showing the goddess surrounded by animals, the beautiful nude figure had presided over the main entrance gate of Anet Castle. But some sansculottists got all excited about this. Not that they were shocked by the nudity, but the stag accompanying the goddess and obviously representing hunting, a particularly detested feudal symbol, should be destroyed, in their view. The worried mayor of Anet tried to convince the over-zealous patriots that "Bronze stags are not covered by the law..." It worked, and the work has been saved.

The "Recumbent Nymph" by Benvenuto Cellini, a scandalous object.

Danton and his friends are arrested

French Republic marries its children

Ain, March 30

On Liberty Square in Ambérieu, the Altar to the Nation had been set up under the tricoloured flag. The National Guards paraded waving their weapons, like a people rising up against the aristocrats. But suddenly some delightful rural music interrupted the martial airs. Several couples came forward, followed by their parents and representatives of the municipality. The weddings were celebrated in succession to cries of "Long live the Republic!" The festivities were then brought to a conclusion with the gift of a dowry of 200 livres to a "poor but virtuous" young woman.

Franco-American relations cool off

Philadelphia, March 28

Franco-American relations have deteriorated ever since the United States proclaimed its neutrality in the war in Europe. After removing Genêt, the French government's envoy, today George Washington decreed a 30-day total embargo on French goods coming into the country. The U.S. President, who has been disgusted by acts of piracy against American ships committed by French privateers, has decided to pound on the table to get the French to put an end to such acts.

There's no meat? Then observe Lent

Mont Blanc, March 28

The needs for fresh meat of the French and Sardinian forces, which have constantly crisscrossed the region, have struck a fatal blow at the cattle herds. Hence the administration of the Arc district, "considering that each citizen must be willing to do for the fatherland what he was led to do for so long by fanaticism and superstition", has ordered "a civic Lent observance in all communes in this district for 60 days". This strict measure ordered by the authorities, which forbids slaughtering or consuming meat, might be endurable except for the fact that cheese is unfortunately also in very short supply.

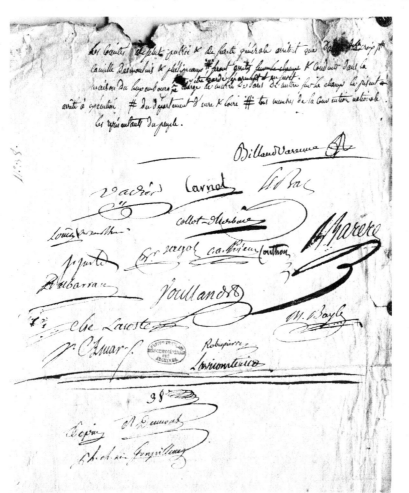

At the end of the indictment of Danton, Delacroix, Desmoulins and Philippeaux, issued by the Committees of Public Safety and of General Security, one sees, from top to bottom and left to right, the signatures of Billaud Varenne, Vadier, Carnot, Le Bas, Louis du Bas Rhin, Collot d'Herbois, Saint Just, Jagot, Prieur, Couthon, Barère, Dubarran, Voulland, Lacoste, Bayle, Amar, Robespierre and Lavicomterie.

Paris, March 31

Who will escape from the terrifying revolutionary justice? Danton and his friends — the deputies Lacroix, Philippeaux and Camille Desmoulins — were arrested last night and have gone to join Hérault de Séchelles in prison. There was great emotion in the Assembly. Deputy Legendre, one of the most ardent demonstrators on August 10th., 1792, refused to believe that Danton had been charged. He spoke to the Convention today to ask that it at least allow the detainees to appear before it to explain themselves, saying: "I think Danton is as pure as I am myself, and I do not think that anybody whosoever can reproach me with having committed any act detracting from the most scrupulous probity." He recalled the heroic behaviour of that Montagnard in 1792, when the fatherland

was in danger, and the formidable impetus his speeches then gave to national defence. But the Assembly refused to listen to him, as it was fascinated by the speech given by Robespierre, who followed him. The Jacobin launched out into one of those patented diatribes of his, beginning in a slow, deliberate fashion only to end up in a formidable crescendo. "The point today is to determine whether the interest of a few ambitious hypocrites should outweigh the interest of the French people," he said at the outset to reject Legendre's proposal and deny Danton the privilege of speaking to the Convention. "We do not want any privileged characters, no, we do not want any idols! What do I care about the fine speeches, the praise people give themselves and their friends? Could what people say about Danton not be applied to

Brissot, to Pétion, to Chabot, even to Hébert, and to so many others who have filled France with pompous noise about their deceitful patriotism? What privilege should he have?" The hypnotised deputies greeted this with a storm of applause. But a shiver went through the gathering when Robespierre came out with this terrifying sentence: "I say that anybody who is trembling at this moment is guilty, for innocence does not fear the public eye." But what are the Dantonists accused of? Before reading the long indictment adopted by the Committee of Public Safety and the Committee of General Security, Saint Just announced: "I have just denounced the last partisans of royalism." He claimed that the accused men had been plotting with the kings in league against the Republic. In his view, they were accomplices of Dumouriez and of the d'Orléans family, and hence traitors to their country, as well as accomplices of Fabre d'Eglantine, who was accused of corruption in the India Company scandal. They will be put on trial along with Fabre. But the arrest of the Dantonists was not unanimously approved within the Committee itself. Some of its members do not understand striking out at such sincere revolutionaries. Actually, the Robespierrists seem to want to demonstrate that nobody has a monopoly revolutionary legitimacy. Hence Saint Just concluded: "The Revolution is in the people, not in a few people's fame. It is a heroic undertaking the authors of which walk between wheel and immortality" (→April 3).

Desmoulins — a traitor to France? ▷

Do we need revolutionary furniture?

A "cupboard-buffet" with inlay work based on revolutionary motifs.

The furniture industry is going through some very hard times. The great cabinet-makers have lost their customers and are reduced to turning out wood rifle parts and munitions crates for the Republican army. Official orders are scarce, and Georges Jacob, thanks to David's friendship, is about the only one to receive orders for seats or rostrums for the room in which Convention meetings are held. The others are having to adjust to customers who prefer furniture made of walnut or fruit-tree wood, rather rustic, decorated with revolutionary motifs, such as Phrygian bonnets, crossed flags, or sculpted or inlaid cocks.

 Convention

1 *(Germinal 12, Year II)*
Paris. Acting on Carnot's proposal, the Convention does away with the Council of Ministers, which is replaced by 12 executive committees coming under the Committee of Public Safety (→19).

1 *(Germinal 12, Year II)*
Paris. The creation of a Police Bureau for the Committee of Public Safety, encroaching on the powers of the Committee of General Security, leads to rivalry between those two governmental authorities.

1 *(Germinal 12, Year II)*
Paris. Euloge Schneider, the former mayor of Strasbourg, is guillotined for having "favoured the hostile plans of domestic and foreign enemies".

1 *(Germinal 12, Year II)*
Paris. Having been unable to convince the judges of the Revolutionary Criminal Court of the innocence of her husband, the Longwy commandant accused of treason, Madame Lavergne decides to die with him and shouts "Long live the King" when the verdict is issued. She is arrested, sentenced and executed.

2 *(Germinal 13, Year II)*
Paris. Establishment of a company of military hot-air balloonists.→

2 *(Germinal 13, Year II)*
Nice. Arrest of General Hoche (→12).

2 *(Germinal 13, Year II)*
Ile de France. The capital, Port Louis, is rechristened Port la Montagne.

3 *(Germinal 14, Year II)*
Paris. While being questioned, Danton defends himself with talent and makes his judges look ridiculous.→

4 *(Germinal 15, Year II)*
Poland. At Raclawice, the Polish insurgents led by Kosciuszko beat back the Russian army.

4 *(Germinal 15, Year II)*
Paris. Saint Just decides to prevent Danton, by any means, from defending himself. He has the Convention approve a decree preventing pleading by any accused person who has insulted national justice.

4 *(Germinal 15, Year II)*
Antilles. The English conquer the island of Sainte Lucie.

4 *(Germinal 15, Year II)*
Maine et Loire. General Crouzat's column devastates Montfaucon sur Moine.

Republican and revolutionary, but suspects as well

Paris, April 2

While getting ready to leave for a tour of northern France, Claire Lacombe and Pauline Léon were arrested on the order of the Committee of General Security. Yet since the closing of their famous Association of Revolutionary Republican Women, the two former presidents had wisely given up all political activity and had resumed acting work. But denunciations came flowing in. They were being called dangerous counter-revolutionaries. With her typical frankness, Citizeness Lacombe is said to have been so reckless as to state she disapproved the September massacres. Much worse, she reportedly claimed that she considered Robespierre "to be a mere individual" and that she did not understand how people could be "infatuated and enthusiastic". Of course, these remarks were very bold, but in any case the arrest of the two young women seemed inevitable in the light of the series of measures that have struck the Enragés in the last few months. In another development, their shared lover, the journalist Leclerc, editor of the *Ami du Peuple*, was arrested at the same time as the two women were.

Reinforcements for the Army: balloons

Paris, April 2

An air force — that is the latest invention made by the Committee of Public Safety. A "balloonists' company" has just been created to use the balloon made in Meudon. These 30 experts, who are able to inflate the device with hydrogen and steer it, will be at the high command's service. To convince the latter that the operation was a serious one, Captain Coutelle, chief balloonist, has been joined by Convention member Guyton Morveau, a well-known chemist and an enthusiastic advocate of the new weapon. His authority as a representative will be welcome. During Coutelle's first mission, despite the Committee's recommendations, he got a bad reception from the generals, who called him a charlatan.

Judges tremble while Danton roars

Danton? A foreign agent!

Paris, April 3

The presiding judge of the revolutionary Tribunal, Herman, is frightened. Is the trial going to turn against the people responsible for it? Herman wants to avoid such a disaster. He absolutely has to find a way to keep Danton from speaking. The latter has just declared that if he and his friends were being charged, it was because they were getting ready to denounce the tyranny of the government committees and of the people exercising it. "Let my accusers show themselves, and I will thrust them back into nothingness... Vile impostors, come forth!" he shouted. And in his tenor's voice, which shook the windows, he demanded the appointment of an investigatory committee. He went so far as to call on 16 deputies as witnesses. The audience dared to applaud him. Outside the hearing room, the crowd was so unruly that a revolt was feared. Yet the government planned a brisk trial, which began yesterday, barely three days after the Dantonists' arrest. All preparations had been made to prevent anything from getting in the way of death sentences for the accused. Prosecutor Fouquier Tinville had been joined by an assistant, the Robespierrist Fleuriot, as the former might prove partial, being a relative of Camille Desmoulins. As to the jurymen, they were drawn by lot behind closed doors. Only a single problem might have come up: no witnesses for the prosecution were mentioned, and the evidence adduced against the Dantonists is singularly thin. The fact is that the prosecution evidence consists of barely more than a single document, the forged decree on the India Company that compromises the main defendant, Fabre d'Eglantine. No matter! To make up for this shortcoming and lend credence to the prosecutors' position to the effect that the Dantonists were implicated in a foreign plot, Desmoulins, Philippeaux, Lacroix and Danton were lumped together with some shady characters: the Frey brothers, Austrian bankers, the Dane Deideriksen, and the Spanish banker Gusman. Delaunay, Chabot, Basire and Jullien of Toulouse have also been charged in connection with the India Company. The accused also include General Westermann, suspected of having helped Dumouriez, and Hérault de Séchelles, too moderate for Robespierre's taste. By mingling common-law prisoners with political detainees, the revolutionary Tribunal is seeking to confuse the reasons for indictment. Even though Danton moved the audience, he appears to have little chance of escaping the guillotine (→ April 5).

Hérault de Séchelles? Moderate!

The administration finds it difficult to get enough officials

Chambéry, April 4

"The people's friend is the man for whom you have to look for a long time to get him to carry out public duties, who withdraws from them as quickly as possible, and who leaves poorer than when he came in." When Carnot gave the Convention this description of a good government member four days ago, he was harbouring illusions. The representative on mission in the Mont Blanc department, Albitte, displays greater realism in this connection. "How, in these areas, can you organise municipalities, find justices of the peace, set up watch committees, and regenerate the administration? Where can you find enough patriots who are pure and not subject to the law against émigrés' relatives?" he complained to the Committee of Public Safety. Regeneration of the department is dragging, due to lack of applicants. In these uncertain times, nobody really wants responsibilities. Hence people who venture to accept them are more brilliant in their Jacobinism than in their professional abilities. The district court is headed by an old trooper, a venal but patriotic fellow, who is helped by a farmer and a shoemaker.

Former Constituent leaves the country

Virginia, April 4

Moreau de Saint Méry, former deputy from Martinique to the Constituent Assembly, never hid his hostility to the Reign of Terror. On November 9th., he left Le Havre with his whole family on the American vessel, the *Sophie*. That turned out to be a good idea. The next day, gendarmes arrived in Paris with orders to arrest all of them. In such troubled times, the United States fortunately offers a providential refuge for the outlawed. But it took no fewer than 120 days at sea for the travellers to reach Virginia. The crossing to Norfolk seemed to take a thousand years. This morning, they finally set foot on this land of liberty. They hoped to be able to leave later for Saint Domingue, where Saint Méry once lived.

Eloquence is Danton's only remaining weapon. He is not afraid to harangue the revolutionary Tribunal.

Danton and his friends are executed

Paris, April 5

It's all over. Desmoulins, Basire, Hérault de Séchelles, Philippeaux and even Chabot, who attempted to commit suicide by drinking poison, were all guillotined this morning along with Danton.

As he was about to climb up to the scaffold, Danton told his executioner: "Don't forget to show my head to the people, it's well worth it." When the man carried out Danton's grisly request, a sudden hush fell over the crowd. The man who dared stand up to the revolutionary Tribunal is dead. His opponents finally decided to get rid of him after his outburst of April 3rd. Robespierre and his backers were aware of the danger of letting the accused speak out and the jury was beginning to show signs of weakness. Trinchard was the only one to fully back the death penalty. Others hesitated, moved by the apparent sincerity of the accused. One of them, Naulin, even asked yesterday that the witnesses be allowed to speak. Terrified by this request, the court's president, Herman, and Fouquier Tinville rushed to ask the Robespierrists to help them out. Saint Just stepped in and got a stunned, but docile Assembly to approve a decree stipulating that "any accused person who resists or voices insults will be silenced". All that remained to be done was for the jury to hand down the expected

On the tumbrel, Danton shouts loudly: "Robespierre will follow me!"

verdict. After a further delay, this was done this morning at 8 o'clock. Trinchard had a tough time convincing his fellow jury members. Despite Danton's renewed protests

and howls of rage from Desmoulins, who embraced Basire and Chabot, the fateful tumbrel was brought up to take the condemned men to the scaffold.

Camille Desmoulins's final letter to his beloved wife Lucile

The Desmoulins couple and their young son Horace during happier times.

Paris, April 5

As he stood on the tumbrel that was taking him to the scaffold, Camille Desmoulins struggled desperately and screamed repeatedly at the assembled crowd: "People, poor people, you are being fooled, they are executing your friends!" His struggles were so fierce that his clothes were in shreds by the time he got to the scaffold. Since his sentencing, he had been mad with sorrow at the thought of leaving his beloved wife Lucile and little Horace behind. In his farewell letter to his wife, he eloquently expresses his despair: "I feel the shores of life receding before me. I can still see Lucile! I see her, my beloved, my Lucile! My bound hands embrace you and my separated head still casts its dying eyes on you."

Music lovers now have their own paper

Paris, April 9

Despite all Sarrette's efforts, the first edition of the *Journal de la Musique* did not appear on the expected date. It was only today, 19 days later than planned, that the newspaper became available. The proud writers and editors gave the Convention a copy of the first edition, in the sincere hope that it would be followed by many others. The 56-page journal contains an overture composed by Catel, a military march, a choral piece written by Gossec, a patriotic, romantic work on Bara's death and a song on the success of the army. The only cloud on the horizon is that Sarrette has been in jail for the past ten days on trumped-up charges.

Political foes share the same scaffold

Paris, April 13

It is a strange sight. The accused do not know each other and some of them were political foes, but they all have to share the same tumbrel taking them to the scaffold. They are charged with trying to crush the Convention and restore the monarchy. The verdict was handed down without witnesses or proof by the feared Robespierrist Dumas. Those to be executed together are: Lucile Desmoulins, found guilty of trying to save her husband, the Commune's prosecutor Chaumette, accused of pro-Hébertist views, the Bishop of Paris, Gobel, who renounced his faith, the royalist Dillon, Lapallus, the executioner of the Lyons royalists, the Hébertist Grammont and the Dantonist Simond. Paris is starting to fear this so-called "justice".

"Pitt's gold paid Chaumette."

A play by Chénier is censored

Paris, April 9

The theatre-goers of Paris have been impatiently awaiting the new tragedy by Marie Joseph Chénier, *Timoléon*, but they will never get to see the play performed. Jullien, the member of the Convention from the Drôme, attended the final rehearsal. He became upset when he saw Timoléon crown the tyrant Timophane without this sparking off a mass uprising. "You always were just a counter-revolutionary in disguise," he cried on leaving the theatre. Chénier was crestfallen. The incident had immediate consequences: the Committee of General Security banned the play. Chénier has been accused of portraying honest monarchs and lukewarm republicans. He was forced to burn his manuscript before Barère and Robespierre. His play *Fénélon* had already been banned by the Committee. His career as a playwright is now in real trouble (→ Sept. 10)

The Great Committee's awesome powers

Paris, April 19

The centralisation and concentration of authority is the order of the day. What little autonomy the departments had retained is just a memory now.

Twenty-one emissaries were recalled today from their missions following the April 1st. demand by Carnot. Moreover, the law of April 16th., backed by Saint Just, orders that all those charged with conspiracy must be tried by the Paris revolutionary Tribunal. This in fact means the abolition of all similar courts in the provinces. Such moves obviously benefit the Committee of Public Safety. This Great Committee, which already controlled political life, has become a veritable government, answerable only to the Convention. Ministers were dismissed on April 1st. Under the terms of the April 16th. law, it can also arrest people, just like the Committee of General Security. The Great Committee has even set up its own police department.

Robespierre visits Rousseau's tomb

Ermenonville, April

Poplar Island is used to seeing illustrious visitors. But few of them are as sombre as Robespierre, who likes to come to Ermenonville to meditate on the teachings of the man who played such a big rôle during his formative years. Soon, however, the ashes of the famous philosopher will leave their resting place. The Convention decreed on April 14th. that Rousseau's remains are to be transferred to the Panthéon in nearby Paris.

War comes to the aid of industry

Le Mans, April 14

The textile industry of the Sarthe region has been hardhit by the Revolution, but it could be saved by the war. The muslin factories which under the Ancien Régime provided cloth for magistrates' and priests' robes are in deep trouble. They have now been requisitioned and placed under the control of Citizen Teste, a Le Mans businessman. The plants will from now on be busy producing red, white and blue cloth for the nation's flags.

David designs curtains for a "sansculottide" play at the Opéra

Paris, April 5

David proclaimed: "The arts must contribute powerfully to the education of the public". He is now organising all of the Republic's festivities. It was David who designed the curtain for a play entitled "The Meeting of August 10th., or the Inauguration of the French Republic", which was performed at the Opéra today. It is billed as a "dramatic sansculottide in verse and five acts", written by P. L. Moline and Gabriel Bouquier and dedicated to the people. The huge curtain shows the people as Hercules on a chariot carrying Liberty and Equality on his lap.

David's Hercules advances on the remains of tyrants, followed by Brutus, William Tell and Marat.

Convention

20 *(Floréal 1, Year II)* Guadeloupe. After having conquered the island of Martinique, the English seize Pointe à Pitre.

20 *(Floréal 1, Year II)* Paris. At the Convention, Billaud Varenne announces that the Committee of Public Safety will end the war as soon as every inch of French territory has been liberated.

21 *(Floréal 2, Year II)* Spain. General Dagobert is killed at Puigcerda after a series of victories over the Spanish forces. An aristocrat, he had refused to emigrate and to those who pressed him to leave the army he replied: "You leave, but the Nation stays."

22 *(Floréal 3, Year II)* Paris. Malesherbes, former minister under Louis XVI, is executed along with Assembly members Thouret, Le Chapelier and d'Eprémesnil.→

22 *(Floréal 3, Year II)* Poland. At Wilno, the Jacobins, under the command of Colonel Jakub Jasiuski, take hold of the town which Kosciuszko will enter on the 23rd.

23 *(Floréal 4, Year II)* Paris. The Convention decrees a new simplification of the divorce procedure: from now on, a six-month separation between spouses will be sufficient grounds.

24 *(Floréal 5, Year II)* Paris. Having become suspect for his "retrograde" artistic ideas, the painter Louis Boilly puts the finishing touch to *Triomphe de Marat* in a more contemporary style.

28 *(Floréal 9, Year II)* Paris. The last lieutenant of police of the capital, Thiroux de Crosne, is sentenced to death and executed at the same time as La Tour du Pin, the former Minister of War responsible for the massacre of the Swiss at Chateauvieux.

28 *(Floréal 9, Year II)* Vendée. The Vendean leaders Stofflet and Charette condemn to death one of their own men, Marigny, who had not applied the terms of the oath sworn on April 22nd. (→July 10, 94).

29 *(Floréal 10, Year II)* Paris. Departure of Saint Just on a mission to the army in the north.

30 *(Floréal 11, Year II)* Northern France. Landrecies surrenders to the Austrians.

The men of 1788 go to the guillotine

Malesherbes, a lawyer to the King.

Paris, April 22

"When we find ourselves on the tumbrel, which one of us will the people be booing?" Le Chapelier asked d'Eprémesnil as they were being driven to the scaffold. "Both of us," the latter replied. In 1788, the two had fought to reinforce the powers of parliaments, just like Thouret and Malesherbes, who are also being taken to the scaffold. Le Chapelier led the unrest that preceded the meeting of the Estates General in Brittany. Thouret played the same role in Normandy. In Paris, d'Eprémesnil was the leader of parliamentary opposition. As for Malesherbes, ex-Secretary of State of the royal household, he tried in vain to push reforms through.

Fraud case involves nation's assets

Avignon, April 22

A big scandal has just come to light. The special envoy from Paris, Maignet, has discovered that a firm grouping between 500 and 600 local people, including a number of administrators, has been buying up national assets sold in the department at very low prices. This well-organised outfit even has its own cashier and treasurer. Whenever a foreign buyer came to a sale, he was shown a piece of string poking out of a pocket. That simple signal was all that was needed for the deal to be clinched!

A united Vendée?

Châtillon, April 22

The four main leaders of Vendée have just sworn a solemn oath under the ruined vaulting arches of the chapel at the La Boulaye castle. Charette, Stofflet, Sapinaud and Marigny swore that from now on all Vendean military operations will be carried out in a well-planned, concerted fashion, but there are doubts that this will be the case. Since the "great army" was crushed, jealousy and rivalry have made agreement difficult between the Vendean chiefs. Charette has always been an extremely independent man. As for Stofflet and Marigny, both touchy and violent men, they have hated each other for a long time (→April 28).

J. B. Say's highly practical philosophy

Paris, April 24

A new journal has been born: *La Décade Philosophique, Littéraire et Politique*. It was founded by Ginguené and its editor in chief is Jean Baptiste Say. Descended from a family of Huguenot traders, Say had seemed destined to follow in his father's footsteps, but his career was ruined by the depreciation of assignats. He came to Mirabeau's attention in 1789 after he wrote a pamphlet on the freedom of the Press. Later, he worked on the *Courrier de Provence* newspaper. In *La Décade*, he tries to show how the Revolution transforms, or should change, all aspects of social and cultural life. Say and his fellow writers believe that philosophy goes beyond books and lives in the Revolution. *La Décade* tries to foster progress by uplifting the awareness of the citizenry and by acting as a bridge between specialists and the public. Although the journal pays homage to the precursors of republican thinking, it stresses the practical aspects of problems. The journal includes, for example, an article on Adam Smith's political economy along with a report on a new machine or industrial process. Its authors see the Revolution as an educational process and hope that they can contribute to it.

André Chénier falls madly in love while sitting in his prison cell

Paris, April

Her name is Aimée Franquetot de Coigny. She is 25 years old and very beautiful.

Her detention has not diminished her zest for life. André Chénier caught a glimpse of her as she was walking with her lover, Casimir de Montrond, in the courtyard of the Saint Lazare jail, where he has been imprisoned since March 7th. The young woman's beauty and smiling face helped him forget his sad fate, at least for a few hours. Chénier has even written an ode dedicated to her, *La Jeune Captive*. But despite all his fiery literary efforts, the obscure poet has not succeeded in capturing the heart of the lively and carefree Aimée.

At Saint Lazare, prisoners meet each other during the exercise period.

1 *(Floréal 12, Year II)*
Pyrénées Orientales. The French troops led by Dugommier and Augereau chase Spanish forces from the town of Boulou, on the River Tech, and make their entry into Spanish Catalonia.

3 *(Floréal 14, Year II)*
Paris. The stockbroker Tassin de L'Etang, who took over from the Duc de Luxembourg as administrator of the Freemason's Grand Orient of France, is beheaded. He had been accused of passing funds to émigré clients.

3 *(Floréal 14, Year II)*
Paris. The government official Payan cancels the ruling banning the use of Ancien Régime titles in pre-revolutionary plays. In future, only new plays must use the terms "Citizen" and "Citizeness".

5 *(Floréal 16, Year II)*
Paris. At the Jacobins Club, Tallien speaks out in favour of the "terrorist" from Avignon, Jourdan Coupe Têtes.

6 *(Floréal 17, Year II)*
Paris. The Opéra Comique shows the first performance of *Mélidor et Phrosine*, a comedy written by Arnaud and Méhul.

7 *(Floréal 18, Year II)*
Colmar. The Committee of Public Education of the Jacobins gets prospective French language teachers to sit an exam.

7 *(Floréal 18, Year II)*
Paris. Robespierre gets the Convention to approve a decree proclaiming that "the people of France recognise the existence of the Supreme Being and of the immortality of the soul". →

7 *(Floréal 18, Year II)*
Ile de France. A battalion called the "Black Couriers of the Republic" is set up. It is made up of 4,250 former slaves and will work to reinforce the island's defences.

8 *(Floréal 19, Year II)*
Paris. The Committee of Public Safety dissolves the revolutionary committees that had been set up in the departments by the special envoys from Paris. Only the committees at Arras and Orange are allowed to continue operating.

8 *(Floréal 19, Year II)*
Paris. The famous chemist Lavoisier is guillotined along with 26 other Farmers General. →

French Republic acknowledges existence of a Supreme Being

Paris, May 7

Atheism has now been outlawed. A little over a month ago, Barère said that the Committee of Public Safety was working on a vast "regeneration plan" aimed at "banishing from the Republic both immorality and prejudice". Today, the final draft of the plan was outlined by Robespierre in a speech on the "links between republican principles and religious and moral concepts". The content of the speech shocked the supporters of de-Christianisation. It argues for the approval of a decree stating that "the people of France recognise the existence of the Supreme Being and of the immortality of the soul". Robespierre sees this as a republican and social proposal based on just retribution. He considers atheism to be basically an aristocrat's invention and believes that only faith can lead to virtue, which is a crucial principle in a democratic

Robespierre imposes a state religion to reinforce the Revolution.

republic. Four new holidays are going to be instituted to "bring man back to divine thought". The new monthly festivities are to replace religious holidays. In a month's time, the capital and the rest of the country are to duly celebrate the Supreme Being (→ June 8).

The chemist Lavoisier is guillotined

Paris, May 8

The 27 Farmers General did not lose their dignity as they were silently packed into tumbrels and driven to Revolution Square. They were executed in the same order as their names had appeared on the charge sheet. Antoine Lavoisier looked on as his father-in-law, Jacques Paulze, was guillotined. Then it was his turn. It was 5 p.m.

The men were tried this morning. It was a case of rough justice. The accused were asked the same questions as yesterday and their replies were ridiculed by the judges. Then, the Tribunal's president, Coffinhal, read out the verdict, which had probably been decided in advance. Charged with helping the enemies of the Republic, they were all sentenced to death.

Joseph Le Bon takes control of Cambrai

Cambrai, May 5

The "Canarian" is coming. Resplendent in his yellow outfit, his

The zealous Le Bon is an ex-priest.

hat crowned with large red, white and blue plumes, the special emissary Joseph Le Bon entered Cambrai today. Ahead of him walked over a dozen of his aides. He had "fierce eyes, a fiery face and was wearing trousers and a carmagnole", the jacket worn by revolutionaries. Robespierre's servant has come with sabre drawn to take up his new posting. His reputation as a bloodthirsty man has preceded him. He will be appointing an executioner and have a guillotine built on the town's main square. Le Bon will stay at the Dechy residence, a pleasant place for guests. Those who dare refuse an invitation had better beware, their heads may roll. His wife Mimie loves to watch the guillotine in action ...

Corsairs versus the Royal Navy

Ile de France, May 5

Two corsair frigates on the way back from Java ran the blockade of the Ile de France. Following a big clash with four ships of the Henry Newcome division, the ship commanded by Jean Marie Renaud was able to get through with all its cargo. This was thanks to the sacrifice of the second corsair frigate, the *Duguay Trouin*, commanded by Julien Tréhouart. This Creole captain withstood English fire for three hours before giving up (→ May 17).

Emigrés celebrate in London

London, May 2

A person can't live in constant fear. This evening, the large society of French émigrés has gathered at the Ranelagh ballroom, one of the fanciest meeting places in the English capital. Some 1,500 of them came, wearing masks and disguises, to poke fun at the Revolution. But the high point of the evening was a short satirical play in which a Charlotte Corday look-alike was seen coming out of a tomb to chase ... Robespierre!

Convention

10 *(Floréal 21, Year II)*
Paris. Pache, the mayor of Paris, is arrested. He used to be closely linked with Chaumette and Hébert. He is replaced by a Robespierrist, Jean Baptiste Fleuriot Lescot.

13 *(Floréal 24, Year II)*
Lyons. According to recent statistics, the toll of repression in Lyons indicates that between November 2nd. 1793 and May 13th. 1794, 1,667 death sentences were handed out and 1,674 buildings were destroyed.

13 *(Floréal 24, Year II)*
Guyana. The abolition of slavery is proclaimed at Cayenne.

14 *(Floréal 25, Year II)*
Paris. The Committee of Public Safety asks David to design national, military and civilian costumes.

15 *(Floréal 26, Year II)*
Paris. At the Jacobins Club, Couthon violently attacks the sectors and people's societies and calls for the Jacobins to resign from such bodies.

17 *(Floréal 28, Year II)*
Northern France. General Moreau captures Tourcoing, thus opening up the route to Belgium for the French army.

18 *(Floréal 29, Year II)*
Vendée. General Vimeux replaces Turreau as commander of the army in the west.

19 *(Floréal 30, Year II)*
Philadelphia. Talleyrand swears allegiance to the Constitution of the United States, where he has been living since being expelled from England.

20 *(Prairial 1, Year II)*
Paris. The deputies Bouquier, Coupé and Thibaudeau submit a draft decree aimed at "revolutionising public education". The plan is to send four students from each district to a central school. After two months, they would go home to teach other student teachers.

22 *(Prairial 3, Year II)*
Paris. Thérésa Cabarrus is arrested (→June 14, 94).

22 *(Prairial 3, Year II)*
Corsica. English forces capture Bastia.

31 *(Prairial 12, Year II)*
Spain. The invasion of Catalonia by the Republic's forces sparks off violent, anti-French rioting, notably at Valencia.

Elisabeth, the King's sister, is beheaded

Deprived of her Bible, Madame Elisabeth is dragged from jail.

Paris, May 10
The sister of Louis XVI recited the *De Profundis* as she was taken to the guillotine. One by one, the 25 others who faced the same fate bowed to her before climbing to the scaffold. A sansculottist was heard to snigger: "Despite all this bowing and scraping, she'll end up just like the Austrian" (Marie Antoinette).

When her turn came, Mme. Elisabeth walked calmly up the wooden steps. As she was being tied to the board, her muslin shawl slipped, baring her shoulders. "In the name of decency, cover me up," she asked her executioner. When her head rolled into the straw basket, the crowd of spectators was surprisingly subdued.

A prison-boat for priests at Rochefort

Rochefort, May 10
The mass of people squeezed aboard the ship *Les Deux Associés* "like herring in a barrel" aren't slaves. They are 800 priests who have been sentenced to deportation from France. They are being held at Rochefort until their departure and have been put aboard the vessel

because there was nowhere else to put them. The conditions on board are beyond description. A letter signed by several of the detainees was sent today to the Committee of Public Safety. In it, they "demand to be provided with some straw, a kindness that is not refused even to common criminals".

Agriculture needs blacksmiths

Paris, May 14
Due to a lack of qualified men, France is short of ploughshares and scythes. Such equipment now has to be purchased abroad, particularly in Switzerland. In order to solve this costly problem, the Convention's agricultural committee has decided to set up a workshop on the Rue de Rueilly in Paris. It will be run by Citizen Molard. Blacksmiths will come from the provinces to learn the latest techniques in metallurgy. The Republic wants French agriculture to prosper.

Barton is named a good citizen.

The "Mother of God" is arrested

Paris, May 17
A strange incident has set tongues wagging. Vadier, the president of the Committee of General Security, had ordered police to raid the home of Catherine Théot, on the Rue de la Contrescarpe. The old woman, who claims to be none other then the "Mother of God", was reported to have been caught red-handed. She is the priestess for a strange, occult sect who regularly held secret meetings at her home and promised her followers immortality in exchange for some hard cash. Such practices are becoming increasingly popular in the capital. Catherine Théot's clients are a bit like the followers of the German doctor Franz Anton, who claimed to have discovered how to use "animal magnetism" to cure all sorts of diseases. However, this evening the "Mother of God" is in jail along with several members of her sect. Among these, policemen were extremely surprised to find Gerle, the former monk who became a deputy in the Constituent Assembly (→June 15).

Toussaint rallies to the Republic

Saint Domingue, May 18
One of the three leaders of the black uprising plans to go over to the Republic's side with his men. This was the content of a secret message that was delivered to General Etienne Laveaux this morning. But before he joins the French, Toussaint Bréda, also known as Louverture, wants to wait for the Convention decree abolishing slavery to reach Saint Domingue. The French general has been hoping for just such a move for several weeks. Laveaux was certain that Louverture's fight for black liberation could not have a better ally than the Republic. What seems to have convinced Louverture to side with the French are the policies of the English, who restored slavery wherever they went. Although he is said to be a cautious man, the black leader chose to help the republicans at a time when they face a desperate situation: some three quarters of the French colony is in the hands of the English and the Spanish.

England now rules the Seychelles Islands

Seychelles, May 17

In order to intimidate the local population, which is on a war footing, English forces have seized Mahé, the main island of the Seychelles archipelago. Yesterday, four of the ships led by Commodore Newcome, which were carrying 1,200 men, arrived off the island and ordered its French commander to surrender. Jean Baptiste Quéau de Quincy, who only had eight cannons and 40 National Guardsmen, chose to capitulate. He was allowed to remain on the island. Newcome this morning handed over to de Quincy the crew of the *Duguay Trouin*, captured on May 5th.

Sophie de Condorcet gets a divorce

Auteuil, May 18

Sophie de Condorcet has had no news from her husband, whom she believes to be living as an émigré in Switzerland. She has been living a quiet life, staying in her house at Auteuil. The divorce she filed for in January, in order to preserve her daughter's inheritance in case her husband's assets are seized, has just been granted by the town council. It was a painful move for her, even though she had told her husband that it was a formality that would be annulled once there was no further risk. But the young woman does not know that she has been a widow for the past two months.

In the spring of 1794, some sector members ask the patriots in their neighbourhood to organise banquets in the street so that they can share their frugal fare fraternally while singing patriotic songs. The atmosphere is very merry, largely due to the torrents of wine that flow.

Robespierre and Collot are attacked

Collot d'Herbois owes his life to his assailant's poor marksmanship.

Paris, May 26

"All that binds me to this fleeting life is the love of motherland and a thirst for justice."

For Robespierre to speak this way before the Convention, he must have been deeply affected by the recent attempt on his life. Yesterday evening, he said at the Jacobins Club: "I feel more distant than ever from the nastiness of mankind." Both Robespierre and Collot d'Herbois have certainly had a run of misfortune. On the night of May 22nd. to 23rd., as he was on his way to his home on the Rue Favart, a man rushed at Collot and fired two gunshots at point-blank range, narrowly missing. The gunman, Henri Amiral, was a neighbour, a former servant and currently unemployed ex-Lottery official who spent much of his time in bars. In fact, it was Robespierre he wanted to kill out of a hatred for the Republic, which he blamed for his predicament. He fired at Collot simply because his many attempts to get close to his intended target had all ended in failure.

The day after that incident, on May 24th., a stationer's daughter, Cécile Renault, was detained. She had gone to the Duplay residence and asked to meet Robespierre. There was something suspicious about this 25 year old woman. She soon admitted to the police that she had come to "kill the tyrant" with the two large kitchen knives she had hidden in her blouse. The two attempted assassinations may be isolated incidents, but people are becoming worried.

A rowdy debate at the Arts Society

Paris, May 20

Founded on February 19th. 1794, the Popular and Republican Society of Arts has been an active participant in the capital's artistic life. Its political contacts have given it a degree of power, particularly when it comes to choosing which works are to be exhibited in museums. All would be fine if some of the artists who belong to the Society did not try to impose their sectarian opinions on others. The debates are often rowdy affairs. Painters such as Topino Lebrun, Lesueur and Isabey, sculptors like Dardel and Détournelle argue about whether artists who spend too long in Italy should be considered as émigrés. Today, for example, Boucher and the Flemish painters were the subject of debate. Some said the Flemish paintings must be banned because they lack "ancient nobility". Others even wanted the works to be destroyed, or at least kept out of museums. As for Boucher, many expressed shock at the licentiousness of his art. The two camps are split between the liberals and the "antiquomaniacs", who hate any attempt at modernity. Luckily the debates held at the Arts Society are just theoretical arguments.

Cécile Renault is arrested: Robespierre thus avoids Marat's fate.

1 *(Prairial 13, Year II)*
Paris. The Mars military academy is founded in Paris.→

2 *(Prairial 14, Year II)*
Brittany. Off Ushant, Admiral Villaret de Joyeuse loses his ships, including *Le Vengeur*, while defending a wheat convoy.→

3 *(Prairial 15, Year II)*
Vaucluse. The village of Bédoin is torched on orders from the criminal tribunal. It had accepted money to provide shelter for many counter-revolutionaries. Maignet, the special envoy from Paris, leads the repression which results in 63 executions (→ Dec. 15, 94).

4 *(Prairial 16, Year II)*
Paris. Robespierre is unanimously elected president of the Convention. His popularity has apparently never been greater.

4 *(Prairial 16, Year II)*
Paris. At the Assembly, Grégoire presents the linguistic policy he believes is necessary to make French a truly national language and to get rid of local dialects.→

5 *(Prairial 17, Year II)*
Paris. The Favart auditorium shows a patriotic opera by Lévrier Champion and Grétry, *Joseph Bara.*

5 *(Prairial 17, Year II)*
United States. Congress in Philadelphia reasserts its position on the conflict in Europe by adopting a neutrality act.

6 *(Prairial 18, Year II)*
Paris. Fouché is elected president of the Jacobins Club. He is seeking to weaken Robespierre's position within the Club and the Convention.

7 *(Prairial 19, Year II)*
Guadeloupe. Victor Hugues, the Commissioner of the Republic, rallies many Blacks and captures Pointe à Pitre after having proclaimed the abolition of slavery.→

8 *(Prairial 20, Year II)*
Paris. Robespierre presides over the celebration of the Supreme Being held on the Champ de Mars.→

9 *(Prairial 21, Year II)*
Paris. The painter David and the chemist Fourcroy publish building projects aimed at improving the capital: a statue of the French people crushing Federalism, Nature reborn on the ruins of the Bastille, a triumphal arch for the feast of October 6th., etc.

The Mars military academy will train competent army officers

Curious passers-by stop to look at the tents that will house the future officers of the republican army.

Paris, June 1

The "Martians", as the students of the Mars military academy are already called, will have to defend the Republic. That is the objective the Convention had in mind when it decided to set up the institution. Known as the Mars School, it will welcome young men aged between 16 and 17, six from each district, three town dwellers and three boys from the country. Priority will be given to the sons of wounded or still serving volunteers. Carnot, who came up with the idea, hopes that the academy will teach students the values and expertise of true republican soldiers. The youths will sleep in tents, remain sober, be unpaid and have no contact with the outside world. To ensure a rounded education, each student will spend some time in each of the various branches of the armed forces. The School, which is to be built on the Sablons plain, opposite the Boulogne park, will focus on teaching its students "fraternity, discipline, frugality, the love of motherland and the hatred of kings".

Naval battle over a convoy of wheat

Off Ushant, June 2

The ship *Le Vengeur* lost all its masts and a third of its crew. The fierce resistance put up by Admiral Villaret de Joyeuse's squadron is now over. However, by delaying the English flotilla, the French commander ensured that a convoy of wheat fom America reached its destination. The sacrifice of the men of *Le Vengeur* and Captain Renaudin was not in vain, but the French tactic of shooting at the masts of enemy ships has once again proved to be disastrous. The reason the English commander, Howe, won is because he fired his cannon from close range (→ June 14).

Both on land and on sea, "liberty or death" is their only motto.

The poet La Harpe is "born again"

Paris, June 1

The committee of the Butte aux Cailles sector may well have made a mistake. Citizen La Harpe, who has just been granted a certificate of good citizenship by the committee, has turned into a "fanatic". La Harpe has been in detention for the past two and a half months. Until recently, he had sworn he was a good patriot and a die-hard republican. But while in jail, he had noted that the only fellow prisoners who seemed to be able to cope were those who had kept or rediscovered their Catholic faith. He had a revelation a few days ago. While reading a passage from *L'Imitation de Jésus Christ,* he was struck by the phrase: "I am here, my son." He was immediately overcome by a deep spiritual joy and this disciple of Voltaire, this friend of the philosophers, was "born again". The poet rediscovered a faith he had abandoned and treated with contempt for most of his adult life. At death's door, La Harpe has found religion.

Port au Prince is captured by the English

Port au Prince, June 4

The siege of Port au Prince is over. The administrative capital of Saint Domingue has fallen into English hands after five days of combat. Its beleaguered defenders had to abandon their positions and flee from the town with the royalists. Following a string of defeats, the republican forces now only control a few parts of the north and the south of the island. Chased out of the west, the commissioners Polverel and Sonthonax fled to Jacmel. Everything seems to be over for the French, unless Toussaint Louverture is true to his word and comes to their aid.

Victor Hugues recaptures Guadeloupe

Pointe à Pitre, June 7

"Our arrival in this colony is something of a miracle." That is how Victor Hugues, the envoy from the Convention and commissioner for the Windward Islands, described the landing of republican forces on the shores of Guadeloupe. They were able to seize stores of arms and ammunition, huge stocks of food and equipment as well as 87 ships. The French ships had sighted the coast of Guadeloupe a week before they actually set foot on dry land. The island was defended by 8,000 well-armed English soldiers and 2,000 royalists. The Convention had even advised the French convoy to head for the United States in case of trouble. But Hugues is a very tenacious man. On the night of June 2nd. to 3rd., some 1,000 Frenchmen silently landed. English forces were caught offguard and withdrew to the Fleur d'Epée fort, which was defended by 900 men and 16 cannons. The French troops only had their bayonets to fight with. Despite this, the French forces were successful due largely to the high morale of the patriots led by Victor Hugues (→July 5).

The intrepid Victor Hugues wears a commissioner's uniform in combat.

Young Robert Surcouf, a master mariner

Ile de France, June 3

At the age of only 19, Robert Surcouf has just passed his master mariner's exam at Port la Montagne. This native of Saint Malo is now qualified to be a naval officer if the governor of the Ile de France agrees to appoint him as a lieutenant. He is in any case ready to take command of a vessel if he can find an owner who trusts him. Robert, the youngest of the Surcouf clan, plans to have an active life. His experience as a lieutenant aboard the *Navigateur*, a slaver operating off the Mozambique coast, will be a big help in his search for suitable employment.

Hundreds are arrested in Avignon

Avignon, June 6

For the past three days, the city has been at a standstill. House-to-house searches are being carried out and nobody is allowed outside. The assassination of a patriot of the Pontet neighbourhood gave the envoy from Paris, Maignet, the excuse he needed to launch the man-hunt. He said he trusts the local commissioners to be able to tell the difference between "a man who loves his country and one who secretly plots its ruin". In all, some 600 people have been arrested in the sweep: known counter-revolutionaries as well as all priests, the parents of émigrés and prostitutes.

A suspect is arrested by a group of sansculottists armed with pikes.

Grégoire lashes out against local dialects

Paris, June 4

The fight to make French the sole language spoken throughout the Republic continues unabated. Now, Grégoire has reminded the Convention of the urgent need to "wipe out local dialects". Basing himself on his wide-ranging linguistic study, he stressed that 12 million citizens are hardly able to speak French, a ridiculous situation for a society that aspires to be on the leading edge of progress. The Convention also has another task before it: replacing archaic terms with revolutionary ones.

Singers rehearsing republican songs prior to a patriotic celebration.

June 8, 1794: France honours the Supreme Being

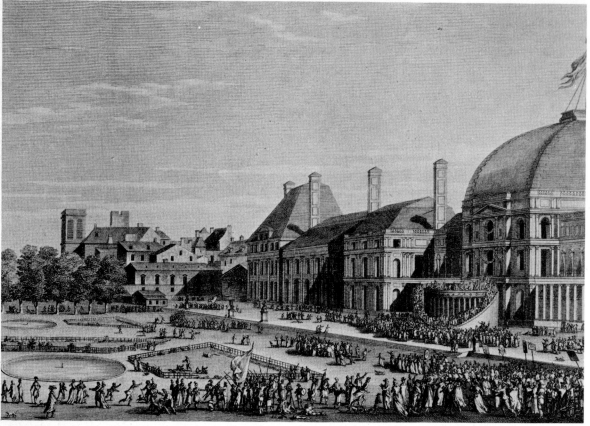

Crowds hurry to the Tuileries carrying huge bunches of flowers, before marching to the Champ de Mars.

Paris

As far as the eye can see, there is nothing but a mass of flowers: on balconies, along streets, on floats and in women and children's arms, all the way from Montmartre hill to the Tuileries. That is where the crowd heads for initially. People have been out in the streets ever since 5 a.m. Outside the palace, a podium has been built for the deputies, who are waiting for Robespierre to arrive. He is the acting president of the Assembly. At last, he arrives in his fancy red-lined, blue suit.

Today's celebration is a major event and the painter David has done his best to make it a memorable one. Carrying an ear of wheat, Robespierre leads the procession which is now heading towards the Champ de Mars. Two columns advance as the drums roll, men on one side, women on the other, behind a mass of youths. One person bearing violets represents Childhood, another wearing a crown of myrtle embodies Adolescence, a third draped in oak leaves represents Virility, while a fourth, with vine and olive leaves, symbolises Old Age. When they stand before the Altar to the Nation, they will pay homage to the Supreme Being by singing hymns for the "virtuous souls and pure hearts". They are not in the least upset or troubled by the sniggers of a few atheists in the crowd who find the whole colourful performance quite absurd.

After the procession, the float bearing the "treasures of France" is exhibited in the National gardens.

The deputies' ceremonial costume.

When the procession reaches the Champ de Mars, thousands of voices sing the hymn to the Supreme Being, as cannons roar and trumpets sound.

France

The French Republic now has a god, the Supreme Being, and this month is to be spent honouring him. That is what Robespierre has decided. He has become the hero, nearly the high priest, of the celebrations. His special message has been distributed from village to village, and city walls are plastered with a proclamation that for a change does not deal with arrests or executions. All citizens were pleased and relieved to hear the news of the celebrations. They are not only preparing to pay homage to the Supreme Being, but also to the nation and the universe itself. The new state religion is to be ushered in with a huge national mass.

A lot of work has gone into the preparations for the feast. There have been countless rehearsals in schools, choirs have been busy practising their songs, while local officials have been drafting long and fiery speeches. Old men and children have been trying on their costumes. Throughout the provinces, local authorities have followed the instructions from Paris telling them to make sure that the celebrations are a solemn and sacred affair. The "patriotic god" will be embodied by a man dressed to look like a hero from antiquity. He will be driven up to the Altar to the Nation, where there will be hymns to virtue, to good citizenship, to the glory of France and to the righteous hatred of kings and all forms of tyranny. Everybody wants to attend the big event.

The inhabitants of the tiny village of Abdelys, in the Eure, sang to the "God of Liberty, Father of Nature" and played Marie Joseph Chénier's hymn based on a score by Gossec. At Angers and at Saint Etienne, large crowds marched behind an ancient chariot bearing a brilliantly decorated, symbolic cart and ear of wheat. People carried hundreds of flags and pikes. At the head of each procession, young girls dressed in white, with red, white and blue ribbons around their waists, walked proudly. Late into the night, heavy artillery rumbled and fireworks thundered. But despite the fervour, the mass rejoicing, many are expressing doubts that the people of France have suddenly and unhesitatingly embraced the new state religion, essentially a mixture of true religion and a citizenship cult.

Each French village marks the new citizenship cult as best it can.

The Great Terror is decreed

Paris, June 10

The day of Prairial 22, Year II, will remain engraved on the memory of Frenchmen for ever. The law named after that fateful date unleashed the bloodiest phase of the Terror.

It was drafted by the Committee of Public Safety, even though some of its members, including Billaud Varenne, were opposed to it. For over a month, Robespierre had been looking for the means to punish the growing number of opponents to his policies more efficiently. He entrusted the drafting of the law to Couthon, a jurist, rather than to one of his close associates such as Saint Just only because he needed a legal expert. It was a matter of radically changing legal procedures relating to "suspects"

by simplifying and speeding them up. The Convention had already allowed the revolutionary Tribunal to limit hearings to three days. In future, there will be no preliminary questioning of defendants or witnesses if the Tribunal states it has enough factual or "moral" proof. From now on, there will be no defence attorneys and the jury's choice of verdict will be simple: acquittal or death. In principle, the revolutionary Tribunal should just confirm the verdict handed down by one of the popular committees set up in May to interrogate those accused. But the committees work slowly, so the "suspects" will go directly before Tribunal, without any prior auditions. The new system of "justice" will be nothing if not speedy (→June 11).

Will this prophesy be true?

Famine avoided thanks to the "Vengeur"

Paris, June 14

The wheat convoy has reached its destination safely. The English warships were unable to intercept the vital cargo.

As usual, Barère has given the good news the largest possible publicity. Large quantities of wheat had been bought in the United States to provide the French army with food. Last April, a convoy of 150 ships set sail for France. It was well known in Paris that Admiral Howe, whose vessels had increased their patrols, was keeping an eye on the convoy. It was vital to ensure that the fleet reached the western port of Brest unscathed.

The Brest squadron was ordered to stop the English from capturing the precious cargo. Three times, ships commanded by Admiral Villaret de Joyeuse tried to block the British fleet.

France's navy, however, could not hope to compete with the British Admiral's know-how and experience. With the exception of a few minor successes, the Republic's recent record on the high seas is pretty poor. Despite the fiery speeches of Barère, in which he claimed that the convoy operation had been a glorious victory, Britain undoubtedly continues to rule the waves.

The French sailors only had their bravery to wield against the English ships.

Tallien is banned by the Jacobin Club

Paris, June 14

Jean Lambert Tallien has good reason to be afraid of finding himself under the guillotine's blade. Robespierre has just openly expressed his hostility by having him ousted from the Jacobins Club. When he had been sent as a special envoy to Bordeaux, Tallien had already been recalled to Paris to explain his actions. He had succeeded in confusing his enemies and believed he was safe at last. But the suspicious Robespierre had ordered his spies to follow Tallien everywhere. Tallien was aware of this. Whenever he left his home, he got his own spies to keep an eye on Robespierre's men. Two days ago, Robespierre found out that the young man had dared to speak out in private against the dreaded law of Prairial 22 giving the revolutionary Tribunal increased powers. That gave him the excuse he needed to attack Tallien and threaten him at the Assembly. Humiliated, but still cautious because his beloved Thérésa is still in jail, Tallien then tried to justify himself by writing a letter reiterating his desire to serve the nation. He got a reply this morning: Robespierre has banned him from the Jacobins Club. Tallien seems to have no other option but to plot to find a way out of his very dangerous predicament.

The guillotine to be moved out of Paris

Paris, June 13

The guillotine is now in the process of being moved out of the capital. It was recently set up by the Trône Renversé toll barrier. For a long time, it had remained on the Place de la Réunion, formely Place du Carrousel, while the one on the Place de Grève was used only for common criminals. But the deputies' meeting at the Tuileries palace could no longer stand seeing executions being carried out before their very eyes. So the guillotine was sent to Revolution Square, only to be moved the day after the celebration of the Supreme Being. Sent to Place Saint Antoine, it only stayed there three days because the ground there could not soak up all the blood.

Has Théroigne gone insane?

Paris, June 27

A few documents and a sabre were all that remained in Théroigne de Méricourt's house to testify to her recent past as a committed revolutionary. The young woman was arrested this morning after having been informed against by the Le Peletier sector committee for allegedly having made "subversive" statements. But when police went to her home, they found her in such a distraught state that they felt she had gone quite insane. However, she was still placed under arrest and her rooms searched. Police have none the less called for a doctor to examine Théroigne.

Mad with hatred for Robespierre.

The French army triumphs at Fleurus

Fleurus, June 26

For the second time since 1792, the road to Belgium is open. The Austrian commander, Prince of Saxe Cobourg, was forced to call for a retreat. The troops of northern France and the Ardennes, a mixture of regular soldiers and volunteers, fought with great bravery all day long. Their officers were equally courageous, in particular during the heroic defence of the Lambusart outpost. The division led by General Joseph Lefebvre, surrounded by flames and thick smoke, for a time seemed about to give way to panic. But, as the men cried "No retreat today", Lefebvre led his men on. Elsewhere, the Republic's soldiers were just as brave: Championnet resisted all the Austrian attacks, while Kléber rushed enemy lines with his usual devil-may-care attitude. During 14 hours, the fighting raged on. The general in command, Jean Baptiste Jourdan, was

For the first time, hot-air balloons have been used during a battle.

killed in combat. Jourdan's repeated charges with three battalions played a decisive role in today's victory. The Austrian Prince was for his part unable to make the best of the complex military situation: he could probably have won the day relatively easily if he had carried out a simple flanking manoeuvre around Jourdan's troops.

Robespierre in hot water over case of Catherine Théot

Paris, June 15

It is becoming more and more obvious that the recent arrest of the "Mother of God" has turned into a political issue. Vadier, the president of the Committee of Public Safety, today stated in a report that the activities of the sect led by Catherine Théot were a "conspiracy" against the Republic. He even claimed that she was linked to a number of groups opposed to the régime. He has therefore requested that she be sent before the revolutionary Tribunal, along with one of her sect, the former member of the Constituent Assembly, dom Gerle. Vadier is in fact aiming even higher. He has spread the rumour that the police found a letter from Catherine Théot in which she thanks Robespierre, whom she calls the "saviour of the world", for having "restored religion". Robespierre was quick to respond to this rumour. This evening, he asked Fouquier Tinville and Dumas, the president of the revolutionary Tribunal, to hand the whole case over to him. It is not easy to see who will win this new trial of strength.

The Girondist leaders' tragic end

Bec d'Ambès (Gironde), June 26

After Barbaroux's execution, the discovery of the bodies of Pétion and Buzot marked the tragic end of the exodus of the Girondist outlaws. Following a grim winter spent in the cellars of Guadet's home, in Saint Emilion, they had managed to flee on the night of June 18th. The small group had split up to avoid being spotted by Jacobin agents. Starving and exhausted, they could go no further. Near Libourne, Barbaroux decided to commit suicide by shooting himself when he realised there was no hope of escaping his pursuers. The bullet failed to kill him and he was taken, badly wounded, to Bordeaux to be guillotined. Buzot and Pétion also killed themselves late on June 20th. Local inhabitants had heard the gunfire, but their bodies were only found today. It was practically impossible to identify the corpses, which had been savaged by wild animals, and the two men were therefore buried on the spot. The fate of other Girondist fugitives was just as sinister: Valady was the first to be arrested, at Périgueux in December 1793, and he was promptly executed. As for Salles and Guadet, they have just been guillotined in Bordeaux. As Salles was strapped down, however, the blade became stuck and would not fall. Salles then calmly explained the problem to his executioner. Moments later, the Girondist's head rolled.

Guadet is found hidden in the attic of his Saint Emilion house.

Convention

1 *(Messidor 13, Year II)* Paris. Robespierre denounces to the Jacobins a conspiracy against his person emanating from the Convention and the Committees.

1 *(Messidor 13, Year II)* Belgium. The troops of the Convention chase the Austrian forces from Ostend (→8).

4 *(Messidor 16, Year II)* Paris. The Friends of the Nation lyric theatre performs *Agricol Viala*, an heroic drama by Adolphe Jadin.

5 *(Messidor 17, Year II)* Paris. The general council of the Commune approves the new maximum ceiling of salaries in the capital.

5 *(Messidor 17, Year II)* Guadeloupe. In spite of the heavy bombardment of Pointe à Pitre for three weeks, the troops of Victor Hugues manage to push the English led by Admiral Jarvis back to the sea.

6 *(Messidor 18, Year II)* Paris. In order to replace the school of engineering, closed in 1790, the Convention creates an agency of engineering.

8 *(Messidor 20, Year II)* Belgium. The French troops commanded by Jourdan and Pichegru meet up and capture Brussels.

10 *(Messidor 22, Year II)* Paris. The Convention decides to nationalise the assets of the hospitals and charitable establishments which had not been included in the transfer of church property.

10 *(Messidor 22, Year II)* Deux Sèvres. At Combrand, Stofflet and his men find and assassinate the Vendean leader Marigny, who had been sentenced to death by the Vendean headquarters for disobeying orders.

11 *(Messidor 23, Year II)* Paris. Dubois Crancé is ousted from the Jacobins Club at Robespierre's request. The latter feels Crancé's hesitant attitude during the siege of Lyons was suspicious.

14 *(Messidor 26, Year II)* Paris. Marie Joseph Chénier's *Chant du Départ*, set to music by Méhul, is sung to mark the fifth anniversary of the fall of the Bastille.

14 *(Messidor 26, Year II)* Paris. After Dubois Crancé, it is Fouché's turn to be kicked out of the Jacobins Club.→

A Jacobin parade on Broadway

New York, July 4

Like every year, the American people are today celebrating their independence. French Jacobins had wanted to join in the celebrations, so a group of them marched down Broadway behind Governor Clinton, as they sang the *Marseillaise* and other republican songs. Many people noted that Genêt, the ambassador of France to the United States, sat among the other officials. However, there were some Frenchmen who stayed away from the celebrations in New York. The émigrés would have nothing to do with anyone involved in the Great Terror. Demonstrators booed as Talleyrand, Beaumetz, Casenove, Moreau de Saint Méry, La Roche and La Colombe watched the colourful Franco-American parade from a window.

Hoche, a well-loved republican general

Paris, July 12

Lazare Hoche loves to fight for the Republic, but for the past three months this 26 year old general has been deprived of his sabre. After having been placed under close observation at the Carmes prison, Hoche is now languishing in the Conciergerie jail. He is accused of being insubordinate and too well-liked by his troops. Now he is forced to share the grim existence of the victims of the Committee of Public Safety's rough justice. It is a boring life. All that happens is the coming and going of prisoners and once in a while the arrival of an unusual detainee. Hoche, the victor of Wissembourg, is such a man. This morning, a simple gesture has made him more popular still. Lazare had had a bunch of roses sent up to cheer up his cell. As the guards were leading one of his loyal soldiers, Thorias, to the guillotine,

Hoche, an exceptional general.

the condemned man gave Hoche his watch "as a souvenir and in exchange for a rose". The general gave him a flower and distributed the rest to other prisoners.

"The death of Joseph Bara" will hang on the Convention's walls

Paris, July 11

The name of Joseph Bara has been added to the long list of martyrs of the Revolution. This young man, still almost an adolescent, is said to have cried "Long live the Republic!" when he was killed by Vendeans who had tried to make him shout "Long live the King!" Robespierre has asked that his body be laid to rest at the Panthéon and Barère wants him to be immortalised "by the hand of the famous David, at the Republic's expense". He wants the painting to be hung at the Convention. Today, David submitted his plan for the work. It will be a straightforward piece with no blood or decorations. Bara will be shown naked, holding the tricoloured cockade on his heart.

David turns Joseph Bara into a symbol of murdered innocence by stressing the martyr's extreme youth.

Purge continues at the Jacobins Club

Paris, July 14

After both Tallien and Dubois Crancé, Robespierre has ensured that Fouché has been expelled from the Jacobins Club. The two men have been at daggers drawn for a long time. They had, however, been friends in 1789 during the merry meetings of the "Rosati" at Arras. But Fouché had become a leader of the opposition to the two Committees and therefore Robespierre's political foe. His influence over the Jacobins had turned him into a dangerous enemy for Robespierre, who has done his best to get Fouché ousted from the Club, of which he was president since June. Robespierre accused him of having been too lenient with the rebels of Lyons, where Fouché had been sent on a special mission. He also lashed out at Fouché's "low cunning" and his "pitiful demeanour". The terrified Assembly has decided to abandon Fouché to his fate.

This wine-grower from Bordeaux deserves his certificate. He plans to drink his wine from patriotic pitchers bearing the effigy of the Nation.

Sex and easy living at the Carmes prison

Paris, July

After a month spent at the Petite Force jail, Thérésa Cabarrus has been sent to the Carmes prison. In her new cell, she met two young women, the Vicomtesse de Beauharnais and the Duchesse d'Aiguillon, who showed her that life at Carmes was quite different from that at the Petite Force. Here, prisoners are allowed to mingle and in certain cells, men and women are even locked up together. The jail guards are not fierce and neither are the female prisoners. Death is always nearby, so virtue is hardly the order of the day. Thérésa had been placed in solitary confinement at the Petite Force on Robespierre's orders. She had been thrown into a cell crawling with bugs. After 25 days without sunlight, without anything to wash with and no change of clothes, Thérésa had fallen ill. Believing her to be at death's door, her guards had allowed her to walk around the courtyard for an hour each day. Compared to such a hell hole, she is beginning to enjoy her stay at Carmes.

Is Robespierre growing weary of power?

Paris, July 13

It has been ten days since Robespierre was last seen in government circles. On July 3rd., he had stomped out of the Committee saying: "Save the homeland without me!" Since then, he has chosen not to take part in the debates. He had been exasperated by Billaud Varenne and Collot d'Herbois, who had dared, on June 28th., to call him a "dictator". Despite his anger and sulking, it is most unlikely that Robespierre is about to retire from politics. He regularly turns up at the Jacobins Club. But his foes are wasting no time during his absence. It may be too late for him to counter their moves (→ July 26).

Robespierre is under attack.

Lazy citizens are also suspect

Niort, July 11

At the request of the special envoy from Paris, Ingrand, the authorities of the district of Niort have decided to mobilise the entire active population for the harvest. In local towns, villages and hamlets, officials have been ordered to draw up lists of all the able-bodied inhabitants who are to be sent to the fields.

Those who "forget" to declare themselves in order to avoid working will be considered as suspect. As for "lazy" people who refuse to do any work on Sundays and holidays, they will be denounced as counter-revolutionaries.

A commissioner on a home visit.

There are many "Marseillaises"

For some time now, the music of the "Marseillaise", or the "beloved song", has been used for many a song. It accompanies this unusual "Hymn to the Guillotine":

O ye, celestial guillotine,
Who shortens king and queen:
By your influence divine,
Our rights we realign.
Support the laws of the nation
Let your wondrous instrument
Be forever permanent
To kill the evil implantation.
Sharpen thy blade
For Pitt and his agents vile,
Fill thy wicker sack divine
With heads of tyrants fine!

Citizen Dunoyer makes the following call for revenge:

To your weapons, my friends!
Let us build scaffolds loftier
Let us the soil of France cover
In blood of heads once jauntier

For his part, Citizen Féraud has composed a "Marseillaise" for labourers. This is it's refrain:

To your ploughs, men
Push the blade along the furrow
March on! March on!
Let the oxen trace it narrow

Citizen Sylvain Maréchal chose the music to ask the French to have babies:

To your beds, happy couples!
Forge your own destiny:
Nine months, nine months
For a fine republican baby.

15 (Messidor 27, Year II)
Hainault. Liberation of Landrecies, one of the last French strongholds to be held by the enemy.

16 (Messidor 28, Year II)
Paris. At the Convention, Barère gets up to protest against the fraternal meals, where, even while toasting the success of the Republican armies, certain of the participants manifest a democratic and royalist opposition.

19 (Thermidor 1, Year II)
Ile de France. The authorities, disturbed about the events in Sainte Domingue, organise a hunt to search for outlawed slaves, whose numbers are on the increase.

19 (Thermidor 1, Year II)
Geneva. Triumph of a democratic and pro-French insurrection.

22 (Thermidor 4, Year II)
Paris. In the absence of Robespierre, Saint Just and Barère organise a joint meeting of the two government Committees in order to try and reach a compromise.

23 (Thermidor 5, Year II)
Paris. Robespierre takes part in a new conciliation meeting of the Committees. A precarious reconciliation is under way.

26 (Thermidor 8, Year II)
Paris. Robespierre, who hasn't spoken for many weeks, demands that the Convention punishes traitors and purges the Committees (→27).

27 (Thermidor 9, Year II)
Paris. The Convention orders the arrest of Robespierre and his followers. The Commune declares itself in revolt and hands them over.→

28 (Thermidor 10, Year II)
Paris. The troops of the Convention, led by Barras, seize control of the city hall and arrest Robespierre. After attempting to commit suicide, he is guillotined along with 21 of his companions.→

29 (Thermidor 11, Year II)
Paris. Seventy of Robespierre's followers are guillotined at the barrier of the Trône Renversé, where the guillotine has been installed since Prairial.

31 (Thermidor 13, Year II)
Paris. Renewal of the Committees of Public Safety and Police, from which all the suspected followers of Robespierre are eliminated.→

Babeuf is retried and found innocent

Laon, July 18

This time, the "case of the forgery" is well and truly over. Babeuf had been proclaiming his innocence ever since January 1793. Now he has finally been freed and his reputation has been restored. In December of the same year, the trial, at which he had been sentenced in absentia to 20 years in irons, had been annulled due to a miscarriage of justice. The annulment was largely due to the efforts of Sylvain Maréchal. Babeuf was then released and he believed that his problems were over at last. But he found out a few days later that he would not be allowed to return to his job as an official of the Paris department of provisions until he had been formally declared innocent. Babeuf therefore decided to settle the issue once and for all and so he turned himself in to the authorities in order to be tried a second time. Today, Babeuf finally won his case. He is a free man. From now on, he plans to spend all his time working to publish his journal, *Le Tribun du Peuple* (→ Feb. 7, 95).

News of a victory is transmitted by semaphore

Paris, July 17

The situation on the northern front is once again becoming favourable to the Republic. The Austrian garrison at Landrecies, one of the last French outposts still held by the enemy, has surrendered. Thanks to the optical semaphore designed by Chappe, the good news reached Barère in record time and he immediately informed the Convention. It is a simple, ingenious system: signals are sent by moving two large arms placed atop towers and operated by pulleys.

Jean Cottereau, alias Jean Chouan, dies

Mayenne, July 28

The Chouans lost more than a leader when Jean Cottereau died. These rebels operating in western France derived their name from him, because his rallying cry was similar to that of the "chat-huant", or hoot-owl. He had become the leader of a group of peasants who repeatedly ambushed and attacked revolutionary forces. Known as Jean Chouan, he used his past experience as a poacher to very good effect. Prior to the Revolution, he made a living by trafficking in salt and his clashes with salt-tax collectors had earned him a death sentence. Jean Chouan was saved by an act of royal clemency that his mother had managed to obtain from Louis XVI. His opposition to the Revolution was partly due to the fact that Paris had cut into his profits by abolishing the salt tax. Caught by patriot soldiers at the Babinière farm, near his village of Saint Ouen des Tiots, he was mortally wounded in the clash.

Jean Chouan, the Vendeans' soul.

Josephine de Beauharnais's husband executed

Paris, July 23

The members of the Committee of Public Safety remained as hard as stone. Alexandre de Beauharnais, deputy of the nobility at the Estates General and former commander in chief of the Rhine army, was beheaded this morning. Neither the desperate pleas of his wife, Josephine, nor the letter Alexandre had sent from his cell at Carmes prison, were any help. His judges refused to believe that he had been trying to "stir up the hatred of kings in his children's hearts".

16 Carmelite nuns are guillotined

Paris, July 17

At eight o'clock this evening, the 16 Carmelite nuns of Compiègne climbed up to the scaffold at the Vincennes toll barrier one after the other.

Before being executed, they sang *Veni Creator* and the psalm *Laudate Dominum Omnes Gentes*. The prioress convinced the executioner to leave her until last so that she could comfort the nuns in their final moments. They had been condemned this very morning both for having corresponded with émigrés and withdrawn their oath of liberty and equality. The crowd attending the execution was impressed by the serene way in which the nuns faced death.

Poet André Chénier is beheaded

Paris, July 25

Barère had not been lying. When André Chénier's father had come to see him three days ago to humbly beg for some news of his son, the powerful Convention member had said pleasantly: "Your son will be out in three days."

Louis Chénier had gone home a happy man, convinced that he had just saved his son's life. But he did not know how ruthless and hypocritical Barère can be. He did not know that the promise was in fact a death sentence. Barère had left out one tiny detail: in fact, it was on the tumbrel that André Chénier left the Tribunal today. Caught up in the turmoil over the so-called prison conspiracy, he had been wrongly accused of having hidden documents belonging to the ambassador of Spain. On the evening of July 24th., only two days after his father's meeting with Barère, André bid a last farewell to the Trudaine brothers, his fellow prisoners, and left Saint Lazare jail for the Conciergerie prison. This morning at 9 a.m., following a farce of a "trial", he was informed of the verdict. André had been sentenced to death. At four o'clock, the young man was taken to the toll barrier at the Trône Renversé. Finally, at six o'clock this evening, the guillotine's deadly blade put an end to the life of a 32 year old poet.

Everyday life in jail under the Great Terror

A dark, grim corridor at Saint Lazare jail during the exercise period.

Paris, July

Each day, more and more suspects are flung into the convents, hospitals and military barracks that have been hastily turned into detention centres. The situation inside these improvised jails is getting worse. Rumours of a plot have led to a strengthening of security measures. There is no longer any question of prisoners being allowed to receive visitors or to send letters. Their mail is censored and newspapers are strictly forbidden. Any gathering outside a jail is quickly dispersed by guards. The detainees are cut off from the outside world, from news about what is going on. They are unable to find out who is slated to be executed on any particular day, even by bribing their guards. A curfew is in force inside the jails. Card games, concerts and reading sessions are all banned. Prisoners can no longer pay guards to bring them food or have their laundry done. There are no rich or poor prisoners as all money has been confiscated. Each detainee is allowed one clean shirt per week. They all eat the same boiled meat or dried fish at a common table. Despite all these hardships, they know that it is better not to complain. At Saint Lazare jail, a young man who had dared throw a rotten herring at

Food supplies are now forbidden.

a guard's head was immediately sent to the revolutionary Tribunal. The only escapes from such living hell are love or death. A number of prisoners have already managed to commit suicide, since property belonging to anyone sentenced to death is automatically seized. Some of the young women have claimed to be pregnant in the hope of being transferred to the Evêché hospice. Their claims are often taken seriously, such has been the promiscuity in some prisons over the past months. Even if they are found to have lied when they are examined by a doctor, they will have gained a few days' respite.

The Conciergerie

The courage of the prisoners
Awaiting trial arouses a lot of admiration. Some of these men compose songs to take their minds off their sad fate. A song, written on the eve of his execution by Nicolas Montjourdain, ex-leader of the Poissonnière sector, moves Parisians deeply:
The time comes I must die;
With faith and honour forth I go,
But with regret my wife I leave
In widowhood and tears of woe;
For her I ought to grieve.
And now I here my life resign.
Adieu to joys, the life coquette,
And free-thinking, and red wine
I cannot but with pain forget.
By tumbrel borne I, unafraid,
Will place my head meek
Neath the new Republic's blade.
O sad lamenting friends so dear,
Bewail no more my lot ingrate,
In these days of doubt and fear
'Tis all too oft a common fate.
Friends, you cannot gainsay,
You oft made me lose my head!

In jails, the daily roll-call of the Tribunal's victims is greeted with horror, pleas or stunned acceptance.

Execution of Robespierre and his friends on Revolution Square, Thermidor 10, Year II of the Republic.

On the evening of Thermidor 10, the mob jeered and spat at the still dripping heads of Robespierre and 21 of his supporters, including Saint Just and Couthon.

It was the final act of a conspiracy whose protagonists, often acting for purely personal reasons, were all Montagnards and part of the Committee of Public Safety: Collot d'Herbois, Billaud Varenne and Barère. The Thermidor 8 speech at the Convention threatening Robespierre has frightened many. The moderates, who had until then been loyal to Robespierre, abandoned him. The plot succeeded because Robespierre had become isolated and the people were tired of the Terror. On Thermidor 9, when the Commune called on the people to save Robespierre, who had been decreed an outlaw, the response was lukewarm. The revolt became bogged down and the Convention was able to crush it with relative ease. Thermidor 9 marked the end of the Terror. It also marked the end of the sansculottist republic and the revolutionary government.

At city hall, there is total confusion. Constable Merda manages to get to Robespierre and hits him in the face with his pistol. When he sees that his friend has been wounded, Le Bas blows his brains out, while Couthon desperately tries to escape.

Collot d'Herbois and Billaud Varenne arrived at the Committee of Public Safety's Paris headquarters at one o'clock in the morning of Thermidor 9.

They had just been violently kicked out of the Jacobins Club, where Robespierre had been cheered for lashing out against the "rogues and scoundrels". He also chastised the Convention for not having backed him the previous day. Barère, Lindet, Carnot, Prieur and, standing alone, Saint Just, were already in the Committee rooms.

Over the past few days, Collot and Billaud had been in contact with a number of deputies, including Tallien, Barras and Bourdon de l'Oise. Many of the Montagnards felt threatened by Robespierre, but it was vital that they rally the moderates of the Plaine, who had until then been fully loyal to Robespierre. Durand Maillane, one of their leaders, agreed to back the plotters if they proved to be winning. In any case, quick action was called for, since Robespierre could count on the support of the Jacobins, of the Commune and of Hanriot, the head of the National Guard. As the meeting was about to end, the Committee members present decided to call for Robespierre's ouster.

Robespierre is accused

At the Convention, the session presided over by Collot d'Herbois had started as usual at 10 a.m. The hall was packed with people who had been called in by the conspirators and nearly all the deputies were present, even right-wing ones. Saint Just, who sought to be conciliating, began to speak: "I belong to no faction, I will fight against all of them." He had barely finished speaking when Tallien cried: "Let the curtain be torn asunder!" This was greeted by wild clapping.

Then Billaud Varenne went up to the podium to speak. Taken aback, Saint Just kept his seat without complaining. Billaud Varenne then launched a violent attack against the "tyrant" Robespierre, who stood up. "Down with the tyrant!" people screamed. The situation at the Convention was getting out of hand. Brandishing a dagger, Tallien jumped up to demand Hanriot's arrest. This proposal was immediately adopted. Twice, Robespierre tried in vain to speak. Then, as he was being repeatedly accused of tyranny, he rose and turned towards the Montagnards, who turned their faces away from him. So, speaking to the moderates of the Plaine, he said: "It is to you, pure-hearted men, that I am speaking, not to the bandits...", but he was unable to go on. "Danton's blood is choking you!" Garnier screamed at him. However, no one had yet uttered the fateful word: arrest. It was Louchet and Lozeau who finally called for Robespierre's arraignment. This was approved as people shouted "Long live the Republic!" Robespierre was then heard to say: "The Republic! It is done for because the bandits are winning." The names of Couthon and Saint Just were added to the decree, as well as those of Le Bas, Dumas and Hanriot. But the ushers refused to lead them away, so all five were taken to the court, then to the Committee of General Security by a group of con-

Barras, the military leader.

Billaud Varenne, the spokesman.

the rule of Robespierre and his friends

Hanriot, National Guard head and loyal Robespierrist, holds firm under the Convention's fire. The moment is decisive, but Hanriot doesn't act.

stables. The crucial session was suspended at 3 p.m. The question now was: how would Paris react to the day's events?

The Commune is threatened

Early in the morning, Hanriot and the mayor, Fleuriot Lescot, had been ordered to go to the Convention to report on the situation in Paris. Worried, Hanriot had refused to obey. Two hours later, having gathered a unit of mounted policemen, he rushed to the Tuileries, but when he got there, the deputy Robin de l'Aube asked the policemen to arrest him. Much to Hanriot's fury, they obeyed. He was therefore not there when the Commune was informed of the arrest of Robespierre. The mayor immediately called for the general council to meet. By around 6 p.m., a quorum was reached and the mayor expressed his support for the five detainees, criticised the enemies of the people and called for an insurrection. At about 7 o'clock, the alarm bells were rung to summon citizens, who decided to set off to free Robespierre and his friends.

Robespierrists are freed

Robespierre had meanwhile been taken to the Luxembourg, but the turnkey refused to lock him up; so Robespierre found himself free by nine o'clock. Saint Just, Le Bas and Robespierre the Younger were also released. Couthon was only freed around midnight. In several parts of Paris, troops were massing, despite the confusion and contradictory orders issued by the Convention and the Commune. Shortly after 8 p.m., Coffinhal, the Robespierrist member of the Tribunal, arrived from the Place de Grève with some 3,000 sector members and 1,000 gunners. The Tuileries were surrounded and the doors of the Committee of General Security knocked down within a few minutes. Coffinhal was able to free Hanriot. When the news spread, a wave of panic hit the deputies. The Convention benches emptied. It was a decisive moment. All that was needed for the enemies of Robespierre to find themselves under arrest was an order from Hanriot.

Paris doesn't react

But, instead of acting right away, Hanriot decided to go to the Commune to receive instructions. The revolt still did not have a true leader. In fact, Robespierre only agreed to join the Commune after delaying for 22 hours out of respect for the Convention and because he still considered himself to be under arrest. Meanwhile, on the other side of the capital, the Convention had stopped hesitating and pulled itself together. It decreed that Hanriot, Robespierre and his friends and the Commune were outlaws. In other words, every citizen had a duty to arrest or kill them. The Convention appointed Barras as head of the National Guard, giving him seven assistants, including Bourdon de l'Oise. A group of several thousand men was gathered thanks to the support of some sectors of central and western Paris. By the time the bells struck midnight, Barras was ready to set off for the Place de Grève. Outside city hall, however, there was still much uncertainty. Many of the sector members were tired of hanging around and started going home. The pro-Robespierre mobilisation was quickly running out of steam just as Barras was preparing to march to city hall. Paris was not about to fight for Robespierre.

Wounded, Robespierre is placed on a large table. Blood is flowing from his jaw. People are jeering at him.

Robespierre: the Incorruptible's final moments

COMMUNE DE PARIS.

The last signature: Ro (bespierre).

Robespierre is wounded

Shortly after one o'clock in the morning, two columns of troops arrived on the nearly deserted Place de Grève without meeting any resistance. Meanwhile, a small unit of constables led by a certain Merda, who was armed with a decree from the Convention, managed to enter city hall.

Inside, there were still about 40 members of the Commune. Couthon and Robespierre had been busy discussing in detail the content of the proclamation they were planning to make to the military. "In whose name?" Robespierre asked, unwilling to act illegally. He was just signing the proclamation when the door of the council chamber burst open. It was Merda and his men. Two shots rang out, creating instant panic and confusion. Robespierre fell to the ground. A bullet had shattered his jaw. Some claimed

Robespierre's head.

that it was a suicide attempt, but Merda said that he was the one who fired. Robespierre the Younger flung himself from a window and suffered a head injury. Couthon tried to flee, but his wheelchair fell down the stairs. He was brought back and left lying on the ground. Le Bas killed himself. Dumas, Fleuriot Lescot and Saint Just were arrested. Hanriot managed to hide, but the area was surrounded and he was found in a courtyard later that day. In one fell swoop, the insurrection had been deprived of its leaders. Meanwhile, the deputy Legendre had had the Jacobins Club surrounded and all those inside expelled. He then triumphantly took the Club's keys to the Convention.

Robespierre is humiliated

While Robespierre was being carried on a stretcher to the chamber of the Committee of Public Safety, Bourdon went to the Convention to report on the total success of his mission and to introduce Constable Merda, the hero of the hour. The other captives were taken to the Committee of General Security. In the morning, the Convention met to work out the details for the execution. Barras was put in charge of keeping order. There would be no trial. The "outlaws" simply had to be identified. During all this, Robespierre lay on the table. Blood was still pouring from his wound, which was only bandaged around 6 a.m. Several of his teeth had to be removed. People claimed that some deputies came to stare at the wounded man, who was unable to speak. Bourdon de l'Oise called him a rascal, while others jeered: "You seem to be at a loss for words." "Is Your Majesty in pain?" Around 11 a.m., Robespierre was sent to the Conciergerie, where his friends had already been taken. At 1 p.m., the hearing at the revolutionary Tribunal got under way.

Sentenced without a trial

Robespierre was the first to be called to the witness box. "Are you Maximilien Robespierre, aged 35, born at Arras and a former deputy at the National Convention?" the court's president asked him. Robespierre could only nod in response. Then the decree naming him as an outlaw was read out. Fouquier

Couthon, Robespierre's shadow.

Saint Just: 22 months of politics.

Tinville, the public prosecutor, asked the court to hand down the death sentence. After that, it was the turn of Couthon, 38, a deputy; La Valette, 40, brigadier; Hanriot, 33, commander of the Paris National Guard; Dumas, 37, president of the revolutionary Tribunal; Saint Just, 26, deputy; Payan, 27, Paris Commune official; Vivier, 50, president of the Jacobins; and Gobeau, 26, town councillor. The session resumed at 4 p.m. Fleuriot Lescot, 39, mayor of Paris; Robespierre the Younger, 30, deputy, and 11 members of the Paris Commune.

The execution

At 6 p.m., a tumbrel came to take them to Revolution Square, where a guillotine had been specially set up on orders from the Convention. Along the way, a large crowd had gathered. Those who could afford it had rented window space and balconies. Jeers and insults rang out as the tumbrel drove by. The condemned men climbed up to the scaffold without saying a word. Over the next few days, the elimination of Robespierre's backers was to continue with the execution of a total of 96 other "outlaws"

Robespierre's second death

Not content with having contributed to Robespierre's fall, the Thermidorians also tried to blacken his name. There were rumours, pamphlets and songs. He was accused of tyranny and oppression. He was made responsible for the Terror, even though the entire Convention had backed him. As his death had to be justified, there was talk of a royalist plot and he was even suspected of seeking the crown. It was also claimed that a small, white leather pouch bearing a fleur-de-lis design had been found on him. People said that he had drawn up a list of some 60,000 citizens who were to be beheaded. There was even a rumour that Robespierre had been planning to marry the daughter of Capet at Lyons before returning to massacre his enemies.

After killing off the nobility and the people, all that remains for the executioner to do is to kill himself.

The victors of Thermidor share power among themselves in the Committees

Paris, July 31

The Convention is once again in control of the Revolution. It had never fully accepted the revolutionary government which had been thrust upon it by popular pressure, the war and a political minority. Following the fall of Robespierre, the Convention would have liked to cut down the Committee of Public Safety's powers, but Barère had been opposed to it.

This supporter of the continuity of power said on the evening of July 28th. that the previous day's events were just a "partial commotion" which did not affect the government's integrity". He also stressed that the Committees were needed to govern the nation as long as the 1793 Constitution could not be enforced. On July 29th., Barère suggested that three new members be appointed to replace the "plotters", namely Saint Just, Robespierre and Couthon. Although Tallien, Thuriot and Legendre were not opposed to keeping the Committees, they also wanted to change the way they operate by making it obligatory for

a quarter of their members to be changed each month, while outgoing members would not be eligible until the following month. But such a move could have harmed the government's stability. Finally, the Convention members named six among them to replace not only the "triumvirs", but also Prieur de la Marne and Jeanbon Saint André, both sent on missions, and Hérault de Séchelles, executed along with Danton.

The six are Tallien, a fierce supporter of the Terror, the Dantonists Thuriot and Bréard, the moderates Laloy and Treilhard and finally Barère's candidate, Eschasseriaux. The Committee of General Security has also been profoundly modified. Three Robespierrists, among them David, have been ousted from it, while four new members, including the Dantonists Merlin de Thionville and Legendre, have been appointed. All this is in fact an act of revenge by the so-called Indulgents who now surround the leaders of Thermidor, Barère, Collot d'Herbois and Billaud Varenne.

The Duplay family are under arrest

Paris, July 31

The Duplay home is empty. The family will never return. These friends of Robespierre have followed him in his downfall. The wife of Le Bas, Elisabeth Duplay, was arrested today. Since her husband's death, she had been living behind closed doors and it was only today that she found out about the death of Saint Just, her sister's fiancé. She also found out about the arrest of many other acquaintances and of

her own mother, who was found dead in her cell the day after her arrest. She was gently told about her father's imprisonment, and that of her two sisters, Henriette and Eléonore, of her brother and of her uncles. All that remained was her five week old son. The unfortunate woman was taken by police to the La Force jail. Before leaving her home, Elisabeth cast one last glance at the place where she had been so happy.

The Great Terror's terrible toll

France, July

Hundreds of thousands of people suffered during the 11 months of bloody revolutionary dictatorship. The Terror came in many forms, ranging from summary executions to the sentencing of "suspects" by the special tribunals and the often deadly activities of local watch committees.

In all, 17,000 people were sentenced and beheaded, while nearly 25,000 French citizens were summarily executed since the start of 1793. The real Terror only spread to the whole country after September of the same year. Events then speeded up to reach a climax during the Great Terror, in June and July 1794, after the law of Prairial 22 came into effect. The Paris

revolutionary Tribunal only handed down 16 per cent of the death sentences, despite the law of April 16th. ordering that all suspects must in future be sent before the Tribunal.

Geographically, it was the west of France, due to the war in the Vendée, and the Rhône valley, because of federalist acti[...] were the hardest hit. O[...] that were affected were [...] areas where military [...] were carried out. In fact, [...] out of every five death [...] were handed down for [...] son or rebellion, while o[...] cent of them were for [...] crimes and nine per cent [...] cal motives. Throughout [...] days, France lived in fea[...]

Gascon dialect, a passport to freedom

Paris, July 27

Childhood friends can be most useful, as the Jacobin Taschereau has just realised. This former official of the Committee of General Security had been working for Robespierre whom he was supposed to spy on. He had double-crossed his employers. He was therefore arrested along with his friends and this evening he wrote a poem in the Gascon dialect for Vadier, to remind him of their childhood in Gascony. Vadier is an extremely tough man, but he likes a good laugh. After reading the poem, he had Taschereau released for being both a Gascon and a man of wit.

Vadier, Pamiers native and deputy.

Santerre is freed, abandons politics

Paris, July 31

Ambition can lead to a man's undoing. Drunk with success, the brewer Santerre had wanted military glory. He was made a general in July 1793 and sent to Vendée, where his incompetence had been clearly noted. The Committee of

Public Safety had summoned him back to Paris and thrown him in jail. He was freed on Thermidor 9, only to find that his wife had left him and that he was ruined. He has learnt his lesson and has just given up his army rank. From now on, he will remain a simple brewer.

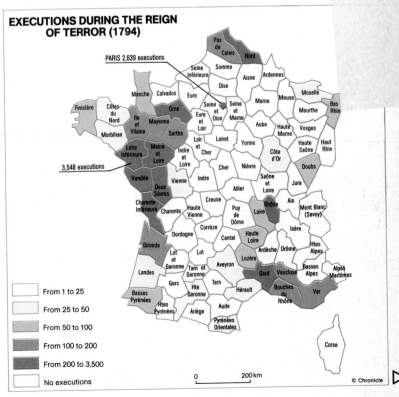

EXECUTIONS DURING THE REIGN OF TERROR (1794)

PARIS 2,639 executions

3,548 executions

From 1 to 25
From 25 to 50
From 50 to 100
From 100 to 200
From 200 to 3,500
No executions

0   200 km

© Chronicle

Corse

The Girondist and Montagnard Convention

The Convention met on September 21st., 1792, a little more than a month after the monarchy's downfall. At its first session, it proclaimed the birth of the Republic. Since the former Constitution had been repudiated, the Convention had to draft a new one. Right from the start, however, disputes between politicians and "parties" took up much time. What was at stake was which group would dominate the Convention and the reins of power. The clash was also between two differing views of the Republic and democracy. On the one hand, the Girondists, who took the upper hand at first, were legalistic, representative, bourgeois. On the other, the Montagnards were more populist, keen on "direct democracy", and backed by the sectors. Between these two groups, there were the numerous representatives of the "Plain", who stood for continuity.

The end of the Girondists

The two groups — they could not yet be called parties as they were far from being fully organised — were fairly similar in social terms: most of the Assembly was bourgeois. However, the Girondists fought with all their might against the dictatorship of Paris, of its sectors and its representatives, particularly Marat and Robespierre, whose influence they wanted to reduce. The Girondists also opposed the sansculottists' demands. The latter wanted to impose taxes on goods and to use terror to impose steps aimed at coping with the war while helping the desperately poor. For their part, the Montagnards, more out of political necessity than for ideological reasons, accepted pressures from the street and the effects of the war. They did not hesitate to call for revolt in order to defeat their opponents. The war, the need for victory which dominated that whole period, was relaunched by the King's trial. Handing over Louis XVI's head to Europe created enemies of France on all fronts and entailed radicalising the Revolution.

During the trial, the Girondists, who were mostly inclined to grant clemency, proved unable to convince the Assembly, and the death sentence, which was carried out on January 21st., 1793, was approved. All Europe was already worried about French successes, and the King's execution brought it into the conflict. After Valmy, the Republic's armies had moved into Savoy, Nice and the east bank of the Rhine. After Jemmapes, in November, Dumouriez had invaded Holland. England, Italy, the German princes and Spain entered the battle in turn and the war became a general conflict in the spring.

But the wider conflict also brought defeat and treason. While the French were losing the east bank of the Rhine, Dumouriez was being defeated in Belgium. He negotiated secretly with the enemy and finally deserted. In France itself, obvious evidence of counter-revolution appeared in the Vendée as of March, as the peasants rebelled to avoid military conscription that the Assembly had just decreed. In this crisis situation, Paris and its extremist sections vehemently denounced the treason of the Girondists, who were attacked by the Montagnard leaders in the Convention every day. They were considered as accomplices of Dumouriez and of the Vendeans, and were suspected of wanting to dismember the Republic. They were unable to resist and had to accept special measures, the setting of grain prices and the establishment of a revolutionary Tribunal and of a Committee of Public Safety. Faced with such dangers, the Girondists hoped to find some effective support against Paris in the French provinces, but events rushed on.

The Convention remained honest and legalistic. Its hand was forced by a power play. The popular sectors and the National Guard, which had just named the extremist Hanriot to head it, surrounded the Assembly, aimed guns at it and forced it on June 2nd., 1793, to decree the arrest of 29 deputies. Insurrection had checkmated national representation, and the "people's coup" had defeated the Girondist party. That marked the end of the first phase of the Convention, which was dominated by the struggle between the two opposing parties and by the mistrust they spontaneously felt for each other.

The Montagnard Convention

The Montagnard victory, which was actually the victory of people's insurrection, had not settled all the problems, far from it. The provincial Girondists' revolt, quickly backed by the royalists, sparked off civil war and a large number of departments seceded. The Republic was in danger all summer, and in the southeast the peril did not disappear until winter, after the recapture of Lyons, then of Marseilles, and finally, in December, of Toulon with its Mediterranean squadron. The situation deteriorated on the borders in the north, Savoy and in the Pyrénées. The economic crisis was worsened by inflation, the assignat's drop, and the price fixing that emptied the markets. Bread was short in Paris and other big cities. The sansculottists wanted the death penalty for hoarders and monopolists, while the "Enragés", led by Jacques Roux, urged the Convention to show firmness, make a strong effort against France's enemies, and make war on the "aristocrats".

To put an end to confusion and inertia, resolve conflicts and impose some effective measures, there apparently had to be a government exercising a kind of dictatorship. That was the rôle of the Committee of Public Safety, set up on April 6th., which eliminated Danton in July, viewing him as too moderate, and transformed itself into a "Grand Committee" in September 1793. It added, in turn, Couthon and Saint Just, Robespierre and Carnot, and other ardent Montagnards. It gradually imposed a war government and was to meet all attacks, foreign and domestic, by resorting to the rule of terror. "Terrorism" was decreed as a continuation and a necessary consequence of the difficulties.

The situation was serious in July. On the borders, Valenciennes and Mainz capitulated. In the west, the Vendeans defeated Santerre's army. Marat was assassinated by Charlotte Corday. The sansculottists demanded special measures, such as the arrest of suspects, mass conscription of soldiers and price controls on food. The Convention had to yield: the suspects were arrested, mass conscription decreed, and price controls imposed on a few products, such as salt and fuels.

In August, popular feeling rose further under the influence of the Enragés, of the shortages that were worsening during that transition period, and of the emotion caused by the betrayal of Toulon, which the royalists had delivered to the enemy on August 27th. The Commune, under pressure from the sansculottists, decided on an "action day". On September 5th., the demonstrators ringed the Convention, which decided to put the Terror "on the agenda". The Terror got organised over the next few days. Foreigners were arrested, prices were set on grains and fodder, a law was passed against suspects that was vague yet threatening because of its very imprecision, and a revolutionary army was created in order to monitor application of all of these repressive measures.

However, the Enragés increased their agitation, and the Committee had their leaders, Roux and Varlet, arrested. At the same time, it decreed the "Maximum", levels of prices and wages, and the big trials got under way. Then, speaking through Saint Just, the Convention declared on October 10th. that the French government would remain a revolutionary one until peace was restored. This meant that enactment of the Constitution voted in June 1793 would be deferred until that time. The revolutionary Tribunal handed down death sentences like hot cakes. The Queen, the Girondists, Bailly and Barnave were executed, while the number of arrests increased. At the end of December, there were more than 4,500 people held in the jails. However, the economic situation was still precarious and rationing cards had to be issued for bread and sugar. Paris was not the only victim of terror, and in the provinces, representatives "on mission" applied the same measures as in the capital. Some of them were responsible for a reign of bloody terrorism, such as Carrier in Nantes and Fouché in Lyons. Still, the sansculottists might indulge in new actions at any time, as they had done in September. Such acts would threaten the authority of the Convention, as well as of the Committee.

Robespierre's dictatorship

The Committee gradually acquired full powers in its attempt to take things in hand. It organised a wartime economy and coped with the religious crisis. Priests had become ever more suspect since August 10th., and a de-Christianisation campaign got under way. Anti-religious masquerades and sacrilege intensified, as did verbal attacks on priests. The Convention had adopted the republican calendar on October 24th. Lay feasts were celebrated in the churches, and Notre Dame Cathedral in Paris was turned into a "Temple of Reason".

Finally, on November 23rd., the Commune decided to close the churches. The Committee was worried by all this, especially Robespierre, who was a deist scandalised by irreligion. Furthermore, some claimed that de-Christianisation masked a plot against the Revolution hatched by the Hébertists. Robespierre and Danton, backed by the Jacobins, got the Convention to adopt decrees aimed at fighting against anti-religious violence. But they often had no effect.

The revolutionary government strengthened itself and intended to draw legitimacy from the nation's danger and counter-revolutionary plotting. Thanks to requisitions and mass conscription, the army had a substantial number of troops and was resupplied, while a purge had renewed the command structure and promoted some young and talented leaders. The invasion was halted everywhere at the end of the year. The last centre of royalist insurrection in the south, Toulon, fell into republican hands on December 19th. The Vendeans had been defeated by Marceau at Le Mans and at Savernay, while Turreau's aptly named "infernal columns" were able to undertake their sinister work of devastation and death.

After all these successes, there was a tendency favouring relaxation of the Terror. Danton and Camille Desmoulins's Le Vieux Cordelier demanded clemency. An "Indulgents' Party" came into being, but Robespierre and the Jacobins were already accusing them. They had to defend themselves from attacks both from the left, where the Hébertists risked forcing them to go farther than they wanted to, and from the right, where the Dantonists still constituted a formidable power bloc. The sansculottists, exasperated by the winter's economic hardships, were pressing for severe measures and the Committee renewed the ones that already existed. Robespierre had the Ventôse decrees voted (February 26th., March 3rd., 1794), which were aimed at distributing property confiscated from the suspects among poor patriots. However, the sansculottists' found that insufficient and there were rumours of insurrection in Paris. The Committee decided on a major attack to neutralise the sansculottists. The Hébertists, accused of plotting, were executed on March 24th. Then Robespierre decided to eliminate the Indulgents. Danton, Camille Desmoulins and everybody else in the way were lumped together with speculators and "brigands" and were given no opportunity to defend themselves. They were executed on April 5th. The Committee did not stop there. It had decapitated popular activism by executing the Hébertists. It now took its resources away from it, closed the clubs and dismissed the revolutionary army. With all authority concentrated in its hands, it did not seem likely to encounter any further obstacles.

Under the pressure of revolutionary nightmares — fear of plots, punitive drives — and in the interest of further strengthening of its power, the Committee then accepted the Great Terror policy. The law of Prairial 22 (June 10th., 1794) shaped it. This extremist law did away with all guarantees. Unless accused persons, who lacked resources for defending themselves, were acquitted, they faced just one verdict: death. The Convention members themselves were now at the mercy of the Committee and of the revolutionary Tribunal that it controlled. Suspects were dragged from their jail cells to be executed. More condemned people were guillotined in six weeks than had been beheaded previously in a whole year. The daily spectacle of the carts carrying people to the bloody guillotine finally moved public opinion, particularly since the so-called "exceptional circumstances" invoked as a justification of the Terror no longer existed. On the borders, the Republic's armies were pushing the enemy back everywhere. They went on the offensive and entered Belgium and the Pyrénées region, as victories followed each other. A victorious peace seemed imminent and counter-revolutionary plots were no longer feared. The sansculottists were annoyed with economic measures providing for greater flexibility in setting food prices, while the middle class worried about the risks involved in dividing up property. There was general dissatisfaction and widespread fear. The Robespierrist dictatorship was attacked in the Convention and was approaching its end as the popular movement declined.

Thermidor

The Convention as a whole had been displeased with the successive purges of which it had been the victim. It was terrified by the prospect of a new bloodbath. There had been rumours of such a danger ever since the fateful Prairial law. Now that the external danger had been dealt with, what was holding it back? Who was preventing it from rebelling against its masters? The representatives who had the most to fear, particularly the ones who had been recalled from their missions, men such as Tallien and Fouché, made efforts to win over their colleagues, all members of the Convention "Plain" who had accepted the dictatorship only out of necessity. The Supervisory Committee did not forgive Robespierre for the purge of the Hébertists and the cult of the Supreme Being that he had imposed against their wishes. Within the Grand Committee itself, Robespierre became ever more isolated, despite Saint Just's loyalty. He was abandoned by the majority of his colleagues, especially by Carnot. The "Incorruptible One" was attacked on every side and withdrew into a meditative isolation that his opponents exploited. Then on Thermidor 8 (July 26th.), he decided to break his silence. He offered some vague denunciations in a speech to the Convention, refused to mention names, caused general alarm and destroyed himself. When he tried to renew his attack the next day, protests broke out. Without being allowed to explain himself, he was charged immediately, as were Couthon, Le Bas and Saint Just. The Commune declared itself to be in a state of insurrection, but the National Guard did not move. It had been deprived of Hanriot, its commander, who had been dismissed.

However, a revolt managed to free Robespierre and the other accused men, who went to City Hall, but failed to act decisively. They were gradually abandoned by the disoriented sansculottists. The Convention's forces carried the day and Robespierre broke his jaw, apparently while trying to kill himself. On Thermidor 10 (July 28th., 1794), he was guillotined along with 21 of his supporters, including Couthon, Saint Just and René François Dumas, presiding judge of the revolutionary Tribunal. There was a vast feeling of relief in the Convention and in the country as a whole. The Terror was waning and a phase of the Revolution was coming to an end. The "Thermidorians" were about to launch a new phase.

Social and cultural assessment

The Convention had been absorbed in immense tasks and particularly in the war that consumed everybody's energy as well as a huge budget. Despite this, it tried to make legislation more democratic in fields still marked by sharp inequalities. Its work, or at least the principles it proclaimed in connection with primary education or aid for the poor, even if implementation of such principles was only begun, was to serve as a standard for the future.

First of all, it attempted to bring about greater equality within the family, to facilitate divorce, which had been instituted by the Legislative Assembly and to restore illegitimate children's rights. Even though the egalitarian principle had often been somewhat neglected, as in relations between men and women, the inheritance system favoured it. The intention was to avoid letting big estates perpetuate themselves and to introduce more justice between heirs. Estates were divided equally among children, including illegitimate children when they were acknowledged and not the fruit of adultery, but the law remained unfavourable to the others.

Assistance for poor and indigent people, under a régime that proclaimed its concern with the fate of unfortunates (whose numbers were increasing due to the crisis), was discussed by members of the Convention, who attempted to organise it. That task had previously been performed by the clergy, but the latter was now deprived of its property and could no longer carry it out. Moreover, doctrine called for the state to be responsible for such assistance. The 1793 Declaration of Rights had defined public assistance (welfare) as a national duty: "Society must provide subsistence for unfortunate citizens, either by providing them with work, or by ensuring that people who cannot work enjoy the means of existence." The Convention decided that the Assembly would vote an annual budget for funding public welfare, and that such payments would be divided among the invalid poor by department, district and canton. Steps were taken to help unmarried mothers and plans were made to rear foundlings in national "hospices" until they reached the age of 12 and then to have them taken on as apprentices. A "Great Book of National Welfare" was also established, containing the names of poor people who could no longer work and they received a pension.

In principle, all of these forms of aid made almsgiving and begging pointless, so they were forbidden, the former being punished by fines and the latter being sharply repressed. People who begged were to be shut up in establishments (the term "charity workshops", which recalled the Ancien Régime, had been banned) in which they would be given work. Only a start was made on implementation of these measures, but they made it possible to help many indigent people all the same.

The Convention had declared that all citizens had a right to education. However, the school system, which had previously been in the clergy's hands, was utterly disorganised. The Assembly was concerned above all with primary education and instructed its Education Committee to see to a reorganisation. There were many projects, especially one developed by Condorcet. First of all, the Convention decreed a principle to be taken up by the Third Republic: schooling was to be obligatory and free. Primary education remained unfettered: anybody, including monks and nuns, could open a school by carrying out a few necessary formalities. In fact, such education was often very basic, as it was hard to recruit primary school teachers due to the low salaries. Free and obligatory schools were not very successful, and were abolished after Thermidor 9. The Convention also had the merit of having worked for the establishment of a central arts museum in the Louvre Palace in Paris.

As a whole, the Convention's work in the social field was considerable, even though it was not to bear fruit until much later.

1 *(Thermidor 14, Year II)* Paris. Reopening of the Jacobins Club, which decides to take back all members banished before Thermidor 9 and to exclude the Robespierrists.

1 *(Thermidor 14, Year II)* Paris. Repeal of the Prairial 22 law, which was responsible for the "Reign of Terror" and arrest of Fouquier Tinville, public prosecutor at the revolutionary Tribunal (→10).

2 *(Thermidor 15, Year II)* Paris. The painter Louis David, a member of the Committee of Public Safety and a fierce Robespierrist, is jailed.→

2 *(Thermidor 15, Year II)* Paris. The new U.S. ambassador, James Monroe, takes up his duties. Unlike Governor Morris, he is a Francophile and a partisan of the Revolution (→15).

3 *(Thermidor 16, Year II)* Corsica. The English begin the siege of Calvi, the last French-held port (→21).

4 *(Thermidor 17, Year II)* Spain. General Moncey seizes San Sebastian.

4 *(Thermidor 17, Year II)* Paris. Creation at the Opéra Comique of *Fête américaine*, a ballet by the dancer Peicam.

4 *(Thermidor 17, Year II)* Paris. Release of General Hoche, arrested in Germinal for being a Cordelier (→21).

6 *(Thermidor 19, Year II)* Paris. The Convention does away with the post of commander in chief of the Paris National Guard.

7 *(Thermidor 20, Year II)* Maine et Loire. From Angers, where it has taken refuge, the administration of the Cholet district sends a letter of protest to the Convention about the negative role of Turreau's "mobile columns", which have merely prolonged the Vendean revolt by the cruelty that is displayed in their actions.

9 *(Thermidor 22, Year II)* Nice. Bonaparte, who was protected by Robespierre's brother Augustin, is arrested as a suspect (→20).

10 *(Thermidor 23, Year II)* Paris. Celebration of the feast commemorating August 10th. in the Palais National gardens. A work by Catel is performed, with words written by Lebrun. The work is known as *The Battle of Fleurus*.

Abbot Grégoire lambasts "vandalism"

Paris, August 1

Grégoire has decided to hunt down the barbarians, the ones who have made looting and destruction the order of the day, savaging the nation's heritage. For it is indeed the nation's heritage that is being squandered, whereas it should be preserved. Waving the report he has just written, he denounced the unworthy attitude of certain sansculottists who have taken orders literally and have not hesitated to wipe out every possible trace of the Ancien Régime. Hence "churches are empty, bell-towers lack bells, cemeteries have no crosses, and the saints are headless". Holy vases have been melted down to make cannon. Much worse is the fact, he said, that some objects not used in religion have been damaged. In Paris, for instance, vengeful hands used a hammer to break the statues of Justice and Prudence that decorated the clock of the Court Building. Similarly, certain castles have been devastated by angry peasants. Following Lakanal in June 1793, he

Grégoire, the heritage protector.

showed that it had become urgent to stop such wanton destruction, and he alluded to the hordes of Visigoths and Vandals who left only ruins and dust behind them. What we have been witnessing is indeed "vandalism", he concluded. "I shall create the word to combat the thing!" (→Sept. 13).

Belgians hit hard for a contribution

Belgium, August 3

After Fleurus, the Committee of Public Safety is not planning to incorporate the Belgian areas into the Republic. Hence there is no reason to spare the country. That is the meaning of the instructions sent by Carnot to the forces in Belgium: "We want neither to lift up the country nor to fraternise with it. It is a conquest that has a lot to pay us back for, and we must hasten to extract all of the resources from it that might help a new enemy invasion." A tax of 60 million was immediately put on the nobles and the big landowners, and some important people were taken as hostages to ensure payment. Moreover, all of the cash in the public cashier establishments will have to be turned over to the military paymaster in exchange for assignats, which will have forced circulation. The commissioners have been asked to requisition food, horses and forage. The French will live off Belgium.

A good pharmacist needs many facts

Ille et Vilaine, August 2

What is ipecacuanha? How does one prepare sweet almond oil? What precautions should one take in using camphor in a medicine? These questions, and many others of the same type, are part of a circular sent to the garrison in Port Solidor, formerly Saint Servan. This is the way checks are being made throughout France on the knowledge of health officers. The reason is that the Revolution also affects chemistry, which is now inseparably linked with therapeutics, thanks to the work of such people as Lavoisier, Berthollet, Glauber and Scheele. Hence the desire to make sure health officers are also good pharmacists. They must be able to write out the process for making antimony butter, rose preserves, or red antimony. The apothecaries have constituted a guild distinct from the grocers since only 1777. Their usefulness was quickly acknowledged. The College and the Masters' Guild of Pharmacy were done away with in March 1791, but were then re-established in April of the same year.

Hubert Robert is getting out of prison

Paris, August 4

Justice had ended by forgetting about the painter in his cell. Or rather, it had no real reason for keeping him in detention, and even lacked serious evidence for putting him on trial. So Hubert Robert is returning to his wife today, and will be able to resume work in the Louvre galleries, where he has his studio. Nine months ago the artist was first taken to Sainte Pélagie, and was then transferred to Saint Lazare prison. The latter, located in the Saint Denis suburb almost in the countryside, is more spacious, making long ballgames possible. This ritual was interrupted only by the one of the guillotine. Ten days ago, the painter witnessed the departure of Chénier and of his great friend, the poet Roucher.

Two prisoners playing cards in their cell, with the help of a candle.

Has justice finally regained serenity?

Paris, August 10

The Reign of Terror is over. The deputies have just radically modified the legal system on which it was based. They abrogated the law of Prairial 22, which did away with all guarantees for detainees in a state based on law. The revolutionary Tribunal itself is being re-organised. Its public prosecutor, Fouquier Tinville, who thought he could redeem himself by turning against Robespierre, has now been thrown into jail. All of the judges will be replaced. Finally, legal proceedings are being transformed by the introduction of the "intentional question": accused persons who cannot be shown to have had counter-revolutionary intentions will be acquitted. Hence the burden of proof is now on the justice authorities, and no longer on the person in the dock, for whom the slightest suspicion during the Reign of Terror was tantamount to conviction. The watch committees are feeling the effect of this reform. The most virulent of the sansculottists are being purged, and their powers are being limited. Furthermore, there will now be only once such committee per district in the provinces, and 12 in Paris, compared with 48 before. But the Convention did not dare carry through completely. It did not touch the law on suspects. It is trying for a moderate, conciliatory position.

A uniformed magistrate waving the country's revolutionary laws.

Prison gates open after Thermidor

Paris, August 10

The unrest has now peaked. Releases of prisoners are collecting crowds in front of the jails, where joyful excitement rivals with a desire for revenge on the Jacobin "tyrants". In just five days, the Convention has freed 478 political detainees out of the 8,500 who populated the Paris jails before Thermidor 9. As soon as news of Robespierre's arrest came out, a rumour spread that all suspects would be freed immediately. To public opinion, the end of the Reign of Terror meant opening the prisons. People imagined that all the convicted were going to be able to get out, being replaced at once by the former masters of the power structure. The prisoners' friends and relatives assailed the watch committees to demand releases. Crowds thronged to sector meetings, and even massed at the door of the Committee of General Security. Deputies were awash with petitions. On the 3rd. the inmates in Saint Lazare prison staged an extraordinary hubbub. They called for wine and demanded that the commissioners come to free them, threatening to slit the guards' throats. Initially, the Convention disavowed these disturbances and Goupilleau denounced general dis-

Reunions are even more moving when captives have escaped death.

order. Yesterday, Barère and Tallien warned their colleagues against the "incorrigible aristocrats" who, in their view, are responsible for the marked agitation around the jail exits. The Convention mistrusts this wave of indulgence, which it had not foreseen. It fears that some real counter-revolutionaries might be freed amidst the general euphoria. But it has already had to give way, in part, to the pressure of menacing street mobs. On August 5th. it decided on the release of poli-

tical detainees who were not covered directly by the law on suspects of September 17th. 1793. Actually, far from calming people down, this measure increased the excitement. The unrest and violence is even greater in some of the provincial cities. In Marseilles and Bourg, as well as in Avignon, the crowds did not wait for any authorisation before they took action. The mobs rushed right to the prisons and broke down the doors in their haste to get the prisoners out.

The capital gets a new Republican Opera House, with benches

Paris, August 7

People who rejected the idea that opera should be "entertainment only for the rich" are now satisfied. The new Arts Theatre, located in "Laws Street", formerly the Rue de Richelieu, has been inspired by the best Republican principles. The spectators who attended the inauguration were struck, first of all, by the house configuration. There are no more proscenium boxes or big boxes in the first balcony, as such things are hated symbols of aristocracy. Instead, there is a vast inclined plane enabling everybody to see the stage. But the main innovation is to be found in the fact that, for the first time in France, benches have been installed in the pit. Thus the delighted audience was able to sit down to hear *The Meeting of August 10*, a sansculottist work with a hymn by Gabriel Bouquier and Pierre Louis Moline, to music by Bernardo Porta.

The decoration is also different: Etruscan motifs on balcony friezes.

New faces are seen in cultural affairs

The painter Jean Baptiste Regnault.

Paris August 2

There are certain signs that do not mislead one. David, the "official" painter of the Jacobin Convention, has just been arrested. As the height of infamy, his name appeared on the same decree as the bloodthirsty Joseph Le Bon. But everything is political, including art and above all art. And the "regeneration" that has been in progress since Robespierre's fall is certainly not sparing cultural domains. The Muséum's curator staff now consists of seven members: Regnault, Langlier and Picault for painting, Duspaquier for sculpture, Varron and Vatté for Antiquity, De Wailly for architecture. As for the Public Education Committee, it has been purged and renewed. Still, it contains such people as Lakanal, Petit, Arbogast, Bourdon, and Abbot Grégoire.

Castles in Périgord are on the way out

Périgord, August 5

Even if Abbot Grégoire in Paris is urging people to respect monuments, Lakanal in Périgord is ordering destruction of the castles. The representative on mission wants to do away with these "citadels that are shameful symbols of slavery and tyranny". All good citizens are urged to spend some of their free time taking part in this project. The demolition will be paid for either by the owners or by the State, which will be reimbursed from the sale of recovered materials. Wood, for instance, will go for shipbuilding.

🏛 **Convention**

11 *(Thermidor 24, Year II)*
Paris. Barère makes the Convention proclaim the persistence of the revolutionary government (→ 24).

15 *(Thermidor 28, Year II)*
Paris. In less than two hours, Chappe's optical telegraph transmits the news of the Austrian garrison's surrender in the city of Le Quesnoy, in the north (→ Sept. 1, 94).

17 *(Thermidor 30, Year II)*
Paris. The first sign of timid opposition: The Muséum sector, at Legray's suggestion, passes a motion demanding freedom of the press and re-establishment of elections for municipal representatives.

20 *(Fructidor 3, Year II)*
Nice. At the request of the representatives on mission and of General Dumerbion, the new commander in chief of the forces in the Alps and Italy, Bonaparte is released in order to reinforce the Army of Italy's general staff.

21 *(Fructidor 4, Year II)*
Paris. General Hoche is appointed commander in chief of the forces on the Cherbourg coast (→ Nov. 9, 94).

24 *(Fructidor 7, Year II)*
Paris. A Convention decree reorganises government operations. →

26 *(Fructidor 9, Year II)*
Paris. Méhée de La Touche denounces the former "terrorists" in a violent pamphlet entitled *Robespierre's Tail.*

26 *(Fructidor 9, Year II)*
Saarland. The Jacobins Club in the city of Saarbrücken requests French annexation of the Saarland.

29 *(Fructidor 12, Year II)*
Paris. While in the Convention Lecointre accuses Barère, Amar, Vadier and others of complicity with Robespierre, gilded youth shows itself in public for the first time. →

30 *(Fructidor 13, Year II)*
Nord. Fall of Condé sur l'Escaut, the last of the territory's strongholds still in the imperial forces' hands (Sept. 1, 94).

31 *(Fructidor 14, Year II)*
Paris. The visionary Catherine Théot, who was widely known as the "Mother of God", dies in prison on the day of the disaster of the Grenelle powder store. Had she not predicted that, on the day of her death, there would be an explosion in Paris? →

Will the Girondists sit in Assembly again?

The Girondists' uncomfortable political position is again the subject of a caricature: half being sansculottist, and half being foppish.

Paris, August

Should the men of June 1793 be allowed to return to the Assembly? That is the question in the current political debate. The right is demanding the return of the deputies excluded for having protested against the events of May 31. But the Thermidorians, and even the Marais, hesitate to approve this amnesty. In their view, that would be tantamount to condemning, after the fact, all of the Convention's actions. The Girondin affair reveals the incongruous nature of the coalition stemming from Thermidor. It brings together some repentant terrorists, such as Tallien and Fréron, Dantonists and Montagnards, who never recanted and intend to keep the spirit of Year II but do away with the excesses. This combine bases itself on rightist deputies, sympathisers with the Girondists or even advocates of constitutional monarchy (→ Nov. 7, 94).

Monroe warmly welcomed by Assembly

Paris, August 15

The Convention had forgotten the new American ambassador. James Monroe had to ask the Assembly president to be so kind as to receive him so that he could show him his credentials. This shortcoming was made up for by the very warm welcome the ambassador got today. The deputies decreed that henceforth the American flag should be on display along with the French flag in the Convention chamber, as a "sign of friendship and eternal alliances". But that is taking things for granted, as the Americans do not approve of the way the Revolution is evolving.

The ambassador of the New World.

Slaves are tracked

Port Louis, August 12

The hunt for runaway slaves is at its peak in Ile de France. Here, the events on Saint Domingue are arousing ever greater fears of a general black revolt. To prevent this, the Colonial Assembly decreed, in July, a major hunt for fugitive blacks living in gangs on the island heights. The result of the first few weeks is promising, as several leaders have been captured, including the ones known as Alexandre and Télémaque. They will be tried by the Committee of Public Safety. They risk the death penalty under the Black Code.

An émigré noble leaves on a mission

Brittany, August 26

Comte Joseph de Puisaye has left on a trip to London. The objective: persuade the English and the émigrés to organise a landing in Brittany. Before his departure, the count, who is now the "federator" of the Chouan revolt, left some instructions for his assistants. He said that absolute priority should go to getting in touch with Charette and reaching an understanding with him. Puisaye is of Norman origin and was not among the first counter-revolutionaries. In fact, he was a deputy to the Constituent Assembly. He also had to make use of all his skill to get himself accepted by the Chouans.

Nation Theatre in Paris is reopened

Paris, August 16

What does it matter if, since its reopening, "their" theatre has become "Equality Theatre", and what does it matter if they now have to share the premises with a lyric troupe? This evening the actors of what used to be known as the Théâtre de la Nation, recently freed from prison, were happy to get back on stage. The actress Louise Contat was so moved that she almost felt ill playing Marivaux's *Les Fausses Confidences*. But she has retained her lucidity. When Talma came to congratulate her, she retorted: "The crowd would have been much bigger to see our heads roll."

French agriculture seen as a disaster

Although the Revolution changed agriculture's structures, peasants kept their age-old working habits.

France, August 19

The review *La Feuille du cultivateur* is very pessimistic. It reports in today's issue on the investigation of the fertiliser situation ordered by the Convention. The results of this probe amount to a sad appraisal of French agriculture, an appraisal that can be called disastrous if it it is compared to the situation in such countries as England. Productivity has been stagnating since 1789, with the wheat yield remaining relatively low nation-wide. Furthermore, many departments show a drop in output. In the poor areas, the yield is even worse. Should one deduce from all this that the Revolution has blocked agricultural progress? All the same, the revolutionaries have shown their interest in, even their fascination for, farm techniques and new crops. But one is forced to the conclusion that French farmers have invested very little in modernising their operations. There is a general lack of interest in improving performance.

The fact is that the Revolution transformed farmers' lives by doing away with feudalism and enabling farmers to become landowners. Hence it has promoted an agrarian individualism that generates a multitude of small farms which are quite unfavourable to the development of profitable crops. Rural mentalities have remained what they were under the Ancien Régime, and it can be said that this is surely one of the causes of France's lag noted in the agricultural sector.

All Corsica is now in England's hands

Corsica, August 21

The citadel of Calvi, the last city still in French hands, has fallen to the English. The Republic now has no authority over the island. It is true that it was a very unequal fight. The garrison was attacked by sea by Captain Nelson's artillery, and was harassed on land by Pascal Paoli's Corsican nationalists, and it probably did well by the country. The fall of Saint Florent last February and Bastia's surrender three months later had left the Republicans with hardly any hope. After six months of fighting, Corsica is in the Paolists' hands, or rather in English hands. A "Constituent Assembly" called into session in June at Paoli's initiative had confirmed the definitive break with France and offered the crown to George III of England. In this way London was upgrading its sea control, the French Mediterranean fleet having been burnt by the English in the city of Toulon. As for Pascal Paoli, he used his age and his infirmities as an excuse to refuse the viceroyalty that was offered to him by Lord Gilbert Elliot, the envoy from England.

Saint Germain abbey is burnt out

Paris, August 19

The Gothic structure fell victim to the flames during the night. The fire, which started accidentally behind the church at around 9:30 p.m., spread very rapidly to the whole building, spewing out thick black smoke. Despite all efforts to get it under control, the blaze destroyed all of the buildings, including the library, which contained priceless mediaeval manuscripts. Only the church and the abbot's palace escaped the disaster. ▷

Difficulty reported for Bidermann firm

French government is reorganised

Winterthur, August 23

The shareholders in the Bidermann textile company in this Swiss city do not want to lose their shirts. They have just set up an association to save their firm. And, if need be, they are ready to kick out the boss, who has really shown poor management of the industrial empire. This Swiss-capital company imports cotton goods from India, which it processes in Geneva and Alsace, and then resells throughout Europe and in the Americas. It prospered until Bidermann had the disastrous idea of speculating in assignats, an activity that represented a considerable burden on his finances. Political uncertainties did not help matters, and the maritime shipping subsidiaries went bankrupt. Investors risk losing their money in this affair.

Carnot escapes being outlawed.

Paris, August 24

Is all this a reform or a kind of dismemberment? The question is pertinent, in view of the scattering effect resulting from the government reorganisation. The fact is that the decree that has just been issued decapitates the Committee of Public Safety, whose powers are reduced to the fields of war and foreign affairs with which it previously concerned itself. Thus the "Grand Committee" is cut back to be on the same level as the other government committees. The number of such committees has been increased from 12 to 16, and each one monitors an executive committee. The prerogatives of the Committee of General Safety are also diminished, even if it maintains supervision of the police and of public order. As for the Legislation Committee, it is taking on new importance, since it is being given the Interior and Justice. This change expresses the spirit of the reform. With Thermidor, legislators took revenge on the executive branch. By dispersing governmental functions, the Convention is showing that it no longer intends to let its authority be frittered away. Cambon, of the Finance Committee, wanted to go even further and dissolve all powers of the Committee of Public Safety. It is true that the latter has always benefited from the relative budget autonomy left by the revolutionary dictatorship. But Barère denounced the "moral federalism" that he said the Convention was trying to impose, referring to the dilution of State powers at the highest level, since authority remains highly centralised in the departments. Actually, the Thermidorians are particularly concerned about staying in office and so have chosen an intermediate solution. But all that remains of the revolutionary government is its name. One of its basic principles is gone: centralisation.

The "terrorists" to be purged in Avignon

Avignon, August 25

Persecution has again changed targets in Avignon. Representative on mission Goupilleau, who replaced Maignet today, will probably punish the Jacobin authorities sharply for their past excesses. For while approving Robespierre's fall, those authorities have gone even further by calling on all patriots to join the ... holy Montagne! In his baggage, Goupilleau brought a report that is very critical of the patriots' actions in the department. It notes Maignet's merciless revolutionary zeal, as well as what it called the "efficacy" of the Orange Special Court. In just a month and a half of busy activity, the Orange Special Court managed to find a total of 332 people for sending to the guillotine.

"Gilded youth" is getting into politics

Paris, August 29

They are young, elegant, and passionately enthusiastic about the Thermidorians. These new-type militants, former detainees, deserters, unemployed artists, or middle-class types with time on their hands, gave Lecointre some noisy support as he was briefing the Convention on his reactionary and repressive programme. He denounced Billaud Varenne, Collot d'Herbois, Barère and Vadier, saying they had been accomplices of the "tyrant" Robespierre. The deputies reacted very violently to these allegations, calling them libellous. But in the meantime, at the Tuileries and the Palais Royal, gilded youth, overexcited and encouraged by Tallien and Fréron, applauded Lecointre's remarks.

Valenciennes is back in French hands

Valenciennes, August 24

The deal was struck by people who keep their word. The Austrian garrison will be able to withdraw without being bothered. Its commander, General Castelly, had pledged to give up the town if the Austrians were allowed to withdraw in dignified fashion. But General Schérer had to consult the Committee of Public Safety before granting the request. The French have everything to gain from this deal. Valenciennes, which had been occupied for over a year, comes back under French control, without any more blood-spilling than necessary. Furthermore, the city is delivering some Austrian-restored fortifications and 227 artillery pieces. After recapture of Le Quesnoy and Landrecies, the situation on the Flanders front is turning to French advantage. Only Condé is still in enemy hands, and continental territory will soon be freed.

General Barthélemy Schérer.

Bonaparte, released on August 20th., spent almost three weeks in jail in Nice. To amuse himself, he worked out a plan for an invasion of Italy.

The Grenelle powder magazine blows up

Paris, August 31

A lot of people this morning thought an earthquake had hit Paris. All it took was a spark to blow up the powder magazine in Grenelle Castle, located near the Military School. The blast was so strong that the houses in the area were shaken and some bridges were cracked. The explosion even broke the seals on the door leading to the Observatory cellars, and the noise carried as far as Fontainebleau. Rescuers dragged hundreds of victims out of the ruins, and the Charité and Gros-Caillou Hospitals are overwhelmed with trying to take care of the injured. In spite of the fact that the disaster was accidental, it was also predictable. Some 2,000 workers were packed into the Grenelle workshop, making powder in overheated surroundings, without any protective measures having been adopted so far. And to date, nobody had expressed any kind of official alarm about this dangerous situation.

Tallien launches a press campaign on behalf of terrorist acts.

France is seizing Flemish art treasures

Paris, August 31

To display all their brilliance, works produced by geniuses must be entrusted to people who are free and will keep them safe. At least, that is the principle espoused by the members of the Temporary Arts Commission who have been sent to The Netherlands and Rhineland areas to make a survey of all treasures suitable for enriching the Republic's collections. The French forces' victories in Flanders have made it possible to seize many paintings by various masters, and the Convention decided today to have them brought to the capital. Thanks to the zeal of the Commissioners Tinet, de Wailly and Leblond — respectively a painter, an architect and an antiquarian — some 5,000 volumes from the Louvain Library will be "repatriated", as will Rubens' famous *Descent from the Cross*, which is kept in Antwerp Cathedral, not to mention many other precious objects considered worthy of interest. As Abbot Grégoire enthusiastically commented: "The Flemish School has risen *en masse* to beautify our museums."

The libretto of Mozart's "Magic Flute", seized in The Netherlands.

"Muscadin" rage starts

France, August

The country is being taken over by a wild new fad. The "Muscadins" among the gilded youth appeared shortly after Thermidor, and they are setting the pace for this fad. These eccentrics roam about in gangs, ostentatiously displaying their bizarre "uniform" -- a tight coat that is bottle-green or dirty beige, worn over close-fitting knee-breeches and decorated with ribbons. They deck themselves out with gigantic monocles, wear wigs under their large, two-pointed hats, and scent themselves with musk, whence their name of "Muscadins". Their girlfriends are equally provocative, strolling about almost naked in sheaths of transparent gauze. These young people affect speaking in a disdainful fashion, dropping their r's. All that would be good clean fun except that the Muscadins are also armed with lead-weighted clubs that they call "rogue-beaters", because they use them on "terrorists", or "executive power" as a derisory reference to the revolutionary régime. They are in the front rank of political reaction and openly display nostalgia for the monarchy. The rust-spotted

Nonchalance is the latest thing.

muslins worn around their necks, the black velvet collars evoking the King's death, and the 17 mother of pearl buttons on their coats recalling the orphan in the Temple are royalist symbols. They gather at the Café de Chartres in Paris, and it is becoming a ghastly place.

Buying and selling freedom in prisons

France, August

Rogues always have an eye out for the main chance and do not even hesitate to traffic in poor people's hopes. They have a simple method. The committees responsible for releasing suspects are overwhelmed and cannot manage to meet demand. Certain individuals take advantage of this general disorder to exploit the prisoners, selling them releases. For instance, the manufacturer Romey, a well-known speculator and an habitué of the Café de Chartres, pretends to be a member of the Committee of General Safety and borrows Commissioner Legendre's name. Others, like Maillol, ask them for money, supposedly for bribing judges or getting their cases to move along faster. Some bailiffs are said to be involved in these shenanigans. Needless to say, these con-men keep the money for themselves. The committees have lost all control.

Revolutionary stir influences Americas

South America, late August

Events in France fascinate even distant continents. Despite the distances and delays in learning the news, revolutionary themes have shaken up the South American states. Cuban walls, for instance, have been plastered with satirical posters proclaiming that "the guillotine will be set up on a public square". There is also mention of a possible uprising against Spain, the symbol of despotism here, whose defeats on the Pyrenean front have been cheered here. In Argentina, nationalistic circles and Masonic lodges are very sensitive to the idea of liberating peoples, which was born in France. In Colombia, the establishment of political-literary clubs has been banned. Their instigator, Narino, has been arrested even though he is a government member. Finally, all Latin America acclaimed the French victory won at Fleurus.

Convention

1 *(Fructidor 15, Year II)*
Paris. Renewal of the Committee of Public Safety. Merlin de Douai joins it, along with Delmas, Barras' assistant for Thermidor 9, the Jacobin chemist Fourcroy, and Cochon de Lapparent. Collot d'Herbois and Billaud Varenne leave the committee.

3 *(Fructidor 17, Year II)*
Paris. Babeuf, using the signature Gracchus for the first time, brings out the *Journal of Press Freedom*.

3 *(Fructidor 17, Year II)*
Paris. Lecointre, Tallien and Fréron are excluded from the Jacobins Club at Carrier's request (→10).

7 *(Fructidor 21, Year II)*
Paris. The Convention extends general price controls and controls on grains for all of Year III.→

7 *(Fructidor 21, Year II)*
Paris. The Favart auditorium is the scene of a musical hoax arranged by the composer Lesueur, who has *Arabella and Vasco, or the Jacobins of Goa* performed as his own work, to help a fellow composer.

10 *(Fructidor 24, Year II)*
Paris. An attack on Tallien gives Merlin de Thionville, speaking to the Convention, the chance to denounce the Jacobins as "knights of the guillotine".

10 *(Fructidor 24, Year II)*
Paris. Marie Joseph Chénier has his tragedy *Timoléon* performed at the Theatre of the Republic. It was banned by the censors last March, but Chénier had kept a copy of the manuscript.

11 *(Fructidor 25, Year II)*
Paris. Stanislas Fréron again brings out *The People's Orator*, in which he displays virulent anti-Jacobinism.

12 *(Fructidor 26, Year II)*
Paris. The Convention votes to shift Marat's remains to the Pantheon, as the Jacobins asked on September 6th. (→21).

13 *(Fructidor 27, Year II)*
Sceaux. The fable-writer Florian dies of exhaustion, shortly after being released from prison.

13 *(Fructidor 27, Year II)*
Paris. Second report by Grégoire to the Convention on the destruction of works due to vandalism.

14 *(Fructidor 28, Year II)*
Paris. Acquittal of 94 Nantais who had been held in the capital since Nivôse 16.

Semaphore telegraph: victory messenger

Paris, September 1
The dispatch riders whipping their steeds to deliver their missives at lightning speed, are on the way out. The news of the capture of Condé reached Paris by way of the Chappe brothers' "optical telegraph", based on semaphore. In a little less than a year, the telegraph engineers managed to instal an initial line between the capital and Lille. The line is 210 kilometres long, goes through Arras, Montdidier and Ecouen, and winds up in Montmartre to get the news to the Flore pavillion at the Louvre. It was tested in July, and seemed to bring good luck: Barère used the telegraph at that time to inform the Assembly of the recapture of Landrecies. With the fall of Condé, the message is taking on more importance. That is why Lazare Carnot, the man of war, wanted to make the announcement personally to the Convention. Thanks to his plans

The winged genius brings news.

and their successful execution, all of the strongholds that are located in the north of the country have now fallen (→Oct. 21).

David's prison view inspires picture idea

Paris, September 2
This time it is a celebrated painter who is going to be able to compare the merits of the various republican jails. David was arrested a month ago because of his relationship with Robespierre and was initially incarcerated in the former headquarters of the General Farm. He has just been transferred to the Luxembourg prison. He was allowed to take his painting equipment along, but what can one paint behind bars, except perhaps a self-portrait? And that has already been done. From his window he can see big trees, with light playing through the foliage. While landscapes are not his favourites, he already has an idea for a painting.

The Luxembourg Garden, as the painter David sees it from his prison.

Indies Company on way to liquidation

Paris, September 3
It is a painful epilogue. The Compagnie des Indes (Indies Company) is finally going to be wound up legally. The Convention has just approved a decree ordering its liquidation under supervision of an impartial committee, with no links with the company. Readers will remember the political-financial scandal stemming from that discount house's speculative operations, the talk of the town last year. Corrupt deputies lost their heads, and investors their money.

Provincial Jacobins

Dijon, September 5
Will the provincial people's associations raise their heads? One must say that the meaning of the Thermidorian reaction is less clear outside Paris. Militants have sometimes not understood that the Reign of Terror is over, and that the vanquished of Year II were bent on revenge. Thus the Dijon Jacobins Club has just sent the Convention a petition. It reaffirms its positions energetically and asks the deputies to put an end to improper releases, to urge citizens to denounce aristocrats, nobles and priests, and to reorganise district revolutionary committees, allowing them to arrest suspects. Similarly, in the Ardèche, Nîmes and Brest, the Jacobins are extremely worried about the progress being made by counter-revolution. But all the same, they are quite isolated (→Oct. 14).

Workers defending their pay packets

Paris, September 5
Workers are thinking about defending their wages. The employees of the paper plants turning out assignats got together to ensure their purchasing power and reached an agreement: wages will vary to reflect labour productivity. The more banknotes a worker turns out, the more he will be paid. In the Pyrénées region, workers are getting together to put pressure on farmers employing them. Farmers will no longer be able to cut wages by competition among workers.

The accused have now become accusers

Paris, September 8

Federalism is still a crime in the Convention's eyes. Robespierre is dead, but a hunt continues for the people he fought, guilty of opposition in Paris and of having tried to secede by winning over the Girondists who were expelled from the Assembly. Thus charges of federalism have put 94 people from Nantes in the dock today before the Revolutionary Court of Paris, to which their cases were referred. They were arrested by representative on mission Carrier, who was the delegate in the department at the time of the disturbances. But the accused have no intention of keeping mum. They appeal to public opinion, which they know they can win over since it now rejects, as a whole, the "tyranny" of the revolutionary dictatorship. The main figure going on trial, Phélippe, known as Tronjolly, demands that certain witnesses appear: namely, the members of the Revolutionary Committee who were also arrested by Carrier, who charges them with being too easy on the federalists. Tronjolly claims that those Jacobins committed a number of atrocious collective murders, sparing neither women nor children. In particular he accuses them of having carried out summary executions by throwing suspects into the Loire. The rest of the trial is impatiently awaited, as it might turn against the accusers (→ Sept. 14).

Peasant anger brings light penalties

Dordogne, September

Grumbling has given way to exasperation in Ribérac. Faced by ever more burdensome requisitions, the farmers have resorted to tricks: hiding their grain reserves. Fortunately for them, the punishments being handed out are light. Jean Faure, a cowherd, got 12 hours in jail for calling the Republic's employees "cads". Others have simply suffered confiscation of the bags they hid, often in places not very hard to find.

Heroes being dethroned by unknowns

Paris, September

Are the great heroes and the great revolutionary actions having to give way to individual acts of brave but unknown Frenchmen? The question arises because the artists chosen to take part in the major competition organised by the Convention are no longer using the themes, dear to Marat or Bara, of July 14th. or August 10th. In fact, there are six paintings illustrating the story of *The Heroine of Saint Milhier*, bravely repulsing an attack by counter-revolutionaries. This virtuous example is taken from the *Collection of Heroic Actions*, a kind of "Republican catechism".

The heroic grocer woman of Saint Milhier threatens to blow up the house.

A plot atmosphere is noted in Mexico

There is always tension between rich Spanish colonists and the Mexicans.

Mexico City, September 8

Rumors suddenly intensified. Fed by the local newspaper, *Noticias de Mexico*, they dealt with the secrets of a conspiracy supposedly hatched by Frenchmen and Creoles against the government. At any time, armed men may surround the National Palace, kill the leaders and cause an uprising in New Spain. That is certainly enough to get the capital all excited as here, more than elsewhere, people can no longer stand the colonial pact with Spain. So whether all this be true or not, the alleged plot has revealed the tensions found in a city living on a powder keg.

Price lids continue but are useless

Paris, September 7

Even though it is doing its best to destroy all the economic measures taken during the Reign of Terror, the Convention has rejected abolition of price controls. It did not dare brave the sansculottists by decontrolling prices. Thermidor is too recent and, in any case, peasants, manufacturers and tradesmen no longer respect the set prices. They refuse to comply with requisitions, as sanctions are no longer applied. All are awaiting adoption of the Lindet Plan, setting rules for economic liberalisation (→ Sept. 20).

The Orléans widow prefers her prison

Paris, September

When the widow of Philippe Egalité was released on September 10th. by the Committee of Public Safety, she was quite disorientated. She pined for the Belhomme home, a delightful jail for privileged detainees, where she had spent many happy hours. After all, had she not encountered true love there? Even though he was just a commoner the Convention deputy Rouzet, who shared her detention, stole away her heart. So she simply returned to the home to ask to stay, and she has opened a salon there.

▷

Reform made of Paris food supply system

Food that is intended for the capital goes by way of Port au Blé.

Paris, September 11

The shortages could not continue any longer. The Convention has now decided to intervene energetically to settle the food problem. Neither wheat nor food generally were lacking. But the eight Paris supply agencies are submerged in so much paperwork and are paralysed by so many bureaucrats that they are almost completely ineffective. The law passed today calls for a reform of those departments that should make up somewhat for their shortcomings. From now on, the capital will have priority over the rest of the country. It will be supplied with grain in the same way as the armies and the forts, thanks to requisitions carried out in 25 districts designated for this purpose. Supply will be a direct responsibility of the central authorities, to which two committees are subordinate: one of them will set the wheat quotas, while the other will see to shipping. Parisians will get their daily bread.

The Marly horses to come to capital

Paris, September

The Convention has just decided to instal the statues of the Marly horses at the edge of the Champs Elysées woods. These rearing horses with flowing manes, held back by two Africans, were ordered in 1740 from the sculptor Coustou to replace the two equestrian groups by Coysevox, which originally embellished the park watering point at Marly, and which were then installed in Paris at the entrance to the Tuileries Gardens. The transfer, which appears to be a complicated question, will take months.

The marble horses are installed at the end of the Champs Elysées.

September 1794
from 15th. to 30th.

 Convention

15 *(Fructidor 29, Year II)* Paris. Maratists Chasles and Lebois bring out a new *Friend of the People.*→

15 *(Fructidor 29, Year II)* Marseilles. The representatives Serre and Auguis, who came here to get the city back into line, are booed by the members of the people's associations (→26).

17 *(1st supplementary day)* Netherlands. Kléber lays siege to Maastricht.

17 *(1st supplementary day)* Pyrénées Orientales. General Dugommier expels the Spaniards from Bellegarde.→

18 *(2nd supplementary day)* Paris. At Cambon's suggestion, the Convention decrees that, in future, the Republic will not pay expenses or salaries for any religion.→

19 *(3rd supplementary day)* Paris. At Palais Egalité gangs of Muscadins, organised by repentant "terrorists" such as Fréron and Tallien, clash with the Jacobins.

20 *(4th supplementary day)* Paris. In the Convention, Robert Lindet explains his economic programme in a report entitled *On the Republic's Situation.*→

21 *(5th supplementary day)* Paris. Burial of Marat's remains in the Pantheon.→

26 *(Vendémiaire 5, Year III)* Marseilles. The representatives Serre and Auguis set up a military committee to press the Jacobin demonstrations (→27).

26 *(Vendémiaire 5, Year III)* Paris. At Théâtre de l'Egalité, Julien Forgeot praises divorce in his comedy *The Double Divorce, or the Law's Benefit.*

27 *(Vendémiaire 6, Year III)* Guadeloupe. Republican troops begin the reconquest of Basse-Terre.

28 *(Vendémiaire 7, Year III)* Paris. Establishment of the Central School for Public Works.→

29 *(Vendémiaire 8, Year III)* Paris. General Turreau, former commander in chief of the Western Army, is arrested. He had made a name for himself by ravaging the Vendée.

30 *(Vendémiaire 9, Year III)* Paris. The composer Jean Baptiste Davaux has just finished a "symphony concerto" mingled with patriotic melodies.

Dugommier moves on into Catalonia

Pyrénées, September 17

There are no more Spaniards in France. After recapturing Bellegarde, General Dugommier was determined to press home his advantage in Catalonia. Since his appointment to the Pyrenean front, the victor of Toulon has recorded a large number of very bold attacks. In June, with Augereau's help, he expelled the enemy from the Boulou camp. Then, resolved to give his opponents no respite at all, he recaptured the famous Montesquiou redoubt the following month, shook up the Spanish garrison at Saint Elme Fort, and harassed the Collioure garrison. Dugommier is not only a bold general, but also a man of principle: he opposed the Convention's decree that no more prisoners should be taken.

Dugommier defeated the Spanish.

Patriots in Nancy suffering a purge

Nancy, September 16

The Nancy Watch Committee has just undergone a severe purge. It had protested against the arrests of patriots ordered by Paris. The population backed the Committee and voiced its noisy support, but the representatives, Pflieger and Michaud, were unyielding. After saying that the Committee needed "men who are more cautious, less given to partiality, and perhaps purer", they renewed it by appointing rural citizens, who are on the whole more moderate than their predecessors had been.

The State will no longer pay the priests

Paris, September 18

"The Republic no longer pays the expenses or the salaries of any religion." The decree proposed by Cambon was immediately adopted by the National Assembly. Cambon had offered the proposal in the name of the Finance Committee. By doing away with the religion budget, the State will be able to make some substantial savings. The reason is that, even at the time of de-Christianisation in Year II, the principle of paying the salaries of "constitutional" priests was not questioned. Even if the actual payments were sometimes problemati-

cal, the principle was uncontested. Actually, without saying so, the decree that has just been adopted marks the end of the Civil Constitution of the Clergy. To Cambon, who had suggested in vain such a measure last year, the State must be independent of all religions. "If the State proclaims any religious principle whatsoever, it will immediately have a clergy to pay. Are the ministers of the cult of the Supreme Being not already requesting salaries?" In any case, this separation of Church and State gives rise to many questions. Are the faithful to be free to pay the pastors they choose?

Marat's ashes transferred to Panthéon

A year after his death, how much glory remains for the people's friend?

Lindet offers liberal economic plan

Paris, September 20

The Jacobins' controlled economy has had its day. Lindet has just explained the outlines of a new programme that partly restores economic freedom, to the extent that certain monetary constraints allow this. Foreign trade will be the first beneficiary of the new pro-

gramme. From now on, there will be no import quotas, and businessmen from neutral countries will be able to deal with customers directly. As for the companies that had been taken over by the State, such as the Gobelins manufacturing group or arsenals, they will return to the private sector (→ Dec. 24).

One way of filling up the prison hours

Paris, September

Prison days are long. But the painter David is not at all the kind of person to get bored. He is working tirelessly, thanks to the brushes and colours he was allowed to take with him. In addition to a self-portrait and the landscape seen from his cell window, which does

not really satisfy him, he has started a project to which he is much attached, and which brings him back to a kind of Neo-Classical inspiration: *Homer Reciting Verses to the Greeks*, of which he has finished a preparatory study and for which he is now asking to be allowed to receive models.

Paris, September 21

The ceremony did not enjoy much success. Yet the Jacobins had organised a rather pompous procession aimed at arousing the kind of enthusiasm that characterised Year II festivities. Léonard Bourdon got the Convention to approve Marat's "Panthéonisation", which had been planned since his death but had never taken place. The remains of the "people's tribune" were first taken from the Cordeliers' enclosure to the Assembly. From there, an imposing procession went to the Panthéon by way of Pont Neuf bridge. It consisted of almost 18,000 people, including Republican authorities. There were the deputies, representatives of the

sectors, the people's associations, the departments and each of the 14 armies, members of the courts, artists, and war orphans as well as wounded veterans. Some cavalry troops and drummers surrounded Marat's carriage, which was some 30 feet high. However, this procession moved through the capital to general indifference. The joy displayed by the organisers seemed totally out of place. The Jacobins hoped to revive the revolutionary fervour and mystique by exalting the memory of one of the most symbolic figures of the Reign of Terror. But it is certain that they failed in their effort to reach this objective: Marat is no longer an idol for the crowd (→ Feb. 8, 95).

Will the steel industry be privatised?

France, September 21

What is to be done with the forges and steelmills controlled by the nation? How can their output be increased? To some people, such as Croquebert, editor of the *Mining Journal*, the system set up during the Reign of Terror proved its efficiency in the war effort for defending the nation. In his view, management can further rationalise in this area by making the districts and departments responsible for administration, and by leaving organisation and control of production up to the Republic. Only the latter, is able to come up with the funding needed to ensure the operation of facilities that are not very profitable, but are useful in the defence effort. The opponents of this policy say that it involves a lot of waste. Together with Carnot, they want freedom of management for the

companies. As for the Weapons Committee, it is opting for privatisation, as practised in the Bas Rhin in the De Dietrich establishments. These are owned by a capitalist-entrepreneur, but can be requisitioned if needed.

Steel: a razor-blade factory.

"Homer Reciting Verses to the Greeks", painted by David in prison.

Abolition of slavery encounters problems

The decree passed by the Convention on February 4th. is a dead letter.

Ile de France, September 20

The slave trade is abolished in the Mascarene Islands. A month apart, the Colonial Assemblies of Ile de France and of Réunion have promulgated a decree banning trade in blacks on their territory. But one must not be taken in. Abolition of the trade does not mean abolition of slavery, and the former is not sure to lead to the latter. The reason is that this decision was made to express the colonists' refusal to apply the Convention's de-cree doing away with slavery. After the arrival of the *Maryland*, an American vessel that left France on April 18th., agitation began among the colonists, as the ship was bringing the "infamous decree"! To quiet them down, and also spare the Convention's feelings, the elec-ted officials decided to abolish only the slave trade. This step is easily accepted by the colonists, since the trade has become clandestine. Without submitting, the islands have not completely disobeyed.

Citizen Ouvrard's influence growing

Paris, September

Less than a year after his arrival in the capital, the Nantes financier Ouvrard enjoys a marked degree of authority and prestige. The Com-mittee of Public Safety compensa-ted him for the fire in his father's paper-mill, which burnt during the Vendée war, paying him an indem-nity of 200,000 francs. To this sum must be added the amount in-volved in speculation on colonial products he set up with a few rich Bordeaux merchants, or 500,000 gold francs. This financial power gives him great influence with the deputies, who often ask him for advice on economic and monetary questions. Ouvrard is a "money-man", and he knows that, in France, fortune and power cannot really be ignored ...

"People's friend" haunts politicians

Paris, September 15

Marat's ghost is still haunting French political life. The first edi-tion of a new *The People's Friend* ap-peared today. The Maratist Chas-les, who intervened in the Assembly a month ago to protest against out-rages perpetrated against the mem-ory of the tribune, defends Jacobin ideas in his publication. The rela-tive freedom of the press that has prevailed since Robespierre's fall benefits both the royalists, who were kept off-stage for a long time, and the Jacobins, even though the latter are currently not in good odour. Along with Barère, Du-quesnoy and Fayau, Chasles is part of the "Cretans", given that nick-name because they sit at the top (*crête*) of the Montagne group, on the far left in the Assembly.

Public works school agreed by deputies

Paris, September 28

The Republic needs scientific and technical personnel. Convinced of this need, the deputies adopted, without debate, the decree intro-duced four days previously by the chemist Fourcroy, a member of the Committee of Public Safety, pro-viding for the establishment of a Central Public Works School. Along with the Paris Bridges and Roads School, this new establish-ment will train young engineers aged 16 to 18. The 400 students will be tested on their scientific know-ledge and selected in a competition, if they have a civic spirit certificate. They will get three months' inten-sive training and then be divided into three levels. They will be paid by the State (→Oct. 22).

The Thermidorians reign in Marseilles

Marseilles, September 27

After the purge, extermination. The representatives Auguis and Serre, sent to the city in order to impose Thermidorian order there, had already released 500 victims of the Reign of Terror, and had re-moved numerous officials. But the trouble began with the arrest of a Jacobin leader who was immedi-ately freed by a mob. Wanting to play a strong hand, the representa-tives found themselves confronted by active opposition on the patriots' part. Yesterday, the latter again gathered for a demonstration. A hundred people were arrested, and five of them were executed today. Nothing daunted, they were singing the *Marseillaise* as they climbed the scaffold.

Saving the Notre Dame Cathedral organ

Paris, September 26

Pipes, keyboard and pedals are all in a pitiful condition. In this cathedral, as in many others, the organ is being ruined because no-body comes in to play it any more. Citizen Godinot, a musician who is fully aware of the value of this mas-terpiece built by François Clicquot, alerted the recently-created Com-mittee for the National Heritage. That panel, with some members who are organists and builders, ap-peared at Notre Dame at 4 a.m. today and talked to the chief bell-ringer Gilbert. After inspecting the instrument, the visitors, impressed by the extent of the damage, ordered that everybody be kept away from the organ until it can be repaired. The Committee will inspect other organs in the capital.

For several years now, no sound has come from this splendid organ.

Convention

2 *(Vendémiaire 11, Year III)* Belgium. The French troops commanded by Jourdan attack and capture the Austrian positions on the other side of the Roer, forcing General Clairfayt to abandon his defence line on the Meuse and to withdraw his forces toward the Rhine.

4 *(Vendémiaire 13, Year III)* Paris. The 73 Girondists in jail write to the Convention to demand their release after Cambon, the previous day, publicly deplored the events of May 31th., 1793.

5 *(Vendémiaire 14, Year III)* Paris. Gracchus Babeuf gives the name *Tribune of the People* to his *Journal of Press Freedom.*→

5 *(Vendémiaire 14, Year III)* Toulouse. A departmental order calls for internment of all priests, even de-frocked ones, unless they are married.

6 *(Vendémiaire 15, Year III)* Paris. Carnot leaves the Committee of Public Safety.

6 *(Vendémiaire 15, Year III)* Paris. Abbot Grégoire resigns from the Assembly's Colonial Committee, on the grounds of the colonists' attitude towards him. They have published more than 500 pamphlets against him, burnt him in effigy, and opened a secret "subscription" to organise his assassination.

6 *(Vendémiaire 15, Year III)* Saint Domingue. André Rigaud's mulatto army expels the English from Léogane and marches on Port au Prince.

7 *(Vendémiaire 16, Year III)* Paris. The Convention allows Ville Affranchie to resume its former name, Lyons.

9 *(Vendémiaire 18, Year III)* Paris. The Convention decides on the list of elementary works for use in the country's primary schools.

10 *(Vendémiaire 19, Year III)* Poland. The Russian General Alexander Vasilyevich Suvorov crushes the Polish army at Maciejowice. The injured Polish leader Kosciuszko is taken prisoner.

10 *(Vendémiaire 19, Year III)* United Provinces. General Pichegru captures Hertogenbosch.

14 *(Vendémiaire 23, Year III)* Paris. The Convention hears a letter from the Dijon Jacobins, who withdraw their petition of September 5th.

School being set up for the "air force"

Paris, October 3

The experimentation has come to an end and, from now on, the young balloonists will be trained at a National Ballooning School. It will be installed in Meudon, and the manufacturer Conté will be its director. The 60 students will be supervised by Captain Coutelle, who becomes commandant of balloonist companies. If funding permits, they will have 13 first-class balloons and ten second-class. To make the studies easier, Conté has set up a system of coloured panels for transmitting information to the ground. The programme will not be limited to military subjects. The young recruits will also learn the telegraph code so as to be able to instruct the ground troops, as well as a few notions of cartography to make surveys, if needed. But Conté also has some other projects in mind. Among other things, he wants to make dirigible balloons, which would be designed with sails or wings. Such devices would be able to bombard enemy positions.

Young handicapped will get assistance

Paris, October

The legislators involved with public education have been guilty of a serious injustice. In their desire for schools open to all, rich or poor, they neglected to adress the issue of the most disadvantaged children of them all: the handicapped. Their infirmities very often mean they are abandoned by their parents at birth. While they are kept in some home or charitable institution until the age of 12, they are then left to their own devices, with no resources and no job. To remedy this terrible situation, The deputy Coupé de l'Oise, a member of the Committee of Public Safety, has submitted a proposal to his colleagues for the establishment in each district of workhouses and shelters. There they would be subsidised by public welfare funds and would take in abandoned and crippled children, training them in arts and sciences with the help of all "industrial machines and inventions". It is high time for the Republic to take care of all its children.

France continues its conquests in north

A tree of freedom has been planted on Royal Square in Brussels.

Paris, October 1

The conquest of the former Austrian Low Countries is continuing. The Committee of Public Safety has ordered representatives on mission Briez and Hausmann to dissolve the revolutionary committees and ban arbitrary arrests. In a nutshell, they are to attempt to have the Republic loved "by a government based on the sacred principles of justice". The improvised nature of the beginnings has been followed by a more regular type of organisation. In each province, neighbourhood administrations have been set up to replace the state assemblies. At the top are two central departments with staff nominated by the representatives on mission.

What's to be done with the Rhineland?

Paris, October 1

The armies of Hoche, Marceau and Championnet have pushed the imperial forces back and are in the process of occupying the whole left bank of the Rhine. But the Convention deputies, who refuse to pay attention to the Rhineland deputies' vote requesting annexation, still hesitate as to the policy to be followed in the conquered areas. While waiting for a settlement deciding the Rhineland's fate, a decree has set up a temporary administration responsible for providing food for the military. Two central agencies, in Kreuznach and Aachen, will be set up for this.

The Rhineland Jacobin clubs have sharp debates on the province's fate.

Three Parisian Jacobin leaders arrested

Paris, October 3

The Thermidorians have just scored a point. They have managed to get three agitators jailed, the ones known as Chrétien, Clémence and Marchand. It was easy to find a pretext for their arrest. Eight Paris sectors had backed the Dijon Jacobins' petition protesting against improper releases of suspects, and four others had signed the manifesto of the Muséum sector demanding free elections in Paris. Pointing to the agitation caused by such moves, and supported by the gilded youth, the deputies approved the indictments. Public opinion, which is tired of political battles, has not reacted.

Collot d'Herbois: in exile since May.

Championnet's men conquer Cologne

Cologne, October 6

The army of Sambre et Meuse certainly deserves the country's gratitude. General Etienne Championnet's troops have entered Cologne. But lassitude, in turn, is conquering the troops, and the only thing the soldiers are thinking about is seeing their communities and families — about going home. Championnet's forces reached the Rhine without difficulty, in view of the enemy's disorganisation after the French victory at Fleurus, but now the troops are really stopped for a time. Neither the capture of Aachen last month nor the victorious entry into Juliers revived the troops' spirits. The revolutionary ideal is gone, even if the Convention still hopes to establish it on this side of the Rhine.

Jail official is the new national hero

Paris, October

The good fellow could not have imagined that his action would be so much talked about. But it took only a few weeks for this unknown citizen to start being recognised and greeted in the street, and for his story to become the subject of stage plays. The hero of this true story is named Cange, and he is a warder at Saint Lazare Prison. His duties brought him into close contact during the Reign of Terror with a large number of detainees who were soon led to the guillotine and were immediately replaced. Feeling sorry for them, he did his best to soften their fate, and on one occasion he visited a husband and wife who were being held in different cells. He took the last 100 francs he had in his pocket and gave half of it to the wife, saying it was from her husband, and the other 50 to the husband "from your wife". The story quickly made the rounds of the capital, and the Parisians were moved by such a display of humanity, which is a very rare virtue these days. Cange has taken the place in their thoughts of a Bara or a Viala.

Toulouse pressures its Masonic lodges

Toulouse, October 5

As from today, the city's four Masonic lodges are going to have to shut up shop. Despite the constant patriotism they have displayed, The deputy Mallarmé, who came from Paris on a mission, put the lodges on a list of "monuments to fanaticism" that he is responsible for destroying. The Toulouse brothers had hoped for better treatment from a lodge brother. But Mallarmé, although himself a Mason, was unable to resist pressure from the city's lower classes; they have pointed out to him that such associations are against the law.

A Masonic seal.

Conservatory voted for arts and trades

Paris, October 10

Painting has its Salon, music its Conservatory, and the natural sciences their Museum. Only the mechanical arts had no school. But thanks to Abbot Grégoire, this shortcoming has just been remedied. On the basis of his report, the Assembly has approved a decree establishing a Conservatory of Arts and Trades, which will contain many collections of machines and scientific instruments for educational purposes. Without being an actual professional or vocational school, the Conservatory will employ three demonstrators and a designer who will do their best to interest visitors and, if need be, they will ensure technological training by means of examples. Since no premises for the Conservatory have yet been set aside, for the time being the machines will remain at the d'Aiguillon mansion, where they are protected from vandalism.

Arguments between Muscadins and sansculottists quickly degenerate into sometimes violent brawls.

Rousseau in Panthéon

The monument put up in the Tuileries to the memory of Rousseau.

Paris, October 11

The hermit of Ermenonville could not have imagined any finer posthumous homage. A huge crowd accompanied his remains to the "Temple of Memory". Actually, the ceremony had got under way three days previously. The philosopher's tomb in Ermenonville was solemnly opened and the metal coffin was placed on a carriage. The next day, the procession set out for Paris. After a night in Mont-morency, which was rechristened Emile because of the stay the writer once made there, it entered the capital yesterday evening. The coffin was displayed in the centre of the Tuileries Basin on a mound representing Peupliers Island. This morning, Parisians, people from Geneva, craftsmen, mothers and children paraded, singing melodies from *Devin de village*, Rousseau's only opera, before taking him to his Panthéon tomb.

The Russians crush the Polish rebellion

Maciejowice, October 10

The Russians have destroyed the Polish Army. This veritable disaster is marked by the loss of a whole army corps, and above all by the loss of the leader, Kosciuszko, who is now a prisoner. The patriots, attacked by the Prussians in June, defended themselves valiantly. But they were defeated at Krakow and fell back to Warsaw, undergoing a two month siege there. The Russians then decided to launch a vast offensive. From the Ukraine, Suvorov moved by forced marches toward the Polish capital. Kosciuszko had hastily recruited 20,000 men to bar the Russians' path to Warsaw, but the enemy's speed kept him from concentrating his forces. For their part, the Polish Jacobins, who are also very hostile to the Prussians, are opposed to the Kosciuszko supporters in the pow-er struggle. They have not recovered from the news, and prefer to wait rather than risk being crushed in their turn.

The patriot Thadeusz Kosciuszko.

Appeasement policy followed in west

Morbihan, October 13

The republicans have taken a further step bearing witness to their desire for pacification. An amnesty has been promised to the Morbihan insurgents who lay down their arms within ten days. On September 24th., an identical measure was adopted for the rebels in the Ille et Vilaine Department. These moves are characteristic of the new policy followed by the Republic with respect to the insurrections in the west. Even before Robespierre's fall, Carrier's recall and the dissolution of General Turreau's "infernal columns" had marked the beginning of a "new course". The clearest-thinking republicans had understood that the only result of the Turreau troops' exactions was to breathe new life into the war. But the most decisive turning point was the Thermidor coup d'état. The new representatives on mission, Bollet, Boursault and Ruelle, as well as Generals Hoche and Canclaux, attempted to bring about proper conditions for pacification. But the situation remains very precarious: in the Vendée, Charette and Stofflet are continuing their warlike activities, while in the area north of the Loire River Chouan-type revolts and banditry are creating a feeling of insecurity.

Babeuf takes position as people's tribune

Paris, October 5

Georges Babeuf founded *The Journal of the Freedom of the Press* just after Thermidor to denounce the Reign of Terror. His opinion-orientated publication is now taking the name of *The People's Tribune or the Defender of Human Rights*. Faithful to his ideals, Babeuf takes a stand in his publication for the Revolution and for the people against reaction. He has chosen the name Gracchus for signing his articles. In addition to a homage to Antiquity, the reference is to the example of the Gracchi brothers, the early Roman democrats and reformers. He sees these tribunes as the revolutionaries' ancestors.

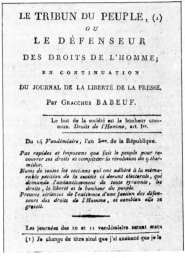

Front page of Babeuf's newspaper.

Sade again being let out of prison

Paris, October 13

Prison doors are again going to open for the former Marquis de Sade. After his sample of the royal jails, the Republican's were almost fatal to him, and it was a miracle that he escaped the guillotine. On July 27th. the court marshal was unable to find him in the many Paris jails, and the tumbril left without him. Two weeks ago, Sade sent the Committee of General Safety a petition for release, referring to his many patriotic works. The request was approved and the former nobleman is now going to get out of prison. He will be able to rejoin the tender and faithful Mme. Quesnet.

Beauty's life saved by love and money

Paris, October 3

Aimée de Coigny, the "young captive" whose radiant beauty inspired one of André Chénier's finest poems, has got out of Saint Lazare Prison. But she does not owe her life to her jailers' pity or their taste for poetry, but more prosaically to the money of her lover, Casimir de Montrond. He bribed the men responsible for drawing up the list of victims for the scaffold with 100 gold louis. Thus both of them escaped death, despite the charges against them of "stinking aristocracy". Their captivity has not lessened their love for each other, and they have even decided to get married.

Convention

15 *(Vendémiaire 24, Year III)*
Germany. The Army of the Rhine wins twin victories: Desaix seizes Frankenthal, while Gouvion Saint Cyr captures Ober Moschel.

16 *(Vendémiaire 25, Year III)*
Paris. The Convention bans any correspondence and any affiliation among associations, thus giving the *coup de grâce* to the Jacobin clubs, which are going to wither.

17 *(Vendémiaire 26, Year III)*
London. Dissension within the coalition. The British Prime Minister, Pitt, has decided to stop financing the Prussian forces, which he holds responsible for the recent defeats suffered by anti-French forces in Germany.

18 *(Vendémiaire 27, Year III)*
Paris. The Assembly decides to establish a fund for aid to artists.→

20 *(Vendémiaire 29, Year III)*
Paris. The deputy Dumont asks the Convention to submit Carrier's "crimes" for the Committees' consideration (→29).

22 *(Brumaire 1, Year III)*
Paris. Opening of the Central Public Works School, the future Ecole Polytechnique.

23 *(Brumaire 2, Year III)*
Germany. General Marceau's army captures Coblentz.

24 *(Brumaire 3, Year III)*
Paris. End of the Ecole de Mars, which was established by a decree of June 1st.

28 *(Brumaire 7, Year III)*
England. Sharper reprisals against the revolutionary elements. After the execution in Edinburgh, on October 15th., of the Scotsman Robert Watt, who had hatched a plot against the crown, a trial opens in London today of the Corresponding Society and of its leader, Thomas Hardy.→

29 *(Brumaire 8, Year III)*
Paris. The Convention sets up a 21-member committee that is to look into prosecutions of deputies proposed by the Committees. The first case to be examined is the one involving Jean Baptiste Carrier, the Nantes tormentor (→ Dec. 16, 95).

30 *(Brumaire 9, Year III)*
Paris. Acting on a proposal made by Lakanal, the Convention decides to create an Ecole Normale responsible for training future teachers, a decision that is also extended to the districts.

Le Bon not living up to his reputation

Paris, October

His new life is not much made for excesses, but in any case the blood-thirsty Joseph Le Bon has become a lamb. The representative on mission was incarcerated in the Luxembourg Prison three months ago, after Robespierre's fall. The man who operated the guillotine for pleasure as much as from a sense of duty now rejoices to be finally "persecuted by evildoers". And he spends his time exchanging letters with his wife, Mimi, who is being held in Arras. She is expecting for the second time, and keeps her husband informed in each letter. Joseph is proving the tenderest of fathers and most loving of husbands.

Joseph Le Bon, the guillotine man.

Cadoudal escapes

Brittany, end of October

The will to fight was stronger. The young Cadoudal and his comrade-in-arms, Mercier, got away from their guards. They had been held in the Brest jail since June 29th., and have now left to rejoin the Whites in the Alréen area between Brittany and the Vendée. Although in despair at what might happen, they left behind Cadoudal's parents, brothers and sisters, who were arrested at the same time as the two men. They set out for the Kerléano house, where their uncle Denis, who died in detention, hid 450 louis intended for the insurgents. From now on, Cadoudal will have no other family than the royalists.

The people celebrate liberation of territory at Champ de Mars

Paris, October 21

An enthusiastic crowd celebrated the end of the occupation of French soil by the coalition troops. Festivities got under way as early as 9 a.m. The centre of the Champ de Mars esplanade was occupied by a platform to which the most seriously wounded veterans of the 14 armies had been assigned. People listened to the speech given by the president of the Assembly and then cheered the hymn composed by Le Sueur. But above all, they admired the simulated attack on an enemy fort very skilfully carried out by the Ecole de Mars students. Then a triumphal march brought them to the foot of the pyramid of the Temple of Immortality, where the names of the Republic's armies and victories have been engraved. A delegation from the Convention appeared in order to lay an oak crown on the urn dedicated to those who died for France. In the evening everyone danced.

The young officer cadets of the Ecole de Mars practise attacking a fortress using a great many fire-crackers.

Carrier's crimes in Nantes are denounced

Paris, October 17

The trial of the 94 Nantais, which ended in their acquittal, is now turning against the city's Revolutionary Committee, which is now accused in turn. The initial witnesses, out of almost 300 who have been called to testify, all denounced the atrocities that were committed. According to Vaugeois, Carrier had "more than 2,400 individuals" shot, including women and children. Phélippe said he was also responsible for 23 group "vertical deportations", sending people to the bottom of the Loire. Others spoke of Vendeans executed after surrendering. Now Carrier himself is threatened (→ Oct. 20).

The sinister Jean Baptiste Carrier.

Has revolution been avoided in England?

England, October 28

Today, the British government has launched a wave of large-scale anti-revolutionary repression, symbolised by the arrest of Thomas Hardy. In 1792 he founded the London Corresponding Society on the model of the Paris Jacobins Club. This very active association established contacts with the French Convention and the Edinburgh Convention in the interests of bringing about parliamentary reform in England. With this in view, the Scotsman Robert Watt even came up with a major plot aimed at overthrowing royalty in Scotland, along the lines of what had happened in France. The movement was then supposed to spread to all England. Frightened by the strength of this revolutionary propaganda, the British government had Hardy and Watt arrested before it was too late. On October 15th. Robert Watt was executed in Edinburgh. As for Thomas Hardy, who is accused of treason, his trial has just opened in London. But that clever politician is in perfect control of his defence. He does not fear to call on public opinion to bear witness for him, and his trial is already much talked about in the British capital.

A juring bishop becomes a turncoat

Alençon, October 31

"I saw an individual come in who had a sanctimonious appearance and an extremely apostolic air about him." These words were spoken by Génissieux, who did not at all appreciate the fact that the former bishop Lefessier dared approach him to request re-establishment of worship. The only response to the former constitutional prelate, who abdicated during the Reign of Terror, was an arrest warrant. It did him no good to protest his attachment to the Republic. He did not convince the inflexible representative, who decided to jail him at once "without paying attention to the flattering things the holy man was saying".

An assistance fund set up for artists

Paris, October 18

The disappearance of the pensions and gratuities paid under the Ancien Régime, combined with the drying up of commissions from the clergy and the nobility, has plunged many artists into misery. Moved by this situation, the Convention, acting on the basis of a report by Grégoire, has voted to set up a 300,000-livre aid fund. Marie Joseph Chénier will be responsible for considering fair ways of distributing this money, by payments of 2,000 to 3,000 livres. His proposals, to which the beneficiaries are eagerly looking forward, will be submitted to the Assembly next January, and concern all the arts, from painting to engraving.

Accelerated courses for training teachers

Paris, October 30

What are called "revolutionary" methods definitely enjoy success. After revolutionary courses in the making of saltpetre, the ones at the Central Public Works School, and the no less revolutionary teaching found at the Ecole de Mars, there is now a revolutionary procedure applied to training primary school teachers. To remedy the shortage of such teachers, Lakanal, in the name of the Public Education Committee, had the idea of training primary school teachers using the model applied to arms-makers and engineers. Thus 1,600 citizens "already trained in the useful sciences" and designated by the district administrators will go to the Ecole Normale in Paris in order to study the "art of teaching". They will be reimbursed for their travel, and will also be paid for the four months of course work. They will also learn how to teach reading, writing, arithmetic, geography, history and grammar; in short, the rudiments of knowledge contained in the primary school programmes covered by the Bouquier Law. At the end of this more intensive training, the new teachers will go back to their respective districts and open improved schools themselves, in order to pass on their knowledge. Thus the gift of learning will spread to the entire nation.

General Marceau seized the city of Bonn on October 8th., leading the Sambre et Meuse forces.

French naval win in the Mascarenes

Ile de France, October 22

Captain Jean Marie Renaud has checkmated the Royal Navy. With two frigates and three privateers, he ventured out to meet the enemy cruising off the Mascarene Islands. This bold sortie surprised and routed two vessels of the English fleet, the *Diomede* and the *Centurion*, each of which carried 50 guns. This win again enables the Indian Ocean islands to fend off the blockade that the British have been trying to put into effect since the fall of Pondicherry.

Thermidorian journalists' panel is set up

Paris, October

The press is again free, at least on a *de facto* basis. Fréron has taken advantage of this fact to bring *The People's Orator* out again. It was once a substitute for Marat's *The People's Friend* and is now definitely anti-Jacobin. This former Terror agent in Southern France turned against Robespierre, and actively contributed to his fall. Fréron claims to be one of the main defenders of the press. He says that if it had not been gagged, it would have "exposed all of Robespierre's crimes and thus done away with tyranny". Faced with a lack of concrete measures on behalf of full press freedom, he has decided to establish a committee consisting of anti-Montagnard journalists to co-ordinate their activity.

Fréron claims to be a Marat pupil.

Convention

1 *(Brumaire 11, Year III)*
Paris. The Convention decides to suspend the order for the sequestration of all property belonging to so-called suspects.

3 *(Brumaire 13, Year III)*
Paris. After the intervention of the new American Minister James Monroe, Thomas Paine is freed.

3 *(Brumaire 13, Year III)*
Metz. Despite the Convention's having decreed on November 1st. that abuses of the local Jews should stop immediately and equality of rights should be strictly observed, the Metz Synagogue is converted into a livestock pen.

4 *(Brumaire 14, Year III)*
Poland. Suvorov seizes the Warsaw suburbs, forcing the city's capitulation two days later.

4 *(Brumaire 14, Year III)*
Germany. Kléber expels the Austrian forces from Maastricht.

7 *(Brumaire 17, Year III)*
Morbihan. A departmental order calls for a payment of 500 livres to anybody turning a non-juring priest over to the authorities.

7 *(Brumaire 17, Year III)*
Paris. In a brochure, the deputy Roederer asks the Convention to re-admit 73 Girondists who had been barred from the Assembly on June 2nd. (→Dec. 8, 94).

8 *(Brumaire 18, Year III)*
United Provinces. General Souham reaches the Rhine and captures Nijmegen.

9 *(Brumaire 19, Year III)*
Paris. The Committee of Public Safety entrusts Hoche with the command of the forces on the Cherbourg and the Brest coasts.→

9 *(Brumaire 19, Year III)*
Paris. Muscadins attack the Jacobins Club, stoning the men and whipping the women (→12).

12 *(Brumaire 22, Year III)*
Paris. The chemist Nicolas Jacques Conté sets up a factory for making carbide pencils in the Rue de l'Université.

12 *(Brumaire 22, Year III)*
Paris. After another raid by the gilded youth on the Jacobins Club, the Convention suspends club meetings (→13).

14 *(Brumaire 24, Year III)*
Paris. Barère tells the Convention that he opposes any compromise with the Coalition, and attacks advocates of a "make-shift peace".

Inventory made of Lavoisier laboratory

Lavoisier spent the major part of his time working in his laboratory.

Paris, November 1

Six months ago, Antoine Lavoisier was led to the scaffold after a mere semblance of a trial. And today Nicolas Leblanc, who has followed the chemist as manager of the Arsenal Laboratory on Madeleine Boulevard, started making an inventory of his predecessor's chemical equipment. He has already counted 6,000 pieces of glassware and pottery, including beakers, crucibles, balloon flasks, funnels and jars. He has also listed 70 litres of mercury, 60 litres of red oxide, and all sorts of chemical products, such as salts, sulphides and compounds of antimony, arsenic and phosphorus, as well as a number of precision instruments making this laboratory a European curiosity. There is a copper pump for creating a vacuum under a bell, thermometers and barometers, and a dozen precision scales. During the inventory, Mme Lavoisier preferred to stay in the Jura region with friends and relatives.

Officers are being thoroughly purged

Paris, November 2

Army cadres are going to be purged. At the order of the Committee of Public Safety, the chiefs of staff and the inspectors-general of depôts are being given the task of making sure everybody stays in line. The point is to exclude dangerous "anarchists" whose high rank makes them an even bigger threat. So the consequences of Robespierre's fall are also being felt in the military, as the exclusions are being accompanied by a reinstatement of officers previously fired for being lukewarm revolutionaries.

Fersen is lionised in Swedish capital

Stockholm, November

A queen's love gives a man a wonderful aura. After returning to his own country, Fersen has become very popular, the hero of the day. When he enters the Opera, all the lorgnettes in the pit and the boxes take aim at him. All the women make eyes at him, and the mothers of marriageable daughters cajole him. But the handsome Axel remains unmoved by such demonstrations. His heart broke with Marie Antoinette's death.

People dancing everywhere, but not all the balls are innocent

Paris, November

Heads are no longer rolling — now they are turning. In wooden shoes or ankle-boots, Parisians are learning the waltz, the new dance from Germany. There is a ball on every street-corner, in the 650 places where people can amuse themselves until morning. People dance at the Carmelites' establishment, where the guillotine blade was the centre of attention not too long ago. One can even hear some frantic *farandoles* from behind the walls of the Carmelite convent. On the right bank, the crowds throng to the Tivoli ball and the Elysée National, which is very popular because of Black Julien's band. On the left bank, the music grates more on the nerves. At Saint Sulpice Cemetery, there is a death's head announcing the Zephyrs' Ball, at which couples waltz on tombs. But the most popular one is the "Victims' Ball", held at home. The only people allowed in are those who have lost a relative on the scaffold.

Men come with the back of the neck shaved and a red thread around the neck. They greet their partner with a motion of a freshly cut-off head.

Two steps forward and one to the side — people also dance to forget.

Jacobins Club closed due to violence

Hoche reorganises Army of the West

Paris, November 9

Promotions also have their bad side. Hoche quickly became aware of this fact when he was given command of the forces on the Brest and Cherbourg coasts. The minister had already taken away the best parts of these two forces to assign them to General Canclaux's army. As a result, the units are disorganised. So Hoche has chosen to use existing abilities as effectively as possible and listen to the helpful indications of the soldiers who have had close contact with the Chouans. The commander knows that success demands appeasement and talks with insurgents (→ Dec. 2).

Lazare Hoche at the age of 26.

Mac Nab is lucky to be alive

Sancerre, November 9

Mac Nab, a native of Berry, is alive and free. But it took a lot of luck. This former royal bodyguard was arrested along with five others in May 1794 for having made uncivic remarks, but he was the only one among them not to have been guillotined. Fouquier Tinville, contrary to his custom, was not satisfied with the evidence and requested more details. The Cher court's evasive answers forced the prosecutor to make another request for more information on the detainee. But, with the help of slow mail, Thermidor arrived before Mac Nab was put in the dock. So now he is again a citizen, and his property has been restored into the bargain.

Paris, November 13

The Jacobins have been dispersed by the Muscadins' clubs. The latter, shouting "Long live the Convention!" and "Down with the Jacobins!", had gathered yesterday evening at the Palais Royal before moving on to the Rue Honoré. The club members were literally besieged and unable to hold out for long. They had blocked the doors, but the young reactionaries simply went in through the windows and sacked the premises. They struck the men and caught and raped the women trying to flee. When the Committee of General Security learnt about the goings on around 1 a.m., it ordered the association to be closed "because of the violence caused by its existence". Actually, it had arranged the operation itself. Or at least it had given the Muscadins their heads. This demonstration offered an ideal pretext. Of course, only a few hundred Jacobins remained, disavowing their support for Robespierre and losing themselves in self-criticism. But a few of them persisted in their beliefs and called for a return

The Jacobin Dominican monastery, which gave its name to the famous club.

to the Reign of Terror. Even the small amount of influence they had was enough to bring about the closure of the club.

Sunday still a sacred day to Auvergnats

Puy de Dôme, November 14

Sunday will not be re-established. Representative on mission Musset issued a formal denial of rumours to the effect that the old calendar will be put back into effect. During his purge tour, he called for severe treatment of people who observe the former holidays and prefer to rest on Sunday, rather than on *décadi*. He called vigourously for obedience to the Republic. But people arond here are not going to be told what to do, and are more determined than ever to fill the taverns on Sunday.

New threat is seen of food shortages

France, November

The 1794 harvests were poor, and people everywhere fear there will not be enough this year to feed the country. The yields are low in Brie as in Beauce, and in the whole Parisian Basin, the areas that are usually a veritable national granary. The harvest will be used to feed the cities, especially Paris, where agitation is feared. The war-devastated North will probably be short. In the fertile Caen plain, the crops are a third below the 1793 level. At Avranches and in the Auxerre region, starving people have already eaten the grain earmarked for the next sowing. The harsh weather does not explain everything. Mass conscription has meant that the fields were short of labour, and military requisition of cattle has also disorganised production. Furthermore, at least a third of the cropland is fallow. Finally, certain farmers, furious at the seizure of their crops, prefer to hide their grain in an attempt to get enough to survive themselves. Others are waiting for prices to start going up. It is certainly going to be a rough winter for the poor.

Habit becomes second nature, and Sunday remains a holiday.

Convention

15 (*Brumaire 25, Year III*) Paris. To prevent a closer relationship between the United States and England, the Committee of Public Safety decides on official abolition of the Navigation Act, thus freeing the sea trade of countries that are neutral towards France (→19).

18 (*Brumaire 28, Year III*) Paris. The Commune orders the suppression of the Board of Directors of the Paris Workshops, dominated by the Jacobins. The authorities fear there may be agitation in the workshops.

19 (*Brumaire 29, Year III*) London. In spite of the existence of the Franco-American Treaty of Alliance of 1778, the United States signs a trade treaty with England aimed at France.→

20 (*Brumaire 30, Year III*) Spain. The Spanish troops are routed after four days of fighting at Black Mountain, during which General Dugommier is killed (→28).

22 (*Frimaire 2, Year II*) Paris. The Convention approves a decree barring payment of pensions to priests who have given up their religious duties.

22 (*Frimaire 2, Year III*) Basel. Arrival of Baron von Hardenberg, sent by the King of Prussia to negotiate a separate peace with France.

23 (*Frimaire 3, Year III*) Paris. The Convention indicts Carrier, with all deputies but two voting in favour.

25 (*Frimaire 5, Year III*) Paris. Mirabeau's body is removed from the Pantheon and thrown into a potter's field.→

26 (*Frimaire 6, Year III*) Paris. Alexandre Lenoir, founder of the Museum of French Monuments, is given the title of Curator of Monuments.

26 (*Frimaire 6, Year III*) Paris. The Convention decides to decontrol all imports not coming from England (→Jan. 2, 95).

27 (*Frimaire 7, Year III*) Paris. Speaking to the Convention, Fourcroy urges the establishment of a central health school (→Dec. 4, 94).

28 (*Frimaire 8, Year III*) Spain. The forces of General Perignon, successor to Dugommier, capture Figueras, in Catalonia.

Paris sectors are in the moderates' hands

Paris, November 30

What remains of the sansculottists? At the Tuileries, Robespierre's sector, known as the "Piques", has just fallen into the moderates' hands. The young reactionary Jullian has been elected its president. Only the Quinze-Vingts and the Gravilliers sectors are holding out and are still dominated by the sansculottists. Others, such as the Temple, are hesitating between being faithful to past beliefs and joining royalist reaction. Since the Jacobins Club was closed, the patriotic bastions have lost their firmest foundation, and everything possible has been done to destroy them. Thus special legal committees have been set up in 37 of the 48 Paris sectors to judge the militants. Nearly 200 of them have been troubled in this way and held up to "public contempt". Furthermore,

Caricature of a sansculottist.

the Convention has asked them to account for themselves. There are forced borrowings and special subscriptions — anything will do as long as it helps ruin the sectors. Neutralised now, they no longer endanger the power structure.

Is French foreign trade under threat?

London, November 19

John Jay, an American lawyer and politician, has just signed a treaty with the British government in his country's name that settles the dispute that has divided the two countries since the American War of Independence came to an end. The conclusion of this alliance has stupefied France. The reason is that the treaty not only calls for the installation of an arbitration commission for settling pending problems between the two nations, but also includes a trade treaty that recognises the British fleet's control of the seas. That fleet will now be entitled to inspect any vessel in areas near American ports, and seize any "war contraband" it may find on them, in exchange for opening the Canadian border and the Antilles to American merchants. Such a rapprochement between its worst enemy and one of its main trade partners is a bad blow to France. The United States has been neutral so far in the war, and has also been one of the few nations whose ships still called at the French ports of Nantes and Bordeaux (→Nov. 26).

General Dugommier was killed on November 17th. in an engagement at Saint Laurent de la Mouga in which his troops defeated the Spaniards.

Volney is back on French public stage

Paris, November 28

A year ago, Volney was thrown in jail. These days, people vie in getting his cooperation. Such are the twists of destiny. Volney has just been appointed to the Executive Committee for Foreign Affairs. He is an expert on the Orient, and is being put in charge of correspondence with the countries of the Ottoman Empire. He is also being asked to re-organise the interpreters' department. Even if he basically owes this position to his knowledge of Oriental languages, the influence of people in the news also has something to do with it. Garat and Lakanal, who are members of the Public Education Committee, intervened on his behalf. He is also going to teach history at the Ecole Normale (→March 4, 95).

Philosopher and historian Volney.

The wretched life of women soldiers

Paris, November 16

The presence of women in the military services has been criticised for months, and these fighters are in a precarious position. The example of Madeleine Petit Jean bears witness to all this. She left Paris in March 1793 at the age of 48 to join her husband, who was a sapper with the 4th Sorbonne Gunners' Company and was involved in fighting the Vendée "brigands". Madeleine was wounded and lives on the modest pension of 636 livres that the Republic grants to those who served bravely (→Dec. 21).

Reforming schools is order of the day

Paris, November 17

The deputies have agreed that they failed. Due to lack of application, the Bouquier Law has remained inoperative. Hence at the suggestion of the deputy Lakanal, they adopted today a group of markedly more realistic decrees on education. There is no attendance requirement this time, but schooling remains free. There is to be one primary school per 1,000 inhabitants, making about 150 pupils per establishment. As for the teachers, they will be housed and paid by the State, 1,200 livres a month, and they will have to use the books prescribed by the Republic.

Assignats rejected in other countries

France, November 26

Assignats have depreciated to such a point that they are no longer accepted abroad. Genoa merchants demanded species (metal money), and the Vaucluse Department's envoy had to pay for the grain he had just bought with silver. To come up with the required amount, the Avignon municipality was forced to call on public generosity. In the ports of Le Havre and Nantes, traders are rejecting the banknotes. Even worse is the fact that in the border areas, everybody demands to receive payment in cold hard cash, meaning in this case in foreign coins.

No confidence means no value.

Is the Republic heading for a new wave of de-Christianisation?

A counter-revolutionary allegory denouncing the Revolution's anti-religious activities and exalting the intervention of Austria and the Pope's armies, which are parading under the gaze of Abundance, Reason and Peace. In the background, under the Concorde arch, angels celebrate the triumph of Religion and Papacy.

Paris, November 20

Besson and Pelletier, who have been sent on a mission to Besançon, think de-Christianisation is still the order of the day. They have just issued an order calling for the arrest of priests who continue to carry out their religious duties, and closing all of the department's places of worship. They are not the only ones to act along these lines. In several departments, representatives have recently taken comparable steps. In the Morbihan, for instance, an order of November 5th. promised a reward of 500 livres to anybody who would turn in a non-juring priest. In Toulouse, it was decided on October 5th. that all ecclesiastics, even those who have been "depriestified", will be concentrated in the district capital, unless they are married. Are these measures the harbinger of a resumption of the de-Christianisation policy, or are they actually a sign of its death struggle? (→ Dec. 21)

Paralysis threatens France's arsenals

Paris, November 24

Tension is rising in the Republic's arms plants. Wages are too low, working conditions are too harsh, and there are far too many idlers. The lazy youngsters that replace the sansculottists are incompetent and anti-Jacobin. They have arranged to be requisitioned to escape military service. The Marat factory, revolted by all these injustices, has just sent a petition to the Assembly demanding enforcement of the conscription law and wage increases. After a stormy discussion, the Committee of Public Safety managed to get its viewpoint across. The arsenals will be transferred to private businessmen who will have full hiring freedom. On its part, the State will guarantee that workers, even young ones, will be exempt from military service. But before all that, all employees of the government-owned arsenals will be fired within six weeks to leave new management free to employ new staff (→ Dec. 12).

Carrier to be tried

Paris, November 23

Many people were amazed that the "Thermidorian terrorist" was still at large, even though the trial of the Nantes Revolutionary Committee was underway. The former envoy from Paris to western France, Carrier, has finally been impeached after pleading his case for three days. His claim that by attacking him the Convention was shooting itself in the foot did not cut much ice with his colleagues, who want to forget the past (→ Dec. 16).

Convention

1 *(Frimaire 11, Year III)*
Paris. Closing of the Salpêtrière Prison. From now on, the facility will take in no more detainees, but only sick, incurable or insane women.

2 *(Frimaire 12, Year III)*
Paris. Hoche gets the Convention to approve an offer of amnesty for the Chouans. →

4 *(Frimaire 14, Year III)*
Paris. Speaking in the Convention, the War Minister, Carnot, praises wooden shoes as substitutes for the *souliers* that are in such short supply in the Army.

4 *(Frimaire 14, Year III)*
Paris. At Fourcroy's suggestion, the Convention decides to establish health schools in Strasbourg, Paris and Montpellier. →

4 *(Frimaire 14, Year III)*
Paris. Triumphant return to the Favart auditorium of actress Rosalie Dugazon, who had been barred from the stage because of her royalist opinions.

8 *(Frimaire 18, Year III)*
Paris. Without debate, the Convention approves re-admission of the 73 Girondist deputies expelled on June 2nd., 1793. →

10 *(Frimaire 20, Year III)*
Paris. The Girondist deputies re-admitted the previous day denounce Pache and Bouchotte.

11 *(Frimaire 21, Year III)*
Guadeloupe. The archipelago is republican again. Victor Hugues, the representative on mission, is mercilessly repressing the royalists turned over to him by the English when the latter surrendered. Some 865 of them are executed in trenches at Berville camp.

12 *(Frimaire 22, Year III)*
Paris. The arsenal workers demonstrate in front of the Convention.

12 *(Frimaire 22, Year III)*
Paris. A Convention decree bars women definitively from serving with the French armed services.

14 *(Frimaire 24, Year III)*
Paris. Abbot Grégoire submits his fourth report on the subject of vandalism.

15 *(Frimaire 25, Year III)*
London. Release of members of the Corresponding Society, which has Jacobin views. Its leader, Thomas Hardy, had been acquitted on November 6th.

Vendeans receive offer of amnesty

A pike's weight rather than wheat.

Paris, December 2

Amnesty may be granted to "all persons known by the names of Vendée rebels and Chouans" who lay down their arms within one month. The decree adopted by the Convention marks a new stage in the policy of pacifying the west. The step was taken at General Hoche's request. He believes that there can be no exclusively military solution to the conflict. There will be no lasting peace without an amnesty and without some measures aimed at calming people's feelings in connection with the religious issue (→Jan. 3, 95).

A Savoyard suffers homeland troubles

Savoy, December 7

People living in border areas sometimes have trouble in deciding on their camp. This was true of Boch, an inhabitant of Saint Jean de Maurienne. As a Francophile in 1792, he was jailed by the Sardinians. He was freed by the French and became a republican official. With the French withdrawal in 1793, Boch again changed sides. Later, Kellermann's successes compelled him to emigrate, following the Sardinian Army, an episode that resulted in jail again when he returned to his village. But now he is French, and free.

France is sacrificing the Dutch patriots

Paris, December 1

The Convention seems to be following a paradoxical policy. At a time when General Pichegru is getting ready to march on Amsterdam, the deputies have indicated that they do not want to help the Dutch patriots in their struggle for power. And to demonstrate this fact, they received Gerard Brantsen, special envoy of the Dutch Stadtholder William V, with all the respect due to his rank. The envoy has every reason to believe in Paris' good faith. The fact is that the patriots' delegates proved unable to persuade the Assembly not to deal with him. Yet the patriots exiled after the failure of the 1787 struggle against William's despotism have long exhorted the French to intervene, since their backers who have remained in Holland are not numerous enough to give rise to a revolutionary current. On the other hand, they will be able to present the French forces as liberators and make it hard for William to move. However, the deputies refused to listen to this appeal. They heard Tallien plead for peace. This new but already influential member of the Committee of Public Safety wants to "bring France back to its old borders". These words, which will please the Stadtholder, show the Dutch patriots' failure with their French counterparts.

Dutch Stadtholder William V.

One law and three schools for medicine

Paris, December 4

"For five years now, the most difficult of the arts has had no master, and the institutions that kept it safe are closed ..." Those were the terms in which the chemist Fourcroy made his appeal to the deputies. This Academy member believes that it is necessary to establish health schools to save medical education. His appeal has been heard, and there will be one such school in Paris, another in Strasbourg, and a third in Montpellier. Moreover, some health officers will be trained in Saint Servan. As much emphasis will be put on practice as on theory at those establishments. A future doctor must learn above all at the bedside.

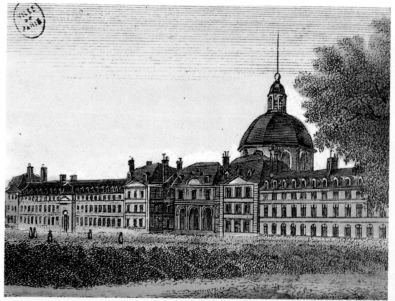

The proposal for medical studies calls for a three-year programme.

The Girondists return to the Convention

Paris, December 8

The moderates' offensive is making headway. The right has just won the re-admission of the 73 protesting Girondists who were expelled from the Assembly on June 2nd., 1793. The Dantonists opposed this decision, and were backed by Tallien, who said that "in a time of revolution, people must not look back". But without debate, the Convention approved the deputies' return. Actually, a total of 78 deputies have been re-admitted. These Girondists are a precious addition to the Thermidorians at a time when the Jacobins and the neo-Hébertists are manifesting themselves. The Montagnards have shown good will, hoping that this concession will sidetrack the threat hanging over Barère and his friends. Hence Merlin de Douai gave the Committees' approval for amnesty. Will the Girondists rejoin the reactionary forces? (→ Dec. 10)

Chouans chalk up propaganda coup

Côtes du Nord, December 15

Boishardy, the leader of the Chouan revolt in the Dinan area, has pulled off a spectacular demonstration of strength. Leading 500 men, he occupied the little town of Jugon without firing a shot. The operation was carefully prepared. During the night, the attackers silently converged on Jugon by way of sideroads. They achieved total surprise, and in the morning, they were able to invest the town without difficulty. To Boishardy, the occupation of Jugon was a propaganda operation above all. He issued safe-conduct passes dated "Year II of Louis XVII's reign" and chopped down the tree of liberty. The point was to prove that the Chouans do indeed control the countryside, and to demonstrate that they do not deserve their sinister reputation. Thus Boishardy had given orders to avoid bloodshed. He went even further, allowing the departure of a food convoy for the Blues: "I do not want any cattle that are intended for those poor republicans who are starving to death," he commented.

The Sacred Heart of Jesus with the Chouan motto "God and King".

Grégoire denounces "floating prisons"

Paris, December 8

Speaking to the Assembly, Abbot Grégoire requested humanitarian measures on behalf of the priests being held in Rochefort. They have been condemned to deportation to Guyana or Africa, and have been shut up in ships that have never sailed because of the danger of such a voyage. The English, after all, control the seas. The crowding of the detainees aboard these floating prisons has led to a very high death rate: out of a total of about 830 priests who were taken to Rochefort, two-thirds have perished (→ May 2, 95).

Workers up in arms over layoffs

Paris, December 12

There were about 15,000 workers marching from the Saint Antoine suburb to the Convention. They were demonstrating, very quietly, against the privatisation of the arsenals and the dismissal of their entire work forces, decided three weeks ago. This step is going to hit 45,000 sansculottists just as winter is coming on. The crowd was so determined that the authorities feared a major uprising. Despite this, the Committee of Public Safety has refused go back on this law, and has decided to be severe, arresting a dozen ringleaders.

"Wonderful women" reign over capital

A style in which classical aspects are set off by a hint of Anglophilia.

Paris, December

These women challenge winter, fashion and morality. They are the ladies known as the "Wonderful Women" in Greek-style scanty attire, with a fan in the belt and a purse in the bosom, followed by young men known as "handkerchief-bearers" who swoon at the sight of their blond wigs. They often leave little to the imagination with respect to their bodies in sheer gauze sheathing, on the grounds that such classical costumes allow any audacity. These ladies attend subscription parties at Wenzell's, where an Altar of Love decorates the rotunda. The essential thing for them is to display "insolent luxury amidst public wretchedness".

Testimony to excesses of Reign of Terror

Paris, December 15

Reporting on the injustices committed during the Reign of Terror often amounts to having Convention decrees revoked. Thus Goupilleau, representative on mission in the Vaucluse, won approval for a delegation of inhabitants of the village of Bédoin to appear at the Assembly to testify to their misfortunes. They recalled the way their town, accused of hiding counter-revolutionaries, was levelled in June at the order of the revolutionary Tribunal, having suffered a wide-ranging purge ordered by Maignet, the zealous representative. Sixty-three villagers were executed, and the others were forbidden ever to return to the village, which in any case was only smoking ruins. Goupilleau felt pity for these people, stricken with a punishment far exceeding the seriousness of their offence. The Convention ratified Maignet's sentences before.

Will it now agree to rehabilitate these unfortunate citizens in the near future?

A young woman saving her family during the fire in Bédoin.

Old people honoured at Angers festivities

Serene in the evening of a full life, the aged patriot typifies experience.

Angers, December 20

The city authorities made a point of following the instructions from the capital: the old people were the heroes of the festivities all day. After married couples and children, they are also entitled to the fatherland's gratitude. There were about 30 of them, men and women, dressed in Roman-style white tunics on Liberty Square, around the tree of the same name. The participants sang songs and put on some entertainment, while the Mayor gave a speech in honour of noble age, experience, and the older people's prestige. Helped by their wisdom, they can instruct future generations to ensure a proper respect for republican virtues.

Controversy erupts on religious freedom

Paris, December 21

"Freedom of religion exists in Turkey, but it does not exist at all in France." The constitutional bishop of Loir et Cher, Grégoire, caused a great hubbub by asking the Assembly to re-establish freedom of worship. The deputy Legendre took it upon himself to respond: "I thought we were sufficiently advanced in revolution that we no longer need to concern ourselves with religion." He then had no difficulty in getting the Convention to reject Grégoire's "dangerous proposal". But all the same, the issue of religious freedom has not finished haunting the debates. The present situation is particularly confused, and the Convention seems hesitant as to the kind of religious policy to follow. Depending on the administrators' personalities and the local balance of forces, there is a range of policies from *de facto* tolerance to the greatest severity. The non-juring priests, many of whom have continued clandestine worship, even during the Reign of Terror, are still subject to the death penalty. Grégoire has started to reorganise the constitutional Church, despite de-Christianisation steps (→ Sept. 29, 95).

Prices decontrolled

Paris, December 24

In accordance with Lindet's recommendations, the Convention has just abolished the "Maximum" price control law. Such a step marks a radical break with the controlled economy instituted during the Reign of Terror. From now on, prices will no longer be set by the administration, but will be determined freely by the interplay of market forces, as has actually been the case since Thermidor. The fact is that, due to lack of sanctions, this law was no longer applied. The farmers, sure of their impunity, have refused to deliver the grain needed for feeding the population in various districts, but they have sold it at very high prices to individuals. The same applied to eggs, butter, meat and vegetables. These articles had disappeared from the shops, and only the fast-growing black market offered a chance to get such things, at prohibitive prices. The people demanded a different economic policy, denouncing speculators who were getting rich. Businessmen also got into the act. Showing the misdeeds of state control, they convinced the deputies that price freedom is a must for any economic recovery.

The Magi creeping back into country

Paris, December 24

The Mayor of Paris cannot get over his anger. And he is not the only one to wax indignant over the behaviour of certain pastry-makers. To attract customers, these worthies have found nothing better than putting Twelfth Night cakes in plain view on their shop counters. On the grounds that Epiphany (Twelfth Night) is approaching, they have gone so far as to beard the police officers and the revolutionary committee members dispatched to the various districts to investigate this behaviour. They dare to celebrate the former kings, stick those painted beans worthy of another age into their dough, and encourage the people to lapse back into superstition. Municipal officers, scenting danger, have decided to take steps against these bad citizens: anybody caught buying or selling such "libertine" delicacies will be rebuked and watched.

Barère and friends to be investigated

Paris, December 27

The Thermidorian Jacobins have been caught in a trap. For several months now, Féraud, Lanjuinais and Tallien have been denouncing the former members of the Committee of Public Safety, demanding their arrest. But the Convention is hesitant: it fears making an open attack on men who are still very popular. It is afraid of having to cope with a popular uprising if it indicts them. Yet the deputies could not continue to ignore the multiple pressures emanating from the vengeance-crazed Muscadins. Hence they have just adopted a compromise solution by setting up a committee to "examine the cases of Barère, Billaud Varenne, Collot d'Herbois and Vadier". This procedure may make it possible to bury this affair until people calm down (→March 2, 95).

Tallien and Cabarrus married by mayor

The beautiful and clever Thérésa.

Paris, December 26

Jean Lambert Tallien, 27, has married Thérésa Cabarrus, 21, the divorced wife of Jean Jacques Devin de Fontenay. Hence the child she conceived shortly after Thermidor, which will be born next May, will be legitimate. But gratitude is the only reason Thérésa agreed to marry the man who saved her from Robespierre's jails, the man whom his enemies accuse of being a "terrorist". She asked M. Gittard, the lawyer, to make a separate property agreement, of which every jot and tittle was checked, because she is rich and Tallien has nothing. Such precautions might prove useful ...

David gets his wife and freedom back

Paris, December 26

The famous painter had nothing with which to reproach himself. So he was not worried as he organised his life in the Luxembourg jail, where he was allowed to install a small studio so as to be able to continue his art-work. His pupil, Delafontaine, even called on him regularly. His imprisonment even brought his wife back to him. They had separated after the King's death, as David's wife disapproved of the painter's being a regicide. But after separating them, politics has now finally brought them back together. And Mme. David did not spare her efforts in trying to get her husband out of jail. She got petitions from the master's students, and was able to interest Boissy d'Anglas in the fate of Louis. In the Assembly, Marie Joseph Chénier cried: "Return David to the arts, to painting and to public education, which wants him. Do not let his talents decay." The authorities finally decided to grant him a conditional release, pending trial. The man who had blamed his lengthy detention on bitter academic grudges and complained that "genius is hemmed in on all sides" is now again out in the world, happily breathing the free air (→Aug. 4, 95).

In prison, David had enough free time to make a portrait of his jailer.

Roving wolves are at gates of Toulouse

The winter is so cold this year that Parisians can even skate at Gentilly.

France, December

The early winter has become a terrible winter. People are digging in at home, and the herds are remaining safely in the shelter of the stables. The wind is coming from the north, and the water has changed to ice. There are no more rivers called Rhine, Meuse, Oise, Seine or Garonne, but only icy expanses where they used to be. In the Vivarais the Loire River carries along chunks of ice, people walk on the Canal du Midi and cross solidified swamps. Trees are dying by hundreds, and the vines as well, even in the South. All of the olive trees have been lost in the Montpellier region. People in Bordeaux are prisoners of the frost, and the charcoal shortage is already making itself felt. Toward Annecy, the snow is so thick that all of the roads are impassable, and inhabitants isolated. For France as a whole, the average temperature ranges between minus ten and minus 15 degrees. In Paris and Rouen, the temperature was below minus 20. Wolves have even been seen roving near Toulouse.

David pupil prefers discretion to valour

Paris, December 30

Just as David is getting out of prison, the Committee of General Security has issued an arrest warrant for his student, Topino Lebrun. As an irony of history, the latter constantly called for the release of his master, who was jailed because of his contacts with Robespierre. Even though Topino Lebrun had been a juror of the Revolutionary tribunal since November 1793, he had not been bothered after Thermidor 9. He had been considered one of the "weak" who did not completely accept Fouquier Tinville's ideas. The painter was involved in the trial of Carrier and of the Nantes Revolutionary Committee. The unfortunate Carrier went to the guillotine, while the committee members were freed. The Thermidorians did not forgive him for this act of semi-clemency and, if he had not gone into hiding, he would now be behind bars ...

La Harpe discusses horrors of the past

Paris, December 31

New converts are the most enthusiastic, and La Harpe is no exception to this rule. He was freed on August 1st., but has not forgotten his prison lessons, and is methodically going about burning what he used to adore. His talk marking his return to the Lycée was very instructive in this connection. He had decided to deal with the stylistic differences between classic writers and the revolutionary language. But these philological reflections were actually only an occasion for some long digressions on the "horrors of the past" and Robespierre's misdeeds. He denounced abuses of words and the "distorted" and excessive nature of the language of "fanaticism". As a sign of the times, his virulent remarks against the Reign of Terror and the "tyrant" brought substantial applause from the audience, even from the former Jacobins.

January 1795

from 1st. to 31st.

 Convention

1 *(Nivôse 12, Year III)*
Rouen. The People's Society is forced to close down after its offices are sacked by a group of wealthy local youths.

2 *(Nivôse 13, Year III)*
Paris. The Convention decides that foreign trade should be totally unrestricted.

10 *(Nivôse 21, Year III)*
Paris. The Convention decrees that January 21st., the "day of the righteous punishment of the last King of the French", is to be a national holiday.

14 *(Nivôse 25, Year III)*
Vannes. In a bid to calm the situation, the representatives Guezno and Guermeur issue a ruling condemning past violence and allowing Catholicism to be practised again in the Morbihan.

19 *(Nivôse 30, Year III)*
Paris. The tenor and composer Pierre Gavaux performs *Le Réveil du Peuple* before the members of the William Tell sector for the first time. The song is to become the anthem of the Muscadins (→24).

19 *(Nivôse 30, Year III)*
United Provinces. General Pichegru marches into Amsterdam.→

22 *(Pluviôse 3, Year III)*
Paris. Death of the organist and composer Michel Corrette. He leaves behind many arrangements for ancient Christmas songs and concertos and several texts teaching how to play various instruments.

23 *(Pluviôse 4, Year III)*
United Provinces. At Helder, General Pichegru's cavalry captures the Dutch fleet, which is blocked by ice.→

25 *(Pluviôse 6, Year III)*
Paris. The capital has its 42nd. consecutive day of frost. The temperature has reached a low of minus 25.5 degrees Celsius.

25 *(Pluviôse 6, Year III)*
Paris. At the Favart auditorium, the singer Antoine Trial, a friend of Robespierre, is forced to read out a poem attacking the "drinkers of human blood" (→ Feb. 5, 95).

30 *(Pluviôse 11, Year III)*
Paris. To mark the conquest of the United Provinces, Kreutzer performs a hymn, *La Hollande Conquise*, at the Théâtre des Arts.

31 *(Pluviôse 12, Year III)*
Rennes. Violent riots sparked off by the lack of food, which broke out on January 30th., force Hoche to call the army in.

A cease-fire is signed in Vendée

Brittany, January 3

Royalists and republicans have agreed to suspend hostilities. A certain Dezoteux, who likes to be called the Baron de Cormatin, negotiated the agreement with General Humbert and the representative Bollet. Dezoteux, an intriguing and controversial figure, claimed he was the Comte de Puisaye's major general. Puisaye is the main royalist leader north of the Loire river. He eloquently described the bravery of his forces and boasted of being able to get all the Chouan leaders to put down their weapons. But he is far from certain of being able to get all the Chouans to follow his lead. In fact, the rebel troops are hardly in a good position: the peasants are weary of the civil war and are finding Hoche's conciliatory policies increasingly attractive.

Frozen potatoes to help feed the hungry

A meat rationing card: just half a pound allowed every five days.

Paris, January 13

In order to combat the famine that is threatening the poor, the Committee of Public Safety has been searching for a cheap and available source of food. It has just published a timely booklet on the "Uses of the Frozen Potato" written by a group of concerned agronomists. It is indeed vital that no scrap of food is wasted, as the temperatures have often hit lows of minus ten degrees Celsius over the past few weeks. But many citizens have been getting rid of frozen potatoes because housewives consider them to be inedible. Now they will know that even rock-hard potatoes are perfectly edible, once they have been thawed and if they are eaten right away, before they have a chance to harden again. At the village of Bar le Duc, the general council found the booklet so interesting that it was read out in public at the temple of Reason for three weeks running. A large number of towns in eastern France have followed that example. Such advice is proving extremely useful during the icy-cold winter months.

"La Vedette" paper ceases publication

Besançon, January 12

La Vedette had been losing a growing number of readers. Today the paper's editors, Briot and Dormoy, announced that the last edition had been printed. The best selling newspaper in the city nowadays is *Le 9 Thermidor*. The day after Robespierre's downfall, *La Vedette* had congratulated itself. It boasted of having forseen the dictatorship of Robespierre two years before the event and of having written a few months before Thermidor: "The aristocrats, priests, fanatics and devout people have found in him an open protector and defender." Despite this, the purged departmental administration cut off the Jacobin paper's subsidies, thus sentencing it to death. The editors then changed tactics. Briot and Dormoy have claimed that they only defended the Terror in principle, while condemning all the violence and not resorting to personal attacks. However, nobody was really convinced by that. The two editors have decided to get out of town. Briot has set off for Paris to see if he can convince officials not to conscript him.

Boulogne Park must be saved!

Paris, January 14

If Parisians continue to cut down trees in the Bois de Boulogne to get their supplies of firewood, there will soon be nothing left of the capital's park. Therefore, a group of artists such as Fragonard, Vernet and Hubert Robert have signed a petition calling for the section of the park that runs by Auteuil to be preserved. Its trees and bushes are exceptionally lovely and continue to inspire a great many amateur landscape artists and nature lovers.

Posthumous poem by Chénier a hit

Paris, January 9

André Chénier's fondest dream has just been fulfilled. Six months after his death, one of his *Odes* has just been published for the first time. It is *La Jeune Captive*, a poem inspired by the beautiful Aimée de Coigny, who was held at Saint Lazare jail at the same time as he was. Its refined tone, so out of favour during the Jacobin Convention, has been warmly welcomed by the men of Thermidor. The poem was published today by Guiguené in his *Décade Philosophique*.

Pichegru's army has crossed the Meuse and the frozen Rhine tributaries.

French troops march into Amsterdam

Secret service held near Béthune

Pas de Calais, January 11

Once again a "travelling priest" has come to the village of Vendin lès Béthune. That is what people are calling the non-juring priests who have been travelling through the provinces to celebrate Mass and administer the sacraments. Their number has grown considerably since Thermidor. They stay at each place barely long enough to say Mass, thus avoiding trouble with the local authorities. By the time the local revolutionary committee finds out about them, they are already long gone. One of these churchmen, who arrived at night, held a secret service at one o'clock in the morning at the home of an elderly lady, Célestine Loison. He then went to visit several bedridden people before resting for a few hours and setting off again. Alerted, the authorities launched a search operation and arrested three people, but they were unable to discover the identity and destination of the ghostly clergyman. The Convention has decided to put a stop to this growing problem. A decree has just been approved ordering public prosecutors strictly to enforce the laws on deported priests who are back in France.

The French conquest of Holland by General Pichegru's troops was helped by the uprisings of Batavian patriots.

Amsterdam, January 19

A short and victorious winter campaign is drawing to a close. The French forces led by Pichegru have arrived in Amsterdam. The Stadtholder, William V, has fled and the republicans were greeted as liberators by the Batavian patriots. French troops crossed the Meuse, Waal and Lek rivers by walking across their frozen waters. Holland's natural borders did not provide much protection. It was easy prey for the French. Since the autumn, patriots had plotted several uprisings. In Amsterdam the Jacobin clubs and reading societies, which have more than 3,000 members, had issued calls for civil and military disobedience. On January 4th. they decided to set up a revolutionary committee grouping ten members. If necessary it could take power. The patriots had already, at the urging of Schimmelpenninck, taken over councils in large cities such as Utrecht and The Hague.

The punishment must fit the crime

Paris, January

Louis Lavicomterie, a deputy at the Convention and former member of the Committee of Public Safety, knows what wrongdoing and morality mean. He feels that few men are frightened enough by the prospect of divine retribution to stop committing crimes. Therefore, he has asked his colleagues to revamp morality and the concept of punishment after death along more down to earth lines. To replace the circles of Hell, he wants a committee of wise men to draw up a new scale of crimes and punishments. Thus, for the first time, a criminal would, according to his crime, face a sentence ranging from a simple fine to capital punishment. This marks the birth of a penal code. But the plan got a cool reception from deputies, who dropped the proposed "calculated morality".

General Pichegru's cavalry captures the ice-bound Dutch fleet

Texel, January 23

The French hussars didn't even have to get their feet wet. All they had to do was to walk across the frozen sea and attack the unsuspecting and ice-bound Dutch fleet. It was a highly daring operation. On January 18th. the French contingent led by Lieutenant Colonel Lahure — three infantry battalions and a unit of the 8th. Hussar regiment — headed towards Helder and Haarlem. There, the Dutch fleet was caught unawares while blocked by the ice from the Texel. Lahure ordered his sharpshooters to ride along with the cavalrymen. Before dawn, he advanced with his troops over the frozen sea. Not one hoofbeat or sabre-rattle could be heard. The silent advance meant that the attack came as a complete surprise. Despite being heavily outnumbered by the Dutch, the French operation was a total success. The entire Dutch fleet was seized without any loss of life. The Dutch admiral and all his crews were captured. Moreover, 14 ships of the line, with their 850 cannons, as well as a number of merchant ships, were taken by the French. All this military equipment will certainly be of use to the Republic's forces.

The French cavalry's unusual charge against the Dutch warships.

Icy cold continues and firewood is low

Paris, January 15

Is is getting harder and harder to keep warm. For the past several weeks, temperatures have remained at around minus ten degrees Celsius. Stocks of firewood have already gone up in smoke. People looking for wood stripped the Boulogne Park and are now scavenging in the Bois de Vincennes. Large logs cost six times more than usual this winter. Wood vendors have sold all they had. Parisians are buying bags of wood shavings on the black market, but these burn too fast. Men fight over twigs, as was the case this morning on the Rue de Bourgogne.

This winter's fashions did their best to cope with the icy weather.

French captives flee from English jail

United Provinces, January 22

The prison guards didn't see or hear anything. The garrison's soldiers were unable to do anything and the inhabitants of Hellevoet Sluis are still stunned. A total of 600 French prisoners who had been captured by the English have managed to break out of jail. They crossed the town and ran to the city walls, where they seized the gates and flung them wide open for the arrival of General Bonneau's conquering troops. The daring prisoners had even been told of the arrival of French forces by the fort's commander himself.

Boissy d'Anglas calls for the Paris stock exchange to reopen

Until now, speculators were able to exchange "gold for paper and paper for gold" with near-total impunity.

Paris, January 29

The Paris stock exchange, known as the Bourse, must be reopened as part of the new policy of economic liberalisation. Such a move has been called for by the deputy Boissy d'Anglas to fight against the wave of stock rigging that is becoming a growing problem for the authorities. He stressed that even though the abolition of the "Maximum" had freed trade, speculators were far from being honest people. Today crooked financiers are openly trafficking in stocks, the price of property and assignats, whose value can vary considerably according to the market. Clever criminals are taking advantage of the confusion in financial circles. Huge fortunes are being amassed thanks to extremely shady deals. A growing number of businessmen are being ruined. The state must take firm action and entrust the stock market to dealers who are both solvent and controllable (→ Mar. 3).

The early days of the Paris Ecole Normale

Paris, January 22

The Museum's amphitheatre is always chock-full. That is where the 1,400 future professors selected to attend the capital's Ecole Normale gather.

The opening ceremony, presided over by the representatives of the Assembly Lakanal and Deleyre, was held there three days ago. After reading out the decrees on the new establishment's founding, Monge, a professor of descriptive geography, spoke. He was followed by Laplace, who has been placed in charge of mathematics courses, along with Lagrange. Lagrange had discovered some minor errors made by Liebniz and the great Isaac Newton. He told his audience that they were very lucky to be called upon to spread learning that is free from prejudice. Moved by such wonderful prospects, the students sent a letter of thanks to the Convention which had been written by their dean, the elderly navigator Bougainville. But it was today's inaugural lesson by the new professor of morality, Bernardin de Saint Pierre, that got the best reception. His first words, "I have a family and live in the country", were greeted by wild cheering and tears. The author told his class that he would be back at the Ecole Normale in three months' time, after he had fully prepared his lessons.

Bougainville, scholar-navigator.

Provinces are hit by economic woes

Dijon, January 19

Times are very hard in the provinces of France. The municipal sectors of Dijon have just sent a message to the Assembly to complain about the critical situation in their city, which is the chief town of the Côte d'Or department. The problem is being caused by both a sharp down-turn in economic and commercial activity and the heavy burden of the war.

In order to breathe new life into the ailing economy of the former capital of the dukes of Burgundy, the sectors have called for local parliamentary activity to resume, or at least for the reopening of the city's prestigious scientific and literary institutions. These had contributed to Dijon's past wealth. The fact is that the Revolution took place mainly in the capital, where power has concentrated. This has meant that Paris has benefited in many areas, while provincial cities are now feeling the pinch.

Seine river floods and the sea rages

France, January 29

France's feet are wet. The storm which has lashed the country, along with some unexpectedly warmer weather, has caused the Seine river to burst its banks. In Paris itself the water level rose by 2.5 metres. The strong current carried along large blocks of ice, which damaged several bridges and destroyed barges tied up along the banks. The bathing houses along the Seine were also badly hit. The muddy water has taken tons of debris all the way to the English Channel, such was the force of the flooding. The worst storm damage was, however, recorded off the western French port of Brest. Despite the terrible weather, the Convention had ordered part of the French fleet to leave the safety of the harbour and set sail for the Mediterranean. But the fleet was quickly dispersed by the high winds and heavy swell and a number of ships sank with all hands.

Dumouriez tries to clear his name

Hamburg, January

Some acts of treason are not easy to justify, but this has not stopped Dumouriez, ex-general of the Republic, from trying to explain his actions in public. He says that all he did was to work for the good of his country: if he was forced to have dealings with Vienna, it was just because the Austrians were the only ones who were capable of restoring the monarchy in France. According to Dumouriez, the Comte de Provence is still the best hope for a nation lashed by a revolutionary storm. That is the argument that this former general of the forces in the north has focused on in his Memoirs, published with the title of *Campagnes du Général Dumouriez dans la Champagne et la Belgique*. However, it appears unlikely that people will easily forget that it was Dumouriez who handed the Minister of War, Beurnonville, over to the Austrians. The latter has been held in Vienna for two years.

Leperdit, mayor of Rennes in 1794-1795, wearing his red, white and blue sash. People respect him for his moderation and opposition to Carrier.

Louis XVI's death still a political issue

Louis Capet, carrying his own head, is greeted in Hell by Charles IX.

France, January 21

France today joyfully celebrated the second anniversary of the death of Louis XVI. In Paris, however, a concert organised by the Convention was interrupted by angry deputies. They felt that the music was being played far too softly, as if it were meant for a funeral. Could the players have some lingering regrets over the execution of Louis Capet, they wondered. Deeply hurt by such unjust suspicions, the members of the National Institute of Music responded by playing such a noisy military march that the audience was forced to shield its ears. Everywhere else the celebrations were happy affairs, marked by the singing of anti-royalist tunes and patriotic verses. In Strasbourg, the ceremonies came to an end after Ignace Pleyel's majestic *Musique du 10 Août* was played.

Talma sings "The People Awake"

Paris, January 24

The Republic Theatre experienced one of its worst ever flops this evening. *La Bayadère*, by Julie Candeille, who also played the heroine, was being performed. The audience had never forgiven her for having taken part in the celebration of Reason, during which she was carried aloft by sansculottists. At the start of the performance a spectator threw the text of *Le Réveil du Peuple,* or The People Awake, onto the stage, forcing the actor Fusil to read it. Fusil was known for his revolutionary acts in Lyons. But the audience was hostile and the actor could not finish the text. Spectators then clamoured first for Madame Dugazon, then for the director, Talma. This former patriot was thus forced to sing the song, which is the hymn of the royalist Muscadins. Fusil knelt on the stage lighting Talma with a torch. The incident was enough to start a war between theatres (→ Feb. 15).

People's Reveille

(Word are by Souriquière, and set to music by Gaveaux)

Ye men of France, kinsmen dear,
With fear see on Gaul's terrain
Crimes raise the banners here
Of fear and massacres profane.
With shame see a scurvy band
Of brigands and assassins base
Smear the name of our fair land.
Our honour their deeds disgrace.

Why this lethargy? Be brave!
Arise ye people, haste and give
To the evils of Tainaron's cave
These beats who by blood live.
To hell the slaves of crime.
The dogs we'll slay! My horror
Share and rage sublime!
They'll not escape or flee away.

Let these traitors meet their fate,
Cruel butchers steeped in villany,
Who bear in their souls a spate
Of crimes, and love of tyranny.
And in your graves you dead,
Rest easy. Vengeance is at hand.
Your butcher's days have fled;
Our revenge they'll not stand.

Already caught in fear's flood
They dare not flee, the evil pack,
The traces they disgorge of blood
Will reveal their faltering track.
Yea, now we swear on your tomb,
What we must all cherish,
To bring them to bloody doom,
To bring them to bloody doom,
Barbarians, they all shall perish.

Convention

1 *(Pluviôse 13, Year III)*
Paris. Babeuf is forced to suspend publication of *Le Tribun du Peuple* (→7).

2 *(Pluviôse 14, Year III)*
Paris. The financier Gabriel Julien Ouvrard marries Elisabeth Tébaud, the daughter of a wealthy merchant of Nantes whose life Ouvrard saved.

3 *(Pluviôse 14, Year III)*
Lyons. Four sansculottists of the Plâtre sector are attacked by "reactionaries". It is the start of a campaign of personal attacks on the former "terrorists" and their supporters.

5 *(Pluviôse 17, Year III)*
Paris. The actor Antoine Trial, an ardent sansculottist, commits suicide in jail by drinking poison. A few days ago he had been forced to read an anti-Robespierrist text on stage.

7 *(Pluviôse 19, Year III)*
Paris. Babeuf is arrested.→

8 *(Pluviôse 20, Year III)*
Paris. The Convention decides to forbid the honour of resting at the Panthéon for ten years after a person has died. It also rules that the ashes of Marat, Bara, Viala and Dampierre are to be removed from the Panthéon.→

8 *(Pluviôse 20, Year III)*
Paris. The Fontaine de Grenelle sector draws up a list of "terrorists" living in the area. This starts off a wave of actions aimed at neutralising neighbourhood political leaders who were influential before Thermidor 9.

9 *(Pluviôse 21, Year III)*
Corsica. The parliament of the Anglo-Corsican kingdom asks Paoli to be its president.

9 *(Pluviôse 21, Year III)*
Paris. A peace treaty is signed between France and the Great Duchy of Tuscany, which affirms its neutrality.

12 *(Pluviôse 24, Year III)*
Vendée. Talks between the Convention's representatives and the Vendean leaders Charette, Sapinaud and Stofflet begin at La Jaunaye (→17).

14 *(Pluviôse 26, Year III)*
Lyons. Joseph Fernex, a judge of the Revolutionary Committee in prison since Thermidor, is killed and thrown into the Rhône river by a mob of "reactionaries". The attack, carried out in broad daylight, causes much public disquiet (→28).

Marat's ashes must leave the Panthéon

Paris, February 8

Poor Marat has suffered a second death. The Convention has decided to put an end to the "Marat cult" and to have his ashes removed from the Panthéon.

The move follows pressure from the growing number of royalist Muscadins who parade around the streets of Paris destroying any statues of Marat they come across. Since last December, the official honours granted to Marat had been coming under strong criticism. The young Thermidorians wanted to wreck his mausoleum at the Tuileries, throw his ashes into the sewers and put those of Charlotte Corday in their place. The Assembly finally decided to have Marat's remains buried at the Saint Etienne du Mont cemetery. Also to be buried there are the ashes of Dampierre, Viala, Bara and Le Peletier. The deputies now want to forget about such famous men. Outraged, the capital's sectors are making their anger felt.

But they are considerably less powerful than the rich young Muscadins. While people were demonstrating in honour of Marat in the Saint Antoine district, a group of Muscadins were dancing a grim jig on his tomb.

Marat's bust is cast into the sewers.

Spelling reforms are being studied

Grammar professor R. A. Sicard.

Paris, February 13

The spelling of the French language has nearly been subjected to major reforms. For a long time people had said that there would be a "linguistic revolution" similar to the one that was rocking politics. Sicard, a professor of grammar at the Ecole Normale who had worked with deaf-mutes, has just suggested a radical reform of the way in which phonemes are noted. For example, why write "eau" when a word is in fact pronounced "o". But others were not convinced.

The "theatre war" rages on

Paris, February 15

For a month now, most of the capital's theatres have been hit by a wave of unrest. Many establishments have been showing moderate plays to their predominantly anti-Jacobin audiences. Texts hostile to yesterday's sansculottists are being read with growing frequency. The Muscadins, who want the actors of Year II to pay dearly for their actions, are always ready to cheer such texts. Despite this, a play mocking the Muscadins, *Le Concert de la Rue Feydeau ou la Folie du Jour,* is the talk of the town. This comedy, written by René Perrin and Cammaille Saint Aubin, caused a riot at the Ambigu theatre. Well-dressed youths interrupted the performance several times before they were arrested as they left by soldiers. The troops had been ordered to surround the theatre by the Committee of General Security (→ Feb. 27).

Gracchus Babeuf is thrown into prison

Paris, February 7

The people's orator did not remain a free man for long. This time, Babeuf has been accused of having criticised the government in his newspaper. After having welcomed Robespierre's downfall, he expressed support for the Thermidorians. But he soon started to criticise their policies openly. He had written of the need for a truly revolutionary government. A warrant for his arrest was issued last January. Babeuf managed to escape and went on the run, but his wife was picked up and imprisoned. The police were hoping that this would force him to turn himself in to the authorities. Now he has been found and taken to the Orties jail.

General Dominique Pérignon, Dugommier's successor, lays siege to and conquers Rosas, in Catalonia, on February 3rd. "Let everybody prepare, for tomorrow I will be at the grenadiers' feast," he said before attacking.

Convention

16 *(Pluviôse 28, Year III)*
Côtes du Nord. At Erquy, the French army intercepts the correspondence of the leaders of the counter-revolution. The Marquis de Pange, the Comte de Vasselot, the Chevalier de La Rosière and the Baron de Boishaudron are arrested. Only the Comte de Frotté escapes.

17 *(Pluviôse 29, Year III)*
Loire Inférieure. Signing at the manor of La Jaunaye of a peace treaty between the Republic and the rebel leaders Charette and Cormartin. →

17 *(Pluviôse 29, Year III)*
Lyons. The royalist journalist Pelzin issues the first number of Le *Journal de Lyon et du département du Rhône.*

18 *(Pluviôse 30, Year III)*
Paris. A delegation from Arras denounces Joseph Le Bon at the Convention, where he had organised the Terror.

19 *(Ventôse 1, Year III)*
Paris. The revolutionary committees are abolished in towns of less than 5,000 inhabitants.

19 *(Ventôse 1, Year III)*
United Provinces. General Macdonald ends the conquest of the country at Groningen.

21 *(Ventôse 3, Year III)*
Paris. Yielding to public pressure, the Convention restores freedom of worship throughout France.→

23 *(Ventôse 5, Year III)*
Paris. The Convention, acting on a proposal from Merlin de Douai, decides to assign a residence in their own parish to all civil or military officers who are destitute or suspended since Thermidor.

24 *(Ventôse 6, Year III)*
Paris. On the advice of Lakanal, the Convention creates central schools in each department.→

24 *(Ventôse 6, Year III)*
Eure. The municipality of Evreux demolishes the post, erected as a mark of shame, on the site of the house of the Girondist deputy Buzot.

26 *(Ventôse 8, Year III)*
Nantes. As a sign of peace, General François de Charette enters the town with General Canclaux and the representative Ruelle.

27 *(Ventôse 9, Year III)*
Paris. After clashes between "reactionaries" and Jacobins in the theatres, the establishments are indefinitely closed.

A central school for each department

Paris, February 24
Lakanal is truly an outstanding educationalist. After launching the prestigious Ecole Normale, he is now hard at work preparing for the establishment of central secondary schools which are to replace the existing colleges. This is a major nation-wide project. There will be one central school for each 300,000 inhabitants. Each will have a library, a natural history department, a garden, a physics department and a collection of machines. The new curriculum will cover all existing knowledge: mathematics, modern languages, political economics and even public health. The ambitious plan has won the support of all the deputies.

Retribution stalks the Rhône valley

Lyons, February 28
The "White Terror" was sparked off by the massacre of jailed Jacobins on February 3rd. Since then a group of deserters and federalists, calling itself the Company of Jesus, or Jéhu, has caused blood to flow along the Rhône valley. The members chase former Montagnards, acting on reports from informants. When they catch their victims, these are killed or thrown into the Rhône River. The list of victims is growing every day. The retribution seekers are motivated by both politics and self-interest. Many of them act for purely personal revenge.

Some teachers score low marks

Puy de Dôme, February
Public education has not been among the Revolution's crowning achievements. That is what the committee in charge of the selection of teachers has concluded. There are some who write badly and know little geography, others who can't add. Others still suffer from speech impediments. To make matters worse, there are only 36 candidates for 70 teaching posts. There are also problems in schools: one woman who has been teaching for 20 years can't do arithmetic.

Republic makes peace with the Vendeans

Loire Inférieure, February 17
The Vendeans did not lose out in the deal that has just been struck with their enemies from Paris. The Vendeans recognised the Republic, which in exchange has granted them freedom of worship, the abolition of conscription and the right to arm a militia partly paid for by the State, as well as substantial cash compensation. The peace talks got under way five days ago at the La Jaunaye castle near Nantes. They have just resulted in a deal that Charette can be doubly proud of:

by signing the treaty with him, the Republic has acknowledged him as the main Vendean leader. He is, moreover, proud of his amorous conquests. Two women played a rôle in establishing contact between the opposing sides: Charette's own sister and one of her friends. The latter, a lovely Creole named Madame Gasnier Chambon, is related to the republican representative Ruelle. Charette found her so attractive that he quickly agreed to open peace negotiations with his long-time enemies (→ Feb. 26).

Dresses worn by the "Merveilleuses" are made fun of by Muscadins.

Freedom of worship is restored in France

Paris, February 21
A page of history has been turned. The Convention has approved a decree restoring freedom of worship, including for Roman Catholics. When he presented the draft bill Boissy d'Anglas stressed, however, that he had no sympathy for the "absurd dogma" of Catholicism. He added that the persecution of "misguided men by fierce men" during the Terror had in many cases simply strengthened the faith of the faithful. "Avoid forcing people to do something underground when it would be met with indifference or even boredom if they did the same thing in a private house," he said. D'Anglas' decree creates a total separation between Church and State: not only will the State not pay clergymen, but no premises are to be provided for

worship, even by town councils. In exchange for this government policy of neutrality, churches will have to remain very discreet. The active search for converts and such public manifestations as the ringing of church bells to summon the faithful will be strictly forbidden. The State is also prepared to do all it can to ensure the security of places of worship. Anyone caught causing a disturbance during a religious service will be sent before the courts. The restoration of freedom of worship had become inevitable since preliminary moves towards that goal had been taken in order to pacify the Vendée and Brittany. Such early moves had been warmly welcomed by the public, and this in time contributed to the Assembly's decision to satisfy the demands of a majority of the population.

Convention

Food shortages turn into a famine

France, March 15

The food crisis has been compounded by the recent terrible winter weather. The poorest in the land are now in a truly desperate situation. In the cities, the ration of bread, which remains a staple food of the poor, is constantly getting smaller: one pound every three days in Lyons and a half pound per day for five days a week at Le Havre. In Paris, where the authorities are afraid that food riots will break out, the ration is theoretically half a pound per day, but there are many who get no bread whatsoever. People start queuing outside shops with bare shelves as early as two or three in the morning. Women and

Long queues form whenever milk is handed out to the poor of Paris.

Empty handed and penniless.

children stand for hours in the icy cold in the hope of getting their hands on a bit of firewood, some oil, or black, smelly dough that is supposed to be bread. Shivering and hungry, entire families huddle in their cold homes. Some people are turning to crime in order to feed themselves. Others prefer to mix soot into their gruel. The frost has made all river and road transport impossible. Bandits are attacking and looting stocks of grain and flour. Peasants who refuse to sell or deliver their produce are causing food prices to rise sharply. All this has contributed to a major crisis for the poor that is made worse by the fact that a lucky few continue to live in luxury. In Paris, for example, fashionable restaurants, such as *Le Veau qui Tète* or *A la Marmite Perpétuelle,* are packed every evening. Those who can afford the prices are offered a choice of over 100 different dishes.

Barère and friends face the Tribunal

Paris, March 2

The Convention intends to judge the men of Year II. Despite protests from the Montagnards, it decided on December 27th. to start legal proceedings against Barère, Vadier, Collot d'Herbois and Billaud Varenne. Today, after Saladin read out his report, the Convention voted for the immediate arrest of all these Jacobins. Cambon, Lindet and the two Prieurs protested against this, but in vain. They wanted to prove that, by condemning the Thermidorians, the deputies were disowning themselves. But the Convention members remain confident in themselves, believing that they are supported by public opinion.

Amsterdam, recently liberated from the Austrians by France, celebrates Freedom on March 4th. A freedom tree has been planted on Revolution Square to mark the birth of the Batavian Republic.

The courtesans are back in town

Paris, March

Courtesans have been returning to Paris high society. They are to be seen at the best spots, including the Variétés Montansier theatre. Its director, Mademoiselle Montansier, has just reopened her establishment after having spent time inside the Terror's jails. Although she is over 60, she is full of plans and wants her theatre to become the new "in" meeting place for the capital's rich and young. In order to please her clients, she has reserved some 50 balcony seats for the courtesans. From their vantage points the ladies of pleasure can eye the richer and handsomer men among the audience. But courtesans can sometimes be difficult to handle, so Mlle. Montansier has hired a young man named Robillard to keep an eye on them. He wears impressive spectacles and shoes with silver buckles. The trusted young man always carries some sweets in his pockets which he generously hands out to the best behaved ladies. But those who cause trouble are punished by being sent to a small room set aside for that purpose. Mlle. Montansier's new theatre specialises in anti-Jacobin plays, much to the delight of the staunchly royalist Muscadin dandies. In the plays, sansculottists are depicted as "assassins" and "tyrants". Not all members of the audience are happy about that.

New Arab-language grammar book

Paris, March 4

The Republic is interested in the East: Volney, a professor of history at the Ecole Normale, has written a 136-page book on Arabic grammar at the request of the Foreign Affairs Executive Committee. This "Simplification of oriental languages, a new method for learning the Arabic, Persian and Turkish languages with European characters" is a practical guide. It deals only with the rules governing everyday use of those languages and is aimed at the Republic's officials who are sent overseas on missions. It is also meant to be of assistance to all the French businessmen and traders who work in the Levant.

The misfortunes of the "red deputy"

Paris, March 6

In public as in private, he is never seen without his bright red revolutionary bonnet. Jean Baptiste Armonville is an ardent Jacobin and he is proud of it. However, this evening at the Payen café, the bonnet nearly cost him his life. As he entered the café, some Muscadins started pointing their fingers at him and jeering. One of the royalists even grabbed his bonnet and waved it around on the end of his cane. The furious deputy summoned his friends and a brawl broke out.

Jean Baptiste Armonville, son of a serge maker and himself a wool carder, was elected the deputy of the Marne at the age of 35. A fan of Marat, he joined the Montagnards and became one of that group's most popular figures.

An accuser with a bad memory

Paris, March 8

Doctor Antoine Hardy is not a particularly grateful man. A former Girondist who has just returned to the Convention, Hardy recently and in public criticised three former Montagnards. He called for the immediate impeachment of the special envoy Maure, of Charlier, Marat's former defender, and especially of Robert Lindet. The latter had saved Hardy's life, as well as that of his family, during the days when the guillotine was kept busy under the Reign of Terror. Whether he is motivated by ambition or revenge, it seems there are some debts of gratitude that Hardy would far rather forget all about.

Unemployment sparks off serious unrest

The unemployed Citizen Mercier advertises in the hope of finding a job.

France, March 10

Such terrible misery has not been seen in France since the devastating winter of 1709. Unemployment has now added its woes to the ravages of cold weather and lack of food. The ice-bound rivers make it impossible for convoys of grain, iron, coal and wood to get through. Production has slumped sharply, due to the lack of raw materials. Many workers have been laid off. In the cities north of the Loire river, the poor no longer know whom to turn to. They are streaming into Amiens, Orléans, Rouen and Paris. Gangs of hungry poor are looting as they pass through Picardy, the Beauce and Normandy. They go to the larger towns hoping to find some form of assistance. In the cities, they just add to the number of starving and jobless beggars. Some die of hunger. Others, who can't feed their children, kill themselves. Apart from certain relatively unscathed regions such as Aquitaine, the Mediterranean coast and Auvergne, death, hardship and unrest are everywhere.

Grégoire calls for church reforms

Paris, March

The constitutional church is far from dead. Although it suffered badly from de-Christianisation and the Terror, it is currently undergoing reforms spearheaded by the tireless Bishop Grégoire. Working with him are four other juring prelates: Gratien, the Metropolitan of the Seine Inférieure, Saurine of the Landes region of southwest France, Royer, from the Ain, and Desbois de Rochefort, from the Somme area. This group, which is to be beefed up soon, has set out some guidelines in a text called "Encyclical letter from the united bishops". The document states that "depriestified" clergymen, namely those who abdicated during the Terror, will be allowed to resume their positions if they make a public apology for their errors in their local churches. As for the clergymen who have married, Grégoire is extremely firm: they will under no circumstances whatsoever be permitted to return to the priesthood (→May 2).

Bloodsuckers

The commoners, who have lost twice as many people on the scaffold as aristocrats, realise that they are the main victims of the Revolution. These bitter verses are going the rounds:

Jacobins and Royalists,
Bloodsuckers and anarchists,
Now from your infernal lists
Let these names be wiped today.
It's your fault we are broke.
While you hunt, while you joke,
Always it is us poor folk
Who must the piper pay.

For the name of democrat,
And for that of aristocrat,
And to wear a smart cravat
Every effort you essay.
Peace and calm is what you need.
To war's needs no more concede.
Austria, England too, indeed,
Will both the piper pay.

With an ever-changing rule,
There are victims pitiful;
Thus prepare we a cesspool
Into which we'll fall some day.
Soon as e'er we change in France
Government or high finance,
Common folk have the assurance
That they'll the piper pay.

16 *(Ventôse 26, Year III)*
Meudon. A fire destroys the castle, already damaged by repeated pillaging.

17 *(Ventôse 27, Year III)*
Paris. Special envoys from the Saint Marceau and Saint Jacques districts demand bread from the Convention (→21).

18 *(Ventôse 28, Year III)*
Maine et Loire. The Vendean leader Stofflet defeats Canclaux's troops at Chalonnes.

21 *(Germinal 1, Year III)*
Paris. Desperately short of bread, the sectors of the district of Saint Antoine come to the Convention to demand immediate action and the enforcement of the Constitution of 1793 (→27).

22 *(Germinal 2, Year III)*
Paris. Opening of the hearing of the Convention members, Barère, Billaud Varenne, and Collot d'Herbois. Vadier has been on the run since March 2nd.

22 *(Germinal 2, Year III)*
Maine et Loire. Defeat of Stofflet near Saint Florent.

25 *(Germinal 5, Year III)*
Paris. Food stocks in Paris have reached their lowest level. Only enough wheat for 115 days is left in warehouses.

27 *(Germinal 7, Year III)*
Paris. Unrest continues in certain sectors, including Gravilliers (→31).

28 *(Germinal 8, Year III)*
Paris. Fouquier Tinville appears before the Paris revolutionary Tribunal (→May 6, 95).

29 *(Germinal 9, Year III)*
Paris. Bonaparte leaves the artillery; he is given the command of an infantry brigade in the Vendée.

30 *(Germinal 10, Year III)*
Paris. Stormy meetings are held in all sectors of Paris.

30 *(Germinal 10, Year III)*
Paris. The Convention decides to create a school of modern oriental languages.

31 *(Germinal 11, Year III)*
Paris. At the Convention, a deputation from the Quinze Vingts sector submits a threatening petition demanding the enforcement of the 1793 Constitution (→April 1, 95).

31 *(Germinal 11, Year III)*
Paris. Auction of the estate of the émigré Talleyrand. A large number of female clothes are found in his wardrobe.

Will the starving people of Paris rise up?

Soup kitchens have become a last resort for many of the hungry poor.

Paris, March 27

"People, awake, the time has come!" For the past ten days, the walls of the suburbs and parts of central Paris have been plastered with posters calling on the capital's population to rise up. Everywhere the message is the same. Two such texts, the *National Tocsin* and the *Address to the Convention and the People,* violently criticise the Committees and the lazy young royalist Muscadins. Patriots can no longer stand watching the insolent way in which the well dressed Muscadins treat them. It is outright provo-

cation, they feel. But before responding they must first become organised. They have been operating clandestinely ever since the abolition of the Society of the Defenders of Human Rights. The patriots remind people that markets were supplied with food and prices were controlled during the Terror. In the Quinze Vingts, Gravilliers and Muséum sectors, the sansculottists are hoping that the current crisis will lead to a new popular uprising. Aware of this danger, the Convention has begun mobilising its supporters and massing its forces.

The Temple of Immortality that stands on the Invalides Square is for the soldiers who died for France. Some remains will go to the Panthéon.

Tribunal president is jailed

Paris, March 20

The president of the revolutionary Tribunal, Martial Herman, has been jailed. He was appointed in October 1793 when the Terror was beginning to make itself felt. Last October, he was placed in charge of keeping an eye on civilian tribunals. Now he has just been impeached and is to be tried as a terrorist. This small man is nothing like the violent Robespierrist Dumas, who had replaced him during the trial of the Hébertists. He is a quiet and cunning man, who was involved in all the major political trials along with Fouquier Tinville. There are few who managed to avoid the parodies of justice that he presided over, which were in fact mere excuses to have suspects beheaded.

Lease will go to highest bidder!

A French general is killed in India

Kardala, March 25

A French army general has just died of his wounds in India. He had defeated the Mahratti and Hindu forces in the Deccan. Leading an Indo-Moslem army, General Michel Joaquim Raymond chased the enemy forces out of Sultan Nizam ali Khan's territory. A former aide de camp for Bussy, General Raymond had been working for the Sultan since 1785. There are many other such French military men devoted to the cause of monarchs at war against England.

April 1795
from 1st. to 15th.

Convention

1 *(Germinal 12, Year III)*
Paris. The sansculottists invade the Convention, demanding bread and the enforcement of the Constitution of 1793 (→). The Convention orders the deportation without judgement of Billaud Varenne, Collot d'Herbois, Barère and Vadier, the latter being still on the run (→ 10).

2 *Germinal 13, Year III)*
Paris. General Pichegru puts down the unrest which is going on in the districts.

2 *(Germinal 13, Year III)*
Maine et Loire. A new defeat for the Vendean leader Stofflet at Chemillé.

3 *(Germinal 14, Year III)*
Paris. The Convention names a commission of seven members. It will prepare the organic laws of the Constitution of 1793 (→ May 6, 95).

5 *(Germinal 16, Year III)*
Basel. François Barthélemy signs a treaty with Ambassador Karl August von Hardenburg. It ends the war between France and Prussia. →

5 *(Germinal 16, Year III)*
Paris. Warrants of arrest are issued for new leftist deputies, among them Cambon, who runs away, Levasseur de la Sarthe and two Thermidorians, Thuriot and Lecointre.

6 *(Germinal 17, Year III)*
Paris. The Convention decides by decree to reduce the powers of the revolutionary Tribunal.

7 *(Germinal 18, Year III)*
Paris. The Convention passes a decree establishing the uniformity of weights, measures and money, using the decimal system.

9 *(Germinal 20, Year III)*
Sarthe. Several hundred Chouans fail in their attack on La Ferté Bernard.

10 *(Germinal 21, Year III)*
Paris. The Convention orders the disarmament of terrorists in all the Republic; this will contribute to the development of the "White Terror" in the south. →

11 *(Germinal 22, Year III)*
Paris. The Convention decides to give back civic rights to all citizens outlawed after May 31st. 1793, with the exception of certain royalists like the leader of the insurrection at Lyons, Précy.

14 *(Germinal 25, Year III)*
Paris. The Convention ratifies the treaty of Basel signed on April 5th.

Paris is again rocked by rioting

Paris, April 1

Screaming "We want bread!", a crowd of furious men and women has invaded the Convention.

Some of the right-wing deputies have given way to panic and fled. Such a popular uprising could, however, easily have been foreseen. Tension had been growing in the suburbs of Paris since the middle of last month. The winter had been particularly hard and the lack of flour, as well as the high price of what little food was available in the markets, led to a terrible scarcity of food. Every morning, long queues of angry and hungry people formed outside Paris bakeries.

The daily bread ration set by the authorities had been getting smaller every day. In February, any citizen having a ration card issued by his neighbourhood's civic committee was entitled to a meagre pound and a half of bread. During March, this was cut to one pound and later to just half a pound. As the bread ration grew smaller, unrest increased. On March 17th., militants of the Finistère, Gobelins and Observatoire sectors had gone to petition the Assembly.

Thibaudeau, the session's president, seemed to greet their demands with utter contempt, saying: "The food issue is just an excuse for causing trouble." By the 27th., the anger of Parisians was set to detonate. Delegations of women went to the Convention, while a riot broke out between Muscadins and sector members at Gravilliers. Several of the capital's sectors decided to hold illegal non-stop meetings.

Yesterday, a new delegation was able to enter the Assembly. Its members stood before the deputies of the Convention, who didn't want to receive them. The speaker of the Quinze Vingts sector, who headed the delegation, told the elected representatives: "Thermidor 9 was supposed to save the people, but they are the victims of all sorts of tricks. We had been promised that the abolition of the maximum was to lead to abundance, but the food problem is worse than it ever was! We stand here now to support both the Republic and liberty." For the militants of Year II, especially for the neo-Hébertists who have put up posters everywhere calling for "the Constitution of 1793 and bread", the food issue is directly

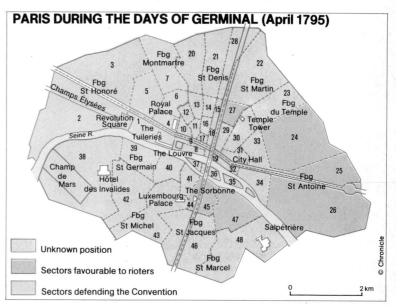

PARIS DURING THE DAYS OF GERMINAL (April 1795)

Fbg Montmartre · Fbg St Denis · Fbg St Martin · Fbg St Honoré · Fbg du Temple · Champs Elysées · Royal Palace · Temple Tower · Revolution Square · The Tuileries · The Louvre · Seine R. · Champ de Mars · Fbg St Germain · City Hall · Hôtel des Invalides · The Sorbonne · Fbg St Antoine · Luxembourg Palace · Fbg St Michel · Fbg St Jacques · Salpêtrière · Fbg St Marcel

Unknown position
Sectors favourable to rioters
Sectors defending the Convention

0   2 km

© Chronicle

Leftist eastern Paris clashes with the move right-coing eastern quaters.

linked to that of republican freedoms. Today it is hunger that sparked off the revolt. However, every single demonstrator out on the streets of Paris is also chanting "1793 Constitution". The uprising was begun by women this morning because they were told that they would only be allowed a quarter of a pound of bread for their children. A group of housewives attacked a guardhouse. They grabbed a drum and summoned others to march on the Convention.

The first crowds began to gather on the Ile de la Cité, near Notre Dame cathedral. There were a lot of starving construction workers among the crowd. Van Heck, a member of the Cité sector, set off for the Assembly at the head of a column of angry citizens. The situation was reminiscent of the revolts of 1792, when the people rebelled to demand their sovereignty. But all those heady days are long gone. The rebels did get into the Convention. They did outline their demands. Van Heck railed against the "jailing of patriots, the impunity of gentlemen with their walking sticks and the speculators who devalue the assignat". They were able to demand the enactment of the Constitution of 1793 and the election of a Commune in Paris. But they dispersed as soon as the security forces showed up. Hurriedly called in by the Committee of General Security, and led by Merlin de Thionville, National Guardsmen moved in from central and western Paris and

quickly took up positions in the gardens of the Tuileries. They were cheered by some rich youths. At the head of a unit of bayonet wielding grenadiers, Legendre marched down the corridors of the Assembly with orders to round up the demonstrators and kick them out of the building. The protesters were not armed. They had neither leaders nor clear plans for action.

This complete lack of prior organisation was the basic reason for the failure of the attempted revolt. By six o'clock in the evening, everything seemed to be over in central Paris. However, the popular unrest has not died down in the suburbs of the capital.

Not a single shot was fired.

▷

Convention takes harsh measures after revolt

Paris, April 10

The open revolt that rocked the capital on Germinal 12 has led the deputies to take harsh action against the rebels and all suspected of siding with them. The deputies have just approved a decree ordering the disarming of all "terrorists" throughout France. The text calls on local authorities to "disarm without delay those men known within their sectors as having been involved in the horrors commited under the tyranny that preceded Thermidor". The decree is aimed at crushing any final Jacobin attempts to resist. The revolt of April 1st. has also given the new leadership an opportunity to get rid of opponents and of its left wing, the Thermidorians. These reformed Robespierrists are under suspicion of seeking to slow down the forces of reaction. On the night of April 1st. to 2nd., the Convention declared martial law in the capital. It called on a senior army officer who happened to be passing through Paris, General Pichegru, the former commander of the northern army. He was on his way to take command of both the Rhine and Moselle armies. He has now been placed in command of Paris troops, with the assistance of Merlin de Thionville and Barras. By April 2nd., unrest was continuing in the Quinze Vingts neighbourhood, as well as in the Panth-

Patriots try to stop a convoy, taking Billaud, Collot d'Herbois and Barère into exile, from leaving.

éon and Cité sectors. Two deputies sent to those areas at the head of a delegation, Pénières and Auguis, even came under fire. The leaderless sansculottists, however, were unable to achieve their goals. To make matters worse, the Montagnard members of the Convention, who could have come to their aid, were quickly neutralised. Making

the best of the panic created by the popular revolt, the Assembly resolved to have done with the "Gang of Four" heading the Committee of Public Safety. They were impeached and their trial was seen as a possible source of embarrassment. The Assembly therefore ruled that they should be deported without a trial to Guyana. For the time being

the four have been sent to Oléron island. On the same day, eight other representatives, including Bourdon and Amar, were detained in Hamm castle. On April 5th., Cambon was ousted from the Finance Committee, along with Levasseur, Thuriot, Lecointre and Maignet. This time, the left wing seems to have been particularly hard hit.

Unrest has spread to Amiens

Amiens, April 3

The representative Blaux, who was sent to Amiens to speed up the supplies of grain to the capital, warned the Convention: "Save our 40,000 fellow citizens from famine. For the past three months, they have only had twelve ounces of bread per day. Tomorrow, they will have nothing." Two days after the capital, it was Amiens' turn to express its rage amid shouts of "Long live the King!" Hunger had been fuelling local unrest. Blaux barely escaped from the people's fury. However, a report on the incident stated that the special envoy from Paris "forgot all about the insults to concentrate on steps aimed at stopping confused people from compounding their errors".

In a tête-à-tête, Merveilleuses and Muscadins are shown by cartoonists as "Invisibles". However, "supreme good taste" remains unsullied.

The downfall of an opportunist

Marseilles, April 5

The oddest aspect of the affair is that Moïse Bayle was not impeached sooner. Elected to the Convention by the Bouches du Rhône thanks to Barbaroux, he betrayed the latter by becoming a Maratist. During Louis XVI's trial he published a pamphlet asking for the people's verdict, as well as another one opposing such a move. When he was sent as a special envoy to Marseilles, his policies caused a revolt. He accused the Marseilles people's tribunal of having "shed the blood of the best patriots", but approved the law on suspects. He was later accused of having fomented counter-revolution, but was a member of the Committee of General Security until Thermidor 9.

Chamfort to be praised posthumously

Paris, April

An important figure has been left out of the process of rehabilitation that followed Thermidor: Nicolas Sébastien de Chamfort. Luckily, the faithful Ginguené is there to watch over the author's posthumous reputation. Ginguené is about to publish a selection of his friend's *Maximes, Pensées et Anecdotes* written over many years by the lucid misanthropist. By spending a lot of time at gatherings of the intellectuals and artists of Paris, Chamfort became a merciless chronicler of the foibles of human nature. In a world where "the heart must either break or harden", this low-born academic, who gave himself a noble name, was able to use all his talents as a moralist. His unbridled use of words led to his arrest. After being released in August 1793, he chose to

The moralist author Chamfort.

kill himself and "die as a free man" rather than face another jail term. He died of his injuries in March 1794.

Prussia sues for peace

Basel, April 5

Austria is isolated. This is largely due to the treaty of "peace, friendship and understanding" signed today between France and Prussia, despite Berlin's refusal to enter into an offensive alliance against Vienna. The treaty of Basel calls for the immediate ending of hostilities between the two sides: France is to occupy the Prussian territories on the left bank of the Rhine "until a general pacification" and, in case French occupation becomes permanent, the Republic undertakes that Prussia will be "justly" indemnified elsewhere. France also agrees to "welcome the good offices" of the King of Prussia on behalf of the States and princes of the German Empire willing to negotiate. The peace does not harm the interests of the two signatories. By leaving the coalition, Prussia leaves the burden of the war on the Rhine on Austria's shoulders, which is to Paris' advantage. The peace treaty with France gives Prussia a chance to resume operations along the Vistula. Prussia has been greedily eyeing Poland and has no intention of allowing Russia and Austria once again to divide up the country by themselves. The Franco-Prussian neutrality also threatens Vienna with the prospect of an alliance between Paris and Berlin. Paris has good reason to welcome Prussia's stance: hostilities are over in the occupied nations, including Holland. Through this agreement the King of Prussia abandons his brother in law, the Stadtholder of Holland and weakens the coalition.

A play about an Arab family is a hit

Paris, April 2

Jean François Ducis, a member of the French Academy since 1778, has just found a new subject to write about. The successful playwright was until recently best known for having been the first to have adapted Shakespearean plays, such as *Hamlet, King Lear, Romeo and Juliet* and *Macbeth*, for the French stage. The tragedy he presents today is particularly exotic. *Abufar ou la Famille Arabe* uses incestuous love to depict a male-dominated society in a desert region. The unusual new play is already being considered as a major literary event by the capital's theatregoers.

A general enlists as a simple soldier

Mainz, April

The desire to see combat once again was far too strong. General Jean Baptiste Aubert Dubayet presented himself today at Kléber's headquarters as a simple enlisted man. This captain in the royalist army, who was later appointed to lead the army on the Cherbourg coast, was elected the deputy of the Isère, then president of the Assembly. He was found responsible for the capitulation of Mainz and jailed before being pardonned. Later sent to fight the Vendeans, the defeat at Clisson cost him his freedom. Robespierre's downfall allowed him to live in Grenoble until now.

Assembly honours the dead Condorcet

Paris, April 12

History can be full of surprises. Almost a year to the day after his mysterious death in a prison cell, Condorcet the outlaw is being honoured by the Assembly. For him, as for so many others, the time for rehabilitation has finally come. As a well deserved posthumous homage, the Convention has ordered that the Nation will pay the entire cost of the publication of 3,000 copies of his *Esquisse d'un Tableau Historique des Progrès de l'Esprit Humain,* the French philosopher's last work before his death. Condorcet did not have sufficient time to get the work published as he was already fleeing with the Republic's police hot on his heels. Despite such dramatic circumstances, the work shows an unshakeable faith in the future of mankind and the progress of enlightenment.

The Innocents' marketplace, located around the fountain of the same name, is a huge tent village. The closure, shortly before the Revolution, of the evil smelling local cemetery has improved the neighbourhood.

Convention

17 (Germinal 28, Year III)
Paris. The National Guard, purged of its revolutionary elements, passes under the control of the military Committee of the Convention. The soldiers will have to equip themselves, which will leave artisans and workers unemployed.

19 (Germinal 30, Year III)
Ain. Six "terrorists" who were being taken to Lons le Saunier are massacred half a league from the town.

20 (Floréal 1, Year III)
Ille et Vilaine. Near Rennes, at La Prévalaye and at the castle of La Mabilais, 121 royalist leaders of Brittany, Maine and Normandy negotiate with the representatives of the Convention. Only 21 agree to lay down their arms, under the same conditions as the Vendeans.→

21 (Floréal 2, Year III)
Paris. The Convention creates two veterinary schools, one at Versailles and the other at Lyons.

21 (Floréal 2, Year III)
Marseilles. Engagement of Bonaparte to Desirée Clary, daughter of a rich merchant.

25 (Floréal 6, Year III)
Morbihan. A violent food riot is contained with great difficulty by the adjutant general Evrard and the representative Brüe.

26 (Floréal 7, Year III)
Paris. Officially sanctioning the collapse of paper money, the Convention annuls the decree forbidding gold and silver trading.

26 (Floréal 7, Year III)
Maine et Loire. Stofflet's camp at Maulévrier is found and destroyed by republican forces (→May 2, 95).

27 (Floréal 8, Year III)
Paris. The Cité Variétés theatre shows Charles Pierre Ducancel's *L'Intérieur des Comités Révolutionnaires ou les Aristides Modernes*, an anti-Jacobin comedy that is a huge hit.

30 (Floréal 11, Year III)
Lyons. In order to avoid a massacre of "terrorists" in the city centre, the representative Boisset orders that all detainees to be tried in Lyons should be held at Mâcon and Roanne (→May 4, 95).

30 (Floréal 11, Year III)
Paris. Abbot Barthélemy, author of *Voyage du Jeune Anacharsis en Grèce*, dies.

Second peace accord between Paris and the Chouans in the west

One of the Chouan leaders places his signature on the peace accord.

Rennes, April 20

The Chouans have agreed to recognise the Republic, abide by all its laws and not take up arms against it again. In exchange, Paris has granted the Bretons freedom of worship and exemption from conscription as well as considerable reparations. Moreover, the ruling on the seizure of the assets of émigrés is to be annulled. The talks which were held at La Mabilais manor, near Rennes, have been most successful. However, only a minority of the Chouan leaders have agreed to recognise the accord. As for General Hoche, he remains very sceptical about the matter, feeling that the peace accord could give the royalists the time they so badly need to regroup.

Antraigues is now a Spanish subject

Venice, April

The Comte d'Antraigues is no longer serving England. He is now working for the Spanish legation in Venice. In January he was granted his naturalisation papers and the cross of Charles III. When he has some spare time, the spy likes to do some writing. He has just published *Observations sur la Conduite des Nations Coalisées*, in which he condemns the oath at the Jeu de Paume as the Revolution's greatest crime. This is already upsetting the close-knit émigré community.

The émigré priests return to France

Ravenna, April 25

Monsignor de Mercy, the nonjuring bishop of Luçon, is still in hiding in Ravenna, in the Papal Estates. Today, he received reports about the return to France of nonjuring clergymen. According to this unconfirmed information, nearly all the priests of the dioceses of both Marseilles and Lyons are planning to return at the request of their parishioners or their church superiors. Twelve non-juring priests are said to have departed from Ravenna, 17 from Rome and many others from Ferrara. Reports from France appear positive, at least as far as the fate of religion is concerned.

Anti-Jacobin police operation in Lyons

Lyons, April 24

The special envoy from Paris can no longer control the situation in Lyons. In a letter sent this morning to the Convention, he reports on the serious events that occurred yesterday. Acting on orders from the Committee of General Security, he had "taken all necessary steps to disarm without delay all the men known within their sectors as having taken part in the horrors committed under the tyranny that preceded Thermidor 9". Police therefore carried out surprise raids on the homes of all such "terrorists". Many of the rounded up suspects were quickly freed, due to a lack of evidence. Despite this, the population is furious and is planning to lynch them. Groups of people have been gathering outside the city's three jails. The number of guards has been doubled, but this has not stopped the menacing crowds from screaming for revenge against the "Jacobin tyrants". Any attempt by the crowd to seize the prisoners must be stopped at all costs, as it could easily get out of hand. Given this, the letter sent by special envoy Boisset is a veritable cry for help. The question is: is it already too late to act? (→April 30).

The Jacobins arrested today will be massacred by the mob on May 4th.

May 1795
from 1st. to 15th.

Convention

1 *(Floréal 12, Year III)*
Paris. Chénier and Louvet, worried by the continual swing to the right by the régime, get the Convention to pass a decree against émigrés and rebels who have returned to France. The decree is also aimed at all those who would call for the restoration of royalty.

2 *(Floréal 13, Year III)*
Maine et Loire. Stofflet, the last original chief of the Vendean revolution, signs the peace accords.→

2 *(Floréal 13, Year III)*
Paris. Bishop Grégoire publishes the first edition of the *Annales de la religion*. This is a weekly of the Christian Philosophy Society that he has just founded with the help of members of the Port Royal school, supporters of a constitutional and Gallican church.→

4 *(Floréal 15, Year III)*
Lyons. Several thousand rioters invade the three jails of the city and massacre 99 Jacobin prisoners, including the actor Dorfeuille, the former president of the revolutionary Tribunal.

6 *(Floréal 17, Year III)*
Paris. Judging it "impossible" to enact the Constitution of 1793, the commission charged with drawing up the organic laws is increased to 11 members and gives itself the task of preparing an entirely new constitution.

7 *(Floréal 18, Year III)*
Saint Etienne. The former Jacobin mayor Johannot is killed by two unknown assailants.

7 *(Floréal 18, Year III)*
Paris. The former public prosecutor Fouquier Tinville, the ex-president Herman and 14 former jurymen of the revolutionary Tribunal are guillotined.

8 *(Floréal 19, Year III)*
Marseilles. Hearing of his appointment in the west, General Bonaparte leaves for Paris in the company of Junot and Marmont, in order to obtain a different posting.

10 *(Floréal 21, Year III)*
Paris. The daily bread ration is reduced to 60 grammes per person. A real famine follows the shortage.

11 *(Floréal 22, Year III)*
Aix en Provence. Thirty Jacobins are assassinated in the prisons of the town.

A former prosecutor in the dock

In the courtroom packed with spectators, guards block all the exits and keep a wary eye on the accused.

Paris, May 6

Fouquier Tinville has at last been given a well-earned lesson in what true justice should be. Probably for the first time in his life, the former public prosecutor has attended an exemplary trial ... his own. It was a not a salutary experience for him. He was sentenced to death along with 15 of his colleagues and he is to be guillotined tomorrow. During the 39 days that the trial lasted, the public galleries remained full of spectators. In order to ensure a fair trial, a special jury of 15 men from the provinces was constituted to try the 33 accused. It was hoped they would be more impartial. Only some of Fouquier Tinville's most scandalous legal rulings were held against him. Lawyers and court officials criticised the Tribunal's sinister use of speeded up proceedings. However, what really moved the spectators were the damning accounts provided to the court by the relatives of the victims. Thus, Madame de Saint Pern told of the execution of her 17 year old son, guillotined in his father's place. The accused did not remain silent, however. In particular, Fouquier Tinville used all the arguments at his disposal to save himself. His extraordinarily precise memory was a considerable help. Despite this, he was unable to save his neck. News of his execution was greeted by an outburst of joy among Parisians. In the capital, groups of citizens have taken to singing a song based on the tune of *La Carmagnole*: "Fouquier Tinville had promised to behead all of Paris, but he lied as he's the one who's lost his head."

Seized assets are being handed back

Paris, May 3

In a moving speech, Doulcet de Pontécoulant asked the Assembly to allow the assets of those who were tried and unjustly executed during the Terror to be returned to the relatives of the victims. Fearing that such a move could be in the interest of counter-revolutionaries, Berliet, speaking on behalf of the moderates, stressed that each case should be examined separately. However, the personal assets of deported priests will be returned unconditionally.

Money crisis hits Paris theatres

Paris, May

The price of seats in the stalls or the dress circle has gone sky high: 1,000 francs for a seat at the Favart auditorium, compared to ten francs a year ago! The capital's theatres have been hard hit by inflation. The lavish productions that audiences seem to like so much are very costly affairs. Although the price of the cheapest tickets has quadrupled in six months, theatres are still losing money. This sobering fact has put a damper on authors' jibes at businessmen and speculators.

This book contains the names of Lyons terrorists and informers.

White Terror sweeps down on France

France, May

The "drinkers of blood" are paying dearly for their past deeds. That is what the reactionaries are calling the revolutionary militants who hunted down and killed political "suspects". Often, however, the term is applied only to ardent republicans who were not directly involved in the Robespierrist Terror. A thirst for revenge has gradually spread through France since Thermidor. In the provinces, reactionaries have been encouraged by the Convention's repressive stance with regard to the Jacobins. By last winter, they had begun to form punitive gangs that "purged" whole villages by carrying out terrible massacres. The White Terror is thus named to differentiate it from the Robespierrist Red Terror. Its spread really got under way at the beginning of May. The events of Germinal gave added impetus by

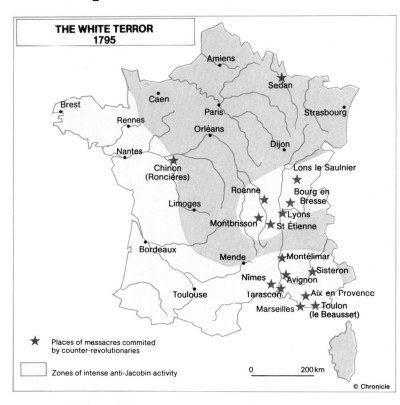

THE WHITE TERROR 1795

★ Places of massacres commited by counter-revolutionaries

☐ Zones of intense anti-Jacobin activity

0   200km

© Chronicle

A "judge" trampling on the Law.

crushing the sansculottists' final attempts to resist. Throughout the southeast of the country and in the Rhône valley, atrocities are being carried out. Lists of citizens known for their republican views are being made public. These then become the targets of the mob's retribution. This entirely new breed of killers, dubbed "assassins in silk stockings", are usually members of the aristocratic élite. They set up secret organisations, such as the Company of the Sun, in Marseilles, or the Companions of Jéhu, in Lyons. They have no qualms about hiring mercenaries to assist them on their bloody missions of revenge. Elsewhere, repression is not quite so severe. It is characterised by a constant harassment of those who have been singled out as victims. Legal action based on reports from countless anonymous informers is being taken against special envoys from Paris, district administrators local and revolutionary tribunal members as well as officials of the watch committees. Muscadins are operating openly in every major town, but local authorities seem to remain indifferent to their activities.

Vendean chief at last signs peace

Maine et Loire, May 2

The most idomitable of all the Vendean leaders, Stofflet, has at last agreed to recognise the Republic. He was the one who had shouted "To Hell with the Republic and Charette!" when the latter signed the peace accord with the republicans at La Jaunaye last February. Backed by his advisor Abbot Bernier, the fierce gamekeeper Stofflet had gone on with the fight against the Republic. The Vendean chief, hunted by General Canclaux, had taken advantage of Charette's neutrality. Finding himself isolated at Saint Florent today, Stofflet had to give up. The accord stipulates that Stofflet's former leader, the Comte de Colbert, will be allowed to return and recover his assets.

French calendar is modified yet again

Paris, May

The calendar drawn up on November 24th. 1793 was not considered to be perfect. There was a discrepancy between the revolutionary year and the astronomical one. The Public Education Committee has therefore decided to set matters right. From now on, years will all have the same number of days, but a supplementary day will have to be added every four, 400 and 4,000 years to compensate. Leap year will be known as "Franciade", and the extra day will be called the "day of the Revolution".

Abbot Grégoire gets unexpected help

Paris, May 2

In the edition of the *Annales de la Religion* that was published today, Abbot Grégoire pays homage to a Protestant. Elie Thomas has given him some unexpected support for the campaign he is waging at the Assembly in favour of improving the lot of the priests still being held aboard ships at anchor in Rochefort. Abbot Grégoire tells his readers about the activities of this descendant of persecuted outlaws, who "on behalf of these unfortunates has called upon all that goodwill and humanity command a generous heart to do".

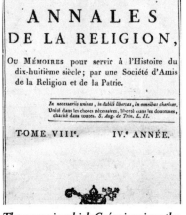

ANNALES DE LA RELIGION,

Ou Mémoires pour servir à l'Histoire du dix-huitième siècle; par une Société d'Amis de la Religion et de la Patrie.

In necessariis unitas, in dubiis libertas, in omnibus charitas. Unité dans les choses nécessaires, liberté dans les douteuses, charité dans toutes. S. Aug. de Trin. L. II.

TOME VIIIe.   IV.[e] ANNÉE.

The paper in which Grégoire sings the praise of the Protestant Thomas.

The Revolution's chronicler is executed

Paris, May 7

The Republic had good reason to spare his life. Jean Louis Prieur, a conscientious and methodical artist, had set himself the daunting task of depicting all the dramatic and memorable events of the past years. His 67 etchings, *Tableaux Historiques de la Révolution Française*, were a lively and extremely vivid chronicle of recent events in France. Despite his considerable talent this ardent Jacobin, who once sat on the jury of the revolutionary Tribunal, has just been executed, thus becoming another victim of the Thermidorian reaction.

Prieur, on the right with Châtelet.

Paris imposes treaty on The Hague

A republican balloon passes over the Rhine. Red bonnets fall on the Austrians from the basket.

The Hague, May 16

The Republic of the United Provinces has been recognised by the French Republic as a free and independent power. However, a high price was paid for this recognition. Under the terms of the peace treaty signed by both sides, the Batavian Estates General will have to help France in its fight against Austria. Also, the United Provinces is to cede Dutch Flanders, Maastricht and Venlo, and commits itself to pay the sum of 100 million florins "in compensation for war costs". Secret clauses state that The Hague will have to pay for the French army of occupation. Such are the terms imposed on the Batavian patriots, who had thought they could deal with the Committee of Public Safety on an equal footing. They had not taken into account the firm stance of Sieyès, who wrote: "The Batavians must in future do as much good for France as the harm they did or tried to do under British influence." The French protectorate closely resembles a subtle form of occupation.

Hungary's Jacobin leader is executed

Budapest, May 20

All the hopes of Hungary's revolutionaries have been dashed. At the end of a lengthy trial, Ignac Martinovics, the founder of the Jacobin movement, was beheaded along with his friends Joseph Hajnocy and Jean Laczkovics. They had secretly founded the "Society of Reformers", grouping enlightened noblemen, and the "Society of the Friends of Liberty and Equality" that included more radical elements. They had planned to start an uprising in Hungary with help from France, Turkey and Poland. Their aim was to overthrow the Hapsburgs and set up a republic.

Churches handed back to faithful

Paris, May 30

The decree approved today at the urging of Lanjuinais is aimed at giving religion true freedom, not the sort of nominal liberty it has had till now. The law on freedom of religion stated that the State and local communes would not provide places of worship. Religious ceremonies had to be held in private homes. From now on, cities and villages will be allowed to let the various religions use churches. However, when more than one faith wants to use a church at the same time, separate services will be held at previously arranged times so that there are no clashes.

Army fails to draw many volunteers

Castelsarrasin, May 21

Out of the 400 men who had been requisitioned, only 179 turned up this morning. Out of these, 36 were sent home because they were either too young or too old to bear arms, or because they were unfit to serve in the army. The remainder did not show great enthusiasm for the military life, while their parents complained about the "harm to business and to affection" done by their sons' enlistment. As for the absentees, of whom there are many in the region, it seems that nothing much can be done, since there are only five constables to police the 100 local communities.

▷

The largest popular mobilisation of the entire Revolution turned into a rout of the sansculottists in the period from Prairial 1 to 4. Motivated by hunger and by the Convention's anti-Jacobin moves, the people of Paris tried in vain to impose a popular republic. However, the lack of determined political leaders and a reluctance to shed blood caused the uprising to fail. The moderate Thermidorians were able to count on support from the army and the bourgeois from the wealthier neighbourhoods, who refused to allow mere sansculottists to impose their will. In their eyes, poverty is blight and the Terror was only made possible because the poor had been granted civil rights. The defeat of the sansculottists became inevitable after the capitulation of the Saint Antoine district. This was followed by widespread purges in both Paris and the provinces. The Thermidorians ordered the immediate disarming of the rebels and the adoption of a constitution that would deny a vast majority of the population the right to vote.

The Assembly's president, Boissy d'Anglas, salutes the head of Féraud, who was murdered moments earlier.

When the alarm bells rang out in the Saint Antoine district, hardly anybody was surprised. Over the past few days, women and workers had been demonstrating their discontent. The bread ration had been cut to 60 grammes per day and people were hungry. The Convention was doing nothing to help, although it was preparing to draft a new constitution. The sansculottists were aware that their civil rights were being threatened. An uprising was their only means of getting bread and preserving freedom. A manifesto circulated on the eve of Prairial 1. It called for bread, the enactment of the Constitution of 1793 and the abolition of the revolutionary government, which was seen as being manipulated by the Thermidorians, as well as the arrest of the members of the Committees, whom the people accused of acts of tyranny against the people.

Paris women rebel

As soon as dawn broke over the capital, groups of women started gathering in the districts of Saint Antoine and Saint Marcel and in central Paris. These were the same women who had been spending several hours a day queuing to buy a measly piece of stale bread. In the Saint Denis district, angry women set off to call their menfolk out of their workshops so that they could all go to the Convention. Elsewhere, women invaded sector committees. Thousands of them headed towards the Tuileries palace, dragging along

A pike is raised on Prairial 1.

other women who were still lining up outside bread shops. Some ladies were even pulled out of their carriages. Near the city hall they seized a drum and beat a call to arms. "It's not up to women to make the law," a shopkeeper was heard to mutter.

The crowd of women, which was being joined by men, some of them armed, reached Carrousel Square around 2 p.m. All demonstrators wore red, white and blue revolutionary cockades, some pinned to hats, others to blouses, on which the twin rallying cries of "Bread or death" and "Constitution of 1793" had been written. The Convention's main hall was soon invaded, but the women were quickly kicked out. Then the National Guard battalions arrived. Throughout Paris, drums had been beating out general quarters all morning long. In the southern and eastern parts of the city it was the insurgents who had mobilised, whereas in the wealthy western areas people had rallied to the Convention's calls. The crowds were heading towards Carrousel Square. There were some incidents, but no major clashes between the two sides.

A severed head is held aloft

Around 4 p.m. the insurgents managed to knock down the Assembly's gates. The deputy Féraud, who seemed to be opposed to the mob, was killed during an exchange of gunfire. He was to be the riot's only casualty. His body was dragged outside and his severed head was stuck on the end of a pike, which was then brandished before the president, Boissy

The Jacobin lowers it on Prairial 4.

480

d'Anglas. The latter withdrew, handing the presidency over to Vernier, and the session continued. Craftily, the moderates stood aside, thus giving the Montagnards a chance to vote for several measures and elect an executive committee grouping Duroy, Romme and Soubrany. It seemed that the time for revenge had struck for the Montagnards. No thought was given to arresting the members of the committees, despite the fact that they were preparing a triumphant return. By nightfall many of the insurgents had gone home because they had been given no clear orders. During the night Tallien and Legendre, who had rallied forces loyal to the Convention in the western areas, went to the gates of the Tuileries and chased the remaining rioters away. Shortly afterwards, arrest warrants were issued for 14 Montagnards.

Soldiers set to open fire on the people of the Saint Antoine district, who are prepared for a confrontation.

Prairial 2: the "fools' day"

News of the arrest of Féraud's killers spread throughout the city, as the Montagnard deputies remained powerless to act. The call to arms rang out in the Quinze Vingts sector at 2 o'clock in the morning of Prairial 2. At 10 a.m., alarm bells were rung in the Hôtel de Ville sector. The Saint Antoine district began mobilising once more.

Then people claimed that the Convention had ordered that all grain stocks in the provinces were to be counted. However, many saw this as just another empty promise. A unit of gunners and sector members meanwhile set off. It was led by Guillaume Delorme from the Antilles. By the time the column reached the Tuileries it had attracted a crowd of 20,000 people, who went up to the closed Assembly gates. This time, there were more than 40,000 uniformed men guarding the gates. The constables and soldiers led by General Dubois began to fraternise with the insurgent sector members, although the demonstrators did not press their advantage home. This could have been due to either tiredness or the hope of victory without bloodshed. The Convention, which was waiting for reinforcements from the regular army, chose to play for time. A few petitioners were listened to and a few reassuring words were exchanged. Then the Assembly's president went outside to greet the crowd. Thus

betrayed, the insurgents let their last chance to succeed slip away.

Prairial 3: the army moves in

The situation had considerably changed by the morning of Prairial 3. Overnight, several thousand horsemen had ridden into Paris and taken up positions around the Tuileries. The Convention was well defended at last, even though more troops were arriving all the time. If there were to be any fighting, a lot of blood would surely be shed.

The Assembly had appointed Delmas to command the troops in the capital. Menou was placed in charge of military operations, while Kilmaine, Brune and Murat were given senior positions. By late morning Kilmaine had marched into the district of Saint Antoine backed by 1,200 soldiers and Muscadins. They had, however, underestimated the rebel forces and quickly found themselves surrounded. The insurgents were, in fact, in complete control of Saint Antoine. Amid jeers and insults, Kilmaine was allowed to retreat. The day passed without any fighting or bloodshed. The only notable incident came when Féraud's killers were set free by the crowd as they were being escorted to the scaffold under heavy guard. This was only a meagre triumph for the rebels.

Prairial 3: the district capitulates

The Saint Antoine district was totally surrounded. The insurgents had set up barricades and were ready for a confrontation. However, their leaders were all in prison and nobody at the scene was able to give orders. Some of the sectors did try to come to the assistance of the besieged rebels, but they were disorganised and had no clear plan of action. An ultimatum was given to the inhabitants: either they put down their weapons and hand over Féraud's killers, or they would be blasted and starved out. Despair set in: the situation was deadlocked. The district capitulated to General Menou and repression began. Some 10,000 sansculottists were arrested.

The martyrs of Prairial

Even before the capitulation of the Saint Antoine district, the Convention set up a special military committee to try the suspected leaders of the uprising as quickly as possible. The chief aim of this move was to destroy the Montagnard party and also get rid of those members who had not been directly involved in the events of Prairial. A total of 36 people was sentenced to death, including Féraud's killers, several constables who had fraternised with rebels, and six deputies — Duquesnoy, Goujon, Romme, Soubrany, Bourbotte and Dubois. The six denounced their judges and chose to commit suicide in their cells. Only the first three died outright. Soubrany died on the way to the scaffold and the last two were beheaded. True to their vow to "live free or die", they chose to become martyrs.

Romme, who chose to die.

1 *(Prairial 13, Year III)* Paris. The Convention impeaches a total of 43 Jacobin deputies.

1 *(Prairial 13, Year III)* Paris. Students of the capital's central school of public works demand the return of the mathematician Monge, who has been in hiding since the days of insurrection. →

2 *(Prairial 14, Year III)* Paris. At the Convention, the composer Gossec plays a funeral song in honour of the deputy Féraud, who was assassinated on Prairial 1 at the Assembly.

2 *(Prairial 14, Year III)* Saint Etienne. During the night, 12 Jacobins are taken from their prison and assassinated.

4 *(Prairial 16, Year III)* Paris. Denounced after Thermidor 9 for extortion, the Convention member Maure commits suicide.

5 *(Prairial 17, Year III)* Marseilles. At the Saint Jean fort, royalists massacre the Jacobin prisoners. →

7 *(Prairial 19, Year III)* Luxembourg. The town capitulates. →

8 *(Prairial 20, Year III)* Paris. Death of the Dauphin, Louis Charles de France (→). Soon the hostilities will start again in Brittany and the Vendée.

12 *(Prairial 24, Year III)* Paris. Start of the trial before the military committee of the deputies involved in the insurrection of Prairial 1 (→17).

12 *(Prairial 24, Year III)* Marseilles. The journalist Ferréol de Beauregard, who had hidden during the Terror, republishes his *Journal de Marseille.*

13 *(Prairial 25, Year III)* Paris. Paris sector workshops which make military uniforms are liquidated to the advantage of private enterprises.

13 *(Prairial 27, Year III)* Vendée. Local municipal officials discover that, despite the pacification of the region, many travellers are still being murdered by bandits between Saint Gilles sur Vie and Sables d'Olonne.

15 *(Prairial 27, Year III)* Paris. General Napoléon Bonaparte has himself put on sick leave, having not received the posting he wanted from his superiors.

Marseilles: "terrorists" are massacred at Saint Jean fort

Marseilles, June 5

A bloodbath took place today at the prison of Saint Jean fort. The killers took advantage of the fact that the number of men guarding the garrison had been reduced, as some soldiers had been sent to Toulon to crush the Jacobin revolt. In all, 700 defenceless "terrorists" were put to death. When the representative Cadroy and his troops got back from Toulon, he took no action. The vengeance of the Company of the Sun is implacable. This group of southern royalists is made up of gangs intent of avenging years of oppression. So-called "terrorists" are no longer safe anywhere, even in jail. On May 11th., 30 Jacobins jailed in Aix were killed. On May 25th., a number of patriots being detained in the castle of Tarascon suffered the same fate.

Bodies of the victims of royalist vengeance at Saint Jean prison.

The theatrical hit of the season

Paris, June

Charles Pierre Ducancel has become a star overnight. His second play has been a smash hit for the past two months. It was first performed on April 27th. at the Ambigu theatre and is now being played at the Cité Variétés. This realistic comedy, entitled *L'Intérieur des Comités Révolutionnaires ou les Aristides Modernes,* has helped the playright forget about the total failure of his *Sainte Omelette,* which was banned during Robespierre's campaign against atheism. His fiercely anti-Jacobin new work is full of anecdotes, jokes and hilarious incidents that poke fun at the Committee members and criticise the way they meted out justice during the Terror. The author got his material from conversations he had overheard during a dinner party. The play is not just a hit in Paris. Many of the play's best lines are being repeated throughout France. The following is among the favourite ones: "Cato — I have just sold my soap for six francs less than the maximum. Aristide — Aren't you worried that the man who bought your soap will now inform on you? Cato — Don't fret, I'll simply have him jailed." Another line, said by a jailer who is pleased to see that a suspect is reading Montaigne, is: "Oh, since it's Montagnard, bravo".

Speculators are being hunted down

Paris, June 6

The National Guard successfully carried out a major operation this evening in the central Paris area of Palais Egalité. A large number of speculators were picked up and arrested on the Rue Vivienne and the Perron passageway near the Bourse. For some time now, police has been hunting down speculators who gamble on the depreciation of assignats and are involved in the illicit trade of various goods. The population holds them responsible for rising prices and the fall in the value of currency. Some speculators have made the best of the liberalisation of trade, making large profits by selling shares after having bought them on credit only hours earlier. Thus, Jean Denis Perrot, a former stockbroker, now owns property in Clichy and houses in Montmartre and the Marais. Monceil and Pyot, who speculated on the price of goods from the colonies, first ruined, then bought up, wholesale groceries in Paris, Bordeaux and Marseilles. The Convention is determined to stamp all this out.

Nobody wants assignats any more; people want to exchange them for cash.

Louis, the former Dauphin, is dead

Paris, June 8

The "Capet son", the orphan of the Temple, died this afternoon around 3 o'clock. His condition had become so serious over the past few days that the Committee of General Security had thought it prudent to ask Doctor Dumangin to assist Pelletan, the child's usual physician. This morning the two men discussed the problem at their patient's bedside. The boy was suffering from repeated vomiting and severe diarrhoea. Although he was still fully conscious, he was no longer able to say a single word. At Pelletan's request, the child was barely able to hold out his hand to be kissed by the doctor. In the afternoon, when the terrified guards urgently called the doctor back because their prisoner was in a desperate condition, Pelletan found that his patient had died. For three years the young Prince had not been allowed out of the Temple, and this lack of the exercise needed by a ten year old boy probably contributed to the spread of his disease. For more than a year little Louis Charles, already a weak and ailing child, had been suffering pain in his

The shoemaker Simon, depicted here as a vile killer of children.

joints. His symptoms were strangely similar to those of the first Dauphin, and the brothers may well have been afflicted with the same disease. The Committee of Public Safety was informed of the death immediately, and it ordered four deputies to look into the case and decide what steps must be taken. Meanwhile, the death of the child must be kept secret. Life at the Temple prison must go on as if nothing had happened so that the people suspect nothing (→11).

The young Dauphin's body is autopsied

Paris, June 11

The four doctors in charge of carrying out the autopsy on the body of young Louis Capet have been hard at work since this morning. The child who was so badly looked after has gathered some highly eminent physicians around him: Dumangin and Pelletan, head doctors of the Unité and Humanité

hospitals, Jeanroy and Lassus, both professors of medicine. Their task is not an easy one, as the child died 72 hours ago. The organs are in a bad state and the stomach is full of a "purulent, yellowish and highly fetid serosity". When their work was done, they sewed the body back together. It was only then that the guards were told of the death.

A schoolteacher faces enraged parents

Anjou, June 5

The schoolteacher of Angerville had a near riot on his hands today. For three hours, he was forced to hide inside his classroom by an enraged mob of parents, who were furious to see him teaching in the village's presbytery. However, the unfortunate teacher was perfectly within his rights, as the Lakanal law of last November states that local communities are to provide free housing for teachers. Presbyteries can be used in cases where they have been deserted by non-juring

priests. The villagers, however, do not agree. Supported by a certain Le Roux, who runs the local "free school", they started off by ordering the poor teacher to hand over the church's pews, which he used as benches for his students. When he turned this demand down, the angry parents broke down the presbytery door and kicked him out. They were shouting that he would be replaced by a priest, Eude. The incident has shown once again that the life of a republican schoolmaster is not an easy one.

Monge has to go into hiding

Paris, June 1

A squad of the Republic's policemen burst into Madame Monge's home two days ago to arrest her husband. However, the scientist had managed to disappear. In order to force his wife to reveal where the mathematician had gone, the police settled down in her home, demanding to be housed and fed for as long as necessary. Since May 29th. an arrest warrant has been out for Monge and his property has been impounded. Some claim that it was his doorman who informed on him to the Unité sector, saying he was in favour of the agrarian law, a supporter of Babeuf and involved in several riots. A neighbour who had attended the sector meeting had warned Monge and advised him to flee. Although he felt he had not committed any crime, Monge left his home right away. He has sought refuge in the country house belonging to his friend, the chemist Berthollet, at Aulnay sous Bois.

Luxembourg falls without a fight

Luxembourg, June 7

The Duchy of Luxembourg, an Austrian possession for the past 82 years, has just surrendered to the French. General Hatry has good reason to be pleased by such an easy success, but he would have preferred a bit more of a fight. In order to add a bit of glory to his lacklustre victory, he sent a detailed inventory of captured equipment to the Convention today: 24 flags, one standard, 377 bronze cannons, six swivel guns, 18 field howitzers, 57 mortars, 14,991 rifles, 2,600 pieces of artillery of various types, 336,857 cannonballs, 47,801 grenades and 11,474 bombs. General Hatry is also hoping that Paris will take due note of the 12,396 prisoners he has taken and justly reward his men's bravery and his own truly outstanding performance.

Emigré nobles are again in the news

Verona, June

Even when they are not busy plotting against the Republic, the émigré nobles like to be talked about. The Comte de Provence is now living on money provided by the English, Italian and Austrian courts. He is often to be seen in the company of Madame de Balbi, his mistress "to the best of his ability". He salutes the Austrian corporals "with abject obsequiousness". His brother, the Comte d'Artois, is to be seen with Madame de Polastron. The Comte d'Antraigues is always with Madame Saint Huberty, a former singer popularly known as "the joker's flower".

The Comte d'Artois, the Comte de Provence and the Prince de Condé.

Convention

Madame de Staël's "salon" reopens

Paris, June

"Jacobsson, my wife is on her way ..." the poor, ailing de Staël whispered to his private secretary when he heard the news that his worthy spouse was coming back to Paris. A month ago Germaine, along with the ever-present Benjamin Constant, decided to return to France regardless of the problems this might cause. Her husband was quite right to be worried. Despite all her solemn promises to behave, she reopened her salon on the Rue du Bac and began plotting as soon as she arrived in the capital. Her new dream is to play a big rôle in this changed France where everything seems possible. Mme. de Staël now claims to be a firm supporter of the Republic, on condition that the reins of power are entrusted to

Mme. de Staël, Necker's daughter.

people who are truly remarkable because of "their talents and virtues". In other words, people of such obvious capabilities as her beloved Benjamin.

Boishardy, the brave Chouan, is killed

Côtes du Nord, June 17

After being hunted for a week, the Chouan leader Boishardy was killed at Moncontour by republican grenadiers. As the main figure in the revolt in the Côtes du Nord, Boishardy had won respect and popularity due to his courage and style. Curiously, he had initially greeted the Revolution reasonably well. It was only after the Terror spread throughout the land that he took up arms. After some major victories, his men began to desert him because of the effect of Hoche's policy of appeasement.

Provence dubs self Louis XVIII

Verona, June 24

The eldest among Louis XVI's brothers will no longer be called "Monsieur". Louis Stanislas Xavier, the Comte de Provence, has just published a manifesto in which he proclaims himself "King of France and Navarre". Following his elder brother's execution he had taken the title of Regent of France. Now he is at it again, claiming to be the heir to the throne. Since the son of Louis XVI, the Dauphin, died on June 8th., it should logically be the Comte de Provence who succeeds the dead sovereign, but the monarchy has been abolished. Many émigrés have said that this latest move by Provence is "madness". Louis Stanislas was probably advised to go ahead by his confidant, the Duc d'Avaray. The manifesto adds that the new "king" plans to restore the Ancien Régime and calls on the French to have faith in his absolute power and his clemency, despite the fact that he plans to punish his brother's executioners. For the time being, Louis Stanislas is spending most of his energy on planning the grandiose ceremony for his coronation.

Celebration of the alliance between Paris and Batavia on June 19th. on Amsterdam's Revolution Square.

Mystery woman's body found

Evry sur Seine, June 28

The body of an unidentified female aged around 35 was found near the Seine river this morning. There were no traces of blows on the body and the victim's muddy clothes and still damp hair pointed to a death by drowning. Investigators rejected the theory of an accident, however, as the river is very shallow and there is practically no current at the spot near a bridge where the body was discovered. Judging by her fine skin and well looked-after hands, the victim was not used to doing manual work. She still wore her jewels. The rings and necklaces seemed to indicate that the victim was well off and that robbery had not been the motive for her death. Investigators were particularly struck by the fact that she wore a fine gold ring engraved with the words "Liberty, Equality, those are our sole divinities". Impressed by the victim's obvious patriotism, the authorities have called on the press to try to find out if the mystery woman had a family. Police officials want to avoid her body being buried in a common grave, as is usually done in such cases.

Convention takes strong action to crush the unrest in Lyons

A monument erected at Brotteaux in memory of the "unfortunate and innocent victims" of the Terror.

Lyons, June 24

People are wondering whether Kellermann will be forced to call on his 12,000 men to march on Lyons. The decree, which is in fact an ultimatum, approved today by the Assembly shows that the deputies mean business. The Assembly is highly concerned by the fact that the Thermidorian reaction in the city of Lyons is becoming clearly royalist in nature. The massacre of about 100 prisoners on May 4th. had brought about a change in policy. Now the time for conciliation is over and the deputies are determined to restore order. The influx of émigrés, the wave of murders and the arming of the National Guard have led the Convention to act firmly to crush the rebels. The decree will mean that administrative powers will be suspended, the National Guard will be disarmed within 24 hours, émigrés will be handed over to the authorities and all foreigners will have to leave.

King's daughter fascinates Paris

Paris, June

Louis XVI's daughter is often to be seen sitting under the chestnut trees in the gardens of the Temple playing with her dog Coco, with her long blond hair spilling down over her shoulders. She also likes to play with her tame goat. The windows of nearby houses are packed with spectators who come each day to watch the former Princess at play in the gardens. It has become fashionable to go on this daily pilgrimmage to the Temple. To keep the young woman's mind occupied, musicians play songs about her misfortunes. A painter equipped with a telescope has even started drawing her portrait. Although she is still a prisoner, Madame Royale is free to move around the jail. She has been allowed to have a lady companion, Madame de Chanterenne. After spending two solitary years, the young prisoner is delighted to have a friend at last.

Artificial limbs for war victims

Paris, June 28

The mechanic Sonneck is to be honoured by the Arts School. The secretary general of the Foundation greeted him solemnly today at a special public session. This newly created institution has been set up to present the latest inventions. Although it has no funds to give inventors, it can at least bring them public recognition. Sonneck has earned the honour. He invented mechanical wooden legs that are exact copies of the real thing. With such artificial limbs, amputees can walk and sit without discomfort or pain. War wounded invited by the Foundation tested the limbs, which they found to be neither too heavy nor too light. These mutilated volunteer "guinea pigs" all seemed very happy with the clever new gadgets that will make life so much easier for them and with which they will at last be able to look just like ordinary men.

Boissy d'Anglas unveils the constitution

Paris, June 23

The defence of property is one of the chief objectives of the new institutions. The president Boissy d'Anglas, has stressed this to the deputies: "You must guarantee the property of the rich at last." The Convention was no longer happy with the Constitution of 1793, viewing it as being too egalitarian. It had initially considered modifying it by using the organic laws, but the events of Germinal convinced the deputies to get rid of this Jacobin text and start from scratch. The new constitution was drafted by a committee made up of true republicans, such as La Réveillière, and a majority of moderates, like Thibaudeau and Lanjuinais. Two moderates, Daunou and Boissy d'Anglas, played a big rôle in the drafting of the text. D'Anglas said that "absolute equality is a pipe dream." Believing that poverty in most cases stems from laziness, he said: "We must be governed by the best, those who have had the best education and have the greatest stake in the enforcement of the law. Such men will be found only among people who own property. A nation that is governed by property owners is a nation where social order exists". Such principles are the basis for a bourgeois republic built on property ownership, which will in future be the sole criterion for citizenship.

François de Boissy d'Anglas.

Convention

1 *(Messidor 13, Year III)*
Paris. Tallien is sent as a special envoy to join Hoche.

3 *(Messidor 15, Year III)*
Quiberon. The army division led by the Comte d'Hervilly captures the Penthière fort.

4 *(Messidor 16, Year III)*
Paris. Opening of the discussions on the first reading by the Convention of the draft of the new constitution.

7 *(Messidor 19, Year III)*
Paris. At the Convention, Thomas Paine defends the principle of universal suffrage which the deputies have decided to abandon in the next constitution.

8 *(Messidor 20, Year III)*
Paris. The Convention decrees that all workers aged between 18 and 25 years, employed in the manufacturing and repair of arms, steel works, forges, foundries and saltpetre factories, will be exempt from military conscription.

9 *(Messidor 21, Year III)*
Paris. The Council of the 500 confirms the status of Val de Grâce as the capital's military hospital.

9 *(Messidor 21, Year III)*
Paris. The proposal made by Rouzet to the Convention to give women the right to vote is rejected by Lanjuinais.

10 *(Messidor 22, Year III)*
Paris. The revolutionary Tribunal sends Joseph Le Bon back to the criminal tribunal of the Somme.

12 *(Messidor 24, Year III)*
Paris. The Convention decides to create an army of the interior with the forces of both the 17th. division and Paris, augmented by those of the departments of the Somme, the Seine Inférieure and the Eure. This new army will watch over the food supplies to the capital and the maintenance of order.

14 *(Messidor 26, Year III)*
Paris. The Convention authorises the launching of a loan of one billion francs, at an annual interest rate of three per cent.

15 *(Messidor 27, Year III)*
Quiberon. In its turn, the division of Sombreuil reaches the coast. It is made up of diverse elements: the remnants of the Condé army who had gone over to England and republican prisoners who are ready to desert at the first opportunity.

"Marseillaise": national anthem

Paris, July 14

It was high time that France paid homage to the *Marseillaise*. This song which had spurred on the soldiers of the Republic, particularly at Jemmapes, where officers saw it as a sort of secret weapon, had gradually fallen from grace. Rouget de Lisle's work was adopted by the Jacobins and had become a symbol of the Terror. The Thermidorians had resolved to replace it by the *Réveil du Peuple*. There had even been frequent brawls between the supporters of the two songs, so the Convention decided to step in to solve the dispute. The musicians of the National Institute went to the Assembly today, as they do on each public holiday, to perform several revolutionary works. In fact, only the *Marseillaise* was played. After the ceremony, a member of the Convention, Jean Debry, spoke of the military glory of the song's words and music. He proposed that the *Marseillaise* be proclaimed the official national anthem.

Martial song as an allegorical figure, sculpted by François Rude in 1836.

Vengeance against the Orange tribunal

Avignon, July 10

After having managed to escape from the people's vengeance several times, the members of the special "terrorist" tribunal of Orange were all executed on June 27th. and their bodies thrown into the Rhône. All, that is, except for one clerk. The court needed more time to reach its verdict. He was finally sentenced today to 20 years in irons and six hours in the stocks. However, the clerk recalled the case of an usher who was killed by the mob as he sat in the stocks. He begged his judges, who agreed, to sentence him to four extra years in irons rather than to the stocks.

An open air market on the Ile de la Cité, facing the main façade of the Grand Châtelet fortress, which serves as both tribunal and prison.

Geography is now a serious business

Paris, July

It used to be said that "geography's first purpose is to wage war". When England is the enemy, efficient compasses become as vital as powerful cannons. On June 25th. the deputies therefore decreed the establishment of a central astronomical office. The Convention decided to entrust a group of ten men with the task of "revealing the true face of the Earth", of ridding astronomy of its old superstitions and giving the nation's sailors "rules that are applicable in all circumstances". Since the start of the month, the specialists have been hard at work. The team is made up of four astronomers and their assistants, two geometricians, one geographer, two former navigators and an artist in charge of the upkeep of the optical instruments. They will all, according to their fields of expertise, be involved in the technical aspects of nautical instruments, the running of observatories, the publication of a maritime almanach and, in a more general way, the advancement of the related sciences of cartography and meteorology.

The Anzin mines are privatised

Northern France, July 10

It was a real windfall for the financiers Berruyer, Perier, Sabatier and Lecouteulx. The usual procedure for the public auction of the State's stake in national assets will not be enforced.

The Committee of Public Safety had decided that only non-émigré owners will be permitted to buy. However, ruined by the way the firm was run during the Terror, the financiers were unable to come up with the 2,418,505 livres needed to buy up the shares that were seized after their former associates emigrated. Therefore, the four bankers offered a loan to the proxy agent, on condition that they were allowed to have a nearly majority share in the firm's capital. Thus, in the name of economic liberty, one of the richest mines in France, which provides some of the highest quality coal, has been indirectly ceded for a considerable sum to businessmen who are closely linked to the government.

Two crooks are arrested in Paris

Paris, July 8

The problem of speculation is getting worse every day. This is causing an increase in fraud. The rate of the louis and of paper currency is regularly and quickly posted on the façades of all neighbourhood grocers' shops. A bourgeois who had tried to exchange 500,000 livres in assignats worth 10,000 livres each against smaller denominations was the victim of a couple of crooks. A certain pensioned-off Benedictine monk, Malvaut, who runs a shop on the Place du Louvre, and a man who claimed to be his uncle, Martel, both knew a good opportunity when they saw one. The "uncle" said he was head of a department at the Treasury and sat at the bourgeois' table. When they had wined and dined, the man was taken to the so-called office. His money was quickly taken and he was given a piece of paper, while the crooks said "Keep that, we'll be in touch". He was still waiting when the banks closed. Luckily, police put an end to the scam and returned the victim's money.

Royalists and patriots cause violent brawls in big city cafés

The Incroyables Café in Paris, where customers come to talk politics and discuss the events of the day.

Besançon, July

The streets of Besançon only appear to be calm; the customers of two cafés facing each other are in a permanent state of alert. The one owned by the widow Douhaint, which is provocatively called Thermidor 9, is a known hang-out for Chouans. Informers often tell the police about the place. It is where young royalists meet to discuss the latest news from Paris and Lyons. The republican soldiers and Jacobins who ventured there to burn the café's sign were badly beaten up. Constables rarely show up there and the city authorities are hesitant about closing the establishment down. The city council has refused to pay for the damage, although the law on public order states that it should. Meanwhile patriots meet at the *Café de la Montagne,* which has been given the new name of *Café de l'Egalité.* When the opposing sides get tired of fighting in cafés, they seek each other out in the town's theatres, where they try to out do their foes by singing songs. Those battles are between the *Réveil du Peuple* and the *Marseillaise,* or between *Ça Ira* and the Vendean song.

Is the Rhine's right bank to be annexed?

Paris, July

At the urging of Reubell and Merlin de Douai, the *Journal de Paris* has asked its readers the following question: "Is it in the interest of the French Republic to push its borders back as far as the banks of the Rhine?" The best replies will be rewarded with a prize. Out of the 56 replies, those of the French diplomat Thérémin and the Belgian Tainturier, a judge at the civil tribunal of Liège, were considered the best. They had both argued for annexation. Only two Rhinelanders were in favour of this policy, but they were émigrés living in Paris. One of them was Dorsch, a Jacobin from Mainz. For his part, the burgomaster of Cologne replied with a violent attack against French territorial claims. The competition's organisers were disappointed by the results of the contest. As heirs to the Girondist policy of natural borders, Merlin de Douai, Sieyès and Reubell are ardent supporters of the annexation of the Rhineland. They stress the economic advantages of such a move for France: the region is rich in raw materials such as coal, wool and iron. It also has a strong industrial base, notably in textiles and metallurgy. Annexation, they say, would be an ideal way to restore France's balance of trade. The Alsatian, Reubell, doesn't see the assimilation of the German speaking population as being a problem. It worked in Alsace, he said.

Assignat values continue to drop

Paris, July

One hundred livres in assignats are now worth only three livres in cash. Such is the disastrous effect of the galloping inflation that has hit France since Thermidor. The end of the Terror, the abolition of the maximum and economic liberalisation measures have led to price rises that the State tried to contain by issuing more assignats. More than three billion assignats were printed in seven months! There are now more than 11 billion livres in paper money in circulation. As there is no guarantee, it loses its value. Currency has lost 68 per cent of its value since December 1794.

18 *(Messidor 30, Year III)*
Evreux. Publication by the printer Chaumont of the first edition of *Memoirs for use in the history of the war in Vendée,* by General Turreau.

18 *(Messidor 30, Year III)*
Morbihan. Following the death of Tinténiac, Georges Cadoudal takes over the leadership of the Breton Chouans.

19 *(Thermidor 1, Year III)*
Spain. General Moncey's army, continuing its advance, seizes Bilbao, after having conquered Vittoria on July 17th. and pushed the Spaniards beyond the Ebro river (→22).

21 *(Thermidor 3, Year III)*
Morbihan. Hoche defeats the royalist defenders of Quiberon, who capitulate.→

22 *(Thermidor 4, Year III)*
Basel. France signs a peace treaty with Spain, which withdraws from the coalition upon seeing its territory invaded.→

24 *(Thermidor 6, Year III)*
Paris. New run at the Feydeau Theatre of *Pamela, or virtue rewarded,* a comedy by François de Neuchâteau, which caused the closing of the Théâtre de la Nation and the arrest of its actors in 1793.

24 *(Thermidor 6, Year III)*
Paris. In the Convention, Marie Joseph Chénier denounces the "White Terror" ravaging Lyons and southern France.

25 *(Thermidor 7, Year III)*
Paris. After re-establishment of the *patente* tax on July 22nd. the Assembly restores the tax on rental income, which the Montagnards had abolished.

27 *(Thermidor 9, Year III)*
Paris. For the anniversary of Robespierre's fall, both the *Marseillaise* and *The People's Awakening* are played. The authorities let the military and Jacobins pursue Muscadins.

28 *(Thermidor 10, Year III)*
Vannes. Execution of the former Bishop of Dol, d'Hercé, and of the Comte de Sombreuil. The Military Committee set up by Tallien cleverly pardons the Chouans taken prisoner at Quiberon, but has no mercy on the émigrés arrested in English uniform. Some 748 of them will be shot.

28 *(Thermidor 10, Year III)*
Paris. In the Assembly, Aubry proposes an amnesty for the many soldiers who have been driven to desertion because of wretched army life.

The royalists capitulate at Quiberon

Republican troops capture Penthièvre fort, on the tip of the peninsula, which was occupied by royalists.

Quiberon, July 21

The Quiberon trap has closed on the émigrés. Amidst an indescribable panic only a few royalists, including the Comte de Puisaye, managed to regain the English ships commanded by Admiral Warren. The fierce waves had prevented Warren's vessels from reaching the shore, and the émigrés threw themselves into the water in an attempt to reach them. But the English artillery, which wanted to protect the fighters fleeing toward the ships, hit both royalists and the Blues. This was the tragic epilogue to an affair that had begun last month. On June 16th., five regiments left Southampton under the orders of Puisay, seconded by Rotalier and d'Hervilly. Three ships of the line with 74 guns each, two frigates with 44, four other vessels with 30 to 36 guns, several gunboats and 60 transport ships set sail for the French coast. It was a major expedition: 80,000 rifles, 80 guns, munitions, powder, uniforms, shoes for 60,000 men, biscuits, salted meat, brandy and counterfeit assignats. The division had 4,000 men, including, along with the émigrés, 2,848 French prisoners-of-war who had been signed up in exchange for a promise of freedom. The plan worked out by the chief of the émigré force was to capture Vannes and Rennes, get the Chouans to join up, and move toward Paris. After making sure there were no republican garrisons along the coast, the division landed on June 27th. on the Carnac beach. But, going against the opinion of Puisaye, Georges Cadoudal and the Bretons,

d'Hervilly refused to move forward, while General Lazare Hoche, the chief of the republican forces, was expelling the Chouans from Auray, Meudon and Landévant, which they had just occupied. On June 28th., d'Hervilly decided to march on the Penthièvre Fort, which closes off the Quiberon Peninsula, and on July 3rd., he captured Major Delise's republican garrison. But in isolating himself on the peninsula in this way, d'Hervilly made a tactical blunder. Three weeks later a second émigré corps arrived from England under Sombreuil's orders and landed near Port Haliguen. Hoche immediately went on the offensive, occupying the Sainte Barbe positions and digging in there. The royalists' and Chou-

ans' attacks aimed at forcing him out were all failures. At midnight on July 21st., with a wild sea, three republican columns moved forward along the cliff, under cover of the storm, to catch the Chouans from behind and push them back from position to position. The royalists found all their hopes in ruins. The émigré chief, Sombreuil, even fell into Hoche's hands. As for England, it backed up the émigrés only weakly, and perfidiously, as it turned out. Thus, even if no English blood was spilt, there are still certain people in London who do not hesitate to emphasise the fact that England's honour has certainly taken a hard knock in this affair of the failed émigré invasion of the French mainland (→July 28).

The royalists surrender to the Blues, after the émigrés' failed campaign.

France and Spain sign a peace treaty

Basel, July 22

France has just signed its fourth peace treaty in three months. The fall of Bilbao and of Vittoria and then the advance to the Ebro River forced the Spaniards to the negotiating table. France is to evacuate the territories it invaded in Spain, and receive the Spanish part of Saint Domingue. It accepts Spanish mediation in connection with Portugal and the Italian states. In exchange Spain is to leave the coalition, and there is a provision for a future offensive and defensive alliance. Thus French policy seems to be bearing fruit. The French government wanted to get Austria to give way by means of separate treaties with Spain, Holland and Prussia. Those treaties have now been obtained, but there is nothing to indicate that Vienna is being forced to make peace. But France is exhausted by war, and its conquests are no help until it can get all its opponents to lay down their arms. Moreover, the transfer of Saint Domingue is all relative, in that fighting against the English is still going on there. Still, the peace frees both countries from a hopeless war and deprives England of a useful alliance (→ Aug. 18, 96).

Jacobins involved in "black collar war" in the French capital

Republicans strip a royalist's black collar off and make him wear a ridiculous, multicoloured one.

Paris, July

Their objective: tangling with the Jacobins. Their slogan: "Long live the Constitution!". They include suspects released from prison, rebels, journalists, artists, clerks, brokers and small tradesmen. The main ringleaders are Fréron, Garat, Pitou, Saint Huruge, Elleviou, Langlois and Martainville. These gangs of young people hunt out what they call "cannibals" and track down the "knights of the order of the guillotine". In their tight-fitting and "dung-coloured" coats with black velvet collars, their "cod-tail" coattails, and their knee-breeches fastened below the knee, they move along in a cloud of musk. In all there are an estimated 2,000 to 3,000 of these "salon soldiers", who ply the new kind of terror aimed at the sansculottists as if it were the latest fashion.

Emigré in Hamburg has odd practices

Hamburg, July 22

At 11 p.m. a man left the home of M. de Brûlepont, a refugee nobleman known to hire émigrés. Just a few steps away from the house, the man collapsed with atrocious stomach pains. He had just been poisoned by his host, who wanted to put him to sleep in order to rob him. This was not the first time the Frenchman had done such things. When his German neighbours learnt about his new crime, they broke the windows in his house to try to lynch him. But the guard was alerted and fired on the attackers, killing two people and injuring another critically. Order was not restored until the city was hit by a hard rain. The poisoner came out of all this unharmed, but people are beginning to wonder when the authorities will throw him in to jail.

French Army recruiting as soldiers desert

France, July

The soldiers of Year II are no longer with us. Young people are ever more reluctant to comply with the requisitions, which frequently give rise to incidents. For instance, in the Ariège, the inhabitants of Mazères prevented the Gendarmerie for a month from getting its hands on deserters. In the Ardèche region as in the Pyrénées Orientales, many mayors have reported the emergence in their communes of gangs of rebels who loot, cut down trees of liberty, attack the regular troops, and even go so far as to put prices on the heads of municipal officials. Such defections mean that the forces are shorter of men than they were only five years ago, just before Valmy. Even worse is the fact that the spirit of patriotism seems to have disappeared among many Frenchmen (→ Nov. 23).

The odious murderer hid in hospital

Paris, July 21

"Kill him!" This unanimous shout going up from the crowd is not aimed at any ordinary condemned man. On Grève Square, Denelle is going to answer for his crimes for the last time. He was a member of the Popincourt sector and of the former Revolutionary Committee, and was found guilty of murdering his wife and three of their children. But he had disappeared after his crime. The police found him by chance, on the basis of a report by a woman visiting somebody at the Hôtel Dieu home. The killer had been admitted as a patient, under his own name! He was taken to the mental ward before he was turned in.

Goodbye assignat

"How ungrateful the French!"
The printer told the assignats.
'Tis, sooth, a sorry state.
By law their block is to be burned
As they're by the people spurned.
'Tis that will compensate.

Tey're forged by William Pitt.
'Tis, sooth, a sorry state.
At Quiberon our men of war
The English bastards beat;
'Tis that will compensate.

When you say these assignats
Enriched the Vendée Chouans,
'Twas, sooth, a sorry state.
Oh, the woes the bills did cause,
'Service rendered' all applause.
'Tis that will compensate.

For Paris these bills did flood,
Deceiving men with wealth dud.
'Twas, sooth, a sorry state.
In future just one single bill
With joy the man in need will fill.
'Tis that will compensate.

2 *(Thermidor 15, Year III)* Vendée. Charette responds to the execution of the émigrés captured at Quiberon by having 300 republican prisoners massacred at Belleville.

3 *(Thermidor 16, Year III)* Paris. Establishment of the National Music Conservatory at Sarrette's initiative. It will replace the National Music Institute, the former Royal Singing School, and the free Music School of the National Guard. Sarrette, who is named government commissioner, is being assisted by five composers: Gossec, Méhul, Grétry, Le Sueur and Cherubini.

4 *(Thermidor 17, Year III)* Paris. David is tried and released. →

5 *(Thermidor 18, Year III)* Paris. The Convention does away with the civic spirit certificate.

9 *(Thermidor 22, Year III)* Paris. The Convention orders Fouché's arrest (→12).

10 *(Thermidor 23, Year III)* Paris. The Committee of Public Safety rejects Austria's armistice proposals.

11 *(Thermidor 24, Year III)* Paris. The keys of Notre Dame are returned to the constitutional clergy, a harbinger of the re-establishment of Catholic worship there.

11 *(Thermidor 24, Year III)* Paris. Creation of a three-member Police Agency.

12 *(Thermidor 25, Year III)* Paris. The Convention finishes the first reading of the draft constitution, and rejects the text proposed by Sieyès.

13 *(Thermidor 26, Year III)* Paris. Under the influence of the attempted royalist invasion at Quiberon, the Assembly adopts an added provision to the draft constitution recalling that French people who have abandoned France since July 15, 1789, and who are not included in the exceptions made to laws against émigrés, may never return to France.

14 *(Thermidor 27, Year III)* Aix en Provence. The "Companions of the Sun" massacre 15 terrorists.

15 *(Thermidor 28, Year III)* Paris. The Convention decides to create a new monetary unit, the franc, with an almost identical value to the Ancien Régime's livre.

Republicans and Muscadins mix it up in street fighting

Paris, August 1

The police are at their wits' end. There has been another battle between the royalist "black collars" and republican soldiers in the gardens of Palais Egalité, formerly known as Palais Royal. On the eve of the opening of the primary assemblies that are to decide on adopting the new constitution, confrontations between Muscadins and sans-culottists have become routine. The gilded youth, which served so well the political reaction launched by the Convention after Thermidor, now embarrasses the deputies. They no longer need it, as the Jacobin danger has been removed for good since the repression of the Prairial working-class riots. They would even be glad to get rid of the gilded youth, since they fear they may be overwhelmed on the right by these young people, who are open monarchists. Even Tallien, who used to encourage them to pursue the former "terrorists", now disowns them. The Convention has tried to disperse these extremist gangs.

It's not a good idea to find yourself alone when the opposing faction is about.

Knowing that they consist primarily of people who have dodged requisitions, it adopted a decree on July 28th. granting deserters amnesty, provided they join the military within ten days. But the Muscadins have no intention of leaving the capital. They want to continue their intimidation efforts to frighten the republicans and with the idea of infiltrating the sectors, the majority of which already actually find themselves in the hands of right-wing forces.

David is acquitted

Paris, August 4

At the end of an exciting trial, the painter David was acquitted. Yet he was in an awkward position, and the charges laid against him were serious ones. Among the most serious accusations, naturally, were his relations with Robespierre and his clan, as well as the rôle he played in the Committee of General Security. Had he not signed many arrest warrants? But his artful speech managed to convince his accusers that he "wanted only the people's cause". He also managed to prove that the list found in his home did not refer to people to be outlawed, but rather to be appointed to the new Arts Jury. He cleansed himself of the libellous accusation of having sent artists to the scaffold because their fame might have damaged his reputation. Finally, in response to the charge that he had been the "tyrant of the arts", he said he had only wanted to destroy the academic institution that oppressed young talent. What did all this amount to in comparison with his eminent role in arranging the Revolution's feasts and his works inspired by events he immortalised? (→Sept., 95).

Fouché escapes arrest by skin of his teeth

Paris, August 12

With Fouché you always have to expect surprises, and he has again lived up to this reputation. Yet this terrorist's fate seemed to have been settled when the Assembly decreed his arrest on August 9th., followed by deportation to Guyana. The "dry guillotine" was a sure thing. But Fouché, who had vanished, did not want to be ignored for long.

This very morning, a letter written by Fouché himself reached the Assembly. He magnanimously agrees to pass over his colleagues' ingratitude in silence, but, in a subtly threatening way, he links their future with his. Recalling their shared past, he refers each of them to memories of an agitated past. The Assembly took fright at such serene threats, and Fouché is still free.

Muscadins, with their carefully careless dress, lord it over the others.

🏛 **Convention**

16 *(Thermidor 29, Year III)*
Paris. The Convention voids "all of the judgements handed down in a revolutionary manner from March 10, 1793, to Nivôse 8 of Year II, against persons who are now living". Thus it refuses to go back on the death sentences issued during the Reign of Terror.

16 *(Thermidor 29, Year III)*
Bas Rhin. At Blotzheim, General Pichegru meets with Fauche Borel, an agent of Louis XVIII and the Prince de Condé, who suggests that the general should agree to serve the King (→20).

18 *(Fructidor 1, Year III)*
Nantes. Nantes inhabitants, exasperated by the Chouans' blockade of the city, massacre 11 prisoners.

20 *(Fructidor 3, Year III)*
Paris. The revolutionary actress Claire Lacombe gets out of prison.→

22 *(Fructidor 5, Year III)*
Paris. The Convention adopts the Constitution of Year III (→Oct. 31, 95), along with the Two-Thirds Decree (→30), and decides to submit them to a referendum for approval.

22 *(Fructidor 5, Year III)*
Paris. In the interest of reducing Jacobin influence, the Convention declares the ineligibility of the 68 deputies indicted or accused since Thermidor 9.

22 *(Fructidor 5, Year III)*
Paris. The Convention does away with the name Department of Paris, which then becomes the Seine Department.

23 *(Fructidor 6, Year III)*
Paris. On the basis of a report by Mailhe, the Convention dissolves people's associations still in existence (→Sept. 1, 95).

27 *(Fructidor 10, Year III)*
Toulouse. The Republic's Museum of the South opens to the public.

29 *(Fructidor 12, Year III)*
Paris. Baron de Staël signs a peace treaty with France in Sweden's name.

31 *(Fructidor 14, Year III)*
Paris. Even though the annexation of Belgium has not been decided, the Committee of Public Safety approves the division that country into nine departments.

31 *(Fructidor 14, Year III)*
England. Death in London of the composer and chess master François André Philidor.→

Majority of the new assembly to consist of same members

Paris, August 30

The present deputies have no intention of being dislodged from their seats. But they are so unpopular that, if nothing were done, they might well lose their hold on power in the next election. Public opinion holds them responsible for both the Reign of Terror, which they initially backed even if they later condemned it, and the very poor condition of the national economy. Hence they have just approved two decrees to avoid defeat. The first one, voted on August 22nd., obliges voters to choose at least two thirds of their future representatives from among the current members of the Convention. The second one, adopted today, says that, if this requirement is not met, the re-elected deputies shall coopt their colleagues so as to reach the desired proportion. This electoral rigging may appear scandalous, as it is aimed more at serving the interest of a political oligarchy than the general interest. But the measure will also prevent the election of a royalist majority, which could not be ruled out in an atmosphere of civil and foreign war. Thus it protects republican institutions. The revolutionary dictatorship did this in suspending the elections 1793 voting (→Oct. 26).

Pichegru is doubted

Illkirch, August 20

The counter-revolutionary network is becoming active. There have been rumours that Pichegru, the commander of the Army of the Rhine, is going over to the Austrians. Fauche Borel, a freemason serving the émigrés, gave him a letter from Montgaillard, a secret agent resonsible for negotiations. Pichegru is offered an enormous amount of money, a promotion to marshal, Chambord Castle and the governorship of Alsace if he agrees to his forces' serving the King and turns Hüningen over to Condé. General Pichegru is ready to accept these offers, but wants enough time to win a few victories to improve his forces' morale. He is ambitious and a pleasure-seeker, and has been disappointed by a state that, in his view neglects its defenders.

Michel offers a new vision of Nature

Paris, August

Georges Michel is not an unknown. He has been able to take advantage of the vogue for Flemish masters by selling his inexpensive imitations of Teniers. But the public does not know every side of this real artist, nor his work as a whole. Michel has given up traditional landscapes, ennobled by the addition of architecture from Antiquity or mythology, in order to paint just what he sees, without prettifying it or falling into an anecdotal approach. His favourite subjects are the simple, harsh Paris suburbs. Yet *The Storm* shows his profound renewal of a vision of Nature.

"The Storm" by Georges Michel shows an artist open to Dutch influence.

Sports in France becoming the latest fad

Paris, August

The French are taking a greater interest in their bodies. For some time now they have imitated the Ancient Greeks by organising foot and horse races that are open to amateurs on the Champ de Mars. The Convention has even tried to introduce physical exercise into the public schools' programmes, "to the extent the localities allow this". But, thanks to Turquin, swimming is the most popular sport. At his school on the island of Saint Louis in central Paris, founded in 1786, he offers his own method of learning. He first teaches the student the required movements by attaching him to a suspension system. Then come the diving exercises, and then the ones for clothed swimming. It is, needless to say, forbidden to outrage good public morals by swimming in the nude!

Current Anglomania is revealed in a marked taste for challenging sports.

Philidor is mourned by opera and chess

Philidor had multiple talents.

England, August 31

One of the most brilliant musicians of our time has just died in London. François André Philidor worked with Rousseau on *Gallant Muses* and *Le Devin de Village*, and he wrote several comic operas marked by a very sure dramatic feeling. He was sensitive to the time's taste, and was able to adapt his style to fashion's requirements: vaudevillian, middle class, imaginative or philosophical. He was also among the greatest chess players of all time, his name being attached to a "Philidor defence". In 1748 he published an *Analysis of the game of chess*, a proof, if one is needed, of the great diversity of this exceptional man's talents.

"Free woman" is freed from prison

Paris, August 20

After 16 months of detention, Claire Lacombe saw the gates of her prison open up today. The former president of the Revolutionary Republican women, who signed her petitions for release "Lacombe, a free woman", is finally going to be able to go home. She was initially incarcerated at the Plessis jail, and finally wound up in the Luxembourg Prison, where she opened a small shop for the detainees in the best middle-class style. Could her imprisonment have quietened her down? She seems to have lost the impetuous part of her nature ... or perhaps faith in the Revolution.

September 1795
from 1st. to 15th.

 Convention

1 *(Fructidor 15, Year III)* Paris. The Convention decides to restore the right to vote in the sectors to the former partisans of the terrorists in order to balance the influence of the royalists, who will do everything possible to prevent the application of this measure.

1 *(Fructidor 15, Year III)* Rodez. In accordance with the decree of August 23rd., the People's Association, already deserted by the majority of its members, closes its doors.

4 *(Fructidor 18, Year III)* Paris. Thanks to Mme. de Staël's intervention, the Convention strikes Tallyrand off the list of émigrés.

5 *(Fructidor 19, Year III)* Paris. The Convention decides to return the property of non-juring priests that has not been sold to their heirs.

6 *(Fructidor 20, Year III)* Germany. The Sambre et Meuse Army crosses the Rhine and pushes the Austrians back beyond Düsseldorf.

6 *(Fructidor 20, Year III)* Paris. The royalist-dominated Le Peletier sector passes a Guarantee Act placing all citizens under the sector's protection.

7 *(Fructidor 21, Year III)* Paris. The Le Peletier sector proposes creation of a sectors' central committee, which the Convention bans at once (→ 10).

9 *(Fructidor 23, Year III)* Franche Comté. At Blamont, people protect deserters from the police.

10 *(Fructidor 24, Year III)* Paris. Gracchus Babeuf is transferred to Plessis Prison, where he meets other opponents of the régime, such as Philippe Buonarroti and William Bodson, who will train cadres involved in the Conspiracy of the Equals (→ Nov. 6, 95).

10 *(Fructidor 24, Year III)* Paris. Fourteen sectors have approved the Le Peletier sector's proposal (→ 15).

13 *(Fructidor 27, Year III)* Châteauneuf en Thymerais. Beginning of a royalist insurrection that will extend as far as Dreux. The rebels send emissaries to Paris to win royalist sectors' support.

15 *(Fructidor 29, Year III)* Paris. The Le Peletier sector decides to send a message to all communes calling on them to mobilise against the Convention (→ Oct. 3, 95).

Monuments Museum builds a reputation

Paris, September 1

The Museum of French Monuments set up by Alexandre Lenoir has already acquired a flattering reputation among the public. For the first time in the history of French art, dozens of works, statues and fragments of monuments found both in Paris and in the provinces are classified strictly by period. Lenoir has taken care to avoid imitating the Museum installed in the Louvre, which has got bogged down in confusing and risky classifications by schools. The visitors, already numerous, appreciate the exceptional quality of the offerings, and artists -- whether they be painters, sculptors or decorators -- are not among the laggards in coming to study trends in the arts and to take lessons from the surest of sources. Sensitive to the quality of the installation, the Interior Minister approved Lenoir's request to use the garden adjoining the museum for putting on displays of statues and monuments.

One of the numerous rooms in the new museum arranged by Lenoir.

Bulk of land tax to be paid in grain

Paris, September 10

After more than ten stormy sessions, the Convention has adopted the proposal submitted by the deputy Dubois Crancé. Three quarters of the land tax will now be payable in grain, rather than in banknotes. Payments may be in wheat, rye, barley or oats. A public granary will be opened in each canton to take the grain, and a "civil servant" will be assigned to maintain custody of it. This law, which seals the failure of assignats, is aimed at restoring public finances by ensuring the value of taxes. The fact is that, since grain is all sold year round at a daily price, the government will benefit from rising prices. That fact has led some people to condemn the policy as speculative.

Vendean soldier is unmanned in battle

Vendée, September 14

During the fighting at Thouars, a good little soldier fell in the midst of the fighting. Was this a soldier like any other? Well, not exactly ... It was only after the battle was over that the other soldiers learnt that their comrade-in-arms was actually a girl named Jeanne Robin. Despite the Vendean leaders' ban on women following the army, Jeanne sneaked into the ranks dressed in men's clothing. Then yesterday she finally revealed her identity to General Lescure, saying: "Once you have seen how I fight, I'm sure you won't send me away." And it was fighting like a lion, or a lioness, that she fell at the general's feet in fighting for the cause she loved.

Jourdan is out to conquer Germany

Constitution is up for voters' approval

Paris, September 6

Today's voting is setting off some violent controversies in the Parisian sectors, as the Constitution and its related decrees are being submitted for the people's ratification. The effervescence in the capital contrasts with the indifference noted in the provinces, where the debate does not much interest the crowds. However, the balloting should interest a very great number of people, since it is being held on the basis of universal suffrage. Incidentally, this is a curious provision when one realises that the point is to approve a Constitution that institutes property qualifications for voting. But the deputies wanted the new institutions to be judged by all so as to ensure their legitimacy. Thus the military and the former terrorists, who recover their civil rights, will be allowed to take part in the vote. On the other hand, émigrés and non-juring priests who do not cooperate are excluded. Eight million people are called on to vote (→ Sept. 23).

Jourdan's men crossed the Rhine by using a bridge built over ships which had been placed across the river.

A doubtful visitor for Madame Royale

Paris, September

Is she an inoffensive spinner of fairy-tales, an unscrupulous adventuress, or an unfortunate victim of the Revolution? Claiming to be the illegitimate daughter of the Prince de Conti and the Duchesse de Mazarin, Stéphanie Louise de Montcairzin had harassed the authorities until, at the beginning of August, she received permission to visit her "unfortunate relative", Madame Royale. The poor Marie Thérèse, who does not remember the members of her family very well, threw herself into the arms of this "cousin" who came out of the blue, and "kisses and embraces had no limits". Stéphanie Louise returned to the Temple every day until August 26th., but on that day, to her great surprise, the guards refused to let her in. Since then all her attempts to try to see the princess have proved vain. In the face of uncertainty as to her real identity, the Convention thought it was better to keep this annoying "cousin" out of the picture.

Düsseldorf, September 5

Boldness paid off. The defenders of the position will certainly meditate on the incredible assault led by Generals Championnet and Legrand. The French first climbed up to attack the positions to shouts of "Long live the Republic!" and "Victory!". Then they found themselves outnumbered three to one in the fighting. The 200 enemy guns that were seized and the 800 members of the Düsseldorf garrison who were killed bear witness to the violence of the battle. However, this success must not make one forget the critical situation on the eastern front. Jourdan's Sambre et Meuse Army and Pichegru's Army of the Rhine are extremely short of supplies. Even though the coalition has been reduced since the defection of Prussia and Spain, it does not intend to give up. The two powerful Austrian armies are ready to exploit the French numerical inferiority. Moreover, in Italy, a third Austrian army is going to reinforce the Piedmontese. Despite tough conditions, Carnot's plans must be carried out exactly: The Jourdan and Pichegru armies will converge on Regensburg, then march toward Vienna. There must be careful coordination, so Jourdan is on the way to Mainz (→ Sept. 6).

Cambacérès defeat

Paris, September

It has been a sharp setback for Cambacérès. The man who loves power so much will be unable to move from the Committee of Public Safety to the Executive Directory. Why on earth did they have to find a letter at Comte d'Antraigues' home attributing royalist views to Cambacérès? He was indignant, offered a long defence of himself, recalling his irreproachable revolutionary past. He finally won the support of the Assembly, which ordered that his speech should be printed. But his colleagues distrust this man, and have decided they will not make him a director.

The Ecole Polytechnique comes into being

Paris, September 1

The original name of the Central School for Public Works seemed a bit long. But, in renaming it Ecole Polytechnique, the Convention did not just simplify the name; it also reorganised the recruiting plan and the programme. From now on the admission examinations are to be held on Brumaire 1 (October 22nd.) every year, and classes will get under way on Nivôse 1 (December 21st. or 22nd.). To pass, the students will have to know arithmetic, algebra, geometry and the physical sciences. They will take an eliminatory examination at the end of each year, especially the first.

The buildings of the new school.

16 *(Fructidor 30, Year III)*
Southern Africa. Following the royal Dutch government's overthrow by France and the local Jacobins, the Stadtholder, William V, invites England to seize the Dutch colonial domain. England begins with Cape Town (→29).

20 *(4th supplementary day)*
Germany. Under the influence of Austrian money, Pichegru prefers to capture Mannheim, rather than join Jourdan. This development seriously compromises the course of the campaign.

23 *(Vendémiaire 1, Year IV)*
Paris. Proclamation of the results of the referendum on the Constitution of Year III (→24).

23 *(Vendémiaire 1, Year IV)*
Paris. The Convention does away with the Arms and Powders Committee.

23 *(Vendémiaire 1, Year IV)*
Paris. The Convention delays the start of voting operations in the electoral assemblies to October 12th.

25 *(Vendémiaire 3, Year IV)*
Vendée. The knight Charette, who has managed to gather 8,000 to 9,000 men, is crushed by the republicans at Saint Cyr.

27 *(Vendémiaire 5, Year IV)*
Paris. In the face of the ever more virulent activity of the sectors that have become royalist, a few sectors from the suburbs appear at the Convention to assure deputies of their support. Five of them will be noted for their faithfulness: the ones of Quinze Vingts, Popincourt, Montreuil, Thermes, and Gardes Françaises.

28 *(Vendémiaire 6, Year IV)*
Avignon. Following an altercation with some soldiers, the local National Guard, the bulk of which is royalist, stages an uprising and forces the representative Boursault and the garrison to leave the city (→Oct. 3, 95).

29 *(Vendémiaire 7, Year IV)*
Batavian Republic. The Estates General start a trial of the Stadtholder William V for high treason.

30 *(Vendémiaire 8, Year IV)*
Vendée. The English forces manage to capture Ile d'Yeu (→Oct. 12, 95).

30 *Vendémiaire 8, Year IV)*
Vendée. General Grovely scatters Charette's troops, and the latter is forced to evacuate Belleville.

Year IV of the Republic has arrived

Proposed calendar for Year IV, designed by citizeness Marguerite Chatte, exalting the free woman, in the likeness of the Republic on a throne in the centre, surrounded by tricoloured symbols and patriotic emblems.

Rebellion in Dreux against Convention

Dreux, September

"The Chouans are beaten!" That was the deputies' cry on hearing the news of the failure of people in Dreux who "were working to set up a Communal Convention in opposition to the National Convention". The Dreux Primary Assembly had already criticised a decree of Sept. 14th. aimed at facilitating wheat shipments to the capital, and it used the terms "tyrannical, absurd and void" in speaking of the decree of Sept. 21st., which banned the relatives of émigrés from public duties. That includes the Mayor. The Convention had decided to send troops against the already armed rebels.

Hunger and grain riots hit Chartres

Chartres, September 17

The representative Tellier could not stand dishonour. "The order that I issued today brings me into disrepute in my own eyes and in those of the Convention. I did not want to use force, as that would have led to bloodshed, which I abhor." He committed suicide by shooting himself with a pistol. The reason was that the inhabitants of Chartres were fed up with seeing their grain go to feed Paris, taken by agents leading a life of insolent luxury, and rose up against Tellier. They invaded the commune house, making him sign an order setting the bread price at the Paris level.

David finds peace and quiet at last in the Sériziat household

Saint Ouen, September

David's worries are over at last. In order to get over the trauma of his detention and trial, he went to the country, to Saint Ouen, near Tournan en Brie, to stay with his wife's parents, M. and Mme. Sériziat. There he found peace of mind and rediscovered the joys of painting. This joy shines forth from the portraits he did of his hosts: Mme. Sériziat and her child are shown in the tradition of the revolutionary portrait, on a dark background that is stripped of all decorations. For his part, Monsieur Sériziat was painted in an outdoor setting with a cloudy sky (→Oct. 7).

Mme. Sériziat and her husband ...

... David's hosts after his release.

Voters approve Year III Constitution

The Constitution got a big majority of those voting, but there are disputes.

What is changing in inheritance law

Paris, September 25

After several months of debate, the Convention is again modifying the inheritance law. From now on, within certain limits set forth in the law, parents may give preferential treatment to some children over others in their wills. The egalitarian legislation adopted during the Reign of Terror is being dropped, but primogeniture and preference to males are being definitively abolished. The new law is retroactive in that it makes it possible to quash the estate divisions governed by the laws of 1793 and 1794, a fact that may cause some dissension ...

A new long novel for divine marquis

Paris, September

The latest novel published by the former Marquis de Sade will not disappoint his readers. *Aline et Valcour* mingles the story of the misdeeds of an incestuous father who is thwarted by a double child switch with the tale of the dangers encountered by his virtuous wife during a trip around the world. The reader will run up against poisoners, cannibals, and a wise man who predicts ... the Revolution! Sade, still absorbed in his social project, exhorts the nobility to "make agriculture bloom, rather than spend all your life under the colours".

With curved leg or stiff posture, posing is the fashion these days.

France, September 24

The referendum is the subject of abundant commentary in today's press. The results were proclaimed yesterday: the new Constitution was approved by 1,057,390 votes to 49,978. This may look like a huge margin, but actually only an eighth of the potential voters expressed a favourable opinion. The other citizens refrained from stating their views. Furthermore, some of the related decrees were barely approved. Thus the decrees known as the "Two Thirds", which reserve two thirds of the seats in the next Assembly for the outgoing Convention deputies, received only 205,498 votes, against 108,784. They were rejected in 19 of the departments and by 47 sectors of the capital out of 48. An article in the newspaper *La Gazette de France* reports on the nation's disillusioned attitude toward the Constitution. It seems, the writer says, that "society consists only of owners. The others are only proletarians who are put in the class of redundant citizens, waiting for the time to come when they, too, can become property owners". This cynical but widely shared judgement on the new institutions that have come into being explains the fact that they have in fact been adopted by default.

Decree passed to calm religious conflict

Paris, September 29

Freedom of religion and separation of the churches from the state -- those are the two major principles inspiring the grand decree on the treatment of religion that the deputies finished approving today. This decree does not break new ground in many respects. The point, as was explained by the "rapporteur", Génissieux, was to collect in the form of a single law the majority of the measures that the Convention had adopted since Robespierre's fall, and spell out the ways they are to be applied. Hence the appeasement policy is confirmed, even if several articles bear witness to a certain distrust of Roman Catholicism. The royalist agitation of the last few weeks has supplied the advocates of vigilance with arguments. If it is now settled that the exercise of the various religions is to be free and that the state

is not to pay for any of them, their ministers must undertake to observe the laws, pronouncing the following formula before the municipality: "I acknowledge that the universality of French citizens is sovereign, and I pledge submission and obedience to the laws of the Republic." In exchange, the law protects free exercise of the various religions. Sanctions are provided against anybody who disturbs a ceremony, and against administrators who force citizens to observe a holiday or, on the contrary, not to observe a holiday on the day of this or that religious feast day or holiday. However, Catholicism remains under suspicion, though not mentioned. Sanctions are provided against people who, during a celebration, speak in favour of royalty, criticise sale of national property, or read writings of a clergyman not residing in France.

The Jacobinière

For the Jacobinière
Sounds the farewell last fanfare.
The death of Robespierre
Puts it out of play
Hey hey hey
The death of Robespierre
Now its rock has turned to sand,
Poor accursed little band;
Plots which it had planned
Now have fallen through
Hoo hoo hoo

Like Tiberius, like Nero,
Barrière, Billaud, Collot,
The same foul traits they show:
Cowardice and fear
'ere 'ere 'ere

Tyrants lacking courage bold
With spilt blood, carnage cold
Manifest rage uncontrolled;
Our spirits affright
Fright fright fright

By this policy so bleak
Robespierre and all his clique
Brought death to the Republic
And its friends did slay
Hey hey hey

Convention

The spectacular trial of Joseph Le Bon, the Arras tormentor

This allegory shows Joseph Le Bon drinking the blood of the victims he has so easily sent to the scaffold.

Amiens, October 16

"Then did you want me to disobey you when you made terror the order of the day?" Everybody was looking forward to hearing Le Bon's defence, but it was unworthy of his reputation as a tormentor. He listened carefully to the proceedings and claimed that he had acted only on the basis of orders. But he was the master of Arras during the Reign of Terror, thanks to Robespierre's protection, and openly took pleasure in making blood flow there. The revolutionary Tribunal was at his orders, since he had a brother in law and three uncles by marriage among the judges and jurors. Le Bon, arrested in August, first tried to pose as having been a Robespierre victim himself. Jurors were not taken in, and the guillotine ended the career of this merciless executioner this morning.

Debate raging about effects of guillotine

Paris, October 1

It is a well-known fact that the guillotine kills. But does the victim die at exactly the moment he is decapitated? A debate on this point has been shaking the medical world for a year now. After all, the *Encyclopaedia* distinguished between "imperfect death" and "absolute death". One remembers the famous anecdote about Mary Stuart's severed head allegedly having spoken. More recently, the witnesses of Charlotte Corday's execution said they saw her flush with indignation when the executioner slapped her. In his *Opinion concerning the guillotine*, the surgeon Sue, who backs the idea that there is a "survival" of feeling in the victim, writes: "What could be more horrible than having a perception of your own execution, and then an afterthought of your own torment?" But the doctors who are disciples of the Enlightenment have taken up arms against this "metaphysical idea", which is only "the fruit of the imagination". In his *Note on the death penalty by guillotine*, Cabanis says the movements ascribed to severed heads are due only to mechanical reflexes. According to him, the vital principle "has no exclusive seat", and "The I exists only in general life". This attenuates the horror ...

Luxembourg is a palace again

Paris, October

The Luxembourg Palace has been reconverted successfully. It became a prison in July 1793, but was taken over by the members of the Directory, who thought the location all the better in that the area is changing rapidly. The fact is that, in the interest of improving the infrastructure on the Left Bank, which has lagged markedly behind the Right Bank, there are eight arteries leaving Observatory Square. This will make the palace and garden more accessible. But the general urbanism project is difficult.

Belgium to become a part of France

Paris, October 1

The Convention has decided to settle the fate of the former Low Countries. After a two-day debate, the deputies finally adopted the decree uniting Liège and the ten Belgian provinces with France. They did not consider it useful to consult the population living in the region about the annexation, knowing, in any case, that the majority are opposed to it. "The people always want the good, but do not always know what it is," commented Portiez, of the Oise. In his speech, Merlin de Douai mentioned the doctrine of natural borders and the need for defending the territory. He said that, if the Belgians were independent, they would be too weak to constitute a real barrier to invasion. The decree provides for dividing the country into nine departments, the borders of which will be determined by the French commissioners alone. The old historical provinces must disappear, and the Belgians have to keep quiet. Only French legislation will have the force of law. The decree also provides for fast installation of departmental and municipal administrations, and of courts, and all officials will have to be elected in accordance with the Constitution.

Various trends in confrontation at the Year IV Exhibition

Paris, October 7

The "Salon" exhibition attracts a greater number of visitors every year. And, incidentally, it is considered a good thing to take an interest in art. Tastes have changed, of course. The Revolution has scattered the artists' traditional clientèle -- clergy, aristocracy -- and brought in tradesmen, manufacturers and politicians to replace it. All these nouveaux riches have a different kind of culture. Great art, i.e., mythological paintings or the portrayal of history, is being neglected for genre painting or portraits of morals, which are easier to instal in middle-class homes. Even if revolutionary iconography still has its

Neo-classicism and its severity.

"Freedom or death", a theme that has inspired Jean Baptiste Regnault.

adepts, and finds one of its most perfect illustrations in Regnault's *Freedom or Death*, portraits are the most appreciated type of paintings, all the same. Thus the pastellist Ducreux shows a portrait of citizen Beauharnais, as well as six effigies from the world of arts and letters. David himself is attracting notice with *M. and Mme. Sériziat*. But the old guard has not given up. Vien is showing an historical painting, even though he has taken care to add four portraits to it!

Return to England for King's brother

Ile d'Yeu, October 12

Monsieur, as the King's brother is called, has decided not to lend his person to the royalist cause. That is the message his envoy the Comte de Grignon has just sent to Charette, who had managed to gather a few thousand peasants on the Vendean coast. Monsieur, also known as the Comte d'Artois, landed on this island on Oct. 2nd., leading an expedition consisting of 4,000 Englishmen and 800 émigrés. He waited a long time without bringing himself to land on the mainland. But contacts with Charette have gradually made him realise that he had overestimated the Vendeans' military resources. With no taste for temerity, Monsieur has resigned himself to going back to England, disappointing all the royalists who had trusted him (→ Nov. 18, 95).

Jacobin reconquest of Toulouse is total

Toulouse, early October

In Toulouse, the Jacobin reconquest is proportional to what the Thermidorian reaction was like, namely total. To be sure, the violence of that reaction was found primarily in words. The newspaper *Anti-terrorist* had published lists of well-known Jacobins, and called for revenge. Representative on mission Laurence had published an *Address to the Toulouse youth* in the newspaper that had brought on a wave of denunciations and clashes. The Muscadins, encouraged, were so bold as to sing *The people's awakening* under the "terrorists'" windows, and did not hesitate to thrash people coming out of the Temple of Reason. The Jacobin Club had been closed and the National Guard purged, with part of it being transformed into a Company of Jesus. But the fear in Paris that the royalists might wind up win-

ning, and the news of an émigré landing at Quiberon, had suddenly raised doubts about the whole process. The Convention sent a moderate Jacobin, Clauzel, to Toulouse with the assignment of putting an end to the Muscadins' domination. Clauzel came in with 3,000 soldiers detached from the Army of the Pyrenees after peace was signed with Spain. And then the hunt for royalists started. The Jacobins, regaining their sense of boldness, suspended *The Anti-terrorist*, dissolved the Companies of Jesus, reorganised the National Guard, and re-opened their club. Hence Toulouse has again become Jacobinism's real citadel in France, a "Red city" in the midst of a region that is still "White". But at least there has not been much bloodshed in these shifts of régime -- just one violent death due to political events since Thermidor.

Knickers On!

Get dressed, Mankind!
Those excesses put behind
Of false prophets woebegone.
Walking unclad is a spoof!
'Tis of virtue no sure proof;
So, put your knickers on!

Wary be of schemers fell
Who the vulgar dress would sell
Of false prophets woebegone.
Don't push Liberty so far's
To show the world your arse!
So then, put your knickers on!

The cowl makes not
The monk, they say.
Clothes do not perforce portray
The false prophets woebegone.
Bankers, merchants rich,
Of artisans would queer the pitch
If they had no knickers on.

Boldly now man's rights defend;
The tenets of the law commend
Like all patriots true anon.
Fellow citizens, I bid
You hide what should be hid;
So then, put your knickers on!
Get dressed, Mankind!

Vendémiaire 13: Royalist revolt

For the second time in just four months, the Convention has stood firm against public pressure. This time, it was the inhabitants of the wealthy neighbourhoods and the young Muscadins who mobilised, and not the poor people of the suburbs, as was the case in Prairial. The royalists attempted to force the Convention to give up its control over the elections, about which the reactionaries were optimistic. They had gambled on the fears of the Paris bourgeoisie, which was still afraid of a resurgence of Jacobinism. The Convention could therefore count only on the army to save a régime which it wanted to be moderate, but truly republican. The Republic has been saved, but it will now have to take the generals into account. Without them, nothing will be achieved in future.

Under Menou's command, the Convention's troops deploy to face the insurgents of the Le Peletier sector.

First light on Vendémiaire 12th. found an extremely agitated Paris. The situation had never occurred since the beginning of the Revolution. This time, the Convention was threatened from the right. This came about because, in breaking up, it wanted to help control the future by forcing the voters electing the future assemblies known as the Five Hundred and the Ancients to make the membership of the two chambers include two thirds of former Convention deputies. But the majority of the sectors, which have been totally controlled since the Prairial days by the middle class owners, refused to accept this measure, which was aimed at limiting the freedom to vote. The fact is that the Convention feared a huge royalist success. To tell the truth, what the middle class was most exercised about was the fact that a few dozen Jacobins, the dreaded "blood-drinkers", might return to the Assembly. The suburbs, which were still threatened by famine and misery, might intervene again. Even though the royalist camp was very much in the minority except in the Le Peletier sector, in the banking district, they thought they could attempt an armed take-over. Preparations were made for an insurrection, and on the morning of October 12th, the Le Peletier sector called the National Guard to arms. For its part the Convention did not remain inactive, but its resources were singularly weak. It had armed about 1,500 patriots from the suburbs, commanded by General Berruyer. Other than this, it had only about 500 men assigned to guarding the Tuileries. That was not much in the face of the 25,000 sector members. The committee set up to coordinate action, with Barras and Merlin de Douai, put all its hopes in General Menou's 4,000 troops, who had been gathered at Sablons, in northwestern Paris.

Menou's treason

Menou had been ordered to go back to the Tuileries by way of the insurgent areas. He did not obey until late in the evening, and when he arrived toward 9 o'clock in the Le Peletier sector it was simply for the purpose of starting talks with the people whose ideas he actually shared. But the insurgents did not seize the opportunity they were being offered. As soon as he arrived at the Convention, Menou was arrested and replaced by Barras, who then had some 5,000 men available, plus some 250 Quinze Vingts sector members. Barras also called on all available generals in Paris: Brune, Carteaux, Dupont and Bonaparte. The latter, who was then struck off the cadre list, received command of the artillery, but without guns since Menou had left them at Sablons. However, without artillery, the battle was lost. In the middle of the night, a column of 300 cavalrymen under Murat's command was ordered to bring the guns back. He only just managed it, coming back

Members of the Convention leaving the Tuileries to fraternise with the soldiers defending the former palace.

against the Convention fails

shortly before a battalion of sector members. At 10 o'clock in the morning of Vendémiaire 13, the 40 Sablons guns were lined up on Revolution Square, along Rue Saint Honoré and the Left Bank docks. Thus all approaches to the Tuileries were controlled. Plans had been made for the Convention to withdraw to Meudon in case of a defeat.

A fierce battle

The first shots rang out near Rue Saint Honoré. A large column of sector members was trying to reach the Tuileries. The fighting was fierce. The sector's troops peppered the Convention's forces at almost point blank range, but then they were decimated in turn by the enfilading fire of the guns. On the Left Bank, General Danican tried to lead 5,000 sector members over Pont Neuf bridge to catch the Convention in a pincer movement. But the artillery, set up on the docks and National Bridge, repulsed them.

The final assault

There were two other resistance centres, one around Palais Royal and the other at Saint Roch church. The former point fell in hand-to-hand fighting. Early in the morning of Vendémiaire 14, General Vachot led the attack in front of Saint Roch. Many sector members were stationed on the church steps, while some of them were even positioned in gaps in the façade. Backed by a Danican column, they at first managed such sustained fire as to make any approach impossible. But then two grapeshot cannons decimated them. Other guns took Neuve Saint Roch street in enfilade, and it was cleared in just a few minutes. Finally, 1,000 men of the patriots' battalion and a regular battalion launched an assault, backed by six guns. The last sector members fled, and the Convention had won.

The Le Peletier sector was occupied and all its inhabitants disarmed, while a few leaders were arrested. The fighting had left 200 to 300 dead on each side. At the Convention, it was claimed that the dead included many fighters wearing shirts embroidered with fleurs-de-lis. Even if Danican and the Le Peletier sector members were indeed royalists, the majority of the rebels seem to have acted more for reasons of social order than for political motives.

A young general named Napoléon Bonaparte was much noticed among the officers working for Barras. He made a strong impression due to his frantic energy and his decisiveness. He was named second in command, but only after the operation.

General Bonaparte has had the cannons brought up. The insurgents are shot at on the steps of the Saint Roch church, where they had taken position.

The work of the Thermidorian Convention

The event known as Thermidor 9 (July 27th., 1794) did not simply mark one man's fall. It also meant the disorganisation of the revolutionary government, the end of the Reign of Terror and the state-managed economy, and a reaction of public opinion against the "terrorist". In the interests of toning down the all-powerful nature of the Committees, especially of the Committee of Public Safety, the Convention adopted a series of measures that destroyed such committees' stability, and hence considerably limited their influence. One-fourth of the Committees' membership was to be renewed every month, and the outgoing members were eligible for a new term only after a one-month interval. The "terrorists" were sidetracked and the Committee of Public Safety no longer had the leading role. It was cut back to its initial concerns: war and foreign affairs. Hence fragmentation succeeded the unity that had prevailed in Year II. The law of Prairial 22 (June 10th.) was deferred, while the Revolutionary tribunal was reorganised. Both had made it possible to institute the Reign of Terror. People who were accused received some guarantees, and it now became necessary to prove an offence in order to sentence them. The special instruments of the Terror, the Watch Committees, were reduced and purged of the majority of sansculottists, and their effectiveness was sharply cut back. Once the organs of the Reign of Terror were liquidated, suspects still had to be freed, and that was soon done under the pressure of public opinion, since the people being held represented very diverse classes and opinions. These releases and the reaction that was getting under way did not fit in with the wishes of the Jacobins, who still had strong positions.

Freedom of the press, which was instituted rapidly, favoured the moderates and the right, who had such talented journalists as Fréron with his *People's Orator.* "Gilded youth" — young middle-class people, clerks, shopkeepers, and so on — took over the streets, invaded the theatres, organised themselves into armed gangs and pursued the Jacobins. As for the sansculottists, they demanded implementation of the Constitution of 1793, which had been buried by the revolutionary government, while the Jacobins urged a resumption of the Reign of Terror.

Purges and recovery of control

The Convention, in a desire for continuity, first adopted some measures for maintaining the situation. In the provinces, reaction triumphed in certain regions, and people who had been in charge in Year II were hounded, while continuity carried the day elsewhere. Public opinion, which had been aroused by the trial of the Nantes federalists revealing the atrocities that Carrier had committed, became angered with the Jacobins and egged on the Convention to greater severity. As of October 16th., the Assembly barred the "people's associations" from affiliating with each other, and the Jacobins Club was closed on November 12. The Montagnards, deprived of their leaders, were silent in the Convention. The Jacobins became ever more isolated and lost control of the sectors. The diehards sought refuge with Babeuf, but did not find the resources for effective action that could come only from popular support. Purges got under way everywhere in the administration. In the Convention, the Girondists, who had been outlawed on June 2nd., 1793, regained their seats in December and strengthened the moderates' camp. The gangs of Muscadins were encouraged and, with more or less open police complicity, they indulged in intimidation, fighting for an end to the Marat cult. Once an idol, he had become a detested symbol. They had already brought about the triumph of the *Réveil du Peuple* (People's Awakening) against the *Marseillaise*, and, after a violent campaing during which they destroyed the Marat busts in the theatres, they got the Convention to "dethrone" Charlotte Corday's victim. The symbolism of sansculottism vanished under the reactionaries' blows, while various societies or associations were formed in the provinces, such as the Companions of the Sun, who hounded the Jacobins and the constitutional priests. The "White Terror" made its appearance in Lyons in February 1795.

Abandonment of the managed economy

The Convention was of the liberal persuasion and the majority of the members had always viewed the managed economy as strictly an expedient. Price fixing was more or less synonymous with shortages as far as public opinion was concerned. People expected freedom to bring abundance. Thus, the Thermidorians gradually came back to supporting free-market principles. This about-face came about rather spontaneously and the Convention followed the producers' initiatives, rather than suggesting them. Farmers avoided requisitions and the factories delayed completing government orders. The Assembly had to follow this liberal current and soon adopted various decontrol measures. Foreign trade was the first beneficiary of this trend. Then the state gave up the "nationalised" sectors, such as the foundries and the arms workshops. Finally, since the farmers had organised a parallel market, a "black" market on which supplies were available at high prices while the official markets were empty, the Convention decided to do away with the "maximum" on December 24th., 1794.

Free trade added its effects to the ones resulting from the crisis affecting subsistence products. The assignat collapsed, plunging from 31 per cent of its nominal value in August 1794 to a mere eight per cent in April 1795. This depreciation and speculation on goods led to higher prices and a recourse to inflationary steps, which further weakened the currency. The lower classes were the first victims of this process, while speculation benefited the profitees, who had enriched themselves.

Some natural causes aggravated shortages, which were becoming dangerous. The Year II harvest had been poor and this was not due to the weather alone. Mass conscription had deprived farmers of indispensable labour, and some fields had not been sown. Moreover, the farmers were hanging onto their stocks as long as possible, hoping for more price increases. The authorities' efforts to supply the cities by purchasing abroad yielded only limited results, and they again had to resort to constraints: farmers were forced to bring their grain to market, soldiers were quartered on farmers at harvest time, and sometimes grain prices were set. At the same time, prices rocketed on the free markets. In Paris, a bread ration of one pound a day had to be instituted in March 1795, and provincial cities got even less. The 1794-95 winter, one of the century's hardest, saw the emergence of immense distress and shortages. Conflict worsened between unfortunates and the people profiting from this crisis. All of the conditions for lower-class uprisings were present, and they broke out in Paris in the spring.

The end of the popular movement

The sansculottists had not lost all their energy or their experience of insurrection. There was murmuring against the rich, the tradesmen and the powerless Convention. Anger rose, and there were daily clashes between the Muscadins and the sansculottists. Revolt was brewing in the Saint Antoine district. March 21st. brought approval of the "grand police" law, which instituted the death penalty for people threatening the Convention. Arms were handed out to loyal citizens. Ways of maintaining order were being organised, but so was the lower-class response. The sectors met, and the ones most affected by shortages, those of the suburbs and of the eastern neighbourhoods, demanded emergency measures to combat the crisis, as well as the release of jailed patriots, the reopening of "people's associations", and implementation of the Constitution of 1793.

These demands could be viewed as a way of giving notice, and the people were again getting ready to swing into action. On Germinal 12 (April 1st.) a crowd invaded the Convention. The Committee of General Safety immediately called on the reliable battalions of the National Guard, which forced the demonstrators to withdraw. The rioters had been dispersed easily, but the Convention took advantage of the opportunity to get rid of some former "terrorists" and to put Paris on a war footing. Troops were brought into the capital under Pichegru's command, and some Montagnards (Billaud Varenne, Collot d'Herbois, Barère) were deported to Guyana, while the cadres of the popular movement were disarmed. However, shortages were worsening, the lower classes' impatience was growing and a new revolt was being prepared quite openly. On Prairial 1 (May 20th., 1795), the suburbs were called to action. Groups of men and women converged on the Convention and invaded it. In the ensuing indescribable chaos, one deputy, Féraud, was killed, and his head was displayed on the end of a pike. The troops and the National Guard were then called in, and the only remaining thing to be done was to arrest the Montagnards, who had been compromised by their involvement with the insurgents and had supported the popular movement.

The next day, the Convention was again endangered when the battalions from the Saint Antoine district aimed their cannons at it, but they left in the evening, leaving the authorities in control of the situation. On Prairial 4 (May 23rd.) troops invested Saint Antoine, which allowed itself to be disarmed after vain resistance. The people's movement was disorganised, lacked leaders and demoralised by its failure. It had lost all vigour. The purges, which eliminated the sansculottists and the Jacobins from the sectors, finished the process of weakening it. The Thermidorians, who had only contempt for the people's movement and contrasted it with the "clean hands" of honest people, had overcome attempts to resist, managing to limit it to a passive role, the type it was to play in future. The Convention had been forced to call on armed force, and it was to depend on it in future.

Repression in the provinces

Repression aimed at the former "terrorists" gave rise to the "White Terror" in the provinces, and particularly in the southeast. The desire for revenge against the Jacobins and the former members of revolutionary courts led to massacres: a hundred in Lyons in May, another hundred in Marseilles in June, a score in Tarascon. The killers benefited from the authorities' weakness and indulgence. In the other regions, people contented themselves with multiplying attempts to vex the Jacobins, without going so far as assassination. If the south and Lyons displayed such a great punitive drive, it was also because those regions had suffered more than the others from the repression of Year II.

Defeat of the royalist émigrés

The royalists, more or less openly backed by ever wider segments of public opinion, worried the Convention's republicans. In the Vendée, the terrible repression of Turreau's "infernal columns" in spring 1794 had pushed the peasants into joining Charette's or Stofflet's troops, while north of the Loire River, especially in the Morbihan region, the Chouans became active and multiplied their attacks. The moderate royalists, who based their hopes for a restoration on Louis XVII, were hit hard when the death of the child in the Temple prison was learnt of in June 1795. A few days later the Comte de Provence, who had taken the name of Louis XVIII, made the mistake of issuing a manifesto in Verona that lined up all the moderates against him. He announced the return to the Ancien Régime "without its abuses" and punishment of the revolutionaries. Such a programme could not satisfy the constitutional monarchists, who were in the majority in France, and pleased only the émigrés. But the pretender's backers were preparing for vigorous action with England's help, in spite of the reluctance felt by Pitt, who would have preferred a legal restoration to a military adventure. However, he allowed himself to be persuaded to attempt an expedition, the main point of which was a landing in Brittany. On June 23rd., the English fleet landed a unit of émigrés at Quiberon, under the orders of Puisaye and Hervilly, but this initial success was soon compromised by the misunderstandings among the leaders and the republicans' craftiness. On July 21st., the latter seized the peninsula, took 9,000 prisoners, and threw the others into the sea. The law punished émigrés captured while bearing arms with death, and despite the hesitations of Hoche, who did not like executions, Tallien's intervention brought the decision: more than 750 prisoners were executed. The defeat at Quiberon, "the inexpiable beach", killed the last hopes of Louis XVIII's supporters to re-establish absolute monarchy by force.

Royalists in France defeated

Meanwhile, yet another danger was taking shape, coming from the moderate monarchists and within France itself. The Convention had been discussing the project for a Year III Constitution since June 23rd., and the Feuillant monarchists' progress in courting public opinion gave rise to a legitimate fear that the next elections would find a majority of legislators favourable to re-establishment of the constitutional maonarchy. To avoid such an outcome, which appeared almost certain, the Convention made some very unpopular, but effective, decisions. Decrees of August 22nd. and 30th. provided that two-thirds of the future deputies would have to be chosen from among the outgoing deputies, and if that proportion were not reached, the newly-elected members would resort to co-opting to fill out their ranks. These measures, questionable in principle, were sujected to ratification and received only doubtful approval, with a very great number of abstentions. Almost all of the Paris sectors (47 out of 48) rejected them. Discontent became a storm and, in the face of an imminent uprising, a hasty decision was made to call troops into Paris. In the hope of blocking the royalists, the former "terrorists" were again authorised to take part in the sectors' meetings, the sansculottists were flattered, and sanctions were voted against people who might suggest re-establishment of the monarchy. Was a return to a revolutionary government in the offing? The sectors feared it was and, taking advantage of the fears, they decided on action. On Vendémiaire 11, seven of them (including the one of Le Peletier, which led the movement) declared themselves to be in insurrection. In response, the Convention set up a five-member commission to assure defence of the Republic. Barras, one of the members, called on Bonaparte, a young Jacobin general, who invested the Tuileries while Murat was bringing up the cannons. On Vendémiaire 13 (October 4th., 1795), the demonstrators heading for the Convention were welcomed by artillery batteries and had to withdraw, leaving 300 dead. The cannonfire came to an end on the steps of the Saint Roch church, and the danger, which had appeared threatening at one time, was past.

Thus the major royalist projects of Year III — both the one of the émigrés and that of the constitutional monarchists still in France — wound up as utter failures, since after Vendémiaire the Thermidorians returned to a more revolutionary policy. Their hostility to counter-revolution was evident in the renewal of the decrees against the non-juring priests and the émigrés. When the Convention broke up on October 26th., 1795, it could believe that it was leaving a healthy and comfortable situation for the Directory. The popular movement had been crushed, the royalists had been defeated, and some new institutions were going to function. But actually, the problems had only been postponed and the economic situation was disastrous.

The Constitution of Year III

The main drafters of the Constitution of Year III, Daunou and Boissy d'Anglas, who was the "rapporteur" for the document, had wanted two principles to dominate the new institutions: liberty and property. Equality, which Year II had extended, was reduced to civil equality, and the distinction between property-owners and proletarians was clearly marked. A declaration of rights, but also of duties, spelt out citizens' obligations. The Constitution dropped universal suffrage, while making a citizen of any man born in France, having lived there for at least one year, and paying a direct contribution. It granted the right to vote only to citizens over 25 years old with an income equal to 200 work-days, a provision that reduced the electorate to around 30,000 people. This tax-based voting system was to remain in effect for a half-century. To avoid a régime dominated by an all-powerful Assembly, two chambers were established. The Council of the Five Hundred had the initiative in proposing laws, while the Ancients approved or rejected the bills developed by the Five Hundred. Executive power was divided among five directors selected by the Ancients on the basis of a proposal from the Five Hundred, and many checks aimed at preventing any attempt at dictatorship were set up. One of the five directors was replaced each year, and an outgoing director could not be chosen again until five years elapsed. The Directory was forbidden to move troops to positions less than 60 kilometres from the two chambers without their express authorisation.

This Constitution, which made property-owners the Republic's political body, was generally approved and the constitutional monarchists themselves backed it in the hope that the Directory could be transformed into a monarchy some day. The document was put up for ratification and was approved on September 23rd. by more than a million "yes" votes, against fewer than 50,000 negative votes. Now it was up to the new régime to assure the proper operation of the new institutions.

Daunou submits enabling law changing public education system

Paris, October 25

A new régime means new policies. Following approval of the Constitution of Year III, the deputies could not remain content with their predecessors' laws governing the school system. Even if the decrees in question, whether framed by Bouquier or Lakanal, were characterised by the generosity of their inspiration, implementation proved to be inefficient. In a concern for regularising an anarchic situation, the Thermidorians have curtailed the great dream of popular education. The free nature of education is dropped in the law adopted today by the Assembly at Daunou's initiative. The teachers will only be housed, and will be paid directly by the pupils' parents in each school "arrondissement". Moreover, it will now be up to the local authorities, and no longer to

Pierre Claude François Daunou.

An allegory celebrating, ancient-style, the enabling act of Brumaire 3.

the state, to decide on setting up schools. As to the higher education levels, Daunou has taken up the essence of the arrangements provided by Lakanal in his law of February 25th., though the provisions are simplified. Each department will have its own central school, whose programme, reorganised so as to be suitable to the students' ages, will no longer include the technical courses previously provided. An Institute will crown the system, bringing together, like the former academies, the greatest savants in physical sciences and mathematics, literature and fine arts, and moral and political sciences (→ Nov. 20).

Vendeans shifting to new war tactics

Brittany, October 22

Cadoudal has changed course, having decided to resume "Chouan" tactics. Since the failure of the Quiberon expedition, major engagements against republican forces seem inappropriate. Hence it has been decided to return to harassment, in order to create a feeling of constant insecurity. In future the royalists will attack only detachments of fewer than 50 men, and will try to cut the enemy's communications by intercepting mail on the roads before it can reach republican forces.

The National Library deprived of a chief

Paris, October 17

The republican régime cannot tolerate the hierarchies of the Ancien Régime. But, as the only exception among the new institutions, the National Library continued to be led by a "chief". So, speaking in the name of the Public Education Committee, Villers appeared in the Assembly today to offer his colleagues a suggestion for a "form of administration better suited to the régime of equality". The post of chief librarian, which had become an object of intrigue and a mark of favour, is going to be abolished. This will preclude such scandalous situations as the one in which Abbot de Louvois was appointed chief librarian at the age of ... eight years! So the library will be adopting the republican form appropriate to the new institutions, inspired particularly by the administration of the Museum. The library will be directed by eight savants or literary men of acknowledged merit, known collectively as the "Conservatoire". Every year they will elect a temporary director, subordinate to the executive branch. There will be two curators for the Publications Department, three for Manuscripts, two for Antiquities, and one for Prints. Each will receive a salary of 6,000 livres per annum.

Jourdan reports on his troops' misery

Near Neuwied, October 22

Jourdan has had to retreat to the left bank of the Rhine. In addition to poor coordination of his movements with General Pichegru's, his troops' weakened condition hardly inclines him to optimism. The report that the victor of Fleurus has decided to send to the Convention presents a terrifying picture of the wretched condition of the Sambre et Meuse Army. He says it is "afflicted by the greatest imaginable shortage of subsistence". And what can one expect from troops trying to fight on an empty stomach? Sometimes they have to fast for 24 hours because food and wine are frozen. Desertions are another reason for worry. They have greatly increased since the summer and, in less than six months, the Republic has lost about a third of its defenders. It is to be feared that the soldiers will steal what they lack. Jourdan, like all other military leaders, knows quite well that looting is the enemy of discipline. The picture grows even darker when the general mentions cavalrymen without horses, horses without forage, and troops without morale. His men forget the reasons for the war, and think only of home.

Barère flees prison

Saintes, October 28

The dark night mentioned by the *Moniteur* is not enough to explain Barère's escape from the Saintes Prison. There are too many possible accomplices: the jailer and the municipal authorities, who saw nothing and heard nothing, his Dutch friends, the Wanderkands, who supplied the rope ladder and pierced the cell walls, the boy who came every morning to sing *The People's Awakening* in front of the prison, and his "tender friend" Mme. de Guibert -- not to mention his cousin Hector, who is hiding Barère in his home. All of them seem to have helped "that nice man Barère". The Convention had already done a lot in separating case from the one involving Billaud Varenne and Collot d'Herbois, deported last May. In helping him flee just before deportation to Guyana, his friends prevented another injustice against him.

A new political landscape in France

France, October 26

The citizens are not at all put out to know that the elections for the Legislature are finally finished. The complexity of the voting procedures and a certain lassitude explain the fact that the turnout was even lower than for the referendum. The balloting opened on October 12th., and closed on October 21st. For all that time the primary assemblies, consisting of "first-degree" voters, meaning only the Frenchmen with citizenship status and property bringing in income at least equal to 150 days' work, were in constant session. But it was only today that the membership of the Councils of the Five Hundred and the Ancients was definitively determined. The reason is that, under the terms of the decrees attached to the Constitution, at least two-thirds of that membership must consist of former Convention deputies. But since only 394 of them were re-elected, it was necessary for them to co-opt 500 of their former colleagues to reach the required proportion. All this is not due primarily to the unpopularity of the former deputies, but rather to the frequency

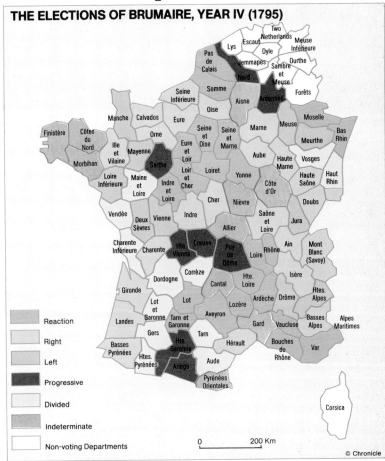

THE ELECTIONS OF BRUMAIRE, YEAR IV (1795)

Reaction
Right
Left
Progressive
Divided
Indeterminate
Non-voting Departments

0   200 Km

© Chronicle

of multiple elections. The candidates were allowed to run in several districts simultaneously, and did not deprive themselves of the opportunity. Thus three leaders of the reactionaries -- Boissy d'Anglas, Henry Larivière and Lanjuinais -- were elected, respectively, 36, 37 and 39 times. Generally speaking the winners were important public figures, traders, farmers, and men of the law, as well as extremely moderate men. The Paris Basin, Normandy, the Loire region and Provence are dominated by the reaction camp. But the Jacobin-trend left is resistant in the North, the Ardennes, Sarthe and Ariège, as well as in the Vendée and Haute Garonne. Still, the new Legislature has only 64 Montagnards, while, on the other hand, there are 158 representatives with royalist views. In the centre, some 305 men are out-and-out republicans, the majority Thermidorians, such as Barras and Tallien. To govern, they will need the backing of undecided members and moderately republican men of divided views. Somehow or other, a majority will have to emerge from these elections.

Deputierter vom Rat der „Fünfhundert". Gala-Kostüm eines Mitglieds des Direktoriums. (1794–

A member of the Council of Five Hundred facing a Director in regalia.

Five Directors are named to govern the Republic

Paris, October 31

The Executive Directory has just been named. The Council of Ancients is furious because it was forced to give way to the will of the Five Hundred in choosing the executive's members. The Council of Five Hundred had drawn up a list of 50 deputies, 45 of whom were not really of Director status, to be sure the other five would be named. Hence Barras, Reubell, La Révellière Lépeaux, Letourneur and Sieyès were chosen. But the latter immediately turned down the job. Perhaps he wants to remain available for a crisis situation. Actually, he has never forgiven the Convention for having rejected his proposed Constitution last August.

Different roads to power

Like Mirabeau, the Vicomte Paul de Barras, a poverty-stricken provincial nobleman disowned by his family, threw himself ardently into the Revolution after a brief career as an officer. This man, who is surrounded by immoral women and by speculators, is said to be greedy and venal. After having been a terrorist, he turned into a Thermidorian in order to save his head. He is the régime's strongman, the man who will not hesitate to carry out any needed repression, as he proved in checkmating the Vendémiaire 13 rebels. On this point he will see eye to eye with the Alsatian Jean François Reubell, who, like Barras, favours the forceful approach. This lawyer sat with the

Paul de Barras.

Montagnards in the Constituent Assembly and in the Convention, but turned against Robespierre when he felt that the latter suspected him of moderatism. He has a reputation for stubbornness and for favouring special revolutionary measures and the annexation policy, especially in connection with the left bank of the Rhine. Short and deformed Louis Marie de La Révellière Lépeaux hates everything with even a remote connection with

Lazare Carnot.

the Reign of Terror. To be sure, this son of a Vendean notary suffered from that phenomenon. He is a jurist by training, though he has never practised law, and sat on the Girondist benches in the Constituent Assembly and the Convention. Hence he was outlawed in June 1793 and had to go underground to avoid being guillotined, as his brother was.

Still, he remains basically republican and anti-clerical. He is also a fierce supporter of the war and of annexations. Louis François Letourneur appears something of a lightweight by comparison with his colleagues. He was an engineering officer, and in 1792 became one of the main members of the Convention's War Committee, also serving as chairman. Close to Carnot, he displayed considerable hostility towards Robespierre and the Jacobins, but also fought against the royalists on Vendémiaire 13.

Louis François Letourneur.

Carnot replaces Sieyès

Lazare Carnot will be named on November 5th. to replace Emmanuel Sieyès. Among the five Directors he is the one with the greatest share of responsibility for the Reign of Terror. Even though he contributed to Robespierre's fall, he barely escaped being outlawed for having fought against the Thermidorian reaction. Still, the fact that his mentality is obviously more middle-class and conservative than Jacobin will reassure the deputies. He was a career officer and responsible for military operations on the Grand Committee, and he will concentrate on getting peace as soon as possible to remove the need for the special measures that impede the establishment of a conservative republic such as he desires. All the Directors are regicides, helped topple Robespierre, and are republicans. But how can they govern, disputing so many other points?

Jean François Reubell.

Louis Marie de La Révellière.

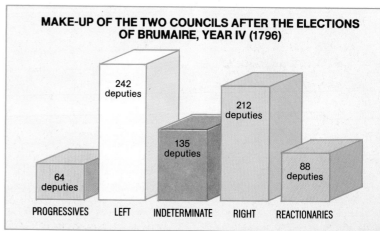

MAKE-UP OF THE TWO COUNCILS AFTER THE ELECTIONS OF BRUMAIRE, YEAR IV (1796)

64 deputies	242 deputies	135 deputies	212 deputies	88 deputies
PROGRESSIVES	LEFT	INDETERMINATE	RIGHT	REACTIONARIES

New power structure is a complicated system

Paris, October 31

The new French power structure is a complicated arrangement. When the Thermidorians drew up the Constitution, they wanted at all costs to avoid any return to dictatorship, whether of a party or a man. Hence, rather than simply separating state functions, they actually fragmented them. Justice is independent of the political authorities, the judges being elected. Legislative power is divided between two Councils, chosen by the same voters, with one-third of the members being elected every year. The latter provision is aimed at preventing the emergence of permanent parties, and the same is true of the rule that the deputies' seats should be determined by lot, so that it will be impossible to distinguish between "right" and "left". The Councils vote funds, but neither they nor the executive have supervisory powers over the Public Treasury. The Councils have exclusive jurisdiction over making laws, but must not seize any executive functions. In particular, they are barred from delegating their authority to representatives on mission. In exchange, the law protects the two chambers against pressures. The executive branch may not, without permission, send armed forces into the "constitutional" premises constituted by the places in which the Councils meet, and the latter have their own guard. The executive communicates with the Councils only in the form of messages, and it has no veto right. Moreover, the Constitution has also provided for protecting the Councils from mob pressures: even if their sessions are open to the public, in principle, the deputies may decide to hold them behind closed doors. Only the Ancients may meet outside Paris. The legislative branch may not act on the executive branch once it has elected the latter. The executive is headed by five collegial Directors. This leadership appoints ministers, responsible only to it. It sees to administration, security and diplomacy. Theoretically, there is no interference between legislative and executive. But there is also no constitutional recourse if they conflict. Does such rigid separation of powers ensure efficient functioning?

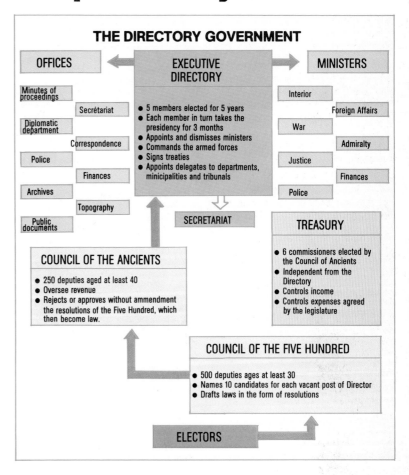

THE DIRECTORY GOVERNMENT

OFFICES
- Minutes of proceedings
- Secrétariat
- Diplomatic department
- Correspondence
- Police
- Finances
- Archives
- Topography
- Public documents

EXECUTIVE DIRECTORY
- 5 members elected for 5 years
- Each member in turn takes the presidency for 3 months
- Appoints and dismisses ministers
- Commands the armed forces
- Signs treaties
- Appoints delegates to departments, minicipalities and tribunals

MINISTERS
- Interior
- Foreign Affairs
- War
- Admiralty
- Justice
- Finances
- Police

SECRETARIAT

COUNCIL OF THE ANCIENTS
- 250 deputies aged at least 40
- Oversee revenue
- Rejects or approves without ammendment the resolutions of the Five Hundred, which then become law.

TREASURY
- 6 commissioners elected by the Council of Ancients
- Independent from the Directory
- Controls income
- Controls expenses agreed by the legislature

COUNCIL OF THE FIVE HUNDRED
- 500 deputies ages at least 30
- Names 10 candidates for each vacant post of Director
- Drafts laws in the form of resolutions

ELECTORS

Medal showing people's representatives in the Five Hundred ...

... and in the Ancients' Council.

The Council of Ancients meets at the Tuileries in the Machines hall, where the Convention used to gather.

David's studio is now the centre of the capital's art scene

Paris, November

David was definitively paroled
by the installation of the Directory,
and enthusiastically went back to
work. Dropping the *Homer Reciting his Verses to the Greeks*, which
he began in prison, he has started an
immense painting known as the
Sabine Women (three metres high
and over five metres wide), which is
an affirmation of the painter's
growing insistence on archaeolo-
gical reconstitution. He has been
given a new and bigger studio in the
Louvre, while retaining the right to
use the ones he already had in the
north corner of the colonnade: a
private studio, which he has lent to
his student and assistant Charles
Moreau, and the studio in which his
students work. All the capital's
young artists have gathered around
the master. Every Monday they
draw lots for places and work from
a nude model, which is becoming
more and more of a requirement.
On some days the students themselves take turns posing. They include Delécluze, Robin, Mulard,
Gautherot, Forbin, Delavergne,

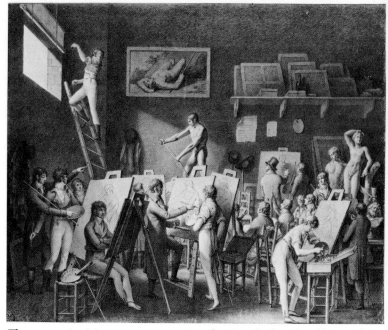

The master is giving a new generation of artists the benefit of his teaching.

Granet and the Franque brothers,
the two shepherds from the Drôme
region whom the Legislative Assembly placed with David in 1792.
The young painters are divided into
"aristocrats" and "crassons" (leftists), making the studio a crucible in
which opinions mix violently, but
with the same passion for Greek
Antiquity.

Val de Grâce becomes military hospital

Paris, November 1

In the former Val de Grâce
Convent, which has been converted
into a military hospital, the nuns
chased away by the Revolution
have been replaced by the Republic's soldiers. The establishment,
formerly devoted to prayer, will
now take in some of the good men
wounded on the battlefield. It took
almost two years for the decision,
made by the Convention on July
31st, 1793, to be implemented, and
for Val de Grâce finally to open its
doors to doctors and patients. Let
us hope that the ghost of its illustrious founder, Anne of Austria,
will not take offence. She is probably still haunting the cloisters of the
abbey she loved so much.

The Val de Grâce Convent, built in 1645, housed some Benedictine nuns.

Bernardin de Saint Pierre finally gets a financial break

Paris, November 10

The Convention has proved its
generosity. Following intervention
by the deputies Grandjean and Ginguené, the author Bernardin de
Saint Pierre has just been awarded a
salary of 12,000 francs for the ethics
courses he gives at the Ecole Normale. Thus the writer's repeated
complaints have not been in vain.
Together with the food allowance
he has just received at the order of
the Committee of Public Safety, the
author of *Paul et Virginie* may
now consider himself as no longer
needy. Unfortunately, the same
cannot be said about everybody,
especially of his most faithful readers. A young teacher in the Seine et
Oise department was found dead of
starvation along the road. The only
thing he had in his pockets that
might have helped him was a copy
of *La Chaumière Indienne*, which
Bernardin de Saint Pierre published
five years ago with great success.
At least he may have been comforted in distress.

Death penalty still matter for debate

Paris, November 14

The deputies thought they had settled the question ... by avoiding any immediate answer. The fact is that on November 5th. they decreed that capital punishment, a "scourge" that, after royalty, "still weighed on mankind", would be definitively abolished throughout the Republic "at the moment of the proclamation of general peace". Today, Savary returned in the Assembly to the question of deserters, which is a tough issue to resolve. Even if their offence deserves the guillotine, in his view, he noted in passing that such a sentence frightened the judges much more than it did the victims. Such remarks are going to relaunch the eternal debate: is there a supreme punishment? Is death justified?

Eight schoolbooks for use in France

Paris, November 5

It is not enough to create schools or train the teachers. The latter also have to be equipped with suitable teaching resources. For two years they have been impatiently awaiting the results of the competition for elementary schoolbooks that began on January 28th. 1794. Today they may well be satisfied, because Lakanal briefed the Council of Five Hundred on the list of the eight works finally selected by the jury. None of the well-known figures the Public Education Committee had in mind for a time for writing the books actually contributed to this educational task. Even if they are not the product of famous scholars, the selected manuals share at least one quality: they are all imbued with the best republican virtues.

Directory chooses new ministerial team

Paris, November 5

The Directory wasted no time in announcing its government programme. It proclaimed that it wanted to "wage active war on royalism, revive patriotism, vigorously repress all factions, and make concord reign". This is indeed a vast ambition, one that is going to force it to remain on its guard to fend off the right close to the royalists, and the left sympathising with the Jacobins. With this in mind, it has chosen a relatively conservative governing team, but one that put in its political apprenticeship under the revolutionary government. Thus the Interior Minister, Pierre Bénézech, was employed by the Committee of Public Safety at the Arms and Powders Agency. But he is said not to be much of a republican. Charles Delacroix, the Foreign Affairs Minister, was a moderate Montagnard. A

Merlin de Douai — Justice Ministry.

former nobleman who sat in the Constituent Assembly, Faipoult, gets the Ministry of Finance, and Reubell's friend Jean Baptiste Aubert Dubayet gets the War Ministry.

Port Louis going to recover original name

Ile de France, November 4

Port de la Montagne is no more. A decree approved by the Colonial Assembly this morning ended its legal existence, so the former Port Nord Ouest, founded by the India Company, is resuming its name of Port Louis. In any case, the Creoles never used any name other than the one that recalled their Breton links. To justify the new decree, the legislators said that "Port de la Montagne" now made people think of a detested faction. Fifteen months earlier, their zealous representative made the same remarks to the Convention to get rid of the name Port Louis.

Le Mans workers have wretched lives

Le Mans, November 15

The textile workers are suffering sharply from price decontrol and the ensuing inflation. Their working and living conditions are becoming ever harder. Since money, even depreciated assignats, is short throughout the region, wages are not always paid. No tradesmen give them credit, so the poorest workers fear starvation. That is why a good number of them are forced to go out into the countryside to offer to work for the peasants in exchange for a bit of food. Exhausted and desperate, they invaded the office of the department's national agent. They are asking for a minimum wage that would be subject to weekly review and revision, in order to be able to buy bread for themselves and their families ...

The Directory

'Tis the latest success
The Mountain can own:
A Directory sits
On the stately top bench.
And it's under this name,
Yet to History unknown,
That the five new-crowned kings
Henceforth govern the French.

Now all talents and virtues,
Are entirely proscribed.
This age does all honour devour.
To achieve supreme rank,
Now bid virtues adieu!
Simply shoot down in flames
All the French people's power.

What deception, sad French!
The Republic for you is the word
Of a rallying clarion call.
But your five ruling kings,
By a road all askew,
Sure will soon lead it safe
To the monument tall.

They Equality sacred degrade.
Cherished Liberty now
By their rule they disdain,
In their minds and their hearts
Blest Fraternity's dead.

At his residence in the Louvre, the painter Gérard has J. B. Isabey as his neighbour. He painted a portrait of Isabey, along with his daughter.

18 *(Brumaire 27, Year IV)*
Ile d'Yeu. The Comte d'Artois returns to England, giving up any hope he may have had of reconquering France by using force.

20 *(Brumaire 29, Year IV)*
Paris. La Révellière Lépeaux draws up a list of the first 48 members of the Institute of France (→Dec. 6, 95).

21 *(Brumaire 30, Year IV)*
Rhineland. Capitulation of the Mannheim garrison, which Pichegru left defenceless after his withdrawal from Landau decided on November 18th.

21 *(Brumaire 30, Year IV)*
Paris. By abrogating the law barring joint stock companies and commercial companies, the new régime completes the process of liberalising the economy.

22 *(Frimaire 1, Year IV)*
Paris. The violinist Pierre Gaviniès is entrusted with the violin classes at the Conservatory. For the pianoforte, the composer and virtuoso Louis Adam is chosen.

23 *(Frimaire 2, Year IV)*
Paris. In the interests of solving the problem of massive desertions from the Army, the Directory creates the post of military agent, "for which it will more particularly choose Montagnards".

23 *(Frimaire 2, Year IV)*
Valenciennes. The discovery of a corpse in an inn revives the fear of gangs of "Hot Feet" who attack isolated dwellings in many areas.

25 *(Frimaire 4, Year IV)*
Italy. The victory of the Army of Italy, commanded by Schérer, at Loano makes it possible to push the Austrians back even behind the Apennines.

25 *(Frimaire 4, Year IV)*
Paris. Multiplication of strikes in the workshops, which are aimed at forcing wage increases.

28 *(Frimaire 7, Year IV)*
Vendée. Hoche captures Charette's camp.

30 *(Frimaire 9, Year IV)*
Paris. In the *People's Tribune*, Babeuf publishes *The Plebeian Manifesto*, which proposes the practice of utopian communism.

30 *(Frimaire 9, Year IV)*
Ile de France. The Colonial Assembly decides to expel the sansculottists who set sail for France.

French capital filled with English spies

Paris, November

The time of the "incorruptibles" is definitely over. It seems that the members of the Directory's departments are easy to bribe. Barras' offices appear to be replete with English spies. After the Comte d'Antraigues' network was broken, the British Foreign Office and its intelligence service, the Record Office, sent an agent to France to establish contacts with a senior official of the Committee of Public Safety, who they knew could be "influenced". But his exclusion after Thermidor obliged the British agent to set up a new network. He got help from the "royalist agency" of Duverne de Presle, Abbot Brottier and La Villeheurnois, who are agents of the Comte de Provence. Other English agents were infiltrated into France by means of corruption. London is no longer ignorant of any details concerning the French economy and finances or the equipment and morale of the armed forces, and is unfortunately all too well informed about the French ministers' activities.

The moderate Panthéon Club is opened

Paris, November 16

The mere fact that they got out of the Directory's prisons did not lead the Jacobin democrats to give up their ideals. They want to choke off the tide of reaction before it is too late. Initially they gathered in public places, where the discussions were lively. Some of them advocated critical support for the Directory. Others, former Robespierrists, wanted to revive "economic terror". But such individual initiatives of a handful of militants quickly proved sterile. The idea of a grouping began to make headway. But should a single association be established, or should one be organised in each arrondissement? Buonarroti and Darthé came out for the first solution. A patriotic association was born from their reflections and the thinking of the former Convention deputy Amar, Lebois, a journalist for *The People's Orator*, and Judge Beaudrais, a spy in the Directory's pay. This association is called the Panthéon Club, and it meets in the former Sainte Geneviève convent. The alliance was concluded on the basis of an extremely moderate programme: bringing the

Buonarroti, Babeuf's companion.

republicans together, and finding them a place for expressing themselves without disturbing public order, under cover of the Constitution of 1795. All the extremists grouped around Babeuf are too small a minority at present to put their views across. Social revolution is not now on the agenda. Since annual dues are set at 50 livres, the membership will be primarily middle class. Hence the club should not frighten the Directory, and Barras allowed it to open.

Outside Saint Germain l'Auxerrois church, jugglers and acrobats are experts at entertaining passers by.

Plebeian Manifesto presents the ideas of agitator Babeuf

Paris, November 30

In the light of the success enjoyed by the Panthéon Club, the revolutionary minority has decided to put itself more in the public eye. It wants to sweep away inequalities and establish a new society. Equality of rights was achieved in 1789. Equality of property, the real equality, is the goal of the revolutionaries of 1795. These ideas are put forward by Babeuf in his *Plebeian Manifesto*. This is a strange revolutionary ideology that goes far beyond the Jacobins' views. Babeuf and his friends, Buonarroti and Darthé, demand pure democracy, perfect and unreserved equality: whence their nickname of "The Equals". These democratic republicans reveal themselves and are swinging into action with their *Manifesto*. Any means will do for the cause: the common happiness, society's final goal (→ Jan. 26, 96).

Bureaucracy growth is still vigourous

Paris, November

The administration continues to beef itself up. The state apparatus began to grow at the end of the Ancien Régime. This phenomenon was speeded up by the war effort and the needs of the controlled economy of Year II. The Directory has not interrupted this trend. The executive branch in the Luxembourg, consisting of a general secretariat, offices for each ministry, and a records department, has no fewer than 80 employees, not to mention the score of Directors' private secretaries. There are 5,500 employees in the various ministries. And local administration is not lagging behind in this process. To be sure, the Directory has a lot of "customers" to take care of. At the lowest level, the administration has become the ideal refuge for a whole population that lost its status in the Revolution. But higher-level and competent officials are in short supply, and salaries are mediocre. One must add that the criteria relating to education and "republicanism" make it difficult to recruit effectively.

Directory facing need for deciding on a new foreign policy

The Directors greet a delegation from abroad in one of the luxurious rooms of the Luxembourg Palace.

Paris, November

Does the Directory want peace? This is actually a complex question, since it inherited a difficult situation from the Thermidorians. Both Prussia and Spain opted out of the coalition opposing France, but in September, Russia, Austria and England put another one together. The latest military campaigns have not been glorious, and money is starting to run short. Yet it is impossible for the Directory to agree to conclude peace without conquest, with France returning to its 1789 borders, as the coalition wants. Only the intransigent royalists advocate this solution. The most common position is that France should extend to its "natural borders", which include the left bank of the Rhine. But certain people would like other annexations, especially in Italy, where Venice and Genoa remain stubbornly neutral. Such people are supporters of the revolutionary propaganda battle, preaching assistance to the patriots abroad and the establishment of sister republics.

Horseman Franconi triumphs in return

Paris, November

Franconi is back. This wonderful horseman, who fled to the provinces for two years to escape the Reign of Terror, is in the limelight and the saddle again. For his return to the Astley Amphitheatre he decided to put on a farce mingling theatre, pantomime and equestrian acrobatics. *Rognolet et Passe Carreau* is a one-act play portraying the misadventures of a tailor and his valet, but above all presenting an amusing horse that jumps through a fake window made in the sets whenever the fancy strikes him. The audience roared with laughter and applauded loudly enough to make the rafters ring in joy at the return of horse master Antonio.

Victories, setbacks in Italy and on Rhine

Paris, November

The military situation is not brilliant, even if the Directory thinks it is rid, for the moment, of war worries. The Army of Italy's victory over the Austro-Sardinian forces at Loano is good news. The southern coastline remains in French hands. The demoralised enemy does not plan to resume the offensive. For his part, General Barthélemy Schérer has decided that the Army of Italy should take up its winter quarters. Hence the enemy has been able to retire in good order, since Schérer did not think it well to exploit an eminently favourable tactical situation. The soldiers' tiredness and extreme shortages of supplies explain this surprising decision. Furthermore, the French may consider themselves as controlling the Apennine peaks. This position enables them to maintain themselves in the narrow strip of territory along the coast. But on the Eastern Front, Jourdan and Pichegru seem to have returned to their point of departure. To be sure, the poor coordination between the Rhine and Moselle and the Sambre and Meuse Armies enabled the Austrians to withdraw to advantageous positions. The French captured Düsseldorf and Neuwied, and then invested Mannheim, but they then had to withdraw and cross back over the Rhine at a time when Clairfayt's Austrians were in difficulty for a moment on the Main River. Still, the campaign revealed some young leaders, such as Masséna, who performed brilliantly at Loano.

Unusual campaign is launched to improve public morality

The foyer at Montmartre theatre: a notorious meeting place where prostitutes go to seek out their clients.

Paris, December 6

The hard-line revolutionaries have fits of indignation about it all. Citizens are neglecting the cockade and noble republican values to go out dancing or to boo at the theatre, or something worse. So the deputies decided to react, and to fight debauchery and indolence by virtue, which will be imposed if necessary. They have approved the establishment of a central office to monitor behaviour. The staff of that office will study reports submitted by police officers sent out into the field. They will keep an eye on the "gilded youth" which shamelessly insults the fatherland's honour, and on the prostitutes who openly solicit on the street; on book-sellers and journalists who hawk royalist ideas, and on actors who turn the theatres into political arenas; on pedlars who unpack their obscene pictures on the pavements, and on clergymen who are reappearing as if miraculously; on charlatans and other buffoons who distract patriots from their civic activities, and even on the keepers of public baths who soften the soul on the pretext of helping the body relax. In a nutshell, they will watch everybody guilty of shamelessly betraying the spirit of the French Revolution.

Director Carnot finds luxurious way of life

Paris, December

Carnot did not expect all this. The instant he expresses the slightest wish, a host of ushers, guards and servants rushes to get his orders. The nation keeps him and his fellow Directors like princes. The new Director has just moved, with his family, into one of the apartments in the Petit Luxembourg, his official residence. The sitting-room has blue and white damask hangings, and from his window he can see the garden of the palace, which used to be a Condé family property. He walks on Raincy carpets, and has a bed in his office for resting. His wife has been assigned an embroidering loom and a pianoforte, which is greatly appreciated when entertaining guests. As the height of luxury, the couple have just lined their personal wine cellar with hundreds of bottles of good wine from Mâcon, Bordeaux, Malaga and Madeira, to help entertain the neighbours, the La Révellière Lépeaux couple.

Carnot: far from military life.

Directory confirms the Institute voters

Paris, December 6

The Convention established the Institute by decree, but it was still necessary to turn it into reality. The Directory has just confirmed the voting third of this group of scholars, some 44 members, the majority of whom are academicians. They will be called on to elect the other 96, and then all will choose their associates. In the section of physical and mathematical sciences, Guyton Morveau and Berthollet were named in chemistry, Daubenton and Lacépède in anatomy and zoology, Des Essartz in medicine and surgery, and Lamarck and Desfontaines in botany. Other famous figures are from moral and political sciences and fine arts.

Bandits in Eure hit inn, killing couple

Nonancourt, December 15

The "Hot Foot" bandits of the Eure region have struck again. They attacked the inn kept by the Du Friche couple. Forcing their way into the house, the bandits tortured the husband to make him talk. He did, enabling the robbers to grab his savings. Finally, since there was no hurry, the "Hot Feet" sat down to carouse at their victims' expense. Egged on by the wine, they raped the woman in her husband's sight and then slit their throats. Then they left, unknown and elusive. For three years now these bandits have been operating with impunity in Normandy and nearby areas, attacking isolated farms. Their modus operandi is always the same. They get in by tricks or force, and torture the occupants to get them to tell where they have hidden their gold. They show great imagination in this process: simulated hangings, burning their victims' feet in the fireplace, beatings. These rough but effective methods have helped them to make off with loot that is estimated at several million francs.

Madame Royale is exchanged for 20 republican prisoners

Madame Royale, the "orphan of the Temple", who is the Emperor's niece, will live at the Austrian court.

Upper Rhine, December 26

"We're losing an angel, and they are giving us some monsters to replace her!" That was what people in the street shouted as they saw the 20 prisoners, who were going to be exchanged for Madame Royale, pass by. The young princess, accompanied by her retinue, arrived in Hüningen on Christmas Eve. But the exchange did not take place until two days later, in a country house near the town. It occurred in the presence of representatives of Austria, France and the city of Basel. The princess was very emotional and murmured: "Gentlemen, I will never forget that I am a Frenchwoman." The republican prisoners exchanged include the former Minister of War Beurnonville, the ambassadors Maret and Sémonville, and Drouet, who handed Louis XVI over in Varennes.

Hunger and discontent in Côte d'Or region

Dijon, December 28

The Côte d'Or authorities have informed the Interior Ministry that in Dijon, as throughout the department, people are suffering from hunger even though the summer harvests have not been exhausted. The farmers refuse to accept assignats, which are now worth only 1.75 francs against 43.50 francs in January, and are keeping their grain. Hence the cities are running short, and there are mutterings of revolt. The authorities particularly fear a monarchical reaction. Many people are nostalgic for the quiet life of the Ancien Régime, and they have no confidence in the new one.

Bonaparte lifts the veil to get a better look at Joséphine de Beauharnais, whom he met last October, dancing naked with Madame Tallien.

"Blue" village lies in a "White" area

Vendée, December

One of the Republic's veterans was there. He saw it all and is still greatly moved. The Grenadier captain had received orders to lead his men through the countryside and the quickset hedges to track down the "Royalist bandits". It was night when the troops reached the edge of the small village of Saint Georges. The silent soldiers scattered, some of them into the nearby woods and the others behind the few hovels in the town. They were sure they would come up with one of those Whites who vanish as soon as they are glimpsed, and then sneak back to cut your throat. Everything was quiet as the grave. But suddenly a door opened and the captain near it stepped back. A farmer eyed him, with a pitchfork in his hand. "Who are you? Death to the King's friends!" Realizing the captain was a "Blue", the farmer told him: "Here you are among your own." The other inhabitants acclaimed the republicans.

Trade has revived at port of Bordeaux

Bordeaux, December

Peace, the liberalisation of the economy and the end of government control of foreign trade have enabled the port of Bordeaux to recover some of its business, if not its former splendour. Once again neutral vessels, Danish, American, Dutch and German from Prussia and the Hanseatic cities, tie up alongside the Bordeaux docks. Most often, they unload grain and take on wine, which they sell in their own country, the colonies, and even in Great Britain. But in spite of a timid recovery in imports of sugar, coffee, chocolate, indigo and cotton, the large-scale colonial trade has not really been re-established. Aware of this trend, many trader families, such as the Gradis, are investing in vineyards, which are now responsible for the region's wealth. Thus the former colonial warehouse is gradually being transformed into a regional port, thanks to the wine-growing areas inland from the city.

Police Ministry set up by government

Paris, January 2

Merlin de Douai is becoming
France's leading policeman. He is
leaving the Justice Ministry to take
over the General Police Ministry, to
which he has just been appointed by
the Executive Directory. This new
institution is being established in
order to relieve the Interior Minister, Bénézech, of the strictly technical questions involved in maintaining order and organising resistance
to "subversive undertakings",
namely, to Jacobin manoeuvres.
Merlin de Douai is a brilliant lawyer
and an opportunistic politician, and
he looks like just the man for this
task. He knows the Jacobins well,
having been one. He favoured terror
until Thermidor, but has been fighting it energetically since then.

Astronomer Laplace details cosmogony

Paris, January

Where does the planet Earth
come from? In his *Presentation of
the World System*, the astronomer
Pierre Simon Laplace offers an explanation of the fascinating history
of the sky for all, without mathematical formulae. In this work, he
develops a radically new hypothe-
sis: that the solar system originated
in a primitive nebula surrounding a
very hot core. He says the rotation
of the whole mass and its cooling
gradually led to the condensation of
a number of superimposed layers,
which then gave rise to the solar
system's planets.

Astronomer Pierre Simon Laplace.

French military is in deplorable condition

ILYPASSERA
Es wird gehen

Despite uniforms in rags, French soldiers want to conquer the world.

Paris, January

The Directory has declared war
on the military suppliers. Rather
than giving in to waste and the administrators' misuse of funds, pro-
curement will now be entrusted to
companies. To realise the urgency
of such a move, one need only consider the extreme shortages with
which the armed forces have to
contend. This is the case of the
Rhine and Moselle Army, about
which one observer made the following comment: "The soldiers are
starving and they can hardly drag
themselves along in their weakened
condition." In the face of such
shortages, the recruits desert in
droves. Some half-brigades have
only 600 men, and there are squadrons with barely a score of cavalrymen. Out of a planned 1.5 million
soldiers, there are no more than
450,000 armed men.

Woman sentenced to knit for the soldiers

Indre et Loire, January 24

Sometimes one only need to twid-
dle one's thumbs to display anti-
revolutionary feelings. That is what
the women of Ligueil recently
dared to do by refusing to carry out
their duty as good citizens: knitting
for the soldiers. This public display
of lack of civic spirit was criticised
by commune leaders, who condemned the most obstinate one of these
ladies to have a pair of men's stockings made at her own expense.
While the punishment may seem
light, the important thing is for it to
be edifying.

"Tribune" Babeuf gives police slip again

Paris, January 26

One can't arrest the "People's Tribune". Babeuf, the spreader of communist ideas, has managed to escape the police again. An arrest warrant had been issued for the firebrand, but the policeman who went to his home to arrest him was alone. As soon as he entered the street, Babeuf called on the people for help. A crowd of curious neighbours immediately gathered around him, and Babeuf took off in the very presence of the representative of powerless authority to find refuge in the Rue Saint Honoré. Even underground, he definitely intends to continue fighting the Directory's policy (→ March 30).

Gracchus Babeuf, eternal opponent.

Paris theatres to be carefully watched

Paris, January 13

One cannot cast doubts on the prestige of the national Army with impunity. Pierre Gardel, the author of *Deserter*, the ballet now featured at the Feydeau Theatre, has learnt this to his cost. Even if people tolerate seeing military men dance on stage like Opera ballet students, it is inconceivable for them to wear white uniforms rather than the regulation national uniforms. Yesterday evening, violent disturbances in the audience forced the actors to interrupt the performance. And when the Police Minister, Merlin de Douai, was informed about the episode, he decided to keep a watch on all Paris stages in future. Napoléon Bonaparte, who has been chief of the domestic army since Vendémiaire, seemed just the man to help the minister in this thankless job. Merlin de Douai has asked him for a report on the main Paris theatres. This army man interfering in the world of culture is starting to worry entertainment people (→ Feb. 14).

Louis XVI's death is commemorated

Paris, January 21

The satisfaction the Directory has given the Jacobins is a matter of form only. In authorising the republicans to celebrate the anniversary of the execution of Louis XVI and in organising the commemoration itself, the Directory was not taking any big political risk, especially since the event was neither grandiose nor one of popular appeal, contrary to Barras' desires. However, this compromise might turn out awkwardly. It annoys the right, which is furious to see a Jacobin demonstration tolerated in this way, yet it does not appeal to the left, which considers the commemoration a trap. The fact is that Reubell seized on the occasion to make a very conservative speech, in which he made efforts to reassure the land-owners.

Cuvier shows fossil study is a science

Paris, January 21

The study of fossils is a science, as has just been proved by the naturalist Georges Cuvier. He briefed his dumbfounded colleagues at the Institute on the results of his research on elephants. According to him, those mammals had ancestors who have disappeared. The study of fossils enables the scientist to prove the existence of vanished animal species, probably wiped out long ago by natural disasters. Once Cuvier's admiring colleagues had managed to get over their surprise, they cheered his *Memoir on living and fossil elephant species*. This marks a new stage for this scientist. In offering his previous scientific work, he laid the foundation for comparative anatomy. He is now beginning to blaze a new trail, the one leading to paleontology.

Stofflet relaunches Vendean agitation

Maine et Loire, January 26

"My good friends, the time has come for you to show yourselves. God, the King, the cry of conscience, the cry of honour and the voice of your leaders call you to combat." That is the proclamation sent by the Vendean General Stofflet to his supporters, asking them to gather near Jallais, on the Cabournes moors. Will many people respond to his appeal? There is nothing more uncertain, as the pacification policy followed by Hoche has proved its effectiveness. Religious freedom and abolition of conscription have satisfied the peasants, who are all the more hesitant about taking up arms again in that they know Hoche has close military control of the region. Stofflet himself thinks the new insurrection has little chance of success. "We are marching toward the scaffold, but that doesn't matter. Long live the King all the same!" he is said to have remarked to his entourage after making his decision. The Comte

Is peace being threatened again?

d'Artois' return to England after the hopes aroused by his arrival at Ile d'Yeu discouraged many people of good will. Yet it is at the order of the prince and his brother that Stofflet, faithful but without illusions, has broken the peace agreed with the Republic (→ Feb. 25).

Heartless Beau François strikes again

Montgon, January 30

The Lejeune farm has been visited by the Orgères gang. Led by "Beau François", 40 bandits invaded the farm and the ordeal began. With their feet held to the fire, the Lejeune couple revealed their secret: the money was in a cask in the cellar. Beau François, leaving the dying husband, went down into the cellar with the wife for her to show him the hiding place, in exchange for her life. But once he got his hands on the money, he stabbed her 18 times. The three valets were decapitated with sabres. In leaving, the gang took along a woman servant, whom they are going to keep in the underground hideout that has so far kept them safe.

For the heartless "Hot Foot" gang, gold is always worth more than life.

Some real bandits fake royalist coup

Eure, February 4

The tax-collector's office in Boissy le Sec was attacked during the evening by "Hot Foot" bandits. They burst into the building and seized the money kept there. Then, to confuse the issue, they pretended to be Chouans and, in exchange for the money, left an IOU signed "18th Henri IV Division". In the interest of making all this more credible, the bandits chopped down the tree of liberty to cries of "Long live the King!". Then they took the road to La Chapelle, where they cleaned out the tax office with the same routine.

Petiet gets ministry

Paris, February 8

Aubert Dubayet is leaving Paris for Constantinople, to be ambassador there. He is being replaced at the War Ministry by Louis Petiet, a deputy to the Five Hundred. There is nothing about military matters that this former royal gendarme does not know. He was the chief *commissaire ordonnateur* of the forces on the Brest coasts and defended Nantes against the Vendean insurrection. He is considered a peerless administrator, a precious asset in the military sphere.

Bonaparte brother military commissar

Paris, February 9

Napoléon Bonaparte's rise has given ideas to Lucien, his younger brother. Lucien requested a position on his brother's general staff, but the young man's myopia tells against trying to command in the field. However, there is no need for perfect eyesight to administer the military, so Napoléon has appointed his brother commissar for the Northern Army. Since Lucien was not yet 20 years old, the minimum age required for that position, he submitted the birth certificate of his brother Joseph, rather than his own. Thanks to this trick, the happy new commissar left this morning to join the forces in Brussels.

A French military commissar.

Bonaparte insists on offensive in Italy

Paris, February 4

"Let him who conceived it come and carry it out." That was the reaction of General Schérer, commander-in-chief of the Army of Italy, to young General Bonaparte's plan. What is basically at stake is the practical application on the tactical level, as conceived by "the General of Vendémiaire", of the general strategic concepts underlying the future campaign, as outlined by Reubell, the Director. The plan calls for attacking the Austrians, pursuing them into the Milan region and occupying the country, not to conquer it, but rather with a view to negotiations. Hence it would be pointless to fight the Sardinians specifically. If Vienna is defeated, the Sardinians will no longer be able to refuse to deal with the French Republic. But Bonaparte has only one idea in mind for implementing the Director's military thinking: an offensive. He thinks the enemy forces can never get together to cope with a sudden attack. And are attacks not always crowned with success in mountainous regions?

Four Beauvais tapestries off to America to top up coffers

One of "The Four Parts of the World", illustrating American independence.

Paris, February

The government needs money, but it so happens that the vestiges of royalty include, at the bottom of the former Furniture Repository, four fine tapestries made by the Beauvais works and known as *The Four Parts of the World*, which particularly illustrate the American Republic's very recent independence. The curator, Villette, first thought of using them to help furnish the Grand Luxembourg Palace, but then suggested it would be much more to the point to put them into the hands of a dealer who would sell them to the United States. This will be a symbol of the French Republic's desire to maintain its relationship with the United States. Moreover, they are "low", and above all "are spoiled by several symbols of feudalism that would be hard to remove ..."

Directory says no to new price controls

Paris, February 9

The Directory has refused to consider a petition from the "Patriots of '89". The signers, grouped around the former Convention deputy Amar, pointed to the fact that, under Robespierre, the people had bread, and urged re-establishment of price controls on basic foodstuffs. Some of them have even suggested that the Republic's taxation system should include a levy on sales and on capital. But the Directory turned all this down, firmly reaffirming its attachment to freedom of trade.

Young Archduke to lead imperial forces

Vienna, February 6

The time for retirement has come: at the age of 63, the Count of Clairfayt has been appointed ambassador to Hungary. The past victories of the Imperial Army's commanding general have never wiped out his defeat against Jourdan and Carnot at Wattignies. Now the Austrian Emperor has decided to bet on youth, as Archduke Charles, the new Army chief and a field marshal, is only 25 years old. But this nephew of Marie Antoinette commanded an army vanguard three years ago.

Charles, one of Leopold II's sons.

General Pichegru is suspected of duplicity

Basel, February 13

The letter that the French ambassador in Basel has just sent to the Directory seems a worrying development. In it Bacher indicates his suspicions about the commanding general of the Army of the Rhine, Pichegru. He decided to alert the government when he discovered that the officer had started talks with royalist agents. Moreover, since Pichegru got leave to go to Paris, Bacher suspects him of having done so to hatch a plot against the Republic. Actually, ever since the general was put in charge of repression of the trouble that broke out in April 1795, during which the Parisians invaded the Convention, Pichegru has considered himself qualified for carrying out a coup d'état. He is helped in all this by his own ambition as well as the marked disorganisation he notes in the military. He thinks conditions are ideal for the royalists' return to power. If his duplicity should be proved, it would show

Has Pichegru been too ambitious?

that the republican régime is indeed threatened by its own military. The armed forces' apparent loyalty may actually be a mere illusion at this point (→ March 14).

"Incredible" men and "Marvellous" women reign over the capital's boulevards

In you everything is incredible
From the head down to the feet
Hat of shape unbelievable
Big feet in shoes so neat.

If, to be in fettle,
Gargantua came to inspire,
Nothing would more settle
Than to borrow your attire.

Booted like Saint George
Trousered like Marlborough,
Waistcoat under throat
Golden tie clip at the neck.

Three marvellous cravats
Have your chin blocked
And the end of your plaits
Form horns that are locked.

I saw another Incredible
Shod like a trollope
To a beauty inconceivable
His white hand doll'd up.

"This incredible hair
Has, said she, such appeal
That on seeing with a stare
I could not with it deal.

For some time now, people have noticed some young men on the boulevards dressed in eccentric fashion and wearing long hair "dog-ear style" under wide hats. They are called the "Incredibles". Their feminine counterpart, the "Marvellous", are young women dressed in generously-slitted muslin tunics worn over flesh-coloured tights that give an impression of nudity. The song-writer Ange Pitou has sketched these young people in these ironic verses.

To match the elegance of the "Marvellous" girls with their costumes from Antiquity, the "Incredibles" must have perfectly-waxed leather boots.

O charming Marvellous!
Mother of love divine,
Of your form fabulous
Nothing can hide it's line.

Of your dress so antique
So beautifully flowing
It is to make a sacrifice
That your stockings are rolled.

In your dress trailing,
When the flounces wave
They forbid the waiting
Of our desire's slave.

I see your light hand
Led by the loves
From mystery's land
We discover the grove.

Heels of a huntress,
Embroidered buckles and shoes
Boots of riding dress
Or stockings so sheer.

Ridiculously in fashion
In all your finery
Of queens and Romans
You search for frippery.

Directory

Vendean chief Stofflet is shot in Angers

Angers, February 25

Two days was all it took to try him and carry out the death verdict. The Vendean leader Stofflet was arrested at night at the Poitevinière farm, probably after being betrayed. He was immediately taken to Angers, and has just been shot there. This marks the disappearance of one of the original leaders of the Vendean insurrection. Stofflet was a former gamekeeper of Comte Colbert de Maulévrier, and was among the first to take in hand the gangs of peasants that took up arms during the great uprising of March 1793. Despite his lack of polish, Stofflet's military abilities quickly made this commoner one of the generals of the Great Catholic and Royalist Army. After recrossing the Loire in 1794, he harassed the re-

The Sacred Heart worn by Stofflet.

publicans in the Mauges area, while Charette, with whom Stofflet was never really on good terms, did the same in the Marais.

Fersen turned down in quest for funds

Vienna, February 24

Axel de Fersen is indignant. At a meeting with the Austrian Emperor and Madame Royale, Marie Antoinette's daughter, Francis II said that any money the late queen may have possessed belonged to her daughter, who would come into it in coming of age. Hence Fersen cannot obtain repayment of the loans he made to Louis XVI for the King's flight to Varennes, nor payment of the 1.5 million livres that the King had promised the count for his help.

Directory considers aid to Irish rebels

Paris, February 29

The Irishman Wolfe Tone has only one goal in life: independence for his country. And the famous patriot does not hesitate to go all out in serving this cause. As soon as he landed upon returning to Europe from the United States, in which he took refuge in 1794, he urged the Directory to authorise French military aid in the effort to free Ireland. He says that all Ireland is ready to follow him and shake off the British yoke. The Directory is interested and will decide soon.

Panthéon Club shut in repression of left

Paris, February 28

The repression launched by the Directory is extending to the entire left. The government has suppressed a few royalist associations to avoid being accused of partiality. But above all, acting in the name of "public tranquillity", it has ordered the closure of the Panthéon Club and has assigned General Bonaparte to see to the application of this decision. This republican association, with headquarters in the former Sainte Geneviève abbey and established by the ex-Maratist Lebois, was set up legally in 1795. Originally moderate, it became extremist under the influence of Babeuf's friends, supporting his cause and demands.

Reconciliation call by Abbot Grégoire

Paris, February 20

What is the greatest wish of the priests who have taken the oath? Reconciliation with the Pope and the non-juring clergy. This fact is revealed in their second *Encyclical of Bishops in Council*, published in Grégoire's newspaper, *Annales de la Religion*. While announcing a summons for a council of the "National", or the "Gallican", Church, which are new names for the former Constitutional Church, the bishops reaffirmed that they are not schismatics in any shape or form.

Free bread, meat hand-outs to continue

The number of beggars is rising.

Paris, February 20

The Directors have had to give in in the face of the people's anger. They have dropped the idea of suspending free hand-outs of bread and meat for the poor, as they had contemplated doing for a time. In the wake of the abolition of price controls and the consequent unfortunate inflation, the new measure would have exacerbated shortages and discontent. The latter is particularly marked since speculators continue their activities even though the people are wretched. Moreover, dropping the free food would have been risky politically: the Jacobins might have used a food riot to launch a popular revolt.

Family court is out on ineffectiveness

Paris, February 28

Aunts and brothers in law will no longer be able to go to the Family Court to try to settle their disputes. This conciliation procedure, which was set up in 1792, has just been abolished. It entailed an attempt to reach friendly settlements of family fights. Each party could represent itself, or have itself represented, without calling in the lawyers. But actually, it was very rare for these proceedings to lead to an agreement settling the dispute. Hence the existence of the Family Court actually complicated justice, rather than simplifying it.

Hated assignat printing plates destroyed

Paris, February 19

The public, furious up about inflation, is delighted. The plates used since November 1789 to print assignats, the Revolution's paper-money, were solemnly burnt on Piques Square. The drop in the currency's value and rocketing prices had become such serious problems that people were demanding urgent solutions.

But people would be wrong to think that this spectacular demonstration sounded the death-knell for inflation and a high cost of living, which have tormented the population for months now. The reason is that the two legislative chambers and the Directory have been unable to agree, apart from this purely symbolic destruction, on the policy that should be followed. They have been clashing for two months now on the thorny currency question. The deputy Eschassériaux opened the debate. Noting the failure of paper money, with a 100 franc note now worth only 15 sous in coins, he proposed at the end of November simply to return to the use of metallic money.

That solution was rejected at that time as too brutal and unrealistic. The point was that under, the Ancien Régime, there were two billion livres in circulation. However, in specie form, only 300 million remain. Hence the 34 billion assignats making up the rest of the money supply are needed for balance and, even if they have lost much of their value, they still help support trade and the economy. Therefore, to increase the currency's value, the former Jacobins

Speculators are compared to gangsters worthy of Cartouche and Mandrin, who have left the forest for the city.

grouped around Lindet suggested reducing the number of assignats by a forced loan of 600 million from the rich. But they had to change their tune after a few days, and the currency continued to depreciate. In the face of this failure, the Directory then adopted a plan submitted by Lebrun and backed by numerous financiers who are creditors of the Treasury. They said they would set up a private bank to have a monopoly on issuing banknotes, the capital of which would be guaranteed by the still-unsold national property. The bank would buy assignats at the daily rate, lend to tradesmen, and make advances to the Treasury in cash, international claims and new banknotes. But there was opposition in the Councils, where there are many former Convention deputies faithful to the revolutionary currency. They think the state must never give financiers control over monetary policy. Hence the Treasury alone is responsible for deflating. That is why, even if they authorised destruction of the assignat plates, the Councils preferred to delay matters when it came to creating a new currency (→ March 18).

Goodbye assignat

The value of the assignat has dropped steadily. The Directory decided to burn the printer's block for printing the bills. The burning took place on the Place Vendôme, giving rise to a song:

"How ungrateful the French!"
The printer told the assignats.
'Tis, sooth, a sorry state.
By law their block is to be burned
As they're by the people spurned.
'Tis that will compensate.

They're forged by William Pitt.
'Tis, sooth, a sorry state.
At Quiberon our men of war
The English bastards beat;
'Tis that will compensate.

When you say these assignats
Enriched the Vendée Chouans,
'Twas, sooth, a sorry state.
Oh, the woes the bills did cause,
'Service rendered' all applause.
'Tis that will compensate.

For Paris these bills did flood.
'Twas, sooth, a sorry state.
In future just one single bill
With joy the man in need will fill.
'Tis that will compensate.

Assignats burnt on Piques Square.

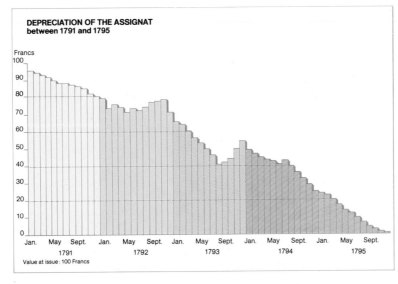

DEPRECIATION OF THE ASSIGNAT
between 1791 and 1795

Francs

Jan.	May	Sept.	Jan.	May	Sept.	Jan.	May	Sept.	Jan.	May	Sept.	Jan.	May	Sept.
1791			1792			1793			1794			1795			

Value at issue : 100 Francs

Another victim of poverty and winter

Paris, March 3

When the police brought the 60-year-old woman back to the police station, she was barely breathing. Once the warmth had restored a bit of her strength, she told the policemen that she had gone to see her husband at the Bicêtre charity hospital, and that she had fallen as she was going toward Saint Denis Gate. Then, tired from talking, she fell silent. A few seconds later, the municipal officer closed her eyes. A roadman had found her lying in the snow near the Fontainebleau checkpoint, at the gates of the capital. She was wearing a poor mended jacket and a tattered *jupon*. The woman is the latest victim of the cold that has tormented the population since the start of the winter. Hunger and exhaustion probably contributed to this unfortunate citizen's death.

Quiet wedding for Bonaparte, Joséphine

The general is 27 years old, while his bride is 33 and has been married.

Paris, March 9

There was no pomp today for the wedding of General Bonaparte to General Beauharnais's widow. The only unusual features of the discreet ceremony were the procedural irregularities. The mayor, supposedly the only official competent to preside, got tired of waiting for the bridegroom and went to bed. A mere assistant united the couple in marriage in the middle of the night. The general's witness, his aide de camp Lemarois, surprised people by his youth. In fact, he is a minor and cannot legally be a witness. The marriage certificate also has some odd mistakes. It ages Bonaparte by 18 months, while Joséphine has got four years younger. The groom said the changes were due to the impossibility of getting the couple's birth certificates quickly. Bonaparte used his brother Joseph's, while Joséphine found one belonging to a sister. Even the bride's name is changed, since Bonaparte refuses to call his beautiful Créole anything but Joséphine, although all her previous lovers called her Rose. This detail made the other witness, Barras, smile. He was happy to see a former mistress married to one of his protegés, and he often makes tender mention of her talent for love (→ March 11).

Carnot authorises new honours for Army

Paris, March 10

Carnot wants to improve military morale. Worried about the Army's general demoralisation, he has just signed a Directory order aimed at resolving this problem. While heaping ridicule on "crosses, ribbons and other baubles of despotism", the order provides for awarding decorations and honorary arms to soldiers who have deserved well of the country. The measure will not feed troops, who are miserably paid in the form of paper money, but at least it has the advantage of not costing anything. Carnot probably thought ironically of the Saint Louis Cross he received in 1792, which he presented to the Convention in 1793.

Batavia Convention meets for first time

The Hague, March 1

The Batavian Convention, elected in February in two-round balloting, is holding its first session. It has very extensive powers, as it can make war and peace, decide on alliances, and impose taxes. It will appoint ministers and may modify legislation by a two-thirds vote. It also has to appoint a commission that will have to draft a constitution.

There are actually two parties in the political arena. On the left, the Unitarians favour a highly centralised state. The most radical among them, including Paul Wreede, demand the abolition of everything reminding people of the old provinces, while Schimmelpenninck's moderates want to maintain the autonomy of certain local administrations. On the right, the Federalists led by Averhoult acknowledge national sovereignty and the principle of unity in general affairs, war and diplomacy, but remain greatly attached to all of the provinces' and municipalities' historic privileges, and particularly to the right they have had of imposing taxes.

Artists still running low on commissions

Paris, March 4

People thought that the lean years had finally gone by. But even though people with property are now reassured, the artists will not recover their vanished customers overnight, all those nobles, clergymen and foreigners who fled from revolutionary agitation. In a letter to Suvée, the future director of the Academy of France in Rome, Ginguené, the Public Education Director, therefore asked for a list of the names of "students entitled to receive bread".

The fact is that the nouveaux riches do not yet constitute a large and regular clientèle. Their portrait orders are hard to get because of tough competition. The majority of artists live very modestly, and often in misery. In order to survive, such a great artist as Prud'hon is reduced to indulging in such activities as painting letterheads, or other types of commercial documents, for use in the business world.

The "Notables" win municipal elections

France, March

The municipal elections marked the triumph of the middle-class order. The results, which firm up the ones obtained during the winter, will strengthen the Directory's conservative policy. In the interest of purging the Jacobin elements from local administrations, the Directory appointed only people who accepted its ideas. When it became possible to hold the balloting, the reduced number of volunteers for municipal office and large-scale abstentions from voting facilitated the local "Notables'" takeover.

Directory removes Pichegru from post

Paris, March 14

The Directory has moved. The "victor of Holland" has been deprived of his command. But one must say that General Pichegru's behaviour in the Rhineland all last autumn was hardly in his favour. Instead of co-operating with Jourdan, he delayed in the Mannheim area. Clairfayt's and Wurmser's Austrians therefore had every opportunity to co-ordinate their efforts. Moreover, informed sources say that his defeats have been due more to lukewarm republicanism than to incompetence.

Petit Trianon is left to its own devices

Versailles, March

Dr. Meyer, a German scholar who visited in Versailles, has given a nostalgic report on the deterioration of the Petit Trianon Palace there. All its furniture has been scattered, and the buildings have been left to their own devices. The English garden in Marie Antoinette's hamlet is only a bramble-overrun wasteland. Yet a year ago the Convention decided to have farming again on land "taken away from agriculture for too many years to be a source of luxury to tyrants and their servants".

Surcouf returns to Port Louis in triumph

Ile de France, March 10

Six prizes, all English and all loaded with rice -- that's the result of Robert Surcouf's cruise on the *Emilie*, with four guns and 30 men. The privateer found his calling on October 8th. off India when an English vessel fired a shot over his bow. That turned out not to be a very good idea, since the Saint Malo native came about and boarded the other ship. Since then, Surcouf has been on the offensive, attacking English convoys without permission. On January 28th., he boldly attacked and captured a three-masted vessel in the dead of night off Calcutta. Finally, he took the liberty of seizing a ship sent to pursue him. All this has delighted Port Louis, saved from starvation by his return (→ March 11).

An English vessel towing a privateer that has just captured her.

A ragged Italy Army awaits its general

Soldiers in Bonaparte's army don't worry about regulation uniforms.

Nice, March

An army in rags. What else could one expect when everything is short? No pay, no bread, poor salted meat as the usual fare and the soldiers are potential sickbay candidates. Men die on straw mats in their huts because of lack of care. Last January, in the 21st. Savona regiment, 600 foot-soldiers died in less than 20 days.

The troop strength is naturally suffering from all this. The Army of Italy now has 61,281 men present out of a planned 116,026. The others are sick, prisoners, on leave, or have deserted. For every ten infantrymen, Bonaparte will be able to count on only one artilleryman. The commanding general will have a hard time sizing up the cavalry, which has had to withdraw to the Durance or the Rhône to find enough to eat.

In this shared misery, a feeling of brotherhood replaces discipline. The way the men are thrown together has brought about excessive familiarity, and the generals drink with the men in the tavern. All authority seems to have vanished. On the eve of Bonaparte's arrival in Nice, the 3rd. Battalion of the 209th. Regiment refused to leave on the ground that it had neither shoes nor money. The officers let it pass.

It is no exaggeration to say that the republican flame, like the troops, is wavering. Last January the 70th. Regiment draped its colours in black crêpe on the anniversary of Louis XVI's execution. Chouan and counter-revolutionary songs make the rounds. One company even went so far as to call itself the "Dauphin's Company". And these are the soldiers Bonaparte is supposed to use to invade Italy. It has a simple mission: in the march toward Vienna, to attract the greatest possible number of enemies to facilitate the advance through the Danube Valley. Bonaparte will soon be at work. But before winning over the enemy, he will have to win over his men.

Directory

520

Territorial mandate replaces assignat

The new banknotes, like the old ones, are backed by national property.

Paris, March 18

A new currency is going to be issued. The reason is that the various plans considered for settling the monetary problem have all failed, especially the one involving a private bank to be given a monopoly on issuing banknotes. As the Councils desired, the state will retain control of monetary policy and will issue territorial mandates to replace assignats, which have lost 99 per cent of their value. But the reform is quite disappointing. The new notes will resemble the old ones to a surprising degree. Like the assignats, the mandates are backed by national property, for which they will be the only means of payment. Moreover, as previously, the rate is set by the administration. Finally, the rate of exchange planned between the two currencies is too favourable to the old one to restore confidence ... In a nutshell, the monetary issue is still open.

Peace talks with England fail; France firm

Paris, March 20

The Franco-British talks have just ended in failure, and peace between France and England now seems out of the question. Yet last December 3rd., it was the British monarch himself who announced his intention to end the war on honourable terms for both sides. At the beginning of March his Prime Minister, William Pitt, sent the Directory in the French capital a message through the intermediary of Wickham, an English agent operating in Switzerland, asking whether France was ready to take part in a conference of European powers to negotiate a lasting peace treaty and, if so, under what conditions. The Directory was extremely contemptuous of these proposals. The French leaders said that they would not even bother to respond to such a semi-official message. If England genuinely wanted to know French intentions, it need only approach the French government directly, in accordance with normal diplomatic practice. The Directory also said that the French Constitution did not allow it to yield any of the Republic's territories, especially Belgium. Negotiations were therefore categorically ruled out. William Pitt, annoyed by such insolence, immediately broke off talks.

Rich wife for liberator of Guadeloupe

Guadeloupe, March 16

The liberator of Guadeloupe, Victor Hugues, is marrying Charlotte Jacquin, the daughter of a rich Martinique lawyer. The bride's dowry is 600,000 livres, half invested in France and half in England and America. The marriage confirms the power exercised in the colony by this Convention commissioner, who has rocketed to prominence. He arrived on June 4th., 1794, with republican troops, and managed to expel the English, who had established themselves on the island. On December 11th. of that year, the tricolour flag was floating everywhere on Guadeloupe. The English surrender proved fatal to the 865 "White" fighters handed over to Victor Hugues. At his order, they were all shot dead. This man often combines the general interest with his own, and quickly built up a nice fortune. Since May 1795, he has been arming the Caribbean privateers for his own profit.

Angers fêtes start of a Central School

Maine et Loire, March 21

Angers will long remember the inauguration of its Central School. At 3 p.m., members of the departmental administration took up their positions at the head of a long procession moving through the city streets, to the sound of the drums of the National Guard and the Music Institute. In front of the former *collège*, which is now going to house the new institution, an enthusiastic crowd heard a reading of the order of February 23rd. appointing the seven professors chosen by the jury. Then, to repeated cries of "Long live the Republic!", three of them spoke in succession to give the inaugural speeches. Barely five months after approval of the Daunou Law establishing central schools, Angers is among the first big cities actually to have one of the new establishments.

Potato populariser Parmentier returns

Paris, March 21

Parmentier has been appointed inspector-general of the Health Department, responsible for all aspects of the department's work relating to disease prevention and treatment. This is a fair about-turn for a man whose friendship with the royal family deprived him, at the start of the Revolution, of his position as apothecary-major, his salary and pension. The Directory is honouring the author of the famous *Treatise on the cultivation and uses of potatoes, sweet potatoes and the Jerusalem artichoke.*

Potato-fancier Antoine Parmentier.

Vendean leader Charette is executed

The execution of the "unfindable" Charette is marked by a show of strength by the Republic's soldiery.

Nantes, March 29

"Abbot, I have defied death a hundred times. Now I am facing it for the last time, without braving it, but also without fear." Charette kept his word. After offering this response to the priest who had thought it well to urge him to be brave as he prepared to take his place in front of the firing squad, he moved forward, his head held high, toward the designated place. But before reaching it, he again surprised the silent crowd that had formed on Farmers' Square to witness the execution. Stopping in front of his coffin, he eyed it care-fully with an ironic smile before nodding with an approving air: yes, it was the right size for him.

Finally, having received permission to die standing and without a blindfold, he gave the order to fire himself. The soldiers carrying out the death sentence, pronounced that very morning by the court, had been chosen from members of the battalion of *chasseurs* that had managed to capture the elusive Charette on March 23rd. in the Chabotterie Woods, after a long hunt led by the Adjutant General Travot. Considered "unfindable" in his Marais region, he had only a

The last refuge, at Chabotterie.

handful of supporters with him, but he still enjoyed immense prestige. Was he not the last leader of the great Vendean uprising of 1793?

Saint Domingue putsch attempt fails

Saint Domingue, March 31

The mulatto putsch attempted at the Cap has failed. The governor of Saint Domingue, General Laveaux, again has the situation in hand. Toussaint Louverture's troops put him back on the job three days after he was removed by a mulatto general. Hence the mulattoes' plot, prepared long in advance to stop the blacks' rise, has turned out to be an utter failure. The result is power for the man the plotters wanted to keep out at any price: the black General Toussaint Louverture. The latter, who only yesterday defeated the Spaniards and the English in the west, now appears as the saviour of the constituted authorities. Laveaux gave him the honorary rank of lieutenant-general at a military ceremony at which the Black Spartacus appeared on a white charger leading 600 horsemen.

A slave who became a general.

Financiers boosting steel firm holdings

Doubs, March 18

This region's forges, former émigré holdings sold as national property, have been bought up by one Antonin, who is acting on behalf of a big banking company. Steel, in fact, is becoming of ever greater interest to the world of finance. The bankers often suggest that the managers of the establishments put up for sale form an association with them. All this results in the emergence of real alliances that display a fortunate pairing of know-how and capital. However, they often have just a fleeting existence, as speculators sometimes buy plants only to resell them.

Three schoolbooks chosen by Ancients

Paris, March 31

The Ancients' legislative chamber is more demanding than the Five Hundred. It selected only three of the eight manuals chosen by Lakanal: *Elements of French Grammar* by Lhomond, Condorcet's *Elements of Arithmetic*, and *Principles of Republican Morality* by La Chabeaussière. On one point, the question is whether the selection was aimed at saving money or was a mere coincidence: of the three winners, only the last one will receive the scheduled reward. Condorcet died in his cell two years ago. Abbot Lhomond, a former non-juring priest, died of old age in December of the same year. As the height of irony, his *Grammar* was written well before 1789 and is already used in schools.

A republican saint "goes to Heaven"

Mayenne, March 23

The royalists have lost their monopoly on saintliness and miracles. The patriots who were present when Perrine Dugué breathed her last said they saw her soul "rise to Heaven on tricoloured wings", and they have decided to build a chapel in her honour. She was a member of a family with ardent republican sympathies, and she helped her brothers fight the Chouans. Her speciality: getting information, until the Whites identified and executed her. Many people already call her "Saint Perrine".

Perrine, a republican saint, is dead.

The Institute holds first session in Louvre

The five Directors facing 312 scientists and artists belonging to the Institute.

Paris, April 4

The Caryatid Room in the Louvre was packed today for the first session of the Institute. The Directors were there in gala costume, accompanied by all of the ministers, many foreign ambassadors, and a generous selection of Europe's savants, thinkers and literary men. They applauded the opening speech given by Daunou. Only the artists seemed to be in a sombre mood. The Fine Arts, associated with Literature within the third class, already look like a poor relation. The Convention decreed today that all members of the Institute would have to vote on the choice of the particular classes. The artists are already imagining seeing the admission of painters depend on the views of philologists or astronomers ... Even Cuvier's paper concerning "the various species of elephants", which was among the reports submitted to the session, did not manage to smooth the artists' troubled brows.

Stormy beginning to marriage in Bourges

Bourges, April 16

The pretty young brides in white, wearing flowers and tricoloured ribbons, proved worthy of the ceremony that had been arranged for them. For their civic festivities, the couples were entitled to an escort of regular troops and homage from old people and children. The marriage ceremony at the Fatherland Altar would have been perfect except for the rain that blew in to interrupt the Chinese-lantern ball, forcing everybody to take refuge in the Etienne building, formerly the cathedral. Some 25 armed men took up positions on pews to keep public decency ...

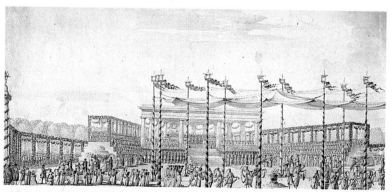

"Married Couples' Day" was celebrated with pomp on Champ de Mars.

Ministers changed to combat Jacobins

Paris, April 3

Carnot is taking the repression of the Jacobins in hand. With this in mind he has just reshuffled the cabinet. Merlin de Douai returns to the Justice Ministry, as this former "terrorist" was suspected of going easy on the left. He is replaced at the Police Ministry by Cochon de Lapparent, a Convention regicide who came over to the right. In the face of growing popular agitation in the country, Carnot wants to be on his guard and have reliable men on the job. In this, he differs from Barras, who is trying to calm the Babeuf faction by displaying a conciliatory approach, and from Reubell, who hesitates to launch repression for fear of giving a signal for more "White terror".

Magazine of Music scores with military

Paris, April 5

Music Magazine has managed to persuade the authorities to renew their subscriptions to the review, which were dropped by the Committee of Public Safety. In the wake of an order from the War Ministry for 2,000 copies for the armed forces, the Navy Ministry has just gone for 600 copies. So publication can now resume, while waiting for better days.

Visit to Sieyès now a must for Germans

Paris, April 11

A visit to Sieyès has become an obligation for any German traveller visiting Paris. Frederic Jean Laurent Meyer did not fail in this obligaation. He followed Sieyès around all day, admiring his calm during a stormy meeting of the Five Hundred, surprised to observe him contemplating the chamber with the help of a *lunette* glass. He then accompanied him to his modest room, in which the only decoration is the feathered legislator's costume hanging on the wall. The sight of Sieyès conversing in bathrobe and night-cap naturally delighted the visitor, who was moved by his hero's philosophical countenance.

Bonaparte scores lightning victories

Masséna and Laharpe study the heights of Montenotte before the attack.

Soldiers of the Army of Italy take an oath to conquer or die trying.

The Austrian forces lost many soldiers at the Battle of Millesimo.

Murat, Bonaparte's right arm.

Piedmont, April 15

Sufficient unto each day is the victory thereof. Now the Dego position is in French hands. The divisions led by Generals Laharpe and Masséna, helped by General Victor's brigade, seized 18 guns from Wukassovitch. The Austrian general's troops fought with remarkable courage, but since Wukassovitch did not see any help arriving, he had to withdraw by way of Spigno, thus losing half of his men.

This new victory comes after earlier wins at Montenotte and Millesimo. As a result of these initial encounters, the Austrians have left about 10,000 dead on the battlefields. So Bonaparte's tactics have paid off. Using the mountainous terrain to his own advantage and relying on the greatest possible speed, the commanding general has managed in each engagement to bring the greatest possible amount of force to bear on the scattered enemy divisions.

Oddly enough, the Austrians do not seem downcast. They have the impression that they have been confronted everywhere by an enemy with two or three times more troops. Dego seems to them to have been a brilliant feat amidst a series of small-scale skirmishes. All of the soldiers think they can easily beat the French in the open countryside. Even if Bonaparte has displayed unprecedented energy and thirst for victory, the Austrian commanding general's strategy has been disconcerting, to say the least. Beaulieu has constantly divided his forces to provoke partial attacks, but in vain. He was outmanoeuvred on each occasion (→ April 21).

Death penalty set on some agitating

Paris, April 16

The Councils have just passed a severe repression measure: anybody who tries to bring about a return to monarchy or to the Constitution of 1793, by agitating among the people will be subject to the death penalty. Actually, this law is aimed at the Jacobins much more than the royalists, and this seems paradoxical since the measure reminds one in many ways of laws during the Reign of Terror. But the Directors' repressive drive is not comparable with that displayed by the power structure in Year II. So they are quite unlikely to apply the law strictly.

Ringing affirmation of anti-bell policy

Paris, April 11

The authorities are stubborn, and the peasants will not have the last word in the "great bell controversy". A decree has been adopted reiterating the ban on any use of bells for summoning people to a religious ceremony. Severe penalties are provided for violators: jail for laymen, and deportation for priests, at least if they are repeat offenders. However, these new provisions do not have much more chance than the previous ones of being applied in rural areas, where people remain attached to their church bells.

A fatherland altar falls apart in town

Cher, April 16

Patriotism is not what it used to be. In Baugy, anybody entering the village for the first time would have trouble recognising "three simple pieces of wood" on the village's public square as the framework of the former fatherland altar. This monument, which was considered sacred just a few months ago, has been abandoned. As for the tree of liberty, once a major symbol of revolutionary fervour, it has now been overgrown and serves to scare away sparrows. Nobody wears a cockade any more. And the people who are threatened with arrest for this openly make fun of it all.

Colli's retreat leaves road to Turin open

The Piedmontese prove unable to contain the French troops near Mondovi.

Mondovi, April 21

Turin is now within range of French guns. Colli, the Piedmontese general, had to withdraw, leaving 1,000 of his men dead. Eight artillery pieces that fell into French hands testify to the hasty nature of this withdrawal. Colli's negligence turned a victory won in advance into a defeat. The fact is that on the eve of the battle, the French forces were in an extremely critical position, so much so that the officers themselves thought the fight was lost. In spite of the troops' tiredness and discouragement, the French had to attempt a new attack quickly to prevent Colli from linking up with the Austrians. So all Colli had to do was withdraw gradually while waiting for help from his Austrian ally, Beaulieu. But the Sardinian troops were too slow in moving back, and Bonaparte's divisions took advantage of the opportunity to throw themselves on the enemy battalions. Near Mondovi, Colli was suddenly attacked by Sérurier's and Meynier's men. His strategic retreat was transformed into a tragic rout. The way things now stand, the Turin Court has no choice but to negotiate with the French (→April 28).

Marguerite Gérard, a pupil of Fragonard

Marguerite Gérard has taken advantage of the lessons she has received from her teacher, Fragonard. Despite an uncompromising Neo-Classicism that makes her a bit different, she joins Labille Guiard, Vallayer Coster and Vigée Lebrun in the ranks of highly respected women painters. She is Mme. Fragonard's younger sister. She was very young when she first came to Paris and moved in with the couple. She posed for Fragonard, who taught her to paint. Her presence in the house caused a great dealof gossip about "love triangles". Marguerite also seems to have helped with some of Fragonard's works, and especially *Le Baiser à la Dérobée*, of which the colour use and the particular sheen make one think of a feminine hand. She is putting the finishing touches to illustrations for the work by the writer Choderlos de Laclos called *Les Liaisons Dangereuses*.

The pupil drawn by the master.

Deserters, bandits may invade Albion

Paris, April 19

Carnot is obsessed with the idea of invading England. To make up for a shortage of troops, Hoche has contemplated gathering all the deserters, bandits and escaped convicts infesting the countryside in the west. Hoche, the "new Du Guesclin", would lead these new "great companies" on an invasion of England, thus also pacifying the west of France. Even if Carnot strongly favours such an operation, the other Directors are rather sceptical. Since there is no fleet for the crossing, the disagreement is unimportant in any case (→July, 6).

Carnot controls military policy.

Unexplained crimes at Vitry sur Seine

Vitry sur Seine, April 19

Unidentified people broke into citizen Petitval's castle during the night and perpetrated a horrible massacre. They killed Petitval, his mother-in-law, two of the latter's sisters, and three chambermaids. The only survivor was a 10-year-old boy found the next morning, trembling, in the castle. Robbery seems ruled out as a motive, as nothing was taken. Tongues are wagging in Vitry. Some people say the survivor is the little Louis XVII, whom the killers wanted to assassinate. Others say a sordid inheritance question is at the bottom of it all. In any case, the thing that most surprises people here is the gendarmes' behaviour. They are making an extremely superficial investigation, and are accused of trying to bury the case.

Bonaparte against Italy troops looting

Italy, April 22

The Army's glory and safety are at stake. Bonaparte has decided to put an end to his forces' looting, by any means. The generals are authorised to order immediate execution of officers and men whose actions "might lead others to indulge in looting, destroy discipline, and sow disorder in the Army". The commanding general of the Army of Italy is greatly afraid that his troops could get used to insubordination. This is particularly the case since lack of discipline could become a political matter in the long run. The effect of the soldiers' actions is to arouse people's hatred for their "liberator".

Bonaparte exceeds orders enforcing an armistice on Sardinians

Piedmont, April 28

The Sardinians have laid down their arms. Upon hearing about Colli's defeat at Mondovi, and in view of the small amount of help to be expected from the Austrians, the Turin Court decided to make peace. A treaty concluded in Cherasco forces the King of Piedmont Sardinia to yield Coni and Tortona, cities that the French will now be able to use as bases for their operations beyond the Alps and the Apennines. By signing this armistice without Paris's agreement, Bonaparte exceeded instructions: he brought all his efforts to bear against the Sardinians, rather than only against the Austrians. But he intends to adapt orders to circumstances and his goals (→ May 15).

Murat offers the Treaty of Cherasco and enemy flags to the Directory.

Publisher has fine idea on Fabre play

Paris, April 22

The Court has enforced respect for literary property rights. The book-seller and publisher Barba has been fined for having published poet Fabre d'Eglantine's comedy *L'Intrigue épistolaire* without permission. This firm, a specialist in such operations, will have to pay the equivalent of the value of the 3,000 copies published, and all of the books will be seized. This is justice for Fabre's widow.

Benjamin Constant scores first success

Paris, April 30

The Directory has found a defender. A young and almost unknown writer, Benjamin Constant, has just published an essay entitled *Concerning the strength of the present government of France and the need to support it*. It appeared in Louvet de Couvray's *La Sentinelle*. But do not look for any exalted feelings or republican ideals. To Constant, the Directory's vast superiority over other forms of government lies in the fact that it is already established. As to men of property nostalgic for the Ancien Régime, they must understand that this "new order" is the best rampart against the people. His mistress, Mme. de Staël, has the same ideas.

Lyons mail coach attacked, two killed — police are on trail

Melun, April 28

The mail coach from Lyons did not arrive. It was discovered yesterday morning near Pont de Pouilly, with the chests empty. The driver's throat had been slit, and the postilion had been killed by sabre blows. The only passenger disappeared, along with a horse, leading one to suppose that he had been an accomplice of the killers.

Despite the shortage of clues, police managed to determine what had happened. On April 27th., four men spent the afternoon in the Montgeron inn, playing billiards and carousing. When evening came, they waited at an agreed spot, near Lieusaint, for the mail-coach to go by. Their accomplice, sitting near the driver, stabbed him, and the four riders seized control of the coach and killed the postilion. Then they simply opened the chests to grab the money and made off for Paris.

The killers rode through the Rambouillet gate toward 4 a.m. and then separated, after leaving the postilion's horse on Carrousel Square. That was a fatal mistake, because there were a number of things about the horse that have already enabled police to get on the track of two of them: Bernard, the sixth man, who simply supplied the horses, and Couriol, who took refuge with his friend Bruer in Château Thierry, with a man called Guesno. Police actually found part of the loot when they arrested Couriol. Now the dénouement of this affair seems imminent, since the police have made so much progress already (→ May 15).

Journeys can be dangerous and the arrival of the mail coach at the Messageries courtyard is greeted with relief.

4 *(Floréal 15, Year IV)*
Paris. The Babeuf Insurrectional Committee meets Ricord, who has a brief from the Montagnard Insurrectional Committee (set up by Amar on April 14th.), to discuss Montagnard demands in connection with joint action against the Directory.

4 *(Floréal 15, Year IV)*
Paris. Captain Grisel reveals the ramifications of the Conspiracy of the Equals to Carnot (→10).

4 *(Floréal 15, Year IV)*
Vendée. The Comte de Vasselot, an agent of the Comte d'Artois who took advantage of his release after the La Jaunaie pact to resume service, is shot at Saint Fulgent.

8 *(Floréal 19, Year IV)*
Paris. The bishops sign a pastoral letter ordering prayers in thanksgiving for the victories won by France.

9 *(Floréal 20, Year IV)*
Italy. The Duke of Parma and Piacenza signs an armistice with Bonaparte. The duke has to make a cash contribution of two million livres, and offer 20 paintings.

10 *(Floréal 21, Year IV)*
Paris. At the Directory's order, police arrest the leaders of the Conspiracy of Equals: Babeuf, Buonarroti, Darthé, Germain, Drouet and Ricord. Altogether, Carnot signs 245 arrest warrants. →

10 *(Floréal 21, Year IV)*
Italy. Brilliant victory for Bonaparte, who attacks the Austrians at Lodi bridge and expels them from Lombardy.

11 *(Floréal 22, Year IV)*
Paris. Another success for Jean François Lesueur, who puts on his new lyric work, *Telemachus on Calypso's Island, or the Triumph of Wisdom*. Joséphine Bonaparte and Madame Tallien are in the audience.

12 *(Floréal 23, Year IV)*
Italy. The Lombardian patriots rise up as the French approach, and almost take over Milan.

13 *(Floréal 24, Year IV)*
Angers. The Vicomte de Scépeaux, leader of the Chouan revolt on the right bank of the Loire River, surrenders to Hoche.

14 *(Floréal 25, Year IV)*
Italy. Masséna, leading the French vanguard, reaches Milan (→15).

Jenner may have conquered smallpox

Thanks to England's Jenner, the younger generation will not get smallpox.

England, May 14

To date there has been only one way of avoiding smallpox: having yourself inoculated with that terrible disease. But thanks to Jenner, this ancient and dangerous method may soon be relegated to the category of barbarous practices. This English doctor seems to have discovered a revolutionary treatment. He had noticed that people who catch cowpox, a mild disease transmitted by cows, no longer had to worry about getting smallpox. After 20 years of effort his research has finally brought a result, and Jenner has managed to inject cox-pox pus into a human being. He says that people immunised in this way will not catch smallpox. If this new kind of treatment works, what people call "vaccination" would seem sure to have a great future, especially because of the total lack of danger in connection with this kind of treatment.

France lays on theft of Italian treasures

Paris, May 14

France is exporting its Revolution and, in exchange, the Directory intends to enjoy some compensation for this effort. The primary target in this connection is Italy's artistic treasures. The French government has been very clear about this. It is convinced that Bonaparte considers "the glory of the fine arts as being attached to the Army's glory". But just in case the commanding general should be in some doubt about this, the Directory has urged him "to seek out, collect and ship the most precious objects to Paris". So nothing seems likely to escape the attention of the French forces. To perform this mission while protecting the works, the Directory has appointed a seven man commission, including the sculptor Moitte and painters Berthelemy and Tinet (→June 18).

An English caricature showing the French forces looting in Italy.

Paris Police Legion dissolved by Carnot

Paris, May 2

Carnot has decided to put an end to the growth of extreme-left agitation. He has just dissolved the Paris Police Legion, the military corps of the security forces. It was suspected of sympathising with Babeuf, and was said to be hatching a plot. Two battalions mutinied on April 28th. following a government decision to transfer them to the border areas to bring a halt to the spread of revolutionary ideas in the armed forces. The leaders of the rebellion have been arrested. These Babeuf agents infiltrated the soldiers' ranks and were getting ready to launch an insurrection, in cooperation with their chief. And it might have succeeded, as the Police Legion contains many "hard line" patriots. Bonaparte put them there after the royalist riot of Vendémiaire 13 in order to ensure the troops' loyalty to the Republic. This dissolution has not caused any strong popular reaction. It bears witness to the fact that the power structure has again stiffened its approach (→May 10).

Franco-Batavians smash guard revolt

Amsterdam, May 10

Franco-Batavian troops commanded by General Beurnonville have crushed the revolt of the National Guard's gunners. In accord with the French government, the Batavian Convention pulled out all the stops, a reaction that was in proportion to the panic caused in its ranks by this rebellion. There had just been a warning of a Babeuf-inspired plot in Paris, and the idea of large-scale conspiracy was in everybody's minds. But actually the reality was more modest. The "Unitary Democrats", in a minority in the Assembly, did not manage to win a hearing in the Constituent Commission, the majority of whose members were hostile to reforms, to say the least, if not actually won over to the cause of the Ancien Régime. That was when the rebels attempted to organise protest movements in several cities in Holland. In Amsterdam, for instance, they managed to win the National Guard to their cause.

Police smash Babeuf plot — leaders are arrested

Paris, May 10

The main leaders of a Babeuf-inspired plot have just been arrested, following a denunciation by one of them, Captain Grisel, an agent acting on behalf of the Directory. Thanks to him, the police managed to catch the "Babouvists" and throw them in jail.

Babeuf, preaching a social and egalitarian revolution and advocating a people's insurrection to overturn the Directory, had become both the sworn enemy and the special target of the government. On March 30th., he set up an Insurrectional Committee to guide a "Conspiracy of the Equals" with the help of his faithful followers Maréchal, Antonelle and Germain, as well as Buonarroti and Darthé, both former Robespierrists who were among the founders of the Panthéon Club.

His organisation has a particularly strong hierarchical bent: under the committee's orders, the Babouvist agents were responsible for propaganda and links with the Paris arrondissements, the Army and the police. This network extended into the distant provinces. The police followed the plot very closely and Carnot had managed to defuse it in the Paris Legion at the start of the month. But he was convinced that an insurrection was still brewing, linked with certain former deputies of the Convention. Grisel confirmed that for him on May 4th.

The Director, deeply mistrusting Barras' Jacobin sympathies, then decided to take the whole operation

France is saved from the dagger of Anarchy by the vigilance of the Spirit which protects the Republic.

in hand himself. The arrests should have taken place on May 7th. when the Babouvist committee was holding a meeting, but the security forces arrived too late. However, that was only a brief delay. Today, at the precise instant that the deputy Doulcet de Pontécoulant was telling the Five Hundred that the government was "informed of the seditious steps being prepared", Babeuf was arrested at his home in the Rue de la Truanderie, in the company of Drouet, an ardent Montagnard who had become a Babeuf agent upon returning from captivity in Austria. Another former Montagnard Convention deputy, Robert Lindet, managed to escape. Immediately after these arrests, the Five Hundred, followed by the Ancients, approved several repressive laws which had been drawn up in advance: one of these allows big cities' central authorities to issue detention orders to offenders, while another expels from Paris former Convention members not domiciled there before their election, dismissed civil servants, milit-

ary men and paroled terrorists. Documents in Babeuf's home led Carnot to issue 245 warrants for Babouvist supporters and leftist republicans not involved in the plot. Carnot plans to use the plot, which had little chance of success, to launch repression (→ Feb. 20, 97).

Babeuf, leader of the conspiracy.

Buonarroti, one of his accomplices.

The Equals' Song

*For too long vile laws we see
All men as slaves unite.
The brigands' rule accursed be!
Let's face full square our plight.*

*That men be equal was thy care,
O kindly Nature free.
Why of wealth and toil is there
Such inequality?*

*And why a thousand slaves
Around a few despots?
Why the knights, the knaves?
Rise up, brave sans-culottes!*

*Through holy, blest equality:
The world a fruitful site
In those days of felicity;
For all the sun shone bright.*

*Alas! for soon ambition rare
With treachery did match;
And loss of rights did dare
The baneful plot to hatch.*

Refrain:
*Our clarion call let all awake!
Come forth from the dark night!
Your rights, people, now retake,
For all the sun shines bright.*

15 *(Floréal 26, Year IV)*
Paris. Signature of the definitive peace treaty between France and the Kingdom of Piedmont Sardinia, which, under the terms of the agreement, cedes Savoy and Nice to the Republic.

16 *(Floréal 27, Year IV)*
Paris. The "Hot Foot" crimes are on the rise, so the Directory decides to establish mobile columns, with units of the National Guard as a basis, for tracking down the criminals.

20 *(Prairial 1, Year IV)*
Lyons. Jacobins and Muscadins again fight each other in violent clashes (→28).

20 *(Prairial 1, Year IV)*
Italy. Bonaparte writes to the Directory to inform it that he plans to give his soldiers half of their pay in cash. The Directory will accept this proposal, which creates personal links between the general and his forces.

23 *(Prairial 4, Year IV)*
Corsica. A thousand peasants gather in Bistuglio to protest against the increase in taxes paid in kind decided on by the Anglo-Corsican authorities.

23 *(Prairial 4, Year IV)*
Pavia. As a result of the process of carving up the Italian states carried out by the Army of Italy, Pavia's people rebel and massacre the French soldiers who have sought refuge in the citadel (→26).

24 *(Prairial 5, Year IV)*
Angers. The Comte Charles d'Autichamp, the last Vendean leader still at large, surrenders. Hoche's clever policy, consisting of giving the peasants their priests back, confiscating cattle to obtain arms, and killing or buying the leaders, has borne fruit.

28 *(Prairial 9, Year IV)*
Lyons. Following the riot on May 20th., the municipality bans the sale of sword-sticks and of lead-loaded and iron-weighted sticks.

31 *(Prairial 12, Year IV)*
Germany. The Sambre and Meuse Army crosses the Rhine with the goal of threatening Vienna while Bonaparte holds down part of the Austrian troops in Italy.

May *(Prairial, Year IV)*
Lausanne. Joseph de Maistre publishes his *Considerations on the French Revolution*, defining the Revolution as a "providential catastrophe".

Bonaparte enters Milan in triumph

"You shall be free and more certain of it than the French," Bonaparte promised the people of Milan.

Milan, May 15

It was a veritable triumph. The Milanese Archbishop and leading figures welcomed the commanding general of the Army of Italy with deference mingled with fear. Three days previously, at the announcement of the French troops' advance, the patriots had seized the Lombardian capital. At present, Bonaparte particularly wants to reassure the population. He has pledged to respect religion and property. In the interests of making his promises more convincing he did not hesitate to move into the crowd, leaving his soldiers behind. If Bonaparte stressed the idea of appeasement in this way, we may view it as the start of a personal policy. The fact is that his military operations of the last few weeks have gone against orders from Paris. Rather than extracting guarantees from the conquered areas and "forcing" the Austrian enemy, Bonaparte came back to the Milan area, thus allowing Beaulieu to withdraw in good order after the fighting at the Lodi bridge. Much more serious is the fact that everything seems to indicate that the Austrian general took advantage of the respite to organise the defence of Mantua under the best possible conditions. The Lombardian citadel now lies between the French and the Austrians. In a man who says "promptness in following up on victory ensures success", this seems hard to justify. Unless he has an "Italian idea" of his own ...

Volney is studying New World society

Philadelphia, May

With a canvas bag on his back, a stick in his hand and a hat on his head, Volney has set out on the American roads in the direction of Baltimore. After six months in Philadelphia, the philosopher-historian is continuing his study trip armed with recommendations from Jefferson and Thornton, who gave him a warm welcome and asked him to brief them on the French Revolution. In a year spent on the U.S. East Coast, he gathered all available information about the customs and behaviour of the New World's inhabitants. He even set about learning English at the American Philosophical Society.

By seizing the Lodi bridge over the Adda on May 10th., the French Army opened the road to Milan, which it reached on May 15th. After a violent battle, and at the cost of heavy losses, Bonaparte expelled the Austrian General Beaulieu from Lombardy. Beaulieu retreated towards Cremona.

Six identified in Lyons mail coach crime

Paris, May 15

Judge Daubenton's investigation of the Lyons mail coach robbery is moving forward fast. Two weeks after the robbery and killings, arrests have come in succession. After Bernard and Couriol were taken into custody, four accomplices still had to be found. Two of them, Bruer and Guesno, were caught at Château Thierry. A third, Joseph Lesurques, was arrested in Paris while accompanying, by chance, his friend Guesno when the latter was summoned to appear in the judge's office. While they were waiting in the anteroom, two women formally identified them as the men who had dined at Montgeron on the evening of the crime. Daubenton thinks the affair is clear, and Lesurques' and Guesno's guilt is obvious. No matter that the two suspects vehemently deny everything. And no matter if Lesurques offers an alibi, saying that he went to see the jeweller Legrand that afternoon. That was not even checked. The judge's view is strengthened by the fact that he has just discovered that Guesno, Lesurques and Couriol had supper together a week before the crime, at the home of a certain Richard. That was certainly their last meeting, held to finalise details of their plan. The sixth man has appeared, in the form of Richard. The judge finally has the six killers (→ Aug. 5).

French troops checkmate revolt in Pavia

The population rebelled against the exactions of the French forces.

Pavia, May 26

Bonaparte has turned the city over to his soldiers. Some houses have just been burnt, bearing witness to the violence with which the general intends to crush any anti-French insurrection. So the conciliation attempts noted 10 days ago in Milan failed in Pavia. On May 23rd., the trees of liberty put up by the patriots were chopped down by peasants, who forced the French garrison out of the castle. Bonaparte was immediately alerted and moved on the city, trying unsuccessfully to force his way through the gate with the help of shelling. He had to remove the peasants posted on the ramparts in order to break the door down with axe-blows. Resistance was to have a short life. The cavalry was soon charging through the streets to disperse some armed groups. The municipal authorities and the clergy, who had carefully fanned the revolt, asked to be pardoned, but in vain. Bonaparte was immovable, and had a tenth of the prisoners shot. The town commander was court-martialled and condemned to death. After the ones in Milan, Binasco and Arquata Scrivia, the resistance movements in Pavia have thus ended in bloodshed. All that shows how difficult it is to liberate a country and hold it to ransom at the same time.

Monge sent to Italy to help find works

Paris, May 23

Monge, a professor at the Polytechnic School and a member of the Five Hundred, has not yet got over his surprise: the Directory has chosen him to accompany a seven-member committee named on May 14th. to visit areas conquered by the Republic's forces in Italy in order to collect all works of art and scientific objects worthy of places in French museums. Monge is a member of the Temporary Arts Commission and of a painting jury, and is a connoisseur of art-works. As for science, that is his favourite field. So he accepted this delicate assignment without any hesitation at all. Equipped with the grand title of "government commissioner", Monge left Paris this morning for Italy and its cities, with the prestigious collections they have to offer (→ June 18).

City of Nantes hit by trade paralysis

Nantes, May 27

The Nantes region is only a shadow of itself. In a letter sent to the Paris Directory the Nantes businessman Treille notes that, due to the war, "trade is in an extremely painful position", and he asks for emergency steps to help revive the economy. Nantes and its region, ravaged by Vendean wars and Chouan revolts, have stopped production. As for the port, which enjoyed big profits from trade with the colonies and the slave trade, now forbidden, its former busy activity is now only a distant memory. No vessel can put in because of the English blockade. And the shippers, who were often ruined by the effects of the Reign of Terror, no longer have either the means or the courage to risk whatever remains of their fortune in some risky venture entailing going to sea ...

Republic's victories celebrated in Paris

Paris, May 29

The Directory was all there, with 2,000 seats reserved for guests, and there was a parade of the National Guard in gala uniforms. Nothing had been neglected for honouring Bonaparte and his soldiers. The festivities took place on the Champ de Mars, renamed "Reunion Field" for the occasion. In the middle was a platform decorated all round with a line of flags and trophies, with access by way of four ramps guarded by lions the symbol of strength and bravery. The centre of the platform featured a statue of Liberty on a pedestal, with one hand resting on the Constitution and the other hand holding a wand topped with William Tell's cap. Around it were the Victories, with bugles in their mouths. The very martial ceremony got under way at exactly 10 a.m., with an artillery salvo greeting the arrival of the ministers and the Diplomatic Corps in front of the Military School. At 11:30, the recruits marched for the veterans and the wounded. Finally, a banquet got under way at noon, which was soon followed by some music and dancing.

Flags and trophies captured from the enemy displayed on the Champ de Mars.

1 *(Prairial 13, Year IV)*
Germany. The army corps commanded by Kléber beats the Austrians at Uckerath.

3 *(Prairial 15, Year IV)*
Italy. The capture of Verona forces the Austrians to retreat toward Tyrol. Only Mantua, which has a central position in the Po plain, remains in their hands (→4).

4 *(Prairial 16, Year IV)*
Altenkirchen. Kléber defeats the Austrians (→15).

5 *(Prairial 17, Year IV)*
Italy. Bonaparte signs an armistice with the Kingdom of Naples.

6 *(Prairial 18, Year IV)*
Paris. The Directory gets the Council of Five Hundred to authorise the entry of 10,000 regular troops into the capital.

8 *(Prairial 20, Year IV)*
Guyana. Death of Collot d'Herbois in penal servitude at Sinnimary, near Cayenne. Due to the climate, a deportation sentence is a kind of "dry guillotine".→

10 *(Prairial 22, Year IV)*
Milan. The Directory commissioners visit the Brera Museum and the Ambrosian Library, where they seize a quantity of paintings, books and manuscripts (→18).

12 *(Prairial 24, Year IV)*
Italy. The French troops enter the Papal States in order to occupy the legations of Bologna (June 19th.) and Ferrara (June 20th.) (→23).

23 *(Messidor 5, Year IV)*
Italy. The Pope signs an armistice with Bonaparte in Bologna. The Directory commissioners, Saliceti and Garrau, do not win withdrawal of the condemnation of the Civil Constitution of the Clergy.→

24 *(Messidor 6, Year IV)*
Paris. In an attempt to gag the press, the Directory decides to increase the postal rate for newspapers to five centimes per copy.

27 *(Messidor 9, Year IV)*
Italy. Violating Tuscan neutrality, Bonaparte's troops occupy Leghorn to force the English forces to evacuate Corsica.

29 *(Messidor 11, Year IV)*
Paris. The main Paris bankers, Desprez, Perregaux and Récamier, open a current account bank in order to collect the savings available in the country.

Austrian forces in Mantua citadel resisting the French attacks

While some units are engaged in combat, others advance. Shown here is the crossing of the Po River at Piacenza.

Mantua, June 4

The city has enough resources to hold out for a long time. There are a 13,000-man garrison, 316 artillery pieces, and enough food for four months. The Austrians in Mantua, galvanised by the presence of their leader, General Canto d'Irles, have no intention of caving in at the initial French attacks. One must say that the terrain does not facilitate General Sérurier's task.

The citadel is bordered by swamps, and is cut off on the north and west by the Mincio. Bonaparte did not think it necessary to pursue the Austrians after Lodi, and now he is paying for the time lost in occupying the Milan area. After evacuating the Mincio, Beaulieu took advantage of the opportunity to retreat to Tyrol at the end of May to reorganise his troops, but during his retreat he left part of his men in Mantua to delay the French advance. Now Bonaparte no longer enjoys the initiative. He can no longer run the risk of pursuing the Austrians, since he is afraid of being attacked in the rear. Moreover, it seems clear that General Sérurier's forces can no longer lay siege to the city by themselves. The conclusion is that the Italian campaign is now being confused with the siege of Mantua (→July 31).

Baby boom noted in the Carnot home

Paris, June 1

There has been a baby boom in the Carnot household. In the immense apartment in the Luxembourg Palace inhabited by Lazare Carnot, his brother Claude, his brother in law Toussaint Colignon and their families, three children have been born over a period of several weeks. A good occasion for bringing up a few bottles from the fine cellar that this tribe of Burgundians had installed! The latest baby is Lazare's son. The proud father will be able to put into practice the lessons learnt during the long sessions of the Public Education Committee. His son's first name, Sadi, arouses curiosity. During his youth in Arras, with his friends Fouché and Robespierre, who were also members of the Rosati Society, Carnot loved the roses praised by the Persian poet Sadi.

Collot d'Herbois dies in Cayenne hospital

Cayenne, June 8

One of the great figures of the Montagnard Convention has just passed on: Collot d'Herbois died, forgotten by all, in a makeshift hospital. He was a former actor, and had a very beautiful voice and perfect diction. The "trumpet of the Revolution" played a leading role during the great Paris days of 1792 and 1793. He joined the Committee of Public Safety, opposing "The Incorruptible One", and it was thanks to his support that the conspirators overthrew Robespierre on Thermidor 9. Collot d'Herbois thus hoped to get through the period of the Thermidorian reaction without bother, but people had not forgotten his behaviour in Lyons during the Reign of Terror, which was comparable to what Carrier did in Nantes. His friends were able to save him from the guillotine by talking about the aid he gave at the time of Thermidor, but he was deported to Guyana. He died there without having ever been able to return to France, tortured by his fevers and living in utterly wretched conditions.

Death of a deportee in Cayenne.

Directory's agents are given the boot in Ile de France

Port Louis, June 22

"Don't touch our slaves!" When René Baco and Pierre Burnel turned a deaf ear to this demand of the Port Louis colonists, they were forced by the crowd to set sail for ... the Philippines. The two Directory agents had arrived on the island on June 18th. with two battalions of soldiers. Their mission: to promulgate the decree of February 4, 1794, abolishing slavery. But Baco and Burnel had neither the time nor the means for acting. Their arrival immediately got the settlers all worked up. When they came face to face with the government agents, nicknamed "nacarats" because of their satin coats, nothing could hold the colonists back, and the two agents were lucky to avoid being lynched by the crowd.

French offensive in Germany grinds to a halt at Wetzlar

Wetzlar, June 15

Operations in Germany have come to a halt. General Jourdan had to retreat, in confusion and disorder. And yet, according to Carnot's plans, the fighting on the left bank of the Rhine was supposed to have priority. The lengthening of communication lines and the absence of a unified command constitute only a partial explanation of the halt of the offensive in Germany. The fact is that, while Bonaparte was overcoming Piedmont and occupying Lombardy, the armies of the Sambre and Meuse and Rhine and Moselle, led by Moreau and Jourdan, remained inactive. They were isolated from each other, and moved forward without co-ordinating their efforts. The general staff is non-existent in Moreau's army. There is a lack of discipline in the units, and the officers are unable to re-establish even a semblance of cohesion. It is hard to tell whether

French troops crossing the Rhine on boats, under cover of night.

it is Jourdan or Moreau who is the more given to contesting the Directory's political initiatives. The vacuum of authority has resulted in constant looting, which has naturally pushed the population into attacking patrols. Thus the endless cycle of retaliation and revolt established itself quickly. And even if

Kléber, at the order of Jourdan, who was finally convinced of the need for an offensive, triumphed on June 4th. at Altenkirchen, Moreau's troops' delay proved disastrous. At Wetzlar, Charles, one of the Empire's best generals, was not about to let such a fine chance slip. The French rout bears witness to this.

Long trip will end in a trying episode

Toulouse, June 3

Vadier is on his way back to the point of departure. The old Jacobin had hardly arrived in Toulouse when he was arrested and thrown into a coach now rolling toward Paris. He will be tried there as an accomplice of Babeuf, who was arrested on May 10th. Yet at the time of the events in question, he was walking along the road from Paris to Toulouse. He has already started thinking out an account of that trip, which constitutes an alibi. To help in the process, he has his accurate memory and his travelling companion, the tailor Fleuré, who planned to collect on a few debts in the Toulouse region and was also arrested. Vadier has a flood of memories: his expulsion from Paris in April, inns always full, feet pinched by his shoes, and then the faces, such as Pierre Latelier's in Vierzon when Vadier took advantage of a chance to ride in his cart, or the coach driver Legrand, who took him in his stage-coach from Rodez to Pompignan. Above all, he remembers the big dog who adopted them in Longjumeau and left them in Toulouse. Vadier says jokingly that the dog was also arrested and will be tried with them.

Uniform approach to entertainment puts several behind bars

Bourges, June 14

If you are short on morality, you should at least display a little discretion. Neglect of this rule led to the denunciation to municipal officers of a woman named Bouillonnet. The constables were not sent in until around 10 p.m. in order to catch this citizeness in full swing. When she opened the door, there were a few young soldiers in her place who all seemed to be having a whale of a time ... The merry grenadiers were arrested on the spot, as well as their hostess. She has been indulging in such social activities for some time now, and neighbours have accused this "criminal" of turning her home into a place of "prostitution and debauchery". But the main reproach expressed by the authorities is the fact that she repeatedly has led men in uniform astray.

This "meat market" shows the fine distinction between so-called society women and common prostitutes.

Cadoudal converted to Republic's cause

Morbihan, June 19

General Quantin could not believe his eyes. Hoche had given him command of the republican forces in the Morbihan, so Quantin was the officer who received Georges Cadoudal's declaration of submission. In the document, the royalist leader and his deputies did not simply content themselves with swearing allegiance to the Republic's laws. Perhaps fearing that the sincerity of their conversion might be doubted, they also made a veritable statement of hatred for their former cause: "We swear that we hate royalty and all of its distinctive signs, and we pledge never to allow anybody to dare appear in our presence wearing or carrying those infamous signs of tyranny."

Hoche will know just how to handle all this. He knows Cadoudal's determination too well to believe in such a conversion. But he has got the essential thing: the man he rightly considered as the most redoubtable of the royalist rebels in the West has submitted. Since he put an end to the last outbreaks in the Vendée with the capture and execution of Charette, Hoche had concentrated all his efforts north of the Loire. The Chouan rebellion was shaken by

The royalist leader Cadoudal.

the failure of the Quiberon expedition, but was still active in several areas. In Lower Normandy, a former noble officer named Frotté had managed to get a few peasants to rise up. In Maine it was the Vicomte de Scépeaux, and between Fougères and Vitré, Boisguy. But the most powerful Chouannerie was the one in the "Kingdom of Bignan", near Josselin. That was where Cadoudal lived. His surrender marks the completion of the pacification of the West, which has been carried out by General Hoche with an effective mixture of firmness and discernment.

Bonaparte signs an armistice with Pius VI

Bologna, June 23

The Pope has had to accept some tough financial conditions. Under the terms of an armistice concluded with General Bonaparte, the Holy See will have to pay France 21 million lire, and will have to turn over some works of art and precious manuscripts. It also pledges to cede Ferrara and Bologna. But despite the severity of the provisions, papal diplomats note with satisfaction that France seems to have dropped the idea of dethroning Pius VI. The search for religious appeasement led the Directory to go easy on the Pope.

Pius VI: armistice with France.

French prepare to celebrate agriculture

France, June 19

Despite the season, cold and rain have continued all month. But fortunately this *décadi* (day off) is offering some fine and even warm weather. The French are getting ready to celebrate the feast of summer, the harvest and the earth. The ripe wheat will soon be cut, and the new month-names appearing on the calendar remind us that June is dedicated to agriculture and to work in the fields. But this national event is not merely a kind of homage to the Nature so dear to Rousseau. If the farmers and the seasonal workers have celebrated it in the countryside with bonfires and elbow-bending, all the same it is above all a civic feast from which every citizen should learn. The mayor of Angers insisted in a speech on the "need for a return to the simplicity of our ancestors' ways". Here, as elsewhere, people walked in procession to the decadal temple, expressing wishes for the return of the "golden age".

France grabbing many Italian art treasures to "protect" them

Parma, June 18

The members of the "Commission for searching for scientific and art objects in Italy" left Paris a month ago. They arrived in Italy on June 9th., and have already toured all the churches of Cremona and Milan, as well as the Brera and the Ambrosian Library, in order to make seizures "aimed at putting mankind's masterpieces under the protection of the French Republic". Every day, a number of paintings, manuscripts and sculptures are carefully inventoried and packed. Today, at the Ducal Gallery in Parma, Correggio's most popular masterpiece, *The Virgin with Saint Jerome*, disappeared into a large packing case to be shipped to the French capital. The Duke of Parma is in despair. He even offered, in vain, to contribute a million francs if he could keep the painting.

The removal of Correggio's "Virgin" from the Ducal Gallery in Parma.

Detail of part of the stolen painting.

Juliette Récamier on summer holiday

Clichy, June

As a favour to his wife, Juliette, Récamier has rented Clichy Castle, at the gates of Paris, for the holiday season. The young woman was delighted by this charming residence, a former lordly hunting lodge surrounded by a park extending along the Seine River bank. The castle is close enough to Paris for Récamier to be able to divide his time between his business and family life. As for Juliette, she can go to a show and then come back for supper. Her "solitude" is quite a relative matter. Her mother, Mme. Bernard, lives with her, as well as Récamier's nephews and numerous friends, among whom the poet La Harpe is a favourite. The nephews are irked by this preference, and they accuse the poet of being more interested in the excellence of Juliette Récamier's fare than in the charms of his delightful companion.

July 1796
from 1st. to 31st.

Amazing: Pope defends the Republic!

Rome, July 5
"French Catholics, you must submit to the constituted authorities, that is, to the Republic." The draft of the papal brief *Pastoralis sollicitudo*, which has just been developed by the Roman Curia, threatens to be a sensation if it is published. For the time being it is only a semi-official text, rather than a document in proper form, but its contents certainly bear witness to an about-turn in the Holy Father's attitude toward France. Following the armistice Bonaparte granted him, the Pope sent an envoy, Abbot Pierachi, to Paris to negotiate peace with the Directory. He was entrusted with the text of the brief. If the French authorities do not disappoint the hopes of papal diplomacy, the Holy Father's envoy will release the contents of the document (→Aug. 14).

General Bonaparte finds love in Italy

Milan, July 13
The French army is relieved *she* has just arrived. "She", of course, is Joséphine, the excessively beloved wife of General Bonaparte. The commanding general, more in love than ever, was languishing in the absence of his beautiful Créole, whose very rare letters could not assuage his melancholy feelings. The Directory became involved because of its concern about its best strategist's morale, and on June 25th., Mme. Bonaparte left for Italy "with a good escort". Actually, Joséphine was not exactly eager to leave Paris and agreed to do so only if young Lieutenant Hippolyte Charles were assigned as escort. He is able to console her.

Joséphine, too far from the general.

English forces retreat to Elba Island

Elba Island, July 9
The English forces are not giving up, and have decided to occupy Elba in order to maintain a position in the Mediterranean. The French takeover of Leghorn (Livorno) forced the English to seek a new naval base. Losing Leghorn is a very serious development for London. Following Genoa's decline, the Tuscan port had become a major warehouse in the western Mediterranean basin. Now English ships will no longer be able to take on supplies there. The Directory hopes to be able to close off all Italian ports to British vessels. Despite all these efforts, the British are maintaining their existing naval superiority in the Mediterranean Sea.

The English land at Portoferraio, after being expelled from Leghorn.

A return to France for Beaumarchais

Paris, July 5
The icy cold mists of Hamburg and cruel solitude are finished. After an absence of three long years, Beaumarchais is finally returning to France from exile. This time the affair of the Holland rifles, which had been the cause of all his problems, has really been buried. Since his fortune has melted like snow in the midday sun, the writer now has to set about remedying the harm done by a trial that lasted three years and the effects of being outlawed. At least he will have the joy of being able to marry his ex-wife, forced to divorce him when his name was on the émigré list.

Nantes Cathedral may be demolished

Nantes, July 2
Something has got to be done. It would be criminal to destroy Saint Peter's Cathedral on the ground that it is a religious building. With its façade and mediaeval towers, and its Renaissance nave, the Cathedral is an architectural masterpiece, in the sense used by the craftsmen who built it. Croleau, the chief engineer at the Bridges and Roads Department, is aware of the danger threatening the church and has just proposed a remodelling plan to the authorities. This calls for an observatory to be built on top and workshops below.

Antiquity is fashionable, as are the light, transparent fabrics.

The Civil war (1793-1796)

The fratricidal war between the royalist "Whites" and the republican "Blues" that lasted for most of 1793 was brought on by a single event, but it was the product of a number of reasons for discontent that made it inevitable. The event was the decree of February 23rd., 1793, ordering the conscription of 300,000 men. On February 1st., the Revolution had declared war on England, which was to be the centrepiece of the first coalition. France needed more men to meet this challenge, as the regular army was too small despite the battalions of volunteers raised in 1791 and 1792. The conscription process was a difficult one, and in many regions it gave rise to resistance and unrest, which were aggravated by disarray and anger when people learnt of the King's execution.

The sharpest reaction came in the west. North of the Loire, it gave rise to guerrilla warfare, an episodic type of small-scale fighting involving ambushes and one-shot operations. This was known as the "Chouannerie". South of that river, there was a merciless civil war that affected four departments: Loire Inférieure, Maine et Loire, Deux Sèvres and the Vendée. This became known as "military Vendée". The inhabitants of that area joined the Catholic and royalist army en masse. That army, which stood up to the Republic's troops until the end of 1793, was not crushed until it had contributed to endangering the Revolution, which was already threatened by foreign dangers. After the defeat, the rebellion took on a new, much less dangerous and intermittent form, similar to the Breton "Chouannerie".

Why the Vendée?

The conscription of 300,000 men, which provoked the explosion, was only a detonator. The Vendée had already been experiencing a few troubles since 1791 and merely needed some outside stimulation to rise up. There was an actual revolt in August 1792 among the Châtillon and Bressuire peasants. The discontent, leading to violence, was caused by the disenchantment and disappointment that had been felt since the start of the Revolution. Actually the Vendeans were no counter-revolutionaries at the outset, and they had even had great hopes for the regeneration in store for France. But they had

been disappointed in their expectations of tax cuts, which did not materialise. The majority of the peasants, who were landless, had hoped to acquire some land in connection with the sale of national properties, but their hopes again came to naught. The land went to others, and they got no benefit from the distribution. The other business groups in the lower classes close to the peasantry, such as craftsmen and weavers, were very numerous and very poor. Poor economic conditions were making them poorer yet, and they linked their cause with rural aspirations. There were other points that created bitterness and anger. Rural inhabitants, among whom religious practices were stronger than elsewhere, grouped themselves around their parish priests, who were generally venerated and constituted the only solid links among communities in areas of dispersed settlements. The Civil Constitution of the Clergy and the reform of the Church annoyed the peasantry, which remained true to its priests and refused to trust the constitutional priests, the "schismatics". Under these circumstances, faith was the cement of the civil war that was triggered by the order for the conscription of 300,000 men.

This war, of course, was waged against the Revolution, but in fact it was also against a less abstract reality: against the people installed by the Revolution, such as administrators, National Guards, land-owners, and purchasers of national assets. Therefore it was above all against the city-dwellers and the middle class, which had benefited from the Revolution, had made themselves the defenders of new ideas, and had become the masters of the administrative apparatus and the economy. The Vendean peasantry felt excluded from all the advantages going to the people it now considered as exploiters and enemies. The civil war was initially a spontaneous revolt, a war of rural people revolting against the city and its privileged classes, even if the nobles soon diverted it from its initial objectives to turn it into an effort at royalist restoration. The Vendean forces, perhaps numbering 100,000 men or more, were grouped in a large number of camps, each of which had a limited number of fighters, but together constituted an impressive force. This Catholic and royalist army consisted primarily of peasants able to mobilise

quickly when the alarm sounded or in response to agreed signals, when they were needed for a given action. On such occasions, the Vendeans dropped whatever they were doing, took along a little food, armed themselves as best they could, and went out to fight, sometimes followed by their wives and children. But they left the army as soon as the operation in question was over.

Such a force was characterised by great indiscipline, and the troops' zeal, which was very real as long as they were winning, fell off markedly when failure came. This army was quite deficient in weapons. The men who did not have any firearms were equipped with farm implements, and one of their objectives was to seize the rifles and cannons of their republican foes. The only cannons available to the Vendeans were a few taken from castles. The army was poorly equipped, poorly supplied, and consisted primarily of footsoldiers from the fields and workshops and an almost non-existent cavalry. It was the result of almost daily improvisation, rather short on material means but with a large number of men, determined, and with excellent knowledge of the theatre of operations. The parish community was the basic building block of this force. Each one had one or more companies which joined up on occasions to form a division. The high command of the Catholic army was in the hands of the nobles. They allowed others to play only a small rôle with the exceptions of Stofflet and Cathelineau, the latter receiving the title of generalissimo. The companies were commanded by non-nobles, who were often low-level "notables" from the towns and villages. These men were acknowledged by the rural masses as leaders.

The year 1793

At the beginning of March 1793, namely, as soon as there were rumours of conscription, the peasants, who were used to their limited world and had never left their own villages, rose up. Bands came into being quickly and, in just a few days, the whole rural world south of the Loire had rebelled. Insurrection was easy in that area. There were no big cities or garrisons of republican soldiers, and the revolt spread fast, encountering very few obstacles. Leaders emerged from the people and took command of the bands. Such men as Stofflet and Perdriau, who had been soldiers, knew something about military manoeuvres. Energetic or professional men, and tradesmen such as Jacques Cathelineau, quickly acquired influence and authority over their troops. But there were too few cadres, and the Vendeans felt a need for more experienced leaders at the top, for former officers, and called on the local nobility for such men. This led quickly to the recruiting of Charette and d'Elbée, and a little later of La Rochejaquelein, Lescure and others. The rebels knew how to use every feature of the terrain, launched surprise attacks where they were least expected, hid and then appeared when no longer looked for, and fired on soldiers who had no experience of such a new and disconcerting type of warfare. The Convention troops, of whom there were few, constantly found themselves in difficult positions, and gave way in the face of unexpected attacks, firing that could not be pinpointed, and ambushes set by elusive enemies.

Under such circumstances the Vendeans won some victories and, made bolder by such successes, they multiplied their efforts. They first attacked the small cities in which the authorities had their headquarters, and in which food and munitions were to be found. In March they quickly captured Machecoul, Chemillé, Montaigu, Mortagne sur Sèvre, Cholet, La Roche sur Yon and Vihiers. While capturing the cities which gave them control of the region, the insurgents pursued another goal in which they were not so fortunate: capturing an Atlantic port from which they could receive reinforcements and arms, either from the émigrés or from the English. They failed to achieve this at Sables d'Olonne, and later at Nantes, which constituted both an opening to the ocean and a city offering contact with the Breton Chouans. Still, the Vendée triumphed initially, and in the face of such success the republican defence was slow to organise.

The first measure adopted by the Convention was very harsh and as if designed to strengthen the insurrection: it declared the insurgents outlaws and liable to the death penalty. That step redoubled the resistance of men who had nothing to lose. In April the republican troops managed, all the same, to recover some positions. Using Sables d'Olonne as a jumping-off point they forced Charette to evacuate Challans, while another column, which had set out from Nantes, entered Machecoul. That, however, was the end of the "Blues'" success. They were beaten at Chemillé and Beaupréau, and their attack was halted. Colonel Quetineau, defeated at Aubiers on April 13th., shut himself up in Thouars, but the Vendeans seized the town on May 5th.. Then on May 25th., the Catholic army took Fontenay le Comte. On June 9th., the Vendeans won their greatest victory, capturing Saumur, the headquarters of the republican general staff. That win opened up the road to Paris for the victors and represented a grave danger to the Convention. However, infighting among the leaders and the troops' lack of enthusiasm led to giving up the bold plan of marching on the capital, and Nantes was designated as the new objective. Unfortunately, the Vendeans encountered such strong resistance there that the siege was quickly lifted.

At that time, the republicans were in a very difficult situation all over France. The Convention had to meet threats from every quarter. Enemies were invading the territory, while the federalist revolt had two-thirds of the French departments up in arms. The Convention thought resistance had to be overcome first in the Vendée, so in August it decided to send an experienced and brave army to the west, one that had proved its discipline and heroism at Mainz. This force, known as the "Mainz Army" and commanded by Kléber, was to be helped by men recruited in the departments neighbouring the Vendée, and the latter was to be sacked systematically, its forests cut down, harvests destroyed, and rebel strongholds rooted out. Despite its bravery, the republican army suffered an initial setback at Torfou on September 19th. The Convention was alarmed and Barère exhorted it to adopt brutal measures. "Destroy Vendée", he urged. The Convention demanded victory and instructed the army to finish the war in a few days. The republicans finally won a success at Cholet on October 17th. The defeated Catholic army fled toward the Loire, crossed the river at Saint Florent, headed for the Normandy coasts under La Rochejaquelein's command, and arrived outside Granville on November 14th. If they had been able to take that town, the "Whites" would have been able to receive aid from England, but Granville was impregnable without siege equipment, and the Vendeans had none. Furious and disappointed, and uneasy so far from home, they demanded to return. The campaign came to a pitiful end with a withdrawal to the Loire river, a failed attempt to seize Angers, a move north, and then the easy capture of Le Mans.

However, a republican counter-attack two days later brought a terrible defeat for the Vendeans and bloody carnage. The survivors fled in disorder and were massacred by Kléber's and Westermann's troops in the Savenay marshes (December 23rd., 1793). The war ended in disaster. Guerrilla warfare continued, to be sure, but it was only a sporadic series of isolated attacks, lacking unity and representing no danger to the Republic. The Vendeans had few true leaders, and the last ones were gradually eliminated: La Rochejaquelein in 1794, Charette and Stofflet in 1796. The Consulate had no difficulty in 1800 in overcoming the last centres of resistance.

The horrors of war

Like all civil wars, this one was atrocious, and fanaticism, the spirit of revenge and anger brought unheard-of acts of cruelty. Murder and looting were daily affairs, and neither side gave quarter to the other. The Catholic army showed no mercy in massacring patriots, particularly in the initial part of the conflict when it was capturing cities and towns. The "Whites" often displayed great ferocity. They developed a cruel practice consisting of making their prisoners walk, tied together two by two, at the head of their columns, subjecting them to enemy fire with no way of defending themselves. Luckily they did not persist for very long in such excesses, brought on by the euphoria resulting from the initial victories. Under the influence of their leaders, who were concerned to protect the image of their cause, both out of humane considerations and as a calculated policy, the "Whites" soon adopted an approach more in keeping with the faith for which they were fighting, and often treated their prisoners with benevolence, even though there were some "mistakes". On the republican side, violence and massacres became a systematic combat method, as did rape and looting, to which civilians fell victim. Particularly toward the end of the war, at Le Mans and Savenay, the "Blues" exterminated the "brigands", as they called the insurgents, in a kind of orgy, and with refined cruelty.

After the Vendean defeat the republican troops organised repression in the largely depopulated region, and the "infernal columns" organised by Turreau criss-crossed the Vendée, burning villages and woods, destroying ovens and mills, and exterminating everybody suspected of having backed the rebellion, including women and children. Of the 80,000 Vendeans who had crossed the Loire river during the last phase of the conflict, only a few were able to return to their villages, and Westermann triumphantly informed the Convention: "The Vendée no longer exists. It died under our free sabre, including its women and children. I have just buried it in the Savenay marshes and woods." Turreau's infernal columns had the task of destroying everything and exterminating everything in an already-weakened Vendée. Those columns carried out their sinister work, without wavering, from January to May 1794. Turreau's removal came late, on May 13th.

The civil war's battles, executions and massacres resulted in a huge number of victims, both among the "Blues" and the "Whites". While the figures are disputed and will probably never be known with accuracy, we may put the Vendean losses at 150,000 to 200,000 people, an impressive proportion (in the order of 20 per cent) of the entire population. The four departments which were directly affected by the revolt suffered enormous losses that left them in a disastrous demographic situation. If we add that the whole economy was destroyed. It was a ruined region that took a long time to recover.

Towards pacification

Even though the Catholic army was annihilated at Savenay, the excesses committed by the "infernal columns" rekindled the anger of many peasants, who joined the remnants of the troops led by Charette, Stofflet and Sapinaud. Fleeing from their villages, they joined up with the Chouan bands operating north of the Loire, and guerrilla warfare continued. But the Convention and military leaders wanted the region to be pacified. Hoche and Canclaux, experienced and humane generals who gradually adapted themselves to the special kinds of actions they had to combat, tried to put a final end to the civil war. Negotiations were held with Stofflet and Charette, which led to the La Jaunaye agreements of February 17th., 1795. An armistice was announced, and free exercise of religion, an essential concession, was authorised. The Vendeans got their priests back, doing away with their main complaint. However, after the landing of some émigrés and Englishmen at Quiberon on June 27th., 1795, which resulted in another disaster, some Chouans resumed fighting, and new engagements led to new repression. Gradually, however, resistance weakened, and confidence slowly vanished. The leaders were captured, as Stofflet and then Charette were ambushed and were soon shot. A few centres of resistance remained until the time of the Consulate, but the civil war was indeed over, and the policy of clemency and moderation followed by Bonaparte brought the survivors of the heroic bands that had taken up arms against the Republic "for God and for the King" back into the fold.

The royalist factions prepare

Paris, July

The monarchists are plotting. They have organised a number of "agencies," both in France and abroad, which serve as assembly centres but can be transformed, if need be, into combat groups to overthrow the Republic.

In Germany the legitimate pretender to the throne, Louis XVIII, and the Prince de Condé are running the Swabian Agency with England and the émigrés. Another agency had been set up in Paris in late 1795 around the Abbot Brottier, a former soldier, Des Pomelles, and an ex-naval officer, Duverne de Presle. The last of these is on good terms with various members of the councils, more than 200 of whom, including Boissy d'Anglas and Pastoret, are in favour of a restoration of the monarchy. They would like to see a constitutional monarchy set up without bloodshed by drawing on the institutions of Year III. They have particularly in mind a short-term union of royalists at the Directory, and demand that a future king give the promise of a Constitution and a general amnesty for all revolutionaries. Louis XVIII is determined, however, to bring back absolute rule and refuses to make any kind of compromise. Negotiations between the constitutional monarchists and the king have thus reached an impasse.

Franco-Irish arms build-up

Paris, July 12

Republican France will help the Irish. Plans for a landing in Ireland are near completion. The patriot Wolfe Tone has managed to convince the French leaders. The opportunity of being a nuisance to the English was too good to be missed. Attacked through Ireland, England will be forced to use its gold and its army for its own defence, and will thus cease its activities against the French. What is more, to liberate a people which for centuries has been dominated by a foreign power is in keeping with the French promise of 1790 to help and protect any country wishing to regain its independence. Since his arrival in France, Wolfe Tone has done all he can to see that his ambitious project is brought to a successful conclusion. The French leaders had almost opted for an alternative project: stir up a Royalist insurrection in England, along the lines of the operations carried out in western France by the Vendean rebels. But the information Wolfe Tone has provided and the energy he has devoted to his cause, have succeeded in keeping his country in the picture. He has just had a three hour meeting with Clarke, Carnot and Hoche. In the event of a success, he has promised that Ireland will opt for the Republic, not the monarchy as some feared. This guarantee won him support for his project. The French intervention in Ireland will go ahead (July 20).

A French King speaks to France

Riegel, July

The pretender to the throne has put on the uniform of the royalist army and joined Condé on the banks of the Rhine. In visiting the posts that have been set up along the river he does more than simply put in an appearance: he denounces the republican forces stationed on the opposite bank. Why should Louis XVIII worry about being taken captive when he has 2,000 noblemen to protect him? He walks confidently forward to where the river is at its narrowest, calling: "It is I who am your king, your father. I have come to put an end to the strife afflicting our country. Those who claim the contrary are deceiving you." But the soldiers stand opposite, quite still.

The Comte de Provence.

General Moreau marches into Stuttgart

Moreau fighting his way through the Black Forest before entering Stuttgart.

Stuttgart, July 18

Moreau has decided to move at last. The Rhine and Moselle Army, particularly inactive these last few weeks, has now entered Stuttgart. General Jourdan has likewise taken up position at Frankfurt at the head of the Sambre and Meuse Army. Instructions from the Directory have, for once, been carried out to the letter by the two generals. Jourdan's earlier defeat at Düsseldorf is felt by all to have been an incredible waste of forces. By hesitating Moreau had, in effect, made it possible for the Archduke Charles to bring together his forces, previously dispersed. In a sudden fit of pride, Moreau decided three weeks ago that it was time to make a move. Yielding to urgent demands from Carnot, Jourdan, for his part, crossed the Rhine once more at the end of June. The two generals have nevertheless compromised the situation in Germany by their delays.

The eventful life of a German patriot

Amsterdam, July

It is not easy being a revolutionary in Germany. *The Complete History of my Persecutions and Sufferings*, which Georg Rebmann has just published in Holland, bears witness to this. As the public prosecutor of Erlangen, he had welcomed the events of 1789 as "the greatest event in recorded history". He had taken up journalism to spread the revolutionary word. His first efforts in Dresden were hardly a success. Threatened with arrest for Jacobinism, he was forced to flee. The same thing happened in Erfurt, Dessau and Altona. Weary, he set off for Paris.

Republican spirit of Jews from Leghorn

Leghorn, July 15

The French occupation is popular. The town's Jewish community gives a particularly warm welcome to the Republican soldiers: not only do they symbolise the defence of the rights of man, they also provide a reassuring sense of security in a town where anti-semitic feelings run high. In order to show their solidarity with the French soldiers, the Jews have made them a "free loan" of 300 mattresses and 50 straw beds. In return for their kindness the commander of the forces, General Vaubois, has gone out of his way to win the support of a community which is quite obviously well-disposed towards his men, and also possesses considerable financial resources. Much to the delight of the ghetto's inhabitants, he was present with great ceremony at the synagogue today. He has even entrusted various members of the town's Jewish community with a number of tricky but profitable missions. One of them has been named administrator of confiscated goods, while another has been made responsible for money obtained from these sales.

The sorry state of French public education

Paris, July 18

If some things need to be destroyed, others need reconstruction. Where public education is concerned, the Revolution has failed. Such is the sad conclusion reached by Pierre Bénézech, the Interior Minister in charge of Arts, Letters and Public Education, in his departmental enquiry. The most disturbing instance concerns primary schools. After commenting on the half-hearted enforcement of the Daunou law, the enquiry draws attention to the appalling conditions in which teaching staff have to work: often they have no lodgings, salary or books, and sometimes no pupils as farmers prefer to send their children to former monks. Things are a little better where central schools are concerned: of the 100 planned, 68 are operational and the rest will shortly follow suit. The ambitious nature of the projects and poor standards among pupils mean that teaching remains inadequate. The courses, oral and free, are not very popular among parents. The only successes are the Polytechnic, the jewel in the Republic's crown, and the Institute, the pride of European learning. But their success is not enough on its own to make up for the rest.

General Sérurier's troops have ended their siege of Mantua

Sérurier has to pull out of Mantua as Masséna lays siege to Verona, but he is pushed back by the Austrians.

Mantua, July 31

The order was without appeal. Just as the town seemed on the point of capitulating, General Sérurier ended the siege. The urgency of the situation has preference over all other considerations: Wurmser has just broken through in Italy with 25,000 men, bringing the total of the Austrian contingent up to 60,000. Bonaparte needs all his forces therefore to break the Vienna offensive. Sérurier, who since June has made up the body of the siege-force with 10,000 men, has even abandoned the 120 items of his heavy artillery in order to lighten the load. Bonaparte can no longer hope to hold the Adige: Quasdanovitch is at Brescia and is threatening to cut off the French line of retreat at Milan (→ Aug. 5).

General Jean Philibert Sérurier.

Sale of estate at Château Lafite

Paullac, July 12

A little over 12,000,000 francs: that was the price paid by the Paris merchant Rozin for the Château Lafite property which produces one of the best Bordeaux wines. In view of inflation, the price is absurd. Since the recent law on the sale of property belonging to the nation, numerous sales have been carried out between private individuals, but this is the most scandalous of them all. The speculator is said to have paid off the experts and all those concerned with overseeing the sale. Having thus disposed of all other potential bidders, a friendly price was agreed upon; the payment, moreover, was made in territorial coupons that are already substantially devalued (→ Sept. 11, 97).

Popular dances are held in this outdoor café. There are more and more such establishments in Paris.

Army suppliers are making a killing

Italy, August 18

Ruined flour for the bread, poor quality meat and sometimes even third-rate rice in the place of meat. If the list drawn up by sub-lieutenant Chauvin reflects badly on the private supplier responsible for feeding the troops, the latter is not alone of his kind. As for those that respect their contracts, the prices they charge are exorbitant. A quintal of corn will often cost half as much again to the army as it would to an individual buyer. As for such things as horses and boots, their prices frequently double. All those concerned, generals, commissioners as well as deputies, firmly denounce the corrupt practices.

A Franco-Spanish treaty of alliance

Spain, August 18

Spain has joined up with the French against England. General Pérignon, ambassador to Madrid, has just concluded a treaty of alliance with Charles IV at San Ildefonso on behalf of the Directory. As was agreed upon in the treaty, Spain is withdrawing support of the British fleet, which has gained access to the Mediterranean for the first time since 1793 thanks to the aid provided by ports along the Iberian peninsula. In exchange, territorial accords have been reached. Once it is won back from the English, Gibraltar will be returned to Spain. This successful piece of diplomacy, which opens Corsica and Italy to the French, was worth making a concession for (→ Oct. 5).

The Spanish Prime Minister, Godoy.

The Austrians driven back at Castiglione

Surrounded by his generals, Bonaparte pays homage to the defeated.

Castiglione, August 5

Austrian fortifications have been pulverised by twelve high calibre cannons. Wurmser, moreover, has only just avoided capture by the French cavalry. After losing 2,000 men, the general in command of the Imperial forces saw no point in any further resistance. Retreating towards the Tyrol, he left 20 cannon and 1,000 soldiers in French hands. Bonaparte's recovery is no less remarkable for all that. At the end of July the enemy's advance had been such that Quasdanovitch was becoming a threat to the French retreat, while Wurmser was marching on Verona. Bonaparte then decided, in an astonishing feat of daring, to attack Quasdanovitch's column before going on to that of Wurmser. A race against the clock, this astonishing risk wwas to be crowned with victory.

News from Lyons: the verdict is given

Paris, August 5

"Death!" Three times the sentence rang out in the courtroom. Lesurques, Couriol and Bertrand will go to the guillotine. Richard, who received part of the booty, has been more fortunate: he has been condemned to 24 years in irons. Guesno and Bruer have gone free. Such is the outcome of a trial centred on a single question: is Lesurques innocent or not? The jury refused, finally, to listen to reason. It had no wish to ask itself why a man with an income of 12,000 livres should make an armed attack from which he has nothing to gain. It allowed itself to be swayed by witnesses for the prosecution who formally identified Lesurques as one of the four men at the inn at Montgeron. The flow of defence witnesses could do nothing to alter that decision. All, however, had unanimously declared that this wealthy young man was honest. For a moment it seemed that their side might win, thanks to the testimony of the jeweller Legrand. The latter, eager to provide his friend with an alibi, had explained that Lesurques had been with him on the afternoon of the crime, helping him carry out purchases entered in the register under the date Floréal 8. At last there was proof of Lesurques' innocence! He couldn't have been in Paris and Montgeron at the same time. When the court examined the register, however, it transpired that the date had in fact been Floreal 9. Legrand had altered the register to get his friend off the hook. Nothing thereafter could have saved the accused. The verdict came as no surprise. The moment that it was passed, Couriol stood up and declared, much to the astonishment of everyone present: "I am the guilty one. My accomplices were Vidal, Rossi, Durochat and Dubosq, whose resemblance to Lesurques has misled the witnesses." But these last-minute avowals did nothing to change the sentence (→ Oct. 30).

Jourdan defeated in Württemberg

Württemberg, August 24

The German campaign is taking a turn for the worse, as a result of continual hesitations on the part of Jourdan and Moreau. The news of Jourdan's defeat at Amberg has lowered the troops' morale. The Sambre and Meuse Army seemed on the point of falling apart. Having abandoned arms and baggage, the soldiers went off marauding. Up until now Jourdan and Moreau's armies have been advancing without any real co-ordination. The archduke Charles has therefore left only a cordon of troops opposite Moreau in order to concentrate his forces against Bernadotte and Jourdan in turn. The victor of Fleurus has had to draw back onto the Main (→ Sept. 11).

Jourdan, the victor of Fleurus.

The Republic pays homage to elders

Paris, August 27

"Time whitens their venerable heads; children, crown them with flowers." At the Théâtre des Arts, the Commune has paid homage to these citizens whom the authorities had previously tended to ignore. Today they are seated in the guest of honour's lodge, among garlands and with oak-leaves crowning their brows. But the heroes turned out to be rather shy. They watched in silence the Sophocles play, Oedipus at Colonus. Then children came to kiss them with the decency and respect that is only fitting when one has just been "set a great example" of wisdom and been able to "set eyes on exemplary figures".

The discreet escape of deputy Drouet

Paris, August 17

One of the principal accused awaiting trial for the Babouvist conspiracy has escaped. The deputy Drouet was due to be tried with other members of the group before the High Court, in keeping with the vote passed by the legislative body on August 13th. Given as a hostage to the Austrians by Dumouriez, he returned from captivity after the Directory exchanged him for Madame Royale. Joining forces with the Babeuf faction, he was arrested at the same time as its leader. The conditions of his escape are shrouded in mystery. Rumour has it that Barras, who has friends on the left, played a part.

The fate of hostile priests divides the Assembly

Paris, August 26

"Force and violence have never worked where religion is at stake": the line argued by Portalis has been effective since, by a very large majority, the Ancients have refused to ratify a resolution of the Five Hundred concerning hostile priests. This text, which was presented by the deputy Drulhe, proposed that priests who had not taken the oath be allowed 20 days in which to leave the territory, after which time they would be grouped with émigrés returning home. Functionaries who persistently dallied over the searching out of such figures would likewise be subject to heavy prison sentences. In the name of tolerance and appeasement, Portalis asked his colleagues on the Council of the Ancients to throw out this resolution. His interest in religious matters is not new: a lawyer at the parliament of Aix, he had been one of the first, under the Ancien Régime, to attend to Protestant affairs. His eloquence and professional standing, however, would not have been enough to win support on their own. But since the discovery of the Babeuf conspiracy the régime has been feeling under threat from the left, and is thus more disposed to make concessions on its right to the defenders of the Roman Catholic Church.

For or against the ransacking of works of art in Italy

Paris, August 27

Appalled by the French armies' systematic ransacking of art works in Italy, a number of artists have signed a petition of protest. They demand an end to the lootings, often hypocritically presented as having noble motives: it is France's duty to remove paintings from nations which are unworthy of them ... David, Girodet, Moreau le Jeune, Pajou, Percier, Fontaine and others have refused to condone this scandalous behaviour. But there is already talk of a counter-petition, favourable to the army, being prepared by Isabey, Gérard, Redouté and Vernet.

Does this imaginary depiction of a museum show what will become of the art treasures stolen from Italy?

1 *(Fructidor 15, Year 4)*
Italy. After a three week rest while awaiting reinforcements from the Vendée, Bonaparte renews his offensive against the Austrians and moves up the Adige. He has split his army into three parts led by Augereau, Vaubois and Masséna.

1 *(Fructidor 15, Year IV)*
Germany. Unhappy about tactical decisions by head-quarters, Kléber resigns his command (→ Oct. 96).

3 *(Fructidor 17, Year IV)*
Paris. At the Five Hundred, Sébastien Mercier advises against the teaching of modern languages at the central school of Paris, on the grounds of the pre-eminence of Republican French.

3 *(Fructidor 17, Year IV)*
London. The Comte de Frotté offers money and a marshal's staff to Hoche if the latter will back Louis XVIII. Hoche declines the offer.

3 *(Fructidor 17, Year IV)*
Germany. Jourdan is again defeated by the Archduke Charles at Wurzburg.

4 *(Fructidor 18, Year IV)*
Italy. At Roverdo, Augereau and Masséna defeat Davidovitch.

4 *(Fructidor 18, Year IV)*
The Hague. The Batavian Convention grants Jews full civil rights, on condition that they agree to be assimilated into the community.

7 *(Fructidor 21, Year IV)*
Italy. Bonaparte defeats Wurmser's rearguard at Primolano.

8 *(Fructidor 22, Year IV)*
Paris. Saint Aubin's *L'Ami du Peuple ou les Intrigants Démasqués* is staged at the Théâtre de la République.

8 *(Fructidor 22, Year IV)*
Italy. Bonaparte defeats the Austrians at Bassano.→

9 *(Fructidor 23, Year IV)*
Paris. Unsuccessful uprising of troops led by Jacobins at the Grenelle camp. Having foreseen it, Carnot lets it follow its course so he can justify reprisals later (→10).

10 *(Fructidor 24, Year IV)*
Paris. The Directory sets up a Military Commission to judge those under arrest for the events at Grenelle.→

11 *(Fructidor 25, Year IV)*
Italy. At Cerea, Bonaparte is again harassing Wurmser.

Tallien household under fire from Royalist satire

Paris, September 2

Former deputies are under attack from Royalist gazettes. A small satirical review, the *Rhapsodies du Jour*, is aiming its darts at the Tallien household. The attacks are particularly intense, for their name appears in practically every issue, notably today's. "There has been talk recently at the Council of the Five Hundred of imposing some kind of tax not only on merchants but also on door to door salesmen, public acrobats, and even prostitutes: Tallien is said to have been violently opposed to any such idea, declaring: You're trying to play a trick on my wife!" Thérésa Tallien could easily put a stop to all the talk she is causing by being more discreet, but she likes to please and cannot resist being the object of so much gossip and applause. The newspapers, by criticising the husband's political past and the wife's behaviour in public, have given a final, crowning touch to the couple's legendary disputes.

Impressive French victory at Bassano

Bassano, September 8

History repeats itself. Wurmser has failed before Bonaparte just as he failed, less than a month ago, at Castiglione. The Austrian general has abandoned 30 cannon and 2,000 prisoners to the French. And just as he had earlier been forced to draw back into the Tyrol, Wurmser now finds himself obliged to withdraw towards Fontania, on the left bank of the Brenta. Meanwhile, General Davidovitch has fled in the direction of Friuli. A complete washout for the Austrians, who had taken up the offensive once again after their defeat at Castiglione. In less than a fortnight, Wurmser had managed to reassemble in the Tyrol an army of some 45,000 men. Once more his plan had been to break through the blockade at Mantua in order to drive the French army back onto the left bank of the Mincio. Despite his numerical inferiority, the general in chief of the Army of Italy has caught the Austrians, as at Castiglione, on the hop.

Four days after Bassano, Augereau and Masséna capture Roverdo.

Thrashing it out in the Malacca Straits

Penang Island, September 8

A nasty surprise was awaiting Admiral de Sercey's French contingent near Penang: two powerful Royal Navy vessels on their way to Malacca had blocked the straits. The French soon realised that they would have to fight if they wanted to get through. The two English ships, the *Arrogant* and the *Victorious*, carried 74 cannons apiece, in other words twice the firepower of the French frigates. A lucky piece of manoeuvring allowed the French flagship *La Forte* to slip between the mastodons taking the rest of the contingent with it in its wake. A noisy affair, but one that went off without serious losses. But Sercey's objective had been attained the day before with the sacking of the English counting-house at Malacca.

Heavy vessels are not always in the right position to attack.

France signs a very lucrative peace with Bavaria

Bavaria, September 5

France has high hopes that its victories over the different German states will help to keep its coffers nicely filled. It has just signed an armistice with the Bavarian Prince Elector in exchange for financial compensation: theoretically, the Directory will shortly be receiving, therefore, ten million livres in hard cash and seven million to be paid in various forms, as well as "the 20 paintings of your choice" that Bavaria has agreed to hand over to the victor. The same principle has been applied in respect of the other states of southern Germany. The various armistices concluded throughout the month of July as the French armies advanced have brought in contributions from the Palatinate, Württemberg (four million livres), the Margrave of Baden (two million livres) and the Swabian Circle which has agreed to pay a total of 12 million in the interests of peace.

Exemplary verdict for villains

Lower Charente, September 5

Haunting the countryside on horseback, gangs of brigands are on the increase and attacking isolated houses at night. In general, they are beggars or ped lars who have turned to pillage and murder. To deal with the new danger, the authorities have decided, through the Charente tribunal, to sentence three of the bandits to 20 years, hard labour, along with the innkeeper who was hiding them. It will be an example to others.

Black general wins promotion

Saint Domingue, September 11

A month ago Toussaint Louverture was named division general. Who could have foreseen that a former slave, having become the liberator of the negroes, would go to the top of the military hierarchy? His support of the Republic in May 1794 decided his destiny. His advancement since then has been a model one: promoted brigadier general in October 1795 and lieutenant general in March 1796, he is today on a par with the governor of Saint Domingue (→ Oct. 19).

Up for sale, the abbey of Jumiège, founded in the eighth century, not far from Rouen, is destroyed along with the adjoining church, added in the 11th. century.

Surprise uprising at Grenelle camp

Paris, September 10

The Directory sees Babouvists at work everywhere. The affair at the military camp at Grenelle, situated at the very gates of the capital, confirms it in its belief that the welfare of the Republic is being seriously threatened by extremist groups. This "mutiny" couldn't have come at a more opportune moment, for it allows the Directory to justify repressive measures against the left. Last night several hundred Jaco bins appeared at the camp at Grenelle, inciting the soldiers to revolt. They succeeded in rallying them to the tune of the *Marseillaise* and by deploying the French flag, the tricolour. A cavalry charge soon put a stop to the activities, however. The demonstrators moved away, leaving some 20 dead scattered about the pavement in their wake. The whole affair has a distinct air of provocation. The Directory members Carnot and Letourneur are said to have had wind, a fortnight ago, of a plot. They said nothing so as to be able to drown the insurrection in blood and make an example of it. They even charged certain of their agents with making sure the mutiny did, in fact, take place. The Marquis de Foissac Latour, in charge of the camp, had been kept informed of the plan. Using the affair as a pretext, the Directory has taken legal action against the rebels and their supposed accomplices arrested in Paris and thereabouts. By playing up its troubles on the left in this way, it risks reinforcing opposition to its policies from the right (→ Sept. 13).

Château made for a love triangle

Dijon, September 4

Who does not dream of owning a château? In order to acquire one near Dijon, Prieur de la Côte d'Or has pooled his resources with those of his mistress, and with those of her husband, Monsieur Vétu. The property, put up for sail in 1793, had not found a buyer up until now. For 33,123 livres, the three partners have become its happy owners. It remains to be seen whether it is the lover or the husband who will be keeping the beautiful Madame Vétu company in the new home.

Caught off guard, officers leap into the saddle to fight off the attack.

The repression aims to set an example: certain leaders are shot on the spot.

The strange retreat of General Moreau

Germany, September 11

The situation is truly disastrous. The Sambre and Meuse Army, defeated at Amberg on August 24th., really only exists now on paper. On top of all this, General Moreau has not sent the Rhine and Moselle Army in pursuit of the Archduke Charles. After beating General La Tour near Augsburg on August 24th, Moreau remained strangely inactive on the banks of the Lech. It is clear now that Carnot's projects will not be realised. The "man of"war" had banked on close co-operation between Jourdan, Moreau and Bonaparte's army. Jourdan, however, who has been defeated yet again, this time at Amberg, is no longer in the game. As for Bonaparte, he is not keen to co-operate with anyone; on the contrary, he now plans to move on to Trieste. Under these conditions Moreau, left to fend for himself, has abandoned any idea of moving towards the Tyrol. His luke-warm republicanism, however, can be said to have played a part in his decision. The émigrés fighting for La Tour's Austrian army have been in frequent contact with the French officers, and Moreau has probably been approached.

13 *(Fructidor 27, Year IV)* Paris. The Military Commission in charge of trying the men accused of involvement in the camp Grenelle incident starts work (→Oct. 10, 96).

14 *(Fructidor 28, Year IV)* Paris. Alexandre Lenoir is authorised by the Minister of the Interior, Bénézech, to extend the Museum of French Monuments as far as the adjoining gardens in the Rue des Petits Augustins.

15 *(Fructidor 29, Year IV)* Italy. General Wurmser is defeated while trying to leave Mantua.

16 *(Fructidor 30, Year IV)* Paris. The Directory draws up plans for the Irish expedition.

16 *(Fructidor 30, Year IV)* Germany. Marceau, leading the rearguard of the Sambre and Meuse Army, stops the Austrians at Limburg.

16 *(Fructidor 30, Year IV)* Rome. The Jacobin Michele Laurora calls for a convention to be established for the whole of Italy.

19 *(3rd supplementary day)* Lyons. Inauguration of the central school.

19 *(3rd supplementary day)* Germany. General Marceau is wounded at Altenkirchen while fighting a rearguard action (→21).

22 *(Vendémiaire 1, Year V)* Paris. The *Manuel des Théophilanthropes* is published by the bookseller Chemin Dupontès.→

22 *(Vendémiaire 1, Year V)* Paris. The Directory reacts favourably to a request from the writer Restif de La Bretonne, now old and without an income, and arranges for the Ministry of the Interior to provide him with five pounds of bread every ten days.

23 *(Vendémiaire 2, Year V)* Germany. Worn out by his series of defeats, Jourdan resigns. He is replaced by Beurnonville at the head of the Sambre and Meuse Army.

25 *(Vendémiaire 4, Year V)* Paris. The artillery's central committee approves plans for organising along military lines those responsible for transporting artillery.

26 *(Vendémiaire 5, Year V)* Paris. The Minister for War confesses to the Directory that he no longer has any authority over the Army of Italy.→

The Directory is without news from Bonaparte

Paris, September 27

Bonaparte's autonomy is starting to worry the government. The Minister for War, General Petiet, has had to face the facts: all contact between the Army of Italy and his ministry has ceased. In his report to the Directory he indicates that he has been unable "to obtain the slightest shred of information from either the chief of staff or from headquarters itself". The Italian campaign is Bonaparte's private sphere. When the latter agrees to write, his account of events is highly personal. When Wurmser beat an orderly retreat after Castiglione, Bonaparte noted: "The Austrian army has faded like a dream."

Quiet, please!

Bordeaux, September 23

The municipality of Bordeaux has decided to put its foot down. Its gilded youth is dissatisfied, it seems, with the existing public holidays, such as the "Married Couples' Day"; it also likes to spend its evenings at the theatre listening to anti-Jacobin plays and its nights singing under the windows of patriots. The central bureau has decreed that it is henceforward illegal to "sing, or to allow to be sung, the song known as *Le Réveil du peuple*, which is an incitement to murder, or to read, or to have read to one, in public theatres before, during or after the performance, any printed paper or manuscript".

Marceau dies in combat

His last words: "My friends, it is sweet to die for one's country."

Altenkirchen, September 21

An Austrian bullet has put an end to the career of General Marceau. The Archduke Charles came in person to pay his last respects to the young general. While the enemy was according him full military honours, the Sambre and Meuse army continued with its retreat. The gift of Marceau's life was not enough to save Jourdan from further defeat. After Wetzlar, Amberg and Wurzburg, the hero of Fleurus found himself once more facing the Archduke Charles. Deprived of the back-up from Moreau that was part of the original plan, Jourdan had to go back across the Sieg and carry out the disastrous retreat during which Marceau was wounded on September 19th. Exhausted, the army's morale is low.

Marceau was 27 when he died.

General Moreau's troops defend the bridge-head at Kehl, on the Rhine, against an Austrian attack.

Italy in search of a good government

Italy, September 27

The French general administration in Lombardy is getting to work. It has just organised a competition where it will select the best model put forward for a free government in Italy. Bonaparte is backing the operation and hopes to find a way of administering the French conquests in the peninsula, for he is not in agreement with the policy of systematic looting of Italian wealth put forward by Carnot. Italy, to Bonaparte, is far more than a piece of booty. It is also more than a road allowing access to the French armies stationed in Germany. What he would like to see is an Italian revolution along the lines of the Jacobin one that would make Italy into a single republic allied to France. Such a vision is starting to win support among the Italians, as can be seen from the propaganda that has been circulating in favour of a unified and Jacobin Italy since last Spring. It is Ranza in Piedmont, Lauberg in Naples and Laurora in Rome who are responsible and Bonaparte has done very little to discourage them. He is aware, moreover, that the ideas championed by these men run counter to those espoused by the Directory, even if certain French government commissioners are keen to encourage Italian independence; Saliceti, for example, commissioner to Lombardy, who would like to make the State into a republic. The future of the Italian peninsula is far from certain...

A manual for the theophilanthropists

Some church ceremonies will be carried out according to the "natural cult".

Paris, September 22

A new religion is born: theophilanthropy. Its founder, Chemin Dupontès, is a Paris bookseller who is both a freemason and a republican, but one who has long preached the virtues of moderation: at the beginning of the Revolution he published a paper called *Le Pour et le Contre*, which aimed to transcend party politics. The manual he has just published lays out the principles underlying the new cult, in particular its two fundamental beliefs: in the existence of God and in the immortality of the soul. For Dupontès, these are "emotional truths that everybody knows deep in their hearts" and are indispensable for a harmonious social existence. It is the duty of all those who subscribe to the cult, therefore, to honour God and love their fellow men by exercising both solidarity and tolerance, and to loving their country (→Jan. 15, 97).

Talleyrand returns from emigration

Paris, September 25

Who could be in the dark about Talleyrand's return? He is hardly known for his discretion. Heralded by the Paris press, his return is not that of a shameful émigré. Ever since he put out from New York, his friends have been impatient for his arrival. What political plans does he have? He, for his part, claims to be in search of peace and quiet, but who would believe him? On arriving in Hamburg, he fell out with his old friend, Madame de Flahaut; on the other hand, he plans to put immediately to good use the contacts and social know-how of another old flame of his, Germaine de Staël, provided she is allowed back into France.

Confession

Anti-régime songs are very popular now. For some days, this one has been secretly going the rounds. It is called "Confession of a Great Lady", who is, of course, the Republic:

My methods cannot be withstood.
I everything did sacrifice
All for the common good
To turn France into Paradise.
'Twas by the threats I did voice
That Liberty a name so fair
Was inscribed in letters choice
On prison portals everywhere.

'Twas fathers brave I first did kill
Next I'll send the children poor
Their blood on lands far to spill,
My men to avenge with gore.
The French faced each new curse,
When Treasury's funds were nix
I emptied every French purse
(An action which the law did fix).

Invoke not now Tainaron's cave,
When my final knell shall toll
In your anger you will rave;
I hear it now, the laughter droll.
All trouble from your soul expel;
I fearless die with unconcern,
For, when called to hell
'Tis to my home I do return.

A show is put on at the Champ de Mars, on September 22nd., to draw crowds to the Republic's anniversary festivities.

Most Academy members have decided to boycott the Salon

The modifications carried out in the Main Gallery of the Louvre continue to preoccupy Hubert Robert.

Paris, October 6

Change always seems shocking to members of the Academy. They have not taken kindly to the Minister of the Interior's decision to hold the two-yearly Salon this year instead of the next. Offended by a decision which runs counter to the traditions they uphold, they have boycotted the event. All the more room is left, therefore, for young artists, 252 of whom have plunged into the fray: 654 works from a wide variety of schools are on show, of which 529 are paintings. There is a noticeable proliferation of genre paintings, and a large number of portraits are also on display, one of the most striking of which is that of the painter Jean Baptiste Isabey with his daughter, by François Gérard. Hubert Robert, meanwhile, remains faithful to his earlier interests and has added a further variation to his series on the modifications being carried in the Main Gallery of the Louvre.

Devoted organist claims his due

Saint Quentin, October

As organist at Saint Quentin since 1787, François Dufour has appealed to the local administration for some kind of pension. Like many in his profession, Dufour found himself "caught up in the measures taken against the chapters and other church bodies throughout the kingdom". Deprived of his 750 livres stipend, Dufour has gradually exhausted his savings. The loyal services he has rendered over the years should win the authorities over to his cause.

Renewed Jacobin activity in Frisia

Friesland, October

The Zeeland and Friesland people seem to be rather fond of extremes. In January 1796, the two provinces joined Groningen in threatening secession. They obstinately refused to summon a national assembly. To try to calm them down a little, Holland threatened at the time to ban all exports of pork and eventually to extend the ban to peat and other materials needed for the construction of dikes. None of this had the slightest impact on events, however. Finally, a riot had to be organised. More recently still, the inhabitants of Leeuwarden, warmly encouraged in their actions by democrats from Holland, decided to invade the State Hall, arrest the members present and organise a new commitee. This new Friesland parliament of sorts has said it will allow the national assembly to be called. For the time being, though, Leeuwarden is a veritable hothouse for every variety of extremist idea. Clubs have been formed which imprison and execute anyone even remotely suspected of federalism. General Dejean, commander in chief of Franco-Batavian troops, has been sent to restore order, if necessary by force.

The birth of the Cispadian republic

Modena, October 16

Bonaparte has killed two birds with one stone. Taking advantage of a popular uprising against the Duke of Modena, he has re-established French authority over the area. The Duke has been removed and the government of the State placed in the hands of the French commissioner, Garrau. The Directory had made Bonaparte responsible for the mission, but the latter made use of the situation to realise a major ambition of his that does not have the consent of the French government and could not have been carried out from Lombardy: the setting up of a unitary Italian republic. With the help of Garrau, he has organised a congress that brings together representatives from the States of Ferraro, Bologna, Reggio and Modena. They have decided between them to form a Cispadian republic, an independent confederation that will be a kind of pilot version of the unitary republic the Italian patriots hope to see created one day. The Cispadian republic has proclaimed civil equality and formed its own legion of 2,500 men. It intends to send a delegation to Paris for recognition of its sovereignty and freedom. But nothing suggests that the Directory approves of this embarrassing move.

Rebel soldiers are sentenced to death

Paris, October 10

A month after the uprising at the Grenelle camp, a swift verdict has been passed by the military Commission which has refused the appeal made by the accused. Thirty-three of the guilty parties have been sentenced to death, two *in absentia*. One of them has committed suicide, and the rest were shot this morning, among them the Convention members Huguet, Cusset and Javogues, and the former mayor of Lyons, Bertrand. They went down crying "Long live the Republic!", which Carnot feared might well have a dangerous influence on the public. Trying civilians before a military commission is, moreover, altogether unconstitutional.

New industrial techniques are developed

Jouy en Josas, October

Although the Revolution has somewhat slowed up production and sales of his printed cloths, Oberkampf has been far from idle. He has taken advantage of the enforced lull to establish new commercial contacts and, with the aid of his assistants, has set about solving production problems. He has recently developed a new kind of press that makes use of a drum for printing: henceforward, an engraved cylinder will take the place of the old bronze plate, thereby allowing designs to be printed one after the other, without the joins being visible.

Rural scenes, meticulously illustrated, are still the most popular of all.

The English decide to abandon Corsica

Corsica, October 19

How could Corsica have remained in English hands at a time when France is passionately following the affairs of General Bonaparte? As he moves from victory to victory in Italy, he has not forgotten his native isle, now Anglo-Corsican. He has selected a number of Corsican officers responsible for retaking the island. Their mission went off with barely a struggle. The English did not intend to oppose the cause. London had asked the viceroy George Elliot to be prepared for a "hasty evacuation" of the island. Napoléon's agents had only to bring to a head the hostilities that have been brewing these last few months. The peasants were full of republican ardour. Officials who had been ousted from power were calling for the head of Pozzo di Borgo. He had taken sole control of the island after having Paoli sent into exile in October 1795: the latter had soon realised that the English alliance was a farce. The small French fleet commanded by Gentili landed at Macinaggio, on the Corsican cape, on October 16th. Bastia fell yesterday. Sir George Elliot and Pozzo left with Nelson's fleet today, having fled to Saint Florent. Thanks to Napoléon's Italian campaign, Corsica has been returned to France.

Corsicans are delighted to be present at the defeat of the English intruder.

Are the Milanese people overzealous?

Paris, October 11

The Directory is worried. It has just written to Bonaparte, asking him to temper the political ardour of the Milanese revolutionaries; the latter have been arguing for the constitution of an independent Lombard republic, as the basis of a future unitary Italian state. To the French government, Lombardy is a bargaining chip: it would agree to return it to Austria if the latter were to recognise in exchange French sovereignty over the left bank of the Rhine. Bonaparte, however, is only too happy to encourage the Italian patriots (→ Oct. 25).

Louis Baraguey d'Hilliers will be responsible for Lombardy.

Institute member is having difficulties

Auteuil, October 16

It is possible to be a member of the Institute and professor emeritus at the Ecole normale and yet still be unable to earn one's living. Cabanis is all too aware of this today. The celebrated doctor, restored to favour after Thermidor, cannot make ends meet with the salary he receives from the Institute, where he is a member of the political and moral science department. His salary, it transpires, is not paid out on a regular basis. As he has a wife and son to feed, Cabanis has had to resort to borrowing three hundred livres from his cousin, who finds the whole situation highly amusing. The times are hard for intellectuals.

Cabanis, a doctor and philosopher.

Overcome with remorse, Kléber resigns

General Jean Baptiste Kléber.

Rhine, late October

After winning the battle of Neuwied, General Kléber was told by the Directory to lead an offensive that would initiate the invasion of Austria. The young commander refused to obey orders. The Sambre and Meuse Army, he explained, lacked boats for crossing the Rhine, and was short on supplies. On top of this, his soldiers were fighting barefoot and with empty stomachs. The government repeated the order. Exasperated by the mindless policy being carried out from Paris, and deeply disturbed by the death a month earlier at Altenkirchen of his companion in arms, Marceau, Kléber has handed in his resignation (→ Dec. 26).

Italy is Bonaparte's privileged domain

Lombardy, October 25

Civil commissioners are just not capable of understanding a war. Such is Napoléon's belief, at least. The commander in chief of the Army of Italy has therefore decided to strip them of their powers, which he intends to hand over to one of his generals, Baraguey d'Hilliers, instead. The Directory had hoped to retain financial control over the occupied territories through the persons of its commissioners, but Bonaparte's ambitions grow with each new success. Having got rid of Kellerman he is the only military chief remaining in Italy, but he has no intention of stopping at that. He now claims to be responsible for all

diplomatic, financial and governmental issues within the provinces he has taken. What is needed, he states in a letter to the Directory, is "a unified military, diplomatic and financial strategy". Bonaparte is also indignant at the government's attempts to interfere in the levies he has been collecting: he can tolerate the commissioners stealing with him, but not their doing so without him! Just the other day, in fact, he warned Paris in terms that, for all their apparent politeness, made no secret of his ambitions: "Every time you act without placing your general squarely at the centre, you will be running a serious risk." The Directory has been warned.

News from Lyons: an error in the court?

Paris, October 30

The heads of Lesurques, Couriol and Bernard have tumbled into the executioner's basket. No pardon was granted. Lesurques was too visibly the guilty man. The attitude of the condemned men, however, as their barrow made its way to the scaffold, made a strong impression on the crowd that had gathered round to watch. Lesurques, dressed all in white, remained dignified and silent, while Couriol cried out at the top of his voice and with tragic sincerity: "I am guilty, but Lesurques is innocent!" He had nothing to lose and his confession is a disturbing one. Two innocent men have perhaps just died on the scaffold: Lesurques and Bernard. The latter, whose only crime was to have provided the horses, has paid a heavy price for it. Four of the murderers have still to be found.

Cambacérès at head of Five Hundred

Paris, October 22

Cambacérès would like to have been a member of the Directory, but, a year later, has had to make do with the presidency of the Five Hundred. It hasn't been easy, for his reputation is far from stainless: his taste for young boys is well known and the cause of much talk among political circles, while his political friendships lead him to fraternise with royalists, something which hard-line republicans find disturbing. His undoubted gifts, however, have won him support from his colleagues. His courtesy and natural authority make him an ideal choice for president, while his legal expertise comes in very handy in debating legislation. He intends, moreover, to renew discussions of his projected civil code, generally considered to be his masterpiece.

The members have already thrown out his first two outlines: will they accept the third?

Cambacérès has a taste for honours.

Although gambling establishments were shut down in 1793, gaming is more popular than ever. At a time when everything is uncertain, dens continue to spring up around the Palais Royal where fortunes are made and lost.

November 1796
from 1st. to 30th.

Alvinczy leads highly successful Austrian offensive at Caldiero

Caldiero, November 12

The Austrian army is tightening its hold. Bonaparte has been forced to withdraw to Verona, leaving some 2,000 dead behind him on the battlefield. Two cannons and 750 men have been left in the hands of the enemy. The French made a dawn attack on Alvinczy's troops, who were concentrated on a high escarpment. After some very fierce fighting, Augereau took the village of Caldiero, while Masséna moved into the hamlet of Cognola. Having decided to fight to the very last, however, Alvinczy descended on Masséna's flank and drove back his left wing. Thereafter, the Austrians had the upper hand. The French troops were having to fight in a blizzard of hail and rain, and Bonaparte finally decided to call a halt to the battle. Even though the commander in chief and his Italian army succeeded in retreating in an orderly fashion, the situation for the French still leaves much to be desired. Very early on in the month

The position at Corona, which Napoléon had asked Vaubois to hold.

of June, General Alvinczy had come down from Frioul with 27,000 men, and Davidovitch had arrived with 18,000 soldiers from the Tyrol. Bonaparte could count on having 26,000 men, 7,000 of whom were caught up in the siege of Mantua. Having defeated Masséna at Bassano, and driven Vaubois back beyond the Corona, will the Austrian army now unite their two columns at Verona? (→Nov. 17)

French bandits are ruthless

Meuse, November 9

It snows through the night. At the chateau of Ville les Pommereul, the notary Lehon and his wife are sitting up by the fire while their while their son sleeps. Suddenly their dog starts barking furiously in the yard. Lehon goes out with his rifle. False alarm. For several long minutes he is on tenterhooks. He has just decided to go to bed when the barking changes to a prolonged howl. It's too late: a silhouette is standing in the doorway. A man is there, with a knife in his belt and his arms folded across his chest: it's Moneuse, the author of the murder at the tavern of la Houlette. Known as "Hot Foot" and feared throughout the region, he has arrived with his gang of killers. "Hand over the 6,000 francs you received if you want your family to live." The wife of the notary is savagely beaten, the son is screaming. The notary is first garrotted, then dragged to the fire. The flames lick his feet. The burns, though unbearable, are not enough to make him confess. The money is no longer in his possession. The brigands leave in the morning, with the police hot on their heels.

Prud'hon: a delicate, sensitive painter

If Pierre Paul Prud'hon all of a sudden decided to take refuge in Arc lès Gray in the Franche Comté in 1794, far removed from the endless turmoil of the capital, it was doubtless through fear of Thermidorian reprisals. Of provincial origin, this ardent partisan of revolutionary ideas had begun life as an art student in Dijon. After three years in Paris, he returned to present his work for the Dijon Academy's annual award, which he won in 1784. This enabled him to leave for Rome, where he met a number of Germans who were passing through the holy city at the time. It was through them that he was exposed to the influence of the Romantic movement, as can be seen in the portraits of local dignitaries he carried out during his stay in the Franche Comté region: the fine portrait of Monsieur Anthony standing beside his horse, and, above all, that of his young wife with her two children, bear witness to his style at the time.

Portrait of Monsieur Anthony ...

... and that of his young wife.

Arcole: 72 hours' combat to secure a bridge

To succeed at Arcole, Bonaparte uses a clever strategy of troop movements which calls for the use of boat bridges over the Alpone River.

Arcole, November 17

Alvinczy's Austrian forces have withdrawn to Vicenza in a state of despair. After three days' intense fighting, the Alpone bridge is still in French hands. Deciding to strike while the iron was hot, Masséna led his forces through the village of Arcole in pursuit of the Imperial troops. Bonaparte, who for two days had laboured to no avail at the stubborn Austrian defences, now gave ample demonstration of his tactical genius. He made the 32nd. battalion hide itself in a small wood to the right of the road leading into Arcole, and then placed three battalions on the same road. Two other battalions were held in reserve on the road to Porcil, ready to attack the Austrian flank when the time had come. Everything was now in place, and Alvinczy walked right into the trap laid for him. The 32nd. battalion attacked the left flank, while the battalions waiting on the Porcil dyke covered the right. Under attack on all sides, the Austrian column yielded to both the force of numbers and the superior planning. Augereau also decided to take advantage of the situation and swung into action. He launched an attack on the Austrian left wing, about a mile or so from the Alpone. But it was precisely at this point that the enemy proved most difficult to displace: its vanguard was perfectly protected by the Alpone and by a stretch of particularly marshy ground. The Austrian position was so strong that, for quite some time, Augereau was unable to launch an all-out attack. Continually harassed by Augereau, Alvinczy could see his columns being wiped out on the roads into Porcil and Alpone. On top of all this, the Austrian general knew that French reinforcements from Legnano could undermine his already precarious position from one moment to the next. The time had come to beat a retreat. In three days, the Austrian army has lost 7,000 men and eleven cannon. It is no longer possible for Alvinczy to relieve Mantua.

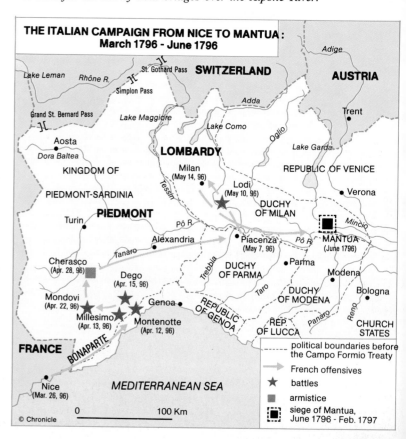

Gold rains down on English brig

Guadeloupe, November 30

Under pursuit from an English brig, Antoine Füet's pirate schooner decided to put up a fight. An artillery duel thus got underway between the *Thérèse* and the *Goddam*. When the English boat's mizzen mast was hit, Füet's cannon commander cried out: "There are no more cannon-balls left!" The schooner was returning from a lenghty cruise in the Antilles, where it had captured a vessel carrying several tons of *moidores*, or Spanish gold pieces. To unmast it, it had bombarded the vessel with cannon-balls chained together in pairs. What could it do now? Prime its cannons with gunpowder and gold! The gold pieces did no damage whatsoever to the enemy's bridge, but they tore its sails to shreds. On boarding the brig Füet recovered some 1,813 pieces of gold.

Suspect card games found in Mexico

Mexico, November 26

The viceroy Branciforte is worried about the dissemination of revolutionary propaganda in the kingdom. A card game has been discovered that originates in Cadiz. The cards are decorated with images showing the deaths of Louis XVI, Marie Antoinette and Madame Elisabeth. At first sight the game doesn't appear to be Jacobin, for the scenes it depicts are more likely to inspire pity for the royal family than anything else. The viceroy is so wary of the French, whom he describes as "given to sedition and the propagation of hideous seed", that he has decided to impose sanctions on anyone who plays the game. Stern measures will be taken towards any Frenchman thought to sympathise with the Revolution.

Is Joséphine likewise on the rampage?

Milan, November 25

Napoléon had imagined that the terrible jealousy from which he suffered would be assuaged once he had Joséphine at his side. Since she joined him in Italy, however, his torment has come to the surface once more with all its old force. For all her amiable indifference, he suspects her of having embarked on a new adventure with a young officer, lieutenant colonel Charles, who never leaves her side. Making a surprise return today from Verona, the poor general discovered his wife missing from the house. She had gone for a walk with Charles, he was told. Bonaparte's disappointment exploded in a note, scribbled in fury: "I arrive in Milan, I rush round to your flat; I have abandoned everything just to be able to see you, to hold you in my arms ... And you are not here!" He is worn out with love and tired from his recent campaigns. He has never looked so pale and wasted

Joséphine during the campaign.

Holland adopts a constitution

The Hague, November 29

After eleven days intense debating in which a total of 78 orators took part, the Batavian constitution was adopted by 76 votes to 52. The principle of unity is invoked early on in the text: the Batavian Republic is now a fully sovereign state, and no longer a confederation of independent provinces. The legislative branch will be in the hands of a Greater Chamber, to be elected by indirect universal suffrage, and the Chamber of the Ancients, the higher of the two authorities. The executive branch will be in the hands of a State Council, made up of seven members renewable one at a time, elected on the basis of a list drawn up by the Chamber of the Ancients. The country is to be organised into departments, administered by a Greater Council and a Committee Council which will retain a degree of financial autonomy. Separation of church and state has also been effected. Dissidents and Catholics are free to act according to conscience. The nation's Jews will also be granted civil rights. Drawn up by the moderate wing, the constitution is very close to the French Constitution of Year III.

New plans for the Louvre's main gallery

Paris, November 20

Refurbishing the main gallery at the Louvre is clearly a delicate business for the man entrusted with the task: he has once more stressed the need for the gallery to be lit from above. As recently as last August, Hubert Robert had the walls painted apple and olive green, with the vault done in "a light sky blue" and the cornices painted over "the colour of Saint Leu stone". This time round, it is the north facing intersections that have had to go. In the enclaves formed where they meet, pediments have been placed on which statues have been set. There are four of these in all, one of the most striking among them being Buchardon's *L'Amour*.

Hubert Robert, the architect and decorator who restored the Louvre.

Teaching methods improve in schools

Grenoble, November

Monsieur Dupuy, a teacher at the central school, is not only a distinguished mathematician: he is also an excellent pedagogue. It did not take him long to realise that it would be impossible to teach the science of numbers to a class made up of a hundred 12 to 16 year old boys. As soon as the winter term got underway, therefore, he decided to take the initiative. He divided his class into roughly 20 groups, each of which contained between five and seven pupils apiece. Each of these groups had a leader that it appointed itself, in general its eldest member. In some cases the arrangement proved very successful; in others it led to a diminished sense of responsibility. In the very first week, Monsieur Dupuy had to demote one such young leader, a boy called Raimonet, who had taken advantage of his height to spit on the smaller members of his brigade! Another of the teacher's inventions is a blackboard he has had constructed for his students where he writes out his equations. With teaching methods of this kind, the central school at Isère seems set for the future.

Royalist spies meet secretly at Venice

Venice, December 4

Royalist émigrés are working busily throughout Europe, in preparation for the restoration. This evening two counter-revolutionary spies met in Venice: the counts of Antraigues and Montgaillard. The latter has won over General Pichegru, head of the Rhine and Moselle Army, to Louis XVIII's cause. To do this, he explains, he had to promise him a marshal's staff, the château of Chambord, two million in hard cash and four cannon! Pichegru, unfortunately, has been sent on "temporary leave" by the Directory. Montgaillard has suggested trying to buy the famous young commander, Bonaparte, in his place. D'Antraigues promises to obtain credit from England and the king. Can Bonaparte be bought?

Where better to plot than in the shadow of a Venetian palace?

Georges Jacob and son, cabinet-makers

Cabinet maker Georges Jacob is tired: he is not as young as he was, and the revolution has been hard for him. He has thus decided to make his sons responsible for the running of the workshop, while he himself will act in an advisory capacity. Continuity is thereby ensured and production will now be carried out under the name of "Jacob brothers". The family will continue to draw on the works of David, Percier and Fontaine for its inspiration, for Antiquity remains fashionable: caryatids, griffins, winged victories, palm leaves and greeks are all popular as supports.

A chair and an armchair, made in the finest Jacob family tradition and in the fashions popular at the time.

La Harpe makes a stunning comeback

Paris, December 1

La Harpe wanted to make the most of his return to the public stage. His emergence, just as the winter term was getting under way, was a spectacular success. He had been in hiding, at the home of a bookseller friend, ever since he was compromised in the Vendémiaire uprisings and condemned by the Directory. He was authorised last month to return to work. Enforced retirement has only deepened his Catholic and royalist feelings, and he launched a violent attack on those very Enlightenment philosophers he had so passionately defended only eight years before.

Miranda is plotting against Spain

Paris, December 22

The former commander in chief of the Dumouriez army is far from idle. Miranda has just signed an agreement with the Peruvian, José del Pozo y Sucre, and the Chilean, Manuel José de Salas, in which he commits himself to finding English equipment for some 25,000 men, which he will then have transported to South America. He has always been concerned with the independence of the Spanish colonies. The Venezuelan knows that he cannot count on help from France, now an ally of Spain, if the conspirators wish to chase the Spanish from their colonies.

Success for Gros

Milan, December 6

In a letter to his mother, the young painter Antoine Jean Gros tells how the Citizeness Joséphine, whom he had met by chance in Genoa, has brought him here to Milan to meet her husband, the hero of the Italian campaigns. It is a real stroke of good fortune for a young painter of talent like himself. Though their meeting was brief, it was more than enough for Gros: he immediately set to work reproducing, with his delicate and lively brushstrokes, the youthful ardour of the victor of Arcole, portrayed dressed all in black and brandishing the standard in his gloved hand.

The French fleet sets sail for Ireland

"The Unbeatable", one of the French vessels heading for the Irish coast.

Brest, December 17

"May the wind be with us; our brows are crowned with gaiety and security, and there is confidence and patriotism in our hearts." It was with these words that General Hoche sent the French fleet on its way to Ireland, where it will help the insurgent nationalists in their struggle with England. The *Rights of Man*, the *Revolution*, the *Unbeatable*, the *Courageous*: these are some of the names among the 48 boat fleet that, to the cries of the crowd, set out from Brest with 25,000 men on board. Originally larger numbers were to have been sent, but General Hoche, who is in charge of the expedition, decided to reduce the effective. Success will depend on the fleet's ability to slip swiftly from the English grasp. In its present state it will be able to stand up to the English, should it have to, and also to impose peace if and when it reaches Ireland. If necessary, the fleet can return for reinforcements. For the moment, everything is in their favour: a fair wind, a calm sea, and sun ... The French forces are feeling joyful (→Dec. 24).

Volney finishes his tour of America

Philadelphia, December 10

Volney is back in Philadelphia after a seven month tour of the East coast. He left the town last May with a few articles of clothing, two razors, an English dictionary and a hairbrush. In the south of Washington, the renowned philosopher met a number of former adventurers from France, whose oaths got on his nerves. He made a note of it in his journal and, meditating, moved on to Richmond, a breezy town without much trade. Heading west, he met rattlesnakes, lamented the condition of bridges and inns, descended the Ohio in a canoe, bought a horse, and then zigzagged north. At Cincinatti he counted 400 wooden houses before going on to Detroit and New York. He is safe and sound but somewhat disappointed by his trip: "The New World is no better than the Old!"

Collapse of Franco-English talks

Paris, December 19

The Directory has just ordered back to London Lord Malmesbury, the English mediator. The failure of the Anglo-French peace talks, that Pitt had re-opened last September, is patent. Malmesbury had initially thought his country would agree to peace at almost any price, and had suggested it forego claims on re-securing Belgium from the French to that end. In exchange, France would cede certain of its colonial claims. The English government would have none of it. Nor did the Directory make any real effort to find grounds for agreement. All through the talks, it continued making preparations for the Irish expedition. As a result, negotiations have been broken off. Because England is none too popular with the French these days, no-one is much troubled by the outcome.

Benjamin Constant goes home incognito

Vaud, December 22

Benjamin Constant is keen to be back in France. The man who had hoped to return head high, and armed with a shining new French citizenship, has had to be content with slipping across the border in the utmost anonymity. He hopes his presence will at least be tolerated on French soil. The request for French nationality he made last July to the Council of Five Hundred, where he drew attention to the family of religious expatriates to which he belongs, was adjourned on December 11th. His celebrated friend, Madame de Staël, is equally impatient to be on her way. She also considers herself "French by virtue of place of birth, residence, property, custom and national feeling", though not, alas! from nationality. The news that the Swedish regent has withdrawn her husband as ambassador to Paris has shaken her to the core, and left her with no more hope than her friend of an official return. In their haste to return to French soil, the two lovers have purchased properties near enough to Paris to provide easy access, yet

Benjamin Constant is of Swiss origin.

sufficiently distant to keep them out of reach of the police. They have decided to risk the adventure, with no real guarantee that they will be allowed to reach their destination. Having bidden a painful farewell to her family, Germaine de Staël stepped into the coach with her friend. Their first stop will be Besançon, where Benjamin wishes to pay a call on his father.

Bonaparte, a brilliant strategist

The two men facing one another in the Italian campaign have absolutely nothing in common. Bonaparte is only 27 years old, while General Beaulieu is at the end of his career. His experience and his unquestionable merit are not enough, however, to pose a serious threat to Napoléon. The commander in chief of the Army of Italy has

The very talented young general.

exceptional will-power and already feels himself to be on a par with the masters of France: was it not due to his "sword" that they survived the events of Vendémiaire 13? As far as tactics go, Bonaparte has a clear advantage over his foe: he knows his way around the Apennines, for he played a very important role there two years earlier. Beaulieu is far from happy with mountain warfare. If Napoléon has always been strong on daring, he shows a remarkable degree of prudence as well. His plans turn on the line of retreat. He begins by attacking whatever enemy forces stand in the way of his retreat: Colli, in April, at Ceva; Quasdanovitch, in July, at Gavardo; and Davidovitch, in September and November, at Trento. For the same reasons, he avoids attacking the main body of the enemy forces. He seeks, instead, to whittle down stray detachments around and about the main army, so that the odds become in his favour.

A truly devastating storm puts an end to the Irish expedition

Monroe recalled to Philadelphia

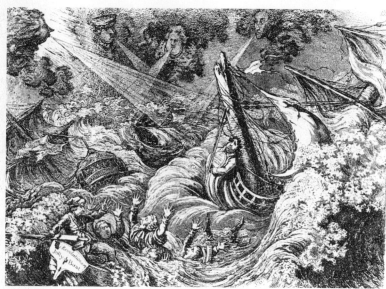

The English chuckle over the destruction of Hoche's French armada.

Cork, December 24

The dream has fallen to pieces: the projected French landing in Ireland has failed. The conditions under which the fleet left Brest on December 17th. couldn't have been better. Sudden winds had scattered enemy vessels, and the fleet was able to put out to sea without meeting the English. Once they arrived level with the island of Ushant, however, they got caught up in a violent storm. Winds were blowing in from the east and the sea was rough. The fleet was broken up and carried wherever the winds and currents decided. General Hoche was left at a considerable distance from the rest of the fleet, and has since disappeared altogether: it is not known whether his ship has gone down with all hands or is drifting on its own somewhere. A few ships succeeded in reaching the bay of Bantry, in southern Ireland, where the fleet had agreed to meet for the landing. As Hoche was no longer present, a council of war was held on board the vessel of General Grouchy, the second in command. But the risks were too great, and morale was low. The fleet set off for home, having failed to liberate Ireland. (→Jan. 13, 97).

Paris, December 30

George Washington felt that a friend of the French Revolution would have more chance than most at keeping France and the United States on friendly terms. When the French government demanded that Governor Morris be called home, on account of his alleged sympathies for the aristocracy, Washington appointed James Monroe to replace him. On arriving in Paris in 1794, the new American minister was warmly received. His support for a conciliatory liberal approach was not popular at home, however, and he was accused of putting his own country's interests second. With every decline in Franco-American relations, Monroe's credit back in Washington fell. To the everlasting regret of the French government, he has finally been relieved of his post.

On December 29th., the Opéra goes traditional by holding a ball during which high society mingles with ladies of pleasure and "nouveaux riches".

January 1797
from 1st. to 31st.

 Directory

4 *(Nivôse 15, Year V)*
Italy. General Bernadotte's division arrives as reinforcements. His soldiers are said to be royalists and have trouble accommodating themselves to the Army of Italy.

7 *(Nivôse 18, Year V)*
Milan. Members of the Arts Commission sent to Italy ask Gros to join them.

10 *(Nivôse 21, Year V)*
Paris. A new triumph for the composer Grétry, whose lyric drama, *Lisbeth*, is staged at the Favart auditorium.

10 *(Nivôse 21, Year V)*
Paris. To speed things up, the Minister of Finance, Ramel Nogaret, suggests to the Council of Five Hundred that fiscal rôles be decided not by the local authorities but by agents of the State.

10 *(Nivôse 21, Year V)*
Germany. Desaix evacuates Kehl after putting up a furious resistance for over two months. Only Hüningen remains in French hands (→ Feb. 5, 97).

14 *(Nivôse 25, Year V)*
Italy. Bonaparte crushes Alvinczy's army at Rivoli. →

16 *(Nivôse 27, Year V)*
Italy. The main body of Provera's Austrian army surrenders to Napoléon at La Favorite.

17 *(Nivôse 28, Year 5)*
Paris. To help out a needy descendant of Corneille, the new proprietors of the Feydeau theatre ask for author's rights to be re-established for *Le Festin de Pierre* and *Le Menteur*.

20 *(Pluviôse 1, Year V)*
Italy. In accordance with a treaty signed with Bonaparte, the Polish general, Dobrowski, calls all Polish patriots to arms, asking them to form a legion with him in Italy.

24 *(Pluviôse 5, Year V)*
Paris. Deciding to have done with Austria, the Directory puts Hoche at the head of the Sambre and Meuse Army. The plan is for him to lead a major offensive in the East.

28 *(Pluviôse 9, Year V)*
Italy. General Joubert takes Trento.

January *(Pluviôse)*
Paris. Profiting from the current vogue for English gothic novels, Le Prieur brings out François Ducray Duminil's *Victor ou l'Enfant de la Forêt,* which will prove to be a remarkable success.

The "Rights of Man" saves the honour of the French fleet

Finistère, January 13

The *Rights of Man* had only one remaining enemy to overcome: the storm which, turned out, alas, to be the stronger of the two. After losing two topmasts and its mizzen mast, it ran aground in the bay of Audierne. Where the rest of the Irish fleet had had to give up on account of the weather, the *Rights of Man* had just put up an extraordinary fight against three English vessels. Its commander had managed to manoeuvre in the midst of a storm; to such a degree, in fact, that he came very close to boarding commodore Pelew's boat. Despite the conditions the French vessel kept up a continual artillery fire, forcing the English to retreat before the sea came between them.

Despite terrible conditions, the Frenchman won the day thanks to his firepower

New plans for reinforced Austrian army

Gen. Josef Alvinczy is 62 years old.

Italy, January 7

The calm here is the calm before a storm. After the defeat at Arcole the Austrians decided to reinforce their army, which now numbers some 65,000 men. The main part of the army is under the command of General Alvinczy, and will attack the French positions at La Corona and Rivoli. According to the plans drawn up in Vienna, a 15,000 man corps will move into the plain in two separate columns: one of 5,000 men will be under the command of Bajalicz and will march on Verona, while the other, with Provera at its head, will move towards Legnano. The corps has been charged with keeping the enemy busy in the Adige, while the main bulk of the army sets about laying waste to the the French division posted in the mountains. The two main columns will then march on Mantua, where they will join up with Wurmser. Here, the French and Austrian armies will be just about equal in terms of military power. Alvinczy, however, has broken his army up into nine corps in a terrain that is far from easy, whereas Bonaparte is in full control of his troops (→Jan. 14).

Some clever thinking from a brigadier

Northern France, January 4

After much running about the countryside to escape the local constabulary, "Hot Foot" Duhem had decided to rest for a while on a friend's farm in the village of Armentières. He arrived with his girlfriend, two acolytes and a lieutenant. While they were having a quiet supper, police slipped into the yard. The brigadier who had come to arrest him had only five men at his disposal, however. He couldn't storm the house under such conditions, for the criminal is very fast with a gun. The gendarme suddenly had an idea: he started shouting out orders all over the place, thereby giving the impression that the police were out in force for the kill. Duhem was terrified and surrendered without a struggle. He will be tried at Lille. Clever thinking is sometimes worth more than force.

Illegal trading at the Palais Royal

Paris, January 6

Trafficking in currency has been a standard practice for some time now on the steps of the Egalité palace. With one eye on *Le Moniteur,* which gives the official exchange rates for Paris, locals barter foreign coin against French. Spanish reales, Austrian thalers or English pounds are exchanged for sols or décimes, which have little value and are produced in insufficient quantities. As the law does not expressly prohibit such practices, they take place in broad daylight, under the eyes of the police.

Proof that elegance does not preclude whimsy.

Abbot Brottier's royalist network is broken up by the police

Paris, January 30

The circle of conspirators known as the Paris Agency has had its day. Most of its agents fell into the trap laid by the police this evening. After an unsuccessful attempt at winning Louis XVIII over to their cause (the restoration of a constitutional monarchy), this English-backed royalist centre decided to try to overthrow the Directory. To do so, it organised an uprising that was to be backed by the police and their like. The Directory guard, led by the royalist agent Ramel Nogaret, and the Paris barracks, whose 21st. regiment was under the orders of another royalist agent, Colonel Malo, were among those involved in the plot. It was Ramel and Malo, moreover, who were responsible for its failure. Knowing that the Prince de Carency, a venal figure and the son of the Duc de La Vauguyon, had gone to warn Barras of the coming

LA PONCELINADE.

AIR: *La bonne aventure, ô gai.*

Quel est ce cul décharné,
    Amis, que l'on fesse ?
Est-ce le cul d'un damné
    Que Pluton carresse ?
C'est du charmant Poncelin,
Le derrière en parchemin,
    Ici qui figure, ô gai,
        Ici qui figure.

Pour payer du grand auteur
    L'éclatant mérite,
C'est à son postérieur
    Que l'on rend visite ;
Qu'il doit être satisfait,
Car on lui prouve qu'il plaît....
    A coups d'étrivières, ô gai,
        A coups d'étrivières !

Cependant, de tant d'honneur
    Son ame est ingrate ;
Plus on va, plus sa fureur
    Contre tous éclate :
Son cul noir comme son cœur,
Jusqu'à certain Directeur,
    En est responsable, ô gai,
        En est responsable.

Il fait procès, baccanal,
    Pour avoir en caisse,
L'intérêt du capital
    Placé sur sa fesse ;
Mais en vain il poursuivra
Pour réconfort il aura
    Nouvelle fessée, ô gai,
        Nouvelle fessée.

Abbot Poncelin, a journalist for the "Courrier", is beaten for his royalism.

Malo, leader of the 21st. dragoons.

upheavals, they thought to clear themselves by going and denouncing their fellow conspirators to Carnot. Thanks to Malo's treachery, Carnot was able to lay a trap for them and, along with their leader, Abbot Brottier, the group was duly arrested. Searches carried out at their homes have provided lists of sympathisers, among them Bénézech, the Minister of Interior, and Cochon, who is in charge of the police force. Given the highly compromising nature of the lists, it is not surprising that the government should be none too keen to start proceedings against the conspirators (→ March 1).

Symphonies are in fashion once more

Paris, January 28

Long fashionable in Germany, the symphony has just returned to France. Méhul, formerly in the forefront of revolutionary music, is now composing more traditional works for a public tired of toeing the line. His first symphony, in G minor, has just been performed with Mozart's 40th at the Feydeau theatre, and was a great success. A revival of the classics was long overdue in France, though it is Germany who leads the way in this field.

A breakthrough in Lyons courier trial

Paris, January 20

Judge Daubenton is lucky. The famous mail-coach passenger who cut the driver's throat has just been handed to him on a plate. On arrest, he made a statement that fully confirmed that of Couriol. He gave the same names and reconstructed the crime in excatly the same way. He only added that it was a post-office employee who had provided the information needed for the attack. He also pointed out, like Couriol, that Lesurques was innocent but confused with Dubosq by witnesses. The only area where his story kept changing was when it came to Bernard: he first of all described him as an accomplice, then as a weak-minded person at the mercy of others more intelligent than he. If what he says is true, three of the genuinely guilty parties are still on the loose (→ April 14).

Violent passions are unleashed by play

Toulouse, January 19

The Jacobins and royalists of Toulouse are no longer content with settling scores on the streets. Their battlefield has recently been extended to the Théâtre de la Liberté. Muscadins regularly applaud Mlle. Cressent, an actress known to have royalist sympathies, while the other side boos her. Those who can shout loudest usually carry the day, with one side chanting *the Réveil du peuple* and the other the *Marseillaise*. More often than not they end up in the street together, but don't do much harm. This time round, however, Mlle. Cressent has gone a bit far. She had arranged for *La Pauvre Femme,* a violently anti-Jacobin play, to be staged once again, even though the local authorities had banned it to avoid trouble. The moment she walked on stage the Jacobins began shouting and brandishing arms. The municipal guard was forced to empty the auditorium, though it was unable to prevent violent brawls breaking out in front of the theatre. More than sixty people were wounded.

Museum is to be completely overhauled

Paris, January 22

Everything was going wrong at the Central Arts Museum. After being reprimanded by the Minister of the Interior for failing to provide the institution with the sense of "order, dignity and public utility" required, the curators have been sent packing. Basically, they have been accused of lacking in method. The new committee is made up of Hubert Robert, Suvée, the sculptor Pajou, Nicolas Jollain and Charles de Wailly. The executive side, for which the artists themselves had been responsible before, has now been put in the hands of a team of administrators, which seems safer. The new team has a clearly defined task: it must decide, during its frequent meetings, everything from which paintings are to be hung to the hours of opening, as well as archival and caretaking matters. Hubert Robert will have assistance from Suvée and Jollain in looking after the painting side. He will be especially responsible for restorations, certain of which have been found to be utterly inadequate.

Masséna rushes to Bonaparte's rescue at Rivoli

Twenty kilometres northwest of Verona, at the foot of the Alps, the plain of Rivoli, where the French would have perished if Masséna had not come.

Rivoli, January 14

The confrontation has occurred. A cavalry charge led by Leclerc and Lasalle has put the final touch to the Austrian torment. Alvinczy's defeat is total. It has to be said, however, that the French side came perilously close to disaster. Going on in advance of the troops he had brought from Verona, Bonaparte had arrived by two o'clock in the morning. He immediately realised that the situation was critical: the Austrians, who had initiated an extraordinary pincer movement, were about to encircle the French. Bonaparte immediately instructed Joubert to put his entire division to engage the enemy. The French general soon found himself out-numbered, however, and it was only by diving into the village of San Giovanni that he was able to save as much as a single division. Only a miracle could prevent a French defeat, it seemed. And the miracle occurred at ten o'clock in the morning. Masséna, stampeding down into the plain of Rivoli, came to the rescue of the unfortunate Joubert and managed to break the enemy hold. The Austrians, who had thought victory imminent, no longer had the resources needed for a decisive counter-attack. Worn out, they dissolved into long lines of snipers scattered about the snow. Alvinczy has lost roughly 14,000 of his 28,000 men, nearly 12,000 of whom have been taken prisoner.

Death of a famous lyric singer

Paris, January 27

The opera singer Jean Baptiste Clairval died today, five years after he had gone into retirement. The public is unlikely to forget the clear tones of a voice that, for 33 years, formed songs that were always in keeping with the expressive needs of the libretto. His lyric insight, moreover, left ample room for an extraordinary dramatic gift that enabled him to sing a wide variety of rôles in one and the same opera: at one moment he would be a rheumatic old man, or a young dandy; at the next, he would be a stuttering lackey or an ugly old lady.

The Theophilanthropists celebrate their first public ceremony

Paris, January 15

It was to the little church of Saint Catherine that the celebrants of the new religion came to take part in their first public ceremony. The service was a sober one, in keeping with the prescriptions laid down by the founder of theophilanthropy, Chemin Dupontès. The priest who presided over the ceremony bears the official title of "head of the family", and began by reading an address to the "Father of Nature", after which the congregation was left in silence for several minutes for the examining of consciences. This was then followed by hymn singing, alternating with readings and "lectures on morals".

The cartoonist has shown only the tedium of the tiny congregation that day.

4 *(Pluviôse 16, Year V)*
Italy. The capitulation of Mantua puts a temporary stop to the Austrian occupation of northern Italy.

4 *(Pluviôse 16, Year V)*
Paris. The Directory confirms the territorial mandate's bankruptcy by declaring the currency invalid.

4 *(Pluviôse 16, Year V)*
Italy. General Victor beats the papal troops near Faenza.

5 *(Pluviôse 17, Year V)*
Germany. The Austrians take the fortified town of Hüningen on the Rhine, defended by General Ferino. The first German campaign is thereby brought to a close.

6 *(Pluviôse 18, Year V)*
United States. Louis Philippe d'Orléans joins his two young brothers in Philadelphia.

9 *(Pluviôse 21, Year V)*
Italy. Bonaparte moves into the Vatican states and occupies Ancona, with a view to forcing Pius VI to negotiate.

12 *(Pluviôse 24, Year V)*
Lyons. Death of the violinist and composer Antoine Dauvergne, author of *Les Troqueurs*, the first comic opera to be performed in France, in 1753.

14 *(Pluviôse 26, Year V)*
Portugal. The Spanish fleet, which is allied to France, is defeated by the English admiral, Jarris, just off the cape of Saint Vincent.

19 *(Ventôse 1, Year V)*
Italy. After executing Carnot's orders to invade the Vatican states, Bonaparte signs the treaty of Tolentino with the Holy See.→

20 *(Ventôse 2, Year V)*
Vendôme. The trial of Babeuf and the 54 "Equals" opens before the High Court of Justice (→ May 27, 97).

25 *(Ventôse 7, Year V)*
Paris. The Directory purges the electoral registers by making it illegal for any citizen on the list of émigrés to take part in primary assemblies. They number some 120,000 in all. The Councils will recover 17,000 of them, however, whose inclusion on the list had earlier been annulled at a departmental level.

27 *(Ventôse 9, Year V)*
Paris. The Academician Jean François de La Harpe publishes an essay entitled *Du fanatisme dans la langue révolutionnaire*.

With the capture of Mantua, Sérurier opens the road to Vienna

The surrender of Mantua has been Bonaparte's chief objective ever since the start of the Italian campaign.

Mantua, February 2

The French victory is decisive. The Austrian general, Wurmser, has capitulated and, as a sign of respect, he has been granted free passage, along with 500 men and six cannons. The rest of the army stationed in the town have had to give up their arms. For 18 months, Mantua had been the very heart of the Italian campaign. Of the 28,000 men who had been stationed there, only 15,000 could be considered fit to fight: 6,000 were in the hospitals from inanition or sickness, and another 7,000 or so had died in one or other of the battles. The victory at Rivoli, by bringing about the fall of Mantua, has opened up the road to Vienna.

Thérésa Tallien starts divorce process

Paris, February 26

Things are not going well in the Tallien household. The court has notified Jean Lambert Tallien that his wife is starting divorce proceedings "for reasons of difference in temperament and character". The news has come as a terrible shock to Tallien. The woman he loves, the woman he had saved from jail during the Terror and married three years ago, now pretends to have given herself to him out of nothing more than "gratitude". As for Thérésa, she scarcely thinks about her husband any more. She is constantly having affairs behind his back and despises his weak nature. He has also become a favourite target of the press, and is as much hated by former Jacobins, as a renegade, as by moderates, as a terrorist. Beautiful, charming and lively, Mme. Tallien is the toast of Paris society, where she makes no secret of her relations with Barras. It is time she got rid of a husband who has become something of a burden.

A great favourite in Paris society.

Mantua's fall

The news of Bonaparte's capture of Mantua on February 2 got to Paris to-day and is arousing great enthusiasm. Naturally, many songs have been composed about it. This one, which mocks the Emperor of Austria, is particularly popular:

Of Mantua and its famed terrain
We now have complete control;
But to get it back again,
The emperor would sell his soul.
He wants to arm, or so they say,
Fol-de-rol dee, fol-de-rol day,
All the women in Hungary,
Fiddle-de-dee,
In the fashion of Barbary.
Yes, sirree!

Now Bonaparte the people cite
As Alexander Number Two,
A living Caesar in the fight.
All enemies he overthrew.
And brave his soldiers, all do say.
Fol-de-rol dee, fol-de-rol day,
He treats all as friends carefree,
Fiddle-de-dee,
In the fashion of Barbary.
Yes, sirree!

His warlike image to retain,
Fair Victory's noble son
A brave warrior will remain;
Bright in glory's fame he's shone.
To the sound of the gunplay,
Fol-de-rol dee, fol-de-rol day,
The enemy will make whoopee,
Fiddle-de-dee,
In the fashion of Barbary.
Yes, sirree!

The Directory goes to war against religion

Paris, February 3

"The Roman church will always be irremediably hostile to the Republic." The Directory's letter to Bonaparte reveals a profound dislike of the Catholic church and its leader. Signed by the three of the five Directory members known as the "Triumvirs", it strongly advises the head of the Army of Italy "to destroy, if possible, the centre of the Roman church's unity" and "to extinguish the flame of fanaticism". Reubell, Barras and, in particular, La Révellière Lépeaux are convinced that priests are a serious threat to the Republic with their sermons, and that some kind of vigorous action should be taken, starting at the top. Nor is this the first time that the Directory has asked the Army of Italy to take Rome as its objective. After French troops had entered Milan, it similary asked Bonaparte to destroy the papal State and "rock the crown of the would-be leader of the universal church". The general declined to do so at the time, however, and it is not at all certain that he will be any more disposed to carry out orders today (→ Feb. 9).

Monsieur Bijou, the eater of animals

Paris, February 23

The serious-minded professor Faujas had to see it to believe it. The natural history specialist went to see the man known as Bijou, whose real name is not known, in the Museum gardens. Bijou could be any age; he sits alone on the same white bench smiling to himself, and takes fright if anyone speaks to him. He spends his life here, watching the animals dying in their cages, while the flies and lizards he lives on come and go before him. He is as fond of the flesh of reptiles and cats as of the eyes of birds; he has a particular predilection, however, for tigers and insects.

Bonaparte imposes peace on the Pope

Tolentino, February 19

Harsh terms have been agreed upon in Napoléon's treaty with the Holy See. Another fifteen million lire must be paid, on top of the twenty one million already agreed upon at the time of the Bologna armistice. Considerable quantities of land have also been sacrificed: the papacy officially confirms that it has yielded Avignon and the Comtat to France, and abandons the Legations and the Marches as far as Ancona. Things could have been worse, however, as far as Cardinal Mattei, who conducted negotiations with the general, is concerned. The papacy had feared that Bonaparte, in accordance with the Directory's recommendations, would push on to Rome and destroy the Holy See altogether. If he did not do so it was because he was in a hurry to have his hands free for Austria. Nor was that the only reason: Bonaparte also wants to appease Rome in the interests of religious peace in France.

Excessive wealth is the principal object of attack in this papal apology.

Mulhouse, heart of the wallpaper trade

A design that is unrelated to the Revolution, ideal for a bourgeois home.

Mulhouse, February

The Mulhouse region is not only known for its textiles: it is also the heart of the wallpaper trade. The man responsible for it all is Jean Henri Dollfus, a manufacturer of printed cloths. Dollfus had set up the industry for his son, but it was bought up in 1795 by one Hartmann Risler. For reasons of customs and excise, Risler has just transferred it to nearby Rixheim which, unlike Mulhouse, is still on French soil. He is hoping the move will facilitate commercial relations with France at a time when the company is rapidly expanding. Two employees in particular should be mentioned: the designer Joseph Laurent Malaine, who used to paint flowers at the Gobelins but whose work has come onto the market since the Revolution; and the young Jean Zuber, scion of one of the town's most important families. The latter has been in charge of the commercial side since 1791 and is in the process of becoming a major shareholder in the company. With men like these two working for them, it seems likely that we shall be hearing more of the firm in the future.

Royalist conspirators are betrayed by one of their own men

Paris, March 1

Duverne de Presle has decided to tell all. He is one of the conspirators involved in the Anglo-royalist Paris Agency plot, currently before the courts. The trial has given rise to heated discussions among the legislative body. The Directory has had the accused hauled up before the Council of War, rather than have them tried by the tribunals, which is in open contempt of normal legal procedures, for the royalist conspirators are civilians. Duverne de Presle either believes that by cooperating in this way he will receive a lighter sentence, or has been overcome with remorse. Whatever his motives, he today told the judges all he knows about the counter-revolutionary activities of the Abbot Brottier, head of the Paris Agency. He also denounced the activities of the Institute of Philanthropy, a veritable hot-bed of royalism, and told the police where they would be able to put their hands on whatever papers concerning the plot they have not already obtained. In the

The bell is the symbol of the traditional church sought by the monarchists.

main, these are lists of plotters that will enable the police to carry out further arrests. The government does not intend to make these papers public, however. It doesn't want the conspirators currently on trial condemned to death; nor does

it wish to see monarchist deputies caught up in a rather embarrassing situation. It is probably waiting for more favourable circumstances in which to take advantage of the wealth of information provided by Duverne de Presle.

The émigrés are gradually returning

It is always possible to come to terms with an administration, especially when it is open to corruption. The French émigrés are taking advantage of the fact in order to return home. Thanks to the information provided by Duverne de Presle, one of the plotters involved in the Paris Agency royalist conspiracy, the police have been able to put their hands on a list of émigrés who

Head high, holes in his clothes.

have returned to France with the help of government employees. The Constitution is formal on this point, however: all émigrés are banished for life and there can be no going back on the fate reserved for them. There are ways round the law, however, for it gives no indication of how an émigré is to be defined. The Convention, what's more, had made provision for certain cases. In particular, it gave all those who had left the country after May 1st. 1793, federalists for the most part, a chance to return to France before a certain date. Likewise, an amnesty of kinds was granted to all those from Alsace who had fled the country in December 1793, from a fear of reprisals now that Pichegru and Hoche had won back the Lower Rhine from the Austrians; and to all those from Toulouse who had fled the Terror when republicans had driven the English from the town. In short, it is now quite easy to get back into France, provided one is neither priest nor aristocrat and has the means of corrupting officials.

The Five Senses

The Directory is being bitterly criticized by a growing number of angry, frustrated or disappointed citizens. Relying on the word play between Council of the "Cinq Cents" (five hundred) and "Cinq Sens" (five senses), an unknown but witty song writer has composed this little satire. The song relies for its impact on the straightforward homonym "l'ouïe" (the sense of hearing) and "Louis", referring naturally to Louis XVIII...

Until today we spoke with pride
Of senses five by man possessed.
But now, my view I do not hide:
France needs one, not the rest.
For to inspire unhealthy air
No need for "smell", I moot,
Now there's hunger everywhere,
What use is "taste" to boot?

For in dire need, bereft of cash,
"Touch" cannot to us redound.
"Sight" does but our lot abash
On seeing misery all around.
But to achieve our dearest goal,
And new prosperity to enjoy,
Of senses five we "Louis" sole,
The king of senses, must employ.

Women writers are attacked by Rivarol

Paris, March

This time round his sarcasm has become venomous, for passions are involved. In *Le Spectateur du Nord,* Rivarol has just published a letter concerning Madame de Staël's *De l'influence des passions.* He clearly is not fond of Baroness de Staël: he has numerous bones to pick with her and her father, the businessman Necker, and has no time for their revolutionary sympathies. He then extends his attack to the novels of Madame de Genlis, the poetry of Chénier, and remarks made by Abbot Sieyès, before turning on women writers, whom he finds abnormal beings with hearts and brains that belong to different sexes: "I like only the definite sexes," he states.

Chateaubriand and the Revolution

London, March 18

Chateaubriand is going to offend a great many people. His *Essai historique et moral sur les révolutions,* published by Deboffe, is pessimistic in its denunciation of all revolutions, with their illusory faith in "good government", whether monarchist or republican. In his view, the only course left open to the wise man is exile, for it was in the heart of the American forests that he found that "natural freedom" that had been lost when men decided to organise themselves as societies. The religion of nature is the only alternative to a defunct Christianity. Few share his views in the little world of those who have emigrated to England.

The Prix de Rome has just been awarded

"The Death of Cato of Utica", which was to be Guérin's passport to Rome.

Paris, March 15

The Prix de Rome has just been re-established, after being discontinued since 1794 on account of the Roman troubles. To make up for the penalising of young artists that was thereby incurred, three major awards have been made this year. The three winning entries, whose theme was *The Death of Cato of Utica,* remained faithful to the neoclassical aesthetic. Pierre Bouillon came first, then Pierre Narcisse Guérin, one of Regnault's students, and finally Bouchet, a disciple of David. The principal award for sculpture went to Lallemand, a student of Pajou.

The young Hegel is taken with politics

Stuttgart, March

Reform is on the agenda for Württemberg. Frederick Eugen will consider his subjects' griefs at the Landtag assembly. Many of them would like to have Württemberg changed into a constitutional state. No-one mentions the principles of 1789, however: all that is asked for is that the institutions be adapted. Such moderation provokes young Hegel, now back in Stuttgart, into writing a violent pamphlet which he addresses not to the Landtag but to "the people of Württemberg". In it he incites them to tear down the outmoded machinery of the state and turn resolutely to the future.

Hegel, who was favour of reform.

Chemists stand up for their profession

Paris, March

Chemists, as apothecaries now wish to be called, have decided that politics are not going to stand in the way of the development of their profession. Their college was shut down in 1793 because it was found to be too conservative in outlook.

The chemists of Paris have thus organised themselves as an independent body, and defend their cause before the public by giving courses in chemistry, botany and natural history. Their foundation has just been recognised by the Directory as a Free School of Pharmacy.

Hoche: also a good administrator

Bonn, March 23

Appointed commander-in-chief of the Sambre and Meuse Army, Hoche found on his arrival a body devastated by famine and worn out from want of even the most basic commodities. In the space of just two months, Hoche has got rid of the suppliers and war commissioners who were fleecing the army. To replace them he has set up a committee of six people, selected in haste. More funds are now available and he just told the Directory he will be raising the soldiers' pay. A stimulus at last!

Division General Joubert pursuing General Kerpen's Austrian forces in the montains of the Tyrol.

Joubert looks set for move on Vienna

Klausen, March 22

General Joubert has got out of a tricky position. The fighting against General Kerpen's Austrians was indecisive for a long time, but finally turned to the French advantage. The enemy army, camping in the village of Klausen, seemed to enjoy an impregnable position, but Joubert gave a convincing exhibition of his talent by getting around the Austrian position by way of the hills. He can now continue his advance toward Vienna, synchronising his progress with Bonaparte's. This is a hard strategy in the Upper Adige Valley, as Austria has raised 10,000 inhabitants for its forces.

Veneto is in hands of the French forces

Tagliamento, March 16

The stream did not have much water in it. The French easily got across the Tagliamento near Valvason, and the outcome was settled quickly. At nightfall the enemy was withdrawing toward Laybach after losing 500 men and six guns. The Archduke Charles, who had collected only 20,000 soldiers, did not want to risk disaster. Since the expected reinforcements from Germany did not arrive, he ordered a retreat in the hope of getting Bonaparte to come after him. The latter, however, preferred winning a small victory to a pursuit with an uncertain outcome (→ March 31).

Chénier falls victim to public's injustice

Paris, March 21

Marie Joseph Chénier has been widely admired, but he is having trouble with the public these days. When the rumour spread that he was the author of *Junius*, a tragedy being performed at Théâtre de la République, the Parisians whistled in disapproval during the entire performance, as if they wanted to punish the poet for the opinions of the same man as a deputy to the Five Hundred. To keep from hurting Monvel, the real author, Chénier had a notice put on the posters that the play was not by him.

Gen. Bonaparte offers Austrians peace

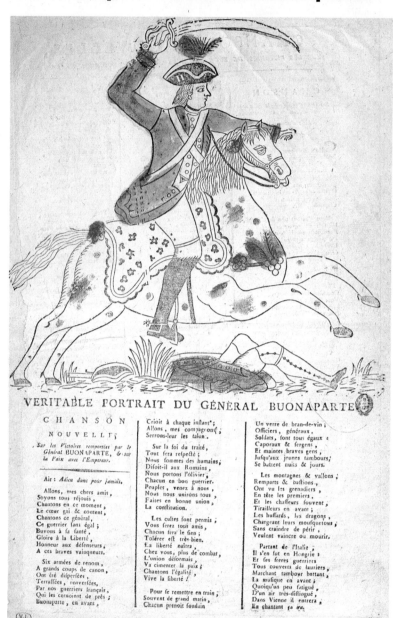

An ode to the glory of General Bonaparte's victories and to peace.

Klagenfurt, March 31

However clever and determined he may be, General Bonaparte was very quick to realize the precarious nature of the situation. Feeling that victory was not yet within rifleshot, he decided to make an overture to the Archduke Charles: "Commanding General, good soldiers make war, but desire peace." Despite Joubert's successes at Bozen and Brixen, the Tyrolean uprising is slowing down, and the road to Vienna is only partly open. But Bonaparte is thinking above all about the woman who will lead him back to the French capital, loaded with honours.

Apothecary boasts a "cure" for terror

Paris, March 30

In the display window of his pharmacy in the Rue du Bac in Paris, M. Lamégie boldly posted a list of names of the members of the committee that had thrown him into jail as a suspect during the Reign of Terror. He headed the list with a sign saying "New drugs". When a police official came to check out the episode, Lamégie explained that it was necessary to know poisons in order to protect oneself against them. His "antidote": a list of "good people" who had made him a sector elector.

Rouget de Lisle's fickleness punished

Paris, March 29

Rouget de Lisle really doesn't seem to know what he wants. After his illustrious performance as a volunteer during the campaign at Quiberon, the famous author of *La Marseillaise* sent in his resignation from the Army to the war minister on March 4th. 1796, without explanation. Carnot then informed him that he was appointing him a major, and this promotion made Rouget change his mind about leaving the military but not for long. On March 29th., he resigned again, and moreover made a violent attack on the war minister in a letter beginning with the aggressive formula "Carnot, I'm your enemy". One can imagine Carnot's surprise when he recently received an official application to rejoin the Army submitted by this same Rouget de Lisle. This time, the request was definitively turned down. After all, one can't make constant fun of the war minister and expect to get away with it.

Revolution was all a Masonic plot!

Hamburg, March

"Everything was foreseen, was thought out and arranged ...," says Abbot Barruel, who has just published his *Memoirs for use in the history of Jacobinism*. He concludes that the French Revolution resulted entirely from a plot hatched by Freemasons. It all began, he says, in 1750 with a meeting of three men Voltaire, d'Alembert and Prusia's King Frederick II, all of whom "were imbued with a profound hatred of Christianity". The conspirators then began a secret correspondence. Eager to offer proof of his accusations, Barruel reveals that Frederick's code-name was "Duluc" that d'Alembert's was "Protagoras", and that the term "Cacouac", synonymous with brother, was used to designate the plotters. The publication of the *Encyclopaedia* and the multiplication of lodges were aimed at widening the conspiracy and enabling the members to reach their goal. The Masons then emerged under the name of Jacobins and moved to topple throne and altar.

Massive election win for royalists

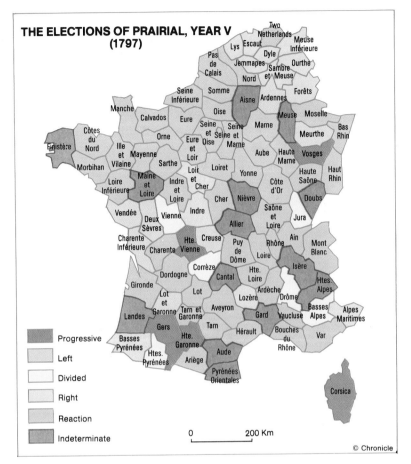

THE ELECTIONS OF PRAIRIAL, YEAR V (1797)

- Progressive
- Left
- Divided
- Right
- Reaction
- Indeterminate

0   200 Km

© Chronicle

POLITICAL LEANINGS OF THE DEPUTIES OF THE TWO COUNCILS ELECTED IN THE POLLS OF PRAIRIAL, YEAR V (1797)

170 deputies — REACTIONARIES
45 deputies — INDETERMINATE
17 deputies — PRO-DIRECTORY
16 deputies — LEFT

France, April 4

Reaction is dominant in French public opinion: at least that is what seems indicated by the results of the elections for renewing a third of the legislature. Out of the 248 deputies elected, a mere 16 are determined leftists and 17 may be regarded as favouring the Directory. About 45 other newly-elected deputies may be considered as hesitant or undecided. However, the majority of the new parliamentarians are definitely on the right. The bulk of them are out-and-out royalists, even if many of them would prefer the restoration of a constitutional king to the return of absolutism. The majority of these new deputies are members of the monarchist group dubbed the "Clichy Union". To this must be added about 30 "camouflaged" royalist deputies who do not speak publicly in favour of the monarchy.

Nevertheless, these results are probably not an accurate reflection of current public opinion. In fact, the organisation of these elections was greatly disturbed by royalist propaganda, and there were a great number of irregularities or "fixes" in connection with the primary assemblies. People who were not entitled to vote, such as servants, and émigrés not struck off the lists, were often allowed to cast ballots. Pavie, one of the Chouan leaders, was even elected in Normandy. The local administrations controlled by royalists were generally involved in obvious frauds. Moreover, propaganda in certain regions gave rise to a resurgence of voter fear of the Jacobins, helping the reactionaries. The latter maintained an atmosphere of extreme hostility toward the republicans, so much so that the latter sometimes did not dare attend the election meetings. This was the case in part of the north and east, in which the non-juring priests who had returned from Belgium or Germany spared no effort in their struggle against the régime.

This phenomenon also explains the very high abstention rate, as a little more than a million out of 6.5 million registered voters cast their ballots. The eastern part of the Massif Central in central France, the Rhône Valley and the Mediterranean south came out for reaction. In particular, Camille Jourdan and Imbert Colomès were elected in the Rhône. For its part, Paris and its region took the royalist road by electing the Comte de La Murinais, Emmery, Boissy d'Anglas, Quatremère de Quincy as well as the Comte de Fleury (→May 20).

A member of the Five Hundred.

Uproar greets failed attack on Sieyès

Emmanuel Sieyès: a close shave.

Paris, April 11

Emotions are running high in the Five Hundred following the shooting of Emmanuel Sieyès. The failed attack by Abbot Poule, a somewhat unbalanced southerner rather than a royalist agent, gave the deputies a chance to display their attachment to "the man who contributed the most to the Republic". A medical report will be read out at the start of each session. The attack offered the deputy Hardy, otherwise not highly regarded, his hour of glory as he gave the shooting victim first aid. While Sieyès' injuries are slight, Hardy described them with dramatic effect.

Writer Marmontel jumping into politics

Paris, April 13

Marmontel, the author of *Moral Stories*, is laying down his pen in order to get into politics. The Directory's position is becoming critical, and opposition is increasing in the provinces. Marmontel, hoping for a royalist victory, accepted the mandate he received from the Eure region voters to serve in the Ancients' Council. He pledged to be zealous in carrying out his duties. He also said he opposed infighting and affirmed his desire to struggle against the enemies of order and to defend his forefathers' religion. His oratorical talent and sincerity gave rise to lively applause.

France confiscates U.S. outlaw vessel

Lorient, April 7

The *Hope* and its cargo have been confiscated. The legal dispute between France and the United States is worsening. The merchant ship had been captured by a French privateer. The Americans demanded her release, but the French refused on the basis of an article of the Maritime Code requiring, since 1778, that a list of crew members be contained in on-board documents in order to check the sailors' nationalities as well as their neutrality in case of conflict. However, the *Hope* captain did not accept this requirement. The court ruled that he might be conniving with England, which is at war with France, and it penalised the ship.

The French port of Lorient bustles with intense business activity.

Occupation in Austria having its troubles

French military leaders are worried about their troops' misbehaviour.

Mauterndorf, April 10

France's reputation abroad is at stake here, and General Saisset, the chief of staff, has had two kinds of posters put up on the walls of this small Austrian village, occupied by his troops. One of them, intended for soldiers and officers, orders them to respect the inhabitants and to protect their property. The other is aimed at reassuring the population by informing it that all necessary steps will be taken to maintain order and discipline, and that it no longer needs to fear the French. Actually, looting is an endemic disease of occupation forces. When the quartermaster does not get there fast enough and troops have to wait too long for their pay, it is very hard to restrain them. Military leaders know that looting and disorder among the troops will lead straight to insubordination.

French improve on English tea ceremony

Paris, April

Parisians have become enthusiastic recently about the beverage from the other side of the Channel, putting in the leaves, pouring on hot water, and letting it steep. In the French capital, you find people everywhere drinking tea ... after dinner. People dress up for a tea party as if they were going to a ball. However, Paris would not be Paris if the French mentality failed to make certain improvements in the tea ceremony. Throwing out the sad pieces of buttered toast accompanying English tea, the French heap up a mountain of pastries and biscuits to heighten the pleasure of the ceremony. A truffle-stuffed turkey is a vital preliminary.

The Lyons courier: double trouble

Lyons, April 14

His name is Dubosq, and he might be the man who robbed the Lyons courier stagecoach. This champion backslider and escapee happened to be in jail for another offence when Judge Daubenton compared descriptions and realised that he might have the killer. The judge sent Lesurques to his death in the case, but now believes in his innocence. He is making every effort to discover his double, who is the real criminal, in the magistrate's view.

Talleyrand is back on the public stage

Paris, April 4

There was a big crowd this afternoon at the Institute. The subject, U.S. relations with England, did not sound very exciting, but the speaker was Talleyrand, who is universally known for eloquence and competence in the foreign relations field. The numerous diplomats in the audience expected him to throw some light on the Directory's policy. He is said to have great influence in this field, and why should he not enjoy a fine future in the government?

April 1797
from 17th. to 30th.

Bonaparte signs armistice with Austrians off his own bat

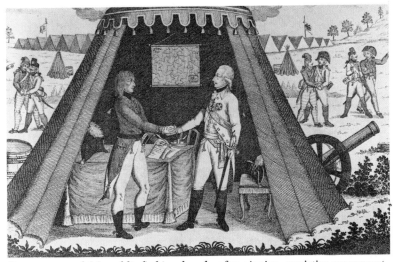

Bonaparte and Merveldt shaking hands after signing armistice agreement.

Leoben, April 18

Bonaparte does just as he likes. He has just signed an armistice at two o'clock in the morning with the representative of the Austrian government, Merveldt, even though the Directory did not empower him to do any such thing. Normally, it would be up to the plenipotentiary Clarke, now in Turin, to conclude such agreements. However, Clarke himself was not informed until the negotiations were completed.

After repulsing the Austrian troops and conquering Veneto, Bonaparte took the step of moving the French advance guard commanded by Masséna forward as far as Leoben, 150 kilometres from the capital. Since Vienna was threatened, the Archduke Charles agreed to the proposal for negotiations that the French general made to him in order to avoid further bloodshed. Moreover, the proposed accord was advantageous to the Austrians. Bonaparte left the choice up to them: they could either agree to cede Belgium and Milan to France, receiving in exchange Mantua, Dalmatia and Venetian Istria, as well as the Venetian mainland territories as far as the Adda, or they could keep Lombardy but would have to yield the left bank of the Rhine, in addition to Belgium, in exchange for the same Venetian provinces, with the exception of the mainland provinces, which Bonaparte awarded to them only as far as the Tagliamento.

The first solution was adopted, for even if the Austrians set great store by Lombardy, they still prefer to keep the left bank of the Rhine in order to maintain their prestige in Germany. They care little about Belgium. The Directory will probably not appreciate these peace terms. Why accept them when Moreau's and Hoche's Rhine forces are moving? Bonaparte wants to impose his own policy (→ April 30).

Championnet avenges Marceau's death

Altenkirchen, April 18

In a war of constant movement, Hoche's takeover of the Sambre and Meuse Army has finally borne fruit. Werneck's Austrians have been beaten at the same place where Marceau was killed a year ago. The winner, Major General Championnet, was not far from Cologne, while his superior, Jourdan, had opened the road from Frankfurt to Nuremberg. Now Championnet is near Neuwied, a major Austrian stronghold. In accordance with the instruction issued by Hoche, the French general is attempting, for the moment, to get the bulk of Werneck's forces to move away in order to make it possible to enter the town of Neuwied.

The second victorious French crossing of the Rhine River, near Neuwied.

Juliette Récamier, Longchamp queen

Paris, April

At the famous Longchamp processions, at which the elegant ladies like to display themselves, Juliette Récamier in her open carriage hit onlookers with all the force of a young goddess coming down from Mount Olympus. Spectators were impressed by the simplicity of her dress, as well as by her ravishing beauty. A halo of white muslin emphasised her svelte body, and the only ornament around her neck was a discreet necklace of delicate pearls. This commitment to naturalness, this refusal to display her wealth, this taste for white give Juliette a style all her own. In our ostentatious age, when everybody parades his wealth, her simple garb surprises and delights Paris. She gives an impression of miraculous purity, on which she capitalises marvellously. Juliette is tall and slender, with a mastery of languid positions, graceful movements, and pleasant expressions. However, her perfectly oval face reminds us of an Italian Renaissance madonna.

Pichegru betrayed by papers found on Austrian general

Rhine, April 22

Pichegru was indeed a traitor. This has just been discovered by General Moreau, who commands the Rhine and Moselle Army. The French troops' advance and their victories sometimes have surprising consequences. When crossing the Rhine two days ago in Hoche's wake, Moreau seized the evidence of this betrayal from Klinglin, a captured Austrian general. The documents now in his possession make out a very serious case against Pichegru. They confirm that the general, who was relieved of his duties a little more than a year ago because he was suspected of cooperating with the enemy, was indeed preparing a royalist move against the Republic. However, it is now a matter of seeing whether Moreau will send this information to the Directory. We are referring to the fact that many people doubt his republican loyalty (→June 1).

Bonaparte's troops put rough end to "Verona Easter" revolt

Verona, April 27

Napoléon Bonaparte's soldiers have put a rough end to the Verona insurrection. The troubles began, especially in Verona, on Easter Monday, April 17th. The population was profoundly exasperated because of the French occupation and the exesses of the soldiers and the Directory's representatives, who did not pass up the chance to loot art treasures. Hostility to France was all the greater amongst the country's aristocratic élite in that the French Jacobins, allied with the Italian patriots, were pushing the people into revolting against their leaders. French agitators brought about revolutions in the cities of Bergamo, Brescia and Crema in March, and thcse upheavals led to a furious reaction on the part of the ruling aristocracy.

That is probably the main explanation for the uprising that led to the massacre of almost four hundred French people in Verona. The villagers living in the surrounding area led the insurgents, and the occupiers had to endure a veritable

"Verona Easter" a spontaneous insurrection or a French provocation?

siege for a week in the citadel. On April 18th., a French vessel entering the harbour at the Lido in Venice was fired on.

It is said that provocations carried out by General Bonaparte's secret agents encouraged this insurrection. That is unlikely, even if the "Verona Easter" gives the general an ideal opportunity for declaring war on the Venetian Republic. The latter had so far sought refuge in neutrality that might have become benevolent vis-à-vis Austria. After suppressing the revolt with some bloodshed and executing the rebels, Bonaparte has a *casus belli* he is going to hold onto, to the point of rejecting the excuses presented by the Venetian Senate.

Princely whiteskins visit the redskins

Tennessee, April 30

A very unusual event took place here recently: some Frenchmen visited an Indian tribe. Indeed, the visitors were princes of the blood. Louis Philippe d'Orléans and his brothers, the Duc de Montpensier and the Duc de Beaujolais, had been forced into exile and had not seen each other since the arrest of their father, Philippe Egalité. They got together in January in Philadelphia. Delighted with the idea of adventure, they decided to set off to discover their host country. Today they reached the goal of their trip, the small village of Pokoma in Cherokee Indian territory. They tried the Indians' *tahuma*, a kind of tobacco made from appona leaves that the men smoke all day while sitting in front of their wigwams. Their women, wrapped in hides, perform their household duties, with their babies wrapped in odd bags they carry on their backs. The three royal brothers are delighted with all this. Could they hope for any greater change of scene to forget their exile?

All kinds of businesses co-exist in the wooden galleries in the Palais Royal. The palace is also a popular meeting point and place for walks. The nearly Tuileries Gardens have been redone and are now open to the public.

May 1797
from 1st. to 31st.

The Belvedere Apollo is awaited in Paris

Rome, May 5

The precious shipment will go by way of the city of Leghorn in order to avoid the bumpiness that would result from going over the Apennines. The Commissioners Moitte, Tinet and Monge, who were asked to inventory Italian art masterpieces, informed the Ministry of Foreign Affairs that they were sending a another shipment of art objects. Among other things, the shipment contains two priceless marble statues, the *Laocoon* and the celebrated *Belvedere Apollo*. The latter is a Roman copy of a Greek original. Its proportions and its classic elegance have made this statue a fine model of the ancient world's concept of virile beauty.

The various ancient statues found in front of the Louvre's Small Gallery include, on the left, one of the three castings in France of the Belvedere Apollo, the original of which will soon be brought back from Italy.

A tree of freedom is planted in India

India, May 15

In Seringapatam, the alliance between France and Mysore was hailed by a fantastic cannonade. Some 2,300 rounds were fired from the Pattane fort to conclude the ceremony marking the event, in the presence of the Indian prince, Sultan Tippoo Sahib, and the privateer captain François Fidèle Ripaud of Montaudevert. The Réunion privateer's visit to the Indian capital has given rise in France's old ally to hope of a landing by troops to support it in its war against the English. The symbol of this pact is a tree of liberty put up on Arms Square. It was planted by the local Jacobin Club, created by Ripaud from among members of the Franco-Indian community which has been living in Mysore serving the citizen-prince since the Treaty of Paris of 1763.

English North Fleet is hit by mutinies

England, May 2

The English crews of the Northern Fleet have defied their leaders and run up the red flag. Their revolt was inspired by Richard Parker, one of them, who is well-known as an active sympathiser of the Irish patriot Wolfe Tone.

The rebellion follows one on April 15th. that hit the Channel Fleet, moored in Portsmouth. The English sailors are tired of the war with France. The British government, which still hopes for an advantageous peace, is still eager for combat. However, its Navy suffered some sharp reverses in the Mediterranean and Puerto Rico last month, and the troops' morale is flagging as a result. Furthermore, the sailors are having trouble getting their pay, and discipline is too strict. All this has set fire to the powder-keg (→June 14).

Americans accuse philosopher Volney as spy for France

Philadelphia, May 2

Things are getting worse every day for the French philosopher Volney. He came to the new world to make a simple study trip west of the Ohio River, but he has involuntarily become an object of suspicion on the part of American public opinion. The main reason for the ostracism he is suffering is simply the fact that he is a French citizen. An aggravating circumstance is his friendship with Talleyrand, who has also attracted attention in a regrettable way. His talks at the Institute have been called subversive, and he is reproached with allegedly having intrigued in the West.

For the time being America has chosen the philosopher Volney as its target, accusing him of being a spy, without any proof. Through its impulsive president, John Adams, it is attacking France, a country it views as having been unable to attain freedom. In the face of growing hostility and in the light of his failure to clear his name, Volney is thinking of leaving. Moreover, he has been disappointed in the country, where he hoped to find real liberty, as he has just written.

Méhul work scores measure of discord

Paris, May 3

At first sight, it would seem another display of audience fickleness. At the Favart theatre the day before yesterday, the audience was so angry and noisy that singer de Saint Aubin, a woman used to appreciation from the public, broke down in tears. But this evening, those same spectators, their hands hurting from long applause, were filled with raving enthusiasm. All this was for the same work, a Méhul opera called *Young Henry*. The sudden about-turn is not due to the composer or the singer. The crowd was annoyed with Bouilly, the libretto author, because of the insipid words and the obscure plot. The audience did not want Méhul to take the booing and whistling as aimed at him. Thus, spectators asked him to repeat the overture to his work at the concert tonight.

Venetian patriots in power, await French

Baraguey d'Hilliers' French troops entering Venice on May 15th.

Venice, May 12

After several agitated days, the Grand Council and the *Conferenza* yielded power. The Venetian patriots led by Pietro Zorzi and Andrea Spada, helped by the secretary of the French Legation in Venice, forced the Doge, Ludovico Manin, to leave the country. Napoléon Bonaparte had concentrated attention on Venice since the revolt in Verona, because he suspected the envoys of the Doge of having fomented that uprising. The Venetian authorities attempted to negotiate, having no way of defending themselves, but Bonaparte was intransigent. The government lost face, so it collapsed under the pressure exercised by the local representatives, who immediately instituted a new municipal government and are now waiting with impatience for the arrival of the French troops.

Privateer privatises piratical prizes

Paris, May 19

His intimidation campaign has just been crowned with success, and the happy epilogue to the *Emilie* affair finds Robert Surcouf recovering the proceeds of his prizes. To win this victory over Malartic, the governor of Ile de France, Surcouf did not hesitate to bring their dispute into the political arena, laying the case before the Directory. Enjoying the prestige resulting from his victories over the English, the privateer came to Paris with the expectation of being able to nullify his opponent's legal arguments. Nevertheless, Surcouf violated the rules of privateer warfare by attacking ships without having prior written authorisation from the Admiralty. Hence he acted as a pirate, not as a privateer. If the English had captured him, he risked losing his prizes and a hanging.

After welcoming Surcouf as a hero, Malartic took his prizes away from him.

The royalists exploit their legislative win

Paris, May 20

The new majority is settling in. The royalists, with a win in the April elections under their belt, have just elected one of their own to preside over the Five Hundred: General Pichegru, who was removed from command in March 1796 because he was suspected of treason, a deputy from the Jura and a member of the Clichy Monarchist Club. As for the Council of Ancients, it has chosen Barbé Marbois as its presiding officer. It is said that he inspired the Duke of Brunswick's Austrian manifesto in 1792.

Now the two Councils have to elect a new Director. Under the Constitution, one of the five Directors must be replaced every year. While the parliamentarians have some room for manoeuvre in selecting presiding officers in line with their wishes, they will be unable to change the Directory majority. It will remain republican, since the triumvirate of Barras, Reubell and La Révellière will stay on the job. The lottery designated Letourneur for replacement. Thibaudeau, a moderate, would like the constitutional monarchists, such as Pas-

Royalist Barthélemy as Director.

toret, to put up a candidate determined to respect institutions, such as Beurnonville. All the same, the royalist deputies from Clichy, where the "White Jacobins" (who advocate re-establishing the old monarchy) dominate, are unlikely to agree to this solution. They have chosen Barthélemy as a candidate, and he is the representative of the Republic in Basel and well-known as a royalist.

An outgoing deputy, having made a mint, gives way to an avid new deputy.

The luck of the draw forces Charles Louis Letourneur to leave the Directory.

Babeuf and Darthé are guillotined

Vendôme, May 27

The jurors in the trial of the Equals issued their verdict yesterday, and Babeuf's main accomplices can call themselves lucky. Antonelle and Félix Le Peletier were acquitted, while Buonarroti and Germain were sentenced to deportation. As for Sylvain Maréchal, he was not even bothered. Only Babeuf and Darthé were sentenced to death for having tried to overthrow the régime and re-establish the Constitution of 1793.

The Directory had infiltrated one of its agents, Grisel, into the ranks of the Equals, and on the night of May 10th., 1796, Barras had more than 50 people suspected of involvement in the conspiracy arrested. Babeuf was found at home, where he was with Buonarroti, working out the final details of the planned insurrection. The trial of the 65 defendants finally began on February 20th., at the High Court of Justice of Vendôme -- and what a

trial! For three months there was an exchange of violent speeches between the prosecution and Babeuf and friends, who sometimes enjoyed considerable support from the public. Their terrible outbursts of anger, free-flowing language and way of rejecting the court's right to try them were in keeping with their fighting image. Germain distinguished himself by his passionate harangues. He particularly attacked Grisel, who said proudly that he deserved a civil crown for his denunciation. "That crown belongs to the victims," Germain cried to the audience's cheers. While Babeuf was limited by the defendants' joint decision to deny the charges, he spoke constantly. Although certain hearings were stormy, others were poignant, as the emotional leader of the plotters explained his doctrine and drew sobs from the audience. In their emotion, the spectators even took up revolutionary songs with them. When the verdict was an-

Babeuf fought to the very end.

nounced, it caused great tumult among the spectators. Buonarroti called on the people, while Babeuf and Darthé stabbed themselves and cried "Long live the Republic!" At dawn they were led, bloody, to pay the penalty on the scaffold.

Spy d'Antraigues on way to prison

Trieste, May 21

The Russian Legation's carriages fled from Venice as Bonaparte's forces approached, but they were soon overtaken at Trieste. The French soldiers invited the travellers to get out and took them to General Bernadotte. Among them was the Comte d'Antraigues, the French spy, who had fled from Venice with some very precious documents concerning his activities. When urged to name the people travelling with him, the count turned to a young woman carrying a baby in her arms: "Gentlemen, let me introduce you to the Comtesse d'Antraigues." So Bernadotte, who had thought he was arresting a dangerous individual, found himself facing a respectable father whose marriage had been kept secret. But no matter! D'Antraigues will be taken alone to the Milan prison. And his wife may follow him, if she really wants to (→June 1).

Venice looted by French troops, officials

Venice, end of May

After all, did Bonaparte himself not want the city to disappear? In spite of its Senate's entreaties, the opulent city of the Doges is suffering from avid hands. As if the troops' looting were not enough, the French commissioners arrived in turn to draw up an inventory of the things they would be taking away. No street, no church, no gallery is

overlooked. Even if the interest they take in the bronze horses on the façade of St Mark's Cathedral does not much disturb the Venetians, who stole them from Constantinople in the year 1204, the same does not apply to the *Martyrdom of St. Peter of Verona*, a Titian masterpiece the Venetians venerate, and one on which the French seem to have designs.

The "Vigier Baths" are very fashionable. In addition to relaxation, these establishments offer the attraction of numerous ladies of pleasure.

Will the Rhineland become independent?

Rhineland, May

The preliminary peace agreement of Leoben, which guaranteed the territorial integrity of the Holy Roman Empire, caused consternation among the Rhineland patriots, who were worried about an imminent return of the Ancien Régime. To ward off this danger, they decided to unite and swore to "live and die as free men". They want to

have the left bank of the Rhine separated from the Empire. The leaders of this movement, Görres, Mathias Metternich and Geich, immediately got into touch with Hoche. The latter received the following order from the Directory: help in the constitution of an independent state on the French side of the Rhine River, to be known as the Cisrhenan Republic.

Removal of the bronze horses from Saint Mark's by the French soldiers.

The moderates establish the Salm Club

Caricature of Salm Club members sharpening knives for use on royalists.

Paris, June 4

The republicans are getting organised in the face of the royalist offensive. Some of them established a "constitutional circle" today that is known as the Salm Club, from the name of the town house in which the meetings will be held. These moderates belong to the "non-terrorist" leftist camp or to the centre-left.

This means that, even if they are far removed from the Jacobins, they are greatly attached to the Republic all the same. This group intends to grow and take in a minority of leftist deputies, as well as some unelected figures. Mme. de Staël and Talleyrand, in particular, as well as Daunou and Tallien, are preparing to join (→July 25).

Bonaparte benefits from spying papers

Italy, June 1

The Comte d'Antraigues' fate is in Bonaparte's hands. The general plans to use to his own advantage the secret papers found on the count when he was arrested. They include a 33 page detailed account of the talk d'Antraigues had with a spy named Montgaillard. During that closed-door interview, the royalist informed d'Antraigues of the treachery of Pichegru, the presiding officer of the Council of Five Hundred. Unlike Moreau, who was warned about this treason as early as April, General Bonaparte now wants to reveal the news. He first took care to have the document "reworked", removing every single reference to himself, to have it signed by d'Antraigues. In the light of the uncomfortable position occupied by this nobleman, who is being held in Milan, it is thought that this signature should come in the rather near future (→Aug. 29).

The Saint Denis suburb: a lively part of the French capital

Paris, June

The lively Saint Denis suburb of the French capital lives, and it lives out of doors. Once people pass under Saint Martin's gate, which has an attic in poor condition and has been deprived of the inscriptions cut into the stone in honour of Louis XIV, and walk along the street, there are workers who have finished their day and embroideresses coming out of their garrets. In Indian sheath dresses and black taffeta aprons, they go along Saint Martin or Saint Denis Boulevard and up through the Percherons district to get to the Saint Laurent market. This market is actually a farm north of Paris. In the same area, there is also a trumpet school in the remains of the former Saint Lazare Convent. When the stroller comes back down the Rue Saint Denis to skirt the Innocents' market, where locals can buy ass's milk among other things, they are walking over what used to be Miracles Courtyard. Going back up to Saint Denis gate, the Courtille café offers some dancing and company.

Paris' Saint Denis suburb is filled with the shouts of hawkers and the rumble of carts going to the Halles market.

Religious freedom still controversial topic

Paris, June 17

"Carillon Jordan, Bells Jordan": these nicknames resulted from the first major speech in Parliament made by the young deputy from Lyons. While the nicknames were invented by his opponents, they may well make him popular among part of the population.

When Camille Jordan stood and went to the podium at the Council of Five Hundred to present the report written by the committee in charge of revising laws on religion, one major feature of his speech was the "bells issue". Current legislation still bans using church bells to summon the faithful to services. Jordan defended the peasants' right to be attached to their church bells. Why deprive them of an "innocent pleasure" found in "one of the most marked sources of enjoyment contained in their religion"?

However, he did not limit himself to this issue, which symbolises the limits on religious freedom as currently practised. He also urged abolition of the oath of acceptance of the Republic's laws demanded of priests. As for laws on the country's non-juring priests, the deputy Dubruel was entrusted with the task of demanding their repeal.

The proclamation of the Ligurian Republic in Genoa on June 14th.

Quiet life is for me, Bonaparte affirms

Milan, June 30

"I need a quiet life", says General Bonaparte. According to his own remarks, all Bonaparte wants is a restful existence with his wife, Joséphine. That is the message of a letter he sent today to the Directory, making sure this would become known. The letter expresses his indignation in response to some statements made on June 23rd. by the deputy Dumoulard, who accused the general publicly of inordinate ambition and of being "much too Jacobin to be honest". The young general has got to parry such attacks, and above all must maintain his popularity. While disclaiming any taste for success and power, Bonaparte is already casting his eyes on Egypt.

Fisticuffs featured in financial fighting

Paris, June 19

A big battle is raging in the Assembly, one that even features fisticuffs between the parliamentarians. Behind the fighting is the leftist deputies' denunciation of the actions of the Treasury, which they view as a "nest of counter-revolutionaries" because it takes advantage of its autonomy to force the Directory to change policy. Indeed, on June 9th., the royalist Gibert Desmolières submitted a report calling for the end of further credits to the government to force it to make peace with England. The right, saying it wants to put an end to the financial traffic between the ministries and the firms supplying the armed forces, actually wants to keep the executive from acting.

Ariège forge-workers on strike for rise

Heat, noise and many dangers make forge-work very exhausting but, above all, the wages that are paid are too low for these inflationary times.

Ariège, June 21

The forge-workers have walked out, demanding a 30 per cent wage boost to enable them to cope with the rising cost of living. They held a general meeting in the village of Tarascon to get organised, and they have just elected a committee to guide and centralise the movement. Each forge-worker will have to contribute one franc and pledge not to become a strike-breaker. Anybody who forgets or breaks his word will be immediately killed and his house will be burnt down. The forge-workers in the Aude and the Pyrénées Orientales took note of this instructive example and decided in turn to go on strike, organising themselves with a view to forcing employers to negotiate or cave in to their demands.

Tapestries tapped to bolster the budget

Paris, June 10

For the second time in less than two months, Villette, the manager of the National Property Office, has just carried out a very special mission: throwing prestigious tapestries into the flames. He explained that "this measure brings in money, without harming the Republic's interests". He then added: "I am even proud to say that it has been advantageous to the country, since the gold and silver materials that are contained in those hangings were unused values".

Last April 18th., he had carried out the same kind of operation successfully, with the interior minister's approval. In the report that was sent to him, which was entitled *A proposal for burning some old tapestries in order to finance government needs*, the official had suggested holding an auto-da-fé of such "old tapestries" on the basis that a large part of them dealt with what he regarded as indecent subjects, a fact that should interest the authorities. Unfortunately, however, it happens that out of the hundred or so works that have already perished in the flames under the programme, some were based on designs created by such artists as Albrecht Dürer, Charles Le Brun and Raphael.

General Bonaparte establishes a Cisalpine Republic in Milan

Banquet in Milan given by the Cisalpine Federation for General Bonaparte.

Milan, July 9

Bonaparte is recasting the map of Northern Italy off his own bat. He has just imposed a constitution inspired by the French model on the brand-new Cisalpine Republic, with a five member executive assisted by a Legislative Council. He plans to appoint the members himself, as he wants to ensure the new state's "loyalty" to France. The time is past when Bonaparte encouraged the Italian patriots to make their own revolution and to rise up against Austrian control, because he needed them to counter the coalition's plans. If he has now created the Cisalpine Republic in accordance with the secret provisions of the preliminary peace accord of Leoben that was signed with Austria, it is more with a desire to firm up his conquests in Italy than a question of spreading the Revolution. As of June 29th., Napoléon Bonaparte had proclaimed the independence of the Cisalpine, consisting of the former Cispadane Republic together with the Duchy of Modena, Carrara and Massa, to which he annexed Lombardy. This cavalier type of procedure, coming before the treaty with Austria has been signed, is forcing the hand of the French Directory, which actually has not yet accepted the peace terms involved in the arrangement.

Economic recovery efforts being made on Saint Domingue

Saint Domingue, July 5

These days, nothing is working on the island. The factories have been abandoned, and the indigenous workers have left. To remedy this situation and stimulate the economy, Colonel Vincent has allocated one of Stanislas Foache's sugar mills, in Jean Rabel, to three blacks working in partnership with a mulatto. Citizens Colas, Saint Pierre, Salomon and Larose got the facility farmed out to them for three years. They committed themselves for an annual income of 54,000 livres. Out of the plantation's 36 hectares, only two are planted with sugar-cane, compared with ten in 1787. Farming it out is part of the recovery plan being applied in the freed regions by Toussaint Louverture. The same approach will be adopted for all of the properties seized for the Republic's benefit. To get them to produce, civilian and military authorities had planned to send the former slaves back to their plantation jobs for one to three years. But for the time being, the black general has dropped that idea and introduced forced farm labour.

When the Director La Révellière Lépeaux reached the peak of his glory, he commissioned the painter Gérard to paint his portrait. The artist shows him in country costume on his Andilly estate, located near Montmorency.

Bonaparte sees self as the last resort

Milan, July 15

"I see that the Club of Clichy wants to walk over my dead body to manage destruction of the Republic," says General Bonaparte in a letter he has just sent to the Directory. The missive from the commanding general of the Army of Italy is a veritable republican profession of faith. Moreover, it leaves no doubt about Bonaparte's intention to intervene militarily if the institutions come under threat. He adds: "If you need force, call in the troops." However, the troops in question are literally galvanised by the speeches they hear from their leader, who fulminates constantly against the royalists. Yesterday the banquet that Bonaparte gave for his soldiers to mark July 14th. long resounded with echoes of toasts made to the Republic: "Mountains separate us from France. You would cross them with eagle speed, if need be, to defend the Constitution ... as well as liberty, and to protect the government and the republicans." When we note this, it would seem that if the military becomes the Directory's last resort, there is a risk of military dictatorship.

Pichegru a member of a Masonic lodge

Paris, July 14

The republicans are annoyed. Furthermore, they indicated this by publishing a violent diatribe against Pichegru today in the *Free Men's Newspaper*. The reason is that this man elected to the Council of Five Hundred, after banning the republicans' public and constitutional meetings, has just joined a Masonic lodge. After all, is this philanthropic organisation not involved in politics? Are its meetings not also an occasion for discussions? Apparently this paradox did not embarrass the general. Nothing else was needed for the republicans to be led to view Freemasonry as a den of royalists. Even if such an attack is unfounded in fact, Pichegru's action in joining the "brothers" proves, all the same, that the present French government can no longer be said to share the Jacobins' bias against the Masons and their lodges.

The generals are called in to rescue the French Republic

Paris, July 18

Republican reaction is in full swing. The Councils were informed that the troops led by General Hoche were moving toward Ferté Alais, near Corbeil, and were inside the "constitutional perimeter", the area around Paris into which the armed forces have no right to move without the Assembly's authorisation. The deputies Jean Pierre Delahaye and Louis Paul Maillard informed the Five Hundred of this development. Camille Jordan then took the floor to denounce what he called a "plot" hatched by the Di-

Talleyrand is replacing Delacroix.

rectory to "assassinate" the Councils. The latter were already worried about the fact that the Police and War Ministers, Cochon and Petiet, were replaced two days ago. It seemed to them that this removal of two of Carnot's close friends, who were favourable to the Clichy meeting of monarchists, presaged an attack by the Directory's republican majority. The triumvirate consisting of Barras, La Révellière and Reubell seem in fact, to have decided to strike a blow against the Catholic and royalist renewal that is taking shape by using forces faithful to the Republic.

However, the monarchists have no intention of letting the other side get the better of them. They are counting on Carnot's backing to counter the triumvirate's initiative. Carnot has already established contact with General Pichegru to consider ways of resisting the republican offensive. After a proposal made by Portalis and Tronson Ducoudray, there is now talk of framing an indictment of Barras, La Révellière and Reubell. One could remove them from power by having them arrested, since they violated the Constitution by allowing troops to enter the safety perimeter set up

Barras, the executive's strongman.

to protect the Assembly. Military power would be turned over to Pichegru, who supports the royalist cause. The local administrations would probably not resist such a move strongly, as they have ignored republican legislation for a long time. Still, such a plan needs Carnot's support, and he is said to be reluctant. People say he has refused to yield to Pichegru's demand that the latter be allowed to name the three new Directors who would replace the triumvirate. Tension remains very strong, for the time being (→July 19).

Fireworks at Tivoli Park over further performances by Ruggieri

Paris, July 17

If one is to believe the public, "three thousand lights in two seconds" lighted up the Paris night thanks to Ruggieri's fireworks magic. However, the show ended on a discouraging note this evening for the famous pyrotechnician. Desrivières, the current manager of Tivoli Park, demanded that the ar-

tist turn over all his receipts, under penalty of not being allowed to perform in the park again.

This park, also known as Folie Boutin from the name of the former owner, who was guillotined during the Reign of Terror, is a paradise. The garden is spread out over 40 *arpents* of greenery at the corner of Saint Lazare and Clichy Streets, in

a district in which the chimneys of the workshops adjoin church bell-towers without spires. There are rare plants, Dutch flowers, exotic fruits in hothouses, an open-air sitting room, a rotunda, and cascades escaping from the Temple of Hercules. The park attracts hundreds of visitors for the band and to see the tightrope walker Cabanel.

Tivoli Park, one of the amusement centres patronised by the "Incredibles", has also been used as a wallpaper motif. ▷

Redouté, Nature's water-colourist

Even though he had been one of Marie Antoinette's teachers, Joseph Redouté had no trouble during the Revolution. Botany is his only passion. An innate feeling for nature and plants, together with a great talent for water-colours, brought him the esteem of the scientific community, as well as commissions. He has worked on the series of *Original Vellums of the Museum*, which adds a dozen plates every year with the most noteworthy plants that flowered during the season in the Museum garden.

"Clematis, pansies, daisies and cyclamen", by Joseph Redouté.

Law passed to close constitutional circles

Paris, July 25

The two Councils have had their way. The Ancients have approved the bill voted two days ago by the Council of Five Hundred that orders suppression of the popular societies, namely, of any private meetings concerning themselves with politics. As was to be expected, the Directory did not make any objection to the measure. It was the Directory, in fact, that had encouraged creation of the constitutional circles, consisting essentially of republicans. In this way it wanted to balance the royalist and Catholic moves, as well as to channel the rebirth of a neo-Jacobin opposition.

Actually, the groups in question brought together a number of moderate republicans, certainly more liberal than extremist, as well as numerous well-known figures such as Mme. de Staël, Tallien, Sieyès and Benjamin Constant. The triumvirate may have accepted the ban because they feared coming under strong attack from the left in the struggle they have begun with the rightist majority in the Assembly. However, it may also be a move aimed at reassuring the royalist deputies and at trying to head off the move that those deputies are now planning to make against the Directory.

Writer Rivarol booked by irate publisher

Hamburg, July 30

Rivarol is as lazy as he is malicious. It was a major effort for him to finish *A preliminary discourse on the new dictionary of the French language*. He has just had it published in Germany, since the slim work is banned in France. One can easily understand that, in view of the fact that Rivarol uses its few pages to curse the Revolution, the cause of his exile, and violently criticises the Reign of Terror while defending Christianity -- all this in rhetoric-laden prose.

He has also begun, with difficulty, to write his new *Dictionary of the French language*, which the Hamburg printer-bookseller Fauche had asked him to write. Fauche became enraged at not getting the manuscript he had been promised a score of times, which was paid for in advance, and he has "jailed" Rivarol in his house in Hamm, posted two guards on the doorstep, and made off with the key. The prisoner can get out only in the evening, after having given his jailers three or four hand-written pages. In spite of having having hired two secretaries, our man is working no faster. He chats with them while smoking aloe and imbibing wine, spouting nonsense to stir up their ideas. Writing gets put off.

Mounier to educate German officialdom

Weimar, July

A man who chose exile in 1790 because the Revolution had rejected the constitutional monarchy for which he hoped is now going to be able to enjoy a better life. The former barrister Mounier has always refused to serve France's enemies, and this has put him in dire financial straits. However, the Duke of Weimar has expressed a desire to settle Mounier on his estates. He has proposed that Mounier should set up a school in one of the ducal castles for training future civil servants and administrators. Mounier will teach philosophy and law, as well as history, in the future establishment.

Bourges is angry with the Directory

Bourges, July 17

"We want bells, not clubs!" The inhabitants of Bourges used this energetic formula to express their anger at the Directory, in general, and municipal authorities in particular. During the night they pasted up a large number of posters with this message. They are fed up with sacrilegious and official remarks made against the former cathedral. They no longer know whether their priests will still be there tomorrow. This is not an isolated instance, and it is a good illustration of the feeling shared by a large number of citizens: the Republic's attitude towards the Church is exaggerated.

Capital carriages are driving too fast

The simple and elegant republican carriages, light as a breeze and fast as lightning, split the air with a thundering noise as they race along. If they were not an appendage of happy times, their uniformity would have something democratic about it. The driver, perched very high, urges the horses on to ever greater efforts. Does his position, above humanity, make him forget that he is driving through an inhabited city, rather than an Olympic arena? The Central Office vainly multiplies orders for carriages to slow down. When a pedestrian is run down, the people, who have a secret admiration for those fine carriages and horses, do not dare complain.

The middle class is wild about high speeds of carriages.

August 1797

from 1st. to 31st.

Bonaparte's "right arm" to command the Paris military

Paris, August 8

The putsch will be a republican one. The Directory has just appointed General Augereau of the army of Italy as commandant of the 17th. Military Division, the Paris division. This officer, fiercely attached to the Republic, is trusted by Napoléon Bonaparte. Already, in July, Barras had had an order approved that authorised part of Hoche's troops to cross the territory, on the basis that they were to be part of an expedition to Ireland. This arrangement, set up with a view to an offensive against the monarchists in Parliament, should be supplemented by the appointment of Chérin, one of Hoche's generals, to head the Directory's guard. Thus the bulk of the army is putting itself at the triumvirate's service.

The Republic finds itself at a crossroads

Augereau supports the Directors.

Paris, August 10

The fifth anniversary of French royalty's overthrow was observed in a tense atmosphere. In a public message, the Directory attacked counter-revolutionaries, and especially their numerous accomplices in the Councils, accusing them of wanting to wipe out the republicans. Carnot, as head of the Directory, read the message. The proclamation appeared paradoxical coming from him, as he and Letourneur disagree with the "triumvirate" consisting of the other Directors. It is even said that the royalists recently persuaded him to support their cause. Today, however, Carnot came down on the republicans' side, describing the "war to the death" that he would not hesitate to launch if there were an attempt to re-establish "the inequality of conditions and the feudal institutions on which monarchies are based". He also reaffirmed the five Directors' solidarity: "The Republic's first magistrates may differ in their opinions, but they will always be united when it is necessary to defend it." He obviously wanted to give a speech on behalf of consensus before consolidating the Republic.

With Sénac de Meilhan, the émigré becomes hero of a novel

Vienna, August

Gabriel Sénac de Meilhan has rediscovered the spirit of Paris salons in the Austrian capital, and he likes it here. Moreover, he has just published an historical novel called *The Emigré*, which draws much of its inspiration from the circles he frequents. One finds several strands in this book. First of all, there is the story of a love affair between a young émigré wounded in fighting the republicans and a young German noblewoman who shelters him in her castle. There is also some social commentary, as Sénac emphasises the Gothic nature of the German nobility and the feeling of solidarity uniting French émigrés in adversity. The work is also a political novel in which the characters have long discussions of events in France. And, finally, it is also an autobiography, in which the author has put a lot of himself into two characters: Comte de Saint Alban, who represents the epicurean he once was, and President de Long-ueil, who incarnates the sage he became. Sénac, now over 60, has already had a long writing career. He was an official of the Paris parliament and royal quartermaster, and became known in the literary world in 1786 by publishing *Memoirs of Anne de Gonzague*. He wrote *Considerations on the mind and manners*, attacking some of Necker's doctrines, and then emigrated in 1791, travelling quite widely in Europe before taking up residence in Vienna.

Boulevard des Italiens, known as "Little Coblentz", where émigrés meet.

An illustration from "The Emigré".

Hoche tired out by illness and infighting

General Hoche, only 29 years old.

Wetzlar, August 2

General Lazare Hoche will not be the man who saves the Republic. When he returned to his headquarters, accompanied by his wife and his one-year-old daughter, his men found him thinner and pale. The commanding general of the Sambre and Meuse Army is obvi-ously exhausted. His tiredness is due both to the progress of his lung disease and to deep disgust with political manocuvring. Heart-sick at the atmosphere of hate and sus-picion reigning in the capital, the pacifier of the Vendée resigned on July 22th. as War Minister, a post he had held for only a week. He ex-plained the move as being due to his youth, but did not fool anybody. The young republican general left the portfolio to General Schérer because the disagreements among the Directors were so obvious that he could not hope to obtain the Directory's backing, much less the support of the Councils. He was sharply accused by Carnot of hav-ing led troops astray on an uncon-stitutional path, and found himself without the means of opposing roy-alists. Yet he accepted Barras' pro-posal that he should lead a new ex-pedition to Ireland, since he under-stood that he could serve the Re-public most effectively on the bat-tlefield, not in Paris. At least, that is the way things are as long as his health lets him work (→ Sept. 19).

"Regent" diamond is pawned for loan

Berlin, August 12

The most beautiful "crown jewel of France" has been pledged as se-curity by the Republic in exchange for a loan from the Berlin banker Treskow. The banker, fearing his client's possible insolvency, insisted on the Regent diamond as a guaran-tee that the loan would be repaid. After some discussion, the Direc-tory agreed to the financier's terms. The diamond is perfectly white, and its only flaws are two slight nicks that are invisible to the naked eye. It weighs a massive 140.5 carats and is estimated to be worth almost 12 million francs.

The money will be used to ensure the financing of some 10,000 Bran-denburg horses for the cavalry. Other valuable diamonds, such as the Sancy, will be used as security for loans from other foreign banks, and some will be sold. Two envoys will be sent to offer some precious stones to the Sultan of Constantin-ople. Thus, to bolster its finances and meet war costs, the Republic has had to resort to using the treas-ures accumulated by the monarchy.

Sonthonax expelled by Saint Domingue

Saint Domingue, August 24

The conflict between General Toussaint Louverture and the Di-rectory's representative, Sontho-nax, came to an end today. Sontho-nax was asked to leave the island on August 17th., and he has just been put on a ship by force by the man who was his friend for three years. The expulsion is explained by the desire expressed by Toussaint Louverture, the current comman-der in chief of the French armed forces on Saint Domingue, to fol-low an autonomous policy, without necessarily taking directives from Paris into account. The violent campaign waged in France against the black and mulatto generals, who are lumped together by the refugee colonists, had annoyed the black general to an ever greater extent. Seen from a distance, the recent events in Paris made him fear a return of the Ancien Régime. Hence he put defence of the black revolution above French interests. Sonthonax was the first target, due to his position. He will return to his seat in the Five Hundred.

Parisian churches divided between the Roman and Constitutional Catholics

Saint Sulpice, one of the churches used by the Constitutional faithful.

Paris, August 16

The parish feast at Saint Roch Church in Paris was celebrated with pomp that had not been seen for years. The ceremony attracted a large crowd, since Saint Roch serves as an unofficial cathedral for Roman Catholics, Notre Dame be-ing assigned to the Constitutional Catholics. The latter have been able to establish themselves in the most important Paris churches, thanks to the relative approval they enjoy on the authorities' part. In addition to Notre Dame, they have obtained Saint Merri, Saint Sulpice, Saint Etienne du Mont and Saint Ger-main l'Auxerrois. The "Papists", who were less fortunate, remained confined to small sanctuaries for a long time, and particularly to cha-pels of former convents, such as the one of the Filles Dieu in Montor-gueil Street and the Christian In-struction Chapel in Pot de Fer Street. However, they recently ob-tained two larger buildings: Saint Thomas d'Aquin Church and Saint Eustache Church. Most of the cler-gy of those two churches have withdrawn the oaths of allegiance they swore.

Jews act on debts

Paris, August 24

No legal measures were adopted to settle the status of the Jewish communities' debts after the com-munities were dissolved by virtue of the Emancipation Decree of Sep-tember 1791. This situation worries the communities as much as it does their creditors. The Jews filed a petition today with the Council of Five Hundred requesting the nationalisation of their debts, since their property has become national property. The Council is favour-able, but wants to be coaxed.

One can be flirtatious without being eccentric at the same time.

Lodoïska mourns for her beloved Louvet

Paris, August 25

"Thank God I'm finishing my life before the Republic" were the last words spoken by Louvet de Couvray, who was carried off today by consumption. He was assisted in his final moments by Marie Joseph Chénier, the only one of his friends to have survived the Reign of Terror. His wife, Lodoïska, was in despair and tried to kill herself by swallowing opium. However, she failed, thus surviving the man she had loved since she was a teenager, the novelist who had made her the heroine of *Amours du chevalier de Faublas*. They returned from exile after Thermidor and accumulated a nestegg by publishing *Quelques notices pour servir à l'histoire de mes périls*, an account of Louvet's banishment. This enabled the couple to open a bookshop in the arcades of Palais Royal, while Louvet became a member of the Five Hundred. Now Lodoïska has decided to give up her business and will supervise a lottery given by the Assembly.

Major survey being made of the French

Paris, August 26

What are the main components of the French population? What is the nature of the inhabitants' business and professional activities? What measures would be appropriate in order to stimulate the economy? These are some of the questions contained in the major statistical survey at national level launched by the Interior Minister, François de Neufchâteau. His colleague, Prony, will analyse the results and interpret the figures. The departmental authorities, assisted by the land register offices, will have to survey people by age and sex in order to calculate growth and fertility rates. It will also be necessary to distinguish between workers and non-workers, and to determine the nature of the workers' jobs, where they work, and the nature of their working and living conditions. Finally, the statistical description, which must display the greatest possible accuracy, will have to lead to economic growth proposals.

D'Antraigues flees from Italian prison

Milan, August 29

The Comte d'Antraigues has just escaped. He had been arrested on May 21th. when he tried to leave Italy, and finally signed the document incriminating Pichegru. In exchange, Bonaparte arranged for considerably better detention conditions for the count in Milan. He was transferred to the Andreotti Palace, where his wife and his son joined him, and only a dozen soldiers were guarding him at the end. He was even allowed to take walks in the city without an escort. However, such privileges were not enough for him. Making use of the make-up talents of his wife, a former actress, d'Antraigues disguised himself as a clergyman and easily got clear of his "gilded cage". Still, his new freedom is actually more like an exile, as he is now quite compromised with the émigré royalists, having given Bonaparte a document betraying royalist secrets. Now, he will have to try to do without the royalists' help (→ Feb. 24, 98).

Republicans, royalists prepare for clash

Paris, August 31

The republicans are arming, and so are the royalists. The republican generals Augereau and Chérin, in violation of the constitutional provision against unauthorised troops in the Paris region, have brought 5,000 to 6,000 troops into the capital, as well as rifles and artillery. They have also authorised some former officers cashiered for Jacobinism to return to Paris, where they are devoting themselves to seeking out royalist "black collars". The enemy camp is also on the alert. The majority of the constitutional monarchists still hesitate to become involved in an open conflict with the Directory, and such moderates as Thibaudeau are trying to calm people down. Others, however, have decided to swing into action, particularly in Pichegru's entourage. Willot has found several thousand volunteers devoted to the monarchist cause, who are ready to march on the Luxembourg Palace. D'André has got arms, thanks to money supplied by the Englishman Wickham. The Directory is multiplying conciliatory measures in order to keep from being elbowed out by the right, and because it trusts neither Carnot nor Letourneur, who could betray it. So it did not protest against the law on the National Guard, which the royalists hope to use for a coup d'état. All the same, a conflict is imminent (→ Sept. 4).

Bookman Barba fined for pirating work

Paris, August 31

The Paris bookseller Barba is not afraid of illegality or being caught out. He published Jean François de La Harpe's *On Fanaticism in the Revolutionary Language* without permission and has been sentenced to pay damages of 1,125 livres but that does not bother him. He had already had some legal problems in the past. Fabre d'Eglantine's widow, for instance, won a law suit she brought against him. However, that warning did not persuade him to put an end to what is a very profitable kind of business.

The authors of genre scenes no longer hesitate to deal with the lower classes. Here, for instance, the artist shows linen maids going to bed, in a style inspired by scenes from antiquity.

1 *(Fructidor 15, Year V)*
Paris. The Directory, informed by Fouché's police, has the royalist deputy Raffet arrested. He was planning to assassinate Barras and Reubell.

3 *(Fructidor 17, Year V)*
Paris. On the eve of the putsch, the Comte de Frotté and the royalist general staff dine at a restaurant in the Rue du Bac. The republican General Augereau eats with his officers on the upper floor.

4 *(Fructidor 18, Year V)*
Paris. Augereau moves before the royalists and has troops occupy the capital. →

5 *(Fructidor 19, Year V)*
Paris. Following a request by the Directory, the Assembly approves a series of repressive laws. →

8 *(Fructidor 22, Year V)*
Paris. Merlin de Douai and François de Neufchâteau are elected Directors, replacing the directors Barthélemy and Carnot.

10 *(Fructidor 24, Year V)*
Paris. General Hoche is given command of all French troops in Germany (→ 19).

18 *(2nd supplementary day)*
Lille. The English diplomat Malmesbury leaves the negotiating table in the face of French intransigence following the triumvirate's victory.

19 *(3rd supplementary day)*
Austria. At the Directory's request, the Austrians release General La Fayette, who was imprisoned in Slovakia in the Olmütz fortress.

22 *(Vendémiaire 1, Year VI)*
Germany. A ceremony is held during which General Marceau's remains are exhumed and cremated in the troops' presence, before being put into a commemorative pyramid on Petersberg designed by his friend Kléber.

23 *(Vendémiaire 2, Year VI)*
Paris. General Moreau, whom the Directory suspects of collusion with the royalists, is dismissed from the Army.

24 *(Vendémiaire 3, Year VI)*
Paris. End of the National Council of the Constitutional Church. The bishops make an appeal for reunification of the Church and suggest the use of French in the liturgy.

30 *(Vendémiaire 9, Year VI)*
Paris. In the interest of a healthier financial situation, the Directory liquidates part of the public debt. →

Army putsch saves French Republic

General Augereau's troops invest the Tuileries Gardens, without any clashes.

Paris, September 4

The Army has just saved the triumvirate and the Republic. This morning at seven o'clock the military operation was over. Yesterday some new troops, commanded by Augereau and called in by La Révellière, Barras and Reubell, moved into the restricted area in and around Paris, from which the military is barred without authorisation, in order to occupy Paris. In just three days there was such a press of events as to do away with the last scruples of the three republicans in the Directory. On September 1st., they discovered the plot being hatched by the deputy Raffet, who planned to have Barras and Reubell killed. The plotter was arrested on the spot, and the next day the government recalled General Moreau, who was suspected of complicity with the royalists. Yet the latter did not give up, and the Club of Clichy decided to go into action at once. On the night of September 2nd., the deputy Vaublanc proposed that the triumvirs be indicted. Some Chouans commanded by La Trémoille were to march on the Luxembourg Palace with the National Guard and some of the dragoon regiments. However, Vaublanc asked to be given enough time to write the speech in which he would denounce the triumvirate.

The delay was fatal. The Directory, informed of these machinations by Fouché's secret police, decided to trigger a preventative military putsch. Carnot was warned of what was in the wind and managed to flee from the capital. However, the main royalist deputies in the Councils, including Barthélemy, Willot and Pichegru, were jailed. The triumvirs had posters put up around Paris reporting on the revelations that Comte d'Antraigues made to Bonaparte, and on others made by Duverne de Presle, a member of a monarchist conspiracy. The posters, indicating royalist contacts with England, may discredit them.

General Verdière arresting Willot (3), Bourdon (4), Rovère (5), Jourdan (6), Pichegru (7) and Boissy d'Anglas (8).

Directory has exceptional measures voted

After his dreams of glory, Pichegru is experiencing the reality of prison.

Neufchâteau: Interior Minister.

Paris, September 5

The consequences of the putsch are wide-ranging. The Directory has just had its power-play ratified by getting the Councils to approve a series of exceptional measures of very debatable legality. The few deputies attending the session were hardly powerful enough to put up the slightest resistance. In addition to the arrests of 65 journalists and right-wing leaders, and of the Directors Carnot and Barthélemy, the government has arranged for the banishment of 11 members of the Five Hundred and of the same number of Ancients' members. Every single one of them is to be deported. The second portion of this law of Fructidor 19 concerns the last elections for the Assembly. They were quashed in 49 departments which chose a royalist majority. On the other hand, when the elections were contested but favourable to the re-publicans, they were systematically upheld. Altogether, the Councils are losing 177 deputies. The elections for judges and departmental and municipal authorities were also ruled invalid in 53 of the departments. The Directory will appoint replacements for these officials until Year VI.

Furthermore, the law of Brumaire 3, Year IV, concerning émigrés and non-juring priests, has been re-established. What is now to be expected is a veritable "terrorist" offensive aimed against the Catholics and émigrés who have come back to France. All the laws that the right passed on behalf of the Church have been abrogated. By taking discretionary police powers, the Directory has, in fact, instituted a kind of republican dictatorship.

Merlin is replacing Barthélemy.

The republican government is refurbished

Paris, September

The republicans are consolidating their power. They have had two republicans elected to replace the Directors Barthélemy and Carnot. In accordance with the Constitution, this choice was made by the Ancients on the basis of a list of candidates, drawn up by the Council of Five Hundred, on which two faithful friends of General Bonaparte were also listed: Generals Augereau and Masséna. Finally, François de Neufchâteau and Merlin de Douai were designated. The former had been at the Interior Ministry for six weeks. He is a secondary figure, somewhat odd, but a triumvirate supporter. As for Merlin de Douai, who has been a minister since the beginning of the Directory, he has experience as an eminent jurist, even if he has never displayed a lot of personality. The right and the moderates hate him because he drew up the 1793 law on suspects, on which the Reign of Terror was based. Still, he did not remain a Jacobin, all the same, and makes it a point of honour to fight his former friends. The Belgian Lambrechts was appointed to his position at Justice, while Letourneux, a former Directory commissioner in Loire Inférieure, succeeds François de Neufchâteau.

For the rest, the government had been reshuffled last July 16th. to the republicans' benefit and did not need to be modified. Talleyrand had already proved his ability at Foreign Affairs, although he still has a reputation as a highly devious operator. The former Admiral Pléville Le Pelley, who is more a technician than a politician, is appointed to the Navy Ministry. Sotin de La Coindière had replaced Lenoir Laroche at the Ministry of Police on July 26th. A former Nantes revolutionary leader, he helped in the putsch. General Schérer became Minister of War on July 23rd. The republican Directory is ensured.

Barras, Reubell and La Révellière shown as "saviours of the fatherland".

Republic saved by putsch, press claims

Paris, September

The putsch of Fructidor 18 was the only way of saving the Republic, which was threatened by a royalist plot. At least, that is the version of events that the Directors are trying to get across by way of a certain press serving the power structure's interests. The main instrument in this campaign is an effective one. It is a letter from the man calling himself Louis XVIII, or rather, from his trusted agent, the Comte d'Avaray. The letter, addressed to Joseph de Maistre, the royalist author of *Considerations on France* living in Turin, was intercepted by Bonaparte's general staff in Milan. It mentions Louis XVIII's satisfaction with the book, which predicts that he will soon come to the throne. It also says that he has taken good note of the desire expressed by the Savoyard writer, who is now a Sardinian subject, to "become French and serve the King of France". Is this not irrefutable proof of the plot?

Château Lafite sold to Batavian envoy

Pauillac, September 11

The previous buyer was insolvent, and Jean de Witt, the Batavian Republic's ambassador to the Swiss authorities, took advantage of the reappearance of the Château Lafite estate on the market to purchase it. This rich Dutchman had expected to spend up to six million francs, but he actually obtained the famous estate for only a third of that. He will pay only a fifth in cash, the rest being in the form of territorial mandates, which depreciate day by day. It is a fine deal for him. Oddly enough, there was very little competition, and certain people suspect the diplomat of having had some gratuities handed out to his competitors. In any case, the sale increases the number of foreigners owning leading vintages in the Bordeaux region.

Decree sets harder terms for divorces

Paris, September 17

The public opinion campaign carried on against divorce is bearing fruit. The deputies have had to accept the fact that the "tutelary god of marriage", to use the term employed in 1792, actually turned out to be more the libertines' god. Since the law of December 1793 made procedures even easier, people have been separating and remarrying as their fancies strike them. In an attempt to save republican virtues, the Council of Five Hundred has just promulgated a new decree. From now on, divorce for incompatibility of temperament can be pronounced only six months after the last of the three reconciliation attempts required by the law of 1792. This measure will primarily affect women, who file two-thirds of all divorce petitions.

Lazare Hoche dies at 29

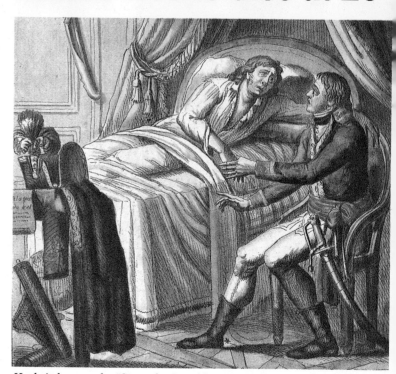

Hoche's last words: "Since the Republic is triumphant, I die content."

Wetzlar, September 19

The stupefying news spread fast throughout the army: this morning at four o'clock, after a final attack of suffocation, Lazare Hoche died. The officer his men had nicknamed "the booted angel" and "the Bonaparte of the North" has passed on at the age of 29 years, three months. His career was devoted entirely to the Republic's service. He was a sergeant in the National Guard at the time of the fall of the Bastille, and was on the northern front at the start of hostilities with Austria. At that time, he distinguished himself at Thionville and Namur. Promoted to general a year later, he took command of the combined Rhine and Moselle Army and freed Alsace by beating the Austrians at Woerth and Landau. Finally, he acquired a reputation for tolerance in the West, overcoming the Vendean insurrection more by dialogue than suppression. The memory of this prestigious leader will be saluted every 30 minutes today and for several more days by the sound of cannonfire.

"Jéhu's companions" terrorise the south

Bouches du Rhône, September 18

The coach was robbed close to Cugnes, and the "companions of Jehu" were responsible. This is the name used by a gang of criminals who have used politics as a cover for terrorising the region for the last three years. The Jehus are ready for any crime: assassination, torture and armed robbery. At Beaudinard, led by the former baker La Calade, they assassinated Julien, a republican, as well as his two children. The parish priest Jauffret, one of the bandits, kept his victim's ears as a souvenir. La Calade sometimes displays a macabre sense of humour. On one occasion, after robbing a lone shepherd, the gangster paraded through the streets of Gémenos wearing the victim's own clothes. The Jehus are feared and respected, and are never turned in. In any case, that would do little good, since it is known that they have accomplices in the police informing them about all military movements and fund transfers. The men earn their living by attacking coaches. Such attacks are so frequent that travellers always put a small amount aside and hasten to turn it over to the Jehus when their coaches are stopped. In this way, unmasked and with complete impunity, these gangsters have shown their ability to subject the Aubagne region to regular tribute.

The funeral ceremony in honour of General Hoche, on the Champ de Mars.

A disguised Carnot gets out of capital

Paris, September 21

Carnot has managed to get out of Paris, and that was no mean feat. He had been sought by the police since the coup d'état, and put out rumours of his death while some faithful Burgundian friends gave him a hideout in the capital. He did not rely on his compatriots to get out of Paris, since they were being watched closely, but called on a friend in the Engineers' Corps. He set off for Switzerland in the man's carriage, disguised as a coachman. Exile is hard when one has never left the country, but the main thing is to escape deportation.

A case of distress

Paris, September 30

She left her garret in Petit Carreau Street, handed out her last sous to the poor, and set off for the "brook". Anne Gravier is 20 years old, and she wanted to die. She works, and has lived apart from her family for six years due to "unpleasant experiences" with her father and because her mother struck her. Since then she has lived in her employer's house, in regret and solitude. Citizen Duchorsel found her on Egalité Bridge, staring with wild eyes. He took her home to comfort her, before taking her to a police station, where the staff on duty took care of her.

Will the "two-thirds bankruptcy" save the French treasury?

Each to his own bankruptcy. Here, a cobbler has declared a 50 per cent bankruptcy, making one boot per creditor.

Paris, September 30

The Council of Five Hundred and then the Ancients have finally approved some sleight of hand with the public debt in order to solve the Treasury's problems. The minister Ramel is in charge of the liquidation process, which calls for only one-third of the borrowings made under the Ancien Régime and to date, and not yet repaid, to be entered in the "great public debt book", and so guaranteed. The remaining two-thirds are arbitrarily converted into securities to be added to government issues made since 1789. It is planned to issue four billion francs' worth of such certificates, which it will be possible to use to pay for national property. They will compete with assignats and territorial mandates, which have depreciated greatly. It seems likely that the new notes will suffer the same drop as the others. Thus bankruptcy is to save the Treasury by harming security-holders.

Restif de La Bretonne reveals his heart

Paris, September 21

This is a unique work, first of all because the author himself has been using an old, creaky press for seven years to crank out the proofs of his novel's 16 volumes. Secondly, because in this summing up, called *Mr. Nicolas, or the human heart revealed*, Restif de La Bretonne unveils his own life, and particularly his love life, in a way nobody before him even Rousseau had dared to do. By delivering himself in this way for public viewing with a sincerity that is sometimes mixed with self-satisfaction, Restif supplies us with a report on his perversions, his loves, his weaknesses and his vices, holding up a mirror to the readers in which more than one individual will recognise himself.

Nicolas Restif de La Bretonne.

Pichegru is deported to Guyana

Rochefort, September 22

General Pichegru, convicted of treason, left France this morning for the Sinnamary convict prison, near Cayenne. He had been arrested at the time of the putsch of Fructidor 18. At that time his friendships with royalists had long been known, but since he had been elected presiding officer of the Council of Five Hundred he could not be arrested without proof. The latter came with the discovery of a letter compromising him, a coded missive written in his handwriting and found by Moreau in baggage belonging to the Austrian general Klinglin. The proof was confirmed by papers found on the Comte d'Antraigues. The traitor has now been hauled off on the *Vaillante*.

Pichegru, an outlawed general.

Dutch fleet ruined in English Channel

England, October 11

France's ally Holland has lost its fleet at Camperdown. The second French intervention in Ireland involved a double operation: a Dutch attack on the Clyde, in Scotland, to get the English to recall their troops from Ireland, and using that diversion to get French troops to Ireland. However, the lack of preparation of De Winter's fleet made it possible for the British admiral, Duncan, to dominate the struggle and send the Batavian vessels to the bottom of the sea.

Catel devotes self to chamber music

Paris, October

The Revolution caused upsets in many different fields, including music. Compositions, particularly Gossec's, were primarily aimed at exalting patriotic ideals. Catel felt this trend keenly, and he is now attempting to react. Taking advantage of the financial security he has been fortunate enough to obtain from his position as a professor at the Conservatory, he is now devoting himself to chamber music, composing some quintets and a number of piano sonatas, which he hopes to have performed.

French parachute advocate jumps for joy

Paris, October 22

André Jacques Garnerin has just made a four year old dream come true. When he was the Convention's Commissioner to the Army of the North, he was taken prisoner by the Austrians in 1793. Having witnessed experiments carried out by Blanchard, who dropped animals from his balloon in a basket hanging from a parachute, Garnerin quickly came up with the idea of trying to escape in that way. Unfortunately his preparations were discovered, but when he was finally released he did not give up his dream. His parachute has changed from a way of escape to a means of saving aeronauts in distress. He gave a convincing demonstration of this fact today.

At five o'clock in the afternoon, before a big crowd, he took off from Monceau Park in an hot air balloon carrying a gondola that had a folded parachute on top. When he reached 1,000 metres, he unhitched the balloon gondola. There were shouts from the ground when the gondola, hanging from a corolla of taffeta 10 metres in diameter, began swinging. Once on the ground, he went up in the air again, on spectators' shoulders (→ July 14, 98).

Some bad luck dogs an escape attempt

Bicêtre, October 13

The escape will have to be put off to another time, and François Vidocq will be staying in the Bicêtre fort. Yet the attempt was well prepared. He and 34 companions took 10 days to dig a tunnel that brought them to a conduit running under the prison. All they had to do was come up in the courtyard of the neighbouring hospital and then get over the wall. The plan was simple and efficient, but the unexpected presence of a watchdog forced them to take refuge in a room in which guards then found them.

Work if you want to become French...

Guadeloupe, October 25

Victor Hugues has issued an order saying that only people working in agriculture can obtain French nationality. In this way, the Republic's commissioner intends to force the former slaves to return to the plantations. He justifies this step by pointing out that he has not received any order from the government to distribute land to the people he freed upon his arrival. Actually, he is going to use any means available to solve the labour shortage that is due to the blacks' preference for military service.

Project by Charles de Wailly for remodelling the Square Courtyard in the Louvre, with an inside portico added.

Bonaparte forces Austria to make fragile peace

Passariano, October 17

Five months of tough negotiations have just resulted in a fragile peace. For Napoléon Bonaparte, the essential point is that he has forced the Austrians to stop fighting. Even if the peace is a precarious one, at least it has the considerable advantage of enablng the

commanding general of the Army of Italy to satisfy his political ambitions. The signature of what is called the Treaty of Campo Formio fits in with his strategy of being, in France, the man who has brought peace. For their part, the Austrians have used diplomatic means to restore a situation that was disadvan-

The treaty was actually signed at Passariano, Bonaparte's residence.

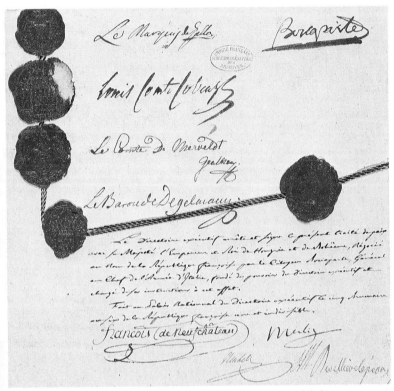

A peace treaty putting an end to more than five years of fighting.

tageous from the military viewpoint. It was the pressure exerted by the movement of General Bonaparte's forces towards Vienna that made Austria decide to sign. The Austrian commander-in-chief, the Archduke Charles, probably considered the enemy movements highly threatening, as Austria lacked the resources needed for a counteroffensive.

The treaty calls for Austria to cede Belgium to France, but it does not make any arrangements for the left bank of the Rhine, the fate of which is to be discussed at a con-

gress attended by German princes with possessions there. So the issue of recognition of the French border on this side of the Rhine is unsettled. Vienna also cedes Lombardy to the Cisalpine Republic, whose independence it recognises. Austria receives Venice and mainland territory as far as the Adige. France annexes the Ionian islands, and obtains Brescia and Bergamo for the Cisalpine Republic. However, in yielding Venice Bonaparte is taking a huge risk, for he has acted in contradiction to the instructions issued by the Directory (→ Oct. 26).

Bonaparte: "a humble servant ..."

Does Bonaparte really have only moderate ambitions? If one is to believe the victor of the Italian campaign, the answer is as simple as it is luminous. In a letter sent to the Directory and very carefully worded, the general says he wants to confine himself to the military sphere. All he wants is to "give an example of respect for magistrates and of aversion to the kind of military régime that has destroyed so many republics". The general is trying to reassure the Directory about the intentions of a young, ambitious officer. If he dispatched Augereau to Paris in connection with the putsch of Fructidor 18, the purpose was only to strengthen the powers of a Directory that was threatened

by enemies of the Republic. Such modesty is hardly credible when Bonaparte is changing Italy's political landscape around to match his own ideas.

General Napoléon Bonaparte.

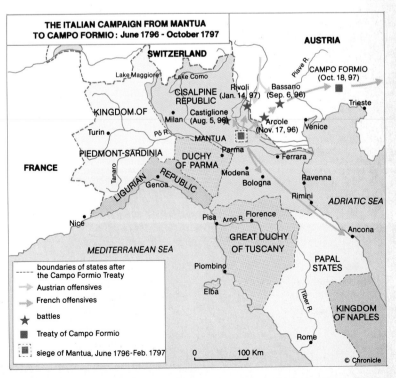

THE ITALIAN CAMPAIGN FROM MANTUA TO CAMPO FORMIO : June 1796 - October 1797

Directory

1 *(Brumaire 11, Year VI)* Paris. Gaspard Monge marries his daughter Louise to Joseph Eschassériaux, the deputy from Charente Inférieure to the Council of Five Hundred.

4 *(Brumaire 14, Year VI)* Rhineland. The Directory drops the idea of creating a Cisrhenane Republic and approves division of the left bank of the Rhine into four departments.→

7 *(Brumaire 17, Year VI)* Adriatic. The Ionian islands, which became French with the Treaty of Campo Formio, are divided up into three departments.

12 *(Brumaire 22, Year VI)* Paris. Creation by decree of a direct taxation agency, responsible for helping departmental directories and municipalities with drawing up tax registers.

12 *(Brumaire 22, Year VI)* Rouen. An earthquake causes more panic than damage.

16 *(Brumaire 26, Year VI)* Berlin. Death of Prussian King Frederick William II.

19 *(Brumaire 29, Year VI)* Ancona. The Italian patriots take up arms and proclaim a republic as the French watch.

21 *(Frimaire 1, Year VI)* French Guyana. Arrival of the Fructidor 18 deportees, interned in Sinnamary fort.→

21 *(Frimaire 1, Year VI)* Paris. The Directory issues a formal statement saying it intends to "seek peace in London".

24 *(Frimaire 4, Year VI)* Paris. Creation of the Trade Discount Bank.

25 *(Frimaire 5, Year VI)* Paris. The Directory issues a decree outlawing the Belgian teaching and hospital orders that had been maintained to date.

29 *(Frimaire 9, Year VI)* Paris. A law adopted at Sieyès' initiative deprives nobles of their civil rights and puts them on the same footing as foreigners.

29 *(Frimaire 9, Year VI)* Saint Etienne. The municipality urges citizens to celebrate the benefits of Fructidor 18.

30 *(Frimaire 10, Year VI)* Rouen. Theophilanthropists, who bill themselves as friends of God and man, begin to worship at Saint Patrice.

Four departments set up in Rhineland

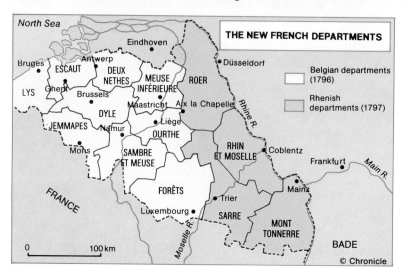

Paris, November 4

The Cisrhenane autonomous republic will never see the light of day. Hoche's death and the Fructidor putsch left the annexationists a free hand. In application of new directives, Bonaparte demanded under the Treaty of Campo Formio that Austria give up the entire left bank of the Rhine. The Alsatian Rudler has been appointed general commissioner for the Rhine and is responsible for introducing French laws and for establishing some new departments. The Directory has accepted his plan for a division into four departments, even if French forces have not yet retaken Mainz and the treaty does not define the status of Cologne. The Cisrhenane republicans are giving up their independence whims without regret. Exchanging the green and white Cisrhenane cockade for the tricolour, they are already pushing the new policy (→April 98).

"In a pig's eye," says Cochon and flees

The cunning Charles Cochon de Lapparent refrained, while he was in the Convention, from taking a stand in favour of any of the various factions. When he was appointed Police Minister in April 1795, he resumed this balancing act, dismantling both the Babeuf conspiracy and Abbot Brottier's "Royalist Agency" plot. He made a major mistake in leaving himself open to charges of complicity with royalists before Fructidor 18. When banned, he was heard to cry "In a pig's eye", and fled.

The Republic's enemy is swept away, and the freedom tree straightened.

World made safe for money presses

Paris, November 20

At last! The engraver Nicolas Gatteau has just developed a press that makes it impossible to counterfeit plates used for printing banknotes. The process calls for the formes to be shaped cold, not hot as before, using a die made from a silver alloy and attached to a press equipped with a powerful balance beam. The printer Firmin Didot, who has financed this research since 1793, rejoices at this success. It will be useful to the Republic, which still issues paper money in the form of territorial mandates, even if it has dropped the assignats.

Republican bandits with fine principles

Villejuif, November 7

With horses galloping smartly, the Sens coach was on its way when an unscheduled stop spoiled the end of the trip. Some robbers in hats and black coats had arranged some ropes and branches on the road and awaited the coach. With pistols in their belts, these individuals very politely forced the travellers to get out one by one and relieved them of their purses. Yet the leader did not monopolise the pretty louis contributed by the travellers. He spread the booty out on the grass and, turning towards his men, shared out the "community property" in equal amounts, "as the Republic would want us to do".

Capital fog-bound

Paris, November 13

A thick layer of fog has covered the capital, so dense that coach drivers have to move along blind. The chests of their horses emerge only as vague spots, and carriages collide or wind up in the boulevard ditches. Pedestrians do not walk in this opaque layer drowning the ground, they float, attempting to find their way with the help of the dim illumination offered by the street lamps. One cannot make out the Seine from the bridges, and the sky has never been so low. What is the explanation of all this? Is it a harbinger of an earthquake, such as hit Rouen yesterday?

Bonaparte, or the taste for power

Turin, November 19

"If I can't be the master, I'll leave France." Some 20 months spent far from Paris have not assuaged Bonaparte's drive to rise. Thus, after dispatching Augereau to re-establish the Republic when it was menaced at the time of the Fructidor putsch, the ambitious general did not hesitate to offer a severe judgement of the executive branch in the following terms: "Those lawyers in Paris they put on the Directory understand nothing about government." Does he perhaps mean that they should be replaced by men with more foresight and energy?

Execution in Nantes of non-juring priest

Nantes, November 27

The most terrifying punishments again threaten non-juring priests. A clergyman has just been executed in Nantes in application of the law of Fructidor 19. Abbot de Gruchy had emigrated after refusing to take the oath. At the time of the initial appeasement measures, he returned to France. Arrested after being denounced as a "returned deportee", he was ordered to swear the oath of hatred for royalty. Upon his refusal to comply with this order, he was tried and executed.

16 in royalist plot in Guyana to serve prison terms

Cayenne Island, November 21

The transit camp for the banished is surrounded by plantations on which French colonists have lived since 1664. Sixteen people involved in the royalist putsch disembarked there from the *Vaillante*. For Pichegru, Barbé de Marbois, Bourdon de l'Oise and their companions, the rough crossing was finally over. The Directory's agent, one of Danton's nephews, entrusted the prisoners to the hospital sisters. Despite this welcome, they are forbidden to move around the colony. They will be incarcerated at Sinnamary Fort, where Billaud Varenne is jailed (→June 3, 98).

The fate of Europe is at stake at the Congress of Rastatt

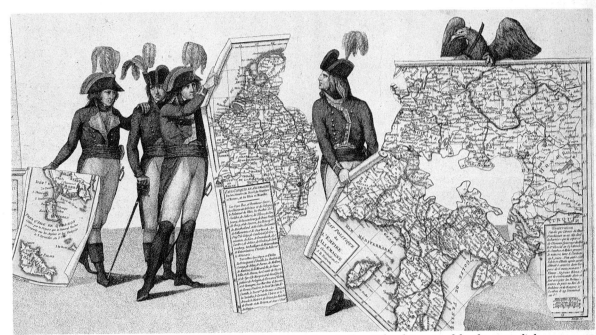

Bonaparte, in the centre, holds Europe's future in his hands, whether it be determined by force or diplomacy.

Rastatt, November 28

The Congress of Rastatt opened in a tense atmosphere. The Swedish delegate, Axel de Fersen, got an extremely chilly welcome from General Bonaparte: "The French Republic will not allow men who are too well known to it because of their connections with the former court of France to flout the ministers of the world's leading people." In addition to Bonaparte, the ministers in question are former Montagnard Treilhard, and Bonnier, the head of the Directory's Diplomatic Office. Austria is represented by Cobenzl and the young Count Metternich. The Prussians have sent three emissaries. The main French objective will be to get the Rhine river accepted as the border, and that will present some serious problems. In return for recognition of the Rhine border, Vienna might demand additional territorial compensation. Actually, this is authorised by a secret provision in the Treaty of Campo Formio, which was signed last month. Logically, Austria might find such compensation in Italy, but an Austrian return to the peninsula, in any form whatsoever, is the last thing the French government wants.

The same clause is also likely to worry Prussia's rulers, who are not fully informed about the exact contents, but who are at least aware of the fact that they are sure to be to their country's disadvantage. Real peace in Europe therefore depends on the results of this diplomatic set to, in which defiance of the enemy is matched only by mistrust of possible allies.

Bonaparte's entry into Basel on November 24th.: a stop along the road leading him from Italy to Rastatt, in Germany.

Victorious Napoléon is welcomed back to Paris in great style

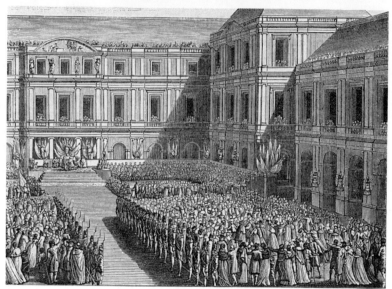
Dignitaries awaiting Bonaparte in the courtyard of the Luxembourg palace.

On December 20th., a banquet for Bonaparte in the Louvre gallery.

Paris, December 10

A lavish ceremony is being held today in the courtyard of the Luxembourg palace: Paris is toasting Napoléon's return after the treaty of Campoformio. The Directory has done a good job. Since dawn, an eager crowd has been lining the streets around the palace, while a second, more privileged crowd is to be found in the main courtyard. An "altar" to the Nation has been set at the centre, while at the head of the steps can be seen the five Directors in official dress: plumed hats and red coats with gold brocade. For all their apparent good humour, they are clearly racked with jealousy. Beside them stand ministers and high-ranking officials grouped around Talleyrand, who is wearing wine-coloured silk and will be making the welcome-home speech on the government's behalf. Two hundred musicians break into *the Chant du Retour*, and Bonaparte, in full general's dress, makes his entry to the cheers of the crowd. He seems little moved by the tribute that is being paid. His reply to Barras's glowing welcome is brusque and staccato. It is difficult to make out what he is saying, for his voice is rough and his Corsican accent is pronounced. One phrase stands out, however, for it bears on the Constitution: "Europe will be free when the happiness of the French people has been founded on more adequate organic laws." With his speech done, Napoléon makes a show of listening to the accolades from the Directors, then abruptly returns home, indifferent to the acclamations of Paris.

Spain censors the philosophers

Madrid, December 3

The Spanish Inquisition has been adding to its list of banned foreign books. Montesquieu's *De l'Esprit des Lois* and Condorcet's posthumous *Esquisse d'un Tableau Historique des Progrès de l'Esprit Humain* are among those works considered to be subversive. As any criticism of religion or of the divine right of kings is forbidden in Spain, the Inquisition constitutes one of the sturdiest of ramparts against the advance of philosophical or revolutionary ideals.

Chénier celebrates the hero's return

Paris, December 10

The composer responsible for the *Chant du Départ* has also written a *Chant du Retour*. This was the title of Marie Joseph Chénier's hymn to the glory of Bonaparte that 200 musicians would perform at the reception given by the Directory in honour of the victorious general's return. The irony of the situation was not lost on Chénier's enemies, for the career of this last-minute Bonapartist is remarkable for its sudden shifts in political sympathies. Had he not begun as a member of the Jacobins Club and an admirer of Robespierre? It was then that he would scale the heights of fame. His plays were performed throughout Paris, and the extremely popular *Chant du Départ* was the official commemoration of the storming of the Bastille. Chénier would fall from grace during the Terror. After his brother André was sent to the scaffold, people accused Chénier of having done nothing to save him. Impervious to slander, he would deny Robespierre after Thermidor. He had no intention of giving up politics. Since joining the Five Hundred in 1795, he has become one of Napoléon's most fervent admirers.

Wurtemberg thirsty for reforms

Stuttgart, December

Frederic Wilhelm II was unable to put a stop to the constitutional upheavals troubling Wurtemberg before he died. His successor, Duke Frederic IV, is a hard-driving man who wishes to sweep away the outmoded edifice and transform the duchy into a centralised, modern state. Uncertain of its future, the Landtag is divided between a deep-rooted traditionalism and a vague desire for reform. In a search for outside support, a representative has been sent to Paris to ask the Directory to pressurise the duke into "a new constitutional act based on the legislation passed by France in Year III".

16 royalist papers come under ban

Paris, December 17

There will soon be nothing left for royalists to read. Sixteen Paris papers have once more been banned in a recent decree by the Directory. For the last two years, the Press had been free. The royalists, who stood to gain most from such a situation, had always managed to block the Assembly's attempts at restricting the Press. The coup carried out on Fructidor 18 put an end to all that. The very next day, a law was passed that placed the entire Press under police surveillance for a year. Then, three days later, a second law was passed, this time to facilitate the deportation of contributors to 44 royalist papers.

Directory torpedoes submarine dream

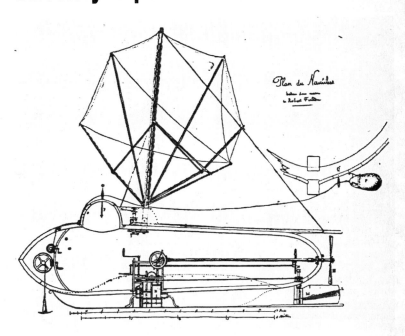

The "Nautilus" submarine invented by Fulton; it measures 6.5 by 2 metres.

The future of Paris porcelain is assured

Porcelain-maker Christophe Dihl.

Paris, December

It was certainly not part of the contract. Ever since the death of Antoine Guérhard, his associate, Christophe Dihl, has been helping Mme. Guérhard run the famous porcelain manufacturer of the same name. Not content with fixing a 19-year term to their partnership, however, the couple have recently decided they will get married. All of which is highly amusing when you bear in mind that the original agreement stipulated Dihl "could live in the Guérhard home, at a cost of some 800 pounds per annum, but would be expected to move out, should he decide to marry...".

Paris, December 13

An invisible vessel hidden away under the ocean and impossible to locate: as a means of defeating the English, the project Robert Fulton has put forward to the Directory is an ambitious one. To the Directors, it appeared more like a pipe dream, and Fulton was sent on his way. The American scientist is far from a beginner in the field, however. On an invitation from the United States ministry, he moved to Paris in 1796, and has since been working on an improved maritime defence system. A few months ago, he put the final touches to an underwater bomb called a *Torpedo*, which he recently tried out in the Seine. He has just hit on the idea of a submarine vessel, known as a *Nautilus*. When he tried it out for the first time, it remained underwater for three hours without a change of oxygen. The next time round, it emerged at a distance of some five leagues from its point of departure. Armed with a *Torpedo*, his *Nautilus* could wreak havoc on the English fleet. Undeterred by the lack of interest shown by the Directory, Fulton has decided to continue with his experiments, and dearly hopes he will be able to renew his offer before a peace treaty is signed with England.

Tax collectors team up with the police

Paris, December 3

The Councils have decided to use strong-arm tactics. To ensure that people start paying their taxes on time, the mounted constabulary have been called in and will assist the tax collectors in their task. If a demand for payment is ignored, members of the force will move into the relevant household and live there at the occupants' expense. If, after ten days, the "wicked" citizens have still not paid their dues, their "tenants" will be instructed to seize their belongings forthwith, and put them up for auction on the public highway.

Ballroom dress for the elegant.

Man of science holds general in esteem

Paris, December 31

Napoléon is visiting the *Ecole polytechnique* today. For Monge, who has just taken over as the head of the school, the general's presence is a great honour and sets the seal on his success. For Bonaparte, it is a way of showing the high opinion he has of his friend. Monge had singled the general out in 1793, during the siege of Toulon. He was present at the ceremony celebrating Napoléon's victorious return from Italy, and will certainly have played a part in his recent election to the Institute. The general and the man of science are clearly inseparable.

Drawing classes go down well in school

Paris, December

Though the Revolution has done away with academies and degrees, it has left arts teaching largely unharmed. It has even enriched it in certain respects, by instituting extremely popular drawing classes in all of the central schools. From Soissons to the Jura, pupils are everywhere eager to take part. As one chronicler puts it, the courses "cultivate the sense of Beauty". At prize-giving time each summer, an exhibition of drawings by the best students from the central schools is held, and the winners are then chosen by the painter Vien.

▷

A French general assassinated by the Pope's guards at Rome

Rome, December 28

In the struggles between local patriots and followers of the Pope, a French victim has been claimed:

Pius VI has been Pope since 1775.

General Duphot, killed by papal guards during a riot. The young officer was a guest of the French ambassador to Rome, Joseph Bonaparte. Some time after midday, local patriots, who are in favour of ejecting the Pope and setting up a Roman republic, attacked a group of papal guards during a patrol. Initially outnumbered, the guards would finally get the upper hand and were able to pursue the rioters, who had meanwhile taken refuge in the French embassy. The "Pope's boys" then decided likewise to enter the premises, at which point Joseph asked both sides to leave, for he did not want a clash taking place inside the palace. France could hardly abandon the patriots to their fate, however, when it had previously been taking such a lively interest in their activities. Indignant at the very sight of the papal guards, the ambassador and Duphot decided to accompany the rioters outside, by

way of protection. And it was then that the young general was killed. His death could prove very costly to the papal state: despite apologies from Cardinal Doria, Secretary of state to the Holy See, Joseph Bonaparte has decided to leave Rome. His sister-in-law, Désirée Clary, was the general's fiancée. Several years ago, a romance sprang up between this beautiful young lady from Provence and Bonaparte. Her family, however, urged her to break off the engagement after Thermidor: The young Jacobin general was an embarrassment and would not go far, they thought. Time passed, bringing changes in fortune and new affections in its wake. Désirée had been about to marry Duphot, a less illustrious figure now than the man who had won at Arcole, but a much stauncher Jacobin. It was the passionate nature of his beliefs that would be responsible for his tragic fate (→ Feb. 15, 98).

The armies of the Republic are on all the war fronts

As agreed on in the treaty of Campoformio, the French have evacuated the Austrian states. In Germany, they have drawn back behind the Rhine, and in Italy, behind the Adige. The Austrian army, meanwhile, has gone in to occupy Venice and the Lombardy provinces. The troops from Vienna have been divided into three main groups:

The flag is the symbol of victory.

Plans for a national Arts Theatre opposite the Tuileries

Paris, December

François Bélanger is an old hand at pulling off the impossible. He was the one who, 20 years ago, built the *Château de Bagatelle* in just 64 days for the Comte d'Artois. This time round, he plans to construct a

national Arts Theatre, or Temple to Apollo, opposite the Tuileries. His outlandish project has been drawn up on neo-classical lines: a long flight of steps with stone lions on either side, a Corinthian peristyle, and a pediment and dome in the

same style as the Panthéon. To either side of the main building, two wings will open out in a half-moon around the enormous square. At the centre, there will be a column in celebration of republican Science, Commerce, Art and Virtue.

one is on the Adige in Italy; another in the Tyrol; while a third, referred to as the Empire contingent, is between the Isar and the Lech. In keeping with the accords, the Austrians left Mainz on December 28th., while the French, in exchange, moved out of Venice. Bonaparte had chosen to negotiate just as the advance of his troops on Vienna was beginning to present a serious threat. A number of military "scenarios" had been considered, and all came to the same conclusion: the time to deal is when one has the upper hand. The French general was perfectly aware that Archduke Charles could decide to dig in, rather than face a pitched battle, the outcome of which was easy to foresee. He also knew that, with 120,00 men between them, Bohemia, Moravia and Hungary could provide an exceptionally strong reserve.

The architect Bélanger used antiquity as inspiration for his plans for the national Arts Theatre.

January 1798

from 1st. to 31st.

Directory

1 *(Nivôse 12, Year VI)*
Saint Etienne. The mayor is attacked by royalists who continue to spread terror in the town (→ March 28, 98).

4 *(Nivôse 15, Year VI)*
France. The Directory orders searches throughout the country, with a view to seizing all English goods.

5 *(Nivôse 16, Year VI)*
Paris. In the hope of restoring a semblance of safety on the roads, the Five Hundred vote a law making highway robbery punishable by death.

9 *(Nivôse 20, Year VI)*
Paris. The Théâtre de la République stages Billardon de Sauvigny's *Scipion l'Africain*, a typical anti-British play.

11 *(Nivôse 22, Year VI)*
Paris. The executive Directory orders Berthier, commander of the army of Italy, to seize Rome (→ Feb. 15, 98).

12 *(Nivôse 23, Year VI)*
Paris. General Jourdan suggests creating an auxiliary army of 100,000 men, to be recruited by pulling names from a hat.

12 *(Nivôse 23, Year VI)*
Paris. Bonaparte presents his plans for the invasion of England to the Directory (→ Feb. 8, 98).

18 *(Nivôse 29, Year VI)*
Paris. Increasing pressure on English trade, the Directory passes a law authorising the seizure of any neutral vessel carrying English goods. →

24 *(Pluviôse 5, Year VI)*
Pays de Vaud. The Vaudois proclaim the Republic of Leman. The Swiss cantons have been in a state of ferment since mid-January: on the 17th., Basel peasants attacked the castles, and on the 20th. citizens planted a tree of Liberty in front of the cathedral.

26 *(Pluviôse 7, Year VI)*
Rouen. François Duramé, leader of a band of "Hot Feet", is executed.

27 *(Pluviôse 8, Year VI)*
Paris. Brune is named head of French troops in Switzerland. The latter went in yesterday to back the Vaudois's revolt against the authorities of Berne.

29 *(Pluviôse 10, Year VI)*
Paris. Alexandre Duval and Pierre Della Maria's comic opera, *Le Prisonnier ou la Ressemblance*, is staged at the Favart theatre.

Bonaparte's first session at the Institute

Napoléon makes his official entry to the Institute on December 25th., 1797.

Paris, January 5

Right now, it is his election to the Institute that Napoléon is most proud of, not his victories in Italy. He is deeply flattered by the nomination and has his official title of commander in chief immediately followed by that of "member of the Institute". The general has never made a secret of the admiration he feels towards the members of this prestigious institution. As soon as he was back, he opened his doors to scholars, writers and philosophers, and would talk mathematics with Lagrange, metaphysics with Sieyès or poetry with Chénier. He can hardly be said to have impressed them with his knowledge, but he would at least listen to them with respect. All agreed he should be given a place among them, which has now been done. In December, he was elected to the mechanics section of the class of Sciences. In the first session he attended at the Institute, he would find himself between Monge and Berthollet. "A great honour for the Institute," said the Press. "I will be their student long before I become their equal," replied Napoléon.

Angers celebrates the décadi

Angers, January 9

The first décadi was celebrated in "a spirit of decency and quiet, and with the respect that should always be shown republican institutions". The civil and military authorities accompanied the teachers and their classes as far as the Maurice temple, where soldiers were standing on guard. The eldest citizen then read various legal and moral texts, along with extracts from the Natural Code in praise of courage, frugality and obedience, the three main virtues. For the décadi is not only a day of rest in the revolutionary calendar, it is also the day on which citizens are instructed in their duties. And attendance is compulsory.

Saving the cockade

Bourges, January 6

The only way of restoring the national emblem to its former glory is by making it obligatory. Anyone who deliberately omits to wear it will be sent before the courts. The same applies to those who wear their hair "with braids and curls" or who wear Muscadin-style frock coats. For the authorities are in no doubt that good morals and good citizenship depends largely on how one is dressed.

Will a Victory column be constructed on the Pont Neuf?

Design for a national column...

Bernard Poyet, architect to the city of Paris and a disciple of Charles de Wailly, has recently submitted plans for a gigantic column to the authorities. Three hundred feet high, it would celebrate the Republic's glorious victories and be raised on the Pont Neuf. This outlandish edifice, resting on a rustic stylobate, would comprise a circular colonnade forming the base of the column proper. The column itself would be topped with a tripod, from which a flame would emerge. The monument could be lit up from inside for important ceremonies. The Pont Neuf is a major source of inspiration for artists, for Poyet is not alone in the field: Prud'hon has visions of a column "to commemorate the nation's victories".

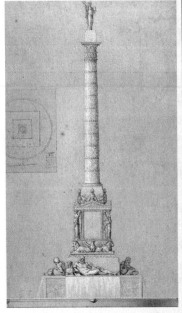

... and another one by Prud'hon.

The guillotine at the service of science

The anatomist's latest supplier.

Paris, January

There are different categories of dead, it appears. Last November, a young doctor, Xavier Bichat, was hauled up before the tribunals for stealing corpses from a Parisian cemetery, which he then used to carry out experiments in anatomy. He has recently been allowed to receive the bodies of guillotine victims, within half an hour of their death. He will thus be able to continue on humans the experiments that the Italian doctor, Galvani, has been carrying out on flayed frogs. A physiologist whose main interest is in the detemination of organic properties passing through the nerves, Bichat is fascinated by the debate between Galvani and his fellow Italian Volta, concerning the causes of muscular contraction as manifested under stimulus from the nerves. Are they the expression of an "animal electricity" or are they caused by the action of the instruments employed?

Mme. de Staël fails to impress general

Paris, January 3

The meeting of minds dreamed of by Germaine de Staël was not to be. The woman renowned for her capacity to win the attention of those around her failed to extract so much as a single remark from the toast of Paris, Napoléon Bonaparte. For the first time in her life, she was ill at ease. She was not the only one, moreover. In the foreign ministry, which Talleyrand had filled with flowers for the occasion, all eyes were on the prestigious figure, with his puny silhouette and pale face, who was to remain distant and impenetrable throughout. Even the presence of his delightful young wife, Joséphine, was powerless to distract the spellbound company.

A secret mission short on discretion

Ile de France, January 19

Malartic, the governor of the Mascarene archipelago, has made a blunder. When the two ambassadors from Tippoo Sahib arrived, he had the troops present arms and deliver a salute, thereby rendering null and void the precautions that had been taken to keep the mission secret. Having arrived incognito yesterday aboard a vessel run by the privateer Ripaud, the two men are here to find out about French intentions and to recruit the 10,000 volunteers promised by Ribaud to help fight the English in India. Malartic, who has received no directive, has revealed that Ripaud is probably an impostor.

A Franco-Batavian coup in Holland

The Hague, January 22

The unitarian democrats have pulled off a coup. With the aid of Joubert's French troops, who have just entered Holland, they have managed, by using force, to do away with the Constitution set up on May 30th. Under the influence of the French ambassador, Charles Delacroix, they had earlier signed the *Manifesto of the 43* and are partisans of a régime founded on the French Constitution of Year I. The National Guard rounded up the moderates at their homes at dawn. Conspirators and parliamentarians newly won over to the cause at once put together a new Assembly and called for a provisional executive.

Talleyrand is discovered to be corrupt

Paris, January 21

Talleyrand's market value is high these days: the Prussian kingdom's representative in Paris puts it at a million livres in gold. That is how much Talleyrand was paid during the recent negotiations with Austria, in exchange for agreeing to one or two secret clauses. For an additional million, he agreed to reveal them to the Prussian government and prevent their being put into effect. During another series of negotiations, the Portuguese and Spanish authorities clubbed together to offer him one and a half million. Only the Americans are shocked at having to pay out 50,000 in gold louis to settle a maritime dispute. As for the foreign minister, his view is that the "perks" come with the job: his position is far from stable and who knows what tomorrow will bring? Talleyrand can be bought, like everyone else: he is just more expensive, that's all.

A new oath is sworn against the royalty

Paris, January 21

It is five years to the day since the traitor Louis Capet was executed. The Directory has made sure that "the anniversary of the last king of France's just punishment" is duly celebrated. It has decided for the occasion that all members of both the Five Hundred and the Ancients must swear individually before the Tribune an oath of hatred against royalty. The same oath must be taken by priests, the majority of whom remain to this day among the staunchest supporters of the Ancien Régime.

Citizen Palloy's antiroyalist song, which was inspired by the new oath.

Harsh new measures taken in France's trade war with England

Shortage is such that illegally imported English goods go for large sums.

Paris, January 18

The law that has just been passed allows French vessels to delay for inspection, even far out at sea, any neutral ship engaged in trade with England. From now on, republican sailors need only discover so much as a single item of British origin, whether it be a sailor's knife or the captain's bedspread, to be entitled to seize the entire cargo! This new measure, which amounts to little less than piracy, is not going to improve relations between England and France. Its sole purpose is to prevent the powerful British lion from exporting its goods. Backed by its Spanish and Dutch allies, the French fleet hopes in this way to contest its enemy's mastery of the seas. There is a widespread fear, however, that it will be France, not England, that suffers as a result. In major ports like Bordeaux, Nantes and Marseilles, where the effects of the war have been most marked, it was the French traders who were the first to suffer. At present, the entire country is having to bear the brunt of the slump in international trade. Is it altogether wise, under such delicate conditions, to ensure by the use of force that the whole of Europe takes part in an embargo on English products?

Mulhouse decides to be part of France

Paris, January 28

Alsace is now entirely French. The Directory has just confirmed the results of the plebiscite carried out in Mulhouse on January 3rd. apropos annexation. The ancient city that, three centuries earlier, had decided to abandon the league of Alsatian towns in favour of an alliance with the Swiss cantons, has returned to its original province at last. The Directory's decision was also influenced by economic and strategic factors. The town is rich. With financial backing from Basel, the Koechlin and Dolfuss families have set up a chintz industry which is the most advanced of its kind in Europe. On top of this, after talks between Reubell, Bonaparte and Ochs from the Vaude, armed intervention in Switzerland is now on the cards. The territory is essential.

The "Magasin de Musique" is empty

Paris, January 21

Patriotic music is no longer in fashion. An investigation carried out by the Ministry of the Interior has revealed that the *Magasin de Musique*, originally founded for the propagation of revolutionary work, is now faced with the painful task of reconversion. Most of Sarette's friends abandoned the publisher in favour of the Conservatoire. The loyal few who stayed behind must choose between publishing classical scores or helping with musical instruction in the form of *Etudes*.

A brawl at Garchi's ice-cream shop

Paris, January 17

The most fashionable lemonade and ice-cream shop in Paris will not be opening again in a hurry. Around 10 o'clock this evening, a group of men wearing greatcoats and long-haired caps turned up. They were looking for Fournier, one of Augereau's aides-de-camp, who they then started threatening. Some 30 in all, the agitators began waving their fists and swords and soon had a fight going. The owner was among the two men wounded.

A denunciation puts a stop to the ravages of the Orgères gang

Beauce, January 30

Luck can prove quite effective at times. The housing marshal Vaseur was busy chatting with a peasant when a tattered old tramp walked up. The peasant at once identified him as the One Eyed Man from Jouy, a member of the "Hot Foot" gang. Arrested on the spot, the villain decided to save his skin by handing over the names of the rest of the gang. The sudden torrent of speech yielded the names of both the notorious Handsome François and of his assistant, the Redskin from Aneau. The information he has provided will allow the police to cast an enormous net round the area in which the gang operates; an area extending from Chartres to Estampes, via Paris, Châteaudun and Epernon. The police will also be counting on the prodigious memory of the One Eyed Man from Jouy to identify his 300 accomplices: behind the amiable façade put up by an innkeeper or a peasant, there could be an informer or a fence. What the police most hope to be able to do, thanks to his co-operation is to lay siege to the bandits' underground hide-out on the outskirts of Orgères.

The "Hot Foot" gang at work: they loot, torture and kill, mainly attacking the well-off and isolated farms.

Directory

The Republic of Rome is proclaimed

Gathered on Vatican Hill on February 11th., a silent crowd watches the arrival of French forces in Rome.

Rome, February 15

The republican family has a new member in its midst, the Republic of Rome. The new proclamation is an advance for the Directory on the Italian chess-board, and one in the eye for the Pope, whose remaining papal states have now been reduced to dust. The French government used the assassination of General Duphot last December as a pretext for sending its troops into the Holy City. After talks with Bonaparte, the Directory decided to take action and sent in General Berthier. Turning the presence of French troops to advantage, a handful of patriots succeeded in proclaiming Rome a republic. While claiming to have played no part in the move, the French general would soon be on excellent terms with the leaders of the provisional government that had been set up. Berthier had, of course, the Constitution of the Republic of Rome immediately to hand, drawn up by Merlin de Douai. It is exactly the same as the Constitution of Year III, with a bit of antiquity thrown in for luck: the Directors are Consuls; the Ancients, Senators; and the Five Hundred, Tribunes (→Feb. 20).

General Alexandre Berthier.

Earth tremor felt in western France

Western France, February 5

Accidents come in groups, they say. At all events, the earth has been undergoing a series of upheavals since some time last month. First in the Deux Sèvres and the Charente, now in Anjou and the Loire Atlantique. A brief tremor was felt in Nantes and Angers, not violent but enough to have left a marked soil subsidence in its wake.

Pope finds himself forced to leave Rome

Rome, February 20

It was in the hour before dawn that a small convoy slipped out by the Porta Angelica. In one of the vehicles could be found an almost impotent old man of 84, Pope Pius VI. Under orders from Berthier, who, for the time being, has had to dispense with his religious instincts, the Pope has been forced to leave Rome and take up exile in the town appointed to him, Sienna. On being told of the arrival of the French forces, the Holy Father had shown a stubborn determination to remain in Rome, come what may, in the hope of establishing some kind of compromise with the Directory. The military authorities turned a deaf ear to his proposals. As for Masséna, who has taken over from Berthier as the head of the French forces, he is likely to spark off trouble: this hot-tempered citizen of Nice is none too popular with the rest of the army (→Feb. 24).

New outfit designed for parliamentarians

Paris, February 19

It is only to be expected that those who represent the nation take care about the way they dress and go about with the dignified air of Roman senators. The deputies' new outfit comprises a dark-blue frock-coat, with a scarf in the three colours of the Republic by way of a belt, the whole being hung with gold cords and fringes. Over the top of that they will wear a full-length scarlet coat which closes over the left shoulder by means of a gold button. In this way, their arms will be free to gesture at will before the speaker's platform. On their heads they will wear a blue-violet square velvet cap. Hung with gold tassels, the cap carries a flame-coloured band at the front, from which a tricolour feather curves up. So as to make sure the people are presented with a suitable vision of all who legislate in the Assembly, members will be required to wear the full regalia whenever they appear in public. There can be no exceptions to the rule.

One of the Council of the Elders.

Classical simplicity is fashionable again

Paris, February

Wearing a linen dress that leaves her arms bare and scarcely conceals her figure, the elegant young lady of today resembles a nymph who has just been woken in her morning dress. Everything changes in the afternoon, however: draped in a red shawl and with her hair up "à la Bérénice", she has the powerful majesty of an antique queen. Come evening, in a tucked-up dress and with a crescent of diamonds in her hair, it is Diana the huntress she recalls. Greek and Roman dress is back in fashion. Even the working-class girls put on a long pleated robe on Sundays and pile their hair up in curls. Women have put away the narrow corsets of their mothers' generation and are virtually naked under a thin layer of muslin that leaves their bodies free. Wigs of every possible description are also the rage among women, whether rich or poor. Some will even change them several times a day, free to be a blonde or a redhead at whim.

What could be simpler than this?

Napoléon opposes the idea of an away match with England

Paris, February 23

There's no point trying to fight England on her home ground. The report drawn up by Napoléon is clear: any frontal attack will lead to defeat. The idea of attacking the "pirates" on their own island had widespread support, however. A police report, dated October 30th., described popular enthusiasm for the project in the following terms: "An invasion of England is keenly desired. The people would like to see the British government receive punishment for the machiavellian way in which it has torn our nation apart." As commander in chief of the Army of England, Napoléon would begin by studying the plans made for the invasion. Some 50,000 men would be drawn from the Army of Italy, while 63 vessels and 50 frigates were to be assembled at Brest. The banker Ramel had even arranged a loan. Napoléon's report came as a surprise, therefore. What he does favour, however, is waging economic war on London, with help from Talleyrand. In the East, for instance... (→ March 2).

The plans for a French invasion of England have been definitely shelved.

Over to England!

Paris is rife with talk of an imminent attack on England Bonaparte left this morning for Calais to study an invasion plan. The people of the capital are already singing these verses called "Over to England":

We'll have yet one ball more,
You soldiers, who love to dance!
The one with Germany is o'er;
With England next we'll prance.
The French who will participate
Rejoice, or so the rumour tells,
For if the English men they hate,
They love the English belles.

The French will give the ball
And truly splendid it will be.
The English provide the hall
And pay cash the musicians' fee.
We shall make the hall to ring
With tunes set to French words.
We'll make Englishmen to sing.
And to dance, the English birds.

By Dover, we'll get there
A-rolling we will set the ball.
Instruments of France will blare
And mark the rhythm out for all.
Since the English at this fête
Know how the English dance,
Our Bonaparte will demonstrate
Just how we do it in France!

D'Antraigues is cast out by his peers

Vienna, February 24

The Comte d'Antraigues has been abandoned by the royalists. Holed up in Vienna since his escape from prison in Italy, he has just received a letter from the Comte de Provence informing him of his sudden fall from grace. On top of this, Louis XVIII has banned the publication of certain papers of his left in the hands of Napoléon at the time of his arrest in May 1797. The very first thing d'Antraigues had done on escaping, however, had been to write to the Comte de Provence to inform him that nothing that might prove compromising had changed hands. He also explained that the text of a conversation he had had with the royalist spy Montgaillard, which proved Pichegru's guilt and had been made public to justify the coup that September, was a fake and had been written by Napoléon himself. Having assured him that he believed the story, the Comte de Provence asked him to publish the original, which would compromise Napoléon and certain officers. The fact that d'Antraigues showed no desire to do so, only confirmed the royalists' suspicions. Since he had betrayed them, he could fend for himself. D'Antraigues is well and truly out for the count.

▷

The urucu plant is no help to an émigré

Guyana, February 20

If you don't happen to live in Guyana, inheriting a plantation is not as straightforward as it might appear. Bordeaux trader Charles Lemesle has found this out to his cost. On the death of his brother in 1789, he found himself with a large plantation of urucu, a plant rich in red dye, on his hands. As he was absent at the time, his lands were sequestered: in order to recover his goods, he had to prove that he still lived there. He is now happily back on his estate, while the market price of urucu has multiplied...by eight.

Put up for sale by the Directory, the 17th. century château of Sceaux passes by adjudication to citizen Lecomte, who will have the waterfalls pulled down and the Le Nôtre gardens transformed into land for grazing.

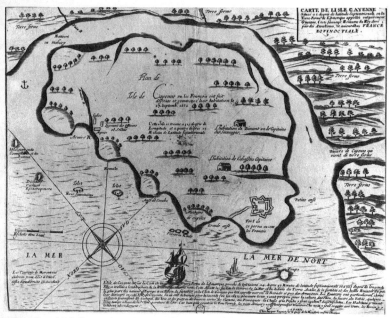

The island of Cayenne opposite Guyana is known as the "guillotine's edge".

Peace banquet organised by Freemasons

Toulouse, February 28

Nearly 400 guests took part in the "brothers' banquet" which was recently held by the Freemasons of Toulouse "to celebrate continental peace". At the outset of the Revolution, the lodges lost members to the clubs. After almost collapsing during the Terror, they finally decided to "recognise only the national convention for Grand Lodge", at which point initiates started arriving once more. Shut down after Thermidor, they have reopened to great success under the Directory. Nobility and clergy, and all but a few notaries, have given way to merchants and clerks.

Benjamin Constant asks property owners to give their support to the Republic

Paris, February 27

The Directory is doing its best to win the support of property owners. That was the idea behind the speech made by Benjamin Constant to the constitutional circle. After getting himself named an elector by buying up certain national properties, the young writer hopes, with a little help from Barras, to launch himself in politics. His speech was felt to be a warning to all those who, come the elections in May, might feel tempted to vote against the republican deputies. "The Revolution is over," he declared, but "let this be a warning to property owners: by siding with counter-revolutionaries or royalists, they risk the same fate that befell the nobility when they persisted in upholding the Ancien Régime". In other words, the only real rampart against the assault on property is the Republic. If, on the contrary, property owners allow themselves to be seduced by the monarchists, they may well end up losing the lot. Benjamin Constant is alluding here to the faction known as "the red-cap royalists": unlike the "white-cockade royalists", who are on the side of the pretender Louis XVIII and absolutism, the "red-caps" back the Duc d'Orléans and hope to win the support of the bourgeoisie by rhetorical means. The Directory, meanwhile, is trying to steer a course between the two.

After Bélanger's project last December, Charles de Wailly has now proposed a different plan for the Arts Theatre opposite the Tuileries.

French Republic's troops seize Berne

A clash between Bernese troops and French republican forces near the Saingine bridge, close to Berne.

Switzerland, March 6

Brune and Schauenburg have led their troops into Berne. What the Directory claims to be doing is helping the Vaude region get free of the yoke that the canton of Berne has imposed on it. Since December, the Directory member Reubell has been in close contact with Vaude patriots Laharpe and Pierre Ochs, who wanted French help in starting a revolution. Napoléon was keen to intervene, for it would open up a road to Italy via the Simplon. What the Republic hopes to be able to do is make Switzerland into a "sister republic", a unitary state that it would control and furnish with a constitution like that of France. For the time being, the storming of the treasury at Berne is a wise move financially (→ March 22).

Brune and Schauenburg's men make a triumphal entry into Berne.

Reinforcements for Tippoo Sahib

Ile de France, March 8

Captain L'Hermitte's frigate, *La Preneuse*, has set sail from Port Louis on its way to the Indian state of Mysore. It is transporting the 26 volunteers that the ambassadors from Tippoo Sahib succeeded in recruiting for the struggle against the English in India. It isn't much compared with the numbers that the privateer Ripaud had promised before the court of the oldest of France's Indian allies.

Private schools placed under surveillance

Paris, March 7

Even in the field of education, the Directory has no intention of letting things go. It has just adopted a series of measures with a view to stemming the proliferation of private schools, which are hotbeds of reactionary fervour. To make sure that none of these establishments escapes his control, the Minister of the Interior, Letourneux, sent out a circular on February 5th., asking all municipal delegates to carry out both monthly inspections and spot checks on the various schools now under surveillance. Officially, these visits will be carried out to make sure teachers are using the proper republican manuals; in fact, they will be made in the company of a commissioner from the executive Directory and a member of the departmental jury of education. In the belief that one can never be too careful, however, Letourneux has sent out a second circular in which municipal officials are encouraged to step up their visits, and doubly so when it is a private school that is under consideration.

Six-year delay for a diploma sent by post

Friedrich Schiller, the poet.

Iena, March 1

The German poet Schiller will have waited six years to receive his diploma. In August 1792, he was awarded a certificate of honorary citizenship of the French Republic by the legislative Assembly. The precious document was put in the post at once but has only recently arrived at its destination. It had got lost somewhere near Strasbourg. For Schiller, the delay is one of history's little ironies, for his views about the Revolution have changed in the meantime. Shocked by the king's execution, he now feels that the principles laid down in 1789 were correct, but that the people are not yet ripe for political reform.

A pair of elephants arrive at the Museum

Paris, March 27

They are impressive and scarce, and their arrival has excited the curiosity of the Parisian people. Born in Ceylon, they are 15 years old, seven feet tall and have very short, broken tusks. They lived in Holland before and would spend the earlier part of the winter at Cambrai, before moving into their new home at the Museum. This evening, the two elephants met up for the first time since starting out on their voyage, and it was a joy to see. The male entered the private "hut" that has been built for him behind a wall and began running his trunk along the bars. He then used his trunk to remove the railing separating him from his companion and, with much trumpet blasting and ear waving, went to join her.

A holiday is named in honour of youth

Grenoble, March 30

Civic virtues are not only taught in the classroom. To make sure the patriot has them by heart, national holidays are needed, like those each county seat organises several times a year in honour of Marriage, Old Age or Agriculture. Youth Day, which is being celebrated today in Grenoble, is easily one of the most important. It honours adolescents between 16 and 21 years old, and marks their entry into adult life. They have various symbolic acts to carry out, such as breaking through a circle formed around the national altar by a gathering of elders. They go in with a rose but must leave with a sword. This rite of passage from one age to another is also a form of social initiation for, during the ceremony, they will be given their card of citizenship and be entered in the register. They can even be given oak or olive branches that symbolise citizenship. The rite is a tribute to that Roman republic whom the Revolution and its lead-ers have always had a soft spot for. The most important thing, though, is to make sure, by appealing to their taste for pleasure, that the young people of today are pointed in the right direction: the road to be followed is, of course, that of politics.

"Young Man", painted by Girodet.

Rivalry between Berthier and Masséna

Rome, March 18

Masséna is as brave as he is greedy. The Directory's envoys did not have very far to look to find a pretext for relieving him of his post. What counted most in the decision, however, was not so much his greed as his avowed Jacobinism. Though it was well known, no one had been very troubled by it thus far. The person who has taken the most pleasure in Masséna's setback is General Berthier. The rivalry between the two men began a month ago. After being disowned by Paris, Berthier was forced to hand over command of the Army of Italy to Masséna. The latter, referred to by Napoléon as "victory's favourite child", would find his predecessor less impressed by his skills when it came to the fight. Now that his pride was up, Berthier saw even less reason for having to abandon the beautiful Signora Visconti. All the elements were there for a war between brothers. No sooner had Masséna arrived than the most violent events broke out. Firstly, all those cardinals who had decided to stay behind were thrown out of the city or clapped in irons. Next, the troops, who had been left destitute by their leaders, took to pillaging in

Masséna's position is none too sure.

great quantities, with the tacit consent of Masséna. At that point, the priests decided to launch a revolt against the French. The commander in chief managed to quell the insurrection, but by then certain of his officers had turned violently against him. Having remarked to the Directory on Masséna's inability to maintain discipline, Berthier would quickly turn the situation to his advantage.

Horse races are won before courts

Paris, March 22

The Paris tribunal has settled a long-standing disagreement in the sporting world. Racehorse owner Vilatte and equerry Carbonnel have been fighting it out in court for two years now. On July 28th. 1796, Carbonnel took part in a race at the Champ de Mars on a horse Vilatte, uncertain of his own abilities, had lent him. Carbonnel won the race. Vilatte had walked off with the prize, however, on the grounds that he was the owner of the winning horse. After two years of litigation, the tribunal has finally decided for the equerry. As the judges see it, the prize goes to the jockey, not to the horse. As the loan was a friendly one, moreover, it is thus Carbonnel who should take the prize. What's more, Vilatte has not only to return the horse and carriage that went to the winner, but must also pay 600 francs in damages and interest to Carbonnel.

Talleyrand gets his lover off the hook

Paris, March 23

Talleyrand's private life was on the Directory's agenda today. The minister had put in a request that Mme. Grand, arrested for spying on England's behalf, be freed. The reason for his request is simple and comes as a surprise: he is in love. This moving confession had little effect on the Directory, who have none of Talleyrand's tact when it comes to so delicate an issue. La Révellière saw this shameful liaison as a resurgence of vices condemned in the former clergy; Merlin de Douai thought it indicative of the minister's treachery; and Reubell found in it grounds for reaching harsh conclusions about sensuality. It was only when the circumspect François de Neufchâteau pointed out the need to respect privacy, that it was decided to free the lady and drop the issue. One thing this odd affair has shown is that Talleyrand is capable of falling in love.

🏛 **Directory**

2 *(Germinal 13, Year VI)*
Ile de France. Two battalions of line infantry mutiny and proclaim freedom for blacks (→4).

3 *(Germinal 14, Year VI)*
Philadelphia. In a message to Congress, President Adams makes public minister for foreign affairs Talleyrand's attempt at securing a pay-off during negotiations with the Americans.

9 *(Germinal 20, Year VI)*
France. Year IV elections begin. Their purpose is to renew a third of the deputies named to the legislative councils (→18).

12 *(Germinal 23, Year VI)*
Switzerland. 121 deputies from 12 cantons have gathered at Aarau, where they proclaim a united Swiss Republic.

12 *(Germinal 23, Year VI)*
Paris. The Directory decides to form an army of the East that will be run by Napoléon.→

15 *(Germinal 26, Year VI)*
Vienna. General Bernadotte, the French ambassador to Vienna, leaves the Austrian capital after anti-French rioting.

15 *(Germinal 26, Year VI)*
Paris. The electoral assembly for the Seine area splits in two; electors close to the Directory leave the Orator's assembly where the left is in the majority.

17 *(Germinal 28, Year VI)*
Paris. The English industrialist William Robinson takes out an import patent on machines for spinning linen. Because French industry lags behind the rest, the Directory is giving its support to any project that encourages an exchange of technology.

21 *(Floréal 2, Year VI)*
Paris. Naval officer Sir William Sydney Smith makes a spectacular escape from the Temple prison.

26 *(Floréal 7, Year VI)*
Geneva. The Directory, keen to assure safety on the road to Milan via le Valais, annexes the Republic of Geneva. The Republic was invaded by French troops on April 15th.→

29 *(Floréal 10, Year VI)*
Rome. The Italian opera has been making innovations: in Giusseppe Mosca's *Chi si Contenta Gode*, the women's parts, previously the work of castrati, were sung for the first time by real women.

All citizens must now conform with the revolutionary calendar

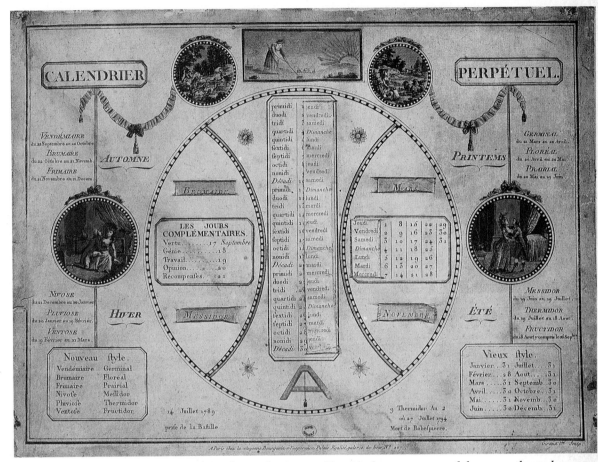

This perpetual calendar will help people who are having trouble with the new names of days, months and years.

Paris, April 3

As from today, quartidi (Sunday) Germinal 14, Year VI and day of the beech tree, everyone is obliged to conform with the ten-day week. What used to be Sunday will no longer be a day of rest, and the relevant authorities, tribunals and town councils will have only every tenth day off. Deeds drawn up by notaries, as well as newspapers and posters, will have to abide by the new terminology. The Directory's decree aims at taking the wind out of the sails of traditional religious practices. It is for this reason that local authorities have been asked to use the new calendar in choosing the days for fish-markets, making sure that they do not coincide with what used to be Fridays.

Jacobin mutiny in the Ile de France

Ile de France, April 4

The soldiers of the 107th. and 108th. line divisions have mutinied. In order to show their hostility to the government's plan to send them to Batavia, they staged an insurrection 48 hours ago, proclaiming the abolition of slavery. Since then, Port Louis has risen up in arms and the white and mulatto populations, fierce supporters of slavery, are laying siege to the barracks. The two battalions, finding themselves surrounded, are trying to negotiate a surrender: stationed in the island since June 1796, they have asked to return to France. The authorities are willing and have put the frigate *Seine* on stand-by (→June 29).

Curates involved in weird transactions

Paris, April 1

There are strange goings-on in the oratory of the Abbaye au Bois. As usual this Sunday, the more self-respecting women would place their louis in the curate's wooden bowl. The man of God claims that these alms are the price that must be paid to cleanse them of their sins: otherwise, they will become daughters of Satan. The priest who officiates at the nearby church of Saint Sulpice, who himself is rather short on funds, has openly accused his colleague of behaving in a far from Catholic manner. He thereby hopes to persuade the sinful lady parishioners to join his flock; and perhaps help with restorations...?

The Echo Song

A new song in which rulers are denigrated is is vogue. It is called the "Echo Song" due to the repetition of the last syllable of each verse:

Hear the story, great and small,
Of governors who reign supreme
Who by their laws have given all
Established with faith devout.
Out! Out! Out!

We know they came
From lands poor. With acumen
They'd laws to help their claim,
The people made their heroine.
Ruin! Ruin! Rhin!

Hear what these Solons declared,
We now are ready and prepared
To take in hand your high finance,
For we are trusty democrats.
Rats! Rats! Rats!

France's purpose fast iron-bound
Demands with vigour in this hour
These governors be rewarded.
Dead! Dead! Dead!

The Directory forms an army in secret: its destination, the East

Paris, April 12

Napoléon's dream is beginning to shape up. In the utmost secrecy, the Directory has just passed a decree allowing him to prepare an army of the East. On March 5th., Napoléon had presented the Directory with a detailed report on the manpower, firepower and financial backing needed to carry out a successful expedition in Egypt. Ten days later, Merlin de Douai recommended to the Ministry of the Interior that "the engineers, artists and other subordinates needed for the expedition he will lead, be put at General Bonaparte's disposal". As commander in chief, General Napoléon aims to drive the English from their various Eastern colonies and smash their trade counters on the Red Sea. The government has thus found an excellent pretext for getting the General, who is far too dangerous a rival to have around, away from the capital. As for Bonaparte, he hopes that Egypt will

A naval drum major and a gunner.

Sergeant-major and aide-de-camp.

bring him the glory that is needed if his increasingly transparent political ambitions are to be satisfied. Talleyrand is also satisfied at the outcome, for he had pleaded the

young general's cause. By backing Napoléon, the Minister for Foreign Affairs hopes finally to arrive at the Directory. Napoléon's promotion is therefore appreciated by all sides.

A new first scored for surgery

Paris, April 12

Health officer Imbert Delonnes has just pulled off a new first in surgery: he has removed a huge tumour from the groin of former foreign affairs minister, Charles Delacroix. The operation, a tricky one with a patient who is in his fifties, took two and a half hours. The patient, who was awake during it all, is doing well and need no longer fear for his manhood.

The tearful loyalty of Lodoïska Louvet

Chancy, April 17

Lodoïska will never abandon her beloved Louvet de Couvray. The inconsolable widow has arranged for him to go with her when she leaves Paris to take up residence in the peace and calm of the Loiret. She has had her loved-one's body transferred to the memorial she has had erected for him at Chancy. There, she bought the small farm they once dreamed of as a home for their love. Lodoïska has decided to break off all contact with Paris and

doesn't in the least regret abandoning the lottery office she used to run. She fully intends to see to her husband's works, and in particular, his *Les Amours du Chevalier Faublas* which is so fashionable in Paris these days as to need reprinting, now that stocks have been exhausted. Alone, and withdrawn from the world, Lodoïska waits peacefully for the death that will at last enable her to return to the arms of her one true love, the handsome Chevalier de Faublas.

Bernadotte causes scandal in Vienna

Vienna, April 14

Bernadotte almost got himself lynched. It was not by accident, however, that the French ambassador decided to provoke the most powerful court in Europe. To show that he had by no means abandoned his republican beliefs, the diplomat hoisted a huge French tricolour in full view of an exceptionally large market-day crowd. The crowd at once rushed in to tear the object of their wrath to shreds, and then set about threatening the ambassador who, to save his skin, was obliged to brandish his pistols. Hypnotised with fear, the crowd began crying: "Death to all Frenchmen, not one of them is any good." (→April 15).

Republican feasts

In Paris republican banquets, or "gamelle", are again being held. The citizen-guests eat from the same dish and sing this song to the tune of "La Carmagnole";

Why we are all so joyful here:
Because a meal in homely style
Is the only one worthwhile.
Long live the pot,
Eat together from the stew-pan.
Long live our communal cocotte.

In order to live free from care
"Tis here you should repair;
Long live the pot,
Eat together from the stew-pan.
Long live our communal cocotte.

The girl so passionate, who's
Endeavouring a lover to choose,
To any caddish proud poseur
A jolly fellow will prefer
Long live the pot,
Eat together from the stew-pan.
Long live the communal cocotte.

The jail that thrives on suicides

Paris, April 13

Louis Delaunay, formerly the republican consul in Philadelphia, has drowned himself in the Seine. His body was identified by one of his neighbours, telegraph engineer François Chappe, in the morgue at the Basse Geôle. The morgue is run by Daude and Boille, who act as both caretakers and specialists in the rag-trade: they examine body and dress, locate bandaging and use wounds to identify the cause of death. They can also tell at a glance the victim's social background.

The Abbaye de Cluny, which became a national asset, was auctioned off to a Mâcon businessman on April 21st. 1798.

Elections rigged by men working for the Directory

While the deputy, having made his fortune, drives off in his elegant tilbury...

... his successor arrives, with a good way to go before finding the good life.

France, April 18

The Directory did not want to risk losing its majority. To be sure of victory, it would have to get the royalists out of the way and then win massive support from moderate republican deputies sympathetic to the cause. It therefore decided to supervise at first hand the elections that have just been carried out to replace a third of the legislative body. And no holds were barred. It would have no qualms, for instance, about using municipal and departmental pressure to achieve its ends. The primary assemblies were too difficult to manipulate on account of their number: the Directory thus decided to concentrate its efforts on the secondary ones. It selected for the task a number of commissioners who owed their promotion entirely to intervention from the Directory. Their job was to make sure electors chose "the right vote" by paying hard cash, if need be. Failing that, the police would make preventative arrests, take over opposition papers and, as actually happened in certain towns, even go so far as to close down republican clubs. Just to be on the safe side, Sotin, thought to harbour Jacobin sympathies, would be replaced on February 13th. as Minister of the Constabulary by Dondeau. The most effective strategy, however, was the one Merlin de Douai put together: government agents were posted to any electoral assembly where there was a chance the vote might "go the wrong way". Their task was to stir up dissension.

Dissident meetings would choose their own deputies, along the same lines as those by which they were chosen. When faced with two lists for a single constituency, the legislative body would choose the one most in the Directory's favour. It is clearly difficult for citizens to say what they really think under such conditions (→ May 11).

In Paris, there is no longer any scaffold on the Place de la Révolution.

Kléber is defeated at home in Alsace

Colmar, April 18

His friends voted for him, but that wasn't enough. Accused of royalism in Paris and of Jacobinism by the people of Alsace, Kléber has not been elected. On learning that legislative elections were to be held, he decided to present his candidacy for the Upper Rhine region. For, after resigning his position in the Sambre and Meuse army, he had returned as an ordinary citizen to Colmar. His only political ambition had been "to make a fool of those imbeciles at the Directory", whom he considers to be "hypocrites and amateurs".

Monge's honesty is starting to pay off

Italy, April 16

It was by post that Monge would learn of the supreme homage paid to his honesty and moderation. He has recently been appointed to a three-year post on the Council of Elders by the colony of Cayenne and the departments of les Bouches du Rhône and la Seine. He has also been named to the Council of the Five Hundred by the Côte d'Or. A member of the Academy of Science and a former First Lord of the Admiralty, this son of a street vendor is an ardent republican. Napoléon has entrusted him with founding the new Italian Republic.

The "terrorist's" return: Barère is back

Tarbes, April 18

Revenants exist. The electors of Tarbes have just sent one off to join the Council of the Five Hundred: Barère. He had disappeared off the face of the earth, after escaping from the de Saintes prison two years ago. Nor had anyone ever thought he would be the subject of a recent amnesty. Only the people of Tarbes, who had been hiding him, knew anything about the man who was once so popular. Deeply moved, Barère has expressed his gratitude at the rehabilitation. All is not yet settled, however. How will the members feel about this "terrorist", who in Paris is known as the "monster"?

Barère is back under the spotlights.

The Rhineland communes are not keen to unite with France

Annexation of the Geneva Republic

Rhineland, April

The Cisrhineland republicans are in mourning: the communes of the Rhineland do not want to become part of France. The republicans had assured the Directory, however, of their compatriots' desire to assume French nationality. Meanwhile, an endless round of talks was dragging on at Rastatt, apropos the treaty of Campoformio and the ins and outs of transferring sovereignty from the territories along the east bank of the Rhine. The Directory had likewise ordered Rudler, as commissioner general for the Rhine, to get the local populations to sign petitions demanding union with France. The Austrian plenipotentiaries would not quarrel with the general wishes of the people. The Rhineland patriots also did everything in their power to assure the campaign was a success. They made use of their newspapers, subsidised by France, to manipulate public opinion. In Bingen, Mathias Metternich would publish his *Entretiens Politiques des Bords du Rhin*; while, at Trèves, J. J. Haan edited the *Journal pour le Département de la Sarre*. Görres ran *La Feuille Rouge* at Coblentz, where his gift for polemic and his mordant irony were directed at the aristocracy, the clergy and the Holy Roman Empire's many outmoded institutions. Rudler, for his part, made any number of promises: the abolition of feudal dues, an end to crippling commercial bonds and a reduction in the costs occasioned in maintaining a military presence. For all their good work, 75 per cent of voters declined to take part. In both Bonn and Coblentz, politically the twin heart of the area, very few people would sign the petition.

Rhineland patriots planting a tree of Liberty at Spire on March 21st., 1798.

Leading Vaude patriot Pierre Ochs.

Geneva, April 26

The Republic of Geneva must renounce its sovereignty and its various alliances: a treaty, ratified with only a tiny majority by the town's council, has annexed it to France. Since 1792, when the city became an enclave with the annexation of the Savoy, it was only a matter of time. Hemmed in by the French blockade, Geneva was more or less cornered, for the French ambassador, Desporges, would do anything to get what he wanted. He harangued the people, opened the magistrates' mail and had a finger in just about every pie in the town.

A new cult spreads through Paris

Paris, April 29

Theophilanthropy has moved to a new temple known as the "City". The building is none other, in fact, than Notre Dame, which followers of the new cult now share with the Catholics. The celebrated basilica is the seventeenth sanctuary to be adopted by the theophilanthropists of Paris, who also frequent Saint Eustache, the temple of the "Social Contract"; Saint Gervais, that of "Fidelity"; and Saint Sulpice, that of "Harmony". The relative simplicity of the movement, along with its moral and political values, have conferred a certain popularity on the new cult. It also enjoys the support of the Directory, via La Révellière Lépeaux, known for his violent anti-Catholicism.

At the Directory's public sessions, citizens hand the ushers petitions or written requests in the hope of having their demands met. This gives the government officials a chance to show off their finery.

Just what is Napoléon doing at Toulon?

Toulon, May 10

The news has spread like wildfire through the town: Bonaparte is in Toulon. Though he checked in to the Naval Hotel last night in the utmost secrecy, he was recognised by a marine lieutenant. His arrival immediately boosted the morale of the troops from the army of Italy. Left to fend for themselves by the Directory, they have been living on their wits ever since, and have taken to looting and pillaging. The arrival of Bonaparte can mean only one thing: things will soon be getting under way. But Napoléon intends to keep quiet for the moment about the objective he has been working towards for a full six weeks. He has had his hands full assembling crew and fleet, and recruiting the various admirals and generals. It is crucial that the whole operation be kept a secret: London must not get wind that Napoléon is putting together an Egyptian expedition.

Napoléon, as sketched by David.

Toussaint Louverture scatters the English

Saint Domingue, May 14

The capital of Saint Domingue gave a royal welcome to the man who had liberated them from the English, when he arrived in Port Républicain. Prancing at the head of his 600-strong cavalry of blacks, whites and mulattoes, the Negro general stunned the crowd. Riding slowly between two rows of soldiers presenting arms, and to the sound of a salute fired from the forts nearby, he made his way from the Intendance Square to the temple, where priests and officials stood in waiting before moving inside for the Te Deum. The general had taken great care over his arrival.

The very first day after the English surrender, he had granted a general amnesty for all Creoles who had served the English authorities. The increasing esteem in which he is held by the people is due to the fact that he has always gone out of his way to avoid bloodshed and make sure discipline is observed. In the areas under his control, order has been restored and the labourers have returned to their fields. The French presence in the island will have cost the English 40,000 livres. If ever the Directory went back on its plans to abolish slavery, Saint Domingue could proclaim its independence from one day to the next.

The sunny season is back in Bordeaux

Bordeaux, May 4

There's nothing like a good party to whip up a flagging patriotism. The central office at Bordeaux has just invited citizens to "spend the month of Floréal celebrating the return of the sunny season and its munificence towards the whole of nature". They are asked to decorate their homes and sing and dance "as they once did on Sundays", no doubt in the hope that some kind of sun worship will remind people of the old rites carried out in honour of the Marian month; and thus prove more successful than the cult of the Supreme Being...

Will Restif make a good teacher?

Allier, May 3

The central jury of republican education has made its decision. The best-qualified candidate for the History chair at the central school of Moulins is the writer Restif de La Bretonne. Until now, he was best known for his contributions to literature. The jury was dazzled, however, by the acute historical sense shown in the dissertation Restif presented to the department's administrative body. All agreed that his application for the post was the best, which leaves the writer in a quandary: he has just been sent off to the Police Ministry. Will he want to leave Paris for Moulins? (→ Dec. 98)

Carnot ripostes and points the finger

Augsburg, May

Carnot's most recent work is wreaking havoc. As soon as it came out, booksellers rushed to lay in stocks of his *Réponse à Bailleul,* where the former member of the Directory, exiled since Fructidor 18, tears his old colleagues and one of their henchmen apart. His gift for polemic and the violence of his sarcasm more than justify the success of Carnot's work, which will soon be available in France, despite being banned. Smugglers and pirate publishers will between them make sure this sensational text gets read.

A prominent and wealthy Swiss has one of his servants hand over his little "contribution to the war" to a detachment from the French army.

Isabey's studio is one of the main meeting-places for artists

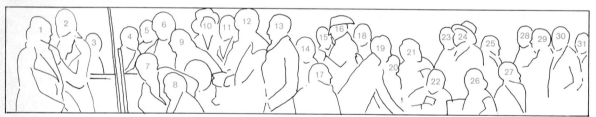

1. E.H.H. Méthul, composer; 2. Hoffmann, art critic; 3. Unknown; 4. Charles Louis Corbet, sculptor; 5. Martin Drolling, genre painter; 6. Jean Louis Demarne, landscape artist; 7. J. B. Isabey, "painter of external relations"; 8. François Gérard, historical painter; 9. Nicolas Taunay, genre and historical painter; 10. J. F. Swebach, painter of battles; 11. Charles Bourgeois, miniaturist; 12. Guillon Lethière, historical painter; 13. Carle Vernet, painter; 14. Duplessis Berteaux, engraver; 15. P. F. L. Fontaine, architect; 16. Charles Percier, architect; 17. Baptiste the elder, of the Comédie Française; 18. J. T. Thiébaut, painter and architect; 19. J. F. Van Daël, flower painter; 20. P. J. Redouté, flower painter; 21. Talma, actor; 22. Charles Meynier, historical painter; 23. L. L. Boilly, genre and portrait painter author of this work; 24. Chenard, artist at the Italian theatre; 25. Xavier Bidault, landscape artist; 26. Girodet, historical painter; 27. Denis Chaudet, sculptor; 28. Maurice Blot, engraver; 29. F. F. Lemot, sculptor; 30. Giovacchino Serangeli, historical painter; 31. Unknown. (After J. Mayor, Review of Napoleonian Studies, 1914).

Paris, May

The painter Jean Baptiste Isabey is pleasant to have around. Not only is he handsome and well built, as revealed by the elegant portrait his colleague Gérard made a few years ago, in which Isabey can be seen holding hands with his little daughter; he is also an excellent host. He likes to bring together, in his studio at the Louvre, the wide circle of friends his natural kindness has attracted. If the painting Boilly has made of them is anything to go by, these get-togethers, at which people from widely differing backgrounds are present, are a tribute to Isabey's open mindedness. All the major disciplines are represented: architecture by Percier and Fontaine, who have decorated his studio in the classical style; music, by the composer Méhul; the theatre, by the two actors Talma and Chénard, the famous portrait of the latter as standard-bearer and sansculotte during a civic banquet also being the handiwork of Boilly; engraving by Duplessis Bertaux, who aims to record all the high points of the Revolution; genre painting by Martin Drolling; war painting by Swebach; landscape by Jean Louis Demarne; and history painting by François Gérard and Girodet. Then there is Redouté, who paints flowers in such minute detail, and, equally prominent, the man who painted *l'Atelier,* Louis Léopold Boilly in person. For many years, Boilly would specialise in semi-erotic subjects but, accused of indecency by his compatriot Wicar, he suddenly started treating more strictly republican themes: it was his *Triomphe de Marat* that would help him out of a tricky situation, bringing him a certain amount of success or, at the very least, the peace of mind needed for a painter to be able to work at all. His *Atelier d'Isabey,* which he is intending, moreover, to present publicly at the forthcoming Salon, also reveals his gifts as a portraitist. Before arriving at the final version of the painting, Boilly would look long and hard at each of the various figures, as well as making a large number of preliminary sketches.

Mme. de Staël is a citizen of France

Switzerland, May 17

There is always a flaw in one's happiness. Despite her passionate desire to be a citizen of France, Mme. de Staël was disturbed to learn that the Five Hundred and the Elders had ratified the French annexation of Geneva. She fears her father may, as a result, be classed retroactively as an émigré and have his goods sequestered. Above all, however, she would have liked the Republic to have opened its arms to her, in recognition of her amazing literary genius. She can at least console herself with the fact that she can now return to her beloved Paris whenever she likes.

Food-stalls down on the Seine

If you walk down by the Seine any night around seven, you will notice a strong smell of herrings in the air. The pavements are lined on both sides with stalls that offer simple dishes at very reasonable prices to the poor. For 15 sols, you can buy three herrings sprinkled with chives and dipped in vinegar. A rickety table is piled up with plates of stewed prunes, lentils swimming in a clear gruel, leaves of salad or even grilled fish. Further down the quays, a tradesman displays a plate of black-pudding, eggs and a piece of either meat or fish. In front of his stall, a huge pot, supported by a pair of stones, is bubbling away while garlands of herrings are hung out to dry in the sun. The customers eat these modest dishes, whose portions are small, standing up. They are often so hungry that they will swallow the lentils without even bothering to chew them, or wolf down the herrings in a single mouthful, without stopping to remove the bones. The caterers who provide these dishes are clearly not going to get rich in the process. Their one reward, however, is the gratitude of the city's many down-and-outs: for without the help of these men and women, many of the poor would perhaps have died from starvation by now.

Floréal 22, Year VI elections have been rigged

Paris, May 11

The Directory has just pulled off what might be called a "coup". The law passed by the Five Hundred on May 8th., and today approved by the Council of the Elders, excludes 106 recently elected deputies from the legislative body. The measure would appear to be quite legal since it stems from the validation process which is one of the Council's rights. In reality, however, the deputies who have been excluded turn out all to have been on the left, while all the members who have been chosen to replace them seem to have been paid off by the Directory. The whole thing smacks of large-scale corruption, aimed at reinforcing the majority. Moreover, as soon as the Councils began verifying the electoral proceedings, department by department, three weeks ago,

the Directory immediately stepped in to inform them that no former "terrorists" could be allowed to take part in the Assembly. Deputy Creuzé Latouche even went so far as to say he would not permit "wild beasts" like these to represent the nation. Despite opposition from deputies Lamarque and Jourdan, the Councils have now annulled the elections in 48 departments. In 19 others, they have chosen candidates elected by minority splinter groups, whose internal divisions had been provoked by government agents. Their argument is that they could not allow candidates to be elected when it knew perfectly well they had no intention of respecting the oath of loyalty to the Constitution. In short, it is the very principle of national representation that is now under threat.

Four of the five practising Directors, the missing one being La Révellière.

A theatre has been destroyed by fire

Paris, May 30

The Variétés Amusantes theatre has been reduced to ashes. Given the number of highly inflammable stage sets it contained for major productions, it comes as no great surprise. The manager Lazzari had been alternating harlequinades with *Il Comitato di Pietra*, an anonymous pastiche of Molière's *Dom Juan ou le Festin de Pierre*, in which a lot of stage sets were used: Na-

ples, Marseilles, la Castille, even a hell where the public watched the hero being tortured before vanishing in a river of fire. Some time after the show had finished, the manager returned to the main hall and found the stage filled with smoke. The building's water supply was all but empty. Even though an actor went off at once to find help, the fire was too far advanced to do anything by the time it arrived.

Napoléon is steadily making his way East

Mediterranean, May 31

The voyage is getting dull. Two weeks after leaving Toulon, the crew still have no idea where they are going and are getting restless. The appalling heat, the promiscuity and the lack of food are beginning to get to them. Fights are frequent and the only other distraction is cards: some even go so far as to

stake the shoes they are wearing. On the flagship, Napoléon wiles away the evenings in conversation with the scholars and artists who have joined him on the voyage. He enjoys talking about chemistry with Berthollet and physics with Monge, while with Quesnot he can discover all kinds of things about the way in which the sky is organised.

Paris linked to Strasbourg by telegraph

A description of a telegraph signal.

Paris, May 31

The articulated arms of Chappe's optical aerial telegraph system will be able to transmit coded messages from the French government to its ambassadors at the congress of Rastatt. A 25-word telegraph will now take only six hours to travel along the 480 kilometres of cable connecting Paris to Strasbourg. In July 1793, as a result of the war on the northern frontiers, the minister for war, Carnot, decided to set up a link between Paris and Lille. This time round, it was the negotiations to be held on the other side of the Rhine that brought the realisation of Chappe's second project, which had been forgotten up until then, to fruition. The telegraph, it would seem, exists only to help fill a very particular kind of deadline.

On May 19th., Bonaparte's squadron left the slipway at Toulon for Malta.

Parisians see unusual solar phenomenon

Paris, May 24

The sky is full of rare surprises just now. Around eleven o'clock this morning, the sun changed its appearance. The fiery sphere was suddenly surrounded by a luminous circle. After observing it through

their glasses from the Observatory, Joseph de Lalande and his nephew Michel, renowned as astronomers, are still uncertain as to how the phenomenon, remarkable for both being both unheard of and sudden, is to be explained.

Sieyès is the new ambassador to Berlin

Deputy for la Sarthe on the Council of the Five Hundred and now diplomat.

Berlin, June 6

The new French ambassador to Prussia is creating a stir. Sieyès, it's true, is already well known in the country: his writings have been translated into German and he is said to be in correspondence with the philosopher Kant. Though the Prussians are impressed by him, they are also a little distrustful: his past record on regicide is not likely to endear him to a Court where émigrés are plentiful. Nor is Sieyès much given to compromise. When the Chief of Protocol wanted to know his rank and nobility, Sieyès made it quite clear that he would make do with being a citizen of France. Today, when it came to paying formal homage to the King, Sieyès, dressed sombrely by comparison with the usual gold braids to be found on uniforms, asked to be exempted from carrying a sword in the King's presence, on account of his former church status and his love of peace. The request was granted, but it did not go down well, it seems, for no one spoke to Sieyès during the long ceremony.

The endless voyage of the convict priests

Cayenne, June 9

There are 500 priests on board the frigate *Décade*, which has just arrived in Guyana. They originally left Rochefort on board a different vessel, the *Charente*, but the boat ended up with the English fleet hot on its trail and had to turn back. The convicts were then transferred to the *Décade*. They received their sentence as a result of the law passed on Fructidor 19. Their ranks include both "the rebellious" and "the constitutionals": the law states, in effect, that any priest who is found guilty of "a breach of the public peace" can, without further need of evidence as to his crime, be arrested on the spot and sent for deportation.

Cadoudal's English mission has failed

Brittany, June

The time is not right, he must wait. That is the frustrating advice Cadoudal brought back with him from his trip across the Channel. On behalf of the Chouan leaders, he had gone to try and convince the Comte d'Artois that, if he did not come and assume command of the royalist forces in western France, they would no longer have even the remotest chance of overthrowing the Republic. "General Georges", however, was unable to persuade the prince, who contented himself with subsidising their efforts.

A new régime is in place at The Hague

The Hague, June 12

First the Jacobins, and now the moderates have resorted to force. Taking advantage of his military prestige and his reputation as a faultless patriot, General Daendels, who also has the French general, Joubert, on his side, has gathered all the malcontents into his ranks. Backed up by troops, he disarmed the National Guard, drove out the deputies and arrested Vreede, the man responsible for the coup last January. Discredited by the makeshift Constitution they assembled in two days, by a rigged referendum and arbitrary arrests, the Jacobin authorities have been replaced by an interim directory and 44-man assembly, pending new elections.

Schimmelpenninck, a lawyer and a republican moderate, represents the Batavian Republic in France.

Napoléon takes possession of Malta

Valletta, June 11

The island's batteries remained silent. A parliamentarian bearing the scarlet flag with the white cross of the Knights of Saint John, moved along the roadstead towards Napoléon's ship. It was the end for Malta. Supposedly inviolable, the capital would not hold out for long under French fire. Three days ago, Napoléon gave orders to surround the island with a vast armada of floating cannons: the unusual use he made of Admiral Brueys's vessels in this way, immediately plunged the good knights into the most terrible confusion. Rather than put up a fight, they locked themselves away in the capital, Valletta, thereby leaving the rest of the island to the French. The next day, Napoléon's army went ashore to little more than an occasional cannon fire from the fort. The victims under siege had not entirely surrendered their dignity, however, and, under orders from the Bailiff of Bellemont, would attempt an escape, albeit in vain. Marmont was able to drive them back into Valletta, however, with such force that the Maltese abandoned all further idea of resistance on the spot. The rest of the day passed quietly, to the pitiful small sound of cannon fire. The evening was a little more eventful: in the belief that the French had started an attack, the soldiers on guard at Senglea took to their boats. The people of Malta, thinking it was an enemy attack, opened fire on their own soldiers. The confusion was soon total. The belief that Gen. Napoléon had launched a night attack spread like wildfire and sentinels started picking one

The cannon fire was not enough to counter the assault of the French forces.

Napoléon prepares to lead his forces ashore during the invasion of Malta.

another off. There was obviously only one real alternative now, and that was to make an unconditional surrender. At midnight, the barons of the island gathered in the palace of the grand master. The secular order had finally collapsed.

Ireland, June 16

The Irish are sick of waiting for the French. Nevertheless, the plan in Paris had been that Wolfe Tone would not give the signal to begin the revolt before the French fleet had landed. The Irish, however, decided to take up arms on May 23rd. in the hope that they might thereby speed up the French. It would not take long, however, for England to snuff out the revolt, and O'Connor, one of its leaders, has now been arrested. The situation is critical and the Irish have appealed to the Directory for help (→ July 14).

The "Seine" goes down into the sea

Rochefort, June 29

Soldiers and sailors fought for nearly two days without a break. Their courage, however, was not enough to stave off defeat. Three English frigates had pursued, and finally caught up with, the *Seine*. That vessel was on its way home with, on board, all those who had tried to free the slaves on the isle de France last April. They put up a good show: to the very last, the captain, Lhermitte, had refused to strike the colours. The vessel went down off the Vendée coast.

The order of the Knights of Malta

By the time Napoléon makes its acquaintance, the order of the Knights of Malta is already on the decline. In many respects, it is a relic from the Middle Ages lost among the waves. All that remains of the time when the island was first given to Saint John of Jerusalem by Charles V, are the fortifications of Valletta. Behind those walls, some 500 brave knights continue to live off the wealth accumulated over the years. The majority of these knights are French and support the monarchy. They are led by a Bavarian grand master, Ferdinand de Hompesch. After the surrender of Valletta, the French troops put their hands on some 1,200 cannon, 30,000 rifles, 7,000 barrels of powder, two vessels and four galleys. The order's treasures are thought to be worth around twenty million livres. Their resources, however, have substantially diminished since the Revolution which, in 1791, abolished all orders of chivalry: being founded on principles of birth, all such orders were, by definition, fundamentally hostile to the very concept of equality. For Napoléon, however, the real source of interest in the island is strategic, on account of the privileged position it occupies in the Mediterranean. There can be no question of allowing the English to get so much as a foot inside the door as this would put an end to any further communications between Napoléon and France.

The English despair on hearing that Malta has been taken by the French.

Late honours for a writer of the future

Paris, June 10

After hearing his earlier plays booed off the stage, time and again, René Charles de Pixerécourt is at last reaping the honours. His three-act play, *Victor ou l'Enfant de la Forêt,* is so successful that every Paris theatre now cries out for his works. The play is set in a chateau in Bohemia. Victor, a child found in a forest, is in love with Clémence, daughter of the baron of Fritzierne who had originally found Victor. A series of adventures then ensues. Grandiloquent in the extreme, this spectacular piece of theatre marks a new arrival on the scene.

Pixerécourt, the author of the play.

Napoléon prepares for his new campaign

Mediterranean, June 22

The *Orient* sails towards Egypt. Nearly a month and a half after leaving Malta, Napoléon has drawn up three proclamations in readiness for the landing. The first is for the ground forces, the second for the Arab population, the third for the Pasha of Egypt, Abu Bekr. All three were printed whilst on board, thanks to Arab lettering provided by former Vatican equipment. In the message to be delivered to the local populations, France is cast in the role of liberator. Napoléon has come to deliver the Egyptians from the tyranny of the Turks: "If Egypt is their farmland, let them produce the lease God gave them." After a few more honeyed phrases of the same kind, Napoléon addresses all those who might be tempted to fight on the wrong side: "A curse on all who take up arms with the mamelukes to oppose our forces". In his letter to the pasha, he assures him that he need have nothing to fear from France, which has come to deliver him from abject slavery. As for his declaration to the troops, in it Napoléon enthuses about the grandeur of their historical mission and asks them to respect the Koran and the local populations.

Prussia votes against abolishing serfdom

Königsberg, June

The Prussian nobility may enjoy reading Voltaire and Kant but it has no intention of sacrificing its own interests to those of Reason. An anonymous pamphlet, calling for the abolition of serfdom, was passed round during a session of the Landtag for western Prussia. When billed at the Assembly, the motion was unanimously rejected: by both wealthy and bourgeois deputies, that is to say. Prussia, nevertheless, thinks of herself as a very bastion of reason, and claims to have the most enlightened public administration in Europe. For this reason, certain intellectuals, and in particular the jurists of Königsberg, are hoping their new king, Frederick William III, will soon carry out the reform. A modern-day state cannot allow such a morally and economically ruinous state of affairs to continue.

The leader of the Jéhus is to be beheaded

Lyons, June 10

The Court of Appeal has upheld the verdict passed by the criminal tribunal of the Haute Loire: Jean Storkenfeld will go to the scaffold. A wanted man for three years in the region, this émigré and deserter was born in Chambéry and, for a short time, would make his living as an actor at the Théatre de Lyon. He would later make his name as leader of the Jéhu group. Convinced that the "liberty cap was the source of all ills and that it was time to have done with it", he gathered a group of bandits with the fleur-de-lis. The accused was on trial for two attempted murders, one on a vinegar-maker, the other on a housing marshal. Duport, a former deputy for Mont Blanc, was delighted: "His friends will now know that, sooner or later, the author of the crime must also pay."

Prieur de la Côte d'Or retires from political life

Paris, June 26

Prieur de la Côte d'Or is going back to the army he abandoned eight years ago. The only politician from Year II still to have a seat in Year IV, Prieur has decided not to complete his term. He hopes in this way to avoid hostilities from the Directory, which is out to get any of Robespierre's alleged accomplices. His career began when, as a young officer at Belfort, he was named to the Legislative chamber. He then moved to the Convention where he was made responsible for public education. At the height of the Terror, he sat on the Committee of Public Safety as the equivalent of armaments minister. Appointed to the Legislative body, he later joined the Council of the Five Hundred where he oversaw gunpowder production. His appointment to the Fortifications Committee signals the end of his political career.

The Festival of Agriculture is one of the most popular feasts. Young farm girls and pastry-makers march from the Halle to the temple of Cérès, on the Champs Elysées, carrying baskets of goods.

July 1798
from 1st. to 31st.

The French forces go ashore in Egypt

While the landing is being completed, the governor of Alexandria hands over the keys of the city to Bonaparte.

Alexandria, July 1

Dawn was just coming up, when the formidable armada sailed into view. The sea appeared to have vanished: there were only boats and sky. Never before had so many sails graced the Mediterranean: 13 line vessels with 1,026 cannon on board, 9 frigates, 11 corvettes and dispatch-boats, 232 store ships and over 300 transport vessels presented the inhabitants of Alexandria with an impressive spectacle. Having spent the day considering where best to anchor, Napoléon gave the order to go ashore, in spite of a heavy swell. The situation was too urgent to have time to stop and consider: only 24 hours earlier, Nelson and the English fleet had been cruising these selfsame waters in search of the French. General Menou's men are the first to set foot on the shores where Pompey died. The landing, however, looks set to be a lengthy and delicate affair: 24,000 infantry, 4,000 cavalry and 3,000 gunners have to be got ashore, along with 17,000 sailors. Transferring all the equipment needed for the journey will also prove an arduous task. Apart from 1,000 artillery guns, 12,000 spare rifles, 100,000 bullets and cartridges, 467 vehicles, 680 horses and considerable reserves of gunpowder, there is also a printing press, a library, and enough food and water to last forty people a hundred days, to be attended to. Napoléon is present to spur the operations on. The young commander in chief plans to hide his divisions behind the high ramparts of Alexandria as soon as the opportunity presents itself. His Egyptian dream, after all, might very well go up in smoke if Nelson and his men were to turn up at the very moment the French forces were engaged in getting their forces ashore.

Relations between France and the United States deteriorate

Philadelphia, July 7

Relations are increasingly uneasy between France and the United States. The American Congress has just unilaterally rescinded all the treaties it has signed with France since the Independence. It has also decided to expel anyone belonging to a country at war with the United States, foremost among them being France, of course. These measures are the more recent additions to a long list of attacks on the French government. As early as last June, Congress made clear its intentions by authorising commercial vessels to carry arms in case of French attacks. At the same time, a law was passed requiring a person to have lived for fourteen years in the country to obtain citizenship. Next, Congress authorised the expulsion of any foreigner considered to be a threat. This whimsical measure was aimed, of course, at France. With the abrogation of the treaties, the break seems complete. Given the current climate, Paris is not quite sure how it should go about trying to improve relations.

▷

The tomb of Diane de Poitiers, crowned by "Diana with stag", in the garden of the museum of French monuments.

A home is found for "Diana with stag"

Paris, July

Alexandre Lenoir is a happy man. The courageous and indefatigable founder of the museum of French monuments has just noted down in his journal the arrival of a number of packing cases from the central authorities for the Eure et Loire. They contain some of the stained-glass windows from the château of Anet and, above all, the gorgeous "Diana with stag" which used to adorn a fountain in the grounds and has somehow miraculously escaped destruction. It will be one of the jewels in the Elysée gardens' crown, where several of the monumental sculptures that were saved from the upheavals of the Revolution have already been housed. In September 1796, Lenoir was allowed by the Ministry of the Interior to extend his museum as far as the adjoining garden in the Rue des Petits Augustins, now open to the public. The minister, who made an official visit the following June, is pleased with the results.

A bumpy first flight for Célestine and her balloon

Seine, July 14

The sky was clear and a good crowd had turned out. The balloon rose slowly into the air, then found the ascending currents that would allow it to turn several times on its axis. In the cockpit sat Garnerin, a seasoned navigator, with Citizeness Henry on her first flight. To be allowed to take part, Célestine Henry had to get past the central bureau for conduct, for her participation alongside an airborne adventurer struck the authorities as suspect. As it turned out, she was very well behaved. She limited herself to a quick drop of eau-de-cologne to dispel her nausea as the balloon reached the 3,000-metre mark. Then, all of a sudden, the balloon started pitching about and went into an abrupt descent. Garnerin at once opened the safety-valve and threw the anchor out on to the ground for a smooth landing. The heroes were somewhat surprised, however, when a policeman walked up and asked to see their passports!

A hard and scarifying march through the burning sands of Egypt

Damanhur, July 7

After five days heavy marching under the Egyptian sun, the good humour of Desaix's men has largely evaporated. Fourteen leagues of stifling heat separate Alexandria from Damanhur. Each miserable village they go through presents the same depressing array of dried-up wells, and the soldiers have had to make do with the odd puddle of mud. For the "old hands" from the Italian campaign, the lush plains of Lombardy are little more than a memory. Here, reality has only one name: the desert. An infinity of sand dunes, exhausting marches under the attentive eyes of vultures, and none of the joy they felt on setting out. Anyone who had hoped to get a good night's sleep after the day's torments, will have been in for a shock. The dew that settles at sunset cuts through their clothes as swiftly as any mameluke spear. The shifts in temperature have caused so much conjunctivitis that Larrey, the chief surgeon, has been unable to attend to them all. Three days after setting out from Alexandria, Desaix has alerted Napoléon to the appalling conditions to be met with during the march to Damanhur: "Should the army fail to cross the desert at less than lightning speed, it will be sure to perish."

Right after leaving their ships, the French soldiers led by Desaix had to face the hardships of the desert.

Victory at the Pyramids opens the road to Cairo

Despite their utter exhaustion, the French soldiers had to face nineteen hours of continuous attacks from the fearsome mameluke forces.

Gizeh, July 21

The entire Nile valley seems to have caught fire. On the right bank of the river, Bey Ibrahim's vessels are engulfed in flames. To prevent the French forces crossing the river and continuing their pursuit, the Bey has had to sacrifice his fleet. The bravest of the Moslem knights have rushed headlong into death in this Ottoman version of Agincourt. Two thousand mamelukes, led by Murad, have fallen to Napoléon's army. Their leader himself, his face covered with blood, only narrowly escaped being captured. On the left bank of the Nile, the French soldiers are an extraordinary sight. Lit up by the flames sent up by Ibrahim's burning fleet, they are celebrating victory with a vengeance. Some are draped in black sable cloaks or tunics of gold; others sport turbans running with enemy blood. The pillaging is chaotic. Grouped around the bodies of dead mamelukes, the soldiers are en-

gaged in a particularly macabre form of bartering. As the cavalry had arrived in battle bearing their entire wealth, as is the custom, there is a lot of gold changing hands just now. A cashmere shawl can be had for fifteen francs, a camel or a magnificent Arab thoroughbred for thirty.

When, on the morning of the battle, the French discovered the enemy massed near the Pyramids at Gizeh, they were suddenly terrified. The sight was enough to freeze the blood of the most hardened warrior. The entire mameluke cavalry was there, gleaming almost, under the early light of the sun. The armoured steel, the gold on their clothes and the pearl and precious stones adorning their horses: there was just this one long line of fire and light. Murad had lined his cavalry up along the left bank of the Nile. Nearby, in the village of Embabeh, 12,000 fellaheen, armed to the teeth, and 40 cannons lay ready

in support. More than 50,000 men were calmly waiting for the French army to emerge. Ibrahim, however, would turn out to be a less reliable ally. By no means certain of the outcome of the impending battle, he decided to stay put on the opposite bank. His flotilla, loaded with baggage and gold, lay at anchor just south of the port of Boulaq: in the event of a defeat he would have no trouble escaping. On seeing the enemy formation, Bonaparte at once decided his plan of attack and gave out instructions. Each division was to arrange itself into a square and place its artillery at each of the four corners. In the event of an enemy charge, they would be able to defend themselves on all fronts. The troops were then informed that on no account was the formation to be broken since the mamelukes, trained in hand-to-hand combat, would soon get the better of their French counterparts under such conditions. Anticipating that Na-

poléon would want to try and break through at the very centre, Murad unleashed his cavalry on Dugua's division and then, swiftly changing direction, turned to face Desaix. Fortunately, the French general's division had been able to form itself into a square beforehand.

Not one of his men moved as, in a tide of horse-backed warriors, 4,000 cavalrymen came surging in. Suddenly, an order snapped out, and the sign to open fire. A volley of musket-fire, swiftly followed by a crescendo of artillery, would slow the onrush of cavalry, who would continue to be torn apart by the French guns. This terrible spectacle would last all day. Ibrahim, meanwhile, had fled at the first shot, thus ruling out any chance Murad might have had of a victory. The people of Cairo are distressed to learn of the mameluke defeat. The cry goes up: "Disaster! We are prisoners of the French." Egypt now belongs to Bonaparte (→July 24). ▷

Directory bans the "Annals of Religion"

Despite government bans, worship is increasingly well thought of in society.

Paris, July 5

Anti-Catholic measures taken by the Directory apply as much to the Constitutional church as to the rest. Even though it gave its support to the Fructidor coup, and its clergy take the oath of hatred against the royalty, it is still an object of suspicion with certain members of the Directory, who accuse it of "hypoc-risy". The ban on Bishop Gré-goire's paper, *The Annals of Religion*, comes as no surprise, therefore. The authorities have not forgiven the leader of the juring priests for refusing to give up Sundays in the interests of the ten-day week, or decadi. Equally intolerable is the bishop's desire to effect a reconciliation with the Pope.

Seizure of General Menou's goods upheld

Paris, July 15

General Menou had debts to pay off. Unlucky on the battlefield, and increasingly harassed by creditors, the drawing-room general ended up with his goods sequestered. In a desperate last move to save at least his geographical charts, he argued that the maps were vital if he were to carry out his work as a general. Unfortunately, however, the tribunal has just upheld the decision to sequester his affairs. He will be informed of the decision on his return from Egypt, where he has gone as a member of Napoléon's expedition.

Division General J.F. Menou.

Violent upheavals in the Latium region

Circeo, July

The troubles that were brewing in the area have begun to look like a crusade, with the priests leading the local peasants out to battle. The mood of disgruntlement had not been alleviated by the decision to discontinue draining the Pontine marshes. What finally triggered off the revolt were the twin yokes of political and religious oppression: the suppression of brotherhoods, various administrative squabbles and, above all, the tax collectors' greed. In Circeo, the violence is such that General Macdonald has had to impose martial law and call for reinforcements.

Italian art treasures in

Paris, July 28

The authorities had decided to spare no expense for the second year of their annual celebrations in honour of Liberty. This time round they organised, for the greater glory of the government, a magnificent parade of art works seized in Italy. Only the weather interfered, from time to time, with the otherwise smooth functioning of the ceremonies. For two days there was a continuous medley of speeches with song and dancing. At two o'clock yesterday afternoon, the government was present to a man for the official ceremony at the Champ de Mars. Lebrun had composed an ode for the occasion which was performed by musicians from the Conservatory to a setting by Le Sueur. In the evening, dancing was organised. Today the crowd was present at three o'clock for what promised to be a memorable sight. With a cavalry detachment leading the way, the Directory moved once more towards the Champ de Mars with, in its wake, a long line of prominent public figures, museum curators, art school professors and commissioners in full regalia. They all then assembled in an amphitheatre set up in the middle of the esplanade. An altar to Liberty had been placed at the centre, with a bust of the founder of the Republic of Rome, Brutus, beneath it.

A spectacular parade

After the artillery had sounded a salute, the Conservatory performed *L'Invocation à la Liberté*. Everyone stood up and removed their hats. It was at this point that the 29 floats entered the Champ de Mars, with their Italian booty fully on display. The parade lasted several hours and the crowd was ecstatic. For the first time in their lives, thousands of Parisians were able to set eyes on such sculptures as the *Apollo of Belvedere*, the *Laocoon*, the *Venus of the Capitol*, the *Discus Thrower* , or the horses of Saint Mark's, as well as paintings such as Raphael's *The Transfiguration*. These were then

Among the treasures seized in Italy there are masterpieces from antiquity and works by Old Masters: the "Laocoon" suffocating with his sons, the "Apollo of Belvedere", a model of masculine beauty, and Raphael's "The Transfiguration". Facing page: "Calvary", at the top Mantegna's "Christ in the garden of Gethsemane" (detail), and Perugino's "The Virgin's Marriage".

Liberty day parade: an eye-opener for Parisians

Allegorical parade of Italian treasures amidst which can be seen the horses of Saint Mark's. The mountains in the background symbolise the Alps.

followed by vehicles heaped with a variety of vegetable and mineral objects, medals, books and precious manuscripts. The crowd was particularly fascinated by the exotic creatures on display: bears from Switzerland, lions and camels from Africa. The floats then formed into a semi-circle before the officials, while the four commissioners who had chosen the treasures presented the Minister of the Interior with a formal list of them all. "A spectacle on this scale has no parallel, even in ancient Rome, and no victorious emperor has ever returned home with such an astonishing army of captives in his wake." The military then went through a number of manoeuvres, after which a balloon covered with flowers, after a few initial problems with the wind, finally got airborne. The delayed flight seemed a fitting symbol for France, as it at last lifts free of the troublesome currents of History.

The art works brought back from Italy were unpacked with great care.

French naval catastrophe at Aboukir

Aboukir, August 1

The French fleet of the East has just been wiped out. Only four vessels survived the massacre, while eleven others fell into the hands of the English. A further five, with more than 4,000 men on board, have sunk. A deathly silence has replaced the screaming of missiles as they tore through the air, the sound of planks sundering under gun-fire and the cries of wounded sailors. Nelson had been searching for the French fleet since last May, and finally found them this morning, lying at anchor outside Aboukir. In open violation of all the rules of naval tactics, which forbid launching an attack on a fleet at anchor, Nelson had colours run up on his flagship, *Vanguard*, ordering his captains to attack the enemy at the centre and vanguard. It was a tricky manoeuvre to pull off: one part of his squadron had to find a path between the coast and Napoléon's boats, while the other attacked directly from the open sea. At 6:30 a.m., the *Goliath* opened fire under the command of Captain

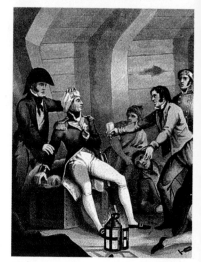

Nelson was wounded in the battle.

Foley. The deluge of fire and iron lasted long into the night. From their position in the shoals, the French vessels were incapable of making an effective riposte, for their decks were piled up with all kind of materials that got in the way. The English, meanwhile, were firing and re-loading with the most amazing speed, and the French sailors were simply unable to keep up. Now that his entire fleet has been destroyed, Napoléon is well and truly trapped in Egypt, at least for the time being.

The English attack takes the anchored French fleet completely by surprise.

Napoléon is keen to get on good terms with the people of Cairo

Cairo, August 18

The crowd rushed down to the waters of the Nile. Women soaked large pieces of linen, that will one day be used as grave-clothes, in the scared river. Napoléon made a point of being present in person at the annual celebrations for what is Egypt's most important feast-day. The gold pieces he awarded to the winning team of a boat-race will only have increased his popularity. Moreover, he particularly enjoys being addressed as "Sultan Kébir" by a people he already considers as his subjects. Since setting foot on Egyptian soil, the commander in chief of the army of the East has done everything in his power to see that his soldiers respect local customs and beliefs. In Alexandria, he made a point of restoring Mohammed El Koraïm to his former position, by naming him governor for the town boroughs. In Cairo, he likewise intends to pursue his policy and leave the Arabs plenty of leeway in home affairs. To that end, he has passed a decree which will allow a government council to be set up, the diwan. It will consist of nine members and will be responsible for keeping order in the town. It will also see to the general running of the markets and decide what stocks are to be provided. It is haped to set up other diwans throughout the provinces.

Bonaparte surrounded by staff on the summit of the pyramid at Giza.

Artists are selected for this year's Salon

The public was particularly delighted to discover at the Salon François Gérard's version of "Psyche and Love", a remarkably modern piece of work.

Paris, August 18

Organising this year's Salon has proved a rather delicate business for the officials involved. Faced with an extraordinary number of submissions, the government had to appoint a 15-member jury for the first time in the history of the Salon: five representatives each for painting, sculpture and architecture. This caused an uproar, for the jury had not been elected by the artists themselves, as had originally been suggested. Things quietened down, however, for it soon became clear that the jury was carrying out its duties to perfection. Any artist who had received a prize from the one-time Academy, for instance, or from the special School of Painting and Sculpture, was able to bypass the jury, as were those who had been given an award for promise. The jury let through a total of 529 works, nearly 450 of which were paintings; many more, in short, than anyone had hoped for. Once the best works have been selected, the winners will be announced at the Vendémiaire 1 celebrations on the Champ de Mars. Lebrun's *The Death of Caius Gracchus* and Gérard's *Psyche and Love* are two of the most outstanding works.

"The Ice-Skater" by Delafontaine.

The Egyptian Institute gets down to work

Cairo, August 22

The Age of Enlightenment is extending its faith in progress to Egypt. Such at least is one of the goals Napoléon has set himself by founding the Institute of Arts and Sciences. Its president, Monge, is only too keen to support the project. A short time before leaving France, the scholar had expressed his wish "to carry the torch of reason to the country that, for so long now, had been deprived of its light". Napoléon has therefore asked the scholars and artists in his company to set to work without further delay: there is urgent need for "research into, and study and publication of, all natural, industrial and historical data concerning Egypt". The commander of the French expedition has had the Institute divided up into four main departments: mathematics, physics and natural history, political economy, arts and literature. He has asked the Institute to study ways in which water from the Nile might be led into the citadel, and wells be dug in the desert. Among the subjects the scholars have to consider, is the following: "Is there anything that might replace hops in brewing beer?" (→ Aug. 99).

The draughtsman Vivant Denon, among the artists and scholars taking part in Napoléon's expedition, greets the general at the new Egyptian Institute.

Directory decides to save the Château of Fontainebleau

Paris, August 5

The château built by François I has been spared: the Directory had been a little hasty, no doubt, in its desire to have it demolished, and has reversed its decision, thanks to the Institute's architecture class. The latter made a plea so powerful and new in favour of Renaissance architecture, that the authorities began to have doubts. The art of the time was not merely a mixed genre, then, imported from abroad; a base amalgam of gothic and classical styles with an excessive taste for ornamentation. With any luck, the petition will mean the Directory pays more attention in the future to protecting the national heritage, whatever the form it takes.

The sorry condition of property rented out by the State

Gironde, August 30

A recent report by the director of registration, La Cressonière, shows rented national properties to be in the most appalling state. Various farmers in the Bec d'Ambès region have not only not paid their rent, they have even set about selling anything that comes to hand. Trees have been cut down, fences torn away, cattle dispersed. Fields are left untilled. The buildings fare no better. Sometimes it is the roofing or timberwork that has been sold; on other occasions doors, windows and even floorboards. In many cases the tenant is not a farmer at all, but a speculator attracted by the short-term leases and keen to make the most of the situation.

Directory

The French landing in Ireland turns out to be a fiasco

Ireland, September 15

The French invasion of Ireland finally took place. Though it had been due for some time now, the event itself was a complete disaster. After a desperate appeal for help from the Irish rebels, the Directory decided on July 6th. to come to their rescue. The English moved swiftly, however. A few days later the last remaining rebels, torn by war, surrendered their arms. It was at this point that General Humbert set out from Rochefort with a reconnaissance force of three frigates and 1,000 men. He landed on the Irish coast on August 22nd. and got off to a good start. Without any kind of reinforcements, however, in a country now once more back under control, he had no choice but to surrender to the English, which he did today. The collapse of his preliminary front means that the two expeditions due to follow have now been cancelled. The Irish patriots can no longer count on any further assistance from France.

Military service is now made compulsory

Paris, September 5

Every Frenchman is a soldier and must come to the defence of his country. The early passages of the law passed by the Council of Five Hundred draw attention to the principle once enunciated to the Convention by Dubois Crancé. On the basis of a report drawn up by Jean Baptiste Jourdan, it has now been decided that "the land army is to be formed by means of voluntary enrolment and by conscription". Volunteers can sign up between the ages of 18 and 30. Conscription applies to all young men between 20 and 25 years of age. Military service will last five years. Conscripts are divided into five classes, each of these corresponding to the year in which the young man was born. The first class to be called up will therefore be that of all young men reaching the age of 20 during Year VI. Conscripts will have to pass a medical checkup before a review council, before being admitted into the army. The call-up is by name and based on lists drawn up by the municipal authorities. In theory, it is illegal for someone to have his place taken by another (→Sept. 24).

A paper to promote knowledge of Egypt

Cairo, September

Under fire for years from the Paris press, Tallien at last has a chance to get even. Napoléon has given him the editor's chair at the *Décade égyptienne, journal littéraire et d'économie politique*, the official organ of the Egyptian Institute. In his capacity as a former journalist, and editor of the *Moniteur* prior to the Revolution, it is Tallien who writes the foreword to each issue; and he takes advantage of this to lash out against his Parisian colleagues, to whom he attributes his failure to get elected to the Five Hundred, and thus his more or less voluntary exile in Egypt. The new journal is printed on the army's presses and is supposed to promote knowledge of Egyptian matters, not only among officers and scholars on the spot, but also among the people of France and Europe generally.

Well-to-do youths playing the latest game, an early form of tennis, on the lawn of the Champs Elysées.

Pichegru escapes from Guyana

London, September 22

Four escaped prisoners have just reached England. Among them is the notorious General Pichegru, who was charged with plotting against the Republic and forming an alliance with an enemy power, and deported after the coup on Fructidor 18. Embarked on scarcely more than a canoe, the prisoners were cast up onto the coast of Dutch Guyana during a storm, where settlers then came to their rescue and provided them with a vessel. Pursued by pirates, they took refuge with the English. A war-ship then handed them over to traders, till finally they reached London on Captain Loop's frigate.

A patrol in the marshes of Guyana.

Paris celebrates the sixth anniversary of the French Republic

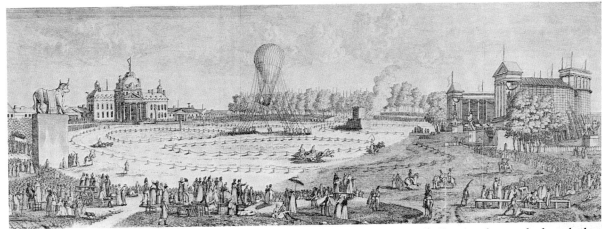

On the Champ de Mars, festivities are in full swing. The races are ending and a balloon is about to be launched.

Paris, September 22

The daughter of the Revolution is six years old. She came under attack almost at once, but, stood her ground and saw her ideals spread far beyond her own frontiers. She has taught her citizens that they have a country, and that they must serve that country with unity and virtue. Such were the terms used in the speech given by the President of the Council of Five Hundred to celebrate the Republic's birthday. Her name was synonymous, he pointed out, with 30 million men equal before the law, and living freely in a free land where the authorities are distinct and people and property sacred. He then invited the people to proceed to the Champ de Mars for racing and hymn-singing. Holidays, after all, are part of the Republic.

Sports such as racing and wrestling bring numerous competitors together.

There are too many nuns teaching

Troyes, September 11

Municipal visits carried out in schools since the law passed on February 5th. have revealed that lay teaching is a myth. In Troyes, for instance, 13 out of every 24 schoolmistresses are former nuns, while the remaining 11 would appear to have "strong religious feelings". The degree varies from "pure bigotry" to what is described as "the more honeyed kind". A former Converse sister, who does nothing more than teach her pupils the catechism and prayers, elicits the following brief response: "Has no more brains than a cow, and is in charge of small children who say their prayers to God-like angels."

Authorities at Rome shown to be corrupt

Rome, September 17

The consuls Visconti and Panazzi have been removed from office and ordered not to leave Rome, pending further instructions. The two men had been having doubts about the economic side of the policy carried out by Duport and Bertolio, the French civil commissioners. They were particularly troubled by the re-introduction of scrip, or paper money, with compulsory rates that could only benefit speculators. As for Angelucci, Reppi and Mathesis, the remaining consuls who were forced to resign after the press had denounced them as corrupt, they have been appointed senators.

Cairo caught up in republican festivities

Cairo, September 22

They may be far from home, but the Republic is written in their hearts. The people of Cairo could hardly fail to notice this. French enthusiasm for the occasion of the Republic's sixth anniversary was overwhelming, and any number of events were organised: races, horse shows, and a variety of dazzling military manoeuvres filled the local population with astonishment. By involving the people of Cairo in the festvities in this way, Napoléon hopes to reinforce his policy of appeasement and good-will.

The Institute pays homage to Didot

Paris, September

The Institute Commission has just paid public homage, in the shape of a report carried out by a certain Camus, to the famous line of publisher-printers, Didot. As long ago as 1783 they had made their name with a new typeface designed by Firmin Didot. His brother Pierre Didot has decided to carry on the editorial policy that made the company's name, and has used the typeface as the basis for a prestigious new collection of works by classical authors, the *Editions du Louvre*, the first volume of which, *Virgil*, has just been published, much to the delight of book-lovers everywhere.

Directory

Independence soon for Saint Domingue?

Saint Domingue, October 22

Hédouville's mission is a total flop. Five months after arriving in Saint Domingue with full civil and military powers, the general has been driven back into the sea by Toussaint Louverture. Hopefully France has got the message: it is the black general who presides over the island! The Directory had sent Hédouville to see that Toussaint was cut down to size and, if need be, driven out. He soon discovered, however, that Saint Domingue is not the Vendée. Piqued at being excluded from Toussaint's talks with the English at the time of their retreat, he tried to eliminate black officers from the army. Sensing a threat, Toussaint marched on the Cape and drove Hédouville out. Before leaving, the commissioner freed the mulatto generals, who are not wild about independence, from the subordinate role imposed on them by the hierarchy.

Pamphleteer Rivarol holds court in Berlin

Berlin, October

Men of letters, representatives from foreign courts and eminent Germans make a point of visiting Berlin to see Rivarol. The celebrated pamphleteer, an émigré since 1792, first lived in Holland and then England before settling in Germany. Many of his old friends are émigrés like himself and form part of his audience. He holds open house each day, and his guests enjoy something of the atmosphere of the Paris salons as they engage in the customary pleasures of intellectual sparring.

Royalist guerrillas in the south-west

Haute Garonne, October 6

The "guerrillas" have gone into action. Is southern France around Toulouse threatened with another Vendée? Just as levying 300,000 men once sparked off revolts in the west of France, the Jourdan draft law is the cause of anger sweeping through the south-west of France, where more than a third of those concerned have refused to come forward. To escape the police, the recalcitrant formed "guerrilla" groups, and soon were be joined by officers from a secret royalist organisation, the Philanthropical Institute. One of the gangs today attacked a police detachment at Escalquens, killing its commander and wounding four others. Some 350 soldiers and two cannons have been sent in to try to "clean up" the department.

Manufactured goods are on display for the first time in Paris

Paris, October 15

Interior Minister François de Neufchâteau has just opened the first national exhibition of manufactured goods. Having proposed the project in the first place, he hopes it will lead to a widespread use of modern methods in industry and the crafts, which are still run along traditional lines and need to be updated. To arouse the interest of manufacturers he has had model workshops installed. Visitors can admire mechanical looms made in England and known as "spinning jennies". Then there is a machine made by Richard and Lenoir for their new cotton mill. Meanwhile, the ministry's arts and crafts office hopes to initiate the French public into recent techniques by means of a series of brochures that it will be distributing throughout France. In keeping with his policy, which is to encourage and inform the people, François de Neufchâteau has also recently launched a new prize, its aim being to reward innovators and the spirit of invention generally, wherever they are found at work.

Plans by the Englishman Edward Bowry for a steam machine of a new type, here powering a flour-mill.

The uprising in Cairo is stamped out

Once the initial shock was over, French troops acted firmly and crushed the rebellion with much bloodshed.

Cairo, October 22

Today, the gutters of the Flower Mosque are running with blood. Every district in the city has been cleaned up thanks to the energetic efforts of the light brigades. After two days of rioting, calm has been restored. A few days ago, rebel factions, encouraged by English and Turkish agents, surfaced in Alexandria and were soon winning support in towns throughout the delta. It was in Cairo, however, that the violence reached its height. Yesterday, the muezzins used their minarets to call the people not to prayer but to a holy war. Numerous soldiers and officers, taken in by the indolence of the local populace, died from rebel knives before a riposte could be organised. Attacks then spread like wildfire, first to French traders in the town, then to Moslems known to be sympathetic to the Napoleonic cause. In the space of an hour the entire town

Bonaparte has decided to exercise clemency and has pardoned the rebels.

was swept by fire and blood. No-one was interested in trying to reconcile interests any more. On account of the enormous scale and violence of the uprising, every single piece of available artillery has had to be used in restoring law and order in the ravaged town.

Belgian peasant population is up in arms against conscription

Luxembourg, October 30

The Belgian peasants' revolt has spread to the Luxembourg villages in the Forêts region. At Stavelot and Clervaux there were tough clashes with French troops. The call-up imposed by France is at the origin of the troubles. The first incident occurred at Overmere, in Flanders, on October 12th. The Waes region was the next to be hit, followed by the departments of Escaut and Lys, and then the Campine and Brabant. The rebels are highly organised. Their tiny army comprises nearly 3,500 men and military discipline could not be more strict. In any number of cities, they have overthrown Francophile magistrates, to replace them with new committees. They destroy civil registers, pillage public treasuries and levy contributions. As legitimists, they carry out their attacks in the name of the Emperor François and William of Orange. The French army, most of which is stationed to defend the coasts and borders, was rather slow in reacting. Its commanders, initially caught off guard by the scale of the movement, soon pulled themselves together. Law and order were quickly restored in the Waes region, where 41 of the rural insurgents were executed by firing-squad (→ Nov. 4).

The Austrian army is looming large in the Alps

Switzerland, October 19

France faces a new threat: the Austrian advance in the Alps. The rival power also has troops massed on the border, which means it can move towards either the Cisalpine or Piedmont regions if it wishes. The three leagues that together form the Grisons confederation, which had chosen to remain outside the Swiss Republic, would welcome the Viennese troops without a fight: the political struggle between the pro-French democratic party and the pro-Austrian conservatives had shifted in the latter's favour in late summer. While the French continue their negotiations with Austria in Rastatt, events in the Grisons look very much like an armed vigil on Austria's part. The news of the French fleet's annihilation in Egypt has provoked new interest in the concept of a Prussian, German and English coalition against France. The Directory is no more keen for a war than Austria is, however. There is, nonetheless, no chance of reconciling the desires of the two sides: Paris refuses to make any changes where the current status quo in Italy is concerned, while Vienna is still intransigent in its desire to lay hands on either the papal legations or the left bank of the Po as far as Oglio.

Rhône region home of hideous crime

Rhône, October 24

The autumn night proved fatal for the Pregay family. In the course of the evening, strangers slipped quietly into their farm at Mornant and then set about looting it. Not content with stealing, they also decided to slit the couple's throats, along with those of their five children and two domestics: a massacre intended, presumably, to prevent their victims identifying them. Still worse is the fact that the murders might have been avoided. Around 11 o'clock, a neighbour returning home heard cries coming from the Pregay household. He did the cowardly thing, however, and instead of fetching the police hid himself away in his farm.

Directory

The architect Charles de Wailly is dead

One of de Wailly's designs for the auditorium at the Comédie Française.

The Théâtre Français in 1782, which became the Théâtre de l'Odéon in 1797.

Paris, November 2

The death of Charles de Wailly deprives architecture of one of its master practitioners. Winner of the first prize in the Prix de Rome in 1752, he studied, like Boullée, with Legeay and Blondel, and thereafter led a brilliant career. Elected to the Academy in 1761 and, still more remarkably, to the Academy of Painting in 1771, he was regularly invited to show his projects at the Salon. His first important work was the Château of Montmusard, near Dijon, in 1764. It was marked by a modernism that would finally become systematic with Ledoux and Boullée. De Wailly also designed the town of Port Vendres, along with a number of Paris buildings, such as the Théâtre de l'Odéon. He developed an original style that did away with neo-classical austerity in favour of full, colourful forms.

New commissioner takes over in Guyana

Cayenne, November 5

A new civil commissioner has arrived in Cayenne. Burnel takes over from the nephew of Danton, Jeannet Oudin. In 1793, the latter was sent to set up a republic in Guyana, a colony made up of less than 2,000 whites as against 12,000 blacks. Thanks to Oudin, the black population was freed on May 13th.

1794. A reformatory was built at the same time for those who did not wish to work. It was also Oudin who, in November 1797, received the Fructidor 18 deportees, some 16 in all, and, in 1798, the two convoys of priests and commoners whom he decided to instal in Sin-namary and on the banks of the Counamama river.

Belgian priests are coming under fire

Belgium, November 4

From now on, priests are banned in all Belgian departments: 7,000 clergy are up for deportation. The agents of the Directory have made the "saintly knaves" responsible for the unrest currently troubling the Waes region, part of Flanders and the Ardennes, where the peasants have risen up in arms against the call-up. Making the most of the general disarray, most priests have managed to flee the country, with the help of a population that is sympathetic to their cause. The authorities have only been able to arrest four or five hundred.

Ten million franc loan to the State

Paris, November

With its coffers empty, France has been forced to borrow. After a request from his good friend and protector Barras, the businessman Ouvrard, known for his wealth, has agreed to lend the State 10,000,000 francs in coin, which will, in part, go to paying off earlier debts. As arms supplier to the French navy, he is responsible for seeing that it has everything it needs and presents the ministry with a heavy bill for his services. He is said to have made more than 15,000,000 francs in this way. The terms on which he has agreed to the loan are likewise said to involve his being named supplier to the entire military in exchange. By making himself indispensable in this way, Ouvrard has emerged as the new régime's most outstanding financier.

The businessman Gabriel Ouvrard.

Wolfe Tone takes his own life in prison

Dublin, November 19

Wolfe Tone was with General Humbert for the abortive invasion of Ireland. Taken prisoner by the English after an heroic struggle, he was thrown into a Dublin gaol and sentenced to death by hanging by the military court. After asking in vain to be sent before a firing squad, he slit his throat in his cell and today died from the wounds. Wolfe Tone had devoted his life to the Irish cause, and was the cause of the French intervention in Ireland. The legendary patriot was unable to make his dream come true before he died: an independent Ireland, that would at last be free of the British yoke.

Wolfe Tone in his French uniform.

Paris restores order to the Army of Italy

Paris, November 25

Generals should stick to military affairs and keep out of politics. To make sure they do, the Directory has decided to bring back military commissioners. Though civilians, each will have the rank of generals and be invested with full financial and political powers. Their field of activity will be extended to include supplies, requisitions and taxes, as well as responsibility for political conventions. The Directory has appointed Rapinat to Switzerland, Amelot to Milan and Faipoult to Rome. It looks as if the going will be rough, however, for the generals seem to have grown rather fond of their new independence.

Commissioners are greedy men.

The Neapolitans arrive in Rome

Rome, November 27

The people of Rome welcomed the Neapolitan army as a force for freedom. What with pillaging and war taxes, the French rapidly lost whatever popularity they had once enjoyed. Ferdinand IV, King of the Two Sicilies, and thus of Naples, who two years ago was forced to sign a peace treaty with France, is now revelling in his new success. It was on hearing last month of the Austrian occupation of the Grisons that Naples decided to renew its struggle with France. Ferdinand IV's powerful army rapidly revealed itself as more than a match for Championnet's.

Fouché is dismissed from his post

Milan, November 26

Fouché is still a threat. That much is clear from his activities as ambassador to Milan. The zeal with which he would get to grips with Cisalpine Jacobins who had earlier been his friends; the speed with which he would restore order to the young republic; his friendship with General Joubert, commander of the French forces: they didn't look good. To put an end to his success, his enemies, whether Italian patriots or French sharks, asked the Directory to dismiss him. This it promptly did, happy to show its authority over this influential man.

A painting by Topino Lebrun is offered to the city of Marseilles

Paris, November

The Minister of the Interior has just acquired a large painting by Jean Baptiste Topino Lebrun, *The Death of Caius Gracchus*. The work won a prize at the last Salon and will be presented to the commune of Marseilles, where the artist first set eyes on the world. Dedicated to Gracchus Babeuf, whose friend the painter was, the work celebrates by allusion Babeuf's martyrdom as leader of the Conspiracy of Equals. Like the famous Roman tribune, Gracchus, Babeuf had defended plans for an agricultural reform that would benefit the people; and, like him, died a violent death, abandoned by the very people whose cause he had been defending. The Directory has announced that it intends to make more donations of this kind. The next town on the list is Toulouse, which has had a museum of its own since 1795. "As a token of thanks for the patriotism the town has shown throughout the Revolution", the government will present the town with a work of great renown "by one of its most able painters". The work on this occasion will be François André Vincent's *William Tell*.

Thanks to his friend Topino Lebrun, Babeuf will live on as the tribune Caius Gracchus, whose name he borrowed.

The revolution is over in the Ile de France

One of the more recent maps that have been made of the Ile de France.

Ile de France, November 7

The dissolution of the colonial Assembly and deportation of 14 of its members: out of loyalty to the principles of the Revolution, such were the terms dictated by the rebel battalions who took control of the government building on November 4th. Their demands were passed on to the colonial Assembly through Governor Malartic, whom they had taken hostage. While the latter set about complying, and arranged for new elections to be held a week from now, the settlers organised themselves and freed the occupied capital. The leaders of the rebels, among them a certain Bernardin from the 12th. infantry battalion, were at once embarked for France on board the *Nathalie*. For the time being, the destiny of the Ile de France is entirely in the hands of its settlers, who have decided to break off relations with the mainland government (→ Feb. 14, 99).

A revolution in the way women behave

Paris, November

"Society is at home away from home": women have applied the slogan to the letter and overturned the world. It is the fair sex that has brought about a revolution in the way people behave. From actresses to wives of Directory members, from spouses to courtesans, they have decided to have done with the old ways and, arm in arm, have invaded the streets in droves. They claim to want to free themselves from their husbands and children, so as to be able to give themselves up to desire. "When you pick up their fans, they don't bother thanking you; when you greet them, they don't bother returning the gesture; they stare at you if you are handsome and laugh in your face if you are ugly." These "amazons" pass the time at balls, where they dance breast to breast, and at the theatre, where they pick up on the slightest play on words, which they then go about repeating. They eat a lot of meat, and couldn't care less if they put on weight or end up with swollen arteries. Some even do

Dances are ideal for meeting girls.

men's jobs, like Mme. de Rivarol. Avid readers of *The Guide to Marriage*, these elegant women dream of making a good catch, preferably an aristocrat who lives abroad, as in *Le Mariage de Nanon*, Maillot's opera which was staged last year.

A tax on windows and doors goes through

Paris, November 25

To restore public funds, a new tax has been decided on. The idea is certainly an original one: a tax will be paid for every window and door a building possesses. After a long debate over what constitutes equity in fiscal affairs, Legrand's suggestion won the Council of Ancients over by its simplicity. All a tax inspector would have to do was position himself in the appropriate street, courtyard and garden, and then tot up the number of openings in house, barn or workshop. And there would be no way anyone could contest their contribution. Those who oppose this "hideous and absurd" system are reminded that it does more than any other tax to keep the peace. As it affects everybody equally, whether rich or poor, there is no chance of the new measure causing dissension among the populace. And, short of walling up every opening in the house, and thereby condemning oneself to a life of darkness, there is no way of getting round it.

A Sorry Tale

The new tax on all doors and windows which was announced this morning seems quite ridiculous to the common people. "Why not a tax on beds and chairs?" the bewildered and angry people cry. A new song echoes this sentiment:

A brand new tax, they so apprise,
Has just been born today,
Taxed will be surprise! surprise!
Each window and doorway.
No! That can't be true
As luxury these things construe.
What a sorry tale, alas!
What a sorry tale!
And next with fiscal acumen
A similar tax they'll make
On lofts and loos, and then?
On door-knobs, real or fake!
Our leaders must have overspent,
They've never been to this extent.
What a sorry tale, alas!
What a sorry tale!
So to avoid this tax, I fear,
All doors we must destroy,
Air-holes and windows clear;
We'll baffles not employ.
To enter? What a handicap!
We'll crawl through the cat-trap!
What a comic tale, alas!
What a comic tale!

Mme. Hamelin, wife of the arms supplier and a star of Paris society.

Art under the Directory

An armchair reduced to essentials.

Mme. Récamier likes her furniture and dress in the antique manner.

The interior of a bourgeois home.

The Revolution is well and truly over: to realise this, one need only consider current tendencies in the arts and crafts. Classical values are more and more popular, and are being adapted to a new, less hurried way of life. Themes from Greek, Etruscan or Roman art are to be found side by side, but are treated with a greater freedom and ease. People not only dress and arrange their hair in the classical fashion, as can be seen from portraits such as

David's *Madame Récamier*; above all, one finds no end of porticos, pilasters, columns, cornices, foliated mouldings, classical vases, winged figures, female sphinxes, griffins or chimeras bordered with palmettes, Greek key-patterns or acanthus. If few of these motifs can be said to be new, the ways in which they are used an original, both in fabrics and wall-papers, and in furniture design, the leaders in this last field being the Jacob family.

Much use is made of stucco ornaments, imitation marble and geometric forms: panels in the form of lozenges with a point facing downwards, circular or oval medallions decorated with figures in monochrome or grey, in imitation of cameos or bas-reliefs. Architects take as their inspiration the frescoes discovered at Herculanum and Pompeii, when decorating houses belonging to their wealthy clients. The strident, martial colours of

recent years have been dispensed with, once and for all. If white is still very much the fashion where women's wear is concerned, it is for the contrast it provides with heavier, more sombre tones such as Etruscan brown, classical green, bright turkey red, violet or black. Each one of these colours is made abundant use of by a variety of celebrities, such as Bélanger, Percier or Fontaine, as they decorate their clients' houses.

Egyptian motifs on Jouy cloth.

This bathroom has been decorated with designs based on those at Pompey.

Design for an ornamental clock.

Restif appointed censor in "Black office"

Paris, December

Restif de La Bretonne has begun a new career at more than 64 years of age. Thanks to the intervention of a friend, he had been working as a deputy chief clerk in the general police's headquarters, and earning 4,000 francs a year, since April 20th. With his fluent knowledge of English and Spanish he was soon noticed by his superiors, who have now promoted him to the "Intercepted Letters" department. It is none other than the famous "Black office" of the monarchy, abolish-ed by the Legislative Assembly and restored under the Terror. It is here that, for reasons of state, the government orders letters to or from émigrés or foreign agents to be opened before they arrive at their destination. On the part of a man who had written only a few years earlier "Whatever is under seal and posted is sacred. To break that seal is an undying crime", it is somewhat surprising that he should have accepted. For the good of one's country, and to earn a living, sacrifices must always be made ...

A female soldier arrives at the Invalides

Parios, December 14

Soldier Duchemin has gone into retirement at the Invalides. She is 28 years old. Badly wounded at the siege of Calvi, she has no choice but to retire from the army for good. This courageous soldier, with seven years' service, seven campaigns and numerous acts of bravery behind her, is a young woman by the name of Angélique. She would, in fact, change her name for one that is less subdued and more heroic: Liberty. She is one of a small number of women who were allowed to stay on in the army after a decree was passed excluding them in April 1793. On account of her valour, an exception was made for this widow who comes from a military family.

Napoléon enjoys a well-earned rest

Egypt, December 10

She was a woman of easy virtue and he was Bonaparte. He didn't have much trouble seducing her, and forgot about Joséphine for a night. It all began in Cairo, where the evenings are long for soldiers. As a result, they get together at the *Tivoli Egyptien*, a ballroom whose reputation allows even Napoléon to wander down there from time to time. It was there he met Marguerite Pauline Bellisle, a former milliner from Carcassonne. The wife of a cavalry officer, Fourès, like many women she disguised herself as a soldier to follow her husband to Egypt. She has been nicknamed "Bellilotte". This evening, though, she abandoned her Spartan green cloth jacket for a stunning gauze gown. And Napoléon was unable to resist. Fourès turned a blind eye, and Joséphine will not get to hear of it. For, though Napoléon rules Egypt, Marguerite Pauline does not have the ambitions of a Cleopatra.

A glorious episode in the war between French and English privateers: on December 14th., off Rochefort, the French corvette "La Bayonnaise", back from Cayenne, meets the English frigate "Ambush", which is captured after some violent hand-to-hand fighting.

New coalition formed against France

The French are too easily convinced of the decline of England, which they see as being in a miserable state.

London, December 29

England has just put together a second military alliance against the French, and today signed a treaty to that effect with Russia. Pending agreement from Austria, Russia has promised to send a sizeable military contingent into Italy. It also plans to join England in an invasion of Holland, and to send an expeditionary force into Brittany, by way of Jersey. In exchange, the English will contribute 225,000 pounds towards the costs of preparing the war, as well as a further 75,000 pounds each month for the duration of the war. The British government has pulled off a major diplomatic coup. The first coalition fell to pieces after France and Austria signed a peace treaty at Campo Formio, which left England alone in its struggles with the Directory. Czar Paul I thought long and hard before cementing the alliance. What decided him was France's recent incursions into the Mediterranean. Nelson's win at Aboukir has proved that France was not invincible. Convinced of this, Russia had already allied itself to Turkey to drive Napoléon out of Egypt, and now joins forces with England. The new coalition also has backing from Naples. Nelson had visited the town after his victory at Aboukir and persuaded Ferdinand IV to launch an attack on France in Italy. On November 22nd. the Neapolitans began their march on Rome, and on December 6th. the Directory declared war on them. In order to have any real effect, however, this three-

Monarchist Europe makes a new alliance against the French Republic.

party alliance will need to win Austrian support for its cause. It is Austria, after all, which has control over the roads leading into France. Without some kind of assistance

from that quarter, therefore, there is no real chance for either England or Russia of achieving anything of lasting consequence in their struggles with France.

A very good year for the theatre

Paris, December 28

The theatrical profession has had a particularly good year. This is notably true of the Odéon, which has enjoyed more success than at any time since the Revolution. It is Sageret's production of August von Kotzebue's play, *Misanthropie et Repentir*, the first to be staged at the theatre since it re-opened, that is responsible. The real triumph of the season has been the Favart auditorium with musicals: Derval and Della Maria's comic opera, *Le Prisonnier ou la Ressemblance*, and *Zoraïme et Zulnare*, by Gauberd de Saint Just and Boieldieu. The singer Jean Baptiste Gavaudan made a brilliant début in Hoffmann and Méhul's *Euphrosine et Coradin*.

The Medical School and its first degree

Paris, December 18

French doctors are becoming more and more knowledgeable. The teaching of medicine has vastly improved since the central medical schools were set up in December 1794, bringing together for the first time medical and surgical instruction, both on a theoretical and a practical plane. A student today presented the first degree thesis. His dissertation was focused on "the differences that occur in individual health, from birth to puberty, as a result of the way in which public health is organised and taught".

Privateers furious at new decree

Guadeloupe, December 31

General Desfourneaux is not too popular just now at *Le rendez-vous des sans-culottes*. The governor's decision to outlaw privateering has not been well-received in the club at Le Morne au Caille, where the island's sea-dogs like to meet. As far as they are concerned, Victor Hugues' successor is hell-bent on ruining the colony, whose recent prosperity is largely the result of privateering: from 1794 to 1798, they have captured more than 800 vessels. Their most famous member is Fuët.

Revolutionary France and foreign relations

The Revolution claimed to be universal from the very outset. Its conception of patriotism, and of the nation, did not seem framed for France alone, but also for its neighbours suffering from the oppression of "tyrants". While it initially took a pacifistic line, it quickly showed itself to be bellicose and expansionist. The threat it represented to the European states and those countries' drive to resist the revolutionary ideology soon led France into a general and long-lasting war, during which the Revolution changed from a desire to crusade for liberating the world's oppressed peoples to carrying on a war of conquest and annexation.

The revolutionary virus

Certain social categories everywhere in Europe, such as peasants hoping for abolition of feudal dues and "patriots" imbued with philosophical ideas, were sensitive to revolutionary propaganda. But none of those groups were ever in a position to put through a revolution in their own countries, and only brought on reaction on the part of worried authorities. Furthermore, revolutionary violence was to lead rather quickly to a shift of opinion. In all of Europe's enlightened circles, the storming of the Bastille had aroused a wave of enthusiasm running from England to Russia. The day after the "glorious day", the British ambassador expressed his reaction in these terms: "From now on, we may consider France a free country." In Germany, despite some reticence, the French Revolution initially caused delighted surprise in the bourgeoisie and among the intellectuals. The revolutionary newspapers were widely distributed, and the gazettes kept their readers informed of what was going on in France. The Declaration of Human Rights was translated into many languages and was read as far away as Latin America. Englishmen, Russians and Germans visited Paris, frequented the clubs, attended meetings of the Constituent Assembly, and wrote informatory and often enthusiastic letters to their compatriots. Great writers and philosophers, from Kant to Goethe, became excited as events in France unfolded and at the mention of the principles of freedom. Italians, Poles and even Greeks followed developments in France.

The contagion was the strongest in the countries adjoining France, and in foreign enclaves, such as Avignon which was still under papal control. Avignon demanded to be attached to France. In the Austrian Netherlands, the Belgians, who had long demanded freedom, revolted in 1789 when they learnt about the revolution in France, while Liège rose up against its prince-bishop a year later. Those movements were put down. When the French armies later entered Belgium, after the battle of Jemmapes (November 6th., 1792), they were welcomed as liberators. Riots multiplied in 1789 along the Rhine, in Basel and Geneva, in Savoy and in Florence. The Irish Catholics compared their national and religious cause to the French Revolution. Even further away, in Hungary and Russia, demands spread in liberal circles. In Poland the patriots won a new constitution on May 3rd., 1791. Such agitation naturally alarmed European princes. All continental Europe came out against the Revolution, from Austria, which disapproved of any revolutionary innovations, including the abolition of feudal dues, and Spain, which set up an armed "cordon sanitaire" to avoid contamination, to the Vatican, which lined up the Catholic states against France by condemning the Civil Constitution of the Clergy (April 13th., 1791). The German intellectuals themselves, from Fichte to Goethe, eventually disowned the French example and denounced the radicalisation of the Revolution. But it was England that cemented the European counter-revolution, from the ideological standpoint. As early as 1790, Edmund Burke supplied the arguments that were to inspire England by denouncing the Revolution's inconsistencies and by calling on Europe to make war on France. Until at least 1791, the various countries had other concerns that hardly left their hands free. Prussia and Austria, which were warring against the Ottoman Empire, were more interested in dividing up Poland than in the French Revolution, which they thought of as Louis XVI's business, while Russia was bogged down in conflicts with Sweden and the Ottoman Empire. In France, bellicose ideas were spreading in the clubs and the newspapers. When Austria and Russia managed to disengage themselves from the Turkish conflict (Treaty of Yassy, January 9th., 1792), they were in a position

to think about a counter-revolutionary crusade, which the humiliations forced on Louis XVI made even more urgent. The very existence of monarchical régimes, threatened by the Revolution, was at stake. War seemed all the more inevitable when the Legislative Assembly took the initiative.

War

By the end of 1791, war seemed, in France, to be the best way of consolidating the Revolution, and it was declared to general enthusiasm on April 20th., 1792. After that, neither the invasion of the territory of August 1792 nor the victory in September could lead to peace. People who might be tempted to demand it risked being immediately found guilty of counter-revolution. In November, the Convention promised aid to all peoples wanting to get rid of their masters and recover their freedom. The annexation of Savoy on November 27th., 1792, was accompanied by the introduction of the revolutionary laws in the conquered countries. France installed administrations favourable to the Revolution in the Austrian Netherlands and on the east bank of the Rhine, both of which were occupied following French successes. The dangers this policy represented for all Europe, for its traditional balance of power, as well as the risk of ideological contamination, pushed England, Holland, Spain and Piedmont into entering the coalition alongside the Empire and Prussia in the spring of 1793. The Montagnard dictatorship had to make immense efforts in the face of this threatening coalition and the danger of invasion of French territory, but it intended to get compensation as soon as victory was won. It was no longer a question of freeing peoples, but of getting all possible financial, economic and even artistic resources from the enemy countries and of putting them at the Republic's service.

The Thermidorian Convention and the Directory followed this doctrine to its logical conclusion by applying a policy of annexation and by creating satellite states on the basis of the principle set forth by the Convention in 1795: "In the interest of compensation for the evils and the expenditures involved in the most just of all wars, and to put itself in a position to prevent new ones by means of defence, the Republic must either retain as conquests or acquire by treaties countries that may be at its disposal, without consulting their inhabitants." All this was far from the promises of liberation that the Convention claimed to offer in 1792 to all "peoples desiring freedom".

The Revolution had resumed the offensive in the summer of 1794. It had re-occupied the east bank of the Rhine, the Austrian Netherlands and Savoy, which had been briefly retaken by the Piedmontese (August-September 1793). Then it invaded Holland. In 1795, Tuscany (February 9th.), Prussia (April 5th.) and Spain (July 22nd.) sued for peace. Holland, which became the Batavian Republic, had the status of a sister republic (July 9th.). In 1797, the Milanese became another, known as the Cisalpine Republic. But it was still necessary to eliminate England, against which the Directory organised the Egyptian expedition (1798), which immediately brought Turkey, suzerain of Egypt, and Russia into the war, and led to the formation of the Second Coalition. The French victories over the Russians and the English and then Bonaparte's successes in Italy brought peace with Russia, Austria and finally with England (Treaty of Amiens, March 25th., 1802). During the decade of constant war, France had incorporated Belgium, the east bank of the Rhine and Savoy, and had acquired the added protection of satellite states in the form of the sister republics.

Annexations and sister republics

The Revolution's policy of conquest followed between 1794 and 1799 resulted in the annexation of substantial territories, which were incorporated into the Republic as departments (the number of which rose from 83 to 102) and in the creation of satellite states, sister republics, from Holland to Naples. Thus the political geography of a large part of Western Europe was changed in just a few years, along with its political and social status. Certain neighbouring countries, such as Switzerland, the Austrian Netherlands and Holland, had affinities with the Revolution that are explained by the presence in those countries of a capitalistic middle class accustomed to economic and cultural relations with France. Some revolutionary movements were evident in such areas even before 1789, and after their failure the protesting forces had put their hopes in the French Revolution and in its intervention, though regretting it when such intervention was accompanied by violence and exploitation.

France annexed 17 departments between 1795 and 1798, from Lys to the Alpes Maritimes. To these must be added the papal state of the Comtat Venaissin, which became French in 1791. (It was initially incorporated into the neighbouring departments of Bouches du Rhône and the Drôme, and then became the Vaucluse department on June 25th., 1793.) Savoy, Léman, the Rhineland and Belgium were also incorporated into the Republic in just a few years. Before annexation the democratic backers of the Revolution were only a minority there, while public opinion as a whole was rather hostile and did not share the French views of liberating occupation.

Furthermore, the French government had other concerns in 1794 than supporting revolutionary minorities. The annexation of Belgium on October 1st., 1795 led to a policy of assimilation that caused popular resistance, particularly because of the secularisation of the Churchand conscription, and this led to the "Peasants' War" in October 1798. The area did not settle down until the Consulate. But the annexation of Belgium, which had long been a French dream, had finally come about.

Annexation and departmentalisation of the conquered areas were not the only means available to the Republic to ensure control and obtain help from states that it turned into vassal states, which the Directory was to call sister republics. Holland was the first to be given this original status. Led by the Stadtholder William V, Holland, which was then part of the First Coalition, had been invaded initially by Dumouriez's armies, but they had to leave it very quickly following the defeat at Neerwinden (May 18th., 1793). Pichegru again invaded it during the winter of 1794-95. Holland, abandoned by Prussia, which had just signed the Treaty of Basel, had to accept the Treaty of The Hague (May 16th., 1795), by which France forced it to accept an offensive and defensive alliance. The Stadtholder had to leave the country, which then received a constitution similar to the Year III Constitution, with two chambers and five directors. This marked the birth of the Batavian Republic. The Directory decided to turn the Helvetic Confederation into a sister republic (April 12th., 1795) primarily in order to assure control of the roads to Italy. The wave of sympathy aroused by the French Revolution lasted for only a time. The massacre of the Swiss guards at the Tuileries on August 10th., 1792, and then the annexation of Savoy and Basel were a source of considerable worry. In 1797 the Directory wanted to take over the region to protect Bonaparte's Italian conquests. The only thing needed was to use the friends of France (there was a Helvetic Club in Paris) to cause trouble in the areas of Vaud, Basel and Lausanne to justify French intervention, and that was done without delay. The Confederation was dissolved and replaced by the Helvetic Republic, while Geneva (April 15th., 1798), Mulhouse and the Jura valleys were annexed.

The Italian case

What is known as Italy's "French period" begin in 1796 with the Directory. The special and effective influence of the Revolution in the Italian peninsula, even before the conquest, is explained by its antecedents. Since the mid 18th. century, rural society had been transformed to various degrees, depending on the regions. Feudalism there had been generally attacked, and middle-class and intellectual élites attuned to the Enlightenment and to new ideas had developed there to a considerable extent. Certain decisive phenomena had occurred that had destabilised traditional society, such as the proletarisation of a large part of the peasantry in Piedmont, which demanded attachment to France in 1790. Italy had been the theatre of many rural insurrections, even before the French troops' intervention. And even if the abolition of seigneurial dues and tithes as well as nationalisation of ecclesiastical property were among the first measures adopted by the sister republics, the peasants did not profit from such steps, even to a limited extent, as the new distribution of land benefited the bourgeoisie alone. It is true that the new governments installed by the Directory based on the French model were not much concerned with the fate of the peasant masses. Disappointed and discontented, they turned against the French in 1799. The intellectual circles, who admired the Revolution and strongly supported French intervention, had already organised republican insurrections in 1794 and 1795 in Turin and Naples, but they failed because the rural and urban masses did not follow their lead and did not help them in their efforts. Bonaparte was clever enough to use those republicans to facilitate his conquest, then constituting republics that were receptive to their democratic wishes, basing themselves primarily on the forces of order and conservatism that were strongly dependent on France.

But under pressure from such "Jacobins", Bonaparte decided to set up the sister republics of Italy; first of all the Cispadane Republic (October 10th., 1796), consisting of the duchies of Modena, Reggio, Ferrara and Bologna, with Ancona added a bit later. In 1797 he organised the Cisalpine Republic north of the Po, with Lombardy, with which he united the Cispadane Republic before later adding part of Veneto (July 9th.). Its government was modelled directly on France's. A five-member Directory headed the new state, and some very tough conditions were imposed on it, to the benefit of its protector: maintaining a large occupation force, and a tribute of 18 million francs. In August it was Genoa's turn, and it was organised into the Ligurian Republic. It had the status of a vassal state, the independence of which was strictly nominal. At the start of 1798, after the assassination in Rome of General Duphot, the Directory had the papal city occupied, and it was immediately transformed into a Roman Republic with backing from the local Jacobins. The Pope was deported and died in France. But French violence, taking the form of looting and excessive contributions, annoyed the Romans, who threw themselves into the arms of the troops of the King of Naples, Ferdinand IV. However, General Championnet's counter-attack enabled him to restore the Roman Republic temporarily. Continuing his effort, he seized Naples on January 23rd., 1799, and established the Parthenopean Republic there. It lasted for barely five months. The Bourbons, backed by Nelson's British fleet, retook Naples in June 1799.

Looting and cultural influence

The Revolution's influence was not limited to remaking the map of Europe. By means of the spread of ideas, and even more through military occupation, it attempted to impose cultural supremacy on many countries, with relative success. It spread the French language in such countries as Italy, despite the hostility of the patriots who viewed the national language as the cement of unity, and in the Batavian Republic, in which French works were read by the middle class. In those same countries, as well as in the Rhineland, France made a far from-negligible propaganda effort.

The metric system was adopted by the sister republics and education improved in the French-controlled regions. But apart from these few positive aspects, the occupied countries were hardly likely to hail a systematic policy of spoliation in the artistic domain. Churches and abbeys were looted in Belgium, and in Italy Bonaparte made the theft of art works a diplomatic rule. Hence discontent and hostility were apparent in many areas in 1799. One of the Consulate's tasks was to be lowering the temperature in areas in which the Directory had multiplied the risks.

Should the Republic choose a general in place of the Directory?

General Napoléon Bonaparte's many victories allow the Directory to bring peace to a grateful French people.

Paris, January 1

Ten years after the Revolution, the country is no longer what it was. Freedom was achieved at the price of much bloodshed, despite numerous attempts at opposition over the last ten years. If civil war, with its burden of exacting and draconian mesures, is no longer a threat today, there is still much ill-feeling and resentment throughout the country. The violence of the political struggles in which, on both left and right, the various factions are engaged weakens the authority of the legislative powers, despite the Directory's determination to do all it can to strengthen its position at the expense of the two Councils. One solution which is making a lot of headway, and which would call a halt to the squabbles, would be to put one of the Republic's dazzling military leaders in charge. With Joubert, Brune and Bonaparte, the army is not short on officers rich in political skill.

Laplace's version of universal gravity

Paris, January

The only revolution which the Marquis de Laplace, also known as Pierre Simon, is interested in is that of the planets. This former mathematics teacher, and now a member of the Institute, who led the delegation set up in 1796 by the Council of Five Hundred to look into the state of the sciences at the time, has just published the first two volumes of his *Traité de mécanique céleste*. At once mathematician, astronomer and physician, he has assembled the discoveries of Halley, d'Alembert, Clairaut and Euler, along with his own, which aim at complementing the work of Newton by introducing into the theory of universal gravity facts which had seemed previously to contradict it. He explains the rules governing the interaction of satellites around Jupiter and how to calculate the heights of tides several years in advance; he also proves that the moon will not come crashing down onto the earth, and works out how long the ring round Saturn takes to complete revolution. It is all very reassuring.

To adapt his army to the needs of the desert, Napoléon has created a regiment of dromedaries.

Naples taken after bitter struggles

Paper soon to be produced in bulk

Seine et Oise, January 18

Can industrial methods be used in making paper? Up until now the paper base, made from scrap rags left to soak in water, has been shaped by hand, one sheet at a time. Nicolas Louis Robert, however, a worker at the paper mill at Essones belonging to the Didot family, has just taken out a patent on a machine for making paper in quantity. The base is spread out in a thin layer over a revolving cloth, where it dries out before being pressed by a series of cylinders. Once dry, the sheet can be stocked on a roll. Robert's new machine still has a long way to go before it is perfected, but one of the most adventurous paper-making firms, Didot, has already shown an interest in what will prove to be an important step forward.

Are the Freemasons secret royalists?

Paris, January 17

The *Journal des hommes libres* has given a cry of alarm: the guild of Freemasons is nothing more than a cover for royalist plotters. The author of the article draws public attention to the fact that, shocking to say, a lodge has been re-opened at Laval. It is composed entirely of parents of émigrés, Chouans who have come out of hiding, members of the Clichy Club and clerks made destitute for royalism at the time of Fructidor. Apparently, it is a beehive of clandestine activities, and good republicans in the area are more and more concerned. Charges against Freemasonry vary widely: for the Abbot Barruel, it is a cover for the Jacobin plotters who organised the Revolution.

Taking advantage of ten days of unrest in Naples, General Championnet marched into the city as a victor ...

Naples, January 25

After three days' fierce fighting, General Championnet has got the town under control at last. And he could probably not have done so without the precious aid provided by the Neapolitan Jacobins. The troubles began roughly a fortnight ago, when King Ferdinand IV was obliged to evacuate the town at very short notice, after the French had carried out a successful offensive against the Neapolitan troops at Civitacastellana. The sovereign's departure was followed by a week of anarchy which literally swept away the established order. First of all there was a popular insurrection against the bishop and the municipal authorities, charged with wanting to compromise with the French forces then marching on Naples. The rioters then turned on the better-off, suspected of treason. Next came the strongholds, notably the one at Saint Elme. Aristocrats

... but he clearly benefited from having the support of the town's Jacobins.

were massacred, and even members of government had to go into hiding to escape the fury of the people. Championnet took advantage of the chaos and the Jacobin recapture of the fort of Saint Elme to reduce the

hopes of the Republic's enemies to rubble. Contrary to the directives given by Paris, the French general wants to proclaim the Neapolitan republic, also known as the Parthenopian republic (→ Jan. 26).

Republican oath for the Ile de la Réunion

La Réunion, January 21

The revolt of the sansculottists in April 1798, led by the priest Lafosse and Sergeant Belleville, suggests further troubles may be in store for the island. To minimise the likelihood, therefore, the new members of the colonial Assembly have sworn a double oath before Governor Jacob: to remain loyal to the French Republic, and also

to maintain slavery in the colony. The sansculottists, who have a large majority in the south of the island, were not taken in by the ceremony. No-one believes that a monarchist like the Comte de Villèle was being sincere when he raised his right hand and said "I swear hatred to royalty and anarchy, and affection and loyalty to the French Republic one and indivisible ..." (→ Feb. 13).

Peasants will sometimes side with priests

Doubs, January 25

Two dead, two badly wounded. It was nothing less than a pitched battle that took place between some sixty peasants and the constables of Ornans today. The police were on their way to Besançon with a pair of priests sentenced to deportation under the law passed on Fructidor 19. It was not the first time a local population had come to the rescue

of condemned priests, either by hiding them or helping them to escape. The mounted constabulary had thus been sent reinforcements in the form of several infantrymen from the 29th. half-brigade. This was why the assailants, who had initially managed to free the priests, finally failed. The troop went in pursuit and ended up recapturing the two condemned men.

Paris and outlying regions under floods

Seine, February

Floods have been breaking out in the department of the Seine since the beginning of the month. The waywardness of nature has come to seem a veritable scourge in the eyes of the local authorities. On February 2nd., with the ice breaking up, the river left its bed and rose to a level of 23 feet or more. The road to Versailles has been cut off, and on half of the Quai de la Vallée in Paris people are going about in boats. Part of the capital is flooded out, moreover. The Seine has burst its banks, and can be seen along the Champs Elysées avenue. Down by the river itself, the washer-women can be seen squatting under the trees, as they work barefoot in wet skirts, for the washing-barges are out of reach. Worse still, the sewers have washed out into the streets, obliging the local authorities to alert the people to the precautions needed, if an terrible epidemic is to be avoided. They should cover their heads and avoid direct contact with planking by using mats instead. They should also wash their hands and feet and brush their hair every day. The Council of Five Hundred has, moreover, freed special funds for helping towards repairs.

In Naples, General Championnet decides to throw out the Directory commissioner

Opponents of the French occupation forces blend religion and politics.

Naples, February

General Championnet isn't the slightest bit interested in power-sharing. He thus had no qualms whatever when it came to throwing the Directory's envoy, Faipoult, out of town. Relations between the two men were such that a rupture was inevitable. The commissioner's job, on arriving in Naples, was to make sure the military authorities remained within the scope of their duties. In short, the Directory had sent the commissioner to warn the generals to stick to military affairs. They seriously underestimated the "appetite" of the man who has been called the Bonaparte of southern Italy, however. Championnet did indeed proclaim the Neapolitan Republic last January, in complete violation of all that the Directory had instructed. In Paris there were fears that the proclamation would start the war going again. On top of this Championnet, busy with his own personal affairs, has been turning a blind eye on looting carried out by his subordinates. In a letter to the Directory, Faipoult had suggested that the cumbersome general who "is assertive and sequesters shops so as to sell them and get rich" should be called back to Paris. He was not allowed to wait around for the response.

A lavish new home for Madame Tallien

Paris, February

The financier Ouvrard has just offered Thérésa Tallien a stunning private house with grounds in the Rue de Babylone. The building was put on sail as confiscated émigré property, and then bought up by an old spinster who never even lived in it. The financier is said to have been walking there with his mistress, the beautiful Thérésa, one day, when she remarked on how much she liked the property. Ouvrard then hands her the keys, with the words "It is yours to have, Madame". She has just left Barras, whose corrupt lifestyle and royalist intrigues are notorious and are beginning to cost him his popularity. She divorced her first husband under similar circumstances, prior to his fleeing the Terror, and likewise left Tallien just before his fall. Ouvrard, who has made his money as a trader on behalf of the State, has the same knack for wriggling out of difficult situations. Both figure prominently in fashionable Paris society.

The divine marquis is living in misery

Versailles, February

If prison seemed tough going to Citizen Sade, freedom is scarcely any better. Ridden with poverty and illness, he has taken refuge at Versailles where the cost of living is less onerous than in Paris, and where he has found employment in the local theatre. His pitiful salary of 40 sols a day is barely enough to live on, however. He shares the back of an attic with a servant and the son of Mme. Quesnet, while the mother herself has had to move in with friends. To save himself from dying of hunger and cold, he eats carrots and beans and warms himself with a few faggots obtained on credit. Just to compound his misery, his eye infection has got worse, filling him with fear that he might go blind. He also suspects he will be unable to have his name removed from the list of émigrés, on account of having used different Christian names on his residence permits: the ministry of police will not recognise *Louis Sade* as the Louis Donatien Alphonse François, one-time Marquis de Sade.

The death of a great visionary architect

Paris, February 6

Architecture is in mourning once again: first there was the death of Charles de Wailly in November 1798, now it is the turn of Louis Etienne Boullée. Apprenticed first with Blondel, like de Wailly, then later with Legeay, his work was distinguished from the outset by the double star of a French classicism married with the Roman tradition. His buildings are few, however: the Hôtel de Brunoy in Paris in 1773, conceived as a temple to Flora, and, in the same year, the conversions carried out on the Hôtel d'Evreux for the financier Beaujon. From 1780 onwards Boullée gave himself over entirely to teaching, and to his treatise on architecture, while at the same time working on projects such as the extraordinary cenotaph to Newton. With Lequeu and, above all, Ledoux, Boullée would argue passionately for an architecture at once rational and utopian, as demonstrated by his constant concern for simple and austere forms that are nonetheless fantastical in their novelty. The future will surely learn much from this visionary, for so long as art and architecture are considered to be sister disciplines.

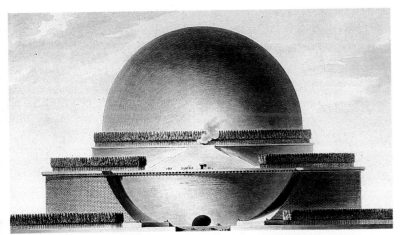

Newton's cenotaph (1784), one of Boullée's most sensational concepts.

A cross-section of the tomb, which illustrates the principles of gravity.

A fire destroys the Théâtre de l'Egalité

Paris, February 18

Was it done out of spite? No-one knows. The fact remains that the Théâtre de l'Egalité has been ruined by a fire. Only the walls are left. The fire broke out at seven o'clock in the morning. It took the heroism of the firemen, two of whom died in the flames, plus soldiers from a nearby barracks and a quantity of civilians, before the fire could be brought under control. Thanks to the courage of grenadiers from the legislative body, all the busts in the main hall, along with the statue of Voltaire, have happily been saved.

Napoléon suddenly leaves Cairo for Syria

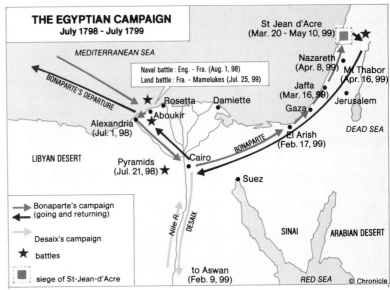

Cairo, February 10

Things don't look too good. A 50,000-strong Turkish army is at present marching towards Egypt. Napoléon immediately sized up the situation. If the pasha of Saint Jean d'Acre, Djezzar, blocks the isthmus at Suez, any hope of marching on the Indies will be destroyed. The loss of their fleet at Aboukir had stopped the French army in their tracks: if the redoubtable pasha also pulled off a victory at this point they would be all but throttled.

Leaving General Destaing to look after Cairo, Napoléon has set out for Syria, in the intention of joining the 13,000 troops who have gone on ahead at Katyeth. For use in future sieges, various artillery have been embarked on a dozen vessels with three frigates for escort: the latter are then to proceed to Jaffa, where they will join up with the land army. The Syrian campaign looks risky: the hatred Djezzar feels for the French is only equalled by his legendary ferocity (→ March 17).

Grouchy snuffs out rebellion in Piedmont

Piedmont, February 16

General Grouchy planned to see that the vote was respected, and has now done so. He has ordered the firing of villages in the Asti, Alba and Mondovi regions, and more than 40 rebels have died before the firing-squad, for having questioned the outcome of the vote. The referendum organised here on Feburary 8th. is the origin of these tragic events. The people had been invited to state whether they would prefer to become part of France, or to form an independent republic. The electors came came out in favour of annexation to France. The patriots, however, organised as *raggi*, or cells, along Babouvist lines, and partisans of an Italian republic one and indivisible, contested the validity of the vote.

A plan to settle the Jews in Palestine?

Paris, February 17

"Is it the second coming you're awaiting?" someone is supposed to have asked a Jew the other day. "No", he is said to have replied, "it has already taken place. Haven't you heard that Napoléon has taken the Holy Land?" Hardly had the Syrian expedition got under way than a rumour started going round that Napoléon was intending to establish a Jewish State in Palestine. On the basis of the rumour, an Irish officer serving in the French army today submitted a plan to Barras, by which all European Jews would be transferred to the Holy Land. Their colony would be a valuable ally for France and could ensure the free circulation of shipping in the Red Sea. What are these dreams based on? Napoléon says nothing on the issue, nor is there any sign that he has ever even thought about it.

A plague descends on the victors of Jaffa

At the risk of contagion, Napoléon visits the stricken and dying in Jaffa.

Jaffa, March 10

There is no longer any reason to
doubt. A violent fever, bubes, then
death: the plague is devastating the
French garrison. Army morale has
been seriously disturbed. Even the
soldiers who have not been touched
thus far are near to despair. All
scrutinise their bodies, waiting for
the deadly bubes to appear. And
every day there are thirty dead. The
plague first appeared in Alexandria
and then spread to Rosetta and
Damiette, pursuing the army across
the desert. The French soldiers
who, on the day after the siege of
Jaffa, took part in a savage massacre
of the local population interpret
the calamity that has befallen them
as a form of divine justice that has
been sent to punish them for their
sins. Nor will the doctors, who are
powerless to help them, be able to
persuade them otherwise.

Sinister project set up to provide work for poor children

Paris, March

There is certainly no shortage of
ideas as far as youth education is
concerned. Few, however, can be
quite so outlandish as the project
put forward to the Ministry of the
Interior by the 79-year-old former
swimming teacher Turquin. Given
the poor state of Paris chimneys, he
proposes that children who come
from areas "where long-standing
poverty has accustomed them to
difficult and poorly-paid work of
this kind" be assigned to sweeping
them out. By way of compensation,
the State would feed and house
them and even teach them to swim,
if they wished. After two years,
they would be offered the following
deal: either they could set up on
their own or, alternatively, become
teachers in their turn; or they could
opt for the more appetising alternative of joining the republican navy,
with a gratuity of 350 francs, with
the alternative this time of contributing the same sum towards doing an
apprenticeship in some technical
discipline that would be useful to
the French navy.

*The "cozy" is a heated room in which gentlemen chat with ladies, read their favourite newspapers and
especially play cards. The latest craze in card games in France is a form of three-of-a-kind.*

Saint Jean d'Acre is truly impregnable!

Saint Jean d'Acre, March 28

It is not for nothing that the town has the reputation it does. Thanks to its immense crenellated towers, heavy bastions and battlements, Acre resists. Every attempt made by Napoléon's soldiers for more than a week now has failed. Ready for action by March 21st., the warlord's labourers began by digging a ditch about a hundred yards from the town. The artillery, meanwhile, set up eight batteries. Bombarded for two solid days, the eastern face of the main tower collapsed. For a moment the assailants thought the town would be surrendering that very evening, as had happened at Jaffa. You could hear them crying out with joy over the cannon-fire. But the sappers who had rushed in where the breach had been opened were brought up short before a wall forming a counterscarp. They struggled in vain. Nor could Napoléon count on the stronghold surrendering. The story of the way the French troops massacred their prisoners at Jaffa has come even as far as Acre. The town is convinced that the same fate awaits it in the event of a defeat. All Napoléon can do is wait for his artillery to arrive from Alexandria (→ April 1).

War declared once more on Austria

Paris, March 12

The Directory has chosen its moment for an attack on Austria. Since a second coalition was formed between England, Russia and the kingdom of Naples, it was only a matter of time. Paris could hardly declare war on Austria, however, when the country had not signed any treaty with a European power openly hostile to France. Officially, the two countries are still involved in negotiations at Rastatt. After the discussions fell through at Seltz, however, Austria soon realised that no acceptable compromises would be reached with a country as hellbent on expansion as France. It thus turned to Russia, asking it to lend support in the event of a new war with the Directory. It was at this point that the Czar joined the second coalition with England. The Viennese authorities were not keen to reach an accord with the two partners, and made do with turning a blind eye to Russian troops on their way through Galicia. The French government then accused Austria of abetting the coalition. More than once it demanded some kind of explanation, while at the same time it did not want to stir things up. Vienna, however, refused to make any kind of real comment on the situation. In the absence of any clear co-operation, therefore, the Directory has just declared war on Austria, as well as on the Austrian Archduke of Tuscany. In reality, the die was cast long ago. France's territorial demands, which were upped still further last December, left Austria with little choice: it could either make an unconditional surrender to France and thereby secure peace, or it could decide to take up arms once more in a war with France.

This English cartoon makes fun of French starvelings who claim they are perfectly happy but, in fact, have only a miserable little frog between them.

A covert revival for the slave trade

Senegal, March 13

Can negroes be found in Africa who will work voluntarily in the colonies? The French commander in Senegal, Blanchot de Verly, finds the question a puzzling one. The instructions he has just been given by the Directory require him, it seems, to arrange the slave trade so that the Africans who join up do so of their own free will. In fact, of course, the Republic has not done away with slavery at all. At the beginning, the Convention put a stop to the bonus paid by the State to encourage the practice. Today, however, the colonies moan about the shortage of manpower. What is to be done? The commissioners of Guadeloupe and Guyana have all English slave ships boarded by their privateers. They then set free any negro who will agree to work on the plantations.

Defeat of Jourdan's troops at the battle of Stokach, on March 25th., by the soldiers led by the Archduke Charles.

An endless succession of French defeats in the north of Italy

Magnano, April 5

General Schérer is no substitute for Napoléon. For the soldiers who fought under the "little corporal" in Italy three years ago, the retreat tastes bitter. Leaving some 4,500 prisoners and 23 cannons in the hands of the Austrians, General Schérer has had to abandon any idea of crossing the Adige. French morale could not be worse. The right wing of Schérer's troops had already succumbed at Legnano, 11 days earlier. The most recent of the Italian campaigns has not got off to a very good start. French manpower is inferior to that of the coalition forces: Schérer has at his disposal 32,000 men, if that; the Austrians have 95,000, and Russia at least 20,000 on the Piava and in Tuscany. Moreover, many French troops are being kept back in the rear for work in the garrisons and general surveillance duties. Under the circumstances, it seem unlikely that the Directory will be able to pull off the full-scale offensive it had been planning (→April 29).

The French soldiers were unable to hold off the Austrian cavalry charges.

The ubiquitous Napoléon to the rescue of his troops in Palestine

Mount Tabor, April 16

The impossible has occurred: Napoléon is here! It came as as much of a surprise to the Turks, who thought he was at Saint Jean d'Acre, as to Kléber's army, who had given up all hope of rescue. Kléber's position was desperate. Surrounded by more than thirty thousand men, the 3,000 French troops expected to be wiped out from one minute to the next. Napoléon, however, had been put in the picture by a dispatch, and had immediately set off to come to Kléber's aid. Riding through the night with a division of infantry and a reserve battery, Napoléon found the enemy army at dawn. Dividing his division up into three columns, he made his way forward with the greatest possible stealth. Concealed by the corn that grows all over the plain of Esdraelon, his soldiers threw the pasha's men into a panic, for they seemed to have turned up out of nowhere, as did the general, who has succeeded in defeating an enemy whose forces considerably outnumbered his own.

Bonaparte's tactical genius and speedy action allowed him to defeat a foe who was better adapted to local conditions.

Assassination of top French diplomats at Rastatt

Le 9 Floréal de l'an 7, à neuf heures du soir, le Gouvernement Autrichien a fait assassiner par ses troupes les Ministres de la République française, BONNIER, ROBERJOT et JEAN DEBRY, chargés par le Directoire exécutif, de négocier la paix au congrès de Rastadt. VENGEANCE!!!

France has condemned the attack.

Paris, April 30

Indignation is widespread, for France has just discovered that two of the Directory's emissaries were killed two nights ago in Rastatt. The Congress where the discussions were being held had been dissolved after war was declared on Austria. Bonnier, Jean Debry, Treilhard's successor since the latter's election to the Directory, and Roberjot, the stand-in for Napoléon since he left for Egypt, were preparing to leave. There were already Austrian troops encircling the town when the carriages carrying the three French diplomats were suddenly attacked by a detachment of hussars. Bonnet and Roberjot were killed on the spot. Only Jean Debry, seriously wounded, managed to avoid certain death by pretending to be already dead. This outrageous attack has provoked strong reactions. It is still not clear for the moment whether

In the middle of the night, French officials are attacked and massacred by a unit of Hungarian hussars.

or not the Viennese government had a hand in it, and the Archduke Charles has ordered an enquiry to be held. The French, however, have no doubts whatsoever about who is to be held responsible. If any justification was needed for a war with Austria, they now have it. In effect, the event makes abundantly clear that the European counter-revolution is once more on the war-path against regicidal and republican France. In the public's eyes, and whatever the diplomatic origins of the affair might be, it is a clear indication of the inextinguishable hatred that kings and aristocrats feel for the Revolution (→ June 8).

A volcano awakens with fire and mud

Guadeloupe, April 4

The volcano in Guadeloupe has awoken from its slumber. In the middle of the night, a whole series of explosions unleashed a torrent of gas, steam and mud, then débris and rocks, driving the people of the Basse Terre from their homes. Even the Créoles, who are well-versed in these tiresome, volcanic upheavals, were somewhat taken aback by the violence of it all. In the space of a few hours, thousands of square feet of coffee, cocoa and vanilla plantations were devastated by torrents of mud. Taking advantage of the widespread disorder, many negroes have fled the forced labour camps and gone into the hills of Goyave. Here they will join the "maroons", former slaves who prefer to live as free men in camps of their own.

A "panorama" of Paris from Montmartre

Paris, April

It's just like the real thing! In a hall on the Boulevard Montmartre children gaze goggle-eyed, while old men start polishing their glasses: before them is a painted canvas attached around a curved wall and lit up from above, depicting Paris. With a single sweep of the eye, you can take in the river, parks, prisons, avenues, gates and chimneys of the city. The painter responsible for the work has made perfect use of all the effects of perspective and trompe l'oeil to give a feeling of depth and height. Known as a "panorama", the method was devised in 1792 by the Englishman Robert Baker and set up in London in 1796. It is an American engineer, Robert Fulton, who has brought it over to France. All the major capitals of Europe have now acquired one of these magical devices.

Wedding of wealth toasted in La Réunion

La Réunion, April 13

It had to end in marriage sooner or later. Ever since he took refuge in La Réunion, the young Jean Baptiste Guillaume Joseph, Comte de Villèle, a naval officer with no money to his name and the protégé of the Marquis de Saint Félix, hasn't let a day go by without a visit to the Panon Desbassayns family. With their help he has acquired a coffee plantation at Bras Panon and a seat in the island's Assembly. Today, with his wedding to Mélanie Barbe, he gives a name and a title to one of the richest families in the island.

Religious overtones divide audience

Paris, April 15

Whistling and applause vied with one another in the Favart auditorium during the première of Dejaure and Bertin's *Montano et Stéphanie*. The numerous allusions to Catholicism soon had the audience in a fever. The second act takes place, it turns out, in a church complete with high altar, crucifix, angels, tabernacle and lighted candles; all that you need, in short, to fire partisan passions and have people at each other's throats. The whistling was rapidly drowned out by the cheering of sympathisers. "The altar is back!" said one man contentedly. "Those who don't like it can leave!" cried another. Nor did the arrival of a bishop on stage, singing a canticle and performing the wedding sacrament, help much.

Seringapatam falls to the British forces

India, May 4

Seringapatam has fallen to the British, after a 30-day siege. The Sultan of Mysore, Tippoo Sahib, died bravely, defending his capital. He had stood up to Wellesley since January, hoping for help from the French. In February, when the British troops were moving toward Mysore, he had sent a new delegation to Paris with this in mind. However, his hopes that the French troops involved in the expedition to Egypt would come to his assistance proved vain.

La Harpe publishes his courses at Lycée

Paris, May

La Harpe is getting back to literature — not his own, which never enjoyed success except among critics, but rather to the authors he got students to discover and love during the 13 years he taught at the Lycée. After his retirement, he requested the Agesse booksellers to publish the first eight volumes of his courses under the title *le Lycée*. Thus, even though hiding since he was outlawed, in other words since Fructidor 18, he will again become a prominent figure in literature.

Sieyès is made new Director; Reubell out

Sieyès in his Director's regalia.

Paris, May 16

A very serious event has just occurred. Reubell, who was chosen by lot to become a Director, has seen his election ruled invalid by the Council of Ancients, which elected Sieyès by 118 out of 205 votes. Previously, in 1795, Sieyès had rejected that post because he opposed the Constitution of Year III, which was adopted instead of his own proposal. The Councils are aware of this, and if they have picked him, it means that they intend to have the Constitution revised. So they have chosen Sieyès to intervene in government policy and modify the balance of power with the Directory, as well as the one existing among the Directors themselves. This move will probably be considered provocative towards the executive.

Bonaparte's enemy de Phelippeaux dead

Acre, May 1

Antoine de Phelippeaux has died of sun-stroke. He and Bonaparte were students together at the Brienne Military Academy, and they were made lieutenants in the artillery the same year. Phelippeaux emigrated to Coblentz after 1789, but the whims of fate brought the two men face to face again on opposite sides of the ramparts of the old Byzantine fortress. When Napoléon Bonaparte reached the Acre walls, Phelippeaux had already organised the defence of the site on behalf of the English. At his orders the Turks had built a new defence line and strengthened the surrounding walls. The successive failures of the French attacks bear witness to de Phelippeaux's abilities as a fine strategist (→ May 17).

Early on May 6th., the people of Arezzo and the surrounding area in Tuscany revolted against the French occupiers.

An isolated victory for Lecourbe forces

Monte Cenere, May 13

In spite of their fine formations, the Austrian troops have been battered. The French General Lecourbe easily got rid of their leader, the Prince de Rohan. This nobleman, who emigrated very early, suffered big losses and had to withdraw under French pressure behind the Tresa, which connects Lake Maggiore with Lake Lugano. The Austro-Russian forces used in the campaign are finding that their advance in Switzerland is in some difficulty due to having put too much faith in the prince. However, it would appear that this victory will not be enough to reverse the Lombardian situation, which remains a source of serious concern to the French forces involved.

General Lecourbe, hero of the day.

French forces suffer defeats in Grisons

Chur, May 14

The Austrians have won a routine victory, as General Ménard's division was crushed after fighting a force five times bigger. The division abandoned 15 guns and 21 munitions vehicles, while losing more than 3,000 prisoners. The same thing happened several kilometres away, near Davos, where the Austrians outnumbered French forces and easily defeated the Republic's conscripts. The Directory's plans have again turned out to be unrealistic. Actually, the excessive scattering of the French forces was an indication that victory could be ruled out.

Bonaparte's unlucky forces are forced to lift the siege of Acre

Syria, May 17

Acre will not be the expeditionary corps' grave. Three months of failed attacks have led Bonaparte to lift the siege. The French forces seem dogged by hard luck. The English intercepted the artillery pieces expected from Alexandria. The result was that not only was Bonaparte deprived of his precious cannon, but the enemy even turned them against him! Moreover, by immobilising the French outside the city, the defenders gave the Rhodes army enough time to arrive. More than 10,000 Anglo-Turkish troops brought in by 30 Ottoman ships have already landed at the port, bringing arms and munitions with them. When the plague joined in, it became clear that the city would never fall. The commanding general was so annoyed that he ordered a final assault, using all his remaining firepower. Bombs, cannon-balls and shells rained

The English and the Turks repulse the French outside the Acre stronghold.

down on Acre as a farewell present. Adopting a scorched-earth policy, Napoléon Bonaparte ordered the burning of the harvests in the surrounding area. However, all these fireworks cannot conceal the extremely precarious nature of the situation in which the French forces in Egypt currently find themselves (→ May 21).

Beaumarchais, the creator of Figaro, dies

Paris, May 18

Words spoken by Figaro, created by Beaumarchais, might well be used to describe the playwright himself, who just died at the age of 65: "Ambitious by vanity, hardworking by necessity, but taking great pleasure in idleness! An orator when danger threatens, a poet in the interest of relaxation, a lover at frenzied intervals, I have seen everything, done everything, consumed everything." With Beaumarchais, it is the famous barber of Seville, Figaro himself, who disappears.

Since Beaumarchais came back from exile in 1796, he had cut his standard of living considerably in view of his crushing debts. He was tired of the daily struggle against neediness. However, what he most regretted at the age of 65, was being forced to give up all the delights that had made him love life. Yesterday he dined with friends and spoke of his youthful memories, his only remaining pleasure. When the servant opened his bedroom door this morning, he found the playwright dead.

Comédie Française gets act back together

Paris, May

The Comédie Française is being reborn from its ashes. This event occurred during a dinner given by the actor Dazincourt. The idea was to reconcile the actors of the former Comédie Française in order to reconstitute it. The break dated back to 1791, when political events led to a split within the Théâtre de la Nation troupe between the monarchists and the advocates of new ideas. The latter camp included Talma, who took several of his friends with him to the Théâtre Français, in the Rue de Richelieu. So it was Talma who used his

warm, vibrant voice in taking the initiative of reciting a particularly appropriate passage from *Athalie* for his comrades, who listened with great emotion: "What New Jerusalem is coming forth from the end of the desert, in shining brightness and bearing, on its forehead, an immortal mark? Oh heavens, pour down your dew, and may the earth bring forth its saviour!" "That saviour's Molière!" Fleury then shouted. Following his example, they all surrounded and then kissed Molière's bust, and then fell into each other's arms in tears. It was a very touching scene (→ May 31).

Free and Easy!

The return of artists to the school of David and the study of antiquity is influencing fashion. Women are dressing in Greek or Roman style. People wear nothing under light, close fitting, transparent dresses. This has just inspired Despréaux to write these ironical verses:

Thanks to fashion's sway
Folk have no more hair;
Folk have no more hair.
That's practical, I say.
Folk have no more hair.
It's much more debonair.

Thanks to fashion's sway
Pockets now are out;
Pockets now are out.
That's practical, I say.
Pockets now are out,
'Cos money we're without!

Thanks to fashion's sway
Corsets are non-U;
Corsets are non-U.
That's practical, I say.
Corsets are non-U,
And a good thing too!

Thanks to fashion's sway
One shirt is quite enough;
One shirt is quite enough.
That's practical, I say.
One shirt is quite enough,
That's anything but tough!

Thanks to fashion's sway
We're practically unclad;

We're practically unclad.
That's practical, I say.
We're practically unclad.
It makes me hopping mad!

The Directory's work

The Year III Constitution had set up a régime in which executive power was shared by five Directors (the first ones were Barras, who remained on the job for the entire Directory period, Reubell, Carnot, La Révellière Lépeaux and Letourneur), while legislative power was given to two assemblies, the Ancients and the Five Hundred. Conflicts between the two branches quickly multiplied. The Directory was installed on October 26th., 1795, and lasted until November 10th., 1799 (Brumaire 19, Year VIII). The Republic ended on that day. For its entire life, the régime was hindered in its operations by poor economic conditions and by war, and it was gradually completely discredited.

From inflation to deflation

The crisis was of a monetary nature initially. Over a four-month period, the Directory had to put 16 billion assignats into circulation. The assignat's value depreciated and the Directory had to drop it. Paper money was abandoned in the summer of 1796 and the country came back to metallic money, but precious metal was scarce. Part of it had left France, while another part was hoarded. Deflation of payment means was no more favourable to economic recovery than inflation had been, and the inflation rate had risen constantly since 1791. Despite the creation of the Current Accounts Fund in 1796 and the Trade Discount Bank in 1797, credit remained extremely limited and business stagnated, while foreign trade, hurt by war and the loss of the Antilles market, fell off. Then the years 1796 to 1798 brought abundant harvests, prices collapsed, and the drop in the price level was accelerated by deflation. Speculation triumphed, giving rise to fast fortunes. People preferred to invest in property and war supplies. The demand for luxury goods did not offset the generally depressed conditions noted in industry. The State could not count on a regular income, since tax collections were poor. However, after the coup d'état of Fructidor 18, some improvement in finances was seen. The Directory declared bankruptcy for two-thirds of the debt, which was cut from 250 to 83 million, and it reorganised the tax system. Still, the Directory had to resort to getting loans from individuals and depended on contributions imposed on the "allied" countries.

The monetary and economic crisis had social consequences. First of all, it worsened the wretchedness of the lower classes, and then, when those classes' condition improved, it caused discontent among the middle class (bourgeoisie). The poor 1795 harvest and galloping inflation until the summer of 1796 had led to higher prices, from which the poor suffered particularly. The Directory had to resort to austerity measures and re-establish requisitions for supplying markets, with only small success since the municipalities generally rejected this policy. Then came deflation, with the good harvests of 1796 and the following years, which brought lower prices. The people got cheap bread, while wages remained relatively high. Discontent then affected land-owners, whose profits fell, and entrepreneurs, who experienced difficulties because of scarce money and credit. The middle class' dissatisfaction was a serious development since it constituted the régime's political basis. First the leftist opposition and then the rightists exploited, in turn, the resentment caused by the crisis.

The Babouvist plot

This plot actually had little chance of bringing in outsiders, even from the lower classes, who could not be won over to its programme. Of course, the poverty that prevailed in the spring of 1796 offered fertile ground, but the kind of communism preached by Babeuf did not find favour, and the sansculottists had no liking for a doctrine that would do away with property and inheritance. Babeuf tried to take advantage of the favourable circumstances created by the Directory itself. At the latter's very outset it had freed many patriots, and the neo-Jacobin movement had been able to reconstitute itself. It had its newspapers and its popular associations, which came back into being in many provincial areas and in Paris. In the capital, where the lower classes remained amorphous, militants met at the Panthéon Club, which attracted such former "terrorists" as Amar, who had been a member of the Committee of General Security, and such foreign refugees as Buonarroti, whose ideas were close to Babeuf's. But the members as a whole were rather moderate. Still, Gracchus Babeuf's propaganda attracted support from part of the club's clients. Babeuf was a reader of Rousseau, and above all of Morelly. He wanted absolute equality. He was convinced of the need for guiding the popular movement. He wanted to abolish property and inheritance, which could be accomplished only by a temporary dictatorship, of which "The Equals" would be the artisans. If he were to succeed Babeuf needed the help of the sansculottists, but they paid scant attention to his arguments, and moreover they were dispersed.

The Directory was frightened, or pretended to be frightened in order to gain support from everybody afraid of the agrarian law. It got Bonaparte to close the Panthéon Club in June 1796. Babeuf's supporters then began meeting clandestinely and hatched a plot. This "conspiracy of the equals" was headed by a directory consisting of Babeuf, Antonelle, Maréchal, Le Peletier and Buonarroti. It was based on a network of agents recruited in all Paris districts, as well as from among garrison soldiers. Babouvism also won a few supporters in the provinces. The themes were discussed in the press and public talks, and appeared in song, but they hardly affected anybody except tradespeople and Paris craftsmen, the sansculottists' recruiting source.

The "conspiracy of the equals" aimed at overthrowing the government, and when one of the conspirators revealed it the Directory decided to act. It had no difficulty in ending the agitation that was developing in the Army, and on May 10th. it had the plot leaders arrested. They were not tried until the next year. Babeuf was sentenced to death and executed, while Buonarroti was deported. The Equals had not managed to evoke any real popular response and were only a secondary threat to the Directory, which it easily overcame.

Fructidor 18

The same could not be said about another peril that the Directory had to fight on the right. Both the Ancients and the Five Hundred contained a ubstantial monarchical right wing, which strengthened itself considerably in new elections. The anti-Jacobin purge carried out in the administration after the "conspiracy of the equals" had weakened the republican party a little more, while the royalists, constitutionals and absolutists gained ground. In the provinces, the returned émigrés and the non-juring priests carried on active propaganda.

Elections were planned for April 1797, and the royalists made very active preparations for their campaign to ensure their control of both chambers. "Philanthropic institutes" in each department played the essential rôle. The Directory multiplied its initiatives to organise a counter-offensive, but the elections were a success for the royalists all the same. Only 11 of the 216 outgoing members of the National Convention were re-elected, while the new deputies included such counter-revolutionaries as Pichegru and such agents of Louis XVIII as Imbert Colomès.

The Directory was divided in the face of this republican failure. Reubell wanted the elections to be quashed, but was opposed by Carnot. The royalists immediately exploited their victory by electing Pichegru president of the Five Hundred and by having Barthélemy appointed as a Director, replacing Letourneur. However, all this did not markedly modify the balance of power, and the Directory retained a republican majority. But the two chambers adopted some measures, such as abrogation of the law barring the parents of émigrés from public duties and dropping repression of non-juring priests, which worried the republican Directors. Part of the army came to support royalism, and the reorganisation of the National Guard, which was decided in August, and the tax-based formation of élite companies, gave people who wanted to topple the régime a devoted armed force.

Barras, La Révellière Lépeaux and Reubell were worried and decided to speed up a takeover bid. They won help from Hoche, who massed troops near Paris, and from Bonaparte, who was then in Italy and dispatched Augereau. On the evening of September 3rd., 1797 (Fructidor 17), they ordered troops to enter the capital, made the army occupy the palace in which the chambers were sitting, and had Pichegru and Barthélemy arrested, while Carnot, warned by Barras, managed to flee. On September 5th., the republicans rounded off their victory: the April elections were annulled in more than half of the departments; 177 deputies' mandates were ruled invalid. Fifty three of them were sentenced to deportation to Guyana. The émigrés who were not struck off the lists had to leave France or be subject to the death penalty, and voters were required to swear an "oath of hatred for royalty". Thus the republican Directors carried the day, though at the price of an attack on legality and of a call on the military, who thus became participants in the political arena.

Directory discredited

The collusion between the Directory, which was always short of money, and bankers, speculators and suppliers, who often lived in insolent luxury, contributed to discrediting a régime that seemed to be falling apart. After Fructidor the Directory indulged in some mild repression: administrative purges, deportations, censorship, and arrests of émigrés and priests. From this the Jacobins gained new energy, which seemed to endanger the conser-

vative Republic. The Councils (chambers) received proposals aimed at bringing the poor back into the electoral assemblies. Fears then arose of a rebirth of egalitarianism and of Babouvism.

In March 1798 the government had the Jacobin clubs closed and tried to organise the Year VI elections for its own benefit. Those elections sent numerous republicans to the two chambers -- including Barere and Lindet -- and they were enough on the Jacobin side to worry the Directory, even though the majority remained favourable to it. The Councils voted a law on May 11th. (Floréal 22) that made it possible to exclude undesirable deputies. Actually, this coup d'état only resulted in lowering the Directory's prestige, since the opposition in the two chambers had not disappeared. The discredited Directory also felt threatened by the popularity of the generals, whose prestige was growing. One might well fear Augereau, who had hoped to join the Directory after Fructidor and had been disappointed in that expectation, and above all Bonaparte, whose glory was becoming worrying. The clever Barras had declared: "We will all perish because of our generals."

The Directory thought it could avoid this danger by allowing Bonaparte, the most ambitious and the boldest of the generals, to launch into an adventure in Egypt that was to last for a year and a half. That adventure led to the formation of the Second Coalition against France, containing the Russians and the Ottoman Empire along with England and Austria. In the spring of 1799 the Austrians won victories in Bavaria and Lombardy, and the Russians occupied all of northern Italy. These defeats accelerated the breakup of the Directory, while the Year VII elections were being prepared.

Sieyès' role

Many deputies turned away from the régime. The elections were a failure for the Directory, as only a third of the official candidates were elected. There was a huge number of abstentions, as the French were losing interest in political life. The new Councils (chambers) immediately displayed their opposition to the Directory. On May 9th., they replaced the outgoing Reubell with a member of the former Constituent Assembly, Sieyès, a determined opponent of the Constitution of Year III and eager to revise it, or else to bring down the régime. The deputies, who wanted to take revenge on a Directory that had humiliated them, forced Treilhard, and then Merlin and La Révellière Lépeaux, to resign. Sieyès was the beneficiary of this operation, together with the military, and especially Bonaparte, whose friends came into the government: Bernadotte at the War Ministry and Cambacérès at Justice.

Sieyès struck indiscriminately at the opposition camps, royalist and Jacobin, depriving them of newspapers. Victory finally came after a number of military failures, enabling the Directory to hold off the Jacobins, while the republican troops finished off the Chouan rebels in the west, who had appeared threatening for a time. But despite these successes, which helped it gain time, the Directory was losing ground in public opinion, in the Councils, and in the business world. The Constitution of Year III, which had functioned very poorly, had lost all credibility. The representative system, which the Directors had mistreated, seemed condemned, while the Directory appeared impotent. Sieyès proved to be the theoretician of a constitutional

revision supported by a large fraction of the "notables", but the republicans and the Councils were not inclined to accept such a revision without resistance. Another takeover seemed necessary, and Sieyès prepared for it carefully. He needed the army to succeed and thought of Joubert, but that general was killed at the battle of Novi, just as he was getting ready to return to Paris. On October 9th., 1799, Bonaparte landed at Fréjus after returning from Egypt. He enjoyed immense prestige. His reputation for republicanism and his victories brought him favour in the eyes of the middle class, which viewed him as the sword it needed to struggle against both counter-revolutionary Europe and Jacobinism. His trip from Fréjus to Paris was a triumph. He quickly understood that the power structure was tottering, and he got in touch with Sieyès through his brother Lucien, who was a member of the Five Hundred and was utterly devoted to the young general's interests. Sieyès had to accept the conditions set by Bonaparte, whose only thought was getting him out as quickly as possible, and the plot was worked out.

Brumaire 18

Bonaparte won the help of bankers, such as Ouvrard, but had greater difficulty in winning over the generals, except for Moreau. Paris was his. The operation was carried out in two phases. On Brumaire 18 (November 9th., 1799) the Councils were informed that a Jacobin plot was being hatched against the Republic, and they decided to move to Saint Cloud, while Bonaparte was appointed commander of the Paris garrison. Sieyès and Ducos, who were in the plot, resigned, and Barras was forced to follow suit. The other two Directors, who refused to bow out, were placed in Moreau's custody. The Directory no longer existed.

The next day the Councils met at Saint Cloud, which was occupied by the Legislative Guard and, understanding that they had been fooled, they got ready to act. Bonaparte then made the decision to intervene personally and speak to the deputies. He got a bad reception at the Ancients, and had to flee from the Five Hundred in the face of threats from the Jacobin deputies, who outlawed him. Sieyès then persuaded the general to resort to force. Bonaparte and his brother Lucien addressed the soldiers, convincing them that an attempt had been made to assassinate the saviour. Murat marched with his men against the Five Hundred, chasing them out of the Orangery, in which they were sitting. In the evening a few fugitives were gathered together at the Ancients, and they docilely agreed to replace the Directory had begun, and not without success: reconciliation of the notables, and the triumph of the middle-class revolution. Thus the Directory had collapsed following a predictable coup d'état. Election manipulation and violations of the Constitution had shown that the representative system functioned poorly. It had proved impossible to create any real governmental party that would back the Directory wholeheartedly, and the various forms of opposition had never been recognised. The interminable war and the formation of the Second Coalition against France had contributed to undermining the system. In a France concerned with both the danger of royalist counter-revolution and Jacobin attempts to outdo others, the Consulate offered reassurance and the guarantees of safety, and of enjoyment of property, to which the country aspired.

June 1799
from 1st. to 30th.

Directory

1 *(Prairial 13, Year VII)*
Maine et Loire. An attack on a mobile column by peasants near Vern confirms that the Chouan rebellion is now re-awakening.

4 *(Prairial 16, Year VII)*
Switzerland. The Austrian forces attack the French positions from the Lake of Zurich to the Limmat.

5 *(Prairial 17, Year VII)*
Paris. The legislative Councils ask the Directory to explain the defeats suffered by French forces over the last three months.→

6 *(Prairial 18, Year VII)*
Switzerland. Masséna digs in on the left bank of the Limmat, allowing the Archduke Charles to enter Zurich.

10 *(Prairial 22, Year VII)*
Russia. The daughter of Louis XVI, Marie Thérèse, marries her cousin, the Duc d'Angoulême, in Mittau.

14 *(Prairial 26, Year VII)*
Egypt. Bonaparte returns to Cairo.→

16 *(Prairial 28, Year VII)*
Paris. The Council of Five Hundred calls on the Directory to answer the questions asked on June 5th., and goes into permanent session (→17).

17 *(Prairial 29, Year VII)*
Paris. The Councils win an initial victory in their conflict with the Directory by declaring the Director Treilhard's election unconstitutional and hence invalid. He is replaced by Gohier, who was Justice Minister in Year II and is considered a Jacobin (→18).

18 *(Prairial 30, Year VII)*
Jura. Saint Claude is destroyed by fire.

18 *(Prairial 30, Year VII)*
Paris. The legislative Councils dismantle the Directory.→

19 *(Messidor 1, Year VII)*
Italy. Macdonald is defeated on the banks of the Trebbia river by Suvorov.→

20 *(Messidor 2, Year VII)*
Paris. After Roger Ducos on June 18th, General Moulin is elected to the Directory.

24 *(Messidor 6, Year VII)*
Naples. Admiral Nelson refuses to include the Neapolitan Jacobins in the capitulation of the city's garrison (→29).

28 *(Messidor 10, Year VII)*
Paris. The Directory imposes a forced borrowing of 100 million livres on the rich.

Deputies hit Directory on military defeats

Paris, June 5

Relationships between legislators and the executive branch are becoming tenser. The Council of Five Hundred has just sent the Directory a demand for an explanation of the Republic's military situation. The fact is that the French defeats in Italy, Switzerland and Holland give the opposition an ideal handle for attacking the government. It accuses the latter of being lax, and says that the War Minister Schérer is corrupt and has used government contracts to line his own pockets. This kind of ultimatum is indicative of the rising tide of opposition in the two Councils. The Jacobins, recently led by Napoléon Bonaparte's brother, Lucien, are raising their heads again and they are said to enjoy support from Sieyès and Barras. They are demanding public safety measures on the basis of military dangers and the revival of royalist agitation in France. What is called "leftist" criticism is increasing constantly (→June 16).

Naturalists sail to see South America

Spain, June 5

The frigate *Pizzaro* left Corunna at dawn. There were two naturalists on board, Alexander von Humboldt and Aimé Bonpland, heading a mission that is to explore South America. Von Humboldt was born in Berlin in 1769, receiving a good education there and then attending the University of Göttingen. At the age of 18 he began making plans for long trips, and sold several pieces of property to raise the money. He went to Paris to buy scientific equipment and met such scientists as Laplace and Berthollet. He also became acquainted with the naturalist Aimé Bonpland, with whom he went to Spain last year. In Madrid, the two men got the Spanish Navy Ministry to issue passports enabling them to visit the Spanish possessions in the Americas, and now they are on their way aboard the *Pizzaro*.

King's aunt is dead

Trieste, June 8

"Will I be going up there?" asked Louis XVI's aunt, Madame Victoire, raising her eyes to Heaven. And a few minutes later she passed on, in her sister's presence. Since the two were obliged to leave Rome in May 1796, they had had several homes-in-exile: Caserta, Corfu, and finally Trieste. Mme. Victoire's condition was already considered alarming when she arrived here. Mme. Adélaïde's health is also a cause of concern.

Bonaparte retreats to Cairo, after Acre

The French retreat through the Syrian desert, moving toward Cairo.

Egypt, June 14

The minarets of Cairo are in view. The city's inhabitants, their arms loaded with all kinds of presents, came out to greet General Bonaparte's soldiers. When the commanding general of the Army of the Orient left Acre a month ago, he sent emissaries ahead with announcements of victory to make a favourable impression on the people. However, the reality is a less glorious one. About 2,300 men died in Syria, killed by the enemy or carried off by the plague. Above all, and this is the first time it has ever happened, Bonaparte has been forced to retreat.

Austro-Russian forces defeat Macdonald

General Alexander Suvorov.

Emilia, June 19

The Austro-Russian forces remained in control of the battlefield after three days' fighting, depriving the French of their last chance to stage a recovery in Italy. The battle hung in the balance for a long time, but eventually General Suvorov got the upper hand, as he proved himself to be the best tactician. The lack of coordination between Moreau and Macdonald was the major flaw in the French operations. The latter, isolated, was hit with full force by the coalition troops. Realising he could not get through, he fell back toward the Apennines.

French homage to two slain diplomats

Bordeaux, June 8

All French theatres were urged to remain closed today in remembrance of the two French plenipotentiaries assigned to negotiate for peace terms at Rastatt and assassinated last April, reportedly at the Austrian government's order. The funeral ceremony turned out to be a dignified one. The only feature of the occasion that caused some disappointment was the small turnout of the National Guard for this commemoration, which scandalised many citizens.

Legislative Councils force Directors out of office

Paris, June 18

A coalition of deputies has just won the trial of strength with the Directory. It consisted of Jacobins allied with dissident "directorials", referring to former supporters of the régime who had felt the wind change and joined the opposition. This coalition has forced the resignations of the triumvirate of the most anti-Jacobin Directors: Merlin de Douai, La Révellière Lépeaux, and Treilhard.

The crisis began in an atmosphere of an impending coup d'état. The legislative Councils feared that the Directors might foment such a coup against them, while the Directors were convinced that the opposition deputies were preparing one with the armed forces' help.

On June 16th., noting that the Directory had not replied to the request for explanations concerning the military situation sent to it by the Council of Five Hundred on June 5th., the deputy Poullain Grandprey demanded that the request be repeated. The same evening, the Directory indicated that it was going into permanent session until it could complete its response to the Councils. The leftist opposition immediately interpreted this statement as a provocation: if the Directory was going into permanent session, it must be because it was preparing a new Fructidor 18.

Directors La Révellière Lépeaux and Merlin de Douai being urged to resign by a delegation of deputies.

The Councils' committees were already in the process of deciding that the Councils should also go into permanent session. Moreover, on the basis of a proposal by the deputy Bergasse, the Five Hundred passed a motion during the night to remove Treilhard, on the grounds that he had been elected a Director in violation of the Constitution, having left the Assembly less than a year previously. Probably under pressure from Sieyès, Treilhard agreed to leave the Directory, which thus lacked a majority, being divided equally between left and right wing republicans. Today, the Councils moved against Merlin and La Révellière, and a group of deputies went to see them, urging them to resign to avoid bloodshed. This evening Merlin finally capitulated, followed by La Révellière.

The question now is, since the Directory has been dismantled, who is going to govern France in future?

Violent anti-Jacobin reactions shake whole Italian Peninsula

The Italian Jacobins being condemned and consigned to the flames of Hell.

Naples, June 29

The Neapolitan patriots are suffering now for their cooperation with the French troops. Since the French evacuated Naples on June 19th., the patriots have undergone terrible repression. Today, Admiral Nelson even hanged the Jacobin Admiral Caracciolo from the mast of his own ship. On June 24th., Nelson refused to approve the capitulation agreement proposed by Cardinal Ruffo, which called for allowing the patriots to leave at the same time as the French garrison. Nelson preferred to leave them to the people's vengeance. The entire peninsula is experiencing such violent reactions. Yesterday, in Siena, the *Viva Maria* counter-revolutionaries massacred some Jacobins and burnt 13 Jews alive on suspicion of complicity with republicans.

French page turned into a blackmailer

Philadelphia, June 11

Alexandre de Tilly is a model for unscrupulous adventurers. He was once among Marie Antoinette's pages, and emigrated early on. He seduced and then married a daughter of the American Senator William Bingham without her father's consent. Bingham, a former trader who got rich from military business, wanted to avoid a scandal and have the marriage dissolved. After long negotiations, Tilly submitted terms yesterday: he would agree to a divorce in exchange for an annual payment of 500 livres, a sum of 5,000 livres to pay off his debts and an amnesty for the crime of seduction. The senator agreed to all this this morning, and the cynical Tilly now has no financial worries.

Oh mercy, Mercier!

Mercier, a true dabbler.

Paris, July 3

Louis Sébastien Mercier was already known as the author of *Tableau de Paris*, but nobody had imagined that he was a speaker as well. His colleagues at the Institute became aware of this fact today, at their expense. Mercier had previously attracted little attention, as he confined most of his remarks to the Council of Five Hundred, where he spoke with equal enthusiasm for teaching foreign languages and in opposition to divorce. Mercier, a sort of jack of all trades, surprised his audience by unexpectedly launching into a speech about the Roman philosopher Cato of Utica, about whom he went on and on. Even though he had promised before starting to limit his remarks to 10 minutes, it took him no less than an hour and a half to convey his thinking. Neither protests nor catcalls could stop the flood of words.

Pope on way to new residence in Valence

Grenoble, July 6

"Citizen Pope, the horses are harnessed." These are the words used every morning by one of the escorts to inform the Holy Father that it is time to get on the road. The pope is then lifted into his carriage, a process causing him some pain as his paralysis is progressing. The Directory decided that Briançon, where Pius VI had been held since May 1st., was too close to the border, and the pope should be moved to Valence. Today's drive took him from Vizille to Grenoble. The pontiff was very tired, but pleased to be welcomed by a big crowd (→ July 14).

The Pope receiving a warm welcome from the French, to his surprise.

Reinvigorated Jacobins set up new club

Paris, July 6

The left, reinvigorated by its victory over the Directory, is being born again from its ashes. Its supporters have just created the Union of Friends of Liberty and Equality, which meets in the Manège hall, where the Constituent and Legislative Assemblies and the Convention met in turn. It is headed by Drouet, who was one of Babeuf's friends. Such former "terrorists" as Bouchotte and Prieur de la Marne, and such generals as Augereau and Marbot, have hastened to sign up. At a time when preparations are being made to pass a series of special measures reminiscent of the public safety laws, this club is reminiscent of Year II (→ July 14).

Joubert appointed to Italian command

Paris, July 5

General Joubert is going to return to the Army of Italy. The decision was made by Sieyès. The Director hopes that Joubert will be the military leader on whom he may rely in order to topple the Directory. To manage this, Sieyès needs a devoted man who is both a sensitive politician and a great soldier. Joubert has already acquired the coup technique in Holland, but he needs a few more victories to his name. That is why Sieyès has decided to let the general "sharpen his sabre" by sending him to fight on the Italian Peninsula.

Young women of easy virtue, with admirers, getting ready for a masked ball at the Tivoli Garden, on the corner of Saint Lazare and Clichy streets.

Bonaparte beats Turks at Aboukir

Aboukir, July 25

Bodies are drifting in Aboukir Bay. The Turkish force was destroyed in only a few hours. All the tents, the pasha's baggage, 400 horses, 100 flags and 32 artillery pieces have fallen into the French force's hands. A week previously, Bonaparte had received alarming news in Cairo: a force of 18,000 Turks had landed. He immediately recalled his generals, who were scattered around Egypt, and in just a few days all units converged on Aboukir to constitute an army of some 20,000 men and 3,000 horses. Everything was in readiness for a major battle. For a moment the infantry fighting was indecisive, but then Bonaparte had an idea of genius: throwing the French cavalry against the Turkish infantry, which was not very good at manoeuvring, despite its bravery. These tactics were the reverse of those used at the Battle of the Pyramids. The only thing remaining to be done was for Murat to carry out the operation, which he did with his usual dash.

Bonaparte (in foreground) ready to send his cavalry to attack the Turkish camps on the Aboukir peninsula.

Use of hostages is passed by Ancients

Paris, July 12

Now the rebels had better behave, as "terrorist" measures are again the order of the day. With a view to repressing royalist agitation, a rebirth of which is particularly apparent in Bordeaux, Toulouse, Narbonne and Montpellier, the Council of Ancients approved a law instituting a hostage system today. In departments in which troubled conditions are proclaimed, local administrations will have to draw up lists of former nobles, relatives of émigrés and known counter-revolutionaries who might be held hostage in order to put pressure on armed royalist gangs. In the event of the assassination of officials of the Republic, or even of constitutional priests, four of those hostages will be deported. Moreover, they will be held responsible for damage caused by royalists and will have to compensate the families of victims or peasants harmed by looting and attacks (→Nov. 13).

The Rare Birds

The people are beginning to learn of the underhand dealings of which Barras and his friends have been guilty. And some malicious person has added two verses to the famous satirical song "The Rares Ones".

Here soon, or so they say,
A company's on its way,
Better than yesterday,
Of people recherché.
Go and see if they've come, John,
Go and see if they've come.

A doctor whose words sparse
A knowledge deep reveal,
Resorting ne'er to spas.
("Thyself, physisian, heal!")
Go and see if they've come, John,
Go and see if they've come.

A canon truly sick
Of last October's brew;
A writer benefic,
A grave musician too.
Go and see if they've come, John,
Go and see if they've come.

A directory member, free,
Honest and serious,
Who lives as all can see
The life of a recluse.
Go and see if they've come, John,
Go and see if they've come.

A Barras pure and chaste,
A Ducot, loved by all,
A Sieyès who God's embraced,
And a Gohier laudable.

Go and see if they've come, John,
Go and see if they've come.

French in Mantua give up to Austria

Mantua, July 30

General Foissac has given up. The Austrians allowed the French garrison to withdraw freely, on condition of not serving against the allies for one year. As a guarantee, the French general staff will be held hostage in Austrian provinces. It took General Kray a mere three weeks to wear down French resistance. To be sure, one could hardly call Foissac's defence stubborn. The Austrians fired only 14,000 cannon rounds, a third as many as they fired in just a week against Alexandria, in Piedmont. In any case, the French capitulation means that Kray's 20,000 Austrians are now available once again for use in other areas.

Petition submitted for artist's return

Paris, July 26

Will Mme. Vigée Lebrun be one of the few émigrés prevented from returning to France? To be sure, her links with the counter-revolution hardly incline the Directory to letting her come back. Still, Barras met a group of 12 artists who brought him a petition signed by 255 people urging that the artist be given permission to return. All of the leading names are on it, such as the painters David, Fragonard, Girodet, Greuze, Isabey and Prud'hon, the sculptor Pajou, and the architects Brongniart, Chalgrin and Fontaine. There are also musicians, Méhul and Gossec, while the writers are duly represented in the petition by Marie Joseph Chénier.

Rosetta stone may solve hieroglyphics

Egypt, July 19

The *Courrier d'Egypte* has reported a surprising bit of news: while the defences of a fort on the left bank of the Nile, at Rosetta, were being strengthened, an engineering officer named Bouchard found a big stele made of black basalt and containing three texts. One is in hieroglyphic characters, one in Demotic, and the third in Greek. The latter was immediately translated, and turns out to be a decree of the second century B.C. reporting that Ptolemy V had had all of the Egyptian canals reopened, a project that cost enormous sums and many lives, and took eight years. If the texts are the same, this may be the key to deciphering hieroglyphics.

August 1799
from 1st. to 31st.

Joubert killed in French defeat at Novi

Novi, August 15

The Army of Italy has lost its commanding general. Joubert is dead, and the French have suffered a serious defeat. The left wing has been completely scattered, and only remnants remain of the right. The battle was murderous. It cost the French forces 37 guns, 28 powder chests, 1,500 dead, about 5,000 wounded and 3,000 prisoners, including the generals Grouchy and Pérrignon. The fact that Joubert gave Suvorov time to collect his forces right after the siege of Alexandria, in Piedmont, deprived him of the opportunity of beating the Russian general. The French are being expelled from Italy.

General Joubert was 30 years old.

Joubert's heroic death under the coalition's fire while leading his troops.

Royalist insurrection shakes southwest

Toulouse, August 10

General Aubugeois has saved Toulouse from a royalist attack. As commander of the region's military division, he has led a successful offensive during the last two days against the armed gangs totalling 5,000 to 6,000 men who have besieged the city since August 5th. The rebels' first attack, a night operation, failed. Royalists armed with pitchforks, scythes and hunting rifles were waiting outside the ramparts for accomplices to open the gates for them. However, the Directory's departmental commissioner had been tipped off about the plan and the insurgents were repulsed. All the same, the republican troops were unable to disperse the gangs completely and it was at that point that the Toulouse resistance was exemplary. The authorities drew up lists of hostages, who were immediately arrested to put pressure on the rebels. They also set up a defence committee consisting of Jacobins determined to fight the rebels, who were trying to get the whole region to rise up.

The bordering departments of Ariège and Lot and Garonne are also being affected by insurrections, as are the cities of Montpellier and Narbonne. The Royal Council of Montesquiou and Royer Collard and the Swabian Agency, which is led by d'André and Imbert Colomès, are the two royalist centres coordinating these actions. The danger is a very real one. However, these counter-revolutionaries lack competent military leaders and the exactions they carry out have the effect of reviving the Jacobin resistance in the region.

Ancients ratify law on press freedom

Paris, August 1

The opposition newspapers are no longer banned. The Council of Ancients has just ratified the law lifting suspension of freedom of the press. However, newspapers did not wait for this authorisation in order to multiply, and many of them have come into being since the end of June. The bulk of them are counter-revolutionary newspapers competing with the press favourable to the Directory, such as *L'Ami des lois* and *Le Moniteur*. The few Jacobin publications, such as *Journal des hommes libres*, are attacked very violently when they dare to demand revision of the Year III Constitution. Moderates and royalists compare them to *Père Duchesne* and say they want new September massacres (→ Sept. 3).

Neo-Jacobins' club is closed by Fouché

Paris, August 13

The neo-Jacobins' final hour of glory is past: the Director Sieyès has just had the Manège Club closed by the new Police Minister, Fouché. The reason for this is that their cult of the Year II Revolution had led to a violent anti-Jacobin reaction among Parisians, who have not forgotten the Reign of Terror. Sieyès accused the club of violating the Constitution. He suspected it above all of actually helping out the royalists by keeping alive the idea that leftist extremism was not dead. As for Fouché, a former Jacobin recalled from his diplomatic duties in Holland specifically for the police job, he now seems to be a hatchetman for Sieyès and Barras.

Fouché recanted his Jacobin past.

Guérin triumphs at Salon with "Marcus Sextus"

"The return of Marcus Sextus", an historical work by Pierre Narcisse Guérin.

Paris, August 18

The Salon art show has again opened its doors to a public that is ever more curious about artistic activity. A total of 241 artists, including 187 painters, 23 sculptors, 13 architects and 18 engravers, are offering a total of 489 works. Some 36 women displayed works at the show this year. The most note-worthy portraits are the one of *Comtesse Regnault de Saint Jean d'Angély* by François Gérard and the standing portrait of *Alexandre Lenoir*, the tireless creator of the Museum of French Monuments, painted by Pierre Maximilien Delafontaine. Visitors were also attracted by the strangeness of Bonnemaison's *Girl surprised by a storm*, in which the classic serenity of genre scenes gives way to a dramatised vision of fear and solitude.

The landscapes are also highly interesting, in particuler the *Snow Landscape* by César van Loo, who is acquiring new fame with this subject, which is an unusual one for him. This popularity of landscapes is easy to explain. Middle-class art-lovers are particularly fond of things familiar to them. Next to portraits, their favourite type of work, they feel reassured by faithful representations of simple aspects of nature, such as they see in their surroundings. That was not the case with the idealised landscapes seen in classical canvases.

However, the most unexpected triumph was chalked up by historical painting, which also has its fervent admirers, thanks to Pierre Narcisse Guérin's painting called *The Return of Marcus Sextus*. This work, which even put David's canvases in the shade, was a sensation — more because of the political context than due to its intrinsic artistic qualities. The public viewed the image of Marcus returning from exile to find his wife dead and his daughter plunged into grief as a symbol of the French émigrés' misfortunes. The considerable number of émigrés who have already returned, and the personal influence on public opinion exercised by a number of them, have led to a kind of fad for émigrés. This sympathy, discreetly but effectively kept alive by the royalist camp, turned to fresy in this case. Crowds clustered in front of the painting all day, and that will no doubt continue during the coming weeks.

Guérin's sensitivity has suffered a lot from all this to-do. Everybody wanted to hail the genius. Bankers, aristocrats, people in the limelight and civil servants all wanted to entertain him. This success is all the more depressing for this naturally modest painter in that he is aware of the strictly political reason for his triumph. Hence he prefers to steer clear of all this, avoiding the temptation to take advantage of events to seek artificial glory.

The naked truth about a painting

Mlle Lange as Danaë — Girodet.

The painting *Marcus Sextus* was not the only major attraction at the Salon. There was a slight incident that greatly amused visitors. One canvas by Girodet had to be taken down almost as soon as it went on view. It showed Mlle. Lange, a famous actress, nude, as Danaë receiving a shower of gold, with an ugly, concupiscent turkey resembling her rich husband at her feet. Girodet turned out this defamatory work at top speed in order to punish the actress for having refused, for obscure reasons or perhaps just as a whim, to let him show a portrait which he had made of her.

"Portrait of Alexandre Lenoir" by Delafontaine, and "Girl surprised by a storm" by Bonnemaison.

Impatient Bonaparte quits Egypt for Paris

English engraving with humorous interpretation of departure from Egypt.

Alexandria, August 23

Pushed by a favourable breeze, *La Muiron* has left Egypt, carrying General Bonaparte, who was unable to hide his impatience to get to Paris. In spite of his victory over the Turks at Aboukir in July, Bonaparte knew that his army, now consisting of little more than 10,000 soldiers, could not cope with an invasion by coalition forces. Yet the Republic's military reverses in Europe deprived him of any hope of assistance. Bonaparte was kept informed of all this by the press, which British agents in Egypt took care to send to him for the sole purpose of demoralising the general. Italy is lost, Mantua has fallen, the Russian and Austrian forces have defeated Jourdan on the Danube, Schérer on the Adige and Moreau on the Adda, and finally more than 60,000 Russians are threatening the border in the Alps. Furious at not having been called back to save the Republic, Bonaparte remains angry with the Directory. The idea of staying in Egypt when the destiny of France was being decided in Flanders did not make sense to the general.

Vadier on the road leading to freedom

Cherbourg, August 26

Vadier is almost free. He was acquitted two years ago and paroled last year, but had been in detention in the port of Cherbourg. The Directory has put an end to this improper imprisonment and ordered the release of the former head of the Committee of General Security. In fact, his prestige as a martyr and the worrying popularity he enjoyed among the officers of the Cherbourg garrison made him a dangerous prisoner. He is still not completely free, being under house arrest in Chartres.

Vadier out of prison at age 63.

French scientific expedition is criss-crossing Upper Egypt

Egypt, August

The members of the French Institute are certainly not taking it easy. The wide divans in Hassan Cashef's palace, in which they are housed, do not keep them for very long. Between two sessions, they prefer to satisfy their curiosity. Their enthusiastic investigations extend to almost every region in Egypt. At present three commission of scientists are exploring Upper Egypt. The first one, led by Pierre Simon Gérard and consisting of seven engineers, left Cairo on March 19th. The other two, which started out this month, notably include the naturalist Geoffroy Saint Hilaire and the painter Redouté. They went up the Nile in "djerms", with tents for camping. They were dazzled by their first stop, Antinopolis, a city founded by Emperor Hadrian. They then went to Sheikh el Haridy, a pilgrimage site visited by sick people who pray for healing at the tomb of a sheikh who was reincarnated in the form of a snake. A snake-charmer there twined the snake around the neck of the expedition leader, Fourier, foretelling that he would be protected in this way from sickness. In exchange, the Institute secretary purchased the animal, which will now become a valuable addition to the collections that have been gathered by Geoffroy Saint Hilaire.

View of temple of Edfu, taken from V. Denon's "Description of Egypt".

Masséna crushes Russians at Zurich

Brune beats British at battle in Bergen

Batavian Republic, September 19

Thanks to General Brune, the threat of an invasion of Belgium by the coalition allies has been sidetracked. The commanding general of French forces in Holland, helped by Daendels' Batavian contingent, won a brilliant victory over the Anglo-Russian forces commanded by the Duke of York, giving the Directory a precious respite.

The allied forces, which landed on the Dutch coast in August, represented a serious threat to the Republic. However, the Russian, British and Austrian sovereigns paid dearly for their political differences. The Austrians take a dim view of Russian advances in Italy and Russian support for the unity of the Kingdom of Piedmont and Sardinia in opposition to the Austrians. Moreover, since their victory at Novi, they do not want to have Belgium under English influence in exchange for a free hand in Italy. Czar Paul I is eager for conquests in the Mediterranean.

Chouans preparing to do battle again

Calvados, September 23

Comte Louis de Frotté is going to take up arms again. He finally left England, where he was depressed by his inactivity, and has just landed near Bayeux, accompanied by about 15 officers.

His return is not an isolated event. The majority of royalist leaders who took refuge in England after the Fructidor coup have already come back and are getting ready for a new insurrection. Circumstances seem to be in their favour, as republican defeats in foreign battles have forced a reduction in the size of garrisons in the west. Those military setbacks have also enabled the royalists to get subsidies and arms from the British government. On September 15th., on the initiative of Bourmont, Châtillon, d'Andigné and La Prévalaye, the ringleaders met at La Jonchère castle. Despite their deep-seated differences, they decided to resume the civil war, coordinating the operations that are to be carried out in Brittany, the Vendée, Maine and lower Normandy.

Zurich, September 27

Masséna has broken through between the Suvorov and Korsakov forces. Under French pressure, the retreat of Korsakov's Russians along the road from Bulach to Eglisau turned into a débâcle. The coalition forces lost 100 artillery pieces and all their baggage, including a large quantity of military supplies, as well as 8,000 men who were killed, wounded or taken prisoner. With nothing else to gain from Korsakov, Masséna left the Lorges and Ménard divisions to face him and turned against the Russians commanded by Suvorov. Thus the French general managed to take effective advantage of the lack of real coordination between the Austrian and Russian forces (→ Sept. 30).

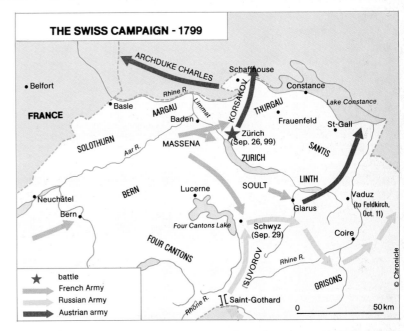

THE SWISS CAMPAIGN - 1799

One of the most spectacular episodes in the "Alps War": the battle at Pont du Diable, in the Saint Gothard Pass.

Directory moves against left and right opposition newspapers

Paris, September 3

The Directory has just taken some radical steps against both leftist and rightist opposition newspapers. Yesterday, acting under the law of Fructidor 19, Year IV, and on the grounds of a counter-revolutionary danger to a number of departments, the Directory ordered deportation to Oléron island of the owners, managers and editorial staff of 34 royalist newspapers. In addition, it had their presses sealed. In particular, the move affected the *Mémorial*, the *Messager du soir*, the *Eclair* and *Courrier républicain*.

Ten more newspapers suffered seizure today, including the two main Jacobin papers, *Journal des hommes libres* and *Le Défenseur de la patrie*. This new repressive act is to be credited to Sieyès. After a summer spent in protesting against the leftist press and denouncing a conspiracy that seems to have existed only in his speeches, he is striking at both the royalists and the Jacobins. Actually, the latter are the primary target. He hopes in this way to make a leftist danger credible, and the Directory is much more obsessed with that than with the royalist danger. He thinks all this will leave him with a free hand reach to his goal discretely: revision of the Constitution.

Napoléon is welcomed home in triumph from Egypt at Fréjus

Napoléon, the victorious general, setting foot on his beloved French soil.

Fréjus, October 9

The quarantine cordon set up by the health authorities was unable to prevent the local inabitants rushing down to the port for Napoléon's arrival. They would let nothing stand in the way of their joy, it seemed. "Come!" they cried, "we would rather have the plague than the Austrians." Napoléon was thus able to dispense with quarantine, thanks to the enthusiasm of the people. After leaving Alexandria on August 23rd., Napoléon was impatient to be back in Paris. If he had been entirely preoccupied, at the time of his departure for Egypt, by Moslem affairs, he was no less concerned, during his return, with the situation he would find back in Paris. Convinced that the era of the Directory is over, he has every intention of becoming the foremost figure in French politics (→ Oct. 17).

Dupont de Nemours sets sail for America

La Rochelle, October 1

The *American Eagle* has set sail. On board are Dupont de Nemours and his family on their way to America. Sent on behalf of the government, the economist intends to settle down and make his fortune in a country where he knows the leaders well. He plans to buy up large amounts of land in Virginia, and then set up one of the main trading companies to import goods from France. His son, Irénée, who studied chemistry with Lavoisier, wants to continue his researches there and apply them to industry.

Back from Egypt

The announcement of Gen. Napoléon Bonaparte's return from Egypt (he landed four days ago at the southern port of Saint Raphaël) is arousing much enthusiasm in the capital. Many people, disheartened by the decline in morals and the scandals of the Directory, are saying: "Here is our saviour!" A song by Citizen Poirier expresses the same sentiments:

He's come back! All is well!
Pay Bonaparte the homage due;
He's come back! All is well!
He is here! We'll win through!

Unite we all to sing his praise;
With ardour France says:
He's come back! All is well!
So all will sing in those fine days.
Hail the name which we adore,
That man beloved by France;
'Tis he will save us evermore.

Our hero's fame let's spread afar,
Bold general and soldiers' star;
He's come back! All is well!
The absence of our avatar
Hurt our hearts, but he is here!
In Turkey, Egypt and in France,
His exploits they cheer.

Let Sultans, viziers, pashas all
His virtue hail, his power recall.
He's come back! All is well!
Each foe will soon be in his thrall.
The Directory he will remake,
And peace on earth will reign;
Then mightily will flourish trade.

Musicians have changed since the "society concerts" have taken over from "republican concerts".

Orgères gang is brought before the court

Chartres, October 3

The Orgères gang is no more. Forty "Hot Feet" will be spending their time in the convicts' cells, and 23 have gone to the scaffold. This is the outcome of an endless trial which brought to light several years worth of heinous crimes. The 84 accused were not the only guilty parties, however. Those who had carried out more minor crimes had finally to be dismissed, though, on account of their number. Only the most virulent members of the gang would stand trial. The Deaf Cat, The Rat Killer, The Dry-Arsed Breton, Shiver-in-the-Wind and Thorn Blossom will no longer be pillaging farms and killing. Only Handsome François, who managed to escape, will continue haunting minds ... and deserted pathways.

It is episodes like this that have earned the "Hot Feet" their nickname.

Lucien Bonaparte heads the Five Hundred

Paris, October 23

The coup is beginning to take shape. With the appointment of his brother, Lucien, to the presidency of the Five Hundred, Napoléon has the future firmly in hand. He is counting on his younger brother's skills as an orator to win over, when the time comes, the Republican members. He has already secured the support of the Ancients, and of their President, Lemercier. To be sure of coming to power, he still needs to win solid backing from the Directory. Though he hates him, Sieyès is vital fo that reason.

Lucien, Napoléon's young brother.

The Revolution's impact on the language

Paris, October 23

Cabanis has just presented the Council of Five Hundred with a *Supplement* to the *Dictionary of the Academy*, listing words that have entered the language since 1789. Emigrés returning to France no longer speak the same language as those who stayed behind. Any number of words have now fallen into disuse: those for bailiff or salt smugglers, for instance. Scientific terminology, however, has grown and become more exact. The names of the months have changed, and foreign words like *club*, which the *Dictionary* pronounces *clob*, have been adopted. The Revolution has also created *département*, *arrondissement* and *commune*.

The English forces driven out of Holland

The Duke of York's Anglo-Russian troops evacuating the coast of Holland.

Batavian Republic, October 18

The bad weather benefited the French. A storm in the North Sea made any support for the Duke of York's Anglo-Russian troops impossible. General Brune made use of the lull in hostilities to fill his divisions with reinforcements from France. The Duke of York had to face the facts: it would be better to negotiate, rather than embark on a battle he would be sure to lose. After his bloody defeat at Bergen last month, then at Castricum a fortnight later, the Duke of York has had to resign himself to the idea of signing an evacuation agreement with France. The coalition forces have also been plagued by illness: over 100,000 of their men are laid up in makeshift hospitals. The re-embarkation of the Duke of York's troops comes as a finale after the long series of victories over the Austro-Russians since early autumn. Paris has had the benefit of inadequate strategy on the enemy's part and, in general, inept handling of the majority of operations they carried out.

Napoléon seeks support from the military

Paris, October 28

The commander in chief of the Army of Egypt has just had talks with Bernadotte, the former Minister for War. He wanted to be sure, if not of his support, at least of his neutrality in the event of a coup. Since arriving back in Paris twelve days ago, Napoléon has been trying to find out whether or not the army would intervene if he were to seize power. On October 22nd. he met Moreau, who agreed to help him out of hatred for the régime. The other major military leaders pose no threat as they are part of his own armies. As for General Augereau and the Jacobin general, Jourdan, both of whom are in Paris, the first has no real standing, while the second has lost the popularity he once had after winning at Fleurus. Neither, therefore, is a threat.

The celebrated General Bernadotte.

Royalist armies defeated in the Vendée

An armed republican patrol passing through a village in the west of France.

Maine et Loire, October 29

The royalist uprising has failed. The Comte d'Autichamp, who had put together a little army in the Beaupréau region north of Cholet, has been beaten by a column of republican troops. At more or less the same moment, the Comte de Suzannet, who was fighting in the former sector of Charette, was also defeated. Only the troops led by the Marquis de Grignon are still in one piece, but they are unlikely to pose a serious threat to the republicans. The situation is little better in the rest of the western provinces: the royalists have not got very far in the uprising they had mapped out at La Jonchère in mid-September. Bourmont's occupation of Le Mans on October 15th., Châtillon's of Nantes on the 20th. and Mercier's of Saint Brieuc on the 25th. were spectacular enough successes but not in any way decisive: the Whites would remain in the different towns for no more than a few hours at a time.

Goodbye Chouans

The Chouans' defeat, marking the end of the long-running royalist revolt in the Vendée, has inspired a song which is being sung by soldiers of the Republic as they bivouac in the evening:

The aristocrat can go to hell,
The brigands of Poitou as well;
Their army is done, so let's yell
We have won!

When we saw them in the sun,
We gave a salute and made run:
We fired with cannon and gun;
We have won!

You should have seen them roll
And drop at the sound,
You should have seen them roll
And drop at the sound of the gun.

The bloody Carmagnole
Let them all dance,
The bloody Carmagnole.
Be f...d to the sound of the gun!

"Madame Easy-Going" is taken prisoner

Italy, October 31

Thérèse Figueur, also known as "Madame Easy-Going", has fallen into enemy hands, a victim of her own courage and devotion. She had accompanied a wounded soldier to the hospital at Busca and was taken prisoner on her way back from there. After signing up with the Allobroges legion in 1793, this vi-

rago proved so courageous that General Dugommier decided to keep her on as a soldier, even though a decree had banned women from the army. In 1795, after peace had been made with Spain, she joined the army of Italy and took part in all the campaigns. It is widely hoped that she will not be kept prisoner for long.

November 1799
from 1st. to 30th.

Directory

1 *(Brumaire 10, Year VIII)* Paris. Napoléon meets Sieyès, who believes he is just the man needed for the coup (→6).

1 *(Brumaire 10, Year VIII)* Egypt. General Verdier drives back into the sea 4,000 Turkish Janissaries who had come ashore near Damietta on the delta.

3 *(Brumaire 12, Year VIII)* Paris. Napoléon has talks with Fouché, whose neutrality is vital if the coup is to be a success.

6 *(Brumaire 15, Year VIII)* Paris. The legislative Councils hold a banquet with 750 guests in honour of Bonaparte and Moreau. The more Jacobin among the generals are notable for their absence. →

9 *(Brumaire 18, Year VIII)* Paris. In response to a supposed terrorist plot, Napoléon begins his coup. →

10 *(Brumaire 19, Year VIII)* Saint Cloud. After a rather confused session of the Council of Five Hundred, Napoléon and his brother Lucien disband the Council with help from the armed forces. →

11 *(Brumaire 20, Year VIII)* Saint Cloud. At four o'clock in the morning, Napoléon, Sieyès and Roger Ducos, who have been appointed temporary consuls, take the oath before the Ancients and the Five Hundred. →

12 *(Brumaire 21, Year VIII)* Paris. *Premier Rayon de Soleil*, an "allegorical" play in honour of the author of the recent coup, is staged at the Théâtre des Jeunes Artistes.

13 *(Brumaire 22, Year VIII)* Paris. The law concerning the hostages of Messidor 24, Year VII, is repealed.

14 *(Brumaire 23, Year VIII)* Egypt. At Aboukir, Kléber gets in touch with commodore Sydney Smith to see how best to go about evacuating Egypt.

22 *(Frimaire 1, Year VIII)* Paris. Talleyrand resumes his post as Minister for Foreign Affairs.

23 *(Frimaire 2, Year VIII)* Paris. Masséna is given the command of the Army of Italy. His job is to attend at once to the defence of Genoa.

30 *(Frimaire 9, Year VIII)* Venice. The conclave charged with appointing a successor to Pope Pius VI gets under way.

Championnet loses to Mélas at Genola

Genola, November 4

The Austrians are not far now from the border. Since last August, the French have been forced to abandon their positions, one by one. The Republic has once again failed to make the right decisions. General Championnet could not grasp the significance of Austrian manoeuvres: he thought Mélas was withdrawing when the Austrian general was, in fact, preparing to launch the most rapid offensive possible. The pasting Championnet received was in keeping with his surprise at the attack, roughly 7,000 dead or wounded, which is nearly half of the two divisions employed. The Austrians lost 2,200 men, and took 4,000 prisoners.

A division general in full uniform.

A factory is sold for next to nothing

Haute Saône, November 4

The iron-works at Pont de Bois has at last found a serious bidder. First there was a Parisian banker, then a penniless individual; now Rochet has proposed to buy the factory for a mere 185,000 francs. Having received no better offer, the department has decided to accept. It is also the fifth time in two years that the national property has been put up for sale. Such occurrences are not infrequent, either because of the insolvency of buyers or because the property has been bought up by a speculator out to make a fast profit by re-selling quickly.

Bonaparte, Sieyès and Fouché prepare to carry out the coup

A banquet at the former Saint Sulpice church attended by Bonaparte and the man who made way for him, Moreau.

Paris, November 6

The plan for the coup has been drawn up. During the reception he held this evening, Napoléon had last-minute discussions with Sieyès and Fouché, the Minister of the Police, to make sure no detail had been overlooked. The method that has been adopted is a simple one. The plotters plan to make use of the Councils so that they bring about their own downfall. Napoléon and Sieyès had reached an agreement on November 1st. The two men detest one another, but know that each has need of the other. Their temporary pact is nonetheless based on a misunderstanding: Sieyès is convinced he is manipulating the general, while the latter is merely making use of him to make sure he gets into power. He has no desire to be associated with a specific party, and certainly not with the left, whose support he refuses for fear of a subsequent Jacobin upsurge that would prove too difficult to control. Nor, on the other hand, does he want to stir up the counter-revolution. He has thus made sure he has on his side the former "terrorist", Fouché, who has likewise decided to fall in with the rest.

Following the final surrender of the Duke of York, the Anglo-Russian expeditionary force is forced to leave Egypt. The highly efficient loading and evacuation procedure takes twelve days.

A group of bankers has underwritten the conspirators

Paris, November 9

Organising a coup costs money. Bonaparte entrusted Collot, who used to run supplies for the Army of Italy, with securing funds from the bankers. If Lecoulteux, Pérégaux and Récamier were eager to support the general, it was because they were unhappy with the current régime, on account of a law which has already been passed by the Council of Five Hundred, and which will be ratified by the Council of the Ancients today: the abolition of "delegations". This system allowed the Treasury's creditors to be payed off by collecting certain taxes. If they are deprived of this finacial guarantee, bankers fear they will no longer get back their investment. In the belief that the régime has turned its back on them, they thus decided to take part in the conspiracy. In exchange for their services, they have been promised secrecy, thus ensuring that no-one else comes to the aid of victory. By backing the coup in this way, they intend to have the lion's share of profits under the new régime. Someone as wealthy as Ouvrard has thus been kept in the dark. And when, at dawn this morning, he saw Bonaparte and his troops on their way to Saint Cloud, he realized, though too late this time, that putting his money on Barras and snubbing the general had been a mistake ...

Santerre is not safe under Bonaparte

Paris, November 8

Santerre is no wiser, ten years later. The famous brewer, who had led the revolt of the Faubourg Saint Antoine in 1789, is today stirring up the same suburb on behalf of the Jacobins. As Napoléon had threatened to have him shot if he did not cease his political activities, Santerre has been forced to take refuge in a lodging-house on the Rue de Rohan. He still remembers, however, the popular song of 1793 where he is said to be "The king of the suburbs, their Agamemnon, one of those whose name the people adore". It isn't easy to return to the brewery when you've been a star!

On the morning of Brumaire 20, the three Consuls take the oath before dozens of deputies of the Five Hundred hastily gathered by the army.

Brumaire 18: General Bonaparte seizes

On the evening of Brumaire 19, a coup put the fate of the Republic in Napoléon's hands: the Directory simply collapsed, along with the system it represented. Sieyès, who merely wanted the executive to be reinforced, seems rapidly to have been taken hostage by the man to whom he had given his support. It is clear to many that Napoléon has started out on an era of individual authority, with backing from the army. The Directory had lost all support: the workers despised it and the bourgeoisie was calling for order. The soldiers were ready to fall in with one of the Republic's most prestigious generals. Only the neo-Jacobins could have stopped him, but though they had a majority in the Five Hundred they had no real clout. The Council's resistance merely destroyed the air of legality which Napoléon wanted to create.

A chorus of indignant protests at the Council of Five Hundred, where Napoléon is greeted by cries of "Outlaw!"

The coup was to be staged in three perfectly co-ordinated acts, and above all with an appearance of legality. It was mainly based on a parliamentary-style manoeuvre led by partisans of Sieyès, who wanted to see the constitution overhauled. On Brumaire 18 a decree passed by the Ancients, on the basis of a non-existent Jacobin conspiracy, was supposed to put the troops of Paris under Napoléon's command and have the Councils moved to Saint Cloud, where they could get on with their work undisturbed. In Act II, the Directory was to stand down. In Act III, now that the executive seat was empty and the Republic itself under threat, the Councils would appeal to citizens Bonaparte and Sieyès to save the nation and the cause of freedom.

Peerless Napoléon
No-one had given much thought to resistance to the coup. The people, shut out from power since 1794, would not rush to the defence of a régime that had been taken over by the bourgeoisie. Soldiers were still necessary, however, though ideally they would not be too noticeable. They were mostly republicans, but admired their leaders and could be counted on to obey orders. How would the generals behave, though? Many were already on Napoléon's side: Lannes, Marmont, Leclerc, Berthier ... Others would toe the line: Augereau, Lefèvre ... Moreau, Jourdan and Bernadotte might pose problems on the left. Napoléon convinced them, in varying degrees, of the need for institutional reform and gave his word that republican principles would be respected. If, finally, most of the Ancients had been won over, there was still the powerful republican party in the Five Hundred and, above all, the Directory members to face. Sieyès

At eight o'clock in the morning, Napoléon leaves his hotel on the Rue de la Victoire and heads for the Tuileries to enthusiastic cries from his generals.

Napoleonic legend would have it that, on arriving at the orangery of Saint Cloud, the hero of the Italian and Egyptian campaigns, instead of being spat upon by Jacobin deputies from the Council of Five Hundred and getting a few bruises, was in fact the object of an assassination attempt which he only escaped thanks to the loyal defence provided by his private guard.

power after a military take-over

and Roger Ducos were obviously no problem, as they were in on the plot. Moulin and Gohier were not very important. As for the left-wing deputies, they could always be bullied into silence, while any scruples the moderates might have could soon be reduced to rubble if the right payment was made. What had happened to all those millions the bankers and businessmen put up? No-one really knew, though persistent rumours suggested Barras might be able to throw some light on the matter.

A good start

On the morning of Brumaire 18, the deputies from the Council of Ancients received notice at their homes of a special assembly to be held at eight o'clock. Some of them, said to be on the left, were most conveniently "overlooked". Troops were massed near the Tuileries. Napoléon had gathered about him some 20 generals and a number of officers. The assembly of the Ancients was held at high speed: some members were already in the know, others pretended to believe in the plot denounced by the president, Lemercier. A decree was passed: the Councils would meet at Saint Cloud the following day, while Napoléon was put in command of the troops of Paris, including the Directory guard and those of the different Councils. As soon as he was told the vote had gone through, the general set off for the Tuileries. Applauded by soldiers along the way, he there swore to save the Republic. He had won the first round. While Napoléon was busily appointing his officers to key posts, proclamations were being posted up all over Paris: the threatened order must be preserved. Meeting under the presidency of Lucien Bonaparte, the Council of Five Hundred found itself faced with a *fait accompli*. The move to Saint Cloud could only be decided by the Ancients. The session was closed without a word being pronounced.

Two Directory members resist

What was the Directory doing in the meantime? Barras had been bullied into resigning by Talleyrand who had helped organise the coup, and, come nightfall, had already retired to his magnificent house at Grosbois. Sieyès and Ducos laboured in vain, however, trying to convince their colleagues Moulin and Gohier to concede. They had to be locked up in the Luxembourg Palace before they would quieten down. Everything had been carried out with great efficiency and Paris was utterly undisturbed. Was it time to take over? Under the conditions, the assemblies of the Councils tomorrow would be little more than a formality.

The neo-Jacobins protest

On the following day, Brumaire 19, the deputies found the château of Saint Cloud filled with soldiers on their arrival there. When sessions got under way, around two o'clock, things suddenly started hotting up. The Ancients, who were all present this time round, were uncertain. Those who had been "overlooked" the day before began protesting. At the Council of Five Hundred, the general uncertainty turned to a fierce desire to defend the Republic. In a roll-call, a vast majority of deputies rallied to the Constitution and vowed to combat tyranny. The setback unsettled Napoléon and, escorted by various officers and soldiers, he decided to visit the Councils in person, just to make sure the right decision was made.

Napoléon, a rotten orator

When he arrived, the Ancients, who were wearing their dignified tricoloured uniforms, remained silent. Napoléon then launched into

Lucien Bonaparte helps his brother.

The château of Saint Cloud, where the Councils arrived on Brumaire 19.

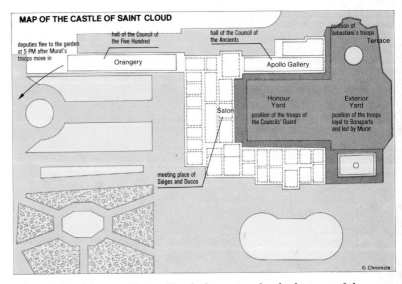

MAP OF THE CASTLE OF SAINT CLOUD

Plan of the château of Saint Cloud, the setting for the last act of the coup.

an incoherent and unclear address that was both an encouragement and a threat. The speech was anything but fluent, and he was interrupted on several occasions. Accustomed to speaking as a leader to soldiers who were already on his side, he was unable to win the support of the assembly which, though it was not hostile, was certainly taken aback. Abashed, Napoléon left the hall, having failed to get what he was after, and went to talk to the Five Hundred. As soon as he appeared, with a few grenadiers with loaded rifles and bayonets at his side, a general uproar broke out: "What's going on? Armed men! Down with the dictator! Outlaw! Outlaw!" Cries like these, traditionally used for enemies of the Republic, had often led men to the guillotine. Jacobin deputies rushed forward to block his path. They were later said to have been wield-

ing knives. A grenadier, so legend has it, was wounded defending Napoléon. His head down, the general left the auditorium.

The only solution is force

In view of the hostility shown by the Councils, force would have to be used. The soldiers were told that Napoléon had almost been killed. Lucien Bonaparte then denounced "those who wield knives" on behalf of the nation's enemies. The soldiers were incensed. Murat's column entered the chamber of the Ancients. Most of the deputies were able to escape by the windows. That same night, the Ancients and a few of the Five Hundred who had been forced to attend appointed Napoléon Bonaparte, Sieyès and Ducos consuls. The Councils are to be replaced by a legislative body. By four a.m. it was all over.

▷

PROCLAMATION

DU GÉNÉRAL EN CHEF

BONAPARTE.

Le 19 Brumaire onze heures du soir.

A mon retour à Paris, j'ai trouvé la division dans toutes les Autorités, et l'accord établi sur cette seule vérité, que la Constitution était à moitié détruite et ne pouvait sauver la liberté.

Tous les partis sont venus à moi, m'ont confié leurs desseins, dévoilé leurs secrets, et m'ont demandé mon appui; j'ai refusé d'être l'homme d'un parti.

Le Conseil des Anciens m'a appelé; j'ai répondu à son appel. Un plan de restauration générale avait été concerté par des hommes en qui la nation est accoutumée à voir des défenseurs de la liberté, de l'égalité, de la propriété: ce plan demandait un examen calme, libre, exempt de toute influence et de toute crainte. En conséquence, le Conseil des Anciens a résolu la translation du Corps législatif à Saint-Cloud; il m'a chargé de la disposition de la force nécessaire à son indépendance. J'ai cru devoir à mes concitoyens, aux soldats périssant dans nos armées, à la gloire nationale acquise au prix de leur sang, d'accepter le commandement.

Les Conseils se rassemblent à Saint-Cloud; les troupes républicaines garantissent la sûreté au dehors. Mais des assassins établissent la terreur au dedans; plusieurs Députés du Conseil des Cinq-cents, armés de stylets et d'armes à feu, font circuler tout autour d'eux des menaces de mort.

Les plans qui devaient être développés, sont resserrés, la majorité désorganisée, les Orateurs les plus intrépides déconcertés, et l'inutilité de toute proposition sage évidente.

Je porte mon indignation et ma douleur au Conseil des Anciens; je lui demande d'assurer l'exécution de ses généreux desseins; je lui représente les maux de la Patrie qui les lui ont fait concevoir: il s'unit à moi par de nouveaux témoignages de sa constante volonté.

Je me présente au Conseil des Cinq-cents; seul, sans armes, la tête découverte, tel que les Anciens m'avaient reçu et applaudi; je venais rappeler à la majorité ses volontés et l'assurer de son pouvoir.

Les stylets qui menaçaient les Députés, sont aussitôt levés sur leur libérateur; vingt assassins se précipitent sur moi et cherchent ma poitrine: les Grenadiers du Corps législatif, que j'avais laissés à la porte de la salle, accourent, se mettent entre les assassins et moi. L'un de ces braves Grenadiers (*Thomé*) est frappé d'un coup de stylet dont ses habits sont percés. Ils m'enlèvent.

Au même moment, les cris de *hors la loi* se font entendre contre le défenseur *de la loi.* C'était le cri farouche des assassins, contre la force destinée à les réprimer.

Ils se pressent autour du président, la menace à la bouche, les armes à la main; ils lui ordonnent de prononcer le hors la loi; l'on m'avertit; je donne ordre de l'arracher à leur fureur, et six Grenadiers du Corps législatif s'en emparent. Aussitôt après, des Grenadiers du Corps législatif entrent au pas de charge dans la salle, et la font évacuer.

Les factieux intimidés se dispersent et s'éloignent. La majorité, soustraite à leurs coups, rentre librement et paisiblement dans la salle de ses séances, entend les propositions qui devaient lui être faites pour le salut public, délibère, et prépare la résolution salutaire qui doit devenir la loi nouvelle et provisoire de la République.

Français, vous reconnaîtrez sans doute, à cette conduite, le zèle d'un soldat de la liberté, d'un citoyen dévoué à la République. Les idées conservatrices, tutélaires, libérales, sont rentrées dans leurs droits par la dispersion des factieux qui opprimaient les Conseils, et qui, pour être devenus les plus odieux des hommes, n'ont pas cessé d'être les plus méprisables.

Signé BONAPARTE.

Pour copie conforme : ALEX. BERTHIER.

In his proclamation, General Bonaparte paints a highly favourable picture of his coup d'état, presenting himself as the "man of the moment".

General Mounier surrenders to the coalition forces at Ancona

Ancona, November 16

With honours or not, it is still a surrender. The Austrians were led by General Fröhlich, who had set out for Ancona after the fall of Rome on September 26th., and had at his disposal 585 cannon and ten war-ships, three of which were capital ships. All things considered, General Mounier's surrender was only to be expected: the French were assailed by 4,000 insurgents from Rome and 9,000 Austrian and Neapolitan troops. On top of this, roughly 1,300 Russians and 2,000 Turks were keeping up the siege from the seaward side. Mounier will have had the bitter satisfaction of seeing the Turks, the Russians and the Austrians arguing among themselves over who is to take the credit for the victory.

The Italian Jacobins fall to pieces before the power of the coalition forces.

Would-be Royalists but real villains

Allier, November 29

The Lyons mail-coach has been attacked again. There were 25 of them this time round, and they all claimed to be on the side of Louis XVIII, the pretender to the throne. After cleaning out the stage-coach, and wanting to do a good job of it, they went through the mail and found nine louis and ... two shirts.

Harsh new guide-lines for the theatres

Paris, November 17

Napoléon would like the theatres to fall into line, as can be seen from the guide-lines Fouché, the Minister of the Police, has sent round to all the main offices: "With one party after another taking its turn in office, the theatre has often been filled with gratuitous insults against the losers, and base flattery for the winners. The present government has no time for factions, which it despises. It does not work for them, it works for the Republic. The people of France must be with them in this, and the theatres must see to it that it wins their support. Only peaceful feelings, expressions of moderation, and wisdom and the language of great and generous passions, should be heard on stage. Nothing that might separate people from one another and cause dissension is to be tolerated."

The solitary life of philosopher Volney

Paris, November

Wealth has not altered his way of life. He has been living in his little room on the Rue Saint Nicaise since moving back to Paris earlier this month. He is now very comfortably off, however: the sale of his house and land at Craonnais, which he inherited from his father who died recently, brought in over 40,000 francs. He prefers a studious and retiring life, however. A convicted misogynist, he lives alone and holds the view that "women's groups and associations are unfortunate institutions, fertile in poor results". His health, it has to be said, is not good. His "troublesome digestive system, filled with acids", and a skin that is "always breaking out in sweat", do not make him attractive to women. It is his failures that have caused him the most bitterness: his journey round the United States was as pitiful as his experience as a planter in Corsica. Such memories have done little to soften up this hardened bachelor.

Brumaire 18

Yesterday's events at Saint Cloud have inspired many song writers. Two songs are circulating in Paris. Here is the first:

After Bonaparte took the road
Back to France, on his homeland
A gift from Egypt he bestowed:
A saint, of stature grand.
Saint Cloud it was named;
He changes radical proclaimed.
By the bay bay bay,
By the yon yon yon,
By the bay, by the yon,
By the bayonet,
Which we will not forget.

To separate the chaff and wheat
Good men from a vile squad,
This saint, with mien discreet,
Gave one holy, blessèd nod.
More agile than a puppet, soon
He made them dance to his tune.

These gentlemen, you know,
Elected Bonaparte, 'tis true,
But the saint was no wise slow
To boot 'em out; good thing too!
Indeed, with virtue none surpass
He kicked them up the arse.

The second turns on a pun based on the word "bon", meaning "advantage" or "benefit":

Musing by myself apart,
I ask'd when our ills would end.
A voice replied to me apart,
"Right soon: a hero I will send
To cleanse your fair city
Of all the brigands it now hoards,
And give you back tranquility."
God! 'Tis a blest "bon apart"!

The decree of Brumaire 29, concerning the enrolment of French conscripts is perfectly clear: "Your country needs you; let both honour and liberty be your guides. Conscripts, to arms!"

1 *(Frimaire 10, Year VIII)*
Paris. Napoléon turns down Sieyès' projected constitution (→4).

4 *(Frimaire 13, Year VIII)*
Paris. Napoléon asks the former Thermidorean, Daunou, to draw up a constitution more to his liking (→12).

5 *(Frimaire 14, Year VIII)*
Italy. Austrian troops take Coni.→

7 *(Frimaire 16, Year VIII)*
Paris. Henri Berton's *Délire ou les Suites d'une erreur* is performed at the Opéra Comique by Jean Baptiste Gavaudan. It is the actor's first major success.

12 *(Frimaire 21, Year VIII)*
Paris. Napoléon invites the two constitutional committees to his home, and gets them to adopt Daunou's project. He then has the three consuls elected on the spot: himself, Cambacérès and Lebrun (→13).

14 *(Frimaire 23, Year VIII)*
United States. Death of George Washington in his residence at Mount Vernon in Virginia. Initially favourable to the Revolution, he had later lost faith in it out of conservatism, but would never formally condemn the régime.

15 *(Frimaire 24, Year VIII)*
Paris. Proclamation of the Year VIII Constitution (→24).

22 *(Nivôse 1, Year VIII)*
Egypt. Kléber breaks off negotiations at Aboukir with Commodore Smith, after the latter refuses to guarantee repatriation for the army.

24 *(Nivôse 3, Year VIII)*
Paris. Before it has even been passed by a plebiscite, the Year VIII Constitution takes effect.

27 *(Nivôse 6, Year VIII)*
Paris. The Senate is set up: Sieyès is appointed president and is entitled to appoint the first 31 members.

27 *(Nivôse 6, Year VIII)*
Paris. Napoléon puts the Secretary of State, Maret, in charge of relations with the press; in particular, with *Le Moniteur* which the First Consul wishes to make the Republic's official organ.

30 *(Nivôse 9, Year VIII)*
Paris. Napoléon orders funeral honours to be administered at the burial of Pope Pius VI.→

31 *(Nivôse 10, Year VIII)*
Eure. The writer Jean François Marmontel dies at his home in Ablonville.→

The Consulate replaces the Directory

Paris, December 13

The Year VIII Constitution was signed today, twenty-four hours after the members were elected to the executive. After naming himself First Consul, Napoléon had Lebrun and Cambacérès "elected" as second and third consuls. The two men have radically different political pasts. Cambacérès is a former pro-regicide Convention member, and Lebrun a former royalist member of the Constituent Assembly. The choice of the two men shows that Napoléon has no desire to continue the see-saw politics that became the norm under the last régime. The institutions he has had adopted, moreover, will ensure that his own authority is not seriously disturbed. On December 4th. he assembled the two constitutional committees chaired by Sieyès and set up the day after the coup. He then got the former Thermidorean, Daunou, to draw up a project which he adopted in the place of the more democratic model that Barère had come forward with on December 10th. Daunou's project does, nonetheless, restore universal suffrage: the legislative assemblies will be elected, but by means of a three-tier process that will involve the entire nation, some 8,000,000

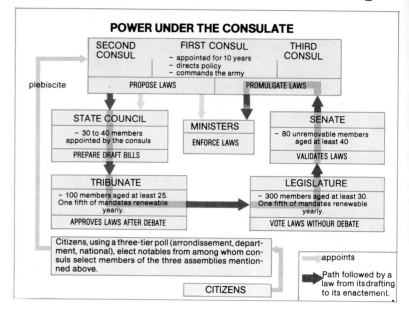

citizens in all. The executive power will be in the hands of three people. It is, in fact, the First Consul who has the real power. He alone can initiate laws and see that they are enacted. He also decides diplomatic and military affairs as well as public spending, and appoints ministers, ambassadors, senior civil servants and judges. The legislative power is divided between two assemblies: a 100-member Tribune, which will debate laws but will not be able to

pass them; and a 300-member legislative body which will pass laws but will not be able to debate them. This structure will be completed by a "conservative Senate" which will be made up of eighty "irremovable and co-opted" members. It will appoint the three consuls for a duration of 10 years and draw up "confidential lists" of secondary electors. Significantly, there is nothing in the preamble to the Constitution about rights (→Dec. 15).

The people of France approve of the new Constitution: everybody's wishes will be fulfilled. Businessmen, men of letters, gamblers, women from the provinces, husbands, plotters, talented people, Parisian ladies and ageing rakes: all of them will celebrate on January 1st., 1800!

Louis David celebrates the return of public peace

Scandal played a large rôle in the success of David's painting: people wondered which famous ladies had posed as models for the Sabine women.

Paris, December 21

"Where will you find a painting that better expresses the stillness that precedes movement, or rather a supreme absence of activity in the place of a bewildered fury?" was the comment of one observer when faced with the huge *Sabines*. David, who has just finished the painting, has hung it in the main hall of the former Academy of Architecture at the Louvre. The entry fee was 1,80 francs. He has decided to depict the arrival of peace in the midst of the most violent combat; the very moment, in other words, when the Sabine women drag their children into the fray and beg their husbands and brothers to cease killing one another; the moment, then, when "Romans and Sabines are about to embrace as a single people". The public is a bit disconcerted by the heroes' nakedness, which David has explained to them in a brochure handed out to visitors. Everyone has understood, however, that the painter was keen to celebrate the triumph of peace in an historical allegory where figures treated with a high realism rub shoulders with more abstract and idealised ones.

French forces defeated once again in Italy

Coni, December 5

The garrison has been captured. Melas' Austrian troops needed just eight days to force the town into surrendering. Some 14,000 quintals of gun-powder and 187 cannons are now in the hands of the enemy. The Austrians are not surprised by the rapidity with which they achieved victory: the soldiers are aware of the difficult situation in which the French find themselves. Fatigue and low morale have overcome the republican armies in Italy. A series of defeats over the last year has broken the most optimistic among them. The French troops console themselves with the fact that Melas decided not to pursue his offensive any further.

Sade performs in one of his own plays

Versailles, December 13

Perhaps Sade is about to have the theatrical success he has dreamed of so long. He has the satisfaction of having his *Le Comte d'Oxtiern* performed by the Drama Society, and also of himself performing in the play. Rather than act the play's "hideous and revolting" hero, the lordly libertine Oxtiern, he chose the role of honest Fabrice, a virtuous inn-keeper who rescues the unfortunate Ernestine from the clutches of the monster and gets her lover out of prison. For Sade, who had had nearly all his plays turned down at one time or another, the change in fortune tastes sweet, and all the more so for the enthusiasm the public has shown for his work. ▷

The Consulate pays tribute to Pius IV

Paris, December 30

The new régime has once again shown itself keen to appease where religious matters are concerned. It has decided that the Republic will accord full funeral honours to Pope Pius VI. Forced to leave Rome under orders from the Directory, the elderly pontiff died at Valence last August. The gesture is not the only one that the First Consul has made: he had already allowed back clergy who had been exiled without trial. Likewise, three decrees passed on December 28th. open the way for the restitution of churches that had not been sold to those who ran them before Year II. They can open outside the décadi.

Marmontel, writer of moral tales, dies

Eure, December 31

His goodness ran deep and was characterised by a candour and optimism that protected him from despair. The writer Jean François Marmontel passed away on the last day of the century, aged 76. He was certainly not an artist of the first rank, and his celebrity was greater than his gift deserved; yet he was a kind man with an open mind and tolerant. The author of *Bélisaire* and *Contes Moraux* retired to Ablonville, near Evreux, for the last years of his life, and it was there that he wrote *Mémoires d'un père pour servir à l'instruction de ses enfants*. The older generation will miss their philosopher and friend.

Surcouf cruising off the coast of Bengal

Bengal, December 17

Privateers are plucky creatures. After meeting in the delta of Bengal, Robert Surcouf and Jean Marie Dutertre are living it up at the expense of the English. The two men, one from the Saint Malo and the other from Lorient, almost ended up fighting after failing to recognise one another. Once they had, however, Dutertre boarded *La Clarisse* for some heavy carousing with Surcouf. In three months in the Indian Ocean aboard his 200-ton vessel from Nantes, with his brother Nicolas for mate, Surcouf has taken five boats, while Dutertre has four to his credit since August. The English must try harder!

France has freed its American prisoners

Bordeaux, December 30

The American consul Barnet has his work cut out for him. As Paris and Philadelphia are now back on good terms, the Franco-American "war" can be considered over. The French have therefore freed all the Americans imprisoned during the freeze, leaving Barnet with 200 of his compatriots to attend to. There is much to be done: he must feed and house them, reassure them and, above all, see that they are sent home as soon as possible. Barnet is so overrun with work that he is beginning to think that he would have been better off if Franco-American relations had continued just as they were before!

France asking the Genius of Painting to hand down to future generations the glory of the French army's many victories and conquests.

sion of the purchasability of offices and privileges. Annuities and rents, paid in assignats, destroyed property-based fortunes. The majority of the shippers and port traders were ruined by war and the interruption of maritime trade. Thus, from 1789 to 1800, entire sections of the middle class lost the advantages of the business conditions that had been so favourable to them in the early 18th. century. On the other hand, other parts of the bourgeoisie were the main beneficiaries of the Revolution, and were in a particularly favourable position at the outset of the Consulate. They were led by the people who had acquired national property, especially near the big cities, where they were able to compete effectively with the peasantry and build up land-based fortunes, as did some members of the former nobility who, in certain regions, and above all in the Paris basin, were among the most active purchasers of national assets. The speculators, profiting from the assignat's devaluation, also got rich, as did the military suppliers. Some of the latter were able to build up enormous fortunes, sometimes unscrupulously, which enabled them to live the high life under the Directory. The bankers prospered, and the iron and steel industry enjoyed a spectacular takeoff.

Finally, society now had to allow for the existence of two social groups which had not been ignored under the Ancien Régime, but were tending to play ever more important roles in the state: the army and the bureaucracy. The army was well aware of its power. Thanks to its victories and the contributions levied from the conquered countries, it supplied the state with money. The generals were involved in coups, and one of them took spectacular advantage of this fact in Brumaire. His army was directly attached to him much more than to the state. The revolutionary government and centralisation had increased the bodies of civil servants, who were becoming ever more numerous and present, and Bonaparte found an influential administration when he came to power. Thus the relationship of forces within society was, if not upset, at least remodelled to the benefit of new categories of rich, powerful and useful people, on whom the consular régime was to rely.

Clergy and nobility: On the other hand, the privileged classes of the Ancien Régime had suffered severely. The clergy was ruined by the nationalisation of its property, and lost the bulk of the functions that had ensured its power and prestige: civil status and charitable activities. It was divided over the subject of the Civil Constitution, and juring and non-juring priests had clashed. The clergy was persecuted, the churches were closed, and some priests were massacred while others were deported. The separation of Church and State had killed the clergy's influence. Due to a shortage of pastors, a substantial part of the population had fallen away from religious observance, despite the brave resistance of the non-juring priests, who had maintained a clandestine church as far as possible. The nobility had been less affected than the clergy, and was rather quick to recover an often-comfortable social position, if not the position it has enjoyed under the Ancien Régime. It had lost its privileges and the benefit of seigneurial dues. Emigration, which part of the nobles chose, brought brutal reprisals. Their property was confiscated, and the law on suspects soon hit at the nobles who had not emigrated.

However, the nobles constituted only a small fraction of the victims of the Reign of Terror (nine per cent) and many of them served the Revolution. They were not excluded from the army. The law of December 1797, which was to deprive them of their civil rights, was not applied, and did not prevent the noble Barras from leading France under the Directory. While certain nobles lost all or part of their fortunes, many others managed in various ways, such as using straw-men, or fictitious divorces, to keep theirs, or even to increase them by buying the clergy's property. They are found in the forefront of the richest land-owners under the Empire, which integrated them into the new régime. But the nobility had lost the political and moral pre-eminence that had made it the most powerful order under the Ancien Régime.

The working class: The former privileged classes were not the only ones to suffer from the Revolution. At the other end of the social spectrum, the condition of the working class actually worsened. Freedom of work was instituted, and the guilds were abolished. The Le Chapelier law prohibited craftsmen and journeymen from banding together and concerting to obtain wage increases, for instance.

The workers were also the first victims of all of the revolutionary economic measures. The institution of wage controls, which were much more carefully monitored than price controls, worsened their position and, when decontrol came, inflation caused terrible misery that resulted in insurrections which were put down mercilessly. Business had suffered greatly, the luxury goods industries had been ruined, and textiles, the decline of which had begun by way at the end of the Ancien Régime, collapsed. Unemployment was even higher than before, while the clergy's charity institutions had disappeared. The working class was in a difficult situation just after the Revolution, and the steps taken by the First Consul with respect to a scorned class definitely did not contribute to improving it. As a whole, the society that Bonaparte found at the end of 1799 was very different from that of 1789. The old orders had disappeared, and individualism was triumphant. People who had managed to put their money into land, or to profit from the new sources of enrichment stemming from war, along with the nobles who had kept or reconstituted their holdings, were to constitute the body of "notables" on which the imperial régime was to rely, while the administration and the army would constitute its two powerful pillars.

A contrasting appraisal

The France that the Revolution passed on to Bonaparte had some bright spots, although darker areas were not lacking. The territorial picture was positive, even highly positive. The kingdom of 1789 had become the "great nation" with the addition of 18 departments made up from the Comtat Venaissin, Savoy and the county of Nice, and taken from Switzerland, Belgium, Holland and the east bank of the Rhine. The sister republics, which were not annexed but were actually vassal countries, must also be added. Some 82 million inhabitants, 113 departments, and bases in foreign territory offered Bonaparte a point of departure that enabled him to establish the "Grand Empire", at least for a time.

The demographic changes were also positive. To be sure, there were executions, massacres, civil war, food shortages, and above all foreign war, all of which together claimed hundreds of thousands of victims. But as the 18th. century population surge continued, the number of births was maintained or increased, and population growth took place. If we consider the population within the borders of 1789, disregarding the annexations, it grew despite the many victims. From about 26 million on the eve of the Revolution, it rose over a decade to nearly 28 million, and it remained young, even though a dip in fertility noted in 1797 represented a still-distant threat for the future. Napoléon was able to call amply on a plethora of youth to renew his armies when they exhausted themselves on the European battlefields.

All this during the revolutionary decade was generally favourable, and the 15 years to follow could not be explained without mentioning the dynamism of a population that continued to grow despite the Revolution, even though the latter promoted a greater imbalance between the countryside and city-dwellers, who were hit harder. Elsewhere, however, results were rather generally disappointing, marked by stagnation or even recession. While the agricultural sector benefited from some legislative measures, such as the abolition of feudal dues, and from an extension of crops due to liberation of common property, it did not enjoy increased yields, as in England. Indeed, yields actually dropped and the area of arable land was reduced, as were the forests. The revolutionary troubles in regions affected by civil war did not help improve output. Animal husbandry declined, and the number of cattle and horses fell off. Yet France was not devastated, except in the Vendée, and the only regions seriously affected by war were along the borders. But the agricultural results of 1800 show no progress in comparison with the situation before the Revolution, which had mostly negative effects on rural production and made it lag considerably behind England, its most fearsome adversary.

Nor did industry benefit from the upheavals. Despite a few efforts at adaptation, particularly in Paris, and in spite of the success of a few manufacturers, traditional activities (by far the most important) developed in hesitant fashion. The textile industry went through a dramatic crisis until 1794, cutting output and the number of employees in that business by two-thirds. Then a recovery, due primarily to the ban on English imports, made it possible to return to the 1789 level in 1800, but without any large-scale modernisation. The spinning wheel and home weaving were still much more important than mechanical spinning. While cotton made progress, wool was in full decline, and the major cloth centres, such as Sedan, Reims and Louviers, saw the number of their looms drop off to a dangerous extent. Lyons was very sorely tested. The metallurgical industry, which had tried to take off in the 1780s, was hit before the end of the Ancien Régime. But it maintained itself, though with great regional differences, during the Revolution, thanks primarily to military orders. It is quite difficult to make an objective general assessment of the gains and losses in the industrial sector stemming from the Revolution, since historians are divided. Some of them see slight growth by comparison with the pre-1789 situation, while others think there was a decline, sometimes even a considerable decline. In any case, if there was any progress, it was almost negligible, and the growth that began under Louis XVI, which might have enabled France to catch up with England, was held back by the Revolution.

The heritage

The revolution was innovative in many respects, but also showed historical continuity with the monarchy, and it strengthened the nation's unity, physically and morally. Within French territory, which had previously been divided up into isolated regions that were relatively impermeable to each other, all of the borders that impeded human contacts and trade were knocked down.

All citizens, who had previously enjoyed highly diverse statuses and rights, became equal before the law, and subject to the same centralised administration. The unanimity of the Third Estate in 1789, the defence of the fatherland and the great number of men mobilised to defend the country against other nations increased the population's psychological cohesion and the feeling, strengthened by danger, of belonging to the same community. While there had previously often been only provinces, with their particularities and their awareness of constituting an irreducible entity, there was now only *one* France. Of course, there was still a lot to be done to achieve unity, beginning with the question of the language, which had to compete with local dialects which took a long time to disappear, and the opinions bringing traditionalists and progressives into conflict were to divide the country on a lasting basis, and were to remain a divisive factor. But divine right and personal royal rule had yielded to a new conception of the State, a lay conception based on the fact that the State is subject to a Constitution, and that its task, as the agent of those it is to govern, is to reconcile the necessary authority of the power structure with the equally necessary freedom of the citizens.

There were to be setbacks and upsets, but this concept finally won acceptance and travelled well beyond the borders of France and of the European continent. The Revolution, which had often had only limited results, or even results contrary to its initial objectives, had explored many paths all the same. It had opened up new prospects, which were to find their fulfilment later in France itself, or in the rest of the world. The principle of national sovereignty, which was proposed by Rousseau and was forcefully asserted at the outset of the Revolution, underlies all democratic régimes.

The Republic, which is based on a meticulous observance of this principle, was born of long reflection on this Revolution, which was the centre of a passionate and continuous debate during the 19th. century. All social thought of the great bourgeois century fed on the efforts of Year II: public education for all, the right to work, welfare and the utopia of social equality that fertilised all socialist thought were inspired by models that the Revolution, which the thinkers always had in mind, had sketched out without managing to make them into realities. Its practises also initiated people and prepared them for the future. It did not content itself with leaving it the ideas of national unity and ideological consistency, which have been pursued without any great success under all régimes down to our own time. It familiarised the people with voting practices, thus preparing them for exercising democracy. Its influence went much further than that: it taught the people to intervene in other ways than the ballot box in political and social life. The example of an insurgent people and of active minorities served as a model for all 19th. and 20th. century revolutionaries.

The Revolution was the origin of the division between left and right, the source of parliamentary democracy and of socialism, and it remains the necessary standard for political action. Parties are judged by reference to it, even if certain things it accomplished appear irreversible. It gave future generations a feeling of respect for basic freedoms, even if its aberrant practices also taught governments how to restrict the exercise of those freedoms. The Republic that was instituted in the last third of the 19th. century is indeed the daughter of the Revolution, which it considers - neglecting everything that preceded the upheaval - as the time when modernity and freedom were founded. The year 1789 is the initial date of a new period in human history, and also served as a model for the Revolution. It inaugurated the concept of total revolution, if not the term itself. Such a revolution marks a decisive break with the past and the dawn of an era of hope, and the world's revolutions have originated in it, and have taken from it the nationalistic idea from which they stemmed. Thus it spread from Europe to Latin America, and later to many other areas in various continents as the result of decolonisation movements.

In the first half of the 19th. century, European intellectuals considered themselves the true heirs of 1789, or even of 1793, and had the feeling that they were continuing an uncompleted revolution, with a will to fill a gap. German nationalism, and the Italian national unification movement to an even greater extent, considered themselves as the heirs of the French Revolution, and the republics born at the start of the 19th. century in Latin America, which also owed much to the example of the nearby United States, were the enthusiastic disciples of 1789 France. In Russia in 1917, in the African countries during the second half of the 20th. century, revolutions were still made under the protective shadow of the great French Revolution, an innovative and unavoidable model.

What became of them?

Actors and witnesses, all of the men and women who participated, directly or indirectly, in the revolutionary adventure and whom the reader has come to know. Some died during the Revolution, while others lived on in the sometimes surprising circumstances outlined here.

Adélaïde, Madame
Born at Versailles, May 3, 1732
Died at Trieste, February 18, 1800

Mme. Adélaïde and her sister Victoire emigrated to Rome in 1790. The two princesses then went to Caserta (1796) and Trieste (1799). Adélaïde died there a few months after her sister.

Amar, Jean Baptiste
Born at Grenoble, May 11, 1755
Died in Paris, December 21, 1816

During the entire era of the Empire, Amar led a very obscure life, well away from politics and the public eye. He became a devout mystic, and was fascinated by the works of Swedenborg. When the Bourbons returned to power, he was not banished like other members of the Convention.

Antraigues, Alexandre de Launay, Comte d'
Born at Antraigues (Ardèche), December 27, 1754
Assassinated at Barnes (England), July 22, 1812

After having lived for a time in Vienna and Dresden, he went to Russia, where Tsar Alexander I appointed him State Councillor in 1803. Following several incidents, he learnt of the secret clauses of the Treaty of Tilsit, passing them on to the English in exchange for a generous pension. He and his wife were murdered by an Italian servant in the village of Barnes, near London. The killing was said to have been ordered by the British government.

Artois, Comte d'
see Charles X

Babeuf, *alias* Gracchus
Born at Saint Quentin, November 23, 1760
Guillotined in Paris, May 25, 1797

Bailly, Jean Sylvain
Born in Paris, January 15, 1736
Guillotined in Paris, November 12, 1793

Barbaroux, Charles Jean
Born in Marseilles, March 6, 1767
Guillotined in Bordeaux, June 25, 1794

Barère de Vieuzac, Bertrand
Born at Tarbes, October 10, 1755
Died at Tarbes, January 13, 1841

Following the *coup d'état* of Brumaire 18, Barère gave his support to Bonaparte and tried in vain to get himself elected to the legislature. He had to await the Hundred Days to become a deputy. Banished as a regicide on July 25th., 1815, when the Bourbons returned to power, he lived in exile in Belgium until the revolution of 1830. Once again elected to represent the Hautes-Pyrénées at the Chamber of Deputies, his election was annulled for fraud. He was, however, a member of the General Council till 1840. Then, no longer having an active political rôle to play, he spent the final year of his life in poverty.

Barnave, Antoine Joseph
Born at Grenoble, October 22, 1761
Guillotined in Paris, November 29, 1793

Barras, Paul François Jean Nicolas
Born at Fox Amphoux, June 20, 1755
Died in Paris, January 29, 1829

Barras's political career was ended by the *coup d'état* of Brumaire 18. He withdrew to his castle at Grosbois. Bonaparte, who did not trust him, offered him an ambassadorship in Saxe, then in the United States. He was also offered the command of the forces in Saint Domingue. His repeated refusals deeply angered Bonaparte. After a voluntary exile in Belgium, Barras got the Emperor to allow him to retire to Provence in 1805 for health reasons. Five years later, he was placed under house arrest in Rome, and only returned to France in 1815. He lived peacefully until his death.

Basire, Claude
Born in Dijon, October 21, 1764
Guillotined in Paris, April 5, 1794

Beauharnais, Joséphine de
Born at Trois Ilets (Martinique), June 26, 1763
Died at Malmaison, May 29, 1814

Joséphine de Beauharnais led a dissolute life while her husband, General Napoléon Bonaparte, was busy fighting for France in Egypt. When he became First Consul, Joséphine shared his rapid rise until his coronation. She became Empress of France on December 2nd., 1804. However, in 1807, Napoléon, to whom she had given no heirs, decided to repudiate her. Their divorce was granted on December 16th., 1809. Despite this, the Emperor gave his former wife a large pension and allowed her to keep her title of Empress. Joséphine then lived at the Malmaison, where Napoléon often visited her, even though he was by then married to Archduchess Marie Louise. In 1814, Joséphine had several foreign sovereigns to stay at the Malmaison. She was to die just two and a half months after Napoléon's first abdication.

Beaumarchais, Pierre Augustin Caron de
Born in Paris, January 24, 1732
Died in Paris, May 18, 1799

Bernardin de Saint Pierre, Jacques Henri
Born at Le Havre, January 19, 1737
Died at Eragny, January 21, 1814

Appointed professor of morality at the Ecole Normale Supérieure in 1794, Bernardin de Saint Pierre continued teaching during the Consulate and the Empire. Napoléon, who admired him, showered him with gifts and granted him a pension, an apartment at the Louvre and a chair at the French Academy. In 1800, Bernardin de Saint Pierre remarried at the age of 63 with the young Désirée de Pelleporc. He died leaving unfinished work behind. One book, *Les Voeux d'un Solitaire*, was published posthumously.

Berthollet, Claude Louis
Born at Talloires, December 9, 1748
Died at Arcueil, November 6, 1822

In 1801, Berthollet published his *Recherches sur les Lois d'Affinités* in which he presents new concepts that revolutionised chemistry. Two years later, he developed his theories in a work entitled *Essai de Statistique Chimique*. He then founded the "Arcueil Society", which from 1807 to 1817 published his other books on chemistry. While carrying on his research, he also became a senator and was made a member of the Legion of Honour. Although he was ennobled during the Empire, he voted for Napoléon's dismissal in 1814. During the Restoration, he was made a peer of France by Louis XVIII. Berthollet worked on his research until the last.

Billaud Varenne, Jacques *alias* Nicolas Billaud
Born at La Rochelle, April 23, 1756
Died at Port au Prince, June 7, 1819

Sentenced in 1795 as a "terrorist", Billaud Varenne was deported to the penal colony at Cayenne. Despite being amnestied by the First Consul after the events of Brumaire 18, he steadfastly refused to acknowledge the new régime and remained in Guyana, where he cultivated some land. In 1817, when Guyana was returned to France by Portugal, Billaud Varenne, fearing Bourbon reprisals for his past activities, set off by ship to New York and finally decided to settle in Haiti.

Boissy d'Anglas, François Antoine
Born at Saint Jean Chambre, December 8, 1756
Died in Paris, October 20, 1826

Appointed to the Tribunal after Brumaire 18, Boissy d'Anglas became a senator in 1804, member of the Legion of Honour and count of the Empire in 1808, then Grand Officer of the Legion of Honour in 1810. In 1814, he learned of the Emperor's downfall, who had showered him with favours. He accepted a peerage of France from Louis XVIII. During the Hundred Days, the Emperor pardoned him and named him peer of the Chamber, which, on the return of the Bourbons, earned him a three-week exclusion from the peerage. Back in favour, he died far from politics.

Bonaparte, Lucien
Born at Ajaccio, March 21, 1775
Died at Viterbe, June 29, 1840

Younger brother of Napoléon, Lucien Bonaparte joined the Tribune after Brumaire 18, then he was named Grand Officer of the Legion of Honour. After quarrelling with his brother, who disapproved of his remarriage to Madame Douberthon, Lucien left for Italy to live in Canino, a new principality, then he stayed in England for three years. Returning to France during the Hundred Days, he was elected by the department of the Isère as representative to the ▷

Chamber in 1815, but refused this mandate, having also been named peer of France by his brother. After the Battle of Waterloo, Lucien Bonaparte retired to Neuilly, then, re-exiled, lived near Viterbe in Italy, where he died.

Bonaparte, Napoléon
Born at Ajaccio, August 15, 1769
Died at St. Helena, May 5, 1821

As First Consul, Napoléon Bonaparte secured all power, reorganised finance, administration, justice, created the lycées, the Bank of France, the Legion of Honour, proclaimed the Civil Code in 1804 and signed the Concordat in 1801 with Pope Pius VII in order to reconcile the Catholics. Abroad, he fought the English and the Austrians and forced them to sign the peace treaty of Lunéville in 1801. On August 2nd. 1802, Bonaparte had himself named Consul for life. Then he eliminated all domestic opposition: royalist deportations and the execution of the Duc d'Enghien. He proclaimed himself Emperor of the French under the name of Napoléon I on May 18th., 1804. He created a nobility of the Empire and placed members of the Bonaparte clan at the head of conquered countries. As from 1805, he undertook a policy of conquest. However, England, allied with Austria and Russia, took up arms. Then Napoléon won a series of victories in 1805 and ended the second coalition. A new campaign against Prussia and Russia began in 1806. Napoléon was the victor of Jena in 1806 and signed the peace treaty of Tilsit with Tsar Alexander I in 1807. Hell-bent on the pursuit of the ruin of his neighbour, England, who refused peace, he applied the continental blockade. At the same time, he invaded Portugal in 1807, the Papal States and Spain in 1808, then went on to annex Holland and part of north Germany in 1810. However, Napoléon also dreamed of his succession: after dissolving his marriage with Joséphine, who was incapable of giving him an heir, he married Marie Louise of the house of Hapsburg in 1810. Their son, born in 1811, was proclaimed King of Rome. The Empire was then at its peak although, as from 1812, the policy of Napoléon came to an end with a series of failures. France capitulated in Spain after exhausting itself in an unwinnable war. Soon after, Alexander I demanded that France evacuate Pomerania and

Prussia; Napoléon had to engage in a new war. His army penetrated Russia, but it was rapidly forced into a retreat in 1812. Prussia, Germany, Sweden and Austria then formed an alliance with Russia. The allies crossed the Rhine and entered Paris in 1814. The Emperor was pronounced dethroned. He abdicated and was forced to leave for the island of Elba, of which he became sovereign. After nine months, he returned to France and reassumed power for the Hundred Days in 1815, but Europe formed a new opposition coalition against him. After the defeat of Waterloo in 1815, he abdicated again and the English exiled him to Saint Helena.

Bouillé, François Claude Amour, Marquis de
Born at Saint Eble,
November 19, 1739
Died in London, November 14, 1800

After having tried in vain to help Louis XVI and his family escape in June 1791, the Marquis de Bouillé fled to Luxembourg for safety. Once there, he placed himself at the service of Condé and fought with the royalist army in 1792, before seeing combat with the Duke of York's troops in 1793. He then lived in London until his death.

Boullée, Etienne
Born in Paris, February 12, 1728
Died in Paris, February 6, 1799

Brissot de Warville, Jacques Pierre
Born at Chartres, January 14, 1754
Guillotined in Paris, October 31, 1793

Buzot, François Nicolas
Born at Evreux, March 1, 1760
Committed suicide at Sainte Magne, June 20, 1794

Cabanis, Pierre Georges
Born at Cosnac, June 5, 1757
Died at Rueil, May 5, 1808

Appointed senator by Bonaparte in 1799, Cabanis then became a member of the Legion of Honour. The First Consul, however, did not fully trust him because of his links with the "ideologues" opposed to all authoritarian power and to the restoration of religion. After the so-called Senate Plot (1807), his poor

health and the climate of suspicion forced him to withdraw from politics and live in semi-retirement, while engaged in scientific research. He settled at Rueil, where he died of an apoplexy attack. His ashes were later placed in the Panthéon.

Cabarrus, Thérésa
see Tallien, Thérésa

Cadoudal, Georges
Born at Kerléano Auray,
January 1, 1771
Executed in Paris, June 25, 1804

Cadoudal, the last leader of the Chouans in Brittany, continued to fight for his cause. In 1800, he attempted to revolt against the First Consul with assistance from the Comte d'Artois and Pichegru. After the failure of the attempt, he fled to London, where the Comte d'Artois appointed him Lieutenant General. He returned secretly to France in 1803 and contacted Pichegru and Moreau again to try to topple the First Consul. The plot was discovered in 1804. He was arrested in Paris, sentenced to death and executed. His family was later ennobled by Louis XVIII.

Calonne, Charles Alexandre de
Born at Douai, January 20, 1734
Died in Paris, October 29, 1802

From London, where he fled into exile prior to 1789, Calonne, the former Minister of Finance to Louis XVI, followed the Revolution very closely. Working for the émigré princes, he joined them in Turin in 1790 and spent all his fortune on them. During the Consulate, he got Bonaparte to allow him to return to Paris.

Cambacérès, Jean Jacques Régis de
Born at Montpellier, October 18, 1753
Died in Paris, March 8, 1824

Although Cambacérès was not directly involved in the coup d'état of Brumaire, he was one of its main beneficiaries, as he became Second Consul and played a major rôle at Bonaparte's side, particularly in the preparation of the Concordat and the Civil Code (1802-1804). Bonaparte showered him with honours, naming him president of the Senate, high officer of the Legion of Honour,

then Duke of Parma in 1808. His loyalty was such that it was tantamount to servility. He adored being awarded civilian or military decorations, wearing official dress uniforms and going to military parades at the drop of a hat. Following the fall of the Empire, Cambacérès was appointed president of the Regency Council. He was able to convince Marie Louise to take the King of Rome to safety beyond the Loire river before sending his senatorial go-ahead for the Emperor's dismissal. However, when Napoléon returned from exile on Elba in 1815, he forgave Cambacérès this betrayal and even made him a peer of France, and later Minister of Justice. Under the Restoration, he was banished as a regicide. He was therefore forced to go to Brussels. In 1818, Louis XVIII gave him permission to return to Paris, where he lived out the rest of his life quietly.

Cambon, Pierre Joseph
Born at Montpellier, June 10, 1756
Died at Saint Josse Ten Voode, February 15, 1820

Following the events of Prairial, in May 1795, Cambon withdrew from politics and settled on some property he owned near Montpellier until the end of the Empire in 1815. During the Hundred Days, he was elected president of the Chamber by the department of Hérault. When the Bourbons returned, he was sentenced to banishment as a regicide. He died in exile in Belgium.

Carnot, Lazare Nicolas
Born at Nolay, May 13, 1753
Died at Magdeburg, August 2, 1823

After Brumaire 18, Bonaparte appointed Carnot Minister of War in 1800, but was unable to get on with him and forced him to resign. As a Tribune, Carnot remained just as stubborn, voting against lifetime membership of the Consulate and against the Empire. This again cost him dearly. However, during the Hundred Days, Napoléon made him Minister of the Interior, a move which caused him to be exiled when Louis XVIII returned. He died in poverty in Prussia.

Carrier, Jean Baptiste
Born at Yolet, March 16, 1756
Guillotined in Paris,
December 16, 1794

Cazalès, Jacques Antoine de
Born at Grenade sur Garonne,
February 1, 1758
Died at Engalvin,
November 24, 1805

After having emigrated to London, where he was associated with Burke, Cazalès returned to France in 1803. He settled near Grenade, in the Haute Garonne, and kept away from politics. He died two years after returning to France.

Cazotte, Jacques
Born in Dijon, October 7, 1719
Guillotined in Paris,
September 25, 1794

Chabot, François
Born at Saint Geniez,
October 23, 1756
Guillotined in Paris, April 5, 1794

Chalier, Marie Joseph
Born at Suze in 1747
Guillotined in Lyons, July 16, 1793

Chamfort, Sébastien Roch
Known as **Nicolas**
Born at Clermont en Auvergne,
April 6, 1740
Died in Paris, April 13, 1795

Chappe, Claude
Born at Brûlon, December 26, 1763
Committed suicide in Paris,
January 25, 1805

Asked by the Convention to oversee the installation of new telegraph lines, his competitors, in particular the clock-maker and mechanic Abraham Breguet, later claimed that Chappe was not the sole inventor. He threw himself into a well out of despair.

Charette de La Contrie,
François Athanese de
Born at Couffé, April 21, 1763
Executed at Nantes, March 29, 1796

Charles X
Born at Versailles, October 9, 1757
Died at Gorizia, November 6, 1836

The Comte d'Artois, younger brother of Louis XVI, emigrated in 1789, soon after the fall of the Bastille. He then visited the various courts of Europe, where he led a dissolute life. After the Emperor's downfall, he returned to Paris in April 1814, but fled to Ghent during the Hundred Days (1815). Back in France during the Restoration, he became leader of the ultra-royalist party. He acceded to the throne when his brother Louis XVIII died in 1824 and was consecrated at Reims on March 29th. 1825, under the name of Charles X. A supporter of absolute monarchy, he brought back censorship, the law of primogeniture, dissolved the Chamber and, after the fall of the Martignac government, appointed an ultra, Prince Jules de Polignac, head of government in 1829. In 1830, a revolt in July caused by public discontent forced him to abdicate on August 2nd. The ousted sovereign fled to England, then to Austria (1832) and to Gorizia, in the Friuli (1836), where he died of cholera.

Charles Louis
see Louis XVII

Chaumette, *alias* **Anaxagoras**
Born at Nevers, May 24, 1763
Guillotined in Paris, April 13, 1794

Chénier, André de
Born in Constantinople,
October 28, 1762
Guillotined in Paris, July 25, 1794

Chénier, Marie Joseph de
Born Constantinople, Aug. 28, 1764
Died in Paris, January, 1814

Although he supported Bonaparte after his coup d'état, Chénier then refused to accept his authority and made a show of his republican views. This caused him to be stripped of all his political positions as from 1802. However, he was made inspector general of education in 1803, but was dismissed three years later following the publication of his *Epistle to Voltaire* attacking the régime. His last tragedy, *Cyrus,* also displeased the Emperor and his plays were therefore banned from all theatres. Since he could no longer make a living from writing plays, Chénier began to teach literature in order to survive.

Clavière, Etienne
Born in Geneva, January 29, 1735
Committed suicide in Paris,
December 8, 1793

Cloots, Jean Baptiste du
Val de Grâce (Baron de)
Born at Clèves, June 24, 1755
Guillotined in Paris, March 24, 1794

Collot d'Herbois,
Jean Marie
Born in Paris, June 19, 1750
Died in Cayenne, June 8, 1796

Condé, Louis Joseph
Prince de
Born at Chantilly, August 9, 1736
Died in Paris, May 13, 1818

A prince of the blood and career soldier, the Prince de Condé emigrated to Turin, then to Worms, as soon as the Revolution broke out. After having set up an army to serve England, Austria and Russia, he offered his services to the Tsar in 1799. Following the 1801 Lunéville Treaty, his army was disbanded and he went to live in England. Upon the return of the Bourbons, he went back to France and became Grand Master of the King's household.

Condorcet, Marie Jean
Antoine de Caritat, Marquis
de
Born at Ribémont, Sept. 1, 1743
Committed suicide at Bourg la
Reine, March 29, 1794

Condorcet, Marie Louise
Sophie, Marquise de
Born at Villette castle, near
Meulan, spring of 1764
Died in Paris, September 8, 1822

Following her husband's death in 1794, Madame de Condorcet lived in poverty before buying a lingerie shop. She managed to recover part of her property in 1799 and issued a first edition of her husband's works (1801-1804). She then re-opened her salon and associated with Tracy, Cabanis and Mallia Garat. She met with ideologues opposed to the Empire and made no secret of her atheism or her republican views. This got her into trouble with the imperial authorities. When she died, she was buried at Père Lachaise cemetery, in Paris, with no religious ceremony

Corday d'Armont, Charlotte
alias **Charlotte Corday**
Born at Saint Saturnin des Ligneries,
July 28, 1768
Guillotined in Paris, July 16, 1793

Couthon, Georges Auguste
Born at Crest, December 22, 1755
Guillotined in Paris, July 28, 1794

Danton, Georges Jacques
Born at Arcis sur Aube,
October 28, 1759
Guillotined in Paris, April 5, 1794

David, Jacques Louis
Born in Paris, August 30, 1748
Died in Brussels,
December 25, 1825

David became an enthusiastic supporter of Bonaparte and painted several portraits of him. This gained him much honour: in late 1803, he was made a knight, and, in 1808, was promoted to an officer of the Legion of Honour. In 1804, he was appointed the First Painter to the Emperor, before he started work on the huge *Sacre* (1805-1807). Louis David then painted the *Distribution des Aigles* in 1810. He reigned over the art world during the Empire with as much glory as he had during the Revolution. He was, however, forced to go into exile during the Restoration, as he had been one of the signatories of the supplementary act to the Empire's Constitution. David settled in Brussels, where he painted his final works. Among these are *L'Amour et Psyché,* as well as several fine portraits.

Desmoulins, Camille
Born at Guise, March 2, 1760
Guillotined in Paris, April 5, 1794

Desmoulins, Lucile
Born in Paris in 1770
Guillotined in Paris, April 13, 1794

Drouet, Jean Baptiste
Born at Sainte Menehould,
January 8, 1763
Died at Mâcon, April 11, 1814

While a commissioner of the Directory in the Marne region, Drouet supported the Brumaire coup d'état. This led to his appointment as Assistant Prefect of Sainte Menehould, a position he kept until the end of the Empire. During the Hundred Days, he was elected representative of the Marne at the Chamber, but when the Bourbons returned in 1815, he was exiled as a regicide. He returned to France using a fake name, living at Mâcon until his death.

Dubois Crancé, Edmond Louis *alias* Dubois de Crancé
Born at Charleville, Oct. 14, 1747
Died at Réthel, June 28, 1814

After the insurrection of Brumaire, in which he took no part, Dubois Crancé ceased all political activity and retired to his property in Champagne.

Dumouriez, Charles François *alias* du Périer
Born at Cambrai, January 25, 1739
Died at Turville Park, England, March 14, 1823

After having allied himself with the opposition, he roamed Europe before settling in Hamburg. In 1800, he left for Saint Petersburg to offer his services to the Tsar, but he was rejected and he moved to England. From 1812 to 1814, he was an adviser to the Castlereagh government, who paid him a large pension. The Bourbons would not authorise his return to France because of the advice he had given to Wellington during the Spanish war; thus he finished his days, forgotten by all, in England.

Dupont de Nemours, Pierre Samuel
Born in Paris, September 14, 1739
Died at Eleutherian Mills, United States, August 6, 1817

Under threat of deportation after Fructidor 18, he left for the United States and founded a business with its headquarters both in New York and Paris. In 1802, he returned to France, where he became secretary, then vice-president of the Paris Chamber of Commerce. In 1814, after the abdication of Napoléon Bonaparte, he was named secretary of the provisional government. In the same year, King Louis XVIII appointed him both councillor and knight of the Legion of Honour, then administrator of the navy at Toulon. Before the Hundred Days, Dupont left for America and died there from an attack of gout.

Dupont, Adrien
Born in Paris, February 5, 1759
Died in Paris, March 18, 1829

Elisabeth de France, *alias* Madame Elisabeth
Born at Versailles, May 3, 1764
Guillotined in Paris, May 10, 1794

Eprémesnil, Jean Jacques Duval d'
Born at Pondicherry, December 5, 1745
Guillotined in Paris, April 22, 1794

Estaing, Charles Henri, Comte d'
Born at Ravel, November 24, 1729
Guillotined in Paris, April 28, 1794

Fabre d'Eglantine, Philippe *alias* François Fabre
Born at Limoux, December 28, 1755
Guillotined in Paris, April 5, 1794

Fersen, Hans Axel, Comte de
Born in Stockholm, Sept. 4, 1755
Assassinated in Stockholm, June 20, 1810

Fersen returned to Sweden, his native country, after having tried in vain to help the royal family when it was detained at the Temple. King Charles XIII of Sweden, whose trust he had by then earned, appointed him Chancellor of the University of Uppsala. Later, Fersen was accused without any solid proof of having poisoned the heir to the Swedish throne, Christian Augustus, Duke of Augustenborg. He was massacred by a mob on the day of the prince's funeral. After his death, his *Correspondance et Journal Intime Inédits* was published. It contained his many letters to Marie Antoinette.

Florian, Jean Pierre Claris de
Born at Sauve, March 6, 1755
Died at Sceaux, September 13, 1794

Fouché, Joseph
Born in Nantes, May 21, 1759
Died at Trieste, December 26, 1820

Following his appointment as Minister of Police in 1799, Fouché craftily set up a network of spies throughout France. This made him an extremely powerful man working for Bonaparte. Despite being the strong man within the government, Fouché was temporarily replaced (1802-1804) after joining the Senate in 1802. Bonaparte then named him Comte of the Empire and Duc d'Otrante before again giving him the Ministry of Police in 1810. When the Emperor abdicated in 1814, Fouché offered to serve the Bourbons. He was Minister of Police yet again during the Hundred Days. In

the wake of Waterloo, he was made president of the Provisional Council. He was involved in plotting with the Bourbons and contributed to the return of Louis XVIII, who sent him back to the Ministry of Police. The same year, he was elected deputy of Seine et Marne and Corrèze. When he found himself a target of the law on regicides, he was forced to resign from the ministry and leave France. He fled to Trieste, where he died leaving a huge fortune behind.

Fouquier Tinville, Antoine *alias* Quentin Fouquier
Born at Hérouël, June 12, 1746
Died in Paris, December 16, 1809

Fourcroy, Antoine François de
Born in Paris, June 15, 1755
Died in Paris, December 16, 1809

Appointed Councillor of State after Brumaire 18, Fourcroy was to become director general of Public Education in 1801. He was made Comte of the Empire and member of the Legion of Honour in 1804. When the Imperial university was set up, he fell into disfavour and was dismissed from the education post. This sudden dismissal affected his health and he died following an attack of apoplexy.

Fragonard, Jean Honoré
Born at Grasse, April 5, 1732
Died in Paris, August 22, 1806

After 1799, Fragonard, who was no longer painting, stopped playing a rôle in the art world. In June 1800, the Minister of the Interior informed him that he had been dismissed from his official duties. On April 1, 1805, a decree from Napoléon ordered all artists still living at the Louvre to leave. Fragonard therefore settled at the nearby Palais Royal and on July 9th. was granted a special pension as compensation. Fragonard died in August 1806 after having eaten an apparently fatal ice-cream on the Champs Elysées.

Franççois de Neufchâteau, *alias* Nicolas Louis
Born at Saffais, April 17, 1750
Died in Paris, January 10, 1828

Minister of the Interior until June 1799, François de Neufchâteau was one of the first to back Bonaparte after Brumaire 18. He became a

member of the Senate in 1800 and its president from 1804 to 1806. He became Comte of the Empire in 1808, and withdrew from politics at the Restoration. He spent his final years working on agronomy, poetry *(Fables et Contes en Vers)*, history *(Histoire de l'Occupation de Bavière)* and various other erudite tasks.

Fréron, Stanislas Louis
Born in Paris, August 17, 1754
Died at Cayes, Saint Domingue, July 15, 1802

Considered as being one of the so-called wealthy young "golden boys", Fréron became the lover of Pauline Bonaparte after the Brumaire 18 uprising. However, the First Consul only appointed him an administrator of alms-houses, a post he did not keep for long. To get rid of him, Pauline had him sent to Saint Domingue as Assistant Prefect. He died there of yellow fever just two months after his arrival.

Genlis, Stéphanie Félicité du Crest (Comtesse de)
Born at Champcéri, January 25, 1746
Died in Paris, December 31, 1830

Having emigrated in 1792, Madame de Genlis returned to France in 1800. She obtained from Bonaparte, who appreciated her talents as a writer, the house of the Arsenal librarian, along with a 6,000 livre pension. Already the author of many novels, she had a new success with *Contes Moraux* in 1802, and the novels *La Duchesse de la Vallière* in 1804, *Mme. de Maintenon* in 1806 and various historical and moral works. In 1825, she published the ten volumes of her *Mémoires*, which caused a scandal.

Gensonné, Armand
Born in Bordeaux, August 10, 1758
Guillotined in Paris, Oct. 31, 1793

Gobel, Jean Baptiste
Born at Thann, September 1, 1727
Guillotined in Paris, April 13, 1794

Gossec, *alias* Joseph Gossé
Born at Vergnies, Hainaut, January 17, 1734
Died in Paris, February 16, 1829

After having been official composer for revolutionary festivals, Gossec took a very active part in the organisation of the Academy of Music and held the chair of composer until 1824. At this date, the government closed the Academy. He then retired to Passy, where he lived until the end of his life.

Gouges, Marie Gouze, alias Olympe de
Born at Montauban, May 7, 1748
Guillotined in Paris,
November 3, 1793

Grégoire, Henri Baptiste
Born at Vého, December 4, 1750
Died in Paris, May 26, 1831

Member of the legislative body during the Consulate, Abbot Grégoire was an opponent of the First Consul and disapproved the drawing up of the Concordat. Having been named Senator in December 1801, he was excluded from the new clergy after the signing of the Concordat and lost his bishopric in Lorraine. Whilst voting against life Consularship, against the Empire, against the re-establishment of an hereditary nobility, he none the less accepted from Napoléon the title of Comte in 1808. Although he had been among the first to call for the Emperor's downfall, he was sidelined by the Bourbons at the Restoration and excluded from the Institute in 1816. In 1819, the department of the Isère sent him to the Chamber as an opposition deputy, but his election was invalidated by the royalists. When he died, the Archbishop of Paris refused him a Christian burial. His *Mémoires* were published in 1837.

Grétry, André Ernest Modeste
Born at Liège, February 8, 1741
Died at Montmorency,
September 24, 1813

Upon the creation of the Academy in 1795, the dramatic composer Grétry was named inspector of that institution. At the end of his life, he retired to the Ermitage, where Jean Jacques Rousseau had lived. He left behind him as his legacy 53 operas, instrumental music, a few revolutionary hymns and a *Mémoire ou Essai sur la Musique*.

Guadet, Marguerite Elie
Born at Saint Emilion, July 20, 1758
Guillotined in Bordeaux,
June 15, 1794

Guillotin, Joseph Ignace
Born at Saintes, May 28, 1738
Died in Paris, March 26, 1814

Imprisoned under the Terror, Doctor Guillotin was released after Thermidor and withdrew from political life. Professor of anatomy at the Paris faculty, he continued medical research and devoted himself to the propagation of vaccination.

Guyton Morveau, Bernard alias Guyton
Born at Dijon, January 4, 1737
Died in Paris, January 2, 1816

During the Consulate era, Guyton Morveau continued his research work in physics. When the Ecole Polytechnique was founded, he became professor of mineralogy and later the school's director. He was much honoured by Bonaparte, who admired him. In 1803, he was made a member of the Legion of Honour, a knight of the Empire in 1809 and Baron in 1811. From 1799 to 1814, he remained administrator of the Treasury. However, under the Restoration he was not forgiven for having supported the Revolution and was dismissed from his posts.

Hanriot, François
Born at Nanterre, December 3, 1759
Guillotined in Paris, July 28, 1794

Hauy, Valentin
Born at Saint Just, November 13, 1745
Died in Paris, March 19, 1822

While continuing to dedicate himself to the education of young blind people, during the Consulate Hauy opened a private establishment, the museum for the blind, which, badly managed, was soon in jeopardy. Even so, his reputation had spread abroad and he was given the task of opening the same type of institution at Saint Petersburg in 1806. During a brief stay in Berlin, he inspired the creation of a similar establishment. He returned to France in 1817.

Hébert, Jacques René
Born in Alençon, November 15, 1757
Guillotined in Paris, March 24, 1794

Hérault de Séchelles, Marie Jean
Born in Paris, October 20, 1759
Guillotined in Paris, April 5, 1794

Hoche, Lazare
Born at Montreuil, June 24, 1768
Died at Wetzlar,
September 19, 1797

Houdon, Jean Antoine
Born at Versailles, March 23, 1741
Died in Paris, July 15, 1828

Having voluntarily stood aside due to his previous dealings with the royalists, Houdon came out of the sidelines at the time of the Consulate. Appointed knight of the Legion of Honour in 1800, he received official commissions, including a bust of Napoléon and of Tsar Alexander I. During the last years of his life, he taught at the school of Fine Arts.

Jeanbon Saint André, alias André Jeanbon,
Born at Montauban, Feb. 25, 1749
Died at Mainz,
December 10, 1813

A prisoner of the Turks from 1798, Jeanbon Saint André was liberated in 1800. He was then named commissioner general of the departments of the Rhine in 1801, then administrator of Mont Tonnerre at Mainz in 1802. In recognition of his services, Napoléon made him a member of the Legion of Honour in 1804, then a Baron of the Empire in 1809. He died of typhoid in 1813.

Jussieu, Antoine Laurent de
Born in Lyons, April 12, 1748
Died in Paris, September 17, 1836

Jussieu joined the Academy of Science under the Directory. He kept the chair of botany after Brumaire 18. In 1800, he ferociously defended the independence of the Natural History Museum. He had contributed to its organisation in 1790. Named member of the university council in 1808, he then devoted himself to his botanic work.

Kellermann, François Christophe
Born in Strasbourg, May 28, 1735
Died in Paris, September 12, 1820

Appointed Senator in the wake of Brumaire 18, Kellermann was given the Legion of Honour in 1801 before being made a Marshal of France by Napoléon in 1804. He then took command of the Rhine army's reserve corps (1805-1806) and was

given the title of Duc de Valmy in 1808. In 1813, he led the Rhine observer corps and organised reinforcements for Germany. When the Empire fell, he joined the Bourbons. Made a peer of France in 1814, Kellermann sat among the liberal deputies in the upper Chamber until his death.

Kéralio, Louise Felicité de
see Robert, Louise

Laclos, Pierre Choderlos de
Born in Amiens, October 18, 1741
Died at Taranto, September 5, 1803

The author of *Les Liaisons Dangereuses* was among those who welcomed Bonaparte's rise to power. A former soldier, Choderlos de Laclos rejoined the army on January 16th. 1800, at the request of the First Consul. He was given the rank of brigadier. He was sent to the army of the Rhine, where, acting under Moreau's orders, he commanded the artillery. After his return to Paris, he was promoted in 1803 to inspector general of artillery in the Naples army. He died of dysentery on his arrival in Italy.

Lacombe, Claire alias Rose
Born at Pamiers, March 4, 1765
Died in Paris, circa 1820

After she was released from jail in 1795, Claire Lacombe ceased all political activity. She took up acting once again and performed in various small theatres in the provinces. Nothing is known about her after the year 1798.

La Fayette, Marie Gilbert Motier, Marquis de
Born at Chavaniac, Sept. 6, 1757
Died in Paris, May 20, 1834

Removed from the list of émigrés after Brumaire 18, La Fayette came back to France in June 1800, but refused all official positions and withdrew to his castle at Grange Bléneau. He stayed there until the Hundred Days and was elected deputy of Seine et Marne in 1815. He called for Napoléon's abdication. Under the Restoration, he was elected deputy of the Sarthe (1818-1824), then of Meaux (1827). He joined the French Carbonari in 1821 and remained in the opposition, protesting against the war in Spain.

▷

In 1830, he joined the revolutionary forces. Named commander of the National Guard in July 1830, he imposed himself effectively as the head of the provisional government. However, he went over to the Bourbons and had a new moment of glory when he received the Duc d'Orléans at city hall and presented him to the people on July 31st. 1830. He was then elected a deputy of the majority, but ended up by distancing himself from the government. He openly opposed the Casimir Perier government and died in opposition.

Lagrange, Joseph Louis
Born in Turin, January 25, 1736
Died in Paris, April 10, 1813

After Brumaire 18, Lagrange entered the Senate in December 1799, keeping his post as professor at the Polytechnic School. As a protégé of Bonaparte, who admired his scientific work, he was made a member of the Legion of Honour in 1804, then Comte of the Empire in 1808. At his death, the mathematician was buried in the Panthéon.

Lakanal, Joseph
Born at Serres, July 14, 1762
Died in Paris, February 14, 1845

At the time of Brumaire 18, he was commissar general of the departments of the left bank of the Rhine; Lakanal was recalled to Paris by Bonaparte. After having obtained the chair of ancient languages at the Central School in 1800, he was finally named Inspector General of Weights and Measures in 1807. Dismissed from his functions under the Restoration, he went into exile in America. He returned to France in 1834 and taught at the Academy of Moral Science until his death.

Lamballe, Marie Thérèse de Savoy Carignan, Princesse de
Born in Turin, September 8, 1749
Killed in Paris, September 2, 1792

Lameth, Alexandre, Comte de
Born in Paris, October 28, 1760
Died in Paris, March 18, 1829

Exiled to Hamburg in 1798 along with his brother Charles, Alexandre de Lameth returned to Paris after Brumaire 18. He joined Bonaparte, working for him in the administration. In 1810, he was made a Baron of the Empire. In 1816, the War Ministry granted him his retirement as a Lieutenant General after 40 years' service. He became a liberal opposition deputy. In 1820, he was elected deputy for the Loire Inférieure and in 1827 he became deputy of Seine et Oise. He died before the end of the second legislature.

Lameth, Charles de, Comte de
Born in Paris, October 5, 1757
Died in Paris, December 28, 1832

A refugee in Hamburg in 1792, Charles de Lameth returned from exile after Brumaire 18, at the same time as his brother Alexandre. Appointed Brigadier General in 1809, he fought in the Spanish war, before being named Governor of Wurzburg. Promoted to Lieutenant General under the Restoration in 1814, he retired in 1819 and stayed on the sidelines until his brother's death, whom he replaced as deputy for the Seine et Oise in 1829. He was one of the 221 deputies hostile to the Polignac ministry. He was a partisan of the Louis Philippe monarchy and stayed, until his death, a defender of conservative ideas.

Laplace, Pierre Simon
Born at Beaumont sur Auge, March 22, 1749
Died in Paris, March 5, 1827

Laplace joined Bonaparte the day after Brumaire 18. Appointed Minister of the Interior in 1799, he was rapidly replaced by Lucien Bonaparte and became vice president of the Senate in 1803 before being made a Comte of the Empire in 1806. An ardent partisan of Bonaparte, he none the less voted the downfall of the Emperor. Louis XVIII made him a Marquis and a peer of France in 1814. He entered the Academy of Science and the Academy of France in 1816. He founded the Société d'Arceuil with his friend Berthollet.

La Révellière Lépeaux, Louis Marie de
Born at Montaigu, August 24, 1753
Died in Paris, March 27, 1824

A member of the Institute, La Révellière refused to swear loyalty to Bonaparte after Brumaire 18. Having done that, he was constrained to leave his post and from then on withdrew from public life until his death.

La Rochejaquelein, Henri du Vergier, Comte de
Born at La Durbellière, Aug. 3, 1772
Killed at Nouaillé, Jan. 28, 1794

Lavoisier, Antoine Laurent de
Born in Paris, August 26, 1743
Guillotined in Paris, May 8, 1794

Le Bas, Philippe François
Born at Frécent, November 4, 1764
Killed himself, Paris, July 28, 1794

Le Bon, Joseph
Born in Arras, September 25, 1765
Guillotined at Amiens, October 7, 1795

Le Chapelier, Isaac René Guy
Born at Rennes, June 12, 1754
Guillotined in Paris, April 22, 1794

Ledoux, Claude Nicolas
Born at Dormans, 1736
Died in Paris, November 20, 1806

Jailed during the Revolution for his royalist sympathies and made unpopular by the building of the toll barriers around Paris between 1783 and 1789 ("the wall surrounding Paris is the talk of Paris"), the architect Ledoux stopped all building activity. Even so, the daring of his architectural conceptions inspired a new fashion. Ledoux made an attempt to justify himself in an illustrated treatise entitled *De l'Architecture Considérée Sous le Rapport de l'Art, des Mœurs et de la Législation,* which he started to write in prison. The first volume of this work was published in 1804.

Le Peletier de Saint Fargeau, Louis Michel
Born in Paris, May 29, 1760
Assasinnated in Paris, Jan. 20, 1793

Lindet, Jean Baptiste Robert
Born at Bernay, May 2, 1746
Died in Paris, February 4, 1825

Following Brumaire 18, Lindet refused to serve under Bonaparte. He left the Ministry of Finance, where he had been appointed in July 1799, re-starting his job as a lawyer which he had abandoned at the Revolution. He retired from politics and devoted himself for the remaining years of his life to being a magistrate.

Lindet, Robert Thomas
Born at Bernay, November 14, 1743
Died at Bernay, August 10, 1823

Profoundly attached to republican institutions, Lindet refused to serve under Bonaparte after Brumaire 18 and withdrew to Bernay, where he practised as a lawyer. Outlawed for regicide under the Restoration, he stayed in Switzerland in 1816 and in Italy, then he went back to the town of his birth where he spent the rest of his days.

Loménie de Brienne, Etienne Charles de
Born in Paris, October 9, 1727
Died at Sens, February 16, 1794

Louis Joseph, Dauphin de France
Born at Versailles, October 22, 1781
Died in Paris, June 21, 1793

Louis XVI
Born at Versailles, August 23, 1754
Guillotined in Paris, January 21, 1793

Louis XVII
Born at Versailles, 1785
Died in Paris, at the Temple, June 8, 1795

Louis XVIII
Born at Versailles, Nov. 16, 1755
Died in Paris, September 16, 1824

At the time of Brumaire 18, the Pretender to the throne, an émigré since 1793, was at Mitau (Yelgava) in Russia. After spending several months in Sweden, he settled in England in 1807. He had to wait until 1814 to return to France. Called by the Senate, he agreed in the declaration of Saint Ouen (May 2nd., 1814) to form a constitutional government. More than a year later, Napoléon regained power and Louis XVIII hid at Ghent until the end of the Hundred Days. On returning to the throne of France in July 1815, he established a policy of national reconciliation embodied by his minister Decazes. However, after the assassination of the Duc de Berry in February 1820, Louis XVIII was overtaken by the reaction of the ultra-royalists. He had to dismiss Decazes and appoint Villèle. The latter represented a victory for the right, who increasingly kept the King out of decision making.

Louis, Nicolas, *alias* Victor
Born in Paris, May 10, 1731
Died in Paris, 1811

After having been a rich man, the architect of the Grand Théâtre of Bordeaux was completely ruined by fraudulent dealings which hastened his death. Apparently he died in hospital, abandoned by all. His name was forgotten until 1846, when, quite by chance, a magnificent collection of drawings and blueprints were found in an attic, a last testament to the brilliant and productive imagination of the architect Victor Louis.

Loustalot, Elisée
Born at Saint Jean d'Angely, August 12, 1762
Died in Paris, September 19, 1790

Louvet de Couvray, Jean Baptiste *alias* Louvet
Born in Paris, June 12, 1760
Died in Paris, August 25, 1797

Malesherbes, Chrétien Guillaume de Lamoignon de
Born in Paris, December 15, 1721
Guillotined in Paris, April 22, 1794

Marat, Jean Paul
Born at Boudry, principality of Neufchâtel, May 24, 1743
Assassinated in Paris, July 13, 1793

Marceau, François Séverin
Born at Chartres, March 1, 1769
Died in battle, Altenkirchen, September 21, 1796

Maréchal, Sylvain Pierre
Born in Paris, August 15, 1750
Died at Montrouge, January 18, 1803

After the condemnation of Babeuf and of the Egaux and his own acquittal in 1796, Maréchal devoted himself to writing. Apart from a *Dictionnaire des Athées*, published in 1800, he also published, before his death, *Histoire de Russie* in 1802, critical of the Emperor.

Marie Antoinette, Josèphe Jeanne de Lorraine
Born in Vienna, November 2, 1755
Guillotined in Paris, October 16, 1793

Marie Thérèse (Mme. Royale)
Born at Versailles December 18, 1778
Died at Frohsdorf, October 19, 1851

Exchanged in 1795 by France for Convention prisoners of the Austrians, Madame Royale married her cousin, the Duc d'Angoulême in 1799 and lived in exile until 1815. On her return to France under the Restoration, she exercised an undeniable influence on her uncle Louis XVIII before being again forced into exile in 1830.

Maury, Jean Siffrein
Born at Valréas, June 26, 1746
Died in Rome, May 11, 1817

Ambassador to Rome acting for the Comte de Provence from 1799, Maury joined Napoléon after he was crowned. Appointed Archbishop of Paris in 1810, without a canonical investiture, he defended the Emperor against Pius VII at the synod of 1811. At the fall of the Empire he was rejected by Louis XVIII and fled to Rome in 1814. The Pope jailed him. Freed, he resigned from episcopal functions in 1815, retiring from public life.

Méhul, Etienne Nicolas
Born at Givet, June 24, 1763
Died in Paris, October 18, 1817

Inspector of the Academy of Music at the time of Brumaire 18, Méhul pursued his brilliant career. Official musician of the Consulate and the Empire, he led the great orchestras and composed several operas, including *Irato* in 1801 and *Joseph* in 1807.

Mercier, Louis Sébastien
Born in Paris, July 6, 1740
Died in Paris, April 25, 1814

The Revolution inspired Mercier to paint *Nouveau Paris* in 1800. A member of the Institute, he demonstrated a belief in republican ideas until the time of his death.

Merlin de Douai, Philippe *alias* Antoine Merlin
Born at Arleux, October 30, 1754
Died in Paris, December 26, 1838

Forced to resign from the Directory in 1799, Merlin de Douai returned to politics after Brumaire 18. Knowing his competence as a jurist, Bonaparte appointed him Attorney General of the Supreme Court of Appeal, 1801-1814 and made him Comte of the Empire in 1810. At the Restoration he hid in Brussels. He returned to France in 1830, and died far from public life.

Merlin de Thionville, Antoine *alias* Christophe Merlin
Born at Thionville, September 13, 1762
Died in Paris, September 18, 1833

Merlin de Thionville lived on the income from his property during the Consulate and the Empire. In 1814, he defended Peronneat, the head of a commando, then retired and died whitout going back to business.

Mique, Richard
Born at Nancy, 1728
Died in Paris, July 7, 1794

Mirabeau, Honoré Gabriel Riqueti, Comte de
Born at Bignon, near Montargis, March 9, 1749
Died in Paris, April 2, 1791

Momoro, Antoine François
Born at Besançon, 1756
Guillotined in Paris, March 4, 1794

Monge, Gaspard
Born at Beaune, May 10, 1746
Died in Paris, July 28, 1818

Joining Bonaparte after Brumaire 18, Monge was appointed Senator in 1800, then Peer of France during the Hundred Days in 1814. At the same time, he became the director of the Polytechnic School in 1802 and published *Précis des Leçons sur le Calorique et l'Electricité* and *Application de l'Algèbre à la Géométrie* in 1809. Stripped of his functions by Louis XVIII in 1815, he devoted the last years of his life to scientific research.

Montansier, Marguerite *alias* Mlle. Brunet
Born at Bayonne, December 19, 1730
Died in Paris, July 13, 1820

Marguerite Montansier, director of the National Theatre, was given by Bonaparte, after Brumaire 18, the task of reorganising the Italian opera. Then she established herself at the Olympique theatre in 1801, then at the Favart theatre in 1803. She died at the age of 90, having dominated Parisian theatre life for over 50 years.

Mounier, Jean Joseph
Born at Grenoble, Nov. 12, 1758
Died in Paris, January 27, 1806

A refugee in Germany where the Grand Duke of Weimar had given him a school directorship in 1797, Mounier ended his ten-year exile and returned to France after Brumaire 18. Bonaparte appointed him administrator of Ile et Vilaine in 1802, then Councillor of State in 1805, a post he held until his death.

Necker, Jacques
Born in Geneva, August 31, 1730
Died at Coppet, April 10, 1804

Necker, who had retired to his property at Coppet in 1790, devoted himself to the writing of works in order to justify his ministries. He stopped writing around 1800 and finished his life peacefully, cherished by his daughter, Madame de Stäel.

Oberkampf, Christophe Philippe
Born at Wiesenbach, June 11, 1738
Died at Jouy en Josas, Oct. 4, 1815

The factory at Jouy en Josas suffered a great deal under the Revolution, but the owner, Oberkampf, managed to redress the situation under the Consulate. In 1805, he had such huge profits that he was able to install a cotton mill at Essonnes. Napoléon decorated him with his own Cross of the Legion of Honour in 1806. At his death, the peace of 1815 re-established English competition which considerably weakened his business.

Orléans, Louis Philippe, Duc de
Born at Saint Cloud, April 13, 1747
Guillotined in Paris, November 6, 1793

Pache, Jean Nicolas
Born in Paris, May 5, 1746
Died at Thin le Moûtier, November 18, 1823

Having retired to the Ardennes from 1795, Pache died there.

Paine, Thomas
Born at Thetford, England,
January 29, 1737
Died in New York, June 8, 1809

Disgusted by French politics, Thomas Paine led a retiring life under the Directory. He returned to America for good in 1802.

Palloy, Pierre François
Born in Paris, January 13, 1755
Died at Sceaux, January 19, 1835

Palloy, who made a fortune during the Revolution selling the stones of the Bastille, finished his days quietly at Sceaux, where he had retired in 1794. Until the end of his life, at each change of régime, he honoured the new leader of France by sending homages in both poem and prose.

Palm, Etta Lubina Johanna
Born at Groningen, 1743
Date and place of death unknown

Etta Palm left for Holland in 1793. At the proclamation of the Batavian Republic in 1795, suspected of supporting the fleeing Stadtholder, she was arrested as an Orangeist and spent three years in prison. Nothing more was heard of her after her liberation.

Pétion de Villeneuve, Jérôme
Born at Chartres, January 3, 1756
Committed suicide, Saint Emilion,
June 20, 1794

Pichegru, Jean Charles
Born at Planches, near d'Arbois,
February 16, 1761
Died in Paris, April 5, 1804

Deported to Guyana in 1797, Pichegru escaped from the convict prison of Sinnamary and lived in hiding in London from 1798. There, he joined Georges Cadoudal and became the leader of a conspiracy to assassinate Bonaparte. He came in secret to Paris in 1804 to carry out the plot. In February 1804, he was denounced, arrested and jailed in the Temple. He was found strangled in his cell, either a suicide or murder.

Polignac, Yolande Gabrielle de Polastron, Duchesse de
Born in Paris, 1749
Died in Vienna, December 9, 1793

Prieur de la Côte d'Or, *alias* Claude Prieur Duvernois
Born at Auxonne, December 2, 1763
Died in Dijon, August 11, 1832

Having been a member of the Council of the Five Hundred until the year 1798, Claude Prieur Duvernois only obtained the post of brigade leader under the Consulate. He then left the administration and took his retirement, devoting himself to the wallpaper factory that he had founded in the city of Dijon.

Prieur de la Marne, Pierre Louis *alias* Prieur
Born at Sommessous, August 1, 1756
Died in Brussels, May 30, 1827

Arrested in May 1795, Prieur de la Marne managed to escape pursuit and lived away from political life until the end of the Empire. He was forced into exile as a regicide in 1816 and died in Brussels without ever returning to France.

Provence, Comte de
see Louis XVIII

Rabaut Saint Etienne, *alias* Jean Paul Rabaut
Born at Nîmes, November 14, 1743
Guillotined in Paris,
December 5, 1793

Restif de La Bretonne, *alias* Nicolas Edme Rétif,
Born at Sacy, October 23, 1734
Died in Paris, February 3, 1806

Ruined by the bankruptcy of the assignat at the beginning of the Revolution, Restif did not manage to make a living as a writer, despite his reputation. His post in the boxroom of the Ministry of Police was abolished under the Empire and the versatile writer died shortly after, in penury, at the age of 72.

Reubell, Jean François
Born at Colmar, October 8, 1747
Died at Colmar,
November 23, 1807

Reubell opposed Bonaparte at the time of the Italian campaign and was forced to leave politics after Brumaire 18. From then on, he withdrew from a public life. He died, completely ruined by the squanderings of his son.

Robert, Hubert
Born in Paris, May 22, 1733
Died in Paris, April 15, 1808

Until 1802, Hubert Robert was a member of the administrative body of the Central Museum of the Arts. Forced to retire in 1802, the painter was, at the same time, obliged to leave his lodgings in the galleries of the Louvre. He settled in the rue Neuve du Luxembourg, where he died in his studio.

Robert, Louise Félicité (née de Kéralio)
Born in Paris, August 25, 1758
Died in Brussels, 1821

After Brumaire 18, Louise de Kéralio devoted herself to literature, while her husband, François Robert, pursued his business activities. She published, under the Consulate and the Empire, several novels, including *Amélie et Caroline* in 1808. After the return of the Bourbons, she went into exile in Belgium with her husband, who opened a liquor business in Brussels.

Robespierre, Maximilien Marie Isidore de
Born at Arras, May 6, 1758
Guillotined in Paris, July 28, 1794

Rochambeau, Jean Baptiste Donatien de Vimeur, Comte de
Born at Vendôme, July 1, 1725
Died at Thoré, May 10, 1807

Retired to his property, Rochambeau obtained a Field Marshal's pension in 1803 and lived away from public life until his death.

Roederer, Pierre Louis
Born at Metz, February 15, 1754
Died at Bois Roussel,
December 17, 1835

Having joined Bonaparte, Roederer played an important role in the coup d'état of Brumaire 18, writing a speech for Parisians. Member of the Council of State, Minister of Finance of the Kingdom of Naples in 1806, Minister of State of the Grand Duchy of Berg in 1810, Commissioner to Strasbourg in 1814 and Peer of France in 1815, he lost his positions at the second Restoration, but found his place at the Institute and in the Chamber of Peers in 1832 under the July monarchy.

Roland de La Platière, Jean Marie
Born at Thizy, February 19, 1734
Committed suicide, Bourg Baudoin,
November 10, 1793

Roland de La Platière, Manon, née Phlipon, *alias* Mme. Roland
Born in Paris, March 17, 1754
Guillotined in Paris,
November 8, 1793

Romme, Gilbert
Born at Riom, March 26, 1750
Killed himself, Paris, June 17, 1795

Ronsin, Charles Philippe
Born at Soissons, December 1, 1745
Guillotined in Paris, March 24, 1794

Rouget de Lisle, Claude Joseph
Born at Lons le Saunier
May 10, 1760
Died at Choisy le Roi,
June 26, 1836

Responsible for diplomatic relations between France and the Batavian Republic from 1798, Rouget de Lisle was dismissed from his functions in 1803. Mixed up with food trafficking along with Joséphine de Beauharnais, he fell into disgrace and misery. In 1826, he was even jailed for debt after having celebrated, without success, the return of the Bourbons. It was only in 1830, that the *Marseillaise* earned him a small pension from Louis Philippe. He then retired to Choisy le Roi, where he died six years later.

Roux, Jacques
Born at Pranzac, August 23, 1752
Killed himself, Paris, Feb. 10, 1794

Sade, Donatien Alphonse François Marquis de
Born in Paris, June 2, 1740
Died in Paris, December 2, 1814

The scandal caused by the publication of *Justine* in 1791 and *Juliette* in 1797 led to the arrest of the Marquis de Sade under the moral order code enforced by the Consulate in 1801. After a stay of two years at the prison of Saint Pélagie, then at Bicêtre jail, he was interned at the hospice of Charenton where he rejoined his mistress Marie Constance Quesnet. It was there that he organised, until 1808, the theatrical shows which became famous in Paris. He then devoted himself to writing his last novels, including: *Les Journées de Florbelle* in 1807, *L'Histoire Secrète d'Isabelle de Bavière* in 1813 and *La Marquise de Gange* in 1813. He died in 1813, having spent more than 30 years in jail.

Saint Just, Louis Antoine de
Born at Decize, August 25, 1767
Guillotined in Paris, July 28, 1794

Santerre, Antoine Joseph
Born in Paris, March 16, 1752
Died in Paris, February 6, 1809

Ordered by the government to buy horses abroad in 1797, Santerre was re-enlisted with his former rank of general following Brumaire 18. Entangled in various ill-fated speculations, he died, a ruined man, at the age of 57.

Sieyès, Emmanuel Joseph
Born at Fréjus, May 3, 1748
Died in Paris, June 20, 1836

Sieyès joined Bonaparte after the death of Joubert in August 1799. After Brumaire 18, he became one of the three provisional Consuls, but he did not manage to impose his constitutional ideas. Bonaparte having modified, for his own benefit, his project of the Constitution of Year VIII, Sieyès was forced to retire from the Consulate in 1800. He entered the Senate in 1800, then was made a Comte of the Empire in 1809, Grand Officer of the Legion of Honour and a Peer of France in 1815. Condemned for regicide at the Restoration in 1815, he went into exile in Brussels and did not go back to Paris until after the Revolution of 1830. It is said that some time before his death, having lost his mind, he said to his valet: "If M. de Robespierre calls, tell him I'm not here."

Staël Holstein, Germaine *alias* Necker, Baronne de
Born in Paris, April 22, 1766
Died in Paris, July 14, 1817

After Brumaire 18, Mme. de Staël would have liked to have become the muse of Bonaparte, but *De la Littérature Considérée dans ses Rapports avec les Institutions Sociales* published in 1800 and *Delphine* in 1802, angered the First Consul. Ex-iled 40 leagues from Paris in 1803, she visited Germany, Italy and Prussia, before settling at Coppet, where she held a salon renowned under the Empire. After *Corinne ou l'Italie* in 1807, which became a beacon for the romantic generation, she published *De l'Allemagne in 1810*. This work was seized and burnt by the Imperial police and she was then kept under house-arrest at Coppet. Widowed in 1802 and having split up with Benjamin Constant, she married, in 1811, a young officer, M. de Rocca. In 1812, she left Coppet in secret and roamed Europe, plotting against Napoléon. When she returned to Paris at the time of the Restoration, she prepared two works which were both published posthumously: *Considerations sur la Révolution Française* in 1817 and *Dix Années d'Exil* in *1821*

Talleyrand Périgord, Charles Maurice de
Born in Paris, February 13, 1754
Died in Paris, May 17, 1838

Talleyrand associated himself with the coup d'état of Bonaparte and became once more Minister for Foreign Affairs after Brumaire 18. From then on, he took part in all international negotiations under the Consulate. Grand Chamberlain in 1804, Prince of Bénévent in 1807, he tried to limit the ambitions of Napoléon by suggesting an alliance with Austria; this cost him his ministry in 1807. He then entered the opposition and was finally disgraced in 1809. In April 1814, he had the downfall of the Emperor proclaimed and joined Louis XVIII, who named him Minister of Foreign Affairs and sent him as representative to the Congress of Vienna in 1815. A member of the opposition during the Hundred Days and during the Restoration, Talleyrand finally accepted the post, offered to him by Louis Philippe in 1830, of Ambassador to London. After having laboured over the Franco-English Treaty in 1834, he returned to France in 1835 and withdrew from political life until his death.

Tallien, Jean Lambert
Born in Paris, January 23, 1767
Died in Paris, November 16, 1820

Tired of political life, Tallien had accompanied Bonaparte to Egypt. Land administrator and editor of *Décade Egyptienne*, he decided to return to France after Brumaire 18. However, the English captured his boat and kept him prisoner until 1802. Upon his return to Paris, his wife Thérésa, who had become the acknowledged companion of Ouvrard, got a divorce. He then left for Alicante where Napoléon had appointed him Consul, but, desperately ill, he was forced to return to France for good. The Emperor kept him on a Consul's pension, as did Louis XVIII in 1815. Struck down by elephantiasic leprosy, he finished his life in agony.

Tallien, Thérésa (née Cabarrus)
Born at Carabanchel, 1773
Died at Hainault, January 15, 1835

During the absence of her second husband, Jean Lambert Tallien, who had accompanied Bonaparte to Egypt, Thérésa Cabarrus became the mistress of the financier, Ouvrard. She obtained a divorce on the return of Tallien, after he had been liberated by the English in 1802. In 1805, she remarried the young Comte of Caraman who was later to become Prince of Chimay. Under the Restoration, she lived in the Rue de Babylone, in the house given to her by Ouvrard. Already the mother of seven children, from her previous unions, Thérésa had four more by her last husband and died at the Château of Chimay, in Belgium, at the age of 72

Talma, François Joseph
Born in Paris, January 15, 1763
Died in Paris, October 19, 1826

In 1799, Talma returned to the Comédie Française which he had left in 1791, after the shocking scandal of *Charles IX* by Marie Joseph Chénier. He then became the favourite actor of Napoléon and enjoyed a huge, well-deserved success. He managed to give back to theatrical productions the historical veracity, which had been hitherto lacking, especially in the area of costume. Having married for the first time in 1791, he then obtained a divorce in 1801 and married Charlotte Vanhove, a shareholder in the Comédie Française, who afterwards published a volume of memoirs of her husband. A year before his death, Talma presented his theories about the theatre in a treatise entitled *Réflexions sur Lekain et l'Art Théâtral* in 1825.

Target, Guy Jean Baptiste
Born in Paris, December 6, 1733
Died at Molières, September 9, 1806

Appointed Judge of the Appeal Tribunal in 1797, Target stayed in this post until his death. A jurist appreciated by Bonaparte, he collaborated notably in the drawing up of the Civil and Criminal Codes.

Théroigne de Méricourt, Anne *alias* Josèphe Terwagne,
Born at Marcourt, Belgium, 1762
Died in Paris, May 9, 1817

After having been publicly whipped in May 1793, Théroigne de Méricourt became insane. In 1800, she left the hospital of the Faubourg Saint Marceau where she had been locked up for seven years, only to be interned at the Salpêtrière. She died without recovering her sanity.

Treilhard, Jean Baptiste
Born at Brive, January 3, 1742
Died in Paris, December 1, 1810

After the events of Brumaire 18, Treilhard joined Bonaparte, who appointed him president of the Paris Court of Appeals in 1802. That same year, he joined the Council of State and became head of its legislative branch. Violating the oath to hate the royalty he took in 1795, he argued before the court in favour of a declaration of an hereditary Empire. Napoléon was grateful for this, naming him a Comte in 1808 and Senator in 1809. When he died, his ashes were taken to the Panthéon on orders from Napoléon.

Vadier, Marc Guillaume
Born at Pamiers, July 17, 1736
Died in Brussels, December 14, 1828

Arrested for having been involved in the plot of the Equals and jailed at Cherbourg in 1796, Vadier was freed in September 1799. He then withdrew from politics, living in Paris and later Toulouse for the duration of the Consulate and the Empire. Elected a deputy in 1815, he voted for the supplementary act during the Hundred Days. Under the Restoration, he went into exile and lived in Brussels from 1816. There, he met up with Buonarroti again and forged good relations with the Convention members living in exile in Holland.

What became of them?

Vergniaud, Pierre Victurien
Born in Limoges, May 31, 1753
Guillotined in Paris, Oct. 31, 1793

Victoire, Madame
Born in Versailles, May 11, 1733
Died in Trieste, June 8, 1799

Vigée Lebrun, Marie Louise Elisabeth Vigée, Mme.
Born in Paris, April 16, 1755
Died in Paris, March 30, 1842

When she returned to Paris from her comfortable life in exile in various European courts, Marie Louise Elisabeth Vigée Lebrun only stayed for a short time in the capital in 1802. She quickly left for London, where she stayed until 1805. After a brief stay in Switzerland, where she painted *Mme. de Staël en Corinne* in 1808, she returned to France and lived in her property at Louveciennes, which she hardly left again. An attempt at a new career in art under the Restoration, during which she painted *La Duchesse de Berry* in 1824, came to nothing. She gave up art and focused on writing her *Mémoires* between 1835 and 1837. In this work, she described her yourth.

Volney, Constantin François de Chasseboeuf, Comte de
Born at Craon, February 3, 1757
Died in Paris, April 26, 1820

Volney returned to France in 1799 after visiting the United States. His book, *Tableau du Climat et du Sol des Etats Unis d'Amérique*, was published in 1803. He supported Bonaparte. A member of the Senate, commander of the Legion of Honour (1804) and Comte of the Empire (1808), he abstained from a vote on the dismissal of Napoléon Bonaparte in 1814. That same year, he was appointed a peer of France by Louis XVIII and became involved in the Hundred Days. Following the battle of Waterloo, he remained a member of the upper Chamber and published a great many works, including *Recherches Nouvelles sur l'Histoire Ancienne, Alphabet Européen Appliqué aux Langues Asiatiques* (1819), *Discours sur l'Etude Philosophique des Langues* (1820) and *L'Hebreu Simplifié*.

Wailly, Charles de
Born in Paris, November 9, 1729
Died in Paris, November 2, 1798

672

The governments of France from 1789 to 1799

Government in power on January 1, 1788, until July 12, 1789

Chancellor, Keeper of the Seals: Barentin; *Director General of Finances:* Necker; *War:* Puységur; *Navy:* La Luzerne; *Foreign Affairs:* Montmorin; *King's Household:* Villedeuil.

Government in power from July 12 to 16, 1789

Head and President of the Royal Council of Finances: Breteuil; *War:* de Broglie; *Keeper of the Seals:* Barentin; *Foreign Affairs:* La Vauguyon.

Government in power from July 16, 1789 to March 15, 1792

Keeper of the Seals then *Justice:* Barentin,
Champion de Cicé (August 4, 1789)
Dupont Dutertre (Nov. 21, 1790)
King's Household then *Interior:* Saint Priest (July 19, 1789)
Montmorin (December 24, 1790)
De Lessart (January 25, 1791)
Cahier de Gerville (Nov. 27, 1791)
Finances: Necker,
Lambert (November 4, 1790)
De Lessart (November 30, 1790)
Public Revenue and Taxes: Tarbé (May 28, 1791)
Foreign Affairs: Montmorin,
De Lessart (November 20, 1791)
War: La Tour du Pin,
Duportail (November 16, 1790)
Narbonne (December 7, 1792)
Grave (March 11, 1792)
Navy: La Luzerne,
Claret de Fleurieu (Oct. 26, 1790)
Thévenard (May 17, 1791,
De Lessart (September 17, 1791)
De Molleville (October 2, 1791)

Girondist government, from March 15 to June 15, 1792

Foreign Affairs: Dumouriez,
De Naillac (June 13)
Justice: Roland,
Duranthon (April 14)
Interior: Roland,
Mourgue (June 13)
Public Revenue and Taxes: Clavière,
Duranthon (June 13)
War: Grave,

Servan (May 9)
Dumouriez (June 13)
Navy: Lacoste

Feuillant government, from June 15 to August 10, 1792

Justice: Duranthon,
Hector de Joly (July 4)
Interior: Terrier de Monciel,
Hector de Joly (July 17)
Champion de Villeneuve (July 20)
Public Revenue and Taxes: Beaulieu,
Leroux de la Ville (July 29)
Foreign Affairs: Chambonas,
Du Bouchage (July 23)
Bigot de Sainte Croix (August 1)
War: Lajard,
Franqueville d'Abancourt (July 23)
Navy: Lacoste,
Du Bouchage (July 20)

Provisional Executive Council appointed on August 10 by the Legislative Assembly and kept until the abolition of ministries on April 1, 1794 (Germinal 12, Year II)

Justice: Danton,
Garat (October 9, 1792)
Gohier (March 20, 1793)
Interior: Roland,
Garat (January 23, 1793)
Paré (August 20, 1793)
Public Revenue and Taxes: Clavière,
Destournelles (June 13, 1793)
War: Servan,
Lebrun (October 5, 1792)
Pache (October 19, 1792)
Beurnonville (February 4, 1793)
Bouchotte (April 4, 1793)
Navy and Colonies: Monge,
Dalbarade (April 10, 1793)
Foreign Affairs: Lebrun,
Deforgues (June 21, 1793)

Governments under the Directory, from the first cabinet formed on November 3 and 4, 1795 (Brumaire 12 and 13, Year IV), until Brumaire 18, Year VIII

Justice: Merlin de Douai,
Génissieu January 5, 1796 — Nivôse 15, Year IV)
Merlin de Douai (April 3, 1796 — Germinal 14, Year IV)
Lambrechts (September 24, 1797 — Vendémiaire 3, Year VI)

Cambacérès (July 20, 1798 — Thermidor 2, Year VII)
Interior: Benézech,
François de Neufchâteau (July 16, 1797 — Messidor 28, Year V)
Letourneux (September 14, 1797 — Fructidor 28, Year V)
François de Neufchâteau (June 17, 1798 — Prairial 29, Year VI)
Quinette de Rochemont (June 22, 1799 — Messidor 4, Year VII)
Finances: Gaudin,
Faipoult (November 8, 1795 — Brumaire 17, Year IV)
Camus (January 5, 1796 — Nivôse 15, Year IV)
Ramel Nogaret (February 14, 1796 — Pluviôse 25, Year IV)
Robert Lindet (July 23, 1799 — Thermidor 5, Year VIII)
War: Aubert Dubayet,
Petiet (February 8, 1796 — Pluviôse 19, Year IV)
Hoche (July 16, 1797 — Messidor 28, Year V)
Schérer (July 23, 1797 — Thermidor 5, Year V)
Milet de Mureau (February 21, 1799 — Ventôse 3, Year VII)
Bernadotte (July 2, 1799 — Messidor 14, Year VII)
Dubois Crancé (September 14,1799 — Fructidor 28, Year VII)
Navy and Colonies: Truguet,
Pleville le Peley (July 16, 1797 — Messidor 28, Year V)
Bruix (April 27, 1798 — Floréal 8, Year VI)
Bourdon de Vatry (July 3, 1799 — Messidor 15, Year VII)
Foreign Affairs: Delacroix,
Talleyrand (July 16, 1797 — Messidor 28, Year V)
Renhard (July 20, 1799 — Thermidor 2, Year VII)
Police (this post was created on January 2, 1796 — Nivôse 12, Year IV): Merlin de Douai,
Cochon de Lapparent (April 3, 1796 — Germinal 14, Year IV)
Lenoir Laroche July 16, 1797 — Messidor 28, Year V)
Sotin de la Ciondière (July 26, 1797 — Thermidor 8, Year V)
Dondeau (February 13, 1798 — Pluviôse 25, Year VI)
Lecarlier (May 16, 1798 — Floréal 27, Year VI)
Duval (November 1, 1798 — Brumaire 2, Year VII)
Bourguignon Dumolard (June 22, 1799 — Messidor 4, Year VII)
Fouché (July 20, 1799 — Thermidor 2, Year VII)

Table of Illustrations

General Index

- The people
- Names of towns and provinces
- Main revolutionary themes

Table of illustrations

Index of maps and charts

Each page reference is followed by a letter (a, b, c, d,) indicating the column containing the required information. When the information is in a chronology column, the reference is in italics.

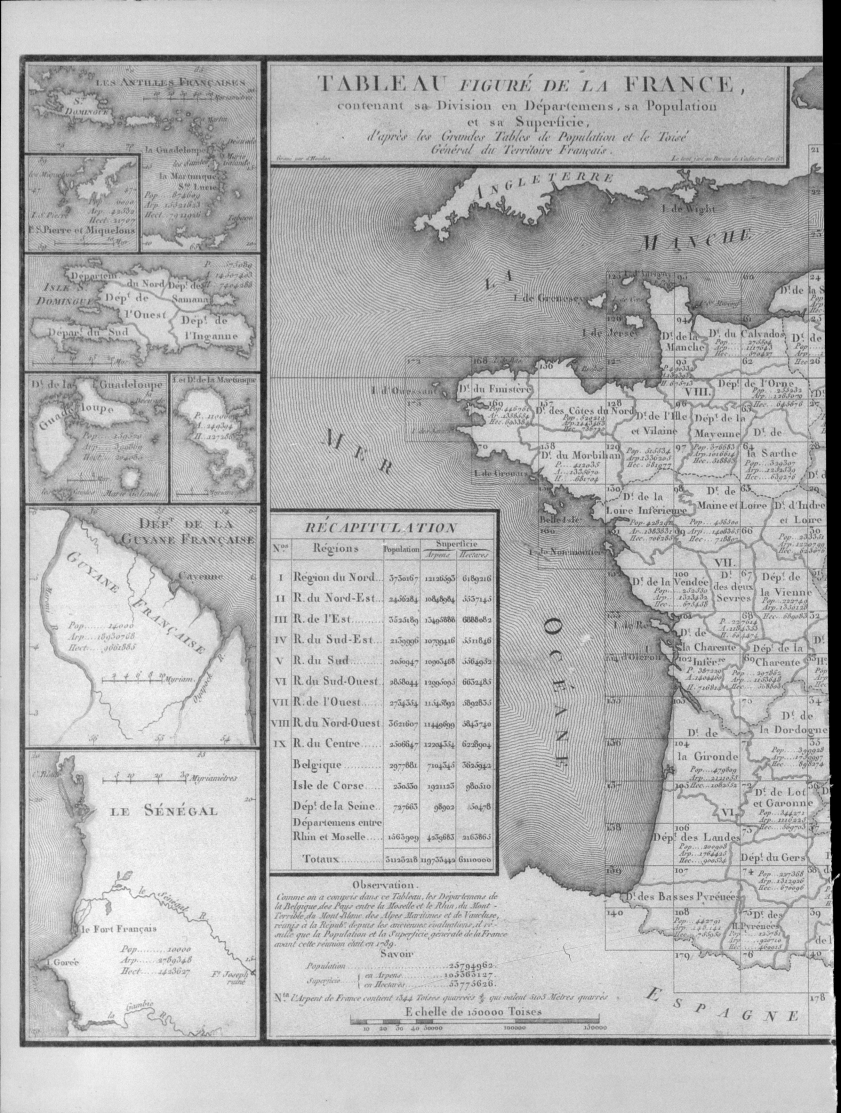

TABLEAU *FIGURÉ DE LA FRANCE*,

contenant sa Division en Départemens, sa Population et sa Superficie,

d'après les Grandes Tables de Population et le Toisé Général du Territoire Français.

Gravé par d'Houdan

Le tout fait au Bureau du Cadastre l'an 6.°

LES ANTILLES FRANÇAISES

ISLE S.* DOMINGUE
Départem. du Nord — Dép.t de Samana
Dép.t de l'Ouest — Dép.t de l'Inganne
Dépar.t du Sud

D.t de la Guadeloupe

D.t et D.t de la Martinique

DÉP.t DE LA GUYANE FRANÇAISE
Cayenne
Pop....14000
Arp....18930768
Hect....9661885

LE SÉNÉGAL
le Fort Français
Pop....10000
Arp....2789348
Hect....1423627
I. Gorée

RÉCAPITULATION

N.os	Régions	Population	Superficie	
			Arpens	Hectares
I	Région du Nord...	3750167	12126593	6189216
II	R. du Nord-Est...	2456284	10848984	5537145
III	R. de l'Est...	3525189	13495888	6888082
IV	R. du Sud-Est...	2159996	10799416	5511846
V	R. du Sud	2050947	10905468	5564952
VI	R. du Sud-Ouest	2858044	12995095	6632485
VII	R. de l'Ouest	2734354	11548892	5892835
VIII	R. du Nord-Ouest	3621607	11449699	5843740
IX	R. du Centre	2506647	12204354	6228904
	Belgique	2977881	7104545	3625942
	Isle de Corse	230330	1921123	980510
	Dép.t de la Seine	727663	98902	50478
	Départemens entre Rhin et Moselle	1563909	4239683	2163865
	Totaux	31125218	119753442	61100000

Observation.

Comme on a compris dans ce Tableau, les Départemens de la Belgique, des Pays entre la Moselle et le Rhin, du Mont-Terrible, du Mont-Blanc, des Alpes Maritimes et de Vaucluse, réunis à la Repub.e depuis les anciennes évaluations, il résulte que la Population et la Superficie générale de la France avant cette réunion était en 1789.

Savoir

Population ....25794962.
Superficie { en Arpens ....105365127.
{ en Hectares ....53775626.

N.ta L'Arpent de France contient 1344 Toises quarrées ⅘ qui valent 5103 Mètres quarrés

Echelle de 150000 Toises
10 20 30 40 50000   100000   150000

ANGLETERRE — MANCHE — LA — MER — OCÉANE — ESPAGNE